The Social Construction of Difference
and Inequality

The Social Construction of Difference and Inequality

Race, Class, Gender, and Sexuality

EIGHTH EDITION

Tracy E. Ore

Saint Cloud State University

NEW YORK   OXFORD

OXFORD UNIVERSITY PRESS

Oxford University Press is a department of the University of Oxford.
It furthers the University's objective of excellence in research, scholarship,
and education by publishing worldwide. Oxford is a registered trade mark of
Oxford University Press in the UK and certain other countries.

Published in the United States of America by Oxford University Press
198 Madison Avenue, New York, NY 10016, United States of America.

For titles covered by Section 112 of the US Higher Education
Opportunity Act, please visit www.oup.com/us/he for the
latest information about pricing and alternate formats.

Library of Congress Cataloging-in-Publication Data

Names: Ore, Tracy E., author.
Title: The social construction of difference and inequality : race, class,
  gender, and sexuality / Tracy E. Ore, Saint Cloud State University.
Description: Eighth edition. | New York, NY : Oxford University Press,
  [2022] | Revised edition of the author's The social construction of
  difference and inequality, [2019] | Includes bibliographical references
  and index.
Identifiers: LCCN 2021050779 (print) | LCCN 2021050780 (ebook) | ISBN
  9780197618967 (paperback) | ISBN 9780197618981 (epub)
Subjects: LCSH: Cultural pluralism—United States. | Equality—United
  States. | Minorities—United States—Social conditions. | Social
  classes—United States. | Women—United States—Social conditions. |
  Gays—United States—Social conditions. | Discrimination—United States.
  | United States—Social conditions—1980- | United States—Race
  relations. | United States—Ethnic relations.
Classification: LCC HN59.2 .S585 2022 (print) | LCC HN59.2 (ebook) | DDC
  305.800973—dc23/eng/20211201
LC record available at https://lccn.loc.gov/2021050779
LC ebook record available at https://lccn.loc.gov/2021050780

9 8 7 6 5 4 3 2 1
Printed by Marquis, Canada

This book is dedicated to the memory of my mother, Virginia Maxine Barton Ore—the smartest woman I have ever known.

I also dedicate this book to my brother, Brian Curtis Ore, and to all others lost in the continuing crisis of AIDS.

About the Author

Tracy E. Ore is a professor of sociology and the Faculty Director of the Community Garden at St. Cloud State University. She received her PhD in sociology from the University of Michigan, is an active member of the American Sociological Association and the Southern Sociological Society, and is past president of Sociologists for Women in Society. Her teaching areas include social inequality, race and ethnicity, social movements, and the global politics of food. She does research in the areas of poverty, food insecurity, food apartheid, and food justice. She serves as a consultant for multicultural education and curriculum to a variety of organizations and agencies and conducts workshops and trainings related to issues of inequality. In addition to this work, Professor Ore is a long-time activist and community organizer. The connections between her scholarly work and activism are made real in the St. Cloud State University Community Garden, which she established in 2005.

About the Cover

In May of 2020, George Floyd was murdered by actions of the Minneapolis police. This act prompted one of the largest protest movements in the United States, with up to 26 million people participating in demonstrations. Floyd's death is in a larger context of a history in the U.S. of Black men and women killed at the hands of police. The officers charged, however, have rarely been arrested, prosecuted, or convicted for excessive use of force. Black and other people of color experience differential justice at all levels of the criminal justice system, whether at the time of arrest, indictment, conviction, sentencing, or parole. Many argue that this is illustrative of a history of systemic racism, where the policies and practices of social institutions and structures perpetuate the oppression of people of color. As we work to address the problems of racial inequality, it will be important to move beyond individual issues of prejudice and discrimination, focusing on changes necessary in our systems and structures.

Contents

** *Indicates New Reading*

Preface xiii

PART I: CONSTRUCTING DIFFERENCES 1
Examining what categories are constructed, how this is done, and why such categories of difference are constructed.

Race and Ethnicity 15

1. Racial Formations 15
   Michael Omi and Howard Winant

2. Optional Ethnicities: For Whites Only? 23
   Mary C. Waters

3. Learning to be Illegal: Undocumented Youth and Shifting Legal Contexts in the Transition to Adulthood 33
   Roberto G. Gonzales

Social Class 49

**4. The Asset Value Of Whiteness: Understanding the Racial Wealth Gap 49
   Amy Traub, Laura Sullivan, Tatjana Meschede, and Tom Shapiro

5. Media Magic: Making Class Invisible 59
   Gregory Mantsios

**6. Latinos are Each of Us: Fair and Just Immigration Policies for All 65
   Noreen M. Sugrue and Sylvia Puente

Sex and Gender 71

7. The Social Construction of Gender 71
   Judith Lorber

**8. Giving Sex: Deconstructing Intersex and Trans Medicalization Practices 77
   Georgiann Davis, Jodie M. Dewey, and Erin L. Murphy

9. "Ain't I a Woman?": Transgender And Intersex Student Athletes In Women's Collegiate Sports 91
   Pat Griffin

Sexuality 102

10. Naming All the Parts 102
    Kate Bornstein

11. "If You Don't Kiss Me, You're Dumped": Boys, Boyfriends, and Heterosexualised Masculinities in the Primary School 110
    Emma Renold

12. What's so Cultural About Hookup Culture? 122
    Lisa Wade

PART II: MAINTAINING INEQUALITIES: SYSTEMS OF OPPRESSION AND PRIVILEGE 125
Examining what elements of social structure work to maintain systems of stratification based on constructions of difference.

Social Institutions: Family   145

13. Why Won't African Americans Get (and Stay) Married? Why Should They?   145
    Shirley A. Hill

**14. "Willing to Do Anything for My Kids": Inventive Mothering, Diapers, and the Inequalities Of Carework   157
    Jennifer Randles

15. Illegality as a Source of Solidarity and Tension In Latino Families   177
    Leisy J. Abrego

16. Marriage and Family: LGBT Individuals and Same-Sex Couples   193
    Gary J. Gates

Social Institutions: Education   205

**17. Mind the Gap: COVID-19 And Learning Loss— Disparities Grow and Students Need Help   205
    Emma Dorn, Bryan Hancock, Jimmy Sarakatsannis, and Ellen Viruleg

18. Civilize Them with a Stick   217
    Mary Crow Dog and Richard Erdoes

**19. Black Girls and School Discipline: The Complexities of Being Overrepresented and Understudied   223
    Subini Ancy Annamma, Yolanda Anyon, Nicole M. Joseph, Jordan Farrar, Eldridge Greer, Barbara Downing, and John Simmons

Social Institutions: Work and Economy   234

20. Black Men and the Struggle for Work: Social and Economic Barriers Persist   234
    James M. Quane, William Julius Wilson, and Jackelyn Hwang

21. Racializing the Glass Escalator: Reconsidering Men's Experiences With Women's Work   239
    Adia Harvey Wingfield

**22. The Threat of Poverty Without Misery   251
    Alyosha Goldstein

Social Institutions: The State and Public Policy   268

23. Jezebel at the Welfare Office: How Racialized Stereotypes of Poor Women's Reproductive Decisions and Relationships Shape Policy Implementation   268
    N. Tatiana Masters, Taryn P. Lindhorst, and Marcia K. Meyers

**24. Race, Place, and Effective Policing   281
    Anthony A. Braga, Rod K. Brunson, and Kevin M. Drakulich

25. The Treacherous Triangle: Justice, Immigration Enforcement, and Child Welfare   300
    Seth Freed Wessler

Social Institutions: Media   308

26. The Digital Reproduction of Inequality   308
    Eszter Hargittai

27. Winnebagos, Cherokees, Apaches, and Dakotas: The Persistence of Stereotyping of American Indians in American Advertising Brands   317
    Debra Merskin

**28. Asian American Media Representation: A Film Analysis and Implications for Identity Development   326
    Tiffany Besana, Dalal Katsiaficas, and Aerika Brittian Loyd

Language and Culture   346

29. How the Right Made Racism Sound Fair—And Changed Immigration Politics   346
    Gabriel Thompson

**30. "Strong Black Woman": African American Women With Disabilities, Intersecting Identities, and Inequality   354
    Angel Love Miles

31. The Florida State Seminoles: The Champions of Racist Mascots   365
    Dave Zirin

Violence and Social Control   368

32. Climate of Fear   368
    Southern Poverty Law Center

**33. "Rape is a Man's Issue": Gender and Power in The Era of Affirmative Sexual Consent   373
    Julia Metz, Kristen Myers, and Patricia Wallace

34. Cyberbullying, School Bullying, and Psychological Distress: A Regional Census of High School Students   387
    Shari Kessel Schneider, Lydia O'Donnell, Ann Stueve, and Robert W. S. Coulter

PART III: EXPERIENCING DIFFERENCE AND INEQUALITY IN EVERYDAY LIFE   399

Examining the impact of constructions of difference and maintaining inequalities on members of society.

35. Making Systems of Privilege Visible   402
    Stephanie M. Wildman with Adrienne D. Davis

36. You May Know me From Such Roles as Terrorist #4   407
    Jon Ronson

**37. Dying to be Competent   413
    Tressie McMillan Cottom

38. The Story of My Body   420
    Judith Ortiz Cofer

**39. Two Hate Notes: Deportations, COVID-19, and Xenophobia Against Hmong Americans in the Midwest   427
    Kong Pheng Pha

40. "Gee, You Don't Seem Like an Indian From the Reservation"   431
    Barbara Cameron

41. The Transgender Crucible   436
    Sabrina Rubin Erdely

42. Nickel-And-Dimed: On (Not) Getting By in America   445
    Barbara Ehrenreich

43. Not Poor Enough   456
    Susan Sheehan

**44. The Miseducation of the American Boy   464
    Peggy Orenstein

PART IV: RESISTANCE AND SOCIAL CHANGE   475

Examining how people working within individual and institutional contexts transform difference from a system of inequality to a system of liberation.

45. Toward a New Vision: Race, Class, and Gender as Categories of Analysis and Connection   485
    Patricia Hill Collins

**46. #Feministantibodies: Asian American Media in the Time of Coronavirus   496
    Rachel Kuo, Amy Zhang, Vivian Shaw, and Cynthia Wang

47. Seeing More than Black and White: Latinos, Racism, and the Cultural Divides   511
    Elizabeth Martinez

48. Reform or Transformation? the Pivotal Role of Food Justice in the U.S. Food Movement   516
    Eric Holt-Giménez and Yi Wang

49. Voices of a New Movimiento   528
    Roberto Lovato

50. The Next Civil Rights Movement?   532
    Fredrick C. Harris

Preface

Teaching about issues of inequality in a culture that focuses on individualism can be a daunting task. Having been raised in such a culture, students in my classes often arrive with little knowledge of the systemic nature of inequality in society. While they may be aware of their own experiences of disadvantage (and perhaps privilege), they are generally not aware of how structural arrangements in society result in systems of difference and inequality. This book, which focuses on how race, class, gender, and sexuality are socially constructed as categories of difference and are maintained as systems of inequality, is an effort to help students move toward a more systemic understanding.

Why Another Race, Class, Gender (And Sexuality) Reader?

With the plethora of readers on race, class, and gender currently on the market, one may wonder why another is needed. Indeed, some excellent anthologies are available that can be effective in demonstrating the impact of race, class, and gender inequality on the life chances of various individuals and groups in our society. However, few of these texts thoroughly explain how such categories of difference are created, and even fewer demonstrate how social institutions work to maintain systems of inequality. The text here is structured in a way that examines how and why the categories of race, class, gender, and sexuality are socially constructed, maintained, and experienced.

This anthology is divided into four parts. Each part begins with an introductory essay that offers a conceptual framework illustrating concepts and theories (which are designated by boldface type) useful for understanding the issues raised by the readings in that section. These essays are not merely introductions to the readings; rather, they provide material that will enable students to move beyond them. Part I provides a thorough discussion of what it means to think critically, as well as an extensive overview of how and why categories of difference are socially constructed. Part II discusses in greater detail how categories of difference are transformed and maintained as systems of inequality by social institutions. Part III examines how categories of difference and systems of inequality impact the everyday experiences of individuals in our society. Finally, Part IV offers a useful look at perspectives on social change and provides examples of barriers to and opportunities for transforming systems of oppression and privilege into systems of equal access to opportunity.

In each section, the readings and examples were selected to cover a variety of racial and ethnic groups as well as experiences of multiracial identity and immigration. In addition, issues of sexuality are incorporated throughout each part of this book. While a few anthologies incorporate readings that address inequality on the basis of sexuality, the majority do so on only a superficial level. With the continuing political and social debate regarding civil rights and sexuality, it is important that texts provide sufficient material to address this area of inequality. Overall, the readings represent myriad individuals with various perspectives and life experiences. Such diversity will aid students' ability to understand perspectives and experiences that differ from their own. Finally, the part introductions as well as many of the readings selected demonstrate the intersections of race, class, gender, and sexuality and stress the importance of viewing them as interlocking systems of oppression and privilege. By moving beyond traditional additive models of examining inequality, students will be better able to see how forms of inequality are interconnected.

A Note on Language

As discussed in Part II, language serves as a link between all the different forms of culture in a society. Although language enables us to communicate with and understand one another, it also incorporates cultural values. Thus, the words we use to describe ourselves and others with regard to race, class, gender, and sexuality reflect not only our own values but also those of the dominant ideology and popular discourse.

In discussing the experiences of different groups, issues of language can become particularly problematic. For example, as discussed in Part I, categories of race and ethnicity are socially constructed. In addition, the externally created labels for these categories are not always accepted by those viewed as belonging to a particular group. For example, individuals of Latin American descent may not accept the term *Hispanic*. Similarly, those who are indigenous to North America may not accept the term *American Indian*. However, there is rarely agreement among all members of a particular racial or ethnic group regarding the terminology with which they would like to be identified.

Recognizing the problems and limitations of language, I have attempted to be consistent in the terminology I have used in each part introduction. For example, I use the term *Latina/o/ x*[1] to refer to those of Latin American descent, although not all people in this group may identify themselves in this way. I also use the terms *black* and *African American* interchangeably, as I do with *American Indian* and *Native American*. In using such terms it is not my intention to homogenize divergent experiences. Rather, it is done in an effort to allow discussion of common experiences within as well as across groups. The terminology used by the authors of the readings was not altered, however. It is important that readers be mindful of the limitations of my language use as well as that of the other authors within this anthology.

Changes to this Edition

With this eighth edition, I have continued to cover a variety of racial and ethnic groups and to incorporate sexuality throughout. In addition, I have maintained the focus on the intersections of race, class, gender, and sexuality as interlocking systems of oppression. To keep the text current with regard to economic conditions, issues of gender and sexuality, the political and social discourse on race, and recent events in our country and world, I have updated all relevant statistics and changed many readings, adding fifteen new readings, several with a more empirical focus. These readings include articles discussing issues of immigration and documentation; updated discussions of the relationship between the growing racial wealth gap and social policy in the United States; examinations of health and educational inequalities, particularly in the context of the COVID-19 pandemic; structural racism and its maintenance through the institutions such as education and the criminal justice system; and the increasing role of hate crimes and other forms of violence in marginalizing and silencing already oppressed groups. As with the seventh edition, I have selected readings that are engaging for students and that reflect a variety of experiences. I welcome any feedback that instructors and students may have.

Online Resources

An instructor's manual to accompany this text is located on the Oxford Learning Link. The instructor's manual contains guidelines for discussion for each reading, short-answer and essay questions, suggestions for classroom activities, and recommendations for films/videos. These items were compiled to help instructors further student comprehension of the issues addressed in this volume.

Acknowledgments

The inception and completion of this project were made possible through the efforts of many people. Foremost among these, I would like to acknowledge the students at the University of Illinois (1995–98) and their efforts in lobbying for a class on multiculturalism and inequality that would incorporate students doing service in the community. Without their perseverance and commitment, I would likely not have had the opportunity to teach a course that provided such a wonderful foundation for this book. As has been the case throughout my teaching career, my students are my best teachers. Thanks go to all of my students at the colleges and universities where I have taught. I continue to learn from each of them.

I also would like to acknowledge the work of a wonderful team of reviewers: Jodi Burmeister-May, St. Cloud State University; Denise M. Dalaimo, Mt. San Jacinto College; Sharon Elise, California State University at San Marcos; Kristin G. Esterberg, University of Massachusetts at Lowell; Susan A. Farrell, Kingsborough Community College; Lisa M. Frehill, New Mexico State University; Melinda Goldner, Union College; Kelley Hall, DePauw University; Melissa Herbert, Hamline University; Eleanor A. Hubbard, University of Colorado at Boulder; Melissa Latimer, West Virginia University; Betsy Lucal, Indiana University South Bend; Anne Roschelle, State University of New York at New Paltz; Steve Schacht, State University of New York at Plattsburgh; Susan Shaw, Oregon State University; and Brett Stockdill, California State Polytechnic University at Pomona. Their insights, comments, and suggestions served me greatly in clarifying the direction of this project. I value the contribution each of them made to its completion.

For the second edition, I would like to thank the following team of reviewers: Peter Meiksins, Cleveland State University; Jackie Hogan, Bradley University; Philip A. Broyles, Shippensburg University; Heather E. Dillaway, Michigan State University; Elizabeth J. Clifford, Towson University; Tom Gershick, Illinois State University; Susan A. Farrell, Kingsborough Community College; Kristin G. Esterberg, University of Massachusetts-Lowell; and Eleanor A. Hubbard, University of Colorado at Boulder.

For the third edition, I would like to thank the following reviewers: Kristin Esterberg, University of Massachusetts-Lowell; Susan Farrell, Kingsborough Community College; Eleanor Hubbard, University of Colorado at Boulder; and Peter Meiksins, Cleveland State University. Again, their suggestions and comments enabled me to continue to improve this project.

For the fourth edition, I would like to thank the following team of reviewers: Tiffany Davis, University of Minnesota; Spencer Hope Davis, Elon University; Mary Ferguson, University of Missouri-St. Louis; Christina M. Jimenez, University of Colorado at Colorado Springs; Peter Meiksins, Cleveland State University; Chadwick L. Menning, Ball State University; and Tracy Woodard Meyers, Valdosta State University. Their suggestions and comments were incredibly helpful in continuing to produce a text that will be useful to others.

For the fifth edition, I would like to thank the following team of reviewers: Christina Accomando, Humboldt State University; Rose Brewer, University of Minnesota-Twin Cities; Edith Brotman, Towson University; Julie Rauli, Wilson College; and Mark Rauls, College of Southern Nevada. Their thoughtful reviews helped to guide me in providing a text that will continue to be useful to instructors in the field.

For the sixth edition, I appreciate the work of the following team of reviewers: Debora Barrera Pontillo, Cascadia Community College; Catherine Felton, Central Piedmont Community College; Timothy Pippert, Augsburg College; Yvonne Moody, Chadron State College; Jason Martin, University of Missouri at Kansas City; Ann Wood, University of Missouri at Kansas City; Linda Bynoe, California State University-Monterey Bay; Daniel Egan, University of Massachusetts-Lowell; Lynn Jones, Northern Arizona University; Leslie Richards, University of the District of Columbia; Lissa Yogan, Valparaiso University; Nicole Hendricks, Houston Community College; and Adrianna Bohm, Delaware County Community College. Their input was helpful in assisting me in developing an edition that is timely and relevant.

For the seventh edition, I would like to thank the following team of reviewers: Karen Hossfeld, San Francisco State University; Hortencia Jimenez, Hartnell College; Diane McMahon, La Roche College; Deinya Phenix, St. Francis College; Michael Polgar, Pennsylvania State University; Alfred Prettyman, Ramapo College of New Jersey; Dominick Quinney, Albion College; Rosemary Shinko, American University; Nivedita Vaidya, California State University-Los Angeles; and Christi Young, Southwestern Michigan College. Their invaluable feedback helped me to make the revisions necessary to continue to provide a tool that will be beneficial to educators.

For the eighth edition, I would like to thank the following team of reviewers: Mary Burke, Carlow University; Kaitlyn Creasy, California State University, San Bernardino; Elaina M. Johns-Wolfe, University of Cincinnati; Melinda D. Kane, East Carolina University; E. Brooke Kelly, University of North Carolina at Pembroke; Santiago Pinon, Texas Christian University; Michael Stewart, Adams State University; and Barbara Vann, Loyola University Maryland. Their comments were particularly useful as I navigated one of the most complicated revisions I have experienced.

The production of the first edition of this book and its adherence to schedule was due to the work of many people. Specifically, I would like to thank Jan Fisher, Kathryn Mikulic, and Dave Mason at Publication Services for their excellent copyediting and other support. At Mayfield Publishing I would like to thank Mary Johnson, April Wells- Hayes, Marty Granahan, and Jay Bauer. My deepest thanks go to Serina Beauparlant for believing in this project and for supporting me throughout. With her vision and perseverance, I couldn't have asked for a better editor.

The creation of the second edition is due to the work of Jill Gordon, Sally Constable, Amy Shaffer, Ruth Smith, Lori Koetters, Jenny El-Shamy, Nathan Perry, and Dan Loch at McGraw-Hill. I appreciate your patience, creative efforts, and attention to detail.

The creation of the third edition is due to the work of Sherith Pankratz, Trish Starner, Larry Goldberg, Jill Gordon, Kim Menning, Melissa Williams, and Randy Hurst at McGraw-Hill. I appreciate your work, imagination, and thoroughness.

The creation of the fourth edition is due to the work of Gina Boedeker, Amanda Peabody, Leslie Oberhuber, Rich DeVitto, and Margarite Reynolds at McGraw-Hill. I am in great appreciation of your patience and commitment.

The creation of the fifth edition is due to the work of Andrea Edwards and Meghan Campbell at McGraw-Hill. I am grateful for your persistence and excellent work.

The production of the sixth edition was supported by Sara Jaeger at McGraw-Hill. I greatly appreciate all that she did to assist me with the completion of the project.

The production of the seventh edition was the result of the most able assistance of Grace Li at Oxford University Press. I am especially appreciative of her patience as the project was delayed because of unforeseen circumstances. Her professionalism and commitment went beyond all my expectations.

Appreciation for this most recent edition goes to Maeve O'Brien at Oxford University Press. Her diligence and attention to detail is much appreciated. In addition, I would like to thank Sherith Pankratz at Oxford for her time and thoughtfulness as she helped me think through editing this edition in the time of a global pandemic, economic crisis, ongoing racial conflict, and political change. Whew!

Completing this project was also made possible through the support and caring of a wonderful community of friends. I could always count on them for unconditional support, and I am thankful to them for sharing their knowledge and insight. Thanks also go to my fellow activists who help me to always keep one foot in reality so that I do not lose perspective. Finally, I am incredibly grateful to my partner Kramer, a consistent and stable force in my life. Her love, support, and understanding continue to be all I need to get by.

Tracy E. Ore

Note

1. While it has become common for academics, activists, students, and journalists to utilize the term Latinx to replace the use of Latina/o in effort to be gender neutral and inclusive of all genders, there remains concern about the inclusivity of this terminology. See Rodriguez (2017) and Vidal-Ortiz and Martínez (2018) for further exploration of these issues.

References

Rodríguez, Richard T. 2017. "X Marks the Spot." *Cultural Dynamics* 29 (3): 202–13.
Vidal-Ortiz, Salvador, and Juliana Martínez. 2018. "Latinx Thoughts: Latinidad with an X." *Latino Studies* 6 (3): 384–95.

PART I

Constructing Differences

Introduction

In the United States, the Census Bureau attempts to conduct a complete accounting of all residents every ten years. The data gathered by the Census Bureau are extremely important because they serve to determine the distribution of federal dollars to support housing assistance, highway construction, employment services, schools, hospital services, programs for the elderly, and other funding targets. In the year 2000, persons filling out census forms were given a unique opportunity. For the first time, those with mixed racial heritage were permitted to select more than one racial category. As a result of new governmental policy, the category *multiracial* then became a new reality in the United States.

Does this mean that people who are multiracial had never before existed in this country? Of course not. Even a superficial exploration of US history will show that multiracial people have been present throughout. A study using DNA tests to confirm that Thomas Jefferson was the father of at least one child by his slave Sally Hemings (Foster et al. 1998) is but one example of how the history of slavery in the United States has contributed to the existence of people of multiracial descent. However, until 2000, government policies in the United States had not allowed for the recognition of a multiracial identity. Rather, they enforced policies such as the rule of **hypodescent**—one drop of black blood makes you black—to maintain distinct racial categories.

The preceding example clearly illustrates that the categories we use to describe ourselves and those around us are the product of social rather than biological factors. Biologically, people who are multiracial certainly exist throughout the United States. Indeed, it is unlikely that anyone has a singular ethnic or racial lineage. Nevertheless, it is the social recognition, definition, and grouping of these factors that make them culturally significant in our daily interactions. Our reliance on such distinct categories is made clear when we ask someone whose race is not immediately discernible to us, what are you?

These culturally defined classifications are also significant in that they are structured as categories that are fundamentally different from one another. Thus, we expect people to be black or white, never in between.[1] It is important to point out, however, that difference is not necessarily a negative quality. On the contrary, the existence of categories of difference adds a great deal of richness to our lives. The presence of different cultural traditions, types of food, forms of music, and styles of dance serves to make society more interesting. It is not the differences that are the causes of inequality in our culture. Rather, it is the meanings and values applied to these differences that make them harmful. For example, it is not that Black, Indigenous, and People of Color are defined as different from whites in the United States, but that whites are viewed as superior and as the cultural standard against which all others are judged that transforms categories of race *differences* into a system of racial *inequality*.

The readings in this text explore how categories of difference with regard to race/ethnicity, social class, sex/gender, and sexuality are constructed and then transformed into systems of inequality. We will investigate what creates these categories and how they are constructed, and we will consider some explanations about why these categories are created. It is important that we understand how the processes that construct these categories simultaneously create structures of **social stratification**—a system by which society ranks categories of people in a hierarchy—and how social stratification results in systems of inequality. The readings in this text will aid us in understanding the effects that categories of difference have on all members of our society and how this inequality can be addressed. By examining closely the processes that construct categories of difference, we will better understand how they impact our lives. Furthermore, by recognizing how systems of inequality are socially created, we can gain a greater understanding of how to transform such systems into ones of equality.

Critical Thinking

A fundamental component in examining constructions of difference and systems of inequality is critical thinking about the social constructs on which systems of inequality rely. This requires us to examine how the social structure has affected our values, attitudes, and behaviors. The object of this text is not to negate your current belief system and provide you with a new one, but rather to provide the tools that will allow you to think critically about the attitudes and opinions you have been given. By thinking critically, we are better able to develop a belief system that we can claim as our own.

Many of us are unsure of what is meant by critical thinking. According to various scholars, critical thinking can involve logical reasoning, reflective judgment, exploring assumptions, creating and testing meanings, identifying contradictions in arguments, and determining the validity of empirical findings and generalized conclusions. For the purposes of this text, to think critically is to ask questions about what is assumed to be real, valued, and significant in our culture. Stephen Brookfield (1987) offers a useful framework for asking these questions. He sees critical thinking as having four primary elements.

First, we must identify and challenge assumptions. We should try to identify the assumptions that are at the foundation of the concepts, values, beliefs, and behaviors that we deem important in our society. Once we have identified these assumptions, we need to explore their accuracy and legitimacy, considering whether what we take for granted does indeed reflect the realities we experience. For example, a common assumption in the United States is that women are inherently more nurturing than men and that men are inherently more aggressive than women. When thinking critically, we ask whether such assumptions reflect reality or simply shape what we observe in the behaviors of women and men. In other words, do we observe women indeed being more nurturing, or do we make note of only their nurturing behavior? In addition, we need to ask whether our expectations of women and men shape the ways in which they act. For example, do men behave in a more aggressive manner because that is what is expected of them? Through identifying and challenging assumptions, we become more aware of how uncritically examined assumptions shape our perceptions and our understanding of our environment.

Second, thinking critically involves awareness of our place and time in our culture. When asking questions about aspects of our culture, we need to be aware of our own **standpoint**—the position from which we are asking these questions. In other words, we need to be aware of our location at a particular intersection of culture and history; how that is influenced by our race/ethnicity, social class, sex/gender, sexuality, ability, age, and other factors; and how these in turn influence the questions we ask and the answers we accept. For example, a millionaire examining the strengths and weaknesses of the US economic system would likely see different problems and solutions to these problems than would a working-class individual. Their respective class standpoints (as well as their race/ethnicity, sex/gender, sexuality, etc.) affect the ways in which they examine the world.

One's standpoint also influences what one sees as normal or ordinary behavior. This relates to the concept of **enculturation**—immersion in our own culture to the point where we assume that our way of life is natural or normal. Because we are so enculturated into our own societal standards and practices, we often assume that they are the only options and, as a result, we are unaware of alternatives. Furthermore, we often view those who have other cultural standards or practices as behaving in a strange or unnatural manner. For example, people raised in a culture with strict religious teachings based on the idea of a supreme being may be so enculturated that they view those with different notions of religion (or none at all) as strange or odd. As a consequence of the depth of our enculturation, we also often possess some level of **ethnocentrism**—the practice of judging another culture using the standards of one's own. Such judging is based on the assumption that one's own group is more important than or superior to other groups (Sumner [1906] 1959). Thus, we may judge those who possess religious beliefs different from ours not only as strange but also as wrong. For example, many non-Muslim Americans, fueled by media stereotypes, view the practices of those who follow Islam as inappropriate, if not un-American.

It is important to point out, however, that ethnocentrism is not in and of itself problematic. Every social system to some degree promotes its ideas and standards. Ethnocentrism becomes a problem when such ideas are used as a basis for treating people in an unequal manner. An alternative to ethnocentrism is **cultural relativism**—judging a culture by its own cultural rules and values. By being cultural relativists, we can gain a better understanding of the real meaning of another culture's ideas and standards. In thinking critically it is important that we recognize the depth of our enculturation and how it is manifested in our ethnocentrism, so that we can become aware of our own standpoint and be better able to judge other cultures by their own values and ideas.

Third, when thinking critically we need to search for alternative ways of thinking. This means examining the assumptions that form the basis of our ideas and ways of behaving. For example, the United States is currently a society based on the notion of **civil rights**—a system based on majority rule. When we vote, the will of the majority becomes the will of all. This system is designed to bring the greatest good for the greatest number. In addition, there is a fundamental belief that if one is a good citizen, one earns rights within society, such as liberty. In a civil rights system some people inevitably do not benefit. Implicit in the statement "the greatest good for the greatest number" is the assumption that society cannot provide for everyone. To think critically about a civil rights system, we must imagine an alternative to this reality. For example, what might it be like to live in a society that operates under a **human rights** framework? Such a system recognizes each person as an individual and as valuable. It is based on the belief that everyone has inalienable rights to housing, food, education, and health care and that society must provide these rights to people who are unable to provide for themselves.

What structural changes are necessary to bring about such a society? Furthermore, if we were to create such a society, how might our own lives be transformed? Considering alternatives to current ways of thinking can provide us with new insights about widely accepted ideas.

Fourth, to think critically one must develop a reflective analysis. Such an analysis requires that we be skeptical, not in the sense that we do not believe anything we see, but rather that we question rigid belief systems. For example, once we become aware that it is possible to have a society that operates under a human rights framework, we come to question those who claim that a system based on civil rights is the only way to operate. A reflective analysis requires that we challenge dominant ideas and popularly held notions regarding solutions to social problems.

Thinking critically frees us from personal, environmental, and institutional forces that prevent us from seeing new directions (Habermas 1979). Furthermore, once we become critical thinkers, we are no longer passive recipients of knowledge and products of socialization. Rather, through practicing thoughtful scrutiny and continuously asking questions, we become active participants and arrive at our own ideas and commitments. As a result, we ground our ideas on a solid and informed foundation, all the while realizing that we may still be wrong. When we face challenges to our ideas, we are better prepared to provide justification and evidence in their support. The readings in this text provide us with many essential tools for becoming discerning critical thinkers.

Essentialism and Social Construction

As mentioned earlier, in the United States we have a system of stratification that is based on many categories of difference, including race/ethnicity, social class, sex/gender, and sexuality. We tend to view this system as fixed because of our assumptions that these categories are unchangeable. Such assumptions are often based on a belief of **essentialism**—the tenet that human behavior is natural, predetermined by genetic, biological, or physiological mechanisms and thus not subject to change. Human behaviors that show some similarity are assumed to be expressions of an underlying human drive or tendency. In the United States, gender and sexuality are among the last realms to have their natural or biological status called into question. For most of us, essentialism informs the way we think about such things as gender and remains the **hegemonic** or culturally dominant belief in our culture. For example, many of us attribute great importance to what we perceive as biological differences between females and males and see them as central to the organization of human society. Essentialism guides the way we order our social world and determines what we value as well as what we devalue.

This text proceeds from a different perspective, however. As you read the selections in Part I, you will note that they all begin with the premise that categories such as race/ethnicity, social class, sex/gender, and sexuality are socially constructed. Peter Berger and Thomas Luckmann, on whose work this premise is based, state that "social order is not part of the 'nature of things,' and it cannot be derived from the 'laws of nature.' Social order exists *only* as a product of human activity" (1966, 52). **Social construction theory** suggests that what we see as real (in this case, cultural categories of difference and systems of inequality) is the result of human interaction. Through such interaction we create aspects of our culture, objectify them, internalize them, and then take these cultural products for granted. A suitable companion to critical thinking, social construction theory encourages us to ask new questions but does not imply a particular answer. Using a critical thinking framework based on the notion of social construction requires that we be committed to asking questions and challenging assumptions that impair our ability even to imagine these questions.

Adopting a framework based on social construction theory means understanding that we are not born with a sense of what it means to be identified based on or sex; with a disability or not; Black, *Latina/o/x*, Asian, white, or Indigenous; gay, straight, asexual, or bisexual; or rich, working class, poor, or middle class. We learn about these categories through social interaction, and we are given meanings and values for these categories by our social institutions, peers, and families. What we learn depends on the culture in which we live as well as on our place within that culture. Further, how we are defined by our culture often determines how we experience our social world. As W. I. Thomas noted, if we "define situations as real, they are real in their consequences" ([1931] 1966, 301). For example, when we define one group as inferior to another, this does not make that group inferior, yet it may result in the group being experienced as inferior. To illustrate this, consider the vicious cycle that results from the assignment of substandard resources to people who are poor. For example, low-income housing is generally located in geographic areas that lack quality resources such as good public schools and access to adequate health care. Lacking such quality resources results in further social disadvantage, which can perpetuate the poverty of this group. Thus, although reality is initially *soft* as it is constructed, it can become *hard* in its effects. We will examine these effects throughout this text.

According to Berger and Luckmann (1966), reality is socially constructed in three stages. In the first stage, **externalization**, we create cultural products through social interaction. These cultural products may be material artifacts, social institutions, or values or beliefs concerning a particular group. When these products are created, they become "external" to those who have produced them; they become products outside ourselves. For example, as Judith Lorber describes in Reading 7, "The Social Construction of Gender," the construction of gender identity starts at birth with placement within a sex category (male or female). Through dress and adornment, others become aware of the sex of the child and they treat the child according to the gendered expectations they have for that particular sex. Children then behave and respond differently because of the different treatment they receive. A situation defined as real thus becomes real in its consequences. Girls and boys are taught to act differently from each other and thus *do* act differently. As a result, boys and girls are seen as *being* different from each other.

A second example of externalization can be found in the first reading, "Racial Formations," by Michael Omi and Howard Winant. They note that the concept of race has varied over history and is subject to a great deal of debate. Using the term **racial formation**, they describe "the process by which social, economic, and political forces determine the content and importance of racial categories, and by which they shape racial meanings." The example cited at the beginning of this essay clearly illustrates the social forces involved in determining racial categories. The recognition of a multiracial identity involves more than individuals being identified as multiracial. Rather, interaction that takes place at the social, economic, and political levels serves to construct such categories of race.

The second stage, **objectivation**, occurs when the products created in the first stage appear to take on a reality of their own, becoming independent of those who created them. People lose awareness that they themselves are the authors of their social and cultural environment and of their interpretations of reality. They feel as if the products have an objective existence, and they become another part of reality to be taken for granted. For example, most of us take race categories for granted, employing an essentialist perspective that views race categories as the result of biological or genetic factors. However, as mentioned earlier, a variety of social, economic, and political forces are involved in the construction of race categories. When we forget our part in the social construction of race or fail to recognize the social forces that operate to construct race categories and the meanings associated with them, these categories take on objective realities.

The objective realities that many of us attribute to racial categories can be seen in the findings of the 2010 census conducted by the US Census Bureau. Nationwide, just under 3 percent of respondents identified themselves as being of mixed race. The reasons for such a low response rate vary from a lack of knowledge of the options to a strong identification with one race, regardless of one's multiracial heritage. These findings demonstrate that most respondents hold on to what they see as the objective reality of clear and mutually exclusive race categories.

In the final stage, **internalization**, we learn the supposedly objective facts about the cultural products that have been created. This occurs primarily through **socialization**, the process of social interaction in which one learns the ways of the society and one's specific **roles**—the sets of rules and expectations attached to a social position (or **status**) in that society. In this stage we make these facts part of our subjective consciousness. Because of the process of internalization, members of the same culture share an understanding of reality and rarely question the origins of their beliefs or the processes by which the beliefs arose. For example, as Gregory Mantsios discusses in Reading 5, "Media Magic: Making Class Invisible," the mass media serve as a powerful tool for shaping the way we think. A significant part of our culture, mass media operate as an extremely important socialization mechanism. What we see presented in the mass media, as well as how it is presented, delivers important messages about who and what is or is not valued. Specifically, mass media help us to internalize certain constructs about class in our society, perpetuating a variety of myths. Among these myths are that poverty is not a significant problem in this country, that those who are poor have only themselves to blame, that we are a middle-class society, and that blue-collar and union workers are to blame for declining economic security. As mass media present us with these images, we develop a particular view of the class structure in our country. In addition, we internalize beliefs about members of a specific class (e.g., the poor are lazy) as if they were objective facts. The role of the media in maintaining constructions of difference and the resulting systems of inequality will be explored in Part II of this text.

It is important to note here that viewing cultural products as being produced in stages does not imply that the creation of reality occurs in a neat and overt progression. In some cases, the process of externalization in the creation of a social category is clear. However, the construction of reality is not always such a clear process. Thinking in terms of a cultural product as produced in stages, however, provides a general understanding of how the knowledge that guides our behavior is established and how it becomes a part of culture and common sense. In addition, it is important to be aware that while categories of difference are being constructed and subsequently transformed into systems of inequality, such systems of inequality are often being maintained by the same social forces and practices. To clearly understand how categories of difference become systems of inequality, we begin by examining the processes that construct them. The social factors that serve to maintain these constructs and their corresponding systems of inequality will be examined in detail in Part II.

What Constructs Categories of Difference?

The readings in this text explore how the categories of race, class, gender, and sexuality are socially constructed and transformed into systems of inequality. The preceding in-depth explanation of social construction theory was intended to give us an understanding of how these categories are socially constructed. To thoroughly comprehend this process, however, it is important to understand what social factors are at work in creating these categories.

Simply put, categories of difference are the result of human activity guided by the values of our culture. When parents teach their child how to behave like a lady or act like a gentleman, when one child labels another gay as discussed in the reading "'If You Don't Kiss Me, You're

Dumped': Boys, Boyfriends and Heterosexualised Masculinities in the Primary School" (Reading 11), or when a girl decides to stop playing rough to avoid being labeled a tomboy, each is engaged in the process of creating categories of difference. We take these everyday actions for granted, but they play a fundamental role in how we view the world. The kinds of categories we create, as well as the meanings we give to them, are guided by our cultural values regarding who or what is important.

The process of creating these categories occurs in a variety of contexts that we encounter every day. Perhaps the most significant of these is the **institutional context**. An **institution** is the set of rules and relationships that govern the social activities in which we participate to meet our basic needs. The major social institutions that we will examine are as follows:

The family: responsible for reproducing and socializing and protecting the young, regulating sexual behavior, and providing emotional comfort and support for each of its members

Education: responsible for teaching members of society the knowledge, skills, and values considered most important for survival of the individual and society

The economy: creates, controls, and distributes the human and material resources of a society

The state: possesses the legal power to regulate the behavior of members of that society, as well as the relationship of that society to others

The media: responsible for supplying members of society with information, for reinforcing the policies of other institutions, and for socializing members of society with regard to appropriate ways of behaving and accepted cultural values

From the policies and practices of each of these institutions, influenced by our cultural values, categories of difference are created. Thus, when parents teach their child how to behave like a lady or act like a gentleman, they create categories of difference within the institutional context of the family.

Another context in which we create categories of difference is the **interpersonal context**— our daily interactions with others. In these interactions we rely on common guidelines for behavior (**norms**) to define situations and create these categories. For example, when an individual, operating on stereotypes based on race and ethnicity, labels another a foreigner, she or he is relying on what are assumed images of what is an American. As a result, she or he creates categories of difference within an interpersonal context.

Finally, we create categories of difference in **internal contexts** by internalizing the values and beliefs established in institutional and interpersonal contexts. When a girl decides to stop playing rough to avoid being labeled a tomboy, she is internalizing the ideas of what it means to be a girl that were taught to her by her family as well as her peers.

Constructing Race and Ethnicity

The institution of the state, which determines how the census should be taken and how individuals should be counted, plays an integral role in defining race categories in an institutional context. **Race** denotes a group of people who perceive themselves and are perceived by others as possessing distinctive hereditary traits. **Ethnicity** denotes a group of people who perceive themselves and are perceived by others as sharing cultural traits such as language, religion, family customs, and food preferences. As Omi and Winant illustrate in "Racial Formations," what is important about the construction of race categories is not necessarily our perception of our own race, but the recognition by social institutions of our membership in that race category. Furthermore, racial and ethnic categories are significant in that they are constructed in a hierarchy from superior to inferior. Additionally, as illustrated by Roberto Gonzales in "Learning to Be Illegal" (Reading 3), a person's position in the racial stratification system may shift as policies define and redefine which groups are granted legal status.

Racial categories are also constructed in interpersonal contexts. As Waters discusses in "Optional Ethnicities" (Reading 2), many of us, particularly whites, will ask someone whose race or ethnicity is not immediately apparent, what are you? We do not, however, generally ask such a question of those whom we perceive to be white. Thus, in our efforts to define others we not only attempt to construct distinct racial categories but also create white as an unmarked category and as a standard against which all others are judged.

Finally, race is constructed in internal contexts, where we reinforce those categories and the meanings associated with them within ourselves. This process is particularly evident when a Black, Indigenous, or person of color who is light skinned attempts or desires to "pass" as a white person. Through internalizing the idea that to be other than white is to be less valued, they participate in constructing race categories as well as the meanings associated with them.

Constructing Social Class

The categories of social class are also constructed within institutional contexts. Although we may view social class as a result of how much **income** (wages and salaries from earnings and investments) and **wealth** (the total amount of valuable goods) a person possesses, it is in fact more than this. What class we belong to is determined not only by how much money we have or the material possessions we own, but also by the institutions of our society, including state policies and the structuring of the economy. For example, definitions of poverty created by the government affect the access some members of our society have to certain important resources. The Thrifty Food Plan—the least costly of four nutritionally adequate plans designed by the Department of Agriculture, based on their 1955 Household Food Consumption Survey—demonstrates how the establishment of the **poverty line**, an annual income level below which a person or family was defined as poor and therefore entitled to certain benefits, creates who is seen as poor. The poverty line is problematic, however, in the way it is determined because it relies on material standards of the 1950s rather than contemporary standards. For example, expenses for items we consider essential today—for things such as transportation, childcare, and technology—were not essential costs for families of the 1950s. As a result, while the government determined in 2021 that the poverty line for a family of four was $26,500, a more accurate calculation, employing contemporary standards, would have been closer to $45,000. The more accurate figure would result in doubling if not tripling the number of individuals defined as poor. Additionally, it is important to note that measures such as the poverty line miss a significant aspect of what it means to be poor. Poverty is more than how much money one has; it is also a process of social exclusion (Neal 2004). According to the United Nations, "poverty is more than a shortage of income. It is the denial of opportunities and choices most basic to human development—to lead a long, healthy, creative life and to enjoy a decent standard of living, freedom, dignity, self-esteem, and respect of others" (Townson 2000). When institutions establish definitions and measures, they determine a person's access to resources (i.e., the ability of people living in poverty to receive aid from the government). In this way, constructions of class provide the foundation for a system of inequitably distributed resources. The impact of such a system will be discussed in greater detail later in this text.

In addition to establishing who is poor, institutions such as the economy and its related public policies also function to create a social class stratification system that is increasingly divided by a "wealth gap," as illustrated by Amy Traub, Laura Sullivan, Tatjana Meschede, & Thomas M. Shapiro in "The Asset Value of Whiteness" (Reading 4). Finally, the values that we place on members of social classes are further influenced by social institutions such as the media, as explained by Gregory Mantsios in "Media Magic: Making Class Invisible" (Reading 5). According to Mantsios, those who control the media (i.e., the upper class) can use this institution to create class divisions and to define our attitudes about members of different social classes. Both these articles clearly illustrate that the rules, practices, and policies of social institutions serve to construct categories of class differences and establish a system of class inequality.

Categories of social class are also constructed in interpersonal contexts. We define who is rich, poor, middle class, and so forth in our interactions with others. In addition, we attach meanings to each of these categories. For example, if we see a well-dressed, clean-cut individual driving an expensive car, we not only may judge the individual as belonging to the upper class but also admire them and the class position we assume they have achieved. However, if we observe people purchasing groceries with food stamps and then taking the bus, we not only judge them as poor but also are likely to think less of them as a result of their presumed class. In each instance, we rely on **stereotypes**—rigid, oversimplified, often exaggerated beliefs that are applied both to an entire category of people and to each individual in that category. As a result of stereotypes, we treat individuals according to the values we attribute to these classes.

The individuals in the preceding examples likely would be aware of the assumptions made about them on the basis of their social class. Mantsios illustrates that such stereotypes about class dominate our media. As these individuals internalize these messages, their sense of self-worth is impacted. In addition, these individuals aid in creating categories of class and the meanings associated with them.

Constructing Sex and Gender

Categories of sex and gender are also socially constructed in institutional contexts. This claim may, at first glance, seem strange. A person's sex is generally seen as a biological condition. However, as Judith Lorber in "The Social Construction of Gender" (Reading 7) and Georgiann Davis, Jodie M. Dewey, and Erin L. Murphy in "Giving Sex" (Reading 8) discuss, the categories of male and female are not always sufficient to describe the variety of sexes that exist in reality. For example, individuals born **intersex**—the physical manifestation of genital/genetic/endocrinological differentiation that is viewed as different from the norm—may constitute as many as 4 percent of live births. However, these infants are placed in a program of hormonal and surgical management almost immediately after birth so that they can become "normal" males or females in society. Thus, the institutions of science and medicine and advances in physiology and surgical technology aid in constructing a reality in which there are only two sexes.

What is significant about **sex**—the genetic (and sometimes scientific) determination of male and female—is the corresponding expectations that we place on people occupying these categories with regard to **gender**—the socially defined roles expected of males and females. As Lorber and others clearly explain, gender constructs are created and justified by a variety of institutions, including the family, the state, and the economy. Thus, gender constructs are transformed into a **gender system** in which men and masculinity are at the top of the hierarchy and women and femininity are at the bottom. Our ideas about gender therefore influence the way people are sorted into social positions. For example, our expectations of women to be feminine and our corresponding assumptions about their ability to handle certain kinds of strenuous or stressful work contribute to the underrepresentation of women as chief executive officers and heads of governing bodies. Similarly, our expectations that males be masculine and our corresponding assumption that they are less able to be nurturing contribute to their being less likely to pursue careers as nurses or elementary school teachers, for example. Because such a gendered division of labor is established in a society that is based on **patriarchy**—a form of social organization in which males dominate females—what results is not only a gendered division of labor but also an occupational hierarchy in which the work of men is valued over that of women.

Further examples of how we construct categories of sex and gender are found in interpersonal contexts. We construct these categories by acting out the two polar sex categories and fulfilling the corresponding gendered expectations that have been constructed by the social institutions of the family, education, and others. As West and Zimmerman (1987) note, we do gender through our attempts to define others and through our expectations that others display appropriate gender identity. Similar to the ways in which we view race, we are often frustrated with ambiguities of sex and gender. If the sex/gender of another individual does not fit our expectations of opposite sex categories with corresponding gendered behavior, we often seek to define the person, again asking, what are you? In so doing we aid in the process of constructing a sex/gender system that allows for only two sexes and requires gender categories to be distinct and polar opposites.

Finally, gender is also created in internal contexts. As sociologists studying masculinity have illustrated, males often insecure in their manhood will thus act as bullies to prove their manhood, not only to others but also to themselves. Furthermore, feelings of **alienation** (a sense of not belonging to the culture or the community, as is the case with males fearing they will be labeled sissy if they do not act like men) as well as feelings of **self-alienation** (hatred for one's own position and oneself) play a significant role in how we create these categories within ourselves. As a result, we often perpetuate the ways in which these categories are constructed in other contexts.

Constructing Sexuality

Categories of sexuality are also constructed within institutional contexts. Claims that sexuality is constructed may at first appear as strange as claims of sex being a social construct. Just as we generally recognize only two categories of sex, we often recognize sexuality as existing in only two opposing categories: gay and straight. Furthermore, we tend to see these categories as polar opposites, with one fundamentally different from the other. However, current notions of sexuality are but one way of imagining the social relations of the sexes. Like all of the previously discussed categories, sexuality is a complex yet culturally defined construct. **Sexuality** can involve attraction on a physical, emotional, and social level as well as fantasies, sexual behaviors, and self-identity (Klein 1978). However, just as we may be required to distill our variations in racial and ethnic heritage into one of a few categories, we are often required to place all the varying aspects of our sexuality into one of two categories. Thus, a complex part of who we are becomes socially defined within rigid and limiting constructs.

What is significant about categories of sexuality is that they are transformed into systems of inequality, where one form of sexuality is valued and viewed as more appropriate than others. In the United States, the policies and practices of the federal government have historically recognized some forms of sexuality and not others. For example, the Defense of Marriage Act allowed some states to exclude same-sex couples from the right to marry. Despite the existence of such an act, thirty states had constitutional amendments that banned civil unions, marriage equality, and, in a few instances, any and all legal protection for lesbian and gay families. In 2008, the voters of California passed Proposition 8, the California Marriage Protection Act, which designated that only marriage between a man and a woman is valid or recognized in California. Such actions served to grant access to resources to heterosexuals but deny that access to lesbians and gays, thus creating systems of inequality. In 2015, the US Supreme Court ruled that same-sex couples have the right to marry in all fifty states, nullifying these institutional policies.

We also create different sexuality categories in interpersonal contexts. As Emma Renold notes in "'If You Don't Kiss Me, You're Dumped': Boys, Boyfriends and Heterosexualised Masculinities in the Primary School" (Reading 11), in addition to Kate Bornstein's discussion in "Naming All the Parts" (Reading 10), constructions of sexuality are culturally linked to constructions of gender. Each of these readings illustrates not only how constructions of difference in institutional contexts are reflected in interpersonal interactions, but also how the social construction of one category of difference is generally dependent on the social construction of another. The interrelatedness of various constructions of difference will be addressed later.

We also create categories of sexuality in internal contexts. Again, this is generally done in response to the ways sexuality is defined in the larger society. Our descriptions of sexuality divisions and our own membership in them are determined by the sexual landscape of the culture and what are viewed as appropriate or available categories. As we define ourselves, we perpetuate the ways in which these categories are created in other contexts.

In summary, the construction of categories of difference occurs within a variety of contexts. The readings in Part I illustrate this process. In addition, they demonstrate how the meanings we attach to these categories result in structures of inequality.

Why Categories of Difference?

Often the most difficult aspect of understanding the construction of categories of difference is not the how or the what, but the *why*. We have difficulty understanding why such categories are created and transformed into systems of inequality. Many explanations regarding why categories of difference and their corresponding hierarchies are constructed have been offered from several perspectives.

The readings in Part I offer a variety of explanations. For example, Michael Omi and Howard Winant in "Racial Formations" discuss some of the reasons European explorers created separate categories for the people who were indigenous to the lands that they "discovered." They explain that when the European explorers came upon people who looked different from them, their assumptions about the origin of the human species were called into question. As a result, religious debates regarding creation and whether God created a single species of humanity led to questions about whether the natives of the New World could be "saved," as well as about how they should be treated. By deeming the European settlers children of God and indigenous people *other*, the European settlers not only were able to maintain their worldview but also were able to justify systems of mistreatment, including slavery, coercive labor, and extermination.

Social theorists also offer explanations regarding why elements of social structure work to create systems of stratification. For example, Kingsley Davis and Wilbert Moore (1945) assert, in what has come to be known as the **Davis–Moore thesis**, that social stratification is a universal pattern because it has beneficial consequences for the operation of society. This is the case, they reason, because societal inequality has important functions for social organization. They note that society is a complex system of occupational positions, each of which has a particular importance. Some jobs, they argue, are easy to do (with a little instruction) and can be performed by just about anyone. Others are far more challenging and can only be accomplished by certain people who possess certain scarce talents. Functionally speaking, according to Davis and Moore, the latter positions of high day-to-day responsibility are the most important.

Other social theorists argue, however, that such a perspective is too conservative and fails to point out the inequality and exploitation of such systems of stratification. Thus, they argue that social stratification is a system by which some people gain advantages at the expense of others. Karl Marx ([1859] 1959), for example, contended that systems of class stratification involve inequality and exploitation and are created so that capitalists can maximize their profits. He went on to say that the economy has primary importance as the social institution with the greatest influence on the rest of society. Other institutions also create systems of stratification but do so, in general, to support the operation of the economy.

Still other theorists, such as Marilyn Frye (1983), argue that the social construction of difference is initiated with the purpose of discrimination and **oppression**—a relationship in which the dominant group benefits from systematic abuse, exploitation, and injustice directed at a subordinate group. Thus, the construction of difference is not arbitrary but systematically created and transformed into systems of inequality in an effort to advantage some at the expense of others. The roles of domination and subordination in the construction of difference and the maintenance of inequality will be addressed in greater detail in Part II.

Categories of Difference within a Matrix of Domination

Candace West and Sarah Fenstermaker (1995) note that, although gender, race, and class (and sexuality) involve different attributes and effects, they are comparable devices for creating social inequality. To this point in our discussion we have looked distinctly at the construction of each category of difference—race/ethnicity, social class, sex/gender, and sexuality—yet the similarities in the processes of construction serve to provide a foundation for understanding how their subsequent systems of oppression interconnect. To fully understand the process of transforming difference into inequality, it is necessary to recognize the interrelationships between these systems.

What we have discussed as distinct categories of difference and systems of inequality are, according to hooks (1989), systems of oppression that interconnect in an overarching structure of domination. She argues that oppression based on race, class, gender, and sexuality is part of an interlocking politics of domination which is "a belief in domination, and a belief in the notions of superior and inferior, which are components of all of those systems" (175). Patricia Hill Collins (1991) refers to this interlocking system as a **matrix of domination**. This model provides the framework for our efforts in this text in seeking to understand how categories of difference are transformed into systems of inequality and maintained as systems of oppression. Such a framework will allow us to move beyond simply describing the similarities and differences between various systems of oppression and will help us to focus on how they interconnect. We will thereby be better able to see how each system of oppression relies on the others. The ways in which these systems of oppression rely on each other to maintain inequality will be discussed in detail in Part II.

The matrix of domination also provides a framework that permits us to avoid additive analyses of systems of oppression (e.g., a black woman being viewed as doubly oppressed as a white woman). Such analyses are problematic in that they suggest that oppression can be quantified. Attempts to do this would result in our placing ourselves in competition with one another, arguing over who is more oppressed and which form of oppression is the worst. Such debates generally divide us and prevent us from working toward equality. Viewing oppression and inequality in the form of a matrix of domination enables us to see commonalities in the sources of inequality and thus provides a clearer perspective on how these inequalities should be addressed.

Viewing constructions of difference and corresponding systems of inequality as interconnected also helps us to see how all groups experience both privilege and oppression in one socially constructed system. Each of us has had a life experience that is unique, and each of us has likely experienced both oppression and privilege. As Collins (1991) notes, a person may occupy the position of oppressor, oppressed, or both. The matrix of domination permits us to understand how we all experience both oppression and privilege.

Just as categories of difference are constructed in a variety of contexts, so, too, is the matrix of domination. To thoroughly understand the process of social construction, as well as to understand the matrix of domination, it is important to understand what is constructed, what does the constructing, how these constructs are created, and how their corresponding systems of inequality intersect. As you read the selections in Part I, note the explanations provided by each of the authors and be aware of your reactions to them. These readings will provide you with a framework to better understand contemporary constructions of race/ethnicity, social class, sex/gender, and sexuality in the United States. In addition, by understanding the process of social construction we can be more optimistic in working toward positive social change. If we recognize the processes by which systems of inequality are constructed as interlocking systems of oppression, we can gain a greater understanding of how to deconstruct these systems while constructing systems of equality.

A Final Comment

As stated earlier, this text will help us begin the process of understanding contemporary constructions of race/ethnicity, social class, sex/gender, and sexuality in the United States. A fundamental component to examining these constructs is to think critically. In addition, it is important to employ **empathy**—the ability to identify with the thoughts and experiences of another, although you have not shared those thoughts and experiences. Thus, it is important to remain aware of your own standpoint—your location in society and how that is impacted by your race/ethnicity, social class, sex/gender, sexuality, ability, age, and other personal qualities. As you read about experiences that you have not had or are challenged by perspectives offered by the authors, try not to shut yourself off to what they have to say. Rather, use this challenge as an opportunity to better understand your own ideas. As the process of critical thinking indicates, becoming aware of alternative experiences and perspectives can result in a greater understanding of why we think what we do. Finally, you may find that you come away from this text with more questions than you had on entering. If so, see this as a positive outcome, because it is not only a sign of success in learning to think critically, but also an indication that the process of critical thinking will continue beyond this text.

Note

1. This is most notable in public discourse about the racial identity of the former US president Barack Obama. As the child of Ann Dunham, a white woman from Kansas, and Barack Obama Sr., a man of Lou ethnicity from Nyanza Province, Kenya, former President Obama's multiracial identity is a well-known fact. Nevertheless, he is predominantly recognized as an African American, not a person with a multiracial identity.

References

Berger, Peter L., and Thomas Luckmann. 1966. *The Social Construction of Reality: A Treatise in the Sociology of Knowledge.* New York: Doubleday.

Brookfield, Stephen D. 1987. *Developing Critical Thinkers: Challenging Adults to Explore Alternative Ways of Thinking and Acting.* San Francisco: Jossey–Bass.

Collins, Patricia Hill. 1991. *Black Feminist Thought: Knowledge, Consciousness, and the Politics of Empowerment.* New York: Routledge.

Davis, Kingsley, and Wilbert Moore. 1945. "Some Principles of Stratification." *American Sociological Review* 10 (2): 242–49.

Foster, Eugene A., M. A. Jobling, P. G. Taylor, P. Donnelly, P. De Knijff, Rene Mieremet, T. Zerjal, and C. Tyler-Smith. 1998. "Jefferson Fathered Slave's Last Child." *Nature* 396: 27–28.

Frye, Marilyn. 1983. *The Politics of Reality: Essays in Feminist Theory.* Trumansburg, NY: Crossing Press.

Habermas, Jurgen. 1979. *Communication and the Evolution of Society.* Translated by Thomas McCarthy. Boston: Beacon Press.

hooks, bell. 1989. *Talking Back: Thinking Feminist, Thinking Black.* Boston: South End Press.

Klein, Fritz. 1978. *The Bisexual Option.* New York: Arbor House.

Marx, Karl. (1859) 1959. "A Contribution to the Critique of Political Economy." In Karl Marx and Friedrich Engels, *Marx and Engels: Basic Writings on Politics and Philosophy*, edited by Lewis S. Feurer, 42–46. Garden City, NY: Anchor Books.

Neal, Rusty. 2004. *Voices: Women, Poverty and Homelessness in Canada.* Ottawa: National AntiPoverty Organization.

Sumner, William Graham. (1906) 1959. *Folkways.* New York: Dover.

Thomas, W. I. (1931) 1966. "The Relation of Research to the Social Process." In *W. I. Thomas on Social Organization and Personality*, edited by Morris Janowitz, 289–305. Chicago: University of Chicago Press.

Townson, Monica. 2000. *A Report Card on Women and Poverty.* Ottawa: Canadian Centre for Policy Alternatives.

West, Candace, and Sarah Fenstermaker. 1995. "Doing Difference." *Gender & Society* 9 (1): 8–37.

West, Candace, and Don H. Zimmerman. 1987. "Doing Gender." *Gender & Society* 1 (2): 125–51.

Race and Ethnicity

RACIAL FORMATIONS

* *Michael Omi and Howard Winant*

In the following reading, authors Michael Omi and Howard Winant examine the sociohistorical processes that are involved in constructing what we know as race in the United States. This excerpt from their book *Racial Formations in the United States: From the 1960s to the 1980s* (1986) illustrates the process of social construction explained in the introduction to this section. It is important to note that their explanation of the process of racial formation involves the actions of groups and individuals, as well as changes in social structures and institutions, in constructing racial differences while simultaneously establishing racial inequalities.

In 1982–83, Susie Guillory Phipps unsuccessfully sued the Louisiana Bureau of Vital Records to change her racial classification from black to white. The descendant of an eighteenth-century white planter and a black slave, Phipps was designated "black" in her birth certificate in accordance with a 1970 state law which declared anyone with at least one-thirty-second "Negro blood" to be black. The legal battle raised intriguing questions about the concept of race, its meaning in contemporary society, and its use (and abuse) in public policy. Assistant Attorney General Ron Davis defended the law by pointing out that some type of racial classification was necessary to comply with federal record-keeping requirements and to facilitate programs for the prevention of genetic diseases. Phipps's attorney, Brian Begue, argued that the assignment of racial categories on birth certificates was unconstitutional and that the one-thirty-second designation was inaccurate. He called on a retired Tulane University professor who cited research indicating that most whites have one-twentieth "Negro"

ancestry. In the end, Phipps lost. The court upheld a state law which quantified racial identity, and in so doing affirmed the legality of assigning individuals to specific racial groupings.[1]

The Phipps case illustrates the continuing dilemma of defining race and establishing its meaning in institutional life. Today, to assert that variations in human physiognomy are racially based is to enter a constant and intense debate. *Scientific* interpretations of race have not been alone in sparking heated controversy; *religious* perspectives have done so as well.[2] Most centrally, of course, race has been a matter of *political* contention. This has been particularly true in the United States, where the concept of race has varied enormously over time without ever leaving the center stage of U.S. history.

What Is Race?

Race consciousness, and its articulation in theories of race, is largely a modern phenomenon. When European explorers in the New World "discovered" people who looked different than themselves, these "natives" challenged then existing conceptions of the origins of the human species, and raised disturbing questions as to whether *all* could be considered in the same "family of man."[3] Religious debates flared over the attempt to reconcile the Bible with the existence of "racially distinct" people. Arguments took place over creation itself, as theories of polygenesis questioned whether God had made only one species of humanity ("monogenesis"). Europeans wondered if the natives of the New World were indeed human beings with redeemable souls. At stake were not only the prospects for conversion, but the types of treatment to be accorded them. The expropriation of property, the denial of political rights, the introduction of slavery and other forms of coercive labor, as well as outright extermination, all presupposed a worldview which distinguished Europeans—children of God, human beings, etc.—from "others." Such a worldview was needed to explain why some should be "free" and others enslaved, why some had rights to land and property while others did not. Race, and the interpretation of racial differences, was a central factor in that worldview.

In the colonial epoch science was no less a field of controversy than religion in attempts to comprehend the concept of race and its meaning. Spurred on by the classificatory scheme of living organisms devised by Linnaeus in *Systema Naturae*, many scholars in the eighteenth and nineteenth centuries dedicated themselves to the identification and ranking of variations in humankind. Race was thought of as a *biological* concept, yet its precise definition was the subject of debates which, as we have noted, continue to rage today. Despite efforts ranging from Dr. Samuel Morton's studies of cranial capacity[4] to contemporary attempts to base racial classification on shared gene pools,[5] the concept of race has defied biological definition. . . .

Attempts to discern the *scientific meaning* of race continue to the present day. Although most physical anthropologists and biologists have abandoned the quest for a scientific basis to determine racial categories, controversies have recently flared in the area of genetics and educational psychology. For instance, an essay by Arthur Jensen which argued that hereditary factors shape intelligence not only revived the "nature or nurture" controversy, but raised highly volatile questions about racial equality itself.[6] Clearly the attempt to establish a *biological* basis of race has not been swept into the dustbin of history, but is being resurrected in various scientific arenas. All such attempts seek to remove the concept of race from fundamental social, political, or economic determination. They suggest instead that the truth of race lies in the terrain of innate characteristics, of which skin color and other physical attributes provide only the most obvious, and in some respects most superficial, indicators.

Race as a Social Concept

The social sciences have come to reject biologistic notions of race in favor of an approach which regards race as a *social* concept. Beginning in the eighteenth century, this trend has been slow and uneven, but its direction clear. In the nineteenth century Max Weber discounted biological explanations for racial conflict and instead highlighted the social and political factors which engendered such conflict.[7] The work of pioneering cultural anthropologist Franz Boas was crucial in refuting the scientific racism of the early twentieth century by rejecting the connection between race and culture, and the assumption of a continuum of "higher" and "lower" cultural groups. Within the contemporary social science literature, race is assumed to be a variable which is shaped by broader societal forces.

Race is indeed a pre-eminently *sociohistorical* concept. Racial categories and the meaning of race are given concrete expression by the specific social relations and historical context in which they are embedded. Racial meanings have varied tremendously over time and between different societies.

In the United States, the black/white color line has historically been rigidly defined and enforced. White is seen as a "pure" category. Any racial intermixture makes one "nonwhite." In the movie *Raintree County*, Elizabeth Taylor describes the worst of fates to befall whites as "havin' a little Negra blood in ya'—just one little teeny drop and a person's all

Negra."[8] This thinking flows from what Marvin Harris has characterized as the principle of *hypo-descent:*

> By what ingenious computation is the genetic tracery of a million years of evolution unraveled and each man [sic] assigned his proper social box? In the United States, the mechanism employed is the rule of hypo-descent. This descent rule requires Americans to believe that anyone who is known to have had a Negro ancestor is a Negro. We admit nothing in between. . . . "Hypo-descent" means affiliation with the subordinate rather than the superordinate group in order to avoid the ambiguity of intermediate identity. . . . The rule of hypo-descent is, therefore, an invention, which we in the United States have made in order to keep biological facts from intruding into our collective racist fantasies.[9]

The Susie Guillory Phipps case merely represents the contemporary expression of this racial logic.

By contrast, a striking feature of race relations in the lowland areas of Latin America since the abolition of slavery has been the relative absence of sharply defined racial groupings. No such rigid descent rule characterizes racial identity in many Latin American societies. Brazil, for example, has historically had less rigid conceptions of race, and thus a variety of "intermediate" racial categories exist. Indeed, as Harris notes, "One of the most striking consequences of the Brazilian system of racial identification is that parents and children and even brothers and sisters are frequently accepted as representatives of quite opposite racial types."[10] Such a possibility is incomprehensible within the logic of racial categories in the U.S.

To suggest another example: the notion of "passing" takes on new meaning if we compare various American cultures' means of assigning racial identity. In the United States, individuals who are actually "black" by the logic of hypo-descent have attempted to skirt the discriminatory barriers imposed by law and custom by attempting to "pass" for white.[11] Ironically, these same individuals would not be able to pass for "black" in many Latin American societies.

Consideration of the term "black" illustrates the diversity of racial meanings which can be found among different societies and historically within a given society. In contemporary British politics the term "black" is used to refer to all nonwhites.

Interestingly this designation has not arisen through the racist discourse of groups such as the National Front. Rather, in political and cultural movements, Asian as well as Afro-Caribbean youth are adopting the term as an expression of self-identity.[12] The wide-ranging meanings of "black" illustrate the manner in which racial categories are shaped politically.[13]

The meaning of race is defined and contested throughout society, in both collective action and personal practice. In the process, racial categories themselves are formed, transformed, destroyed, and re-formed. We use the term *racial formation* to refer to the process by which social, economic, and political forces determine the content and importance of racial categories, and by which they are in turn shaped by racial meanings. Crucial to this formulation is the treatment of race as a *central axis* of social relations which cannot be subsumed under or reduced to some broader category or conception.

Racial Ideology and Racial Identity

The seemingly obvious "natural" and "common sense" qualities which the existing racial order exhibits themselves testify to the effectiveness of the racial formation process in constructing racial meanings and racial identities.

One of the first things we notice about people when we meet them (along with their sex) is their race. We utilize race to provide clues about *who* a person is. This fact is made painfully obvious when we encounter someone whom we cannot conveniently racially categorize—someone who is, for example, racially "mixed" or of an ethnic/racial group with which we are not familiar. Such an encounter becomes a source of discomfort and momentarily a crisis of racial meaning. Without a racial identity, one is in danger of having no identity.

Our compass for navigating race relations depends on preconceived notions of what each specific racial group looks like. Comments such as, "Funny, you don't look black," betray an underlying image of what black should be. We also become disoriented when people do not act "black," "Latino," or indeed "white." The content of such stereotypes reveals a series of unsubstantiated beliefs about who these groups are and what "they" are like.[14]

In U.S. society, then, a kind of "racial etiquette" exists, a set of interpretive codes and racial meanings which operate in the interactions of daily life. Rules shaped by our perception of race in a comprehensively racial society determine the "presentation of self,"[15] distinctions of status, and appropriate modes of conduct. "Etiquette" is not mere universal adherence to the dominant group's rules, but a more dynamic combination of these rules with the values and beliefs of subordinated groupings. This racial "subjection" is quintessentially ideological. Everybody learns some combination, some version, of the rules of racial classification, and of their own racial identity, often without obvious teaching or conscious inculcation. Race becomes "common sense"—a way of comprehending, explaining, and acting in the world.

Racial beliefs operate as an "amateur biology," a way of explaining the variations in "human nature."[16] Differences in skin color and other obvious physical characteristics supposedly provide visible clues to differences lurking underneath. Temperament, sexuality, intelligence, athletic ability, aesthetic preferences and so on are presumed to be fixed and discernible from the palpable mark of race. Such diverse questions as our confidence and trust in others (for example, clerks or salespeople, media figures, neighbors), our sexual preferences and romantic images, our tastes in music, films, dance, or sports, and our very ways of talking, walking, eating, and dreaming are ineluctably shaped by notions of race. Skin color "differences" are thought to explain perceived differences in intellectual, physical, and artistic temperaments, and to justify distinct treatment of racially identified individuals and groups.

The continuing persistence of racial ideology suggests that these racial myths and stereotypes cannot be exposed as such in the popular imagination. They are, we think, too essential, too integral, to the maintenance of the U.S. social order. Of course, particular meanings, stereotypes, and myths can change, but the presence of a *system* of racial meanings and stereotypes, of racial ideology, seems to be a permanent feature of U.S. culture.

Film and television, for example, have been notorious in disseminating images of racial minorities which establish for audiences what people from these groups look like, how they behave, and "who they are."[17] The power of the media lies not only in their ability to reflect the dominant racial ideology, but in their capacity to shape that ideology in the first place. D. W. Griffith's epic *Birth of a Nation*, a sympathetic treatment of the rise of the Ku Klux Klan during Reconstruction, helped to generate, consolidate, and "nationalize" images of blacks which had been more disparate (more regionally specific, for example) prior to the film's appearance.[18] In U.S. television, the necessity to define characters in the briefest and most condensed manner has led to the perpetuation of racial caricatures, as racial stereotypes serve as shorthand for scriptwriters, directors and actors, in commercials, etc. Television's tendency to address the "lowest common denominator" in order to render programs "familiar" to an enormous and diverse audience leads it regularly to assign and reassign racial characteristics to particular groups, both minority and majority.

These and innumerable other examples show that we tend to view race as something fixed and immutable—something rooted in "nature." Thus we mask the historical construction of racial categories, the shifting meaning of race, and the crucial role of politics and ideology in shaping race relations. Races do not emerge full-blown. They are the results of diverse historical practices and are continually subject to challenge over their definition and meaning.

Racialization: The Historical Development of Race

In the United States, the racial category of "black" evolved with the consolidation of racial slavery. By the end of the seventeenth century, Africans whose specific identity was Ibo, Yoruba, Fulani, etc., were rendered "black" by an ideology of exploitation based on racial logic—the establishment and maintenance of a "color line." This of course did not occur overnight. A period of indentured servitude which was not rooted in racial logic preceded the consolidation of racial slavery. With slavery, however, a racially based understanding of society was set in motion which resulted in the shaping of a specific *racial* identity not only for the slaves but for the European settlers as well. Winthrop Jordan has observed: "From the initially common term *Christian*, at mid-century there was a marked shift toward the terms *English* and *free*. After about 1680, taking the colonies as a whole, a new term of self-identification appeared—*white*."[19]

We employ the term *racialization* to signify the extension of racial meaning to a previously racially unclassified relationship, social practice, or group. Racialization is an ideological process, a historically specific one. Racial ideology is constructed from pre-existing conceptual (or, if one prefers, "discursive") elements and emerges from the struggles of competing political projects and ideas seeking to articulate similar elements differently. An account of racialization processes that avoids the pitfalls of U.S. ethnic history[20] remains to be written.

Particularly during the nineteenth century, the category of "white" was subject to challenges brought about by the influx of diverse groups who were not of the same Anglo-Saxon stock as the founding immigrants. In the nineteenth century, political and ideological struggles emerged over the classification of Southern Europeans, the Irish, and Jews, among other "non-white" categories.[21] Nativism was only effectively curbed by the institutionalization of a racial order that drew the color line *around*, rather than *within*, Europe.

By stopping short of racializing immigrants from Europe after the Civil War, and by subsequently allowing their assimilation, the American racial order was reconsolidated in the wake of the tremendous challenge placed before it by the abolition of racial slavery.[22] With the end of Reconstruction in 1877, an effective program for limiting the emergent class struggles of the later nineteenth century was forged: the definition of the working class *in racial terms*—as "white." This was not accomplished by any legislative decree or capitalist maneuvering to divide the working class, but rather by white workers themselves. Many of them were recent immigrants, who organized on racial lines as much as on traditionally defined class lines.[23] The Irish on the West Coast, for example, engaged in vicious anti-Chinese race-baiting and committed many pogrom-type assaults on Chinese in the course of consolidating the trade union movement in California.

Thus the very political organization of the working class was in important ways a racial project. The legacy of racial conflicts and arrangements shaped the definition of interests and in turn led to the consolidation of institutional patterns (e.g., segregated unions, dual labor markets, exclusionary legislation) which perpetuated the color line *within* the working class. Selig Perlman, whose study of the development of the labor movement is fairly sympathetic to this process, notes that:

> The political issue after 1877 was racial, not financial, and the weapon was not merely the ballot, but also "direct action"—violence. The anti-Chinese agitation in California, culminating as it did in the Exclusion Law passed by Congress in 1882, was doubtless the most important single factor in the history of American labor, for without it the entire country might have been overrun by Mongolian [sic] labor and *the labor movement might have become a conflict of races instead of one of classes.*[24]

More recent economic transformations in the U.S. have also altered interpretations of racial identities and meanings. The automation of southern agriculture and the augmented labor demand of the postwar boom transformed blacks from a largely rural, impoverished labor force to a largely urban, working-class group by 1970.[25] When boom became bust and liberal welfare statism moved rightwards, the majority of blacks came to be seen, increasingly, as part of the "underclass" as state "dependents" Thus the particularly deleterious effects on blacks of global and national economic shifts (generally rising unemployment rates, changes in the employment structure away from reliance on labor intensive work, etc.) were explained once again in the late 1970s and 1980s (as they had been in the 1940s and mid-1960s) as the result of defective black cultural norms, of familial disorganization, etc.[26] In this way new racial attributions, new racial myths, are affixed to "blacks"[27] Similar changes in racial identity are presently affecting Asians and Latinos, as such economic forces as increasing Third World impoverishment and indebtedness fuel immigration and high interest rates, Japanese competition spurs resentments, and U.S. jobs seem to fly away to Korea and Singapore.[28] . . .

Once we understand that race overflows the boundaries of skin color, superexploitation, social stratification, discrimination and prejudice, cultural domination and cultural resistance, state policy (or of any other particular social relationship we list), once we recognize the racial dimension present to some degree in every identity, institution, and social practice in the United States—once we have done this, it becomes possible to speak of *racial formation*. This recognition is hard-won; there is a continuous temptation to think of race as an *essence*, as something

fixed, concrete and objective, as (for example) one of the categories just enumerated. And there is also an opposite temptation: to see it as a mere illusion, which an ideal social order would eliminate.

In our view it is crucial to break with these habits of thought. The effort must be made to understand race as *an unstable and "decentered" complex of social meanings constantly being transformed by political struggle.* . . .

Notes

1. *San Francisco Chronicle*, 14 September 1982, 19 May 1983. Ironically, the 1970 Louisiana law was enacted to supersede an old Jim Crow statute which relied on the idea of "common report" in determining an infant's race. Following Phipps's unsuccessful attempt to change her classification and have the law declared unconstitutional, a legislative effort arose which culminated in the repeal of the law. See *San Francisco Chronicle*, 23 June 1983.
2. The Mormon church, for example, has been heavily criticized for its doctrine of black inferiority.
3. Thomas F. Gossett notes:

    Race theory . . . had up until fairly modern times no firm hold on European thought. On the other hand, race theory and race prejudice were by no means unknown at the time when the English colonists came to North America. Undoubtedly, the age of exploration led many to speculate on race differences at a period when neither Europeans nor Englishmen were prepared to make allowances for vast cultural diversities. Even though race theories had not then secured wide acceptance or even sophisticated formulation, the first contacts of the Spanish with the Indians in the Americas can now be recognized as the beginning of a struggle between conceptions of the nature of primitive peoples which has not yet been wholly settled. (Thomas F. Gossett, *Race: The History of an Idea in America* [New York: Schocken Books, 1965], p. 16.)

    Winthrop Jordan provides a detailed account of early European colonialists' attitudes about color and race in *White over Black: American Attitudes toward the Negro, 1550–1812* (New York: Norton, 1977 [1968]), pp. 3–43.
4. Pro-slavery physician Samuel George Morton (1799–1851) compiled a collection of 800 crania from all parts of the world which formed the sample for his studies

    of race. Assuming that the larger the size of the cranium translated into greater intelligence, Morton established a relationship between race and skull capacity. Gossett reports that:

    In 1849, one of his studies included the following results: The English skulls in his collection proved to be the largest, with an average cranial capacity of 96 cubic inches. The Americans and Germans were rather poor seconds, both with cranial capacities of 90 cubic inches. At the bottom of the list were the Negroes with 83 cubic inches, the Chinese with 82, and the Indians with 79. (Ibid., p. 74.)

    On Morton's methods, see Stephen J. Gould, "The Finagle Factor," *Human Nature* (July 1978).
5. Definitions of race founded upon a common pool of genes have not held up when confronted by scientific research which suggests that the differences *within* a given human population are greater than those *between* populations. See L. L. Cavalli-Sforza, "The Genetics of Human Populations," *Scientific American* (September 1974), pp. 81–89.
6. Arthur Jensen, "How Much Can We Boost IQ and Scholastic Achievement?" *Harvard Educational Review*, vol. 39 (1969), pp. 1–123.
7. Ernst Moritz Manasse, "Max Weber on Race," *Social Research*, vol. 14 (1947), pp. 191–221.
8. Quoted in Edward D. C. Campbell, Jr., *The Celluloid South: Hollywood and the Southern Myth* (Knoxville: University of Tennessee Press, 1981), pp. 168–70.
9. Marvin Harris, *Patterns of Race in the Americas* (New York: Norton, 1964), p. 56.
10. Ibid., p. 57.
11. After James Meredith had been admitted as the first black student at the University of Mississippi, Harry S. Murphy announced that he, and not Meredith, was the first black student to attend "Ole Miss." Murphy

described himself as black but was able to pass for white and spent nine months at the institution without attracting any notice. (Ibid., p. 56.)

12. A. Sivanandan, "From Resistance to Rebellion: Asian and Afro-Caribbean Struggles in Britain," *Race and Class*, vol. 23, nos. 2–3 (Autumn-Winter 1981).

13. Consider the contradictions in racial status which abound in the country with the most rigidly defined racial categories—South Africa. There a race classification agency is employed to adjudicate claims for upgrading of official racial identity. This is particularly necessary for the "coloured" category. The apartheid system considers Chinese as "Asians" while the Japanese are accorded the status of "honorary whites." This logic nearly detaches race from any grounding in skin color and other physical attributes and nakedly exposes race as a juridical category subject to economic, social, and political influences. (We are indebted to Steve Talbot for clarification of some of these points.)

14. Gordon W. Allport, *The Nature of Prejudice* (Garden City, New York: Doubleday, 1958), pp. 184–200.

15. We wish to use this phrase loosely, without committing ourselves to a particular position on such social psychological approaches as symbolic interactionism, which are outside the scope of this study. An interesting study on this subject is S. M. Lyman and W. A. Douglass, "Ethnicity: Strategies of Individual and Collective Impression Management," *Social Research*, vol. 40, no. 2 (1973).

16. Michael Billig, "Patterns of Racism: Interviews with National Front Members," *Race and Class*, vol. 20, no. 2 (Autumn 1978), pp. 161–79.

17. "Miss San Antonio USA Lisa Fernandez and other Hispanics auditioning for a role in a television soap opera did not fit the Hollywood image of real Mexicans and had to darken their faces before filming." Model Aurora Garza said that their faces were bronzed with powder because they looked too white. "I'm a real Mexican [Garza said] and very dark anyway. I'm even darker right now because I have a tan. But they kept wanting me to make my face darker and darker" (*San Francisco Chronicle*, 21 September 1984). A similar dilemma faces Asian American actors who feel that Asian character lead roles inevitably go to white actors who make themselves up to be Asian. Scores of Charlie Chan films, for example, have been made with white leads (the last one was the 1981 *Charlie Chan and the Curse of the Dragon Queen*). Roland Winters, who played in six Chan features, was asked by playwright Frank Chin to explain the logic of casting a white man in the role of Charlie Chan: "The only thing I can think of is, if you want to cast a homosexual in a show, and you get a homosexual,

it'll be awful. It won't be funny . . . and maybe there's something there . . ." (Frank Chin, "Confessions of the Chinatown Cowboy," *Bulletin of Concerned Asian Scholars*, vol. 4, no. 3 [Fall 1972]).

18. Melanie Martindale-Sikes, "Nationalizing 'Nigger' Imagery Through 'Birth of a Nation,'" paper prepared for the 73rd Annual Meeting of the American Sociological Association, 4–8 September 1978 in San Francisco.

19. Winthrop D. Jordan, op. cit., p. 95; emphasis added.

20. Historical focus has been placed either on particular racially defined groups or on immigration and the "incorporation" of ethnic groups. In the former case the characteristic ethnicity theory pitfalls and apologetics such as functionalism and cultural pluralism may be avoided, but only by sacrificing much of the focus on race. In the latter case, race is considered a manifestation of ethnicity.

21. The degree of antipathy for these groups should not be minimized. A northern commentator observed in the 1850s: "An Irish Catholic seldom attempts to rise to a higher condition than that in which he is placed, while the Negro often makes the attempt with success." Quoted in Gossett, op. cit., p. 288.

22. This analysis, as will perhaps be obvious, is essentially DuBoisian. Its main source will be found in the monumental (and still largely unappreciated) *Black Reconstruction in the United States 1860–1880* (New York: Atheneum, 1977 [1035]).

23. Alexander Saxton argues that:

> North Americans of European background have experienced three great racial confrontations: with the Indian, with the African, and with the Oriental. Central to each transaction has been a totally one-sided preponderance of power, exerted for the exploitation of nonwhites by the dominant white society. In each case (but especially in the two that began with systems of enforced labor), white workingmen have played a crucial, yet ambivalent role. They have been both exploited and exploiters. On the one hand, thrown into competition with nonwhites as enslaved or "cheap" labor, they suffered economically; on the other hand, being white, they benefited by that very exploitation which was compelling the nonwhites to work for low wages or for nothing. Ideologically they were drawn in opposite directions. *Racial identification cut at right angles to class consciousness.* (Alexander Saxton, *The Indispensable Enemy: Labor and the Anti-Chinese Movement in California* [Berkeley and Los Angeles: University of California Press, 1971], p. 1, emphasis added.)

24. Selig Perlman, *The History of Trade Unionism in the United States* (New York: Augustus Kelley, 1950), p. 52; emphasis added.
25. Whether Southern blacks were "peasants" or rural workers is unimportant in this context. Some time during the 1960s blacks attained a higher degree of urbanization than whites. Before World War II most blacks had been rural dwellers and nearly 80 percent lived in the South.
26. See George Gilder, *Wealth and Poverty* (New York: Basic Books, 1981); Charles Murray, *Losing Ground* (New York: Basic Books, 1984).
27. A brilliant study of the racialization process in Britain, focused on the rise of "mugging" as a popular fear in the 1970s, is Stuart Hall et al., *Policing the Crisis* (London: Macmillan, 1978).
28. The case of Vincent Chin, a Chinese American man beaten to death in 1982 by a laid-off Detroit auto worker and his stepson who mistook him for Japanese and blamed him for the loss of their jobs, has been widely publicized in Asian American communities. On immigration conflicts and pressures, see Michael Omi, "New Wave Dread: Immigration and Intra-Third World Conflict," *Socialist Review*, no. 60 (November-December 1981).

Questions for Critical Thinking

1. Does Omi and Winant's discussion of race as a social rather than biological concept help you to see issues of race in new and different ways? If so, how? If not, why not?

2. How does your membership in a particular race category influence your understanding of or level of agreement with the authors' discussion?

3. Considering the authors' discussion, do you think it is possible or desirable to move beyond racial divisions?

OPTIONAL ETHNICITIES

For Whites Only?

- *Mary C. Waters*

This second reading, by sociologist Mary C. Waters, illustrates how, like race, ethnicity is a social construct, not a biological one. Drawing on her field research with suburban whites, she explains the concept of symbolic ethnicity—an ethnicity that is individualistic in its origin and without real social cost for the person. However, as she explains, such a choice is not available to all, and understanding ethnicity as an individual choice may make us unaware of the ongoing discrimination experienced by people of color.

Ethnic Identity for Whites in the 1990s

What does it mean to talk about ethnicity as an option for an individual? To argue that an individual has some degree of choice in their ethnic identity flies in the face of the common sense notion of ethnicity many of us believe in—that one's ethnic identity is a fixed characteristic, reflective of blood ties and given at birth. However, social scientists who study ethnicity have long concluded that while ethnicity is based in a *belief* in a common ancestry, ethnicity is primarily a *social* phenomenon, not a biological one (Alba 1985, 1990; Barth 1969; Weber [1921] 1968, p. 389). The belief that members of an ethnic group have that they share a common ancestry may not be a fact. There is a great deal of change in ethnic identities across generations through intermarriage, changing allegiances, and changing social categories. There is also a much larger amount of change in the identities of individuals over their life than is commonly believed. While most people are aware of the phenomenon known as

"passing"—people raised as one race who change at some point and claim a different race as their identity—there are similar life course changes in ethnicity that happen all the time and are not given the same degree of attention as "racial passing."

White Americans of European ancestry can be described as having a great deal of choice in terms of their ethnic identities. The two major types of options White Americans can exercise are (1) the option of whether to claim any specific ancestry, or to just be "White" or American (Lieberson [1985] called these people "unhyphenated Whites"), and (2) the choice of which of their European ancestries to choose to include in their description of their own identities. In both cases, the option of choosing how to present yourself on surveys and in everyday social interactions exists for Whites because of social changes and societal conditions that have created a great deal of social mobility, immigrant assimilation, and political and economic power for Whites in the United States. Specifically, the option of being able to not claim any ethnic identity exists for Whites of European background in the United States because they are the majority group—in terms of holding political and social power, as well as being a numerical majority. The option of choosing among different ethnicities in their family backgrounds exists because the degree of discrimination and social distance attached to specific European backgrounds has diminished over time.

The Ethnic Miracle

When European immigration to the United States was sharply curtailed in the late 1920s, a process was set in motion whereby the European ethnic groups already in the United States were for all intents and purposes cut off from any new arrivals. As a result, the composition of the ethnic groups began to age generationally. The proportion of each ethnic group made up of immigrants or the first generation began to gradually decline, and the proportion made up of the children, grandchildren, and eventually great-grandchildren began to increase. Consequently, by 1990 most European-origin ethnic groups in the United States were composed of a very small number of immigrants, and a very large proportion of people whose link to their ethnic origins in Europe was increasingly remote.

This generational change was accompanied by unprecedented social and economic changes. The very success of the assimilation process these groups experienced makes it difficult to imagine how much the question of the immigrants' eventual assimilation was an open one at the turn of the century. At the peak of immigration from southern and central Europe there was widespread discrimination and hostility against the newcomers by established Americans. Italians, Poles, Greeks, and Jews were called derogatory names, attacked by nativist mobs, and derided in the press. Intermarriage across ethnic lines was very uncommon—castelike in the words of some sociologists (Pagnini and Morgan 1990). The immigrants and their children were residentially segregated, occupationally specialized, and generally poor.

After several generations in the United States, the situation has changed a great deal. The success and social mobility of the grandchildren and great-grandchildren of that massive wave of immigrants from Europe has been called "The Ethnic Miracle" (Greeley 1976). These Whites have moved away from the inner-city ethnic ghettos to White middle-class suburban homes. They are doctors, lawyers, entertainers, academics, governors, and Supreme Court justices. But contrary to what some social science theorists and some politicians predicted or hoped for, these middle-class Americans have not completely given up ethnic identity. Instead, they have maintained some connection with their immigrant ancestors' identities—becoming Irish American doctors, Italian American Supreme Court justices, and Greek American presidential candidates. In the tradition of cultural pluralism, successful middle-class Americans in the late twentieth century maintain some degree of identity with their ethnic backgrounds. They have remained "hyphenated Americans." So while social mobility and declining discrimination have created the option of not identifying with any European ancestry, most White Americans continue to report some ethnic background.

With the growth in intermarriage among people of European ethnic origins, increasingly these people are of mixed ethnic ancestry. This gives them the option of which ethnicity to identify with. The U.S. census has asked a question on ethnic ancestry in the 1980 and 1990 censuses. In 1980, 52 percent of the American public responded with a single ethnic ancestry, 31 percent gave multiple ethnic origins (up to three were coded, but some individuals wrote in more than three), and only 6 percent said they were American only, while the remaining 11 percent gave no response. In 1990 about 90 percent of the population gave some response to the ancestry question, with only 5 percent giving American as a response and only 1.4 percent reporting an uncodeable response such as "don't know" (McKenney and Cresce 1992; U.S. Bureau of the Census 1992).

Several researchers have examined the pattern of responses of people to the census ancestry question. These analyses have shown a pattern of flux and inconsistency in ethnic ancestry reporting. For instance, Lieberson and Waters (1986, 1988, p. 93) have found that parents simplify children's ancestries when reporting them to the census. For instance, among the offspring in situations where one parent reports a specific single White ethnic origin and the other parent reports a different single White origin, about 40 percent of the children are not described as the logical combination of the parents' ancestries. For example, only about 60 percent of the children of English-German marriages are labeled as English-German or German-English. About 15 percent of the children of these parents are simplified to just English, and another 15 percent are reported as just German. The remainder of the children are either not given an ancestry or are described as American (Lieberson and Waters 1986, 1993).

In addition to these intergenerational changes, researchers have found changes in reporting ancestry that occur at the time of marriage or upon leaving home. At the ages of eighteen to twenty-two, when many young Americans leave home for the first time, the number of people reporting a single as opposed to a multiple ancestry goes up. Thus while parents simplify children's ancestries when they leave home, children themselves tend to report less complexity in their ancestries when they leave their parents' homes and begin reporting their ancestries themselves (Lieberson and Waters 1986, 1988; Waters 1990).

These individual changes are reflected in variability over time in the aggregate numbers of groups determined by the census and surveys. Fairly (1991) compared the consistency of the overall counts of different ancestry groups in the 1979 Current Population Survey, the 1980 census, and the 1986 National Content Test (a pretest for the 1990 census). He found much less consistency in the numbers for northern European ancestry groups whose immigration peaks were early in the nineteenth century—the English, Dutch, Germans, and other northern European groups. In other words each of these different surveys and the census yielded a different estimate of the number of people having this ancestry. The 1990 census also showed a great deal of flux and inconsistency in some ancestry groups. The number of people reporting English as an ancestry went down considerably from 1980, while the number reporting German

ancestry went up. The number of Cajuns grew dramatically. This has led officials at the Census Bureau to assume that the examples used in the instructions strongly influence the responses people give. (Cajun was one of the examples of an ancestry given in 1990 but not in 1980, and German was the first example given. English was an example in the 1980 instructions, but not in 1990.)

All of these studies point to the socially variable nature of ethnic identity—and the lack of equivalence between ethnic ancestry and identity. If merely adding a category to the instructions to the question increases the number of people claiming that ancestry, what does that mean about the level of importance of that identity for people answering the census? Clearly identity and ancestry for Whites in the United States, who increasingly are from mixed backgrounds, involve some change and choice.

Symbolic Ethnicities for White Americans
What do these ethnic identities mean to people and why do they cling to them rather than just abandoning the tie and calling themselves American? My own field research with suburban Whites in California and Pennsylvania found that later-generation descendants of European origin maintain what are called "symbolic ethnicities" Symbolic ethnicity is a term coined by Herbert Gans (1979) to refer to ethnicity that is individualistic in nature and without real social cost for the individual. These symbolic identifications are essentially leisure time activities, rooted in nuclear family traditions and reinforced by the voluntary enjoyable aspects of being ethnic (Waters 1990). Richard Alba (1990) also found later-generation Whites in Albany, New York, who chose to keep a tie with an ethnic identity because of the enjoyable and voluntary aspects to those identities, along with the feelings of specialness they entailed. An example of symbolic ethnicity is individuals who identify as Irish, for example, on occasions such as Saint Patrick's Day, on family holidays, or for vacations. They do not usually belong to Irish American organizations, live in Irish neighborhoods, work in Irish jobs, or marry other Irish people. The symbolic meaning of being Irish American can be constructed by individuals from mass media images, family traditions, or other

intermittent social activities. In other words, for later-generation White ethnics, ethnicity is not something that influences their lives unless they want it to. In the world of work and school and neighborhood, individuals do not have to admit to being ethnic unless they choose to. And for an increasing number of European-origin individuals whose parents and grandparents have intermarried, the ethnicity they claim is largely a matter of personal choice as they sort through all of the possible combinations of groups in their genealogies.

Individuals can choose those aspects of being Italian, for instance, that appeal to them, and discard those that do not. Or a person whose father is Italian, and mother part Polish and part French, might choose among the three ethnicities and present herself as a Polish American. With just a little probing, many people will describe a variety of ancestries in their family background, but do not consider these ancestries to be a salient part of their own identities. Thus the 1990 census ancestry question, which estimated that 30 percent of the population is of mixed ancestry, most surely underestimates the degree of mixing among the population. My research, and the research of Richard Alba (1990), shows that many people have already sorted through what they know of their ethnic ancestries and simplified their responses before they ever answer a census or survey question (Waters 1990).

But note that this freedom to include or exclude ancestries in your identification to yourself and others would not be the same for those defined racially in our society. They are constrained to identify with the part of their ancestry that has been socially defined as the "essential" part. African Americans, for example, have been highly socially constrained to identify as Blacks, without other options available to them, even when they know that their forebears included many people of American Indian or European background. Up until the mid-twentieth century, many state governments had specific laws defining one as Black if as little as one-thirty-second of one's ancestors were defined as Black (Davis 1991; Dominguez 1986; Spickard 1989). Even now when the one-drop rule has been dropped from our legal codes, there are still strong societal pressures on African Americans to identify

in a particular way. Certain ancestries take precedence over others in the societal rules on descent and ancestry reckoning. If one believes one is part English and part German and identifies in a survey as German, one is not in danger of being accused of trying to "pass" as non-English and of being "redefined" English by the interviewer. But if one were part African and part German, one's self-identification as German would be highly suspect and probably not accepted if one "looked" Black according to the prevailing social norms.

This is reflected in the ways the census collects race and ethnic identity. While the ethnic ancestry question used in 1980 and 1990 is given to all Americans in the sample regardless of race and allows multiple responses that combine races, the primary source of information on people defined racially in the United States is the census race question or the Hispanic question. Both of these questions require a person to make a choice about an identity. Individuals are not allowed to respond that they are both Black and White, or Japanese and Asian Indian on the race question even if they know that is their background. In fact, people who disobey the instructions to the census race question and check off two races are assigned to the first checked race in the list by the Census Bureau.

In responding to the ancestry question, the comparative latitude that White respondents have does not mean that Whites pick and choose ethnicities out of thin air. For the most part people choose an identity that corresponds with some element of their family tree. However, there are many anecdotal instances of people adopting ethnicities when they marry or move to a strongly identified neighborhood or community. For instance Micaela di Leonardo (1984) reported instances of non-Italian women who married into Italian American families and "became Italian." Karen Leonard (1992) describes a community of Mexican American women who married Punjabi immigrants in California. Some of the Punjabi immigrants and their descendants were said to have "become Mexican" when they joined their wives' kin group and social worlds. Alternatively she describes the community acknowledging that Mexican women made the best curry, as they adapted to life with Indian-origin men.

But what do these identities mean to individuals? Surely an identity that is optional in a number of ways—not legally defined on a passport or birth certificate, not socially consequential in terms of societal discrimination in terms of housing or job access, and not economically limiting in terms of blocking opportunities for social mobility—cannot be the same as an identity that results from and is nurtured by societal exclusion and rejection. The choice to have a symbolic ethnicity is an attractive and widespread one despite its lack of demonstrable content, because having a symbolic ethnicity combines individuality with feelings of community. People reported to me that they liked having an ethnic identity because it gave them a uniqueness and a feeling of being special. They often contrasted their own specialness by virtue of their ethnic identities with "bland" American-ness. Being ethnic makes people feel unique and special and not just "vanilla," as one of my respondents put it.

Because "American" is largely understood by Americans to be a political identity and allegiance and not an ethnic one, the idea of being "American" does not give people the same sense of belonging that their hyphenated American identity does. When I asked people about their dual identities—American and Irish or Italian or whatever—they usually responded in a way that showed how they conceived of the relationship between the two identities. Being an American was their primary identity; but it was so primary that they rarely, if ever, thought about it—most commonly only when they left the country. Being Irish American, on the other hand, was a way they had of differentiating themselves from others whom they interacted with from day to day—in many cases from spouses or in-laws. Certain of their traits—being emotional, having a sense of humor, talking with their hands—were understood as stemming from their ethnicity. Yet when asked about their identity as Americans, that identity was both removed from their day-to-day consciousness and understood in terms of loyalty and patriotism. Although they may not think they behave or think in a certain way because they are American, being American is something they are both proud of and committed to.

Symbolic ethnicity is the best of all worlds for these respondents. These White ethnics can claim to be unique and special, while simultaneously finding the community and conformity with others that they also crave. But that "community" is of a type that will not interfere with a person's individuality. It is not as if these people belong to ethnic voluntary organizations or gather as a group in churches or neighborhoods or union halls. They work and reside within the mainstream of American middle-class life, yet they retain the interesting benefits—the "specialness"—of ethnic allegiance, without any of its drawbacks.

It has been suggested by several researchers that this positive value attached to ethnic ancestry, which became popular in the ethnic revival of the 1970s, is the result of assimilation having proceeded to an advanced stage for descendants of White Europeans (Alba 1985; Crispino 1980; Steinberg 1981). Ironically, people celebrate and embrace their ethnic backgrounds precisely because assimilation has proceeded to the point where such identification does not have that much influence on their day-to-day life. Rather than choosing the "least ethnic" and most bland ethnicities, Whites desire the "most ethnic" ones, like the once-stigmatized "Italian," because it is perceived as bringing the most psychic benefits. For instance, when an Italian father is married to an English or a Scottish or a German mother, the likelihood is that the child will be reported to the census with the father's Italian ancestry, rather than the northern European ancestries, which would have been predicted to have a higher social status. Italian is a good ancestry to have, people told me, because they have good food and a warm family life. This change in the social meaning of being Italian American is quite dramatic, given that Italians were subject to discrimination, exclusion, and extreme negative stereotyping in the early part of the twentieth century.

Race Relations and Symbolic Ethnicity

However much symbolic ethnicity is without cost for the individual, there is a cost associated with symbolic ethnicity for the society. That is because symbolic ethnicities of the type described here are confined to White Americans of European origin. Black Americans, Hispanic Americans, Asian Americans, and American Indians do not have the option of a symbolic ethnicity at present in the United States. For all of the ways in which ethnicity does not matter for White Americans, it does matter for non-Whites. Who your ancestors are does affect your choice of spouse, where you live, what job you have, who your friends are, and what your chances are for success in American society, if those ancestors happen not to be from Europe. The reality is that White ethnics have a lot more choice and room to maneuver than they themselves think they do. The situation is very different for members of racial minorities, whose lives are strongly influenced by their race or national origin regardless of how much they may choose not to identify themselves in terms of their ancestries.

When White Americans learn the stories of how their grandparents and great-grandparents triumphed in the United States over adversity, they are usually told in terms of their individual efforts and triumphs. The important role of labor unions and other organized political and economic actors in their social and economic successes is left out of the story in favor of a generational story of individual Americans rising up against communitarian, Old World intolerance, and New World resistance. As a result, the "individualized" voluntary, cultural view of ethnicity for Whites is what is remembered.

One important implication of these identities is that they tend to be very individualistic. There is a tendency to view valuing diversity in a pluralist environment as equating all groups. The symbolic ethnic tends to think that all groups are equal; everyone has a background that is their right to celebrate and pass on to their children. This leads to the conclusion that all identities are equal and all identities in some sense are interchangeable—"I'm Italian American, you're Polish American. I'm Irish American, you're African American." The important thing is to treat people as individuals and all equally. However, this assumption ignores the very big difference between an individualistic symbolic ethnic identity and a socially enforced and imposed racial identity. When White Americans equate their own symbolic ethnicities with the socially enforced identities of non-White Americans, they obscure the fact that the experiences of Whites and non-Whites have been

qualitatively different in the United States and that the current identities of individuals partly reflect that unequal history.

In the next section I describe how relations between Black and White students on college campuses reflect some of these asymmetries in the understanding of what a racial or ethnic identity means. While I focus on Black and White students in the following discussion, you should be aware that the myriad other groups in the United States—Mexican Americans, American Indians, Japanese Americans—all have some degree of social and individual influences on their identities, which reflect the group's social and economic history and present circumstance.

Relations on College Campuses

Both Black and White students face the task of developing their race and ethnic identities. Sociologists and psychologists note that at the time people leave home and begin to live independently from their parents, often ages eighteen to twenty-two, they report a heightened sense of racial and ethnic identity as they sort through how much of their beliefs and behaviors are idiosyncratic to their families and how much are shared with other people. It is not until one comes in close contact with many people who are different from oneself that individuals realize the ways in which their backgrounds may influence their individual personality. This involves coming into contact with people who are different in terms of their ethnicity, class, religion, region, and race. For White students, the ethnicity they claim is more often than not a symbolic one—with all of the voluntary, enjoyable, and intermittent characteristics I have described above.

Black students at the university are also developing identities through interactions with others who are different from them. Their identity development is more complicated than that of Whites because of the added element of racial discrimination and racism, along with the "ethnic" developments of finding others who share their background. Thus Black students have the positive attraction of being around other Black students who share some cultural elements, as well as the need to band together with other students in a reactive and oppositional way in the face of racist incidents on campus.

Colleges and universities across the country have been increasing diversity among their student bodies in the last few decades. This had led in many cases to strained relations among students from different racial and ethnic backgrounds. The 1980s and 1990s produced a great number of racial incidents and high racial tensions on campuses. While there were a number of racial incidents that were due to bigotry, unlawful behavior, and violent or vicious attacks, much of what happens among students on campuses involves a low level of tension and awkwardness in social interactions.

Many Black students experience racism personally for the first time on campus. The upper-middle-class students from White suburbs were often isolated enough that their presence was not threatening to racists in their high schools. Also, their class background was known by their residence and this may have prevented attacks being directed at them. Often Black students at the university who begin talking with other students and recognizing racial slights will remember incidents that happened to them earlier that they might not have thought were related to race.

Black college students across the country experience a sizeable number of incidents that are clearly the result of racism. Many of the most blatant ones that occur between students are the result of drinking. Sometimes late at night, drunken groups of White students coming home from parties will yell slurs at single Black students on the street. The other types of incidents that happen include being singled out for special treatment by employees, such as being followed when shopping at the campus bookstore, or going to the art museum with your class and the guard stops you and asks for your I.D. Others involve impersonal encounters on the street—being called a nigger by a truck driver while crossing the street, or seeing old ladies clutch their pocketbooks and shake in terror as you pass them on the street. For the most part these incidents are not specific to the university environment; they are the types of incidents middle-class Blacks face every day throughout American society, and they have been documented by sociologists (Feagin 1991).

In such a climate, however, with students experiencing these types of incidents and talking with each other about them, Black students do experience a tension and a feeling of being singled out. It is unfair that this is part of their college experience and not that of White students. Dealing with incidents like this, or the ever-present threat of such incidents, is an ongoing developmental task for Black students that takes energy, attention, and strength of character. It should be clearly understood that this is an asymmetry in the "college experience" for Black and White students. It is one of the unfair aspects of life that results from living in a society with ongoing racial prejudice and discrimination. It is also very understandable that it makes some students angry at the unfairness of it all, even if there is no one to blame specifically. It is also very troubling because, while most Whites do not create these incidents, some do, and it is never clear until you know someone well whether they are the type of person who could do something like this. So one of the reactions of Black students to these incidents is to band together.

In some sense then, as Blauner (1992) has argued, you can see Black students coming together on campus as both an "ethnic" pull of wanting to be together to share common experiences and community, and a "racial" push of banding together defensively because of perceived rejection and tension from Whites. In this way the ethnic identities of Black students are in some sense similar to, say, Korean students wanting to be together to share experiences. And it is an ethnicity that is generally much stronger than, say, Italian Americans. But for Koreans who come together there is generally a definition of themselves as "different from" Whites. For Blacks reacting to exclusion, there is a tendency for the coming together to involve both being "different from" but also "opposed to" Whites.

The anthropologist John Ogbu (1990) has documented the tendency of minorities in a variety of societies around the world, who have experienced severe blocked mobility for long periods of time, to develop such oppositional identities. An important component of having such an identity is to describe others of your group who do not join in the group solidarity as devaluing and denying their very core identity. This is why it is not common for successful Asians to be accused by others of "acting White" in the United States, but it is quite common for such a term to be used by Blacks and Latinos. The oppositional component of a Black identity also explains how Black people can question whether others are acting "Black enough." On campus, it explains some of the intense pressures felt by Black students who do not make their racial identity central and who choose to hang out primarily with non-Blacks. This pressure from the group, which is partly defining itself by not being White, is exacerbated by the fact that race is a physical marker in American society. No one immediately notices the Jewish students sitting together in the dining hall, or the one Jewish student sitting surrounded by non-Jews, or the Texan sitting with the Californians, but everyone notices the Black student who is or is not at the "Black table" in the cafeteria.

Institutional Responses

Our society asks a lot of young people. We ask young people to do something that no one else does as successfully on such a wide scale—that is to live together with people from very different backgrounds, to respect one another, to appreciate one another, and to enjoy and learn from one another. The successes that occur every day in this endeavor are many, and they are too often overlooked. However, the problems and tensions are also real, and they will not vanish on their own. We tend to see pluralism working in the United States in much the same way some people expect capitalism to work. If you put together people with various interests and abilities and resources, the "invisible hand" of capitalism is supposed to make all the parts work together in an economy for the common good.

There is much to be said for such a model—the invisible hand of the market can solve complicated problems of production and distribution better than any "visible hand" of a state plan. However, we have learned that unequal power relations among the actors in the capitalist marketplace, as well as

"externalities" that the market cannot account for, such as long-term pollution, or collusion between corporations, or the exploitation of child labor, means that state regulation is often needed. Pluralism and the relations between groups are very similar. There is a lot to be said for the idea that bringing people who belong to different ethnic or racial groups together in institutions with no interference will have good consequences. Students from different backgrounds will make friends if they share a dorm room or corridor, and there is no need for the institution to do any more than provide the locale. But like capitalism, the invisible hand of pluralism does not do well when power relations and externalities are ignored. When you bring together individuals from groups that are differentially valued in the wider society and provide no guidance, there will be problems. In these cases the "invisible hand" of pluralist relations does not work, and tensions and disagreements can arise without any particular individual or group of individuals being "to blame." On college campuses in the 1990s some of the tensions between students are of this sort. They arise from honest misunderstandings, lack of a common background, and very different experiences of what race and ethnicity mean to the individual.

The implications of symbolic ethnicities for thinking about race relations are subtle but consequential. If your understanding of your own ethnicity and its relationship to society and politics is one of individual choice, it becomes harder to understand the need for programs like affirmative action, which recognize the ongoing need for group struggle and group recognition, in order to bring about social change. It also is hard for a White college student to understand the need that minority students feel to band together against discrimination. It also is easy, on the individual level, to expect everyone else to be able to turn their ethnicity on and off at will, the way you are able to, without understanding that ongoing discrimination and societal attention to minority status makes that impossible for individuals from minority groups to do. The paradox of symbolic ethnicity is that it depends upon the ultimate goal of a pluralist society, and at the same time makes it more difficult to achieve that ultimate goal. It is dependent upon the concept that all ethnicities mean the same thing, that enjoying the traditions of one's heritage is an option available to a group or an individual, but that such a heritage should not have any social costs associated with it.

There are many societal issues and involuntary ascriptions associated with non-White identities. The developments necessary for this to change are not individual but societal in nature. Social mobility and declining racial and ethnic sensitivity are closely associated. The legacy and the present reality of discrimination on the basis of race or ethnicity must be overcome before the ideal of the pluralist society, where all heritages are treated equally and are equally available for individuals to choose or discard at will, is realized.

References

Alba, Richard D. 1985. *Italian Americans: Into the Twilight of Ethnicity.* Englewood Cliffs, NJ: Prentice-Hall.

Alba, Richard D. 1990. *Ethnic Identity: The Transformation of White America.* New Haven, CT: Yale University Press.

Barth, Frederik. 1969. *Ethnic Groups and Boundaries.* Boston: Little, Brown.

Blauner, Robert. 1992. "Talking Past Each Other: Black and White Languages of Race." *American Prospect* (Summer) 61(10):55–64.

Crispino, James. 1980. *The Assimilation of Ethnic Groups: The Italian Case.* Staten Island, NY: Center for Migration Studies.

Davis, F. James. 1991. *Who Is Black. One Nation's Definition.* University Park: Pennsylvania State University Press.

di Leonardo, Micaela. 1984. *The Varieties of Ethnic Experience: Kinship, Class and Gender among Italian Americans.* Ithaca, NY: Cornell University Press.

Dominguez, Virginia. 1986. *White by Definition: Social Classification in Creole Louisiana.* New Brunswick, NJ: Rutgers University Press.

Fairly, Reynolds. 1991. "The New Census Questions about Ancestry: What Did It Tell Us?" *Demography* 28:411–29.

Feagin, Joe R. 1991. "The Continuing Significance of Race: Antiblack Discrimination in Public Places." *American Sociological Review* 56:101–17.

Gans, Herbert. 1979. "Symbolic Ethnicity: The Future of Ethnic Groups and Cultures in America." *Ethnic and Racial Studies* 2:1–20.

Greeley, Andrew M. 1976. "The Ethnic Miracle." *Public Interest* 45 (Fall):20–36.

Leonard, Karen. 1992. *Making Ethnic Choices: California's Punjabi Mexican Americans.* Philadelphia: Temple University Press.

Lieberson, Stanley. 1985. "Unhyphenated Whites in the United States." *Ethnic and Racial Studies* 8:159–80.

Lieberson, Stanley, and Mary Waters, 1986. "Ethnic Groups in Flux: The Changing Ethnic Responses of American Whites." *Annals of the American Academy of Political and Social Science* 487:79–91.

—————. 1988. *From Many Strands: Ethnic and Racial Groups in Contemporary America.* New York: Russell Sage.

—————. 1993. "The Ethnic Responses of Whites: What Causes Their Instability, Simplification, and Inconsistency?" *Social Forces* 72(2):421–50.

McKenney, Nampeo R., and Arthur R. Cresce. 1992. "Measurement of Ethnicity in the United States: Experiences of the U.S. Census Bureau." Paper presented at the Joint Canada-United States Conference on the Measurement of Ethnicity, Ottawa, Canada, April 1–3.

Ogbu, John U. 1990. "Minority Education in Comparative Perspective." *Journal of Negro Education* 59(1): 45–57.

Pagnini, Deanna L. and S. Philip Morgan. 1990. "Intermarriage and Social Distance among U.S. Immigrants at the turn of the Century." *American Journal of Sociology* 96 (2): 405–32.

Spickard, Paul R. 1989. *Mixed Blood.* Madison: University of Wisconsin Press.

Steinberg, Stephen. 1981. *The Ethnic Myth: Race, Ethnicity, and Class in America.* Boston: Beacon Press.

U.S. Bureau of the Census. 1992. *Census of Population and Housing, 1990: Detailed Ancestry Groups for States. Supplementary Reports CP-S-1-2.* Washington, D.C.: U.S. Government Printing Office.

Waters, Mary C. 1990. *Ethnic Options: Choosing Identities in America.* Berkeley and Los Angeles: University of California Press.

Weber, Max. [1921] 1968. *Economy and Society: An Outline of Interpretive Sociology*, edited by Guenther Roth and Claus Wittich, translated by Ephraim Fischoff. New York: Bedminster Press.

Questions for Critical Thinking

1. What are some of the reasons whites may choose to identify with a particular ethnicity? What purpose does belonging to a particular ethnicity serve?

2. How does the freedom to include or exclude ancestries differ for whites and people of color?

3. How do "optional ethnicities" differ from ethnicities that result from exclusion and oppression? What are some of the advantages and/or disadvantages of each?

LEARNING TO BE ILLEGAL

Undocumented Youth and Shifting Legal Contexts in the Transition to Adulthood

· *Roberto G. Gonzales*

In the reading that follows, Roberto Gonzales discusses how the transition to adulthood among the children of undocumented immigrants in the United States involves moving from a status of legal protection to one of considerable vulnerability. Based on research involving 150 interviews with undocumented 1.5-generation young adult Latinos in Southern California, the author illustrates the profound consequences of access to opportunity and social equality for those who experience this shift from de facto legal to illegal status.

During the past 25 years, the number of undocumented immigrants in the United States has grown substantially, from an estimated 2.5 million in 1987 to 11.1 million today (Passel 2006; Passel and Cohn 2010).[1] Scholars contend that this demographic trend is the unintended consequence of policies designed to curb undocumented migration and tighten the U.S.-Mexico border (Nevins 2010), transforming once-circular migratory flows into permanent settlement (Cornelius and Lewis 2006; Massey, Durand, and Malone 2002). Making multiple migratory trips back and forth became increasingly costly and dangerous throughout the 1990s and the first decade of the twenty-first century, so more unauthorized migrants began creating permanent homes in the United States. And they brought their children with them. According to recent estimates, there are more than 2.1 million undocumented young people in the United States who have been here since childhood. Of these, more than a million are now adults (Batalova and McHugh 2010). Relatively little is known about this vulnerable population of young people, and their unique circumstances challenge assumptions about the incorporation patterns of the children of immigrants and their transitions to adolescence and adulthood.

Building on prior scholarship about immigrant incorporation and the life course, this article offers an up-close examination of the ways in which public schooling and U.S. immigration laws collide to produce a shift in the experiences and meanings of illegal status for undocumented youth at the onset of their transition to adulthood. I am interested in how these young people become aware of, and come to understand, their status under the law—that is, when they begin to notice their legal difference and its effects, and how they experience this shift as they move through late adolescence and young adulthood. The multiple transformations that undocumented youth

Republished with permission of Sage Publications Inc, Journals, © 2011. "Learning to Be Illegal: Undocumented Youth and Shifting Legal Contexts in the Transition to Adulthood," by Roberto G. Gonzales, from *American Sociological Review*, 76(4), 602–19; permission conveyed through Copyright Clearance Centre, Inc.

experience have important implications for their identity formation, friendship patterns, aspirations and expectations, and social and economic mobility, and they also signal movement of a significant subset of the U.S. immigrant population into a new, disenfranchised underclass. In developing a conceptual and theoretical map of how undocumented youth learn to be illegal, this article identifies important mechanisms that mediate transitions to adulthood for the children of immigrants. Therefore, it helps us understand the consequences of non-legal status for undocumented youth as they move from protected to unprotected status, from inclusion to exclusion, and from de facto legal to illegal, during their final years of secondary schooling.

Undocumented Youth and Shifting Contexts

Assimilation and Public Schooling

As today's children of immigrants come of age, contemporary immigration scholarship challenges the conventional expectation that they will follow a linear generational process of assimilation into mainstream U.S. life (Gans 1992; Portes and Rumbaut 2006; Portes and Zhou 1993). Much current theorizing has moved away from a singular focus on human capital toward nuanced approaches that more fully appreciate the context of reception (Portes 1981; Portes and Bach 1985; Portes and Rumbaut 2006). This approach stresses that multiple factors channel the children of immigrants into different segments of society (Portes and Rumbaut 2001, 2006; Portes and Zhou 1993). Studies suggest that increasing fault lines of inequality along race and ethnicity, poor public schools, and differential access to today's labor market may cause recent immigrants' children to do less well than the children of previous waves (Gans 1992; Portes and Rumbaut 2001, 2006; Portes and Zhou 1993; Rumbaut 1997, 2005, 2008; Zhou 1997).

Given the changes in the U.S. economy and labor market, educational attainment has become critical to the social mobility of all children, and the link between school outcomes and future success is a thread that runs throughout much of the literature (Kasinitz et al. 2008; Portes and Rumbaut 2001, 2006; Suàrez-Orozco and Suàrez-Orozco 1995;

Suàrez-Orozco, Suàrez-Orozco, and Todor-ova 2008; Waters 1999; Zhou and Bankston 1998). While some young people with modest levels of education manage to find skilled blue-collar jobs, most need a college degree to qualify for jobs that offer decent wages, benefits, job security, and the possibility of advancement. Children from poor and minority families, however, have historically experienced difficulty attaining significant levels of education (Alba and Nee 2003; Portes and Rumbaut 2001; Telles and Ortiz 2008). Disadvantaged students are particularly harmed by highly differentiated curricula and de facto tracking (Lucas and Berends 2002; Oakes 1985), although scholars have found that supplementary educational programs (Zhou 2008), extrafamily mentors (Portes and Fernandez-Kelly 2008; Smith 2008), and positive support networks (Stanton-Salazar 2001) can help overcome these disadvantages.

For generations, the public school system has been the principal institution that educates and integrates the children of immigrants into the fabric of U.S. society. This is especially true today, as more immigrant children spend more waking hours in school than ever before. Suàrez-Orozco and colleagues (2008:2–3) identify public schools' critical role in shaping immigrant youths' understanding of their place in society: "It is in school where, day in and day out, immigrant youth come to know teachers and peers from majority culture as well as newcomers from other parts of the world. It is in schools that immigrant youth develop academic knowledge and, just as important, form perceptions of where they fit in the social reality and cultural imagination of their new nation." Certainly, the role of public schools is increasingly critical, as the returns on education have sharply increased over the past few decades. But public schools' socialization mechanisms are also powerful catalysts for promoting the acculturation processes of the children of immigrants. Schools foster what Rumbaut (1997:944) calls a "unity of experiences and orientation" among their pupils that aid in the development of a "community of purpose and action" with "primary social contacts." This assimilating experience is profoundly different from what most adult immigrants encounter. While their parents may be absorbed into low-wage labor markets and often work with co-ethnics who speak their language and share their cultural practices, children are integrated into the school system, where they grow up side-by-side with the native-born (Gleeson and Gonzales 2012). Their "unity of experiences" with friends and classmates promotes feelings of togetherness and inclusion (Rumbaut 1997:944), and these feelings, in turn, shape immigrant youths' identification and experience of coming of age.

Today's Children of Immigrants Come of Age

Scholarly consensus on contemporary transitions to adulthood suggests that the process of coming of age is taking much longer today (Furstenberg et al. 2002). In particular, young people are spending more time in postsecondary schooling and are delaying exit from the parental household, entry into full-time work, and decisions about marriage and children (Settersten, Furstenberg, and Rumbaut 2005).

Life-course scholars traditionally define the transition to adulthood in terms of five milestones or markers: completing school, moving out of the parental home, establishing employment, getting married, and becoming a parent. The developmentally dense period of transition entails a large number of shifts out of roles that support and foster childlike dependence and into roles that confer adulthood in a relatively short time (Rindfuss 1991). Drawing from Erikson's (1950) early work, life-course scholarship views the transition to adulthood as composed of adolescence (ages 12 to 17 years) and young adulthood (ages 18 to 35 years). Yet recent decades have brought significant shifts in the roles of social institutions as well as changes in the opportunities for entry into the labor market. By delaying entry into the workforce in favor of additional education, young adults build human capital that will make them more competitive in the high-skilled labor market. Some parents aid this process by assisting children over a longer period and using financial resources to help pay for college, providing down payments for their children's first homes, or defraying some of the costs associated with having children (Rumbaut and Komaie 2010). Theorists have responded to these changes by conceptually disaggregating young adulthood into shorter periods of time that better define contemporary transitions and permit a better understanding of the relationship between broader contexts and life transitions. Arnett (2000) adds emerging adulthood, a stage between adolescence and young adulthood, roughly between ages 18 and 25 years, and Rumbaut (2005) differentiates between the early transition (18 to 24 years), the middle transition (25 to 29 years), and the late transition (30 to 34 years).

Within the larger national context of coming of age, scholars have uncovered key differences by social class, country of origin, nativity, and immigrant generation (Mollenkopf et al. 2005; Rumbaut and Komaie 2010). Many youngsters from less-advantaged immigrant households put off postsecondary schooling because their parents are not able to provide financial assistance or because they carry considerable financial responsibilities in their households that make it impossible for them to make tuition payments (Fuligni and Pedersen 2002; Suárez-Orozco and Suárez-Orozco 1995). Many of the 1.5 and second generations of certain immigrant groups are in reciprocal financial relationships with their parents, often even supporting them (Rumbaut and Komaie 2010). As a result, they do not enjoy the same degree of freedom from the stresses and responsibilities of adult roles. These differences suggest that we should expect the children of immigrants—documented and undocumented alike—to experience coming of age differently from the native-born.

Conceptualizing the Transition to Illegality for Undocumented Youth

For undocumented youth, the transition into adulthood is accompanied by a transition into illegality that sets them apart from their peers. Undocumented youngsters share a confusing and contradictory status in terms of their legal rights and the opportunities available to them (Abrego 2008; Gonzales 2007). On the one hand, because of the Supreme Court ruling in *Plyler v. Doe* (1982), they have the legal right to a K to 12 education.[2] Furthermore, the Family Educational Rights and Privacy Act prevents schools from releasing any information from students' records to immigration authorities, making school a protected space in which undocumented status has little to no negative effect. On the other hand, undocumented young adults cannot legally work, vote, receive financial aid, or drive in most states, and deportation remains a constant threat. Unauthorized residency status thus has little direct impact on most aspects of childhood but is a defining feature of late adolescence and adulthood and can prevent these youth from following normative pathways to adulthood. Therefore, coupled with family poverty, illegal status places undocumented youth in a developmental limbo. As family need requires them to make significant financial contributions and to assume considerable responsibility for their own care, they become less likely to linger in adolescence. At the same time, legal restrictions keep them from participating in many adult activities, leaving them unable to complete important transitions.

Researchers studying immigrant incorporation and the life course have not systematically considered the effects of the legal context on the children of immigrants, that is, the specific challenges facing undocumented immigrant youth and their complex and contradictory routes to adulthood. Current scholarship is limited to conjecture based on what is known in general about children of immigrants from low-skilled groups. Failure to focus on legal status also limits what we know about the linkages between important mechanisms such as education and social mobility. K to 12 schooling certainly plays an important role in the development and integration of immigrant children, but significant questions remain about how undocumented status shapes educational trajectories and how, in turn, it affects the link between educational attainment and social and economic mobility. The scant existing research on undocumented youth notes that undocumented status depresses aspirations (Abrego 2006) and sensitizes them to the reality that they are barred from integrating legally, educationally, and economically into U.S. society (Abrego 2008).

For conceptual help, I turn to recent advances in the literature that move beyond the binary categories of documented and undocumented to explore the ways in which migrants move between different statuses and the mechanisms that allow them to be regular in one sense and irregular in another. In describing the experiences of Salvadoran migrants caught in the legal limbo of Temporary Protected Status, and their feelings of being legally and socially

in-between, Menjívar (2006) introduced the concept of liminal legality. This phrase underscores that documented and undocumented categories do not adequately capture the gray areas experienced by many migrants. Menjívar's analysis builds on Coutin's (2000) exploration of the contradictions that lie between migrants' physical and social presence and their official designation as illegal. Several other scholars have called for a shift from generally studying unauthorized migrants and migrations to a more deliberate investigation of the mechanisms that produce and sustain what they term migrant illegality (Coutin 2000; De Genova 2002; Ngai 2004; Willen 2007). This deliberate shift in focus allows us to pay attention to the effects laws have on migrants' day-to-day lives, revealing the ways in which undocumented persons experience inclusion and exclusion and how these experiences can change over time, in interactions with different persons, and across various spaces. It also points to the two-sided nature of citizenship, which can allow the same person, citizen or not, to experience belonging in one context but not in another.

Portes and Rumbaut (2006) emphasize that it is the combination of positive and negative contexts that determines the distinct modes of immigrants' incorporation. While school contexts foster expectations and aspirations that root undocumented youngsters in the United States (Abrego 2006), they leave these young people grossly unprepared for what awaits them in adulthood. This article focuses on the interactions between such favorable and unfavorable contexts during what I call the transition to illegality. I conceptualize this process as the set of experiences that result from shifting contexts along the life course, providing different meanings to undocumented status and animating the experience of illegality at late adolescence and into adulthood. The transition to illegality brings with it a period of disorientation, whereby undocumented youth confront legal limitations and their implications and engage in a process of retooling and reorienting themselves for new adult lives. But this process is not uniform among undocumented youth. Previous qualitative work on youth populations coming of age has uncovered key mechanisms within the school setting that shape divergent trajectories (MacLeod 1987;

Willis 1977). Because comparisons between differently achieving youth may help to more clearly identify mechanisms that mediate undocumented status during the transition to adulthood, I compare the experiences of college-going young adults (i.e., college-goers) with those who exit the education system after high school graduation or earlier (i.e., early-exiters).

Methods

While many recent immigrants have dispersed to new destination states in the South and the Midwest (Marrow 2009; Massey 2008; Singer 2004; Zuniga and Hernandez-Leon 2005), California remains home to the largest undocumented immigrant population in the country. The numbers of undocumented immigrants from countries outside of Latin America have risen slightly since 2000, but immigrants from Mexico continue to account for the majority. In fact, no other sending country constitutes even a double-digit share of the total (Passel and Cohn 2009). I thus focus on Mexican-origin immigrants in California, drawing on 150 individual semi-structured interviews with 1.5-generation young adults ages 20 to 34 years (who migrated before the age of 12). The interviews focused on respondents' experiences growing up in Southern California without legal status. Such close study of the 1.5 generation permits an examination of the unique ways in which undocumented status is experienced in childhood and adolescence (Rumbaut 2004; Smith 2006).

Until very recently, it has been difficult to study undocumented young adults like those interviewed for this study because their numbers have been prohibitively small. Researching hard-to-reach populations adds layers of difficulty, time, and cost to any study. While previous large-scale efforts have been successful at locating and interviewing undocumented Mexicans on both sides of the U.S.–Mexico border, and have provided useful direction for random sampling,[3] today's anti-immigrant climate and localized immigration enforcement present challenges to finding respondents in the United States. These conditions lead many unauthorized migrants to be more fearful in their everyday lives, thus posing significant challenges to random sampling efforts. Data collection for this study involved nearly four

and a half years of field work in the periods 2003 to 2007 and 2008 to 2009, during which I conducted interviews and did additional ethnographic research in the Los Angeles Metropolitan Area.[4] I began conducting interviews after spending lengthy periods of time in the field gaining a rapport with respondents and community stakeholders. I recruited respondents from various settings, including continuation schools, community organizations, college campuses, and churches. After gaining trust, I accompanied respondents throughout their school and work days, volunteered at local schools and organizations, and sat in on numerous community meetings. I built on the initial group of respondents by using snowball sampling to identify subsequent respondents.

All 150 1.5-generation respondents interviewed spent much of their childhood, adolescence, and adulthood with undocumented status. With the exception of eight Central Americans (Guatemalan and Salvadoran), all were born in Mexico. I drew the sample from the five-county Los Angeles Metropolitan Area, and respondents come from all five counties. Most had parents who were undocumented (92 percent) and had fewer than six years of schooling (86 percent). Most respondents were also raised by two parents; one-quarter were raised by single parents and six were raised by other family members.

I designed the sampling process to include relatively equal numbers of males and females (71 males and 79 females) and equal numbers of individuals who dropped out of or completed high school (73) and those who attended some college (77). Of the 77 college respondents, nine had advanced degrees at the time of the interview, 22 had earned bachelor's degrees, 26 were enrolled in four-year universities, and 20 were enrolled in or had attended community college. The majority attended a California public college or university. Of the 73 respondents who exited school at or before high school graduation, 31 had not earned a high school degree at the time of interview, and 42 had high school diplomas.

The life history interviews included questions regarding respondents' pasts and their present lives as well as future expectations and aspirations. Interviews ranged in length from 1 hour and 40 minutes to 3 hours and 20 minutes. To analyze interview transcripts, I used open coding techniques. I placed conceptual labels on responses that described discrete events, experiences, and feelings reported in the interviews. Next, I analyzed each individual interview across all questions to identify meta-themes. Finally, I examined responses for common meta-themes across all interviews.

The Transition to Illegality

To better conceptualize the ways in which legal status affects the transition to illegality, I focus on three transition periods—discovery (ages 16 to 18 years), learning to be illegal (ages 18 to 24 years), and coping (ages 25 to 29 years). While the life-course literature defines the early and middle transitions as ages 18 to 24 and 25 to 29, respectively, I add an earlier period to capture the awakening to newfound legal limitations, which elicits a range of emotional reactions and begins a process of altered life-course pathways and adult transitions. Next, as undocumented youth enter early adulthood, they engage in a parallel process of learning to be illegal. During this period, many find difficulty connecting with previous sources of support to navigate the new restrictions on their lives and to mitigate their newly stigmatized identities. At this stage, undocumented youth are forced to alter earlier plans and reshape their aspirations for the future. Finally, the coping period involves adjusting to lowered aspirations and coming to grips with the possibility that their precarious legal circumstances may never change.

Discovery: Ages 16 to 18

Most life-course scholars focus on age 18 as a time of dramatic change for young people. In the United States, 18 is the age of majority, the legal threshold of adulthood when a child ceases to be considered a minor and assumes control over his actions and decisions. This is traditionally the time when young people exit high school and enter college or full-time work. Yet young people adopt semi-adult roles, such as working and driving, while still in high school. Most respondents in this study began to experience dramatic shifts in their daily lives and future outlooks around age 16.

Because public schooling provided respondents with an experience of inclusion atypical of undocumented adult life in the United States (Bean, Telles, and Lowell 1987; Chavez 1991, 1998), respondents spent their childhood and early adolescence in a state of suspended illegality, a buffer stage wherein they were legally integrated and immigration status rarely limited activities. Through school, respondents developed aspirations rooted in the belief that they were part of the fabric of the nation and would have better opportunities than their parents (Gans 1992). They learned to speak English, developed tastes, joined clubs, dated, and socialized—all alongside their U.S.-born and legal resident peers. During this period, school-based relationships with peers and adults provided key sources of support and identity formation (Portes and Fernandez-Kelly 2008). As Marisol, a college-goer, explained, relationships with teachers and friends provided a comfortable space for many like her to learn and develop: "School was an escape from home. I felt happy, calm. . . . I could be myself. I could be recognized at school. My teachers encouraged me to keep going. And my friends, we believed in education and pushed each other. We helped each other with homework and talked about college."

Such positive relationships, however, were not uniformly experienced by respondents. Many early-exiters (those who left the school system at or before completion of high school) recounted feeling disconnected from school and lacking significant relationships with teachers or counselors. They felt they were left to fall through the cracks and cut off from important services; they also reported having limited visits with counselors. Juan, for example, did not meet with a college counselor until late in his junior year. "I wanted to go to college," he told me, "but the counselors didn't let me know the requirements for four-year colleges. I tried to go to see them, but they didn't have time for me" Nevertheless, even respondents who reported having trouble in school believed they would have more options than their parents. Eric, an early-exiter who grew up in Riverside County, told me he had grown up thinking he was going to have a "better life": "I saw my older [U.S.-born] cousins get good jobs. I mean, they're not lawyers or anything like that, but they're not in restaurants or mowing lawns. I thought, yeah, when I graduate from school, I can make some good money, maybe even go to college."

Respondents uniformly noted a jolting shift at around age 16, when they attempted to move through rites of passage associated with their age. Life-course scholars refer to critical events in one's life as "turning points" that "knife off" past from present and restructure routine activities and life-course pathways (Elder 1987:452). These turning points can enable identity transitions and set into motion processes of cumulative advantage and disadvantage (Rumbaut 2005). For undocumented youth, the process of coming of age is a critical turning point that has consequences for subsequent transitions. Finding a part-time job, applying for college, and obtaining a driver's license—all markers of new roles and responsibilities—require legal status as a basis for participation.

As respondents tried to take these steps into adult life, they were blocked by their lack of a Social Security number. These incidents proved to be life changing and were often accompanied by the realization that they were excluded from a broad range of activities. Rodolfo, an early-exiter who is now 27 years old, spoke of his first experience of exclusion:

> I never actually felt like I wasn't born here. Because when I came I was like 10 and a half. I went to school. I learned the language. I first felt like I was really out of place when I tried to get a job. I didn't have a Social Security number. Well, I didn't even know what it meant. You know Social Security, legal, illegal. I didn't even know what that was.

Until this time, Rodolfo had never needed proof of legal residency. The process of looking for a job made the implications of his lack of legal status real to him for the first time. Like Rodolfo, many early-exiters (a little over 68 percent) made such discoveries while applying for jobs or for driver's licenses.

On the other hand, most college-goers (almost 60 percent) reported finding out they were undocumented in the course of the college application process. Jose, for example, was on the academic decathlon and debate teams. He did well in school and was well-liked by teachers. During his junior year, he attempted to enroll in classes at the community college to earn college credits. But without a Social Security number, he could not move forward.

While most respondents did not know of their unauthorized status until their teenage years, some reported knowing in childhood. This was more true of early-exiters (almost 30 percent, compared with a little over 9 percent among college-goers), many of whom lived in households where older siblings had gone through the process of discovery before them. But even these respondents did not realize the full implications their illegal status would have for their futures until much later. Being undocumented only became salient when matched with experiences of exclusion. Early-exiter Lorena started cleaning houses with her mother and sisters at age 12. Even before she began working, reminders from her mother made her aware that she did not have "papers." But she explained to me that "it really hit home" when she tried to branch out to other work in high school and was asked for her Social Security number.

Discovery of illegal status prompted reactions of confusion, anger, frustration, and despair among respondents, followed by a period of paralyzing shock. Most respondents conveyed that they were not prepared for the dramatic limits of their rights. They struggled to make sense of what had happened to them, many feeling as though they had been lied to. "I always thought I would have a place when I grew up" David, an early-exiter, told me. "Teachers make you believe that. It's all a lie. A big lie" They often blamed teachers and parents for their feelings of anger and frustration. Cory, a college-goer, locked herself in her bedroom for an entire week. When she finally emerged, she moved out of her parents' house, blaming them for "keeping [her] in the dark during childhood" Cory said: "They thought that by the time I graduated I would have my green card. But they didn't stop to think that this is my life. . . . Everything I believed in was a big lie. Santa Claus was not coming down the chimney, and I wasn't going to just become legal. I really resented them."

Respondents reported that soon after these discoveries, they experienced a second shock as they came to realize that the changes they were experiencing would adversely affect their remaining adult lives. As they came to grips with the new meanings of unauthorized status, they began to view and define themselves differently. Miguel, a college-goer who has been caught in the part-time cycle of community college and work for six years, told me: "During most of high school, I thought I had my next 10 years laid out. College and law school were definitely in my plans. But when my mom told me I wasn't legal, everything was turned upside down. I didn't know what to do. I couldn't see my future anymore" Miguel's entire identity was transformed, and the shift placed him, like many other respondents, in a state of limbo. Cory put it this way: "I feel as though I've experienced this weird psychological and legal-stunted growth. I'm stuck at 16, like a clock that has stopped ticking. My life has not changed at all since then. Although I'm 22, I feel like a kid. I can't do anything adults do"

Respondents' illegality was paired with a movement into stigmatized status that reinforced their legal exclusion. While laws limited their access to grown-up activities and responsibilities, fears of being found out curbed their interactions with teachers and peers. Ironically, while many respondents believed they had been lied to in childhood, they adopted lying themselves as a daily survival strategy that separated them from the very peer networks that had provided support and shaped a positive self-image. Many reported they were afraid of what their friends would think or how they would react if they learned of their illegal status. These fears were validated by observations of friends' behavior. Chuy, a college-goer who played sports throughout school, explained that after he saw a teammate on his high school soccer team berate players on an opposing team as "wet-backs" and "illegals," he was reticent to disclose his status even to good friends. "I grew up with this guy," he said. "We had classes together and played on the same team for like four years. But wow, I don't know what he would say if he knew I was one of those wetbacks"

Frustration with the present, uncertainty about the future, and the severing of support systems caused many respondents to withdraw, with detrimental effects on their progress during the last half of high school (see also Abrego 2006; Suárez-Orozco et al. 2008). In my interview with Sandra, an early-exiter, she recalled her struggles during junior year: "I felt the world caving in on me. What was I going to do? I couldn't ask my parents. They didn't know about college or anything. I was kind of quiet in school, so I didn't really know my teachers. Besides, I was scared. What would they do if they knew? I was scared and alone." Throughout high school, Luis, an early-exiter, hoped to attend college. During the latter part of his sophomore year, his grades fell considerably. As a result, he did not meet the requirements to gain entrance into the University of California system. His girlfriend convinced him to apply to the lower-tier California State University, but when he found out he was not eligible for financial aid, he gave up: "It took a while to get accepted. But I ended up not going (because of) financial aid. . . . It just kinda brought down my spirit, I guess" Like Sandra and Luis, many respondents had done moderately well in school before the cumulative disadvantages resulting from the transition to illegality caused them to lose motivation to continue. Lacking trusting relationships with teachers or counselors who could help them, they ended up exiting school much earlier than they had planned (Gonzales 2010).

Nationally, 40 percent of undocumented adults ages 18 to 24 do not complete high school, and only 49 percent of undocumented high school graduates go to college. Youths who arrive in the United States before the age of 14 fare slightly better: 72 percent finish high school, and of those, 61 percent go on to college. But these figures are still much lower than the numbers for U.S.-born residents (Passel and Cohn 2009). The combination of scarce family resources and exclusion from financial aid at the state[5] and federal levels makes the path to higher education very steep for undocumented high school students. Estimates reveal that as few as 5 to 10 percent of all undocumented high school graduates ever reach post-secondary institutions (Passel 2003), and the vast majority attend community colleges (Flores 2010). In several states, laws allowing undocumented students to pay in-state tuition have increased the number of high school graduates matriculating to college over the past decade (Flores 2010). Nonetheless, steep financial barriers prohibit many undocumented youth from enrolling in college.

While depressed motivation contributed to many respondents' early exit from the school system, limited financial resources within their families and a general lack of information about how to move forward also played a part in causing early departures.

Karina, an early-exiter, maintained a B average in her general-track high school classes. When she applied to college, she had no guidance. Unaware of a California provision that should have made it possible for her to attend school at in-state tuition rates, Karina opted not to go to college: "I didn't know anything about AB 540.[6] Maybe if I knew the information I could have gotten a scholarship or something. That's why I didn't go. I don't know if my counselors knew, but they never told me anything."

The experiences of successful college-goers, by contrast, unlock a key variable to success missing from the narratives of early-exiters: trusting relationships with teachers or other adults. Portes and Fernandez-Kelly (2008:26) find evidence linking school success to the presence of what they call "really significant others" who "possess the necessary knowledge and experience" and "take a keen interest in [their students], motivate [them] to graduate from high school and to attend college." When Marisol began to exhibit decreasing levels of motivation, for instance, her English teacher was there to intervene. Although Marisol felt embarrassed, she was able to talk frankly with her teacher because they had developed a trusting relationship. As a reward for her trust, Marisol's teacher helped her obtain information about college and also took up a collection among other teachers to pay for her first year of tuition at the community college.

Most college-goers reported they had formed trusting relationships with teachers, counselors, and other mentors in high school. These respondents were concentrated in the advanced curriculum tracks in high school; the smaller and more supportive learning environments gave them access to key school personnel. Compared to early-exiters, they disclosed their problems more easily and were able to draw on relationships of trust to seek out and receive help. At critical times when the students' motivations were low, these relationships meant the difference between their leaving school or going to college. When difficulties arose during the college admissions process for college-goer Jose, for instance, he went straight to his counselor, with positive results. The counselor called the college and found out about the availability of aid through AB 540, which neither he nor Jose had been aware of.

Learning to Be Illegal: Ages 18 to 24

For the children of unauthorized parents, success means improving on the quality of jobs and opportunities. Many youths end up only a small step ahead, however. Lacking legal status and a college degree, early-exiters confront some of the same limited and limiting employment options as their parents. Economic circumstances and family need force them to make choices about working and driving illegally. Nearly all respondents contributed money to their families, averaging nearly $300 per month. After high school, early-exiter Oscar, who at 27 still gives his parents $500 a month, moved through a string of short stints in the workforce, not staying in any one job more than six months at a time. He quit jobs because he was dissatisfied with the meager wages and generally uneasy about the ways in which employers treated him. Each new job proved no better than the previous one. Over time, Oscar realized he had few job choices outside of physical labor: "I wasn't prepared to do that kind of work. . . . It's tough. I come home from work tired every day. I don't have a life. . . . It's not like I can get an office job. I've tried to get something better, but I'm limited by my situation."

> [At first] I thought, "I'm not gonna bust my ass for someone who can be yelling at me for like $5.75, five bucks an hour." Hell no. If I get a job, I wanna get paid 20 bucks an hour. I speak English. But actually I didn't have any experience. So, it's really hard to get a job. Especially now, because those kinds of jobs . . . they're looking for a more experienced person who knows how to work in the field and ain't gonna complain.

Respondents also recounted difficulty negotiating precarious situations because their undocumented status forced them to confront experiences for which K to 12 schooling did not prepare them. Pedro found himself in legal trouble when, after completing a day job, he tried to cash his check at the local currency exchange. A teller called Pedro's employer to verify its legitimacy, and he denied writing the check and called the police. When the police arrived, they found multiple sets of identification in Pedro's possession and took him to jail for identity fraud. This incident awoke Pedro to the reality that his inexperience with undocumented life could have grave consequences, including arrest and even deportation.

Given the limited employment options available to undocumented youth, moving on to college becomes critical. Making a successful transition to postsecondary schooling requires a number of favorable circumstances, however, including sufficient money to pay for school, family permission to delay or minimize work, reliable transportation, and external guidance and assistance. Respondents who enjoyed such conditions were able to devote their time to school and, equally important, avoid activities and situations that would place them in legal trouble. As a result, they suspended many of the negative consequences of unauthorized status.

When I met Rosalba, she had associate's, bachelor's, and master's degrees. Her parents had prohibited her from working, thus allowing her to concentrate fully on school. Throughout her time in school, she benefited from assistance from a number of caring individuals. "I've made it because I've had a support system," she said:

> At every step of my education, I have had a mentor holding my hand. It's a thousand times harder without someone helping you. Being undocumented, it's not about what you know, it's who you know. You might have all of the will in the world, but if you don't know the right people, then as much as you want to, you're gonna have trouble doing it.

When I interviewed Nimo, he was in his final year of college and considering graduate school. His college years had been enjoyable, lacking many of the stressors of legal limitations. A financial sponsor paid his tuition and fees and provided money for books. Nimo worked only minimally, because his mother did not ask for his financial assistance. He was usually able to secure rides to and from school; on other days, he took the bus. Although the two-hour commute each way was time consuming, the time allowed him to "read and think" Nimo's case is exceptional, but it is also instructive. Without the various barriers of financing college, supporting family, and having to work and drive, he was able to concentrate on school. As a result, he maintained a positive attitude and has high aspirations for his future.

Many other respondents, however, found postsecondary education to be a discontinuous experience, with frequent stalls and detours. Several took leaves of absence, and others enrolled in only one school term per year. Faced with the need to work, few scholarships, debt, and long commutes, these respondents managed to attend college, but completing their schooling was an arduous task that required them to be creative, keep their costs low, and in many cases join early-exiters in the low-wage labor market. Several respondents' dreams of higher education did not materialize because financial burdens became too overwhelming. Margarita, for example, aspired to be a pharmacist, but after two years of community college, her mother started asking her to pay her share of the rent. She left school to clean houses, which she had been doing for almost four years when I met her.

Coping: Ages 25 to 29

The impact of not having legal residency status becomes particularly pronounced for respondents in their mid-20s, when prolonged experiences of illegality force them to begin viewing their legal circumstances as more permanent. By this time, most young adults in the United States have finished school, left the parental home, and are working full-time. They have also started to see the returns on their education in better jobs and have gained increased independence from their parents. Although sharp differences in educational returns persist among legal young adults, I found a high degree of convergence among college-goers and early-exiters as they finished the transition to illegality. By their mid-20s, both sets of respondents held similar occupations. While both groups were also starting to leave the parental home, early-exiters were already settled into work routines. Years on the job had provided them with experience and improved their human capital. Many had let go of hopes for career mobility long ago, opting instead for security and stability. While college-going respondents spent much of their late teens and early 20s in institutions of higher learning, by their mid-20s most were out of school and learning that they had few legal employment options, despite having attained advanced degrees.

In his study of working-class youth in Clarendon Heights, MacLeod (1987) chronicled the experiences of two groups of differently achieving working-class students as they came to realize their limitations in the job market. As their aspirations flattened over time, they put a "lid on hope" (p. 62). For my respondents, day-to-day struggles, stress, and the ever-present ceiling on opportunities similarly forced them to acknowledge the distance between their prior aspirations and present realities. The realization was especially poignant for those who managed to complete degrees but ultimately recognized that the years of schooling did not offer much advantage in low-wage labor markets—the only labor markets to which they had access.

These are young people who grew up believing that because their English mastery and education surpassed those of their parents, they would achieve more. Instead, they came face-to-face with the limits on their opportunities—often a very unsettling experience. Early-exiter Margarita underscored this point:

> I graduated from high school and have taken some college credits. Neither of my parents made it past fourth grade, and they don't speak any English. But I'm right where they are. I mean, I work with my mom. I have the same job. I can't find anything else. It's kinda ridiculous, you know. Why did I even go to school? It should mean something. I mean, that should count, right? You would think. I thought. Well, here I am, cleaning houses.

Others conveyed a tacit acceptance of their circumstances. When I interviewed Pedro, he had been out of school for nine years. He had held a string of jobs and was living with childhood friends in a mobile home. He was slowly making progress toward his high school diploma but was not hopeful that education would improve his opportunities or quality of life. I asked him what he wanted for himself. He replied:

> Right now, I want to take care of my legal status, clean up my record for the stupidity I committed and get a decent job. I'm thinking about five years from now. I don't want to extend it any longer. I wish it could be less, you know, but I don't want to rush it either, because when you rush things they don't go as they should. Maybe 10 years from now. I like where I live, and I wouldn't mind living in a mobile home.

Other respondents had similarly low expectations for the future, the cumulative result of years of severely restricted choices. When I first met Gabriel, he was 23 years old. He was making minimal progress at the community college. He had moved out of his mother's home because he felt like a financial burden, and he left his job after his employer received a letter from the Social Security Administration explaining that the number he was using did not match his name. He was frustrated and scared. When I ran into him four years later, near the end of my study, he seemed to be at ease with his life. He was working in a factory with immigrant co-workers and participating in a community dance group. He told me he was "not as uptight" about his situation as he had once been:

> I just stopped letting it [unauthorized status] define me. Work is only part of my life. I've got a girlfriend now. We have our own place. I'm part of a dance circle, and it's really cool. Obviously, my situation holds me back from doing a lot of things, but I've got to live my life. I just get sick of being controlled by the lack of nine digits.

Undoubtedly, Gabriel would rather be living under more stable circumstances. But he has reconciled himself to his limitations, focusing instead on relationships and activities that are tangible and accessible.

Such acceptance was most elusive for respondents who achieved the highest levels of school success. At the time of their interviews, 22 respondents had graduated from four-year universities, and an additional nine held advanced degrees. None were able to legally pursue their dream careers. Instead, many, like Esperanza, found themselves toiling in low-wage jobs. Esperanza had to let go of her long-held aspiration to become a journalist, in favor of the more immediate need to make ends meet each month. In high school, she was in band and AP classes. Her hopes for success were encouraged by high-achieving peers and teachers. Nothing leading up to graduation prepared her for the reality of her life afterward. Now three years out of college, she can find only restaurant jobs and factory work. While she feels out of place in the sphere of undocumented work, she has little choice:

> The people working at those places, like the cooks and the cashiers, they are really young, and I feel really old.

Like what am I doing there if they are all like 16, 17 years old? The others are like senoras who are 35. They dropped out of school, but because they have little kids they are still working at the restaurant. Thinking about that makes me feel so stupid. And like the factories, too, because they ask me, "Que estas haciendo aqui? [What are you doing here?] You can speak English. You graduated from high school. You can work anywhere."

Discussion and Conclusions

The experiences of unauthorized 1.5-generation young adults shed some important light on the powerful role played by immigration policy in shaping incorporation patterns and trajectories into adulthood. Contemporary immigration theory has made great strides in its ability to predict inter-generational progress. In doing so, however, it has paid less attention to the here-and-now experiences and outcomes of today's immigrants and their children. As Portes and Fernandez-Kelly (2008) point out, focusing exclusively on inter-generational mobility contributes to a failure to uncover key mechanisms that produce delayed, detoured, and derailed trajectories. Indeed, by focusing on individuals they call the "final survivors"—two to three generations out—we neglect the struggles of individuals today who end up disappearing from view. Many respondents in this study possess levels of human capital that surpass those of their parents, who tend to speak little English and have fewer than six years of schooling. We may be tempted to see this outcome as a sign of inter-generational progress. But these young men and women describe moving from an early adolescence in which they had important inclusionary access, to an adulthood in which they are denied daily participation in most institutions of mainstream life. They describe this process as waking up to a nightmare.

While life-course scholars note that most U.S. youngsters today face some difficulty managing adolescent and adult transitions, undocumented youth face added challenges. Their exclusion from important rites of passage in late adolescence, and their movement from protected to unprotected status, leave them in a state of developmental limbo, preventing subsequent and important adult transitions. Their

entry into a stigmatized identity has negative and usually unanticipated consequences for their educational and occupational trajectories, as well as for their friendships and social patterns. Unlike documented peers who linger in adolescence due to safety nets at home, many of these youngsters must start contributing to their families and taking care of themselves. These experiences affect adolescent and adult transitions that diverge significantly from those of their documented peers, placing undocumented youth in jeopardy of becoming a disenfranchised underclass.

Positive mediators at the early (discovery) and middle (learning to be illegal) transitions help cushion the blow, and a comparison of early-exiters and college-goers reveals a lot about the power, and the limitations, of these intermediaries. The keys to success for my respondents—extrafamilial mentors, access to information about postsecondary options, financial support for college, and lower levels of family responsibility—are not very different from those required for the success of members of other student populations. For undocumented youth, however, they take on added significance. In adult mentors, they find trusting allies to confide in and from whom to receive guidance and resources. The presence of caring adults who intervene during the discovery period can aid in reducing anxiety and minimizing barriers, allowing undocumented youth to delay entry into legally restricted adult environments and to make successful transitions to postsecondary institutions. Eventually, however, all undocumented youth unable to regularize their immigration status complete the transition to illegality.

My findings move beyond simply affirming that immigrant incorporation is a segmented process. Analyses of this group of undocumented young adults also suggest that successful integration may now depend, more so than ever before in U.S. history, on immigration policy and the role of the state. Historically, assimilation theory has been concerned with the factors that determine incorporation into the mainstream. Scholars argue that human capital is a key determinant for upward mobility (Zhou 1997). However, as I demonstrate here, blocked mobility caused by a lack of legal status renders traditional measures of inter-generational mobility by educational progress irrelevant: the assumed link between educational attainment and material and psychological outcomes after school is broken. College-bound youths' trajectories ultimately converge with those who have minimal levels of schooling. These youngsters, who committed to the belief that hard work and educational achievement would garner rewards, experience a tremendous fall. They find themselves ill-prepared for the mismatch between their levels of education and the limited options that await them in the low-wage, clandestine labor market.

The young men and women interviewed for this study are part of a growing population of undocumented youth who have moved into adulthood. Today, the United States is home to more than 1.1 million undocumented children who, in the years to come, will be making the same sort of difficult transitions, under arguably more hostile contexts (Massey and Sanchez 2010). These demographic and legal realities ensure that a sizeable population of U.S.-raised adults will continue to be cut off from the futures they have been raised to expect. Efforts aimed at legalizing this particular group of young people have been in the works for more than 10 years without success. Political experts believe there will not be legislative movement at the federal level for at least two more years. In the meantime, proposals aimed at ending birthright citizenship for U.S.-born children of undocumented immigrants and barring their entry to postsecondary education threaten to deny rights to even greater numbers. These young people will very likely remain in the United States. Whether they become a disenfranchised underclass or contributing members to our society, their fate rests largely in the hands of the state. We must ask ourselves if it is good for the health and wealth of this country to keep such a large number of U.S.-raised young adults in the shadows. We must ask what is lost when they learn to be illegal.

Acknowledgments
Joanna Dreby, Cecilia Menjívar, Rubén G. Rumbaut, Celeste Watkins-Hayes, the *ASR* editors and reviewers, and audiences at Brown University, Cornell University, UC-Berkeley, the University of Michigan, the University of Kansas, and the University of Washington provided helpful comments on previous versions of this article.

Funding
This project was supported by the National Poverty Center using funds received from the U.S. Department of Health and Human Services, Office of the Assistant Secretary for Planning and Evaluation, grant number 1 U01 AE000002-01. The opinions and conclusions expressed herein are solely those of the author and should not be construed as representing the opinions or policy of any agency of the Federal government. To protect confidentiality, all names of individuals have been replaced with pseudonyms.

Notes

1. The Immigration Reform and Control Act (IRCA) of 1986 provided the last large-scale legalization program. The 1987 estimate represents the undocumented population after many of the 2.7 million estimated illegal immigrants had moved into legal categories under IRCA.
2. Under *Plyler*, the Supreme Court ruled that undocumented children are entitled to the equal protection under the law afforded by the 14th Amendment of the Constitution and therefore cannot be denied access to public elementary and secondary education on the basis of their legal status (see Olivas 2005).
3. See, in particular, the Mexican Migration Project (MMP), a bi-national research effort co-directed by Jorge Durand (University of Guadalajara) and Douglas S. Massey (Princeton University). Since 1982, the MMP has collected economic and social data from more than 140,000 Mexicans including many migrants; most of the households in the MMP random samples were interviewed in Mexico.
4. Given the respondents' immigration status, I went to great lengths to ensure confidentiality. Having gone through a thorough Human Subjects process, I took several measures to avoid any identifiers that would directly link data to specific respondents. I gave pseudonyms to all respondents at the time of the initial meeting, and I never collected home addresses. Because of these precautions, personal information does not appear anywhere in this research.

Respondents provided verbal consent rather than leaving a paper trail with a written consent form. I destroyed all audio tapes immediately after transcription. I conducted all interviews in English, and I gave respondents gift cards for their participation.

5. Only New Mexico (SB 582) and Texas (HB 1403) allow undocumented students to apply for state aid.

6. Assembly Bill 540 (2001) gives undocumented youth in California who have gone to a state high school for three years and graduated the ability to pay tuition at in-state rates. Many undocumented immigrant students have benefited from this provision.

References

Abrego, Leisy J. 2006. "I Can't Go to College Because I Don't Have Papers: Incorporation Patterns of Undocumented Latino Youth." *Latino Studies* 4: 212–31.

Abrego, Leisy J. 2008. "Legitimacy, Social Identity, and the Mobilization of Law: The Effects of Assembly Bill 540 on Undocumented Students in California." *Law & Social Inquiry* 33:709–34.

Alba, Richard and Victor Nee. 2003. *Remaking the American Mainstream: Assimilation and Contemporary Immigration.* Cambridge: Harvard University Press.

Arnett, Jeffrey J. 2000. "Emerging Adulthood: A Theory of Development from Late Teens through the Twenties" *American Psychologist* 55:469–80.

Batalova, Jeanne and Margie McHugh. 2010. "*DREAM vs. Reality: An Analysis of Potential DREAM Act Beneficiaries.*" Washington, DC: Migration Policy Institute (http://www.migrationpolicy.org/pubs/DREAM-Insight-July2010.pdf).

Bean, Frank D., Edward Telles, and B. Lindsey Lowell. 1987. "Undocumented Migration to the United States: Perceptions and Evidence." *Population and Development Review* 13:671–90.

Chavez, Leo R. 1991. "Outside the Imagined Community: Undocumented Settlers and Experiences of Incorporation." *American Ethnologist* 18:257–78.

Chavez, Leo R. 1998. *Shadowed Lives: Undocumented Immigrants in American Society.* Fort Worth, TX: Harcourt Brace College Publishers.

Cornelius, Wayne A. and Jessa M. Lewis, eds. 2006. *Impacts of Border Enforcement on Mexican Migration: The View from Sending Communities.* Boulder, CO: Lynne Rienner Publishers and Center for Comparative Immigration Studies, UCSD.

Coutin, Susan B. 2000. *Legalizing Moves: Salvadoran Immigrants' Struggle for U.S. Residency.* Ann Arbor: University of Michigan Press.

De Genova, Nicolas. 2002. "Migrant 'Illegality' and Deportability in Everyday Life." *Annual Review of Anthropology* 31:419–47.

Elder, Glen H., Jr. 1987. "War Mobilization and the Life Course: A Cohort of World War II Veterans." *Sociological Forum* 2:449–72.

Erikson, Erik. 1950. *Childhood and Society.* New York: Norton.

Flores, Stella M. 2010. "State Dream Acts: The Effect of In-State Resident Tuition Policies and Undocumented Latino Students" *Review of Higher Education* 33:239–83.

Fuligni, Andrew J. and Sara Pedersen. 2002. "Family Obligation and the Transition to Young Adulthood." *Developmental Psychology* 38:856–68.

Furstenberg, Frank, Thomas Cook, Robert Sampson, and Gail Slap. 2002. "Early Adulthood in Cross National Perspective." *ANNALS of the American Academy of Political and Social Science* 580:6–15.

Gans, Herbert J. 1992. "Second Generation Decline: Scenarios for the Economic and Ethnic Futures of the Post-1965 American Immigrants." *Ethnic and Racial Studies* 15:173–92.

Gleeson, Shannon and Roberto G. Gonzales. 2012. "When Do Papers Matter? An Institutional Analysis of Undocumented Life in the United States." *International Migration* 50: 1–19.

Gonzales, Roberto G. 2007. "Wasted Talent and Broken Dreams: The Lost Potential of Undocumented Students." *Immigration Policy: In Focus* 5:13. Washington, DC: Immigration Policy Center of the American Immigration Law Foundation.

Gonzales, Roberto G. 2010. "On the Wrong Side of the Tracks: The Consequences of School Stratification Systems for Unauthorized Mexican Students." *Peabody Journal of Education* 85:469.

Kasinitz, Philip, John H. Mollenkopf, Mary C. Waters, and Jennifer Holdaway. 2008. *Inheriting the City: The Children of Immigrants Come of Age.* Cambridge: Harvard University Press.

Lucas, Samuel R. and Mark Berends. 2002. "Sociodemographic Diversity, Correlated Achievement, and De Facto Tracking." *Sociology of Education* 75: 328–48.

MacLeod, Jay. 1987. *Ain't No Makin It: Aspirations and Attainment in a Low-Income Neighborhood.* Boulder, CO: Westview Press.

Marrow, Helen B. 2009. "Immigrant Bureaucratic Incorporation: The Dual Roles of Professional Missions and Government Policies." *American Sociological Review* 74:756–76.

Massey, Douglas S. 2008. *New Faces in New Places: The New Geography of American Immigration.* New York: Russell Sage Foundation.

Massey, Douglas S., Jorge Durand, and Nolan J. Molone. 2002. *Beyond Smoke and Mirrors: Mexican Immigration in an Era of Economic Integration.* New York: Russell Sage Foundation.

Massey, Douglas and Magaly Sánchez R. 2010. *Brokered Boundaries: Creating Immigrant Identity in Anti-Immigrant Times.* New York: Russell Sage Foundation.

Menjivar, Cecilia. 2006. "Liminal Legality: Salvadoran and Guatemalan Immigrants' Lives in the United States." *American Journal of Sociology* 111:999–1037.

Mollenkopf, John H., Mary Waters, Jennifer Holdaway, and Philip Kasinitz. 2005. "The Ever-Winding Path: Ethnic and Racial Diversity in the Transition to Adulthood." Pp. 454–97 in *On the Frontier of Adulthood: Theory. Research, and Public Policy*, edited by R. Settersten Jr., F. F. Furstenberg Jr., and R. G. Rumbaut. Chicago: University of Chicago Press.

Nevins, Joseph. 2010. *Operation Gatekeeper and Beyond: The War on "Illegals" and the Remaking of the U.S.-Mexico Boundary.* New York: Routledge.

Ngai, Mae. 2004. *Impossible Subjects: Illegal Aliens and the Making of Modern America.* Princeton, NJ: Princeton University Press.

Oakes, Jeannie. 1985. *Keeping Track: How Schools Structure Inequality.* New Haven, CT: Yale University Press.

Olivas, Michael A. 2005. "The Story of *Plyler v. Doe*, the Education of Undocumented Children, and the Polity." Pp. 197–220 in *Immigration Stories*, edited by D. Martin and P. Schuck. New York: Foundation Press.

Passel, Jeffrey S. 2003. *Further Demographic Information Relating to the DREAM Act.* Washington, DC: The Urban Institute.

Passel, Jeffrey S. 2006. "*The Size and Characteristics of the Unauthorized Migrant Population in the U.S.: Estimates based on the March 2005 Current Population Survey.*" Washington, DC: Pew Hispanic Center (http://pewhispanic.org/files/reports/61.pdf).

Passel, Jeffrey and D'Vera Cohn. 2009. "*A Portrait of the Unauthorized Migrants in the United States.*" Washington, DC: Pew Hispanic Center (http://pewhispanic.org/files/reports/107.pdf).

Passel, Jeffrey and D'Vera Cohn. 2010. "*U.S. Unauthorized Immigration Flows Are Down Sharply Since Mid-Decade.*" Washington, DC: Pew Hispanic Center (http://pewhispanic.org/files/reports/126.pdf).

Portes, Alejandro. 1981. "Modes of Structural Incorporation and Present Theories of Labor Immigration." Pp. 279–97 in *Global Trends in Migration: Theory and Research on International Population Movements*, edited by M. M. Kritz. New York: Center for Migration Studies.

Portes, Alejandro and Robert Bach. 1985. *Latin Journey: Cuban and Mexican Immigrants in the United States.* Berkeley: University of California Press.

Portes, Alejandro and Patricia Fernandez-Kelly. 2008. "No Margin for Error: Educational and Occupational Achievement among Disadvantaged Children of Immigrants." *ANNALS of the American Academy of Political and Social Science* 620:12–36.

Portes, Alejandro and Rubén G. Rumbaut. 2001. *Legacies: The Story of the Immigrant Second Generation.* Berkeley: University of California Press.

Portes, Alejandro and Rubén G. Rumbaut. 2006. *Immigrant America: A Portrait*, 3rd ed. Berkeley: University of California Press.

Portes, Alejandro and Min Zhou. 1993. "The New Second Generation: Segmented Assimilation and its Variants." *ANNALS of the American Academy of Political and Social Science* 530:74–96.

Rindfuss, Ronald R. 1991. "The Young Adult Years: Diversity, Structural Change and Fertility." *Demography* 28:493–512.

Rumbaut, Rubén G. 1997. "Assimilation and its Discontents: Between Rhetoric and Reality." *International Migration Review* 31:923–60.

Rumbaut, Rubén G. 2004. "Ages, Life Stages, and Generational Cohorts: Decomposing the Immigrant First and Second Generations in the United States." *International Migration Review* 38:1160–205.

Rumbaut, Rubén G. 2005. "Turning Points in the Transition to Adulthood: Determinants of Educational Attainment, Incarceration, and Early Childbearing among Children of Immigrants." *Ethnic and Racial Studies* 28:1041–86.

Rumbaut, Rubén G. 2008. "The Coming of the Second Generation: Immigration and Ethnic Mobility in Southern California." *ANNALS of the American Academy of Political and Social Science* 620:196–236.

Rumbaut, Rubén G. and Golnaz Komaie. 2010. "Immigration and Adult Transitions." *The Future of Children* 20:39–63.

Settersten, Jr., Richard A., Frank F. Furstenberg, and Rubén G. Rumbaut. 2005. *On the Frontier of Adulthood: Theory, Research, and Public Policy.* Chicago: University of Chicago Press.

Singer, Audrey. 2004. "*The Rise of New Immigrant Gateways.*" Washington, DC: The Brookings Institution (https://www.brookings.edu/research/the-rise-of-new-immigrant-gateways/).

Smith, Robert Courtney. 2006. *Mexican New York: Transnational Lives of New Immigrants.* Berkeley: University of California Press.

Smith, Robert Courtney. 2008. "Horatio Alger Lives in Brooklyn: Extrafamily Support, Intrafamily Dynamics, and Socially Neutral Operating Identities in Exceptional Mobility among Children of Mexican Immigrants." *ANNALS of the American Academy of Political and Social Science* 620:270–90.

Stanton-Salazar, Ricardo. 2001. *Manufacturing Hope and Despair: The School and Kin Support Networks of U.S.-Mexican Youth.* New York: Teachers College Press.

Suárez-Orozco, Carola and Marcelo Suárez-Orozco. 1995. *Transformations: Migration, Family Life, and Achievement Motivation among Latino Adolescents.* Stanford, CA: Stanford University Press.

Suárez-Orozco, Carola, Marcelo M. Suárez-Orozco, and Irina Todorova. 2008. *Learning a New Land: Immigrant Students in American Society*, Cambridge: Harvard University Press.

Telles, Edward E. and Vilma Ortiz. 2008. *Generations of Exclusion: Mexican Americans, Assimilation, and Race.* New York: Russell Sage Foundation.

Waters, Mary C. 1999. *Black Identities: West Indian Immigrant Dreams and American Realities.* New York: Russell Sage Press.

Willen, Sarah S. 2007. "Towards a Critical Phenomenology of 'Illegality': State Power, Criminalization, and Abjectivity among Undocumented Migrant Workers in Tel Aviv, Israel." *International Migration* 45: 7–38.

Willis, Paul. 1977. *Learning to Labour: How Working Class Kids Get Working Class Jobs.* New York: Columbia University Press.

Zhou, Min. 1997. "Segmented Assimilation: Issues, Controversies, and Recent Research on the New Second Generation." *International Migration Review* 4:825–58.

Zhou, Min. 2008. "The Ethnic System of Supplementary Education: Non-profit and For-profit Institutions in Los Angeles' Chinese Immigrant Community." Pp. 229–51 in *Toward Positive Youth Development: Transforming Schools and Community Programs*, edited by B. Shinn and H. Yoshikawa. New York: Oxford University Press.

Zhou, Min and Carl L. Bankston III. 1998. *Growing Up American: How Vietnamese Children Adapt to Life in the United States.* New York: Russell Sage Foundation.

Zúñiga, Victor and Rubén Hernández-León, eds. 2005. *New Destinations: Mexican Immigration in the United States.* New York: Russell Sage Foundation.

Questions for Critical Thinking

1. How does Gonzales's discussion of the transition to adulthood for undocumented Latino young adults impact your understanding of the impact of social policy on one's identity?

2. As the author illustrates, youth today are taking longer to transition to adulthood. How is this transition different for youth based on class immigration status?

3. How does the author's discussion impact your perspective on the need for immigration policy reform?

Social Class

THE ASSET VALUE OF WHITENESS

Understanding the Racial Wealth Gap

• Amy Traub, Laura Sullivan, Tatjana Meschede, and Tom Shapiro

As discussed in Part II of this text, the racial wealth gap continues to grow ever wider. In the following essay, authors Amy Traub, Laura Sullivan, Tatjana Meschede, and Tom Shapiro examine popular explanations for the wealth gap, looking at education, family structure, employment patterns, and spending and consumption habits. Their analyses demonstrate that explanations for the wealth gap that focus on individual behavior and choices are not sufficient to eliminate decades of accumulated wealth. Rather, racial inequality in wealth is embedded in structural racism.

Introduction

Issues of racial inequity are increasingly at the forefront of America's public debate. In addition to urgent concerns about racial bias in law enforcement and the criminal justice system, activists highlight deeply connected issues of economic exclusion and inequality. No metric more powerfully captures the persistence and growth of economic inequality along racial and ethnic lines than the racial wealth gap. According to data from the Survey of Consumer Finances, the median white household possessed $13 in net wealth for every dollar held by the median black household in 2013. That same year, median white households possessed $10 for each dollar held by the median Latino/a household.

Research probing the causes of the racial wealth gap has traced its origins to historic injustices, from slavery to segregation to redlining.[1] The great expansion of wealth in the years after World War II was fueled by public policies such as the GI Bill, which mostly helped

white veterans attend college and purchase homes with guaranteed mortgages, thus building the foundations of an American middle class that largely excluded people of color. The outcomes of past injustice are carried forward as wealth is handed down across generations and are reinforced by ostensibly "color-blind" practices and policies in effect today. Yet many popular explanations for racial economic inequality overlook these deep roots, asserting that wealth disparities must be solely the result of individual life choices and personal achievements. The misconception that personal responsibility accounts for the racial wealth gap is an obstacle to the policies that could effectively address racial disparities.

This chapter explores a number of these popular explanations for the racial wealth gap, looking at

"The Asset Value of Whiteness: Understanding the Racial Wealth Gap," Amy Traub, Laura Sullivan, Tatjana Meschede, and Tom Shapiro, https://www.demos.org/research/asset-value-whiteness-understanding-racial-wealth-gap.

individual differences in education, family structure, full- or part-time employment, and consumption habits. In each case, we find that individual choices are not sufficient to erase a century of accumulated wealth: structural racism trumps personal responsibility. Drawing on data from the 2013 Survey of Consumer Finances, we find that white adults who don't graduate high school, don't get married before having children, and don't work full time still have much greater wealth at the median than comparable black and Latino adults—and often have more wealth than black and Latino households that have married, completed more education, or work longer hours. Differences in consumption habits also cannot explain the wealth gap; we look at academic research finding that white households spend more than black households of comparable incomes, yet still have more wealth.

The racial wealth gap matters because of the central role wealth plays in enabling families to both handle current financial challenges and make investments in their future. Families that have accumulated some wealth are better equipped to manage unanticipated expenses like an emergency medical bill, or disruptions in household income such as a layoff, without falling into debt or poverty. Over the longer term, wealth can expand the prospects of the next generation, helping to pay for college, provide a down payment for a first home, or capitalize a new business. As long as a substantial racial wealth gap persists, white households will continue to enjoy greater advantages than their black and Latino neighbors in meeting the financial challenges of everyday life and will be able to make greater investments in their children, passing economic advantages on. We can only create a more equitable future by confronting the racial wealth gap and the public policies that continue to fuel and exacerbate it.

Terminology

This report analyzes data on white, black, and Latino households. The terms 'black' and 'white' are used to refer to the representative respondents of a household who identified as non-Latino black or white in the Survey of Consumer Finances (SCF).[2] Latinos include everyone who identified as Hispanic or Latino and may be of any race.

Throughout this report, we use the term 'racial wealth gap' to refer to the absolute differences in

wealth (assets minus debt) between the median black and white households as well as between the median Latino and white households. All dollar figures are in 2013 dollars.

Attending College Does Not Close the Racial Wealth Gap

Higher education is associated with greater household wealth for Americans of every race and ethnicity, yet going to college isn't enough to overcome racial disparities in wealth.[3] Among households under age 55, the median white high school dropout has similar wealth to the median black adult who graduated high school and attended at least some college, according to data from the Survey of Consumer Finances.[4] Similarly, the median Latino adult who attended college has similar wealth to the median white high school dropout. The median white adult who attended college has 7.2 times more wealth than the median black adult who attended college and 3.9 times more wealth than the median Latino adult who attended college.

As Figure 1 shows, black adults with at least some college—a group that includes any amount of college education, from students who attended college but attained no degree to those with associate's or bachelor's degrees—had $11,100 in wealth at the median, while Latino adults with at least some college had $20,500 in wealth at the median. These figures are dwarfed by the $79,600 in median wealth held by whites who attended at least some college.

In effect, to gain wealth comparable to white high school dropouts, black and Latino students must not only complete high school, but also attend college.[5] Higher education is valuable—but when it comes to wealth, white privilege is equally, if not more valuable.

Attending college is associated with wealth in a number of ways. A college education has long been heralded as a ladder of social mobility: graduates who earn a bachelor's degree or other college certification are more likely to be employed and generally have higher earning power than high school graduates or dropouts; they can use their higher incomes to build savings and wealth. Indeed, research consistently finds that college graduates of every race and ethnicity have greater income and wealth than their counterparts who did not graduate college.[6] Yet wealth also plays a

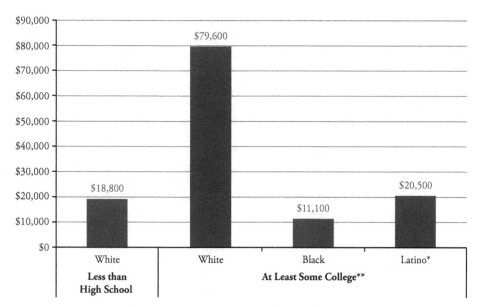

FIGURE 1. Median Wealth by Educational Attainment for Working Households under Age 55

Source: Authors' calculations of the Survey of Consumer Finances, 2013

* Latino refers to anyone who identified as Hispanic or Latino on the Survey of Consumer Finances and may be of any race.

**This group includes households who attended college but attained no degree as well as those with associate's or bachelor's degrees. Households with graduate and professional degrees are not included.

role in determining who attends college in the first place, and how much debt students must take on to get a degree. [7] In effect, education can generate a "wealth feedback loop," as parents' level of education and wealth significantly predicts the level of education their children will complete.[8] Thus, the educational and wealth-building opportunities directly denied to people of color in past generations continue to reverberate in the lives of their children, even those whose educational achievements open up opportunities for well-paid employment opportunities.

Having left high school without a diploma and never pursued further education, white dropouts do not gain the wealth-building opportunities offered by a college education. Yet advantages such as greater access to gifts and inheritances offer white households more opportunities to gain and build wealth, even when they have completed less education. Because white families accumulated more wealth over a history in which black and Latino families were excluded from many wealth-building opportunities through discriminatory policies in housing, banking, education, and other areas, white families today have,

in general, greater resources to pass on to their offspring. As a result, white families are 5 times more likely than black or Latino families to receive large gifts and inheritances, and the amounts they receive are far greater.[9] An analysis of data from the Panel Study of Income Dynamics finds that white recipients collect $5,013 more than black families on average over a two-year period.[10] Not only do these funds add up to a substantial amount over time, but they can also be used to jump-start further wealth accumulation, for example, by enabling white families to buy homes and begin acquiring equity earlier in their lives and to make larger down payments on a first home, thereby reducing interest rates and lending costs.[11]

For black and Latino households with at least some college education, the high cost of college is another reason why pursuing higher education—and even attaining a degree—is not more effective at reducing the racial wealth gap. Our earlier research finds that even if black and Latino students graduated college at the same rate as white students, the reduction in the racial wealth gap would be modest: cut by just 1 to 3 percent at the median.[12] Because of the existing racial wealth gap, white college students dis-proportionately come from wealthier family back-grounds than black and Latino students. As a result, the research finds that black students borrow at much higher rates, and in higher amounts, to receive the same college degrees as their white counterparts.[13] The higher rate of borrowing may in turn contribute to other disparities, including college dropout and com-pletion rates. With less student loan debt to pay off over their working years, the typical white college graduate has a head start on building wealth com-pared to their black peers. The picture is different for Latino households, which attend and graduate from college at lower rates than both black and white households. Evidence suggests that Latino students may be more averse to taking on student loans even when they face substantial financial need for school.[14]

The result is that whites with little formal educa-tion still benefit disproportionately from social net-works that help them attain jobs, and inheritances and gifts that help them build wealth. Black and Latino households that have pursued higher educa-tion often lack access to these networks and resources, but black college-goers in particular carry a dispro-portionate burden of student loan debt that saps their resources and diminishes their ability to build wealth. While attending and graduating college is associated with greater wealth for all American households and

is a boost to lifetime earnings and wealth, it's not enough to overcome historic and accumulated white advantages in building wealth. An individual's striv-ing to get a degree is not sufficient to close the racial wealth gap.

Raising Children in a Two-Parent Household Does Not Close the Racial Wealth Gap

Raising children is expensive. The high cost of child care and difficulty of supporting a family on a single income make it particularly difficult for single par-ents to get by, much less build wealth. Not surpris-ingly, single parent households have much higher poverty rates and significantly lower wealth than two-parent households. Yet, raising children in a two-parent household isn't enough to overcome racial disparities in wealth. According to data from the Survey of Consumer Finances, the median white single parent has 2.2 times more wealth than the median black two-parent household and 1.9 times more wealth than the median Latino two-parent household.

As Figure 2 shows, black couples with children had $16,000 in wealth at the median, while Latino couples with children had $18,800 in wealth at the median. For each group, this is significantly more than the wealth of single-parent households. Yet it is a fraction of the $161,300 in median wealth held by

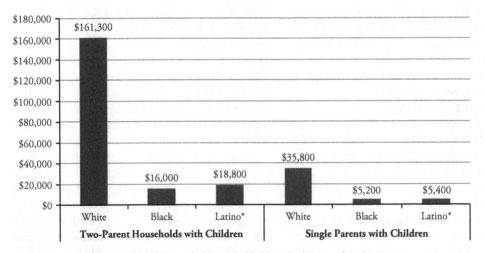

FIGURE 2.   Median Wealth of Households with Children by Partnership Status

Source: authors' calculations of the Survey of Consumer Finances, 2013

* Latino refers to anyone who identified as Hispanic or Latino on the Survey of Consumer Finances and may be of any race.

white couples with children—and is still significantly less than the $35,800 in median wealth held by white single parents. Despite the financial benefits of marriage and partnership, including the opportunity to share expenses, provide child care within the family, or have two adult earners, the median white single parent is $19,800 wealthier than the median black couple with children, and $17,000 wealthier than the median Latino couple with children. It's clear that raising children with two parents is not enough to overcome the racial wealth gap—or even to pull families out of poverty. In 2014, black children with married parents were 3 times more likely to be living in poverty than white children with married parents, while Latino children with married parents were 4 times more likely to be living in poverty than their white counterparts.[15]

In 1965, Senator Daniel Patrick Moynihan's report, *The Negro Family: The Case for National Action*, attributed racial inequality as well as poverty and crime in the black community to family structure, particularly the prevalence of families headed by single mothers.[16] Not only did research at the time cast doubt on this causality, but evidence over the last the 50 years demonstrates that rates of child poverty, educational attainment, and crime do not track rates of single parenthood.[17] Thus, even though the share of children living with a single mother rose for all racial and ethnic groups through the mid-1990s and has remained high since then, school completion and youth arrests for violent crimes have declined significantly, while poverty rates have fluctuated according to economic conditions. Family structure does not drive racial inequity, and racial inequity persists regardless of family structure. The benefits of intergenerational wealth transfers and other aspects of white privilege discussed above benefit white single mothers, enabling them to build significantly more wealth than married parents of color.

Working Full Time Does Not Close the Racial Wealth Gap

Full-time work is critical to the economic security of most American households. Full-time jobs generally pay more per hour than comparable part-time work and are more likely to offer benefits such as employer-provided health coverage, paid sick time, and workplace retirement plans that can provide greater opportunities for employees to build wealth. At the median, households in which at least 1 member works full time (35 or more hours per week) have greater wealth than households where the only jobs held are part-time positions (less than 35 hours per week). But working full time isn't enough to close the racial wealth gap. According to data from the Survey of Consumer Finances, the median white household that includes a full-time worker has 7.6 times more wealth than the median black household with a full-time worker. The median white household that includes a full-time worker also has 5.4 times more wealth than the median Latino household with a full-time worker. Even white households that include only part-time workers—with at least 1 person in the household employed but not working more than 35 hours a week—have statistically indistinguishable levels of wealth as black households with a member employed full-time.[18]

As Figure 3 shows, black households with at least 1 worker employed full time had $10,800 in wealth at the median, while Latino households with at least 1 worker employed full time had $15,300 in wealth at the median. For both groups, this is significantly more than the wealth of households where workers held only part-time jobs. Yet it is nowhere near the $82,400 in median wealth held by white households with a full-time worker. Working full time is far from enough for households of color to catch up to white wealth. Despite all the wealth-building benefits of full-time employment, median black and Latino households with full-time workers had essentially the same level of wealth as the median white household with only part-time employment.

Americans of all races and ethnicities work hard: among working white, black, and Latino households with a head under age 55, all work at least 40 hours a week at the median and 80 percent or more have an adult employed full-time.[19] Yet work effort does not pay off equally: in 2012, white workers employed full time earned a median wage of $792 a week, compared to $621 for African Americans and $568 for Latinos. Considering gender makes the pay disparities even more glaring: Latina women employed full time earned median weekly wages equal to just 59 percent of the wages earned by white males, while black

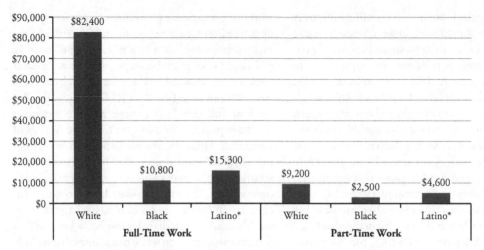

FIGURE 3.   Median Wealth of Full- and Part-Time Workers, for Working Households under Age 55
Source: authors' calculations of the Survey of Consumer Finances, 2013
* Latino refers to anyone who identified as Hispanic or Latino on the Survey of Consumer Finances and may be of any race.

women earned just 68 percent as much.[20] However, even if households earned the same income, the racial wealth gap would persist. Previous research from Demos and Institute on Assets and Social Policy at Brandeis University finds that if the distribution of incomes for black and Latino Americans was similar to that of white households (with a median equal to $50,400 in 2011), the wealth gap between black and white households would shrink just 11 percent at the median and the wealth gap between Latino and white households would shrink just 9 percent. An individual's striving to get a higher paid job or work more hours is not enough to close the racial wealth gap.

Spending Less Does Not Close the Racial Wealth Gap
Personal finance experts abound with advice on how to build wealth by moderating personal spending and shifting a greater share of income into savings and investment. Yet evidence from a recent Duke University study suggests that reduced spending is not enough to close the racial wealth gap between black and white households. Drawing on data from the 2013 and 2014 Consumer Expenditure Surveys, researchers find that the average white household spends 1.3 times more than the average black household of the same income group.[21] In general, little research has been published on racial and ethnic

differences in spending patterns and no findings were available on consumer spending among Latino households.

The Duke study divided households into low-, medium-, and high-income groups and found that white households in every income group spent more on average than black households in the same group. On average, white households spent $13,700 per quarter, compared to $8,400 for black households. Even after accounting for factors such as family structure, income, occupation, and geography, as well as wealth and homeownership, white households at all income levels continued to spend more than comparable black households, with low-income white households spending $1,200 more per quarter than low-income black households and high-income white households spending $1,400 more than their black counterparts.

The study also looked at specific categories of spending, finding that white households spend about twice as much as black households on entertainment among all income groups and that white households, especially those with low incomes, spend more than black households on cars. The researchers note that "for clothing, jewelry, personal care, entertainment, eating out, and other non-essential spending, our findings show that black consumers in fact spend the same or much less than whites, at all income levels."[22] The only category in which black households were found to consistently spend more was for utilities, including payments for electricity, heating fuel, water, sewer, and telephone service; this may be due to the common utility company practice of risk-based pricing, which requires a deposit or other form of additional payment from customers with low credit scores, without stable employment, or with criminal records. While technically color-blind, risk-based pricing can have a disproportionate impact on black consumers, causing them to be charged more than white households for the same service.[23]

Differences in spending habits cannot explain the racial wealth gap: white households spend more than black households with similar incomes, yet also have more wealth. While spending less and saving more may be excellent advice for individuals, the evidence suggests that personal spending habits are not driving the racial wealth gap and cannot succeed in closing it.

Conclusion

In order for our nation to begin addressing disparities in wealth and opportunity, we must recognize that the racial wealth gap exists and clearly understand its causes. Public polling data suggest that there remains much work to be done. When asked in a 2016 opinion survey to assess "the financial situation of blacks compared with whites today," just half of Americans (including 47 percent of white respondents, 58 percent of black respondents, and 49 percent of Latino respondents) recognized that white households were better off financially.[24] No comparable question was asked comparing the finances of Latino and white households. Similarly when the same survey asked about "reasons why black people in our country may have a harder time getting ahead than whites," majorities of black, white, and Latino Americans endorsed explanations such as "lack of motivation to work hard" and "family instability"—factors which the data reveal cannot account for the growth and persistence of the racial wealth gap. Although 77 percent of respondents also identified "racial discrimination" as a reason that black Americans might have a harder time economically, 66 percent asserted that "discrimination that is based on the prejudice of individual people" was a greater problem than "discrimination that is built into our laws and institutions."

Racial inequality in wealth is rooted in historic discrimination and perpetuated by policy: our analyses show that individual behavior is not the driving force behind racial wealth disparities. Typical black and Latino households that attend college and live in two-parent households still have much less wealth than similarly situated white households. Black and Latino households that include a full-time worker have much less wealth than white households with a full-time worker, and only slightly more wealth at the median than white households where the only person employed works part time. Differences in spending habits also fail to explain wealth disparities between black and white households.

Building a more equitable society will require a shift in focus away from individual behavior towards addressing structural and institutional racism. To aid in that effort, the Institute on Assets and Social Policy developed the Racial Wealth Audit™ as a framework to evaluate public policy proposals for their potential to reduce the racial wealth gap. When policymakers explicitly consider the racial wealth gap in developing policy, the Racial Wealth Audit can provide information to achieve greater racial wealth equity.

Methodological Appendix

In this report, we present key descriptive statistics of household wealth for specific subgroups of interest. Data derive from the Survey of Consumer Finances (SCF) from 2013, the most recent available year for the data, which is among the best national sources of data on household wealth in the United States.

We calculated medians and their confidence intervals for wealth of white, black, and Hispanic [the term used by SCF] households by education, family structure, and full-time employment. For the analysis of households by educational level and full-time employment status, only households who reported any positive work hours and whose head was less than 55 years of age were included in the analysis to focus on working households in their prime workforce years.

Because of the highly skewed nature of wealth, the median is the preferred statistic, as it is not affected by extremely high values. Confidence intervals indicate the range in which we are 95 percent confident the true median value in the population lies. Overlapping confidence intervals between 2 groups indicate that the values for the groups cannot be statistically distinguished; conversely, if the confidence intervals for 2 groups do not overlap, we have sufficient statistical evidence to indicate that the values of the 2 medians are distinct in the true population.

Analysis by race/ethnicity is shaped by the available data in the SCF on the US resident population. Whites are defined for this analysis as non-Hispanic whites. Hispanics may be of any race. There are insufficient data in the SCF to produce this analysis for Native Americans and Asians.

Analysis Results
Education: Median wealth is compared among race/ethnicity subgroups for households whose heads have not completed high school and those whose heads have completed some college or hold an undergraduate

degree. Those households with no work hours, with heads greater than 54 years old, and with heads with more than 16 years of education (i.e. those who started or completed graduate school) have been excluded from the analysis.

Since this report focuses on median wealth, 95 percent confidence intervals for all median point estimates are provided. Confidence intervals are calculated using a dataset which averages the data from the 5 implicates that are provided in the SCF data for every survey household in the survey due to multiple imputation (see the SCF website for further information on the survey design of the SCF). Median point estimates vary slightly when the dataset is averaged across implicates; however, these confidence intervals provide a conservative estimate of the confidence intervals while adjusting for the structure of the publicly available data.

95 Percent Confidence Intervals for Median Wealth of Households < 55 by Education

| | Less than High School | | At Least Some College | |
	Number of Observations	95% Confidence Interval	Number of Observations	95% Confidence Interval
All US Households	225	$6,934 $12,706	1464	$42,237 $63,463
White, Non-Hispanics	79	$5,675 $31,877	1009	$64,095 $97,505
Black/African Americans	21	* *	223	$6,623 $15,897
Hispanics	115	$6,674 $10,766	120	$12,239 $31,033

Note: Households with positive work hours only. Those households with heads with at least some graduate school excluded. *Insufficient number of observations to report wealth for African American households with less than a high school degree.

Family Structure of Parents: Median wealth is compared for parent households—who have children of the head or spouse of any age living in the household—by marital status of the household head among

white, black, and Latino households. Households who are married or living with a partner are included in the married sample.

95% Confidence Intervals for Median Wealth of Parent Households by Marital Status

| | Married/Partnered with Kids | | Single with Kids | |
	Number of Observations	95% Confidence Interval	Number of Observations	95% Confidence Interval
All US Households	1963	$79,590 $107,102	636	$10,308 $18,172
White, Non-Hispanics	1361	$138,888 $184,712	303	$23,530 $48,510
Black/African Americans	164	$9,151 $23,289	207	$1,748 $8,900
Hispanics	256	$10,930 $23,470	80	$2,855 $9,637

Full-Time and Part-Time Work of Households: Lastly, median wealth is examined by race/ethnicity for working households categorized by whether a household has an adult employed full time or has only workers employed part time. Households that have at least 1 full-time working adult (at least 35 hours per week) are selected into the group of households working full time, while those with positive work hours but no individual working at least 35 hours per week are included in the group of part-time working households. Households with no work hours and those with heads greater than 54 years old have been excluded from the analysis to focus on working households in their prime years and avoid the inclusion of part-time workers transitioning into retirement.

95 Percent Confidence Intervals for Median Wealth of Households < 55 by Full-Time and Part-Time Employment Status

	Full-Time			Part-Time		
	Number of Observations	95% Confidence Interval		Number of Observations	95% Confidence Interval	
All U.S. Households	2694	$46,162	$61,782	332	$2,630	$7,570
White, Non-Hispanics	1766	$73,694	$92,510	183	$2,220	$15,781
Black/African Americans	339	$7,587	$15,085	67	$74	$4,386
Hispanics	354	$10,637	$19,223	48	$972	$8,628

Notes

1. For more on the causes of the racial wealth gap, see Melvin Oliver and Thomas Shapiro, *Black Wealth, White Wealth: A New Perspective on Racial Inequality* (New York: Routledge, 1997).

2. For more on SCF, see the Federal Reserve website, which provides detailed information and documentation about the survey, https://www.federalreserve.gov/econresdata/scf/scfindex.htm.

3. Darrick Hamilton, William Darity Jr., Anne E. Price, Vishnu Sridharan, and Rebecca Tippett, *Umbrellas Don't Make It Rain: Why Studying and Working Hard Isn't Enough for Black Americans*, Insight Center for Community Economic Development, April 2015, https://gallery.mailchimp.com/bf2b9b3cf3fdd8861943f-ca2f/files/Umbrellas_Dont_Make_It_Rain8.pdf.

4. Since wealth accumulation tends to increase with age and is influenced by the time period when a worker is employed, our analysis looked exclusively at households where someone is currently employed and looked only at heads of households under age 55. Our analysis also excludes households with a graduate or professional degree.

5. We analyze households with at least "some college" rather than college graduates because the sample size in the Survey of Consumer Finances was not large enough to make statistically significant comparisons of college graduates of color.

6. William R. Emmons and Bryan J. Noeth, *Why Didn't Higher Education Protect Hispanic and Black Wealth?* Federal Reserve Bank of St. Louis, December 2015, https://www.stlouisfed.org/publications/in-the-balance/issue12-2015/why-didnt-higher-education-protect-hispanic-and-black-wealth#table2.

7. Dalton Conley, "Capital for College: Parental Assets and Postsecondary Schooling," *Sociology of Education*, 74, no. 1 (January 2001): 59–72, http://www.jstor.org/stable/2673145?seq=1#page_scan_tab_contents.

8. Mark Huelsman, Tamara Draut, Tatjana Meschede, Lars Dietrich, Thomas Shapiro, and Laura Sullivan, *Less Debt, More Equity: Lowering Student Debt While Closing the Black-White Wealth Gap*, Demos, November 2015, http://www.demos.org/publication/less-debt-more-equity-lowering-student-debt-while-closing-black-white-wealth-gap.

9. Signe-Mary McKernan, Caroline Ratcliffe, Margaret Simms, and Sisi Zhang, *Do Financial Support and Inheritance Contribute to the Racial Wealth Gap?* Urban Institute, Opportunity and Ownership Facts no. 26, September 2012, http://www.urban.org/sites/default/files/alfresco/publication-pdfs/412644-Do-Financial-Support-and-Inheritance-Contribute-to-the-Racial-Wealth-Gap-.PDF.

10. McKernan et al., *Do Financial Support and Inheritance Contribute to the Racial Wealth Gap?*

11. Thomas Shapiro, Tatjana Meschede, and Sam Osoro, *The Roots of the Widening Racial Wealth Gap: Explaining the Black-White Economic Divide*, Institute on Assets and Social Policy, February 2013, http://iasp.brandeis.edu/pdfs/Author/shapiro-thomas-m/racial-wealthgapbrief.pdf.

12. Amy Traub and Catherine Reutschlin, *The Racial Wealth Gap: Why Policy Matters*, Demos, 2015, http://www.demos.org/publication/racial-wealth-gap-why-policy-matters.

13. Huelsman et al., *Less Debt, More Equity.*

14. Alissa Cunningham and Debra Santiago, *Student Aversion to Borrowing*, Institute for Higher Education Policy and Excellence in Education, 2008, https://www.edexcelencia.org/research/publications/student-aversion-borrowing-who-borrows-and-who-doesnt

15. *U.S. Census Current Population Survey*, Bureau of Labor Statistics, 2014, https://www.bls.gov/cps/cps_aa2014.htm

16. *The Negro Family: The Case for National Action*, U.S. Department of Labor, Office of Policy Planning and Research, 1965, http://www.dol.gov/oasam/programs/history/webidmeynihan.htm

17. Jeffrey Hayes and Phillip Cohen, *Moynihan's Half Century: Have We Gone to Hell in a Hand Basket? Council on Contemporary Families*, March 2015, https://contemporaryfamilies.org/moynihan-half-century-brief-report/.

18. Differences in wealth may be influuenced by a greater share of households that include 2 adults working full time. Sample sizes were too small to permit separate analysis of single- and dual-earner households. Additional analysis of single-earner households suggests similar work patterns by race/ethnicity to those found among both single and couple households. To avoid including households on the brink of retirement who are a working part time as they transition out of the workforce, this analysis includes only households headed by an adult under age 55.

19. Authors' calculations based on the 2013 Survey of Consumer Finances.

20. *Current Population Survey*, Bureau of Labor Statistics. Weekly and hourly earnings data from the Current Population Survey, 2014.

21. Raphaël Charron-Chénier, Joshua J. Fink, and Lisa A. Keister, "Race and Consumption: Black and White Disparities in Household Spending," *Sociology of Race and Ethnicity*, May 2016, https://www.ncbi.nlm.nih.gov/pmc/articles/PMC6641572/

22. Raphaël Charron-Chénier, Joshua J. Fink, and Lisa A. Keister, *Racial Inequality and Consumption: Exploring Disparities in White and Black Household Expenditures*, Duke University, May 2015, https://wealthinequality.org/content/uploads/2015/10/Racial-Inequality-and-Consumption.pdf.

23. Jonathan S. Spader, "Beyond Disparate Impact: Risk-based Pricing and Disparity in Consumer Credit History Scores, *The Review of Black Political Economy* 37, no. 2 (June 2010): 61–78, https://www.researchgate.net/publication/226802620_Beyond_Disparate_Impact_Risk-based_Pricing_and_Disparity_in_Consumer_Credit_History_Scores; Racial Justice and Equal Economic Opportunity Project, *Past Imperfect: How Credit Scores and Other Analytics 'Bake In' and Perpetuate Past Discrimination*, National Consumer Law Center, May 2016, https://www.nclc.org/images/pdf/credit_discrimination/Past_Imperfect050616.pdf.

24. Pew Research Center, *On Views of Race and Inequality, Blacks and Whites Are Worlds Apart*, Pew Research Center, June 2016, http://www.pewsocialtrends.org/files/2016/06/ST_2016.06.27_Race-Inequality-Final.pdf.

Questions for Critical Thinking

1. How does the authors' discussion of the wealth gap help you understand the importance of addressing economic inequality in the United States?

2. How does your personal experience with regard to class influence your understanding of or level of disagreement with the authors' discussion?

3. The idea of the American Dream (if a person works hard, they will get ahead) is still common in the United States. How does this idea perpetuate misconceptions of those who are poor? Of those who are wealthy?

MEDIA MAGIC

Making Class Invisible

° *Gregory Mantsios*

The mass media serve as a powerful tool for shaping the way we think. A significant part of our culture, mass media operate as an extremely important socialization mechanism. In the following article, Gregory Mantsios explains how the media influence the values that we learn to place on members of social classes. According to Mantsios, those who control the media (i.e., the upper class) can use this institution to create class divisions and to define our attitudes about members of different social classes.

Of the various social and cultural forces in our society, the mass media is arguably the most influential in molding public consciousness. Americans spend an average twenty-eight hours per week watching television. They also spend an undetermined number of hours reading periodicals, listening to the radio, and going to the movies. Unlike other cultural and socializing institutions, ownership and control of the mass media is highly concentrated. Twenty-three corporations own more than one-half of all the daily newspapers, magazines, movie studios, and radio and television outlets in the United States.[1] The number of media companies is shrinking and their control of the industry is expanding. And a relatively small number of media outlets is producing and packaging the majority of news and entertainment programs. For the most part, our media is national in nature and single-minded (profit-oriented) in purpose. This media plays a key role in defining our cultural tastes, helping us locate ourselves in history, establishing our national identity, and ascertaining the range of

national and social possibilities. In this essay, we will examine the way the mass media shapes how people think about each other and about the nature of our society.

The United States is the most highly stratified society in the industrialized world. Class distinctions operate in virtually every aspect of our lives, determining the nature of our work, the quality of our schooling, and the health and safety of our loved ones. Yet remarkably, we, as a nation, retain illusions about living in an egalitarian society. We maintain these illusions, in large part, because the media hides gross inequities from public view. In those instances when inequities are revealed, we are provided with messages that obscure the nature of class realities and blame the victims of class-dominated society for their own plight. Let's briefly examine what the news media, in particular, tells us about class.

About the Poor

The news media provides meager coverage of poor people and poverty. The coverage it does provide is often distorted and misleading.

The Poor Do Not Exist

For the most part, the news media ignores the poor. Unnoticed are forty million poor people in the nation—a number that equals the entire population of Maine, Vermont, New Hampshire, Connecticut, Rhode Island, New Jersey, and New York combined. Perhaps even more alarming is that the rate of poverty is increasing twice as fast as the population growth in the United States. Ordinarily, even a calamity of much smaller proportion (e.g., flooding in the Midwest) would garner a great deal of coverage and hype from a media usually eager to declare a crisis, yet less than one in five hundred articles in the *New York Times* and one in one thousand articles listed in the *Readers Guide to Periodic Literature* are on poverty. With remarkably little attention to them, the poor and their problems are hidden from most Americans.

When the media does turn its attention to the poor, it offers a series of contradictory messages and portrayals.

The Poor Are Faceless

Each year the Census Bureau releases a new report on poverty in our society and its results are duly reported in the media. At best, however, this coverage emphasizes annual fluctuations (showing how the numbers differ from previous years) and ongoing debates over the validity of the numbers (some argue the number should be lower, most that the number should be higher). Coverage like this desensitizes us to the poor by reducing poverty to a number. It ignores the human tragedy of poverty—the suffering, indignities, and misery endured by millions of children and adults. Instead, the poor become statistics rather than people.

The Poor Are Undeserving

When the media does put a face on the poor, it is not likely to be a pretty one. The media will provide us with sensational stories about welfare cheats, drug addicts, and greedy panhandlers (almost always urban and Black). Compare these images and the emotions evoked by them with the media's treatment of middle-class (usually white) "tax evaders," celebrities who have a "chemical dependency," or wealthy businesspeople who use unscrupulous means to "make a profit." While the behavior of the more affluent offenders is considered an "impropriety" and a deviation from the norm, the behavior of the poor is considered repugnant, indicative of the poor in general, and worthy of our indignation and resentment.

The Poor Are an Eyesore

When the media does cover the poor, they are often presented through the eyes of the middle class. For example, sometimes the media includes a story about community resistance to a homeless shelter or storekeeper annoyance with panhandlers. Rather than focusing on the plight of the poor, these stories are about middle-class opposition to the poor. Such stories tell us that the poor are an inconvenience and an irritation.

The Poor Have Only Themselves to Blame

In another example of media coverage, we are told that the poor live in a personal and cultural cycle of poverty that hopelessly imprisons them. They routinely center on the Black urban population and focus on perceived personality or cultural traits that doom the poor. While the women in these stories typically exhibit an "attitude" that leads to trouble or a promiscuity that leads to single motherhood, the men possess a need for immediate gratification that leads to drug abuse or an unquenchable greed that leads to the pursuit of fast money. The images that are seared into our mind are sexist, racist, and classist. Census figures reveal that most of the poor are white, not Black or Hispanic, that they live in rural or suburban areas, not urban centers, and hold jobs at least part of the year.[2] Yet, in a fashion that is often framed in an understanding and sympathetic tone, we are told that the poor have inflicted poverty on themselves.

The Poor Are Down on Their Luck

During the Christmas season, the news media sometimes provides us with accounts of poor individuals or families (usually white) who are down on their luck. These stories are often linked to stories about soup kitchens or other charitable activities and sometimes call for charitable contributions. These "Yule time" stories are as much about the affluent as they are about the poor: they tell us that the affluent in our society are a kind, understanding, giving people—which we are not.* The series of unfortunate circumstances that have led to impoverishment are presumed to be a temporary condition that will improve with time and a change in luck.

Despite appearances, the messages provided by the media are not entirely disparate. With each variation, the media informs us what poverty is not (i.e., systemic and indicative of American society) by informing us what it is. The media tells us that poverty is either an aberration of the American way of life (it doesn't exist, it's just another number, it's unfortunate but temporary) or an end product of the poor themselves (they are a nuisance, do not deserve better, and have brought their predicament upon themselves).

By suggesting that the poor have brought poverty upon themselves, the media is engaging in what William Ryan has called "blaming the victim."[3] The media identifies in what ways the poor are different as a consequence of deprivation, then defines those differences as the cause of poverty itself. Whether blatantly hostile or cloaked in sympathy, the message is that there is something fundamentally wrong with the victims—their hormones, psychological makeup, family environment, community, race, or some combination of these—that accounts for their plight and their failure to lift themselves out of poverty.

But poverty in the United States is systemic. It is a direct result of economic and political policies that deprive people of jobs, adequate wages, or legitimate support. It is neither natural nor inevitable: there is enough wealth in our nation to eliminate poverty if we chose to redistribute existing wealth or income. The plight of the poor is reason enough to make the elimination of poverty the nation's first priority. But poverty also impacts dramatically on the nonpoor. It has a dampening effect on wages in general (by maintaining a reserve army of unemployed and underemployed anxious for any job at any wage) and breeds crime and violence (by maintaining conditions that invite private gain by illegal means and rebellion-like behavior, not entirely unlike the urban riots of the 1960s). Given the extent of poverty in the nation and the impact it has on us all, the media must spin considerable magic to keep the poor and the issue of poverty and its root causes out of the public consciousness.

About Everyone Else

Both the broadcast and the print news media strive to develop a strong sense of "we-ness" in their audience. They seek to speak to and for an audience that is both affluent and like-minded. The media's solidarity with affluence, that is, with the middle and upper class, varies little from one medium to another. Benjamin DeMott points out, for example, that the *New York Times* understands affluence to be intelligence, taste, public spirit, responsibility, and a readiness to rule and "conceives itself as spokesperson for a readership awash in these qualities"[4] Of course, the flip side to creating a sense of "we" or "us" is establishing a perception of the "other" The other relates back to the faceless, amoral, undeserving, and inferior "underclass" Thus, the world according to the news media is divided between the "underclass" and everyone else. Again the messages are often contradictory.

The Wealthy Are Us

Much of the information provided to us by the news media focuses attention on the concerns of a very wealthy and privileged class of people. Although the concerns of a small fraction of the populace, they are presented as though they were the concerns of everyone. For example, while relatively few people actually own stock, the news media devotes an inordinate amount of broadcast time and print space to business news and stock market quotations. Not only do business reports cater to a particular narrow clientele, so do the fashion pages (with $2,000 dresses), wedding

---

* American households with incomes of less than $10,000 give an average of 5.5 percent of their earning to charity or to a religious organization, while those making more than $100,000 a year give only 2.9 percent. After changes in the 1986 tax code reduced the benefits of charitable giving, taxpayers earning $500,000 or more slashed their average donation by nearly one-third. Furthermore, many of these acts of benevolence do not help the needy. Rather than provide funding to social service agencies that aid the poor, the voluntary contributions of the wealthy go to places and institutions that entertain, inspire, cure, or educate wealthy Americans— *art museums, opera houses,* theaters, orchestras, ballet companies, private hospitals, and elite universities. (Robert Reich, "*Secession of the Successful New York Times Magazine,*" February 17, 1991, p. 43.)

announcements, and the obituaries. Even weather and sports news often have a class bias. An all-news radio station in New York City, for example, provides regular national ski reports. International news, trade agreements, and domestic policies issues are also reported in terms of their impact on business climate and the business community. Besides being of practical value to the wealthy, such coverage has considerable ideological value. Its message: the concerns of the wealthy are the concerns of us all.

The Wealthy (as a Class) Do Not Exist

While preoccupied with the concerns of the wealthy, the media fails to notice the way in which the rich as a class of people create and shape domestic and foreign policy. Presented as an aggregate of individuals, the wealthy appear without special interests, interconnections, or unity in purpose. Out of public view are the class interests of the wealthy, the interlocking business links, the concerted actions to preserve their class privileges and business interests (by running for public office, supporting political candidates, lobbying, etc.). Corporate lobbying is ignored, taken for granted, or assumed to be in the public interest. (Compare this with the media's portrayal of the "strong arm of labor" in attempting to defeat trade legislation that is harmful to the interests of working people.) It is estimated that two-thirds of the U.S. Senate is composed of millionaires.[5] Having such a preponderance of millionaires in the Senate, however, is perceived to be neither unusual nor anti-democratic; these millionaire senators are assumed to be serving "our" collective interests in governing.

The Wealthy Are Fascinating and Benevolent

The broadcast and print media regularly provide hype for individuals who have achieved "super" success. These stories are usually about celebrities and superstars from the sports and entertainment world. Society pages and gossip columns serve to keep the social elite informed of each others' doings, allow the rest of us to gawk at their excesses, and help to keep the American dream alive. The print media is also fond of feature stories on corporate empire builders. These stories provide an occasional "insider's" view of the private and corporate life of industrialists by suggesting a rags

to riches account of corporate success. These stories tell us that corporate success is a series of smart moves, shrewd acquisitions, timely mergers, and well thought out executive suite shuffles. By painting the upper class in a positive light, innocent of any wrongdoing (labor leaders and union organizations usually get the opposite treatment), the media assures us that wealth and power are benevolent. One person's capital accumulation is presumed to be good for all. The elite, then, are portrayed as investment wizards, people of special talent and skill, whom even their victims (workers and consumers) can admire.

The Wealthy Include a Few Bad Apples

On rare occasions, the media will mock selected individuals for their personality flaws. Real estate investor Donald Trump and New York Yankees owner George Steinbrenner, for example, are admonished by the media for deliberately seeking publicity (a very unupper class thing to do); hotel owner Leona Helmsley was caricatured for her personal cruelties; and junk bond broker Michael Milken was condemned because he had the audacity to rob the rich. Michael Parenti points out that by treating business wrongdoings as isolated deviations from the socially beneficial system of "responsible capitalism," the media overlooks the features of the system that produce such abuses and the regularity with which they occur. Rather than portraying them as predictable and frequent outcomes of corporate power and the business system, the media treats abuses as if they were isolated and atypical. Presented as an occasional aberration, these incidents serve not to challenge, but to legitimate, the system.[6]

The Middle Class Is Us

By ignoring the poor and blurring the lines between the working people and the upper class, the news media creates a universal middle class. From this perspective, the size of one's income becomes largely irrelevant: what matters is that most of "us" share an intellectual and moral superiority over the disadvantaged. As *Time* magazine once concluded, "Middle America is a state of mind."[7] "We are all middle class," we are told, "and we all share the same concerns": job security, inflation, tax burdens, world peace, the cost of food and housing, health care, clean air and water, and the safety of our streets. While the concerns of the wealthy are quite distinct from those of the middle class (e.g., the wealthy worry about investments, not jobs), the media convinces us that "we [the affluent] are all in this together"

The Middle Class Is a Victim

For the media, "we" the affluent not only stand apart from the "other"—the poor, the working class, the minorities, and their problems—"we" are also victimized by the poor (who drive up the costs of maintaining the welfare rolls), minorities (who commit crimes against us), and by workers (who are greedy and drive companies out and prices up). Ignored are the subsidies to the rich, the crimes of corporate America, and the policies that wreak havoc on the economic well-being of middle America. Media magic convinces us to fear, more than anything else, being victimized by those less affluent than ourselves.

The Middle Class Is Not a Working Class

The news media clearly distinguishes the middle class (employees) from the working class (i.e., blue collar workers) who are portrayed, at best, as irrelevant, outmoded, and a dying breed. Furthermore, the media will tell us that the hardships faced by blue-collar workers are inevitable (due to progress), a result of bad luck (chance circumstances in a particular industry), or a product of their own doing (they priced themselves out of a job). Given the media's presentation of reality, it is hard to believe that manual, supervised, unskilled, and semiskilled workers actually represent more than 50 percent of the adult working population.[8] The working class, instead, is relegated by the media to "the other"

In short, the news media either lionizes the wealthy or treats their interests and those of the middle class as one in the same. But the upper class and the middle class do not share the same interests or worries. Members of the upper class worry about stock dividends (not employment), they profit from inflation and global militarism, their children attend exclusive private schools, they eat and live in a royal fashion, they call on (or are called upon by) personal physicians, they have few consumer problems, they can escape whenever they want from environmental pollution, and they live on streets and travel to other areas under the protection of private police forces.[9],**

The wealthy are not only a class with distinct lifestyles and interests, they are a ruling class. They receive a disproportionate share of the country's yearly income, own a disproportionate amount of the country's wealth, and contribute a disproportionate number of their members to governmental bodies and decision-making groups—all traits that William Domhoff, in his classic work *Who Rules America*, defined as characteristic of a governing class.[10]

This governing class maintains and manages our political and economic structures in such a way that these structures continue to yield an amazing proportion of our wealth to a minuscule upper class. While the media is not above referring to ruling classes in other countries (we hear, for example, references to Japan's ruling elite),[11] its treatment of the news proceeds as though there were no such ruling class in the United States.

Furthermore, the news media inverts reality so that those who are working class and middle class learn to fear, resent, and blame those below, rather than those above them in the class structure. We learn to resent welfare, which accounts for only two cents out of every dollar in the federal budget (approximately $10 billion) and provides financial relief for the needy,[†] but learn little about the $11 billion the federal government spends on individuals with incomes in excess of $1,000,000 (not needy),[12] or the $17 billion in farm subsidies, or the $214 billion (twenty times the cost of welfare) in interest payments to financial institutions.

Middle-class whites learn to fear African Americans and Latinos, but most violent crime occurs within poor and minority communities and is neither interracial[‡] nor interclass. As horrid as such crime is, it should not mask the destruction and violence perpetrated by corporate America. In spite of the fact that 14,000

** The number of private security guards in the United States now exceeds the number of public police officers. (Robert Reich, "*Secession of the Successful*," *New York Times Magazine*, February 17, 1991, p. 42.)

† A total of $20 billion is spent on welfare when you include all state funding. But the average state funding also comes to only two cents per state dollar.

‡ In 92 percent of the murders nationwide the assailant and the victim are of the same race (46 percent are white/white, 46 percent are black/black), 5.6 percent are black on white, and 2.4 percent are white on black. (FBI and Bureau of Justice Statistics, 1985–1986, quoted in Raymond S. Franklin, *Shadows of Race and Class*, University of Minnesota Press, Minneapolis, 1991, p. 108.)

innocent people are killed on the job each year, 100,000 die prematurely, 400,000 become seriously ill, and 6 million are injured from work-related accidents and diseases, most Americans fear government regulation more than they do unsafe working conditions.

Through the media, middle-class—and even working class—Americans learn to blame blue-collar workers and their unions for declining purchasing power and economic security. But while workers who managed to keep their jobs and their unions struggled to keep up with inflation, the top 1 percent of American families saw their average incomes soar 80 percent in the last decade.[13] Much of the wealth at the top was accumulated as stockholders and corporate executives moved their companies abroad to employ cheaper labor (56 cents per hour in El Salvador) and avoid paying taxes in the United States. Corporate America is a world made up of ruthless bosses, massive layoffs, favoritism and nepotism, health and safety violations, pension plan losses, union busting, tax evasions, unfair competition, and price gouging, as well as fast buck deals, financial speculation, and corporate wheeling and dealing that serve the interests of the corporate elite, but are generally wasteful and destructive to workers and the economy in general.

It is no wonder Americans cannot think straight about class. The mass media is neither objective, balanced, independent, nor neutral. Those who own and direct the mass media are themselves part of the upper class, and neither they nor the ruling class in general have to conspire to manipulate public opinion. Their interest is in preserving the status quo, and their view of society as fair and equitable comes naturally to them. But their ideology dominates our society and justifies what is in reality a perverse social order—one that perpetuates unprecedented elite privilege and power on the one hand and widespread deprivation on the other. A mass media that did not have its own class interests in preserving the status quo would acknowledge that inordinate wealth and power undermines democracy and that a "free market" economy can ravage a people and their communities.

Notes

1. Martin Lee and Norman Solomon, *Unreliable Sources*, Lyle Stuart (New York, 1990), p. 71. See also Ben Bagdikian, *he Media Monopoly*, Beacon Press (Boston, 1990).
2. Department of Commerce, Bureau of the Census, "Poverty in the United States: 1992," *Current Population Reports, Consumer Income*, Series P60–185, pp. xi, xv, 1.
3. William Ryan, *Blaming the Victim*, Vintage (New York, 1971).
4. Benjamin Demott, *The Imperial Middle*, William Morrow (New York, 1990), p. 123.
5. Fred Barnes, "The Zillionaires Club," *The New Republic*, January 29, 1990, p. 24.
6. Michael Parenti, *Inventing Reality*, St. Martin's Press (New York, 1986), p. 109.
7. *Time*, January 5, 1979, p. 10.
8. Vincent Navarro, "The Middle Class—A Useful Myth," *The Nation*, March 23, 1992, p. 1.
9. Charles Anderson, *The Political Economy of Social Class*, Prentice Hall (Englewood Cliffs, N.J., 1974), p. 137.
10. William Domhoff, *Who Rules America?*, Prentice Hall (Englewood Cliffs, N.J., 1967), p. 5.
11. Lee and Solomon, *Unreliable Sources*, p. 179.
12. *Newsweek*, August 10, 1992, p. 57.
13. *Business Week*, June 8, 1992, p. 86.

Questions for Critical Thinking

1. What assumptions do you have about members of different socioeconomic classes? Does Mantsios's discussion help you to understand the sources of these assumptions?
2. How do media representations influence our understandings of the sources of economic inequality? According to these representations, who is to blame for such inequality?
3. How do media representations of class influence policies that are created to respond to economic inequality? In your opinion, do these policies effectively address the source of the problem? Why or why not?

LATINOS ARE EACH OF US

Fair and Just Immigration Policies for All

* *Noreen M. Sugrue and Sylvia Puente*

Public policies in the United States increasingly are reflecting distorted, inaccurate, and terrible images of the Latina/o/x communities within our borders. Relying on research evidence, authors Noreen M. Sugrue and Sylvia Puente demonstrate the reality that, like all other past and present immigrant groups, Latinas/os/x living in the US—be they documented or undocumented immigrants, native-born or naturalized citizens—contribute significantly to the stability and health of the country.

Fair and just policies centering on immigrants and immigrations must reflect the data as well as values and ideals of words inscribed on the Statue of Liberty:

> Give me your tired, your poor, Your huddled masses yearning to breathe free, The wretched refuse of your teeming shore. Send these, the homeless, tempest-tost to me, I lift my lamp beside the golden door!

The Problem

According to the [former President Trump], many members of Congress, numerous state and local officials, and an embarrassingly large percentage of the general public, Latinos are immigrants and just do not belong here. These views and beliefs persist in spite of the fact that in 2017, there were about 56.8 million Latinos in the US, 19.7 million or 34 percent of whom were immigrants, leaving 39.1 million or just under two thirds of whom were US citizens.

Current immigration policies, ICE raids, and deportation activities, as well as the descriptions of Latinos coming to or currently living in the US, would lead one to believe that most Latinos in this country are foreigners, very few are citizens, and they do not contribute to the social good. In fact, they are too often described as being a social problem, exacerbating violence, ruining communities, taking handouts, and contributing little, if anything, to the social, political, and economic stability and health of the US. Public policies increasingly are reflecting this distorted, inaccurate, and hateful discourse. That is, public policies continue to take aim at Latinos as if they are out to destroy the US economy and way of way life by eroding the country's social and cultural DNA. The reality is that Latinos, like every other immigrant group past and present, be they asylum seekers, documented immigrants, undocumented immigrants, naturalized citizens, or native born, are making significant and essential contributions to the wellbeing of all residing in the US.

Noreen M. Sugrue and Sylvia Puente. (2020). "Latinos are Each of Us: Fair and Just Immigration Policies for All." In Glenn W. Muschert, Kristen M. Budd, Michelle Christian, and Robert Perrucci (Eds.), *Agenda for Social Justice: Solutions for 2020* (pp. 13–20). Policy Press. ISBN 978-1- 4473- 5461-1.

The Research Evidence

We cannot ignore that it is the hateful bigotry that seems to be the foundation for far too many discussions and policy decisions regarding immigration and immigrants generally, and Latinos specifically. Therefore, we turn to facts about who Latinos are and what they are contributing to the US, all with the intent of providing a foundation of truth in order to better explore fairer and just social policies for immigration, all immigrants, and each of us living in the US.

Today, more than 321 million people live in the US; slightly more than 44 million are immigrants, making immigrants about 14 percent of the total US population. In 2000, approximately 40 percent of Latinos were foreign born; today, according to Pew Research, about 34 percent are foreign born. There are over 56 million Latinos living in the US which translates into almost 18 percent of the US population being Latino; that percentage will only continue to grow for the foreseeable future.

A common ugly untrue charge that is far too often leveled against all Latinos, especially the undocumented, and is used as a justification for public policies such as the change in the definition of public charge, is that Latinos are taking advantage of the system and "getting all kinds of government support and free stuff" paid for by hardworking "real" Americans. One way to document that this charge is false is to examine labor force and economic data.

According to the Bureau of Labor Statistic (BLS), in 2017, the labor force participation rate for Latinos was 66.1 percent, regardless of country of origin, while the rate for non-Latinos was 62.2 percent.

According to other reports, another way to understand the economic contributions of Latinos in the US is: If US Latinos were their own nation, they would have the world's seventh-largest gross domestic product (GDP), at $2.13 trillion. According to a research center at the University of Georgia, this year Latino purchasing power will top $1.7 billion.

Finally, in 2019 earning an income that was 200 percent of the federal poverty level translated into an annual salary of $24,980 for one person or $51,500 for a family of four. Forty percent of undocumented workers earn at or above 200 percent of the federal poverty level. This means that even if they were

legally entitled to apply for government benefits and subsidies, which they are not, their incomes would make them ineligible; simply put, they earn too much.

It is commonly noted, or at least implied, that only Latinos are undocumented. Another claim we hear all too often is that undocumented Latinos are poor, they are now crossing the border in the largest numbers ever to do bad things, and they are using US-born children for "chain migration." All of these charges are untrue.

And, while it is true that Latinos are a significant share of undocumented workers, their numbers have been dropping since 2008. At the same time, significantly measurable numbers of undocumented workers from other parts of world are living in the US (e.g., 16 percent are from Asia and 13 percent are from every other region in the world, including Europe, Canada, and Africa).

Robert Sampson, a sociologist at Harvard points out that communities with high numbers of Latino immigrants, regardless of status, have far lower rates of crime than similar communities that are dominate by native-born people.

It should also be noted that undocumented Latinos in the US, far from recently arriving to get "free stuff from the government" or having children here to function as "anchor babies," are long term working age residents who have high rates of employment. Specifically, 62 percent have been in the US for more than 10 years and 21 percent have been living in the US for more than 20 years. Of the 66 percent who are between the ages of 25 and 54, 67 percent of this group are employed, compared to only 58 percent of the US born in the same age group.

Another untrue charge that drives unjust and unfair policies is that undocumented Latino immigrants are almost all males who speak no English and live in horrible conditions that are detrimental to neighborhoods. Almost half (47 percent) of undocumented immigrants are female and only about 44 percent of the undocumented speak no English or do not speak it very well. At the same time, almost 10 percent of undocumented Latinos speak only English and 34 percent of them own their own home.

Latino immigrants and their American children are the catalyst for creating immigration reform. And those reforms must be framed in terms of social justice, fairness, and equity. In other words, immigration policies must not reflect the misrepresentations, fear peddling, vilifications, and lies currently perpetuated by words and the misuse of data.

Addressing the language used in public discourse is necessary but difficult. How we speak of something or someone reveals our values and underlying views; it shapes how we define problems and structure solutions. Too much of today's discourse surrounding immigration and immigrants gives rise to policies that are unfair and unjust, to say the least. While language use cannot be legislated, every one of us has the moral responsibility to counter and challenge all distortions, lies, and attacks that are verbally hoisted onto immigrants. Each of us must speak truth to power and hate. It is when that occurs that we have the best chance of designing and implementing fair and just social policies.

Recommendations and Solutions

Policies related to immigration and immigrants must be built on two principles. The first is that immigration reforms and policies should be tied to the economic and social needs of the US, most notably economic growth and development. There is no disputing that immigration is a necessary condition for the US to secure both economic and population growth. Without growth in those two areas, the long-term stability and security of the country is not guaranteed. The second principle is the US's humanitarian and moral responsibilities to those seeking opportunity, safety, and protection; the US has a moral duty to these people. The US has these duties and obligations because of its power, wealth, and history. It is a national noblesse oblige.

Policy solutions are not easy. Immigration is complicated but if approached from the framework of social justice and fairness, there are many options available to states and the federal government. However, before embracing specific solutions, it must be underscored that the first step in addressing anything related to immigration or any immigrant is that all discussions and proposed solutions and policies must be grounded in the data. Further, the lies and vitriolic disdain for immigrants that all too often dominate the public discourse today must stop. It is a truism to

note that without a change in that discourse there will be no policy changes because the two are inexorably linked. Truth, facts, and fairness must be what shape our words so that our policies also can be shaped within the same context.

Although the data here are primarily Latino based, it is important to remember that immigration policies are written for all immigrants. The horrific treatment targeted at and vicious attacks on Latinos coming, or who have come, to the US through the southern border are driving the need for policy changes and recommendations that will restructure how immigrants are treated. These policy changes are required in order to redress the unspeakably immoral treatment of Latino immigrants as well as their US families. Latinos have borne an unconscionable amount of abuse and discrimination; rectifying those through improving immigration policies will benefit all immigrants and all native-born Americans. And, such reforms and policies will go a long way in ensuring that each of us lives not in a perfect union, but rather in a country that continually strives to be a more perfect union.

The following are specific policy recommendations that should be instituted immediately because they are just. In addition, these policy proposals will benefit the nation and all living within its borders, regardless of where they or their ancestors were born.

1. All Immigration and Customs Enforcements (ICE) raids must stop for at least four years.
   There are two exceptions to this:
   i. National security risks, which must be demonstrated to a judicial panel of three federal judges. All evidence presented for such cases must meet the criminal standards of collection, chain of command, and constitutional protections for alleged criminals.
   ii. Conviction of violent criminal offense. Any convictions used as a basis for deportation must have exhausted the constitutionally guaranteed appellate processes, which are open to all who come before the criminal justice system.

2. There must be an allocation of whatever money and resources are required in order to guarantee adequate numbers of appropriately

trained staff so that there is a timely processing of applications for all who are seeking entry into the US.

   i. There needs to be a determination of specifically how much time is required for the "timely processing of applications for all seeking entry into the US."

3. The number of immigration judges must be increased to meet the demand for fair and just processing of all applications.

4. There must be a fair and reasonably easy path to citizenship for all undocumented immigrants who have not met the exception to deportations criteria.

5. All money for the erection of a border wall must be frozen for five years. This will provide enough time for fair and just immigration policies to be enacted. In addition, it will provide a short-term period for the evaluation of how these policies are working and living up to the two principles that guided their development and implementation.

6. Any legal challenges to the policies suggested here, or any other policy initiatives that meet the two principles laid out earlier, must be given expedited hearings and reviews in the courts.

7. All detention centers, camps, or holding facilities of any kind must be dismantled immediately.

8. There will be no family separation. This policy will be disbanded and legislation must be enacted to ensure such horrors can never again occur.

9. There must be both the personnel and monetary resources necessary to reunite separated families immediately.

   i. The necessary medical and mental health needs of these separated families will be met and costs will be absorbed by the federal government.

   ii. Any adoption of children separated from families at the border will be null and void. Those children will be reunited with their family in the US.

   iii. How children that are not reunited with families will be cared for will be determined not by a government agency but rather by groups put together by an array of experts in the areas of trauma, family, and abandonment. These groups will be constituted and monitored by the American Academy of Pediatrics and any other non-governmental agencies with the requisite expertise in addressing and mitigating the horrors and traumas associated with family separation.

10. We must reaffirm and ensure that we provide the constitutional guarantees that are, or should be, afforded anyone, regardless of immigration status, in the US who are confronting legal structures or institutions. In addition, there must be the creation and formalization of processes for application, review, adjudication, and appeal of request for entry into the US. And these processes must be afforded to all who seek entry, regardless of whether they enter the country by land, air, or sea. Further, those processes must differentiate between immigrants, refugees, and asylum seekers. Each of these categories carries special circumstances and needs to be treated as a sui generis category.

   i. This approach to those seeking entry into the US will ensure fairness and due process while also building trust in the system. Those three components are necessary especially since some cases will be denied.

11. There should be no laws, orders, or policies that in any way intimidate, call into question, or drive underground immigrants who live with family members who are US citizens. In the case of Latinos, because this community is really a community of US citizens and immigrants, all policies targeting immigrants or any family members must reflect and respect this reality.

12. Those who are residing in the US, regardless of status, require a path to stability and security. As the data document, the contributions of immigrants, regardless of status, are enormous. Those contributions must be acknowledged. Public policies must be a set of incentives for supporting the continuation of such contributions.

13. Currently, public support for immigrants is both restricted and dependent upon where immigrants and their families live. The goal is to have immigrants integrate into US life—be vital and contributing members of communities, states, and the nation. If that goal is to be met, then public policies need to reflect that sometimes people need a safety net to succeed. There should be no time constraints or conditions on assisting people with food, housing, health care, transportation, language acquisition, or educational needs. This assistance should be seen as investment in the human capital and capacity that will benefit all who live in the US, regardless of where they or their parents were born.

    i. Safety net policies that are accessible with no artificial time barriers are squarely on top of the two foundational components for fair and just immigration policies.

Immigration is here to stay; immigrants, although there has been a discernible decline in numbers, will continue to come to the US. It is, therefore, incumbent upon each of us to ensure that our immigration policies are fair and just. These issues are complex, morally challenging, and any public action or response must be grounded in the realities of who immigrants are and why they immigrate, not stereotypes, purposeful lies, fear mongering, or misinformed emotional hyperbole.

Every sovereign nation has a right to control its own borders and set immigration policies. At the same time, the US and 47 other countries are signatories to the 1948 Universal Declaration of Human Rights, which notes that people have a right to migrate. This means the US, up to this point, believed that every human being had a right to move, seek shelter or refuge, but also that no nation was obligated to take all who came to and/or through their borders. Assuming each nation addresses requests for immigration, shelter, or asylum in a fair and even-handed manner, there would be trust in the process. Nations adhering to such processes become beacons and standard bearers for how to work with people moving from one nation to another. And it is with that in mind as well as a commitment to data-driven social-justice-oriented policies that a fair, humane, and workable immigration system is possible in the US. Such a system benefits the society overall as well as the immigrants and their descendants, and that is what is fair and just in a democracy.

Key Resources

Davis, Julie Hirschfeld, and Michael D. Shear. 2019. *Border Wars: Inside Trump's Assault on Immigration.* New York: Simon and Schuster.

DeParle, Jason. 2019. *A Good Provider Is One Who Leaves: One Family and Immigration in the 21st Century.* New York: Penguin Random House.

Hendricks, Kasey, et al. 2017. *A Tale of Three Cities: The State of Racial Justice in Chicago.* Chicago: Institute for Research on Race and Public Policy, University of Illinois at Chicago. Retrieved July 7, 2019. (https://stateofracialjusticechicago.com/a-tale-of-three-cities).

McDermott, Monica. 2006. *Working Class Whites: The Making and Unmaking of Race Relations.* Berkeley: University of California Press.

Noe-Bustamante, Luisard and Antonio Flores. 2019. *Facts on Latinos in the U.S.* Washington D.C.: Pew Research Center Hispanic Trends. Retrieved September 20, 2019. (https://www.pewresearch.org/hispanic/fact-sheet/latinos-in-the-u-s-fact-sheet/).

Sandoval-Strausz, A. K. 2019. *Barrio America: How Latino Immigrants Saved the American City.* New York: Basic Books.

Sawhill, Isabel. 2018. *The Forgotten Americans: An Economic Agenda for a Divided Nation.* New Haven: Yale University Press.

Shapiro, Thomas M. 2017. *Toxic Inequality: How America's Wealth Gap Destroys Mobility, Deepens the Racial Divide, and Threatens Our Future.* New York: Basic Books.

Vissek, M. Anne, and Edwin Melendez. 2015. "Working in the New Low Wage Economy: Understanding Participation in Low-Wage Employment in the Recessionary Era." *The Journal of Labor and Society,* 18: 7–29.

Zepeds-Millan, Chris. 2017. *Latino Mass Mobilization: Immigration, Racialization, and Activism.* Cambridge: Cambridge University Press.

Questions for Critical Thinking

1. How does the authors' discussion of the research data on the contributions of Latinas/os/x impact your understanding of this issue?
2. As the authors discuss, strict enforcement of immigration law would have a profound effect on our economy. What would be the impact on consumers if there were suddenly fewer immigrant workers?
3. What changes are necessary to immigrant policy in the United States that would counter the inequality and economic exploitation often faced by immigrant workers?

Sex and Gender

THE SOCIAL CONSTRUCTION OF GENDER

· *Judith Lorber*

In the following essay, sociologist and gender scholar Judith Lorber describes how the process of gender identity construction begins at birth with placement within a sex category (male or female). As Lorber clearly explains, gender constructs are created and justified by a variety of institutions, including the family, the state, and the economy, thereby transforming them into a gender system in which men and masculinity are at the top of the hierarchy and women and femininity are at the bottom.

Talking about gender for most people is the equivalent of fish talking about water. Gender is so much the routine ground of everyday activities that questioning its taken-for-granted assumptions and presuppositions is like thinking about whether the sun will come up.[1] Gender is so pervasive that in our society we assume it is bred into our genes. Most people find it hard to believe that gender is constantly created and re-created out of human interaction, out of social life, and is the texture and order of that social life. Yet gender, like culture, is a human production that depends on everyone constantly "doing gender" (West and Zimmerman 1987).

And everyone "does gender" without thinking about it. Today, on the subway, I saw a well-dressed man with a year-old child in a stroller. Yesterday, on a bus, I saw a man with a tiny baby in a carrier on his chest. Seeing men taking care of small children in public is increasingly common—at least in New York City. But both men were quite obviously stared at—and smiled at, approvingly. Everyone was doing gender—the men who were changing the role of fathers and the other passengers, who were applauding them silently. But there was more gendering going on that probably fewer people noticed. The baby was wearing a white crocheted cap and white clothes. You couldn't tell if it was a boy or a girl. The child in the stroller was wearing a dark blue T-shirt and dark print pants. As they started to leave the train, the father put a Yankee baseball cap on the child's head. Ah, a boy, I thought. Then I noticed the gleam of tiny earrings in the child's ears, and as they got off, I saw the little flowered sneakers and lace-trimmed socks. Not a boy after all. Gender done.

Gender is such a familiar part of daily life that it usually takes a deliberate disruption of our expectations of how women and men are supposed to act to pay attention to how it is produced. Gender signs and signals are so ubiquitous that we usually fail to note them—unless they are missing or ambiguous. Then we are uncomfortable until we have successfully placed the other person in a gender status; otherwise, we feel socially dislocated. In our society, in addition to man and woman, the status can be *transvestite* (a person who dresses in opposite-gender clothes) and *transsexual* (a person who has had sex-change surgery). Transvestites and transsexuals construct their gender status by dressing, speaking, walking, gesturing in the ways prescribed for women or men—whichever they want to be taken for—and so does any "normal" person.

For the individual, gender construction starts with assignment to a sex category on the basis of what the genitalia look like at birth.[2] Then babies are dressed or adorned in a way that displays the category because parents don't want to be constantly asked whether their baby is a girl or a boy. A sex category becomes a gender status through naming, dress, and the use of other gender markers. Once a child's gender is evident, others treat those in one gender differently from those in the other, and the children respond to the different treatment by feeling different and behaving differently. As soon as they can talk, they start to refer to themselves as members of their gender. Sex doesn't come into play again until puberty, but by that time, sexual feelings and desires and practices have been shaped by gendered norms and expectations. Adolescent boys and girls approach and avoid each other in an elaborately scripted and gendered mating dance. Parenting is gendered, with different expectations for mothers and for fathers, and people of different genders work at different kinds of jobs. The work adults do as mothers and fathers and as low-level workers and high-level bosses, shapes women's and men's life experiences, and these experiences produce different feelings, consciousness, relationships, skills—ways of being that we call feminine or masculine.[3] All of these processes constitute the social construction of gender.

Gendered roles change—today fathers are taking care of little children, girls and boys are wearing unisex clothing and getting the same education, women and men are working at the same jobs. Although many traditional social groups are quite strict about maintaining gender differences, in other social groups they seem to be blurring. Then why the one-year-old's earrings? Why is it still so important to mark a child as a girl or a boy, to make sure she is not taken for a boy or he for a girl? What would happen

if they were? They would, quite literally, have changed places in their social world.

To explain why gendering is done from birth, constantly and by everyone, we have to look not only at the way individuals experience gender but at gender as a social institution. As a social institution, gender is one of the major ways that human beings organize their lives. Human society depends on a predictable division of labor, a designated allocation of scarce goods, assigned responsibility for children and others who cannot care for themselves, common values and their systematic transmission to new members, legitimate leadership, music, art, stories, games, and other symbolic productions. One way of choosing people for the different tasks of society is on the basis of their talents, motivations, and competence—their demonstrated achievements. The other way is on the basis of gender, race, ethnicity—ascribed membership in a category of people. Although societies vary in the extent to which they use one or the other of these ways of allocating people to work and to carry out other responsibilities, every society uses gender and age grades. Every society classifies people as "girl and boy children," "girls and boys ready to be married," and "fully adult women and men," constructs similarities among them and differences between them, and assigns them to different roles and responsibilities. Personality characteristics, feelings, motivations, and ambitions flow from these different life experiences so that the members of these different groups become different kinds of people. The process of gendering and its outcome are legitimated by religion, law, science, and the society's entire set of values.

Gender as Process, Stratification, and Structure

As a social institution, gender is a process of creating distinguishable social statuses for the assignment of rights and responsibilities. As part of a stratification system that ranks these statuses unequally, gender is a major building block in the social structures built on these unequal statuses.

As a *process*, gender creates the social differences that define "woman" and "man." In social interaction throughout their lives, individuals learn what is expected, see what is expected, act and react in expected ways, and thus simultaneously construct and maintain the gender order: "The very injunction to be given gender takes place through discursive routes: to be a good mother, to be a heterosexually desirable object, to be a fit worker, in sum, to signify a multiplicity of guarantees in response to a variety of different demands all at once" (J. Butler 1990, 145). Members of a social group neither make up gender as they go along nor exactly replicate in rote fashion what was done before. In almost every encounter, human beings produce gender, behaving in the ways they learned were appropriate for their gender status, or resisting or rebelling against these norms. Resistance and rebellion have altered gender norms, but so far they have rarely eroded the statuses.

Gendered patterns of interaction acquire additional layers of gendered sexuality, parenting, and work behaviors in childhood, adolescence, and adulthood. Gendered norms and expectations are enforced through informal sanctions of gender-inappropriate behavior by peers and by formal punishment or threat of punishment by those in authority should behavior deviate too far from socially imposed standards for women and men.

Everyday gendered interactions build gender into the family, the work process, and other organizations and institutions, which in turn reinforce gender expectations for individuals.[4] Because gender is a process, there is room not only for modification and variation by individuals and small groups but also for institutionalized change (J. W. Scott 1988, 7).

As part of a *stratification* system, gender ranks men above women of the same race and class. Women and men could be different but equal. In practice, the process of creating difference depends to a great extent on differential evaluation. As Nancy Jay (1981) says: "That which is defined, separated out, isolated from all else is A and pure. Not-A is necessarily impure, a random catchall, to which nothing is external except A and the principle of order that separates it from Not-A" (45). From the individual's point of view, whichever gender is A, the other is Not-A; gender boundaries tell the individual who is like him or her, and all the rest are unlike. From society's point of view, however, one gender is usually the touchstone, the normal, the dominant, and the other is different, deviant, and subordinate. In Western

society, "man" is A, "woman" is Not-A. (Consider what a society would be like where woman was A and man Not-A.)

The further dichotomization by race and class constructs the gradations of a heterogeneous society's stratification scheme. Thus, in the United States, white is A, African American is Not-A; middle class is A, working class is Not-A, and "African-American women occupy a position whereby the inferior half of a series of these dichotomies converge" (P. H. Collins 1990). The dominant categories are the hegemonic ideals, taken so for granted as the way things should be that white is not ordinarily thought of as a race, middle class as a class, or men as a gender. The characteristics of these categories define the Other as that which lacks the valuable qualities the dominants exhibit.

In a gender-stratified society, what men do is usually valued more highly than what women do because men do it, even when their activities are very similar or the same. In different regions of southern India, for example, harvesting rice is men's work, shared work, or women's work: "Wherever a task is done by women it is considered easy, and where it is done by [men] it is considered difficult" (Mencher 1988, 104). A gathering and hunting society's survival usually depends on the nuts, grubs, and small animals brought in by the women's foraging trips, but when the men's hunt is successful, it is the occasion for a celebration. Conversely, because they are the superior group, white men do not have to do the "dirty work," such as housework; the most inferior group does it, usually poor women of color (Palmer 1989).

Freudian psychoanalytic theory claims that boys must reject their mothers and deny the feminine in themselves in order to become men: "For boys the major goal is the achievement of personal masculine identification with their father and sense of secure masculine self, achieved through superego formation and disparagement of women" (Chodorow 1978, 165). Masculinity may be the outcome of boys' intrapsychic struggles to separate their identity from that of their mothers, but the proofs of masculinity are culturally shaped and usually ritualistic and symbolic (Gilmore 1990).

The Marxist feminist explanation for gender inequality is that by demeaning women's abilities and keeping them from learning valuable technological skills, bosses preserve them as a cheap and exploitable reserve army of labor. Unionized men who could easily be replaced by women collude in this process because it allows them to monopolize the better-paid, more interesting, and more autonomous jobs: "Two factors emerge as helping men maintain their separation from women and their control of technological occupations. One is the active gendering of jobs and people. The second is the continual creation of sub-divisions in the work processes, and levels in work hierarchies, into which men can move in order to keep their distance from women" (Cockburn 1985, 13).

Societies vary in the extent of the inequality in social status of their women and men members, but where there is inequality, the status "woman" (and its attendant behavior and role allocations) is usually held in lesser esteem than the status "man." Since gender is also intertwined with a society's other constructed statuses of differential evaluation—race, religion, occupation, class, country of origin, and so on—men and women members of the favored groups command more power, more prestige, and more property than the members of the disfavored groups. Within many social groups, however, men are advantaged over women. The more economic resources, such as education and job opportunities, are available to a group, the more they tend to be monopolized by men. In poorer groups that have few resources (such as working-class African Americans in the United States), women and men are more nearly equal, and the women may even outstrip the men in education and occupational status (Almquist 1987).

As a *structure*, gender divides work in the home and in economic production, legitimates those in authority, and organizes sexuality and emotional life (Connell 1987, 91–142). As primary parents, women significantly influence children's psychological development and emotional attachments, in the process reproducing gender. Emergent sexuality is shaped by heterosexual, homosexual, bisexual, and sadomasochistic patterns that are gendered—different for girls and boys, and for women and men—so that sexual statuses reflect gender statuses.

When gender is a major component of structured inequality, the devalued genders have less power, prestige, and economic rewards than the valued genders. In countries that discourage gender discrimination, many major roles are still gendered; women still do most of the domestic labor and child rearing, even while doing full-time paid work; women and men are segregated on the job and each does work considered "appropriate"; women's work is usually paid less than men's work. Men dominate the positions of authority and leadership in government, the military, and the law; cultural productions, religions, and sports reflect men's interests.

In societies that create the greatest gender difference, such as Saudi Arabia, women are kept out of sight behind walls or veils, have no civil rights, and often create a cultural and emotional world of their own (Bernard 1981). But even in societies with less rigid gender boundaries, women and men spend much of their time with people of their own gender because of the way work and family are organized. This spatial separation of women and men reinforces gendered differences, identity, and ways of thinking and behaving (Coser 1986).

Gender inequality—the devaluation of "women" and the social domination of "men"—has social functions and social history. It is not the result of sex, procreation, physiology, anatomy, hormones, or genetic predispositions. It is produced and maintained by identifiable social processes and built into the general social structure and individual identities deliberately and purposefully. The social order as we know it in Western societies is organized around racial, ethnic, class, and gender inequality. I contend, therefore, that the continuing purpose of gender as a modern social institution is to construct women as a group to be the subordinates of men as a group.

The Paradox of Human Nature

To say that sex, sexuality, and gender are all socially constructed is not to minimize their social power. These categorical imperatives govern our lives in the most profound and pervasive ways, through the social experiences and social practices of what Dorothy Smith calls the "everday/evernight world" (1990). The paradox of human nature is that it is *always* a manifestation of cultural meanings, social relationships, and power politics; "not biology, but culture, becomes destiny" (J. Butler 1990, 8). Gendered people emerge not from physiology or sexual orientations but from the exigencies of the social order, mostly from the need for a reliable division of the work of food production and the social (not physical) reproduction of new members. The moral imperatives of religion and cultural representations guard the boundary lines among genders and ensure that what is demanded, what is permitted, and what is tabooed for the people in each gender is well known and followed by most (C. Davies 1982). Political power, control of scarce resources, and, if necessary, violence uphold the gendered social order in the face of resistance and rebellion. Most people, however, voluntarily go along with their society's prescriptions for those of their gender status, because the norms and expectations get built into their sense of worth

and identity as [the way we] think, the way we see and hear and speak, the way we fantasy, and the way we feel.

There is no core or bedrock in human nature below these endlessly looping processes of the social production of sex and gender, self and other, identity and psyche, each of which is a "complex cultural construction" (J. Butler 1990, 36). *For humans, the social is the natural.* Therefore, "in its feminist senses, gender cannot mean simply the cultural appropriation of biological sexual difference. Sexual difference is itself a fundamental—and scientifically contested—construction. Both 'sex' and 'gender' are woven of multiple, asymmetrical strands of difference, charged with multifaceted dramatic narratives of domination and struggle" (Haraway 1990, 140).

Notes

1. Gender is, in Erving Goffman's words, an aspect of *Felicity's Condition:* "any arrangement which leads us to judge an individual's . . . acts not to be a manifestation of strangeness. Behind Felicity's Condition is our sense of what it is to be sane" (1983:27). Also see Bem 1993; Frye 1983, 17–40; Goffman 1977.
2. In cases of ambiguity in countries with modern medicine, surgery is usually performed to make the genitalia more clearly male or female.

3. See J. Butler 1990 for an analysis of how doing gender is gender identity.
4. On the "logic of practice," or how the experience of gender is embedded in the norms of everyday interaction and the structure of formal organizations, see Acker 1990; Bourdieu [1980] 1990; Connell 1987; Smith 1987.

References

Acker, Joan. 1990. "Hierarchies, jobs, and bodies: A theory of gendered organizations," *Gender & Society* 4: 139–58.

Almquist, Elizabeth M. 1987. "Labor market gendered inequality in minority groups," *Gender & Society* 1: 400–14.

Bem, Sandara Lipsitz. 1993. *The Lenses of Gender: Transforming the Debate on Sexual Inequality.* New Haven: Yale University Press.

Bernard, Jessie. 1981. *The Female World.* New York: Free Press.

Bourdieu, Pierre. [1980] 1990. *The Logic of Practice.* Stanford, Calif.: Stanford University Press.

Butler, Judith. 1990. *Gender Trouble: Feminism and the Subversion of Identity.* New York and London: Routledge.

Chodorow, Nancy. 1978. *The Reproduction of Mothering.* Berkeley: University of California Press.

Cockburn, Cynthia. 1985. *Machinery of Dominance: Women, Men and Technical Know-how.* London: Pluto Press.

Collins, Patricia Hill. 1990. "The social construction of black feminist thought," *Signs* 14: 745–73.

Connell, R. [Robert] W. 1987. *Gender and Power: Society, the Person, and Sexual Politics.* Stanford, Calif.: Stanford University Press.

Coser, Rose Laub. 1986. "Cognitive structure and the use of social space," *Sociological Forum* 1: 1–26.

Davies, Christie. 1982. "Sexual taboos and social boundaries," *American Journal of Sociology* 87: 1032–63.

Dwyer, Daisy, and Judith Bruce (eds.). 1988. *A Home Divided: Women and Income in the Third World.* Palo Alto, Calif.: Stanford University Press.

Frye, Marilyn. 1983. *The Politics of Reality: Essays in Feminist Theory.* Trumansburg, N.Y.: Crossing Press.

Gilmore, David D. 1990. *Manhood in the Making: Cultural Concepts of Masculinity.* New Haven: Yale University Press.

Goffman, Erving. 1977. "The arrangement between the sexes," *Theory and Society* 4: 301–33.

Haraway, Donna. 1990. "Investment strategies for the evolving portfolio of primate females," in Jacobus, Keller, and Shuttleworth.

Jacobus, Mary, Evelyn Fox Keller, and Sally Shuttleworth (eds.). (1990). *Body/politics: Women and the Discourse of Science.* New York and London: Routledge.

Jay, Nancy. 1981. "Gender and dichotomy," *Feminist Studies* 7: 38–56.

Mencher, Joan. 1988. "Women's work and poverty: Women's contribution to household maintenance in South India," in Dwyer and Bruce.

Palmer, Phyllis. 1989. *Domesticity and Dirt: Housewives and Domestic Servants in the United States, 1920–1945.* Philadelphia: Temple University Press.

Scott, Joan Wallach. 1988. *Gender and the Politics of History.* New York: Columbia University Press.

Smith, Dorothy. 1987. *The Everyday World as Problematic: A Feminist Sociology.* Toronto: University of Toronto Press.

_____. 1990. *The Conceptual Practices of Power: A Feminist Sociology of Knowledge.* Toronto: University of Toronto Press.

West, Candace, and Don Zimmerman. 1987. "Doing gender." *Gender & Society* 1: 125–51.

Questions for Critical Thinking

1. In what ways do you see yourself "doing gender"?
2. Lorber argues that gender is a social rather than a biological construct, yet the dominant notion in our society is that gender is linked to biological factors. What do you see as the reasoning behind assertions that gender is biological? What would be the implications of accepting the notion that gender is socially constructed and therefore mutable?
3. Lorber discusses many reasons why a culture maintains constructions of gender differences. What are your own ideas regarding why we maintain such constructs?

GIVING SEX

Deconstructing Intersex and Trans Medicalization Practices

° *Georgiann Davis, Jodie M. Dewey, and Erin L. Murphy*

The following reading illustrates the institutional power held by medicine, particularly as it creates and obfuscates notions of sex, gender, and sexuality. Authors Georgiann Davis, Jodie M. Dewey, and Erin L. Murphy argue that medical providers who specialize in intersex and trans medicine "give gender" by "giving sex." Yet these providers fail to take responsibility for their medicalization practices. Rather, they project blame onto parents in the case of intersex, or adult recipients of care in the case of trans persons.

Medicine is a powerful institution in countless ways, but it holds particular sway in producing and obscuring ideologies about sex, gender, and sexuality. When providers define bodies that defy sex, gender, and sexuality binaries as morbidities in need of corrective treatments (see Foucault [1973] 1994), they not only perpetuate but produce the notion that a healthy body is identifiably male or female, masculine or feminine, and heterosexual. Sociologist Catherine Connell argues that every setting has a "particular constellation of interactive practices and consequences" that interpret and reinterpret embodiment (2010, 50). This article compares how providers approach intersex and trans bodies in order to show how the "practices and consequences" of the medical profession actively work to align embodiment with binary constructions of sex, gender, and sexuality.

Public and intellectual discourse often conflates intersex and trans terminologies, experiences, and embodiments, but the two have important differences as well as similarities.[1] Intersex generally describes the presence of both male and female sex traits (genital, gonadal, and/or chromosomal). Trans is commonly used as "an abbreviated term" for "transgender" (individuals "whose gender identity or expression, or both, does not normatively align with their assigned sex") and "transsexual" (individuals who align their physical bodies with their gender identities via medical intervention; Pfeffer 2010, 167). While intersex and trans people disrupt binary understandings about sex and experience some of the same struggles with some identifying as both intersex and trans, our research suggests that they have significantly different experiences with medical providers, especially when it comes to surgery.[2,3]

Even after years of criticism from intersex people, many providers are quick to perform surgery on bodies of babies and young children that they consider abnormal (Davis 2014b; Davis and Murphy 2013; Holmes 2008; Karkazis 2008; Preves 2003).

GENDER & SOCIETY, Vol 30 No. 3, June 2016 490–514
DOI: 10.1177/0891243215602102

At the same time, they hesitate to act in cases where trans individuals request surgery (Dewey 2013; Lev 2009; Speer 2006), instead requiring them to undergo lengthy diagnostic processes according to codes in *The Diagnostic and Statistical Manual of Mental Disorders, Fifth Edition* (DSM-5) (American Psychiatric Association 2013), and guidelines outlined in the World Professional Association of Transgender Healthcare's *Standards of Care for the Health of Transsexual, Transgender, and Gender Nonconforming People* (SOC-7) (Coleman et al. 2012). This difference generates our discussion here, in which we ask why and how providers respond quickly to intersex but slowly to trans, and, in turn, is a crucial step in better understanding how intersex and trans embodiments are medicalized as problematic bodies. Specifically, we compare two qualitative datasets—one of medical providers who treat intersex people, and the other of medical providers who serve trans people—to explore how both kinds of providers articulate and address these issues.

Our fundamental claim is that providers often approach intersex and trans bodies through essentialist ideologies about sex, gender, and sexuality, which hold that sex is a binary biological phenomenon correlated with gender identity and sexuality. The majority of providers we spoke with base their medical recommendations on what they believe a patient's gender identity to be. This applies equally to situations in which they are determining whether an intersex individual needs intervention and situations in which they are responding to a trans individual's request for intervention. In 2010, sociologist Jane Ward theorized the process of "giving gender" as a way to understand how femmes in sexual relationships with transmen perform "gender labor" through various "emotional, physical, and sexual caretaking" acts that serve to authenticate their partner's gender (Ward 2010, 236). In 2011, sociologist Tey Meadow deployed the notion of "giving gender" to illustrate how parents of gender-variant children "engage in affective, intellectual and bodily projects to assist their children in securing their desired gender identities" by simultaneously drawing on "scientific and social knowledge in their accounts of their children's identities" (Meadow 2011, 730). We join this conversation by arguing that medical providers for both intersex and trans people also engage in this process of "giving gender," but they do so by "giving sex." We theorize giving sex as the process where providers validate (the construction of) heteronormative bodies and invalidate intersex and trans embodiments according to their interpretations of appropriate gender expectations. In this circular struggle over gendered embodiments and identities, sex assignments become profoundly gendered markers, as the institution of medicine acts as a gatekeeping site, deploying normative ideologies of sex, gender, and sexuality to map sex onto gender for embodiments that do not fit existing sex, gender, and sexuality binaries.

The Medical Gaze and "Morbid" Bodies

Since the nineteenth century, medical thinking has been based on a "medical polarity of the normal and the pathological" which results in a "healthy/morbid opposition" (Foucault [1973] 1994, 35). In this context, intersex and trans bodies have been—and unfortunately still are, despite some changing beliefs—constructed as abnormal, which is to say, in Foucault's terms, "pathological" and "morbid." In the case of intersex, the medical profession precipitously medicalizes healthy bodies as pathological without conferring with the intersex person (or with their parents if they are too young for consultation); in the case of trans, this medical pathologization occurs slowly due to the numerous steps required by the current SOC guidelines that slow down any requested medical interventions, regardless of the desires of trans people. We believe that medicalization is "a fluid and mutable dynamic whose causes and effects must be analyzed rather than assumed" (Tone 2012, 319), that "medicalization and diagnosis represent sites of struggle," and that the relationship between diagnosis and medicalization is rarely unidirectional but rather results in diverse and sometimes contradictory effects (Burke 2011, 188). Thus, we are determined to look closely at the connections providers make between normative sex embodiments and the possibilities for intersex and trans embodiments.

We are all, regardless of our genitalia, gonads, and chromosomes, subjected to the "medical gaze," which is the process by which medical professionals approach, diagnose, and judge bodies with uncontested authority in ways that frame one's body as either healthy or morbid (Foucault [1973] 1994). While providers could affirm intersex and trans as healthy differences on a continuum of normative sexed embodiments, instead, our data suggest, they often frame intersex and trans embodiments as pathologies on the basis of a belief that people are either male or female. Their judgments, in turn, can be a powerful incentive for intersex and trans folks—or their parents—to seek sexed embodiments via medicalized intervention so that normative sex, gender, and sexuality expectations do not disassociate them from their bodies. It is important to note here that regulation and normativity are not necessary outcomes of medicalization. Meadow (2011) uncovers moments when parents of gender variant youth use medical discourses to construct understandings of gender variance that resist the binary gender framework and create new spaces for their children; in essence, these parents use language and meanings derived from regulatory discourses in biomedicine and psychiatry to give gender to their children by affirming their gender variant identities. Similarly, Rahilly (2015, 358) finds parents of gender variant and transgender children disrupt the gender binary with their parenting styles, but "they do not refute presocial understandings of gender, which are often considered the converse of gender-progressive parenting."

Providers may very well be unaware of their role in constructing normatively sexed embodiments as healthy. McGann (2011, 337) discusses the diagnostic imaginary as "a way of thinking which conceals the presence of the social in diagnosis, closing off critical analysis of the complex ways they are structured by history, culture, politics, and value judgments." But conscious or not, this diagnostic imaginary and its privileging of normative sexed embodiments has powerful consequences. The construction of normative sexed embodiments has played a significant part in the history of medicalizing diverse sexed embodiments, to the point that we question whether the majority, rather than a minority, of medical providers can even imagine healthy gender identities for their gender variant intersex and trans patients. Moreover, pushing for and policing interventions that modify

bodies to fit within gender expectations itself disparages intersex and trans embodiments (Sadjadi 2013), in essence culturally disciplining them through medical technologies. In these cases, there is no clear division between cultural expertise and medical expertise (Rose 2007): Providers treat intersex and trans people because society awards them authority to "fix" bodies that deviate from normative expectations (Foucault [1973] 1994).

Medical responses to intersex and trans reflect the bureaucratic and ideological work sparked by the categorical crisis these groups incite (Davis and Murphy 2013; Meadow 2010). Clearly, intersex and trans undermine the idea that biological sex is a fixed, unitary characteristic. When providers determine whether intersex and trans individuals need treatment, they exercise biopower (Foucault [1973] 1994), managing and regulating bodies to foster the normatively gendered and disallow the gender or sex variant (Mills 2007). The physician's medicalized gaze determines a patient's health and treatment solely on the basis of the presence of the intersex trait or the individual's desire for a different sex to match their gender. This assessment begins when providers construct an intersex trait as an emergency that necessitates immediate attention (Davis and Murphy 2013) or an individual seeks medical services to address their trans embodiment (Dewey 2008; Winters 2006). A provider's perception of the patient's identity development plays a key, if often unstated, role in their interpretation of the best course of treatment. In the absence of a clear scientific test of sex, although they run many tests, providers often rely on an identity-based gender ideology and engage in a negotiated process of authenticating the patient's gender to ensure that the body harmonizes with what is perceived as a stable, coherent identity (Meadow 2010; Westbrook and Schilt 2014). Providers thus tend to engage in "gender naturalization work" as they balance the "ideological collision" between identity- and biology-based ideologies of gender (Westbrook and Schilt 2014).

In this way, providers contribute to a proliferation of "advances" in biomedicine and psychiatry that provide ways we can "know" the appropriate binary embodiment of sex, through questionable scientific approaches. Drawing on Bourdieu and Wacquant's (1992) discussion of "symbolic violence," Bourgois and Schonberg (2009) theorize the symbolic violence embedded in public health policies by showing how medical practices and policies that are disguised as dissemination of medical information to better facilitate choice-making can further disempower marginalized recipients of care. Similarly, in our discussion of responsibility for treating intersex and trans people, we explore how providers enact symbolic violence by claiming that they only offer information to their patients (or patients' families), while, consciously or not, pathologizing bodily variance.

Sociologist Raewyn Connell (2012) refers to the ontology of sex in relation to gender as "ontoformative": We enter into an existing gender structure that shapes us at the individual level as others react to us and treat us at the interactional level in ways that are themselves shaped by historical gendered dynamics (see Risman 2004). Sexed embodiments, especially intersex and trans, can challenge the gender structure by disrupting ideas about sex and gender correlation, but only if non-normative sexed embodiments are allowed rather than pathologized. When providers instead pathologize intersex and trans embodiments, they establish the claim that they can surgically relieve societal anxieties associated with being differently bodied. Surgery thus functions as a tool for aligning sex with gender, where the ultimate success is the enactment of a gender normative heterosexual identity. In this way, providers not only give gender, but regulate sexed embodiments by giving sex.

Although the process we have just described applies to all kinds of nonnormative sexed embodiments, differences between intersex and trans medicalization illuminate the social construction of sex, gender, and sexuality as arbitrary and correlated binaries (Butler 1993; Fausto-Sterling 2000; Foucault [1973] 1994; Kessler 1990). With these theoretical and empirical insights in hand, we compare the experiences of each group under the medical gaze.

Deconstructing Intersex and Trans Medicalization Practices

Our analysis revealed four key themes in the medicalization of intersex and trans embodiments as "problems." These themes, which represent the thinking and work of the majority of providers interviewed,

involve (1) defining the problem, (2) responding to the problem, (3) markers of successful treatment and perpetuation of the problem, and (4) responsibility for treating the problem.

Defining the Problem

When providers define intersex and trans embodiments as problems, they do so because they believe, consciously or unconsciously, in sex, gender, and sexuality as binary ideologies, which in turn underpin a problematic distinction between healthy and morbid bodies. In this binary framework, a healthy embodiment, to use Foucault's term, neatly aligns sex, gender, and sexuality: A healthy woman has a vagina, a healthy man has a penis, and both engage in heterosexual relations, specifically penilevaginal penetration. Any deviation from this alignment results in a morbid embodiment that is pathologized in providers' accounts. While some intersex and trans people may also believe that sex, gender, and sexuality are binaries, their beliefs are less consequential for they reside outside the medical gaze. They do not, for example, self-perform surgeries on their bodies.

Armed with the medical authority to surgically modify intersex bodies, many of the providers who treat intersex people relied on a binary understanding of sex, gender, and sexuality, which disallows unaltered intersex bodies to be viewed as healthy. Their accounts articulated naturalized views of sex and gender that they believed demonstrated how sexed embodiments should be regulated. Dr. ID explained:

> My experience with girls with CAH [congenital adrenal hyperplasia] suggests to me that [gender is] pretty hardwired. A lot of the CAH girls are significant tomboys. . . . I think some of those behaviors are absolutely hardwired.

If under the medical gaze gender is assumed to be a "hardwired" or inherent characteristic, the intersex body can never be considered healthy, for its natural sex ambiguity cannot be aligned with a singular gender. Some providers who treat intersex also correlate androgen exposure during gestational fetal development with sexual behaviors later in life. Dr. IA pointed to research on monkeys to suggest that "androgen levels during fetal development pro-duce male-typical behavior later on . . . humping behaviors and things like that . . . how they engage in intercourse." Here Dr. IA's account correlates sex traits with gendered behaviors that seems as much based on ideology—"male-typical . . . humping behaviors"—as the biological predispositions he presumes.

It is an easy jump from these essentialist and cor-related conceptions of sex, gender, and sexuality to the assumption that the uncorrelated intersex em-bodiment is a socially problematic morbidity. Dr. IC, for instance, insisted that life would be difficult for a child without a "normal" penis, who would not "see himself as most other males" and would not "be able to function as most other males." Despite—or per-haps because of—years of experience with intersex, Dr. IC could not disentangle the body, especially the genitals, from gender identity and sexual practices, in essence insisting that a "normal" penis is essential to being a man. This accounting of intersex embodi-ment as a morbid sex variation justifies surgical in-tervention and establishes it as a reasonable response to intersex.

One major difference between intersex and trans treatment is the timing of diagnosis, which in turn makes a difference in how providers consider the iden-tity development of their patients. Yet providers who treat trans adults, often interpret trans embodiments through a similar essentialist lens of male/female, masculine/feminine, gay/straight. Using the same lan-guage as Dr. ID, Dr. TM, a surgeon, articulated that gender identity is intertwined with biology: "First of all, it's not psychological. . . . People are telling me that this is the way they've felt since they were three, four, and five years old . . . so it quickly became ap-parent to me that [gender is] something that is hard-wired in the individual." Providers who serve trans people enact the medical gaze, establishing a narrative about patient identity grounded in biology to relieve the liability in providing treatments that are in opposi-tion to binary views of sex, gender, and sexuality and to justify the interventions they employ.

Moreover, looking at childhood to construct a giving gender narrative serves as a necessary, yet prob-lematic, proxy for proving that gender is biologically determined. At the same time, this framing explicitly

aligns with what Judith Butler (2004, 76) labels the complicated "instrument of pathologization," better known as the Gender Identity Disorder (GID) criteria in the DSM-IV-TR (American Psychiatric Associa-tion 2000), and which is also implied in the criteria for Gender Dysphoria in the DSM-5 (American Psy-chiatric Association 2013). Butler (2004, 76) reminds us that the diagnostic pathologization may offer access to insurance coverage for trans people request-ing interventions, but it does so at the cost of con-structing trans people as "ill, sick, wrong, out of order, abnormal, and to suffer a certain stigmatiza-tion as a consequence of the diagnosis."

Providers for trans people tend to be sensitive to the fact that a giving gender narrative that medical-izes trans can help legitimate it in the eyes of families, insurance companies, and the like and validate giving sex. This is why Dr. TE sees value in the DSM: "I think we need it [in the DSM], otherwise how would you get insurance to pay for it? How could you ex-plain it to family members?" In other words, medi-calization becomes a tool for empowerment that can facilitate sex embodiment. But the irony is that when providers use medicalization in a progressive way to support their patients' wishes, they do so by perpetu-ating the claim that sex, gender, and sexuality are natural, fixed phenomena whose pathological devia-tions can be medically corrected (see Butler 2004). Dr. TM, a surgeon, provided his giving sex account using intersex as a frame: "[Trans] . . . is basically an intersex condition. . . . It just happens to be brains that are intersexed, not genitalia that are inter-sexed . . . and it should not be in the DSM . . . be-cause it's certainly nothing psychological."[4] Ironically again, while a diagnosis is required for insurance coverage, insurance companies often exclude psychi-atric diagnoses related to gender from coverage, so providers who serve trans people often use alternative diagnoses, such as depression or anxiety, even as they continued to support GID's place in the previous DSM-IV-TR, presumably because of their belief in diagnostic power.

Although providers for trans people attempt to depathologize trans embodiment through biomedical explanations, they still often view trans people as morbid, pathologizing their condition in order to offer treatment (see Butler 2004). Like providers who treat intersex people, providers who serve trans people leave little, if any, room for an understanding of trans embodiments as healthy. In this sense, providers intervene with embodiment processes by giving gender to their patients through the process of giving sex.

Responding to the Problem

Although many providers similarly define intersex and trans as morbid deviations from normative expectations of sex, gender, and sexuality, providers who treat intersex people often frame intersex as a medical emergency—a morbidity that needs to be fixed immediately. While trans people may feel they are in an emergency situation, their providers tend to do everything they can to avoid such framing. Because of the power of the medical gaze (Foucault [1973] 1994), how providers frame these conditions as problems matters in that these pathologizing frames produce "knowledge" with authority for treatment (Butler 2004). In other words, in both instances, providers maintain control and authority over the body with the power to assert the need for medical interventions.

Dr. ID accounts for the necessity of running emergency tests, explaining, "We try to find out as much biochemical and genetic data as we can, *as fast as we can*" [emphasis added] in order to predict "what is likely to happen to them at puberty." Dr. II elaborated: "We let the family know that the emergency, which would have been a salt-wasting CAh, is or is not the concern. Once you say there's no medical emergency here, then we say, let's get some more data." In this case, there is a possible "medical emergency"—"salt-wasting CAh," which is potentially life-threatening—but ruling out that possibility does not end the medical investigation. Rather, the perception of an emergency situation is sustained by searching for "more data" in order to make questionable predictions about future gender (discussed in the next section). The sense of emergency is further heightened when a medical team treats intersex. In theory, the team model is in the best interest of the patient, but, as Dr. II explained, medical teams often meet to "help the family reach a decision *as soon as possible*" [emphasis added], thus perpetuating the creation of the emergency situation.

Similar to providers who treat intersex, providers who serve trans people often work within an emergency framework, but trans people are the ones who define their situation as urgent. In the trans case, providers try to minimize the emergency their patients created. Dr. TF explains: "If [trans patients] do not get what they want, surgery *now*, hormones *now*, they will go elsewhere" [emphasis added]. Therefore, he deflects the emergency by telling his patients that "this is not the way it works. . . . There are a lot of steps that you have to go through before we can say you need hormones [or other transitioning services]." Dr. TF references here the assessments with which many professionals begin the process of transitioning a patient. These assessments, under both the 6th and 7th versions of the SOC, include both physical examinations and mental health evaluations, an element of the decision-making process that is substantially different from that of intersex.

Providers who serve trans people report that the goal of assessment, which may last months or even years, is to ensure that the patient is mentally stable before undertaking irreversible treatments. Just as Dr. ID accounted for running tests on intersex patients which establishes an emergency situation, Dr. TO accounts for the screening process to assess the appropriateness of the patient's sense of urgency for medical interventions, with another reference to the male penis as a fundamental part of a man's identity:

> Plastic surgeons don't just do anything that anyone asks them to, they screen patients. . . . And it is very common when people have a vasectomy or an abortion that they have to have counseling first. So this is really a big myth that no one else has an evaluation. A total myth. If you have weight loss surgery, you have [a] psychological evaluation. And in most cultures, if you remove somebody's penis it is the worst possible thing that could happen.

In comparing their treatment of trans patients to other medicalized groups, Dr. TF and Dr. TO fail to acknowledge a key difference, which is that "screening" for trans patients, often taking months or years, includes more than a medical or psychiatric diagnosis, but also a social one where patients' lives, from their work to family relationships, are scrutinized to reduce what is perceived as a significant risk for providers in administering treatments for trans people. Whereas surgeries on intersex bodies continue despite a medical consensus advising otherwise (Lee et al. 2006), the considerations of the medical board become relevant for providers who serve trans people. Allowing sex and gender variants could be considered abuse on the otherwise healthy bodies of trans patients. Dr. TF shared the fear of giving sex upon the patient's request:

> I said [to my patient], "Every time I [administer hormones] my license takes a little walk onto the precipice because it is not in the mainstream. If I just put you on hormones . . . any medical board looking at this . . . would call me a nut. They could file child abuse charges against me."

Although it hadn't happened to any of them, providers for trans people were concerned that they could lose their medical licenses if they did not adhere to standards for providing treatment, especially administering the screening process that slowed the time between diagnosis and administering hormonal and surgical treatments.[5]

When providers view medical guidelines as protection for themselves and benevolent assistance for their patients, they may frame patient impulsivity as noncompliance because of the power of the medical gaze to legitimately determine how to separate or incorporate one's sex identity with one's gender identity. According to Dr. TA, "[Usually] a person is being too impulsive and too pushy, not patient. . . ." Yet as providers slow down their patients' requests, they ignore the fact that by the time trans individuals seek out medical services, they have likely been contemplating their decision for a long time (see Green 2004).

One additional important difference between intersex and trans medicalization is the role of psychosocial providers. Mental health professionals are less involved in intersex than trans medicalization. Current medical protocols for the treatment of intersex highlight the importance of psychosocial care (see Lee et al. 2006), yet mental health professionals are rarely meaningfully included in intersex medical decisions. In contrast, trans medicalization almost always begins with mental health professionals. One reason for this difference may be that while providers tend to pathologize intersex bodies as morbid because of ambiguous sex development, this is not an ethically viable view of trans bodies, so mental illness must be ruled out before proceeding with requested interventions, lest providers find themselves physically treating problems of the mind, which most would agree is unethical.

Though there are some differences between the framing of emergency in intersex and trans situations, both reflect the power of providers who control access to medical interventions. Although most intersex bodies are healthy, providers often respond to them as morbid emergencies that require intervention. Meanwhile, when trans patients seek medical treatment, providers with the power of the medical gaze slow the pace of treatment, redefining the situation from an emergency to a process designed to guarantee the persistence of their patient's desire to transition. While providers in both cases might see themselves as guarantors of health, they tend to reinforce the pathologization of intersex and trans embodiments in their decisions to give sex.

Markers of Successful Treatment and Perpetuation of the Problem

In intersex and trans cases, providers view successful medical interventions as those that align sex, gender, and even sexuality, according to the binary ideology that upholds heteronormativity. This measurement of success perpetuates the assumption that intersex and trans embodiments are problems and fuels essentialist ideologies about sex, gender, and sexuality.

Providers for intersex people commonly referred to gender assignments as successful or unsuccessful—an outcome they could ensure if they had the right data. Dr. IC explained that achieving the correct gender assignment starts with figuring out "who the child [will] think they're going to be later." This prediction about gender identity that attempts to appropriately give gender reflects the belief that intersex is not a true sex, and thus that intersex individuals must, with the medical help to give sex, end up male or female. To figure out whether to give an intersex person a male or female sex, Dr. IC asks questions hunting for biological data: "Did the child have significant testosterone exposure? . . . And then once that's been established, discuss [with the parents] the issues such as fertility, functional success of surgery," especially as it pertains to future penilevaginal penetration. According to Dr. IC's accounting for surgery, which pathologizes intersex, "Nature . . . just about got it right," but armed with more "knowledge" the surgeon "can complete . . . the last few steps or last step [of development]" in the operating room.

Many providers who treat intersex people feel their giving sex interventions are successful when the intersex person lives in the gender they were assigned at birth. Of course, their assessment of gender presentation is deeply rooted in cultural understandings of femininity and masculinity. When Dr. ID was asked whether incorrect gender assignment was possible, she answered:

> Yes. When an individual who's been raised as a female gender assignment comes to the office having totally cut off all her hair, wearing army combat boots and fatigues—it sounds very stereotypical, but it really happens—wearing combat boots and fatigues, saying, "Oh God, I hate having periods, it doesn't make any sense for my life, I don't like this." Or they threaten to commit suicide or they're institutionalized with substance abuse, and part of what comes out of their therapy through that substance abuse is that they don't know who they are or they think they weren't assigned to the way they feel now. And those are not always permanent, by the way . . . one of my fatigue-wearing persons came in a couple weeks later wearing a miniskirt, makeup, and having dyed her hair.

Although Dr. ID unwittingly acknowledged that gender presentation is fluid, she still tied a patient's gender presentation to her assessment of whether a correct gender assignment had been made at birth. She could have said it is impossible to evaluate the success of gender assignment or tied success in a more central way to gender self-identification rather than gender presentation, but she instead focused on gender presentation.

Among providers who serve trans people, criteria for the successful treatment of giving sex vary, especially among most physical and mental health providers. Many mental health workers define success as therapeutic progress. For Dr. TG, a mental health

therapist, successful treatment involves patients being "engaged in the process" of the therapy, in which they "try to understand [themselves], feel better, and make changes." This self-understanding and change also entails moving into the gender the trans person wishes to express. Dr. TG offered an example of a patient still in the process of achieving this goal:

> Sometimes he feels like he really is a woman and would like to transition into more of being a woman. Sometimes he talks about pursuing it medically in terms of hormone therapy, looking at surgery, but hasn't gotten that far, but has, from time to time, varying degrees of cross-dressing, body hair removal, makeup, and haircuts. So he sort of plays with it. He dabbles.

Reducing the patient's identity to a playful, childlike confusion, Dr. TG reinforces the idea that a successful adult ready to physically transition would embrace a steady stereotypical display of gender.

For surgeons, and some therapists, the success of giving sex is based on how well the medically altered body functions and allows the patient to have a "normal" life, defined as living in a gender aligned with physiological sex and a heterosexual identity. This is demonstrated in Dr. TJ's account of "beautiful" success:

> I have [a] patient who I met when she was 16. I thought she was a natural female. She was a male to female. When she turned 18 she came to me for surgery, male to female surgery. I saw her again about three weeks ago at the age of 23. [She] had signed [up] for a modeling job in Los Angeles, a very lucrative modeling career, and she's getting married, has a modeling career, and is perfectly female in every way. No complications, a beautiful thing.

A modeling career and marriage to a man confirm her social acceptance, and even excellence, as a woman whose sexuality maps appropriately onto gender.

One central marker of success is the engagement of heterosexual intercourse, specifically penile-vaginal penetration. Socially, heterosexuality marks success in giving sex through medicalization because it reflects socially acceptable relationships with the "opposite" sex. Physically, it is additional evidence of successful compliance with medical directives, which is addressed in Dr. TE's account: "Vaginoplasty is not always good because [patients who underwent vaginoplasty] don't use dilators enough, don't have sex enough. Many are not in a sexual relationship with a man. They need to get dilators out or there is a chance [the] canal can close. They cannot find a partner. Major problem." When sex, gender, and sexuality align properly, with the achievement of a boyfriend who serves any number of purposes including keeping the vaginal canal open, patients succeed not only at being "normal," healthy individuals, but also at being good, compliant patients under the authority of the medical gaze. When the heteronormative alignment between sex, gender, and sexuality fails to emerge, providers who serve trans people were inclined to shift the blame to trans patients for failing to comply with their requests—by not using "dilators enough," for instance.

Defining success for giving sex by shaping patient-sexed embodiments to fit into binary categories further pathologizes intersex and trans embodiments, while leaving the medical system, its agents, and the cultural investment in those binaries unchallenged (Sadjadi 2013). Medical decisions reflect the bureaucratic and ideological work of a medical gaze that makes gender recognizable while perpetuating essentialist ideologies about sex differences, allowing some, but not all, intersex and trans bodies to exist by giving sex in order to give gender.

Responsibility for Treating the Problem

Despite the power providers for intersex and trans people clearly hold, neither group tends to accept responsibility for their authority in shaping intersex and trans medical experiences or responsibility in giving gender by giving sex. Instead, providers often see themselves as facilitators, rather than decision makers, and describe their role as educating patients (or their parents). This description may sound empowering, but in fact what is missing is an acknowledgement of providers' powerful role to frame the appropriate "knowledge" of each condition, "knowledge" focused through the medical gaze that encourages self-regulated decisions. Ignoring this dynamic, providers shift decision-making responsibility onto patients and families without owning their active role in the decision-making process. Providers tend to

argue that medicalized discourse educates, with the "knowledge" they create and frame, and empowers their patients, but this argument masks the symbolic violence inherent in aligning patient decision making to existing medical and cultural standards (see Bourgois and Schonberg 2009). When patients and families lean toward options that providers consider unacceptable, they find themselves pushed to make the "right" decision, as providers promote "disciplined subjectivities that self-impose responsible behavior" (Bourgois and Schonberg 2009, 106).

Although providers for intersex people enact interventions, they tend to frame their actions as a response to parental desires. Dr. IA's account articulates this rhetoric: "[S]ome families, for cultural, religious, or psychological reasons, may feel very strongly about the importance of trying to have their child look more typically male or female." Because intersex is often diagnosed in infancy or childhood, it makes sense that providers look to parents to grant medical consent. But in focusing primarily on consent, they evade responsibility for their role in framing medically unnecessary interventions as the best response to intersex, which can have a powerful and authoritative effect on the parental decision-making process. When providers define intersex to parents as a medical problem, providing medical discourses to interpret and recommendations on potentially life-altering courses of treatment, they essentially script parental response. When Dr. IB explained that providers "do the initial education with families . . . and get parents pretty actively involved . . . 'cause they make the decision," she is occluding a powerful set of influences that shape that decision.

Some parents do question medical recommendations, but they often are met with resistance from providers who hold tight to their medical authority. Dr. IC illustrated this resistance in an account of a consultation:

> The father said . . . "Why should we do anything?" And I acted physically surprised, I'm sure I did. . . . [The father went on to say], "Well, in our family we like to celebrate our differences and not try to all be the same and feel the social pressure to do everything like everyone else does." . . . I said, "I do have to say one thing, and I think it's of key importance, that you both see a psychiatrist."

If parents challenge providers, they may find themselves referred to a psychiatrist not for psychosocial care but because they have been pathologized for not adhering to medical recommendations. Such incidents paint providers in our analysis as far more than the mere facilitators of health care that they claim to be, further undermining the claim that providers are presenting parents with objective choices. When providers respond to intersex as an emergency, they frame it as a medical abnormality that must be treated, thus upholding essentialist understandings about sex, gender, and sexuality. Without medical expertise and in the face of these powerful imperatives, parents have little, if any, room to slow down irreversible, medically unnecessary surgical decisions designed to give their children sex.

Providers who serve trans people similarly assume little responsibility for their role in giving gender by giving sex. Since trans embodiments are more likely to be diagnosed in adulthood than childhood,[6] providers shift responsibility for decisions to patients themselves, on the basis of their ability to formulate coherent gender identities. They also accounted for themselves as facilitators and educators. Dr. TJ explains their role in "education": "If you look in the Oxford English Dictionary for the word doctor, it's Latin for teacher. My job is to provide enough education that people can make good choices based on sound understanding of the variable." Dr. TA elaborated, "My role is really a consultant to the patient. . . . I view my role now not as gatekeeper but helping them understand what their options are and making a careful, thoughtful decision." By highlighting patient desire, however, providers obscure their power in regulating the transition process and keep gender coherence as the standard criterion for moving transition forward. They tend to be skeptical of trans people who do not adhere to stereotypical displays of their chosen gender, and are more wary of providing them with transitioning services. Dr. TB explained the notion of responsibility: "[I] want to make sure that [I] appropriately identify individuals in my mind that would benefit from surgery. It's still a matter of making an accurate diagnosis and formulating an appropriate treatment plan."

Not wanting to appear as gatekeepers, providers who serve trans people point to DSM criteria and SOC guidelines to defend slowing down patient requests for gender transitioning services. They also not so subtly blame their patients for forcing them to slow things down. Dr. TH explained that when her patients have what she considers a reasonable "timeline in mind," she doesn't "feel any pressure, like oh my God, I am going to have to be a gatekeeper here," but when a patient's timeline differs from hers, she pushes back and has a more difficult time offering medical services. While providers may feel they are giving their trans patients agency and embracing the widespread belief that medicine ought to move away from paternalistic care in favor of more patient-centered care, they award full agency only to those who make decisions that align with their own treatment preferences, thus keeping pronounced barriers to agency in place in the process of giving sex.

While ostensibly transferring responsibility for giving sex to parents (intersex) or patients (trans), providers continue to frame the discussion and control the pace of intervention, pulling strings by controlling where and how to give sex, and thereby evading accountability for the symbolic violence they enact (see Bourgois and Schonberg 2009). Providers may speak to their deference to the decisions of parents and patients, but in doing so they obscure their own power in constructing possible treatments for inter-sex and trans that maintain the binaries of sex, gender, and sexuality.

Conclusion

Medical providers in our comparative analysis are often quick to respond to intersex with medically unnecessary and often irreversible interventions, but they are slow to approve and provide similar practices when trans people request them. This noticeable difference can be explained through Foucault's ([1973] 1994) theorization of the medical gaze. More specifically, Foucault allows us to understand that providers, like all of us, are members of society who operate under the widespread heteronormative institutionalization of sex and gender binaries. however, providers have a unique power to either perpetuate or challenge prevailing assumptions about sex, gender, and sexuality. unfortunately, the accounts providers gave in our interviews lead us to conclude that those who are positioned (because of their intersex and trans expertise) to disrupt stereotypical binary understandings of sex, gender, and sexuality by not approaching intersex and trans embodiments as abnormal in fact often perpetuate the binary rhetoric that pathologizes variance. They do so unreflexively and uncritically through their control and regulation of the interventions by which they give gender by giving sex, creating what they consider to be heterosexual and healthy male men and female women.

We have reached this conclusion by deconstructing intersex and trans medicalization practices. First, we argued that providers for intersex people and those for trans people similarly define intersex and trans embodiments as problems to be solved, rather than as healthy human variations. To put it another way, providers' medicalization practices often construct intersex and trans embodiments as morbidities by viewing them through a lens that maintains normatively correlated sex, gender, and, although perhaps to a lesser extent, sexuality as indicators of ideal health. We then turned to the construction of intersex and trans as emergency situations, the one by providers eager to embark on medical intervention, purportedly to assuage parental anxiety, the other by patients eager for transition, who are slowed down by anxious providers. In other words, providers for intersex and trans people differ on whether and when to frame the situation of giving sex in order to give gender, but in both cases they tend to enact and maintain their authority over the body and the medical tools they use to irreversibly shape it.

Both sets of providers determine the success of their medicalization efforts on the basis of signs that their patients are living heteronormatively gendered lives. These markers of success further reify socially constructed binaries, perpetuating binary ideologies and impediments to better care for intersex and trans people. Yet providers for both intersex and trans people commonly evade responsibility for their roles in perpetuating these problems, presenting themselves as facilitators, not decision makers, for patients (or parents) who have responsibility for their own decisions about medicalization. This false perception of medical autonomy obscures the ways in which the health care system is not just unreflexive and uncritical but also creates self-discipline in parents and patients through medicalized scripts that enacts a symbolic form of violence (see Bourgois and Schonberg 2009).

While our deconstruction of intersex and trans medicalization has revealed the medical and social power providers hold, it has also identified spaces where they could make very different choices. In light of this analysis, we suggest that providers need to be more self-critical and aware of their powerful influence. They can do this by creating a welcoming and supportive institutionalized space for those who want to enact sex, gender, and sexuality as multifaceted rather than binary phenomena. In doing so, providers could approach their intersex and trans patients as healthy people who have the right to make autonomous decisions about their bodies.

One step in this direction may be the new Medical College Admission Test (MCAT), approved in 2012. According to the Association of American Medical Colleges (AAMC), the new MCAT will "require aspiring doctors to have an understanding of the social and behavioral sciences, in addition to a solid background in the natural sciences" (Mann 2012). AAMC President and CEO Darrell G. Kirch, M.D. said, "We all know America is becoming much more diverse. . . . These changes to the exam have been done with a very clear eye toward the changes that are occurring in health care and the kinds of physicians we will need" (Mann 2012). We are hopeful this change to the MCAT will affect intersex and trans medical care. Future generations of providers will hopefully have, and rely more on, knowledge from the social and behavioral sciences when they see intersex and trans patients; however, we fear providers may instead still cling to the power to give sex to their patients in a binary way, given the inertia of medicalization and the medical gaze.

***

Georgiann Davis is assistant professor of sociology at the University of Nevada, Las Vegas. She has written numerous articles on intersex in various venues ranging from *Ms. Magazine* to the *American Journal of Bioethics*. Her book, *Contesting Intersex: The Dubious Diagnosis*, is available from NYU Press.

Jodie M. Dewey is associate professor of sociology and director of the criminal justice program at Concordia University-Chicago. She has published several articles on trans-identified patients' impact on the health care process. Her work focuses on medicalization and psycho-pathologization in transgender health.

Erin L. Murphy is an independent scholar and graduate of the Sociology Doctoral Program at the University of Illinois at Urbana-Champaign. Her work has previously appeared in *Gender & Society*, *Feminist Formations*, *Critical Sociology*, and the *Journal of Historical Sociology*. She is working on a book tentatively titled *Exceptions of Empire: Anti-Imperialist Protests during the Philippine-American War*.

Notes

The authors wish to thank Joya Misra and Maxine Craig for their editorial direction and the insightful reviews they secured. We also wish to thank Rachel Allison, Pallavi Banerjee, and Amy Brainer for their helpful comments on earlier iterations of this paper. And, lastly, we'd like to thank Ranita Ray for lending us her breadth of knowledge during the revision process. Direct correspondence to Georgiann Davis, University of Nevada, Las Vegas, Box 455033, 4505 S. Maryland Parkway, Las Vegas, NV 89154-5033; e-mail: georgiann.davis@unlv.edu.

1. Although intersex and trans are contested terms, as are other terminologies across these communities, such as disorder of sex development (DSD), transgender, and transsexual, we have chosen to use intersex and trans in this article because they are easily recognizable and because they represent our preferred terms. In particular, we use intersex rather than DSD language because not all individuals with intersex traits embrace DSD terminology (Davis 2014a), including Davis, who is intersex and prefers intersex language.
2. We suspect that people who are both intersex and trans historically faced the most stigmatization from providers, given that intersex people were expected to strictly adhere to the gender that providers assign (in the case of infants) or validate (in the case of children and young adults) when intersex was diagnosed (Reis 2009). When intersex people deviated from that gender, providers viewed them as noncompliant patients. This may be changing, although such is an empirical question beyond the scope of this article.
3. Regardless of specialty, all providers are labeled "Dr." to further protect participant anonymity.
4. In *Brain Storm*, Jordan-Young (2010) challenges the widely held medical claim that gendered behaviors are hardwired into the brain.
5. According to the SOC-6 (Meyer et al. 2002), patients must be formally diagnosed as having a gender identity disorder by a qualified mental health worker, engage in a period of psychotherapy or live in their chosen gender, also called the real-life experience, for at least three months prior to accessing hormones, and have at least one year of the real-life experience before undergoing gender confirmation surgery.
6. This may be changing as children, with the support of their parents, express gender variance. See Meadow (2011) and Rahilly (2015).

References

American Psychiatric Association. 2000. *Diagnostic and statistical manual of mental disorders*, 4th ed. Washington, D.C.: American Psychiatric Association.

American Psychiatric Association. 2013. *Diagnostic and statistical manual of mental disorders*, 5th edition. Washington, D.C.: American Psychiatric Association.

Bourdieu, Pierre, and Loïc J. D. Wacquant. 1992. *An invitation to reflexive sociology*. Chicago: University of Chicago Press.

Bourgois, Philippe, and Jeffrey Schonberg. 2009. *Righteous dopefiend*. Berkeley: University of California Press.

Burke, Mary. 2011. Resisting pathology: GID and the contested terrain of diagnosis in the transgender rights movement. In *Sociology of diagnosis*, edited by P. J. McGann and David J. Hutson. Wagon Lane, Bingley, UK: Emerald.

Butler, Judith. 1993. *Bodies that matter: On the discursive limits of "sex."* New York: Routledge.

Butler, Judith. 2004. *Undoing gender*. New York: Routledge.

Coleman, Eli, Walter Bockting, Marsha Bozer, Peggy Cohen-Kettenis, Griet DeCuypere, Jamie Feldman, Lin Fraser, Jamison Green, Gail Knudson, Walter J. Jeyer, Stan Monstrey, Righcard K. Adler, George R. Brown, Aaron H. Devor, Randall Ehrbar, Randi Ettner, Evan Eyler, Rob Garofalo, Dan H. Karasic,

Arlene Istar Lev, Gal Mayer, Geino Meyer-Bahlburg, Blaine Paxton Hall, Friedmann Ffafflin, Katherine Rachlin, Bean Robinson, Loren S. Schechter, Vin Tangpricha, Mich Van Trotsenburg, Anne Vitale, Sam Winter, Stephen Whittle, Kevan R. Wylie, and Ken Zucker. 2012. *Standards of care for the health of transsexual, transgender, and gender-nonconforming people, 7th version*. Minneapolis, MN: World Professional Association for Transgender Health.

Connell, Catherine. 2010. Doing, undoing, or redoing gender?: Learning from the workplace experiences of transpeople. *Gender & Society* 24:31–55.

Connell, Raewyn. 2012. Transsexual women and feminist thought: Toward new understanding and new politics. *Signs* 37:857–81.

Davis, Georgiann. 2014a. The power in a name: Diagnostic terminology and diverse experiences. *Psychology & Sexuality* 5:15–27.

Davis, Georgiann. 2014b. "Bringing intersexy back"? Intersexuals and sexual satisfaction. In *Sex matters: The sexualities and society reader*, 4th ed., edited by Mindy Stombler, Dawn M. Baunach, Wendy Simonds, Elroi J. Windsor, and Elisabeth O. Burgess. New York: Norton.

Davis, Georgiann, and Erin Murphy. 2013. Intersex bodies as states of exception: An empirical explanation for unnecessary surgical modification. *Feminist Formations* 25:129–52.

Dewey, Jodie. 2008. Knowledge legitimacy: How trans-patient behavior supports and challenges current medical knowledge. *Qualitative Health Research* 18:1345–55.

Dewey, Jodie. 2013. Challenges of implementing collaborative models of decision making with trans-identified patients. *Health Expectations* doi:10.1111/hex.12133.

Fausto-Sterling, Anne. 2000. *Sexing the body: Gender politics and the construction of sexuality*. New York: Basic Books.

Foucault, Michel. ([1973] 1994). *The birth of the clinic: An archaeology of medical perception*. New York: Vintage Books.

George, Alexander L., and Andrew Bennett. 2005. *Case studies and theory development in the social sciences*. Cambridge: MIT Press.

Green, Jamison. 2004. *Becoming a visible man*. Nashville: Vanderbilt University Press.

Holmes, Morgan. 2008. *Intersex: A perilous difference*. Selinsgrove, PA: Susquehanna University Press.

Jordan-Young, Rebecca M. 2010. *Brain storm: The flaws in the science of sex differences*. Cambridge: Harvard University Press.

Karkazis, Katrina. 2008. *Fixing sex: Intersex, medical authority, and lived experience*. Durham, NC: Duke University Press.

Kessler, Suzanne J. 1990. The medical construction of gender: Case management of intersexed infants. *Signs* 16:3-26.

Lee, Peter A., Christopher P. Houk, S. Faisal Ahmed, and Ieuan A. Hughes. 2006. Consensus statement on management of intersex disorders. *Pediatrics* 118:488–500.

Lev, Arlene Istar. 2009. The ten tasks of the mental health provider: Recommendations for revision of the World Professional Association for Transgender Health's standards of care. *International Journal of Transgenderism* 11:47–99.

Mann, Sarah. 2012. *AAMC approves new MCAT® exam with increased focus on social, behavioral sciences. AAMC Reporter*, Association of American Medical Colleges, https://www.aamc.org/newsroom/reporter/march 2012/276588/mcat2015.html.

McGann, P. J. 2011. Troubling diagnoses. In *Sociology of diagnosis*, edited by P. J. McGann and David J. Hutson. Wagon Lane, Bingley, UK: Emerald.

Meadow, Tey. 2010. "A rose is a rose": On producing legal gender classifications. *Gender & Society* 24:814–37.

Meadow, Tey. 2011. "Deep down where the music plays": How parents account for childhood gender variance. *Sexualities* 14:725–47.

Meyer III, Walter J., Walter Bockting, Peggy Cohen-Kettenis, Eli Coleman, Domenico DiCeglie, Holly Devor, Louis Gooren, J. Joris Hage, Sheila Kirk, Bram Kuiper, Donald Laub, Anne Lawrence, Yvon Menard, Jude Patton, Leah Schaefer, Alice Webb, and Connie Christine Wheeler. 2002. The Harry Benjamin International Gender Dysphoria Association's standards of care for gender identity disorders, sixth version. *The International Journal of Transgenderism* 13:1–30.

Mills, Catherine. 2007. Biopolitics, liberal eugenics, and nihilism. In *Giorgio Agamben: Sovereignty and life*, edited by Matthew Calarco and Steven DeCaroli. Stanford, CA: Stanford University Press.

Pfeffer, Carla. 2010. "Women's work"? Women partners of transgender men doing housework and emotion work. *Journal of Marriage and Family* 72:165–83.

Preves, Sharon. 2003. *Intersex and identity: The contested self*. New Brunswick, NJ: Rutgers University Press.

Rahilly, Elizabeth P. 2015. The gender binary meets the gender-variant child: Parents' negotiations with childhood gender variance. *Gender & Society* 29:338–61.

Reis, Elizabeth. 2009. *Bodies in doubt: An American history of intersex*. Baltimore, MD: Johns Hopkins University Press.

Risman, Barbara. 2004. Gender as a social structure: Theory wrestling with activism. *Gender & Society* 18:429–50.

Rose, Nikolas. 2007. Beyond medicalisation. *The Lancet* 369:700–2.

Sadjadi, Sahar. 2013. The endocrinologist's office—puberty suppression: Saving children from a natural disaster? *Journal of Medical Humanities* 34:255–60.

Speer, Susan. 2006. Gatekeeping gender: Some features of the use of hypothetical questions in the psychiatric assessment of transsexual patients. *Discourse & Society* 17:785–812.

Tone, Andrea. 2012. Medicalizing reproduction: The pill and home pregnancy tests. *Journal of Sex Research* 49:319–27.

Ward, Jane. 2010. Gender labor: Transmen, femmes, and collective work of transgression. *Sexualities* 13:236–54.

Westbrook, Laurel, and Kristin Schilt. 2014. Doing gender, determining gender: Transgender people, gender panics, and the maintenance of the sex/gender/sexuality system. *Gender & Society* 28:32–57.

Winters, Kelley. 2006. Gender dissonance: Diagnostic reform of gender identity disorder for adults. *Journal of Psychology & Human Sexuality* 17:71–89.

Questions for Critical Thinking

1. Given the devastation many experience as a result of the medical practices illustrated here, what do you see as the responsibility of medical providers to alter their practices with regard to the treatment of intersex and trans people?

2. As the authors note, medical providers for trans and intersex people determine the success of their medicalization efforts based on signs that their patients are living heteronormatively gendered lives. Why do you think this is? What would be an effective way to change such a practice?

3. Currently, medical providers maintain their authority over intersex and trans bodies and the medical tools they use to shape them. Why do you think this is? What do you see as the likelihood of this practice changing?

"AIN'T I A WOMAN?"

Transgender and Intersex Student Athletes in Women's Collegiate Sports

- *Pat Griffin*

Athletics is an aspect of U.S. society that is significantly involved in maintaining the idea that males and females are distinct groups. In this essay, Pat Griffin, the founding director of Changing the Game (a project of the Gay, Lesbian, and Straight Education Network), addresses the barriers transgender athletes face that keep them from full participation in sports and offers solutions that would work toward equality for all.

The title of this chapter is borrowed from Sojourner Truth's powerful demand that white feminist abolitionists in the nineteenth century expand their awareness to include the needs of black women in their fight for race and sex equality. Her question, "Ain't I a Woman," seems fitting for the twenty-first century also with regard to the inclusion in women's sports of transgender women and men and women who have intersex conditions. Increasing numbers of athletes who are transgender or have intersex conditions are challenging gender boundaries in sports as they insist on their right to participate according to their self-affirmed genders. Recent controversies surrounding the eligibility of South African runner Caster Semenya to compete in women's events and the participation of transgender athletes, such as George Washington University basketball player, Kye Allums and professional golfer Lana Lawson, challenge the traditional boundaries of sex and gender in sport.

This chapter explores how the gender and sex binary assumptions upon which the organization of sports competition is based can create problems when people whose gender identities or variations in sexual development do not conform to these assumptions assert their right to participate. I discuss how transgender and intersex athletes challenge assumptions about the essential nature of the category "woman." At the same time, I show how sexist and heterosexist stereotypes converge to affect the gender performance of all women in sports, with a particularly limiting effect on people whose gender identity, gender expression, biological sex, and/or sexual orientation do not conform to cultural norms.

After a description of relevant language related to this topic, I review selected historical events describing concerns about women athletes' sex, femininity, and heterosexuality. I then explore how these concerns and the gender-binary assumptions undergirding them affect policies governing the eligibility of transgender and intersex athletes to participate in women's collegiate athletic events. I conclude the chapter with a discussion of current efforts to provide transgender and intersex athletes with opportunities to participate in school-based women's athletic competitions.

A Word about Words

The language of sex and gender can be confusing and complicated. Many of the concepts feminist scholars and gender activists use challenge conventional notions about gender and sex. Moreover, the language is evolving, and many feminist scholars and gender activists disagree about how the language should be used. For example, the terms "sex" and "gender" are used interchangeably by some writers, while others find it useful to provide specific and separate definitions for each of these terms. I find it helpful, at least on a conceptual level, to define these two key terms separately.

According to Gender Spectrum, an education and advocacy organization for gender-variant children and teens, "sex" is biological and includes physical attributes, such as sex chromosomes, gonads, sex hormones, internal reproductive structures, and external genitalia. At birth, individuals are typically categorized as male or female based on the appearance of their external genitalia. This binary categorization ignores the spectrum of biological sex characteristics that confound attempts to fit everyone neatly into either male or female categories. The term "gender" is similarly complicated. According to Genderspectrum.org, "Along with one's physical traits, it is the complex interrelationship between those traits and one's internal sense of self as male, female, both or neither as well as one's outward presentations and behaviors related to that perception." I find it helpful to make this differentiation, especially when discussing these terms in relationship to sports, where physical attributes are integral aspects of the discussion.

Gender is not inherently related to sex. A person who identifies as transgender has a gender identity (an internal sense of gender: being male or female, trans, or other gender sensibility) that does not match the sex (or gender) they were assigned at birth based on an inspection of their physical characteristics.

A transgender woman or girl may be born with a body identified as male and, on the basis of that body, assigned to the gender category "boy," even though she identifies as a girl. The reverse is true for a transgender man or boy. Transgender people choose to express their genders in many ways: changing their names and self-referencing pronouns to better match their gender identities; choosing clothes, hairstyles, or other aspects of self-presentation that reflect their gender identities; and generally living and presenting themselves to others consistently with their gender identities. Some, but not all, transgender people take hormones or undergo surgical procedures to change their bodies to better reflect their gender identities. Transgender encompasses a vast range of identities and practices; however, for the purposes of this essay, I use the term "transgender" more specifically to refer to women who have transitioned from their assigned male gender at birth to their affirmed gender as women and to men who have transitioned from their assigned female gender at birth to their affirmed gender as men.

People with intersex conditions may be born with chromosomes, hormones, genitalia, or other sex characteristics that do not match the patterns that typify biological maleness or femaleness. Many intersex people are not aware of their intersex status unless it is revealed as part of a medical examination or treatment. People with intersex conditions are assigned a gender at birth; many live and identify with that assigned gender throughout their lives, although many do not. In this essay, I use "intersex women" to refer to women with intersex conditions who have always identified as women (for more information about intersex conditions, go to www.accordalliance.org).

The participation of transgender and intersex women poses related but different challenges to gendered divisions in sports. Transgender women and intersex women are viewed by many sports leaders, women competitors, and the general public as men or as "not normal" women whose participation in women's sports threatens the notion of a "level playing field." In the context of sex-segregated women's sports, these athletes' bodies are viewed as male, and they are often perceived to have an unfair competitive advantage over non-intersex or non-transgender women athletes. But trans and intersex visibility and participation belies the myth of the level playing field and the myth of binary gender on which it rests.

Sports and the Gender Binary

Although some school athletic teams, such as sailing, are composed of men and women who compete without regard to the sex or gender of participants, mixed-sex competition is the exception at all levels of sports. In most sports that women and men play, schools sponsor separate men's and women's teams—basketball, volleyball, swimming, track, and field, lacrosse, or soccer, for example. This sex division is based on the assumption that sex-separate competitive opportunities are the best route to equal opportunity and fair competition for all. Title IX, the 1972 landmark federal legislation prohibiting sex discrimination in education, includes guidelines for providing comparable school-based athletic opportunities for girls and women and boys and men on sex-separate teams to provide equal participation opportunities (Brake 2010; Hogshead-Makar and Zimbalist 2007).

Dividing participants into sex-separate teams is based on two assumptions: (1) Sex and gender are binary and immutable characteristics, and (2) salient physical differences between males and females substantially affect athletic performance to the advantage of males in most sports.

Rather than a binary of athletic performance based on sex, it would be more accurate to describe sex differences as a spectrum, with females and males occupying overlapping positions. Although it is fair to say that most adult male athletes are bigger, taller, and stronger than most adult female athletes, some female athletes outperform their male counterparts in sport. So, even among athletes who are not transgender or intersex, sex-separated teams do not always adequately accommodate the diversity of skill, motivation, and physical characteristics among female and male athletes. Some boys or men might find a better competitive match competing on a girls' team, and some girls' athletic performances are more comparable to those on a boys' team.

Some girls and boys have been allowed to participate on teams designated for the other sex, particularly if a school only sponsors a team in that sport for one sex. For example, girls sometimes compete on boy's wrestling or football teams, and boys sometimes compete on girls' field hockey or volleyball teams. However, cross-sex participation on sports teams is always an exception and is often greeted with skepticism by other competitors, parents, and fans. Even among prepubescent girls and boys where size and strength are similar or where girls are often taller, stronger, and faster than boys, sports are typically divided by sex. Such is the entrenched nature of the belief in a static and immutable gender and sex binary in sports.

For most athletes whose gender identity is congruent with their gender assigned at birth or whose physical sex anatomy is congruent with their sex assigned at birth, the answer to the question of which team to play for is simple. However, for athletes whose gender identity does not match the gender they were assigned at birth or for athletes with differences of sexual development, the separation of sports into participation categories based on binary sex has often resulted in humiliation and discrimination. Transgender and intersex athletes challenge the gender binary in sports and force sports leaders to reflect on how and where to draw gender boundaries for the purposes of identifying on which teams an athlete is allowed to compete.

Because women athletes have always challenged the hegemonic notion of athleticism as a masculine trait and because sports participation has historically been a male privilege to which girls and women were not entitled, the fight for equal sports opportunities for women is ongoing. Gendered expectations for girls and women have not comfortably included such characteristics as "competitive," "athletic," or "muscular"; as a result, women athletes have always had to prove their "normalcy" based on socially constructed assumptions about femininity, heterosexuality, and an unquestioned acceptance of a gender binary. Women who excel in sports *and* whose appearance, behavior, and/or identity does not conform to traditional notions of who is a woman, how a woman should look and act, and who a woman should be sexually attracted to are viewed with suspicion and as illegitimate participants in women's sports competitions (Cahn 1994; Festle 1996; Griffin 1998).

History of Gender Anxiety in Women's Sport

During the early twentieth century, women participating in athletic competitions were subjected to white middle-class criticism from medical doctors, media commentators, psychologists, and others who warned of a range of catastrophic effects of athletic competition they believed would cause physiological and psychological damage. Based on the belief that white women were physically and psychically frail, sports participation was viewed as dangerous to their health and well-being. The prevailing medical and social perspective was that women who did compete in sports were subjected to a number of "masculinizing" effects on their appearance, behavior, and sexual interests that would prevent them from living as "normal" women whose proper roles were wives and mothers. Thus, the early seeds of gender suspicion about women athletes were planted. Advocates for women's sports participation and women athletes themselves often responded defensively to these criticisms by highlighting their femininity (according to racially white heteronormative standards) and heterosexual interests, and by portraying their sports interest as a complement to their focus on motherhood and marriage (Cahn 1994).

These fears are best illustrated in public reaction to Babe Didrikson, a multisport athlete who won Olympic medals in track and field and played baseball, basketball, and tennis before later focusing on professional golf. Didrikson was a well-known cultural icon whose brash manner, quick sense of humor, and competitive fire always made for a good story. Unfortunately, Didrikson was treated as a gender freak and ridiculed for her lack of femininity, her "masculine" appearance, and her athletic prowess. Called a "muscle moll" and worse, it is no wonder that by midcentury, Didrikson initiated an international public-relations campaign to reassure the American public that she was a "normal" woman after all, despite her athletic achievements. (Cayleff 1995). She began wearing dresses and talking about her love of cooking, and, to seal the deal, she married wrestling champion George Zaharias. These efforts succeeded in quieting the concerns of male sports reporters and the general public about Didrikson's femininity and heterosexuality.

As women's competition in Olympic sports and professional golf and tennis became more visible in the 1940s through the 1970s, another wave of suspicion about the gender and sexuality of women athletes prompted some women's sports advocates and athletes themselves to take an apologetic stance by focusing on disproving sexist assumptions about the "masculine" lesbian women who lived in the sports world. These efforts included the institution of feminine dress codes, instructions about makeup application and hair styling, and direction of media attention to the "pretty ones," who served as goodwill ambassadors who contradicted the unsavory image of "masculine" women athletes (Gerber, Felshin, and Wyrick 1974).

These fears, coupled with the belief that women are inherently athletically inferior to their male counterparts, caused increased gender suspicions about outstanding athletic performances by female athletes. These questions were raised in the 1964 Olympics by Russian hammer-throwers and shot-putters Tamara and Irina Press, whose muscular appearances and medal-winning performances provoked suspicion that they were actually men posing as women.

In 1976, Renée Richards, a transgender woman, was denied entry in the Women's U.S. Open by the U.S. Tennis Association (USTA) on the basis that she was not a "born woman." The New York Supreme Court ruled against the USTA and enabled Richards to compete in the women's event. Despite this court ruling, the Ladies Professional Golf Association (LPGA) maintained a "born woman" requirement for membership until 2010; when faced with a lawsuit by transgender woman golfer Lana Lawson, the LPGA dropped its prohibition against transgender participants. Transgender women, such as Richards and Lawson, are viewed by some suspicious tennis players and golfers as illegitimate women who have male bodies that confer an unfair competitive advantage when competing against so-called "natural" women.

In 1966, in response to fears of male cheaters competing as women, the International Olympic Committee (IOC) instituted mandatory "gender" verification testing of all female competitors. (The tests were called "sex tests," and their purpose was to confirm that competitors were female-bodied and, later, that their chromosomal makeup was female.) The first such tests required all Olympic competitors entered in women's events to appear naked before a panel of "experts," who, by visual inspection, determined whether the prospective competitors were eligible to compete as female.

Not surprisingly, athletes and other sports observers criticized this humiliating process. Medical experts also criticized the process, because, in addition to the invasive and voyeuristic nature of the "gender test," it was also a crude and ineffective means of determining whether a competitor was female.

Eventually, more "scientific" procedures were developed in which women athletes were subjected to buccal smear tests in which mouth swabs yielded cellular samples from which the chromosomal makeup could be identified. Athletes whose chromosomal makeup was other than XX were determined to be ineligible to compete as women. Women who "passed" the test were given "certificates of femininity" and allowed to compete.

These supposedly more-scientific tests also failed to achieve their intended goal. Rather than identifying male imposters, the only competitors who were ever disqualified were women with atypical chromosomal makeup who had lived their entire lives as women and were not attempting to gain an unfair competitive advantage. The resulting traumatic and public shaming that followed their identifications as "not women" not only terminated their athletic careers but damaged their personal lives as well.

Current Policy Governing the Participation of Transgender and Intersex Athletes

These "gender" tests revealed the folly of identifying a simple and fair, not to mention respectful, means of determining who is a woman. Nonetheless, although mandatory "gender verification" testing was discontinued prior to the 2000 Olympic Games, individual women athletes who trigger suspicions about their sex are now tested on a case-by-case basis. Unfortunately, these sex challenges are typically triggered by such ambiguous and culturally biased gender criteria as short hair, small breasts, preferences for "masculine" clothes, deep voices, muscular physiques, and excellence of athletic performance. Thus, the challenge of identifying who is and is not a woman for the purpose of determining eligibility to compete in women's sports events continues to be controversial.

During the 2009 Track and Field World Championships, South African runner Caster Semenya astounded the international track establishment with her gold-medal performance in the women's eight-hundred-meter run, leaving her competition far back on the track. Semenya was identified as a female at birth, has always identified as a woman, and is accepted as a woman by her family and friends. However, unconfirmed speculations are that she has an intersex condition. Immediately following her victory, some of her competitors and race officials from other countries filed challenges to the International Association of Athletics Federation (IAAF) under the IAAF's case-by-case "gender-verification" policy. (Mirroring the IOC, the IAAF policy had replaced mandatory "gender" verification testing of women athletes in favor of a case-by-case process.)

After months of subjecting Semenya to medical examinations, public speculation about whether she is a woman, public humiliation, and egregious breaches of confidentiality by the IAAF, she was allowed to keep her gold medal. Eleven months later, after secretive IAAF deliberations, she was cleared for competition in women's events. The IAAF released this decision without an explanation of its process, criteria, or reasoning. When Semenya won her first two races after returning to competition and finished third in another, some of her competitors again began complaining that they were unfairly forced to compete against a man or, at the very least, a "woman on the fringe of normalcy," as one competitor described Semenya.

Whether being intersex confers any performance advantage is open to speculation. No scientific data are available to indicate that it does or does not. However, Semenya's competitors assume that she is a man or not a "normal" woman and that she has an unfair competitive advantage that should disqualify her from competing in women's events. These objections to Semenya's eligibility to compete as a woman are based on her margin of victory over the other women in the 2009 World Championships and on her "masculine" physical appearance, clothing, and deep voice. All these characteristics challenge the gender binary upon which sports competition is based as well as binary assumptions about who is a woman and therefore eligible to compete in women's events.

In 2004, in a surprisingly proactive decision by a typically conservative organization, the IOC adopted a policy outlining criteria enabling transgender athletes to compete in IOC-sponsored events:

- The athlete's gender must be legally recognized on official identity documents.
- The athlete must have completed genital reconstructive surgery and had his or her testes or ovaries removed.
- The athlete must complete a minimum two-year postoperative hormone treatment before she or he is allowed to compete.

The IOC policy is the first attempt by a mainstream sports organization to identify specific criteria governing the participation of transgender athletes. However, transgender-rights advocates criticize the policy, noting the class and sex bias built into the policy as well as problems related to privacy and medical confidentiality. Moreover, some transgender medical experts have provided some data indicating that a one-year waiting period is adequate for the athletes' hormonal levels to be within the range of non-transgender women and men. To date, no transgender athlete has competed in the Olympic Games under this policy.

Despite its considerable flaws, USA Track and Field, the U.S. Golf Association, and a few state high school athletic governing organizations have adopted the IOC policy (for example, those in Colorado, Connecticut, and Rhode Island). The participation criteria identified in the IOC policy would make it virtually impossible for transgender student athletes to compete in high school sports. The requirements of genital reconstructive surgery, mandatory sterilization, and changing the sex indicated on official identity documents impose financial and legal burdens that even many adult transgender athletes cannot or choose not to pursue. The two-year waiting period is

not supported by medical data and is not practical in school sports, where a student athlete's eligibility is already limited to four or five years.

As of 2011, no national governing organization for high school sports has adopted a policy concerning the participation of intersex athletes in school-based sports events. However, in 2008, the Washington State Interscholastic Activity Association (WIAA) adopted the most progressive policy to date governing the participation of transgender student athletes on high school sports teams. This policy requires neither surgery nor change of identity documents. Transgender students can participate in their affirmed genders after appealing to the state interscholastic activities association and providing written documentation of the student's gender from the student and parent/guardian and/or a health-care provider. To date, the policy has been used successfully to enable transgender students to participate on sex-separate teams.

At the collegiate level, the National Collegiate Athletic Association (NCAA) released a statement in 2004 clarifying that the organization does not prohibit transgender student athletes from competing in NCAA-sanctioned events but that student athletes must compete in the sex identified on their official identity documents. NCAA legal advisers believed that this provision was a simple solution to addressing the question of transgender participation in NCAA athletic programs. Because of significant differences among state requirements for changing the sex indicated on official identity documents, however, this requirement is discriminatory and creates complications when athletes from different states compete against each other. More recently, the NCAA has recognized the need for a more nuanced and inclusive policy. In 2011, it adopted the first-ever national policy regarding transgender athletes in collegiate athletics; the policy allows transgender athletes to compete in sex-segregated sports if, and only if, their hormonal treatment is consistent with current medical standards—standards that themselves suggest different treatment requirements for trans men and trans women (Lawrence 2011).

As of 2010, only two collegiate openly transgender student athletes had competed in NCAA-sponsored events. Keelin Godsey competed on the women's track and field team at Bates College and in the Olympic trials in the women's hammer throw. Allums currently is a member of the George Washington University women's basketball team. Godsey and Allums are female-bodied transgender men who are not taking testosterone so they can continue to compete in women's events. Because they are not taking testosterone, an NCAA-banned substance, and are competing in the sex identified on their official identity documents as specified by the NCAA and IOC, Godsey and Allums are eligible to compete on women's teams.

Whether the perceived threats to women's sports are identified as male imposters, transgender women, transgender men not taking testosterone, intersex women, butch-looking straight women, or lesbians, protecting the boundaries of women's sports from these gender transgressors by upholding the gender binary has become increasingly difficult as the myth of the gender binary and the myth of the level playing field have been exposed.

The Myth of the Level Playing Field

Just as some people view lesbians as threats to women's sports because they fear association with the stereotypes of lesbians as unsavory, so, too, do many athletes and the general public view transgender and intersex women athletes with particular suspicion. Although lesbians may be viewed as women who look or act like men, some people view transgender and intersex women as actually *being* men, in most places making them ineligible to compete in women's sports. The most-often-cited concern about the participation of transgender or intersex women in women's sports is that they threaten a "level playing field." Many competitors, coaches, and parents assume that transgender and intersex women, because of their male bodies, have an unfair competitive advantage over women who are not perceived to be trans or intersex.

Even without the participation of transgender or intersex women in women's sports, the playing field is hardly level. The entire focus of sports competition is to gain a competitive advantage, as long as that advantage is defined as being within the rules. Training hard to gain a competitive advantage is fair. Taking performance-enhancing drugs is not fair.

Competitive advantages in women's sports come in many different forms; social, economic, environmental, psychological, and physiological, to name a few. Some women grow up in cultures where girls' sports participation is supported by social norms. These girls have a competitive advantage over other girls whose cultures restrict female athleticism. Girls whose families have the financial resources that enable them to train with the best coaches, to use the best equipment, to have access to good nutrition and health care, and to compete with the best athletes have a competitive advantage. Girls who live in places with clean air and water and safe streets have a competitive advantage. Girls who have inner resources of mental toughness and competitive drive have a competitive edge over physically talented but less mentally tough opponents. Some women have competitive advantages over opponents in their sports because of their genetics. Even some genetic conditions, such as Marfan syndrome, which results in unusual height, can be a competitive advantage in some sports where being tall is an advantage. All these competitive advantages are viewed in sports as fair and part of the game. All these advantages expose the myth of the level playing field even among women who are not transgender or intersex.

Why then is it that all these competitive advantages are accepted as fair variations among women athletes that can account for athletic-performance differences, but the competitive advantages that may or may not be enjoyed by some transgender or intersex women are viewed as unfair and threats to a level playing field warranting banishment from women's competition?

Competitive advantages assumed to be conferred by perceived maleness or masculinity are viewed as unfair competitive advantages. Transgender women, intersex women, or any women who do not conform to social expectations of femininity and heterosexuality are threats to the image of athletic women as gender conformists. As long as women athletes can be cast as feminine, heterosexual women, they do not pose a threat to the dominance of men in sports and male privilege in sports. This is the price of acceptance that women in sports have had to pay since the early twentieth century, when they began participating in sports in large numbers.

Gender Binary Meets Transgender and Intersex Athletes: What Is the Way Forward?

Women who by their inability or refusal to conform to binary gender norms in sports also challenge the mythical gender binary altogether. Given that athletics as an institution has been built on sexist assumptions about the natural superiority of men's sports performance over that of women and that the gender binary forms the basis for how sports are structured into sex-separate participation categories, how should women's sports address the question of including transgender and intersex athletes?

Policy development designed to address this question can take several forms: (1) Protect the gender binary by using sex-verification testing to exclude "non-women," (2) address challenges to the gender binary on a case-by-case basis, (3) eliminate gender as a sport-participation category, and (4) expand gender categories to include participants whose bodies and/or gender identities do not conform to the gender binary.

Protect the gender binary with mandatory sex-verification testing of all female participants. This policy has been discredited as impractical, discriminatory, invasive, and ineffective. The IOC abandoned this policy in 1999, and nothing suggests that any improvement of testing procedures will bring it back as a mandatory process.

Use sex-verification testing on a case-by-case basis as challenges to individual female participants arise. This is the IOC/IAAF policy now in effect. The controversy surrounding the challenge to Semenya's eligibility to compete in women's events illustrates many of the problems with this policy. The criteria for challenging an individual athlete's gender are based on a combination of sexist assumptions about female athletic performance and bodies, socially constructed-gendered expectations for appearance and behavior, and a selective belief in the level playing field in sports in which some competitive advantages, particularly those based on genetic differences, are viewed as fair while others are not. Testing on a case-by-case basis eliminates the impracticality of testing all competitors entered in women's events and avoids the mass anxiety inherent in the process. However, the sex testing of individual competitors on a case-by-case basis is based on myths about gender and a level playing field that subject the athletes who are targeted to an invasive and humiliating, and often public, process. The effects of these tests are questionable given the arbitrary nature of determining when a woman's physiological makeup crosses a socially constructed line to become "too" male to qualify to compete against other women.

The IOC policy for determining the eligibility of transgender women athletes on a case-by-case process includes criteria that require surgical intervention and legal documentation of transition that create insurmountable obstacles for most transgender people. The policy also requires an excessive waiting period once hormone treatment has begun that is not supported by current medical research.

Eliminate sex and gender as sports-participation categories. Some LGBT legal advocates believe that eliminating men's and women's sports in favor of other criteria for determining sports participation is the only way to address the complexities and challenges of including transgender and intersex athletes. These advocates argue that dividing sports participation on the basis of a sex and gender binary is inherently unfair. Some feminist legal critics of Title IX believe that the law, by assuming that sex-separate teams are the best route to equality for women in sport, has enshrined sex inequality and relegated women's sports to a permanent second-class status. Their assumption is that Title IX establishes a "separate but equal" goal even though this legal concept has been discredited in lawsuits challenging racial and disability discrimination (McDonagh and Pappano 2008).

The logic and goals of such legalistic arguments for the elimination of sex-separate sports as a way to address the myth of the gender and sex binary, inequality in women's sports, and the inclusion of transgender and intersex women athletes are appealing in some ways. Dividing sports by such performance-related physical criteria as height, jumping ability, or weight might be a reasonable strategy to eliminate discrimination based on sex and gender identity. Using actual performance in sports, such as running or swimming speed, agility, balance, points scored, or batting averages, also provides alternatives for dividing competitors into teams to level the playing field.

Although is it true that the gender binary creates a questionable division between the athletic interests, talent, and performance of men and women, it is also accurate to say that, for adults, most male athletes are bigger and stronger than most women athletes. As a result, dividing school teams by such "non-gendered" criteria as physical characteristics and athletic performance at this point in the history of women's sports would likely result in most athletic teams consisting of men and a few select women (including trans and intersex athletes). Second teams, if schools chose to field them, would probably consist of men and women in more equal numbers (including trans and intersex women). Third teams, in the unlikely event that schools chose to expand their support for more than two teams per sport, would probably consist of mostly women (including men and some trans and intersex athletes) and some men.

It is also questionable whether these performance-based criteria are really non-gendered. Many of the physiological differences between male and female bodies do give men a competitive advantage over women, depending on the sport. However, gendered social and cultural expectations still encourage and reward male athletes more than they do female athletes. Sexism in sports still limits women athletes' access to sports and the resources that support athletic teams. Much like the rationale behind affirmative action as a way of correcting past race and sex discrimination, sex-separate sports enable women to overcome past sex discrimination in sports. Studies documenting the impressive increases in girls' and women's participation in sports and the increasing quality and quantity of women's sports experiences since the passage of Title IX demonstrate the law's undeniable positive effects (Carpenter and Acosta 2004). At the same time, despite these successes, resistance to Title IX compliance and persistent sexism are still obstacles to full women's equality in sports.

I worry that eliminating women's sports in favor of "non-gendered" sports opportunities will, at this point in the development of women's sports, relegate the majority of women athletes either to the junior varsity or to the sidelines. Sport is gendered by social and cultural expectations. Even criteria meant to be "gender-free" are still embedded in historical and contemporary societal structures of sex inequality

that disadvantage female athletes while advantaging male athletes. I keep imagining an incredibly talented athlete, such as the University of Connecticut women's basketball player Maya Moore, sitting on the bench for a varsity college team made up of mostly taller, stronger men or starting on a junior varsity team that receives less attention and fewer resources than the varsity team. Moreover, Moore is an exceptional athlete. How does the elimination of women's teams benefit the majority of college women athletes (including trans women and intersex women) who are not as talented as she is?

Expand gender categories to include participants whose bodies and/or gender identities do not conform to the gender binary. I believe that, despite compelling criticisms of the problems posed by dividing sports participation into sex-separate participation categories, this structure is the best way, at this point in women's sports history, to achieve sex equality in sports. Sex-separate sports teams provide the most participation opportunities for the most girls and women. Title IX, although not perfect, has demonstrated that, when opportunities are available, girls and women come to play in increasingly larger numbers with every successive generation. I do not believe that this would be so if girls and women were competing not only against each other but also against boys and men for these opportunities.

If sex-separate sports are indeed the best route to sex equality, the question is how can we expand our criteria to include competitors in women's sports who challenge the rigidity of the gender binary? Can we respect the self-affirmed gender identities of transgender athletes and the differences of sex development in intersex women by including them in our definitions of "woman" so their right to participate on women's teams is also protected?

Current Efforts to Create Inclusive Collegiate Athletic Policy Governing the Participation of Transgender and Intersex Athletes

In October 2009, the National Center for Lesbian Rights and the Women's Sports Foundation co-sponsored a national think tank titled "Equal Opportunities for Transgender Student-Athletes." The attendees were legal, medical, athletic, and advocacy leaders with expertise in transgender issues. The think tank's goal was to develop recommended policies for high school and collegiate athletic programs. The report from this think tank, *On the Team: Equal Opportunities for Transgender Student-Athletes*, includes a comprehensive discussion of issues, policy recommendations for high school and college athletics, and a list of best practices for sport administrators, coaches, student athletes, and parents (Griffin and Carroll 2010).

The following guiding principles served as a foundation for the think tank's discussions and the policy recommendations included in the report:

1. Participation in interscholastic and intercollegiate athletics is a valuable part of the education experience for all students.

2. Transgender student athletes should have equal opportunity to participate in sports.

3. The integrity of women's sports should be preserved.

4. Policies governing sports should be based on sound medical knowledge and scientific validity.

5. Policies governing sports should be objective, workable, and practicable; they should also be written, available, and equitably enforced.

6. Policies governing the participation of transgender students in sports should be fair in light of the tremendous variation among individuals in strength, size, musculature, and ability.

7. The legitimate privacy interests of all student athletes should be protected.

8. The medical privacy of transgender students should be preserved.

9. Athletic administrators, staff, parents of athletes, and student athletes should have access to sound and effective educational resources and training related to the participation of transgender and gender-variant students in athletics.

10. Policies governing the participation of transgender students in athletics should comply with state and federal laws protecting students from discrimination based on sex, disability, and gender identity and expression.

To maintain the integrity of women's sports while including transgender and intersex women athletes on women's sports teams requires that sports-governing organizations at all levels develop policies enabling women who challenge the gender binary to play. These policies must be focused on providing equal opportunities to a broad spectrum of women and be based on current medical and legal information rather than on unchallenged acceptance of the gender binary, female athletic inferiority, and a selective view of what constitutes a level playing field. This endeavor will require confronting our anxieties about blurring gender and sexuality boundaries and recognizing the arbitrary manner in which we define who is a woman to maintain a comfortable but oppressive understanding of gender and sexuality. We must recognize that the enforcement of exclusionary definitions of who qualifies as a woman denies some students the opportunity to play on school sports teams. We must understand that enabling transgender and intersex students to participate on women's sports teams is an important step toward greater equality for all women and strengthens women's sports in the same way that addressing the needs of lesbians, women with disabilities, and women of color strengthens the broader social movement for women's equality.

Most colleges and universities include as part of their education missions commitments to equality and fairness. As reflected in nondiscrimination statements and educational programming focused on social justice and diversity, schools endeavor to invite students and staff to think more critically about privilege and disadvantage based on social and cultural identities. Policy development in collegiate athletics should reflect the broader goals and values of the schools they are part of and not allow competitive goals or financial gain to shape policies (Buzuvis 2011). Policies governing the inclusion of transgender and intersex student athletes must be based on a commitment to providing all students with equal opportunities to participate on school sports teams, while at the same time protecting the integrity of women's sports as the best strategy for achieving sex equality in sports.

References

Brake, Deborah. 2010. *Getting in the Game: Title IX and the Women's Sports Revolution.* New York: New York University Press.

Buzuvis, Erin E. 2011. *The Feminist Case for the NCAA's Recognition of Competitive Cheer as an Emerging Sport for Women,* 52 B.C. L. REV. 439.

Cahn, Susan. 1994. *Coming on Strong: Gender and Sexuality in Twentieth-Century Women's Sport.* New York: Free Press.

Carpenter, Linda Jean, and R. Vivian Acosta. 2004. *Title IX.* Champaign, IL: Human Kinetics.

Cayleff, Susan E. 1995. *Babe: The Life and Legend of Babe Didrikson Zaharias.* Urbana, IL: University of Illinois Press.

Festle, Mary Jo. 1996. *Playing Nice: Politics and Apologies in Women's Sports.* New York: Columbia University Press.

Gerber, Ellen W., Jan Felshin, and Waneen Wyrick. 1974. *The American Woman in Sport.* Reading, MA: Addison–Wesley.

Griffin, Pat. 1998. *Strong Women, Deep Closets: Lesbians and Homophobia in Sport.* Champaign, IL: Human Kinetics.

Griffin, Pat, and Helen J. Carroll. 2010. On the Team: Equal Opportunities for Transgender Student-Athletes. National Center for Lesbian Rights and Women's Sports Foundation. Available at: http://www.nclrights.org/site/DocServer/TransgenderStudentAthleteReport.pdf?docID=7901.

Hogshead-Makar, Nancy, and Andrew Zimbalist, eds. 2007. *Equal Play: Title IX and Social Change.* Philadelphia, PA: Temple University Press.

Lawrence, Marta. 2011. Transgender Policy Approved. September 13, NCAA.org. Available at http://www.ncaa.org/wps/wcm/connect/public/NCAA/Resources/Latest+News/2011/September/Transgender+policy+approved.

McDonagh, Eileen, and Laura Pappano. 2008. *Playing with the Boys.* New York: Oxford University Press.

Questions for Critical Thinking

1. How does the notion of transgender challenge the ways that you view gender? Does it encourage you to see issues of gender in new and different ways? Why or why not?

2. How does your gender identity influence your understanding of or level of agreement with the author's discussion?

3. Considering Griffin's discussion, do you think it is possible or desirable to expand or eliminate socially defined gender roles, particularly in the field of athletics?

SEXUALITY

NAMING ALL THE PARTS

Kate Bornstein

The first reading of this section by playwright and gender scholar Kate Bornstein links constructions of gender to those of sexuality. She notes that, although gender is a social construct, we typically assume that it is biological. As a result, we marginalize other ways of conceptualizing and experiencing gender. Additionally, she discusses the problems that result from conflating concepts of gender and sex with those of sexuality. By doing so, we construct ideas of what is normal sexuality and what is not, and we limit the dynamic aspects of our sexual identities.

For the first thirty-or-so years of my life, I didn't listen, I didn't ask questions, I didn't talk, I didn't deal with gender—I avoided the dilemma as best I could. I lived frantically on the edge of my white male privilege, and it wasn't 'til I got into therapy around the issue of my transsexualism that I began to take apart gender and really examine it from several sides. As I looked at each facet of gender, I needed to fix it with a definition, just long enough for me to realize that each definition I came up with was entirely inadequate and needed to be abandoned in search of deeper meaning.

Definitions have their uses in much the same way that road signs make it easy to travel: they point out the directions. But you don't get where you're going when you just stand underneath some sign, waiting for it to tell you what to do.

I took the first steps of my journey by trying to define the phenomenon I was daily becoming.

There's a real simple way to look at gender: Once upon a time, someone drew a line in the sands of a culture and proclaimed with great self-importance, "On this side, you are a man; on the other side, you are a woman." It's time for the winds of change to blow that line away. Simple.

Gender means *class*. By calling gender a system of classification, we can dismantle the system and examine its components. Suzanne Kessler and Wendy McKenna in their landmark 1978 book, *Gender: An Ethnomethodological Approach*, open the door to viewing gender as a social construct. They pinpoint various phenomena of gender, as follows:

Gender Assignment

Gender assignment happens when the culture says, "This is what you are." In most cultures, we're assigned a gender at birth. In our culture, once you've been assigned a gender, that's what you are; and for the most part, it's doctors who dole out the gender assignments, which shows you how emphatically gender has been medicalized. These doctors look down at a newly-born infant and say, "It has a penis; it's a boy." Or they say, "It doesn't have a penis; it's a girl." It has little or nothing to do with vaginas. It's all penises or no penises: gender assignment is both phallocentric and genital. Other cultures are not or have not been so rigid.

In the early nineteenth century, Kodiak Islanders would occasionally assign a female gender to a child with a penis: this resulted in a woman who would bring great good luck to her husband, and a larger dowry to her parents. The European umbrella term for this and any other type of Native American transgendered person is *berdache*. Walter Williams in *The Spirit and the Flesh* chronicles nearly as many types of *berdache* as there were nations.

> *Even as early as 1702, a French explorer who lived for four years among the Illinois Indians noted that berdaches were known "from their childhood, when they are seen frequently picking up the spade, the spindle, the ax [women's tools], but making no use of the bow and arrow as all the other small boys do."*
>
> —Pierre Liette, *Memoir of Pierre Liette on the Illinois Country*

When the gender of a child was in question in some Navajo tribes, they reached a decision by putting a child inside a *tipi* with a loom and a bow and arrow—female and male implements, respectively. They set fire to the *tipi*, and whatever the child grabbed as he/she ran out determined the child's gender. It was perfectly natural to these Navajo that the child had some say in determining its own gender. Compare this method with the following modern example:

> *[The Montana Educational Telecommunications Network, a computer bulletin board,] enabled students in tiny rural schools to communicate with students around the world. Cynthia Denton, until last year a teacher at the only public school in Hobson, Montana (population 200), describes the benefit of such links. "When we got our first messages from Japan, a wonderful little fifth-grade girl named Michelle was asked if she was a boy or a girl.*

> *She was extraordinarily indignant at that, and said, 'I'm Michelle—I'm a girl of course.' Then I pointed out the name of the person who had asked the question and said, 'Do you know if this is a boy or a girl?' She said, 'No, how am I supposed to know that?' I said, 'Oh, the rest of the world is supposed to know that Michelle is a girl, but you have no social responsibility to know if this is a boy or a girl?' She stopped and said, 'Oh.' And then she rephrased her reply considerably."*
>
> —Jacques Leslie, *The Cursor Cowboy*, 1993

Is the determination of one another's gender a "social responsibility"?

Do we have the legal or moral right to decide and assign our own genders?

Or does that right belong to the state, the church, and the medical profession?

If gender is classification, can we afford to throw away the very basic right to classify ourselves?

Gender Identity

Gender identity answers the question, "Who am I?" Am I a man or a woman or a what? It's a decision made by nearly every individual, and it's subject to any influence: peer pressure, advertising, drugs, cultural definitions of gender, whatever.

Gender identity is assumed by many to be "natural"; that is someone can feel "like a man," or "like a woman." When I first started giving talks about gender, this was the one question that would keep coming up: "Do you feel like a woman now?" "Did you ever feel like a man?" "How did you know what a woman would feel like?"

I've no idea what "a woman" feels like. I never did feel like a girl or a woman; rather, it was my unshakable conviction that I was not a boy or a man. It was the absence of a feeling, rather than its presence, that convinced me to change my gender.

What **does** a man feel like?

What does a woman feel like?

Do **you** feel "like a man?"

Do you feel "like a woman?"

I'd really like to know that from people.

Gender identity answers another question: "To which gender (class) do I want to belong?" Being and belonging are closely related concepts when it comes to gender. I felt I was a woman (being), and more importantly I felt I belonged with the other women (belonging). In this culture, the only two sanctioned gender clubs are "men" and "women." If you don't belong to one or the other, you're told in no uncertain terms to sign up fast....

> ... I remember a dream I had when I was no more than seven or eight years old—I might have been younger. In this dream, two lines of battle were drawn up facing one another on a devastated plain: I remember the earth was dry and cracked. An army of men on one side faced an army of women on the other. The soldiers on both sides were exhausted. They were all wearing skins—I remember smelling the untanned leather in my dream. I was a young boy, on the side of the men, and I was being tied down to a roughly-hewn cart. I wasn't struggling. When I was completely secured the men attached a long rope to the cart, and tossed the other end of the rope over to the women. The soldiers of the women's army slowly pulled me across the empty ground between the two armies, as the sun began to rise. I could see only the sun and the sky. When I'd been pulled over to the side of the women, they untied me, turned their backs to the men, and we all walked away. I looked back, and saw the men walking away from us. We were all silent.
>
> I wonder about reincarnation. I wonder how a child could have had a dream like that in such detail. I told this dream to the psychiatrist at the Army induction center in Boston in 1969—they'd asked if I'd ever had any strange dreams, so I told them this one. They gave me a 1-Y, deferred duty due to psychiatric instability.

Gender Roles

Gender roles are collections of factors which answer the question, "How do I need to function so that society perceives me as belonging or not belonging to a specific gender?" Some people would include appearance, sexual orientation, and methods of communication under the term, but I think it makes more sense to think in terms of things like jobs, economic roles, chores, hobbies; in other words, positions and actions specific to a given gender as defined by a culture. Gender roles, when followed, send signals of membership in a given gender.

Gender Attribution

Then there's gender attribution, whereby we look at somebody and say, "that's a man," or "that's a woman." And this is important because the way we perceive another's gender affects the way we relate to that person. Gender attribution is the sneaky one. It's the one we do all the time without thinking about it; kinda like driving a sixteen-wheeler down a crowded highway ... without thinking about it.

In this culture, gender attribution, like gender assignment, is phallocentric. That is, one is male until perceived otherwise. According to a study done by Kessler and McKenna, one can extrapolate that it would take the presence of roughly four female cues to outweigh the presence of one male cue: one is assumed male until proven otherwise. That's one reason why many women today get "sirred" whereas very few men get called "ma'am."

Gender attribution depends on cues given by the attributee, and perceived by the attributer. The categories of cues as I have looked at them apply to a man/woman bi-polar gender system, although they could be relevant to a more fluidly-gendered system. I found these cues to be useful in training actors in cross-gender role-playing.

Physical cues include body, hair, clothes, voice, skin, and movement.

> I'm nearly six feet tall, and I'm large-boned. Like most people born "male," my hands, feet, and forearms are proportionally larger to my body as a whole than those of people born "female." My hair pattern included coarse facial hair. My voice is naturally deep—I sang bass in a high school choir and quartet. I've had to study ways and means of either changing these physical cues, or drawing attention away from them if I want to achieve a female attribution from people.

Susan Brownmiller's book, *Femininity*, is an excellent analysis of the social impact of physical factors as gender cues.

Behavioral cues include manners, decorum, protocol, and deportment. Like physical cues, behavioral cues change with time and culture. *Dear Abby* and other advice columnists often freely dispense gender-specific manners. Most of the behavioral cues I can think of boil down to how we occupy space, both alone and with others.

Some points of manners are not taught in books of etiquette. They are, instead, signals we learn from one another, mostly signals acknowledging membership to an upper (male) or lower (female) class. But to commit some of *these* manners in writing in terms of gender-specific behavior would be an acknowledgment that gender exists as a class system.

Here's one: As part of learning to pass as a woman, I was taught to avoid eye contact when walking down the street; that looking someone in the eye was a male cue. Nowadays, sometimes I'll look away, and sometimes I'll look someone in the eye—it's a behavior pattern that's more fun to play with than to follow rigidly. A femme cue (not "woman," but "femme") is to meet someone's eyes (usually a butch), glance quickly away, then slowly look back into the butch's eyes and hold that gaze: great hot fun, that one!

In many transsexual and transvestite meetings I attended, when the subject of the discussion was "passing," a lot of emphasis was given to manners: who stands up to shake hands? who exits an elevator first? who opens doors? who lights cigarettes? These are all cues I had to learn in order to pass as a woman in this culture. It wasn't 'til I began to read feminist literature that I began to question these cues or to see them as oppressive.

Textual cues include histories, documents, names, associates, relationships—true or false—which support a desired gender attribution. Someone trying to be taken for male in this culture might take the name Bernard, which would probably get a better male attribution than the name Brenda.

Changing my name from Al to Kate was no big deal in Pennsylvania. It was a simple matter of filing a form with the court and publishing the name change in some unobtrusive "notices" column of a court-approved newspaper. Bingo—done. The problems came with changing all my documents. The driver's license was particularly interesting. Prior to my full gender change, I'd been pulled over once already dressed as a woman, yet holding my male driver's license—it wasn't something I cared to repeat.

Any changes in licenses had to be done in person at the Department of Motor Vehicles. I was working in corporate America: Ford Aerospace. On my lunch break, I went down to the DMV and waited in line with the other folks who had changes to make to their licenses. The male officer at the desk was flirting with me, and I didn't know what to do with that, so I kept looking away. When I finally got to the desk, he asked "Well, young lady, what can we do for you?"

"I've got to make a name change on my license," I mumbled.

"Just get married?" he asked jovially.

"Uh, no," I replied.

"Oh! Divorced!" he proclaimed with just a bit of hope in his voice, "Let's see your license." I handed him my old driver's license with my male name on it. He glanced down at the card, apparently not registering what he saw. "You just go on over there, honey, and take your test. We'll have you fixed up soon. Oh," he added with a wink, "if you need anything special, you just come back here and ask old Fred."

I left old Fred and joined the line for my test. I handed the next officer both my license and my court order authorizing my name change. This time, the officer didn't give my license a cursory glance. He kept looking at me, then down at the paper, then me, then the paper. His face grim, he pointed over to the direction of the testing booths. On my way over to the booths, old Fred called out, "Honey, they treating you all right?" Before I could reply, the second officer snarled at old Fred to "get his butt over" to look at all my paperwork.

I reached the testing booths and looked back just in time to see a quite crestfallen old Fred looking at me, then the paper, then me, then the paper. **Mythic cues** include cultural and sub-cultural myths which support membership in a given gender. This culture's myths include archetypes like: weaker sex, dumb blonde, strong silent type, and better half. Various waves of the women's movement have had to deal with a multitude of myths of male superiority.

Power dynamics as cue include modes of communication, communication techniques, and degrees of aggressiveness, assertiveness, persistence, and ambition.

Sexual orientation as cue highlights, in the dominant culture, the heterosexual imperative (or in the lesbian and gay culture, the homosexual imperative). For this reason, many male heterosexual transvestites who wish to pass as female will go out on a "date" with another man (who is dressed as a man)—the two seem to be a heterosexual couple. In glancing at the "woman" of the two, an inner dialogue might go, "It's wearing a dress, and it's hanging on the arm of a man, so it must be a woman." For the same man to pass as a female in a lesbian bar, he'd need to be with a woman, dressed as a woman, as a "date."

> I remember one Fourth of July evening in Philadelphia, about a year after my surgery. I was walking home arm in arm with Lisa, my lover at the time, after the fireworks display. We were leaning in to one another, walking like lovers walk. Coming towards us was a family of five: mom, dad, and three teenage boys. "Look, it's a coupla faggots," said one of the boys. "Nah, it's two girls," said another. "That's enough outa you," bellowed the father, "one of 'em's got to be a man. This is America!"

So sex (the act) and gender (the classification) are different, and depending on the qualifier one is using for gender differentiation, they may or may not be dependent on one another. There are probably as many types of gender (gender systems) as could be imagined. Gender by clothing, gender by divine right, gender by lottery—these all make as much sense as any other criteria, but in our Western civilization, we bow down to the great god Science. No other type of gender holds as much sway as:

Biological gender, which classifies a person through any combination of body type, chromosomes, hormones, genitals, reproductive organs, or some other corporal or chemical essence. Belief in biological gender is in fact a belief in the supremacy of the body in the determination of identity. It's biological gender that most folks refer to when they say *sex*. By calling something "sex," we grant it seniority over all the other types of gender—by some right of biology.

So, there are all these *types* of gender which in and of themselves are *not* gender, but criteria for systemic classification. And there's sex, which somehow winds up on top of the heap. Add to this room full of seeds the words *male, female, masculine, feminine, man, woman, boy, girl*. These words are not descriptive of any sexual act, so all these words fall under the category of gender and are highly subjective, depending on which system of gender one is following.

But none of this explains why there is such a widespread insistence upon the conflation of *sex* and *gender*. I think a larger question is why Eurocentric culture needs to see *so much* in terms of sex.

> It's not like gender is the *only* thing we confuse with sex. As a culture, we're encouraged to equate sex (the act) with money, success, and security; and with the products we're told will help us attain money, success and security. We live in a culture that succeeds in selling products (the apex of accomplishment in capitalism) by aligning those products with the attainment of one's sexual fantasies.
>
> Switching my gender knocked me for a time curiously out of the loop of ads designed for men or women, gays or straights. I got to look at sex without the hype, and ads without the allure. None of them, after all, spoke to me, although all of them beckoned.

Kinds of Sex

It's important to keep *gender* and *sex* separated as, respectively, *system* and *function*. Since function is easier to pin down than system, sex is a simpler starting place than gender.

Sex does have a primary factor to it which is germane to a discussion of gender: *sexual orientation*, which is what people call it, if they believe you're born with it, or *sexual preference*, which is what people call it if they believe you have more of a choice and more of a say in the matter.

> *[W]e do not need a sophisticated methodology or technology to confirm that the gender component of identity is the most important one articulated during sex. Nearly everyone (except for bisexuals, perhaps) regards it as the prime criterion for choosing a sex partner.*
>
> —Murray S. Davis, *Smut: Erotic Reality/Obscene Ideology*, 1983

The Basic Mix-Up

A gay man who lived in Khartoum
Took a lesbian up to his room.
They argued all night

Over who had the right
To do what, and with what, to whom.
—Anonymous limerick

Here's the tangle that I found: sexual orientation/preference is based in this culture solely on the gender of one's partner of choice. Not only do we confuse the two words, we make them dependent on one another. The only choices we're given to determine the focus of our sexual desire are these:

- *Heterosexual model:* in which a culturally-defined male is in a relationship with a culturally-defined female.
- *Gay male model:* two culturally-defined men involved with each other.
- *Lesbian model:* two culturally-defined women involved with each other.
- *Bisexual model:* culturally-defined men and women who could be involved with either culturally-defined men or women.

Variants to these gender-based relationship dynamics would include heterosexual female with gay male, gay male with lesbian woman, lesbian woman with heterosexual woman, gay male with bisexual male, and so forth. People involved in these variants know that each dynamic is different from the other. A lesbian involved with another lesbian, for example, is a very different relationship than that of a lesbian involved with a bisexual woman, and *that's* distinct from being a lesbian woman involved with a heterosexual woman. What these variants have in common is that each of these combinations forms its own clearly-recognizable dynamic, and none of these are acknowledged by the dominant cultural binary of sexual orientation: heterosexuality/homosexuality.

Despite the non-recognition of these dynamics by the broader culture, *all these models depend on the gender of the partner.* This results in minimizing, if not completely dismissing, other dynamic models of a relationship which could be more important than gender and are often more telling about the real nature of someone's desire. There are so many factors on which we *could* base sexual orientation. The point is there's more to sex (the act) than gender (one classification of identity).

Try making a list of ways in which sexual preference or orientation could be measured, and then add to that list (or subtract from it) every day for a month, or a year (or for the rest of your life). Could be fun!

Sex without Gender

There are plenty of instances in which sexual attraction can have absolutely nothing to do with the gender of one's partner.

> *When Batman and Catwoman try to get it on sexually, it only works when they are both in their caped crusader outfits. Naked heterosexuality is a miserable failure between them. … When they encounter each other in costume however something much sexier happens and the only thing missing is a really good scene where we get to hear the delicious sound of Catwoman's latex rubbing on Batman's black rubber/leather skin. To me their flirtation in capes looked queer precisely because it was not heterosexual, they were not man and woman, they were bat and cat, or latex and rubber, or feminist and vigilante: gender became irrelevant and sexuality was dependent on many other factors….*
>
> *You could also read their sexual encounters as the kind of sex play between gay men and lesbians that we are hearing so much about recently: in other words, the sexual encounter is queer because both partners are queer and the genders of the participants are less relevant. Just because Batman is male and Catwoman is female does not make their interactions heterosexual—think about it, there is nothing straight about two people getting it on in rubber and latex costumes, wearing eyemasks and carrying whips and other accoutrements.*
>
> —Judith Halberstam, "Queer Creatures," On Our Backs, Nov./Dec., 1992

Sexual preference *could* be based on genital preference. (This is not the same as saying preference for a specific gender, unless you're basing your definition of gender on the presence or absence of some combination of genitals.) Preference could also be based on the kind of sex *acts* one prefers. But despite the many variations possible, sexual orientation/preference remains culturally linked to our gender system (and by extension to gender identity) through the fact that it's most usually based on the gender of one's partner. This link probably accounts for much of the tangle between sex and gender.

The confusion between sex and gender affects more than individuals and relationships. The conflation of sex and gender contributes to the linking together of the very different subcultures of gays, lesbians, bisexuals, leather sexers, sex-workers, and the transgendered.

> A common misconception is that male cross-dressers are both gay and prostitutes, whereas the truth of the matter is that most cross-dressers that I've met hold down more mainstream jobs, careers, or professions, are married, and are practicing heterosexuals.

A dominant culture tends to combine its subcultures into manageable units. As a result, those who practice non-traditional sex are seen by members of the dominant culture (as well as by members of sex and gender subcultures) as a whole with those who don non-traditional gender roles and identities. Any work to deconstruct the gender system needs to take into account the artificial amalgam of subcultures, which might itself collapse if the confusion of terms holding it together were to be settled.

In any case, if we buy into categories of sexual orientation based solely on gender—heterosexual, homosexual, or bisexual—we're cheating ourselves of a searching examination of our real sexual preferences. In the same fashion, by subscribing to the categories of gender based solely on the male/female binary, we cheat ourselves of a searching examination of our real gender identity. And now we can park sex off to the side for a while, and bring this essay back around to gender.

Desire

I was not an unattractive man. People's reactions to my gender change often included the remonstrative, "But you're such a good-looking guy!" Nowadays, as I navigate the waters between male and female, there are still people attracted to me. At first, my reaction was fear: "What kind of pervert," I thought, "would be attracted to a freak like me?" As I got over that internalized phobia of my transgender status, I began to get curious about the nature of desire, sex, and identity. When, for example, I talk about the need to do away with gender, I always get looks of horror from the audience: "What about desire and attraction!" they want to know, "How can you have desire

with no gender?" They've got a good point: the concepts of sex and gender seem to overlap around the phenomenon of desire. So I began to explore my transgendered relationship to desire.

> About five months into living full-time as a woman, I woke up one morning and felt really good about the day. I got dressed for work, and checking the mirror before I left, I liked what I saw—at last! I opened the door to leave the building, only to find two workmen standing on the porch, the hand of one poised to knock on the door. This workman's face lit up when he saw me. "Well!" he said, "Don't you look beautiful today." At that moment, I realized I didn't know how to respond to that. I felt like a deer caught in the headlights of an oncoming truck. I really wasn't prepared for people to be attracted to me. To this day, I don't know how to respond to a man who's attracted to me—I never learned the rituals.

To me, desire is a wish to experience someone or something that I've never experienced, or that I'm not currently experiencing. Usually, I need an identity appropriate (or appropriately inappropriate) to the context in which I want to experience that person or thing. This context could be anything: a romantic involvement, a tennis match, or a boat trip up a canal. On a boat trip up the canal, I could appropriately be a passenger or a crew member. In a tennis match, I could be a player, an audience member, a concessionaire, a referee, a member of the grounds staff. In the context of a romantic involvement, it gets less obvious about what I need to be in order to have an appropriate identity, but I would need to have *some* identity. Given that most romantic or sexual involvements in this culture are defined by the genders of the partners, the *most* appropriate identity to have in a romantic relationship would be a gender identity, or something that passes for gender identity, like a gender role. A gender role might be butch, femme, top, and bottom—these are all methods of acting. So, even without a gender identity per se, some workable identity can be called up and put into motion within a relationship, and when we play with our identities, we play with desire. Some identities stimulate desire; others diminish desire. To make ourselves attractive to someone, we modify our identity, or at least the appearance of an identity—and this includes gender identity.

I love the idea of being without an identity; it gives me a lot of room to play around; but it makes me dizzy, having nowhere to hang my hat. When I get too tired of not having an identity, I take one on: it doesn't really matter what identity I take on, as long as it's recognizable. I can be a writer, a lover, a confidante, a femme, a top, or a woman. I retreat into definition as a way of demarcating my space, a way of saying "Step back, I'm getting crowded here." By saying "I am the (fill in the blank)," I also say, "You are *not*, and so you are not in my space." Thus, I achieve privacy. Gender identity is a form of self-definition: something into which we can withdraw, from which we can glean a degree of privacy from time to time, and with which we can, to a limited degree, manipulate desire.

Our culture is obsessed with desire: it drives our economy. We come right out and say we're going to stimulate desire for goods and services, and so we're bombarded daily with ads and commercial announcements geared to make us desire things. No wonder the emphasis on desire spills over into the rest of our lives. No wonder I get panicked reactions from audiences when I suggest we eliminate gender as a system; gender defines our desire, and we don't know what to do if we don't have desire. Perhaps the more importance a culture places on desire, the more conflated become the concepts of sex and gender.

As an exercise, can you recall the last time you saw someone whose gender was ambiguous? Was this person attractive to you? And if you knew they called themselves neither a man nor a woman, what would it make you if you're attracted to that person? And if you were to kiss? Make love? What would you be?

Questions for Critical Thinking

1. Bornstein discusses how constructs of sex and gender are connected to sexuality. Do her ideas challenge the way in which you view gender and sexuality? Why or why not?

2. How does your own gender and sexual identity influence your understanding of or level of agreement with the author's discussion?

3. To many of us, it is important that we are able to identify the sex of another individual. When there is ambiguity, we often have a sense of frustration. Why do you think this is? If we were to have a greater tolerance for such ambiguity, how might that impact our level of tolerance for ambiguity with regard to sexuality?

"IF YOU DON'T KISS ME, YOU'RE DUMPED"

Boys, Boyfriends, and Heterosexualised Masculinities in the Primary School

• *Emma Renold*

In the essay that follows, author Emma Renold, professor of childhood studies, explores how the primary or elementary school serves as a site for constructing heterosexual identities. Drawing from her ethnographic research with ten- and eleven-year-old boys, she illustrates how these constructions of sexuality are often linked with normative assumptions of gender and sexism as well as homophobia.

Introduction

The sanctioning and institutionalisation of heterosexuality within school arenas has been empirically explored in a now growing volume of US, UK and Australian research (Mahony & Jones, 1989; Thorne, 1993; Mac an Ghaill, 1994, 1996; Laskey & Beavis, 1996; Epstein, 1997a, b; Kehily & Nayak, 1997; Epstein & Johnson, 1998; Letts & Sears, 1999; Epstein *et al.*, 2001). Schools and schooling processes are now recognised as key social sites in the production and reproduction of male heterosexualities and boys' sexual cultures (Kehily, 2000). Researchers have extended their understanding of "heterosexual" practices, from sexual activity, to a wide range of discourses and performances, through which boys (and girls) define, negotiate and essentially construct their gendered selves. For example, Mac an Ghaill (1994) and Connell (1995) have shown how hegemonic masculine performances are inextricably tied to dominant notions of heterosexuality. They and others have argued that by problematising and interrogating the "heterosexual presumption," within educational organisations, its "normalisation" and subsequent "dominance" is made visible (Epstein & Johnson,

1994). This has led to a number of school-based investigations into the processes by which heterosexual identities are produced and desired and how that dominance is secured and maintained.

Overwhelmingly, these investigations have focused upon the production of older male heterosexualities (Mac an Ghaill, 1994, 1996; Epstein & Johnson, 1994; Kehily & Nayak, 1996, 1997, 2000; Nayak & Kehily, 1997; Haywood, 1996; Redman 2000, 2001; Frosh *et al.*, 2002). Little research attention has been paid to (hetero)sexualised pupil cultures within the primary school (although see Wallis & VanEvery, 2000; Redman, 1996) and in particular the diversity and ambiguities surrounding boys' heterosexual cultures within primary/elementary school research (see Skelton 2001, pp. 149–154). This paper hopes to offer some insight into the different ways in which Year 6 boys (aged 10/11) engage with, practice and occupy "heterosexualities" and how integral, yet complex and contradictory heterosexual performances are to the production of "proper" boys. It foregrounds children's own accounts and constructions of dominant notions of heterosexualised masculinities which were, for some boys, produced through the precarious and fragile subject position of "boyfriend" but also through heterosexual fantasies/sex-play, homophobic, anti-gay and misogynistic talk and behaviour and the sexualised harassment of female classmates.

The Study: Researching and Theorising Children's Gender and Sexual Relations

The data and analyses presented in this paper derive from doctoral research in the form of a year-long ethnography exploring the construction of children's gender and sexual identities in their final year (Year 6) of primary school (Renold, 1999). The fieldwork was conducted during the academic year 1995/1996 in two primary schools, Tipton Primary and Hirstwood (both pseudonyms) situated in a small semi-rural town in the east of England [1]. Fifty-nine children from two Year Six classes participated in the research [2]. Alongside observation, unstructured exploratory friendship group interviews was the main method used to explore children's gender and sexual relations because it maximised children's ability to create spaces (physical and discursive) from which they could freely discuss what they felt to be important and significant to them. As discussed elsewhere (Renold 2000, 2002a) I did not set out to study children's sexual cultures. However, as in many qualitative studies, the reflexivity and flexibility of the ethnographic process, combined with the longitudinal element of the research, led to a progressive focusing of ideas. From examining gender relations, I found myself increasingly witnessing a complex, interactive and daily network of heterosexual performances by both boys and girls as they negotiated their gendered selves. And from the first few weeks in the field, the inter-connectedness of sexuality and gender was becoming increasingly visible and I began exploring how dominant notions of heterosexuality underscore much of children's identity work and peer relationships as they "live out" the categories "girl" and "boy."

I also began to disrupt the myth of the primary school as an "asexual" environment and explore how young children are each subject to the pressures of "compulsory heterosexuality" (Rich, 1980) and "the heterosexual matrix" (Butler, 1990)—where to be a "normal" boy and girl involves the projection of a coherent and abiding heterosexual self:

> I use the term *heterosexual matrix* ... to designate that grid of cultural intelligibility through which bodies, genders, and desires are naturalised ... a hegemonic discursive/epistemological model of gender intelligibility that assumes that for bodies to cohere and make sense there must be a stable sex expressed through a stable gender (masculine expresses male, feminine expresses female) that is oppositionally and hierarchically defined through the compulsory practice of heterosexuality. (Butler, 1990, p. 151)

This paper seeks to examine the acting out of Butler's (1990) "heterosexual matrix" in which the "real" expression of masculinity and femininity is embedded within a presupposed heterosexuality. It explores how boys, multiply positioned through generational ("child") and gendered discourses ("boy"), make sense of the oppositionality of sex/gender through the often hierarchical heterosexualised economies of classroom and playground relations.

The Social World of Boyfriends and Girlfriends: A Case of Mixed Messages

A number of studies have explored the salience of (hetero)sexualities and the discursive practices of dating, dumping and two-timing within a boyfriend/girlfriend network that permeates and structures most upper primary school children's social relations[3] (Thorne, 1993; Hatcher, 1995; Redman, 1996). This study was no exception (see Renold, 2000). For example, simple mixed-sex interactions like borrowing a pencil or helping with a class-task could be (hetero) sexualised (usually by teasing the boy/girl involved that they "fancy" each other). What became apparent, however, was that having a girlfriend and being a boyfriend seemed to be an increasingly *overt* "compulsory" signifier for the public affirmation of a boy's heterosexuality, and a further performative signifier of their hegemonic masculinity. [4] The following group interview extract goes some way to highlight the pressures, pleasures and fears of the heterosexual matrix at work via a ritualised, yet diverse language of "fancying," "going-out," "love" and "embarrassment":

ER: OK, you can talk about what you like … .

MARTIN: Erm erm erm erm cool … erm Jenna fancies Michael, Michael fancies Jenna

MICHAEL: No I don't

MARTIN: Only joking

ER: How do you/feel about Jenna fancying you Michael?

MARTIN: I was only joking

MICHAEL: Not very good

ER: Why not?

MARTIN: She's a fat cow

COLIN: She put, she put on his dictionary, erm, "good luck, I love you"

ER: Really? … (he nods) Have you spoke to her at all?

MICHAEL: (shakes his head to signify "no")

MARTIN: He's shy … he's getting embarrassed

COLIN: I'll speak for him, "no"

MARTIN: She's a cow

Despite the ubiquitous presence, and often highly desirable status of boyfriend, actually "going out" with a girl created conformative pressures for boys and girls. Indeed as the latter extract illustrates "coming out" as heterosexual in this way, was often a complex and contradictory process. Despite the connection, heterosexual performances, or "having a girlfriend," did not automatically signify hegemonic masculinity. It was usually only the boys who were good at sport (usually football), and who were deemed "hard," "tough," "cool" or "good-looking" by their peers, who were reported to be the most romantically desirable. While more gentle and non-sporting boys invested and participated in the heterosexual network of boyfriends and girlfriends, they were more often positioned as "heterosexual failures" and subject to much teasing and ridicule, usually for pursuing or being pursued by "non-desirable" girls (see Renold, 2002b). For the majority of girls in this study, the most sought after boys constituted the "A" team (football). Heterosexual hierarchies were thus produced and the cycle of heterosexuality, sport and hegemonic masculinity reinforced.

I have discussed elsewhere how competing discourses surrounding the sexually innocent child and the sexual adolescent created contradictions and conflicts for many girls in ways that were not reported or observed in boys' sexual cultures (Renold, 2000). Rather, boys' contradictions lay in their ambivalent attitude towards proximity to girls. This could give rise to teasing behaviours associated with fear of the "feminine" (often via a language of pollution, disease and contamination) or could publicly represent and confirm a boy's heterosexual masculinity. In sum, physical or emotional closeness to girls could be both masculinity confirming and masculinity denying. Indeed, teasing and ridicule, as illustrated in the extract above, predominantly occurred when boys, like Martin, rarely located themselves in heterosexual/romantic discourses and when there was a lack of boys in the group who were "going out" or who previously had a "girlfriend." Furthermore, attempts to re-secure "masculinity," often led boys to draw on alternative hegemonic discourses such as misogynist comments which usually involved the objectification of girls ("she's a cow"). The fine line between romance and sexual harassment (Skelton, 2001) is discussed in more detail later in the paper.

"It's Always the Girls That Use You": Heterosexual/Romantic Delusions

With a few exceptions, most of the boys who were observed to fleetingly engage in the subject position "boyfriend" and the heterosexualised practices of "fancying" and "going out" rarely felt at ease or reported any sustained pleasure. Many boys described their experiences in a less than positive light:

MARTIN: If you have a girlfriend you have everyone saying "oh can you come and kiss me/, can you come and kiss meee" (singsong)

COLIN: Yeah it's all that/and the next day

MARTIN: Will you kiss me, will you kiss me, will you kiss me?

ER: And you don't want to?

COLIN: NO and Harriet/is like

MARTIN: Jane and Hayley, they'll be going, if you don't kiss me you're dumped

While some boys were teased for not having a girl-friend, those that did, like Martin and Colin, were often overwhelmed by girls' expectations of boys to express their commitment in a physical way ("will you kiss me," "if you don't kiss me, you're dumped"). Indeed, Martin's concern over kissing further emphasises the ambiguity surrounding the desire for yet resistance of sexual maturity and "older child identities" (Redman, 1996). Alternatively, other boys (below) experienced what they considered to be more than their fair share of "dumping" (i.e. when a "relationship" is terminated). Indeed, it seemed that a great deal of power could be exercised and experienced by being able to "dump" relationships and girls were more ready to and more frequently changed their boyfriends than boys[6]:

> PETE: I used to be going out with Fiona but I didn't like having a relationship with her because she always used to dump me
> DARREN: Yeah that's what Victoria used to do—what she used to do when I was in a stress was she used to get in a bigger stress and then dump me ... and then about five minutes later she always comes back to me and thinks it's all right again, "do you still love me" and she expects everything to be all right again
> ER: And what does that make you feel like?
> DARREN: They just use you ... it's not fair

Indeed, the feelings of powerlessness embedded in Darren and Pete's frustration at being "always dumped" and "used" and the pressures of engaging in "older" sexual activities suggest that neither one of these boys experienced the dominant subject position and power relations associated perhaps with the more traditional heterosexual discourses of patriarchy. At best, most boys experienced heterosexual relationships as fragile, ambiguous, and with a mixture of unease and tension. Given these experiences, it seems difficult to understand why many boys continued to pursue girls for "girl-friends" or subject themselves to the precarious role of "boyfriend." A possible explanation could be that the pressures of "compulsory heterosexuality" (i.e. their investment at all costs to perform as heterosexual subjects), the status attached to "older (sexually mature) identities" and the wider media/cultural discourses that bind heterosexuality with hegemonic masculinity (from TV to magazines) leave boys little discursive space for

any systematic resistance without throwing into doubt their "masculinity."

"I'm Waiting until the Comp": Delayed (Hetero) Sexualities and Re(a)lationships

Some boys, however, did actively resist "being a boy-friend" and avoid engaging in the heterosexualised discourses and practices of "going-out." As the extracts below illustrate, they either expressed a desire for a "proper" relationship proceeding primary school, which involved intimate sexual activities. Or, they stressed that they were "too young" or "not ready" to have a girlfriend:

> DAVID: We don't really care about the girls in our school
> RYAN: Yeah
> ER: At other schools?
> DAVID: In Year Seven, but they're too old for us
> ER: Why's that?
> SEAN: Coz we don't want to
> JAKE: I'm waiting until the comp
> ER: You're waiting until the comp are you?
> RYAN: Yeah, and I'm waiting till my brother brings one home then I'll know what to do
> [responding to a discussion on the lack of sexual activity amongst boyfriends and girlfriends in their class]
> RYAN: They don't do anything, they just hold hands
> DAVID: Yeah, real boyfriends and girlfriends kiss properly and stuff and go around each other's houses

Drawing upon developmental discourses of childhood innocence (i.e. sexual immaturity), and exposing and positioning their peers' "relationships" as phoney (not "real"), Ryan, David, Jake and Sean provide a legitimate rejection to be part of the heterosexualised culture of their peers, whilst simultaneously confirming their imagined, and perhaps superior ("proper"), albeit delayed heterosexualised trajectories as older "comprehensive" boys. It also allowed them to position boys who "just sit and talk" with their girlfriends as subordinate and (hetero) sexually inferior [7]. However, it was not an easy position to maintain. Their "heterosexuality" could be called into question if they failed to successfully demonstrate hegemonic forms of masculinity in other ways (usually through "fighting" or "football"). As I have reported in earlier papers (Renold, 1997, 2000) and as others have noted (Connolly, 1994) the two routes through which boys defined their hegemonic masculinity were usually girlfriends and sport. For example, Ryan's positioning, as successful "sports-man," immediately follows his negative response to having a girlfriend:

> ER: So what about you three, any girlfriends, David? (shakes his head), Ryan? (shakes his head), Jake? (shakes his head) … so no girlfriends/
> RYAN: I got up to novice two in [go]carting.

However, the need for boys to outwardly per-form their heterosexualised masculinity to others could not solely be achieved by demonstrating their sporting skills. Indeed, in the pursuit of a hegemonic heterosexual masculinity, which seemed to be increasingly undermined by the re-fusal of girls to occupy passive sexual subject posi-tions in "real" boyfriend/girlfriend relationships (Renold, 2000), heterosexual identifications were displayed in ways that were not directly under-mined or challenged.

"God, I Wish I Could Have Sex": Heterosexual Fantasies, "Sex Talk," Misogyny and Sexualised Harassment

Boys who did not regularly "go-out" or form hetero-sexual relationships with girls and even some of those who did, would define and construct their "hetero-sexuality" through publicly projecting their hetero-sexual fantasies and desires. They located themselves firmly as (hetero)sexual subjects both within and outside classroom spaces in a variety of ways from public and private declarations for greater sexual knowledge to the sexual objectification of girls and women.

Public Desire for Sexual Knowledge
(comments follow from a sex education lesson)

> PETE: We want to know more about the girls
> ER: OK, so what did you want to know more about the girls? … (few seconds silence and embarrassed looks)

> PETE: We are interested because when you get older you've got to sometime er er … coz when I'm older I won't be able to do it will I, I won't be able to/
> COLIN: Yeah sometime or other you'll have to do something beginning with "s" and ending in "x"/
> ER: Sex
> COLIN AND DARREN: Yeah
> TIMOTHY: You wouldn't know how to would you/
> PETE: What's the point of having sex education if you, if it's not really showing it and it's just showing your genitals and all that stuff
> PETE: Yeah it hasn't got enough detail, it hasn't got enough details/
> ER: So you want more detail
> PETE AND TIMOTHY: Yeah
> PETE: We want to know we want to have a man and a lady, real, having it off/
> TIMOTHY: Today when that bloke was shaving naked they had him on for about three minutes and had the girl on/
> DARREN: For three seconds bathing this other girl
> PETE: All it shows was their boobies
> ER: So you wanted to see more?
> DARREN: More breast stroke (they all laugh)

Sexualising Lyric

The bell rings, signalling the end of break-time. Adrian walks across the playground singing out loud his version of Michael Jackson's *Earth Song* which has a number of lines beginning "what about …" He changes the end of the line with "what about erections?," "what about sex?," "what about masturbation?"

Sexualising Classroom Talk

Mrs. Fryer tries to quieten the class down. She asks them to put their lips together. Adrian shouts out "oo err, I'm not kissing everyone in this class." Many of the boys and girls start laughing. Mrs. Fryer looks at me, smiles, rolls her eyes and gives Adrian a long look (of disapproval?).

Sexual Objectification of Girls and Women

David and Sean prepare the tables for group artwork by covering them in old newspapers. As they spread the newspapers around David comes across a picture of three topless women posed in an intimate embrace. "Cor—look at this—I wouldn't mind a bit of that" and he shows up the picture to Sean and a number of boys crowd round. The boys start giggling and Mrs Fryer walks over, saying "what's the fuss, they're just naked, haven't you seen naked ladies before?" She takes the paper from them and goes back to her marking.

Sexualisation of Body Parts

TIMOTHY: Stuart gets erections
COLIN: Yeah (they all laugh) he was talking when the video was on and goes "I've got a stiffy" (more laughter)

Positioning themselves as dominant sexual subjects was achieved in a number of ways. David's public declaration of his sexual desires for super-models (in this case, topless models) and Darren's sexualisation of the girl in the sex education video through his call for more "breast stroke" illustrates how some boys overtly located themselves as heterosexual using dominant discourses in which "women are represented as passive objects of male sexual urges, needs and desires" (Mac an Ghaill, 1994, p. 92). Other (hetero)sexualised performances were maintained through more light-hearted engagements, such as altering song lyrics to sexualise the content or introducing sexual innuendo to everyday pedagogic relations. Moreover, the first extract highlights how some boys' thirst for hetero/sexual knowledge far exceeded official sex education programmes. Like Mac an Ghaill's (1994, p. 92) findings amongst older teenage boys, the boys' "sex-talk" seemed "publicly to validate their masculinity to their male friends." All the extracts to some extent reveal boys' experimentation with sex and sexuality as a means of regulating their hetero/sexualities, transcending "official" (school) sexual discourses and releasing sexual tension through humour (last extract). Pete's fear of being caught-out, not knowing what to do (when the time comes) in future sexual relationships, however, does suggest that some boys could communicate their private insecurities.

Positioning themselves as dominant sexual subjects was also achieved, however, through overt and covert forms of sexualised harassment to their female classmates and peers.

Symbolic Sexual Gestures

The class have been told they can go out—it is now break-time. Neil gets up and as he is walking out, he stops at Carrie's table. Carrie is still sitting down. Neil bends over in front of her so that his face is parallel with hers and wags his tongue up and down directly in front of her face, then walks off. Carrie looks confused and unsettled for a moment and then continues to chat with her friends.

Sexual Swear Words

ER: So what about you Darren?
PETE: Well he's been out with Mandy, I mean, not Mandy, I mean er er Victoria about three times in the past three months init? or something like that and once he went out with her for about a month didn't ya?
DARREN: Mmm
ER: What happened, why aren't you seeing her anymore?
PETE: Because she, because he called her a fucking bitch

Physical Sexual Harassment

ER: Do boys pick on you like they do to their friends?
TRUDY: They punch you in the boobs
ANABEL: Yeah they punch you in the boobs sometimes and pull your bra and that really kills/
TRUDY: Yeah, they go like that (shows me)
ER: Who does that?
ALL: Stu
ANABEL: And Ryan and that
ER: So what do you do to that/
ANABEL: Nothing, we just walk away going like this (hugging chest), "don't touch me"

Heterosexualised harassment usually took the form of denigrating girls through sexually abusive and aggressive language, gestures or behaviours and in most cases were not reported to teaching (or non-teaching) staff (see Renold, 2002b, for a fuller discussion of sexualised bullying and harassment). On two occasions, a group of boys also took to positioning their class teacher as sexually subordinate (see Walkerdine, 1981) by calling her a "slag" and a "bitch" (in an interview): first, when football was banned on the playground and second, when they felt they were receiving unnecessary disciplinary treatment in the classroom. These forms of sexualised harassment/offensive sexualised behaviours were often engaged in by boys who were located lower down the heterosexual hierarchies (Darren for example was continuously "dumped" in a string of relationships).

What I hope these extracts go some way to illustrate are the overt ways in which boys "perform" their heterosexuality in a need to confirm their hegemonic heterosexual masculinity and how such performances, particularly the sexual objectification of women and the sexualised harassment (verbal and physical) of their female classmates, re-instated boys' heterosexual dominance, often undermined and denied through conventional and "real" boyfriend/girlfriend relationships, as Mac an Ghaill explains:

> Externally and internally males attempt to re-produce themselves as powerful within social circumstances which remain out of their control. (1996, p. 200)

With many boys coupling heterosexual activity with maturity and "older boys," these sexualised performances could also be interpreted as a direct challenge to the perceived "asexuality" of the primary school environment and discourses of "childhood innocence." They could also be one of the ways in which boys "collectively explore(d) the newly available forms of authority and autonomy conferred by their position at the 'top of the school'" (Redman, 1996, p. 178). Indeed, their entry into heterosexuality and heterosexual discourses/practices could have thus been further reinforced by their chronological positioning within the school.

Anti-gay Talk and "Homophobic" Narratives

As many secondary school-based studies have illustrated, "homophobic" [8] discourses and anti-gay/lesbian talk and behaviours saturate boys' peer-group cultures, social relations and masculinity-making activities. However, as some primary school-based research (Letts & Sears, 1999) is beginning to uncover, younger children are *also* drawing upon the term "gay" either as a general form of abuse, where

the intention is to unsettle or upset their (usually male) peers, or to target particular boys who fail or choose not to access hegemonic masculine discourses or practices. I would argue, from my own research, that towards the end of children's primary school years, boys outwardly demonstrate a fear and loathing of homosexualities and are highly aware of how anti-gay talk/behaviours (labelling and teasing other boys as "gay") can police and produce acceptable heterosexual masculinities. I stress "also" because some authors (Redman, 1996) suggest that "homosexual anxieties" are not employed as a means of defining and constituting "normal" heterosexualities until boys are at least 12 to 13 years of age. The following extracts provide a rare discussion of how "homosexuality" was perceived negatively, with a mixture of fear and disgust:

RYAN: There was a programme on the other day [it is AIDS week] I turned it off after a while, it was disgusting/

ER: Why?

RYAN: Because it showed these er two men who dressed up as women and they were er they were having sex and it was really horrible

ER: And you didn't like it, so you turned it off?

RYAN: Yeah

ER: OK ... why do you think you didn't like it?

RYAN: Well like if you see a women and a man doing it I don't really care and er/

DAVID: Coz everyone does it, every night

RYAN: You see you see people doing it that way then you don't really mind coz that's what most people do and then you see like two men doing it and you know that's horrible, disgusting

ER: When you say gay Jake what do you mean by that?

JAKE: You know, like/really sad

SEAN: A bender (Sean, Ryan and Jake laugh)/

RYAN: And you can sound gay can't you/

DAVID: Simon/he sounds gay

RYAN: Our next door neighbour/

JAKE: You know that "supermarket sweep" (game show)?

ER: Yeah

JAKE: Well there was this man on there/

DAVID: And he (host of show) goes, "you're really pretty aren't you"

JAKE: Yeah and he won it right, about 2000 pounds and he goes up to him and he can't stop kissing him (laughing) he kisses him about 2000 times/

RYAN: Yeah that's like Michael Barrymore/

JAKE: Yeah and/he smacked Michael Barrymore in the other day/Sean and Ryan: Yeah (they all cheer and clap)/

DAVID: Who did?

ER: Why is that good?

SEAN: Coz he's gay

Anti-gay talk and homophobic performances were expressed more often by boys who did not engage in overt heterosexual boyfriend/girlfriend relationships and more frequently than boys who *did* "have girlfriends" and who *were* "going out." Indeed, the powerlessness experienced by many boys participating in the boyfriend/girlfriend cultures (i.e. being dumped or being used), the precarious position of "boyfriend" and indeed the ambiguity of initiating physical or emotional intimacies with girls at all, produced some very confusing messages and some rather contradictory heterosexual identities.

Processes of differentiation (from "homosexualities") and subordination (of alternative masculinities) were all ways in which these boys asserted and attempted to make coherent their heterosexual identities, which Mac an Ghaill and others (Kehily & Nayak, 1997; Redman, 2000) suggest involve external (social) and internal (psychic) processes:

> Heterosexual male students were involved in a double relationship of traducing the Other, including women and gays (external relations), at the same time as expelling femininity and homosexuality from within themselves (internal relations). (Mac an Ghaill, 1994, p. 90)

However, the differences in attitudes and homophobic behaviours in my study, seemed not to be based not on "class" (as in Mac an Ghaill's research) but on their success at being "tough," "sporty" and "cool," and in particular their sustained participation in heterosexual relationships. Unfortunately, what this study does lack, is a detailed discussion of boys' views towards homosexuality. Because of the sensitivity of discussing non-heterosexualities with primary school children, only the boys' perspectives who instigated discussions on homosexuality were recorded.

This is surely an area which would benefit from further investigation.

Conclusions

> Young children, according to commensense understandings, are innocent. They neither do, nor should they, know anything about sexuality. The fear is that contemporary children "grow up too soon" or are "not yet ready" for sexual knowledge. (Epstein *et al.*, 2001, p. 134)

This paper is situated within a growing recognition that primary schools are far from asexual environments and primary school children cannot be presumed (sexually) innocent (Thorne & Luria, 1986; Davies, 1993; Thorne, 1993; Redman, 1996; Connolly, 1998; Hatcher, 1995; Wallis & VanEvery, 2000; Skelton, 2001). Rather, as Wallis and VanEvery argue, "sexuality (especially heterosexuality) is not only present but crucial to the organisation of primary schools, both explicitly and implicitly" (2000, p. 411) and thus in ways similar to secondary and further education sectors, a key social and cultural site for the production of children's sexual relations and identities. Primarily, the purpose of this paper has been to make visible and thus break the silence around young children's (hetero)sexual cultures and shed some analytic light on a specific aspect of the organisational heteronormativity of the primary school—boys' sexual cultures and in particular how hegemonic masculinities involve the "heterosexual presumption." That is, how being a "proper boy" involves establishing or at least investing in and projecting a recognisable (and hegemonic) heterosexual identity.

Throughout the paper I have highlighted how all boys are to some extent subject to the pressures of "compulsory heterosexuality" (most evident in the boyfriend/girlfriend cultures of the school, which even if they were not directly engaged in, were forever positioned in relation to it). I have also shown how boys can feel confused, anxious, and powerless because of the contradictions involved in constructing heterosexualised masculinities through boyfriend/girlfriend discourses (i.e. that intimacy with girls could be simultaneously contaminating *and* masculinity confirming). In an attempt to make coherent ultimately fragile masculinities I argue that the majority of boys come to define and produce their heterosexualities through various public projections of (hetero)sexual fantasies, imagined (hetero)sexual futures, misogynistic objectifications of girls and women and homophobic/anti-gay performances towards boys and sexualised forms of harassment towards girls. Furthermore, all of these "performances" permeated and thus ultimately affected everyday classroom and playground interactions and as such became a significant site of learning as Kehily (2002) highlights in her discussion of gender, sexuality and pedagogy in the secondary school:

> Students develop an understanding of the meanings and implications of sex–gender categories and also create their own meanings in a range of informal encounters. (2002, p. 125)

Indeed, some boys drew upon discourses of "childhood innocence" and "older sexualities" to legitimate delaying their active role in boyfriend/girlfriend networks, where others (see Renold, 2002) readily took up the subject position "boyfriend" to maintain close friendships with female classmates.

Most disturbing, however, was how the regulation of hegemonic heterosexualities through the policing and shaming of gender (Butler, 1993) which usually occurred when investment in overt heterosexual practices (girlfriends) did not automatically signify hegemonic masculinity. In these cases, such performances have real social and emotional consequences which are damaging for both boys and girls. For example, homophobic/anti-gay performances not only had the effect of subordinating alternative masculinities and non-hegemonic sexualities, but implicitly subordinates femininities and all things "feminine" (i.e. majority of girls/"girl's activities"). However, in a moral and political climate where children's sexuality and moreover sex/uality education is a contested and contentious space (see the numerous and competing struggles in the UK over the repeal of Section 28 [9]), schools are "legitimately anxious about the reactions of some parents and worse, the popular press if they stray into territory considered to be too risky" (Epstein et al., 2001, p. 136). Headteachers and teachers are thus placed in a difficult position to openly discuss children's emerging gender and sexual identities and knowledges in ways that can challenge the more prevailing heteronormativity of boys' (and girls') peer group cultures and indeed draw upon the services or formulate the policies needed to support children's more painful and oppressive practices of gender-based and sexualised forms of harassment.

On a more positive note, primary headteachers and teachers committed to creating an anti-oppressive environment that strives for gender equity and celebrates and supports diversity within gender/sexual relations can be encouraged in a number of ways:

- First, there has been a shift in UK education policy under the Local Government Act 2000 (Section 104) stating that teachers must take steps to "prevent any form of bullying," including "homophobic bullying" (Social Inclusion: Pupil Support Circular 10/99). This circular also includes a specific reference to peer bullying as a result of "or related to sexual orientation" (1.32) and includes strategies to address sexual and racial harassment (4.47). Furthermore, the government's anti-bullying pack for schools (DfE, 2000) also offers detailed advice and guidance to prevent bullying because of perceived or actual sexual orientation. The phrasing, "related to their sexual orientation" is an important one in relation to the findings of this study insofar as much of the homophobic/anti-gay insults directed at boys are more often related to their gender deviance (from recognisable "masculine" traits) than their perceived or actual sexual orientation [10]. For those primary headteachers and governers wary of incorporating the term "sexuality" into their bullying policies, conceptualising and including gender-based harassment as a form of "bullying" will go some way to raising awareness and challenge the heteronormative status quo (because of the ways in which gender is mediated by and embedded within sexuality).
- While governing bodies have no legal obligation to provide sex education for primary school pupils, the vagueness of primary sex education guidelines creates gaps which any school can harness to tackle the more oppressive forms of gendered and sexualised harassment and bullying and develop a broader

understanding of sex/uality education (Redman, 1994). For example, Brown (1997) suggests that the National Curriculum Council's (NCC) recommendations on primary sex education which stress *positivity, self-image, bodies, sexuality and relationships* and most importantly, in relation to children, *agency* and *responsibility* can be effectively deployed to construct a more comprehensive and inclusive sex/uality education policy.

• Third, as this research and other studies illustrate, many boys (and girls) are aware of the contradictions and difficulties of securing a hegemonic heterosexual masculinity and respond to "gentle challenges about the effects of narrowly constructed masculinities" (see Frosh et al., 2002, p. 262). Indeed, group discussions provide a forum for some boys to openly, and sometimes critically, discuss the constraining nature of hegemonic masculinities and can thus be deployed by teachers as one way to explore the "knock-on effect" of "doing boy" in hegemonic ways (see MacNaughton, 2000).

Group-based activities, if sensitively handled, can also be useful "starting points" (see Kenway et al., 1997) for those teachers creating policies that are grounded in children's own experiences. This is especially important given the increasing recognition that pupils be more involved and active in the policy making process (Alderson, 2000). As Skelton (2001) notes, however, any specific strategy (whether it be to tackle homophobic bullying or sexualised harassment more widely) must be integrated within a whole-school approach to gender equity and one that focuses on gender relations—girls *and* boys, masculinities *and* femininities and the power relations at play in their often oppositional construction.

While there are obviously no quick-fix solutions there are opportunities and developments (and gaps) in both policy and practice for committed teachers to support pupil's emerging gender and sexual identities and combat the damaging consequences of negotiating a heteronormative world.

Notes

1. Tipton Primary's catchment area served white "working" and "middle" class families, while Hirstwood served predominantly white "middle" class families.

2. Each child participated in a series of group interviews/discussions (six times in total) over the period of a year. Indeed, I visited each school for 2/3 days every fortnight during that year.

3. Other studies have highlighted how even 4- and 5-year-olds "practice heterosexuality" through dating games and kiss chase (Epstein, 1997a; Connolly, 1998; Skelton, 2001).

4. The subject positions of "boyfriend" and "girlfriend" were discursively reproduced and maintained daily via "messengers" (usually female) who mediated and relayed love letters, dumping letters and requests to be X's boyfriend or girlfriend.

5. Despite the active connotation of the phrase "going out," couples rarely went anywhere. "Going out" was a particular discourse which signified and made available the subject position "boyfriend" or "girlfriend" and could range from a "couple" spending time together in their lunch break (holding hands, chatting,

kissing) to simply *saying* you were "going out" with someone.

6. I have argued elsewhere how some girls reported experiencing a great deal of power from being able to terminate relationships. For some, it seemed the only domain in which they could "get one over the boys."

7. Indeed, I argue in another paper how some boys draw upon the discourses and engage in the practices of the boyfriend/girlfriend culture to maintain close friendships with girls and avoid the macho-making activities associated with fighting and football free (almost) from ridicule and speculation over their gender/sexual identities (Renold, 2002a, 2002b).

8. I am using the term "homophobic" to define those behaviours and practices which signify a fear of "homosexuality" and the term "anti-gay" to define talk and behaviour that signifies any negative sentiment regarding same-sex identities, practices or relationships. While there is obviously some overlap, differentiating "homophobia" from "anti-gay" sentiment offers a way of situating the realm of the unconscious within wider social and cultural relations (see Redman, 2000, for a

fuller discussion of the usefulness of the term "homophobia" as an analytic tool).

9. Section 28 of the 1988 Local Government Act prohibits local education authorities from "promoting" the teaching of "homosexuality as a pretended family relationship." While Section 28 has been repealed in Scotland it has undergone two defeated repeals in England and Wales (see Redman, 1994; Epstein, 2000; and Moran, 2001, for a wider discussion of Section 28).

10. However, advice and guidance to date have centred on older children and teenagers.

References

Alderson, P. (2000). Children as Researchers. In *Research with Children*, P. Christensen & A. James (eds.). London: Falmer Press, pp. 241–57.

Brown, T. (1997). Sex Education. In M. Cole, D. Hill & S. Shan (eds.). *Promoting Equality in Primary Schools*. London, Routledge.

Butler, J. (1990). *Gender Trouble: Feminism and the Subversion of Identity*. London: Routledge.

Butler, J. (1993). *Bodies That Matter: On the Discursive Limits of Sex*. London: Routledge.

Connell, R. W. (1995). *Masculinities: Knowledge, Power and Social Change*. Cambridge: Polity Press.

Connolly, P. (1994). Boys Will Be Boys? Racism, Sexuality and the Construction of Masculine Identities amongst Infant Boys. In J. Holland & M. Blair (eds.), *Debates and Issues in Feminist Research and Pedagogy*. Clevedon: Multilingual Matters.

Connolly, P. (1998). *Racisms, Gendered Identities and Young Children: Social Relations in a Multi-ethnic, Inner-city Primary School*. London: Routledge.

Davies, B. (1993). *Shards of Glass: Children Reading and Writing beyond Gendered Identities*. New Jersey: Hampton Press.

DfE (2000) *Bullying—Don't Suffer in Silence—An Anti-Bullying Pack for Schools* (64/2000). Great Britain: Department for Education.

Epstein, D. (1997a). Cultures of Schooling/Cultures of Sexuality. *International Journal of Inclusive Education*, 1, pp. 37–53.

Epstein, D. (1997b). Boyz' Own Stories: Masculinities and Sexualities in Schools. *Gender and Education*, 9, pp. 105–17.

Epstein, D. (2000). Promoting Homophobia: Section 28, Schools and Young People. *ChildRight*, 164, pp. 14–15.

Epstein, D. & Johnson, R. (1994). On the Straight and Narrow: The Heterosexual Presumption, Homophobias and Schools. In D. Epstein (ed.), *Challenging Lesbian and Gay Inequalities in Education*. Buckingham: Open University Press.

Epstein, D. & Johnson, R. (1998). *Schooling Sexualities*. Buckingham, Open University Press.

Epstein, D., O'Flynn, S., & Telford, D. (2001). "Othering" Education: Sexualities, Silences and Schooling. *Review of Research in Education*, 25, pp. 127–79.

Frosh, S., Phoenix, A., & Pattman, R. (2002). *Young Masculinities*. (Hampshire, Palgrave).

Hatcher, R. (1995). Boyfriends, Girlfriends: Gender and "Race" in Children's Cultures. *International Play Journal*, 3, pp. 187–97.

Haywood, C. (1996). Out of the Curriculum: Sex Talking, Talking Sex. *Curriculum Studies*, 4, pp. 229–51.

Kehily, M. J. (2000). Understanding Heterosexualities: Masculinities, Embodiment and Schooling. In G. Walford & C. Hudson (eds.), *Genders and Sexualities in Educational Ethnography*. New York: Elsevier.

Kehily, M. J. (2002) Issues of Gender and Sexuality in Schools. In B. Francis & C. Skelton (eds.), *Investigating Gender: Contemporary Perspectives in Education*. Buckingham, Open University Press.

Kehily, M. J. and Nayak, A. (1996). Playing It Straight: Masculinities, Homophobias and Schooling. *Journal of Gender Studies* 5, pp. 211–29.

Kehily, M. J. and Nayak, A. (1997). Lads and Laughter: Humour and the Production of Heterosexual Hierarchies. *Gender and Education*, 9, pp. 69–87.

Kehily, M. J. and Nayak, A. (2000) Schoolgirl Frictions: Young Women Sex Education and Social Experiences. In G. Walford & C. Hudson (eds.), *Genders and Sexualities in Educational Ethnography*. New York: Elsevier.

Kenway, J. & Willis, S., with Blackmore, J. & Rennie, L. (1997). Are Boys Victims Of Feminism In Schools?: Some Answers from Australia. *International Journal of Inclusive Education*, 1, pp. 19–35.

Laskey, L. & Beavis, C. (1996) *Schooling and Sexualities: Teaching for a Positive Sexuality*. Geelong, Victoria: Deakin University Centre for Change.

Letts IV, W. & Sears, J. T., eds. (1999). *Queering Elementary Education: Advancing the Dialogue about Sexualities and Schooling*. New York: Rowman and Littlefield.

Mac an Ghaill, M. (1994). *The Making of Men: Masculinities, Sexualities and Schooling*. Buckingham: Open University Press.

Mac an Ghaill, M. (1996). Deconstructing Heterosexualities within School Arenas. *Curriculum Studies*, 4, pp. 191–207.

MacNaughton, G. (2000). *Rethinking Gender in Early Childhood Education*. London: Paul Chapman.

Mahony, P., & Jones, C. (eds.) (1989). *Learning Our Lines: Sexuality and Social Control in Education*. London: Women's Press.

Moran, S. (2001). Childhood Sexuality and Education: The Case of Section 28. *Sexualities* 4, pp. 73–89.

Nayak, A., & Kehily, M. J. (1997). Masculinities and Schooling: Why Are Young Men So Homophobic? In D. L. Steinberg, D. Epstein & R. Johnson (eds.). *Border Patrols: Policing the Boundaries of Heterosexuality*. London: Cassel.

Redman, P. (1994). Shifting Ground: Rethinking Sexuality Education. In D. Epstein (ed.), *Challenging Lesbian and Gay Inequalities in Education*. Buckingham: Open University Press.

Redman, P. (1996). Curtis Loves Ranjit: Heterosexual Masculinities, Schooling, and Pupils' Sexual Cultures. *Educational Review*, 48, pp. 175–82.

Redman, P. (2000). Tarred with the Same Brush: Homophobia and the Unconscious in School-Based Cultures of Masculinity. *Sexualities*, 3, pp. 483–99.

Redman, P. (2001) The Discipline of Love: Negotiation and Regulation in Boys' Performance of a Romance-Based Heterosexual Masculinity. *Men and Masculinities*, 4, pp. 186–200.

Renold, E. (1997). All They've Got on Their Brains Is Football: Sport, Masculinity and the Gendered Practices of Playground Relations. *Sport, Education and Society*, 2, pp. 5–23.

Renold, E. (1999). Presumed Innocence: An Ethnographic Investigation into the Construction of Children's Gender and Sexual Identities in the Primary School. Unpublished Doctoral Dissertation.

Renold, E. (2000). "Coming Out": Gender (Hetero)Sexuality and the Primary School. *Gender and Education*, 12: 309–27.

Renold, E. (2002a). *Primary School Studs: (De)Constructing Heterosexual Masculinities in the Primary School*, paper presented at British Association Annual Conference, 25–27 March 2002, University of Leicester.

Renold, E. (2002b). "Presumed Innocence": (Hetero) Sexual, Homophobic and Heterosexist Harassment amongst Children in the Primary School. *Childhood*, 9, pp. 415–33.

Rich, A. 1980. Compulsory Heterosexuality and Lesbian Existence. *Journal of Women's History*, 15, Autumn 2003, pp. 11–48.

Skelton, C. 2001. *Schooling the Boys: Masculinities and Primary Education*. Buckingham: Open University Press.

Thorne, B. 1993. *Gender Play: Boys and Girls in School*. Buckingham: Open University Press.

Thorne, B., & Luria, Z. (1986). Sexuality and Gender in Children's Daily Worlds. *Social Problems*, 33, pp. 176–90.

Walkerdine, V. (1981). "Sex, Power and Pedagogy." *Screen Education*, 38, pp. 14–24.

Wallis, A., & VanEvery, J. (2000). Sexuality in the Primary School. *Sexualities*, 3, pp. 409–23.

Questions for Critical Thinking

1. Renold discusses the ways in which children in primary schools construct heterosexual identities, even at very early ages. What are some of the ways that you have witnessed the gendered behaviors of girls and boys that later influence the construction of their sexuality as women and men?

2. The experiences of the children in this article indicate that heterosexual behavior does not necessarily come naturally to girls and boys but is constructed. In your opinion, how does this challenge everyday representations of heterosexuality as the norm?

3. Do you think it is possible that we can deconstruct sexuality? What would be the implications for society if we were to be successful in doing so?

WHAT'S SO CULTURAL ABOUT HOOKUP CULTURE?

Lisa Wade

The following essay by sociologist Lisa Wade explores the norms and practices that make up college students' experience of hookup culture. Connected with her research for her book *American Hookup: The New Culture of Sex on Campus*, Wade illustrates that sex on college campuses is more than just what people do and that hookup culture is a phenomenon that impacts all students, whether they participate or not.

Arman was 7,000 miles from his family, one of the roughly million international students who were enrolled in U.S. colleges last year. Dropped into the raucous first week of freshman year, he discovered a way of life that seemed intensely foreign, frightening, and enticing. "It's been a major shock," he wrote.

The behavior of some of his fellow students unnerved him. He watched them drink to excess, tell explicit sexual stories, flirt on the quad, and grind on the dance floor. He received assertive sexual signals from women. It was, Arman wrote, "beyond anything I have experienced back home."

By his second semester, Arman's religious beliefs had been shaken. He was deeply torn as to whether to participate in this new social scene. "Stuck," he wrote, "between a sexually conservative background and a relatively sexually open world." Should he "embrace, accept, and join in?" Or, he wondered, using the past tense like a Freudian slip, "remember who I was and deprive myself of the things I actually and truly want deep down inside?"

He struggled. "Always having to internally fight the desire to do sexual things with girls is not easy," he wrote. One night, he succumbed to temptation. He went to a party, drank, and kissed a girl on the dance floor. When the alcohol wore off, he was appalled at his behavior. "How much shame I have brought onto myself," he recalled with anguish.

A few months later, he would lose his virginity to a girl he barely knew. His feelings about it were deeply ambivalent. "I felt more free and unbounded," he confessed, "but at the same time, guilt beyond imagination."

For my book, *American Hookup: The New Culture of Sex on Campus*, I followed 101 college students through a semester of their first year. They submitted weekly journal entries, writing about sex and dating on campus however they wished. In total, the students wrote over 1,500 single-spaced pages and a million words. I dovetailed their stories with 21 follow-up interviews, quantitative data from the Online College Social Life Survey, academic literature, hundreds of essays written by students for college newspapers, and 24 visits to campuses around the country.

Arman was an outlier. Very few students are strongly motivated to abstain from sex altogether, but it's typical for students to report mixed feelings about the opportunity to have casual sex. Thirty-six of the 101 students I studied reported being simultaneously attracted to and repelled by hookup culture upon arrival at college, compared to thirty-four who opted out entirely, twenty-three who opted in with enthusiasm, and eight who sustained monogamous relationships.

For students like Arman, who are unsure of whether they want to participate, hookup culture has a way of tipping the scales. Its logic makes both abstaining from sex and a preference for sex in committed relationships difficult to justify, and its integration into the workings of higher education makes hooking up hard to avoid.

The Logic of Hookup Culture

Hooking up is immanently defensible in hookup culture. Students believe, or believe that their peers believe, that virginity is passé and monogamy prudish; that college is a time to go wild and have fun; that separating sex from emotions is sexually liberating; and that they're too young and career-focused for commitment. All of these ideas are widely circulated on campus—and all make reasonable sense—validating the choice to engage in casual sex while invalidating both monogamous relationships and the choice to have no sex at all.

For the students in my study who were enthusiastic about casual sex, this worked out well, but students who found casual sex unappealing often had difficulty explaining why, both to themselves or others. Many simply concluded that they were overly sensitive or insufficiently brave. "I honestly admire them," wrote one Latina student about her friends who enjoyed casual sex, "because I just cannot do that." A White middle-class student implored herself to not be so "uptight." "Sometimes I wish I could just loosen up," she wrote. A sexually sophisticated pansexual student wondered aloud if she was a "prude." "I'm so embarrassed by that," she confessed. "I feel as if by not voluntarily taking part in it, I am weird and abnormal."

If culture is a "toolkit" offering culturally competent actors a set of ideas and practices with which to explain their choices, to use Ann Swider's metaphor from her article "Culture in Action," then hookup culture offers students many tools useful for embracing casual sex, but few for articulating why they may prefer other kinds of sexual engagement, or none at all. Faced with these options, many students who are ambivalent decide to give it a try.

The New Culture of College

In the colonial era, colleges were downright stodgy. Student activities were rigidly controlled, curricula were dry, and harsh punishments were meted out for misbehavior. The fraternity boys of the early 1800s can be credited with introducing the idea that college should be fun. Their lifestyle was then glamorized by the media of the 1920s and democratized by the alcohol industry in the 1980s after *Animal House*. Today, the reputation of higher education as a place for an outlandish good time is second only to its reputation as a place of learning.

Not just any good time, though. A particular kind of party dominates the social scene: drunken, wild, and visually titillating, throbbing with sexual potential. Such parties are built into the rhythm and architecture of higher education. They occur at designated times, such that they don't interfere with (most) classes, and are usually held at large, off-campus houses (often but not always fraternities) or on nearby streets populated by bars and clubs. This gives the institutions plausible deniability, but keeps the partying close enough to be part of colleges' appeal.

Almost all of the students in *American Hookup* were living in residence halls. On weekend nights, dorms buzzed with pre-partying, primping, and planning. Students who stayed in were keenly aware of what they weren't doing. Eventually residence halls would empty out, leaving eerie quiet; revelers returned drunker, louder. Students were sometimes kicked out of their own rooms to facilitate a roommate's hookup. A few had exhibitionistic roommates who didn't bother to kick them out at all.

The morning after, there would be a ritual retelling of the night before. And the morning after that, anticipation for the next weekend of partying began. Being immersed in hookup culture meant being surrounded by anticipation, innuendo, and bragga-docio. As one of the African-American men in my study wrote: "Hookup culture is all over the place."

For students who went to parties, hookups felt, as several put it, "inevitable." Sooner or later, a student had one too many drinks, met someone especially cute, or felt like doing something a little wild. For young people still learning how to manage sexual desire, college parties combining sex with sensory overload and mind-altering substances can be over-whelming. Accordingly, anyone who regularly partici-pates in the routine partying built into the rhythm of higher education will likely find themselves opting in to hooking up.

Sex on college campuses is something people do, but it's also a cultural phenomenon: a conversation of a particular kind and a set of routines built into the institution of higher education. When students arrive on campus, they don't just encounter the op-portunity to hook up, they are also immersed in a culture that endorses and facilitates hookups. Ceding to or resisting that culture then becomes part of their everyday lives.

"Even if you aren't hooking up," said an African-American woman about her first year on campus, "there is no escaping hookup culture." Residential colleges are what sociologist Erving Goffman called "total institutions," planned entities that collect large numbers of like individuals, cut them off from the wider society, and provide for all their needs. And because hookup culture is totally institutionalized, when students move into a dorm room on a college campus, they become a part of it—whether they like it or not.

Students wish they had more options. Some pine for the going-steady lifestyle of the 1950s. Many mourn the utopia that the sexual revolution promised but never fully delivered. Quite a few would like things to be a lot more queer and gender fluid. Some want a hookup culture that is kinder—warm as well as hot. And there are still a handful who would prefer stodgy to sexy. Satisfying these diverse desires will re-quire a shift to a more complex and rich cultural life on campus, not just a different one.

Questions for Critical Thinking

1. How does Wade's discussion of the prevalence of hookup culture on college campuses reflect your own experiences? How do you think this culture impacts your interactions with others?

2. Wade argues that everyone is impacted by hookup culture, whether they participate in it or not. What evidence have you seen to support or refute this argument?

3. Do you think it is possible or even necessary to eliminate hookup culture on college campuses? If so, how so? If not, why not?

PART II

Maintaining Inequalities

SYSTEMS OF OPPRESSION AND PRIVILEGE

Introduction

On April 6, 2016, Khairuldeen Makhzoomi, an Iraqi asylee and student at the University of California, Berkeley, was removed from a Southwest Airlines flight and questioned by the FBI. He had recently attended a speech by United Nations secretary general Ban Ki-moon and was excited to call his uncle to tell him about the event. While on the phone, he told his uncle about the chicken dinner they were served and the moment when he got to stand up and ask the secretary general a question about the Islamic State. A nearby passenger overheard the conversation and reported him to the crew for making "potentially threatening comments." Makhzoomi had ended his call with his uncle with a common phrase in Arabic, *inshallah*, meaning "god willing."

Since the events of September 11, 2001, passengers who are perceived to be Arab or followers of Islam—which has included people who are South Asian, Latino, Indian, and Mexican—have been removed from airplanes because of the refusal by crew members and passengers to fly with them. Calling it "flying while Arab," Michel Shehadeh, former West Coast regional director of the American-Arab Anti-Discrimination Committee, asserts that any Arab (or person perceived to be Arab) is thought to be a terrorist. This form of racial profiling is certainly nothing new.[1] Rather, it is based on a long history of US government anti-Arab programs and policies. However, racial profiling of people perceived to be Arab or Muslim increased greatly as the result of a September 12, 2001, directive from the Federal Aviation Administration to the nation's airlines instructing security to immediately conduct "random identification checks," stating,

> Extremist groups, with a history of targeting civil action, are actively targeting U.S. interests, particularly in the Middle East. They retain a capability to conduct airline bombings, hijackings, suicide attacks, and possess surface-to-air missiles.

Such a directive is reinforced by other federal policies, such as the National Security Entry Exit Registration System, which was established in 2002 and required the special registration of all male nationals over the age of fifteen from twenty-five countries (with the exception of North Korea, all countries were Arab and Muslim). This registration obligated these males to report to the government to register and be fingerprinted, photographed, and questioned. Those failing to register were subject to detention and/or immediate deportation (American Civil

Liberties Union 2004). Because of the ineffectiveness of this policy, the US Department of Homeland Security delisted the countries under the system in April 2011, although the regulatory structure stayed largely intact until December 2016.

Such profiling is similar to that experienced by blacks and Latinos for some time. For example, in May 1992 the Maryland State Police stopped a car in the early morning hours just outside of Cumberland, Maryland. The occupants—Washington, D.C., attorney Robert Wilkins and members of his family—were questioned, ticketed, and made to stand in the rain while a dog sniffed for drugs in their car. Mr. Wilkins sued, and the resulting litigation uncovered a memorandum instructing police to watch for "predominantly black" drug couriers.

In Illinois, a defense attorney hired a Latino private investigator to drive across certain counties to test the validity of assertions that the state police stopped Latinos and African Americans in disproportionate numbers. Peso Chavez, a twenty-year veteran investigator and a former elected official from Santa Fe, New Mexico, was followed by an assistant to verify the legality of his driving. Although the assistant saw no violation, state police officers stopped Chavez for a traffic offense. They asked him for permission to search his car and, when he asked whether he had to allow the search, a drug-sniffing dog was brought to the scene. Despite Chavez's unmistakable objection and his request that he be permitted to leave, the police used the dog on his car. The officers then told Chavez that the dog had alerted them to the presence of drugs. Chavez was put into the back of a patrol car and probed with questions as he watched the police search every part of his vehicle, open his luggage, and go through all of his personal possessions.

These are examples of a practice known as **pretext stops**—the use of traffic stops as an excuse to stop African Americans, *Latinas/os/x*, and other people of color to search their cars and question the occupants about possession of drugs. Traffic stops are, in fact, the most common interaction members of the U.S. population have with police. On a typical day, police pull over more than 50,000 drivers—more than 20 million people a year. According to a recent study, undertaken by faculty at the Stanford Open Policing Project, in a dataset of nearly 100 million traffic stops across the United States, black drivers were about 20 percent more likely to be stopped than white drivers relative to their share of the residential population. The study also found that once stopped, black drivers were searched about 1.5 to 2 times as often as white drivers, while they were less likely to be carrying drugs, guns, or other illegal contraband compared to their white peers (Pierson et al. 2020). As an additional example, we can look to a statewide investigation in California of **racial profiling**—the practice of police and other officials targeting people of color for traffic stops because they believe that people of color are more likely to be engaged in criminal activity. This study revealed that police stopped African American drivers at a rate disproportionate to their percentage of the population and searched them at a rate 2.9 times the rate at which they searched white drivers, even though contraband was generally found on white individuals at higher rates than individuals from all other groups. (Racial & Identity Profiling Advisory Board Annual Report, 2020). Pretext stops are so common that members of black and *Latina/o/x* communities refer to them as DWB: driving while black or driving while brown (Fletcher 1996).

These examples illustrate the way in which institutions maintain inequality based on categories of difference. Police officers and airline crew members, acting not on the basis of their own attitudes but on institutional policies (e.g., memorandums instructing to watch for predominantly black drug couriers, directives to conduct random checks mentioning "extremist groups … particularly in the Middle East"), help to maintain racial inequality.

As the 2009 *Climate of Fear* report from the Southern Poverty Law Center illustrates (Reading 32), practices of racial profiling can exacerbate anti-immigrant sentiments. In Suffolk County, New York, a largely white suburban area of Long Island, *Latinas/os/x* make up roughly 14 percent of the population. Yet they comprise nearly half of the defendants appearing in court for traffic violations. Laws, such as Arizona's SB 1070, further support these racial profiling practices. This law requires officials and agencies at the state and local levels to make "a reasonable attempt to determine the immigration status of a person" if they come into contact with someone they have reasonable suspicion to believe is undocumented. Such a perpetuation of a stereotype of *Latina/o/x* immigrants as criminals is often used as a justification for violence that is directed toward members of the *Latina/o/x* community.

Individuals are stopped because of their **status,** the socially defined position that they occupy in society. Note that only one status is important here. Although Mr. Wilkins occupied different statuses (lawyer, spouse, father, etc.), as did Mr. Chavez (investigator, former elected official, etc.), what mattered to the police was their presumed membership in a racial or ethnic group. Thus, their **master status**—the most important status they occupied—was their race or ethnicity.

Each of us occupies a variety of statuses at any given moment in terms of our race, class, gender, sexuality, age, religion, (dis)ability, height, weight, and so on. While we may feel that one status is more important to ourselves than another, we do not always get to pick which is most important to others. Just as Mr. Wilkins and Mr. Chavez were singled out for their race, each of us has likely been singled out by other individuals for some aspect of ourselves. In this section we will investigate how institutions—family, education, economy, the state, and media—support this practice and thus maintain inequality based on categories of difference.

Categories of Difference Maintained as a System of Oppression and Privilege

The value of the statuses that we occupy is determined by how they have been defined. When our statuses are defined as having value within the social structure, we experience **privilege**—a set of (not necessarily) earned rights or assets belonging to a certain status. If our statuses are devalued, the result is **oppression**, defined in Part I as a relationship of domination and subordination in which the dominant group benefits from the *systematic* abuse, exploitation, and injustice directed at a subordinate group. Oppression occurs in three forms: **institutionalized oppression**, that which is built into, supported by, and perpetuated by social institutions; **interpersonal oppression**, that which is manifested between individuals; and **internalized oppression**, that which is directed at oneself.

The Role of Ideology

Maintaining systems of inequality relies on a foundation constructed of several components. Central to this foundation is the presence of an **ideology**—a set of cultural values, beliefs, and attitudes that provide the basis for inequality and thus, in part, endorse and justify the interests of the dominant group. Systems of racial inequality in the United States rely on ideologies that include judgments about racial differences to maintain white privilege. Similarly, systems of class inequality rely on ideologies that include valuing the rich over the poor to uphold class privilege. Furthermore, ideologies based in **androcentrism**—the notion that males are superior to females—preserve systems of sex and gender inequality. Finally, an ideology that includes moral or religious judgments about what is and is not an appropriate sexual orientation is used to justify a system of inequality on the basis of sexuality.

The readings in this section demonstrate that the ideologies that maintain systems of inequality are built into the rules, policies, and practices of our social institutions. In addition, these ideologies often depend on one another, further illustrating the matrix of domination discussed in Part I. For example, as several of the readings in this section illustrate, the foundation of class inequality in the United States is an ideology based in capitalism. More than just the private ownership of goods, capitalism, according to some social theorists, involves exploitation because those who control the ownership of goods use the labor of workers to make a profit. Profit making, they argue, is based on paying workers less than the full value of what they produce. To justify paying one group less than another, we establish ideologies in which one group is viewed as less valuable than others. Thus, ideologies justifying inequality in terms of race/ethnicity, sex/gender, and sexuality perpetuate class inequality.

These interdependent ideologies and the resulting interlocking systems of inequality illustrate that oppression is *systematic*. According to Marilyn Frye, **oppression** involves

> a system of interrelated barriers and forces which reduce, immobilize and mold people who belong to a certain group, and effect their subordination to another group. (1983, 33)

Thus, our circumstances are shaped not by accidental or avoidable events but by systematically related forces. To illustrate how pervasive and institutionalized oppression is, Frye offers the following analogy:

> Consider a birdcage. If you look very closely at just one wire in the cage, you cannot see the other wires. If your conception of what is before you is determined by this myopic focus, you could look at that one wire, up and down the length of it and be unable to see why a bird would not just fly around the wire any time it wanted to go somewhere. ... There is no physical property of any one wire, *nothing* that the closest scrutiny could discover, that will reveal how a bird could be inhibited or harmed by it except in the most accidental way. It is only when you step back, stop looking at the wires one by one, microscopically, and take a macroscopic view of the whole cage, that you see why the bird doesn't go anywhere; and then you will see it in a moment. ... It is perfectly *obvious* that the bird is surrounded by a network of systematically related barriers, no one of which could be the least hindrance to its flight, but which, by their relations to each other, are as confining as the walls of a dungeon. (Frye 1983, 35)

As this analogy illustrates, comprehensive systems of oppression maintain the inequality that many experience in our culture. To fully comprehend this system, we must employ a macro- rather than microscopic perspective, using a systemic frame of analysis to understand how each form of oppression is interrelated and maintained by our social institutions.

Defining Forms of Oppression

Employing a systemic frame of analysis requires that we redefine the ways we categorize issues of discrimination. To label unjust ideas and actions, many of us usually think in terms of **prejudice**, a negative attitude toward members of a group or social category, and **discrimination**, the unequal treatment of people determined by their membership in a group. However, these concepts do not acknowledge the ways in which inequality is institutionalized. The definitions of forms of oppression that follow incorporate a more systematic perspective.

To understand issues of racial oppression within the United States, we must examine **institutional or systemic racism.** This refers to the systematic and institutionalized policy or practice by which people of color are exploited or controlled because of their perceived physical characteristics. Racism is part of our institutional structure, not simply the product of individual actions. In the previous examples, racism does not simply consist of the actions of the individual officers. Rather, it is the fact that these actions are supported by police *policy* that defines them as racist behaviors.

Furthermore, to fully understand racism we need to see how white people in the United States benefit from institutionalized racism regardless of their own individual actions. For example, as Dave Zirin discusses in "The Florida State Seminoles: The Champions of Racist Mascots" (Reading 31), some institutions of higher education make use of Native American images and symbols in creating mascots for their sports teams. Despite the protest of a substantial number of American Indian individuals and organizations, places such as the University of Illinois, the home of the Fighting Illini, institutionalize racist notions of American Indians by continuing to use these images.[2] White students at that university benefited from this practice, regardless of their participation in it, by not having their race objectified and dehumanized at each sporting event and on numerous university souvenirs.

Similar to racism, oppression based on social class also relies on the rules, policies, and practices of social institutions. As discussed in Part I, social class is a great deal more than individual characteristics. Rather, it is determined by a variety of factors in our social structure. Social institutions, including the state and the economy, that rely on a capitalist system create class structures that benefit some at the expense of others. The result is a heavily skewed distribution of income and wealth. According to the US Census Bureau's Current Population Survey, the median household income in 2019 was $68,703. The 20 percent of households with the highest earnings (with mean earnings of about $213,941) received 51.9 percent of all income, while the bottom 20 percent (with mean earnings of $14,042) received only about 3.1 percent. The distribution of income is illustrated in Figure 1. The distribution of wealth is even more concentrated than the distribution of income. According to economist Edward Wolff (2021), in 2019 the top 20 percent of the population of the United States owned 88.9 percent of the financial wealth—total net worth minus the value of one's home. As Figure 2 illustrates, 1 percent of the United States owned 38.2 percent of the financial wealth (with their average net worth over $10 million), while the bottom 80 percent possessed just 11.1 percent of the nation's financial wealth. What makes this unequal distribution even more significant is the difference in kind of wealth at various places in the social class system. For example, the majority of the net worth of the bottom 90 percent consists of assets tied up in the family home and trusts, while the distribution of stocks, financial securities, and business equity is concentrated in the richest 10 percent of the population (see Figure 3). Government policies that disproportionately tax workers while granting tax breaks to the wealthy perpetuate a skewed distribution of income and wealth. Indeed, since 2000, tax cuts have reduced federal revenue by trillions of dollars and disproportionately benefited well-off households. For example, from 2001 through 2018, such tax changes reduced government revenue by $5.1 trillion, with nearly two-thirds of that flowing to the richest fifth of Americans. As can be seen in Figure 4, the wealthiest 20 percent of the country received 65 percent of tax cuts between 2001 and 2018. By the end of 2025, the tally of tax cuts will grow to $10.6 trillion. Nearly $2 trillion of this amount will have gone to the richest 1 percent (Institute on Taxation and Economic Policy 2018).

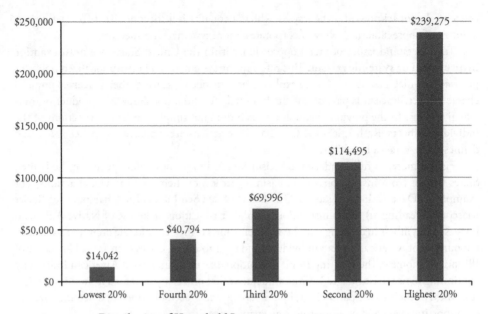

FIGURE 1.   2019 Distribution of Household Income

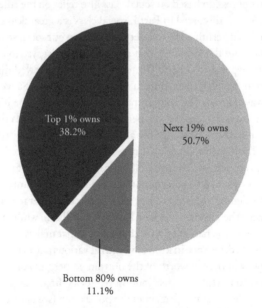

FIGURE 2.   Distribution of Wealth, 2019: Share of Total Net Worth

Meanwhile, payroll taxes have significantly increased since 1980, disproportionately affecting workers. The overall impact of such a shift can be seen in the sources of federal revenues, with individual taxes accounting for 85 percent in 2020, while they only accounted for 77 percent in 1962 (see Figure 5). According to Collins et al. (2004), such a shift of the tax burden from investment to wage income means that a wealthy person relying on earnings from dividends paid a marginal tax rate of approximately 15 percent in 2003, while a person such as a

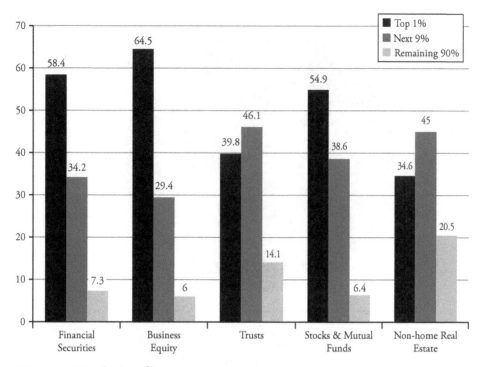

FIGURE 3. **Distribution of Assets**

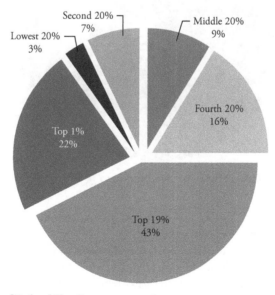

FIGURE 4. **Shares of Federal Tax Cuts, 2001–2018**

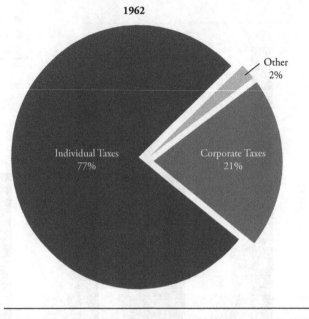

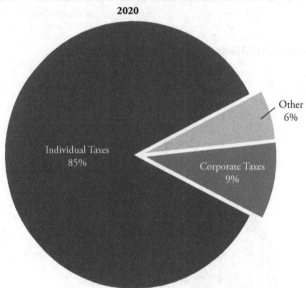

FIGURE 5.   **Sources of Federal Revenues, 1962 and 2020**

schoolteacher earning $28,400 paid a payroll tax of 15.3 percent as well as a marginal tax rate of 25 percent, for a total tax rate of over 40 percent.

Such systematic class inequality is defined as **classism**—a system of beliefs rooted in the institutions of society where the wealthy are privileged with a higher status at the expense of the oppression of the poor. The ways in which this system is maintained, as well as how issues of class intersect with race/ethnicity and sex/gender, will be discussed later.

Using a systemic analysis to understand issues of sex/gender oppression and privilege requires that we incorporate the role of institutions in definitions of sexism. Thus, for the purposes of this discussion, **sexism** is a systematic and institutionalized policy or practice in which women are exploited or controlled because of perceptions that their sex or gender characteristics are inferior. Again, in recognizing that sexism is systematic, we acknowledge that it is a product of our institutional structure, not necessarily individual actions. As a result, men do not need to individually behave in a sexist manner to benefit from a sexist system. For example, many physical requirements for occupations (such as height) advantage men while they disadvantage women, although they may have little to do with the actual requirements for the job. Additional ways in which sex and gender inequality is reinforced by social institutions will be discussed later.

Finally, inequality with regard to sexuality is also institutionalized. Thus, privilege experienced by heterosexuals and the oppression experienced by those who are or are perceived to be lesbian, gay, bisexual, or transgender (LGBT) is perpetuated through the practices and policies of social institutions. For example, the failure to pass the Employment Non-Discrimination Act—a bill to prohibit employment discrimination on the basis of sexual orientation—perpetuates the advantage experienced by heterosexuals and the stigma experienced by LGBT individuals.[1] Additionally, as mentioned in Part I, the passage of state constitutional amendments—and the campaign by President George W. Bush for a nationwide constitutional amendment—that banned civil unions, marriage equality, and legal protections for lesbian and gay families for decades denied access to resources for lesbian, gay, bisexual, and transgender families.[3] **Heterosexism,** as defined by Cherríe Moraga (1983), applies directly to this example:

> The view that heterosexuality is the "norm" for all social/sexual relationships and as such the heterosexist imposes the model on all individuals through homophobia (fear of homosexuality). S/he supports and/or advocates this continued institutionalization of heterosexuality in all aspects of society—including legal and social discrimination against homosexuals and the denial of homosexual rights as a political concern. (1983, 105)

Moraga indicates here that a person who is heterosexist is an active participant in oppressing those who are or are perceived to be lesbian, gay, bisexual, or transgender. However, as with all other forms of oppression, it is not necessary to actively participate in discrimination against others to benefit from their systematic exploitation. For example, mainstream media continue to perpetuate stereotypes of LGBT people. According to the Gay and Lesbian Alliance against Defamation, representation of lesbian, gay, bisexual, and transgender individuals account for just over 9 percent of all scripted-series regular characters in the 2020–2021 broadcast television schedule. This figure is up from just under 3 percent in 2011 and 1.1 percent in 2007, although it is a decrease of the previous year's record high percentage of 10.2 percent. While such characters may be more present on streaming services and cable programs, as well as on more widely accessible network programs (although these numbers have declined in recent years), lesbian, gay, bisexual, and transgender people and families are nearly

---

Although a bill supporting this act was passed with bipartisan support in 2013, The House Rules Committee voted against it. Since 2015, supporters of rights for lesbian, gay, bisexual, and transgender individuals have supported the Equality ACT, which would be more comprehensive, prohibiting discrimination on the basis of sexual orientation and gender identity not only in employment, but also housing, public accommodations, public education, federal funding, credit, and jury service. On June 15, 2020, the Supreme Court that Title VII of the Civil Rights Act of 1964 protects employees from discrimination based on their sexual orientation and gender identity. While this was an important ruling, advocates still support the passage of the Equality Act, observing that as of 2020, 29 states do not have the full protections the Equality Act would provide for the LGBT community.

invisible (Macias 2004). Additionally, efforts to present messages inclusive and accepting of lesbian, gay, bisexual, and transgender persons are often excluded by broadcast networks. For example, a 2004 advertisement by the United Church of Christ portrayed a gay couple (along with other members of marginalized groups) being kept out of a church by two bouncers. The message was "Jesus didn't turn people away, neither do we." Major broadcasting networks, including CBS and NBC, rejected this advertisement. A heterosexual seeking to find images in the media of someone who represents her or his own sexuality is likely to find numerous examples. This ability to find representations of self is a benefit that not only is often overlooked by those who are privileged but also does not require any direct discrimination on the part of the individual who benefits.

As each of these examples illustrates, oppression on the basis of race, class, gender, and sexuality does not require the overt discrimination of bigots that we often think of when examining issues of inequality. Acts of oppression in interpersonal contexts maintain systems of inequality by engaging in oppressive practices that are a reflection of oppressive social institutions.

In summary, our experiences of oppression and privilege occur within a comprehensive system of interconnected social institutions. Thus, issues of prejudice and discrimination are transformed into experiences of institutionalized *oppression*. The remainder of this section will explore the ways in which the social institutions of family, education, work and the economy, the state, and media, along with the social forces of language and social control, maintain systems of inequality. As you consider the following, remember to keep in mind how the ideologies depend on one another, forming interlocking systems of oppression.

Social Institutions: Maintaining Systems of Oppression and Privilege

As an intangible aspect of the social structure, the role of social institutions in maintaining inequality often goes largely unnoticed. Rather, we tend to view institutionalized oppression or privilege as the way things are. For example, when we hear of racist acts on the part of individuals, such as in the brutal killing of James Byrd in Jasper, Texas,[4] we are often rightfully outraged and horrified. At the same time, however, few of us likely to notice the residential segregation that systematically excludes blacks from certain neighborhoods. Although the federal government eliminated overtly racially biased housing, tax, and transportation policies in the 1960s, as an analysis of data from the US Department of Education documented, a high level of racial segregation nevertheless continues to exist (Orfield, Kucsera, and Siegel-Hawley 2012). Feagin and Sikes (1994) note that practices such as redlining (the systematic refusal on the part of some lenders to make loans in certain areas because of racial composition), racial steering, animosity on the part of whites, and discriminatory practices by mortgage lenders help maintain this segregation. The impact of such segregation influences not only wealth, but also access to important resources, such as education, employment, and good health. In this section we will examine the practices and policies of institutions to understand the ways in which they maintain systems of oppression.

As discussed in Part I, social institutions play a significant role in creating inequality. They define race, class, gender, and sexuality not only in terms of what does and does not exist, but also in terms of the values that we associate with each category. Thus, they confer privilege on some while oppressing others. This is done through the establishment and enforcement of policies constructed by these institutions.

The readings in this section illustrate how social institutions maintain systems of oppression and privilege and how they, in turn, impact access to resources. Ranging from money and property to medical care and education, **resources** are anything that is valued in society. Resources are generally considered scarce because of their unequal distribution among different groups. For example, the unequal distribution of income and wealth, as illustrated earlier, results in the perception that resources such as money and property are scarce.

The ways in which resources are distributed greatly impact an individual's **life chances**—the material advantages or disadvantages that a particular member of a social category can expect to receive based on his or her status (Weber 1946; Dahrendorf 1979). One of the most significant life chances is the distribution of health care and the resulting impact on one's quality of life. For example, according to an article in the *New York Times* by Erica Goode (1999), social class is one of the most powerful predictors of health—more powerful than genetics and even more than smoking. As a result of an unequal distribution of resources, the lower one's rung on the socioeconomic ladder, the greater the likelihood of negative health effects that have long-ranging consequences. Furthermore, experiences of being marginalized, residing in racially segregated areas, and other forms of institutionalized racism were also found to magnify the impact of social class on health.

This example illustrates that social institutions, with their unequal distribution of valuable resources, perpetuate a cycle of disparate life chances. If someone experiences poor health as a result of occupying a lower social class or living in a racially segregated neighborhood, she or he is going to be less able to fully participate in the social system and less able to develop skills and achieve career goals than is someone who belongs to a higher social class with correspondingly better health.

Family

As a primary social institution, the family is central to maintaining systems of oppression and privilege based on race, class, gender, and sexuality. In addition, because it is so closely connected with other social institutions, such as the state and the economy, the structure of the family significantly influences and is influenced by the structure and actions of these institutions. While many of the ways systems of inequality are maintained are interconnected, perhaps the strongest connection is the relationship of family to the social structure.

For example, Jennifer Randles in "Willing to Do Anything for My Kids" (Reading 14) illustrates how lack of a social safety net for the poor and limited support for fundamental aspects of childcare results in what she terms as "inventive mothering." Out of economic necessity, many poor mothers devise distinctive childrearing strategies and logics to carry out carework for their children. Randles research illustrates that social institutions such as the economy and the state have not responded in ways that support poor mothers and their families. As a result, they maintain systems of class inequality.

Notions of citizenship also maintain systems of oppression in a variety of ways. As Leisy J. Abrego explains in "Illegality as a Source of Solidarity and Tension in Latino Families" (Reading 15), the status of illegal impacts all members of a family, even when only one person or a few people are categorized as undocumented or only temporarily protected. This results in tensions for people whose disadvantages are heightened by structural inequality because of immigration laws.

Education

The institution of education also maintains systems of oppression and privilege. This institution reproduces the existing race, class, and gender structure through a variety of mechanisms, including the distribution of cultural capital and the existence of a hidden curriculum. In "Mind the Gap: COVID-19 and Learning Loss" (Reading 17), Emma Dorn and her co-authors clearly illustrate how the pandemic's impact on education has exacerbated already existing race and class inequities in education, over fifty years after *Brown v. Board of Education*. As this article illustrates, whether a student attends a resource-rich or a resource-poor educational system will impact his or her access to **cultural capital**—social assets that include beliefs, values, attitudes, and competencies in language and culture. A concept proposed by Bordieu and Paseron (1977), cultural capital consists of ideas and knowledge people draw on as they participate in social life, including proper attitudes toward education; socially approved dress and manners; and knowledge about books, music, and other forms of high and popular culture. Because cultural capital is essential for succeeding, children with less cultural capital often have fewer opportunities. In addition, the dominance of white, patriarchal, affluent class notions of what counts as cultural capital generally excludes the ideas and beliefs of the poor and people of color. Schools with fewer economic resources, which are often disproportionately attended by African American, Latina/o/x, or Native American students, are less able to provide students with what is viewed by the dominant culture as important cultural capital, thus affecting their opportunities in the future. As a result, the educational system, with its unequal distribution of cultural capital, perpetuates a system of stratification based not only on race but also on class.

The institution of education also maintains race and class inequality through the existence of a **hidden curriculum**—the transmission of cultural values and attitudes, such as conformity and obedience to authority, through implied demands found in rules, routines, and regulations of schools. Because of the existence of a hidden curriculum, the values and attitudes that are reinforced in one school are not necessarily those that are promoted at another. For example, curriculum directed toward working-class students often focuses on rote memorization without much decision making, choice, or explanation of why something is done. Curriculum directed at middle-class students, however, emphasizes figuring and decision making in getting the right answer. The curriculum directed at affluent students often stresses the expression of ideas and creative activities, while that directed at elite students stresses critical thinking skills and developing analytical powers to apply abstract principles to problem solving. As the readings in this section illustrate, our education system is largely segregated on the basis of class. In addition, there is also significant evidence of de facto racial segregation. As a result, the hidden curriculum maintains class as well as racial inequality.

Mary Crow Dog and Richard Erdoes further illustrate in "Civilize Them with a Stick" (Reading 18) the ways policies in the institution of education perpetuate racial inequality. As a result of these policies, in combination with policies of the state, Native American children were forced to leave their reservations and attend boarding or day schools. These efforts to assimilate members of this group are but one example of how the institution of education maintains racial inequality.

The institution of education also constructs and perpetuates categories of difference on the basis of sex and gender as well as race. In the reading "Black Girls and School Discipline: The Complexities of Being Overrepresented and Understudied" (Reading 19), Subini Ancy Annamma and her coauthors examine the ways urban schools perpetuate intersectional violence against Black girls through disproportionate frequency of out-of-school suspensions, law enforcement referrals, and expulsions. Their work goes on to indicate that schools as sites of racialized and gendered violence are not only urban schools. Rather, these disparities existed wherever children of color go to school, whether the districts be defined as urban, suburban, or rural. Such patterns maintain clear sex, gender, and race divisions that contribute to differential ways of viewing and valuing Black girls in our culture as well as the inequalities that Black girls experience in our society.

Finally, the policies and practices of the institution of education can also maintain a system of stratification in which students who are perceived to be heterosexual are deemed more important and are thus more embraced by the institution than those who are perceived to be lesbian, gay, bisexual, or transgender. Examples of heterosexism can even be found in what may be viewed as harmless school traditions (e.g., proms and other social events), but it can also be seen in more overt and meaningful ways. For example, at various times the US Congress has voted on proposals to eliminate federal aid to schools that "promote" homosexuality. In addition, a policy enacted by the Merrimack, New Hampshire, School Board stated,

> The Merrimack School District shall neither implement nor carry out any program or activity that has either the purpose or effect of encouraging or supporting homosexuality as a positive lifestyle alternative. A program or activity, for purposes of this item, includes the distribution of instructional materials, instruction, counseling, or other services on school grounds, or referral of a pupil to an organization that affirms a homosexual lifestyle.

Although this policy was later repealed, similar policies have been passed in other school districts. Some of the policies are phrased more bluntly than the one above and simply forbid any discussion of homosexuality at all—be it positive or negative. Regardless, the ramifications of official policies such as these, as well as implicit practices based on heterosexism, are severe.

Such overt and covert ways of valuing heterosexuality result in **heteronormativity**—the ways in which the practices of social institutions prescribe heterosexuality as the norm. This can have a profound effect on those who do not fit into such a norm. As a result of heterosexist school traditions and policies like those described above, lesbian, gay, bisexual, transgender, or questioning students are likely to experience feelings of alienation and self-alienation. For example, according to the Centers for Disease Control, gay youth are four to five times more likely to have attempted or seriously considered suicide than their heterosexual peers. Lesbian, gay, and bisexual youth, as well as students who are questioning their sexuality, often need counseling that is only available in schools. Official and unofficial policies and practices based on heterosexism ignore these concerns and maintain inequality based on sexuality.

Work and the Economy

The institution of work and the economy is perhaps the most fundamental in maintaining systems of inequality. As already noted, changes in the structure of the economy significantly impact other institutions. At times, these changes offer new opportunities and privilege to some, and at other times, these changes foster continued oppression. In "Black Men and the Struggle for Work: Social and Economic Barriers Persist" (Reading 20), James M. Quane and others illustrate that continued structural barriers to opportunity disproportionately prevent economic self-sufficiency for poor black men and, as a result, poor black families. Indeed, increases in the jobless rate disproportionately affect those who are on the low end of the economic spectrum because they are less likely to have other sources of support (e.g., savings or social networks leading to new jobs).

Additionally, through selective recruitment and biased hiring strategies, employers favor white applicants at the expense of others. As Figure 6 indicates, there is a significant wage gap with regard to race in the United States. Policies impacting employee recruitment, hiring, promotion, and termination maintain this gap. Finally, policies of the social institution of work and the economy also perpetuate inequality with regard to sex and gender. As research of men's underrepresentation in predominantly female professions has illustrated, sex segregation continues to exist within the US labor force (Williams 1992). This research also reveals policies and practices with regard to hiring and supervising. These policies maintain a gap in the incomes of women and men, as illustrated in Table 1, and as a result, they maintain a system of inequality.

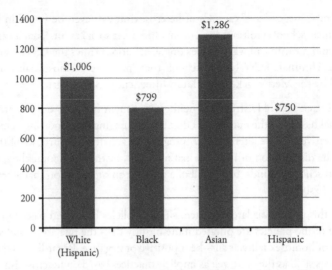

FIGURE 6. **Median Usual Weekly Earnings of Full-time Wage and Salary Workers by Race**

TABLE 1.1 **Median Usual Weekly Earnings of Full-Time Wage and Salary Workers by Sex and Age, 2021 1st Quarterly Average**

Age	Males	Females	Female Income as Percentage of Male Income (%)
All workers, 16 years and older	$1,089	$900	82.6
16–24	$634	$593	93.5
25–34	$950	$850	89.5
35–44	$1,232	$999	81.1
45–54	$1,334	$1,002	75.1
55–64	$1,224	$964	78.8
65 years and older	$1,102	$911	82.7

Source: U.S. Department of Labor, U.S. Bureau of Labor Statistics, Economic News Release, April 16, 2021, https://www.bls.gov/news.release/pdf/wkyeng.pdf

The State and Public Policy

The state and public policy is another social institution that contributes to inequality. Often confused with the government, the state acts as a blueprint for how various procedures of the government should be carried out. In maintaining inequality, the state acts in the interest of the dominant group or groups in society, reinforcing policies that work in their favor.

Currently, social policies regarding welfare reform have been the subject of much debate. As a result of the myths and stereotypes regarding people who receive aid within the welfare system, US policies regarding Aid to Families with Dependent Children and similar entitlement programs have undergone considerable change in recent years. State policies often ignore how issues of race and class intersect. As Figure 7 illustrates, poverty is unequally distributed according to race, with people of color disproportionately representing those who are poor. Issues of poverty are exacerbated by stratification on the basis of sex, with women being more likely to be poor than men (11.5 percent compared to 9.4 percent according to 2019 census data). In addition, female-headed households with children are also disproportionately poor, with 22.2

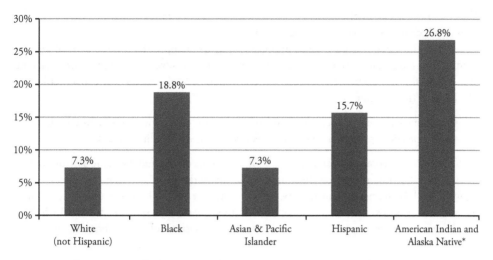

FIGURE 7.   **Poverty Rates by Race, 2019.**

percent living in poverty compared to 11.5 percent for male-headed families with children. Recent changes in welfare reform only maintain these economic inequalities.

The criminal justice system, also ruled by state policies, reinforces inequality, particularly with regard to race and class, especially as it depends on unequal racial and class patterns in prosecution and incarceration. The evidence of such continuing institutionalized racism can serve as justification of the need for corrective programs such as affirmative action. While such programs have often been accused of discriminating against those in the majority, such policies rarely do this. Rather, they tend to enhance productivity and encourage improved employment practices.

Finally, as stated earlier, public policies established by the state maintain the interest of the majority. For example, state policies prohibiting concepts of multiraciality were established during the colonial period to sustain the distinction between master and slave. These and other public policies were created to maintain the control of whites over others. This motivation is reflected in contemporary policies as well, and whites continue to benefit from such a system in the United States.

Media

Like other social institutions, the media convey dominant ideologies about systems of inequality. Often the images reflected in the media represent the policies, practices, and prevailing attitudes of other social institutions. We can see policies of inclusion and exclusion regarding lesbian, gay, bisexual, and transgender individuals reflected in our television media. For example, when the Employment Non-Discrimination Act failed, denying lesbian, gay, bisexual, and transgender individuals the right to be free from employment discrimination on the basis of sexual orientation, *Ellen*, the first prime-time series to feature an out lesbian as the main character, was canceled. As mentioned earlier, television has failed to accurately reflect the diversity of sexuality in the United States.

Television is perhaps the most influential form of media today—viewers in the United States watch approximately thirty-four hours a week. As a result, this form of media possesses the power not only to influence but also to maintain our perceptions of reality, as the distorted images perpetuate not only our stereotypes of these groups but also their continued oppression. Further, the media engage in practices of **media framing**—the process by which information and entertainment are put together by the media to convey a particular message to an audience.

Thus, we are less able to distinguish between the realities of class in the United States and the ways in which it is portrayed in the mass media.

The institution of the media also maintains systems of oppression on the basis of sex and gender. For example, images in music, movies, television, and advertising degrade women. One of the ways this is accomplished is through the process of **objectification,** which Catharine MacKinnon (1982) defines as

> the primary process of subjugation of women. It unites act with word, construction with expression, perception with enforcement, myth with reality (1982, 541).

Through such a process, the media support the privileges of men and the oppression of women.

As the preceding discussion illustrates, social institutions, often acting in tandem, play a significant role in maintaining inequality. As you read the selections in this section, keep in mind the earlier discussions of the matrix of domination and look closely to see the ways in which these social institutions work together to maintain interlocking systems of oppression and privilege.

Language and Maintaining Inequality

One significant, yet often unexplored mechanism for maintaining inequality is language. Functioning in a manner similar to a social institution, the ways in which we use language can maintain the values, roles, norms, and ideologies of the dominant culture. The readings on language in this section demonstrate that it is a powerful tool of culture, determining how members of a society interpret their environment. According to social construction theory, our social world has no inherent meaning. Rather, the meaning of the social world is constructed, in part, through language. Language serves as the link between all of the different elements of culture and maintains a system of inequality.

There are those who feel that examining the role of language in the maintenance of inequality is trivial or misplaced. However, as illustrated in "How the Right Made Racism Sound Fair" (Reading 29), issues of language are particularly significant, especially in framing how we think of groups that are different from ourselves. In addition, one of the significant functions of language is to serve the purpose of **cultural transmission**—the passing of culture (values, beliefs, symbols, behaviors) from one generation to the next. Through language, children learn about their cultural heritage and develop a sense of personal identity in relation to their group. In addition, language also helps them learn about socially constructed categories of difference and the meanings associated with them.

Language consists of words that are symbols with meaning and serves as a tool for interpreting our environment. The power of words lies in the fact that the members of a culture share their meanings and valuations. It is our common language that allows us to communicate and understand one another, and this makes for order in society. Philosopher Ernst Cassirer (1978) identified several different functions of the ability of humans to use symbols, explaining that they help to define, organize, and evaluate experiences of people. Julia Wood (1997) uses the assertions of Cassirer to illustrate the ways in which we use language to indicate cultural values and views of women and men, thereby maintaining inequality.

First, Wood argues that language *defines sex and gender.* It serves to define women and men as well as what can and cannot exist. For example, generic language (e.g., using the pronoun *he* to refer to all sexes or using words like *fireman, mankind, man-hour,* etc.) excludes women and dismisses their importance. As a result, men and their experiences are presented as the norm while women and their experiences are seen as deviant. In addition to establishing *who* exists, Wood argues that language defines *what* exists. For example, since we use the masculine word as the base to make compounds in the English language, it might appear that women's ability to rule or own may seem impossible in that we can have a kingdom but not a queendom. Does this mean that only men can have land over which they rule? Certainly not. Rather, it illustrates that we attend to what we name and tend not to recognize that which we do not name. For example, words like *sexual harassment* or *date rape* are recent creations. That does not mean that these are new phenomena; rather, they are phenomena that we have only recently attended to and been willing to acknowledge.

Additional ways that language is used to define our perceptions of women and men can be seen in how women are defined by their relationships. Consider, for example, the commonly used titles of respect for men and women in our society. Men are addressed as Mr., which reveals nothing about their relationship to women. But how are women typically addressed? The titles Miss and Mrs. define women in terms of their relationship to men. Even when a woman has earned a higher-status title, such as Dr., she is still likely to be addressed as Miss or Mrs. On an interesting note, many states in the United States have required women to take their husband's name on marrying. It was only in 1975 that a Hawaiian statute requiring women to give up their birth names on marriage was ruled unconstitutional.

The second way that language illustrates our perceptions of women and men, according to Wood, is that it *organizes our perceptions of sex and gender*. The ability of language to organize our experiences and perceptions enables us to express cultural views of sex and gender by stereotyping men and women. In addition, the ways in which we talk about women and men in the English language encourage dualistic notions of sex and gender. For example, when we stereotype women as emotional and men as rational, we limit our abilities to recognize rationality in women and men's abilities to express emotion. Furthermore, because of the heavy emphasis that the English language places on polarity (good–bad, wrong–right, male–female), it is often difficult for us to think of things such as gender as existing along a continuum. In reality, few of us fit on the polar ends of what a male or female is supposed to be. Rather, most of us are somewhere in the middle, and many people identify as non-binary with regard to gender. Yet we are all expected to conform to the two polar ends or suffer the consequences for not being seen as gender appropriate.

Third, Wood argues that language *evaluates our perceptions of women and men*. Language is ideological, reflecting the values that are important in our culture. In the case of our use of the English language, we can find a great deal of evidence of **linguistic sexism**—the ways in which a language devalues members of one sex, almost invariably women. To illustrate this concept, consider the following word pairs: *brothers* and *sisters, husband* and *wife, men* and *women, hostess* and *host, madam* and *sir, Eve* and *Adam*. As you read these word pairs, it is likely that those in which the female term preceded the male term sounded awkward or incorrect. This is not coincidental; rather, it is a practice based on a long tradition. As Baron (1986) notes, eighteenth-century grammarians established the rule precisely to assert that "the supreme Being . . . is in all languages Masculine, in as much as the masculine sex is the superior and more excellent" (3). According to these grammarians, to place women before men was to violate the natural order.

In addition, the English language often trivializes or diminishes women and things defined as feminine. There has often been a debate in college athletic associations regarding whether the names generally applied to female sports teams trivialize or diminish the role of women in sport. While male teams are generally set as the standard, being assigned team names with little or no gender meaning (e.g., the Polar Cats, the Volunteers), female teams generally receive feminized team names (e.g., the Polar Kittens, the Lady Volunteers). Many argue that such a practice devalues the role of women in sport and thus in society.

An additional example of how language trivializes things that are feminine is in the use of diminutive suffixes for occupations held by women (e.g., actress, waitress, stewardess) and through the use of terms like *girls* for adult females. Furthermore, when we consider word pairs like *governor* and *governess*, *master* and *mistress*, or *bachelor* and *spinster*, it becomes clear that the words associated with men have different implied meanings than those associated with women, with the latter consistently negative or demeaning. The male words suggest power or positively valued status, whereas the female words have negative connotations. Although many of these words originally had neutral connotations, over time these words declined in value, a process known as **semantic derogation.** Smith (1985) notes that "once a word or term becomes associated with women, it often acquires semantic characteristics that are congruent with social stereotypes and evaluations of women as a group" (1985, 48). Because such values about women are reflected in our language, our perception that women have less value than men is perpetuated. According to the **Sapir–Whorf hypothesis,** "people perceive the world through the cultural lens of language" (Sapir 1949, 162). Thus, language shapes our reality.

As the preceding discussion illustrates, language plays a significant role in maintaining inequality. The readings in this section expand on this illustration. For example, Angel Love Miles argues in "'Strong Black Woman': African American Women with Disabilities, Intersecting Identities, and Inequality" (Reading 30) the ways African American women with disabilities responded to the controlling images associated with the trope "Strong Black Woman." The notion itself is embedded in an ableist ideology that values independence over interdependence and caregiving over self-care and tends to include a narrow conception of strength and resilience that devalues and pathologizes those that are perceived as weak. As her research illustrates, African American women with disabilities exhibit and identify with Strong Black Women characteristics of resilience, independence, sacrifice, and endurance, yet such expectations can be simultaneously an asset and hindrance to their empowerment. In addition, Dave Zirin discusses in "The Florida State Seminoles: The Champions of Racist Mascots" (Reading 31) the use of American Indian names and images in sports. Their discussion explains that such a practice maintains a system of stratification in which Native Americans are not only seen as less valuable than whites but also often objectified and seen as less than human. Each of the readings demonstrates that language is a pervasive tool of culture. In maintaining cultural values, roles, norms, and ideologies, language maintains inequality.

Violence and Social Control

Increasing violence in the United States—particularly evident in the recent surge in campus gun violence has resulted in considerable discussion regarding the causes of and solutions to this problem. Even though thousands of elementary, middle and high schools remain partially or entirely closed due to the pandemic, there were 14 school shootings between March and mid-June, 2021—the highest total over that period since 1999 (Cox and Rich, 2021). While some have been quick to blame the media or lax gun-control laws, focusing on violence as an act of individuals, it is important that we understand violence as a pervasive form of **social control**—the regulation of human behavior in any social group. As the findings of a May 1999 Gallup Poll linking antigay and racist attitudes with student-on-student violence illustrates, violence used as a mechanism for social control maintains inequality.

Several of the readings in this section illustrate how violence is used as a means of social control. For example, the Southern Poverty Law Center's report *Climate of Fear* (Reading 32) exposes the practice of *beaner hopping*, where youth in suburban areas go out looking for a Hispanic to beat up. This practice has resulted in most Latino immigrant families living in fear. The role of violence in controlling women is further demonstrated in the article "'Rape Is a Man's Issue:' Gender and Power in the Era of Affirmative Sexual Consent" (Reading 33). Through their research, Julia Metz, Kristen Myers, and Patricia Wallace illustrate that affirmative consent policies—laws and policies that require the affirmative, conscious, and voluntary agreement to engage in sexual activity—are not sufficient to dismantle systems of power that foster sexual violence against women. Each of these examples illustrates that violence is used as a mechanism of social control to reinforce interlocking systems of oppression. All forms of violence have a severe impact on an individual's ability to participate fully in society. As a result, violence perpetuates inequality.

Examining violence and social control further illustrates the interconnectedness of race, class, gender, and sexuality oppression. In working to understand the escalating violence within the United States and the world, it is important also to understand how systems of oppression interconnect. In so doing, we will gain a better understanding of how violence is used to maintain interlocking systems of inequality.

Conclusion

As discussed in this section, constructions of difference regarding race, class, gender, and sexuality are transformed into interlocking systems of oppression and privilege. As a result, it is important that we understand how one system relies on another. The readings in this section examine the ways in which the social institutions of family, education, the economy, the state, and the media work together with language and violence and social control to maintain inequality. Once we are aware of this process, we will have a greater understanding of how to transform systems of inequality.

Notes

1. The phrase "flying while Arab" or "flying while Muslim" was likely coined at the June 1999 meeting of the American Muslim Political Coordination Council.
2. Because of pressure from the National Collegiate Athletic Association, officials at the University of Illinois decided to end the Chief Illiniwek tradition. The chief made his last performance on February 21, 2007.
3. On July 8, 2010, this denial of resources was recognized through the finding of a federal judge in Massachusetts who ruled that the Defense of Marriage Act, a law that barred the federal government from recognizing same-sex marriage, was unconstitutional, ruling that gay and lesbian couples deserved the same federal benefits as heterosexual couples. Additionally, the US Supreme Court struck down the Defense of Marriage Act as unconstitutional on June 26, 2013, and dismissed California's Proposition 8 appeal. In 2015, the US Supreme Court ruled that same-sex couples have the right to marry in all fifty states, nullifying these institutional policies.
4. James Byrd, forty-nine, was beaten unconscious and then dragged by a chain to his death from the back of a pickup truck after accepting a ride from three white men in Jasper, Texas, in June 1998. One of the men, John William King, was found guilty and given the death penalty for his role in the killing. Another man, Lawrence Brewer, was also found guilty and sentenced to death. The third suspect, Shawn Berry, was sentenced to life in prison. Byrd's body was dismembered in the assault, and many of his body parts were found about a mile from his torso. When he was found, his body was so badly disfigured that Byrd had to be identified by his fingerprints.

References

American Civil Liberties Union. 2004. *Sanctioned Bias: Racial Profiling since 9/11*. New York: American Civil Liberties Union.

Baron, Dennis E. 1986. *Grammar and Gender*. New Haven, CT: Yale University Press.

Bordieu, Pierre, and Jean-Claude Paseron. 1977. *Society, Culture, and Education*. Beverly Hills, CA: Sage.

Cassirer, Ernst. 1978. *An Essay on Man*. New Haven, CT: Yale University Press.

Cole, David. 1999. *No Equal Justice: Race and Class in the American Criminal Justice System*. New York: New Press.

Collins, Chuck, Chris Hartman, Karen Kraut, and Gloribell Mota. 2004. *Shifty Tax Cuts: How They Move the Tax Burden off the Rich and onto Everyone Else*. Boston, MA: United for a Fair Economy.

Cox, John Woodrow and Steven Rich. 2021 "As School Shootings Surge, A Sixth-Grader Tucks His Dad's Gun in His Backpack." *Washington Post*, June 24, https://www.washingtonpost.com/education/2021/06/24/school-shootings-2021-increase/

Dahrendorf, Ralf. 1979. *Life Chances*. London: Weidenfeld & Nicolson.

Department of Justice. 2012. "Justice Department Releases Investigative Findings on the Alamance County, N.C., Sheriff's Office." September 18. http://www.justice.gov/opa/pr/2012/September/12-crt-1125.html.

Feagin, Joe R., and Melvin P. Sikes. 1994. *Living with Racism: The Black Middle-Class Experience*. Boston: Beacon Press.

Fletcher, Michael A. 1996. "Driven to Extremes: Black Men Take Steps to Avoid Police Stops." *Washington Post*, March 29, A1.

Frye, Marilyn. 1983. *The Politics of Reality: Essays in Feminist Theory*. Trumansburg, NY: Crossing Press.

Goode, Erica. 1999. "For Good Health, It Helps to Be Rich and Important." *New York Times*, June 1, D-1, D-9.

Harris, David A. 1998. "The Use of Traffic Stops against African Americans: What Can Be Done?" American Civil Liberties Freedom Network. http://www.aclu.org/issues/policepractices/harris_statement.html.

Institute on Taxation and Economic Policy. **"Federal Tax Cuts in the Bush, Obama, and Trump Years."** July 11, 2018. https://itep.org/federal-tax-cuts-in-the-bush-obama-and-trump-years/

Macias, Stephen. 2004. *Reality Check: GLAAD Examines the 2004–2005 Primetime Television Season*. New York: Gay and Lesbian Alliance against Defamation.

MacKinnon, Catharine A. 1982. "Feminism, Marxism, Method, and the State: An Agenda for Theory." *Signs* 7 (3): 515–44.

Moraga, Cherríe. 1983. *Loving in the War Years*. Boston: South End Press.

Orfield, Gary, John Kucsera, and Genevieve Siegel-Hawley. 2012. *E Pluribus … Separation: Deepening Double Segregation for More Students*. Los Angeles: Civil Rights Project.

Pierson, Emma, Camelia Simoiu, Jan Overgoor, Sam Corbett-Davies, Daniel Jenson, Amy Shoemaker, Vignesh Ramachandran, Phoebe Barghouty, Cheryl Phillips, and Sharad Goel. 2020. "A Large-scale Analysis of Racial Disparities in Police Stops Across the United States." *Nature Human Behaviour.* 736 (4): 736–45.

Racial & Identity Profiling Advisory Board. 2020. *Annual Report*. California Department of Justice.

Sapir, Edward. 1949. *Selected Writings of Edward Sapir in Language, Culture, and Personality*, edited by David G. Mandelbaum. Berkeley: University of California Press.

Shora, Kareem. 2002. "Guilty of Flying While Brown." *Air and Space Lawyer* 17, no. 1 (Summer).

Smith, Philip M. 1985. *Language, the Sexes, and Society*. New York: Blackwell.

U.S. Census Bureau Current Population Reports. 2019. P60-270. Income and Poverty in the United States: 2019.

Weber, Max. 1946. *From Max Weber: Essays in Sociology*, edited and translated by Hans Gerth and C. Wright Mills. New York: Oxford University Press.

Williams, Christine L. 1992. "The Glass Escalator: Hidden Advantages for Men in the 'Female' Professions." *Social Problems* 39 (3): 253–67.

Wolff, E. N. (2021). *Household Wealth Trends in the United States, 1962 to 2019: Median Wealth Rebounds … But Not Enough*. National Bureau of Economic Research Working Paper No. 28383. Cambridge, MA: National Bureau of Economic Research.

Wood, Julia T. 1997. *Gendered Lives: Communication, Gender, and Culture*. 2nd ed. Belmont, CA: Wadsworth.

Social Institutions: Family

WHY WON'T AFRICAN AMERICANS GET (AND STAY) MARRIED? WHY SHOULD THEY?

• *Shirley A. Hill*

In this essay by sociologist Shirley Hill, the author examines the impact of historical and class, racial, and gender inequalities on marriages among African Americans. Despite the additional burdens placed on these marriages, there continues to be strong ideological support for marriage in the African American community. To increase the rate of successful marriages among African American families, Hill argues that it is essential to address the racial, class, and gender inequality experienced by African Americans.

The extent to which African American families conform to mainstream family ideologies was the focus of much scholarly debate throughout the twentieth century, with the prevalence of single-mother families being at the center of that debate. Early research explained single-mother families as a legacy of slavery and offered a class analysis of black families that characterized them as matriarchal, dysfunctional, and a barrier to socioeconomic mobility. This work, however, was thoroughly challenged during the civil-rights era of the 1960s as revisionist scholars studied the family lives of enslaved black people (Blassingame 1972; Gutman 1976) and drew parallels between the family systems of precolonial Africans, slaves, and contemporary African American families (Nobles 1974). Social historians studying enslaved families argued that two-parent families were and had always been the statistical norm among African Americans, even during slavery, and that persistent racism was more responsible for

single-mother families than slavery (Gutman 1976). This broader scholarship led those who were studying contemporary African American families to shift their focus from their deficiencies to their cultural strengths, often highlighting the adaptive strategies (e.g., extended families) that had enabled them to survive slavery, economic exclusion, and institutional racism (Allen 1978; Billingsley 1968; 1972; Stack 1974).

This cultural-strengths framework still informs much research on African American families, but it is not without critics. More recent researchers, for example, have contested the notion that two-parent families were the norm among enslaved African Americans, asserting that this assumes a universality in their family experiences that simply did not exist.

Instead, social-structural factors produced a diversity of family forms among slaves (Dunaway 2003; Franklin 1997). The decline in the quality of life for low-income African American families during the 1980s, as seen in weaker extended family ties, a decrease in marriage, and the rise in nonmarital childbearing and welfare dependency, also seemed to assert the primacy of social-structural forces, namely the rise of the postindustrial economy (Wilson 1978), in shaping families. Cultural theorists were at a loss to explain why the cultural traditions that had enabled black families to survive centuries of slavery and racial oppression were so weakened by economic restructuring. Moreover, the historic focus on the strengths of *families* had never offered much analysis of African American *marriages*, yet by the 1990s black women were the *least* likely to marry and the *most* likely to become single mothers.

Between 1930 and 1944, black men married at an earlier age than white men (23.3 compared to 24.3) (Koball 1998). Heather Koball notes that during this era black men, mostly as tenant-farmers, were more likely to be employed full-time than white men and benefited from the labor of their wives and children. But even more important, she argues, was the fact that their life options were constrained by their low levels of education and concentration in the poor, rural South. Despite this high rate of marriage, very little is known about the quality and resilience of African American marriages during this era, but it is likely that both cultural traditions (e.g., female-centered families) and structural forces (e.g., racism, economic hardship, northward migration) converged to heighten their risk of marital separation and divorce (Frazier 1957; Marks 1989).

By 1945 a racial crossover in marriage had occurred, with blacks marrying later and less often than whites (Koball 1998). By the 1950s, 88 percent of African American and 95 percent of white American women entered marriage (Cherlin 2008). The marriage decline continued at an accelerated rate for African Americans in the ensuing decades. During the 1970s, the rate of marriage among women under the age of twenty fell for all racial groups, but much more dramatically for African American women (Fitch and Ruggles 2000). Moreover, the rate of non-marriage among African American women more than doubled between 1970 and the 1990s, rising from 17 to 40 percent. By the late 1990s, only about 15 percent of black women between the ages of twenty and twenty-four had married, compared to one-third of white women; by the age of forty, 93 percent of white women had married, compared to only 65 percent of black women (Cherlin 2008; Huston and Melz 2004). Thus, marriage rates among African American women reached a historic low during the latter decades of the twentieth century, sparking concern over the welfare of children and the impact of social-welfare policies on families.

In this chapter, I begin with a historical overview of African American marriages that shows how centuries of slavery compromised African marriage traditions, yet precluded African Americans from embracing American traditions. As noted, the extent to which enslaved black families formed two-parent families has now become a matter of some debate; however, it seems clear that most sought to legalize their marital unions after slavery was abolished. Their ability to reap the benefits of marriage, however, was curtailed by racist policies and dominant gender ideologies, thus undermining the viability of their marriages and perpetuating a strong tradition of single-mother and extended families. Next, I show how social scientists have characterized African American families, arguing that theorists have often ignored marriage and the demands of the traditional marriage contract, which were inconsistent with the cultural traditions and economic resources of African Americans. I explore how the intersection of race, gender, and class inequalities continue to affect African American families and relationships adversely, and I conclude with a look at the future of marriage for African Americans.

Marriage among African Americans: A Historical Perspective

Although marriage and families are universal institutions that are often seen as the bases for societal stability, the rules and norms that govern these institutions are a product of differing cultural ideologies and economic forces. In West African societies, marriage was often arranged and polygamous and, given the importance placed on fertility, was sometimes preceded by the birth of children (Cherlin

2008). Both American and African marriages embraced patriarchal traditions, but the implications of male authority were muted in African societies by the economic roles of women, the primacy of the mother–child relationship, female-centered kin relationships, and the fact that blood relationships were often seen as more important than marital relationships (Caldwell 1996; Young 1970). Thus, Africans brought to the United States their own marital and family traditions, some of which were destroyed by the demands of slavery (e.g., polygamy), while others were reinforced by slavery (e.g., female work roles, extended families). Enslaved blacks undoubtedly merged West African and American family traditions in ways that enabled them to survive, but faced formidable obstacles to conforming fully to either family system. For example, the marriages of enslaved blacks had no legal sanction and were often unstable, and slavery coerced and controlled their labor and lives in ways that undermined family life. Black families were often defined as mothers and their children. Equally arduous labor was required for men and women, and men, even when present in families, were neither the primary providers nor heads of their families. These factors made it impossible for marriage to become thoroughly institutionalized among African Americans, but also freed them from rigid gender norms and the notion that love, sexuality, and family had to be centered in a legally sanctioned marriage contract (Hill 2005).

Emancipation had a destabilizing effect on African American families, often resulting in starvation, migration, marital separation, and the desertion of spouses and children. During the Civil War, armies invaded and disrupted plantation life, setting thousands of black people adrift and leading many to abandon their spouses and children (Frazier 1957). Resisting the loss of cheap labor, white southerners sometimes refused to allow black soldiers returning from war to claim their wives and children (Landry 2000), and some states passed laws allowing whites to "indenture" (or re-enslave) the children of black couples who were unmarried or unemployed (Scott 1985). As racism intensified, African American men lost many of the skilled jobs they had held during slavery. Frequently charged with crimes like vagrancy and rape, they increasingly faced the prospects of

being lynched, incarcerated, or forced into labor contracts (Booker 2000). As Booker has explained, many southerners argued that slavery had a civilizing influence on black people, but without it they were regressing to their primitive state, such as giving in to their natural tendency toward sexual immorality.

Amid myths of dangerous, unbridled sexuality among African Americans, a campaign was waged to legalize their marital unions, with marriage described as elevating "freedpeople to a new level of civilization" (Giddings 1984; Higginbotham 1993; Schwalm 1997). Former slaves were sometimes forced to legalize fairly casual sexual relationships; Frankel, for example, found an 1870 Mississippi law declaring all African American couples "who have not married, but are now living together, cohabiting as man and wife, shall be taken and held, for all purposes in the law, as married" (Frankel 1999). The legalization of marriage was also urged for economic reasons—the need to reorganize the labor of black people for the sharecropping system.

Evidence suggests that the majority of African Americans married after slavery ended; however, a significant minority remained single and/or formed single-mother families. There was, for example, much regional variation in marriage rates. Dabel found that two-thirds of free black women living in New York City between 1850 and 1870 did not marry (Dabel 2002); perhaps they were live-in domestics or had fewer potential marriage partners, since most blacks lived in the South. Indeed, in earlier research (Hill 2005, 2006), I have argued that while most African Americans married after slavery ended, there was also a nonmarriage ethos among a significant minority of black women, since the costs of being married outweighed the benefits. For example, many had developed a tradition of self-reliance during slavery, could perform labor that was still in demand, and were participants in female-centered kin networks that were not easily abandoned in favor of marriage. But even those who married did not necessarily adhere to mainstream family ideologies or abandon black cultural traditions such as relying on extended families and fostering children to other families. The latter may account for the fact that Steven Ruggles found that in 1850 nearly half of all free black children lived with one or neither of their parents, and by the 1880s (a few years after slavery was abolished) parental absence was five times more common among blacks than whites (Ruggles 1994).

Northward migration further diminished marital stability among African Americans, as many migrants failed to gain the economic foothold they had expected. The tradition of working wives was simply transferred from rural to urban areas (Landry 2000), where the tendency of white families to insist on live-in maids threatened the ability of African American women to prioritize caring for their own families (Marks 1989). Efforts to create married couple families were also countered by growing rates of unemployment among African American men during the 1950s (Billingsley 1992), the same decade that marriage rates began to decline. In fact, the birthrate among single African American women tripled between 1940 and 1957 (Franklin 1997), which suggests that nonmarital parenting, although neither normative nor the ideal, was not strongly stigmatized among blacks. Still, the growing concentration of single-mother families in urban areas and on welfare rolls made them more visible and controversial, thus setting the stage for twentieth-century debates about African American families.

Theorizing African American Families

The early sociological study of families was guided by the theoretical premises of structural functionalism, which saw the breadwinner–homemaker family model as ideal for social mobility in the rapidly industrializing economy. Centuries of slavery and racism had made it difficult for most African Americans to form such families; yet racist thinking often led scholars to explain the "deficiencies" in black families using theories of biological inferiority. Even those at the Chicago School of Sociology, which was known for its focus on the primacy of social and environmental forces, sometimes fell sway to the belief that different human populations were "endowed with different *biologically transmitted* cultural capacities" (Hall 2002). Among those opposing such reasoning was E. Franklin Frazier, an influential black scholar who argued that African American families had been shaped by social structural forces. Like other liberal scholars of the era, Frazier essentially

offered a class analysis of African American families.

The Class (or Social Deficit) Perspective

Early twentieth-century sociologists focused heavily on processes of assimilation among racial–ethnic minorities who were moving into urban areas, and most sought to refute biological theories of racial inequality by emphasizing the impact of social structural forces on families. Thus, they often highlighted the similarities between middle-class black and white families that had assimilated into mainstream society, but provided dire portrayals of poor black families that had been unable to do so, especially those headed by single mothers (Davis and Havighurst 1946; Kardiner and Ovesey 1951). Frazier also emphasized class diversity among African American families (Frazier 1957), and he thought slavery had destroyed their African culture and was responsible for fostering single-mother families. He argued that single-mother (or matriarchal) families among African Americans had often worked well in the South, but they impeded socioeconomic mobility in a rapidly modernizing society. Never doubting the premises of the dominant theory of his era, structural-functionalism, or the merits of assimilating into the dominant culture, Frazier saw single-mother families as a legacy of slavery and two-parent, patriarchal families as ideal. This theme resonated with most African American activists and leaders throughout the 1950s; however, when reiterated in the Moynihan Report, it became the catalyst for a new genre of research on black families (Moynihan 1965).

The Cultural (or Family Strength) Perspective

The revolutionary era of the 1960s and 1970s produced research that was more critical of hegemonic family, marital, and gender ideologies, and of the social deficit perspective on African American families. The Moynihan Report, although it emphasized that there was significant class diversity among African Americans, was seen during the civil-rights era as attributing the blame for black economic disadvantage to single-mother families rather than racism. The report was widely criticized among activists and scholars, including feminists who bristled at the notion of patriarchal families as inherently superior to those headed by women. In their efforts to refute depictions of African American families as pathological and matriarchal, it became common to valorize the strength and family support networks of single mothers (Stack 1974) and argue that black married couples had created egalitarian relationships (Scanzoni 1977).

Two important themes emerged in the field of African American families studies among these revisionist scholars. First, social historians—in work that ultimately tended to "humanize" slave owners and "masculinize" the study of black families—argued that strong, stable, two-parent families were the norm among enslaved African Americans (Gutman 1976). According to revisionist researchers, enslaved black men exercised considerable authority over their families; indeed, "slaves created impressive norms of family life, including as much of a nuclear family norm as the conditions allowed," and slave owners "rarely if ever denied the moral content of the [marriage] relationship" between slaves (Genovese 1974). More recent scholars have challenged this work by emphasizing the diversity of experiences among enslaved African Americans, even describing revisionist accounts of family life under slavery as being nothing more than "Disney scripts" (Dunaway 2003).

Second, revisionist scholars rejected the idea that African cultural traditions had been destroyed by slavery. Walter Allen, for example, argued that African American families are best described as "culturally variant" rather than "culturally deviant" (Allen 1978), and Robert Hill described their cultural traditions as including religiosity, extended kin networks, the primacy of blood over marital relationships, multiple parentage, and flexible or egalitarian gender roles (Hill 1972). The premise that African American families were simply culturally different from white families and that most were supported by extended family networks deflected some of the criticism of single-mother families and sparked a virtual cottage industry of studies on the nature, extent, and consequences of their extended family networks.

But the cultural perspective also inadvertently fostered a monolithic depiction of *the* black family as governed by an immutable set of cultural traditions, and failed to offer many insights into African American marriages. In addition, it was at a loss to explain the decline of poor families and their traditions during the post–civil rights era, when, arguably, opportunities for African Americans had expanded. Meanwhile, the political discourse on culture among low-income African Americans had begun to focus on the urban underclass and their lack of family values, with some arguing that escalating rates of nonmarriage and single-mother families were the direct result of generous welfare policies (Murray 1984).

Criticism of the "urban underclass" helped reignite the class perspective on African American families, with William J. Wilson arguing that the rise of the postindustrial economy had severely diminished the employment prospects of young men and produced significant class polarization among African Americans (Wilson 1978). Wilson theorized that class had become more important than race in predicting the life chances of African Americans, and linked the decline in marriage to growing joblessness among men. His narrow focus on the employment–marriage connection, however, failed to place the marriage dilemma of African Americans in historical context or acknowledge the impact of multiple forms of social inequality on marriage.

African American Marriages: A Contemporary Perspective

Scholarly inquiry into the demise of marriage has produced a host of studies showing that attitudinal support for marriage among African Americans has remained strong; indeed, blacks often express greater support for traditional ideals about sexuality, marriage, and family than do white Americans. Despite living lives that contradict their expressed ideals, African Americans are as likely as white Americans to idealize marriage (Edin 2000; Harknett and McLanahan 2004) and are less accepting of nonmarital sex, cohabitation, and divorce than whites (Huston and Melz 2004). How, then, does one explain the discrepancy between their support for marriage and their lived experiences? I argue that marriage has traditionally been based on social norms and ideologies that were at odds with the cultural traditions and economic resources of African Americans, and thus has never been as firmly institutionalized among black people. I use an intersectionality framework to show that class, race, and gender inequalities have made and continue to make it difficult for many African Americans to conform to mainstream marital expectations, and that these structural inequalities have fostered their participation in cultural patterns (such as nonmarriage and single motherhood) that contradict their professed ideals. Neither cultural nor structural theorists have adequately dealt with the intersection of these inequalities, and thus have offered at best partial explanations of the marriage decline.

The traditional marriage contract is rooted in notions of patriarchy, female subordination, distinct roles for men and women, the protection of property, and the production of legitimate children—all of which were negated for African Americans for centuries by the dictates of slavery. Slavery, as noted earlier, demanded diversity and flexibility in the family arrangements of black people, depending on factors such as the type of economy, region, size of the plantation, and solvency of the slave owner (Dunaway 2003; Franklin 1997). At best, slavery nearly always undermined the economic basis for male authority in families, fostered female independence, prevented blacks from owning much property, and defined families primarily as mothers and their children. Most evidence suggests that a majority of African Americans married and formed two-parent families after slavery ended. Clearly, however, a significant minority either remained single (Hill 2005, 2006) or lived in informal or cohabiting relationships (Frankel 1999), at least partly because it was difficult for them to reap the benefits and privileges of married life. For example, most former slaves entered the sharecropping system that demanded the labor of men and women, and that criticized black women who tried to exempt themselves from such work as "aspiring to a model of womanhood that was considered inappropriate for them" (Dill 1988). This labor system made it difficult for black men to claim head-of-household status based on economic provisioning or for wives to prioritize caring for their children and homes. Marriage neither exempted women from productive labor nor substantially improved their standards of living, yet those who married sometimes found their husbands eager to assert patriarchal

power in their families—a factor blamed for high rates of domestic violence and marital separation among the newly freed slaves (Franklin 1997). Indeed, mainstream gender expectations, economic marginalization, and racism continued to make it difficult for African Americans to create stable marriages.

The Intersection of Class, Gender, and Racial Inequality

Intersectionality refers to understanding the "interconnectedness of ideas and the social structures in which they occur, and the intersecting hierarchies of gender, race, economic class, sexuality, and ethnicity" (Collins 1999). In applying this concept to the study of marriage, I focus on how structural factors shape cultural ideas and how multiple forms of inequality affect the challenges of marrying and staying married. For example, class matters a great deal as a factor in whether people will get and stay married: researchers have consistently found that higher income and educational attainment predict marriage and marital stability (Cherlin 2008). The rate of poverty among African Americans remains twice as high as that of white Americans, and much of that poverty is related to joblessness among black men (Wilson 1978). Low-income women, although struggling alone to make ends meet, are unwilling to marry men who cannot contribute much to their economic support (Edin 2000). Moreover, joblessness and poverty help push young African American men from mainstream society, and in their pursuit for manhood and respect many embrace behaviors (e.g., violence, hypersexuality) (Anderson 1999) that do not bode well for marriage and often lead to criminal behavior. Indeed, Western and Beckett (1999) have argued the racially motivated sentencing has made the penal system a major strategy in regulating the labor market, with more than 1.6 million people (disproportionately male and black) incarcerated by the late 1990s.

Economic restructuring has lessened the demand for unskilled labor, but racism in the labor market also undercuts the economic position of African Americans. Data from the Bureau of Labor Statistics reveal that among men twenty-five years of age or older in 2005, black men (7.6 percent) were more than twice as likely as white men (3.5 percent) to be unemployed (U.S. Department of Labor, 2008). Moreover,

African American men are discriminated against by employers for numerous reasons (Wilson 1987), including the notion that they simply lack the "soft skills" that are now in demand, such as "skills, abilities and traits that pertain to personality, attitude and behavior rather than formal or technical knowledge" (Moss and Tilly 1996). As Moss and Tilly have noted, employers often describe black men as being unmotivated, defensive, and hostile. Similar stereotypes undermine the ability of black women to find work. They are twice as likely as white women to be unemployed, and employers often stereotype them as unreliable single mothers (Browne and Kennelly 1995).

Neither the end of legalized racial segregation nor the gains made since the civil-rights era have eliminated racism or racial inequality; white Americans still endorse a spate of racist assumptions about African Americans and their families (Bobo, Kluegel, and Smith 1997). Racism and racial exclusion adversely affect the feelings of African Americans about their place in society and their quality of life. Hughes and Thomas, for example, found racial disparities in life quality between black and white Americans, and they argued that racism produces identity problems and a sense of rage and resentment among African Americans. Even when age and social class were considered, "African Americans were less satisfied, less happy, more mistrustful, more anomic, had less happy marriages, and rated their physical health worse than whites" (Hughes and Thomas 1998). This sense of being disrespected and disvalued in the larger society can adversely affect the quality of intimate relationships and the likelihood of marriage.

Persistent class and race inequalities intersect with and shape gender ideologies, making it difficult for African Americans to conform to traditional gender expectations or embrace the evolving ideal of gender-egalitarian marriages. For example, their long tradition of work and socioeconomic gains makes it difficult for many African American women to "marry up," or even marry men whose educational and economic position is comparable to their own. Although African American men earn more than black women, mostly because they hold male-typed jobs and more high-paying professional positions, the gains since the 1950s have been greater for black women. African American women, for example, are more likely than men to hold managerial and professional jobs (albeit in areas such as social work and teaching), more likely to have bachelor and especially graduate degrees, and more likely to feel integrated into the values of the dominant culture. This has created an important status gap between black women and men—and numerous books and movies that suggest the problem could be solved if middle-class black women would accept and marry working- or lower-class black men (Hill 2005). But class matters in forming viable marriages and marrying men of a lower class or status may help explain why black women feel less benefited by marriage than white women (Goodwin 2003). Indeed, the ideology of "marrying up" also affects low-income women, who are concerned about the loss of respectability associated with marrying poor and often jobless men (Edin 2000).

These structural inequalities foster cultural practices and behaviors that militate against marriage and marital success. Economic exclusion and persistent racial inequality, for example, ultimately creates an "oppositional culture that devalues work, schooling, and marriage" (Massey and Denton 1993). The courtship practices of young African American men who lack decent jobs or respect in mainstream society are often characterized by deceit, violence, and a general disrespect for women (Anderson 1990). The skewed gender ratio of men to women favors men and shapes their attitudes toward marriage and women; for example, Harknett and McLanahan found that "when men are in short supply, partner quality and relationship quality tend to be worse, and parents place less emphasis on the two-parent, male breadwinner norm" (Harknett and McLanahan 2004). African American men who marry tend to bring to their relationships more conservative gender beliefs than white men (Blee and Tickamyer 1995) and, despite being more accepting of employed wives, their marriages are characterized by more work–family conflicts, especially when the wife has a career (Bridges and Orza 1996). Gender traditions also persist in the division of domestic work: African American men spend only about half as much time doing housework as their partners (John and Shelton 1997). Overall, black couples are less satisfied in their marriages than white couples; they report sharing fewer activities and experiencing more conflict and distrust (Harknett and McLanahan 2004).

The Marriage Decline: Can (Should) It Be Reversed?

The strongest arguments for marriage are that married couples have higher levels of health and well-being than singles, that marriage reduces poverty, and that children fare better in two-parent families. For these reasons, the 1996 Personal Responsibility and Work Opportunity Act (PRWOA) declared that marriage "is the foundation of a successful society" and "is an essential institution that promotes the interests of children" (Jayakody and Cabrera 2002). Proponents of marriage contend that married people are happier, healthier, and wealthier than single people (Waite and Gallagher 2000). Still, the extent to which this applies to African American couples is debatable. As indicated earlier, there is a racial gap in marital satisfaction, with married African American couples experiencing more conflict and distrust in their relationships than white couples. Although their lower level of marital satisfaction cannot be explained away by noting class differences between blacks and whites, it is undoubtedly exacerbated by the fact that African Americans are more likely to be in the working and lower classes, where divorce and domestic violence are more common. Staying in unhappy marriages correlates with adverse health outcomes, such as elevated levels of psychological distress and poor health (Hawkins and Booth 2005). There is also evidence that marital unhappiness takes a greater toll on the health of wives than of husbands, with unhappy wives having high levels of depression and substance abuse (Coontz 2005).

From an economic standpoint, black married couple families fare better than single-mother families, although their 2001 median household income ($55,618) was much less than that of white married couple families ($71,155) (Conrad and King 2005). Linda Waite has found that several factors reduce the economic benefits of marriage for African Americans, such as lower wage gap between black men and women, the lower returns black women receive for investing in their husband's earnings, and the expense of raising children, who are more likely to be present in the homes of black couples (Waite 1995). For lower-income couples, where the prospects of unemployment, divorce, and domestic violence are high, the economic benefits of marriage may prove even more meager. D. T. Lichter and colleagues report that poverty rates would still be more than twice as high among African American women if they had the same family background and rates of marriage and unwed childbirth as white women (Lichter, Graefe, and Brown 2003). They also found that among economically disadvantaged black women, marriage is associated with downward educational mobility, and those who marry and divorce have higher rates of poverty than those who never married.

Although the growth in single-mother families has leveled off in recent years, nearly 41 percent of American children live in such families, with African American children (53 percent) more likely to do so than white children (22 percent) (Sigle-Rushton and McLanahan 2004). Children benefit from having the emotional and financial support of their fathers; indeed, many studies have shown that children living with single mothers, regardless of their race or social class, are more likely than those living with two biological parents to experience academic failure, behavioral and psychological problems, delinquency, and illegal drug use (Ellwood and Jencks 2004; Sigle-Rushton and McLanahan 2004). Still, single-mother families and extended family relationships are more institutionalized among African Americans and may have fewer adverse consequences for black children. A study comparing male adolescents living in white and black single-mother families found that lack of involvement with fathers elevated the risk of problematic behaviors only for white sons—at least partially because they were more likely to live in *divorced* single-mother families and were more likely to have lost a father with whom they had a relationship (Thomas, Farrell, and Barnes 1996). For African Americans, the risks of single-mother families may be more the result of the demise of extended family relationships and higher rates of poverty and extreme poverty; for example, in 2001 the median household income for black single mothers was less than $21,000, compared to $29,650 for white single mothers (Conrad and King 2005).

So, should African Americans get married? There are clearly benefits to be gained from marriage, although most evidence suggests that those benefits are not as great for blacks as for whites. But given the diminishing support single mothers are receiving from the state and their extended families, marriage may become more appealing. Moreover, there is strong ideological support for marriage among African Americans; the majority would like to get married, and they equate marriage with respectability, endorsing more traditional marital, gender, and sexual norms than white Americans. Still, a gap has always existed for African Americans between their endorsement of mainstream family values and their lived experiences. As I have argued, many African Americans have historically lacked the economic and cultural resources to conform to the traditional marriage contract, which was based on male-domination, gendered roles, and property. Today, these institutional aspects of marriage have now given way to marriage as a personal relationship based on gender equality and emotional satisfaction (Amato 2004). Such marital expectations should, at least arguably, make it easier for African Americans to achieve marital success, since the emphasis on economics has declined. Still, these new marital expectations are more likely to be embraced by middle-class couples, and African Americans have primarily been in the working and lower classes, where traditional values are more apparent. For example, as Landry has pointed out, employed wives have always been acceptable among African Americans, but "[it] remained for the upper-middle-class black wives to elevate the *acceptable* to the *desirable* in the early decades of the twentieth century" (Landry 2000).

Conclusion
In this chapter, I have argued that multiple forms of social inequality, both historically and currently, have created an important gap between the marital ideals of African Americans and the resources needed to live those ideals. This has made marriage seem less attainable, and thus has fostered cultural alternatives to marriage, such as high rates of single-mother families and nonmarital cohabitation. Mainstream marital traditions, for example, have supported patriarchal marriages headed by men earning the family wage, but exempted African American men from such jobs. These marital traditions have also been based on the primacy of marriage-centered families, but African Americans have often had to rely on extended family networks in order to survive. It has also been traditionally based on a gender division of labor that makes women economic dependents by placing them in the home, yet since slavery African American women have always combined productive and domestic work. Thus, despite high levels of attitudinal support for marriage among black Americans, dominant marital traditions have been at odds with their experiences. In this sense, marriage has never been fully institutionalized among African Americans.

Multiple social inequalities are responsible for the erosion of marriage among African Americans during the twentieth century, and addressing those inequalities is the key to restoring marriage as a vital institution. For example, workshops have sprung up to teach African American men the value of being involved in their children's lives, but less has been done to bring them into the economic mainstream or enhance their employment skills or educational achievement—both of which are important if they are to participate consistently in family life. Similarly, both politicians and religionists who trumpet the value of marriage and two-parent families have not always acknowledged the gender inequities in those arrangements, which women increasingly refuse to tolerate. Welfare-related marriage-promotion programs have more leverage over poor, young mothers than they do the fathers, and some research suggests that such programs place the responsibility on mothers to "swallow their rage and grievances against men" and bring them into the cultural mainstream of marriage (Huston and Melz 2004). Failing to resolve basic gender issues, though, will not lead to successful marriages. Finally, marriages have changed for all Americans over the past few decades, with more employed wives, more dual-income families, more economic independence, and more couples unwilling to stay in marriages that are emotionally unsatisfying. These changes in marriage have made issues such as gender equity in the home, adequate childcare, and family-friendly practices by employers key factors in the maintenance of families.

References

Allen, W. R. 1978. The search for applicable theories of black family life. *Journal of Marriage and the Family* 40, no. 1:117–29.

Amato, P. R. 2004. Tension between institutional and individual views of marriage. *Journal of Marriage and Family* 66 (November); 959–65.

Anderson, E. 1990. *Streetwise: Race, class, and change in an urban community.* Chicago: University of Chicago Press.

_____. 1999. *Code of the street: Decency, violence, and the moral life of the inner city.* New York: Norton.

Billingsley, A. 1968. *Black families in white America.* Englewood Cliffs, N. J.: Prentice-Hall.

Billingsley, A. and J. M. Giovannoni. 1972 *Children of the Storm: Black Children and American Child Welfare.* New York: Harcourt Brace Jovanovich.

_____. 1992. *Climbing Jacob's ladder: The enduring legacy of African-American families.* New York: Simon & Schuster.

Blassingame, J. W. 1972. *The slave community: Plantation life in the antebellum south.* New York: Oxford University Press.

Blee, K. M., and A. R. Tickamyer. 1995. Racial differences in men's attitudes about women's gender roles. *Journal of Marriage and the Family* 57, no. 1: 21–30.

Bobo, L., J. R. Kluegel, and R. A. Smith. 1997. Laissez-faire racism; The crystallization of a kinder, gentler, antiblack ideology. In S. A. Tuch and J. K. Martin, eds., *Racial attitudes in the 1990s: Continuity and change,* 15–42. Westport, Conn.: Praeger.

Booker, C. B. 2000. *"I will wear no chain!" A social history of African American males.* Westport, Conn.; Praeger.

Bridges, J. S., and A. M. Orza. 1996. Black and white employed mothers' role experience. *Sex Roles* 35, nos. 5–6: 337–85.

Browne, I., and I. Kennelly. 1995. Stereotypes and realities: Images of black women in the labor market. In I. Brown, ed., *Latinas and African American women at work: Race, gender, and economic inequality,* 302–26. New York: Russell Sage.

Caldwell, J. C. 1996. The demographic implications of West African family systems. *Journal of Comparative Family Studies* 27:331–52.

Cherlin, A. J. 2008. *Public and private families: An introduction.* New York: McGraw Hill.

Collins, P. H. 1999. Moving beyond gender: Intersectionality and scientific knowledge. In M. M. Ferree, J. Lorber, and B. B. Hess, eds., *Revisioning gender,* 261–84. Thousand Oaks, Calif.: Sage.

Conrad, C. A., and M. C. King. 2005. Single-mother families in the black community: Economic context and policies. In C. A. Conrad, J. Whitehead, P. Mason, and J. Stewart, eds., *African Americans in the U.S. Economy,* 163–74. Lanham, Md.: Rowman & Littlefield.

Coontz, S. 2005. *Marriage, a history: From obedience to intimacy, or how love conquered marriage.* New York: Viking Penguin.

Dabel, J. E. 2002. African American women and household composition in New York City, 1827–1877. In J. L. Conyers Jr., ed., *Black cultures and race relations,* 60–72. Chicago: Burnham.

Davis, A., and R. J. Havighurst. 1946. Social class and color differences in child-rearing. *American Sociological Review* 2:698–710.

Dill, B. T. 1988. Our mothers' grief: Racial ethnic women and the maintenance of families. *Journal of Family History* 13, no. 4: 415–31.

Dunaway, W. A. 2003. *The African American family in slavery and emancipation.* New York: Cambridge University Press.

Edin, K. 2000. What do low-income single mothers say about marriage? *Social Problems* 47, no. 1: 112–13.

Ellwood, D. T., and C. Jencks. 2004. The spread of single-parent families in the United States since 1960. In D. P. Moynihan, T. M. Smeeding, and L. Rainwater, eds., *Future of the family,* 25–65. New York: Russell Sage Foundation.

Fitch, C. A., and S. Ruggles. 2000. Historical trends in marriage formation: The United States 1850–1990. In L. J. Waite, Bachrach, M. Hindin, E. Thomson, and A. Thornton, eds., *The ties that bind: Perspectives on marriage and cohabitation.* New York: Aldine de Gruyter.

Frankel, N. 1999. *Freedom's women: Black women and families in Civil War–era Mississippi.* Bloomington: Indiana University Press.

Franklin, D. L. 1997. *Ensuring inequality: The structural transformation of the African-American family.* New York: Oxford University Press.

Frazier, E. F. 1957. *The Negro in the United States.* New York: Macmillan.

Genovese, E. D. 1974. *Roll, Jordan, roll: The world the slaves made.* New York: Pantheon.

Giddings, P. 1984. *When and where I enter: The impact of black women on race and sex in America.* New York: Bantam.

Goodwin, P. Y. 2003. African American and European American women's marital well-being. *Journal of Marriage and the Family* 65 (August): 550–60.

Gutman, H. G. 1976. *The black family in slavery and freedom, 1750–1925.* New York: Pantheon.

Hall, R. L. 2002. E. Franklin Frazier and the Chicago school of sociology. In J. E. Teele, ed., *E. Franklin Frazier and the black bourgeoisie,* 47–67. Columbia: University of Missouri Press.

Harknett, K., and S. S. McLanahan. 2004. Racial and ethnic differences in marriage after the birth of a child. *American Sociological Review* 69 (December): 790–811.

Hawkins, D., and A. Booth. 2005. Unhappily ever after: Effects of long-term, low-quality marriages on well-being. *Social Forces* 84, no. 1: 451–71.

Higginbothan, E. B. 1993. *Righteous discontent: The women's movement in the black Baptist church, 1880–1920.* Cambridge, Mass.: Harvard University Press.

Hill, R. B. 1972. *The strengths of black families.* New York: Emerson Hall.

Hill, S. A. 2005. *Black intimacies: A gender perspective on families and relationships.* Walnut Creek, Calif.: AltaMira.

_____. 2006. Marriage among African Americans: A gender perspective. *Journal of Comparative Family Studies* 37, no. 3: 421–40.

Hughes, M., and M. E. Thomas. 1998. The continuing significance of race revisited: A study of race, class and quality of life in America, 1972 to 1996. *American Sociological Review* 63 (December): 785–95.

Huston, T. L., and H. Melz. 2004. The case for (promoting) marriage: The devil is in the details. *Journal of Marriage and Family* 66 (November): 943–58.

Jayakody, R., and N. Cabrera. 2002. What are the choices for low-income families? Cohabitation, marriage, and remaining single. In A. Booth and A. C. Crounter, eds., *Just living together: Implications of cohabitation on families, children, and social policy,* 85–95. Mahwah, N. J.: Erlbaum.

John, D., and B. A. Shelton. 1997. The production of gender among black and white women and men: The case of household labor. *Sex Roles* 36, nos. 3–4: 171–93.

Kardiner, A., and L. Ovesey. 1951. *The mark of oppression: Explorations in the personality of the American Negro.* New York: Meridian.

Koball, H. 1998. Have African American men become less committed to marriage? Explaining the twentieth century racial cross-over in men's marriage timing. *Demography* 35, no. 2: 251–58.

Landry, B. 2000. *Black working wives: Pioneers of the American family revolution.* Berkeley: University of California Press.

Lichter, D. T., D. R. Graefe, and J. B. Brown. 2003. Is marriage a panacea? Union formation among economically disadvantaged unwed mothers. *Social Problems* 50, no. 1: 60–86.

Marks, C. 1989. *Farewell—we're good and gone: The great black migration.* Bloomington: Indiana University Press.

Massey, D. S., and N. A. Denton. 1993. *American apartheid: Segregation and the making of the underclass.* Cambridge, Mass.: Harvard University Press.

Moss, P., and C. Tilly. 1996. "Soft" skills and race: An investigation of black men's employment problems. *Work and Occupations* 23, no. 3: 252–76.

Moynihan, D. P. 1965. *The Negro family: The case for national action.* Washington, D.C.: Office of Policy Planning and Research.

Murray, C. 1984. *Losing ground: American social policy, 1950–1980.* New York: Basic Books.

Nobles, W. W. 1974. Africanity: Its role in black families. *Black Scholar* 5, no. 9: 10–17.

Ruggles, S. 1994. The origins of African-American family structure. *American Sociological Review* 59 (February): 136–51.

Scanzoni, J. 1977. *The black family in modern society: Patterns of stability and security.* Chicago: University of Chicago Press.

Schwalm, L. A. 1997. *A hard fight for we: Women's transition from slavery to freedom in South Carolina.* Urbana: University of Illinois Press.

Scott, R. J. 1985. The battle over the child: Child apprenticeship and the freedmen's bureau in North Carolina. In N. R. Hiner and J. M. Hawes, eds., *Growing up in America: Children in historical perspective,* 193–207. Chicago: University of Chicago Press.

Sigle-Rushton, W., and S. McLanahan. 2004. Father absence and child well-being: A critical review. In D. P. Moynihan, T. M. Smeeding, and L. Rainwater, eds., *Future of the family,* 116–55. New York: Russell Sage Foundation.

Stack, C. 1974. *All our kin: Strategies for survival in a black community.* New York: Harper & Row.

Thomas, G., M. P. Farrell, and G. M. Barnes. 1996. The effects of single-mother families and nonresident fathers on delinquency and substance abuse in black and white adolescents. *Journal of Marriage and the Family* 58 (November): 884–94.

U.S. Department of Labor, Bureau of Labor Statistics. Household data and annual averages. Retrieved January 25, 2008, from www.bls.gov/cps/cpsaat24.pdf.

Waite, L. 1995. Does marriage matter? *Demography* 32, no. 4: 483–507.

Waite, L., and M. Gallagher. 2000. *The case for marriage: Why married people are happier, healthier, and better off financially.* New York: Doubleday.

Western, B., and K. Beckett. 1999. How unregulated is the U.S. labor market? The penal system as a labor market institution. *American Journal of Sociology* 104, no. 4: 1030–60.

Wilson, W. J. 1978. *The declining significance of race: Blacks and changing American institutions.* Chicago: University of Chicago Press.

_____. 1987. *The truly disadvantaged.* Chicago: University of Chicago Press.

Young, V. H. 1970. Family and childhood in a southern Negro community. *American Anthropologist* 72, no. 2: 269–88.

Questions for Critical Thinking

1. Hill's discussion of the history of African American families demonstrates the importance of examining race, social class, and gender simultaneously when we examine the institution of family. Do you think that this is important? Why or why not?

2. How do the policies of other institutions (e.g., economy, education, the state) result in additional strains on the family for African Americans that white families do not experience? What policies can you think of that might alleviate some of these strains?

3. How is your own definition of family inclusive or exclusive of a diversity of race, class, or gender experiences?

"WILLING TO DO ANYTHING FOR MY KIDS"

Inventive Mothering, Diapers, and the Inequalities of Carework

• *Jennifer Randles*

The following essay by sociologist Jennifer Randles introduces the concept of ***inventive mothering***, emphasizing the complexity and agency of mothers who are poor as they develop innovative pathways to ensure children's access to resources, protect them from the harms of poverty and racism, and present themselves as fit parents in the context of intersecting gender, class, and race stigma. The ability of the mothers to manage the needs of their children while also handling disrespectful attitudes towards their families reflects a level of creativity and inventiveness that demonstrates how mothers in poverty conceive of distinctive childrearing strategies and logics to perform carework that results from deprivation, discrimination, and the lack of an adequate social safety net.

Mothers across social classes express similar beliefs in support of the ideology of "intensive mothering" (Hays 1996), which characterizes good parenting as child-centered, time-consuming, and self-sacrificing (Christopher 2012; Gunderson and Barrett 2015; Ishizuka 2019; Lee 2008). Yet intensive mothering assumes class and race privileges, specifically that children's needs are satisfied and their human dignity recognized (Elliott, Powell, and Brenton 2015; Verduzco-Baker 2017); it emphasizes parenting labor, logics, and strategies that protect or promote children's high-class status (Milkie and Warner 2014). These ideas overlook the distinctively rigorous and often invisible forms of carework marginalized mothers do to ensure their children's basic needs are met. Prior research highlights how poor mothers aspire to poverty-adjusted versions of intensive parenting compatible with their socioeconomic constraints (Edin and Kefalas 2005; McCormack 2005; Weigt 2018). Less attention has focused on the parenting ideas and practices poor mothers devise as they strenuously, meticulously, and creatively manage components of carework demanded by deprivation and a meager social safety net.

To fill this gap, I theorize *inventive mothering* as an ideology of parenting that accounts for the physical, cognitive, and emotional labor poor mothers perform. In addition to being child-centered, time-consuming, and self-sacrificing in specifically classed ways, inventive mothering is innovatively resourceful, harm-reducing, and stigma-deflecting. Focusing on the case of how mothers in poverty manage diaper need—lacking sufficient diapers to keep an infant dry, comfortable, and healthy—I develop the concept *diaper work* as a previously unanalyzed form of childcare labor that reveals the complexity, agency, and inventiveness of low-income mothers' parenting.

Jennifer Randles is Associate Professor and Chair of Sociology at California State University-Fresno. Her research focuses on family policy, low-income parenting, and gender, class, and race inequalities. She is the author of *Proposing Prosperity: Marriage Education Policy and Inequality in America* (Columbia 2017) and *Essential Dads: The Inequalities and Politics of Fathering* (University of California Press 2020).

As the first to conceptualize diapering as a social arrangement shaped by gender, class, and race inequalities, this study answers three key questions: How do poor mothers manage the material and emotional conflicts that arise around children's diapering needs, specifically in a sociopolitical context that does not recognize diapers as necessities? What does this reveal about low-income mothers' childrearing logics and strategies? Consequently, how should we expand sociological theories of parenting to encompass the ways marginalized mothers do much more than try to live up to poverty-adjusted versions of intensive mothering? Drawing on 70 in-depth interviews with mothers who experienced diaper need, I show how parents use diapering and diaper access strategies to claim a good-mother status in the context of poverty, racism, welfare state curtailment, and limited public support for basic hygiene needs.

These findings reveal that diapering involves much more than the physical labor of purchasing or procuring diapers and disposing of or cleaning used diapers. It entails classed and racialized forms of emotional and cognitive labor necessary to oversee limited diaper supplies, invent and utilize diaper-stretching strategies, and manage stigma and threats to a "good" parent identity. Mothers' narratives capture the complexity and rigor of coping with diaper need and claiming identities as good, worthy parents through diaper work.

More broadly, inventive mothering draws necessary theoretical attention to how the taken-for-granted, if tedious, tasks of middle-class mothering—such as diapering, feeding, and housing children—are often judged as less rigorous and consequential than parenting tasks intended to promote children's upward mobility and high-class status. With implications for sociological understandings of parenthood, poverty, and welfare policies, this study reveals that focusing on childrearing practices experienced as "intense" from the point of view of more affluent, white mothers perpetuates inequalities by obscuring the complex labor poor mothers perform to secure children's basic needs. In the context of extreme and growing inequality and a shrinking social safety net in the United States (Collins and Mayer 2010; Edin and Shaefer 2015), these findings compel us to revise existing frameworks of how structural inequities intensify parenting.

Background and Justification
Mothering Ideologies Intersecting with Gender, Class, and Race Inequalities

Based on her study of an economically diverse group of mothers, sociologist Sharon Hays (1996:8) theorized "intensive mothering" as a gendered ideology of parenting that compels women to engage in "child centered, expert-guided, emotionally absorbing, labor-intensive, and financially expensive" childrearing practices. "Intensity" in parenting has come to mean what sociologist Annette Lareau (2011) termed "concerted cultivation," whereby parents deliberately develop children's abilities and dispositions as part of "status safeguarding" (Milkie and Warner 2014) through methods such as enrolling children in organized activities and consciously developing their language skills. Education, occupation, and income are associated with distinct parenting strategies (behaviors and skills) and logics (interpretive frames for understanding those strategies) (Calarco 2014; Lareau 2011), and higher-SES parents are more likely to practice the tenets of intensive mothering and concerted cultivation (Cheadle and Amato 2011). This is more structural than cultural, as lower-SES parents espouse the same beliefs but do not have the same means to enact them (Bennett, Lutz, and Jayaram 2012). Some mothers' class and race privileges enable them to manage, if not entirely meet, intensive mothering expectations (Gunderson and Barrett 2015; Lee 2008; Walls, Helms, and Grzywacz 2016), especially as they work to protect and promote children's status and security (Cooper 2014; Nelson 2010; Villalobos 2014).

The parenting labor of working-class and poor mothers, who often adopt an "accomplishment of natural growth" logic focused on meeting children's basic needs and providing love and limits (Lareau 2011:3), is often presumed to be less demanding and consequential for children's status. Given equitable opportunities, economically vulnerable mothers would presumably parent much like their middle-class counterparts, implying that poor women cannot be equally good mothers until they are able to access the resources required of intensive parenting (Verduzco-Baker 2017). As Hays (1996) and Lareau (2011) suggest, this results in a deficit lens of low-income parenting that obscures how marginalized women work at least as hard—and often harder—to develop parental self-efficacy and meet their children's needs within the context of deprivation and discrimination.

Complex considerations of inequality inform low-income mothers' parenting decisions, such as when they spend some of the little money they have on "non-essential" items that give children access to valuable mainstream cultural experiences (Pugh 2009). Elliott and Bowen (2018) theorize how low-income mothers try to avoid criticisms through "defensive mothering" tactics of rejecting negative assessments, conveying a favorable impression of their choices, and differentiating themselves from "other" neglectful parents. Elliott and colleagues (2015) and Verduzco-Baker (2017) similarly find that low-income mothers' parenting strategies not only align with intensive mothering ideologies, but these mothers perform additional rigorous and innovative labor intended to promote upward mobility and help children avoid and cope with poverty and racism. Low-income mothers tend to emphasize more concrete parenting goals attuned to these inequities, such as ensuring children get to school safely, rather than abstract parenting values and beliefs (Tsushima and Burke 1999). Research also shows how poor mothers creatively manage meager resources and perceptively weigh the costs and benefits of marriage, legal work, underground money-making activities, welfare receipt, and monetary and in-kind support from kin and friends (Edin and Kefalas 2005; Edin and Lein 1997).

Despite how its tenets reflect the objectives and opportunities of white, middle-class, able-bodied, highly educated parents, intensive mothering remains the universal standard for all mothers (Johnson 2014). Sociological literature has documented how differentially positioned mothers adhere to, adapt, and resist intensive mothering ideologies, including research on mothers of color (Christopher 2013), employed mothers (Christopher 2012, 2013), incarcerated mothers (Lockwood 2018), mothers with disabilities (Frederick 2017), and mothers who receive welfare (McCormack 2005; Weigt 2018). Theorizing the work that low-income mothers do as their "own, equally valid, form of intensive mothering and cultivation

strategies," Verduzco-Baker (2017:1034) argues that sympathetic scholars underestimate the sophistication of poor mothers' attempts to adapt middle-class parenting logics to their children's needs.

Yet inequitable access to opportunities and resources requires lower-income mothers and mothers of color to engage in unique forms of high-intensity parenting that privilege renders obsolete. A primary example is that white mothers do not need to deliberately cultivate children's pride in their racial identity when society already valorizes and privileges whiteness (Collins 1987; Dow 2019). Ensuring children's physical and psychic survival has long been among the most demanding and consequential components of parenting for mothers of color who creatively strive to generate a sense of dignified security for their children (Collins 1994; Glenn 1994). Low-income mothers engage in strategic "security projects," which Cooper (2014) theorizes as the remarkably adaptive economic and emotional labor of creating and maintaining notions of security amidst precarity.

The tendency to essentialize and universalize intensive mothering belies how caregiving demands, in both degree and kind, emerge in response to where families live at the intersection of gender, class, race, and other structural inequities. The intensive mothering lens frames marginalized mothers' parenting as deficient and defensive, rather than as a form of resistance among women who work hard to overcome controlling images and shape positive self-definitions of their parenting abilities (Collins 2000). An intersectional lens on mothering instead reveals the complexity of what sociologist Patricia Hill Collins (1994) termed "motherwork," that is, the extensive labor involved in nurturing, preserving, and protecting children steeped in poverty and racism. Motherwork involves innovative approaches that valorize marginalized mothers' parenting, such as how Black mothers have long integrated paid work into conceptions of good motherhood and relied on "other mothers" to provide communal childcare (Collins 1994; Dow 2016).

Yet the laborious and creative parenting tactics poor mothers and mothers of color devise to manage the challenges of poverty and racism are, at worst, seen as pathological adaptations that perpetuate their disadvantages (Roberts 1993), and at best as derivative "survival strategies rather than productive practices" (Verduzco-Baker 2017:1015). Intensive mothering ideologies have particularly high physical, cognitive, emotional, and social costs to poor mothers, who must often sacrifice their own basic needs to provide for their children's (Elliott et al. 2015; Henderson, Harmon, and Newman 2016).

Poor women, especially poor women of color, suffer punitive consequences for deviating from intensive mothering expectations due to how gendered and racialized economic constraints limit their ability to provide and compel their participation in public assistance programs (Collins and Mayer 2010; Hays 2003; Roberts 2002). Welfare aid policies provide too little for mothers to meet normative criteria for "good" motherhood and place little value on the unpaid care labor consistent with ideas of intensive parenting (Turgeon 2018). The racialized controlling image of the "welfare queen" has contributed to further retrenchment of the U.S. social safety net for poor mother-headed families in recent decades (Collins 2000; Roberts 1997). Yet poor mothers on welfare still construct themselves as good mothers working within a "poverty-adjusted version" of intensive mothering to deflect stigma that could lead to separation from their children (Weigt 2018).

Heightened state surveillance of poor families of color by law enforcement and child welfare agencies subjects them and their parenting practices to extra layers of scrutiny. The child welfare system is designed to detect and punish parents when they cannot provide for children's basic needs, but it largely ignores the failings of middle-class and affluent parents whose shortcomings are not defined as "neglect" or "child maltreatment" (Roberts 2002). Being deemed careless or unfit can have disastrous consequences for poor mothers of color whose children are more likely to enter the foster system and receive inferior services within it (Roberts 2002).

Intensive mothering ideologies (Hays 1996), combined with sacred views of childhood (Zelizer 1985), task mothers with protecting children from dirt, defilement, and outward signs of defecation. Children's appearances are a core part of mothers' own self-presentations as fit parents, as varying levels of cleanliness among children differentiate "normal" and "neglectful" mothers (Collett 2005). Poor mothers therefore devote vigilant attention to their children's hygiene and keeping them publicly clean to ward off critiques of their parenting abilities and not risk losing children to state custody (Edin and Kefalas 2005; Roberts 2002). In this context, diapering becomes uniquely important as mothering ideologies intersect with growing inequality, a meager social safety net, heightened scrutiny of poor parents, and mothers' strategic efforts to provide children cleanliness, comfort, and security.

Inventive Mothering through Diaper Work

Diaper need is a problem of inequality experienced by one in three mothers in the United States (Smith et al. 2013), and disproportionately by poor mothers of color (Raver et al. 2010). All parents must dispose of children's waste, but affording and managing limited diapering supplies is a complex physical, cognitive, emotional, and social process for poor parents who must plan, calculate, save, stretch, sacrifice, and innovate regarding diapers. Following Collins's (1994) theory of "mother-work" as the extensive racialized parenting labor needed to preserve children's dignity, and Marjorie DeVault's (1991) concept of "feeding work" as the feminized, often invisible, labor of producing family meals, I term this process *diaper work*. No prior research has analyzed diapering, specifically managing diaper need, as a distinct form of care labor that marginalized parents must perform.

Despite how children, and ultimately many adults, require diapers for numerous years throughout their life course, diapering is almost completely absent from the sociological literatures on parenting, carework, and welfare policies. There are only brief references to diapers as expenditures in budgets for families with young children (Edin and Lein 1997); common items that nonresidential fathers provide through informal child support (Edin and Nelson 2013; Kane, Nelson, and Edin 2015); part of maintaining a consistent supply of household toiletries and paper goods (Daminger 2019); and one task among many that mothers do to feed, clothe, and clean their children (Hays 1996).

Moreover, U.S. social policy does not systematically recognize diapers as a need of early childhood. Diapers are categorized as "unallowable expenses" by public food programs, including the Supplemental Nutrition Assistance Program (SNAP) and Women, Infants, and Children (WIC). Parents can use Temporary Assistance for Needy Families (TANF) cash aid to purchase diapers, but benefits often do not cover other needs, and only one in four U.S. families in poverty receives TANF (Edin and Shaefer 2015). The $75 average monthly diaper bill would alone use 8 to 40 percent of the average monthly state TANF benefit (Safawi and Floyd 2020). One state, California, offers diaper vouchers for TANF recipients, but only as a work support for parents with approved welfare-to-work plans. Cloth diapering in poverty is prohibitively difficult due to lack of personal washers and dryers, laws against washing diapers in public laundry facilities, and daycare center requirements for disposables.

As with menstrual hygiene products, most states still tax diapers as a "discretionary" expense. Research on menstrual politics has analyzed how the "tampon tax" reflects social stigma and taboos that prevent policy-makers from recognizing menstrual hygiene needs (Bobel 2010). Diapers similarly touch on issues of marginalized identities related to poverty, gender, and race. Low-income women disproportionately perform low-status carework involving feces and urine (Jervis 2001), a form of labor that is socially invisible due to how bodily products deemed disgusting and contaminated transgress personal boundaries and adult dignity (Isaksen 2002). Diapering has also historically fallen outside the purview of intensive mothering ideologies, in large part because the labor of containing children's waste often falls to low-paid, hired women of color (Hays 1996).

Prior research has analyzed how the provision of food (Elliott and Bowen 2018; Fielding-Singh 2017; Wright, Maher, and Tanner 2015) and housing (Berger et al. 2008; Guo, Slesnick, and Feng 2016) is central to women's identities as good parents. Because most parents in poverty lack public diaper support, diaper need is individualized in ways that food and housing insecurity are not, with stark consequences for mothers' experiences and self-efficacy. Mothers who experience diaper need are almost twice as likely to struggle with postpartum depression, with diaper need being a stronger predictor of maternal mental health than food insecurity or housing instability (Austin and Smith 2017; Smith et al. 2013). Even limited public support for food and housing validate poor parents' struggles with procuring these essentials.

The case of diaper work illuminates how gender, class, and race inequalities obscure significant aspects of parenting labor, especially their emotional (Hochschild 1979) and cognitive (Daminger 2019) dimensions. In addition to the physical labor of acquiring, changing, and disposing of diapers, diaper work involves the cognitive labor of anticipating children's diapering needs, identifying options for meeting them, making decisions, and monitoring results (Daminger 2019). It also involves extensive emotional labor for poor parents when options for meeting diapering needs are limited, deciding among options means forgoing other basic needs, and monitoring results involves managing gendered and racialized stigma associated with constrained parenting choices. Existing theories of parenting ideologies and strategies (Hays 1996; Lareau 2011) do not fully account for how class-based forms of childcare labor, like diaper work, are created specifically by conditions of gendered and racialized poverty and welfare policies that do not recognize families' full needs.

Diaper work is therefore a particularly apt case to expand theories of intensive mothering by conceptualizing what I call *inventive mothering*. U.S. welfare policies do not systemically cover diapers despite their unique practical and symbolic significance for early childcare. How parents manage diaper work and its physical, cognitive, and emotional components reveals how poverty and policy vacuums around basic needs intensify parenting. Rather than understand the strategies and logics low-income mothers devise as deviant, derivative, or mostly about deflecting stigma, it is crucial to theorize them as reasonable, responsible, and resourceful tactics shaped by the precarious and perilous conditions of their parenting.

Inventive mothering adheres to all the criteria of intensive mothering by being child-centered, time-consuming, emotionally absorbing, labor-intensive, self-sacrificing, and expert-guided (Hays 1996).

Beyond this, inventive mothering draws necessary theoretical attention to how gender, class, and race inequalities shape how parenting practices are called on to meet these criteria. For example, while middle-class mothers may invest significant time and labor in children's educational enrichment and sacrifice personal energy and time to do so (Lareau 2011), poor mothers, as I will show, must often devote extensive time and labor to managing diaper need through sacrificing their own basic needs and personal comfort. Poor mothers may not spend as much in absolute dollars on diapers as more affluent mothers spend on children's extracurricular activities, but they often spend a greater proportion of the resources they have.

"Expert-guided" from the point of view of middle-class intensive mothering typically means consulting child-rearing manuals and seeking advice from trusted teachers and doctors (Hays 1996). Poor mothers of color subject to increased surveillance must instead direct their actions to avoiding claims of child maltreatment and neglect as defined by other experts, namely child welfare professionals (Roberts 2002). Poor mothers do not merely adapt intensive mothering strategies and logics to their constrained circumstances: gender, class, and race inequities shape different experiences and meanings of parenting as laborious, expensive, sacrificial, and directed by experts.

Inventive mothering centers the experiences of poor mothers to underscore their initiative and ingenuity in realms of childrearing not required of white, middle-class motherhood. This reduces the tendency to depict low-income mothers as engaging in less rigorous or less consequential parenting practices, while highlighting how they must work harder to acquire or compensate for what more privileged parents already have or can simply buy. Whereas intensive mothering operates on a logic of maximizing children's potential and protecting their class status, inventive mothering operates on a logic of maximizing children's access to basic needs and protecting their humanity. Using diapering as a previously unexplored lens, this analysis illuminates a larger social phenomenon that has received insufficient sociological attention: inequalities and inadequate social safety nets intensify parenting in gendered, classed, and racialized ways that demand different, not just adaptive or reactive, parenting practices.

Findings: The Inventive Labor of "Living Diaper to Diaper"

Patricia, a 32-year-old Black mother of three, bought the 120-count box of supermarket brand diapers for $30 within hours of receiving her cash aid check on the 2nd of each month. Neither the cheapest nor highest-quality diapers she could find, this brand was the best balance of price per diaper, minimal leakage, and less skin irritation for her 1-year-old daughter, Sofia. Patricia devoted exacting attention to stretching that box as far as possible until next month's check. She kept a careful diaper log and closely monitored the toddler's liquid intake to optimize each diaper's capacity. Patricia also sold food stamps, aluminum cans and glass bottles, and her blood plasma for diaper money. When at home, she sometimes used paper towels secured with duct tape around Sofia's waist as makeshift diapers. Patricia knew to save her limited diaper supplies for times when Sofia was seen in public, especially by welfare case workers and healthcare providers. She feared that a baby without what others recognized as a legitimate, clean diaper was grounds for having Sofia taken into state custody and away from a mother who had been diagnosed with post-traumatic stress disorder as a victim of intimate partner violence. She told me: "Providing those diapers means I'm a good mom who keeps them away from my trauma and our money problems. For diapers, I'm willing to do anything for my kids." Patricia went without food, toilet paper, and tampons to save diaper money and prevent the diaper rashes that she knew could trigger suspicion of a poor Black mother's parental fitness.

As Patricia's experience suggests, diaper work becomes a central form of care labor for mothers in poverty and involves three primary components as a case of inventive mothering: (1) creatively meeting children's basic needs through remarkable resourcefulness; (2) productively protecting children from the harms of poverty and racism; and (3) strategically presenting themselves as fit parents in the context of intersecting gender, class, and race stigma. Drawing on mothers' narratives to illuminate these components of inventive mothering reveals that diaper work exceeds the criteria of intensive mothering as child-centered, labor-intensive, financially expensive, self-sacrificing, and expert-guided (Hays 1996). More than a survival strategy, inventive mothering as a productive class-based logic of parenting prioritizes protecting children from the physical and psychological harms of deprivation and discrimination and staking a good-mother status in the context of scarcity and stigma.

Inventing Diaper Supplies and Diaper Need Management Strategies

Mothers described diaper work as a particularly demanding form of care labor they performed to meet their infants' specific basic needs, which included milk and diapers. Sonia, a 33-year-old Latina mother of two, described diapers as "part of babies' developmental and physical needs, which means it's really scary for a mom not to have diapers, not to be able to provide this basic thing for your child." Over half of respondents told me diapers were the household expense they worried about most, more than food, housing, or electricity. According to Cora, a 30-year-old Black mother of five: "I worry about diapers more than food because we can portion our food. We get some food stamps, always have at least a can of something. You can't really portion your diapers in the same way and say, 'Okay, I'm going to use only three diapers today.' What if your kid goes poop four times?" Diapers were the bigger concern for mothers like Cora in part because they received public aid, including food stamps and housing assistance, to offset the costs of other necessities. Few mothers received public diaper assistance, and all struggled to cover costly diaper expenses with limited cash aid and low wages earned from work.

Mothers thus prioritized diapers in their accounting of household and personal expenses and devised strategies for managing diaper need that were necessarily laborious, self-sacrificial, and child-centered. Like Patricia, many pursued side jobs and other money-making activities specifically for diapers. Half had used diaper banks or pantries, but few could access enough to fill their diaper gaps. Mothers'

strategies for getting or making diapers and diaper money also included couponing; writing diaper companies for free samples; asking nurses in doctors' offices for diapers; trading food stamps for diapers; collecting and selling recyclables; crafting makeshift diapers from household items; panhandling; theft; writing fraudulent checks; selling household furniture and electronics; selling blood plasma; babysitting other families' kids or cleaning other people's homes in exchange for diapers; participating in research studies or market surveys for diaper incentives; taking parenting classes for which they could earn "mommy money" to buy diapers; asking for diapers through social media posts; holding diaper raffles; hosting baby showers where diapers were the preferred gift; and attending diaper give-a-ways at food banks, churches, and social service organizations. The three most common diaper work strategies mothers developed involved extensively tracking and managing diaper supplies, asking others in their social networks for diapers or diaper money, and forgoing or minimizing their own needs to save diaper money.

Mothers' descriptions of these strategies highlighted the physical, cognitive, and emotional labor of stretching diapers and diaper money, devising diaper alternatives, and managing diaper need anxiety and stigma. Tellingly, most mothers described with great specificity how many diapers they had and exactly how long those diapers would last for their children. Patricia explained: "I have seven in the house, two in my purse, and one I've hidden for an emergency. Based on how often [Sofia] goes to the bathroom and that she pees twice as much as she poops, I know those diapers will last me about 36 hours before I run out and have to figure out how to get more." Like Patricia, most mothers paid very close attention to their diaper supplies, where diapers could be purchased for change in a pinch, and who specifically among their family members and friends could help with diapers or diaper money on short notice. Many noted walking or bus routes timed to the minute that enabled them to get individual diapers or mini packs, allowing them more time to collect money for a bigger package.

Most mothers knew their children's elimination schedule so well they could predict within a few hours, depending on the child's current health and how much they recently had to drink and eat, when their last available diaper would be too full or dirty to use. Maria, 30, Latina, and a mother of four, logged each diaper change on a chart, tracked her son's urine output by the ounce, and set a daily diaper quota with different limits for when her son had diarrhea and when he was healthy. Based on this data, she kept a strict diaper budget to predict the date and hour when she would need to open a new box and how long that box should last. Maria's thorough track-and-budget diaper work technique allowed her to stretch her diaper supply while accounting for her son's needs:

> Diapers are lasting longer because I know when my son pees, how many times, how much he pees each time, and how many times fill up a diaper. ... Diapers is the number one concern for me right now because I don't want to struggle more, so I have to think about this stuff in this way, and I can't go over my daily limit. It's hard living pay-check to paycheck, living diaper to diaper. But I budget, compare, stretch things, figure out prices, the best deal for the most diapers. I'm a pro at this now with my fourth child.

"[L]iving diaper to diaper" necessitated specific strategies and logics—having to "think about this stuff in this way"—that involved interpreting diaper work as a skillful ability and form of childcare expertise. Like Maria, most mothers took pride in their resourcefulness around managing limited diaper supplies. More than a survival strategy, they conceived of diaper work as a productive practice based on hard-earned experience and knowledge.

Mothers' extensive management of diaper supplies profoundly shaped the daily rhythms of family life, including interactions with children and how mothers planned their work and social schedules. A third of mothers had reduced their work hours or time their children spent in childcare facilities due to lack of diapers, and over half had forgone running errands, attending social events, or otherwise leaving their homes because of diaper need. Most mothers had at least once completely run out of diapers, which required creative tactics for constructing makeshift diapers out of more readily available household materials, including paper towels, dish cloths, pillow-cases, t-shirts, toilet paper, menstrual pads, adult incontinence products, and napkins.

Some respondents, like Christine, a 52-year-old Black custodial grandmother of three, devised clever games that required observation, coordination, and persuasion. When Christine ran out of diapers, she had her three grandchildren, ages 1, 2, and 3 and all in diapers, play while diaperless on the linoleum kitchen floor as she waited the three hours it usually took for her sister to arrive with an emergency pack. The children received a piece of candy every half hour for sitting on the toilet during the affectionately dubbed "potty game." Determining if any of the children showed signs of urinating or defecating before their turn in the bathroom required Christine's constant, careful attention, but it hid the gravity of the situation from the kids, who never knew they ran out of diapers. What troubled Christine most was that her sister could usually afford only a single diaper pack, which meant she had to choose the one size that could best accommodate her barely walking 1-year-old granddaughter and her 3-year-old grandson who weighed twice as much.

Christine, like most respondents, kept close tabs on who in her social network could afford to offer diaper assistance, and especially who would be willing to do so with little or no judgment. In the absence of a public safety net for diapers, mothers necessarily relied on their private safety nets, especially fellow mothers who had similarly struggled and empathized with diaper need. Almost two-thirds of mothers had received financial or in-kind diaper support from friends or family, more commonly Black respondents. Compared to white mothers, Black and Latina mothers were more likely to describe seeking diaper support as a strategy that solidified social ties, rather than as an embarrassing last resort measure that subjected them to shame or unattainable expectations of reciprocity. Natasha, a 35-year-old Black mother of four, explained how neighbors on her street helped struggling moms with diapers by buying in bulk when they found sales. Although most of the neighbors did not currently have children in diapers, they experienced diaper need when their children were younger and knew the value of being able to reach out to those living nearby when diaper supplies ran low. Natasha explained: "My neighbors help with diapers because they know I'm trustworthy. If you don't have a job, then you won't be able to get Pampers, and you need someone to love you, help you get them."

Black mothers' more positive experiences receiving diaper support likely reflected a history and valorization of "other mothering," whereby members of the Black community provide communal childcare and support for carework (Collins 1994). Similarly disadvantaged family members and friends, even those who struggled to afford their own needs, were often the most willing to help with diapers. Black mothers were also more likely to have shared some of their own very limited diaper supplies with others in need. Yet Black mothers were also the most likely to report facing stigma when seeking diapers from public aid offices, charities, churches, and social service organizations. They believed racist assumptions led to more extensive questioning and doubt in these spaces about the legitimacy of their diaper need, their spending habits, and whether they had pursued other options to get diaper money.

White mothers, employed mothers, and mothers with more education reported facing greater social censure when asking for diapers or diaper money from family and friends, despite the fact that people in their social networks typically had more resources. Because their jobs and degrees presumably prevented diaper need, employed and college-educated mothers feared that others attributed their need to bad budgeting. Yet insufficient diapers thwarted mothers' efforts to be upwardly mobile through higher education. A third of the 30 mothers with some college were still pursuing their degrees, and several reported that diaper need prevented them from attending classes or affording tuition and books. Of the seven mothers in the sample with college degrees, only one was employed, and she made less than $40,000 a year as a store manager and was supporting a family of four. The other six college-educated mothers, including one with a graduate degree, had struggled to find jobs that paid enough to offset the cost of daycare. Perpetual conflicts between education, employment, and childcare necessitated their diaper work. The most highly educated respondent, Raquel, a 42-year-old multiracial mother of one with a master's degree in policy, explained: "If I got a job, we'd have more money for diapers, but then most of the rest would go to childcare. I'd rather be home with my daughter if what I'd make would just go to someone else to take care of her."

Before Raquel's daughter was born, she stocked up on clearance sale diapers at all stores within a 20-mile radius and attended weekly parenting classes at the hospital where she received obstetric care in exchange for diapers. After her daughter's birth, she sought out breastfeeding classes and three parent support groups that gave away diapers for attendance. She devoted an entire closet in her small apartment to stocking diapers, many she could not use because they were already too small. Raquel planned to exchange them for bigger ones with other mothers through online support groups that existed solely for that purpose. She shared with me: "I was just thinking before you called that I'm running out of size fours. I've been so focused on being ahead with size fives so I could stretch that supply that I didn't realize I'm running out. I just have to tell myself, 'I gotta go through some of those fives before I can trade or buy some more fours.' I can only imagine if someone doesn't have diapers how they feel because it's even constantly on my mind right now." Raquel was the most educated respondent in the sample, but her family of three still struggled to live on less than $25,000 a year.

Mothers with less education pursued these same diaper work techniques, and mothers from higher and lower socioeconomic backgrounds devised similar strategies to manage diaper need. This suggests inventive mothering is shaped more by mothers' commitments to manage childcare exigencies created by the structural conditions of poverty than any deeply engrained, class-based cultural beliefs about appropriate childrearing techniques. Affluent mothers can more obviously practice the tenets of what others recognize as intensive mothering, not because they hold fundamentally different parenting values, but because they can call on greater economic and social resources. Put another way, poor mothers must inventively compensate when they are not in a financial position to, as Raquel put it, "just buy your way out of the diaper problem."

A primary way mothers met their diaper needs was by sacrificing their own needs. A quarter of respondents reported they had gone without food to save diaper money, and many others ate only cheap foods—tortillas, dry cereal, packaged soups—as part of their diaper work. Melissa, 32, Asian, and a mother of three, noted: "I just need to worry about the girls having enough diapers and food because I can go on a diet and deal. Well, when I was breastfeeding and I didn't eat, I would get really bad headaches with all the pumping, but I made it work." Half of mothers described not buying new clothing, shoes, makeup, or hair products so they could afford diapers. Many said they wore the same shoes or clothing they wore while pregnant months or even years earlier.

The extent of mothers' sacrifices was evident in their accounts of things they "bought for myself" with severe guilt. Aisha, a 20-year-old Black mother of one, confided: "Well, I did buy myself a pair of socks yesterday. Honestly, I'm wearing the same clothes I wore when I was pregnant with her, even the same flip flops in the winter. To think about myself is so selfish." When I met Aisha in person to give her the interview stipend, she pointed to her new socks and pregnancy flip flops that had thinning soles and a hole where the strap attached. She said, "See, I wasn't lying. My daughter needs diapers, so I have to make these work. With the new pair of socks, I can stretch them another winter." Other mothers talked about the difficulties of buying their own menstrual supplies, toilet paper, medicine, and underwear. Toni, 29, Latina, and a mother of four, explained: "When I get paid, I pay my bills and then go to Walmart and get whatever my kids need, like the diapers. If there's any money left over, then I can think about if I need shoes, socks, or underwear, like, 'Crap, my underwear is all holey, or my bra broke.'" Diaper work required mothers to decide what their households, and especially they, could do without.

Yet mothers emphasized their inventiveness and resourcefulness in managing diaper need even more than what they sacrificed. Tracy, a 25-year-old multiracial mother of three, was already coping with trauma associated with the murder of her 10-month-old son's father a few weeks before the baby was born. Beyond her deep grief, this meant she could not count on him for financial support. Tracy underscored her ability to reconfigure her household budget on a moment's notice based on her son's diapering needs:

I always figure things out. With my bills and diapers, it's a picking and choosing game. You have to reserve the rent space, so that's a priority. Your child needs this, so you use food stamps when you can, instead of paying cash. You think, "How much do I have for this box of diapers for this day? I don't have to pay taxes when I use my food stamps. How much of that can I put on the diapers for today? What will that leave for tomorrow? Is there something I need that I can put back to buy the diapers?"

Most days Tracy felt confident about her ability to play this skilled "picking and choosing game," but an emergency could throw her for a financial loop. Diarrhea meant more than a sick baby; it meant more diapers and picking something else for herself that she had to put back.

These strategies for stretching diaper supplies were informed by parenting logics that involved vigilant attention to babies' bodily rhythms, social behaviors and connections that could alleviate diaper need, and accounting for every cent of household expenditures. Beyond the practical tasks of containing children's bodily waste while on limited budgets, mothers' diaper work was also deeply rooted in the inventive mothering strategy of containing the effects of economic deprivation and racism.

Inventing a Sense of Security and Status for Children through Diaper Work

Unlike the intensive parenting strategies of middle-class mothers, the intent of diaper work is not to promote children's ascent up the class ladder. It is, however, an equally child-centered parenting tactic informed by the classed and racialized logic that a mother's job is to protect children from the injuries and indignities of poverty and racism. Diaper need conjures up images of babies left hours or days in the same dirty diaper. Yet the ones shouldering the ill effects of diaper need are often poor mothers working rigorously and creatively within their limited means to provide their children comfort, security, and a sense of dignity, all through diapers.

Many mothers admitted they did not change their babies immediately after urination, but only when they knew exactly how much urine could be wicked away from the absorbent layer in direct contact with infants' skin. Yazmin, a 28-year-old Latina mother of three, said: "As long as I know she's not going to get a rash, I'll hold off for about an hour or so until it's time to change her. If I bathe her, and she hasn't used the diaper, I reuse the same one she had before the bath, so I don't waste a diaper." Mothers like Yazmin invested significant cognitive labor into learning which diaper brands and sizes could hold the most without causing discomfort or pain for children.

The primary criterion that dictated mothers' diaper brand preferences was whether they irritated their babies' skin, with price a secondary consideration. Although they could barely afford to buy any diapers at all, mothers frequently bought the most expensive ones because they held more while keeping their children drier, rash-free, and more comfortable. Mothers often covered the extra costs by buying the cheaper versions of their own hygiene items or household products. Audra, 33, white, and a mother of five, explained: "You can't just get the cheapest diapers because kids would get rashes. … I don't smoke cigarettes, I don't do drugs, and I don't drink. I can't think of the last time I bought something for myself. Well, I bought tampons yesterday, but I got the cheap brand so the kids can have their good diapers. You work around your stuff, not theirs." Aware of stereotypical controlling images of low-income mothers, especially mothers of color, as "welfare queens" who spend money irresponsibly on vanity items and vices like hair styling and cigarettes, respondents stressed that their diaper need was not a result of reckless personal spending. They also developed a logic of their own basic needs—food, clothing, menstrual products—as discretionary items they could forgo if it meant affording and providing more comfort for their children.

Mothers specifically described access to clean diapers as a necessity of early childhood that transcended class and race lines and ensured children's health, security, and personhood. Patricia explained: "Diapers are a need because that's a bodily function they have. Every child needs diapers, from the poorest of the poor to the richest of the rich. Even the richest babies poop, and even the poorest babies deserve a clean butt." Fatima, a 32-year-old Black mother of two, prioritized diapers over her medical care and internet access, the only means of communication

with her family in Africa, because she believed that "babies need diapers as people. They are not a luxury. They are about being human."

Providing diapers suited to infants' personal needs was a way mothers believed they preserved their children's human dignity. They rationalized not buying a lot of toys or books, but they could not justify having their children smell, sit in urine or feces, or look dirty. Trina, 29, white, and a mother of two, said: "It doesn't bother me to go without food to buy more diapers. I'm weird about my kid sitting in a diaper that has any pee in it. Any time I use a diaper, I always panic honestly. My brain is on a constant loop of, 'Am I gonna run out? Where am I gonna get more diapers?'" Trina knew she could stretch her diaper supply if she let her daughter urinate a few times between changes. Yet, for Trina, a clean diaper was not only about vigilant hygiene; it represented a baby who was well cared for and comfortable, despite other scarcities the family, and especially she herself, faced.

Respondents thus conceptualized diaper work as a strategy for shielding their children from the trauma of material deprivation. Yazmin confided: "My kids, their comfort, come first. I don't want them to be traumatized by certain events. If you really knew my backstory, I still try to keep my kids away from it. That's why the diapers, the kids, come first." Yazmin's conflation of "diapers" and "kids" pointed to the practical and symbolic significance of mothers' diaper work as about living up to a child-centered, self-sacrificial ideology of parenting in the context of poverty. Yet unlike intensive mothering that focuses on children's enrichment through surrendering maternal time, energy, and work and leisure opportunities, the mothers I studied spoke of inventive mothering as necessarily prioritizing their children's base humanity and security, often at the cost of meeting their own physical and psychological basic needs.

Mothers' diaper work also involved creative efforts to mitigate the effects of inequalities on older children. Juana, a 29-year-old Latina mother of two, explained how her 7-year-old daughter learned about scarcity through their family's experience with diaper need: "Sometimes we have a little bit of extra money, and I'll try to buy her a toy. But just recently she was like, 'Oh, no, it's okay, Mama, I don't want it. Save it for when the baby needs some diapers.'" Likewise, Lisa, 30, Latina, and a mother of four, shared:

> I had to break the two oldest ones' piggy bank. I cried, "I'm so sorry I have to do this." My son, my oldest, he understood: "It's okay, Mama. I know you'll put it back." But my 5-year-old daughter, she's like, "Mommy, what do you need all those diapers for?" I just tell her, "Baby, your sister needs to be changed, and I can't let her sit in pee. She'll get sick and get rashes." But the next time I get any money, and it's not for diapers, I go back and reward them with something small in the store for being so understanding about the diapers. My son will say, "Mama, it's okay that you have to, I know my sister needs diapers. I remember when I was a baby, and I wore diapers, too." I cried and say, "Son, yes you did." I couldn't be prouder of him.

For these mothers, diaper work specifically, and parenting generally, involved resourcefully managing children's experiences with and understandings of deprivation and sacrifice.

Mothers described diapers as more than mere pieces of plastic and cotton when articulating their perspectives on childrearing and childhood inequities. Ramona, a 21-year-old Latina mother of one, took great pride in being a young mother, but lamented: "I see other parents who are not much older than me. They have their life together, and my daughter's the same age as their kid, but she's not wearing the [expensive] Honest Company brand. She's wearing these $4 diapers that I can barely afford. It's right in my face that their kids' future will probably be better than mine, especially if I don't get it together fast." Ramona "splurged" whenever possible on name-brand Huggies or Pampers when she had money. This strategy made her feel like she was giving her daughter the chance to experience one small part of a middle-class lifestyle by wearing softer, more absorbent diapers with popular mainstream cartoon characters imprinted on them. This example was telling of how diapers became practically and symbolically important for mothers' inventive efforts to provide opportunities they felt equalized early childhood experiences of comfort, consumption, and status.

This was a major reason why mothers chose not to use cloth diapers. In addition to the prohibitively expensive start-up costs and money and labor associated with cleaning soiled cloth diapers, mothers were reluctant to use a type of diaper they believed others would stereotypically associate with filth, racialized poverty, and maternal unfitness. When describing cloth diapering, mothers did not envision colorful, reusable diaper covers with smooth snaps and washable inserts, the kind commonly used by affluent mothers. Instead, they imagined using prickly diaper pins to secure cheap pieces of stained thick fabric that could be purchased in bulk at discount stores, what many mothers used as burp cloths.

Mothers feared that using cloth would involve leaky urine and feces on their children's bodies and foul smells that did not go away with washing. These were the same reasons mothers became hyper-focused on having their children in clean diapers and changing them perhaps more frequently than affluent mothers with greater access to diapers. Aisha described why she could not be seen in public as a Black mother with her daughter wearing a cloth diaper: "Nope! If you start walking around with your kid that way, they might see it as a kid in rags. … If you go in front of a judge and be like, 'Well, I didn't have diapers or diaper money, so I used cloth,' and your kid pees and soaks right through it, they'll say you're not taking care of your kid. The last thing we want in our life is [Child Protective Services], especially when we've been in the foster care system before." Part of diaper work was an overwhelming, reasonable desire among many mothers to keep their children in dry, powder scented, disposable diapers that could be readily changed and immediately discarded.

Mothers ensured that their children had access to disposable diapers as both a material need and a status symbol that was less a marker of middle-class affluence and more about deflecting classist and racist criticisms of their children as unhygienic and not well cared for. Although they were not in a financial position to give their children everything that more privileged parents could provide, mothers reasoned that they could at least offer clean, comfortable diapers as part of a secure and dignified early childhood experience. Understood in this way, diaper work became a powerful strategy for staking a positive maternal identity in a socioeconomic and political context that often denies marginalized mothers' agency and status as "good" parents.

Inventing and Claiming a Good-Mother Status through Diaper Work

Respondents' diaper work deliberately defied stereotypes of poor mothers as promiscuous, lazy, and irresponsible. Solange, a 24-year-old Black expectant mother of four, described the contempt she faced when trying to access diapers for her youngest child while visibly pregnant with her fifth: "Welfare people say, 'They're fed, and you get money.' When I go to sign up for services, they don't ask about diapers, the children themselves. But there's more to raising a child than just clothes, food, and lights. No one seems to care about the under stuff of raising a baby." Solange speculated that the lack of public diaper aid was as much about diapers' association with the unspeakable and unacknowledged needs of young children's bodies as it was about the assumption that poor women, especially poor women of color, should avoid having children they cannot afford. Other unmet household needs certainly compounded the stresses of diapering in the context of stretched family budgets. Still, mothers emphasized the unique challenges and meanings of diaper work within a sociopolitical context characterized by sexist, classist, and racist stereotypes of parental unfitness. Consequently, providing diapers became especially significant for their maternal self-efficacy and efforts to deflect stigmatizing assumptions about poor women's childbearing choices and parenting abilities.

The stigma surrounding diaper need was particularly acute, mothers reasoned, because people were more sympathetic to other forms of need and yet more apt to judge mothers who could not procure hygiene items necessary to care for infants' most vulnerable body parts. Yesenia, a 28-year-old Latina mother of two, said: "People just judge you more. If we needed help with housing or food, people get that, but what does it say about you as a mother if you can't provide diapers, the one simple thing only your child needs?" Respondents believed diapers are so taken for granted as parents', particularly mothers', responsibility that they receive little public recognition and support when they struggle to get enough.

Diaper work required careful consideration of intersecting gender, class, and race stereotypes of parental fitness as mothers weighed the risks of diaper need against the potential consequences of their efforts to prevent it. Some respondents noted that presumptions of good parenting for affluent white mothers would lead others to give them the benefit of the doubt that they were simply waiting for the next convenient diaper change opportunity if their babies wore dirty diapers. Yet Latina and Black mothers described fearing lost custody if their children wore soggy or smelly diapers because others assumed they were negligent and had babies to collect additional state aid. Jocelyn, a 31-year-old Black mother of two, told me: "I don't get my hair or nails done, none of that. I just stay in the house and spend money on the kids. I even went out and stole diapers, risked my freedom for my kids. I don't have to do that all the time, but if I have to, I will. I never take the whole pack, but just open one and get the couple she really needs until I know we can get more money for diapers. I know to never leave diapers on too long, to prevent rashes, and who might see." Jocelyn knew that diaper theft risked her incarceration, especially as a poor Black woman. She was also acutely aware that a baby with rashes assumed to be caused by a mother who did not adequately change her risked equally disastrous claims of child maltreatment and maternal neglect.

Several mothers—all Black—had grown up in or lost custody of older children to the child welfare system. They emphasized the importance of having babies in clean diapers, especially for daycare or while in public, and not asking for additional government aid via WIC or TANF that could raise suspicion about their parenting capabilities. The ever-present threat of family separation compelled them to develop inventive mothering strategies for managing the outward appearance of diaper need.

Several Black mothers talked about having ample publicly visible diaper supplies in their homes, where they were more likely to be under surveillance. Lila, a 32-year-old Black mother of five who was pregnant with her sixth child, lost custody of her children through CPS due to inadequate housing. The social worker had documented "dirty housing unfit for kids," but according to Lila, the house was merely cluttered due to packing for an upcoming move. Claiming there were already plans to revoke custody of her newborn, Lila explained: "They're making every excuse to take her. We're trying to get everything, really the diapers and wipes, to make sure they don't take her. We get food stamps and basically Housing Authority is paying the full rent. We're keeping our head afloat, but we need lots of diapers so they don't take her away." Lila was counting on her food and housing aid to convince social workers of her ability to provide these basic needs for the new baby. But because she had no comparable direct public support for diapers, and Lila did not qualify for cash aid until after the baby was born, she believed that maintaining custody was contingent on her ability to have a "huge stack of diapers" during the social worker's next home visit. Mothers' diaper work necessarily included these types of strategies for presenting a fit mother status in the context of a racially biased child welfare system where poor mothers of color were considerably more likely to experience diaper need as part of racialized poverty.

Like Lila, many respondents believed that procuring sufficient diapers was a primary strategy for proving their worth, respectability, and perseverance as good mothers, despite the severe hardships they faced. Gina, 16, Latina, and a mother of one, had struggled with postpartum depression and intermittent homelessness since her daughter's 1st birthday. However, seeking diaper assistance through diaper banks and parenting classes meant she was "a parent who didn't give up on taking care of my baby. If a person really wants the help, they're going to get those diapers." Similarly, Christine, the grandmother who devised the "potty game," emphasized that her ability to inventively manage diaper need proved her love and commitment to caring for her grandchildren, despite her age and single-parent status:

> Keeping diapers is the hardest part, but none of us did anything wrong to be in this position, and we love each other. I can't cry, fuss, and holler about it, and I can't let these kids walk around here bare butt all day. So what do you do? You get creative, and you figure it out. I make my own wigs, budget gas in the car, know exactly where I have to go this day, this week, how far we have to travel, if the gas already in my car can get us there. I stretch the budget to cover diapers. I'm just determined not to fail.

As the youngest and oldest respondents in the sample, Gina and Christine repeatedly mentioned their diaper work to challenge stereotypes that their age undermined their parenting ability.

Respondents anchored virtuous maternal identities in their creative approaches to diaper work when recalling stigma they faced as parents who fell outside the normative bounds of "proper" motherhood, including those defined by age, marital status, class, education, and race. Alexis, a 23-year-old Asian American mother of four, explained:

> As a teen mom, people would look down on me all the time, while I'm over here paying myself through school with a minimum wage job trying to fend for myself and my kids. I ask for help with diapers, and then judgment gets thrown on us like, "Oh, you should stop having kids." I was on birth control with my last one. They're blessings, and people try to look at them as curses. If I didn't ask for help with diapers, they would just pee and poop everywhere. Then people look at you the wrong way for that. Moms, we figure it out with the diapers. We just mold into these people that make it work.

Respondents described common criticisms lodged at poor mothers, principal among them that they just need to get a job, budget their income or government benefits more effectively, and stop having kids. Performing self-sacrificial diaper work was a very practical, but also profoundly moral, way they deflected these criticisms. As Alexis noted, mothers without privilege must be innovative and adaptable in ways more affluent parents do not, often by "mold[ing] into these people" who make parenting in poverty work. They do so by working low-wage jobs, scrupulously managing limited resources, devising creative and laborious strategies to meet families' needs, and embracing children, planned or not, as gifts rather than liabilities.

Respondents also developed inventive mothering strategies for modeling to children how to be resilient and resourceful in the face of poverty and unmet household needs. Mothers sometimes worried they were not setting good examples because they lacked college degrees and high-paying jobs, but they felt they compensated by demonstrating innovation, sacrifice, and moral determination through their diaper work. Winona, 29, Black, and a mother of two, shared: "I can't be down, knowing I got these kids looking up to me to see how I can handle the diapers. It's challenging, but I'm not letting it break me. Every time I don't go out because I need to save that money for diapers, they see that."

Part of setting a good example for children is asking for assistance, which often meant, as several mothers put it, "swallowing my pride." Jackie, 35, Black/Latina, and a mother of three, humbly noted: "I don't have too much to say about myself, but I can tell you this. I dedicate all my time and everything I am to my children. Becoming a mother was the best thing that happened to me, and sometimes you have to learn not to worry about getting diapers from a pantry, asking for help so your kids have their diapers." Tanya, a 25-year-old Black mother of four, explained how her willingness to do anything necessary to get enough diapers was core to her identity as a parent who taught her children about the contextual nature of right versus wrong: "If you see yourself getting low on diapers, you should be able to come up with a solution. One time, a long time ago, I didn't have no diapers, and my mom wasn't helping me then. So I had to go inside a store, open a bag of diapers, put a few in my diaper bag, and hurry out. I felt awful, but I got no support, no welfare, so I had to do what I had to do for my baby." As a Black mother, diaper need forced Tanya into a perilous bind, one that compelled her to risk arrest and incarceration for diaper theft or potentially suffer other severe consequences if someone reported her for child endangerment or neglect for lack of diapers. Tanya's inventive mothering involved reconciling these impossible choices and rationalizing that providing her child diapers in times of dire need was a stronger moral imperative than any restriction against stealing. She hoped her children learned that letting one's baby go without diapers would have been the bigger ethical transgression.

Other respondents similarly explained how inventive mothering was about balancing the absolute needs and occasional valid wants of all their children. Protecting them from the indignities of poverty meant sometimes buying the "extras" children desired, even if it left less money for diapers. Ciara, 38,

Latina, and a mother of two, explained: "Sometimes I want to buy them something just because they want it, like take them to the movies. ... I'm trying to do something for both my kids. One needs diapers, and one just wants to have a little fun. I'm working, trying to get off welfare, trying to get my own place and save money, but I also need diaper money. ... I hear people say, 'Well, why did you have children?' She's my little miracle. I'm happy to have her. I'm going to take care of her, get the diapers. She's mine."

For mothers like Ciara who managed low-wage work, the racialized stigma of welfare, and the daily stress of deprivation including diaper need, the symbolism of diapers was a double-edged sword. Ensuring access to clean diapers represents providing children a comfortable lifestyle as much as a comfortable bottom. Yet, as mothers described, their strategic efforts to address diaper need can evoke the worst stereotypes of poor mothers of color, notably that they deliberately have too many kids they neglect, become irresponsibly dependent on public aid, and engage in reckless, imprudent behaviors. Respondents' descriptions of their inventive mothering practices, particularly diaper work, intentionally challenged these sexist, classist, and racist assumptions through compelling counter-narratives of ingenuity, hard work, and maternal sacrifice and pride.

These diaper work narratives reaffirmed respondents' parental self-efficacy. A third of mothers reported that they struggled with anxiety, depression, or post-traumatic stress disorder (PTSD). Their resourceful efforts to manage diaper need during times of desperation were a bulwark against affronts to their self-esteem and sense of security. Diaper need was likely a contributing factor to their mental health challenges. Nonetheless, they referenced their diaper work as proof of their deservingness as good mothers when they felt self-doubt or dehumanized by others. Brenda, a 25-year-old Asian American mother of three, told me:

> Sometimes I feel hopeless, like I can't do much at all. But I know I've tried to provide as much as I can for my kids, times when I've gone without or would push a bill out because my son really needed diapers, and I had nobody and nothing else. ... My PTSD definitely comes out over the diapers. As much as I need

electricity, to keep my kids out of the dark, I need even more to make sure they're comfortable so they won't see my struggle. ... They saw it once and are still traumatized. My older son won't go near a police officer, and my middle child is like, "Oh, Mommy, be careful, I hear sirens." ... Diapers are one thing I can do to protect them from that.

For Brenda and others, diapers represented the more secure life unburdened by the trauma of poverty and racism they wanted to give their children. Other basic needs like food, housing, and electricity were certainly no less significant for families' well-being. Yet as an item tailored to a fundamental bodily need of their youngest family members, especially one so closely tied to ideas of cleanliness, comfort, respectability, and class status, diapers had a unique moral import for mothers. Diaper work therefore became a core strategy of inventive mothering through which respondents developed a sense of themselves as good parents with agency who had at least some power to resist and counteract the inequalities that shaped their children's life chances.

Discussion and Conclusions

Conveying the middle-class presumptions of what makes parenting intensive, Hays (1996:5) notes that "modern American mothers do much more than simply feed, change, and shelter the child," and intensive mothering refers to the "more." Dominant ideologies of mothering tend to center the experiences of white, middle-class mothers by assuming children's physical and psychic survival are not at stake and their basic needs are met (Collins 1994). These ideologies marginalize poor mothers and mothers of color, not just by setting an impossibly high bar for good parenting, but by failing to account for how class and race privileges absolve white, middle-class mothers from forms of carework demanded by poverty and racism. Intensive mothering problematically defines "intensity" from the perspective of mothers with a high relative degree of economic security, personal autonomy, and freedom to parent without state interference. Focusing on how marginalized mothers express and strive to meet intensive parenting standards will inevitably frame them as deficient in terms of goals and outcomes, if not beliefs and attitudes. This contributes to the invisibility of classed and

racialized forms of childcare labor, like diaper work, that compel lower-income mothers, especially poor mothers of color, to develop appropriately distinctive parenting logics and strategies, not merely lower-cost adaptations of intensive mothering.

Inventive mothering avoids the pitfalls of treating marginalized mothers' parenting as efforts to live up to a poverty-adjusted version of intensive mothering. Just as intensive mothering is concerned with securing children's class position, equally important and rigorous carework strategies and logics focused on accessing crucial needs and protecting children's basic humanity become central to many mothers' experiences of and claims to "good" mothering. Even "defensive mothering" (Elliott and Bowen 2018) misses how marginalized mothers use class-specific forms of childcare labor, such as diaper work, to construct and facilitate a strong sense of parental self-efficacy, not merely defend against threats to a good mother identity.

Diaper work is a particularly relevant case to develop inventive mothering as a distinct theoretical framework of parenting. It illuminates how certain mothers face pressures to parent in ways that prioritize mitigating the consequences of inequality and how they respond with initiative and ingenuity in realms of childcare not required of white, middle-class motherhood. All parents must attend to their children's elimination needs, but diaper work more broadly accounts for the physical, cognitive, and emotional labor of coping with lack of access to diapers. As mothers noted, diapers are a need, not a luxury; yet the ability to buy ahead, stock up, and not give much thought to running out certainly is. Children across the class spectrum require diapering, but the labor required to meet that universal need is significantly stratified. As a case of inventive mothering, diaper work goes beyond being self-sacrificial, time-consuming, and child-centered to include strategies that are necessarily resource-stretching, dignity-protecting, and stigma-deflecting. These strategies are just as deliberate, complex, and attuned to inequalities and providing children opportunities as are concerted efforts to develop talents and skills deemed valuable in schools and workplaces (Lareau 2011).

Yet, whereas intensive mothering cultivates entitlement, inventive mothering cultivates innovation as mothers make strategic calculations about how to provide for their children while preventing the potential harms of scarcity. If intensive mothering focuses on pushing children up the socioeconomic ladder, inventive mothering is about protecting them from the indignities and injuries of growing up on the lowest rung. In this way, diaper work specifically, and inventive mothering generally, are akin to the "security projects" theorized by Cooper (2014), who found that, in an era of growing socioeconomic insecurity, parents pursue resourceful strategies to maintain notions of security, including downscaling families' basic needs to align with extremely limited budgets. The mothers I studied minimized their own needs, but they viewed diaper need as a more objective form of precarity that cannot be downscaled, despite budget limitations. Inventive mothering becomes particularly important in these instances when mothers struggle to align their children's needs with what they can afford.

Although diapering applies to a limited period of a child's life, diaper work reveals an overlooked human toll of the dismantling of the U.S. social safety net. Mothers' inventive diaper work is a necessary response to the distinctively American confluence of strict hygiene norms; minimal public support for childcare; a growing low-wage labor market; dwindling redistributive policies that vilify childbearing among poor women; exceedingly high rates of racialized childhood poverty; and a child welfare system that defines conditions of that poverty as parental neglect. Existing public programs for food and housing fail to meet families' full needs, but their existence is public acknowledgment that these needs exist. The focus on diapering illuminates how accessing basic needs that are neither formally recognized as necessary nor systematically subsidized via policy demands inventive mothering. It also shows how the core components of inventive mothering—the physical, cognitive, and emotional labor involved in accessing key resources, protecting children's dignity, and constructing a positive and valued maternal identity in the face of gender, class, and race stigma—become deeply entwined in a sociopolitical context that stigmatizes anyone, but especially poor mothers of color, for needing public aid. This is especially true when mothers silently struggle to meet a need that no one officially recognizes their children have.

Inventive mothering is also a useful theoretical framework for understanding other forms of carework parents perform to mitigate the effects of limited access to critical resources, including those related to food insecurity and housing instability. This involves reframing how we understand parenting tactics developed in response to deprivation, not as survival strategies, but as rigorous, innovative, and productive practices ingeniously cultivated to address stratification. Sociological theories have long attributed these intentions to more privileged mothers, largely because their intensive efforts to promote their children's life chances align with the "more" of middle-class mothering that obscures how privilege de-intensifies the labor involved in feeding, sheltering, and changing children. The inventive mothering framework applies a class lens to cognitive labor (Daminger 2019), which entails understanding how marginalized parents anticipate children's unacknowledged needs, identify options for meeting them with insufficient resources, and make difficult choices to provide other household necessities—and all in ways that protect children's dignity and parents' self-efficacy. Mothers' comments about ensuring adequate food and housing point to similarly inventive tactics.

This suggests areas for future research on parents' inventive efforts to cope with various forms of deprivation. I did not recruit according to demographic characteristics such as income or education, so subsequent studies could analyze how these factors shape inventive parenting practices. A comparative approach analyzing diaper need in the United States with that in other countries would further illuminate how social, economic, and political conditions, such as level of state support for caregiving, influence incidence of diaper need and diaper work techniques. The inventive mothering strategies and logics involved in performing diaper work have likely become more important as parents cope with growing precarity during the COVID-19 crisis. Diapers were among the most sought-after store items in early 2020 when shelter-in-place orders began, and many diaper banks across the country reported three-fold and greater increases in diaper requests.

Lifting the veil on diaper work shows how limited public support for care labor can have disastrous social, economic, and psychological ripple effects throughout entire families. It also helps dismantle deficit perspectives of marginalized parents and shows how carework is a primary aspect of social life where gender, class, and race are created and reproduced. Diapers deserve a place in the social safety net, but not only because they are a basic need for infants. Including diapers in family support policies would validate mothers' struggles to provide them. Sociological theories of parenting must account for how those struggles involve extensively inventive efforts to protect children from the dire consequences of inequality.

Poor mothers are often regarded with pity and contempt, rather than admiration and respect. When mothers must manage wide gaps between income and expenses, sociologists tend to focus on how they are deficient in resources, not how they rarely lack resourcefulness. Yet mothers' abilities to manage diaper need and affronts to their families' dignity reflect agency and ingenuity, not merely attempts to live up to intensive mothering ideologies. Diaper work and inventive mothering are responses to our collective failure to recognize some items—and parenting practices—as necessary for children's survival and well-being. They also powerfully remind us that, when it comes to what parents in poverty are willing to do for their children, necessity is indeed the mother of invention.

Acknowledgments
I am grateful to Daisy Rooks, Jennifer Sherman, Jennifer Utrata, Laurel Westbrook, and Kerry Woodward for their constructive feedback on previous drafts of this manuscript.

Funding Information
This research was generously supported by the American Sociological Association Fund for the Advancement of the Discipline.

References

Austin, Anna E., and Megan V. Smith. 2017. "Examining Material Hardship in Mothers: Associations of Diaper Need and Food Insufficiency with Maternal Depressive Symptoms." *Health Equity* 1(1):127–33.

Bennett, Pamela R., Amy C. Lutz, and Lakshmi Jayaram. 2012. "Beyond the Schoolyard: The Role of Parenting Logics, Financial Resources, and Social Institutions in the Social Class Gap in Structured Activity Participation." *Sociology of Education* 85(2):131–57.

Berger, Lawrence M., Theresa Heintze, Wendy B. Naidich, and Marcia K. Meyers. 2008. "Subsidized Housing and Household Hardship among Low-Income Single-Mother Households." *Journal of Marriage and Family* 70(6):934–49.

Bobel, Chris. 2010. *New Blood: Third-Wave Feminism and the Politics of Menstruation*. New Brunswick, NJ: Rutgers University Press.

Calarco, Jessica McCrory. 2014. "Coached for the Classroom: Parents' Cultural Transmission and Children's Reproduction of Educational Inequalities." *American Sociological Review* 79(5):1015–37.

Cheadle, Jacob E., and Paul R. Amato. 2011. "A Quantitative Assessment of Lareau's Qualitative Conclusions about Class, Race, and Parenting." *Journal of Family Issues* 32(5):679–706.

Christopher, Karen. 2012. "Extensive Mothering: Employed Mothers' Constructions of the Good Mother." *Gender & Society* 26(1):73–96.

Christopher, Karen. 2013. "African Americans' and Latinas' Mothering Scripts: An Intersectional Analysis." Pp. 187–208 in *Notions of Family: Intersectional Perspectives, Advances in Research*, Vol. 17, edited by M. Kohlman, D. Krieg, and B. Dickerson. Bingley, UK: Emerald.

Collett, Jessica L. 2005. "What Kind of Mother Am I? Impression Management and the Social Construction of Motherhood." *Symbolic Interaction* 28(3):327–47.

Collins, Jane L., and Victoria Mayer. 2010. *Both Hands Tied: Welfare Reform and the Race to the Bottom in the Low-Wage Labor Market*. Chicago: University of Chicago Press.

Collins, Patricia Hill. 1987. "The Meaning of Motherhood in Black Culture and Black Mother-Daughter Relationships." *SAGE: A Scholarly Journal of Black Women* 4(2):3–10.

Collins, Patricia Hill. 1994. "Shifting the Center: Race, Class, and Feminist Theorizing about Motherhood." Pp. 45–65 in *Mothering: Ideology, Experience, and Agency*, edited by E. N. Glenn, G. Chang, and L. R. Forcey. New York: Routledge.

Collins, Patricia Hill. 2000. *Black Feminist Thought: Knowledge, Consciousness, and the Politics of Empowerment.* New York: Routledge.

Cooper, Marianne. 2014. *Cut Adrift: Families in Insecure Times.* Berkeley: University of California Press.

Daminger, Allison. 2019. "The Cognitive Dimension of Household Labor." *American Sociological Review* 84(4):609–33.

DeVault, Marjorie L. 1991. *Feeding the Family: The Social Organization of Caring as Gendered Work.* Chicago: University of Chicago Press.

Dow, Dawn Marie. 2016. "Integrated Motherhood: Beyond Hegemonic Ideologies of Motherhood." *Journal of Marriage and Family* 78(1):180–96.

Dow, Dawn Marie. 2019. *Mothering While Black: Boundaries and Burdens of Middle-Class Parenthood.* Oakland: University of California Press.

Edin, Kathryn, and Maria Kefalas. 2005. *Promises I Can Keep: Why Poor Women Put Motherhood Before Marriage.* Berkeley: University of California Press.

Edin, Kathryn, and Laura Lein. 1997. *Making Ends Meet: How Single Mothers Survive Welfare and Low-Wage Work.* New York: Russell Sage.

Edin, Kathryn, and Timothy J. Nelson. 2013. *Doing the Best I Can: Fatherhood in the Inner City.* Berkeley: University of California Press.

Edin, Kathryn, and H. Luke Shaefer. 2015. *$2.00 a Day: Living on Almost Nothing in America.* Boston: Mariner.

Elliott, Sinikka, and Sarah Bowen. 2018. "Defending Motherhood: Morality, Responsibility, and Double Binds in Feeding Children." *Journal of Marriage and Family* 80(2):499–520.

Elliott, Sinikka, Rachel Powell, and Joslyn Brenton. 2015. "Being a Good Mom: Low-Income, Black Single Mothers Negotiate Intensive Mothering." *Journal of Family Issues* 36(3):351–70.

Fielding-Singh, Priya. 2017. "A Taste of Inequality: Food's Symbolic Value across the Socioeconomic Spectrum." *Sociological Science* 4:424–48.

Frederick, Angela. 2017. "Risky Mothers and the Normalcy Project: Women with Disabilities Negotiate Scientific Motherhood." *Gender & Society* 31(1):74–95.

Glenn, Evelyn Nakano. 1994. "Social Constructions of Mothering: A Thematic Overview." Pp. 1–29 in *Mothering: Ideology, Experience, and Agency,* edited by E. N. Glenn, G. Chang, and L. R. Forcey. New York: Routledge.

Gunderson, Justine, and Anne E. Barrett. 2015. "Emotional Cost of Emotional Support? The Association between Intensive Mothering and Psychological Well-Being in Midlife." *Journal of Family Issues* 38(7):992–1009.

Guo, Xiamei, Natasha Slesnick, and Xin Feng. 2016. "Housing and Support Services with Homeless Mothers: Benefits to the Mother and Her Children." *Community Mental Health Journal* 52(1):73–83.

Hays, Sharon. 1996. *The Cultural Contradictions of Motherhood.* New Haven, CT: Yale University Press.

Hays, Sharon. 2003. *Flat Broke with Children: Women in the Age of Welfare Reform.* New York: Oxford University Press.

Henderson, Angie, Sandra Harmon, and Harmony Newman. 2016. "The Price Mothers Pay, Even When They Are Not Buying It: Mental Health Consequences of Idealized Motherhood." *Sex Roles* 74:512–26.

Hochschild, Arlie Russell. 1979. "Emotion Work, Feeling Rules, and Social Structure." *American Journal of Sociology* 85(3):551–75.

Isaksen, Lise Widding. 2002. "Toward a Sociology of (Gendered) Disgust: Images of Bodily Decay and the Social Organization of Care Work." *Journal of Family Issues* 23(7):791–811.

Ishizuka, Patrick. 2019. "Social Class, Gender, and Contemporary Parenting Standards in the United States: Evidence from a National Survey Experiment." *Social Forces* 98(1):31–58.

Jervis, Lori L. 2001. "The Pollution of Incontinence and the Dirty Work of Caregiving in a US Nursing Home." *Medical Anthropology Quarterly* 15(1):84–99.

Johnson, J. Lauren. 2014. "The Best I Can: Hope for Single Mothers in the Age of Intensive Mothering." Pp. 267–79 in *Intensive Mothering: The Cultural Contradictions of Modern Motherhood,* edited by L. R. Ennis. Bradford, Ontario, Canada: Demeter Press.

Kane, Jennifer B., Timothy J. Nelson, and Kathryn Edin. 2015. "How Much In-Kind Support Do Low-Income Nonresident Fathers Provide? A Mixed-Method Analysis." *Journal of Marriage and Family* 77(3):591–611.

Lareau, Annette. 2011. *Unequal Childhoods: Class, Race, and Family Life,* 2nd ed. Berkeley: University of California Press.

Lee, Ellie J. 2008. "Living with Risk in the Age of 'Intensive Motherhood': Maternal Identity and Infant Feeding." *Health, Risk & Society* 10(5):467–77.

Lockwood, Kelly. 2018. "Disrupted Mothering: Narratives of Mothers in Prison." Pp. 157–73 in *Marginalized Mothers, Mothering from the Margins, Advances in Gender Research,* Vol. 25, edited by T. Taylor and K. Bloch. Bingley, UK: Emerald.

McCormack, Karen. 2005. "Stratified Reproduction and Poor Women's Resistance." *Gender & Society* 19(5):660–79.

Milkie, Melissa A., and Catharine H. Warner. 2014. "Status Safeguarding: Mothers' Work to Secure

Children's Place in the Social Hierarchy." Pp. 66–85 in *Intensive Mothering: The Cultural Contradictions of Modern Motherhood*, edited by L. R. Ennis. Bradford, Ontario, Canada: Demeter Press.

Nelson, Margaret K. 2010. *Parenting Out of Control: Anxious Parents in Uncertain Times*. New York: New York University Press.

Pugh, Allison J. 2009. *Longing and Belonging: Parents, Children, and Consumer Culture*. Berkeley: University of California Press.

Raver, Cybele, Nicole Letourneau, Jennifer Scott, and Heidi D'Agostino. 2010. "Every Little Bottom: Diaper Need in the U.S. and Canada" (https://nationaldiaperbanknetwork.org/wp-content/uploads/2019/02/Diaper-Need-in-the-US-and-Canada.pdf).

Roberts, Dorothy. 1993. "Racism and Patriarchy in the Meaning of Motherhood." *American University Journal of Gender, Social Policy & the Law* 1(1):1–38.

Roberts, Dorothy. 1997. *Killing the Black Body: Race, Reproduction, and the Meaning of Liberty*. New York: Vintage.

Roberts, Dorothy. 2002. *Shattered Bonds: The Color of Child Welfare*. New York: Civitas.

Safawi, Ali, and Ife Floyd. 2020. "TANF Benefits Still Too Low to Help Families, Especially Black Families, Avoid Increased Hardship." Center on Budget and Policy Priorities (https://www.cbpp.org/research/family-income-support/tanf-benefits-still-too-low-to-help-families-especially-black).

Smith, Megan V., Anna Kruse, Alison Weir, and Joanne Goldblum. 2013. "Diaper Need and Its Impact on Child Health." *Pediatrics* 132(2):253–59.

Tsushima, Teresa, and Peter J. Burke. 1999. "Levels, Agency, and Control in the Parent Identity." *Social Psychology Quarterly* 62(2):173–89.

Turgeon, Brianna. 2018. "A Critical Discourse Analysis of Welfare-to-Work Program Managers' Expectations and Evaluations of Their Clients' Mothering." *Critical Sociology* 44(1):127–40.

Verduzco-Baker, Lynn. 2017. "'I Don't What Them to Be a Statistic': Mothering Practices of Low-Income Mothers." *Journal of Family Issues* 38(7):1010–38.

Villalobos, Ana. 2014. *Motherload: Making It All Better in Insecure Times*. Berkeley: University of California Press.

Walls, Jill K., Heather M. Helms, and Joseph G. Grzywacz. 2016. "Intensive Mothering Beliefs among Full-Time Employed Mothers of Infants." *Journal of Family Issues* 37(2):245–69.

Weigt, Jill. 2018. "Carework Strategies and Everyday Resistance among Mothers Who Have Timed Out on Welfare." Pp. 195–212 in Marginalized Mothers, Mothering from the Margins, Advances in Gender Research, Vol. 25, edited by T. Taylor and K. Bloch. Bingley, UK: Emerald.

Wright, Jan, Jane Maree Maher, and Claire Tanner. 2015. "Social Class, Anxieties and Mothers' Foodwork." *Sociology of Health & Illness* 37(3):422–36.

Zelizer, Viviana. 1985. *Pricing the Priceless Child: The Changing Social Value of Children*. New York: Basic Books.

Questions for Critical Thinking

1. How do some of the inventive solutions by mothers who are poor to ensure children's access to resources, protect them from the harms of poverty and racism, and present themselves as fit parents challenge some of your assumptions about mothering?

2. How do economic inequalities and the lack of a sufficient social safety net in our society place additional burdens on mothers who are poor?

3. What policy changes in social institutions such as the economy or education would aid mothers who are poor? What would need to occur to bring about such changes?

ILLEGALITY AS A SOURCE OF SOLIDARITY AND TENSION IN LATINO FAMILIES

Leisy J. Abrego

The following article is based on extensive interviews with documented and undocumented Latino immigrants from El Salvador, Guatemala, and Mexico in Los Angeles over a ten-year period. In her analysis of these interviews, Leisy Abrego, a professor of Chicana and Chicano studies, illustrates that the status of illegal impacts all members of a family, even when only one person or a few people are categorized as undocumented or only temporarily protected. As the author notes, this can create tensions for people whose disadvantages are heightened by structural inequality as a result of immigration laws. Alternatively, the presence of a supportive social network can aid families in transforming illegal to a source of solidarity and strength.

I had known 19-year-old Mayra to be a confident, articulate young woman; she was thoughtful and warm in her demeanor, particularly during one-on-one conversations when her shyness usually dissipated.[1] It was surprising, therefore, to witness her sudden fidgeting and eye contact avoidance when we discussed her mother during the interview. Although Mayra was born in the United States and is, as a result, a U.S. citizen, the issue of immigrant legal status (as conferred upon individual migrants through U.S. immigration laws) made her nervous; her mother is an undocumented immigrant from Guatemala. As she explained:

> Talking about my mom is hard. It's like there's this whole cloud of, like, a whole heaviness [motions as though she is carrying weight on her shoulders and above her head], I don't know, of things that I was never allowed to say out loud. If she was ever late, if she wasn't back from church or from work right on time, we all worried. . . . Nobody said anything, but we were all

thinking it: what if she got caught? . . . That weight, it's just fear, I guess . . . it really sucks to grow up like that.

The deeply divisive and largely misinformed U.S. national debate about undocumented immigrants and immigration laws often masks the great complexity and diversity of legal statuses and their repercussions for Latino immigrants and their families. The discourse suggests that the exclusion and deportability associated with undocumented status affects only the 11.2 million undocumented immigrants in the country (Passel & Cohn, 2011). As the record-breaking number of deportations continues to make news, break families apart, and keep immigrants and their loved ones in fear, it becomes ever more clear that harshly restrictive immigration policies are causing violence against individuals and their entire families (Menjívar & Abrego, 2012). Experiences like Mayra's

Previously published in *JOLLAS (Journal of Latino/Latin American Studies)* 8.1 (2016): 5–21.

are proof of the uncontained anguish resulting from the current implementation of U.S. immigration policies. Even though she was born a U.S. citizen, Mayra experienced fear of detention and deportation—some of the gravest repercussions associated with undocumented status—in ways that powerfully affected several aspects of her life.

Despite being a U.S. citizen, Mayra grew up carrying the heavy weight of fear because the law's implementation would have had a direct impact on her, even though, from a legal perspective, she is not the target of these laws. Drawing on Mayra's and others' experiences and narratives, this article sheds light on some of the complexities of "illegality" as they play out within different configurations of Latino families. Having to negotiate these repercussions, families learn to live with tension or to develop strategies for mutual support. These experiences, moreover, have long-term consequences for family communication and well-being.

Illegality and Contemporary Latino Families in the United States

Illegality—the historically specific, socially, politically, and legally produced condition of immigrants' legal status and deportability (De Genova, 2002)—intimately and deeply impacts all immigrants. There is nothing inherent in the common understanding or practices associated with someone's undocumented status. Rather, there are historically specific conditions and cues that establish the term's meaning and its consequences in the lives of those categorized in a tenuous legal status at any given time. For example, there have been moments in this country's history when, in practical terms, undocumented status had little meaning (Ngai, 2004). Even immigrants who arrived in the 1970s in Los Angeles were able to obtain a driver's license and work without the intense fear of deportation that now permeates immigrant communities in the city (Abrego, 2014). Increasingly, over the last few decades and especially since the attacks of September 11, 2001, undocumented status, and illegality more broadly, have gained significance in the public eye (Golash-Boza, 2012; Hernández, 2008). Immigrants categorized as undocumented or temporarily protected have become the target of progressively more harsh laws and ever more hateful

speech, all of which work together to criminalize and dehumanize them and their families (Menjívar & Abrego, 2012), even when immigrants' behavior has not changed.

Arguably, Latinos are disproportionately affected. After 9/11, legal moves to criminalize undocumented immigrants were magnified and accelerated (Hernández, 2007, 2008). Programs such as 287(g) and Secure Communities were implemented to allow more communication between local authorities, the FBI, and Immigration and Customs Enforcement (ICE) agencies.[2] In practice, this has meant increased numbers of detentions and deportations, in part through sweeping workplace raids, but also because even routine traffic stops can quickly lead to ICE involvement and, ultimately, to the tearing apart of hundreds of thousands of families. In fact, in recent years the Department of Homeland Security reports that they have deported over 300,000 and closer to 400,000 immigrants annually.[3] The figures of those who are detained and deported are now, therefore, more likely to include the parents of U.S. citizen children. When parents are deported, children are often then placed in foster care with little regard for principles of family unity that presumably guide both immigration and child welfare policies (Wessler, 2011). These record numbers of deportations, moreover, are taking place alongside a wave of hateful speech and growing animosity against Latino immigrants (Chavez, 2008; Menjívar & Abrego, 2012), all of which inevitably affect families' well-being.

Mainstream media's visual representations and powerful public discourses work to dehumanize Latino immigrants—whether documented or undocumented (Chavez, 2001, 2008; McConnell, 2011). While making immigrants' contributions as workers and community members invisible, these images and discourses also make immigrants' very presence in the country hypervisible—but only through the lens of illegality. Although undocumented status has been and largely continues to be a matter of civil law. mainstream media images tend to portray undocumented immigrants as criminals. For example, one common visual used to discuss undocumented immigrants is the image of them being apprehended, handcuffed, and publicly treated in ways that presume they are dangerous criminals (Santa Ana, 2012).

In a battle against official statistics that confirm the majority of deported immigrants do not have criminal records (see, for example, National Community Advisory, 2011), these repeated images are unfortunately more convincing to a broad audience. Such persistently negative representations shape the general public's view, but also affect how immigrants and their families understand and experience illegality.

In this article, I heed the call of feminist social scientists to move beyond notions of familism associated with Latino families and instead underscore the role of social structures that delimit the experiences of diverse U.S. Latino groups (Alcalde, 2010; Landale & Oropesa, 2007; Zinn & Wells, 2003). In this tradition, I examine the repercussions for Latino families as they deal with issues associated with illegality during a historical moment that criminalizes and dehumanizes them merely for seeking survival. I am guided by the following questions: In such a harsh legal and political climate, how do Latino immigrant families experience illegality in their day-to-day lives? Moreover, how do individuals negotiate illegality when trying to fulfill their family roles? I explore some of the various ways that immigration laws affect Latino family dynamics, particularly as experienced in transnational, undocumented, and mixed-status families.

Latino Families: Transnational, Undocumented, and Mixed Status

Like other members of the working poor, Latino families dealing with various facets of illegality face notable barriers. Geographically, given undocumented workers' job prospects and legal limitations, most families relying on one or two undocumented parents end up in areas of dense poverty (Chavez, 1998). These communities are typically beset with low-performing schools, high rates of crime, and few opportunities for their residents. These realities, in turn, block families and their next generation from integrating positively and thriving in this country. How do various forms of illegality further mediate these experiences?

One experience of illegality among Latino immigrants is long-term separation as members of transnational families, in which core family members live across borders. Unable to survive in their countries—largely as a result of U.S.-funded wars and neoliberal policies, including free-trade agreements—parents opt to migrate to the United States in search of work to support their children from afar (Abrego, 2014; Dreby, 2010). The vast wage inequalities in the region make this a likely strategy. Once they arrive in the United States, however, immigration laws restrict their chances for family reunification, making for prolonged family separations—often at least a decade (Abrego, 2009). It is difficult to enumerate how many people live in these types of arrangements, but it is a notable proportion for groups from various countries throughout Latin America (Abrego, 2009; Dreby, 2010; Hondagneu-Sotelo & Avila, 1997; Pribilsky, 2004; Schmalzbauer, 2005). In El Salvador, for example, it is estimated that anywhere between 16 and 40 percent of children in various regions of the country are growing up without one or both parents due to migration (García, 2012; Martínez, 2006). For these families, illegality is likely to play out differently than for families forced apart through deportation or who live together in fear.

For Latino undocumented families, in which all or most members are undocumented, they are likely more conscious about illegality's role in their everyday life. It is estimated that there are about 500,000 undocumented children in the United States growing up in families with at least one undocumented parent (Taylor, Lopez, Passel, & Motel, 2011). An additional 4.5 million U.S. citizen children are growing up in mixed-status families in which at least one of their parents is undocumented. Significantly, this figure more than doubled between 2000 and 2011 (Taylor et al., 2011). Illegality is likely to play out in different ways for these families as well. As made clear in the introductory case of this article, U.S.-born citizens are not entirely protected from the consequences of anti-immigrant laws—particularly when their loved ones are undocumented. For mixed-status families who experience the deportation of one or more family members, illegality can mean forced separation, in very painful and difficult ways (Dreby, 2012; Human Rights Watch, 2007; Wessler, 2011). Importantly, even when they are not forced into separation through the deportation of one of their members, mixed-status and undocumented families are also likely to deal with and experience illegality in different ways (Menjívar & Abrego, 2012).

In this article, I examine the ways that illegality permeates family life for Latinos whose relatives include at least one undocumented immigrant. My point is to underscore that illegality affects not only those immigrants who are undocumented. Their families must also grapple with the impact of changing laws, their implementation, and perceptions of undocumented immigrants. The consequences of illegality can lead to various types of experiences for Latino families. Here I focus on the potential for tensions and solidarity as responses to illegality at the family level.

Methods

I draw on various research projects for this article. Between June 2004 and September 2006, I conducted 130 in-depth interviews with Salvadoran parents, children, and caregivers who are members of transnational families that have been separated continuously for 3 to 27 years. In the United States, I interviewed 47 parents (25 mothers and 22 fathers) who had been separated from their children for an average of 11 years. The single-session interviews lasted between one and three hours. I recruited participants in various locations and through different entry points mostly in the greater Los Angeles region. As part of the same project, I also conducted interviews with 83 relatives of migrants, mostly adolescent and young adult children, whom I recruited in public and private high schools and colleges in El Salvador. The single-session interviews lasted between 45 and 90 minutes. The average age of participants was 17 years old, with a range from 14–29. The average length of separation from their parents was nine years.

I also draw from a separate longitudinal study conducted between 2001–2006 that focused on access to higher education for Guatemalan, Mexican, and Salvadoran undocumented high school and college students in Los Angeles. This project consisted of 43 interviews with 27 informants, some of whom I interviewed a total of three times.[4] In the first round, from July to November 2001, I conducted 12 interviews with undocumented youth. I located all of the respondents at community-based organizations. About half participated in an immigrant rights' youth organization while the rest were enrolled in an art class for school credit. In the second round, from November 2002–January 2003, I re-interviewed eight of the original respondents, all of whom were still undocumented. The third round of interviews took place between December 2005 and June 2006. In this last round, I also conducted interviews with 15 more undocumented students who were attending various colleges and universities throughout California.[5]

The interview data for all phases of each project were heavily supplemented with participant observation conducted on a regular basis over the course of several years at community organizations and in numerous meetings and events. From 2001–2010, I gained access to strikingly similar stories of many more students, parents, and community members in these interactions. Based on the interviewees' narratives and participant observation notes from my ongoing work with immigrant rights' organizations, the article draws on Latina and Latino immigrants' and their children's voices to highlight some patterns that demonstrate the effects of illegality in their lives, whether or not they are undocumented.

Latino Families Negotiating Illegality

My main argument is that all members of Latino families with one or multiple immigrants who are undocumented or only temporarily protected must negotiate the extensive effects of illegality in their lives. How they experience and cope with illegality, however, will vary depending on their resources and local context. Whether neighborhoods and communities are supportive or hostile toward immigrants mediates families' ability to negotiate illegality and its vast consequences. Even though some families include U.S. citizens and legal permanent residents, the narratives of multiple family members reveal the deep pressures and long-term consequences of illegality in all their members' lives.

Transnational Families

Transnational families may be constituted in a number of different ways. Here I focus on families in which parents migrated to support their children who remain in the home country. In these cases female relatives—mothers, grandmothers, aunts, or older sisters—typically care for children (Dreby, 2010; Schmalzbauer, 2005). Parents work in the United States to send remittances to families who often rely solely on these monies to survive. Each member of the family, then, experiences illegality differently.

Unauthorized migrant parents feel the brunt of the criminalization and exclusion associated with illegality beginning from the moment they leave home. The journey north can be a brutal experience that communicates to the migrants they are not welcome and not valued as human beings (Amnesty International, 2010; Martínez 2010). If they reach the United States, they hope never to go through that process again, nor to put their children through such horrors. Instead, the safest option is to stay separated across borders indefinitely (Abrego, 2014).

Once in the United States, life continues to be difficult if immigrant parents are undocumented or only temporarily protected (Abrego, 2011; Abrego & Menjívar, 2011). Limited work opportunities and widespread forms of exploitation in labor sectors that hire undocumented immigrants result in prolonged separations also because parents rarely earn enough money to help their families thrive back in the home countries (Dreby, 2010). Unable to reach their financial goals, even when they work multiple jobs and overtime, immigrant parents experience illegality as frustration and fear of deportation.

Meanwhile, in the home countries, caregivers and children suffer the migrants' illegality from afar. Spouses, mothers, and siblings of migrants are pained in watching the news and knowing of the great likelihood of violence against their loved ones while en route. As one elderly mother of a migrant told me:

> No, look, I really suffered. She's my daughter and I didn't want her to ever suffer any pain. And it's that thing of wanting to watch the news because she wouldn't call, but then you see so many ugly things on television that sometimes I would say, maybe it's better not to watch anything. No, that whole time was just anguish. I wouldn't even sleep those 15 days. That was really terrible.

The inability to do anything, even to remain informed about their loved ones' whereabouts and well-being, is very challenging for relatives. In this example, the journey took two weeks, while in others, it may take one or several months. As the numbers of kidnappings and abuse of migrants continue to escalate (Amnesty International, 2010; Martínez 2010), this part of the experience for transnational families is also increasingly stressful.

When migrants make it to the United States and remain apart from their families for years, their relatives continue to grapple with the consequences of illegality—even if they do not always locate the source of their struggles within immigration laws and their implementation. Much of the tension for transnational families relying on undocumented or only temporarily protected migrants comes from the limited and rare sums of money remitted. Undocumented immigrants are especially likely to be employed in sectors that are dangerous and exploitative (Holmes, 2007; Milkman, González, & Narro, 2010; Walter, Bourgois, & Loinaz, 2004). For transnational families, this results in limited remittances and little improvement in their lives. Undocumented fathers may be prone to injuries that prevent them from fulfilling their financial goals. I met Mauricio, an undocumented immigrant father, at a day labor site. After suffering an injury at his previous job, he was having trouble finding a job. He had not remitted to his children in a few months and preferred not to call them because he was embarrassed that he was not living up to his promise of sending them money regularly:

> You see that without papers it is very difficult to be hired just anywhere. So my brother-in-law found me a job [at a warehouse]. That is hard work because they don't care if one is tired, if one needs to rest, or if [the weather is] too hot or too cold. And so, since they didn't even let us rest, I messed up my back and when I told them, they pretended not to hear me, they didn't do anything. I kept complaining and in the end they told me that if I couldn't do the work anymore, I should look for another job because they needed someone who could stay on schedule. And after that I still had to fight with them to get my last paycheck because they were saying that I worked too slowly. Up until now I still can't carry anything too heavy, so I haven't been able to find a steady job.

Because of his undocumented status, Mauricio was afraid to apply for worker's compensation or to denounce the employer who fired him when he complained of back pain. Since losing that job, he spent most of his time at a day labor site, trying to get temporary, short-term jobs. Day labor, however, is unstable employment that does not generate sufficient wages to support his family in El Salvador (cf. Valenzuela Jr., 2002). To further exacerbate the situation, rather than blaming the exploitation made possible by strict immigration laws, parents accept responsibility and feel ashamed. As a result, relatives experience illegality's consequences through continued poverty and increased tension when mothers and fathers cannot meet their parental expectations.

Constantly bombarded by negative images of people like themselves and overcome with uncertainty and lack of solidarity in so many facets of their lives, undocumented immigrant parents can internalize illegality as a sense of worthlessness and helplessness. Mauricio describes how he has internalized illegality:

> One comes here thinking that life will be better . . . but without papers, one's life is not worth much. Look at me; I have always been a hard worker . . . but I messed up my back working, carrying heavy things without any protection. . . . What doctor is going to help me if I can't pay? . . . Who's going to hire me now? How will I support my family?

For Mauricio, whose fear of deportation prevents him from applying for workers' compensation, illegality means that he is excluded from basic rights and dignity. Unable to fulfill his role as a father and provider for his family in El Salvador, Mauricio experiences illegality as a personal devaluation when he proclaims that his life is "not worth much." Despite his initially positive migration goals, the sense of being less than a person now pervades him. Moreover, similar situations for undocumented parents in transnational families are especially difficult because the distance across borders further hampers communication between them and their loved ones.

Undocumented immigrants are limited with respect to the kinds of jobs and working conditions they can access. Their unprotected status makes them vulnerable to unscrupulous employers who pay them low wages and withhold health benefits and other basic, legally mandated provisions, such as bathroom breaks, safety training, and protective gear when necessary for the job. Lacking legal recourse, undocumented immigrants can easily fall prey to such dishonest employers and are therefore greatly disadvantaged.

Understanding only that the separation was supposed to lead to financial stability, when this expectation is unmet, children in transnational families can become hurt, confused, and resentful (Abrego, 2009; Menjívar & Abrego, 2009). Sixteen-year-old Lucía in El Salvador, for example, shared her account of how much she had suffered through her mother's absence. Lucía's mother is undocumented, lives in Los Angeles, and, after eight years, has been remitting only about $50 per month due to her limited wages as a nanny. When I asked Lucía what had been the most difficult aspect of being a member of a transnational family, she paused, cried, and shared this thoughtful response:

> You're going to think I'm crazy, but when I was little, I would hear people say that McDonald's was American food so whenever we went downtown by that McDonald's, I would try to peer inside, just look inside the window for as long as I could to see if I could see my mother there. . . . [Crying] Yes, my life has been pure suffering without her. One never really understands why a mother would abandon you, why she would leave you if nothing changes. Nothing is better. Everything is worse.

The severity of Lucía's suffering is based on the sense of abandonment she feels because she has little to show for the family sacrifice of separation. Her undocumented mother, who like other undocumented immigrants is probably hard-pressed to find better employment, remits consistently but insufficiently. Being undocumented, moreover, prevents Lucía's mother from visiting her daughter because doing so would require a dangerous journey to re-enter the United States. As a result, eight years have gone by for Lucía and her mother without personal interactions, further adding tension to their family dynamics.

Importantly, illegality also intersects with gendered parental expectations to further shape the experiences of transnational families. Fathers, who are expected to be economic providers, can minimize tensions when they send sufficient remittances. Mothers, on the other hand, are held to higher expectations of caring, even from afar, and even if they manage to send sufficient remittances (Abrego, 2009; Abrego & Menjívar, 2011). For transnational families relying on undocumented mothers, illegality can have extensively painful and difficult consequences. Unable to fulfill the gendered expectations that require them to care for their children intensively and on a daily basis, transnational mothers live with great sadness, guilt, and deprivation (Miranda, Siddique, Der-Martirosian, & Belin, 2005; Parreñas, 2001, 2005; Pratt, 2012). Such was the case for Esperanza. When I interviewed her, she recalled the hardships she underwent to ensure her family's economic well-being in El Salvador:

> I've always sent $300 [monthly] to my mother and I would get paid $100 weekly [working as a live-in nanny]. I would end up with $90 because I also had to pay the fee to wire the money. . . . It was horrible. . . . Each week I would buy a dozen ramen noodle soups that I don't even want to see anymore, really, . . . so my food was the ramen noodle soup. But I was the happiest woman in the world because my daughter had something to eat!

Like Esperanza, several undocumented mothers in transnational families shared that they had greatly sacrificed themselves and sometimes increased their vulnerability just to be able to remit more money to their children. In the face of great disadvantages as undocumented immigrants, these mothers put themselves on the line to try to attain greater stability for their children. Illegality for them, therefore, meant greater personal risk and deprivation.

For transnational families, more broadly, the consequences of illegality are mostly present through increased tension. Parents suffer the brunt of physical risk and exploitation, but their children and other relatives in the home country experience illegality as stress, poverty, and abandonment. Nonmigrant relatives, moreover, often do not see the source of their suffering in the consequences of illegality. Instead, they blame parents who have not fulfilled their promises and who have been away for too many years.

Undocumented Families

Undocumented families, with all members living together in the United States, are not in the midst of family separation, though many likely spent some time apart, migrating in stages (Suárez-Orozco, Todorova, & Louie, 2002). Illegality, however, plays out differently and in complicated ways for undocumented families. As with transnational families, illegality intersects with gender and other categories to shape individuals' and families' experiences. I now focus on intergenerational relations between members of undocumented families.

Illegality's consequences can create tension and add burdens for undocumented families whose members are already structurally vulnerable. Beyond the usual challenges of communicating and working together across generations, undocumented parents and children may first have to reestablish a family relationship in the likely case they were separated and reunited after years apart (Suárez-Orozco, Bang, & Kim, 2010). Indeed, several undocumented youth mentioned difficult transitions with parents after joining them in the United States. Mario, who came from Guatemala at age six, was 16 when I met him. He still dealt with painful unresolved issues with his father who had migrated when Mario was only a few months old:

> It's not a good feeling. I mean, I knew I had a father, but it was just, he wasn't there. . . . It's still not easy getting along with my dad. We disagree a lot. . . . I was just thinking too highly of my dad, because I never knew him, you know. Things are just not how I figured. . . . I've never been really attached to my dad because of that reason. . . . I guess he expected me to, you know, be like, "Wow, my dad" [in dreamy tone]. But it was just like, how could I show that if he wasn't there? You know?

As Mario explains, being apart from parents over several years can lead to the development of idealized and unrealistic expectations. It is difficult to establish loving bonds and smooth communication when both parents and children expect too much from each other following a painful separation. These experiences of step-migration are especially common among families who travel and live in the United States without authorization (Suárez-Orozco et al., 2010).

Even short separations can be difficult for young children. Luis, whose parents migrated from Mexico to the United States during his early childhood spent only a few months with his grandmother before his own migration at the age of four. He was separated from his father for years, but was apart from his mother for only a few months. Still, in his late teens Luis recalls that through much of his childhood, he felt uneasy about his relationship with his mother:

> Those three months made a huge difference. I didn't remember her. It felt like she wasn't my mom. You know what I mean? It felt like she was someone else. And it was only three months. I remember like when I used to get mad at her, if I was in trouble and she was telling me what to do, in my mind I was like, "What if she's not my mom? What if she's another person?" . . . Yeah, it's just hard. I mean, that's your logic at that age.

Even short separations can confuse children and make them question their parents' authority. As separations are prolonged due to immigrant parents' undocumented status, reunifications are likely to involve difficult transitions that further complicate family dynamics (Suárez-Orozco et al., 2002).

Another challenge for undocumented families is rooted in the vastly different experiences and interpretations of illegality across generations (Abrego, 2011). First-generation immigrants who are usually the parents in these families feel responsible for choosing to migrate, remember clearly the horrific details of the migration journey, and deal with exploitative working conditions on a daily basis. For this generation, illegality is mainly about exclusion from society and great fear of deportation. The 1.5 generation undocumented immigrants, who are usually the children in undocumented families, often remember less about the journey; feel they had little choice in migrating; and enjoy greater levels of membership in U.S. society where they have spent most of their lives (Abrego, 2011). As they learn more details about their status, however, they experience their own forms of exclusion (Abrego, 2008; Gonzales, 2011; Gonzales & Chavez, 2012).

The exclusion associated with illegality can mean different things for various members of undocumented families. For parents, exclusion is most prominent when they are unable to perform the tasks—often gendered—that are expected of them. Mothers often speak of their great worry over their children's well-being if they were to be deported, while fathers feel their lives are worthless if they are unable to access rights, health care, and work to provide for their families. This sense of worthlessness and the fear that pervades undocumented parents are very different from what undocumented children in these families describe as their experience of illegality.

Undocumented immigrants who grow up in the United States and are socialized through schools are more likely to experience illegality as a matter of stigma (Abrego, 2008, 2011). For example, many are embarrassed that they cannot drive a car, go out on dates, go clubbing, or travel abroad like the rest of their peers (see also Gonzales, 2011). Unlike their undocumented parents, moreover, undocumented youth have adapted socially to U.S. social norms and can more easily fit in. This allows them to participate in activities their parents consider too risky, thereby adding tensions to family dynamics when parents disapprove of their children's behavior. This can be frustrating for children because they consider such behavior would, in any other legal context, be perfectly acceptable for someone their age.

Jovani, a 16-year-old undocumented Guatemalan high school student, expressed great resentment toward his parents. His mother, who is also an undocumented immigrant, volunteers at his school and tries to keep an eye on him constantly to keep him out of trouble. Meanwhile, he just wants to get a part-time job and be able to drive like all his friends, but his mother's adamant opposition is challenging for Jovani:

> When I want to get a job, I can't. I want to drive, but I can't. . . . So, most of the time, I just don't think about it, but I mean, there's sometimes when it crosses your mind, you know, you gotta get a job, you want to work, you want to have money. . . . So yeah, it's kind of hard for me. . . . I get mad because my parents brought me. I didn't tell them to bring me, but I get punished for it, for not having the papers.

The consequences of illegality—being excluded from otherwise typical experiences for people his age—deeply frustrate Jovani. But rather than blaming the legal system that prevents him and his family from thriving, he blames his parents. Therefore, despite his mother's best efforts to keep him focused on being a successful student, Jovani rebels. When I met him, he was in danger of failing most of his classes in his second attempt at junior year in high school.

To further complicate intergenerational relations in undocumented families, illegality infused by stigma, as undocumented youth experience it, allows them to develop personal discourses that help them limit the exclusion they feel. For example, undocumented youth try to justify their presence in the country by distancing themselves from negative connotations of illegality. In doing so, they underscore that their liminal status differs from the marginalized and criminalized status of their parents' generation. Most notably, they defend themselves by emphasizing they did not actively choose to come to the United States. Stellar students are especially effective when they can draw on their educational achievements to defend their honor as good people and good citizens of this country. As Isabel states: "The fact that we're students gives us credibility and, in their [anti-immigrant activists] eyes, that's better." This strategy is not available to the more marginalized and publicly targeted undocumented workers and parents in these families and may add greater tension to family dynamics.

Exclusion leads to several other associated experiences of illegality for undocumented immigrants. As Norma, a Mexican first-generation, undocumented immigrant mother, sums it up, "We are here and we know this is not our country. They don't want us here, so you have to be careful. Always be careful." In this experience of illegality, immigrants are made to feel constantly insecure, unaware of who they can trust, and unable to rely even on institutions that should represent safety for all. In such a context, navigating social relationships can be difficult. As Agustín, a first-generation Salvadoran immigrant, shares:

> It just feels like you don't know who you can trust. I tell people that I don't have papers. I feel like I'm not doing anything wrong. I'm not a criminal. But my wife gets mad at me. She tells me to be careful because you never know who could call the migra on you. But I feel like I have nothing to hide.

Most undocumented immigrants feel deeply disconnected from descriptions of themselves as criminals. They migrated in search of work for the sake of their families' survival. But in trying to counter the criminalization of undocumented status, it is difficult to know who they can trust. In this way, illegality and the cloud of distrust around undocumented status cause tension and complicate family dynamics when relatives have different approaches to handling illegality's repercussions in their lives.

Importantly, there are also spaces to build communication and solidarity among members of undocumented families. The following exemplifies this ability to work together to make claims for inclusion in this country. Adela, the undocumented mother of undocumented students who organized a press conference to support the DREAM Act,[6] was one of a few older adults holding signs and standing in support of the event. After 14 years of living in the United States, this was the first time she had participated in such a public and political act and she was nervous, but her children had convinced her to be there. As with undocumented immigrants generally and for various reasons, parents who arrived in the country as adults are less vocal politically than their children's generation (Abrego, 2011). These different forms of socialization have the potential to create tensions, but can also generate possibilities for communication, as evident in the notes from my conversation with Adela that day.

Adela told me she had never been involved in organizations for immigrant rights. She came from Mexico 14 years ago, but she was dedicated to working and taking care of her kids. The thought of going out to protest or draw attention to herself never crossed her mind. But as her kids got older and the oldest went on to college, she realized how much it hurt them to not have papers. When she came from Mexico, she knew she would have to put up with not having papers and it might mean she could only get hard jobs, but she didn't know it would affect her kids this way—she had no idea—and all she wants is for them to achieve their dreams. It has been painful to watch them struggle just to be able to afford college. Both of her children are great students and are now at a community college. They have been participating in marches and meetings at this organization for a few years now, since high school, and they always invite her to come, but she was always too scared. This year, she finally went to one event and liked what she heard. All she wants to do is support her kids, and now she's committed to being present for them at these rallies and events because she knows how much it means to them.

Her children's persistent requests and her own understanding of how illegality was affecting them gave Adela the courage to become politically engaged. In general, because children of immigrants adapt to U.S. society at a faster pace than their parents, it is often the case that they are socialized politically in school and other spaces and they then socialize their parents (Bloemraad & Trost, 2008). This is becoming increasingly evident even in the immigrant rights' movement—particularly among the most vocal and visible sector at a national level.[7] For these undocumented families then, intergenerational communication may also lead to greater political participation.

Families that include multiple generations of undocumented immigrants experience the consequences of illegality in various ways. Many of these families are likely to have migrated in steps, thereby reuniting after some time apart. In these cases, even the negotiation of a family relationship can be difficult. And when these families overcome the challenges of reunification, the different generational experiences of illegality can also lead to tension when parents, spouses, and children disagree about how to approach their lives and their actions in this country. Finally, the shared experience of illegality, even though it plays out differently in their lives, can also lead to greater solidarity among undocumented members of families.

Mixed-Status Families

Mixed-status families include members with multiple statuses. They share many of the same challenges and experiences of illegality as undocumented families, but also have unique tensions and possibilities as a result of legal internal stratification of their members. Illegality can play out in numerous ways, partly depending on the role of the undocumented persons and their relationships to others. For example, illegality will have different repercussions in a family that includes an undocumented parent and U.S. citizen children versus a family that includes undocumented parents and siblings with various statuses.

Beginning in the late 2000s, journalists and researchers have shed light on the experiences of mixed-status families that include U.S. citizen children and their undocumented parents. One of the most compelling cases is that of Encarnación Bail Romero, a Guatemalan immigrant to the United States (Brané, 2011; Thompson, 2009). In 2007, while working at a poultry plant in Missouri, immigration officials detained Bail Romero in a workplace raid. Her son Carlos, who was then only six months old, spent some time with different caretakers, until a couple approached her about adopting him. She was adamantly against this option, but helpless to act from a detention center in another state. Her lawyer, who explained the situation to her only in English (a language she did not understand), failed to protect her. Unable to leave detention, she later learned that a judge used her absence in court for a hearing about Carlos's future as evidence of abandonment. The judge terminated her parental rights and Carlos was adopted. Although Ms. Bail spent many years fighting to regain custody of her son, the laws stood against her. As unjust and bizarre as this story may sound, it reflects an increasingly common experience today: the legal system denies undocumented immigrants the same parental rights guaranteed to other parents.

In fact, among the 4.5 million U.S. citizen children growing up in mixed-status families, the chances of undocumented parents being deported have increased considerably over the last decade. With greater communication between local law enforcement and federal immigration agencies, undocumented parents caught during a routine traffic stop, for example, can be detained and deported—for having a broken taillight or driving without a license (Hagan, Eschbach, & Rodríguez, 2008; Hagan, Rodriguez, & Castro, 2011). By 2011, among the record number of deportees, 22 percent were parents of U.S. citizen children (Wessler, 2011). Parents may be detained for simply driving between home and work or dropping off or picking up their kids at school. Such increased targeting adds great stress for families.

Indeed, this sense of insecurity spreads through entire families, whether or not all members are undocumented (Dreby, 2012; Rodriguez & Hagan, 2004; Suárez-Orozco, Yoshikawa, Teranishi, & Suárez-Orozco, 2011; Yoshikawa, 2011). This is evident in the narratives of children of immigrants who grew up with one or two undocumented parents. In Southern California, just over an hour outside of Los Angeles, 20-year-old Nayeli grew up in the outskirts of an affluent city where the majority of inhabitants are white. Throughout her childhood, Nayeli's mother, who is a documented Mexican immigrant, reminded her and her siblings about the need to keep their father's undocumented status a secret. The vocal anti-immigrant groups in the area instilled great fear in Nayeli, and she grew up painfully aware of her family's vulnerability in the face of the consequences of illegality. When asked what the hardest part of the situation had been, she described how she experiences illegality at a personal level: "The silence . . . when it comes to talking about it with people that I trust, it's hard just to even talk about it. It's hard for me to even admit that my father is undocumented. I've kept it a secret for so long, and I feel like it's my secret and I don't want to tell people about it. It's the way I internalize it. We do it to protect my dad."

Nayeli's burden was heavy and constant; her neighbors' hostility exacerbated the potential for harm against her father if her family's secret were revealed. Emotionally, this crushed Nayeli, who cried throughout the interview: "Just my dad, period, is an emotional subject for me. . . . If he took long to get home from work, I feared that he was caught. It's a scary feeling." Her relationship with her father was damaged when the secret prevented them from having open conversations about such an important topic. And to this day, as a young adult, she has difficulty discussing anything related to her father and her childhood generally because the cloud of illegality has been so deeply hurtful.

Not all mixed-status families with undocumented parents have the same experience. In another part of Los Angeles, 20-year-old Aminta, a U.S.-born child with an undocumented Guatemalan father, explains how illegality affected her father and her family:

> I think when I was a kid I didn't really understand it. But now as an adult, I feel my dad was frustrated and tired with his job and that he wanted to give us more, but he couldn't. Sometimes my dad seemed very quiet and sad. . . . My mom was the emotional backbone, I

think. She always talked about the importance of family, something we had. I'm proud of my parents. They worked hard and that has made me work hard because I know I have something many people wish they had. And one day, hopefully, I can have the money to get a lawyer that will help my dad get his citizenship status. It just hurts because my dad went almost all his life living through economic challenges.

Aminta's family experienced illegality largely as an economic barrier that limited her father's ability to provide for his family. She suggests that his inability to live up to this gendered expectation weighed heavily on him as he seemed "frustrated," "very quiet and sad," much of the time. This weight can easily extend to the rest of the family. It was her mother's ability to live up to her gendered expectation as the "emotional backbone" of the family that held the family together and allowed them to work around the effects of illegality in their lives.

Aminta's experience in a mixed-status family stands in stark contrast to that of Nayeli. Although both had one undocumented parent and both were U.S. citizens by birth, their different communities mediate how their families experience illegality. While Nayeli grew up in an anti-immigrant community, Aminta's family has lived for decades in the same working class neighborhood where mixed status and undocumented families are common enough to make them seem close to the norm. Aminta, therefore, feels comfortable talking about her experiences and discussing how illegality has shaped her family's participation in the community: "It hasn't been easy, but we feel comfortable in our community. We know we're not the only family who is going through challenges and it feels like we are supportive of each other. My family is very close. We all play an important role. We each do something and the challenges seem less that way."

In Aminta's case, illegality added extra challenges to their lives, but her community's ability to integrate mixed-status families was also helpful. Moreover, illegality and the tenuous status of her father's situation led her family to find ways to increase their solidarity with one another by sharing responsibilities and bringing the family closer together.

Beyond intergenerational challenges, mixed-status families also experience other consequences of illegality when siblings do not share the same legal status. Often there is tension and resentment when U.S. citizen children have access to more resources and opportunities than their undocumented or temporarily protected siblings. Such was the case for Mario, whose younger brother was born in the United States, making him the only member of the family with U.S. citizenship. In the following excerpt, Mario describes resentments resulting from the family's mixed statuses:

> Well, basically, I don't have medical insurance. My younger brother, whenever he's sick, they always take him to the hospital, and stuff like that, because the government pays for him. . . . My mom takes him to the dentist yearly, to the doctor, you know, but if I feel really sick, like I have to be dying to go to the hospital. But then, you know, my brother, he feels a stomach-ache—"let's go to the hospital."

Stratified access to health care means that parents have to provide what seems like preferential treatment for some children owing to their legal status. Despite understanding that his brother had legal access to more resources, Mario harbored resentment toward his brother and his mother for what he experienced as limited concern for his well-being.

Furthermore, because immigration laws change and people move between statuses as they become eligible, families may experience illegality differently at different stages. Andrés, a 21-year-old member of a Mexican mixed-status family, was granted legal residency only a month before high school graduation; he was completing his third year of college when I interviewed him. He reflects on how being undocumented shaped his older brother's experience:

> I feel bad for him. He worked even harder than I did in high school, and he should've been graduating from college by now. He even got better grades than me, but just because of his papers he can't go.

LA: What is he doing now?

> He works at a warehouse, packing and unpacking things from a truck all day. It makes me feel really bad, guilty because he deserves it as much as I do, but I'm the only one who gets to go [to college].

The way that families experience illegality, therefore, also depends on when statuses shift and how these shifts affect individuals. In this case, Andrés' older brother aged out of a chance to get legal permanent residency, leaving only Andrés to benefit from the change in status. Consequently, illegality played out as guilt for Andrés, who qualified for financial aid and other privileges that continued to be out of reach for his brother.

Among mixed-status families, however, there is sometimes also the opportunity to share rights and protections of one or multiple members with those who have more tenuous legal statuses. For example, Alisa, a 19-year-old Guatemalan undocumented college student, is thankful that her entire family benefits from the privileges of her sisters who are U.S. citizens. As citizens, they are eligible for government assistance, including public housing that is more spacious than what the family (all the rest of whom are undocumented) could otherwise afford:

> We moved over here because of the twins. I have two smaller twin sisters, they were born here, but when they were five months old, they got epilepsy, both of them, so it damaged their brain. . . . because of them we moved over here because of the housing. We used to live in a smaller apartment so they gave us a larger apartment for them, because of them, so they could have more room to walk around and stuff.

Although her younger sisters' developmental disabilities have taken a physical and emotional toll on the family, Alisa is grateful that as U.S. citizens, they have access to health care and housing. She is aware of the benefits the entire family receives as a result of the twins' legal status. In this case, the consequences of illegality for a mixed-status family are mediated by the benefits of more spacious housing accorded to the U.S. citizens in the family.

The consequences of illegality in mixed-status families are multiple and varied, depending on the status of each family member and their role in the family. When parents are undocumented, this can lead to limited parental rights and fear of accessing resources for their children, even when children have legal rights to various benefits (Menjívar, 2006; Menjívar & Abrego, 2009; Suárez-Orozco et al., 2011; Yoshikawa, 2011). Illegality, moreover, can weigh heavily on all members of these families, even those who are U.S. citizens by birth or naturalization.

Particularly with internal stratification of resources, children can blame each other and develop resentment, but they may also recognize when they benefit from resources given more freely to U.S. citizens in their families. Overall, mixed-status families' experiences of illegality are further mediated by local contexts—whether communities are inclusive or exclusive of immigrants more broadly—and shifts in statuses across time and at different stages in their lives. With these changes, families learn to navigate tensions and solidarity.

Conclusion

Despite the common assumption that immigration laws target only undocumented immigrants, illegality—the historically specific, socially, politically, and legally produced condition of immigrants' legal status and deportability—intimately and deeply impacts a larger proportion of Latinos. Illegality's repercussions are especially present in family dynamics and experiences—forcing parents and children to live across borders over a prolonged period; multiplying families' vulnerability when they are all undocumented and residing together; or complicating family relationships when only one or a few members are in tenuous statuses, but they reside with those who have more rights and protections.

In this article, I examine how illegality encompasses all members of a family, even when only one person is categorized as undocumented. Unsurprisingly, I find that illegality can create tension for people whose disadvantages are heightened by structural limitations related to immigration laws. On the other hand, illegality can be a source of solidarity and strength when families live in welcoming communities. Based on notions of family and solidarity, some are able to pool resources to help the undocumented member(s) of their families. When they have the right context and resources, this strengthens the family, even in the face of illegality's increased barriers and burdens.

Whether families live apart or together, illegality contextualizes their day-to-day lives and long-term relationships. It limits parents' authority while adding responsibilities for parents and children. Immigrant mothers, for example, experience the violence of illegality when they are unable to care for their children as they would like and as is socially expected of them (Abrego & Menjívar, 2011), while immigrant fathers are likely to be blocked from opportunities to provide for their children. This means that children have to carry part of the burden—sometimes financially, often emotionally—to help the family survive despite the limitations. Illegality, moreover, prevents all parents from accessing social services and other resources to help their children achieve optimal well-being.

When combined, all of illegality's repercussions undermine families' efforts to move out of poverty. Like parents in other working poor families, undocumented parents often work in low-paying, unstable jobs for long periods of time. And like other children who grow up in poverty (documented and undocumented), children of undocumented immigrants also face high levels of danger and few educational opportunities. Furthermore, being undocumented also increases the likelihood that families will lack health insurance (Fortuny, Capps, & Passel, 2007) and lowers their chances of accessing bank accounts and other financial services. Their parents' undocumented status is also detrimental to children in numerous, sometimes indirect ways. For example, due to fear of deportation, such families are less likely to apply for food-stamp benefits, even though their children may be eligible. They may be afraid to go into a government agency to apply for their children's health care benefits. Children in these families are thus less likely to seek the services they need (Abrego & Menjívar, 2011). In the longer term, undocumented status keeps families in the shadows, avoiding many of the institutions that have traditionally benefited immigrant families (Menjívar, 2006).

Despite these structural and very real challenges, illegality's consequences are also mediated by the demographics and political nature of their local context. People living in communities with a concentration of undocumented immigrants and mixed-status families are more likely to develop networks and access information that can mitigate the fear and insecurity so often associated with illegality. In cases where members of mixed-status communities are able to develop solidarity, they may be able to create safety nets for children and the most vulnerable members among them. However, in communities where few undocumented immigrants are known to reside and where anti-immigration advocates feel emboldened, immigrants and their families are likely to experience illegality as extreme vulnerability that can penetrate even their most intimate relationships.

In many respects, undocumented immigrants and their families are already important members of U.S. society—even if only on the lower rungs of the economic ladder. They contribute to our economy, children are educated in our schools, and all family members envision their futures here. However, these families currently have no available structural paths out of poverty. In a cruel twist, parents' efforts to secure their families' survival by migrating are met with legal obstacles. Current policies restrict their ability to thrive in this country and, for transnational families, to pull children out of poverty in the home countries as well. Without full legal rights, these families are barred from the very mechanisms that have ensured high levels of economic and social mobility to other immigrants throughout U.S. history (Abrego, 2006; Menjívar & Abrego, 2012). Legalization, therefore, is necessary to give Latino families a chance at success in this country.

Notes

1. The names of individual respondents, locations, and organizations have been disguised to preserve anonymity.
2. See Menjívar and Kanstroom 2013 for details on 287(g) and Secure Communities programs.
3. See Table 38 of the Department of Homeland Security's Yearbook of Immigration Statistics: 2010, retrieved from http://www.dhs.gov/files/statistics/publications/YrBk10En.shtm, for a breakdown of the number of deportees with and without histories of criminal offenses.
4. Twelve informants form the basis of the longitudinal part of the study. The remaining 15 participants were recruited only for the interviews that took place in the last two rounds of interviews.
5. For more detailed information about my role as the researcher in these projects, see Abrego, 2009 and Abrego, 2014.
6. The Development, Relief, and Education for Alien Minors (DREAM) Act (S. 2075, H.R. 5131) is a bipartisan piece of legislation that would provide undocumented students who have grown up in the United States with a pathway to legal permanent residency. It has been unsuccessfully introduced multiple times in the U.S. Congress.
7. See, for example, http://immigrantyouthcoalition.org/undocumented-families-come-out-of-the-shadows/

References

Abrego, L. J. (2006). "I can't go to college because I don't have papers": Incorporation patterns of Latino undocumented youth. *Latino Studies*, 4(3), 212–31. DOI:10.1057/palgrave.1st.8600200

Abrego, L. J. (2008). Legitimacy, social identity, and the mobilization of law: The effects of Assembly Bill 540 on undocumented students in California. *Law & Social Inquiry*, 33(3), 709–34. DOI: 10.1111/j.1747-4469.2008.00119.x

Abrego, L. J. (2009). Economic well-being in Salvadoran transnational families: How gender affects remittance practices. *Journal of Marriage and Family*, 71, 1070–85. DOI: 10.1111/j.1741-3737.2009.00653.x

Abrego, L. J. (2011). Legal consciousness of undocumented Latinos: Fear and stigma as barriers to claims making for first and 1.5 generation immigrants. *Law & Society Review*, 45(2), 337–70. DOI: 10.1111/j.1540-5893.2011.00435.x

Abrego, L. J. (2014). *Sacrificing families: Navigating laws, labor, and love across borders*. Stanford, CA: Stanford University Press.

Abrego, L. J., & Menjívar, C. (2011). Immigrant Latina mothers as targets of legal violence. *International Journal of Sociology of the Family*, 37(1), 9–26.

Alcalde, M. C. (2010). Violence across borders: Familism, hegemonic masculinity, and self-sacrificing femininity in the lives of Mexican and Peruvian migrants. *Latino Studies*, 8(1), 48–68. DOI:10.1057/lst.2009.44

Amnesty International. (2010). "Invisible victims: Migrants on the move in Mexico." Report published by Amnesty International Publications. London, UK.

Bloemraad, I., & Trost, C. (2008). It's a family affair: Intergenerational mobilization in the Spring 2006 protests. *American Behavioral Scientist*, 52(4), 507–32. DOI: 10.1177/0002764208324604

Brané, M. (2011). Delayed justice for Guatemalan mother Encarnación Bail Romero. Retrieved from http://www.huffingtonpost.com/michelle-bran/delayed-justice-for-guate_b_817191.html

Chavez, L. R. (1998). *Shadowed lives: Undocumented immigrants in American society* (2nd ed.). Fort Worth, TX: Harcourt Brace.

Chavez, L. R. (2001). *Covering immigration: Popular images and the politics of the nation.* Berkeley: University of California Press.

Chavez, L. R. (2008). *The Latino threat: Constructing immigrants, citizens, and the nation.* Palo Alto, CA: Stanford University Press.

De Genova, N. P. (2002). Migrant "illegality" and deportability in everyday life. *Annual Review of Anthropology,* 31, 419–47. DOI: 10.1146/annurev.anthro.31.040402.085432

Dreby, J. (2010). *Divided by borders: Mexican migrants and their children.* Berkeley: University of California Press.

Dreby, J. (2012). The burden of deportation on children in Mexican immigrant families. *Journal of Marriage and Family,* 74, 829–45. DOI: 10.1111/j.1741-3737.2012.00989.x

Fortuny, K., Capps, R., & Passel, J. (2007). *The characteristics of unauthorized immigrants in California, Los Angeles County, and the United States.* Washington, DC: The Urban Institute.

García, J. J. (2012, January). *20th anniversary of El Salvador's peace accords and implications for transnational development and voting abroad.* Paper presented at the UCLA North American Integration and Development Center, Los Angeles, CA.

Golash-Boza, T. (2012). *Due process denied: Detentions and deportations in the United States.* New York: Routledge.

Gonzales, R. G. (2011). Learning to be illegal: Undocumented youth and shifting legal contexts in the transition to adulthood. *American Sociological Review,* 76(4), 602–19. DOI: 10.1177/0003122411411901

Gonzales, R. G., & Chavez, L. R. (2012). "Awakening to a nightmare": Abjectivity and illegality in the lives of undocumented 1.5 generation Latino immigrants in the United States. *Current Anthropology,* 53(3), 255–81. DOI: 10.1086/665414

Hagan, J., Eschbach, K., & Rodríguez, N. (2008). U.S. deportation policy, family separation, and circular migration. *International Migration Review,* 42(1), 64–88. DOI: 10.1111/j.1747-7379.2007.00114.x

Hagan, J., Rodriguez, N., & Castro, B. (2011). Social effects of mass deportations by the United States government, 2000–10. *Ethnic and Racial Studies,* 34(8), 1374–91. DOI: 10.1080/01419870.2011.575233

Hernández, D. M. (2007). Undue process: Racial genealogies of immigrant detention. In C. B. Brettell (Ed.), *Constructing borders/Crossing boundaries: Race, ethnicity, and immigration* (pp. 59–86). Lanham, MD: Lexington Books.

Hernández, D. M. (2008). Pursuant to deportation: Latinos and immigrant detention. *Latino Studies,* 6(1–2), 35–63. DOI:10.1057/lst.2008.2

Holmes, S. M. (2007). "Oaxacans like to work bent over": The naturalization of social suffering among berry farm workers. *International Migration,* 45(3), 39–68. DOI: 10.1111/j.1468-2435.2007.00410.x

Hondagneu-Sotelo, P., & Avila, E. (1997). "I'm here, but I'm there": The meanings of Latina transnational motherhood. *Gender & Society,* 11(5), 548–70. DOI: 10.1177/089124397011005003

Human Rights Watch. (2007). *Forced apart: Families separated and immigrants harmed by United States deportation policy.* New York: Human Rights Watch.

Landale, N., & Oropesa, R. S. (2007). Hispanic families: Stability and change. *Annual Review of Sociology,* 33, 381–405. DOI: 10.1146/annurev.soc.33.040406.131655

Martínez, L. (2006, April 28). El rostro joven de las remesas, *El Diario de Hoy.* Retrieved from http://www.elsalvador.com/noticias/2006/04/28/nacional/nac13.asp

Martínez, O. (2010). *Los migrantes que no importan: En el camino con los centroamericanos indocumentados en México.* Barcelona: Icaria.

McConnell, E. D. (2011). An "incredible number of Latinos and Asians": Media representations of racial and ethnic population change in Atlanta, Georgia. *Latino Studies,* 9(2/3), 177–97. DOI:10.1057/lst.2011.17

Menjívar, C. (2006). Family reorganization in a context of legal uncertainty: Guatemalan and Salvadoran immigrants in the United States. *International Journal of Sociology of the Family,* 32(2), 223–45. Retrieved from http://www.jstor.org/stable/23030196

Menjívar, C., & Abrego, L. (2009). Parents and children across borders: Legal instability and intergenerational relations in Guatemalan and Salvadoran families. In N. Foner (Ed.), *Across generations: Immigrant families in America* (pp. 160–89). New York: New York University Press.

Menjívar, C., & Abrego, L. (2012). Legal violence: Immigration law and the lives of Central American immigrants. *American Journal of Sociology,* 117(5), 1380–424. DOI: 10.1086/663575

Menjívar, C., & Kanstroom, D. (Eds.). (2013). *Constructing immigrant "illegality": Critiques, experiences, and resistance.* Cambridge: Cambridge University Press.

Milkman, R., González, A. L., & Narro, V. (2010). *Wage theft and workplace violations in Los Angeles: The failure of employment and labor law for low-wage workers.* Los Angeles: UCLA Institute for Research on Labor and Employment.

Miranda, J., Siddique, J., Der-Martirosian, C., & Belin, T. R. (2005). Depression among Latina immigrant mothers separated from their children. *Psychiatric Services*, 56(6), 717–20. DOI: 10.1176/appi.ps.56.6.717

National Community Advisory. (2011). *Restoring community: A National Community Advisory report on ICE's failed "Secure Communities" program*. Location: National Community Advisory.

Ngai, M. M. (2004). *Impossible subjects: Illegal aliens and the making of modern America*. Princeton, NJ: Princeton University Press.

Parreñas, R. (2001). Mothering from a distance: Emotions, gender, and intergenerational relationships in Filipino transnational families. *Feminist Studies*, 27(2), 361–90. DOI: 10.2307/3178765

Parreñas, R. (2005). Long distance intimacy: Class, gender and intergenerational relations between mothers and children in Filipino transnational families. *Global Networks*, 5(4), 317–36.

Passel, J., & Cohn. D. (2011). *Unauthorized immigrant population: National and state trends, 2010*. Washington. DC: Pew Hispanic Center.

Pratt, G. (2012). *Families apart: Migrant mothers and the conflicts of labor and love*. Minneapolis: University of Minnesota Press.

Pribilsky. J. (2004). "Aprendemos a convivir": Conjugal relations, co-parenting, and family life among Ecuadorian transnational migrants in New York City and the Ecuadorian Andes. *Global Networks*, 4(3), 313–34. DOI: 10.1111/j.1471-0374.2004.00096.x

Rodriguez, N., & Hagan, J. M. (2004). Fractured families and communities: Effects of immigration reform in Texas, Mexico, and El Salvador. *Latino Studies*, 2(3), 328–51. DOI: 10.1057/palgrave.lst.8600094

Santa Ana, O. (2012). *Juan in a hundred: The representation of Latinos on network news*. Austin: University of Texas Press.

Schmalzbauer, L. (2005). *Striving and surviving: A daily life analysis of Honduran transnational families*. New York and London: Routledge.

Suárez-Orozco, C., Bang, H. J., & Kim, H. Y. (2010). "I felt like my heart was staying behind": Psychological implications of family separations and reunifications for immigrant youth. *Journal of Adolescent Research*, 20(10), 1–36. DOI: 10.1177/0743558410376830

Suárez-Orozco, C., Todorova, I., & Louie, J. (2002). Making up for lost time: The experience of separation and reunification among immigrant families. *Family Process*, 41(4), 625–43. DOI: 10.1111/j.1545-5300.2002.00625.x

Suárez-Orozco, C., Yoshikawa, H., Teranishi, R. T., & Suárez-Orozco, M. (2011). Growing up in the shadows: The developmental implications of unauthorized status. *Harvard Educational Review*, 81(3), 438–72. Retrieved from http://www.metapress.com/content/G23X203763783M75

Taylor, P., Lopez, M. H., Passel, J., & Motel, S. (2011). *Unauthorized immigrants: Length of residency, patterns of parenthood*. Washington, DC: Pew Hispanic Center.

Thompson, G. (2009, April 23). After losing freedom, some immigrants face loss of custody of their children *New York Times*. Retrieved from http://www.nytimes.com/2009/04/23/us/23children.html?hpw

Valenzuela Jr., A. (2002). Working on the margins in metropolitan Los Angeles: Immigrants in day-labor work. *Migraciones Internacionales*, 1(2), 6–28.

Walter, N., Bourgois, P., & Loinaz, H. M. (2004). Masculinity and undocumented labor migration: Injured Latino day laborers in San Francisco. *Social Science & Medicine*, 59, 1159–68. DOI: 10.1016/j.socscimed.2003.12.013

Wessler, S. F. (2011). *Shattered families: The perilous intersection of immigration enforcement and the child welfare system*. New York: Applied Research Center.

Yoshikawa, H. (2011). *Immigrants raising citizens: Undocumented parents and their young children*. New York: Russell Sage.

Zinn, M. B., & Wells. B. (2003). Diversity within Latino families: New lessons for family social science. In A. S. Skolnick & J. H. Skolnick (Eds.), *Family in transition* (12th ed., pp. 389–415). Boston: Allyn and Bacon.

Questions for Critical Thinking

1. The author's research illustrates that the status of illegal impacts all members of a family, even when only one person or a few people are categorized as undocumented or only temporarily protected. How does the author's discussion deepen your understanding of the impact of being an undocumented immigrant?

2. Reflecting on the author's discussion, what are some of the ways that families work to reframe the status of being undocumented as a source of solidarity and strength?

3. Considering the analysis offered in this study, what do you see as solutions to the challenges these families face?

MARRIAGE AND FAMILY

LGBT Individuals and Same-Sex Couples

* *Gary J. Gates*

With the recent Supreme Court decision legalizing same-sex marriage, there has been much debate in the public sphere regarding the suitability of same-sex couples to raise children. In the following essay, Gary Gates reviews evidence presented by scholars on both sides of the issue and concludes that same-sex couples are as good at parenting as their different-sex counterparts.

The speed with which the legal and social climate for lesbian, gay, bisexual, and transgender (LGBT) individuals, same-sex couples, and their families is changing in the United States has few historical precedents. Measures of social acceptance related to sexual relationships, parenting, and marriage recognition among same-sex couples all increased substantially in the last two decades. The legal climate followed a similar pattern. In 2005, when the *Future of Children* last produced an issue about marriage and child wellbeing, only one state allowed same-sex couples to legally marry. By June 2015, the Supreme Court had ruled that same-sex couples had a constitutional right to marry throughout the United States.

Analyses of the General Social Survey, a biennial and nationally representative survey of adults in the United States, show that, in the years between 1973 and 1991, the portion who thought that same-sex sexual relationships were "always wrong" varied little, peaking at 77 percent in 1988 and 1991. The two decades since have seen a rapid decline in this figure, from 66 percent in 1993 to 40 percent in 2014.[1] Conversely, the portion of those who say that same-sex sexual relationships are never wrong didn't go much above 15 percent until 1993. From 1993 to 2014, that figure increased from 22 percent to 49 percent. Notably, 2014 marks the first time in the 30 years that the General Social Survey has been asking this question that the portion of Americans who think same-sex sexual relationships are never wrong is substantially higher than the portion who say such relationships are always wrong.

The General Social Survey data demonstrate an even more dramatic shift in support for marriage rights for same-sex couples. In 1988, just 12 percent of U.S. adults agreed that same-sex couples should have a right to marry. By 2014, that figure had risen to 57 percent. Data from Gallup show a similar pattern, with support for marriage rights for same-sex couples increasing from 27 percent in 1996 to 60 percent in 2014.[2] Gallup's analyses document even larger changes in attitudes toward support for adoption by same-sex couples. In 1992, its polling showed that only 29 percent of Americans supported the idea that same-sex couples should have the legal right to adopt children. In a 2014 poll, that figure was 63 percent, even higher than support for marriage among same-sex couples.[3]

Legal Recognition of Same-Sex Relationships

These shifts in public attitudes toward same-sex relationships and families have been accompanied by similarly dramatic shifts in granting legal status to same-sex couple relationships. California was the first state to enact a statewide process to recognize same-sex couples when it created its domestic partnership registry in 1999. Domestic partnership offered California same-sex couples some of the benefits normally associated with marriage, namely, hospital visitation rights and the ability to be considered next of kin when settling the estate of a deceased partner. In 2000, Vermont enacted civil unions, a status designed specifically for same-sex couples to give them a broader set of rights and responsibilities akin to those associated with marriage.

Massachusetts became the first state to legalize marriage for same-sex couples in 2004. In 2013, the U.S. Supreme Court declared unconstitutional the provision of the federal Defense of Marriage Act (passed in 1996) that limited federal recognition of marriages to different-sex couples.[4] That ruling, in *Windsor v. United States*, prompted an unprecedented wave of lawsuits in every state where same-sex couples were not permitted to marry. After numerous rulings in these cases affirming the right of same-sex couples to marry in a series of states, the Supreme Court's June 2015 decision meant that same-sex couples could marry anywhere in the country.[5]

Globally, marriage or some other form of legal recognition through civil or registered partnerships is now widely available to same-sex couples across northern, western, and central Europe, large portions of North and South America, and in South Africa, Australia, and New Zealand.[6] Conversely, homosexuality remains criminalized, in some cases by punishment of death, throughout much of Africa, the Middle East, and Southeast Asia, and in Russia and many Pacific and Caribbean island nations.[7]

Effects on LGBT Relationships and Families

Social norms and legal conditions affect how we live our lives. Psychologists document how social stigma directed toward LGBT people can be quite insidious and damage their health and wellbeing.[8] It can also affect how they form relationships and families. For example, studies from the early 1980s found that same-sex couple relationships were, on average, less stable than different-sex relationships.[9] My own analyses of data from the early 1990s showed that lesbians and gay men were less likely than their heterosexual counterparts to be in a cohabiting relationship.[10] Is this because same-sex couple relationships differ from different-sex relationships in ways that lead to instability? Are lesbians and gay men just not the marrying type? Recent research suggests that the social and legal climate may explain a great deal about why same-sex couples behave differently from different-sex couples in terms of relationship formation and stability. As society has begun to treat same-sex couples more like different-sex couples, the differences between the two groups have narrowed. For example, compared to 20 years ago, proportionately more lesbians and gay men are in cohabiting same-sex relationships, and they break up and divorce at rates similar to those of comparable different-sex couples.[11] As of March 2015, Gallup estimated that nearly 40 percent of same-sex couples were married.[12]

The social and legal climate for LGBT people also affects how they form families and become parents. In a climate of social stigma, LGBT people can feel pressure to hide their identities and have relationships with different-sex partners. Not surprisingly, some of those relationships produce children. Today, most children being raised by same-sex couples were born to different-sex parents, one of whom is now in the same-sex relationship. This pattern is changing, but in ways that may seem counterintuitive. Despite growing support for same-sex parenting, proportionally fewer same-sex couples report raising children today than in 2000. Reduced social stigma means that more LGBT people are coming out earlier in life. They're less likely than their LGBT counterparts from the past to have different-sex relationships and the children such relationships produce.[13]

But that's not the full story. While parenting may be declining overall among same-sex couples, adoption and the use of reproductive technologies like artificial insemination and surrogacy is increasing. Compared to a decade ago, same-sex couples today may be less likely to have children, but those who do are more likely to have children who were born with same-sex parents who are in stable relationships.[14]

Framing the Debate

The legal and political debates about allowing same-sex couples to marry tend to focus on two large themes that can be seen even in the earliest attempts to garner legal recognition of same-sex marriages. These two themes pit arguments about the inherent and traditional relationship between marriage and procreation (including the suitability of same-sex couples as parents) against arguments about the degree to which opposition to legal recognition of same-sex relationships is rooted in irrational animus and discrimination toward same-sex couples or lesbian, gay and bisexual (LGB, used here because these arguments rarely consider the transgender population) individuals more broadly. (Throughout this article, I use LGB rather than LGBT when data or research focuses only on sexual orientation and not on gender identity.)

In the United States, the earliest legal attempt to expand marriage to include same-sex couples began in 1970, when Richard Baker and James McConnell applied for and were denied a marriage license in Hennepin County, Minnesota.[15] They filed a lawsuit that eventually came before the Minnesota and U.S. supreme courts. The Minnesota court ruling observed that the arguments in favor of allowing the couple to marry were based on the proposition that "the right to marry without regard to the sex of the parties is a fundamental right of all persons and that restricting marriage to only couples of the opposite sex is irrational and invidiously discriminatory." The court wasn't persuaded by these arguments, ruling that "the institution of marriage as a union of a man and woman, uniquely involving the procreation of children, is as old as

the book of Genesis."[16] The U.S. Supreme Court dismissed the case on appeal for lack of any substantial federal question.[17]

More than 30 years later, in a ruling from the U.S. Court of Appeals for the Seventh Circuit in *Baskin v. Bogan*, which upheld a lower court's ruling that Indiana's ban on marriage for same-sex couples was unconstitutional, Judge Richard Posner offered a distinctly different perspective from that of the Minnesota court regarding similar arguments made in a case seeking to overturn Indiana's ban on marriage for same-sex couples. He wrote:

> At oral argument the state's lawyer was asked whether "Indiana's law is about successfully raising children," and since "you agree same-sex couples can successfully raise children, why shouldn't the ban be lifted as to them?" The lawyer answered that "the assumption is that with opposite-sex couples there is very little thought given during the sexual act, sometimes, to whether babies may be a consequence." In other words, Indiana's government thinks that straight couples tend to be sexually irresponsible, producing unwanted children by the carload, and so must be pressured (in the form of governmental encouragement of marriage through a combination of sticks and carrots) to marry, but that gay couples, unable as they are to produce children wanted or unwanted, are model parents— model citizens really—so have no need for marriage. Heterosexuals get drunk and pregnant, producing unwanted children; their reward is to be allowed to marry. Homosexual couples do not produce unwanted children; their reward is to be denied the right to marry. Go figure.[18]

As in *Baker v. Nelson*, the U.S. Supreme Court opted not to take *Baskin v. Bogan* on appeal. But this time, the court's inaction prompted a rapid expansion in the number of states that allowed same-sex couples to marry.

This article explores the social and legal debates about access to marriage for same-sex couples, how social and legal change is affecting the demographic characteristics of LGBT people and their families, whether parents' gender composition affects children's wellbeing, and how social science research has contributed to those debates and can track the impact of these social changes in the future.

LGBT Families: Demographic Characteristics

Depending on which survey we consider, from 5.2 million to 9.5 million U.S. adults identify as LGBT (roughly 2–4 percent of adults).[19] An analysis of two state-level population-based surveys suggests that approximately 0.3 percent of adults are transgender.[20] More people identify as LGBT today than in the past. Findings from the 2012 Gallup Daily Tracking survey suggest that, among adults aged 18 and older, 3.6 percent of women and 3.3 percent of men identify as LGBT.[21] Nearly 20 years ago, 2.8 percent of men and 1.4 percent of women identified as lesbian, gay, or bisexual in a national survey.[22] These estimates measure the LGBT population by considering who identifies themselves using the terms lesbian, gay, bisexual, or transgender. Self-identity is not necessarily the only way to measure sexual orientation or gender identity. For example, if sexual orientation is measured by the gender of one's sexual partners or sexual attractions, then population estimates increase. Findings from the 2006–08 National Survey of Family Growth, a national survey of adults aged 18–44 conducted by the National Center for Health Statistics, show that 12.5 percent of women and 5.2 percent of men report at least some same-sex sexual behavior. An estimated 13.6 percent of women and 7.1 percent of men report at least some same-sex sexual attraction.[23]

Estimates for the number of cohabiting same-sex couples in the United States are most commonly derived from U.S. Census Bureau data, either decennial Census enumerations (beginning in 1990) or the annual American Community Survey (ACS). Unfortunately, the accuracy of the Census Bureau figures for same-sex couples has been called into question because of a measurement problem whereby a very small portion of different-sex couples (mostly married) make an error on the survey when recording the gender of one of the partners or spouses, so that the survey appears to identify the couple as same-sex. Findings from various analyses of Census and ACS data suggest that the presence of these false positives among same-sex couples could mean that from one-quarter to one-half of identified same-sex couples may be miscoded different-sex couples.[24]

In 2010, the U.S. Census Bureau released estimates of the number of same-sex couples that were adjusted to minimize the inaccuracies created by the measurement problem. They reported nearly 650,000 same-sex couples in the country, an increase of more than 80 percent over the figure from Census 2000 of 360,000 couples.[25] Same-sex couples represent about 0.5 percent of all U.S. households and about 1 percent of all married and unmarried cohabiting couples. My analyses of the National Health Interview Survey (NHIS), an annual survey of adults conducted by the U.S. Department of Health and Human Services, suggest that there were approximately 690,000 same-sex couples in the United States in 2013, representing 1.1 percent of all couples, a modest increase from the 2010 figures.[26] Gallup estimates from March 2015 suggest that the number of cohabiting same-sex couples may be close to 1 million.[27]

Estimating the number of married same-sex couples in the United States is difficult. Not all states collect administrative marriage data that explicitly identifies same-sex couples. A further complication comes from the measurement issues in Census Bureau data. Estimates of the number of same-sex couples who identify as married are now reported in annual ACS tabulations, but the measurement error that I've discussed likely means that these figures aren't very accurate.[28]

Based on NHIS data, I calculated that there may have been as many as 130,000 married same-sex couples by the end of 2013, approximately 18 percent of all same-sex couples.[29] By contrast, ACS estimates from the same year suggested that there were more than 250,000 married same-sex couples. The NHIS and ACS estimates both were made before the majority of states allowed same-sex couples to marry. Gallup estimates from data collected in March 2015 found 390,000 married same-sex couples.[30] Regardless of the accuracy of these estimates, it's clear that same-sex couples are marrying at a rapid rate. The population of married same-sex couples appears to have doubled or even tripled in just one year.[31]

LGBT and Same-Sex Couple Parents and Families

LGBT individuals and same-sex couples come to be parents in many ways. My own analyses estimate that 37 percent of LGBT individuals have been parents and that as many as 6 million U.S. children and adults may have an LGBT parent.[32] I estimate that while as many as 2 million to 3.7 million children under age 18 may have an LGBT parent, it's likely that only about 200,000 are being raised by a same-sex couple.[33] Many are being raised by single LGBT parents, and many are being raised by different-sex couples where one parent is bisexual. Most surveys find that bisexuals account for roughly half of the LGBT population, and my NHIS analyses suggest that among bisexuals with children, more than six in 10 are either married (51 percent) or partnered (11 percent) with a different-sex partner.[34] Only 4 percent are living with a same-sex spouse or partner.

Data rarely provide clear information about the birth circumstances of children with LGBT parents or those living with same-sex couples. But, as I've already pointed out, my analyses of ACS data suggest that most children currently living with same-sex couples were likely born in previous different-sex relationships. Two-thirds of children under age 18 living with a same-sex cohabiting couple (married or unmarried) are identified as either the biological child or stepchild of one member of the couple. Only about 12 percent of them are identified as adopted or foster children, though that figure has been increasing over time.[35] My research also shows that, among people who have ever had a child, LGB individuals report having had their first child at earlier ages than their non-LGB counterparts.[36] This is consistent with many studies documenting that LGB youth are more likely to experience unintended pregnancy or fatherhood when compared to their non-LGB counterparts.[37] Researchers speculate that social stigma directed toward LGB youth contributes to psychological stress. That stress can sometimes lead them to engage in risky behaviors, including sexual activity that results in unplanned pregnancies.

Analyses of many data sources show that racial and ethnic minorities (particularly African Americans and Latinos) who are LGB or in same-sex couples are more likely to report raising or having had children. The proportion of all same-sex couples raising children tends to be higher in more socially conservative areas of the country, where LGB people may have come out relatively later in life, so were more likely to have children with a different-sex partner earlier in life.[38] These patterns likely also contribute to the broad economic disadvantage

observed among same-sex couples and LGB individuals who are raising children. They have lower incomes than their different-sex couple or non-LGB counterparts and have higher levels of poverty.[39] In fact, same-sex couples with children are twice as likely as their married different-sex counterparts to be living in poverty.

The evidence of economic disadvantage among same-sex couples with children is intriguing given the overall high levels of education historically observed among those in same-sex couples. Nearly all research shows that individuals in same-sex couples have higher levels of education than those in different-sex couples.[40] But this pattern differs among couples raising children. While nearly half of those in same-sex couples have a college degree, only a third of those raising children have that much education. Same-sex couple parents also report higher rates of unemployment than their different-sex counterparts. Individuals in same-sex and different-sex couples with children report similar levels of labor force participation (81 percent and 84 percent, respectively), but those in same-sex couples are more likely to be unemployed (8 percent versus 6 percent, respectively). While in the majority of same-sex and different-sex couples with children, both spouses or partners are employed (57 percent and 60 percent, respectively), same-sex couples are more likely to have neither partner employed (8 percent versus 5 percent, respectively).[41]

The percentage of same-sex couples who are raising children began declining in 2006.[42] As I've said, this may actually be a result of social acceptance and LGBT people coming out (being more public about their LGBT identity) earlier in life today than in the past. In a Pew Research Center study, for example, younger respondents reported that they first told someone that they were LGBT at younger ages than did older respondents.[43] It may be that lesbians and gay men are less likely now than in the past to have different-sex sexual relationships while young and, therefore, are less likely to have children with a different-sex partner. Today, about 19 percent of same-sex couples are raising children under age 18, with little variation in that statistic between married and unmarried couples. Among LGB individuals not in a couple, the figure is also 19 percent.[44]

Social Science and Political Debates

To the extent that social scientists have weighed in on the debate about allowing same-sex couples to marry and the consequences that such a change might have on society and families, they have largely focused on parenting. Questions regarding the extent to which LGBT individuals and same-sex couples become parents, how they come to be parents, and whether and how sexual orientation or gender composition of children's parents might affect their health and wellbeing have all been considered within the framework of the debates about legalizing marriage for same-sex couples.

Social Science on Trial

This dynamic may be best observed in the testimony that emerged from a trial in the case of *DeBoer v. Snyder*, a lawsuit filed in the U.S. District Court for the Eastern District of Michigan that challenged the state's ban on marriage for same-sex couples. The case originated when plaintiffs April DeBoer and Jayne Rowse were denied the ability to complete a joint adoption (where both partners are declared a legal parent to the child) because Michigan allowed such adoptions only among married couples. Judge Bernard A. Friedman ordered a trial, the first such trial in a case involving marriage rights for same-sex couples since a challenge to California's Proposition 8 (a 2008 ballot initiative, later overturned by the courts, that made marriage for same-sex couples illegal). Given the origins of the lawsuit, litigants on both sides assembled expert witnesses from the social sciences, including me, to testify regarding what social science tells us about parenting among same-sex couples. . . .

In the end, Judge Friedman, a Reagan appointee to the federal judiciary, issued a strongly worded opinion in favor of the plaintiffs' right to marry.[45] His opinion was later overturned by the U.S. Sixth Circuit Court of Appeals, but upheld by the Supreme Court. In his ruling, Freidman dismissed arguments suggesting that the limitations of social science research with regard to same-sex couple parents were sufficient to cause concern about how allowing same-sex couples to marry would affect children and families. Though Friedman's judicial ruling hardly settles the debates among social scientists about LGBT and same-sex couple parenting, it has affected legal cases that followed. Judge Posner's words that I cited earlier demonstrate that lawyers defending Indiana's ban on marriage for same-sex couples effectively conceded that same-sex couples make entirely suitable parents. Since the Michigan ruling, it has become very rare for those opposed to allowing same-sex couples to marry to base their arguments partly on questions about the suitability of same-sex couples as parents or on possible negative consequences for children's health and wellbeing.

Married Same-Sex Couples

Substantial evidence shows that marriage promotes stability in couples and families.[46] Stability, and the financial and social benefits that come with it, contribute to better outcomes for children raised by married parents. The widespread acceptance of marriage for same-sex couples comes at a time when more of them are pursuing parenting as a couple through adoption and reproductive technologies and fewer are raising children from prior different-sex relationships. Will marriage have the stabilizing effect on same-sex couples and their families that we've seen in different-sex couples? Evidence suggests that it might, since lesbians and gay men have a strong desire to be married and have views about the purpose of marriage that are similar to those of the general population.

Desire for Marriage

In two recent studies, the Pew Research Center has found that 56 percent of unmarried gay men and 58 percent of unmarried lesbians would like to be married someday, compared to 45 percent of unmarried bisexuals and 46 percent of the unmarried general population.[47] The views of bisexuals and the general population may be similar because the vast majority of coupled bisexual men and women report having different-sex spouses or partners. At the time of the Pew survey, neither marriage nor recognition of a legal relationship through civil union or domestic partnership was yet widely available for same-sex couples in the United States. So it isn't surprising that lesbians and gay men were less likely to be married or in a civil union or registered domestic partnership when compared to bisexuals or the general population. When current marital status was taken into account, approximately 60 percent of LGBT adults in the Pew survey were currently married or said they would like to be married someday, compared to 76 percent of the general population.

Relationship Formation

While desire for marriage may be relatively high among lesbians and gay men, there are differences between the groups, and between LGB individuals and heterosexuals, in patterns of forming relationships. Among LGB men and women, lesbians are the most likely to be in cohabiting relationships, usually at rates very similar to those of non-LGB women. Overall, LGB individuals are less likely than non-LGB individuals to be in a married or unmarried cohabiting relationship. My analyses of the 2013 NHIS show that roughly six in 10 non-LGB adults are living with a partner or spouse, compared to about four in 10 LGB individuals. However, the likelihood of having a cohabiting spouse or partner is markedly higher among lesbians, at 51 percent, than among gay men or bisexual men and women, about one in three of whom are coupled. The difference between lesbians and non-LGB women (58 percent) in the NHIS was not statistically significant.[48] In an older paper, Christopher Carpenter and I also found that cohabiting partnerships were more common among lesbians than among gay men (though the data were from California only) and that lesbians' levels of cohabitation were comparable to those found in heterosexual women.[49]

Findings from a Pew Research Center survey of LGBT adults showed that, consistent with the NHIS analyses, 37 percent of LGBT adults were cohabiting with a spouse or partner. The Pew findings also showed that lesbians were more likely than gay men to have a spouse or partner (40 percent versus 28 percent, respectively). Unlike the NHIS findings, bisexual women were the most likely among LGB men and women to have a spouse or partner at 51 percent, compared to 30 percent of bisexual men. Among the general population, Pew found that 58 percent of adults were cohabiting with a spouse or partner. Regardless of cohabitation, 40 percent of gay men were in a committed relationship, compared to 66 percent of lesbians. Among bisexual men and women, the figures were 40 percent and 68 percent, respectively. In the general population, Pew estimates that about 70 percent were in committed relationships.[50]

As we've seen, lesbians and gay men appear to be partnering at higher rates today than in the past. In analyses of the 1992 National Health and Social Life Survey, a population-based survey of adults focused on sexual attitudes and behaviors, 19 percent of men who identified as gay and 42 percent of women who identified as lesbian reported being in a cohabiting partnership.[51] This suggests that gay men are nearly twice as likely to partner today as they were in the early 1990s. It also confirms that the pattern of higher levels of coupling among lesbians when compared to gay men has persisted over time.

Reasons to Marry

The Pew survey also considered the reasons that people marry. LGBT respondents were no different from the general population in their belief that love, companionship, and making a lifelong commitment were the three most important reasons for a couple to marry. The only substantial difference between LGBT respondents and the general population in this regard was that LGBT people gave more weight to legal rights and benefits as a reason to marry than did the general population.[52] This difference may not be surprising given the substantial media attention focused on the legal rights and benefits that were not available to same-sex couples in places where they could not marry.

The findings also suggested that lesbians and gay men were largely responsible for the fact that rights and benefits were ranked higher among LGBT respondents; lesbians and gay men ranked rights and benefits, as well as financial stability, as much more important than bisexuals did (bisexuals were similar to the general population in this regard, and this portion of the analyses didn't separately consider transgender respondents).[53] Recall that the Pew findings show that most coupled bisexuals are with different-sex partners, while coupled lesbians and gay men are with same-sex partners. Given their more limited access to marriage, rights, benefits, and financial stability might be more important for lesbians and gay men.

Social Impact

When social scientists examine the issue of marriage rights for same-sex couples, they do so largely through the medium of parenting and family studies. Broader public discourse and debate often involves more philosophical (rather than empirical) arguments about marriage as a social and legal institution and the degree to which allowing same-sex couples to marry reflects a fundamental or undesirable change to that institution (a book that pits philosopher John Corvino against political activist Maggie Gallagher, *Debating Same-Sex Marriage*, provides an example of these arguments).[54] However, social scientists certainly have led the way in tracking contemporary changes in patterns of family formation and marriage. Sociologist Andrew Cherlin, for example, has documented many of these changes, including: increases in the age of first marriage; diverging patterns of both marriage and divorce by education, such that those with lower levels of education are less likely to marry and more likely to divorce when compared to those with higher educational attainment; increases in nonmarital births and cohabitation; and increases in the number of children living in families not headed by their married biological mothers and fathers.[55]

Some public debate has emerged regarding the degree to which these social changes are related to allowing same-sex couples to marry. Political commentator Stanley Kurtz argues that marriage for same-sex couples in Europe has contributed to and hastened the institutional decline in marriage, to the detriment of families and children.[56] Journalist Jonathan Rauch disagrees, arguing that allowing same-sex couples to marry will enhance the prestige of the institution and reinvigorate it during a period of decline.[57]

The empirical evidence for a link between the emergence of marriage rights for same-sex couples and broader marriage, divorce, and fertility trends is weak. Economist Lee Badgett has shown that trends in different-sex marriage, divorce, and nonmarital birth rates did not change in European countries after they legalized marriage for same-sex couples.[58] Another study, using data from the United States, found that allowing same-sex couples to marry or enter civil unions produced no significant impact on state-level marriage, divorce, abortion, and out-of-wedlock births.[59] In the Netherlands, where marriage for same-sex couples has been legal for more than a decade, neither the country's domestic partnership law nor the legalization of same-sex marriage appears to have affected different-sex marriage rates. Curiously, however, there appear to be different effects among liberals and conservatives: the introduction of same-sex marriage was associated with higher marriage rates among conservatives and lower rates among liberals.[60]

Conclusions: New Opportunities for Family Research

The demographic and attitudinal data that I've summarized suggest that same-sex and different-sex couples may not look as different in the future as they do today. Already they have similar perspectives on the desire for and purpose of marriage, and increasing numbers of same-sex couples are marrying and having their children as a married couple. Even under the challenging circumstances of social and legal inequality between same-sex and different-sex couples, it's clear that same-sex couples are as good at parenting as their different-sex counterparts, and their children turn out fine. Lesbian and gay parents report outcomes similar to those of their heterosexual counterparts with regard to mental health, stress, and parental competence. Same-sex and different-sex parents show similar levels of parental warmth, emotional involvement, and quality of relationships with their children. So, not surprisingly, few differences have been found between children raised by same-sex and different-sex parents in terms of self-esteem, quality of life, psychological adjustment, or social functioning.[61] As the legal and social playing fields become more equal for same-sex and different-sex couples, we have the opportunity to consider new research questions that can contribute to debates about whether and how parental relationship dynamics affect child wellbeing.

For example, while society has changed in its views about LGBT people and their families, it has also changed in its attitudes about gender and the norms associated with how men and women organize their relationships and families. In 1977, more than half of Americans thought that having a mother who works outside the home could be harmful to children. In 2012, only 28 percent of Americans thought so.[62] Changing social norms concerning gender and parenting likely play a role in explaining the decisions that couples make about how to divide time between work and family. Since those decisions can affect family finances and involvement in parenting, research has considered the effects that family division of labor can have on child wellbeing.[63]

Same-sex couples raising children give us the opportunity to assess how parents divide labor in the absence of gender differences between spouses or partners. However, comparisons between same-sex and different-sex couples are more complicated when same-sex couples don't have access to marriage. Decisions about employment and division of labor among same-sex couples could be directly associated with their inability to marry if, for example, their access to health insurance for each other or their children were contingent on both partners working, because spousal benefits would not be available. But there is also evidence that same-sex couples intentionally favor more egalitarian divisions of labor precisely as a rejection of traditional male/female roles in parenting.[64]

With equal access to marriage among same-sex and different-sex couples and trends toward greater intentional parenting among same-sex couples (as opposed to raising children from prior relationships), the two groups now look more similar in many ways, except, of course, in the couple's gender composition. These are the right conditions for a kind of "treatment" and "control" approach to studying the two groups (or perhaps three, if you think that male and female same-sex couples might behave differently based on gendered behavioral norms) and isolating the influence of gender roles in decisions about how much and which parents work outside the home, how much they interact with their children, and, ultimately, whether any of those decisions affect children's wellbeing. There's already some evidence that children raised by same-sex couples may show fewer gender-stereotyped behaviors and be more willing to consider same-sex sexual relationships (though there is still no evidence that they are more likely than other children to identify as LGB).[65]

The award-winning television program *Transparent* highlights the increasing visibility of parenting among transgender individuals, a relatively understudied subject. In a survey of more than 6,000 transgender individuals in the United States, nearly four in 10 (38 percent) reported having been a parent at some time in their lives.[66] Existing research offers no evidence that children of transgender parents experience developmental disparities or differ from other children with regard to their gender identity or development of sexual orientation. As with LGB people, several studies have shown that people who transition or "come out" as transgender later in life are more likely to have had children than those who identify as transgender and/or transition at younger ages. This suggests that many transgender parents likely had their children before they identified as transgender or transitioned.[67]

Just like comparing same-sex and different-sex parents, studying transgender parents offers another fascinating opportunity to better understand the relationship between gender and parenting. Transgender parenting research could consider whether the dynamics of parent/child relationships change when a parent transitions from one gender to another. In essence, this would give us another "treatment" and "control" group to explore parent–child relationships when the same parent is perceived as and perhaps conforms behaviors to one gender versus when that parent presents and parents as another gender.

While arguments about what drives trends and changes in marriage and family life may continue, it appears that, with the Supreme Court's ruling that same-sex couples have a constitutional right to marry, heated debates about the subject may be drawing to a close, at least in the United States. Polling data suggest that a substantial majority of Americans now support allowing same-sex couples to marry and raise children. For decades, scholarship regarding LGBT and same-sex couple parenting has occurred in a contentious political and social environment that invited unusual scrutiny. For example, publication of the Regnerus study in 2012 prompted unprecedented responses from scholars who both criticized and supported it.[68] LGBT advocates actually initiated legal action amid charges of academic malfeasance and fraud.[69]

This article highlights how research on LGBT and same-sex couple parenting can not only advance our understanding of the challenges associated with parenting in the face of stigma and discrimination, but also contribute more broadly to family scholarship. While robust political and social debates can be critical in allowing social and political institutions to progress and advance, they can make it hard to advance scholarly goals of objectivity and academic freedom. Let us hope that as the debates about LGBT rights and marriage for same-sex couples cool, scholars can work in a less volatile political and social environment and advance much-needed research that includes and explores parenting and family formation among same-sex couples and the LGBT population.

Notes

1. Figures based on author's analyses of General Social Survey data using the University of California, Berkeley's Survey Documentation and Analysis web-based analysis tool (http://sda.berkeley.edu/index.html).
2. Justin McCarthy, "Record-High 60% of Americans Support Same-Sex Marriage," Gallup, May 20, 2015, http://www.gallup.com/poll/183272/record-high-americans-support-sex-marriage.aspx?utm_source=Social%20Issues&utm_medium=newsfeed&utm_campaign=tiles.
3. Art Swift, "Most Americans Say Same-Sex Couples Entitled to Adopt," Gallup, accessed May 20, 2015, http://www.gallup.com/poll/170801/americans-say-sex-couples-entitled-adopt.aspx.
4. Windsor v. United States 570 US___ (2013).
5. Freedom to Marry, "History and Timeline of the Freedom to Marry in the United States," accessed October 10, 2014, http://www.freedomtomarry.org/pages/history-and-timeline-of-marriage.
6. For a current list of the legal relationship status for same-sex couples around the world, see Freedom to Marry, "The Freedom to Marry Internationally," accessed October 10, 2014, http://www.freedomtomarry.org/landscape/entry/c/international.
7. For a current summary of laws regarding homosexuality and gender identity around the world, see the International Lesbian, Gay, Bisexual, Trans and Intersex Association website, http://ilga.org/.
8. Ilan H. Meyer, "Prejudice, Social Stress, and Mental Health in Lesbian, Gay, and Bisexual Populations: Conceptual Issues and Research Evidence," *Psychological Bulletin* 129 (2003): 674–97, doi: 10.1037/0033-2909.129.5.674.
9. Philip Blumstein and Pepper Schwartz, *American Couples: Money, Work, Sex* (New York: William Morrow & Co., 1983).
10. Dan Black et al., "Demographics of the Gay and Lesbian Population in the United States: Evidence from Available Systematic Data Sources," *Demography* 37 (2000): 139–54.
11. Michael Rosenfeld, "Couple Longevity in the Era of Same-Sex Marriage in the United States," *Journal of Marriage and Family* 76 (2014): 905–18, doi: 10.1111/jomf.12141; M. V. Lee Badgett and Christy Mallory,

Patterns of Relationship Recognition for Same-Sex Couples: Divorce and Terminations (Los Angeles, CA: Williams Institute, UCLA School of Law, 2014), http://williamsinstitute.law.ucla.edu/wp-content/uploads/Badgett-Mallory-Divorce-Terminations-Dec-2014.pdf.
12. Gary J. Gates and Frank Newport, "An Estimated 780,000 Americans in Same-Sex Marriages," Gallup, accessed May 20, 2015, http://www.gallup.com/poll/182837/estimated-780-000-americans-sex-marriages.aspx.
13. Gary J. Gates, *LGBT Parenting in the United States* (Los Angeles, CA: Williams Institute, UCLA School of Law, 2013), http://williamsinstitute.law.ucla.edu/wp-content/uploads/LGBT-Parenting.pdf.
14. Ibid.
15. William N. Eskridge and Darren R. Spedale, *Gay Marriage: For Better or for Worse? What We've Learned from the Evidence* (New York: Oxford University Press, 2007).
16. Baker v. Nelson. 291 Minn. 310 (1971).
17. Baker v. Nelson. 409 US 810 (1972).
18. Baskin v. Bogan, 7th Cir. No. 14-2386, 2014 WL 4359059 (2014).
19. Gary J. Gates, *LGBT Demographics: Comparisons among Population-Based Surveys* (Los Angeles, CA: Williams Institute, UCLA School of Law, 2014), http://williamsinstitute.law.ucla.edu/wp-content/uploads/lgbt-demogs-sep-2014.pdf.
20. Gary J. Gates, *How Many People Are Lesbian, Gay, Bisexual, and Transgender?* (Los Angeles, CA: Williams Institute, UCLA School of Law, 2011), http://williamsinstitute.law.ucla.edu/wp-content/uploads/Gates-How-Many-People-LGBT-Apr-2011.pdf.
21. Gary J. Gates and Frank Newport, "Special Report: 3.4% of US Adults Identify as LGBT," October 18, 2012, http://www.gallup.com/poll/158066/special-report-adults-identify-lgbt.aspx.
22. Edward O. Laumann et al., *The Social Organization of Sexuality: Sexual Practices in the United States* (Chicago: University of Chicago Press, 1994).
23. Anjani Chandra et al., "Sexual Behavior, Sexual Attraction, and Sexual Identity in the United States: Data from

the 2006–2008 National Survey of Family Growth," National Health Statistics Reports no. 36 (Hyattsville, MD: National Center for Health Statistics, 2011).

24. Dan Black et al., "The Measurement of Same-Sex Unmarried Partner Couples in the 2000 US Census," Working Paper 023–07 (Los Angeles, CA: California Center for Population Research, 2007), https://escholarship.org/uc/item/72r1q94b; Gary J. Gates and Michael D. Steinberger, "Same-Sex Unmarried Partner Couples in the American Community Survey: The Role of Misreporting, Miscoding and Misallocation" paper presented at the Population Association of America Annual Meeting, Detroit, MI, 2009, http://economics-files.pomona.edu/steinberger/research/Gates_Steinberger_ACS_Miscode_May2010.pdf; Martin O'Connell and Sarah Feliz, "Same-Sex Couple Household Statistics from the 2010 Census," Working Paper Number 2011–26 (Washington, DC: Social, Economic and Housing Statistics Division, US Bureau of the Census, 2011), http://www.census.gov/hhes/samesex/files/ss-report.doc.

25. O'Connell and Feliz, "Same-Sex."

26. Gary J. Gates, *LGB Families and Relationships: Analyses of the 2013 National Health Interview Survey* (Los Angeles, CA: Williams Institute, UCLA School of Law, 2014), http://williamsinstitute.law.ucla.edu/wp-content/uploads/lgb-families-nhis-sep-2014.pdf.

27. Gates and Newport, "780,000 Americans."

28. D'Vera Cohn, "Census Confirms More Data Problems in Sorting out the Number of US Gay Marriages," *Fact Tank*, September 22, 2014, http://www.pewresearch.org/fact-tank/2014/09/22/census-confirms-more-data-problems-in-sorting-out-the-number-of-us-gay-marriages/.

29. Gates, *LGB Families.*

30. Gates and Newport, "780,000 Americans."

31. Ibid.

32. Gates, *LGBT Parenting.*

33. Ibid.

34. Gates, *LGBT Demographics: Comparisons.*

35. Gates, *LGBT Parenting*; Gary J. Gates, "Family Formation and Raising Children among Same-Sex Couples," *NCFR Report* (Winter 2011), F1–4, http://williamsinstitute.law.ucla.edu/wp-content/uploads/Gates-Badgett-NCFR-LGBT-Families-December-2011.pdf.

36. Gates, "Family Formation."

37. Elizabeth M. Saewyc, "Research on Adolescent Sexual Orientation: Development, Health Disparities, Stigma, and Resilience," *Journal of Research on Adolescence* 21: 256–72 (2011), doi: 10.1111/j.1532-7795.2010.00727.x.

38. Gary J. Gates, *Same-Sex and Different-Sex Couples in the American Community Survey: 2005–2011* (Los Angeles, CA: Williams Institute, UCLA School of Law, 2013), http://williamsinstitute.law.ucla.edu/wp-content/uploads/ACS-2013.pdf.

39. M. V. Lee Badgett et al., *New Patterns of Poverty in the Lesbian, Gay, and Bisexual Community* (Los Angeles, CA: Williams Institute, UCLA School of Law, 2013), http://williamsinstitute.law.ucla.edu/wp-content/uploads/LGB-Poverty-Update-Jun-2013.pdf.

40. Black et al., "Demographics"; Lisa K. Jepsen and Christopher Jepsen, "An Empirical Analysis of the Matching Patterns of Same-Sex and Opposite-Sex Couples," *Demography* 39 (2002): 435–53; Gary J. Gates and Jason Ost, *The Gay and Lesbian Atlas* (Washington, DC: Urban Institute Press, 2004); Gates, *American Community Survey*; Gates, *LGBT Families.*

41. Author's analyses of 2012 American Community Survey Public Use Microdata Sample.

42. Gates, "Family Formation"; Gates, *American Community Survey.*

43. Pew Research Center, *A Survey of LGBT Americans: Attitudes, Experiences and Values in Changing Times* (Washington, DC: Pew Research Center, 2013), http://www.pewsocialtrends.org/files/2013/06/SDT_LGBT-Americans_06-2013.pdf.

44. Gates, *LGB Families.*

45. Bernard A. Friedman, "Findings of Fact and Conclusions of Law," *Deboer v. Snyder*, United States District Court, Eastern District of Michigan, Southern Division, 12-CV-10285, 2014, https://www.mied.uscourts.gov/PDFFIles/12-10285DeBoerFindings.pdf.

46. Linda Waite and Maggie Gallagher, *The Case for Marriage: Why Married People Are Happier, Healthier, and Better Off Financially* (New York: Broadway Books, 2001).

47. Pew Research Center, *Survey of LGBT Americans*; Pew Research Center, *The Decline of Marriage and Rise of New Families* (Washington, DC: Pew Research Center, 2010), http://www.pewsocialtrends.org/files/2010/11/pew-social-trends-2010-families.pdf.

48. Gates, *LGB Families.*

49. Christopher Carpenter and Gary J. Gates, "Gay and Lesbian Partnership: Evidence from California," *Demography* 45 (2008): 573–90, doi: 10.1353/dem.0.0014.

50. Pew Research Center, *Survey of LGBT Americans.*

51. Black et al., "Demographics."

52. Pew Research Center, *Survey of LGBT Americans.*

53. Ibid.

54. Jon Corvino and Maggie Gallagher, *Debating Same-Sex Marriage* (New York: Oxford University Press, 2012).

55. Andrew J. Cherlin, "Demographic Trends in the United States: A Review of Research in the 2000s," *Journal of Marriage and Family* 72 (2010): 403–19, 10.1111/j.1741-3737.2010.00710.x.

56. Stanley Kurtz, "The End of Marriage in Scandinavia: The 'Conservative Case' for Same-Sex Marriage Collapses," *The Weekly Standard*, February 2, 2004, http://www.weeklystandard.com/Content/Public/Articles/000/000/003/66ozypwj.asp.

57. Jonathan Rauch, *Gay Marriage: Why It Is Good for Gays, Good for Straights, and Good for America* (New York: Times Books, 2004).

58. M. V. Lee Badgett, "Will Providing Marriage Rights to Same-Sex Couples Undermine Heterosexual Marriage?" *Sexuality Research and Social Policy* 1 (2004): 1–10, doi: 10.1525/srsp.2004.1.3.1.

59. Laura Langbein and Mark L. Yost, "Same-Sex Marriage and Negative Externalities," *Social Science Quarterly* 90 (2009): 292–308, 10.1111/j.1540-6237.2009.00618.x.

60. Mircea Trandafir, "The Effect of Same-Sex Marriage Laws on Different-Sex Marriage: Evidence From the Netherlands," *Demography* 51 (2013): 317–40, doi: 10.1007/s13524-013-0248-7.

61. Abbie E. Goldberg, Nanette K. Gartrell, and Gary J. Gates, *Research Report on LGB-Parent Families* (Los Angeles, CA: Williams Institute, UCLA School of Law, 2014), http://williamsinstitute.law.ucla.edu/wp-content/uploads/lgb-parent-families-july-2014.pdf.

62. Author's analyses of the General Social Survey. Respondents were asked whether they agreed or disagreed with the statement that having a mother working does not harm children. The figures reported represent the portion who disagreed with that statement.

63. Suzanne M. Bianchi et al., "Housework: Who Did, Does, or Will Do It, and How Much Does It Matter?" *Social Forces* 91 (2012): 55–63, doi: 10.1093/sf/sos120.

64. Abbie E. Goldberg, "'Doing' and 'Undoing' Gender: The Meaning and Division of Housework in Same-Sex Couples," *Journal of Family Theory & Review* 5 (2013): 85–104, doi: 10.1111/jftr.12009.

65. Goldberg, Gartrell, and Gates, *Research Report*.

66. Jaime M. Grant et al., *Injustice at Every Turn: A Report of the National Transgender Discrimination Survey* (Washington, DC: National Center for Transgender Equality and National Gay and Lesbian Task Force, 2011), http://www.thetaskforce.org/static_html/downloads/reports/reports/ntds_full.pdf.

67. Rebecca L. Stotzer, Jody L. Herman, and Amira Hasenbush, *Transgender Parenting: A Review of Existing Research* (Los Angeles, CA: Williams Institute, UCLA School of Law, 2014), http://williamsinstitute.law.ucla.edu/research/parenting/transgender-parenting-oct-2014/.

68. Gary J. Gates et al., "Letter to the Editors and Advisory Editors Social Science Research," *Social Science Research* 41 (2012), doi: 10.1016/j.ssresearch.2012.08.008: 1350–51; Byron Johnson et al. "Letter to the Editor," *Social Science Research* 41 (2012): 1352–53, doi:10.1016/j.ssresearch.2012.08.009.

69. Human Rights Campaign, "Judge Overturns Order to Disclose Documents Detailing Publication of Regnerus' Junk Science," news release, April 17, 2014, http://www.hrc.org/press-releases/entry/judge-overturns-order-to-disclose-documents-detailing-publication-of-regner.

Questions for Critical Thinking

1. What do you think constitutes a family? What are its important components? What has led you to define family in the way that you do (e.g., your own family experience, media, friends, other social institutions)?

2. Many things influence the well-being of children. Considering the author's discussion, how might the legalization of same-sex marriage positively impact the children of these relationships?

3. How might same-sex marriages challenge traditional notions of family in the United States? How might recognizing these families lead to greater equality for people of all sexual orientations?

Social Institutions: Education

MIND THE GAP

COVID-19 and Learning Loss—Disparities Grow and Students Need Help

• *Emma Dorn, Bryan Hancock, Jimmy Sarakatsannis, and Ellen Viruleg*

The following article examines the impact of COVID-19 and school shutdowns on student achievement. As the authors illustrate, although states and school districts made significant efforts to close the digital divide and provide access to remote education for all students, as the pandemic continued, Black and Latina/o/x students were still more likely than white students to be attending school remotely and less likely to have access to the necessary resources to successfully participate in virtual learning. The authors offer recommendations of the significant investments that will be necessary to catch up on lost learning, which should improve the educational experience for all students.

When the COVID-19 pandemic prompted a historic shutdown of US schools in the spring, state and district leaders speculated that the disruption could last anywhere from a few weeks to a few months. With a surge in new infections, the pandemic is now likely to keep many students out of the classroom until well into 2021.

Educators, parents, and students know firsthand the high cost of this prolonged period of remote learning, from rising rates of depression and anxiety to the loss of student learning. The COVID-19 pandemic has taken an especially heavy toll on Black, Hispanic, and Indigenous communities. Along with robbing them of lives and livelihoods, school shutdowns could deny students from these communities the opportunity to get the education they need to build a brighter future.

In the spring, we examined how school shutdowns were likely to compound racial disparities in learning and achievement, analyzing the toll on learning, dropout rates, and the overall economy. We now share assessment data from this fall, which show that students, on average, started school about three months behind where we would expect them to be in mathematics. Students of color were about three to five months behind in learning; white students were about one to three months behind. The picture for reading is more positive, with students starting school just a month and a half behind historical averages.

Much has improved since the spring. States and school districts have made significant efforts to close the digital divide and improve remote learning, and the implementation of school-based health and safety precautions enabled some students to return to classrooms in

McKinsey & Company. (2020, December 8). Mind the Gap: COVID-19 and learning loss—disparities grow and students need help. https://www.mckinsey.com/industries/public-and-social-sector/our-insights/covid-19-and-learning-loss-disparities-grow-and-students-need-help.

the fall (although some of these gains are now at risk as COVID-19 cases spike across the country). However, Black and Hispanic students continue to be more likely to remain remote and are less likely to have access to the prerequisites of learning—devices, internet access, and live contact with teachers. Left unaddressed, these opportunity gaps will translate into wider achievement gaps. Looking forward, we consider several different scenarios to estimate the total potential learning loss to the end of this academic year in June 2021. While the worst-case scenarios from the spring may have been averted, the cumulative learning loss could be substantial, especially in mathematics—with students on average likely to lose five to nine months of learning by the end of this school year. Students of color could be six to 12 months behind, compared with four to eight months for white students. While all students are suffering, those who came into the pandemic with the fewest academic opportunities are on track to exit with the greatest learning loss.

It doesn't have to be this way. While we may not be able to control the virus without an effective vaccine, we are more prepared to deal with its consequences. The immediate priority is to prevent further learning loss through a combination of bringing students back to school where it is safe to do so and improving remote learning across the board. However, that is not enough. Much damage has already been done, and even the best-case scenarios have students half a grade-level behind in June. To catch up, many students will need step-up opportunities to accelerate their learning. Now is the time for school systems to prepare postpandemic strategies that help students to meet their full potential.

Autumn Report Card: The High Cost of COVID-19

School systems were understandably overwhelmed and unequipped to respond when COVID-19 began rapidly spreading in the spring. The US education ecosystem is built around an in-class experience, from technology investments in school-level broadband internet and devices to curriculum design and how teachers are trained. In many communities, schools are also the hub for supports such as school meals, mental-health counseling, and childcare. In many homes, especially for low-income families, students lack access to the internet, devices, and a dedicated, quiet place to study.

The disparities in basic conditions for learning are reflected in the results of formative assessments taken this fall. We analyzed assessment data from the Curriculum Associates i-Ready platform[1] and found that students in their sample learned only 67 percent of the math and 87 percent of the reading that grade-level peers would typically have learned by the fall.[2] On average, that means students lost the equivalent of three months of learning in mathematics and one-and-a-half months of learning in reading.[3] The learning loss was especially acute in schools that predominantly serve students of color,[4] where scores were 59 percent of the historical average in math and 77 percent in reading (Exhibit 1).

These results are only a snapshot of a small cross section of students, but, if anything, these students may outperform national averages. These assessments were taken in school by students who had already made it back into the classroom. In addition, because the survey compares results at the school level, it doesn't capture the full scope of student-level opportunity and achievement gaps. The OECD suggests that more than three-quarters of the variance in US student scores typically occurs with children and parents. Grading and testing within schools, not between them.[5] Extrapolating to a student level, these scores suggest that students of color may have lost three to five months of learning in mathematics, while white students lost just one to three months.[6] Four months roughly tracks with the number of months of disrupted learning after schools began closing in March 2020—suggesting that some students didn't learn any new material once the pandemic hit and may have even slipped backward.

The Next Normal: Adapting to the Realities of Remote Learning

Conditions for learning have improved significantly since the spring, even though many students remain remote. Even students who still spend their days online are likely to have a better learning experience this year as schools have adapted their curricula, teacher training, and outreach to boost engagement with children and parents. Grading and testing have been reinstated in most schools, raising expectations for teachers and students.[7]

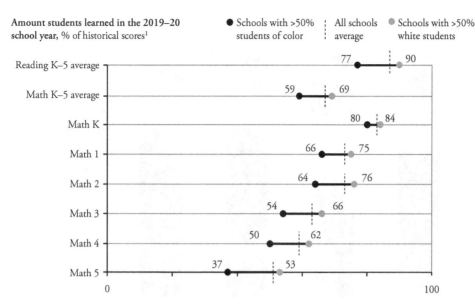

Amount students learned in the 2019–20 school year, % of historical scores[1]

● Schools with >50% students of color ┊ All schools average ● Schools with >50% white students

EXHIBIT 1 Most students are falling behind, but students of color are faring worse.

Percent of an "average" year of learning gained by students in 2019–20 school year, where 100% is equivalent to historical matched scores over previous 3 years. Source: Curriculum Associates

We estimate that about 60 percent of K–12 students started the 2020–21 school year fully remote. Another 20 percent started school with a hybrid model of remote and in-person classes, while the remaining 20 percent headed back full-time to in-person classrooms (Exhibit 2). This reflects a patchwork of modalities across the 13,000 public school districts in the nation.

Students in urban areas and large school districts are most likely to still be learning remotely. Even within the same district, Black and Hispanic students were more likely than white students to have started the school year remote. This partially reflects parental demand, as multiple polls show that Black and Hispanic parents are less likely to want their children to attend in-person classes.[8] The pandemic hasn't just forced schools to remain remote; it has also prompted some students to leave the public school system altogether. Some parents who can afford it have switched their children to private schools, pandemic pods, or homeschooling. Other children lack that option, and older teens may have dropped out of school altogether. The biggest drop appears to be at the starting point for school. While we don't yet have national enrollment data, an NPR survey of more than 60 school districts across 20 states found that kindergarten enrollment is down an average of 16 percent this year.[9] Some parents may be keeping their children in quality preschool programs that promote socio-emotional and academic growth, but others may not have that option. The decision to skip kindergarten is understandable, especially if the kindergarten experience is remote and parents are juggling work and childcare, but it has long-term consequences. Although kindergarten is compulsory in only 19 states and the District of Columbia, it can have a profound impact on children's skill development that influences later academic performance and even long-term life outcomes.[10]

For those children who remain in the K–12 school system, the challenge is having the tools and resources to thrive academically in a remote environment. Over the spring and summer, states and districts made a Herculean effort to distribute devices, connect students to the internet, reconnect with homeless students who had fallen off the radar, and put in place new regulations and benchmarks on remote instruction (Exhibit 3). But gaps remain.

Students receiving each type of instruction (estimate), %

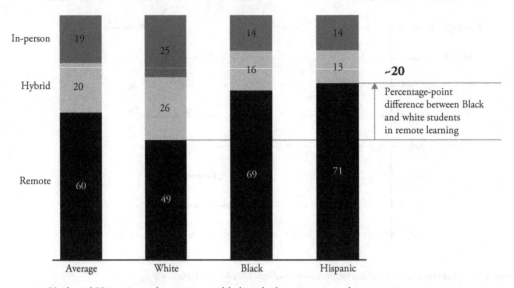

EXHIBIT 2   Black and Hispanic students are more likely to be learning remotely.

Source: Consortium for Policy Research in Education; EdSurge; *Education Week*; National Center for Education Statistics; US public school data

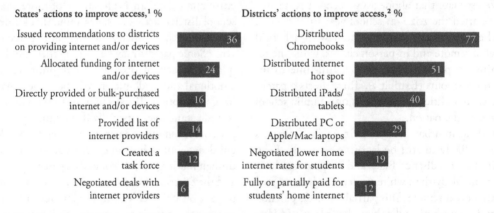

EXHIBIT 3   States and districts mobilized to equip students for remote learning.

[1]Center for Reinventing Public Education (CRPE) Response Database; summary of qualitative responses.

[2]*Education Week Market Brief*, nationally representative survey of 242 district leaders, 251 school principals, July 2020. Conducted by the *Education Week* Research Center. Source: CRPE; *Education Week Market Brief*

The October US Census Bureau Household Pulse Survey shows that 91 percent of households with K-12 students always or usually have access to a device for learning and internet access. Although gaps have narrowed since the spring, Black and Hispanic households are still three to four percentage points less likely than white households to have reliable access to devices, and three to six percentage points less likely to have reliable access to the internet (Exhibit 4).

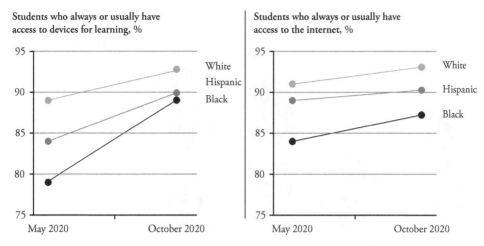

EXHIBIT 4   Gaps in access have narrowed since the spring but still remain.

Source: "Table 3: Computer and internet availability in households with children in public or private school, by select characteristics," US Census Bureau Household Pulse Survey

Access is easy to measure; quality less so. However, most experts agree that without any live instruction, many students will struggle to progress. Although more students may be receiving live instruction this fall than in the spring, significant racial disparities remain. Black and Hispanic students are twice as likely as white students to have received no live contact with teachers over the previous week and are three to six percentage points less likely to be receiving consistent live instruction (Exhibit 5).

Keeping students engaged remotely is a challenge. Data from instructional software provider Zearn show that student participation in online math coursework decreased by 11 percent this fall compared with participation prior to the pandemic. Among low-income students, the drop is 16 percent, while participation by high-income students decreased by just 2 percent.[11] The good news is that this is a substantial improvement from the spring, when participation was 41 percent lower for low-income students.

Beyond access and quality of instruction, students must be in a physical and emotional state that enables them to learn. The COVID-19 pandemic has wreaked havoc on families, leaving many children in precarious situations. Feeding America notes that one in four children is at risk of hunger during the

pandemic.[12] The number of children who are housing-insecure has risen as families struggle to pay rent. Parental supervision and support may be more difficult in families in which both parents need to work outside the home, or in which the parents are English-language learners and cannot directly support their child's learning.

Looking Forward: A High Hurdle to Reduce Learning Loss

While schools have made progress in key areas, the reality is that the 2020–21 school year is going to remain a challenge for every student. The COVID-19 pandemic has upended the US education system, forcing schools to adopt strategies without certainty about the results. Existing remote learning studies are based on virtual charter schools that aren't representative of the full public school population.[13] There are no rigorous studies on the impact of hybrid models—not just on learning, but also on students' emotional and mental health, as well as on limiting disease spread. This makes it tough for schools to design effective learning strategies and makes it difficult for researchers to predict the impact of ongoing disruptions. Guided by pre-COVID-19 studies of the effectiveness of virtual learning and by assessment data collected at the

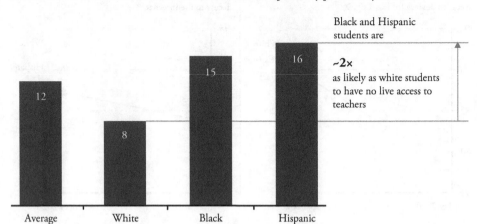

Students who have no live interaction with teachers this fall (in person, by phone, or by video), %

EXHIBIT 5   Black and Hispanic students are twice as likely as white students to have no live access to teachers.

Source: "Table 3: Computer and internet availability in households with children in public or private school, by select characteristics," US Census Bureau Household Pulse Survey, October 2020, census.gov

start of this school year, we created four scenarios to consider:

— *No progress.* As a baseline scenario, this is what students were on track to lose had we continued on the same path as the initial switch to remote learning in the spring.[14] Given the improvements this fall, we hope we have averted this worst-case scenario.

— *Status quo.* This presumes that students stay in their current learning modalities (remote, hybrid, or in-person) until the end of the school year, with a mix of remote learning quality slightly better than historical virtual charter school performance.[15]

— *Better remote.* In this scenario, students stay in their current learning modalities until the end of the school year, but with significant improvements in remote and hybrid learning quality.[16]

— *Back to school.* This scenario is identical to the status quo scenario to the end of 2020, and then students resume a more typical in-person schedule from January 2021 to the end of the school year.[17]

The results are startling. Students on average could lose five to nine months of learning by the end of June

2021. Students of color could be six to 12 months behind, compared with four to eight months for white students (Exhibit 6).

All of these scenarios will have a meaningful impact on existing achievement gaps, but shortening the length of disruption or improving the quality of remote learning can lessen this impact significantly, especially for students of color. If the status quo continues, students of color stand to lose 11 to 12 months of learning by the end of the year, but targeted action could help reduce this to six to eight months.

And this could be just the beginning—we also know from studies of natural disasters, such as the 2005 earthquake in Pakistan, that learning losses are likely to compound over time. Schools can take action right now to minimize further damage and repair what's already been done.

A Path Forward: Curb Losses and Accelerate Learning

With remote classes likely to remain a reality for months to come, school systems could do more to make the online experience more conducive to learning. Along with access to both technology and live teaching, students need a daily schedule that builds in formal opportunities for engagement, collaboration, and feedback. System leaders should also

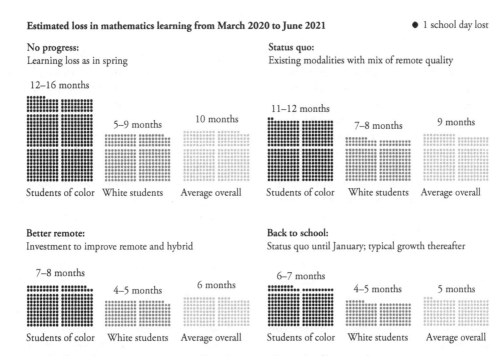

Estimated loss in mathematics learning from March 2020 to June 2021   ● 1 school day lost

EXHIBIT 6 Different learning scenarios significantly impact the scale of learning loss.

Source: *Online charter school study 2015*, Center for Research on Education Outcomes (CREDO), Oct 2015; Curriculum Associates i-Ready Assessment data; Public US district reopening analysis by select characteristics; US Census data, Oct 2020

empower teachers with new ways to share practices and receive professional development in an online format.[18] There are already some bright spots. Recent Curriculum Associates analysis identified a subset of exemplar schools serving low-income students of color that managed to minimize learning loss. These schools eliminated the digital divide; reached out to each family; doubled down on feedback loops of instruction, learning, and assessment; and held everyone accountable while celebrating successes.[19]

Most important, perhaps, schools can take a more holistic view of their role in a student's life, reimagining elements of curriculum, teaching, technology, and supporting infrastructure in ways that go beyond the norm. That could start with a renewed focus on early childhood—integrating healthcare, social services, and education programs to support children to be ready for school cognitively and socioemotionally. It could continue with ensuring high-quality instructional materials in every classroom, integrating best-practice personalized, blended

learning to help students master content. By recognizing teachers as the lifeblood of our education system, the approach could involve a more practicum-based approach to teacher professional development and innovation in unbundling the role of the teacher. For example, Opportunity Culture has been working with several school districts to adopt its multiclassroom leadership model to remote learning—embedding real-time virtual coaching into every classroom.[20] More broadly, schools provide so much more than academics. The pandemic has underscored the importance of investing in mental-health support, motivational coaching, skills training, and new support structures that could lead to an improved education experience.

Even if schools follow the most carefully structured, evidence-based approach to get the most out of remote learning and improve their teaching going forward, the reality is that many months of learning have already been lost. As a result, school systems need to create a step change in student learning if we are to catch up on what has been lost through this pandemic. Systems can start now to create acceleration plans using evidence-based strategies that support students with more time and more dedicated attention, all founded on exposing students to grade-level learning. These strategies can be targeted to the students who need them most, leveraging the best formative assessments and early-warning systems to identify students at risk.[21] These approaches have been road-tested, but will require significant investment to scale (Exhibit 7).

Some of this may only be possible once it is safe to return to in-person learning, but other elements can begin remotely. In a recent survey of district and state leaders conducted in partnership with Chiefs for Change, we found that several districts and states are already experimenting to implement these strategies in the current environment. Some specific examples follow.

— **Expanded learning time: Acceleration Academies**

Given the scope of learning loss so far and the limitations of remote learning, students will likely need additional learning hours to make up the loss. That can come through extended school-day and structured after-school programs, weekend school, and summer school programs that already have proven benefits.[22] The most effective programs strive to reinforce core learning, be culturally relevant, and limit groups to eight to 12 students. While some of these strategies can be implemented now, others should be developed for rapid implementation once in-person instruction is safe.

The summer of 2021 presents a promising opportunity. A recent RAND analysis of 43 summer programs suggests that 75 percent were effective in improving at least one outcome, especially in reading. Promising examples include Acceleration Academies, which has helped students gain up to three months of learning through 25 hours of targeted instruction in a single subject (math or English-language arts) over week-long vacation breaks.[23] California's Aim High organization, meanwhile, reduced chronic absenteeism by 22 percent and suspensions by 37 percent with its project-based summer program.

What might it cost? Examples of scaling existing evidence-based approaches

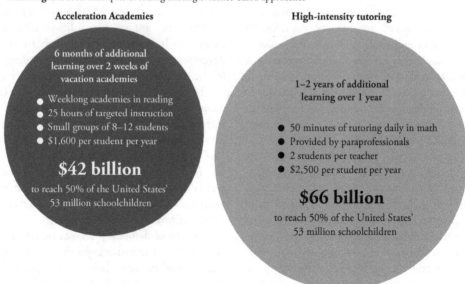

Acceleration Academies

6 months of additional learning over 2 weeks of vacation academies

- Weeklong academies in reading
- 25 hours of targeted instruction
- Small groups of 8–12 students
- $1,600 per student per year

$42 billion

to reach 50% of the United States' 53 million schoolchildren

High-intensity tutoring

1–2 years of additional learning over 1 year

- 50 minutes of tutoring daily in math
- Provided by paraprofessionals
- 2 students per teacher
- $2,500 per student per year

$66 billion

to reach 50% of the United States' 53 million schoolchildren

EXHIBIT 7   Significant investments will be required to catch up on lost learning.

Source: McKinsey projections, based on studies by *Educational Evaluation and Policy Analysis*, EdResearch for Recovery Project, and Hamilton Project

Some districts are already planning for extended learning time. For example, Ector County Independent School District in Texas has extended its school year from 180 to 210 days and will run a summer-long program available for all students.

What this might look like at scale: Governments, foundations, and school districts collaborate to create a national initiative to bring locally driven, evidence-based summer learning programs to every US student who needs it in 2021.

— **Dedicated attention: High-intensity tutoring**

A proven catalyst for accelerated learning is one-on-one support for students. That requires bringing more talent into the system to provide "high dosage" tutoring and coaching.[24] These programs were pioneered by Match Education in Boston and scaled by Saga Education in Chicago to provide students who are behind grade level in mathematics with an individualized 50-minute class period every school day. Tutors work with two students at a time in each session and cover content that not only meets students where they are but also links back to what is being taught in the regular math classroom. These types of student–tutor ratios may seem unachievable, but costs are kept (relatively) low by using paraprofessionals (for example, recent college graduates) to provide the tutoring. Although certified classroom-teaching expertise is required for teaching a class of 25, trained college graduates can effectively tutor a group of two students. The results are impressive: participating students learned one to two additional school years of mathematics in a single year.

These high-dosage programs are much more effective than low-dosage volunteer tutoring provided weekly or on an ad hoc basis, which have not been shown to have any significant effect on academic progression. Broader research on tutoring finds that it has the greatest impact on reading abilities in the early years (especially in kindergarten and first grade) but more impact in math performance in later grades. Tutoring conducted during school hours is more effective than tutoring after school, and tutoring using teachers or paraprofessionals is more effective than that using volunteers or parents.[25]

It's unclear whether remote tutoring can have the same impact as in-person sessions, but several school systems are running experiments. For example, the Broward County Public Schools district is implementing and assessing several remote tutoring programs, including targeted high-intensity algebra tutoring for high schoolers through an external partnership with Saga Education, as well as "Ask BRIA" (Broward Remote Instructional Assistance)—a locally developed, broad-based interactive video homework helpline available to every K–12 student. The National Student Support Accelerator is working to scale quality tutoring nationwide through increased funding, clear quality standards, and communities of practice.

What this might look like at scale: Universities and school districts partner to leverage successful math-tutoring strategies, creating a national education-service program that gives college students credit to tutor K–12 students through a targeted curriculum.

— **Acceleration not remediation: Exposure to grade-level content**

A key factor fueling disparity in achievement is disparity in teaching. Teachers who follow evidence-based best practices in curriculum and pedagogy are most likely to foster academic progression. When helping students catch up on lost learning, it's critical for instructors to keep them immersed in grade-level content. That might seem counterintuitive. Shouldn't teachers "meet students where they are"? However, recent research from the New Teacher Project suggests that well-intentioned approaches that pull students out of grade-level instruction to "reteach" earlier-grade content can reinforce low expectations and create vicious cycles of underachievement.[26] The better approach is for instructors to provide exposure to grade-level content, while scaffolding students with "just-in-time support" so they can access such content.[27] This is a natural way of prioritizing the building-block content from previous grades that is required to progress.

For example, the Mississippi Department of Education has provided professional development and webinars to teachers, shifting from a deficit model toward accelerated learning—starting with teaching grade-level standards. Meanwhile, the Highline Public Schools district in the state of Washington has identified the *essential* "essential standards" to provide just-in-time scaffolding to students, creating sample units demonstrating how to implement this grade-level teaching approach.

What this could look like at scale: Teachers and schools around the country set high expectations for every student, exposing them to grade-level learning with the scaffolding they need to succeed.

The COVID-19 pandemic has both illuminated and magnified the persistent disparities between different races and income groups in the United States. In education, attention has largely focused on the achievement gap, which is widening because of the pandemic. But to address the achievement gap, schools must focus on underlying opportunity gaps. The pandemic has forced the most vulnerable students into the least desirable learning situations with inadequate tools and support systems to navigate them. In the spring, that was perhaps an inevitable consequence of being thrust into a sudden unpredictable crisis. With the knowledge and systems we now have in place, allowing this to continue is unacceptable.

One of the distinguishing drivers of US success is Americans' ability to innovate and mobilize around ambitious goals. That drive made the country spend $250 billion to put a human on the moon in 1969 and has made the United States a magnet for talent from around the world. A similar investment and focus on innovation is needed now in education—with deeper collaboration across public, private, and social sectors. Currently, the United States ranks 36th in math and 13th in reading in the Programme for International Student Assessment (PISA) rankings. With many other OECD countries having resumed in-person learning, the United States risks falling further behind relative to other nations. Even more important than national competitiveness, of course, is the imperative to provide every child with an opportunity to succeed. While the COVID-19 pandemic has forced this generation of students to face challenges that could shape the rest of their lives, it could also inspire a new moonshot to bring excellence and equity to an education system that's already left too many students behind.

Emma Dorn is the global education practice manager in McKinsey's Silicon Valley office; **Bryan Hancock** and **Jimmy Sarakatsannis** are partners in the Washington, DC, office; and **Ellen Viruleg** is a senior adviser based in Providence, Rhode Island.

Notes

Acknowledgments: The authors wish to thank their collaborators Chiefs for Change for their partnership and contribution and Curriculum Associates for the essential data on student performance to date. They also wish to thank Sophia Autor, Katie Kettering, and Mike Munroe for their contributions for this article.
Designed by McKinsey Global Publishing.

1. Curriculum Associates i-Ready Assessment, taken in schools across 25 states, by 357,731 K–5 students in math and 255,018 students in reading, from the beginning of the school year until October 15, 2020. For more research information, see, "New data from Curriculum Associates quantifies impact of COVID learning loss; raises questions about at-home testing," Curriculum Associates, October 5, 2020, curriculumassociates.com.

2. Specifically, we compared the growth of students between the fall 2019 and fall 2020 assessments with historical matched average growth for fall-to-fall over the previous three years. For more information, see "Appendix A: Detailed methodology and sample characteristics," in *Understanding student needs: Early results from fall assessments*, Curriculum Associates, October 2020, curriculumassociates.com.

3. Although the conversion to "months of learning" can be problematic, it provides an intuitive sense of how

much learning has been lost. We recognize that these are approximate values and should not be regarded as precise metrics.

4. Students of color include students who identify as American Indian/Alaskan Native, Asian, Black/African American, Hispanic/Latino, Native Hawaiian/Pacific Islander, or two or more races.

5. *Programme for International Student Assessment (PISA) 2012 results: Excellence through equity: Giving every student the chance to succeed (volume II),* OECD, 2013; United States between-school versus within-school data (2012 was the last year that PISA focused on mathematics, the focus of our analysis).

6. To extrapolate from the school to the student level, we applied the historical ratio of between-school and within-school student score variance to provide a range of learning loss at the student level. The range for students of color was 3.4 to 4.6 months of lost learning (an average of about four months), the range for white students was 1.4 to 2.6 months of lost learning in mathematics (an average of about two months).

7. Comprehensive data is elusive, given the fragmentation of decision making, so we combined data from the Center on Reinventing Public Education (CRPE), Chalkbeat, EdSurge, and *Education Week* to create a holistic picture.

8. "July 24–31, 2020, Washington Post–Schar School poll of parents," *Washington Post,* August 17, 2020, washingtonpost.com.

9. According to an NPR survey of 60 districts: Anya Kamenetz et al., "Enrollment is dropping in public schools around the country," National Public Radio, October 9, 2020, npr.org.

10. See, for example, Raj Chetty et al., "The effects of kindergarten classroom on earnings in the United States," Abdul Latif Jameel Poverty Action Lab (J-PAL), povertyactionlab.org; "Chicago Longitudinal Study," University of Minnesota, 2020, innovation.unm.edu; "Home page," Heckman Equation, 2020, heckmanequation.org.

11. See Opportunity Insights Economic Tracker, tracktherecovery.org, for updated charts. Data accessed November 15, 2020.

12. "The impact of coronavirus on food insecurity," Feeding America, October 30, 2020, feedingamerica.org.

13. *Online charter school study 2015,* Center for Research on Education Outcomes (CREDO), October 2015, credo.stanford.edu.

14. Learning loss equivalent to March-June 2020 learning loss, which is based on school-level in-school assessment data from mid-October from Curriculum Associates, with historical within-school and between-school ratio to estimate range of student-level loss.

15. No instruction for the portion of students who receive no live contact with teachers (from census data), equivalent to losing half a month of learning each month (less than summer slide, but still significant); high-quality remote learning (equivalent to the top quintile of CREDO's *Online charter school study 2015*) providing 90 percent of typical growth for the top quintile of students; low-quality remote learning (equivalent to average of CREDO's *Online charter school study 2015*) providing 0 percent of typical growth for the remainder of remote students. Hybrid learning assumed to be the average of in-person and remote learning as a proxy (given lack of any academic study results).

16. All students get instruction. High-quality remote learning (equivalent to the top quintile of CREDO's *Online charter school study 2015*) providing 90 percent of typical growth for the top quintile of students; above-average quality remote learning (equivalent to the top half of CREDO's *Online charter school study 2015*) providing 50 percent of typical growth for the remainder of remote students. Hybrid learning assumed to be the average of in-person and remote learning as a proxy (given lack of any academic study results).

17. Same assumptions as status-quo scenario based on CREDO's *Online charter school study 2015,* but with typical instruction resuming in January 2021.

18. For example, Doug Lemov recently released a compendium of best practices in online teaching, *Teaching in the Online Classroom: Surviving and Thriving in the New Normal* (Jossey-Bass, October 2020), based on several months of study of videos of effective teachers at work online.

19. *Overcoming the digital divide: Distance-learning successes during the pandemic,* Curriculum Associates, September 2020, curriculumassociates.com.

20. "At-home/hybrid teaching and learning," Opportunity Culture, last accessed December 2, 2020, opportunityculture.org.

21. Early warning systems that track attendance, assignment completion, grades and behavioral data can help schools identify students that need intervention. For example, see William Corrin et al., *Addressing early warning indicators: Interim impact findings from the Investing in Innovation (i3) evaluation of Diplomas Now,* MDRC, June 2016, mdrc.org.

22. Linda Darling-Hammond et al., *Restarting and reinventing school: Learning in the time of COVID and beyond,* Learning Policy Institute, August 2020, learningpolicyinstitute.org.

23. David J. Deming, Joshua S. Goodman, and Beth E. Schueler, "Can states take over and turn around school districts? Evidence from Lawrence, Massachusetts," *Educational Evaluation and Policy Analysis*, June 2017, Volume 39, Number 1, pp. 311–32; and Elaine Allensworth and Nate Schwartz,"School practices to address student learning loss," EdResearch for Recovery Project, June 2020, annenberg.brown.edu.

24. Roseanna Ander, Jonathan Guryan, and Jens Ludwig, *Improving academic outcomes for disadvantaged students: Scaling up individualized tutorials*, Hamilton Project, March 2016, hamiltonproject.org.

25. Andre Nickow, Philip Oreopoulos, and Vincent Quan, *The impressive effects of tutoring on preK-12 learning: A systematic review and metaanalysis of the experimental evidence*, National Bureau of Economic Research working paper, number 27476, July 2020, nber.org.

26. *The opportunity myth: What students can show us about how school is letting them down—and how to fix it*, TNTP, September 2018, opportunitymyth.tntp.org.

27. "Learning acceleration guide: Planning for acceleration in the 2020–2021 school year," TNTP, April 2020, tntp.org.

Questions for Critical Thinking

1. The authors' research illustrates that the educational gap worsened during the COVID-19 pandemic. How does their discussion deepen your understanding of the factors that create and exacerbate the educational divide in the United States?

2. Reflecting on the authors' discussion, what do you think of their recommendations to narrow the educational gap? What do you see as the likelihood of these investments being made?

3. Considering the analysis offered in this study, what additional solutions can you offer?

CIVILIZE THEM WITH A STICK

* *Mary Crow Dog and Richard Erdoes*

The following essay is taken from the autobiography of Mary Crow Dog, Lakota Woman, written with Richard Erdoes, which recounts her experiences growing up Sioux in a white-dominated society. In this excerpt, she reflects on her personal experiences as a student in a boarding school run by the Bureau of Indian Affairs.

> . . . Gathered from the cabin, the wickiup, and the tepee, partly by cajolery and partly by threats; partly by bribery and partly by force, they are induced to leave their kindred to enter these schools and take upon themselves the outward appearance of civilized life.
>
> —*Annual Report of the Department of Interior,* 1901

It is almost impossible to explain to a sympathetic white person what a typical old Indian boarding school was like; how it affected the Indian child suddenly dumped into it like a small creature from another world, helpless, defenseless, bewildered, trying desperately and instinctively to survive and sometimes not surviving at all. I think such children were like the victims of Nazi concentration camps trying to tell average, middle-class Americans what their experience had been like. Even now, when these schools are much improved, when the buildings are new, all gleaming steel and glass, the food tolerable, the teachers well trained and well intentioned, even trained in child psychology—unfortunately the psychology of white children, which is different from ours—the shock to the child upon arrival is still tremendous. Some just seem to shrivel up, don't speak for days on end, and have an empty look in their eyes. I know of an 11-year-old on another reservation who hanged herself, and in our school, while I was there, a girl jumped out of the window, trying to kill herself to escape an unbearable situation. That first shock is always there.

Although the old tiyospaye has been destroyed, in the traditional Sioux families, especially in those where there is no drinking, the child is never left alone. It is always surrounded by relatives, carried around, enveloped in warmth. It is treated with the respect due to any human being, even a small one. It is seldom forced to do anything against its will, seldom screamed at, and never beaten. That much, at least, is left of the old family group among full-bloods. And then suddenly a bus or car arrives, full of strangers, usually white strangers, who yank the child out of the arms of those who love it, taking it screaming to the boarding school. The only word I can think of for what is done to these children is kidnapping.

Even now, in a good school, there is impersonality instead of close human contact; a sterile, cold atmosphere, an unfamiliar routine, language problems, and above all the maza-skan-skan, that damn clock—white man's time as opposed to Indian time, which is natural time. Like eating when you are hungry and sleeping when you are tired, not when that damn clock says you must. But I was not taken to one of the better, modern schools. I was taken to the old-fashioned mission school at St. Francis, run by the nuns and Catholic fathers, built sometime around the turn of the century and not improved a bit when I arrived, not improved as far as the buildings, the food, the teachers, or their methods were concerned.

In the old days, nature was our people's only school and they needed no other. Girls had their toy tipis and dolls, boys their toy bows and arrows. Both rode and swam and played the rough Indian games together. Kids watched their peers and elders and naturally grew from children into adults. Life in the tipi circle was harmonious—until the whiskey peddlers arrived with their wagons and barrels of "Injun whiskey." I often wished I could have grown up in the old, before-whiskey days.

Oddly enough, we owed our unspeakable boarding schools to the do-gooders, the white Indian-lovers. The schools were intended as an alternative to the outright extermination seriously advocated by generals Sherman and Sheridan, as well as by most settlers and prospectors overrunning our land. "You don't have to kill those poor benighted heathen," the do-gooders said, "in order to solve the Indian Problem. Just give us a chance to turn them into useful farmhands, laborers, and chambermaids who will break their backs for you at low wages." In that way the boarding schools were born. The kids were taken away from their villages and pueblos, in their blankets and moccasins, kept completely isolated from their families—sometimes for as long as ten years—suddenly coming back, their short hair slick with pomade, their necks raw from stiff, high collars, their thick jackets always short in the sleeves and pinching under the arms, their tight patent leather shoes giving them corns, the girls in starched white blouses and clumsy, high-buttoned boots—caricatures of white people. When they found out—and they found out quickly—that they were neither wanted by whites nor by Indians, they got good and drunk, many of them staying drunk for the rest of their lives. I still have a

poster I found among my grandfather's stuff, given to him by the missionaries to tack up on his wall. It reads:

1. Let Jesus save you.
2. Come out of your blanket, cut your hair, and dress like a white man.
3. Have a Christian family with one wife for life only.
4. Live in a house like your white brother. Work hard and wash often.
5. Learn the value of a hard-earned dollar. Do not waste your money on giveaways. Be punctual.
6. Believe that property and wealth are signs of divine approval.
7. Keep away from saloons and strong spirits.
8. Speak the language of your white brother. Send your children to school to do likewise.
9. Go to church often and regularly.
10. Do not go to Indian dances or to the medicine men.

The people who were stuck upon "solving the Indian Problem" by making us into whites retreated from this position only step by step in the wake of Indian protests.

The mission school at St. Francis was a curse for our family for generations. My grandmother went there, then my mother, then my sisters and I. At one time or other every one of us tried to run away. Grandma told me once about the bad times she had experienced at St. Francis. In those days they let students go home only for one week every year. Two days were used up for transportation, which meant spending just five days out of 365 with her family. And that was an improvement. Before grandma's time, on many reservations they did not let the students go home at all until they had finished school. Anybody who disobeyed the nuns was severely punished. The building in which my grandmother stayed had three floors, for girls only. Way up in the attic were little cells, about five by five by ten feet. One time she was in church and instead of praying she was playing jacks. As punishment they took her to one of those little cubicles where she stayed in darkness because the windows had been boarded up. They left her there for a whole week with only bread and water for nourishment. After she came out she promptly ran away, together with three other girls. They were found and brought back. The nuns stripped them naked and whipped them. They used a horse buggy whip on my grandmother. Then she was put back into the attic— for two weeks.

My mother had much the same experiences but never wanted to talk about them, and then there I was, in the same place. The school is now run by the BIA—the Bureau of Indian Affairs—but only since about 15 years ago. When I was there, during the 1960s, it was still run by the Church. The Jesuit fathers ran the boys' wing and the Sisters of the Sacred Heart ran us—with the help of the strap. Nothing had changed since my grandmother's days. I have been told recently that even in the '70s they were still beating children at that school. All I got out of school was being taught how to pray. I learned quickly that I would be beaten if I failed in my devotions or, God forbid, prayed the wrong way, especially prayed in Indian to Wakan Tanka, the Indian Creator.

The girls' wing was built like an F and was run like a penal institution. Every morning at five o'clock the sisters would come into our large dormitory to wake us up, and immediately we had to kneel down at the sides of our beds and recite the prayers. At six o'clock we were herded into the church for more of the same. I did not take kindly to the discipline and to marching by the clock, left-right, left-right. I was never one to like being forced to do something. I do something because I feel like doing it. I felt this way always, as far as I can remember, and my sister Barbara felt the same way. An old medicine man once told me: "Us Lakotas are not like dogs who can be trained, who can be beaten and keep on wagging their tails, licking the hand that whipped them. We are like cats, little cats, big cats, wildcats, bobcats, mountain lions. It doesn't matter what kind, but cats who can't be tamed, who scratch if you step on their tails." But I was only a kitten and my claws were still small.

Barbara was still in the school when I arrived and during my first year or two she could still protect me a little bit. When Barb was a seventh grader she ran away together with five other girls, early in the morning before sunrise. They brought them back in the evening. The girls had to wait for two hours in front of the mother superior's office. They were hungry and

cold, frozen through. It was wintertime and they had been running the whole day without food, trying to make good their escape. The mother superior asked each girl, "Would you do this again?" She told them that as punishment they would not be allowed to visit home for a month and that she'd keep them busy on work details until the skin on their knees and elbows had worn off. At the end of her speech she told each girl, "Get up from this chair and lean over it." She then lifted the girls' skirts and pulled down their underpants. Not little girls either, but teenagers. She had a leather strap about a foot long and four inches wide fastened to a stick, and beat the girls, one after another, until they cried. Barb did not give her that satisfaction but just clenched her teeth. There was one girl, Barb told me, the nun kept on beating and beating until her arm got tired.

I did not escape my share of the strap. Once, when I was 13 years old, I refused to go to Mass. I did not want to go to church because I did not feel well. A nun grabbed me by the hair, dragged me upstairs, made me stoop over, pulled my dress up (we were not allowed at the time to wear jeans), pulled my panties down, and gave me what they called "swats"—25 swats with a board around which Scotch tape had been wound. She hurt me badly.

My classroom was right next to the principal's office and almost every day I could hear him swatting the boys. Beating was the common punishment for not doing one's homework, or for being late to school. It had such a bad effect upon me that I hated and mistrusted every white person on sight, because I met only one kind. It was not until much later that I met sincere white people I could relate to and be friends with. Racism breeds racism in reverse.

The routine at St. Francis was dreary. Six a.m., kneeling in church for an hour or so; seven o'clock, breakfast; eight o'clock, scrub the floor, peel spuds, make classes. We had to mop the dining room twice every day and scrub the tables. If you were caught taking a rest, doodling on the bench with a fingernail or knife, or just rapping, the nun would come up with a dish towel and just slap it across your face, saying, "You're not supposed to be talking; you're supposed to be working!" Monday mornings we had cornmeal mush, Tuesday oatmeal, Wednesday rice and raisins, Thursday cornflakes, and Friday all the leftovers mixed together or sometimes fish. Frequently the food had bugs or rocks in it. We were eating hot dogs that were weeks old, while the nuns were dining on ham, whipped potatoes, sweet peas, and cranberry sauce. In winter our dorm was icy cold while the nuns' rooms were always warm.

I have seen little girls arrive at the school, first graders, just fresh from home and totally unprepared for what awaited them, little girls with pretty braids, and the first thing the nuns did was chop their hair off and tie up what was left behind their ears. Next they would dump the children into tubs of alcohol, a sort of rubbing alcohol, "to get the germs off." Many of the nuns were German immigrants, some from Bavaria, so that we sometimes speculated whether Bavaria was some sort of Dracula country inhabited by monsters. For the sake of objectivity I ought to mention that two of the German fathers were great linguists and that the only Lakota–English dictionaries and grammars which are worth anything were put together by them.

At night some of the girls would huddle in bed together for comfort and reassurance. Then the nun in charge of the dorm would come in and say, "What are the two of you doing in bed together? I smell evil in this room. You girls are evil incarnate. You are sinning. You are going to hell and burn forever. You can act that way in the devil's frying pan." She would get them out of bed in the middle of the night, making them kneel and pray until morning. We had not the slightest idea what it was all about. At home we slept two and three in a bed for animal warmth and a feeling of security.

The nuns and the girls in the two top grades were constantly battling it out physically with fists, nails, and hair-pulling. I myself was growing from a kitten into an undersized cat. My claws were getting bigger and were itching for action. About 1969 or 1970 a strange young white girl appeared on the reservation. She looked about 18 or 20 years old. She was pretty and had long, blond hair down to her waist, patched jeans, boots, and a backpack. She was different from any other white person we had met before. I think her name was Wise. I do not know how she managed to overcome our reluctance and distrust, getting us into a corner, making us listen to her, asking us how we were treated. She told us that she was from New York. She was the first real hippie or Yippie we had

come across. She told us of people called the Black Panthers, Young Lords, and Weathermen. She said, "Black people are getting it on. Indians are getting it on in St. Paul and California. How about you?" She also said, "Why don't you put out an underground paper, mimeograph it. It's easy. Tell it like it is. Let it all hang out." She spoke a strange lingo but we caught on fast.

Charlene Left Hand Bull and Gina One Star were two full-blood girls I used to hang out with. We did everything together. They were willing to join me in a Sioux uprising. We put together a newspaper which we called the *Red Panther*. In it we wrote how bad the school was, what kind of slop we had to eat—slimy, rotten, blackened potatoes for two weeks—the way we were beaten. I think I was the one who wrote the worst article about our principal of the moment, Father Keeler. I put all my anger and venom into it. I called him a goddam wasicun of a bitch. I wrote that he knew nothing about Indians and should go back to where he came from, teaching white children whom he could relate to. I wrote that we knew which priests slept with which nuns and that all they ever could think about was filling their bellies and buying a new car. It was the kind of writing which foamed at the mouth, but which also lifted a great deal of weight from one's soul.

On Saint Patrick's Day, when everybody was at the big powwow, we distributed our newspapers. We put them on windshields and bulletin boards, in desks and pews, in dorms and toilets. But someone saw us and snitched on us. The shit hit the fan. The three of us were taken before a board meeting. Our parents, in my case my mother, had to come. They were told that ours was a most serious matter, the worst thing that had ever happened in the school's long history. One of the nuns told my mother, "Your daughter really needs to be talked to." "What's wrong with my daughter?" my mother asked. She was given one of our *Red Panther* newspapers. The nun pointed out its name to her and then my piece, waiting for mom's reaction. After a while she asked, "Well, what have you got to say to this? What do you think?"

My mother said, "Well, when I went to school here, some years back, I was treated a lot worse than these kids are. I really can't see how they can have any complaints, because we was treated a lot stricter. We could not even wear skirts halfway up our knees.

These girls have it made. But you should forgive them because they are young. And it's supposed to be a free country, free speech and all that. I don't believe what they done is wrong." So all I got out of it was scrubbing six flights of stairs on my hands and knees, every day. And no boy-side privileges.

The boys and girls were still pretty much separated. The only time one could meet a member of the opposite sex was during free time, between 4 and 5:30, in the study hall or on benches or the volleyball court outside, and that was strictly supervised. One day Charlene and I went over to the boys' side. We were on the ball team and they had to let us practice. We played three extra minutes, only three minutes more than we were supposed to. Here was the nuns' opportunity for revenge. We got 25 swats. I told Charlene, "We are getting too old to have our bare asses whipped that way. We are old enough to have babies. Enough of this shit. Next time we fight back." Charlene only said, "Hoka-hay!"

* * *

In a school like this there is always a lot of favoritism. At St. Francis it was strongly tinged with racism. Girls who were near-white, who came from what the nuns called "nice families," got preferential treatment. They waited on the faculty and got to eat ham or eggs and bacon in the morning. They got the easy jobs while the skins, who did not have the right kind of background—myself among them—always wound up in the laundry room sorting out 10-bushel baskets of dirty boys' socks every day. Or we wound up scrubbing the floors and doing all the dishes. The school therefore fostered fights and antagonism between whites and breeds, and between breeds and skins. At one time Charlene and I had to iron all the robes and vestments the priests wore when saying Mass. We had to fold them up and put them into a chest in the back of the church. In a corner, looking over our shoulders, was a statue of the crucified Savior, all bloody and beaten up. Charlene looked up and said, "Look at that poor Indian. The pigs sure worked him over." That was the closest I ever came to seeing Jesus.

I was held up as a bad example and didn't mind. I was old enough to have a boyfriend and promptly got one. At the school we had an hour and a half for ourselves. Between the boys' and the girls' wings were some benches where one could sit. My boyfriend and I used to go there just to hold hands and talk. The nuns were very uptight about any boy–girl stuff. They had an exaggerated fear of anything having even the faintest connection with sex. One day in religion class, an all-girl class, Sister Bernard singled me out for some remarks, pointing me out as a bad example, an example that should be shown. She said that I was too free with my body. That I was holding hands which meant that I was not a good example to follow. She also said that I wore unchaste dresses, skirts which were too short, too suggestive, shorter than regulations permitted, and for that I would be punished. She dressed me down before the whole class, carrying on and on about my unchastity.

* * *

We got a new priest in English. During one of his first classes he asked one of the boys a certain question. The boy was shy. He spoke poor English, but he had the right answer. The priest told him, "You did not say it right. Correct yourself. Say it over again." The boy got flustered and stammered. He could hardly get out a word. But the priest kept after him: "Didn't you hear? I told you to do the whole thing over. Get it right this time." He kept on and on.

I stood up and said, "Father, don't be doing that. If you go into an Indian's home and try to talk Indian, they might laugh at you and say, 'Do it over correctly. Get it right this time!'"

He shouted at me, "Mary, you stay after class. Sit down right now!"

I stayed after class, until after the bell. He told me, "Get over here!" He grabbed me by the arm, pushing me against the blackboard, shouting, "Why are you always mocking us? You have no reason to do this."

I said, "Sure I do. You were making fun of him. You embarrassed him. He needs strengthening, not weakening. You hurt him. I did not hurt you."

He twisted my arm and pushed real hard. I turned around and hit him in the face, giving him a bloody nose. After that I ran out of the room, slamming the door behind me. He and I went to Sister Bernard's office. I told her, "Today I quit school. I'm not taking any more of this, none of this shit anymore. None of this treatment. Better give me my diploma. I can't waste any more time on you people."

Sister Bernard looked at me for a long, long time. She said, "All right, Mary Ellen, go home today. Come back in a few days and get your diploma." And that was that. Oddly enough, that priest turned out okay. He taught a class in grammar, orthography, composition, things like that. I think he wanted more respect in class. He was still young and unsure of himself. But I was in there too long. I didn't feel like hearing it. Later he became a good friend of the Indians, a personal friend of myself and my husband.

He stood up for us during Wounded Knee and after. He stood up to his superiors, stuck his neck way out, became a real people's priest. He even learned our language. He died prematurely of cancer. It is not only the good Indians who die young, but the good whites, too. It is the timid ones who know how to take care of themselves who grow old. I am still grateful to that priest for what he did for us later and for the quarrel he picked with me—or did I pick it with him?—because it ended a situation which had become unendurable for me. The day of my fight with him was my last day in school.

Questions for Critical Thinking

1. As discussed by Crow Dog and Erdoes, policies and practices of educational institutions construct Native Americans and Native American culture as deviant. What other cultures are constructed as deviant by our educational institutions?
2. What are some of the ways that we expect marginalized groups to assimilate? How do the policies and practices of the educational institution foster this assimilation process?
3. What would our culture look like if we included the perspectives of Native Americans rather than requiring them to assimilate?

BLACK GIRLS AND SCHOOL DISCIPLINE

The Complexities of Being Overrepresented and Understudied

• *Subini Ancy Annamma, Yolanda Anyon, Nicole M. Joseph, Jordan Farrar, Eldridge Greer, Barbara Downing, and John Simmons*

The article that follows examines data that provides evidence of disciplinary disparities for Black girls in out-of-school suspensions, law enforcement referrals, and expulsions. Employing **Critical Race Theory**—the idea that systemic racism and structured disadvantages are built into U.S. society and not merely a matter of individual prejudice—the authors demonstrate how the biases and stereotypes teachers hold about Black girls as well as the policies and practices of our public educational system perpetuate the silencing and oppression of this population.

On Monday, October 26, a video of Police Officer Ben Fields entering a classroom and assaulting a young Black girl[1] as she sat quietly at her desk exploded on social media. In the video, Fields, a White male, can be seen grabbing the seated Black girl around her neck, flipping her over in her desk, and dragging her across the floor. Another video of the same incident shows a Black male adult standing idly by and watching the entire incident unfold. Students are seen with their heads down or watching the violence unfold silently. Only one young Black girl, Niya Kenny,[2] stands up to Fields, crying, "What the fuck did she do?" to which Field's responds, "Hey, I'll put you in jail next." Kenny, was the second young Black girl arrested at Spring Valley that day. The #AssaultatSpringValleyHigh highlights how schools can be sites of racialized and gendered terror for Black girls.

In this article, we explore the ways urban schools perpetuate intersectional violence against Black girls through school discipline disparities in Denver

Public Schools (DPS), an urban school district. It is important to note that we are conceptualizing urban based on

> (1) *the size* of the of the city in which the schools are located: dense large, metropolitan areas; (2) *the students* in the schools: a wide range of student diversity, including racial, ethnic, religious, language, and socioeconomic; and (3) *the resources*: the amount and number of resources available in a school, such as technology and financial structures through federal programs as well as property taxes. (Milner & Lomotey, 2014, p. xv)

The city of Denver houses a population of 663,862 and is the largest metropolitan area in Colorado (U.S.

Urban Education
2019, Vol. 54(2) 211–242
. . .The Author(s) 2016
Article reuse guidelines:
sagepub.com/Journals-permissions
DOI: 10.1177/0042085916646610
Journals.sagepub.com/home/uex

Census Bureau, 2015). The total student population of DPS as of October 2014 was 90,150 including 0.6% American Indian, 3.3% Asian, 14.1% Black, 56.7% Hispanic, 3.4% Other, and 21.9% White. The English Language Learning population compromised 38.8% of the total population and 69.69% were on free and reduced lunch[3] (DPS, 2015). The resources of DPS are limited with an average state per pupil spending being US$6,872.87, whereas the wealthy Aspen 1 school district receiving US$8,381.96 per pupil. Therefore, in all ways, DPS qualifies as an urban district.

However, it is important to note that schools as sites of racialized and gendered violence are not only urban schools in the ways Milner and Lomotey (2014) describe. In another study of racialized disciplinary disparities in Colorado, it was found instead that these disparities existed wherever children of color went to school, whether the districts be defined as urban, suburban, or rural (Annamma, Morrison, & Jackson, 2014). Furthermore, when considering the highly publicized assault of a young Black girl at Spring Valley High School, the school itself is not considered urban. Richland County, where Spring Valley High is situated, is described as "in the center of SC. The community is a mixture of suburban, rural and military families" (Richmond School District, 2015). However, the school is 72% minority. Some scholars describe urban areas as a socially constructed place where lower income people of color have been ghettoized, marginalized by Whites (Massey & Denton, 1993). Leonardo and Hunter (2007) note that "the urban is socially and discursively constructed as a place, which is part of the dialectical creation of the urban as both a real and imagined space" (p. 779). Moreover urban areas are largely thought of as a Black space, one that Black people are viewed as carrying with them as they venture into White spaces (e.g., city's public spaces such as parks, middle-class or white-collar work-places, middle-upper class neighborhoods, schools; Anderson, 2015). Understanding how students are considered to be the carriers of "urban" even when they are not in urban places expands ways urban schools are conceptualized. This is not to argue that urban *should* be a proxy for race, only that the two words are often considered synonyms. When students of color are considered to be carrying the ghetto with them, it is

easier to see how they are then hyper-surveilled in spaces such as schools and punished more quickly. We argue in this article that for Black girls, disproportionate surveillance and punishment often occurs through the application of dominant narratives.

School discipline has increased links to criminalization because of a national commitment to a carceral state, one governed by carceral logics of punishment of the disposable (Annamma, 2016; Foucault, 1977). It is important to contextualize punitive school discipline practices and the School-to-Prison Pipeline as part of this larger carceral state, where the mass criminalization and imprisonment of bodies different from the norm is the goal (Alexander, 2012). In view of these racialized patterns of punishment, scholars, educators, and advocates have argued that the goal of equity for students of color in public education cannot be realized without disrupting racial disparities in school discipline practices (Fenning & Rose, 2007; Gregory, Skiba, & Noguera, 2010).

Black Girls Are Invisible in School Discipline Literature

Young men of color have increasingly been the focus of discussions regarding urban school discipline and criminality (Caton, 2012). Although attending to the issues Black males face is indeed important, the dearth of scholarship around Black girls' experiences have rendered them largely invisible in criminalization discussions, even though Black girls are disproportionately affected by the relationships between urban educational and carceral institutions (Losen & Gillespie, 2012; Winn, 2011; Wun, 2014). Specifically, Black girls often experience exclusionary discipline outcomes more than many males across the country, a trend that is paralleled in the criminal legal system (Chesney-Lind, 2010; Tate et al., 2014). Consequently, there is a need for research to better understand Black girls' experiences with discipline in urban schools, particularly studies that demonstrate how national trends occur in local contexts and potential reasons for these patterns.

What is known about Black girls' experience with urban school discipline and the Pipeline is disheartening. In the last decade, Black girls have had the fastest growing suspension rates of all students (Losen & Skiba, 2010). Nationally, Black girls experience discipline rates 6 times higher than White girls; they experience suspension rates higher than 67% of boys as well (U.S. Department of Education Office of Civil Rights, 2014). These trends do not appear to be the result of more serious offending patterns among Black girls. For example, Blake, Butler, Lewis, and Darensbourg (2011) examined the reasons that Black girls were suspended in one urban school district and found that, "Black girls were most often cited for defiance followed by inappropriate dress, using profane language toward a student, and physical aggression" (p. 100). In general, racial disparities in exclusionary school discipline outcomes appear to be driven by minor infractions and subjective categories of student misconduct, rather than more objective and serious behaviors such as bringing a weapon to school (Bradshaw, Mitchell, O'Brennan, & Leaf, 2010; Skiba, Michael, Nardo, & Peterson, 2002; Vavrus & Cole, 2002).

The increased likelihood of suspension among Black girls is also linked to their greater probability of being incarcerated. Wald and Losen (2003) note, "the 'single largest predictor' of later arrest among adolescent females is having been suspended, expelled or held back during the middle school years" (p. 4). Due to increased coordination between urban educational and carceral institutions, the association between exclusionary discipline outcomes and later imprisonment has likely strengthened over time. Nationally, Black girls represent 31% of girls referred to law enforcement by school officials and 43% of those arrested on school grounds, but only constitute 17% of the overall student population (National Women's Law Center & NAACP Legal Defense and Education Fund, 2014). Once entangled in the criminal system, the disparities continue, as Black girls tend to receive harsher sentences than other girls for the same offenses (Crenshaw, Ocen, & Nanda, 2015). Many of these outcomes are linked with lower achievement later in life (Wallace, Goodkind, Wallace, & Bachman, 2008).

These statistics are important but still tell very little about the processes and practices that affect Black girls' experiences with the Pipeline (Ferguson, 2000). Crenshaw et al. (2015) note, "investigations into *why* Black girls are much more likely to be harshly disciplined than other girls have been few and

far between" (p. 26, emphasis added). This study considers whether Black girls are overrepresented in exclusionary disciplinary actions in a local, urban context and through what mechanisms.

Such a focus on Black girls and discipline in urban schools is essential because it can inform urban education research through a more rigorous analysis about the intersectionality of race and gender (Crenshaw, 1989). The field needs an analysis that is simultaneously raced and gendered because discipline reform efforts targeting racial discipline gaps do not usually differentiate strategies by sex (e.g., Morgan, Salomon, Plotkin, & Cohen, 2014; U.S. Department of Education & U.S. Department of Justice, 2014). These "gender-neutral" policy and intervention recommendations appear to reflect two major assumptions that (a) Black male issues of overrepresentation in the Pipeline are the more pressing problem and (b) Black males and females are disciplined for identical reasons and, therefore, need similar interventions (Morris, 2012). Yet, findings from the extant literature on the experiences of Black girls in schools and Black women in society more broadly suggest that social constructions of gender and femininity intersecting with race shape their educational outcomes (Blake et al., 2011; DeBlase, 2003). In particular, issues of U.S. societal gender norms around femininity are important to pay attention to because these norms are oftentimes aligned with White, middle-class values (Annamma, 2015; Ladson-Billings, 1998); consequently Black girls, like Black women, tend to experience excessive surveillance and punishment if their personalities or attire diverge from what society and, by extension, educational institutions expect (Blake et al., 2011; Crenshaw et al., 2015; Richie, 2012). We believe that dominant narratives about Black girls reify the social processes that funnel Black girls out of urban schools and into prisons. These dominant narratives place these already vulnerable girls in danger of pathologization and criminalization (O'Connor, Mueller, & Neal, 2014).

Purpose

This empirical study contributes to the small but growing body of literature about Black girls and school discipline by examining exclusionary discipline outcomes among this group in DPS, a large urban school district. First, we examine descriptive disciplinary data to assess racial group differences in office referrals and whether Black girls are overrepresented in exclusionary discipline outcomes. Next, we use multivariate models to determine whether these patterns hold after accounting for other identity markers. Finally, we use Critical Discourse Analysis (CDA) to consider what mechanisms moved girls into the Pipeline by examining whether disciplinary actions were for subjective or objective behaviors and whether they align with dominant narratives about Black girls.

Specifically, the following research questions guided our investigation:

Research Question 1: Are Black girls (a) disproportionately represented in certain office referral categories and exclusionary discipline outcomes and (b) still disproportionately represented after accounting for other identity markers?

Research Question 2: Do the reasons why Black girls are referred align with (a) subjective or objective behaviors and (b) dominant narratives about Black girls?

Conceptual Framework

Theory grounds how researchers identify, name, interpret, and write about Black girls' experiences with school discipline. Consequently, it is imperative to identify theories that reflect Black girls' historical and social location and that of others with whom they interact in their world. We therefore situate this mixed-methods study within Critical Race Theory (CRT) and Critical Race Feminism (FemCrit) to understand how the nuanced ways in which Black girls are disciplined are affected by dominant narratives about who Black girls are in society—historically and contemporarily.

Fredrick Douglas, Mary Church Terrell, and Bayard Rustin were all intellectual ancestors of CRT, foregrounding race, highlighting the voices of the marginalized, and pushing for an intersectional analysis of oppression. Legal scholars of color developed CRT to counter Critical Legal Studies (CLS) when CLS engaged in a class-based analysis but was absent a race analysis (Bell, 1979; Crenshaw, Gotanda, Peller,

& Thomas, 1995; Matsuda, 1987). Scholars in education took up CRT to address disparities in education resources that led to racialized outcomes (Ladson-Billings & Tate, 1995). CRT transcended disciplines to address racialized intersections with language, immigration status (LatCrit), sexuality (QueerCrit), and more (McKinley & Brayboy, 2005; Misawa, 2010; Solórzano & Bernal, 2001). To address the deep intersections between race and gender, CRT scholars also developed FemCrit (Wing, 2003).

CRT is an important framework for this study because prevailing narratives regarding Black girls are connected to the ways in which race operates in U.S. society and schools (Ladson-Billings, 2006). Black girls, who are a sub-group of Black people in the United States, are a part of a collective that has been positioned historically as inferior simply because of the color of their skin for generations. CRT centers these facts about race and racism, and suggests that there will always be a majoritarian story, a story told by the powerful about the marginalized, about race, and that Black girls are a part of that story (Crenshaw et al., 1995). CRT also exposes how laws, policies, and practices that are considered neutral actually reinforce normative standards of Whiteness, and how these norms problematize bodies that differ from these ideals (Delgado & Stefancic, 2001; Goodwin, 2003). These processes of everyday racism lead to pathologizing individuals who are different, diagnosing differences as inherent deficits instead of socially constructed (Annamma, Connor, & Ferri, 2013). In other words, Blackness is viewed as the problem instead of racism, and specifically, anti-Blackness. CRT is also helpful in thinking about not just theory but also praxis, in practice and policy, for educational reform related to Black girls (Parker & Stovall, 2004).

In addition, Black girls experience multiple marginalized identities, an issue viewed through a single lens (e.g., race or gender) that limits understanding of ways gender *interacts* with race (Wing, 2003). Therefore, we draw on FemCrit to build on CRT by recognizing these multiple identities of women and girls, acknowledging that girls of color have unique experiences different from White girls, White boys, and even boys of color (Crenshaw, 1993; Wing, 2003). In our study, we include comparison data of other girls of color and White girls with Black girls.

Embedded within these numbers are social and educational contexts that are rooted in issues of power, systems of domination, social justice, and gender.

FemCrit highlights how sexism further compounds the ways Black girls are seen as deficit when they do not match standards of White femininity (Evans-Winters & Esposito, 2010; Morris, 2012). One way Black girls are omitted from the right to education is through exclusionary discipline. By channeling Black girls out of schools and into carceral institutions, schools are protecting education for the most privileged (Wun, 2014). Said differently, education is a property right instilled by Whiteness, with the absolute right to exclude those outside of Whiteness (Harris, 1993). Finally, the politics of multiple oppressions Black females experience as a result of their race, class, and gender status are connected to a history of slavery and controlling images, such as the matriarch (Collins, 2000). These controlling images include the (a) Mammy or Matriarch, a woman who is nurturing, loving, and sexless; (b) Sapphire, the emasculating, overly aggressive, unfeminine, or masculine, and loud female; (c) Jezebel, as hypersexualized woman who pursues and initiates sex; and (d) The Welfare Queen, the woman who is conniving, loud, talks back, and is vampiric, sucking off the system by having children and refusing to work (Hancock, 2004; Mullings, 1994; Scott, 1982). Black girls can be shaped by these controlling images, and as we see in our results section, reasons for referrals are deeply connected to the dominant narratives about who Black girls are in society (Spillers, 1987).

As guiding conceptual frameworks, CRT and FemCrit provide several affordances by (a) refuting dominant discourses surrounding Black girls that lack supporting evidence, such as that Black girls are more deserving of incarceration due to their inherently violent nature (Chesney-Lind, 2010); (b) demanding a focus on counter-narratives, contrasted by the master narrative, counter-stories provide an opportunity to see Black girls not as inherently "bad," but as thoughtful young women maneuvering complex lives and institutions; (c) allowing for a better understanding of the experiences of marginalized Black girls to understand how hegemony is enacted and embodied, along with the ways students strive for dignity (Rios, 2011); and (d) problematizing

singular notions of identity such as race or ability or gender (Crenshaw, 1993). These affordances allow us to bring different theories, methods, and questions to bear on racial disproportionality in exclusionary discipline outcomes. . . .

Discussion

Quantitative data analyses revealed there were significant racial differences in several categories of office referral reasons and exclusionary discipline outcomes. In multivariate analyses, findings were statistically significant for Black girls in the categories of disobedient/defiant behavior, drug possession, and out-of-school suspension, even when controlling for other demographic factors. Thus, the quantitative analysis shows that even when Black girls are referred to the office for the same behaviors as others girls, holding for other identity markers, Black girls are punished more harshly. This pattern is reinforced by other research that documented similar patterns for all Black students (Anyon et al., 2014; Skiba et al., 2013; Wallace et al., 2008) and Black girls in particular (Blake et al., 2011).

Qualitatively, Black girls were more likely to experience exclusionary discipline outcomes for subjective reasons, such as disobedience/defiance, detrimental behavior, and third-degree assault, which depend on the judgment of school personnel. White girls were more likely to be suspended for objective reasons, such as drug and alcohol possession, which are often considered more serious. These findings align with other studies on racial disparities in discipline (Skiba et al., 2002). However, our conceptual framework and methodology allowed for deeper qualitative examination of subjective categories to better understand why these patterns may occur. van Dijk (1993) notes, "critical discourse analysis may literally reveal processes of racism that otherwise would be difficult to establish, or that would be formally denied by the majority participants" (p. 119). The dominant discourses that frame Black girls as less innocent and feminine than all other girls likely influence these exclusionary discipline outcomes (Morris, 2012).

Counter-narratives, stories marginalized people tell about themselves and their sociocultural context in which they function, about Black girls are necessary (Harper, 2015). That is because these dominant narratives about Black girls ignore the fact that many young women of color have had to learn to be assertive, take initiative, and show fortitude in the face of historical and contemporary racism (Collins, 1991). Young women of color are also creative, innovative, and thoughtful (Brown, 2009; Jones, 2009; Winn, 2011). Social relationships are always undergirded by invisible ideologies about the least powerful (Fairclough, 1989; van Dijk, 1993). If teachers and school personnel are unaware of the historical and contemporaneous ways racism manifests in the lives of their Black female students, will they be able to perceive behaviors as positive traits or will they mistake these behaviors for threats and non-compliance (Pane, Rocco, Miller, & Salmon, 2014; Wun, 2014)? As Hall and Smith (2012) note, "regrettably, the 'inherited' attributes of Black girls are often interpreted (against the framework of conventional femininity) as obstinate, aggressive, and disobedient behaviors" (p. 225). This is especially important when considering the carceral state, in which the School-to-Prison Pipeline functions. Spillers (1987) notes, the "African-American female's . . . 'strength' come(s) to be interpreted by . . . both black and white, oddly enough-as a 'pathology,'" (p. 74). In this study, we expose the mechanisms for funneling Black girls into the Pipeline using supposedly race-neutral definitions in the name of pathologization and criminalization, making incarceration more likely in their future.

Implications
Findings indicate that Black girls are most often being subjected to discipline based on the judgment of school personnel, many of whom likely have limited understanding of ways race and racism affect Black girls' lives. A direct implication from this study is that all teachers need training on understanding both historical and contemporary racism, equity, and power (Milner & Tenore, 2010). Along with this, teachers need training to understand how racism and White supremacy affect their own biases and stereotypes they hold about Black girls. CRT and FemCrit remind us that because Black girls are a part of an oppressed group in U.S. society, their voices are often silenced (Pratt-Clarke, 2010). Currently, if a Black girl

acts in a way that contrasts normative femininity, she is at risk of being thrown out of the classroom and school, increasing the likelihood that she will interact with the criminal legal system. To remedy this, instead of implementing disciplinary exclusion when Black girls act in ways that do not align with White femininity, educators should take the opportunity to learn new ways of being a woman in the world. In fact, it would benefit all who work in schools to see Black girls as powerful and assertive women who can solve their own problems with savvy and ingenuity.

Solving problems with savvy and ingenuity is a disposition that can be traced back to slavery when Black families were separated and Black women had to assume the position of "head of household" to raise their children alone. Naturally, generations of young Black girls "seeing" and enacting various survival practices have come to be a part of the fabric of who they are and have come to be, young women who are empowered to claim their own lives (Collins, 1989). However, our discussion of Black girls' behaviors is not intended to essentialize, or assume "that a unitary, 'essential' . . . experience can be . . . described" (Harris, 1990, p. 585). Black girls possess varied experiences and skills, all of which need to be viewed as strengths. In other words, there are a multitude of ways of being a Black girl, and no one set of behaviors should be expected or demanded from them to be given equal access to educational opportunity.

Limitations and Future Research
Whereas the strength of this study lies in its conceptual framing and focus on Black girls, the limitation of this study is the reliance on statistical data from one school district to describe their experiences. Findings from this study are only generalizable to other school districts that have similar discipline policies, serving a comparable population of students in an urban setting. Further investigation of these patterns using a larger sample of schools and districts would substantially further knowledge development. Moreover, our data did not include information about the adult who made an office discipline referral. Some scholars have suggested that adults who do not have consistent opportunities to build relationships and trust with students, such as security guards and

administrators, may be "more likely to rely on potentially negative racial stereotypes than individualized knowledge about the specific students" (McIntosh, Girvan, Horner, & Smolkowski, 2015, p. 10). Such data would provide important information about the types of school staff members whose discipline referrals may be most influenced by dominant discourses about Black girls and should be the target of interventions.

Other limitations to study design that should be taken into account include the reliance on an administrative data set and policy documents that were not triangulated with other sources. We explored the outcomes of disciplinary practices and processes, but need more information on the ways discipline occurs in schools from the views of school personnel and students. Additional qualitative studies are, therefore, needed to continue to shed light on the experiences, counter-narratives, and positioning of Black girls.

Finally, this study was correlational and does not provide *causal* evidence of the dynamics that lead to discipline disparities among Black girls. Misbehavior is not a random phenomenon, so there are likely other factors not captured in our data set that may also explain why Black girls were more or less likely to be referred for different types of discipline incidents. Future research in this area should include measure such as the nature of the schools' discipline philosophy or code of conduct, students' access to culturally responsive instruction, and the availability of prevention or intervention programs. In short, our discussion only provides hypotheses about underlying mechanisms behind this phenomenon, using FemCrit as a guide.

Conclusion

Returning to the attack at Spring Valley High by Officer Ben Fields on a Black girl sitting quietly at her desk, this article illustrates how dominant narratives about Black girls can affect the ways Black girls

are disciplined in schools. Seeing a young Black girl obstinately refuse to turn over her cell phone may have conjured narratives of Sapphire's un-ladylike bad attitude, and when she continually declined to leave the classroom, the Welfare Queen trope of being dangerous and threatening. These dominant narratives, along with one of carrying the urban ghetto inside of her, may have been the mechanisms that influenced Fields to view a Black girl sitting at her desk as a threat, one that needed to be forcibly assaulted. Each of these dominant narratives makes Black girls more susceptible to disciplinary disparities in urban schools that can leave them with both emotional and physical scars from their education.

The School-to-Prison Pipeline has received increasing attention as the number of students funneled from urban educational to carceral institutions through exclusionary school discipline practices continues to grow at alarming rates (Kim, Losen, & Hewitt, 2010). Conducted through a partnership with DPS, this study represents an effort to improve policy and practice through research in urban schools. Using FemCrit and CRT, we argue that dominant discourses about Black girls inform the reasons why Black girls enter the school discipline system through office referrals and be punished more harshly for the same behavior. This article seeks justice by expanding urban education research to include and center Black girls, a marginalized population that is often left out of conversations around inequities in school discipline and urban education.

Declaration of Conflicting Interests: The author(s) declared no potential conflicts of interest with respect to the research, authorship, and/or publication of this article.

Funding: The author(s) received no financial support for the research, authorship, and/or publication of this article.

Notes

Corresponding Author: Subini Ancy Annamma, Department of Special Education, University of Kansas, Joseph R. Pearson Hall, Rm. 521, 1122 West Campus Rd., Lawrence, KS 66045-3101, USA Email: subiniannamma@ku.edu

1. The teenage Black girl does have a name; however, the authors believe in her right to privacy considering that she is a minor and has not come forward with her story.

2. Because Kenny has gone on television with her own account of the incident, the authors feel it is appropriate to name her here.

3. Free and reduced lunch is a common indicator for socioeconomic status.

References

Alexander, M. (2012). *The new Jim Crow: Mass incarceration in the age of color-blindness.* New York, NY: The New Press.

Anderson, E. (2015). The white space. *Sociology of Race and Ethnicity,* 1(1), 10–21.

Alim, H. S., & Reyes, A. (2011). Introduction: Complicating race: Articulating race across multiple social dimensions. *Discourse & Society,* 22(4), 379–84.

Annamma, S. A. (2015). Innocence, ability and whiteness as property: Teacher education and the school-to-prison pipeline. *Urban Review,* 47(2), 293–316. doi:10.1007/s11256-014-0293-6

Annamma, S. A., Connor, D., & Ferri, B. (2013). Dis/ability Critical Race Studies (DisCrit): Theorizing at the intersections of race and dis/ability. *Race, Ethnicity and Education,* 16, 1–31. doi:10.1080/13613324.2012.730511

Annamma, S. (2016). Cartographies of inequity. In D. Morrison, S. Annamma, & D. Jackson (Eds.), *The spatial search to understand and address educational inequity to inform praxis.* Stylus.

Annamma, S. A., Morrison, D., & Jackson, D. (2014). Disproportionality fills the gaps: Connections between achievement, discipline and special education in the school-to-prison pipeline. *Berkley Review of Education,* 5(1), 53–87.

Anyon, Y., Jenson, J., Altschul, I., Farrar, J., McQueen, J., Greer, E., . . . Simmons, J. (2014). The persistent effect of race and the promise of alternatives to suspension in school discipline outcomes. *Children and Youth Services Review,* 44, 379–86.

Arcia, E. (2007). Variability in schools' suspension rates of black students. *The Journal of Negro Education,* 597–608.

Bell, D. A., Jr. (1979). Brown v. Board of Education and the interest-convergence dilemma. *Harvard Law Review,* 93, 518.

Blake, J., Butler, B., Lewis, C., & Darensbourg, A. (2011). Unmasking the inequitable discipline experiences of urban Black girls: Implications for urban educational stakeholders. *The Urban Review,* 43, 90–106.

Bradshaw, C. P., Mitchell, M. M., O'Brennan, L. M., & Leaf, P. J. (2010). Multilevel exploration of factors contributing to the overrepresentation of Black students in office disciplinary referrals. *Journal of Educational Psychology,* 102, 508–20.

McKinley, B., & Brayboy, J. (2005). Toward a tribal critical race theory in education. *The Urban Review,* 37(5), 425–46.

Brown, R. N. (2009). *Black girlhood celebration: Toward a hip-hop feminist pedagogy.* New York: Peter Lang.

Caton, M. T. (2012). Black male perspectives on their educational experiences in high school. *Urban Education,* 47, 1055–85.

Chesney-Lind, M. (2010). Jailing "bad" girls: Girls' violence and trends in female incarceration. In M. Chesney-Lind & N. Jones (Eds.), *Fighting for girls.* New York: State University of New York Press, 57–79.

Churchill, K. (2009). Assault Charges in Denver, Colorado. Retrieved from http://www. denvercriminalattorney.com/criminal_charges/assault.html

Collins, P. H. (1989). A comparison of two works on Black family life. *Signs,* 14, 875–84.

Collins, P. H. (1991). *Black feminist thought: Knowledge, consciousness, and the politics of empowerment.* New York, NY: Routledge.

Collins, P. H. (2000). *Black feminist thought: Knowledge, consciousness, and the politics of empowerment* (2nd ed.). New York, NY: Routledge.

Colorado Department of Education. (2015). About the Colorado Department of Education (CDE). UPDATED December 17, 2015. Retrieved from https://www.cde.state.co.us/cdecomm/aboutcde

Crenshaw, K. (1989). Demarginalizing the intersection of race and sex: A black feminist critique of antidiscrimination doctrine, feminist theory and antiracist politics. *The University of Chicago Legal Forum,* 140, 139–67.

Crenshaw, K. (1993). Mapping the margins: Intersectionality, identity politics, and violence against women of color. *Stanford Law Review,* 43, 1241–99.

Crenshaw, K., Gotanda, N., Peller, G., & Thomas, K. (1995). *Critical race theory: The key writings that formed the movement.* New York, NY: The New Press.

Crenshaw, K., Ocen, P., & Nanda, J. (2015). Black Girls Matter: Pushed Out, Overpoliced, and Underprotected. Retrieved from http://www.atlanticphilanthropies.org/app/uploads/2015/09/BlackGirlsMatter_Report.pdf

Creswell, J. W., & Clark, V. L. P. (2007). *Designing and conducting mixed methods research.* Thousand Oaks, CA: Sage.

DeBlase, G. L. (2003). Missing stories, missing lives: Urban girls (re)constructing race and gender in the literacy classroom. *Urban Education*, 38, 279–329.

Delgado, R., & Stefancic, J. (2001). *Critical race theory: An introduction* (1st ed.). New York: New York University Press.

Denver Public Schools. (2015). Facts and Figures. Retrieved from https://www.dpsk12.org/communications/facts.html

Erickson, F. (2004). Commentary: Demystifying data construction and analysis. *Anthropology & Education Quarterly*, 35(4), 486–93.

Evans-Winters, V., & Esposito, J. (2010). Other people's daughters: Critical race feminism and Black girls' education. *Educational Foundations*, 24, 11–24.

Fairclough, N. (1989). *Language and power*. London, England: Longman.

Fairclough, N. (2012). Critical discourse analysis. *International Advances in Engineering and Technology (IAET)*, 7, 452–87.

Fairclough, N., & Wodak, R. (1997). Critical discourse analysis. In T. van Dijk (Ed.), *Discourse as social interaction* (pp. 258–84). London, England: Sage.

Fenning, P., & Rose, J. (2007). Overrepresentation of African American students in exclusionary discipline the role of school policy. *Urban Education*, 42, 536–59.

Ferguson, A. A. (2000). *Bad boys: Public schools in the making of Black masculinity*. Ann Arbor: The University of Michigan Press.

Fordham, S. (1993). "Those loud Black girls": (Black) women, silence, and gender "passing" in the academy. *Anthropology & Education Quarterly*, 24, 3–32.

Foucault, M. (1977). *Discipline and punish: The birth of the prison*. Vintage.

Goff, P. A., Jackson, M. C., Di Leone, B. A. L., Culotta, C. M., & DiTomasso, N. A. (2014). The essence of innocence: Consequences of dehumanizing Black children. *Journal of Personality and Social Psychology*, 106(4), 526.

González, T. (2012). Keeping kids in schools: Restorative justice, punitive discipline, and the school to prison pipeline. *Journal of Law and Education*, 41, 281–35.

Goodwin, M. (2003). Gender, race, and mental illness: The case of Wanda Jean Allen. In A. K. Wing (Ed.), *Critical race feminism: A reader* (pp. 228–37). New York: New York University Press.

Grant, L. (1994). Helpers, enforcers, and go-betweens: Black females in elementary school classrooms. In M. B. Zinn & B. T. Dill (Eds.), *Women of Color in U.S. Society*. Philadelphia, PA: Temple University Press.

Greene, J. C., Caracelli, V. J., & Graham, W. F. (1989). Toward a conceptual framework for mixed-method evaluation designs. *Educational Evaluation and Policy Analysis*, 11(3), 255–74.

Gregory, A., Skiba, R., & Noguera, P. (2010). The achievement gap and the discipline gap: Two sides of the same coin? *Educational Researcher*, 39, 59–68.

Hall, H. R., & Smith, E. L. (2012). This Is Not Reality . . . It's Only TV": African American Girls Respond to Media (Mis) Representations. *The New Educator*, 8(3), 222–42.

Hancock, A.-M. (2004). *The politics of disgust: The public identity of the welfare queen*. New York, NY: New York University Press.

Harris, A. P. (1990). Race and essentialism in feminist legal theory. *Stanford Law Review*, 42(3), 581–616.

Harper, S. R. (2015). Success in these schools? Visual counternarratives of young men of color and urban high schools they attend. *Urban Education*, 50, 139–69.

Harris, C. I. (1993). Whiteness as property. *Harvard Law Review*, 1707–91.

Johnson, R. B., & Onwuegbuzie, A. J. (2004). Mixed methods research: A research paradigm whose time has come. *Educational Researcher*, 33, 14–26.

Jones, N. (2009). *Between good and ghetto: African American girls and inner-city violence*. New Brunswick, NJ: Rutgers University Press.

Kim, C., Losen, D., & Hewitt, D. (2010). *The school-to-prison-pipeline: Structuring legal reform*. New York: New York University Press.

Ladson-Billings, G., & Tate IV, W. (1995). Toward a critical race theory of education. *The Teachers College Record*, 97(1), 47–68.

Ladson-Billings, G. (1998). Just what is critical race theory and what's it doing in a nice field like education? *International Journal of Qualitative Studies in Education*, 11, 7–24.

Ladson-Billings, G. (2006). From the achievement gap to the education debt: Understanding achievement in US schools. *Educational Researcher*, 35(7), 3–12.

Leonardo, Z., & Hunter, M. (2007). Imagining the urban: The politics of race, class, and schooling. In *International handbook of urban education* (pp. 779–801). Netherlands: Springer.

Losen, D. J., & Gillespie, J. (2012). *Opportunities suspended: The disparate impact of disciplinary exclusion from School*. UCLA: The Civil Rights. Retrieved from http://escholarship.org/uc/item/3g36n0c3

Losen, D. J., & Skiba, R. J. (2010). *Suspended education: Urban middle schools in crisis*. Montgomery, AL: Southern Poverty Law Center.

Martin, J. L., & Beese, J. A. (2017). Talking back at school: Using the literacy classroom as a site for resistance to the school-to-prison pipeline and recognition of students labeled "at-risk." *Urban Education*, 52, 1204–32. doi:10.1177/0042085915602541

Matsuda, M. J. (1987). Looking to the bottom: Critical legal studies and reparations. *Harvard CR-CLL Rev.*, 22, 323.

Massey, D. S., & Denton, N. A. (1993). *American apartheid: Segregation and the making of the underclass.* Cambridge, MA: Harvard University Press.

McIntosh, K., Girvan, E. J., Horner, R. H., & Smolkowski, K. (2015). Education not incarceration: A conceptual model for reducing racial and ethnic disproportionality in school discipline. *Journal of Applied Research on Children: Informing Policy for Children at Risk*, 5, Article 4.

Milner, H. R., & Lomotey, K. (2014). *Handbook of urban education.* New York, NY: Routledge.

Milner, H. R., & Tenore, F. B. (2010). Classroom management in diverse classrooms. *Urban Education*, 45, 560–603.

Misawa, M. (2010). Musings on controversial intersections of positionality: A queer crit perspective in adult and continuing education. In V. Sheared, J. Johnson Bailey, S. J. Colin III., S. Brookfield, & E. Peterson (Eds.), *The handbook of race and adult education: A resource for dialogue on racism* (pp. 187–200). San Francisco, CA: Jossey-Bass.

Morgan, E., Salomon, N., Plotkin, M., & Cohen, R. (2014). *The school discipline consensus report: Strategies from the field to keep students engaged in school and out of the juvenile justice system.* New York, NY: The Council of State Governments Justice Center.

Morris, E. W. (2005). "Tuck in that shirt!" Race, class, gender and discipline in an urban school. *Sociological Perspectives*, 48, 25–48.

Morris, E. W. (2007). "Ladies" or "loudies"? Perceptions and experiences of black girls in classrooms. *Youth & Society*, 38, 490–515.

Morris, M. (2012). *Race, gender, and the school-to-prison pipeline: Expanding our discussion to include Black girls.* New York, NY: African American Policy Forum. Retrieved from https://www.academia.edu/7871609/The_SCHOOL-TO-_PRISON_PIPELINE_EXPANDING_OUR_DISCUSSION_TO_INCLUDE_BLACK_GIRLS

Moynihan, D. P. (1965). *The Negro family: The case for national action.* Washington, DC: Government Printing Office.

Mullings, L. (1994). Images, ideology and women of color. In M. B. Zinn & B. T. Dill (Eds.), *Women of color in U.S. society.* Philadelphia, PA: Temple University Press.

National Women's Law Center and the NAACP Legal Defense and Education Fund. (2014). Unlocking Opportunity for African American Girls. Retrieved from http://www.nwlc.org/sites/default/files/pdfs/unlocking_opportunity_for_african_american_girls_final.pdf

O'Connor, C., Mueller, J., & Neal, A. (2014). Student resilience in urban America. *Handbook of Urban Education*, 75–96.

Okonofua, J. A., & Eberhardt, J. L. (2015). Two strikes race and the disciplining of young students. *Psychological Science*, 26(5), 617–24.

Pane, D. M., Rocco, T. S., Miller, L. D., & Salmon, A. K. (2014). How teachers use power in the classroom to avoid or support exclusionary school discipline practices. *Urban Education*, 49, 297–328.

Parker, L., & Stovall, D. O. (2004). Actions following words: Critical race theory connects to critical pedagogy. *Educational Philosophy and Theory*, 36, 167–82.

Payne, A. A., & Welch, K. (2010). Modeling the effects of racial threat on punitive and restorative school discipline practices. *Criminology*, 48, 1019–62.

Pratt-Clarke, M. A. E. (2010). *Critical race, feminism, and education: A social justice model.* New York, NY: Palgrave Macmillan.

Richie, B. (2012). *Arrested justice: Black women, violence, and America's prison nation.* New York: New York University Press.

Richmond School District. (2015). Spring valley high school profile. Retrieved from https://www.richland2.org/svh/Documents/Profile%202015-16.pdf

Rios, V. M. (2011). *Punished: Policing the lives of Black and Latino boys.* New York: New York University Press.

Scott, P. B. (1982). Debunking Sapphire: Toward a non-racist and non-sexist social science. In *All the women are white, all the blacks are men, but some of us are brave* (pp. 85–92).

Safety & Discipline Indicator (SDI). (2013-2014). *Student Submissions Team-Denver Public Schools.* Colorado Department of Education.

Skiba, R. J., Michael, R. S., Nardo, A. C., & Peterson, R. L. (2002). The color of discipline: Sources of racial and gender disproportionality in school punishment. *The Urban Review*, 34, 317–42.

Skiba, R. J., Trachok, M., Chung, C.-G., Baker, T., Sheya, A., & Hughes, R. (2013). Where should we intervene? Contributions of behavior, student, and school characteristics to suspension and expulsion. In D. Osher (Ed.), *Closing the school discipline gap: Research to practice.* Los Angeles: University of California, Los Angeles Civil Rights Project.

Solorzano, D. G., & Bernal, D. D. (2001). Examining transformational resistance through a critical race and LatCrit theory framework Chicana and Chicano students in an urban context. *Urban Education*, 36(3), 308–42.

Spillers, H. J. (1987). Mama's baby, papa's maybe: An American grammar book. *Diacritics*, 17(2), 65–81.

Tate IV, W. F., Hamilton, C., Jones, B. D., Robertson, W. B., Macrander, A., Schultz, L., & Thorne-Wallington, E. (2014). Serving vulnerable children and youth in the urban context. *Handbook of Urban Education*, 3–20.

U.S. Census Bureau. (2015). Quick Facts, Denver City, Colorado. Retrieved from http://www.census.gov/quickfacts/table/PST045215/0820000,00

US Department of Education Office for Civil Rights. (2014). Civil rights data collection data snapshot: School discipline. Retrieved from https://www2.ed.gov/about/offices/list/ocr/docs/crdc-discipline-snapshot.pdf

U.S. Department of Education & U.S. Department of Justice. (2014). *Dear colleague letter on the nondiscriminatory administration of school discipline*. Washington, DC: U.S. Department of Education. Retrieved from www2.ed.gov/about/offices/list/ocr/letters/colleague-201401-title-vi.html

Van Dijk, T. A. (1987). *Communicating racism: Ethnic prejudice in thought and talk*. Sage Publications, Inc.

Van Dijk, T. A. (1993). Principles of critical discourse analysis. *Discourse & Society*, 4(2), 249–83.

Van Dijk, T. A. (2002). Discourse and racism. In *The Blackwell companion to racial and ethnic studies* (pp. 145–59).

Vavrus, F., & Cole, K. (2002). "I didn't do nothin'": The discursive construction of school suspension. *The Urban Review*, 34, 87–111.

Wald, J., & Losen, D. J. (2003). Defining and redirecting a school-to-prison pipeline. *New Directions for Youth Development*, (99), 9–15.

Wallace, J. M., Goodkind, S., Wallace, C. M., & Bachman, J. G. (2008). Racial, ethnic, and gender differences in school discipline among us high school students: 1991-2005. *The Negro Educational Review*, 59, 47–62.

Wing, A. (Ed.). (2003). *Global critical race feminism: An international reader*. New York: New York University Press.

Winn, M. (2011). *Girl time: Literacy, justice, and the school-to-prison pipeline*. New York, NY: Teachers College Press.

Wodak, R. (2002). Aspects of critical discourse analysis. *ZfAL*, 36, 5–31.

Wun, C. (2014). Unaccounted foundations: Black girls, anti-Black racism, and punishment in schools. *Critical Sociology*, 1, 1–14.

Questions for Critical Thinking

1. Reflecting on your own educational experience, in what ways were biases and stereotypes as well as the policies and practices based on race reinforced in your schools? In what ways do you think you were given advantage or disadvantage because of assumptions made about your race? How do you think this has impacted you today?

2. Do you see evidence of racial bias in your educational experience? If so, how do you think this impacts the ways in which Black and Indigenous people of color participate in the classroom?

3. If racial biases in the educational system were eliminated, how do you think this would impact the lives of Black and Indigenous people of color?

Social Institutions: Work and Economy

BLACK MEN AND THE STRUGGLE FOR WORK

Social and Economic Barriers Persist

* *James M. Quane, William Julius Wilson, and Jackelyn Hwang*

The following essay explores the continued structural barriers to opportunity that disproportionately prevent economic self-sufficiency for poor black men and, as a result, poor black families. According to the authors, this necessitates an effective, coordinated response of government-funded institutions to support opportunities for economic self-sufficiency for the poor.

Driven by deep dissatisfaction with the economic and social condition of the black family, Daniel Patrick Moynihan hoped, with the release of his 1965 report, to stimulate a national discussion linking economic disadvantage and family instability. Although Moynihan focused on the structural causes of the fragmentation of the black family, critics associated his report with the "culture of poverty" thesis, which implies that poverty is passed from one generation to the next through learned behavior.

A number of those critics emphasized Moynihan's suggestion that the problem "may indeed have begun to feed on itself." From 1948 to 1962, the unemployment rate among black males and the number of Aid to Families with Dependent Children (AFDC) cases were positively correlated, but after 1962, the number of new AFDC cases continued to rise even as black male unemployment declined. "With this one statistical correlation, by far the most highly publicized in the Report," states historian Alice O'Connor, "Moynihan sealed the argument that the 'pathology' had become self-perpetuation."

Still, Moynihan's main concern in the report involved black exclusion from opportunities that fortify economic self-sufficiency. Unlike conservative analysts, he combined economic and cultural explanations for the persistence of poverty. Nevertheless, the controversy that surrounded the report undermined for decades serious research on the complexity of the problem.

A 1987 study by one of this article's authors, William Julius Wilson's *The Truly Disadvantaged*, rekindled the debate with its discussion of institutional and cultural dynamics in the social transformation of the inner city. Research undertaken since that time has reinforced the need for more coordinated, government-directed efforts to dismantle structures that reinforce racial and class-based biases and

James M. Quane, William J. Wilson, and Jackelyn Hwang, "Black Men and the Struggle for Work: Social and Economic Barriers Persist," *Education Next*, Spring 2015, 15(2). Reprinted with permission of Education Next Institute, Inc., all rights reserved.

inequalities. To this end, Moynihan's call for an expansion of such things as youth employment opportunities, improvements in high-quality education programs, greater housing options, and a broadening of income supplements to combat inequality is as pertinent today as it was in 1965.

Concentrated Disadvantage and Socialization in the Inner City

The Truly Disadvantaged chronicles the rise of poor black single women with children, the decline in marriage among the poor, the increase in concentrated urban black poverty, and escalating joblessness among young black males. It links sociodemographic changes in the inner city to shifts in the labor market, the outmigration of higher-income black and white families, and the concomitant decline in services available to poor black families left behind. The analysis suggests that in such neighborhoods, many households lack the resources necessary to sustain stable family life, but it links that fact to structural factors such as persistent exclusion from employment opportunities, social networks, and institutions that are essential for economic mobility.

Both Moynihan and subsequent researchers have acknowledged the critical significance of the family as the primary socializing influence on children and youth. The data show that the percentage of children growing up in single-parent homes has continued to increase. Trends are similar for all races and classes, but the percentages remain highest among families in poor, minority neighborhoods. Indeed, the issue is so acute that law professors June Carbone of the University of Minnesota and Naomi Cahn of George Washington University have recently opined that "marriage has disappeared from the poorest communities" in the U.S.

The numbers by themselves are stark, but when considered in isolation, they do not provide a comprehensive understanding of the major social and economic forces buffeting inner-city black families. In particular, the dramatic mismatch between skill level and employment opportunities among black males has further undermined marriageability in the inner-city black community. In these neighborhoods, poor black children are increasingly likely to grow up in family units whose dire financial circumstances

affect every aspect of their physical, emotional, and cognitive development. Their caregivers' abilities to envision and execute a concerted strategy to ensure their children escape poverty is constrained by their own social location, economic circumstances, and restricted access to information.

The Role of Institutions

Many of society's intermediary institutions, whether intended to support social and economic advancement or punish antisocial behavior, have a disproportionate impact on poor black families. Such organizations include public schools, social service agencies, and juvenile and criminal justice systems. Even at the earliest stages in their cognitive development, inner-city black children are less likely to be enrolled in a high-quality child-care arrangement, which puts them at an enormous disadvantage compared to their white and better-off counterparts. Low-income caregivers do not have access to a broad range of choices among high-quality providers of this crucial service. Compared to their higher-income neighbors, caregivers in poorer communities have fewer options when it comes to the provision of regulated child care, and these programs are also disproportionately more likely to experience funding cuts during periods of austerity. Child-care choices among poor inner-city residents are also constrained by issues of trust and safety that often outweigh quality. Inadequate preschool education has important implications for the social and academic domains of child development, and the negative ramifications can last well into adulthood.

When they enter primary school, low-income, inner-city black youth are clustered in failing schools. They are more likely to be suspended or enrolled in special education classes, less likely to graduate from high school on time, and, indeed, more likely to drop out of school altogether.

Consequently, as they enter adulthood, many young blacks, particularly males, are less likely to enter the workforce or postsecondary educational institutions. Young black males have experienced unemployment and been disconnected from schools and vocational institutions at rates ranging from 20 to 32 percent. By 2011, after the end of the last recession, more than one-quarter of young black males were neither employed nor enrolled in school or vocational educational training. The rates for white and Hispanic young people were also very high, around 20 percent, but throughout most of the past few decades rates of disconnection among black youth have been higher than for the other two groups.

Furthermore, many government institutions that have an impact on the lives of poor black families focus more on regulating and controlling behavior than on improving skills and providing opportunity. Poor families who qualify for cash or noncash means-tested benefits are disproportionately exposed to rules that inhibit job seeking and discourage two-parent households.

Moreover, black youth are more likely than their peers to be confined in secure detention and correctional facilities. Admittedly, detention rates since 1977 have been steadily declining for all youth. There are a number of plausible explanations for the decline, including the downward shift in the violent-crime rate among youth in recent years. And the juvenile justice system is now more focused on prevention and rehabilitation as opposed to the harsh sentencing approach of prior decades. That said, black youth, in comparison to white youth, are still disproportionately more likely to be arrested. Furthermore, young black arrestees, compared to their white counterparts, are also more likely to have their case formally adjudicated by the courts, and, following a hearing, they are disproportionately more likely to be placed in an out-of-home detention facility. Black youth were nearly five times as likely to be in detention or correctional facilities in 2011 than white youth.

Contact with school-based disciplinary committees and the juvenile justice system is just a harbinger of a much more ominous trend that is gutting low-income minority communities of their male residents. As a group, black men were six times more likely than white men to be incarcerated in 2010, and blacks constitute nearly half of all people jailed and imprisoned in the U.S. today. The difference between black and white incarceration rates for young men varies greatly by education level. Research conducted by sociologists Bruce Western and Becky Pettit shows a dramatic rise in incarceration rates for young black male high-school dropouts over time. By 2008, approximately 37 percent, or three in eight, were behind bars. The one bit of good news is the noticeable drop—from 11 to 9 percent from 2000 to 2008—in the detention rate of young black males with a high school diploma. Among blacks with some college, the rate falls to around 2 percent, similar to that for young men from other racial and educational backgrounds.

As a result of the escalating incarceration rates among less-educated black males, poor black children are more likely than white or Hispanic children to experience a period when at least one of their parents is incarcerated. Rates for black children with an incarcerated parent more than quadrupled from 1980 to 2008. It should also be noted that close to half of black children with fathers who were high school dropouts had an incarcerated father at some point. The overall implications, therefore, are that poor black children and youth in disadvantaged communities are embedded in family and institutional arrangements that result in socialization experiences that are fundamentally different from those of their peers.

The Role of Neighborhoods

Inner-city neighborhoods are often where all of these dynamics collide, yet youth exposed to these influences are expected to share the aspirations and expectations of their counterparts in better-off communities and to acquire the capacity to make the choices necessary to realize them. Low-income parents are often severely constrained in their ability to help guide their children's engagement with critical facilitators of upward mobility, such as schools, and it is left to youth themselves to formulate and exercise strategic choices that might prove to be avenues out of poverty. These youth are seriously impeded, however, as a result of the gap between the knowledge they accumulate in the restrictive social environment in which they operate and the skills and know-how they need to transcend it.

In high-poverty neighborhoods, the effect on negative youth outcomes increases significantly. Chronically poor neighborhoods, those with poverty rates at or above 40 percent, have higher rates of school dropout, teenage pregnancy, and crime, and lower scores on cognitive and verbal skill tests and health indicators among school-age children. Many poor black and Hispanic children remain disproportionately exposed to conditions in high-poverty neighborhoods with all their deleterious impacts on family well-being.

Between 1990 and 2000—a period of economic growth, tight labor markets, and changes in government welfare policies—the percentage of poor black children living in neighborhoods of concentrated poverty declined from 24 percent to 15 percent. The improvement was short-lived, however, and the concentration of poor black children in high-poverty neighborhoods began to increase again in the next decade. Although not as sharp, the trend line for all black children followed a similar pattern, showing the increased likelihood that black children across all socioeconomic strata reside in disadvantaged neighborhoods compared to poor and nonpoor white children.

The residential distribution of poor (and nonpoor) Hispanic children followed a somewhat different pattern from that of blacks, influenced, in part, by a 29 percent growth in this population since 2000 and their subsequent migration to less blighted regions in the U.S. Like black children, however, Hispanic children of any socioeconomic background are disproportionately more likely to live in high-poverty neighborhoods than white children.

Addressing the Need

Confronting poverty and inequality in the inner city requires that we recognize the complex, interrelated problems facing poor black families. This necessitates an effective, sustained, and coordinated mission of government-funded institutions to support opportunities for economic self-sufficiency among the poor, which has yet to be realized. Recently, the Obama administration funded numerous efforts to revitalize poor, underresourced neighborhoods by expanding "ladders of opportunity" for youth of color. For example, Choice and Promise Neighborhoods, Promise Zones, and the Strong Cities, Strong Communities initiatives seek to enhance family and community ties and better embed households in networks of institutional supports to improve the in-school and extracurricular experiences of school-age children. Building on neighborhood-empowerment efforts dating from the 1960s, these initiatives seek to create enhanced social contexts

that extend choice-making capacity and practical opportunities to act on them. Just as importantly, this emphasis on coalition building has motivated the formation of new alliances among important service providers and community-based organizations that recognize the enormous potential that such collaborations can realize.

Many of these initiatives represent innovative attempts by the federal government to bring the combined resources of inter-agency collaboration to bear on tackling intractable social problems. It is therefore surprising that a more concerted effort is not being made by the administration to tout its significant investments and advances in this regard, and articulate an overarching framework that integrates all of these initiatives and formulates a rationale for how they may complement and inform one another in a cohesive, long-range fashion.

Thus far, the Obama administration's efforts to address the social and physical isolation of disadvantaged and disenfranchised poor families of color lack the size and focus that Moynihan vigorously championed. Many of the administration's place-based strategies can best be considered as multisite demonstration programs, since they only reach a fraction of the beleaguered neighborhoods and disenfranchised children and youth that reside in them. Congress has seriously hampered the replication and expansion of these programs by refusing the administration's repeated requests for additional funds.

Fifty years ago, Moynihan worried that too much responsibility was being placed on community-action programs to address the problems of persistent family poverty. Moynihan implied that these initiatives only go part of the way toward influencing the choice sets available to the poor, as well as the actions such choices energize. Indeed, the combined effects of the multiple forces that we touched upon, ones that disproportionately prevail upon too many poor, urban children of color are not going to be solved by incremental approaches. Under current conditions, many societal institutions exacerbate the disadvantaged status of poor families rather than provide pathways to self-sufficiency and equality of opportunity. Increased efforts must be devoted to rectifying the large-scale fragmentation and lack of uniformity in the mission and practice of schools, social service agencies, and workforce development centers that are intended to support the social and economic mobility of disadvantaged families.

Regrettably, the misinterpretation and intense criticism of the implicit "culture of poverty" observations in Moynihan's report precluded a serious public discussion of the need to tackle these impediments to the progress of the poor. Even more regrettable, the need to acknowledge and address them is all the more urgent 50 years later.

Questions for Critical Thinking

1. How does the authors' discussion impact your own understanding of common notions of unemployment and poverty?
2. How does the authors' discussion of the social and economic barriers that persist broaden your understandings of the disproportionate amounts of poverty in African American communities?
3. The authors offer some strategies for addressing the problems of poverty and unemployment. What do you think of their strategies? What strategies would you offer?

RACIALIZING THE GLASS ESCALATOR

Reconsidering Men's Experiences with Women's Work

• *Adia Harvey Wingfield*

Research on the experiences of men in what are usually seen as women's occupations, such as nursing, has long argued that they experience a glass escalator effect where subtle aspects of the professions push men toward higher statuses. This next essay by sociologist Adia Harvey Wingfield further explores this issue, examining how intersections of gender and race work together to shape experiences for men of color in the traditionally feminine field of nursing. What she finds is that this phenomenon is racialized and not necessarily available to all.

Sociologists who study work have long noted that jobs are sex segregated and that this segregation creates different occupational experiences for men and women (Charles and Grusky 2004). Jobs predominantly filled by women often require "feminine" traits such as nurturing, caring, and empathy, a fact that means men confront perceptions that they are unsuited for the requirements of these jobs. Rather than having an adverse effect on their occupational experiences, however, these assumptions facilitate men's entry into better paying, higher status positions, creating what Williams (1995) labels a "glass escalator" effect.

The glass escalator model has been an influential paradigm in understanding the experiences of men who do women's work. Researchers have identified this process among men nurses, social workers, paralegals, and librarians and have cited its pervasiveness as evidence of men's consistent advantage in the workplace, such that even in jobs where men are numerical minorities they are likely to enjoy higher wages and faster promotions (Floge and

Merrill 1986; Heikes 1991; Pierce 1995; Williams 1989, 1995). Most of these studies implicitly assume a racial homogenization of men workers in women's professions, but this supposition is problematic for several reasons. For one, minority men are not only present but are actually overrepresented in certain areas of reproductive work that have historically been dominated by white women (Duffy 2007). Thus, research that focuses primarily on white men in women's professions ignores a key segment of men who perform this type of labor. Second, and perhaps more important, conclusions based on the experiences of white men tend to overlook the ways that intersections of race and gender create different experiences for different men. While extensive work has documented the fact that white men in women's professions encounter a glass escalator effect that

Republished with permission of Sage Publications Inc, Journals, © 2009. "Racializing the Glass Escalator: Reconsidering Men's Experiences with Women's Work," by Adia Harvey Wingfield, from *Gender and Society*, 23(1), pp. 5–26; permission conveyed through Copyright Clearance Centre, Inc.

aids their occupational mobility (for an exception, see Snyder and Green 2008), few studies, if any, have considered how this effect is a function not only of gendered advantage but of racial privilege as well.

In this article, I examine the implications of race-gender intersections for minority men employed in a female-dominated, feminized occupation, specifically focusing on Black men in nursing. Their experiences doing "women's work" demonstrate that the glass escalator is a racialized as well as gendered concept.

Theoretical Framework

In her classic study *Men and Women of the Corporation,* Kanter (1977) offers a groundbreaking analysis of group interactions. Focusing on high-ranking women executives who work mostly with men, Kanter argues that those in the extreme numerical minority are tokens who are socially isolated, highly visible, and adversely stereotyped. Tokens have difficulty forming relationships with colleagues and often are excluded from social networks that provide mobility. Because of their low numbers, they are also highly visible as people who are different from the majority, even though they often feel invisible when they are ignored or overlooked in social settings. Tokens are also stereotyped by those in the majority group and frequently face pressure to behave in ways that challenge and undermine these stereotypes. Ultimately, Kanter argues that it is harder for them to blend into the organization and to work effectively and productively, and that they face serious barriers to upward mobility.

Kanter's (1977) arguments have been analyzed and retested in various settings and among many populations. Many studies, particularly of women in male-dominated corporate settings, have supported her findings. Other work has reversed these conclusions, examining the extent to which her conclusions hold when men were the tokens and women the majority group. These studies fundamentally challenged the gender neutrality of the token, finding that men in the minority fare much better than do similarly situated women. In particular, this research suggests that factors such as heightened visibility and polarization do not necessarily disadvantage men who are in the minority. While women tokens find that their visibility hinders their ability to blend in and work productively, men tokens find that their conspicuousness can lead to greater opportunities for leadership and choice assignments (Floge and Merrill 1986; Heikes 1991). Studies in this vein are important because they emphasize organizations—and occupations—as gendered institutions that subsequently create dissimilar experiences for men and women tokens (see Acker 1990).

In her groundbreaking study of men employed in various women's professions, Williams (1995) further develops this analysis of how power relationships shape the ways men tokens experience work in women's professions. Specifically, she introduces the concept of the glass escalator to explain men's experiences as tokens in these areas. Like Floge and Merrill (1986) and Heikes (1991), Williams finds that men tokens do not experience the isolation, visibility, blocked access to social networks, and stereotypes in the same ways that women tokens do. In contrast, Williams argues that even though they are in the minority, processes are in place that actually facilitate their opportunity and advancement. Even in culturally feminized occupations, then, men's advantage is built into the very structure and everyday interactions of these jobs so that men find themselves actually struggling to remain in place. For these men, "despite their intentions, they face invisible pressures to move up in their professions. Like being on a moving escalator, they have to work to stay in place" (Williams 1995, 87).

The glass escalator term thus refers to the "subtle mechanisms in place that enhance [men's] positions in [women's] professions" (Williams 1995, 108). These mechanisms include certain behaviors, attitudes, and beliefs men bring to these professions as well as the types of interactions that often occur between these men and their colleagues, supervisors, and customers. Consequently, even in occupations composed mostly of women, gendered perceptions about men's roles, abilities, and skills privilege them and facilitate their advancement. The glass escalator serves as a conduit that channels men in women's professions into the uppermost levels of the occupational hierarchy. Ultimately, the glass escalator effect suggests that men retain consistent occupational advantages over women, even when women are numerically in the majority (Budig 2002; Williams 1995).

Though this process has now been fairly well established in the literature, there are reasons to question its generalizability to all men. In an early critique of the supposed general neutrality of the token, Zimmer (1988) notes that much research on race comes to precisely the opposite of Kanter's conclusions, finding that as the numbers of minority group members increase (e.g., as they become less likely to be "tokens"), so too do tensions between the majority and minority groups. For instance, as minorities move into predominantly white neighborhoods, increasing numbers do not create the likelihood of greater acceptance and better treatment. In contrast, whites are likely to relocate when neighborhoods become "too" integrated, citing concerns about property values and racialized ideas about declining neighborhood quality (Shapiro 2004). Reinforcing, while at the same time tempering, the findings of research on men in female-dominated occupations, Zimmer (1988, 71) argues that relationships between tokens and the majority depend on understanding the underlying power relationships between these groups and "the status and power differentials between them." Hence, just as men who are tokens fare better than women, it also follows that the experiences of Blacks and whites as tokens should differ in ways that reflect their positions in hierarchies of status and power.

The concept of the glass escalator provides an important and useful framework for addressing men's experiences in women's occupations, but so far research in this vein has neglected to examine whether the glass escalator is experienced among all men in an identical manner. Are the processes that facilitate a ride on the glass escalator available to minority men? Or does race intersect with gender to affect the extent to which the glass escalator offers men opportunities in women's professions? In the next section, I examine whether and how the mechanisms that facilitate a ride on the glass escalator might be unavailable to Black men in nursing.[1]

Relationships with Colleagues and Supervisors

One key aspect of riding the glass escalator involves the warm, collegial welcome men workers often receive from their women colleagues. Often, this reaction is a response to the fact that professions dominated by women are frequently low in salary and status and that greater numbers of men help improve prestige and pay (Heikes 1991). Though some women workers resent the apparent ease with which men enter and advance in women's professions, the generally warm welcome men receive stands in stark contrast to the cold reception, difficulties with mentorship, and blocked access to social networks that women often encounter when they do men's work (Roth 2006; Williams 1992). In addition, unlike women in men's professions, men who do women's work frequently have supervisors of the same sex. Men workers can thus enjoy a gendered bond with their supervisor in the context of a collegial work environment. These factors often converge, facilitating men's access to higher-status positions and producing the glass escalator effect.

The congenial relationship with colleagues and gendered bonds with supervisors are crucial to riding the glass escalator. Women colleagues often take a primary role in casting these men into leadership or supervisory positions. In their study of men and women tokens in a hospital setting, Floge and Merrill (1986) cite cases where women nurses promoted men colleagues to the position of charge nurse, even when the job had already been assigned to a woman. In addition to these close ties with women colleagues, men are also able to capitalize on gendered bonds with (mostly men) supervisors in ways that engender upward mobility. Many men supervisors informally socialize with men workers in women's jobs and are thus able to trade on their personal friendships for upward mobility. Williams (1995) describes a case where a nurse with mediocre performance reviews received a promotion to a more prestigious specialty area because of his friendship with the (male) doctor in charge. According to the literature, building strong relationships with colleagues and supervisors often happens relatively easily for men in women's professions and pays off in their occupational advancement.

For Black men in nursing, however, gendered racism may limit the extent to which they establish bonds with their colleagues and supervisors. The concept of gendered racism suggests that racial stereotypes, images, and beliefs are grounded in gendered ideals (Collins 1990, 2004; Espiritu 2000; Essed 1991;

Harvey Wingfield 2007). Gendered racist stereotypes of Black men in particular emphasize the dangerous, threatening attributes associated with Black men and Black masculinity, framing Black men as threats to white women, prone to criminal behavior, and especially violent. Collins (2004) argues that these stereotypes serve to legitimize Black men's treatment in the criminal justice system through methods such as racial profiling and incarceration, but they may also hinder Black men's attempts to enter and advance in various occupational fields.

For Black men nurses, gendered racist images may have particular consequences for their relationships with women colleagues, who may view Black men nurses through the lens of controlling images and gendered racist stereotypes that emphasize the danger they pose to women. This may take on a heightened significance for white women nurses, given stereotypes that suggest that Black men are especially predisposed to raping white women. Rather than experiencing the congenial bonds with colleagues that white men nurses describe, Black men nurses may find themselves facing a much cooler reception from their women coworkers.

Gendered racism may also play into the encounters Black men nurses have with supervisors. In cases where supervisors are white men, Black men nurses may still find that higher-ups treat them in ways that reflect prevailing stereotypes about threatening Black masculinity. Supervisors may feel uneasy about forming close relationships with Black men or may encourage their separation from white women nurses. In addition, broader, less gender-specific racial stereotypes could also shape the experiences Black men nurses have with white men bosses. Whites often perceive Blacks, regardless of gender, as less intelligent, hardworking, ethical, and moral than other racial groups (Feagin 2006). Black men nurses may find that in addition to being influenced by gendered racist stereotypes, supervisors also view them as less capable and qualified for promotion, thus negating or minimizing the glass escalator effect.

Suitability for Nursing and Higher-Status Work
The perception that men are not really suited to do women's work also contributes to the glass escalator effect. In encounters with patients, doctors, and other staff, men nurses frequently confront others who do not expect to see them doing "a woman's job." Sometimes this perception means that patients mistake men nurses for doctors; ultimately, the sense that men do not really belong in nursing contributes to a push "*out* of the most feminine-identified areas and *up* to those regarded as more legitimate for men" (Williams 1995, 104). The sense that men are better suited for more masculine jobs means that men workers are often assumed to be more able and skilled than their women counterparts. As Williams writes (1995, 106), "Masculinity is often associated with competence and mastery," and this implicit definition stays with men even when they work in feminized fields. Thus, part of the perception that men do not belong in these jobs is rooted in the sense that, as men, they are more capable and accomplished than women and thus belong in jobs that reflect this. Consequently, men nurses are mistaken for doctors and are granted more authority and responsibility than their women counterparts, reflecting the idea that, as men, they are inherently more competent (Heikes 1991; Williams 1995).

Black men nurses, however, may not face the presumptions of expertise or the resulting assumption that they belong in higher-status jobs. Black professionals, both men and women, are often assumed to be less capable and less qualified than their white counterparts. In some cases, these negative stereotypes hold even when Black workers outperform white colleagues (Feagin and Sikes 1994). The belief that Blacks are inherently less competent than whites means that, despite advanced education, training, and skill, Black professionals often confront the lingering perception that they are better suited for lower-level service work (Feagin and Sikes 1994). Black men in fact often fare better than white women in blue-collar jobs such as policing and corrections work (Britton 1995), and this may be, in part, because they are viewed as more appropriately suited for these types of positions.

For Black men nurses, then, the issue of perception may play out in different ways than it does for white men nurses. While white men nurses enjoy the automatic assumption that they are qualified, capable, and suited for "better" work, the experiences of Black professionals suggest that Black men nurses may not encounter these reactions. They may, like their white counterparts, face the perception that they do not belong in nursing. Unlike their white counterparts, Black men nurses may be seen as inherently less capable and therefore better suited for low-wage labor than a professional, feminized occupation such as nursing. This perception of being less qualified means that they also may not be immediately assumed to be better suited for the higher-level, more masculinized jobs within the medical field.

As minority women address issues of both race and gender to negotiate a sense of belonging in masculine settings (Ong 2005), minority men may also face a comparable challenge in feminized fields. They may have to address the unspoken racialization implicit in the assumption that masculinity equals competence. Simultaneously, they may find that the racial stereotype that Blackness equals lower qualifications, standards, and competence clouds the sense that men are inherently more capable and adept in any field, including the feminized ones.

Establishing Distance from Femininity
An additional mechanism of the glass escalator involves establishing distance from women and the femininity associated with their occupations. Because men nurses are employed in a culturally feminized occupation, they develop strategies to disassociate themselves from the femininity associated with their work and retain some of the privilege associated with masculinity. Thus, when men nurses gravitate toward hospital emergency wards rather than obstetrics or pediatrics, or emphasize that they are only in nursing to get into hospital administration, they distance themselves from the femininity of their profession and thereby preserve their status as men despite the fact that they do "women's work." Perhaps more important, these strategies also place men in a prime position to experience the glass escalator effect, as they situate themselves to move upward into higher-status areas in the field.

Creating distance from femininity also helps these men achieve aspects of hegemonic masculinity, which Connell (1989) describes as the predominant and most valued form of masculinity at a given time. Contemporary hegemonic masculine ideals emphasize toughness, strength, aggressiveness,

heterosexuality, and, perhaps most important, a clear sense of femininity as different from and subordinate to masculinity (Kimmel 2001; Williams 1995). Thus, when men distance themselves from the feminized aspects of their jobs, they uphold the idea that masculinity and femininity are distinct, separate, and mutually exclusive. When these men seek masculinity by aiming for the better paying or most technological fields, they not only position themselves to move upward into the more acceptable arenas but also reinforce the greater social value placed on masculinity. Establishing distance from femininity therefore allows men to retain the privileges and status of masculinity while simultaneously enabling them to ride the glass escalator.

For Black men, the desire to reject femininity may be compounded by racial inequality. Theorists have argued that as institutional racism blocks access to traditional markers of masculinity such as occupational status and economic stability, Black men may repudiate femininity as a way of accessing the masculinity—and its attendant status—that is denied through other routes (hooks 2004; Neal 2005). Rejecting femininity is a key strategy men use to assert masculinity, and it remains available to Black men even when other means of achieving masculinity are unattainable. Black men nurses may be more likely to distance themselves from their women colleagues and to reject the femininity associated with nursing, particularly if they feel that they experience racial discrimination that renders occupational advancement inaccessible. Yet if they encounter strained relationships with women colleagues and men supervisors because of gendered racism or racialized stereotypes, the efforts to distance themselves from femininity still may not result in the glass escalator effect.

On the other hand, some theorists suggest that minority men may challenge racism by rejecting hegemonic masculine ideals. Chen (1999) argues that Chinese American men may engage in a strategy of repudiation, where they reject hegemonic masculinity because its implicit assumptions of whiteness exclude Asian American men. As these men realize that racial stereotypes and assumptions preclude them from achieving the hegemonic masculine ideal, they reject it and dispute its racialized underpinnings. Similarly,

Lamont (2000, 47) notes that working-class Black men in the United States and France develop a "caring self" in which they emphasize values such as "morality, solidarity, and generosity." As a consequence of these men's ongoing experiences with racism, they develop a caring self that highlights work on behalf of others as an important tool in fighting oppression. Although caring is associated with femininity, these men cultivate a caring self because it allows them to challenge racial inequality. The results of these studies suggest that Black men nurses may embrace the femininity associated with nursing if it offers a way to combat racism. In these cases, Black men nurses may turn to pediatrics as a way of demonstrating sensitivity and therefore combating stereotypes of Black masculinity, or they may proudly identify as nurses to challenge perceptions that Black men are unsuited for professional, white-collar positions.

Taken together, all of this research suggests that Black men may not enjoy the advantages experienced by their white men colleagues, who ride a glass escalator to success. In this article, I focus on the experiences of Black men nurses to argue that the glass escalator is a racialized as well as a gendered concept that does not offer Black men the same privileges as their white men counterparts.

Findings

The results of this study indicate that not all men experience the glass escalator in the same ways. For Black men nurses, intersections of race and gender create a different experience with the mechanisms that facilitate white men's advancement in women's professions. Awkward or unfriendly interactions with colleagues, poor relationships with supervisors, perceptions that they are not suited for nursing, and an unwillingness to disassociate from "feminized" aspects of nursing constitute what I term *glass barriers* to riding the glass escalator.

Reception from Colleagues and Supervisors

When women welcome men into "their" professions, they often push men into leadership roles that ease their advancement into upper-level positions. Thus, a positive reaction from colleagues is critical to riding the glass escalator. Unlike white men nurses,

however, Black men do not describe encountering a warm reception from women colleagues (Heikes 1991). Instead, the men I interviewed find that they often have unpleasant interactions with women coworkers who treat them rather coldly and attempt to keep them at bay. Chris is a 51-year-old oncology nurse who describes one white nurse's attempt to isolate him from other white women nurses as he attempted to get his instructions for that day's shift:

> She turned and ushered me to the door, and said for me to wait out here, a nurse will come out and give you your report. I stared at her hand on my arm, and then at her, and said, "Why? Where do you go to get your reports?" She said, "I get them in there." I said, "Right. Unhand me." I went right back in there, sat down, and started writing down my reports.

Kenny, a 47-year-old nurse with 23 years of nursing experience, describes a similarly and particularly painful experience he had in a previous job where he was the only Black person on staff:

> [The staff] had nothing to do with me, and they didn't even want me to sit at the same area where they were charting in to take a break. They wanted me to sit somewhere else…. They wouldn't even sit at a table with me! When I came and sat down, everybody got up and left.

These experiences with colleagues are starkly different from those described by white men in professions dominated by women (see Pierce 1995; Williams 1989). Though the men in these studies sometimes chose to segregate themselves, women never systematically excluded them. Though I have no way of knowing why the women nurses in Chris's and Kenny's workplaces physically segregated themselves, the pervasiveness of gendered racist images that emphasize white women's vulnerability to dangerous Black men may play an important role. For these nurses, their masculinity is not a guarantee that they will be welcomed, much less pushed into leadership roles. As Ryan, a 37-year-old intensive care nurse says, "[Black men] have to go further to prove ourselves. This involves proving our capabilities, *proving to colleagues that you can lead,* be on the forefront" (emphasis added). The warm welcome and subsequent opportunities for leadership cannot be taken for granted. In contrast, these men describe great challenges in forming congenial relationships with coworkers who, they believe, do not truly want them there.

In addition, these men often describe tense, if not blatantly discriminatory, relationships with supervisors. While Williams (1995) suggests that men supervisors can be allies for men in women's professions by facilitating promotions and upward mobility, Black men nurses describe incidents of being overlooked by supervisors when it comes time for promotions. Ryan, who has worked at his current job for 11 years, believes that these barriers block upward mobility within the profession:

> The hardest part is dealing with people who don't understand minority nurses. People with their biases, who don't identify you as ripe for promotion. I know the policy and procedure, I'm familiar with past history. So you can't tell me I can't move forward if others did. [How did you deal with this?] By knowing the chain of command, who my supervisors were. Things were subtle. I just had to be better. I got this mostly from other nurses and supervisors. I was paid to deal with patients, so I could deal with [racism] from them. I'm not paid to deal with this from colleagues.

Kenny offers a similar example. Employed as an orthopedic nurse in a predominantly white environment, he describes great difficulty getting promoted, which he primarily attributes to racial biases:

> It's almost like you have to, um, take your ideas and give them to somebody else and then let them present them for you and you get no credit for it. I've applied for several promotions there and, you know, I didn't get them.... When you look around to the, um, the percentage of African Americans who are actually in executive leadership is almost zero percent. Because it's less than one percent of the total population of people that are in leadership, and it's almost like they'll go outside of the system just to try to find a Caucasian to fill a position. Not that I'm not qualified, because I've been master's prepared for 12 years and I'm working on my doctorate.

According to Ryan and Kenny, supervisors' racial biases mean limited opportunities for promotion and upward mobility. This interpretation is consistent with research that suggests that even with stellar performance and solid work histories, Black workers may receive mediocre evaluations from white supervisors that limit their advancement (Feagin 2006; Feagin and Sikes 1994). For Black men nurses, their race may signal to supervisors that they are unworthy of promotion and thus create a different experience with the glass escalator.

Strong relationships with colleagues and supervisors are a key mechanism of the glass escalator effect. For Black men nurses, however, these relationships are experienced differently from those described by their white men colleagues. Black men nurses do not speak of warm and congenial relationships with women nurses or see these relationships as facilitating a move into leadership roles. Nor do they suggest that they share gendered bonds with men supervisors that serve to ease their mobility into higher-status administrative jobs. In contrast, they sense that racial bias makes it difficult to develop ties with coworkers and makes superiors unwilling to promote them. Black men nurses thus experience this aspect of the glass escalator differently from their white men colleagues. They find that relationships with colleagues and supervisors stifle, rather than facilitate, their upward mobility.

Perceptions of Suitability

Like their white counterparts, Black men nurses also experience challenges from clients who are unaccustomed to seeing men in fields typically dominated by women. As with white men nurses, Black men encounter this in surprised or quizzical reactions from patients who seem to expect to be treated by white women nurses. Ray, a 36-year-old oncology nurse with 10 years of experience, states,

> Nursing, historically, has been a white female's job [so] being a Black male it's a weird position to be in.... I've, several times, gone into a room and a male patient, a white male patient has, you know, they'll say, "Where's the pretty nurse? Where's the pretty nurse? Where's the blonde nurse?."... "You don't have one. I'm the nurse."

Yet while patients rarely expect to be treated by men nurses of any race, white men encounter statements and behaviors that suggest patients expect them to be doctors, supervisors, or other higher-status, more masculine positions (Williams 1989, 1995). In part, this expectation accelerates their ride on the glass escalator, helping to push them into the positions for which they are seen as more appropriately suited.

(White) men, by virtue of their masculinity, are assumed to be more competent and capable and thus better situated in (nonfeminized) jobs that are perceived to require greater skill and proficiency. Black men, in contrast, rarely encounter patients (or colleagues and supervisors) who immediately expect that they are doctors or administrators. Instead, many respondents find that even after displaying their credentials, sharing their nursing experience, and, in one case, dispensing care, they are still mistaken for janitors or service workers. Ray's experience is typical:

> I've even given patients their medicines, explained their care to them, and then they'll say to me, "Well, can you send the nurse in?"

Chris describes a somewhat similar encounter of being misidentified by a white woman patient:

> I come [to work] in my white uniform, that's what I wear—being a Black man, I know they won't look at me the same, so I dress the part—I said good evening, my name's Chris, and I'm going to be your nurse. She says to me, "Are you from housekeeping?"... I've had other cases. I've walked in and had a lady look at me and ask if I'm the janitor.

Chris recognizes that this patient is evoking racial stereotypes that Blacks are there to perform menial service work. He attempts to circumvent this very perception through careful self-presentation, wearing the white uniform to indicate his position as a nurse. His efforts, however, are nonetheless met with a racial stereotype that as a Black man he should be there to clean up rather than to provide medical care.

Black men in nursing encounter challenges from customers that reinforce the idea that men are not suited for a "feminized" profession such as nursing. However, these assumptions are racialized as well as gendered. Unlike white men nurses who are assumed to be doctors (see Williams 1992), Black men in nursing are quickly taken for janitors or housekeeping staff. These men do not simply describe a gendered process where perceptions and stereotypes about men serve to aid their mobility into higher-status jobs. More specifically, they describe interactions that are simultaneously raced *and* gendered in ways that reproduce stereotypes of Black men as best suited for certain blue-collar, unskilled labor.

These negative stereotypes can affect Black men nurses' efforts to treat patients as well. The men I interviewed find that masculinity does not automatically endow them with an aura of competency. In fact, they often describe interactions with white women patients that suggest that their race minimizes whatever assumptions of capability might accompany being men. They describe several cases in which white women patients completely refused treatment. Ray says,

> With older white women, it's tricky sometimes because they will come right out and tell you they don't want you to treat them, or can they see someone else.

Ray frames this as an issue specifically with older white women, though other nurses in the sample described similar issues with white women of all ages. Cyril, a 40-year-old nurse with 17 years of nursing experience, describes a slightly different twist on this story:

> I had a white lady that I had to give a shot, and she was fine with it and I was fine with it, But her husband, when she told him, he said to me, I don't have any problem with you as a Black man, but I don't want you giving her a shot.

While white men nurses report some apprehension about treating women patients, in all likelihood this experience is compounded for Black men (Williams 1989), Historically, interactions between Black men and white women have been fraught with complexity and tension, as Black men have been represented in the cultural imagination as potential rapists and threats to white women's security and safety—and, implicitly, as a threat to white patriarchal stability (Davis 1981; Giddings 1984). In Cyril's case, it may be particularly significant that the Black man is charged with giving a shot and therefore literally penetrating the white wife's body, a fact that may heighten the husband's desire to shield his wife from this interaction. White men nurses may describe hesitation or awkwardness that accompanies treating women patients, but their experiences are not shaped by a pervasive racial imagery that suggests that they are potential threats to their women patients' safety.

This dynamic, described primarily among white women patients and their families, presents a picture of how Black men's interactions with clients are shaped in specifically raced and gendered ways that suggest they are less rather than more capable. These interactions do not send the message that Black men, because they are men, are too competent for nursing and really belong in higher-status jobs. Instead, these men face patients who mistake them for lower-status service workers and encounter white women patients (and their husbands) who simply refuse treatment or are visibly uncomfortable with the prospect. These interactions do not situate Black men nurses in a prime position for upward mobility. Rather, they suggest that the experience of Black men nurses with this particular mechanism of the glass escalator is the manifestation of the expectation that they should be in lower-status positions more appropriate to their race and gender.

Refusal to Reject Femininity

Finally, Black men nurses have a different experience with establishing distance from women and the feminized aspects of their work. Most research shows that as men nurses employ strategies that distance them from femininity (e.g., by emphasizing nursing as a route to higher-status, more masculine jobs), they place themselves in a position for upward mobility and the glass escalator effect (Williams 1992). For Black men nurses, however, this process looks different. Instead of distancing themselves from the femininity associated with nursing, Black men actually embrace some of the more feminized attributes linked to nursing. In particular, they emphasize how much they value and enjoy the way their jobs allow them to be caring and nurturing. Rather than conceptualizing caring as anathema or feminine (and therefore undesirable), Black men nurses speak openly of caring as something positive and enjoyable.

This is consistent with the context of nursing that defines caring as integral to the profession. As nurses, Black men in this line of work experience professional socialization that emphasizes and values caring, and this is reflected in their statements about their work. Significantly, however, rather than repudiating this feminized component of their jobs, they embrace it. Tobias, a 44-year-old oncology nurse with 25 years of experience, asserts,

The best part about nursing is helping other people, the flexibility of work hours, and the commitment to vulnerable populations, people who are ill.

Simon, a 36-year-old oncology nurse, also talks about the joy he gets from caring for others. He contrasts his experiences to those of white men nurses he knows who prefer specialties that involve less patient care:

They were going to work with the insurance industries, they were going to work in the ER where it's a touch and go, you're a number literally. I don't get to know your name, I don't get to know that you have four grandkids, I don't get to know that you really want to get out of the hospital by next week because the following week is your birthday, your 80th birthday and it's so important for you. I don't get to know that your cat's name is Sprinkles, and you're concerned about who's feeding the cat now, and if they remembered to turn the TV on during the day so that the cat can watch *The Price is Right*. They don't get into all that kind of stuff. OK, I actually need to remember the name of your cat so that tomorrow morning when I come, I can ask you about Sprinkles and that will make a world of difference. I'll see light coming to your eyes and the medicines will actually work because your perspective is different.

Like Tobias, Simon speaks with a marked lack of self-consciousness about the joys of adding a personal touch and connecting that personal care to a patient's improvement. For him, caring is important, necessary, and valued, even though others might consider it a feminine trait.

For many of these nurses, willingness to embrace caring is also shaped by issues of race and racism. In their position as nurses, concern for others is connected to fighting the effects of racial inequality. Specifically, caring motivates them to use their role as nurses to address racial health disparities, especially those that disproportionately affect Black men. Chris describes his efforts to minimize health issues among Black men:

With Black male patients, I have their history, and if they're 50 or over I ask about the prostate exam and a colonoscopy. Prostate and colorectal death is so high that that's my personal crusade.

Ryan also speaks to the importance of using his position to address racial imbalances:

> I really take advantage of the opportunities to give back to communities, especially to change the disparities in the African American community. I'm more than just a nurse. As a faculty member at a major university, I have to do community hours, services. Doing health fairs, in-services on research, this makes an impact in some disparities in the African American community. [People in the community] may not have the opportunity to do this otherwise.

As Lamont (2000) indicates in her discussion of the "caring self," concern for others helps Chris and Ryan to use their knowledge and position as nurses to combat racial inequalities in health. Though caring is generally considered a "feminine" attribute, in this context it is connected to challenging racial health disparities. Unlike their white men colleagues, these nurses accept and even embrace certain aspects of femininity rather than rejecting them. They thus reveal yet another aspect of the glass escalator process that differs for Black men. As Black men nurses embrace this "feminine" trait and the avenues it provides for challenging racial inequalities, they may become more comfortable in nursing and embrace the opportunities it offers.

Conclusions

Existing research on the glass escalator cannot explain these men's experiences. As men who do women's work, they should be channeled into positions as charge nurses or nursing administrators and should find themselves virtually pushed into the upper ranks of the nursing profession. But without exception, this is not the experience these Black men nurses describe. Instead of benefiting from the basic mechanisms of the glass escalator, they face tense relationships with colleagues, supervisors' biases in achieving promotion, patient stereotypes that inhibit caregiving, and a sense of comfort with some of the feminized aspects of their jobs. These "glass barriers" suggest that the glass escalator is a racialized concept as well as a gendered one. The main contribution of this study is the finding that race and gender intersect to determine which men will ride the glass escalator. The

proposition that men who do women's work encounter undue opportunities and advantages appears to be unequivocally true only if the men in question are white.

This raises interesting questions and a number of new directions for future research. Researchers might consider the extent to which the glass escalator is not only raced and gendered but sexualized as well. Williams (1995) notes that straight men are often treated better by supervisors than are gay men and that straight men frequently do masculinity by strongly asserting their heterosexuality to combat the belief that men who do women's work are gay. The men in this study (with the exception of one nurse I interviewed) rarely discussed sexuality except to say that they were straight and were not bothered by "the gay stereotype." This is consistent with Williams's findings. Gay men, however, may also find that they do not experience a glass escalator effect that facilitates their upward mobility. Tim, the only man I interviewed who identified as gay, suggests that gender, race, and sexuality come together to shape the experiences of men in nursing. He notes,

> I've been called awful things—you faggot this, you faggot that. I tell people there are three *F*s in life, and if you're not doing one of them it doesn't matter what you think of me. They say, "Three *F*s?" and I say yes. If you aren't feeding me, financing me, or fucking me, then it's none of your business what my faggot ass is up to.

Tim's experience suggests that gay men—and specifically gay Black men—in nursing may encounter particular difficulties establishing close ties with straight men supervisors or may not automatically be viewed by their women colleagues as natural leaders. While race is, in many cases, more obviously visible than sexuality, the glass escalator effect may be a complicated amalgam of racial, gendered, and sexual expectations and stereotypes.

It is also especially interesting to consider how men describe the role of women in facilitating—or denying—access to the glass escalator. Research on white men nurses includes accounts of ways white women welcome them and facilitate their advancement by pushing them toward leadership positions

(Floge and Merrill 1986; Heikes 1991; Williams 1992, 1995). In contrast, Black men nurses in this study discuss white women who do not seem eager to work with them, much less aid their upward mobility. These different responses indicate that shared racial status is important in determining who rides the glass escalator. If that is the case, then future research should consider whether Black men nurses who work in predominantly Black settings are more likely to encounter the glass escalator effect. In these settings, Black men nurses' experiences might more closely resemble those of white men nurses.

Future research should also explore other racial minority men's experiences in women's professions to determine whether and how they encounter the processes that facilitate a ride on the glass escalator. With Black men nurses, specific race or gender stereotypes impede their access to the glass escalator; however, other racial minority men are subjected to different race or gender stereotypes that could create other experiences. For instance, Asian American men may encounter racially specific gender stereotypes of themselves as computer nerds, sexless sidekicks, or model minorities and thus may encounter the processes of the glass escalator differently than do Black or white men (Espiritu 2000). More focus on the diverse experiences of racial minority men is necessary to know for certain.

Finally, it is important to consider how these men's experiences have implications for the ways the glass escalator phenomenon reproduces racial and gendered advantages. Williams (1995) argues that men's desire to differentiate themselves from women and disassociate from the femininity of their work is a key process that facilitates their ride on the glass escalator. She ultimately suggests that if men reconstruct masculinity to include traits such as caring, the distinctions between masculinity and femininity could blur and men "would not have to define masculinity as the negation of femininity" (Williams 1995, 188). This in turn could create a more equitable balance between men and women in women's professions. However, the experiences of Black men in nursing, especially their embrace of caring, suggest that accepting the feminine aspects of work is not enough to dismantle the glass escalator and produce more gender equality in women's professions. The fact that Black men nurses accept and even enjoy caring does not minimize the processes that enable *white* men to ride the glass escalator. This suggests that undoing the glass escalator requires not only blurring the lines between masculinity and femininity but also challenging the processes of racial inequality that marginalize minority men.

Note

1. I could not locate any data that indicate the percentage of Black men in nursing. According to 2006 census data, African Americans compose 11 percent of nurses, and men are 8 percent of nurses (http://www.census.gov/compendia/statab/tables/08s0598.pdf). These data do not show the breakdown of nurses by race and sex.

References

Acker, Joan. 1990. Hierarchies, jobs, bodies: A theory of gendered organizations. *Gender & Society* 4: 139–58.

Britton, Dana. 1995. *At work in the iron cage.* New York: New York University Press.

Budig, Michelle. 2002. Male advantage and the gender composition of jobs: Who rides the glass escalator? *Social Forces* 49 (2): 258–77.

Charles, Maria and David Grusky. 2004. *Occupational ghettos: The worldwide segregation of women and men.* Palo Alto, CA: Stanford University Press.

Chen, Anthony. 1999. Lives at the center of the periphery, lives at the periphery of the center: Chinese American masculinities and bargaining with hegemony. *Gender & Society* 13: 584–607.

Collins, Patricia Hill. 1990. *Black feminist thought.* New York: Routledge.

Collins, Patricia Hill. 2004. *Black sexual politics.* New York: Routledge.

Connell, R. W 1989. *Gender and power.* Sydney, Australia: Allen and Unwin.

Davis, Angela. 1981. *Women, race, and class.* New York: Vintage.

Duffy, Mignon. 2007. Doing the dirty work; Gender, race, and reproductive labor in historical perspective. *Gender & Society* 21: 313–36.

Espiritu, Yen Le. 2000. *Asian American women and men: Labor, laws, and love.* Walnut Creek, CA: AltaMira.

Essed, Philomena. 1991. *Understanding everyday racism.* New York: Russell Sage.

Feagin, Joe. 2006. *Systemic racism.* New York: Routledge.

Feagin, Joe, and Melvin Sikes. 1994. *Living with racism.* Boston: Beacon Hill Press.

Floge, Liliane and Deborah M. Merrill. 1986. Tokenism reconsidered: Male nurses and female physicians in a hospital setting. *Social Forces* 64: 925–47.

Giddings, Paula. 1984. *When and where I enter; The impact of Black women on race and sex in America.* New York: HarperCollins.

Harvey Wingfield, Adia. 2007. The modern mammy and the angry Black man: African American professionals' experiences with gendered racism in the workplace. *Race, Gender, and Class* 14 (2): 196–212.

Heikes, E. Joel. 1991. When men are the minority: The case of men in nursing. *Sociological Quarterly* 32: 389–401.

hooks, bell. 2004. *We real cool.* New York: Routledge.

Kanter, Rosabeth Moss. 1977. *Men and women of the corporation.* New York: Basic Books.

Kimmel, Michael. 2001. Masculinity as homophobia. In *Men and masculinity*, edited by Theodore F. Cohen. Belmont, CA: Wadsworth.

Lamont, Michelle. 2000. *The dignity of working men.* New York: Russell Sage.

Neal, Mark Anthony. 2005. *New Black man.* New York: Routledge.

Ong, Maria. 2005. Body projects of young women of color in physics: Intersections of race, gender, and science. *Social Problems* 52 (4): 593–617.

Pierce, Jennifer. 1995. *Gender trials: Emotional lives in contemporary law firms.* Berkeley: University of California Press.

Roth, Louise. 2006. *Selling women short: Gender and money on Wall Street.* Princeton, NJ: Princeton University Press.

Shapiro, Thomas. 2004. *Hidden costs of being African American: How wealth perpetuates inequality.* New York: Oxford University Press.

Snyder, Karrie Ann and Adam Isaiah Green. 2008. Revisiting the glass escalator: The case of gender segregation in a female dominated occupation. *Social Problems* 55 (2): 271–99.

Williams, Christine. 1989. *Gender differences at work: Women and men in non-traditional occupations.* Berkeley: University of California Press.

Williams, Christine. 1992. The glass escalator: Hidden advantages for men in the "female" professions. *Social Problems* 39 (3): 253–67.

Williams, Christine. 1995. *Still a man's world: Men who do women's work.* Berkeley: University of California Press.

Zimmer, Lynn. 1988. Tokenism and women in the workplace: The limits of gender neutral theory. *Social Problems* 35 (1): 64–77.

Questions for Critical Thinking

1. Harvey Wingfield discusses how sex segregation continues to exist within the US labor force. How do the policies and practices she reveals maintain a gap in the incomes of women and men?

2. What are some ways of correcting gender-biased hiring practices in the workplace? What do you see as the likelihood of such corrective policies being enacted?

3. How does Harvey Wingfield's discussion impact your own expectations for your career?

THE THREAT OF POVERTY WITHOUT MISERY

In the following article, Alyosha Goldstein examines how social policy in the United States worsens conditions for people in poverty rather than relieving them from its conditions. In the decades since government policies established to "end of welfare as we know it," false stereotypes about people in poverty have resulted in making access to public assistance increasingly inaccessible. Through an examination of mandates and sanctions attached to programs such as Temporary Assistance for Needy Families (TANF) and changes to welfare programs resulting from the 1996 Personal Responsibility and Work Opportunity Reconciliation Act, the author argues that such policies are organized around sustaining poor people's misery and denying their enjoyment and pleasure.

United States social policy in the twenty-first century strives to intensify the suffering of impoverished people rather than to alleviate poverty. Measures taken by the Biden administration during the COVID-19 pandemic are responses to the exigencies of economic crisis and mounting precarity rather than new directions in antipoverty policy, with the possible exception of support for children. Since at least 1996, when the Personal Responsibility and Work Opportunity Reconciliation Act heralded the "end of welfare as we know it," this bipartisan aspiration to immiserate, while differing in degree over time, has essentially endorsed the long-standing claim by social conservatives that government welfare programs perpetuate poverty and create dependency. This claim drives the expansion of work requirements under conditions of economic precarity and aspires to make access to public assistance increasingly untenable (Grant et al. 2019; Hamilton 2020; Hatton 2020). Welfare legislated from this perspective casts the pleasures and pastimes of impoverished people as suspect, irresponsible, immoral, and extravagant. For instance, since 2012, federal law explicitly prevents Temporary Assistance to Needy Families (TANF) recipients from using electronic benefits transfer (EBT) cards in "liquor stores, casinos, and strip clubs" (Falk 2020). The Supplemental Nutrition Assistance Program (SNAP—the program that replaced food stamps in 2008) makes the point of insisting that food assistance cannot be used to buy "any food that will be eaten in the store," "hot food," prescription drugs, alcohol, and tobacco (USDA 2019), and pending legislation would also forbid the purchase of "junk food" and sweetened beverages. Social policy as a matter of social control and labor market regulation serves more decidedly as a means to humiliate, punish, and moralize.[1] The consequences of this orientation are compounded by the proliferation of eviction and predatory revenue

©2021 Feminist Formations, Vol. 33 No. 1 (Spring) pp. 117–141

schemes targeting and criminalizing impoverished people of color—including a massive complex of escalating fines, fees, debt, and credit regimes associated with citations, arrest, adjudication, incarceration, probation, bail, and bond payment, as well as direct asset seizure in the form of civil forfeiture (Eubanks 2018; Katzenstein and Waller 2015; Page et al. 2019; Page and Soss 2017; Nopper 2019; Roy, Graziani, and Stephens, 2020).

In the years since the 1996 legislation, US social policy has further institutionalized prescriptive conceptions of marriage and sexuality that imagine poor people themselves—and their familial and sexual lives especially—to be the cause of poverty, and has used the remnants of public assistance as instruments aimed at making poor peoples' lives intolerable through constant surveillance and scrutiny of their most mundane activities. This is not simply a matter of state-administered contempt and condemnation. It is symptomatic of a racialized fantasy that the welfare and well-being of the impoverished not only comes at everyone else's expense, but that any enjoyment poor people may have is in effect an act of theft from the rest of society. his essay thus examines how the normalization of bureaucratic cruelty now relentlessly insists on ensuring the unconditional misery of poverty. Policy imperatives today in effect underscore pleasure and enjoyment—associated with but not limited to sexuality—as arenas of political antagonism. This is not unique to the current historical moment, but it does require the collective mobilization of an insistently nonnormative politics of pleasure specific to the present intensified conditions of impoverishment.

In this essay, I make three interrelated arguments. First, I aim to show how and why US social policy, itself a site of contestation and not the uniform outcome of a single ideological perspective, is in effect organized around sustaining poor people's misery. This policy logic does not preclude deployment of the remnants of the social safety net as a means of labor market and social regulation. But in an era where wageless life proliferates, the spectacle of punishment and immiseration with cruelty as its own objective assumes a new degree of significance. Second, I argue that this orientation toward cruelty is at least partially galvanized by the idea that any aspect of the lives of welfare recipients in excess of bare survival—any

enjoyment and pleasure—is effectively stolen from taxpayers and so-called productive members of society. Third, in this context, I contend that the everyday practices and politics of pleasure articulated by women of color feminism and queer of color critique—often but not exclusively in relation to Audre Lorde's conception of "the erotic as power"—is an indispensable resource and counterforce to the enduring discourse on poverty that distinguishes between the "deserving" and "undeserving" poor (Katz 2013) and the script of heteronormative respectability as equivalent to having value and being worthy. Under these conditions, as Cathy Cohen argued more than twenty years ago, nonnormative, intersectional coalition-building is essential for refusing and dismantling dominant alignments of power and subjection (Cohen 1997).[2]

Rather than assume conformity to and compliance with heteropatriarchal norms to be the regulatory goal of contemporary social policy, I argue that the mandates and sanctions attached to programs such as Temporary Assistance for Needy Families (TANF) tacitly presume conformity and compliance to be ultimately unlikely if not impossible. This impossibility is accentuated by fiscal policies of devolution, state and municipal budget crises, and emergent economies of entrapment and extraction predicated on the desperation and vulnerability of poor people. Concurrently, state programs deploy normativity and normalization as a justification and a means to further brutalize—rather than to assimilate or economically reintegrate—those targeted by such policies. TANF policies are disciplinary not so much in the sense that they aim to teach and inculcate certain behavior; instead, they serve to ensnare and reproach recipients in the performance of uninhabitable standards and impracticable aspirations. In particular, the state-imposed heteropatriarchal sexuality administered by TANF endeavors to justify and accelerate the social disposability of poor women of color. Impoverished white women and their children are in effect also targeted in this regard as a matter of being the majority of the recipient population, but disidentification and denial underwritten by the "wages of whiteness" and the symbolic economy of racism discourage the potential solidarities of this more expansive frame.

The escalation of extreme poverty as a consequence of the accelerated upward redistribution and acute concentration of wealth is among the most significant features of the present moment in the United States (Edin and Shaefer 2015; Nadasen 2017; Pavetti 2017).[3] In December 2017, following an investigative tour of the United States, the United Nations Special Rapporteur on Extreme Poverty and Human Rights reported that "more than one in every eight Americans were living in poverty (roughly 40 million, equal to 12.7 percent of the population). And almost half of those (18.5 million) were living in deep poverty, with reported family income below one-half of the poverty threshold" (Alston 2017). The UN rapporteur concluded that on the brink of new tax legislation that would contribute to making the United States "the most unequal society in the world," the persistence of extreme poverty is "a political choice made by those in power," adding that a "reliance on criminalization" and allegations of welfare fraud were used to "conceal the problem" (Alston 2017). As a legislative drive akin to what Sharon Holland has described as "the erotic life of racism," these political decisions appear to have become the ends as much as the means policymaking (Holland 2012). By June 2020, the number of people in the United States living below the official poverty line grew to 65 million, with the increase vastly disproportionate for people of color (Saenz and Sherman 2020). The economic crisis in the wake of the COVID-19 pandemic only further compounds mass impoverishment while the most affluent class accumulates ever more wealth.

My intention in this essay is to situate TANF's "healthy-marriage promotion" and "responsible fatherhood" initiatives within the broader context of the intensification of means-tested welfare policies designed to punish, shame, and revile poor people—and, as the extraordinary resilience of the Moynihan Report's racism and misogyny suggests, poor Black women especially (US Department of Labor 1965). To be clear, the main point of this essay is not an argument about marriage and parenthood per se; rather, it intends to show how US social welfare policy envisions the enjoyment and pleasure of poor people as a matter of theft and impropriety. I consider social welfare policy as one facet of an expansive punitive institutional network that includes jails, bail, probation, prisons, foster care, and unevenly, but to an increasing extent, public education, as well as regimes of migrant detention and the further precaritization of those without citizenship rights. In order to demonstrate that racialized sexuality and the calculated attribution of perversion and deviance serve as the focal point of present-day policymaking, I begin with an overview of recent legislative changes and then show how initiatives targeting marriage and sexuality have become less about regulation than a means to vilify and punish poor people of color. In conclusion, I turn to engagements with Audre Lorde's conception of "the erotic as power" by women of color feminist scholarship and queer of color critique that elaborate on the erotic to refuse normative economies of the family. Following the lead of Black, Indigenous, and people of color (BIPOC) feminist and queer scholars and activists, exemplified by the work of groups like Queers for Economic Justice and its Welfare Warriors Research Collaborative (Welfare Warriors Research Collaborative 2010), I argue that an expansive politics of the erotic, nonutilitarian, nonnormative pleasure, and the other-than-familial is key to contesting the necropolitical misogyny and racism of present-day state policy against impoverished people. As the activist, filmmaker, and writer Tourmaline (who, when known as Reina Gossett, directed the Welfare Warriors Research Collaborative) declares, "I am envisioning a world in which pleasure isn't a scarce resource, but is something to revel in and share" (Tourmaline 2020).

Demeaning Need

When in 2017 the Trump administration began touting its plans for "ending welfare," relatively little remained of the anemic block grant program TANF, which now stands in rhetorically as the afterlife of AFDC (Aid to Families with Dependent Children)—the program commonly called welfare that the Clinton administration dismantled in 1996. Instead, this rhetoric was an attempt to leverage the protracted bipartisan defamation of so-called welfare toward more expansive ends (Jaffe 2018; Restuccia et al. 2017). In 2017, TANF provided its meager support to only 2.5 million people—mostly children—as compared to the still-inadequate 11 million recipients served at the peak of AFDC provision, a high point only reluctantly extended by the welfare state as a result of the indefatigable efforts of welfare rights activists (HHS 2018; Meyer and Floyd 2020; Office of Family Assistance 2019; Pavetti 2018).[4] This decrease is not indicative of a decline in the number of impoverished people, but is rather a consequence of severe cuts to social spending. Only 23 out of 100 families officially recognized as living in poverty received TANF assistance in 2016, as compared with the already insufficient aid provided to 68 of 100 families in poverty when the program began in 1996. As a consequence of policies intended to discourage participation and purge recipients rather than provide financial relief for the impoverished, a mere 32 percent of eligible families currently receive income assistance. The considerable discretionary leeway of spending guidelines for combined federal and state TANF grants has enabled state governments to divert large amounts of this money as a form of budgetary triage to address fiscal crises. As a result, states on average use only half of such funds on "core welfare reform areas" for eligible recipients—cash assistance for families with children, childcare for low-income families, and work-related programs—with some states allocating less than 20 percent to such areas (Safawi and Schott 2021). Nevertheless, the symbolic and rhetorical value of "welfare" persists as a means to conflate and malign.

The mobilization of long-cultivated racialized and misogynist resentment and contempt toward poor women of color is obviously not a new phenomenon. What is specific to the current moment, however, are the particular ways in which legislative efforts draw on familiar repertoires of anti-Black racism and anti-feminism to dismantle or privatize a broad array of social programs that have not historically been denigrated as programs for the "undeserving" poor. Likewise, the idea of including work requirements as a component of all social programs is not itself new but has gained further prominence as a means of signaling the retributive emphasis of social statecraft today. Thus, for instance, in 2011, Pennsylvania's Secretary of Public Welfare Gary D. Alexander testified before Congress:

> Unfortunately, I think in our other programs like food stamps and Medicaid ... there is a scant work requirement or no work requirement at all. I think what we have learned from TANF from 1996 is that there was a focus on self-reliance, personal responsibility, the focus on work, it was time-limited, and that there was a focus on bringing families together in a healthy marriage. And I think that if we are going to proceed in the future and end dependency, we are going to have to work harder at encompassing all of our programs across the welfare spectrum and bring all of these together" (US House of Representatives 2011, 86).

Indeed, such comprehensive work requirements were the declared goal of the Trump administration, which also attempted to leverage Medicaid work stipulations toward a number of other antagonistic ends, such as undermining Native American tribal sovereignty (Diamond 2018; Federal Register 2018).

Programs such as SNAP, housing assistance, and Medicaid have historically been popular with the US electorate (Dickinson 2020; Gritter 2018; Michener 2018; Tach and Edin 2017). Proposals that attach work requirements and mandate drug testing for otherwise eligible recipients to qualify for these programs cast all impoverished people seeking assistance in the same terms as TANF recipients (Agorist 2015; Delaney 2017). In effect, they presume—despite voluminous evidence to the contrary, such as the statistics recounted by the UN special rapporteur mentioned above—that recipients do not need assistance to meet basic needs for survival and set out to punish the indolence and hedonism they attribute to the impoverished.

Such retaliatory legislation seeks to leverage the neoliberal idea that government welfare programs perpetuate if not create poverty in order to justify policies intended to inflict suffering. Paul Ryan of Wisconsin was a prominent champion of this policy ideology during his time as a congressman and as the House Speaker. Ryan's initiatives exemplify policy-making that advocates expanding work requirements for eligibility. By extending punitive measures from TANF to food assistance and Medicaid, Ryan's policies sought to further poor people's immiseration as the supposed solution to poverty. In July 2013, in anticipation of the fiftieth anniversary of the Economic Opportunity Act and the War on Poverty, the House Budget Committee chaired by Ryan convened a series of hearings compiled in The War on Poverty: A Progress Report (US House of Representatives 2013). In his opening remarks, Ryan insisted, "if you work hard and play by the rules, you can get ahead. That is something that we all believe in and that we all care about. This is the central promise of this country. We want to protect that idea, and we want to preserve it for the next generation" (1). Not surprisingly, the subsequent report on the hearings stated that "Federal programs are not only failing to address the problem [of poverty]. They are also in some significant respects making it worse" (House Budget Commit-tee Majority Staff 2014, 9). Although the authors noted a variety of reasons for poverty's persistence, they nonetheless concluded that "perhaps the single most important determinant of poverty is family structure. … The Moynihan Report identified the breakdown of the family as a key cause of poverty within the Black community. More recent research on Americans of all backgrounds has backed up Moynihan's argument" (US House of Representatives 2013, 4, 5).

Indeed, the Moynihan Report and other versions of the "culture of poverty" thesis argue that single-mother households—as supposed crucibles of deviant Black matriarchy and the emasculation of Black men—propagate intergenerational racial pathology (Katz 2013, 220–30; King 2018; Mayeri 2013; Valentine 1968). This misogynist, heteropatriarchal, and racist narrative appears in a variety of iterations. The 2020 publication of Lawrence Mead's racist screed "Poverty and Culture" in a peer-reviewed academic journal (Mead 2020), even if subsequently retracted by the publisher, is evidence of this enduring argument. A 2012 New York Times Magazine cover story titled "Obama vs. Poverty" similarly maintained that although poor people in the United States are materially better off than they were fifty years ago, what the author calls a "social gap" between poor people and the so-called middle class has become most pronounced. This gap is made and perpetuated, according to the article, by "family dynamics and their effects on child development" (Tough 2012, 345; see also Cohen 2010; Lowrey 2014). Thus, marriage is the happy ending that not only promises to bring closure to inherited social dysfunction but also to transfer the provision of care from the state to the institutions of private life. In this sense, the hetero-normative

two-parent family ostensibly allows for appropriate dependency in the private sphere while ultimately cultivating independence.

When in 2014 Paul Ryan was criticized for comments on poverty, culture, and "inner cities," he responded, "this has nothing to do with race whatsoever. … [I]t's a breakdown of families, it's rural poverty in rural areas, and talking about where poverty exists—there are no jobs and we have a breakdown of the family" (quoted in Lowery 2014). Acknowledging that there are "no jobs" appears to have little impact on the persistent focus on expanding work requirements for eligibility, and as such underscores "work" as detached from employment and job training. In a 2017 memorandum ending TANF work-requirement waivers introduced five years previously, Clarence Carter, the Trump-appointed director of the Office of Family Assistance that oversees TANF, noted that "one of the core goals of the 1996 welfare reform law … was to help needy families end dependency on government benefits through employment" (Office of Family Assistance 2017).[5] Contending that "we cannot achieve the goal of self-sufficiency if meaningful work participation is divorced from welfare cash assistance," Carter's memo insisted that "work creates opportunities for individual growth" and "instills personal dignity" while leaving "meaningful work participation" unspecified beyond the ostensible benefits of "hard work" (Office of Family Assistance 2017). The culture of poverty thesis insinuates that it is a racialized aversion to "hard work" rather than a lack of employment or living wage that ultimately serves as the obstacle to "independence" and "personal dignity."

If the overt insistence here is that "hard work" is the means to supposed self-improvement and economic mobility, I would argue that "hard work"—especially in the form of work requirements in the absence of options for a living wage—increasingly assumes an exclusively malevolent inflection, becoming a demand that the impoverished must suffer more and an assertion that they do not sufficiently experience misery. The rhetoric of "hard work" expresses a desire to inflict pain and anguish. Ryan's initial focus on "inner cities," as well as his continued insistence on "the breakdown of the family" as a consequence of "culture," are precisely the means to speak in anti-Black terms, to fully articulate this malevolence with a racialized desire for the affliction of poor people of color, while disavowing race altogether. An ostensible concern with culture in this sense has served as an enduring basis for the (neo)liberal and social conservative agreement that marriage is the solution to poverty (Cooper 2017).

Just as the so-called culture of poverty supposedly perpetuated by unmarried mothers of color is incessantly "rediscovered" and attributed causal significance over structural conditions of impoverishment, platitudinous mandates for family-oriented social policy are introduced time and again as allegedly untried innovative solutions. Thus, in 2015, the American Enterprise Institute and the Brookings Institution copublished a report asserting a broad consensus on "American values" and advocated what it called the "four cornerstones of a pro-family, pro-opportunity agenda": "1) Promote marriage as the most reliable route to family stability and resources; 2) Promote delayed, responsible childbearing; 3) Promote parenting skills and practices, especially among low-income parents; and 4) Promote skill development, family involvement, and employment among young men as well as women" (AEI/Brookings 2015, 32). Despite this purported consensus, rightwing and conservative pundits and legislators repeatedly decry a lack of programmatic support for the heteronormative conjugal family, even though there has been a steady increase of such policy mandates launched over the past twenty years. For instance, the 2016 report issued by Ryan's Task Force on Poverty, Opportunity, and Upward Mobility once again claimed that "federal programs do little to promote marriage as the most reliable route to economic stability and the setting most likely to yield the best outcomes for children" (Task Force on Poverty 2016, 16). The repetition of such assertions ad nauseam endeavors to establish the perception that social norms are under siege rather than acknowledge how social disinvestment and economies of dispossession make such norms uninhabitable for most people.

Marriage That Punishes

A focus on inculcating and compelling the heteropatriarchal nuclear family norm has long animated social policy in the United States. This was paralleled and reinforced in law more broadly through the persistence of the doctrine of coverture—common-law rules mandating that upon marriage, a woman ceased in effect to have a separate legal personhood from her husband, her rights and obligations becoming fully subsumed by him, and that marriage rendered her dependent and incapable of owning property in her own name or controlling her own earnings. The legal norms of coverture were only partially dismantled with the Married Women's Property Acts during the second half of the nineteenth century. This same logic contributed to the creation of widow's pensions as support for the "deserving poor."

The matrimonial imperative has also worked in conjunction with colonial and racial dispossession, as was overtly evident with the marriage promotion for the formerly enslaved initiated by the Freedman's Bureau during Reconstruction and the "head of household" stipulations of allotment policy for Native peoples. Amid the concerted project of US imperial nation-building following the Civil War, marriage was a key instrument of state power in the making and administration of gendered social and civic statuses. If on the one hand marriage had been denied those enslaved and after emancipation offered advantageous ways in which to claim recognition for family and kinship, on the other hand it served as a means through which to moralize and regulate those no longer enslaved in a context where anti-miscegenation laws likewise policed the permissible racial limits of matrimony (Franke 1999; Hunter 2017; Yamin 2012, 23–46). In the wake of the failures of land redistribution promised under Radical Reconstruction, Priscilla Yamin contends that Republicans increasingly directed the formerly enslaved "toward marriage and working for wages as symbols of freedom, independence, and equality, as opposed to owning land" (Yamin 2012, 26–27). Freedman's Bureau agents sought to enforce marriage and monogamy and touted their importance as resources for dignity and self-reliance so as to discourage further recourse to government support and subsidy. For Native peoples during and after the mid- to late nineteenth century, as Rose Stremlau points out:

> Reformers concluded that kinship systems, especially as they manifested in [non-heteropatriarchal] gender

roles, prevented acculturation by undermining individualism and social order, and they turned to federal Indian policy to fracture these extended indigenous families into male-dominant, nuclear families, modeled after middle-class, Anglo-American households (2005, 265).

That children were systematically removed from Native families under boarding school and later adoption and foster care programs further demonstrates how the imposed disciplinary strictures of marriage could operate untethered from an ethics of caring, filiation, or even privacy for those whom the state sought to pacify, domesticate, and civilize. These are not simply historical examples but enduring normative configurations that continue and have profound consequences.

The refrain of marriage as the solution to poverty enlists as evidence extraneous social facts—that children who grow up in environments where they feel loved and cared for are likely better prepared for the challenges of life—with no direct correlation with marital imperatives. Under circumstances in which such matrimonial norms, whether actually desired or not, are largely impossible to enact due the very economic conditions that they are somehow supposed to redress, an unequivocal insistence on marriage is paternalistic and punitive.

The 1996 Personal Responsibility and Work Opportunity Reconciliation Act (PRWORA) ended "welfare as we know it" by replacing AFDC with TANF block grants. The 1996 act asserted that: "1) Marriage is the foundation of a successful society; 2) Marriage is an essential institution of a successful society which promotes the interests of children; 3) Promotion of responsible fatherhood and motherhood is integral to successful child rearing and the well-being of children." TANF was therefore designed, as stated in the legislation, to (a) "end the dependence of needy parents on government benefits by promoting job preparation, work, and marriage;" (b) "prevent and reduce the incidence of out-of-wedlock pregnancies;" and (c) "encourage the formation and maintenance of two-parent families." Federal guidelines dictate that recipients must engage in work activities and require that states impose sanctions (by reducing or ending benefits) if a recipient fails to

participate. Most states have what are termed "full-family" sanction policies that terminate benefits to the entire family if a parent fails to complete the work requirements (Center on Budget and Policy Priorities 2018).

In addition to marriage promotion and work requirements and sanctions for noncompliance, PRWORA imposed time-limited eligibility. The law prohibited states from using federal TANF funds to assist most families for more than a lifetime total of sixty months (although some states have used their discretionary authority to work around this cutoff point) (Lindhorst and Mancoske 2006). PRWORA not only imposed strict limits on the parsimonious benefits provided to recipients, but also set funding for TANF itself to expire in 2002. The Bush administration announced that one of its highest priorities in "welfare reform" was "healthy" marriage as a condition for renewing TANF. As a consequence of this priority, already minimal funding for income assistance was diverted to faith-based organizations running marriage promotion programs. The reauthorization of TANF and the Personal Responsibility, Work, and Family Promotion Act of 2003 stipulated that among their primary objectives was to "encourage the formation and maintenance of healthy two-parent married families, and encourage responsible fatherhood." That same year, the House and the Senate Finance Committee passed two bills that included marriage provisions. The reauthorization of TANF as part of the Deficit Reduction Act of 2005 included Title IV-A Healthy Marriage and Responsible Fatherhood grants programs—made competitively available to "states, territories, Indian tribes and tribal organizations, and public and nonprofit groups including religious organizations."

Funding for such initiatives has been a continuous feature of TANF since 2005, with Barack Obama as an outspoken advocate for making "responsible fathers" central to social welfare policy and his administration's Fatherhood, Marriage, and Families Innovation Fund further amplifying Bush-era programs.

The legislative precarity of the program mirrors the deliberate provisionality and impermanence of the support provided. Time limits and formidable eligibility requirements hasten attrition, while marriage and heteronormativity ostensibly offer the privatized stability and support no longer available as public welfare (Goldstein 2015). Attending marriage education programs is often a requirement for unwed TANF recipients to access government benefits or services. Directly tied to the terms of compliance and sanctions, the focus on marriage and fatherhood in TANF likewise serves to privatize poverty by shifting the burden of support almost exclusively to families and to enforce heteropatriarchy by punishing single motherhood and nonconjugal familial arrangements (Bentele and Nicoli 2012; Mannix and Freedman 2013; Monnat 2010; Weaver 2014). Marriage promotion—and hence the penalization of nonconjugal families or unwed mothers—has become increasingly central to TANF policy.

The governmental insistence on marriage as the solution to poverty has worked in conjunction with the modes of surveillance and the routine bureaucratic degradation of welfare recipients that have been features of welfare policy at least since the 1950s. The confluence between the penal system and the criminalization of welfare recipients as a means through which to discredit and roll back the gains of the welfare rights movement accelerated during the global economic crisis and neoliberal restructuring of the 1970s. Julilly Kohler-Hausmann has analyzed the strategic fabulation of the so-called welfare queen in this context as key to the integration of policing, penality, and poor discipline. She argues that by casting welfare recipients as lazy, financially comfortable, and criminally suspect, the welfare queen trope made absent the poverty of and the multiple forms of work done by parents receiving state assistance (Gilman 2014; Hinton 2017; Kohler-Hausmann 2017). Ronald Reagan, as both California governor and president, was among the most opportunistic popularizers of the welfare queen myth, which he deliberately linked to misguided social policy as the cause of familial breakdown—for example, when in 1986 he declared that the 1960s War on Poverty had been won by poverty "because instead of helping the poor, government programs ruptured the bonds holding poor families together. Perhaps the most insidious effect of welfare is its usurpation of the role of provider" (Reagan 1986).

The welfare queen trope has proven to be remarkably durable. In Dan Quayle's infamous 1992 campaign speech castigating the fictional television character Murphy Brown for denigrating family values, he declared that "a welfare check is not a husband, the state is not a father. It is from parents that children learn how to behave in society. … [M]arriage is probably the best anti-poverty program of all" (quoted in Heath 2013, 568). A year later, in an *Atlantic Monthly* article titled "Dan Quayle Was Right," Barbara Dafoe Whitehead wrote that "welfare dependency … takes two forms: first, single mothers particularly unwed mothers, stay on welfare longer than other welfare recipients. … Second, welfare dependency tends to be passed on from one generation to the next." Contending that public welfare was eroding the foundation of private life, she asserted that "the family is responsible for teaching lessons of independence, self-restraint, responsibility, and right conduct, which are essential to a free, democratic society" (Whitehead 1993). Thus, according to Whitehead, an extended reliance on public welfare and the intergenerational effects of "broken" homes perpetuating dependency threatened freedom and democracy. During the mid-1990s a number of organizations were established to promote marriage and fatherhood as key to public policy, including the National Fatherhood Initiative, Promise Keepers, the National Marriage Project, Marriage Savers, the Institute for American Values, and the Coalition for Marriage, Family, and Couples Education.

It is significant that much of the political momentum for TANF marriage promotion came from the so-called fathers' rights movement. Indeed, the state's role in marriage has historically been organized to facilitate patriarchy and sanction paternity. Fatherhood initiatives as part of TANF were first proposed with the Fathers Count Act in 1998. Since the 1990s, self-proclaimed fathers' rights advocates—who are specifically anti-feminist—"use the 'language of gender neutrality to attack programs created to ameliorate the outcomes of gendered inequality' and they 'seek to reassert the patriarchal prerogative to define violence and delimit responses to it' " (Baker and Stein 2016, 94–95). For instance, Carrie Baker and Nan Stein note that in 2002, father's rights activists sued the state of Minnesota "claiming that the state's domestic violence laws were sex discriminatory, because they funded battered women's shelters that advocated on behalf of and served women" (Baker and Stein, 93). Marriage promotion policy and programs further entrench patriarchal entitlement and women's vulnerability to domestic violence by presenting marriage as the only viable means to survival and, in effect, pressuring them to marry abusive partners. Baker and Stein observe that "while TANF's Family Violence Option allows states to waive some TANF requirements in the interest of safety, a study by the National Law Center on Homelessness and Poverty argues that poor state and local implementation of this waiver has meant that many intimate partner violence survivors have not had access to support" (Baker and Stein, 91).

Such policy and program priorities further amplify the state as arbiter of heteropatriarchal norms. Jacqueline Stevens argues that, "in its insistence on controlling marriage, the state positions itself as constitutive of intergenerational forms of being. It is the prerogative of the state to distinguish, and hence to constitute, the difference between what is profane (sex as 'fornication,' children as 'illegitimate') and what is sacred (sex within marriage, legitimate children)" (Stevens 1999, 223). According to Stevens, "the very representation of a mother's 'natural' relation with the infant requires a legal system that performs a comparable relation for the husband, if paternity is to be politically institutionalized. The effect of this is to sacralize paternity in comparison with the apparent materiality and indeterminacy of maternity" (Stevens, 223). The state's investment in so-called father's rights serves to shore up the authority of the state itself, to confer legitimacy on itself as the political expression of natural social bonds.[6]

At the same time, it would be a mistake to understand TANF's concern with marriage only in heteropatriarchal and heteronormative terms. Marriage promotion as welfare policy in this sense equivocates between a capacious normative demand and fortifying the heteropatriarchal imperative. In 2013, the US Supreme Court overturned the 1996 Defense of Marriage Act, which had defined marriage as the "legal union between one man and one woman as husband and wife." And in Obergefell v. Hodges (2015), the Court decided that same-sex couples are guaranteed

the right to marry by both the Due Process Clause and the Equal Protection Clause of the Fourteenth Amendment to the US Constitution. Yet, as Kaiponanea Matsumura points out, "dozens of states and scores of municipalities have created nonmarital statuses like civil unions and domestic partnerships for those who (until recently) could not, or chose not to, marry. … Where same-sex couples have won the right to marry, however, jurisdictions have repeatedly treated that legalization as a green light to eliminate existing nonmarital statuses" (Matsumura 2016, 1510). Further-more, Melissa Murray argues that acknowledging marriage as "a vehicle of state-imposed discipline and regulation makes clear that expanding marriage to new constituencies does little to undermine its disciplinary force; it merely expands the state's disciplinary reach to include new subjects" (Murray 2012, 7; see also DeFilippis et al. 2018; Murray 2016; Reddy 2011; Spade 2013). Discussing the example of Lawrence v. Texas (2003), Murray argues that "even as Lawrence creates a new geography for sex, the opinion cannot relinquish the idea that sex must be subject to state discipline" (2012, 56). According to Murray, "Lawrence's language makes clear that the decision is not about protecting sex for sex's sake. Instead, Lawrence's protections are most robust when private, consensual sex occurs between two adults in the context of a monogamous relationship" (2012, 57). She concludes that "the emphasis on marriage-like sex means … that this space has been rendered disciplinary and regulatory because its protections are reserved primarily to those who are willing to live their lives in the disciplined manner of married people" (2012, 58). Murray reads Lawrence in relation to nineteenth-century seduction laws in order to theorize "marriage as punishment," a disciplinary narrowing of allowable possibility and conduct. I argue that marriage in this sense provides the affective and programmatic underpinning of TANF.

Hating Other People's Pleasure

Social statecraft in the United States has historically been preoccupied with imposing racialized sexual, gender, and familial norms (Abramovitz 2017; Katz 1996; O'Connor 2001). Indeed, it often seems as though poverty has been a governmental concern only to the extent to which it has been articulated as a problem of such norms—which helps to explain the durability of the culture of poverty thesis as a means of making the relation between norms and poverty both causal and circular. Labor market participation requirements have been articulated through such norms rather than serving as distinct imperatives. The particular ways in which such concerns shape policy change over time. In the early twenty-first century—with the intensification of the upward redistribution of wealth, unfettered capitalist predation and austerity regimes, and the heightened social expendability of racialized populations—TANF's "healthy-marriage promotion" and "responsible fatherhood" initiatives are increasingly detached from the Keynesian social reproductive project.

Under such circumstances, TANF endeavors to guarantee that the sexual lives of poor people are further policed and purged of pleasure. Diminishing support for those who are impoverished works in tandem with casting poor women of color as participating in what amounts to an iniquitous theft from those who are properly entitled to enjoyment, as somehow ostensibly enjoying promiscuity, indolence, and excess at the expense of hardworking taxpayers. What after all animates the reactionary and racially coded proliferation of the political trope of the "taxpayer"? Who declares "not with my tax dollars," a sentiment bitterly manifest since at least California's 1978 Proposition 13 (Martin 2008)?[7] At least in part, it is resentment toward a fiscal obligation allocated beyond individual will and a response to the threat of something presumably misused, taken, or in effect stolen. I suggest that an important aspect of the outrage expressed is that what is imagined as stolen is pleasure and enjoyment. Often, "my tax dollars" indicates not only that poor people are undeserving, but also that any aspect of their lives not consumed with suffering and misery comes at the taxpayers' expense—a zero-sum equation of theft, loss, and resentment.

The deferred promise of enjoyment is a significant organizing principle in the libidinal economy of racial capitalism. The racialized attribution of suspect and excessive pleasure to those who have ostensibly not properly internalized the virtues of a mythic Protestant work ethic functions as a deflection. Those deemed lazy and indulgent are the root cause of the hardworking citizen's unhappiness rather than capitalist social relations, which prioritize the aspiration to possess and perpetually restage desire as lack.[8] Saidiya Hartman notes further the definitional connection between enjoyment and property, observing that "to take delight in, to use, and to possesses are inextricably linked. ... [E]njoyment entails everything from the use of one's possession to the value of whiteness," with the term "enjoy" defined in law as the exercise or promise of a right, as well as "to have, possess, and use with satisfaction; to occupy or have the benefit of (Hartman 1997, 23–24). Hartman argues that in the antebellum United States, "not only were the rights and privileges of white citizens undergirded by the subjection of blacks but ... enjoyment in turn defined the meaning of subjection" such that "there was no relation to blackness outside the terms of this use of, entitlement to, and occupation of the captive body" (1997, 25). And yet, even under the brutalizing conditions of slavery and racialized abjection, racial subjection was never secure enough to guarantee enjoyment and possession, prompting instead an unsettling white fear of loss or not truly possessing on the one hand, and on the other, the proliferation of fantasies that Black people had some innate access to pleasure beyond the means of whites, fantasies of Black lasciviousness and excessive enjoyment. The fantasy of theft and excess in this sense provides an affective repository for white supremacist deflection and racist hatred.[9]

In this regard, TANF as the hatred of another's enjoyment is related to what Ange-Marie Hancock calls with respect to racialized antiwelfare affect "the politics of disgust" (Hancock 2004), but with greater emphasis on the entwining of repulsion and desire as constitutive of the drive to retribution and abhorrence. The ways in which the fathers' rights movement and the reaffirmation of heteropatriarchy have been the source of current TANF policy similarly express conjugal domesticity and personal responsibility as a response to women ostensibly stealing men's rightful authority. In part because what is at stake is not simply de jure liberal mechanisms of access and equality but rather the sanctioning and distribution of misogynist necropolitical violence, rights claims are insufficient for challenging the presumptions and racialized heteronormative, anti-poor agenda of contemporary state policy. In this sense, TANF, as an instantiation of what Kaaryn Gustafson describes as "degradation ceremonies" (Gustafson 2013), serves as a means of producing what scholars such as Lisa Marie Cacho and Naomi Paik discuss in the context of anti-immigrant campaigns and the criminalization of poor people of color as "rightlessness" (Cacho 2012; Paik 2016).

Relations of Abundance

Under the hateful and hostile conditions discussed in this essay, a nonnormative politics of pleasure and sociality otherwise, a politics that refuses compulsory matrimony, austerity, and asceticism becomes ever more significant. Although the paranoid resentment of a fantasied theft of enjoyment serves as a supposed justification for deliberate cruelty, it also reveals the profound sense in which the other-than-familial and other-than-normatively gendered do in fact threaten heteropatriarchal control. Scholars writing from a range of perspectives, including Grace Kyungwon Hong, LaMonda Horton-Stallings, Jennifer C. Nash, Mireille Miller-Young, Amber Jamilla Musser, and adrienne maree brown, among others, have engaged with and elaborated on Audre Lorde's conception of the erotic as an indispensable resource for collectively living otherwise under intensifying regimes of violence (brown 2019; Hong 2015; Lorde 1984; Miller-Young 2014; Musser 2018; Nash 2014, 2017; Stallings 2015).

In the context of "a racist, patriarchal, and anti-erotic society," what Lorde calls "the erotic as power" for women defies the fearful and "severe abstinence of the ascetic" and "self-abnegation" (1984, 59, 56). For Lorde, the erotic as a "deep and irreplaceable knowledge of my capacity for joy comes to demand from all my life that it be lived within the knowledge that such satisfaction is possible, and does not have to be called marriage." This is a fundamental challenge to "any system which defines the good in terms of profit rather than in terms of human need, or which defines human need to the exclusion of the psychic and emotional components of that need" (1984, 57, 55). Moreover, absolutely indispensable to this challenge is the importance of work grounded in queer, trans, and women of color analysis that troubles Lorde's division between an authentic erotic and

sex as normative instrument of domination. Approaching sexuality and pleasure as not equivalent to but iterations of the erotic, Jennifer C. Nash, for instance, notes the importance of theorizing the complex ways in which "pleasure is a position of ambivalence, that it can electrify and wound simultaneously, that it can excite and harm, that it can arouse and injure" (Nash 2017, 270–71). Rather than a matter of truth or authenticity, such critical elaborations conceive of the erotic as heightened sensing and sensorium, a delirious clarity of embodiment and mind, a relation layered in fantasy that can also feel fraught, shameful, and vulnerable.

In the specific context of this essay, what I want to emphasize is how erotic power, in the expansive ways just suggested, is a multidimensionality of living and feeling that is not simply preempted by the conditions of poverty. For the prevailing order, this evokes the threat of poverty without misery because, as Lorde puts it, "once we begin to feel deeply all the aspects of our lives, we begin to demand from ourselves and from our life pursuits that they feel in accordance with that joy which we know ourselves to be capable of" (1984, 57). Moreover, asserts Lorde, "in touch with the erotic, I become less willing to accept powerlessness" or live under states of "resignation, despair, self-effacement, depression, self-denial" (58). Heteropatriarchy is maintained through the suppression of erotic knowledge. Unsettling this suppression, however, also means grappling with the messy and not always necessarily liberatory dynamics of desire (Holland 2012, 41–64). The heteropatriarchal state aims to secure not only its monopoly on ostensibly legitimate violence but its monopoly on the connection between enjoyment and property, wherein the joy or pleasure of those it judges to be deviant is perceived as coming at the expense of proper, self-possessed citizens organized under normative relations of family and filiation (Hartman 1997). In North America more broadly in this regard, settler colonial violence has incessantly targeted Indigenous relations of kinship as grounded in relations with land and the bodies of Indigenous women (Simpson 2016).

A queer women of color critique, drawing on and critically rethinking Lorde among others, not only rejects the racist misogyny through which the parsimonious hatred of other peoples' pleasure is organized, but also sustains and incites relations of social profusion that resist the intensified suffering and expendability advanced by contemporary necropolitics in the United States.[10] Alexis Pauline Gumbs elaborates on the generative consequences of "radical motherhood" practiced by collectives such as the Sisterhood of Black Single Mothers as a way to refuse "the pathologizing language placed on female-headed families" and affirm the "abundance of mothering" (Gumbs 2016, 30). Gumbs points out that "seeing mothering as a queer collaboration with the future has to do with transforming the parenting relationship from a property relation-ship to a partnership in practice" (2016, 29)—and in this sense to disrupt the normative juridical link between enjoyment and property. Tiffany Lethabo King builds on the work of Kay Lindsey and Hortense Spillers to denaturalize "the family as a normative and humanizing institution to which people should aspire to belong" (King, 2018, 69), a constitutively "white institution, [that] has been held up to Blacks as a desirable but somehow unattainable goal" (Lindsey as quoted in King 2018, 74). King argues that the family as "the geopolitical unit of woman-children-land-slaves is a form of property that can be accumulated" (2018, 74), an accumulation that remains predicated on the theft of Indigenous land and the ongoing consequences of the human property regimes of racialized colonial slavery. To disassemble the family as "an organizing logic of control and state power" (2018, 9) is to reveal the machinations of the family as the exclusive means to protect and provide under the accelerated regimes of neoliberal privatization and predation. It is, of course, not a coincidence that King's essay focuses on the Moynihan Report, and that Spillers's classic 1987 essay "Mama's Baby, Papa's Maybe: An American Grammar Book" turns partially on the critique of Moynihan as well (Spillers 1987). Both provide a genealogy of refusing the entrenched justifications of now-escalating bureaucratic cruelty and resentful paranoia of stolen pleasure. A queer women of color critique therefore not only provides a crucial rejection of state-administered violability, but also offers resources for collectively living otherwise.

The threat of poverty without misery is ultimately the threat of this collective living otherwise as relations of social abundance that unhinge the normative force and enforcement of administrative cruelty. Nonnormative erotic power as sensuous sociality—a life-giving mutuality such as what Amber Musser calls "brown jouissance" (Musser 2018)—is not pleasure stolen from the rest of society but in fact an affirmation of living that may refuse apprehension and appropriation by dominant alignments of power and subjection. Against and beyond capitalist predation and the statecraft of suffering, such relations of abundance make possible something more than survival.

Acknowledgments

Many thanks to Nicole Fleetwood, Sarah Tobias, the anonymous readers for Feminist Formations, Rebecca Schreiber, and participants at the "Poverty and Sexuality" symposium organized and hosted by the Institute for Research on Women at Rutgers University in April 2016, where the initial version of this essay was presented.

Notes

1. On welfare as the regulation of poor women, see Abramovitz 2017; Piven and Cloward 1993; and Smith 2007.

2. See also the important forum on Cohen's 1997 essay in GLQ with incisive contributions by Nic John Ramos, Cathy Cohen, Christina B. Hanhardt, Chandan Reddy, L. H. Stallings, C. Riley Snorton, Marlon M. Bailey, Jih-Fei Cheng, Sarah Haley, Nayan Shah, and Elliott H. Powell ("Twenty Years of Punks" 2019).

3. Extreme poverty is currently defined by the World Bank as earning the equivalent of less than USD $1.90 a day.

4. On the welfare rights movement, see Goldstein, 2012; Kornbluh, 2007; Nadasen 2005.

5. Moreover, as noted by the New York Times, "the resources devoted to increased workforce development in Mr. Trump's 2019 budget … are relatively modest compared with the deep cuts proposed for safety net programs. And the work requirements come in addition to the administration's proposal to drastically cut domestic spending, including a plan to trim food aid by $213 million over the next decade" (Thrush 2018). This divergence is typical of the contemporary

Republican agenda rather than being unique to the Trump administration.

6. For more on the role of marriage promotion initiatives in this regard, see Heath 2012 and Randles 2017. On the relation of these dynamics to moral panic regarding teen pregnancy and the promotion of abstinence-only sex education, see Daniel 2017.

7. In contrast to the prevailing "tax revolt" rhetoric, see Newman and O'Brien 2011 and Henricks and Seamster 2017.

8. Slavoj Žižek contends that "what we conceal by imputing to the Other the theft of enjoyment is the traumatic fact that we never possessed what was allegedly stolen from us" (Žižek 1993, 203; see also Stavrakakis and Chrysoloras 2006; Tomšič 2019). Analyzing nationalism as "a privileged domain of the eruption of enjoyment into the social field," Žižek contends that "we always impute to the 'other' an excessive enjoyment: he [sic] wants to steal our enjoyment (by ruining our way of life) and/or he has access to some secret, perverse enjoyment. In short, what really bothers us about the other' is the peculiar way he organizes his enjoyment, precisely the surplus, the 'excess' that pertains to this way: the smell of 'their' food, 'their' noisy songs and dances, 'their' strange manners, 'their' attitude toward work" (Žižek 1993, 203).

9. Also see Haley 2016 on the carceral constructions of Black female deviance.

10. Also consider emergent anti-capitalist and anti-colonialist movements for radical are. See, for instance Hobart and Kneese 2020 and Kandaswamy 2018.

References

Abramovitz, Mimi. 2017. *Regulating the Lives of Women: Social Welfare Policy from Colonial Times to the Present.* 3rd ed. New York: Routledge.

AEI/Brookings Working Group on Poverty and Opportunity. 2015. *Opportunity, Responsibility, and Security: A Consensus Plan for Reducing Poverty and Restoring the American Dream.* Washington, DC: American Enterprise Institute for Public Policy Research and the Brookings Institution. https://www.brookings.edu/wp-content/uploads/2016/07/full-report.pdf.

Agorist, Matt. 2015. "It's Official: Drug Testing Welfare Applicants FAILS by Costing More Than Twice What It Saves." *Alternet.* October 8, 2015. https://www.alternet.org/2015/10/its-official-drug-testing-welfare-applicants-fails-costing-more-twice-what-it.

Alston, Philip. 2017. "Statement on Visit to the USA, by Professor Philip Alston, United Nations Special Rapporteur on Extreme Poverty and Human Rights." *Office of the High Commissioner for Human Rights, United Nations.* December 15, 2017. http://www.ohchr.org/EN/NewsEvents/Pages/DisplayNews.aspx?NewsID=22533&LangID=E.

Baker, Carrie, and Nan Stein. 2016. "Obscuring Gender-Based Violence: Marriage Promotion and Teen Dating Violence Research." *Journal of Women, Politics and Society* 37, no. 1: 87–109.

Bentele, Keith Gunnar, and Lisa Thiebaud Nicoli. 2012. "Ending Access as We Know It: State Welfare Benefit Coverage in the TANF Era." *Social Service Review* 86, no. 2 (June): 223–68.

brown, adrienne marie, ed. 2019. *Pleasure Activism: The Politics of Feeling Good.* Chico, CA: AK Press.

Cacho, Lisa Marie. 2012. *Social Death: Racialized Rightlessness and the Criminalization of the Unprotected.* New York: New York University Press.

Center on Budget and Policy Priorities. 2018. "Policy Basics: An Introduction to TANF." Washington, DC. August 15, 2018. http://www.cbpp.org/research/policy-basics-an-introduction-to-tanf.

Cohen, Cathy J. 1997. "Punks, Bulldaggers, and Welfare Queens: The Radical Potential of Queer Politics?" *GLQ: A Journal of Lesbian and Gay Studies* 3, no. 4 (May): 437–65.

Cohen, Patricia. 2010. "'Culture of Poverty' Makes a Comeback." *New York Times*, October 17, 2010.

Cooper, Melinda. 2017. *Family Values: Between Neoliberalism and the New Social Conservatism.* Brooklyn, NY: Zone Books.

Daniel, Clare. 2017. *Mediating Morality: The Politics of Teen Pregnancy in the Post-Welfare Era.* Amherst: University of Massachusetts Press.

DeFilippis, Joseph N., Michael W. Yarbrough, and Angela Jones, eds. 2018. *Queer Activism After Marriage.* New York: Routledge.

Delaney, Arthur. 2017. "Food Stamp 'Work Requirements' Are Kind of a Sham." *Huffington Post*, July 12, 2017. https://www.huffingtonpost.com/entry/work-requirements-food-stamps_us_5966475se4b09b587d641625.

Diamond, Dan. 2018. "Trump Challenges Native Americans' Historical Standing." *Politico*, April 22, 2018. https://www.politico.com/story/2018/04/22/trump-native-americans-historical-standing-492794.

Dickinson, Maggie. 2020. *Feeding the Crisis: Care and Abandonment in America's Food Safety Net*. Berkeley: University of California Press.

Edin, Kathryn J., and H. Luke Shaefer. 2015. *$2.00 a Day: Living on Almost Nothing in America*. Boston: Houghton Mifflin Harcourt.

Eubanks, Virginia. 2018. *Automating Inequality: How High-Tech Tools Profile, Police, and Punish the Poor*. New York: St. Martin's Press.

Falk, Gary. 2020. *The Temporary Assistance for Needy Families (TANF) Block Grant: A Legislative History*. Washington, DC: Congressional Research Service.

Federal Register. 2018. "Reducing Poverty in America by Promoting Opportunity and Economic Mobility." *Executive Order. April* 10, 2018. https://www.federalregister.gov/documents/2018/04/13/2018-07874/reducing-poverty-in-america-by-promoting-opportunity-and-economic-mobility.

Franke, Katherine M. 1999. "Becoming a Citizen: Reconstruction Era Regulation of African American Marriages." *Yale Journal of Law and the Humanities* 11, no. 2: 251–09.

Gilman, Michele Estrin. 2014. "The Return of the Welfare Queen." *Journal of Gender, Social Policy and the Law* 22, no. 2: 247–79.

Goldstein, Alyosha. 2012. *Poverty in Common: The Politics of Community Action During the American Century*. Durham, NC: Duke University Press.

_____. 2015. "The Duration of Inequality: Limits, Liability, and the Historical Specificity of Poverty." In *Territories of Poverty: Rethinking North and South*, edited by Ananya Roy and Emma Shaw Crane, 198–24. Athens: University of Georgia Press.

Grant, Kali et al. 2019. *Unworkable and Unwise: Conditioning Access to Programs That Ensure a Basic Foundation for Families on Work Requirements*. Economic Security and Opportunity Initiative Working Paper. Georgetown University Law Center on Poverty and Inequality, Washington, DC. February 1, 2019. http://www.georgetownpoverty.org/wp-content/uploads/2019/02/Unworkable-Unwise-20190201.pdf.

Gritter, Matthew. 2018. *Undeserving: SNAP Reform and Conceptions of the Deserving Poor*. Lanham, MD: Lexington Books.

Gumbs, Alexis Pauline. 2016. "M/Othering Ourselves: A Black Queer Feminist Genealogy for Radical Mothering." In *Revolutionary Mothering: Love on the Front Lines*, edited by Alexis Pauline Gumbs, China Martens, and Mai'i Williams, 19–31. Oakland, CA: PM Press.

Gustafson, Kaaryn. 2013. "Degradation Ceremonies and the Criminalization of Low- Income Women." *UC Irvine Law Review* 3, no. 2 (May): 297–58.

Haley, Sarah. 2016. *No Mercy Here: Gender, Punishment, and the Making of Jim Crow Modernity*. Chapel Hill: University of North Carolina Press.

Hamilton, Leah. 2020. *Welfare Doesn't Work: The Promise of Basic Income for a Failed American Safety Net*. Cham, Switzerland: Palgrave.

Hancock, Ange-Marie. 2004. *The Politics of Disgust: The Public Identity of the Welfare Queen*. New York: New York University Press.

Hartman, Saidiya V. 1997. *Scenes of Subjection: Terror, Slavery, and Self-Making in Nineteenth-Century America*. New York: Oxford University Press.

Hatton, Erin. 2020. *Coerced: Work Under Threat of Punishment*. Berkeley: University of California Press.

Heath, Melanie. 2012. *One Marriage Under God: The Campaign to Promote Marriage in America*. New York: New York University Press.

_____. 2013. "Sexual Misgivings: Producing Un/Marked Knowledge in Neoliberal Marriage Promotion Policies." *Sociological Quarterly* 54, no. 4 (September): 561–83.

Henricks, Kasey, and Louise Seamster. 2017. "Mechanisms of the Racial Tax State." *Critical Sociology* 43, no. 2 (March): 169–79.

HHS. 2018. "HHS FY2018 Budget in Brief." *US Department of Health and Human Services, Administration for Children and Families*. May 23, 2017. https://www.hhs.gov/about/budget/fy2018/budget-in-brief/index.html.

Hinton, Elizabeth. 2017. *From the War on Poverty to the War on Crime: The Making of Mass Incarceration in America*. Cambridge, MA: Harvard University Press.

Hobart, Hi'ilei Julia Kawehipuaakahaopulani and Tamara Kneese. 2020. "Radical Care: Survival Strategies for Uncertain Times." *Social Text* 142 (March): 1–16.

Holland, Sharon Patricia. 2012. *The Erotic Life of Racism*. Durham, NC: Duke University Press.

Hong, Grace Kyungwon. 2015. *Death Beyond Disavowal: The Impossible Politics of Difference*. Minneapolis: University of Minnesota Press.

House Budget Committee Majority Staff. 2014. The War on Poverty: 50 Years Later—*A House Budget Committee Report*. March 3, 2014. https://republicans-budget.house.gov/uploadedfiles/war_on_poverty.pdf.

Hunter, Tera W. 2017. *Bound in Wedlock: Slave and Free Black Marriage in the Nineteenth Century*. Cambridge, MA: Belknap Press of Harvard University Press.

Jaffe, Sarah. 2018. "How the Media Is Abetting the GOP's War on 'Welfare.'" *New Republic*, January 31, 2018. https://newrepublic.com/article/146859/media-abetting-gops-war-welfare.

Kandaswamy, Priya. 2018. "Reflections on Class: Intersectional, Anticapitalist Pedagogies for Our Times." *Feminist Formations* 30, no. 3 (Winter): 16–24.

Katz, Michael B. 1996. *In the Shadow of the Poorhouse: A Social History of Welfare in America.* 2nd ed. New York: Basic Books.

_____. 2013. *The Undeserving Poor: America's Enduring Confrontation with Poverty.* 2nd ed. New York: Oxford University Press.

Katzenstein, Mary Fainsod, and Maureen R. Waller. 2015. "Taxing the Poor: Incarceration, Poverty Governance, and the Seizure of Family Resources." *Perspectives on Politics* 13, no. 3 (September): 638–56.

King, Tiffany Lethabo. 2018. "Black 'Feminisms' and Pessimism: Abolishing Moynihan's Negro Family." *Theory and Event* 21, no. 1 (January): 68–87.

Kohler-Hausmann, Julilly. 2017. *Getting Tough: Welfare and Imprisonment in 1970s America.* Princeton, NJ: Princeton University Press.

Kornbluh, Felicia. 2007. *The Battle for Welfare Rights: Politics and Poverty in Modern America.* Philadelphia: University of Pennsylvania Press.

Lindhorst, Taryn, and Ronald J. Mancoske. 2006. "The Social and Economic Impact of Sanctions and Time Limits on Recipients of Temporary Assistance to Needy Families." *Journal of Sociology and Social Welfare* 33, no. 1 (March): 93–114.

Lorde, Audre. 1984. "The Uses of the Erotic: The Erotic as Power." In *Sister Outsider*, 53–59. Berkeley, CA: Crossing Press.

Lowery, Wesley. 2014. "Paul Ryan, Poverty, Dog Whistles, and Electoral Politics." *Washington Post, March* 18, 2014.

Lowrey, Annie. 2014. "50 Years Later, War on Poverty Is a Mixed Bag." *New York Times, January* 5, 2014.

Mannix, Mary R., and Henry A. Freedman. 2013. "TANF and Racial Justice." *Journal of Poverty Law and Policy* 47, no. 5–6 (September–October): 221–28.

Martin, Isaac William. 2008. *The Permanent Tax Revolt: How the Property Tax Transformed American Politics.* Stanford, CA: Stanford University Press.

Matsumura, Kaiponanea T. 2016. "A Right Not to Marry." *Fordham Law Review* 84, no. 4 (March): 1509–58.

Mayeri, Serena. 2013. "Historicizing the 'End of Men': The Politics of Reaction(s)." *Boston University Law Review* 93, no. 3 (May): 729–44.

Mead, Lawrence M. 2020. "Poverty and Culture." *Society* (July) [retracted].

Meyer, Laura, and Ife Floyd. 2020. *"Cash Assistance Should Reach Millions More Families to Lessen Hardship: Families' Access Limited by Policies Rooted in Racism."* Center on Budget and Policy Priorities, Washington, DC. November 20, 2020. https://www.cbpp.org/research/family-income-support/cash-assistance-should-reach-millions-more-families-to-lessen.

Michener, Jamila D. 2018. *Fragmented Democracy: Medicaid, Federalism, and Unequal Politics.* Cambridge, MA: Cambridge University Press.

Miller-Young, Mireille. 2014. *A Taste for Brown Sugar: Black Women in Pornography.* Durham, NC: Duke University Press.

Monnat, Shannon M. 2010. "The Color of Welfare Sanctioning: Exploring the Individual and Contextual Roles of Race on TANF Case Closures and Benefit Reductions." *Sociological Quarterly* 51, no. 4 (Fall): 678–07.

Murray, Melissa. 2012. "Marriage as Punishment." *Columbia Law Review* 112, no. 1 (January): 101–68.

_____. 2016. "Rights and Regulation: The Evolution of Sexual Regulation." *Columbia Law Review* 116, no. 2 (March): 573–23.

Musser, Amber Jamilla. 2018. *Sensual Excess: Queer Femininity and Brown Jouissance.* New York: New York University Press.

Nadasen, Premilla. 2005. *Welfare Warriors: The Welfare Rights Movement in the United States.* New York: Routledge.

_____. 2017. "Extreme Poverty Returns to America." *Washington Post, December* 21, 2017.

Nash, Jennifer C. 2014. *The Black Body in Ecstasy: Reading Race, Reading Pornography.* Durham, NC: Duke University Press.

_____. 2017. "Pleasurable Blackness." In *The Palgrave Handbook of Sexuality Education*, edited by Louisa Allen and Mary Lou Rasmussen, 261–78. London: Palgrave Macmillan.

Newman, Katherine S., and Rourke O'Brien. 2011. *Taxing the Poor: Doing Damage to the Truly Disadvantaged.* Berkeley: University of California Press.

Nopper, Tamara K. 2019. "Digital Character in the 'The Scored Society': FICO, Social Networks, and Competing Measurements of Creditworthiness." In *Captivating Technology: Race, Carceral Technoscience, and Liberatory Imagination in Everyday Life*, edited by Ruha Benjamin, 170–87. Durham, NC: Duke University Press.

O'Connor, Alice. 2001. *Poverty Knowledge: Social Science, Social Policy, and the Poor in Twentieth-Century U.S. History.* Princeton, NJ: Princeton University Press.

Office of Family Assistance. 2017. "TANF-ACF-IM-2017-01 (Rescinding guidance concerning waiver and expenditure authority under section 1115 of the

Social Security Act).” *Office of Administration for Children and Families, US Department of Health and Human Services*. August 30, 2017. https://www.acf.hhs.gov/ofa/resource/tanf-acf-im-2017-01.

—————. 2019. TANF Caseload Data 2018. *Office of Administration for Children and Families, US Department of Health and Human Services*. April 23, 2019. https://www.acf.hhs.gov/ofa/resource/tanf-caseload-data-2018.

Page, Joshua, and Joe Soss. 2017. “Criminal Justice Predation and Neoliberal Governance.” In *Rethinking Neoliberalism: Resisting the Disciplinary Regime*, edited by Sanford F. Schram and Marianna Pavlovskaya, 141–61. New York: Routledge.

Page, Joshua, Victoria Piehowski, and Joe Soss. 2019. “A Debt of Care: Commercial Bail and the Gendered Logic of Criminal Justice Predation.” *RFS: The Russell Sage Foundation Journal of the Social Sciences* 5, no. 1: 150–72.

Paik, A. Naomi. 2016. *Rightlessness: Testimony and Redress in U.S. Prison Camps Since World War II*. Chapel Hill: University of North Carolina Press.

Pavetti, LaDonna. 2017. “Doubling of Extreme Poverty Belies Welfare Reform Success Claims.” *Huffington Post, December* 6, 2017. https://www.huffingtonpost.com/entry/doubling-of-extreme-pover_b_8177680.html.

—————. 2018. “Work Requirements Don’t Work.” *Center on Budget and Policy Priorities, Washington, DC*. January 10, 2017. https://www.cbpp.org/blog/work-requirements-dont-work.

Piven, Frances Fox, and Richard Cloward. 1993. *Regulating the Poor: The Functions of Public Welfare*. New York: Vintage.

Randles, Jennifer M. 2017. *Proposing Prosperity? Marriage Education Policy and Inequality in America*. New York: Columbia University Press.

Reagan, Ronald. 1986. “Radio Address to the Nation on Welfare Reform.” *February* 15, 1986. https://www.reaganlibrary.gov/archives/speech/radio-address-nation-welfare-reform.

Reddy, Chandan. 2011. *Freedom with Violence: Race, Sexuality, and the US State*. Durham, NC: Duke University Press.

Restuccia, Andrew et al. 2017. “Behind Trump’s Plan to Target the Federal Safety Net.” *Politico, December* 11, 2017. https://www.politico.com/story/2017/12/11/trump-welfare-reform-safety-net-288623.

Roy, Ananya, Terra Graziani, and Pamela Stephens. 2020. *“Unhousing the Poor: Inter- locking Regimes of Racialized Policing.”* Roundtable on the Future of Justice Policy, Square One Project, New York, NY. August 25, 2020.

https://challengeinequality.luskin.ucla.edu/2020/08/25/unhousing-the-poor.

Saenz, Matt, and Arloc Sherman. 2020. *“Number of People in Families with Below-Poverty Earnings Has Soared, Especially Among Black and Latino Individuals.”* Center on Budget and Policy Priorities, Washington, DC. July 15, 2020. https://www.cbpp.org/research/poverty-and-inequality/research-note-number-of-people-in-families-with-below-poverty.

Safawi, Ali, and Liz Schott. 2021. *“To Lessen Hardship, States Should Invest More TANF Dollars in Basic Assistance for Families.”* Center on Budget and Policy Priorities, Washington, DC. January 12, 2021. https://www.cbpp.org/research/family-income-support/to-lessen-hardship-states-should-invest-more-tanf-dollars-in-basic-0.

Simpson, Audra. 2016. “The State Is a Man: Theresa Spence, Loretta Saunders and the Gender of Settler Sovereignty.” *Theory and Event* 19, no. 4.

Smith, Anna Marie. 2007. *Welfare Reform and Sexual Regulation*. Cambridge, MA: Cambridge University Press.

Spade, Dean. 2013. “Under the Cover of Gay Rights.” *NYU Review of Law and Social Change* 37: 79–100.

Spillers, Hortense. 1987. “Mama’s Baby, Papa’s Maybe: An American Grammar Book.” *Diacritics* 17, no. 2 (Summer): 64–81.

Stallings, L. H. 2015. *Funk the Erotic: Transaesthetics and Black Sexual Cultures*. Urbana: University of Illinois Press.

Stavrakakis, Yannis, and Nikos Chrysoloras. 2006. “(I Can’t Get No) Enjoyment: Lacanian Theory and the Analysis of Nationalism.” *Psychoanalysis, Culture and Society* 11, no. 2 (August): 144–63.

Stevens, Jacqueline. 1999. *Reproducing the State*. Princeton, NJ: Princeton University Press.

Stremlau, Rose. 2005. “‘To Domesticate and Civilize Wild Indians’: Allotment and the Campaign to Reform Indian Families, 1875–1887.” *Journal of Family History* 30, no. 3 (July): 265–86.

Tach, Laura, and Kathryn Edin. 2017. “The Social Safety Net After Welfare Reform: Recent Developments and Consequences for Household Dynamics.” *Annual Review of Sociology* 43: 541–61.

Task Force on Poverty, Opportunity, and Upward Mobility. 2016. “A Better Way: Our Vision for a Confident America: Poverty, Opportunity, and Upward Mobility.” *US House of Representatives Republican Conference Task Force on Poverty, Opportunity, and Upward Mobility*. June 7, 2016. https://www.heartland.org/_template-assets/documents/publications/abetterway-poverty-policypaper.pdf.

Thrush, Glenn. 2018. "Trump's Vow on Welfare Faces an Uncertain Future." *New York Times*, March 15, 2018.

Tomšič, Samo. 2019. *The Labour of Enjoyment: Towards a Critique of Libidinal Economy.* Berlin: August Verlag.

Tough, Paul. 2012. "Obama vs. Poverty." *New York Times Magazine*, August 19, 2012.

Tourmaline. 2020. "Filmmaker and Activist Tourmaline on How to Freedom Dream." *Vogue*, July 2, 2020. https://www.vogue.com/article/filmmaker-and-activist-tourmaline-on-how-to-freedom-dream. "Twenty Years of Punks." 2019. *GLQ: A Journal of Lesbian and Gay Studies* 25, no.1 (January): 137–93.

USDA. 2019. "Facts About SNAP." *Supplemental Nutrition Assistance Program (SNAP), US Department of Agriculture.* August 14, 2019. https://www.fns.usda.gov/snap/facts.

US Department of Labor. Office of Policy and Planning Research. 1965. *The Negro Family: The Case for National Action.* Washington, DC: Government Printing Office.

US House of Representatives. 2011. *Improving Work and Other Welfare Goals: Hearing Before the Subcommittee on Human Welfare of the Committee on Ways and Means.* 112th Cong., 1st Sess., September 8, 2011. Washington, DC: Government Printing Office.

US House of Representatives. 2013. *The War on Poverty: A Progress Report—Hearing Before the Committee on the Budget, House of Representatives.* 113th Cong., 1st sess., July 31, 2013. Washington, DC: Government Printing Office.

Valentine, Charles A. 1968. *Culture and Poverty: Critique and Counter-Proposals.* Chicago: University of Chicago Press.

Weaver, R. Kent. 2014. "Compliance Regimes and Barriers to Behavioral Change." *Governance* 27, no. 2 (April): 243–65.

Welfare Warriors Research Collaborative. 2010. *A Fabulous Attitude: Low-Income LGBTGNC People Surviving on Love, Shelter and Knowledge.* New York: Queers for Economic Justice.

Whitehead, Barbara Dafoe. 1993. *"Dan Quayle Was Right."* Atlantic Monthly, April 1993. http://www.theatlantic.com/magazine/archive/1993/04/dan-quayle-was-right/307015.

Yamin, Priscilla. 2012. *American Marriage: A Political Institution.* Philadelphia: University of Pennsylvania Press.

Žižek, Slavoj. 1993. *Tarrying with the Negative: Kant, Hegel, and the Critique of Ideology.* Durham, NC: Duke University Press.

Questions for Critical Thinking

1. How does the authors' discussion impact your understanding of the ways in which the welfare system in the United States perpetuates conditions of poverty for the poor?

2. How does this article broaden your understanding of the ways in which social structures, rather than personal responsibility, perpetuate rather than alleviate poverty?

3. Some argue that we need to grant more assistance to the poor rather than less. What solutions would you offer?

Social Institutions: The State and Public Policy

JEZEBEL AT THE WELFARE OFFICE

How Racialized Stereotypes of Poor Women's Reproductive Decisions and Relationships Shape Policy Implementation

* *N. Tatiana Masters, Taryn P. Lindhorst, and Marcia K. Meyers*

This next essay, by social workers N. Tatiana Masters, Taryn P. Lindhorst, and Marcia K. Meyers, discusses how caseworkers perpetuate negative myths regarding African American women's sexuality and motherhood. Drawing on data from interview transcripts, the authors demonstrate that, regardless of the recipient's individual race, clients were placed into racialized myths through the caseworkers' talk. Their analysis shows that negative ideas about poor women's sexuality persist in welfare policy and are built into its day-to-day implementation.

Welfare workers' conversations with clients about fertility and family formation have the potential to illuminate the discourses on poor women's sexual behavior that are embedded in present-day welfare policy. To understand how poor women's sexuality and fertility are framed during welfare office interviews, this study examined interactions about reproductive decisions and relationships between caseworkers and clients, using transcripts from a multisite study and focusing on caseworkers' language.

A substantial amount of scholarship has grappled with Temporary Assistance to Needy Families (TANF), the program resulting from 1996's welfare reform. Much of this work critically analyzes the policy itself (e.g., A. M. Smith, 2001; Soss & Schram, 2007), assesses the policy's effects (e.g., Burger, 2004;

Corcoran, Danziger, Kalil, & Seefeldt, 2000; De Jong, Graefe, & St. Pierre, 2005; Loeb, Fuller, Kagan, & Carrol, 2003), or examines aspects of the policy's implementation (e.g., Hays, 2003; Meyers, 1998; Meyers & Lurie, 2005). Implementation research like ours focuses on interactions between clients and caseworkers to understand how policy mandates are translated within social welfare systems. Research on policy implementation has shown that street-level workers exercise great discretion in their application of formal policy mandates (Lipsky, 1980; Maynard-Moody, Musheno, & Palumbo, 1990; Watkins-Hayes, 2009). Frontline workers are constrained by policy requirements and able to interpret them in such a way as to facilitate or hinder client access to services (Meyers, 1998; Meyers & Lurie, 2005).

An important element of current scholarship on welfare reform implementation studies these efforts at the ground level, using data from interviews or observation and recording in welfare offices. Hays' 2003 book, *Flat Broke with Children*, uses such data to examine the cultural norms, beliefs, and values embedded in welfare reform. She points out that TANF, as written and as implemented, enforces "family values" by discouraging women from raising children alone. Watkins-Hayes' (2009) work focuses on how welfare workers' professional identities and their race and gender locations interact to influence their implementation of policy as they work with clients. Both of these works use day-today talk in welfare offices to study implementation, but neither focuses on how workers and clients discuss issues of sexuality and reproduction in the context of the welfare interview.

Welfare office talk matters as a measure of policy implementation and as the kind of language in action that can contribute to perpetuating stigmatizing discourses of poor women's sexuality. Reich's study (2005) of clients' interactions with child protective services sheds light on how everyday practices in government offices draw upon and contribute to racialized and gendered stereotypes of bad parenting; no equivalent work has been done using data from welfare offices. Women on welfare have long been the subjects of derogatory stereotypes, and their sexual behavior and reproductive decisions have been a major element of these negative portrayals (Cassiman, 2006; Collins, 1990, 2004; Lens, 2002; Roberts, 1997, 2002). Such myths, as Dorothy Roberts (1997) puts it, are "more than made-up stories" (p. 8). Myths about people (e.g., poor women, welfare mothers, Black women) affect not only the treatment of specific individuals—unjust in and of itself—but also the treatment of everyone in those people's groups: all women, all mothers, all African Americans. As such, these demeaning myths are of concern in the realms of scholarship and citizenship (Harris-Perry, 2011).

Gilens (1999), in his study of national polling data about welfare policies, found that White Americans responded to racially encoded language: they disapproved of "welfare" (something received, as they saw it, by African Americans), but approved of "assistance for the poor." Likewise, Hancock's (2004) study of references to welfare recipients in newspaper reports and the *Congressional Record* showed how the public identity of welfare recipients was cast as sexually permissive African American women, and Cassiman (2006) delineated the social construction of the "welfare queen" as "the embodiment of the deviant ... black, poor, and dependent upon an unearned income" (p. 57). Empirical falsification of such negative myths is often insufficient to diminish their power. For example, the U.S. General Accounting Office (2001) reviewed research on the effect of TANF policies on out-of-wedlock births and concluded that there was no evidence that these policies affected the childbearing choices of women on welfare. In spite of this authoritative statement, the dehumanizing myth of the welfare client having another baby to increase her check persists. Critical analytic descriptions of such myths in action, such as those produced by this study, can potentially contribute to lessening their influence among those who make or implement welfare policy, or who shape it with their public statements or their votes.

The sexual behavior of women and the structure of their families have long been a concern of social policy. The federal Aid to Dependent Children (ADC) program was established in 1935. As the Social Security system was modified in subsequent years, more widowed White women were transferred from ADC to Social Security benefits, and unmarried mothers, particularly African American mothers who were excluded by design from other social assistance programs (Jones, 1995), constituted an increasing percentage of ADC caseloads. ADC became a lightning rod for criticism as this transition occurred, particularly among conservative leaders who believed that providing cash assistance to mother-only families enabled women to avoid the traditional bonds of marriage (Gordon, 1994; Murray, 1984). Poor women were stigmatized by their use of welfare; this stigma was particularly harsh for women of color, as racist attitudes linked the African American women heading these families with irresponsible sexual behavior (Berkowitz, 1991; Collins, 1990; Jones, 1985; Roberts, 1997).

As discriminatory state welfare practices were struck down by the Supreme Court, women previously denied benefits began to receive cash assistance for the care of their children, and welfare rolls grew dramatically (Quadagno, 1994). Cyclically, whenever a system of overtly biased practices was legally overturned, another set of welfare implementation practices seemed to emerge to exclude Black women. Thus as welfare officially became more accessible, state policies also increased scrutiny of poor women's sexual behavior. For example, in 1960, Louisiana discontinued benefits to 95% of its African American clients on the basis of a "suitable home" provision that prohibited welfare benefits for families in which any child had been born out of wedlock (Lindhorst & Leighninger, 2003). Welfare case-workers were also required to conduct raids to find men who were not married to the welfare recipient but were living in the home (Abramovitz, 1996), until legal and administrative challenges by the National Welfare Rights Organization and other groups ended these practices (Neubeck & Cazenave, 2001).

Explanations for welfare use focused increasingly on a "culture of poverty" argument. The culture of poverty thesis, resurrected by Charles Murray (1984), suggests that poverty is caused by the "deviant" values of poor people, particularly poor Black people. One relevant example is his conclusion that poor women, especially African American women, have babies in an entrepreneurial fashion to increase their welfare checks rather than engaging in paid work. Instead of an overtly racist focus on the creation of laws that limit African American women's access to financial assistance, culture of poverty arguments focus on women's transgressive moral and sexual behavior and advocate for conventional gender structures, themes that persist into the current round of welfare reform. Although important refutations of the culture of poverty argument exist (e.g., Katz, 1989; Piven & Cloward, 1971; Quadagno, 1994), it nonetheless continues to exert a powerful influence over U.S. welfare policy.

With welfare reform under the Personal Responsibility and Work Opportunity Reconciliation Act (PRWORA) in 1996, the federal government once again asserted its right to set normative standards for women's sexual behavior, including the prevention of out-of-wedlock pregnancies and the encouragement of marriage. This assertion reinforced welfare's historical devaluing of poor women and women of color as mothers (McCormack, 2005; Roberts 1997, 2002). One example of PRWO-RAs regulation of reproduction is "family cap" policies that allow states to prohibit increasing a family's financial assistance if the mother has another child while receiving welfare. Twenty-two states have currently implemented family cap provisions (R. J. Smith, 2006). This policy and others sought to eliminate any perceived financial incentive for women receiving welfare to have more children, but empirical evidence of their effectiveness has been mixed (Horvath-Rose, Peters, & Sabia, 2008; Jagannathan & Camasso, 2003).

Welfare rolls dropped dramatically after the passage of PRWORA. Debate continues as to whether these declines were due to discontinuation of recipients who would have been eligible under previous welfare rules, improvements in national economic conditions immediately after PRWORA passed, or increases in the stigma associated with welfare receipt (Danziger, 1999). Under the Bush administration, further efforts were made to encourage marriage through the reallocation of TANF monies to marriage and fatherhood promotion efforts that focused on patriarchal, heterosexual marriage as the primary solution to poverty among women and children (Edin & Kefalas, 2005; Hays, 2003; Weigt, 2010).

The Current Study

Based upon this historical context, we would certainly expect the regulation of women's reproductive decisions and relationships to be a substantial element of frontline workers' implementation of TANF. Our objective with this study was to explore the relationship between welfare workers' conversations with clients and dominant discourses regarding sexual behavior and family structures that are embedded in welfare policy, while also attending to the ways in which gendered and racialized assumptions intertwine in workers' implementation of these policies. Our focus was not on connections between worker rhetoric and welfare case outcomes (e.g., whether a client was granted benefits), but on caseworker language itself. We addressed our research questions by examining conversations related to fertility and family formation in worker-client interactions in welfare offices, using transcripts of these conversations from a multisite study. To date, scholarship on welfare reform has not focused directly on interactions between welfare workers and clients in relation to issues of sexuality and fertility.

Method

Data for this study consisted of transcribed interviews between welfare caseworkers and clients applying for TANF benefits at public welfare agencies in three states. Data were originally collected as part of the Frontline Management and Practice Study conducted by the Rockefeller Institute of Government for the U.S. Department of Health and Human Services (see Lindhorst, Meyers, & Casey, 2008; Meyers, Riccucci, & Lurie, 2001, for further description of the study). The goal of the parent study was to investigate the implementation of welfare reform policies in states with diverse administrative and political structures. This research is a qualitative analysis of a subset of data from this larger study.

The research design for the parent study maximized organizational variation by drawing samples in three stages. The first stage used purposive sampling to select states, based on variation in location, political culture, and TANF agency structures. The states chosen were Georgia, Michigan, and Texas. The second stage used purposive sampling to select nine sites (two to three per state) that represented urban and either rural or suburban locations. Each of these states was below the national median in child well-being indicators (Annie E. Casey Foundation, 2003). The lower child well-being ranking of these states indicates that while they differed from one another somewhat in terms of policy and organizational structures, they were similar in terms of their levels of poverty and of underlying need for TANF assistance.

Data Collection

Data collection took place in 1999 to 2000. Front-line welfare workers' encounters with clients were captured either through tape recording and transcription

or through the taking of detailed notes by a trained observer. Informed consent for observation and recording was obtained from the worker in advance and from the client at the start of the encounter. Research assistants tape recorded and transcribed data in Texas and Michigan. In Georgia, we were unable to obtain permission to tape-record encounters, so research assistants were instructed to record verbatim conversation on 25 topics and activities that were of particular interest, including discussions of reproductive decisions and relationships. Comparison of the Georgia transcripts to the recordings in Texas and Michigan showed no meaningful differences in the length of transcripts or the topics discussed.

Sample

Our aim was to characterize the discourses of fertility and family formation reflected in the routine social and linguistic practices of the welfare encounter. Thus, we focused our preliminary analyses on interviews in which these topics were likely to be discussed. In most welfare systems, clients must participate in an "application interview" that determines their eligibility for benefits; after this, they usually have minimal follow-up contacts with caseworkers. It is during these initial applications (or reapplication interviews for clients renewing their benefits) that conversations about sexuality, fertility and family formation are most likely to occur.

This study's sample has limitations. Data were collected over a decade ago and thus may not reflect current welfare office operations, which may be different in ways to which this study cannot speak. Because locations for data collection were purposefully selected in the context of the parent study (Meyers, 1998), they may not be representative of all U.S. welfare offices. Because we worked with written text, nonverbal worker-client communication that may have provided further insight into these transactions was lost, and the presence of research assistants in offices during welfare interviews may have altered worker behavior in unknowable ways. The data from Georgia may differ from the recordings obtained in Texas and Michigan, potentially affecting its trustworthiness. In spite of these limitations, the available transcripts represent a unique opportunity to examine the spoken discourses with which the welfare system contributes to the construction of poor women's gendered positions through talk about reproductive decisions and relationships.

Our initial data set contained 232 observations of TANF interviews between welfare workers and female clients. The sample of interviews involved 60% female workers and 17% male workers; the remaining workers' genders were not recorded. Forty-four percent of workers were African American, 25% White, 4% Latino/a, 1% Asian American, and 25% of unknown race-ethnicity (percentages do not sum to 100 due to rounding). Seventy-eight percent of clients were African American, 21% White, and 1% Latina; all were women.

To select a subset of interviews and data for in-depth analysis, the first author read and reread all 232 interview transcripts and coded conversations on topics of pregnancy, birth control, family planning, conjugal relationships, and sexual behavior. This topic coding resulted in a subset of 72 interviews that included talk of reproductive decisions and relationships. The second author independently coded a subset of transcripts to validate the topic coding; convergence was excellent overall, and disagreements about topic coding were resolved through discussion. The inclusion criterion for child support conversations deserves special mention. Child support enforcement generally involves workers gathering information about the father's description, location, or social security number for use in finding him and compelling him to pay for the care of his child(ren), and these topics were a part of nearly every welfare interview. We differentiated these routine child support conversations from those that included a pronounced focus on the sexual aspects of the relationship, for example, establishment of children's paternity through questions about the client's sexual relationship with the father. We included child support conversations in the in-depth analysis subset of data only when they had this sexual content in addition to routine, nonsexual discussion of enforcement issues.

Analytical Approach

We drew on a discourse analysis framework to investigate how workers' talk with welfare office clients perpetuated or resisted the negative stereotypes of poor women's reproductive decisions and relationships embedded in welfare policy. Discourse analysis operates from a theoretical perspective that treats social realities such as gender and sexuality as being socially constructed through language and social practices (Cameron & Kulick, 2003). It focuses on what people do with their talk: they "produce versions of events, objects, and people" (Horton-Salway, 2001, p. 153). Focusing on the 72 interviews in which workers discussed reproductive decisions and relationships with clients, we conducted across-case analyses and used techniques of data summarization and display (Miles & Huberman, 1994), categorization (Saldana, 2009), and comparative analysis (Strauss & Corbin, 1998). We characterized coded statements with brief descriptive labels and grouped related statements together into categories. We refined, split, or merged categories when associations, divisions, or overlap appeared in the data (Hall & Stevens, 1991). The first two authors worked together iteratively to produce the findings and verify their trustworthiness.

Findings

Only about one third of the 232 interviews between caseworkers and clients included conversations that were directly related to clients' sexual behavior. We identified 72 interviews (31%) in which reproductive decisions and relationships were discussed; these conversations are characterized below. The remaining 160 interviews (69%) involved discussion of other welfare issues such as Food Stamp eligibility, access to child care, work requirement fulfillment, and routine child support enforcement with no discussion of sex or the conjugal relationship. We began these analyses with a focus on how race and gender intertwined in welfare office talk about sex, childbearing, and family organization. Through close reading of the interviews, we identified moments of informal, discretionary talk that focused on moralizing about client behaviors. The more predominant form of talk, however, was a highly bureaucratized exchange of questions and answers. We start with findings related to issues of race and racialized talk within these exchanges, followed by a description of the moralizing and bureaucratic styles of talk.

Race or Racialized Talk?

In the first phase of analysis, we looked at whether race/gender concordance between welfare workers and clients was associated with moralizing or bureaucratic styles of talk. All of the clients and more than one half of the caseworkers in our sample were women. The majority of the clients were African American, as were nearly one half of the caseworkers. The distribution of each of these groups in our sample, as well as our sample size, may have obscured patterns of interaction specific to particular pairings, for example, between a White worker and a Black client, or between two African American women. We did not identify distinct discourses on reproductive decisions and relationships associated with workers' race or gender, clients' race, or the racial or gender makeup of worker-client dyads. Workers were no more likely, for example, to moralize with an African American client, or with a client of a different race or gender than their own. However, the discourse of poor women's reproductive decisions and relationships that emerged from these data on welfare workers' everyday talk with clients was overwhelmingly disrespectful. Regardless of their individual races, clients were subject to the negative myths that arose out of gendered racism against African American women so powerfully characterized by Roberts (1997) and Collins (1990, 2004).

Although we observed an occasional exception—discussed below—in general, workers' language functioned to create negative subject positions for clients. These positions were remarkably congruent with the stereotypes of African American women's sexuality and reproduction discussed in Collins (1990) and further elaborated by Roberts (1997). Some welfare clients were positioned as the immoral "Jezebel," focused on sexual fulfillment without responsibility; others as the devious "welfare queen" who tricked the state into supporting her and her children; some as "matriarchs" who abandoned marriage in favor of asserting dominance within the family; others as "Mammies" who bore children only to neglect them. In the next section, we present examples of exchanges between workers and clients, highlighting moments when these racialized myths are present in the underlying assumptions expressed in the interview. In quotations from transcripts, we have replaced names with initials, and specific dates with spaces, to protect study participants' confidentiality.

When portions of the transcript not relevant to the analysis have been left out, we use this symbol: [...].

Styles of Talk

Our analyses identified two overlapping rhetorical styles that supported the stigmatized positioning of welfare clients, with the occasional exception. We labeled the first of these patterns "discretionary moralizing." This style extended the moralistic "suitable home" talk documented among welfare caseworkers of the 1960s (Lindhorst & Leighninger, 2003) into the present. It comprised workers' personal and optional talk regarding the social riskiness of having babies as a poor woman, and the moral deficiencies they ascribed to women who had children and sought state assistance for their support. Discretionary moralizing was layered over the second style, bureaucratic talk, in roughly one third of the interviews analyzed. The bureaucratic style involved statements through which sex-related policy decisions such as the family cap were implemented in the worker–client transaction, reducing reproductive decision making to issues of verification and rule imposition. Unsurprisingly, given that they were official transactions in government offices, all of the 72 welfare interviews involving fertility and family formation included this type of bureaucratic talk.

The bureaucratic examples we discuss below may seem to make less of a contribution to the perpetuation of negative myths regarding welfare clients' sexual and relational behavior than do the examples involving discretionary moralizing. The distinction between these two styles is important to note, however, so that the more subtle action of the bureaucratic imperative is not overlooked. Both strategies—old-fashioned moralizing and neutral-appearing bureaucracy—functioned toward the same end. Through them, welfare clients were positioned as sexually irresponsible supplicants for aid whose fertility and family structures were in need of governmental regulation, rather than as citizens for whom assistance was a right and whose reproductive decisions and relationships were their own.

Discretionary Moralizing

In these cases, in addition to the policy-mandated bureaucratic language present in all the interviews we studied, workers did what we have called "discretionary moralizing"; they spoke in ways that reflected a personal sense of entitlement to judge and regulate clients' reproductive decisions and relationships. These discussions included talk of clients as negligent of their maternal responsibilities, critiques regarding children's paternity and clients' conjugal choices, and talk in which workers took clients to task for their sexual behavior. The moralistic strategy overtly draws on the dominant discourse of irresponsible reproduction and inappropriate family structure in which PRWORA is embedded.

A prominent feature of workers' moralistic talk is statements that position clients as negligent "Mammies" (Collins, 1990; Roberts, 1997), as in this example from Georgia.

> WORKER: How many children are in the home?
> CLIENT: Five and one on the way.
> WORKER: Why would you go ahead and do that? we can talk to y'all until we're blue in the face. You know you won't get any extra money.

Here we see discretionary moralizing layered on top of the bureaucratic imperative as the worker conveys the substance of the family cap regulation in less neutral, more personally judgmental language.

Another instance of morality talk appears in discussions about the fathers of clients' children during workers' attempts to get information for use in child support enforcement. These examples demonstrate workers' personal normative judgments of clients' reproductive relationships.

> WORKER: Do you have your current ID? Are you getting child support?
> CLIENT: Um, well right now, he's just helping me pay the mortgage so, I guess, yeah.
> WORKER: Is he the father of all your children?
> CLIENT: The other three, no, he's in prison, the father of the other three.
> WORKER: You don't pick them good.

Here the client is talked about as to blame for her own difficulties due to her deficiencies at partner selection and placed in the "Jezebel" role for having children by two different men. The Michigan worker conveys her verdict on the client's partner with the statement, "You don't pick them good." The client is asked to justify the fact that she is not married to the man who

fathered her new baby: PRWORA aims to encourage marriage as part of its perspective on appropriate types of family structure, but the worker's discretionary moralizing takes this conversation to a more personally intrusive level.

Discretionary moralizing can also have a sarcastic quality, as when a worker in Georgia said, "You don't have ANY information on their father?" When the client stated that she and her children's father, "didn't talk," the worker responded "You had to talk sometime, you had three babies" Another worker in Texas expressed disbelief regarding the client's knowledge of her former partner:

> WORKER: What's the father's name?
> CLIENT: I can only think of his first name, that's_____.
> WORKER: How long did you go out with him?
> CLIENT: A while. But he's in denial. Only thing I can think of is his first name.
> WORKER: If you went out with him a while you should know his last name. […] Oh, I'm getting a message [from the computer]. I never got that before. […] I guess the system couldn't believe someone would only know the first name.

In both examples, the workers take a tone of disbelief that the clients would not have certain information about their children's fathers. This language contributes to the workers' positioning of the clients as "Jezebels" who have sex (and children) with men they do not know.

The moralistic rhetorical strategy also occurs in a way that exhorts the client to do better with the kind of tough talk that a coach or parent might use. In Georgia, after discussing tubal ligation with a pregnant client, a worker pointed out that the client's mother worked, saying, "That's probably why she can take care of her children. Like you need to" This quote from a Michigan worker is another minor exception to the overall negativity of caseworkers' positioning of welfare recipients with their moralizing language.

> WORKER: You're going to go on and get your GED [Graduate Equivalency Diploma]?
> CLIENT: Yes.
> WORKER: Because you need that. And you don't need any more children to hinder you. […] You could

go to a trade school and learn how to be a nurse. Don't say "don't know"—you just need to do it. And stop having babies. You're too young.

In both of these examples, the worker exhorts the client to pull herself up by her bootstraps. This coaching language is somewhat supportive of the client, positioning her as a potentially strong person who can succeed at school or a career and take care of herself and her children without assistance. It shows some worker resistance to the overwhelmingly negative perspective on poor women's fertility demonstrated in most other examples, and is also congruent with caretaking aspects of TANF policy. However, this paternalistic tone displays no less of an entitlement by the worker to decide what is best for the client regarding reproduction; it simply combines this entitlement with a more parental interpersonal style.

The Bureaucratic Imperative

The dominant discourse of poor women as sexually irresponsible affected talk in the welfare interview through workers' personal and optional talk, but it did so more frequently through its influence on the policy and regulations workers were mandated to implement. The bureaucratic strategy did not involve overtly judgmental language regarding clients' sexual behavior, merely a rote statement of the rules or a seemingly neutral inquiry for information. Much of the content of welfare office encounters was driven by the worker's task of gathering information to complete welfare forms or cover policy-mandated material. Topics of reproductive decisions and relationships (e.g., family cap, child support enforcement) came up in these contexts. Conversations involving the bureaucratic imperative reinforced negative myths regarding poor women's sexual behavior in a low-intensity way without using language that overtly denigrated clients' reproductive decisions or relationships.

We often saw the bureaucratic imperative in encounters where the worker's goal was to get information about the father of the client's children for use in child support enforcement. In this Texas interview the worker's talk had the tone of an interrogation in a police drama on television.

> WORKER: All right, this part. Do you know who M's father is?

> CLIENT: Nuh-uh.
> WORKER: Do you know anything about him? You never see his face or know where he is? OK. You never did find out who he is? (Client shakes her head.) […]
> WORKER: Do Z and P have the same father? (Client nods her head.) What's his name?
> CLIENT: PM.
> WORKER: OK. Um. When was the last time you had contact with him?
> CLIENT: About a month ago. […]
> WORKER: Did he have any plans to marry you? (Client shakes her head.)
> WORKER: OK, do you know his social security number? Date of birth?
> CLIENT: September ___, 197_.
> WORKER: 197_? Is he white? How tall is he?
> CLIENT: I don't know.

Here the worker asserts her entitlement as a representative of the welfare system to get information from the client about the father of her children. At the same time, her language positions the client as an immoral "Jezebel" who has been sexually involved with men she cannot remember and as an unwed "matriarch" who is building a family outside marriage (Collins, 1990; Roberts, 1997). The worker demonstrates her skepticism about the clients truthfulness (i.e., "You never see his face?"), but the emphasis of the conversation is discovering information to track down the father rather than moral judgment of the woman.

In addition to across-state policies like child support enforcement, some states had their own reproduction-related policies. One state, Georgia, had a specialized fertility policy, the "family cap," that prevented women who were on welfare from receiving additional financial assistance if they had another child. in the encounter below, the bureaucratic imperative led to a conversation bordering on the absurd.

> WORKER: Are you pregnant now?
> CLIENT: No.
> WORKER: You're not having any more?
> CLIENT: No.
> WORKER: Are you using any birth control?
> CLIENT: I've had my tubes tied.

WORKER: I need you to sign this saying that if you have any more, the baby will not be added to your check.

The dominant discourse of welfare that characterizes clients as at best careless, or at worst, entrepreneurial, about their fertility speaks through the worker so powerfully that even after the client states that she has been sterilized and cannot have more children, the worker continues to talk as if the client is imminently likely to conceive a baby and ask the state to support it. The worker's language enacts within the interview the negative view of welfare clients' reproductive decision-making that permeates welfare policy.

The bureaucratic imperative is also visible in the requirement that pregnancy be medically verified. This documentation requirement in and of itself suggests that welfare clients are likely to fake pregnancy to obtain benefits, even in the absence of a negative tone from the worker:

WORKER: How many months pregnant are you?
CLIENT: 7 months.
WORKER: Have you been to the doctor yet?
CLIENT: Yes.
WORKER: Did they give you a due date or a letter with the due date?
CLIENT: Yes, here it is.

Although this Georgia worker uses neutral language, a negative perspective on poor women's fertility-related behavior nonetheless enters this interview through the documentation requirement. The myth of the devious "welfare queen," who uses her fertility to trick the state into supporting her, informs the policy that workers implement in conversation with clients (Collins, 1990; Roberts, 1997).

There were several instances in which workers discussed reproductive issues with clients using bureaucratic language but resisted participating in the demeaning stereotyping of poor women that imbues welfare policy. These instances arose when workers emphasized assisting clients to comply with TANF's requirements while taking into account women's needs during pregnancy or early motherhood, as in this example from Georgia.

WORKER: What kind of work—what do you want to do? Do you have a GED?

CLIENT: No. [...]
WORKER: You may want to work towards the GED while waiting for the baby. [...] We've got a program called New Connections to Work that may be good. Do you know what kind of work you may want?
CLIENT: Nursing. [...]
WORKER: We should do the program. Here's some information. [...] After you have the child, you go to work—you'll be set. It's a very good program.

Discussion

This research indicates that though sexuality-related topics are not discussed in the majority of welfare interviews, the private sexual decisions and relationships of poor women continue to be a focus of intervention in the day-to-day interactions welfare caseworkers have with their clients. Negative myths regarding poor women's reproductive decisions and relationships (Collins, 1990, 2004; Roberts, 1997) are expressed in welfare offices through their influence on welfare policy and regulations and through the effect these myths have on worker behavior. How workers talk with (and implicitly "frame" clients) is prescribed by bureaucratic mandates whose underlying assumptions reflect racialized myths antagonistic to poor women (Collins, 1990; Hays, 2003; Roberts, 1997). Workers' own informal, discretionary conversations with clients reflected moralizing messages that were also shaped by negative perceptions of poor women's sexuality. Although workers' talk expressing personal judgments of clients may seem more offensive than their bureaucratized language, both styles of speech contribute to the dehumanization of welfare clients. The more subtle action of the bureaucratic imperative should not be disregarded; both of these strategies reflect the widely accepted false beliefs that poor women on welfare make careless or financially calculating reproductive decisions and that woman-headed families are not legitimate.

Just as the style of mainstream U.S. talk on race has gradually become less overtly and personally racist, more subtle and bureaucratized in its action (Bonilla-Silva, 2006), so analogously has welfare office talk regarding sexuality. By embedding conversations about sexual matters in bureaucratic talk about child support enforcement and the family cap, these conversations are transformed from overtly intrusive discussions of private issues into normalized outcomes of the need to ask for financial help. Women of other class backgrounds would be unlikely to submit to these interrogations, but the United States' current approach to ensuring a social safety net allows this continued focus for poor women (Hays, 2003). This analysis demonstrates that negative ideas about poor women and their fertility and family formation decisions persist in welfare policy and in its day-today implementation by caseworkers, but that they are often veiled in bureaucratic language.

Our findings regarding the apparent absence of differences in welfare office talk related to the race or gender of workers or clients are congruent with recent work by welfare implementation scholar Watkins-Hayes (2009), who observes that caseworkers' attitudes and behaviors are not determined by their social group membership alone. Rather, we observed workers' fairly consistent application of an ideology of irresponsible fertility to clients regardless of clients' races or their own. We ascribe this pattern to the racialization of welfare through which the state sanctions discourses (bureaucratic scripts and discretionary utterances) which reinforce underlying negative racial stereotypes, and normalizes the application of these myths to all poor women, regardless of race. Although Black and White women constitute roughly equal proportions of total TANF recipients (35.7% and 33.4%, respectively), African American women are disproportionately represented among welfare clients (Hays, 2003; U.S. Department of Human Services, 2006). Welfare has been associated with Blackness in the collective mind of the U.S. public ever since African American women gained access to these programs in the 1960s (Gilens, 1999; Quadagno, 1994; Roberts, 1997); in these findings, we see negative myths regarding Black women's sexuality and childbearing extended to include all women on welfare, regardless of their individual races.

Our findings are based on data that are more than 10 years old, and we cannot be certain that the same racialized discourses we identified are employed in welfare offices today. However, scholars of race and policy such as Michelle Alexander (2010) have illuminated a pattern in which new systems of "racial control" in the United States, which tend to be more overtly "colorblind," emerge to replace those that are overturned. In this analysis, which seems likely to extend to welfare office practices, it is probable that these deep negative myths persist and continue to shape caseworker language, though they may look slightly less racially influenced on the surface.

We also noted differences among the three states studied in the amount and the style of conversations on reproductive decisions and relationships. Caseworker–client interactions in Georgia were more likely than those in Texas or Michigan to include sexuality-related topics, however, these conversations were less likely to involve discretionary moralizing by workers than those in other sampled states. In Texas, though interactions were less likely than in Georgia or Michigan to include discussion of clients' sexuality, when such discussions did occur, they were quite likely to involve moralizing discourses in addition to bureaucratic language; such moralizing was also more likely in Michigan than it was in Georgia. One possible explanation for these findings is that negative myths regarding poor women's fertility have a tendency to enter welfare office conversations, and if they do not do so in bureaucratically mandated ways, they may be more likely to do so through caseworkers' personal moralizing. In states with explicit reproduction-related policies, like Georgia with its "family cap," workers were mandated to discuss sexuality-related topics and thus did so more frequently. Absent such policies in Michigan and Texas, conversations regarding sex and reproduction occurred less often, but because these conversations arose more at workers' discretion, they often included optional, personal moralizing.

In light of these results, it is important to note that individual welfare workers are not solely responsible for talking in ways that position clients negatively (Lindhorst et al., 2008). The actions of these workers reflect a structural reality: Across states and settings, caseworkers are required by law to discuss aspects of the private sexual lives of poor women. Current welfare policy, informed by an ideology that positions poor women as irresponsible in their fertility and illegitimate in their family formation, speaks through these workers.

This study has implications for the theoretical framing of future research on welfare, and for the implementation and creation of welfare policy.

Our findings indicate the importance of careful theoretical attention to race and processes of racialization in any study examining welfare. Roberts' (1997) statement that race "fuels the welfare debate even when it is not mentioned" (p. 215) is exemplified by our finding that racialized myths regarding poor women's sexuality enter the welfare interview across multiple dimensions of potential difference. This dehumanizing framing of poor women was expressed through workers' optional moralizing talk about sexuality-related issues and in their bureaucratized language. Regardless of caseworker race, client race, or racial pairing of the worker–client dyad, these stereotypes affected workers' language in welfare interviews. Viewed one way, this finding might be considered null. However, a theoretical attunement to processes of racialization supports a more convincing interpretation: that the dominant discourse of African American women's irresponsible reproduction and inappropriate family structure in which welfare interviews are embedded acts to "color" all welfare recipients and the language workers use with them.

Regarding policy implications, our analysis suggests that demeaning racialized stereotypes may influence welfare policy's creation and implementation in obvious and subtle ways. Different training and supervision might decrease the amount of discretionary moralizing done by caseworkers. However, such a solution would only address part of the problem. Negative myths regarding poor women's sexuality not only shape workers' optional talk but may also play a role in welfare policy itself. Thus, it is likely that these myths will continue to affect day-to-day talk in welfare offices even if they emerge through the less obviously offensive bureaucratic language mandated by policy. This problem is sustained by tenacious stereotypes that act at many levels.

The pervasiveness of these stereotypes means that attempts to challenge them must focus on depths, not surfaces. To change the discretionary messages welfare workers give their clients, their underlying perceptions of poor women and women of color, and more critically, the perceptions of policy makers, must be changed. This type of deep intervention will not proceed quickly or easily. It will require, at minimum, the kind of open discussion of race and racism that is rare in the United States (Alexander, 2010; Bonilla-Silva, 2006). However, such work has the potential to decrease the influence of negative myths upon those who implement welfare policy as caseworkers as well as reframing these issues for those who make it as elected representatives and those who shape it with participation as citizens.

Current welfare policy emphasizes marriage to "breadwinners" as a way of addressing poor women's need for financial resources for themselves and their children. This policy functions to place women and men into a family structure in which men of severely limited economic means are made financially responsible for women and children, regardless of structural economic factors (e.g., low wages, unemployment) that make meeting this responsibility difficult or impossible (McCall, 2000). It ignores the inconvenient fact that the majority of men who are the would-be husbands of women on welfare, and the fathers of their children, live in poverty as well (McCall, 2000; Roberts, 1997).

Regulating poor women's reproductive decisions and relationships has negative effects on women's freedom and well-being and does not adequately address child poverty (R. J. Smith, 2006; Weigt, 2010). Through regulating sexuality and encouraging marriage, and through other elements of TANF (e.g., work requirements), U.S. welfare policy treats financial provision for children as the almost exclusive responsibility of individual families (Cassiman, 2006). Issues of structural poverty are not considered. Women are made ultimately responsible for ensuring resources for their children by finding husbands who can provide for them financially (Swift, 1995). An alternative policy approach would be for the state to contribute to the support of children regardless of the sexual behavior or gendered positions (i.e. "breadwinner" and "homemaker") of their parents. To take this approach would be to recognize that earners and caregivers are required in families, regardless of whether men or women occupy these roles (Gornick & Meyers, 2009). This perspective could decrease child poverty and the stigmatization of poor women, which in the United States often involves racialized stereotypes that exacerbate existing injustice.

Funding

Data gathering for this work was supported by a grant to Marcia K. Meyers from the Nelson A. Rockefeller Institute of Government, State University of New York. During data analysis and writing, N. Tatiana Masters was partially supported by a fellowship from the National Institute of Mental Health (F31-MH078732), and Taryn P. Lindhorst was partially supported by a career development award from the National Institute of Mental Health (1K-01-MH72827–01A).

References

Abramovitz, M. (1996). *Regulating the lives of women: Social welfare policy from colonial times to the present.* Boston, MA: South End Press.

Alexander, M. (2010). *The new Jim Crow: Mass incarceration in the age of colorblindness.* New York, NY: New Press.

Annie E. Casey Foundation. (2003). *Kids count data-book.* Baltimore, MD: Author.

Berkowitz, E. D. (1991). *America's welfare state: From Roosevelt to Reagan.* Baltimore, MD: Johns Hopkins University Press.

Bonilla-Silva, E. (2006). *Racism without racists: Color-blind racism and the persistence of racial inequality in the United States.* Lanham, MD: Rowman & Littlefield.

Burger, S. (2004). Community health changes under welfare reform. *Journal of Community Health Nursing,* 21(3), 127–40.

Cameron, D., & Kulick, D. (2003). *Language and sexuality.* Cambridge, UK: Cambridge University Press.

Cassiman, S. (2006). Of witches, welfare queens, and the disaster named poverty: The search for a counter-narrative. *Journal of Poverty,* 10(4), 51–66.

Collins, P. H. (1990). *Black feminist thought: Knowledge, consciousness, and the politics of empowerment.* New York, NY: HarperCollins.

Collins, P. H. (2004). *Black sexual politics: African Americans, gender, and the new racism.* New York, NY: Routledge.

Corcoran, M., Danziger, S. K., Kalil, A., & Seefeldt, K. S. (2000). How welfare reform is affecting women's work. *Annual Review of Sociology,* 26, 241–69.

Danziger, S. H. (Ed.). (1999). *Economic conditions and welfare reform.* Kalamazoo, MI: W. E. Upjohn Institute for Employment Research.

De Jong, G. F., Graefe, D. R., & St. Pierre, T. (2005). Welfare reform and interstate migration of poor families. *Demography,* 42(3), 469–96.

Edin, K., & Kefalas, M. (2005). *Promises I can keep: Why poor women put motherhood before marriage.* Berkeley, CA: University of California Press.

Gilens, M. (1999). *Why Americans hate welfare: Race, media, and the politics of anti-poverty policy.* Chicago, IL: University of Chicago Press.

Gordon, L. (1994). *Pitied but not entitled: Single mothers and the history of welfare, 1890–1935.* New York, NY: Free Press.

Gornick, J. C., & Meyers, M. K. (2009). Institutions that support gender equality in parenthood and employment. In J. C. Gornick & M. K. Meyers (Eds.), *Gender equality: Transforming family divisions of labor* (pp. 3–56). New York, NY: Verso.

Hall, J. M., & Stevens, P. E. (1991). Rigor in feminist research. *ANS: Advances in Nursing Science,* 13(3), 16–29.

Hancock, A.-M. (2004). *The politics of disgust: The public identity of the welfare queen.* New York, NY: New York University Press.

Harris-Perry, M. (2011). *Sister citizen: Shame, stereotypes, and Black women in America.* New Haven, CT: Yale University Press.

Hays, S. (2003). *Flat broke with children: Women in the age of welfare reform.* New York, NY: Oxford University Press.

Horton-Salway, M. (2001). The construction of M.E.: The discursive action model. In M. Wetherell, S. Taylor, & S. J. Yates (Eds.), *Discourse as data* (pp. 147–88). London, UK: Sage.

Horvath-Rose, A. E., Peters, H. E., & Sabia, J. J. (2008). Capping kids: The family cap and nonmarital childbearing. *Population Research and Policy Review,* 27, 119–38.

Jagannathan, R., & Camasso, M. J. (2003). Family cap and nonmarital fertility: The racial conditioning of policy effects. *Journal of Marriage and Family,* 65, 52–71.

Jones, J. (1985). *Labor of love, labor of sorrow: Black women, work, and the family, from slavery to the present.* New York, NY: Vintage Books.

Katz, M. B. (1989). *The undeserving poor: From the war on poverty to the war on welfare.* New York, NY: Pantheon Books.

Lens, V. (2002). Welfare reform, personal narratives, and the media: How welfare recipients and journalists frame the welfare debate. *Journal of Poverty,* 6(2), 1–20.

Lindhorst, T., & Leighninger, L. (2003). "Ending welfare as we know it" in 1960: Louisiana's suitable home law. *Social Service Review,* 77(4), 564–84.

Lindhorst, T., Meyers, M., & Casey, E. (2008). Screening for domestic violence in public welfare offices: An analysis of case manager and client interactions. *Violence Against Women,* 14(1), 5–28.

Lipsky, M. (1980). *Street-level bureaucracy: Dilemmas of the individual in public services.* New York, NY: Russell Sage.

Loeb, S., Fuller, B., Kagan, S. L., & Bidemi, C. (2003). How welfare reform affects young children: Experimental findings from Connecticut. *Journal of Policy Analysis and Management*, 22(4), 537–50.

Maynard-Moody, S., Musheno, M. C., & Palumbo, D. (1990). Street-wise social policy: Resolving the dilemma of street-level influence and successful implementation. *Western Political Quarterly*, 43(4), 833–49.

McCall, L. (2000). Increasing inequality in the United States: Trends, problems, and prospects. *Economic and Political Weekly*, 35(21/22), L18–23.

McCormack, K. (2005). Stratified reproduction and poor women's resistance. *Gender & Society*, 19(5), 660–79.

Meyers, M. K. (1998). *Gaining cooperation at the front lines of service delivery: Issues for the implementation of welfare reform*. Albany, NY: Nelson A. Rockefeller Institute of Government.

Meyers, M. K., & Lurie, I. (2005, June). *The decline in welfare caseloads: An organizational perspective*. Paper presented at the Mixed Methods Research on Economic Conditions, Public Policy, and Family and Child Well-Being conference in Ann Arbor, MI.

Meyers, M. K., Riccucci, N. M., & Lurie, I. (2001). Achieving goal congruence in complex environments: The case of welfare reform. *Journal of Public Administration Research and Theory*, 11(2), 165–01.

Miles, M. B., & Huberman, A. M. (1994). *Qualitative data analysis: An expanded sourcebook* (2nd ed.). Thousand Oaks, CA: Sage.

Murray, C. (1984). *Losing ground: American social policy, 1950–1980*. New York, NY: Basic Books.

Neubeck, K. J., & Cazenave, N. A. (2001). *Welfare racism: Playing the race card against America's poor*. New York, NY: Routledge.

Piven, F. F., & Cloward, R. (1971). *Regulating the poor: The functions of public welfare*. New York, NY: Pantheon Books.

Quadagno, J. S. (1994). *The color of welfare: How racism undermined the war on poverty*. New York, NY: Oxford University Press.

Reich, J. A. (2005). *Fixing families: Parents, power, and the child welfare system*. New York, NY: Routledge.

Roberts, D. E. (1997). *Killing the Black body: Race, reproduction, and the meaning of liberty*. New York, NY: Pantheon.

Roberts, D. E. (2002). *Shattered bonds: The color of child welfare*. New York, NY: Basic.

Saldana, J. (2009). *The coding manual for qualitative researchers*. Thousand Oaks, CA: Sage.

Smith, A. M. (2001). The sexual regulation dimension of contemporary welfare law: A fifty state overview. *Michigan Journal of Gender and Law*, 8, 121–18.

Smith, R. J. (2006). Family caps in welfare reform: Their coercive and damaging effects. *Harvard Journal of Law and Gender*, 29, 151–00.

Soss, J., & Schram, S. F. (2007). A public transformed? Welfare reform as policy feedback. *American Political Science Review*, 101(1), 111–27.

Strauss, A., & Corbin, J. (1998). *Basics of qualitative research: Techniques and procedures for developing grounded theory*. Thousand Oaks, CA: Sage.

Swift, K. J. (1995). *Manufacturing "Bad Mothers": A Critical Perspective on Child Neglect*. Toronto: University of Toronto Press.

United States Department of Health and Human Services Temporary Assistance to Needy Families program seventh annual report to Congress. (2006). *Administration for Children and Families, Office of Family Assistance*, Washington, DC.

U.S. General Accounting Office. (2001). *Welfare reform: More research needed on TANF family caps and other policies for reducing out-of-wedlock births (GAO-01-924)*. Washington, DC: U.S. General Accounting Office.

Watkins-Hayes, C. (2009). *The new welfare bureaucrats: Entanglements of race, class, and policy reform*. Chicago, IL: University of Chicago.

Weigt, J. (2010). "I feel like it's a heavier burden… ": The gendered contours of heterosexual partnering after welfare reform. *Gender & Society*, 24(5), 565–90.

Questions for Critical Thinking

1. The authors discuss how caseworkers perpetuate negative myths regarding African American women's sexuality and motherhood. How does their analysis help you to understand how policy, rather than individual or cultural characteristics, perpetuates inequality for recipients of welfare?

2. Reflecting on this reading, what do you believe needs to change with regard to policy and institutional practices to better aid recipients of welfare? What do you see as the likelihood of implementing such changes? What barriers exist that may prevent their implementation?

3. What solutions do you see to poverty in the United States? How are these solutions informed by your own class experience?

RACE, PLACE, AND EFFECTIVE POLICING

• *Anthony A. Braga, Rod K. Brunson, and Kevin M. Drakulich*

The subject of police reform has been one of much public debate, particularly precipitated by the murders of George Floyd, Breonna Taylor, Rayshard Brooks, Jacob Blake, Adam Toledo, and far too many others. In the following article, the authors argue that to be effective in controlling crime and holding offenders accountable, the police need public support and cooperation. While recognizing that there are no simple solutions to address the fractured relationships between the police and the Black and Indigenous people of color communities that they serve, they outline policies and practices that could improve police–community relations and enrich police effectiveness.

> When any part of the American family does not feel like it is being treated fairly, that's a problem for all of us. ... It's not just a problem for some. It's not just a problem for a particular community or a particular demographic. It means that we are not as strong as a country as we can be. And when applied to the criminal justice system, it means we're not as effective in fighting crime as we could be.
>
> —*Remarks made by former President Barack Obama when establishing the*
> *Task Force on 21st Century Policing*, December 18, 2014

Introduction

Policing communities involves a delicate balance (Meares & Kahan 1998). On the one hand, research suggests that the police benefit from the general willingness of community members to cooperate with them to report crimes, identify offenders, assist in open investigations, and address persistent social conditions that might facilitate crime (Reisig 2010, Tyler & Fagan 2008). On the other hand, effective policing invariably involves proactive strategies that bring frontline officers into close and regular contact with community residents. The nature of this contact matters. Frequent contact under zero-tolerance order-maintenance strategies—an aggressive policing strategy that uses misdemeanor arrests to attempt to disrupt disorderly social behavior in the hope of preventing crime (Natl. Acad. Sci. Eng. Med. 2018)—can be viewed by residents as intrusive and unwarranted, leading citizens to doubt whether the police respect their rights and genuinely care about their well-being (Carr et al. 2007, Brunson & Miller 2006, Brunson & Weitzer 2009). Whether or not individuals have personal contact with police officers, their perceptions of officers' legitimacy have

Annu. Rev. Sociol. 2019. 45:535–55

First published as a Review in Advance on April 2, 2019

The *Annual Review of Sociology* is online at soc.annualreviews.org

https://doi.org/10.1146/annurev-soc-073018-022541

important consequences for police effectiveness (Tyler 2003, 2006). Simply put, policing is far more difficult without public support. Therefore, police effectiveness and legitimacy are powerfully influenced by the consequences of specific tactical and policy choices.

Policing policies, practices, and strategies vary across places. For instance, stop, question, and frisk (SQF) encounters are sometimes used by police departments as person-focused crime reduction strategies (Natl. Acad. Sci. Eng. Med. 2018). SQF encounters are grounded in constitutional laws that allow police officers to stop citizens based on reasonable suspicion—rather than the higher standard of probable cause—that they have committed, are in the process of committing, or are about to commit a crime (*Terry v. Ohio* 1968). If officers reasonably suspect that stopped citizens may be armed and possibly dangerous, they may frisk citizens for weapons. Research consistently finds that SQF encounters are disproportionately carried out in communities of color—particularly socioeconomically disadvantaged places—even after controlling for levels of crime and other social characteristics (Fagan & Davies 2000, Fagan et al. 2016, Gelman et al. 2007). Communities of color also struggle with the consequences of delicately balancing their desire for effective crime-control solutions while simultaneously being unsure that the police are truly interested in resolving these problems due to fundamental concerns about the toxic nature of police–minority citizen contact (Bell 2016, 2017; Brunson 2007; Pattillo-McCoy 1999).

Recent events in Ferguson, New York City, Chicago, and elsewhere in the United States have exposed longstanding rifts in police–minority community relations. Some scholars suggest that too many urban police departments engage in excessive surveillance and enforcement practices, contributing to mass incarceration and racial disparities throughout the criminal justice system (see, e.g., Epp et al. 2014, Young & Petersilia 2016). One-dimensional and overly broad police surveillance and enforcement strategies do little to change the underlying dynamics that drive serious urban violence (Braga 2016). Inappropriate police focus on ambiguous people and places—one where the police, in isolation from the community, identify the areas of focus and where

entire neighborhoods are defined as trouble zones—can contribute to racial disparity and mass incarceration problems that further exacerbate disadvantaged neighborhoods. This is particularly true when such an approach is coupled with a crime numbers game managerial mindset that promotes yearly increases in arrests, summons, and investigatory stops as key performance measures (Eterno & Silverman 2012). To restore effective working relationships with minority communities, police must renew their efforts to develop, implement, and sustain crime-control policies that are both fair and effective.

This review begins by summarizing race differences in crime and in the criminal justice system to frame a more focused discussion on race, place, and policing. We then review the existing scientific evidence on specific policing policies and practices with an eye toward their efficacy in controlling crime as well as how communities experience and view these efforts. While certain studies analyze national data sets, studies of policing in urban contexts represent the bulk of the existing research base on the racially disparate impacts and crime-reduction effects of specific police strategies. The fundamental lesson learned from our review is that it greatly matters how the police approach crime problems in places. By coupling problem-oriented crime-control efforts with complementary attempts to increase community engagement and enhance procedural justice in their interactions with the public, police can simultaneously enact effective crime-control practices that minimize harmful racial disparities and improve their legitimacy in disadvantaged minority neighborhoods. The review concludes with a discussion of the current paradox of policing communities of color—that they are simultaneously over- and underpoliced—as well as the critical questions of why police departments have chosen their current policies and practices and what it might take to change them.

Race Differences in Crime and Criminal Justice

Some observers suggest that disproportionate police contact with minorities is simply a function of their increased involvement in criminal behavior (e.g., MacDonald 2016). However, racial differences in criminal offending do not exist for most crime types, with the exception of serious violent crimes. In 2015, for example, just over 13% of the US population was black, but of those murders for which the race of the offender was reported to Uniform Crime Reports, 53% of offenders were black (US Dep. Justice & Fed. Bureau Investig. 2016). Similarly, 53% of race-identified murder victims were black (US Dep. Justice & Fed. Bureau Investig. 2016). The vast majority of these murders were intraracial: In cases where the race of the offender and victim were both known, 91% of black victims were killed by black offenders (US Dep. Justice & Fed. Bureau Investig. 2016). Serious but nonfatal violence also disproportionately affected black citizens. In 2015, black citizens were 40% more likely than non-Hispanic white citizens to be the victims of a rape, robbery, or aggravated assault (Truman & Morgan 2016).

Research on racial differences in violent offending suggests these differences appear rooted in the very different neighborhood contexts in which members of those different racial groups tend to live (McNulty et al. 2013, Sampson & Wilson 1995, Sampson et al. 2005). Serious violent crime is most common in areas experiencing concentrations of socioeconomic disadvantage, where—due to historical and contemporary discrimination and segregation—communities of color and other marginalized groups disproportionately reside (e.g., Peterson & Krivo 2010). Among the multiple ecological mechanisms by which community context matters, empirical evidence suggests that the capacity of neighborhood residents to achieve a common set of goals and exert control over youth and public spaces, termed collective efficacy, protects against serious violence (Sampson et al. 1997). The presence of community-based organizations, drawing membership from individuals within and outside specific neighborhoods, predicts collective efficacy and collective civic action (Sampson 2012). Concentrated disadvantage in urban neighborhoods, which are often populated by black residents, undermines local collective efficacy and gravely limits the ability of residents to address serious violent crime problems (Sampson et al. 2002). As a result, urban homicides, largely committed with guns and perpetrated by and against young black men, tend to concentrate in disadvantaged communities of color.

Theoretical work has made several core claims about why neighborhood context matters in explaining racial differences in offending. One argument is that the environmental causes of crime are identical for both black and white people (e.g., Sampson & Wilson 1995, Shaw & McKay 1942). The available evidence suggests that there is nothing fundamentally different about people based on race and implies that members of more advantaged racial groups living in the same conditions of less advantaged groups would experience similar levels of criminal offending. However, a major critique of this line of reasoning is its inattention to the basic fact that black and white Americans do not, on average, live in the same kinds of neighborhoods, and this reality is not a mere accident or happenstance (Massey & Denton 1993). Instead, a racial order structures the socioeconomic conditions of black versus white communities in fundamental ways (Peterson & Krivo 2010). Some scholars even suggest a direct role of racism in the causation of crime, whether from racial disparities in police practices or through the influence of racial oppression and injustice on a unique African American worldview (DuBois 1899, Unnever & Gabbidon 2011).

Differential offending and victimization rates feed a misperception that crime and violence are pervasive in black communities. Careful within-city research facilitates a deeper understanding of the situations, dynamics, and relationships associated with elevated rates of violent crimes committed by black offenders against black victims. For instance, in Boston, gun violence is driven by gang conflicts and is highly concentrated among a small number of high-risk places and people (Braga 2003). Roughly 5% of Boston's street block faces and intersections generated about 74% of fatal and nonfatal shooting incidents between 1980 and 2008 (Braga et al. 2010). These gun violence hot spots were in and around gang turf and drug market areas, comprising very small geographies within disadvantaged neighborhoods. In 2006, only 1% of Boston's population between the ages of 15 and 24 were members of street gangs involved in gun violence; however, gang-related disputes generated half of all homicides, and gang members were involved as offenders, victims, or both in nearly 70% of nonfatal shootings (Braga et al. 2008). The patterns observed in Boston parallel distributions seen in many other cities (Howell & Griffiths 2016, Weisburd 2015, Wolfgang et al. 1972).

Research generally finds that racial disproportions in the criminal justice system exceed racial differences in offending (e.g., Crutchfield et al. 2010, Rosich 2007). African Americans are overrepresented in every stage of contact with the criminal justice system, among those arrested, sentenced, on probation, in prison, and put to death. These disparities begin early in life: In 2013, the arrest rate for black juveniles was 2.4 times higher than the arrest rate for white juveniles (Puzzanchera & Hockenberry 2016). Particularly strong disparities exist in incarceration. In 2010, black imprisonment rates were 4.1 times higher than white imprisonment rates (Natl. Res. Council 2014). Exposure to incarceration is particularly high at the intersection of race, class, gender, and age (Pettit & Western 2004, Western 2006). In 2010, more than 35% of black men between the ages of 20 and 39 who did not finish high school were incarcerated—the equivalent number for white men was around 12%, and the number for white men with a college education was close to zero (Natl. Res. Council 2014).

Race, Place, and Problematic Policing

The American public has grown progressively interested in attending to allegations of widespread, racially disparate policing practices. This is unquestionably a troubling matter for a nation that tirelessly promotes a commitment to the equitable treatment of all its citizens. Age-old patterns of discriminatory policing, however, strike an especially raucous chord with people of color, who possibly view contemporary policing strategies through historical lenses. For example, historians have uncovered that, in addition to functioning as slave patrols, surveilling and limiting blacks' physical movement, early law enforcement officers were instrumental in a wide range of illegal activities: mob action, torture, and countless killings of freed blacks.

While Southern blacks' experiences with lynching are well-documented in American history (see, e.g., Royster 1997), the general public knows considerably less concerning a myriad of Latino victims. For instance, Richard Delgado (2009, p. 298) noted, "recent research by reputable historians shows that Latinos, particularly Mexican Americans in the Southwest, were lynched in large numbers during roughly the same period when lynchings of blacks ran rampant." Blacks' and Latinos' experiences with lynching are an undeniable and permanent stain on the legacy of early American law enforcement. Moreover, these past atrocities may also serve as the backdrop against which many people of color view contemporary policing practices, holding remnants of horrific misdeeds accountable for continuing police–minority community tensions.

This particularly striking and salient period of history is far from the only problematic reference point for communities of color. The police—as well as the criminal justice system more broadly—have long participated in efforts to suppress and exploit black Americans, including enforcement of the Fugitive Slave Act, Black Codes, Jim Crow laws, and the convict leasing program, as well as enforcing the so-called tough on crime laws that arose in the backlash to the civil rights movement. The police also played important and visible roles in suppressing civil rights activists and clashing with civil rights protestors, not just in the 1950s and 1960s but also in the modern era movement (e.g., Alexander 2010; Beckett 1997; Beckett & Sasson 2004; Blackmon 2008; Drakulich et al. 2017; Wacquant 2003, 2005; Weaver 2007). These moments of widespread visibility, however, represent only the most public and egregious face of the more routine problematic interactions faced by those living in communities of color.

The war on drugs that was initiated during the Nixon administration and expanded by the federal government during the 1980s provides another example of the police being used to tackle emergent crime problems in ways that disproportionately impact communities of color. During the 1990s, African Americans represented only 13% of drug users but accounted for 40% of individuals arrested for drug violations (Langan 1995). The US Drug Enforcement Administration (DEA) developed drug courier profiles that included race/ethnicity based on reports that Jamaican, Haitian, and black street gangs controlled interstate trafficking in crack cocaine (Tonry 1995, Harris 2002). The infamous DEA Operation

Pipeline highway drug interdiction program trained federal, state, and local law enforcement officers to use the race/ethnicity of drivers as one indicator of drug trafficking. These kinds of drug enforcement initiatives fueled African Americans' concerns over racial profiling and driving while black—being stopped, questioned, and even searched based on a pretextual traffic offense when they had committed no crime (Harris 2010).

African Americans experience substantially more contact with police than do whites (e.g., Stewart et al. 2017). African Americans are significantly more likely to be stopped (Baumgartner et al. 2018, Crutchfield et al. 2012), searched (Baumgartner et al. 2015, 2017; Rojek et al. 2012), frisked (Gelman et al. 2007), and arrested (Baumgartner et al. 2017, Kochel et al. 2011, Lytle 2014, Mitchell & Caudy 2015) by police than similarly situated whites. Indeed, the US Bureau of Justice Statistics Police–Public Contact Survey reported black drivers (13%) were only modestly more likely to be pulled over than white drivers (10%); however, black drivers (12%) were much more likely to be searched than white drivers (4%), and a greater percentage of black drivers (5%) were arrested relative to white drivers (2%) (Langton & Durose 2013). In Boston, Fagan et al. (2016) found that neighborhoods with 85% black residents experienced 53 more street stop encounters per month relative to neighborhoods with only 15% black residents, controlling for crime, police resources, and other factors; furthermore, during these encounters with Boston Police, black subjects were 12% more likely to be frisked and/or searched when compared to white subjects. Black suspects are also more likely to be mistreated by the police (Fryer 2016, Ross et al. 2018). Black victims of fatal police shootings are more than twice as likely as white victims to be unarmed (Nix et al. 2017), or via a separate estimate, the probability of being black, unarmed, and shot by the police is about 3.5 times greater than the probability of being white, unarmed, and shot by the police (Ross 2015).

Although establishing the motivations and exact mechanisms by which these disparities are produced can be methodologically challenging (Natl. Acad. Sci. Eng. Med. 2018, Ridgeway & MacDonald 2010), it is clear that they cannot be fully explained by differing rates of offending. Drug arrests, as noted above, are substantially higher among African American and Hispanic youth despite lower overall levels of drug offending (e.g., Mitchell & Caudy 2015). African American teens are more than twice as likely to report having had police contact, even after controlling for rates of criminal involvement (Crutchfield et al. 2012). Higher search rates for black citizens persist despite evidence that searches of white suspects appear more likely to yield contraband or lead to arrest (e.g., Gelman et al. 2007, Jones-Brown et al. 2010).

Experiences with the police differ not just by race but also by place. Communities of color—particularly those that are economically disadvantaged—disproportionately experience police contact and mistreatment (Fagan & Davies 2000, Kane 2002, Mastrofski et al. 2002, Petrocelli et al. 2003, Smith 1986, Terrill & Reisig 2003). Race can also condition the role of place—for instance, frisks of black suspects are more likely when those individuals appear out of place in predominantly white communities (Carroll & Gonzalez 2014, Stewart et al. 2009). In short, communities of color likely view the police through a combination of lenses, including their historical functions supporting slavery, lynchings, and discrimination; their role combatting civil rights protests; a series of highly visible incidents of police abuses of black citizens, both past and present; and the personal and vicarious experiences of interactions with the police.

Nationally televised broadcasts of civil unrest have cast unprecedented light on dubious and longstanding policing practices underway across several US cities. The release of unsettling details and airing of graphic video images capturing officer-involved killings of unarmed black suspects have shaken public confidence in the policing profession; this is especially the case within many communities of color (President's Task Force 21st Century Polic. 2015). In fact, studies examining citizen perceptions of police underscore that racial differences in attitudes toward police have been among the most robust findings in criminal justice research (see, e.g., Taylor et al. 2001). A sizeable body of scholarship finds that African Americans reliably report possessing lower levels of satisfaction with and trust in the police compared to their counterparts from other racial groups (Hurst & Frank 2000, Leiber et al. 1998).

Whites typically describe enjoying better relationships with the police, followed by Latinos and blacks. We caution, however, against assumptions that minority groups hold a uniform view of police officers. On the contrary, scholars have pointed to a racial hierarchy, signifying a descending, Asian/Latino/black scale (Weitzer & Brunson 2015, Weitzer & Tuch 2006). That is, among the three specified racial groups, blacks report having the most strained police relationships, Asians have the greatest likelihood of offering positive evaluations of officers, and Latinos occupy the middle position. The observed group differences are perhaps not surprising, however, when we consider historical differences concerning how certain minorities entered the United States, as well as their past and current treatment at the hands of the police (Solis et al. 2009).

In addition to individual race differences, the racial composition of places appears to matter to views of the police as well. In Seattle, for instance, mistrust of the police is higher in communities of color, especially communities with larger numbers of black residents, but this effect is not exclusive to those black residents (Drakulich 2013, Drakulich & Crutchfield 2013). In other words, white and other residents appear to have greater mistrust of the police when they have larger numbers of black neighbors. The race and class composition of places also conditions the relationship between perceptions of police bias and perceptions of police efficacy: When the police are viewed as biased on race, ethnicity, or class, they are also seen as particularly ineffective at policing those same communities (Drakulich & Crutchfield 2013).

Apart from racial and ethnic group membership, researchers have thoughtfully examined why some individuals hold less positive views of the police than others. For instance, several studies indicate that poor evaluations of the police may actually result from citizens' negative encounters with officers (Brandl et al. 1994, Deby 1980, Hagan et al. 2005, Weitzer et al. 2008). Therefore, the vast majority of research concerning people's appraisals of the police has focused on direct police experiences. Recently, however, scholars have begun to consider that individuals' perceptions of officers are also shaped by how they make sense of friends', relatives', and neighborhood residents' encounters (Brunson 2007). These indirect police interactions are typically referred to as vicarious experiences and have proven especially meaningful for those disproportionately suspected, stopped, searched, and shot by the police—young black men. With that in mind, Feagin & Sikes (1994, p. 16) explained that, "a black victim [of racial discrimination] frequently shares the account with family and friends, often to lighten the burden, and this sharing creates a domino effect of anguish and anger rippling across an extended group." There is also compelling evidence that black parents strategically forewarn their children about looming and inescapable racial animus, particularly in the form of police brutality (Brunson & Weitzer 2011). It is striking, however, that there are no corresponding indications that white elders also warn their youth about the likelihood of police violence.

Scholars have also consistently found that neighborhood social and physical conditions have important implications for understanding police–minority citizen relations (Kane 2002, Klinger 1997). Opponents of aggressive order-maintenance approaches warn that rounding up scores of low-level offenders who are associated with disorderly conditions only serves to exacerbate racial disparities in the ever-expanding criminal justice system, worsening already fragile police–community relations (Gau & Brunson 2010). It stands to reason then, that residents of distressed, high-crime, inner-city communities are more likely to bear the brunt of frequent, heavy-handed crime-control efforts (Boyles 2015). Ethnographic research on zero-tolerance policing in the Skid Row area of Los Angeles suggests that officers sometimes used threats of arrests and citations to coerce homeless citizens to take advantage of social services intended to help them reenter the labor market, secure housing, and improve their health; unfortunately, these services are in short supply, and these vulnerable citizens end up with insurmountable fines and criminal records that disqualify them from work and housing opportunities (Stuart 2016). Moreover, scholars have suggested that the aforementioned findings concerning race and place result from difficulty in separating race and neighborhood social conditions, such that indications of racial bias actually result from officers' tendencies to behave more aggressively in places that they consider more dangerous (Gaston & Brunson 2018, Smith 1986). Regardless of their root causes, however, aggressive policing strategies have been shown to erode police legitimacy in the eyes of community members.

Citizen confidence in the police is critical to sustained public safety; this statement also rings true among residents of impoverished, high-crime neighborhoods. Simply put, most individuals, regardless of race and socioeconomic status, are not antipolice. Many blacks and Latinos, however, disapprove of what they consider overpolicing, coupled with dehumanizing treatment. Research has shown that people are more apt to adopt a moral obligation to obey the law when they believe in the legitimacy of the police (Tyler 2003, 2006). However, adherence to the law is appreciably greater when people genuinely believe in it as opposed to complying simply because they fear being arrested, prosecuted, and sanctioned.

Many of the same environmental conditions related to overpolicing also influence the level of dissatisfaction that residents of high-crime neighborhoods have with the police, leading to claims that certain kinds of neighborhoods are simultaneously over- and underpoliced, and confirming the complex nature of police–minority citizen relations. Allegations of underpolicing center around perceptions of poor service delivery (e.g., slow response times, discourtesy, displays of apathy) and a shared belief that the police are either unable or unwilling to control crime in disadvantaged, minority communities but are seemingly quite effective at doing so in more affluent neighborhoods (Anderson 1999, Bell 2017, Brunson 2007, Gau & Brunson 2010, Pattillo-McCoy 1999, Weitzer & Brunson 2009). Residents of distressed urban communities are sometimes inaccurately portrayed as tolerant of persistent crime and disorder (Drakulich & Crutchfield 2013, Sampson & Bartusch 1998). To the contrary, people of color living in challenging conditions often report feeling unprotected and unsafe, insisting upon more effective public safety initiatives. Moreover, in addition to reporting grave concerns about their own well-being, minority citizens are equally worried that those responsible for implementing crime-control strategies often fail to recognize their humanity, a dimension largely missing from the policing tradition. Indeed, analyses of interviews with black residents, police officers, and video recordings of police–civilian encounters suggest that race shapes police suspicion and bias during the earliest moments of police–civilian interactions, and encounters that begin over seemingly minor infractions, such as jaywalking, can sometimes end with police use of force (Jones 2016).

Unfortunately, the intentional association of blacks with dangerousness (i.e., criminality) has been an enduring feature of American life (Drakulich & Siller 2015). While it is unsettling to consider that everyday citizens might hold this view, it is perhaps even more troubling to consider that criminal justice system decision-makers might, unbeknownst to even themselves, hold racially biased beliefs (Banks et al. 2006). Moreover, because of their reprehensible nature, blatantly discriminatory acts receive considerable attention, allowing for public denouncing and corrective measures. On the other hand, implicit bias operates at a subconscious level, making it difficult to know when and under what conditions we are at risk of being swayed by our preconceived views about others. Because individuals, including police officers, are not aware of their implicit biases does not mean that unconscious prejudice is harmless.

Social psychologists have produced an influential stream of research demonstrating how implicit bias potentially influences various criminal justice outcomes (e.g., SQF, police use of force, sentencing decisions). Jennifer Eberhardt and colleagues' (2004) research team discovered that after being exposed to words associated with violent crime, their study participants, one group composed of white male undergraduate students and another of police officers serving an urban area, were more apt to look at black as opposed to white faces. Furthermore, officers receiving the criminal behavior prime, and who incorrectly remembered black male faces, were inclined to select photographs of persons having more stereotypically black facial characteristics than the images of black faces that they were actually shown. Thus, the more stereotypically black an individual's face, the greater the likelihood that officers associated the image with crime. The results of these experiments, although produced in controlled settings, suggest that officers' decisions regarding who to watch, stop, arrest, and shoot might perhaps be influenced by the physical traits they tend to associate with criminality. Analyses of police body-cam footage also reveal evidence of implicit bias—in particular, that officers treat black community members less respectfully than whites during everyday traffic stops (Voigt et al. 2017).

The ability to lawfully detain suspicious persons is the hallmark of several order-maintenance policing strategies (Fagan & Davies 2000, Spitzer 1999). While undeniably an important tool for officers, these tactics also have the potential to expose law-abiding citizens to frequent and unwelcome police contacts. SQF stops require merely that police have reasonable suspicion that "criminal activity may be afoot" (*Terry v. Ohio* 1968, p. 30). However, a higher legal standard, probable cause, is needed before an officer is justified in making an arrest. Thus, reasonable suspicion provides officers legal standing to temporarily disrupt suspicious persons' movements and, if warranted, conduct protective frisks, despite not yet having probable cause to make an arrest. While officers might be acting within the confines of the law when they decide to detain, interrogate, and search individuals that they deem suspicious, police administrators should be very mindful of the potential for widespread abuse. In fact, the indiscriminate and unbridled use of SQF tactics has consistently been found to undermine citizen confidence (Brunson 2007, Gau & Brunson 2010, Weitzer & Brunson 2009). Irrespective of whether aggressive policing initiatives are legally permissible, citizen views of unequal treatment at the hands of police have dire consequences for already weakened police–minority community relations.

These problematic practices and the mistrust they engender may make crime problems worse. First, they may make citizens less likely to report crimes or cooperate with the police. For instance, when black citizens see the police as racially biased, they are far less likely to expect that their calls for help will elicit quick responses or be taken seriously (Bobo & Thompson 2006). Similarly, after the assault of an unarmed black man in Milwaukee received media attention, residents of local black neighborhoods were far less likely to call 911 to report crimes (Desmond et al. 2016). Second, mistrust of the police may harm other tools that otherwise help control local crime. A lack of faith in the police makes people feel less safe in their own communities (Drakulich 2013)—something that leads residents to withdraw from neighborhood social life or even flee the neighborhood altogether (e.g., Miethe 1995, Skogan 1995)—both of which harm the area's capacity for social capital and collective efficacy, important tools for controlling crime (Coleman 1990, Sampson et al. 1997). This effect may also be more direct: A lack of confidence in the ability of the police to control crime makes residents believe that other informal social controls are also less effective—in fact, this helps explain lower capacities for informal social control in neighborhoods with more black residents (Drakulich & Crutchfield 2013; see also Kirk & Matsuda 2011). Finally, a lack of faith in the police may lead directly to crime. Vulnerable residents of high-violence areas may feel the need to take responsibility for their own personal safety by developing a tough reputation, picking fights, and carrying a gun (Anderson 1999). Recent work describes this as legal cynicism—a cultural orientation in which the law and its agents of control are viewed as ineffective and illegitimate—something that makes people feel freer to violate the law (Kirk & Papachristos 2011).

Communities of color want effective policing; many face real dangers from crime and do not have other places to turn for help (Bell 2016, Hagan et al. 2018). However, these communities—like all communities—also want to be taken seriously; treated with respect rather than suspicion; and not subjected to aggressive, harsh, and seemingly indiscriminate policing tactics (e.g., Bobo & Thompson 2006, Brunson 2007, Weitzer & Brunson 2009).

Reducing Racial Harms in Policing

There are no simple answers to the complex, multi-level problems outlined above. The available scientific evidence suggests that the relationship between race and violent offending varies substantially across ecological contexts. Within disadvantaged neighborhoods, serious violence is highly concentrated among a very small group of highly active offenders who largely commit their crimes at very specific locations. Unfortunately, popular discourse on race and crime differences tends to be poorly conceptualized and highly reactionary. Indeed, some compelling evidence suggests that racial disparities in the administration of justice involve political responses to community and national constructions of moral panics. As Tonry (1995) suggests, the politically charged war on drugs in the late 1980s and early 1990s can be viewed as racially discriminatory in its intent and consequences given its legislative and budgetary emphasis on a specific type of drug (crack cocaine), largely associated with disadvantaged black neighborhoods. As conflict theorists argue, close attention to how crime is defined and how crime problems are socially constructed is essential in the study of racial differences in crime and understanding the nature of racial disparities in criminal justice (Chambliss 1995, Goode & Ben-Yehuda 1994).

The Need for Better Data on and More Sophisticated Analyses of Crime Problems

Poor analyses and inappropriate descriptions of urban violent crime problems can lead to the adoption of problematic policing policies and programs that exacerbate racial disparities in the criminal justice system and diminish confidence and trust in its institutions. Moreover, careless discussions of the nature of urban violence can further alienate law-abiding black residents who need and desperately want to partner with the police and other governmental institutions to create safer communities. For instance, as Braga & Brunson (2015) suggest, the term black-on-black violence, while statistically correct, is a simplistic and emotionally charged definition of urban violence that can be problematic when used by political commentators, politicians, and police executives. To most urban black residents who are not involved in violence or criminal behavior, the term invokes visions of indiscriminate and aggressive police enforcement responses applied to a broad range of black people. The term also seems to marginalize serious urban violence as a black problem that, in the minds of some black residents, may only receive a cursory response or, worse yet, be ignored by police departments entirely.

An important step in enhancing society's ability to diagnose, understand, and respond to race differences in crime and racial disparities in policing would involve the improved collection of race and ethnicity data. Throughout this essay, we focus largely on black

and white comparisons. This crude categorization stems from a lack of crime data that consistently classify information for Hispanics and non-Hispanics as well as for Asians and Native Americans (Lauritsen & Sampson 1998). Investments need to be made in criminal justice data collection systems that facilitate our understanding of differences across a more refined set of race and ethnicity categories. More nuanced theoretical and policy-relevant insights on race and crime differences have been developed by the limited data that do exist. Immigrants have long been accused of disproportionate involvement in criminal and disorderly behavior. However, a growing body of research suggests that neighborhoods characterized by larger concentrations of immigrants, such as Latinos and Asians, tend to have lower levels of violence, controlling for other factors (see, e.g., Kubrin & Ishizawa 2012).

Policing policy debates could be better informed by more careful consideration of the connections between race and underlying ecological variations in neighborhood contexts. The extant research on the nature of urban crime problems suggests effective policing requires a focus on particular people and places. Thus, police departments should pursue strategies that are artfully tailored to specific risks such as hot spots, repeat victims, high-rate offenders, or gang hostilities (Braga 2008). However, how police departments choose to address these recurring problems may either improve or worsen their relationships with minority residents. Police departments can adopt crime prevention strategies that seek to engage the community in changing the underlying conditions, situations, and dynamics that cause violence to recur. Alternatively, police departments can simply put cops on dots through directed patrols or carry out enforcement blitzes aimed at potential offenders in high-violence areas. Unfortunately, these kinds of initiatives sometimes become unfocused in practice, as entire neighborhoods can be defined as hot spot locations and young minority males simply enjoying public spaces can be regarded as would-be criminals (Brunson & Gau 2014).

Careful analysis can lead to clarity in describing urban violence patterns and thus improve police–minority community relations in at least two important ways (see Braga & Brunson 2015). First, police executives can better frame and communicate to constituents the true nature of serious violent crime problems. Second, careful analysis can lead to the development and implementation of effective and appropriately focused crime reduction strategies. The type of crime analysis work described above is well within the reach of most inner-city police departments. Inappropriate framing of urban criminal violence problems and the policies and practices that result constitute substantial obstacles for police departments and for minority communities struggling to solve these critical issues.

Problem-Solving to Reduce Enforcement and Surveillance in Proactive Policing

The US National Academies' Committee on Proactive Policing (Natl. Acad. Sci. Eng. Med. 2018, p. 1) defines proactive policing as referring to "all policing strategies that have as one of their goals the prevention or reduction of crime and disorder and that are not reactive in terms of focusing primarily on uncovering ongoing crime or on investigating or responding to crimes once they have occurred." The Committee concluded that proactive policing strategies do not inherently lead to officer misconduct. However, the Committee did identify specific proactive policing strategies as being at greater risk of possible violations of Fourth Amendment protections against illegal stops, searches, and seizures as well as violations of the Fourteenth Amendment's Equal Protection Clause prohibition against discrimination based on race, religion, national origin, and other personal characteristics. The risks of unconstitutional police practices were identified as especially relevant for SQF strategies that attempt to deter illegal gun carrying by supposed high-risk people, broken windows policing programs that increase misdemeanor arrests to control disorderly conditions associated with more serious crime problems, and hot spots policing interventions that use an aggressive practice of searches and seizures to deter criminal activity in specific places. As described above, numerous quantitative and qualitative studies have identified concerning racial disparities associated with these kinds of efforts.

The existing body of scientific evidence on proactive policing programs generally does not consider how these crime reduction and community perception impacts might vary with the racial composition of communities, the police, and police leadership. Future research studies need to consider how these kinds of racial variations might influence the effectiveness of proactive policing programs. There are a few exceptions, however. During the mid-1990s, an evaluation of the Chicago Police Department's community policing program found that attendance rates at police community meetings were highest in high-crime neighborhoods heavily populated by African Americans and that citizen perceptions of the police grew more positive for white and African American residents but did not change for Hispanic residents (Skogan & Hartnett 1997). The proactive policing programs described here tend to be implemented in disadvantaged minority communities suffering from serious crime problems, and as such, any harm reduction benefits or negative impacts would be experienced by the residents most directly exposed to these policing strategies.

Communities expect the police to control violence, and ineffective strategies will undoubtedly undermine police legitimacy (Tankebe 2013). Effective police crime prevention efforts are characterized by changing the perceptions of potential offenders of apprehension risk and modifying criminal opportunities (Nagin et al. 2015). While arrests are inevitable, the police should be oriented toward preventing crimes from happening in the first place. The adoption of problem-oriented policing principles in designing and implementing proactive crime prevention strategies can help safeguard against the use of overly harsh and indiscriminate enforcement tactics. Problem-oriented policing is a proactive crime prevention strategy that seeks to identify the underlying causes of crime problems and to frame appropriate responses using a wide variety of innovative approaches (Goldstein 1979). The approach challenges police officers to analyze the causes of problems behind a string of crime incidents or substantive community concern. Once the underlying conditions that give rise to crime problems are known, police officers develop and implement appropriate responses. Importantly, problem-oriented policing encourages police officers to think about alternative approaches to crime prevention rather than simply relying on increased surveillance, arrests, and the prosecution of offenders.

The available evaluation evidence suggests that problem-oriented policing is an effective crime reduction strategy in its own right (Weisburd et al. 2010) and may enhance the crime-control efficacy of broken windows policing and hot spots policing strategies.

A recent systematic review of rigorous program evaluations suggests that the types of broken windows strategies used by police departments to control disorder seem to matter (Braga et al. 2015). Zero-tolerance order-maintenance strategies that target enforcement actions on individual disorderly behaviors did not generate significant crime reductions. In contrast, community problem-solving approaches that seek to change social and physical disorder conditions at particular places produced significant crime reductions. These findings suggest that, when considering broken windows policing approaches, police departments should adopt a community coproduction model rather than drift toward a zero-tolerance policing model, which focuses on a subset of social incivilities, such as drunken people, rowdy teens, and street vagrants, and seeks to remove them from the street via arrest (Taylor 2001). In devising and implementing appropriate strategies to deal with a full range of disorder problems, police must rely on citizens, city agencies, and others in numerous ways. Disorder reduction is rooted in a tradition of stable relationships with the community and responsiveness to local concerns. A sole commitment to increasing misdemeanor arrests stands a good chance of undermining relationships in low-income, urban communities of color, where coproduction is most needed and distrust between the police and citizens is most profound.

Furthermore, evaluation evidence finds that hot spots policing programs do generate crime reductions and that these crime-control benefits diffuse into areas immediately surrounding targeted areas (Braga et al. 2014). What is more, Braga and his colleagues (2014) found that problem-oriented policing interventions generated larger crime reduction impacts when compared to interventions that simply increase levels of traditional police actions in crime hot spots. Police presence in crime hot spots can change offender perceptions of risk without generating mass arrests or subjecting large numbers of people to unwarranted stops. While in these places, police can

engage problem-oriented strategies to change the physical and spatial characteristics, such as poor lighting, abandoned buildings, disorderly bars, and the like, that attract potential offenders. These kinds of preventive strategies can reduce the number of young minority men ensnarled in the criminal justice system and, in turn, could diminish the harms associated with mass incarceration in these vulnerable communities.

Problem-oriented policing concepts can also be applied to economize on the use of enforcement in crime-control strategies targeting repeat offenders, gangs, and other kinds of criminally active groups. Focused deterrence strategies are firmly rooted in the problem-oriented policing model and use analysis to ensure that interventions are focused on the small number of high-risk people who generate the bulk of urban crime problems (Braga et al. 2001). Evaluation evidence suggests that focused deterrence is effective at controlling violent crime problems (Braga et al. 2018b). These strategies seek to change offender behavior by understanding underlying crime-producing dynamics and conditions that sustain recurring conditions and implementing an appropriately focused blended strategy of law enforcement, community mobilization, and social service actions (Kennedy 2011). Direct communications of increased enforcement risks and the availability of social service assistance to target groups and individuals are defining characteristics of focused deterrence strategies. Following the focused deterrence model, high-risk people, such as gang members, can be warned of the enforcement consequences associated with continued violent behavior and advised to take advantage of the services and opportunities being offered to them. In the eyes of community members, there is an inherent fairness in offering targeted offenders a choice and providing resources to support their transition away from violent behavior rather than simply arresting and prosecuting them.

Police Legitimacy, Community Policing, and Procedural Justice

Police legitimacy is generally regarded as a view among community members that police departments play an appropriate role in implementing rules governing public conduct. Police depend heavily on the public to execute their law enforcement duties successfully (Meares & Kahan 1998, Tyler 2006). Multiple factors, such as the fair distribution of police resources, police crime-control effectiveness, and procedural fairness, have been shown to be associated with citizen perceptions of police legitimacy (Bottoms & Tankebe 2012, Jackson & Bradford 2009). Procedural justice focuses on how the police treat citizens in their everyday encounters. When citizens view the police as trustworthy, they are more likely to support officers having a wider range of discretion, defer to officer authority, and comply with requests (Sunshine & Tyler 2003, Tyler 2006). The process-based model of police legitimacy suggests that when police are perceived to make fair decisions and treat people with respect, they will be viewed as legitimate authorities (Tyler 2003). As a result, the police will enjoy enhanced citizen cooperation and compliance with the law. A series of studies have found support for key components of the process-based model of police legitimacy (see, e.g., Mastrofski et al. 1996, Mazerolle et al. 2013, Tyler & Wakslak 2004). Police officers should embrace procedural justice principles in their interactions with all citizens.

Community policing should be the foundation of any police-led violence reduction strategy. Community policing strategies attempt to address and mitigate community crime and disorder problems by working with the community to build resilience, collective efficacy, and social infrastructure for the co-production of public safety (Natl. Acad. Sci. Eng. Med. 2018). While community policing programs have not been found to be effective in reducing crime, they have generated positive effects on citizen satisfaction, perceptions of disorder, and police legitimacy (Gill et al. 2014). Moreover, community engagement strategies implemented as part of community policing initiatives can provide important input to help focus problem-oriented policing, hot spots policing, and focused deterrence approaches, which do seem to reduce violence (Natl. Acad. Sci. Eng. Med. 2018). Developing close relationships with community members would help the police to gather information about crime and disorder problems, understand the nature of these problems, and solve specific crimes. Community members can also help with key components of strategies tailored to specific problems by

making improvements to the physical environment and through informal social control of high-risk people. In this way, police strategies focusing on particular people and places would cease to be a form of profiling and instead become a generator of community engagement projects. Indeed, a central idea in community policing is to engage residents so they can exert more control over situations and dynamics that contribute to their own potential for victimization and, by doing so, influence neighborhood levels of violence.

Preventing violence by addressing underlying violent crime–producing situations and dynamics reduces harm to potential victims as well as harm to would-be offenders by not relying solely on arrests and prosecution actions (Braga 2016). Community engagement in developing appropriately focused strategies would help to safeguard against indiscriminate and overly aggressive enforcement tactics and other harmful policing activities, which erode the community's trust and confidence in the police and inhibit cooperation. Collaborative partnerships between police and community members improve the transparency of law enforcement actions and provide residents with a much-needed voice in crime prevention work. Ongoing conversations with the community can ensure that day-to-day police–citizen interactions are conducted in a procedurally just manner that enhances community trust and compliance with the law.

Given the powerful role of neighborhood conditions on race differences in violent behavior and victimization, one clear set of policy implications involves increased community social organization to prevent violence. The key idea here is to change places rather than people. Underlying social and structural characteristics of neighborhoods can be addressed through a variety of interventions such as diminishing economic deprivation through local investment incentives, rehabilitating deteriorating housing, promoting stable housing, ameliorating social and physical disorder, enhancing municipal services, dispersing concentrated public housing, and building human capital through neighborhood-based child development strategies (Sampson 2011). These kinds of community investments can help to reverse concentrated disadvantage and stabilize neighborhoods. The police can serve as key initiators and partners in stimulating these kinds of broader social policy changes.

Neighborhood violence can also be addressed by improving the social organization and capacity of residents to exert informal social control over public spaces. The presence of community based organizations, which draw membership from individuals from within and outside specific neighborhoods, predicts collective efficacy and collective civic action (Sampson 2012). These organizations, which include community newspapers, family planning clinics, alcohol/drug treatment centers, counseling or mentoring services (e.g., Big Brother), neighborhood watch, and other local agencies, typically act to ensure the well-being of larger community areas. For instance, Sampson (2011, p. 226) suggested that the key to fostering informal social controls and collective efficacy "is to increase positive connections among youth and adults in the community" and recommends initiatives such as parent involvement in after-school and nighttime youth programs, adult youth mentoring systems, and organized supervision of leisure time youth activities. These community-based organizations can be potent crime prevention partners for the police.

Conclusion

More than 50 years ago, reflecting on the 1965 Watts riots, Municipal Judge Loren Miller cast light on the wellspring of mutual distrust between police and black citizens (Reddick 1965). An examination of events triggering the Watts riots offers keen insights for making sense of contemporary strained relationships between police and black communities. In particular, following the arrest and alleged beating of Marquette Frye, a 21-year-old black male motorist, several days of rioting resulted in dozens of deaths, hundreds of injuries, and property damage exceeding $100 million. While the historical significance of the Watts riots is clear, modern protests following questionable police actions involving black suspects demonstrate that black citizens' deep-seated feelings of mistrust persist. Some police administrators might question the extent to which communities of color also bear responsibility for repairing frayed relationships with the police. Disadvantaged urban neighborhoods, where blacks disproportionately reside, lack the immense social and political capital required to

marshal change. Police departments, conversely, are formal organizations with established command structures, policies, and mechanisms that, if effectively leveraged, could be geared toward strengthening police–minority community relations (Chevigny 1995, Mastrofski et al. 2002). Therefore, it seems fitting that American police departments should lead the way toward establishing a more equitable criminal justice system.

Looking toward the future, we believe that there are some reasons to be cautiously optimistic. The research evidence reviewed here suggests that so-called high-risk places, high-risk people strategies can actually improve police legitimacy when they are coupled with a strong commitment to community partnership. Community policing is a well-established guiding philosophy in police policy circles. Nevertheless, we believe that modern police departments need to reinvigorate their efforts to embrace the key principles of this important strategic orientation toward their work in all communities. In a community like Ferguson, where mistrust of law enforcement is deep-seated, it may be very difficult to establish strong police–citizen relationships that can lead to much-needed enhanced police legitimacy. Immediate reforms, such as a short-term unilateral reduction in investigatory stops (Young & Petersilia 2016), could be used to smooth the transition to community policing. While not a panacea for police–community relations problems, the introduction of body-worn cameras seems to reduce citizen complaints and reports of police use of force (Ariel et al. 2015, Braga et al. 2018a). The adoption of body-worn cameras should be accompanied by police department policies that facilitate the appropriate public viewing of captured video footage to generate the desired enhancements to transparency and police accountability (see Friedman 2017). Police executives should consider these approaches as possible means to initiate better working relationships in communities characterized by persistently low levels of trust and confidence in the police.

In sum, it matters how we police spaces, especially along racial lines. The path to changing how we police requires an answer to the question of why we have historically pursued the policing policies and strategies that we have. If current practices exist merely because of an innocent ignorance of the harms they cause and the availability of alternative strategies, then the clear identification of those harms and better alternatives—both of which have been accomplished by the work summarized in this article—will suffice.

On the other hand, the racially problematic history and contemporary practices of American policing suggest that the issues may be rooted in more than mere ignorance. In addition to the biased legal and police practices described above, communities of color are subject to an inter-locking system of disparities and bias in a broader system, including schools; health care; and the labor, housing, consumer, and credit markets (e.g., Pager & Shepherd 2008), a phenomenon Barbara Reskin (2012) has referred to as uber- or metadiscrimination. If all of these policies and practices work together to help maintain the existing racial hierarchy (e.g., Peterson & Krivo 2010), then the path to implementing these police reforms is more complicated (e.g., Bell 2017, Vitale 2017) and requires a direct challenge to that hierarchy and the structures that preserve it.

While this work will be difficult, it is also urgently necessary. The policing paradox—that impoverished communities of color feel simultaneously over- and underpoliced—has and continues to produce tragic consequences. The central tragedy is that these communities that are subject to the most aggressive and harmful policing strategies, and who have the least confidence in the police, are also the most dependent on their services. Despite high levels of legal cynicism and estrangement, residents of racially isolated and disadvantaged places continue to call the police to seek help. This is true even when these calls expose partners and children to potentially harmful police contact (Bell 2016), and in fact, calls appear to increase as neighborhoods experience greater levels of racial isolation, incarceration, and economic stressors (Hagan et al. 2018). This overreliance on the police in the absence of alternative strategies highlights the moral imperative to better serve and protect the nation's most vulnerable populations.

Disclosure Statement

The authors are not aware of any affiliations, memberships, funding, or financial holdings that might be perceived as affecting the objectivity of this review.

Literature Cited

Alexander M. 2010. *The New Jim Crow: Mass Incarceration in the Age of Colorblindness*. New York: New Press

Anderson E. 1999. *Code of the Street: Decency, Violence and the Moral Life of the Inner City*. New York: Norton

Ariel B, Farrar W, Sutherland A. 2015. The effect of police body-worn cameras on use of force and citizens' complaints against the police: a randomized controlled trial. *J. Quant. Criminol.* 31(3):509–35

Banks R, Eberhardt JL, Ross L. 2006. Discrimination and implicit bias in a racially unequal society. *Calif. Law Rev.* 94:1169–90

Baumgartner FR, Epp DA, Shoub K. 2018. *Suspect Citizens: What 20 Million Traffic Stops Tell Us About Policing and Race*. Cambridge, UK: Cambridge Univ. Press

Baumgartner FR, Epp DA, Shoub K, Love B. 2017. Targeting young men of color for search and arrest during traffic stops: evidence from North Carolina, 2002–2013. *Politics Groups Identities* 5(1):107–31

Baumgartner FR, Grigg AJ, Mastro A. 2015. #BlackLivesDon'tMatter: race-of-victim effects in US executions, 1976–2013. *Politics Groups Identities* 3(2):209–21

Beckett K. 1997. *Making Crime Pay: Law and Order in Contemporary American Politics*. New York: Oxford Univ. Press

Beckett K, Sasson T. 2004. *The Politics of Injustice: Crime and Punishment in America*. Thousand Oaks, CA: Pine Forge Press. 2nd ed.

Bell MC. 2016. Situational trust: how disadvantaged mothers reconceive legal cynicism. *Law Soc. Rev.* 50(2):314–47

Bell MC. 2017. Police reform and the dismantling of legal estrangement. *Yale Law J.* 126:2054–150

Blackmon DA. 2008. *Slavery by Another Name: The Re-Enslavement of African-Americans from the Civil War to World War II*. New York: Anchor Books

Bobo LD, Thompson V. 2006. Unfair by design: the war on drugs, race, and the legitimacy of the criminal justice system. *Soc. Res.* 73:445–72

Bottoms A, Tankebe J. 2012. Beyond procedural justice: a dialogic approach to legitimacy in criminal justice. *J. Crim. Law Criminol.* 102(1):119–70

Boyles AS. 2015. *Race, Place, and Suburban Policing: Too Close for Comfort*. Oakland: Univ. Calif. Press

Braga AA. 2003. Serious youth gun offenders and the epidemic of youth violence in Boston. *J. Quant. Criminol.* 19(1):33–54

Braga AA. 2008. *Problem-Oriented Policing and Crime Prevention*. Boulder, CO: Lynne Rienner Publ. 2nd ed.

Braga AA. 2016. Better policing can improve legitimacy and reduce mass incarceration. *Harv. Law Rev. Forum* 129(7):233–41

Braga AA, Brunson RK. 2015. *The police and public discourse on "black on black" violence*. New Perspect. Polic. Bull., Natl. Inst. Justice, US Dep. Justice, Washington, DC

Braga AA, Hureau D, Winship C. 2008. Losing faith? Police, black churches, and the resurgence of youth violence in Boston. *Ohio St. J. Crim. Law* 6(1):141–72

Braga AA, Kennedy D, Waring E, Piehl AM. 2001. Problem-oriented policing, deterrence, and youth violence: an evaluation of Boston's Operation Ceasefire. *J. Res. Crime Delinq.* 38(3):195–225

Braga AA, Papachristos AV, Hureau D. 2010. The concentration and stability of gun violence at micro places in Boston, 1980–2008. *J. Quant. Criminol.* 26(1):33–53

Braga AA, Papachristos AV, Hureau D. 2014. The effects of hot spots policing on crime: an updated systematic review and meta-analysis. *Justice Q.* 31(4):633–63

Braga AA, Sousa WH, Coldren JR Jr., Rodriguez D. 2018a. The effects of body-worn cameras on police activity and police-citizen encounters: a randomized controlled trial. *J Crim. Law Criminol.* 108(3):511–38

Braga AA, Weisburd DL, Turchan B. 2018b. Focused deterrence strategies and crime control: an updated systematic review and meta-analysis of the empirical evidence. *Criminol. Public Policy* 17(1):205–50

Braga AA, Welsh BC, Schnell C. 2015. Can policing disorder reduce crime? A systematic review and meta-analysis. *J. Res. Crime Delinq.* 52(4):567–88

Brandl S, Frank J, Worden R, Bynum T. 1994. Global and specific attitudes toward the police. *Justice Q.* 11(1):119–34

Brunson RK. 2007. "Police don't like black people": African American young men's accumulated police experiences. *Criminol. Public Policy* 6(1):71–102

Brunson RK, Gau JM. 2014. Race, place, and policing the inner-city. In *The Oxford Handbook on Police and Policing*, ed. MD Reisig, RJ Kane, pp. 362–82. New York: Oxford Univ. Press

Brunson RK, Miller J. 2006. Young black men and urban policing in the United States. *Brit. J. Criminol.* 46(4):613–40

Brunson RK, Weitzer R. 2009. Police relations with black and white youths in different urban neighborhoods. *Urb. Aff. Rev.* 44:858–85

Brunson RK, Weitzer R. 2011. Negotiating unwelcome police encounters: the intergenerational transmission of conduct norms. *J. Contemp. Ethnog.* 40:425–56

Carr PJ, Napolitano L, Keating J. 2007. We never call the cops and here is why: a qualitative examination of legal cynicism in three Philadelphia neighborhoods. *Criminology* 45(2):445–80

Carroll L, Gonzalez ML. 2014. Out of place: racial stereotypes and the ecology of frisks and searches following traffic stops. *J. Res. Crime Delinq.* 51(5):559–84

Chambliss W. 1995. Crime control and ethnic minorities: legitimizing racial oppression by creating moral panics. In *Ethnicity, Race, and Crime: Perspectives Across Time and Place*, ed. D Hawkins, pp. 235–58. Albany: State Univ. N.Y. Press

Chevigny P. 1995. *Edge of the Knife: Police Violence in the Americas*. New York: New Press

Coleman JC. 1990. *Foundations of Social Theory*. Cambridge, MA: Harvard Univ. Press

Crutchfield RD, Fernandes A, Martinez J. 2010. Racial and ethnic disparity and criminal justice: How much is too much? *J. Crim. Law Criminol.* 100:903–32

Crutchfield RD, Skinner ML, Haggerty KP, McGlynn A, Catalano RF. 2012. Racial disparity in police contacts. *Race Justice* 2(3):179–202

Deby D. 1980. Citizen ratings of the police: the difference contact makes. *Law Policy Q.* 2:445–71

Delgado R. 2009. The law of the noose: a history of Latino lynching. *Harv. Civ. Rights-Civ. Lib. Law Rev.* 44:297–312

Desmond M, Papachristos AV, Kirk DS. 2016. Police violence and citizens crime reporting in the black community. *Am. Sociol. Rev.* 81(5):857–76

Drakulich KM. 2013. Perceptions of the local danger posed by crime: race, disorder, informal control, and the police. *Soc. Sci. Res.* 42:611–32

Drakulich KM, Crutchfield RD. 2013. The role of perceptions of the police in informal social control: implications for the racial stratification of crime and control. *Soc. Prob.* 60:383–407

Drakulich KM, Hagan J, Johnson D, Wozniak KH. 2017. Race, justice, policing, and the 2016 American presidential election. *Du Bois Rev.* 14(1):7–33

Drakulich KM, Siller L. 2015. Presumed danger: race, bias, stigma, and perceptions of crime and criminals. In *Deadly Injustice: Race, Criminal Justice, and the Death of Trayvon Martin*, ed. D Johnson, P Warren, A Farrell, pp. 23–58. New York: NYU Press

Du Bois WEB. 1899. *The Philadelphia Negro*. Philadelphia: Univ. Pa. Press

Eberhardt JL, Goff PA, Purdie VJ, Davies PG. 2004. Seeing black: race, crime, and visual processing. *J. Pers. Soc. Psych.* 87:876–93

Epp C, Maynard-Moody S, Haider-Markel D. 2014. *Pulled Over: How Police Stops Define Race and Citizenship.* Chicago: Univ. Chicago Press

Eterno J, Silverman E. 2012. *The Crime Numbers Game: Management by Manipulation.* New York: CRC Press

Fagan J, Braga AA, Brunson RK, Pattavina A. 2016. Stops and stares: street stops, surveillance, and race in the new policing. *Fordham Urb. Law J.* 43:539–614

Fagan J, Davies G. 2000. Street stops and broken windows: Terry, race, and disorder in New York City. *Fordham Urb. Law J.* 28:457–504

Feagin JR, Sikes MP. 1994. *Living with Racism: The Black Middle-Class Experience.* Boston, MA: Beacon Press

Friedman B. 2017. *Unwarranted: Policing Without Permission.* New York: Farrar, Straus, and Giroux

Fryer RG. 2016. *An empirical analysis of racial differences in police use of force.* NBER Work. Pap. 22399

Gaston S, Brunson RK. 2018. Reasonable suspicion in the eye of the beholder: routine policing in racially different disadvantaged neighborhoods. *Urb. Aff. Rev.* https://doi.org/10.1177/1078087418774641

Gau J, Brunson RK. 2010. Procedural justice and order maintenance policing: a study of inner-city young men's perceptions of police legitimacy. *Justice Q.* 27(2):255–79

Gelman A, Fagan J, Kiss A. 2007. An analysis of the New York City Police Department's "stop-and-frisk" policy in the context of claims of racial bias. *J. Am. Stat. Assoc.* 102(479):813–23

Gill C, Weisburd DL, Telep C, Vitter Z, Bennett T. 2014. Community-oriented policing to reduce crime, disorder and fear and increase satisfaction and legitimacy among citizens: a systematic review. *J. Exp. Criminol.* 10(4):399–428

Goldstein H. 1979. Improving policing: a problem-oriented approach. *Crime Delinq.* 25:236–58

Goode E, Ben-Yehuda N. 1994. Moral panics: culture, politics, and social construction. *Annu. Rev. Sociol.* 20:149–71

Hagan J, McCarthy B, Herda D, Cann Chandrasekher A. 2018. Dual-process theory of racial isolation, legal cynicism, and reported crime. *PNAS* 115(28):7190–99

Hagan J, Shedd C, Payne MR. 2005. Race, ethnicity, and youth perceptions of criminal injustice. *Am. Sociol. Rev.* 70:381–407

Harris D. 2002. *Profiles in Injustice: Why Racial Profiling Cannot Work.* New York: New Press

Harris D. 2010. The stories, statistics, and the law: why "driving while black" matters. In *Race, Ethnicity and Policing,* ed. SK Rice, MD White, pp. 36–83. New York: NYU Press

Howell JC, Griffiths E. 2016. *Gangs in America's Communities.* Newbury Park, CA: Sage. 2nd ed.

Hurst YG, Frank J. 2000. How kids view cops: the nature of juvenile attitudes toward the police. *J. Crim. Justice* 28:189–202

Jackson J, Bradford B. 2009. Crime, policing and social order: on the expressive nature of public confidence in policing. *Br. J. Sociol.* 60(3):493–521

Jones N. 2016. *How things fall apart: race, gender and suspicion in police-civilian encounters.* Lecture presented at the Department of Sociology, Harvard Univ., Boston, MA, March 22

Jones-Brown D, Gill J, Trone J. 2010. *Stop, question, and frisk policing practices in New York City: a primer.* Rep., Cent. Race Crime Justice, John Jay Coll. Crim. Justice, City Univ. N.Y., New York. https://static.prisonpolicy.org/scans/PRIMER_electronic_version.pdf

Kane RJ. 2002. The social ecology of police misconduct. *Criminology* 40:867–96

Kennedy DM. 2011. *Don't Shoot: One Man, a Street Fellowship, and the End of Violence in Inner-City America.* New York: Bloomsbury

Kirk DS, Matsuda M. 2011. Legal cynicism, collective efficacy, and the ecology of arrest. *Criminology* 49(2):443–72

Kirk DS, Papachristos AV. 2011. Cultural mechanisms and the persistence of neighborhood violence. *Am. J. Sociol.* 116(4):1190–233

Klinger DA. 1997. Negotiating order in patrol work: an ecological theory of police response to deviance. *Criminology* 35(1):277–306

Kochel TR, Wilson DB, Mastrofski SD. 2011. Effect of suspect race on officers' arrest decisions. *Criminology* 49(2):473–512

Kubrin CE, Ishizawa H. 2012. Why some immigrant neighborhoods are safer than others: divergent findings from Los Angeles and Chicago. *Ann. Am. Acad. Political Soc. Sci.* 641:148–73

Langan P. 1995. *The racial disparity in U.S. drug arrests.* Rep., US Dep. Justice, Washington, DC

Langton L, Durose M. 2013. *Police behavior during traffic and street stops, 2011.* Rep., US Dep. Justice, Washington, DC

Lauritsen J, Sampson RJ. 1998. Minorities, crime, and criminal justice. In *The Handbook of Crime and Punishment,* ed. M Tonry, pp. 58–84. New York: Oxford Univ. Press

Leiber MJ, Nalla MK, Farnsworth M. 1998. Explaining juveniles' attitudes toward the police. *Justice Q.* 15(1):151–74

Lytle DJ. 2014. The effects of suspect characteristics on arrest: a meta-analysis. *J. Crim. Justice* 42(6):589–97

MacDonald H. 2016. *The War on Cops: How the New Attack on Law and Order Makes Everyone Less Safe*. New York: Encounter Books

Massey DS, Denton NA. 1993. *American Apartheid: Segregation and the Making of the Underclass*. Cambridge, MA: Harvard Univ. Press

Mastrofski SD, Reisig M, McClusky JD. 2002. Police disrespect toward the public: an encounter-based analysis. *Criminology* 40:519–51

Mastrofski SD, Snipes JB, Supina AE. 1996. Compliance on demand: the public's response to specific police requests. *J. Res. Crime Delinq.* 33(3):269–305

Mazerolle L, Antrobus E, Bennett S, Tyler TR. 2013. Shaping citizen perceptions of police legitimacy: a randomized field trial of procedural justice. *Criminology* 51(1):33–63

Meares TL, Kahan DM. 1998. Law and (norms of) order in the inner city. *Law Soc. Rev.* 32(4):805–38

McNulty TL, Bellair PE, Watts SJ. 2013. Neighborhood disadvantage and verbal ability as explanations of the black–white difference in adolescent violence: toward an integrated model. *Crime Delinq.* 59(1):140–60

Miethe TD. 1995. Fear and withdrawal from urban life. *Ann. Am. Acad. Political Soc. Sci.* 539:14–27

Mitchell O, Caudy MS. 2015. Examining racial disparities in drug arrests. *Justice Q.* 32(2):288–313

Nagin DS, Solow RM, Lum C. 2015. Deterrence, criminal opportunities, and the police. *Criminology* 53(1):74–100

Natl. Acad. Sci. Eng. Med. 2018. *Proactive Policing: Effects on Crime and Communities*. Washington, DC: Natl. Acad. Press

Natl. Res. Council. 2014. *The growth of incarceration in the United States: exploring causes and consequences*. Rep., Natl. Res. Council, Natl. Acad., Washington, DC

Nix J, Campbell BA, Byers EH, Alpert GP. 2017. A bird's eye view of civilians killed by police in 2015: further evidence of implicit bias. *Criminol. Public Policy* 16(1):309–40

Pager D, Shepherd H. 2008. The sociology of discrimination: racial discrimination in employment, housing, credit, and consumer markets. *Annu. Rev. Sociol.* 34:181–209

Pattillo-McCoy M. 1999. *Black Picket Fences: Privilege and Peril Among the Black Middle Class*. Chicago: Univ. Chicago Press

Peterson RD, Krivo LJ. 2010. *Divergent Social Worlds: Neighborhood Crime and the Racial-Spatial Divide*. New York: Russell Sage Found.

Petrocelli M, Piquero AR, Smith MR. 2003. Conflict theory and racial profiling: an empirical analysis of police traffic stop data. *J. Crim. Justice* 31(1):1–11

Pettit B, Western B. 2004. Mass imprisonment and the life course: race and class inequality in U.S. incarceration. *Am. Sociol. Rev.* 69(1):151–69

President's Task Force 21st Century Polic. 2015. *Final report of the President's task force on 21st century policing*. Rep., Office Community Oriented Polic. Serv., Washington, DC

Puzzanchera C, Hockenberry S. 2016. *National disproportionate minority contact databook*. Database, US Dep. Justice, Office Juvenile Justice Delinq. Prev., Washington, DC, updated Aug. 22, 2018. https://www.ojjdp.gov/ojstatbb/dmcdb/

Reddick LD. 1965. Trigger of hate. *Time*, Aug. 20, pp. 13–19

Reisig MD. 2010. Community and problem-oriented policing. In *Crime and Justice: A Review of Research*, Vol. 39, ed. M Tonry, pp. 1–53. Chicago: Univ. Chicago Press

Reskin B. 2012. The race discrimination system. *Annu. Rev. Sociol.* 38:17–35

Ridgeway G, MacDonald J. 2010. Methods for assessing racially biased policing. In *Race, Ethnicity and Policing*, ed. SK Rice, MD White, pp. 180–204. New York: NYU Press

Rojek J, Rosenfeld R, Decker S. 2012. Policing race: the racial stratification of searches in police traffic stops. *Criminology* 50(4):993–1024

Rosich KJ. 2007. *Race, Ethnicity, and the Criminal Justice System*. Washington, DC: Am. Sociol. Assoc.

Ross CT. 2015. A multi-level Bayesian analysis of racial bias in police shootings at the county-level in the United States, 2011–14. *PLOS ONE* 10(11):e0141854

Ross CT, Winterhalder B, McElreath R. 2018. Resolution of apparent paradoxes in the race-specific frequency of use-of-force by police. *Palgrave Commun.* 4:61

Royster JJ. 1997. *Ida B. Wells: Southern Horrors and Other Writings*. New York: Bedford

Sampson RJ. 2011. The community. In *Crime and Public Policy*, ed. JQ Wilson, J Petersilia, pp. 210–36. New York: Oxford Univ. Press

Sampson RJ. 2012. *Great American City: Chicago and the Enduring Neighborhood Effect*. Chicago: Univ. Chicago Press

Sampson RJ, Bartusch DJ. 1998. Legal cynicism and (subcultural?) tolerance of deviance: the neighborhood context of racial difference. *Law Soc. Rev.* 32:777–804

Sampson RJ, Morenoff JD, Gannon-Rowley T. 2002. Assessing "neighborhood effects": social processes and new directions in research. *Annu. Rev. Sociol.* 28:443–78

Sampson RJ, Morenoff JD, Raudenbush SW. 2005. Social anatomy of racial and ethnic disparities in violence. *Am. J. Public Health* 95:224–32

Sampson RJ, Raudenbush SW, Earls F. 1997. Neighborhoods and violent crime: a multilevel study of collective efficacy. *Science* 277:918–24

Sampson RJ, Wilson WJ. 1995. Toward a theory of race, crime, and urban inequality. In *Crime and Inequality*, ed. J Hagan, R Peterson, pp. 37–56. Palo Alto, CA: Stanford Univ. Press

Shaw CR, McKay HD. 1942. *Juvenile Delinquency in Urban Areas*. Chicago: Univ. Chicago Press

Skogan WG. 1995. Crime and the racial fears of white Americans. *Ann. Am. Acad. Political Soc. Sci.* 539:59–71

Skogan WG, Hartnett S. 1997. *Community Policing, Chicago Style*. New York: Oxford Univ. Press

Smith DA. 1986. The neighborhood context of police behavior. *Crime Justice* 8:313–41

Solis C, Portillos E, Brunson RK. 2009. Latino youths' experiences with and perceptions of involuntary police encounters. *Ann. Am. Acad. Political Soc. Sci.* 623:39–51

Spitzer E. 1999. *The New York City Police Department's "stop & frisk" practices: a report to the people of the State of New York from the Office of the Attorney General*. Rep., Office Attorney General State N.Y., New York

Stewart EA, Baumer EP, Brunson RK, Simons R. 2009. Neighborhood racial context and perceptions of police-based racial discrimination among black youth. *Criminology* 47(3):847–87

Stewart EA, Warren PY, Hughes C, Brunson RK. 2017. Race, ethnicity, and criminal justice contact: reflections for future research. *Race Justice*. https://doi.org/10.1177/21533687 17738090

Stuart F. 2016. *Down, Out, and Under Arrest: Policing and Everyday Life in Skid Row*. Chicago: Univ. Chicago Press

Sunshine J, Tyler TR. 2003. The role of procedural justice and legitimacy in shaping public support for policing. *Law Soc. Rev.* 37(3):513–48

Tankebe J. 2013. Viewing things differently: the dimensions of public perceptions of police legitimacy. *Criminology* 51(1):103–35

Taylor R. 2001. *Breaking Away from Broken Windows: Baltimore Neighborhoods and the Nationwide Fight Against Crime, Grime, Fear, and Decline*. Boulder, CO: Westview

Taylor TJ, Turner KB, Esbensen FA, Winfree LT. 2001. Coppin' an attitude: attitudinal differences among juveniles toward the police. *J. Crim. Justice* 29:295–305

Terrill W, Reisig MD. 2003. Neighborhood context and use of police force. *J. Res. Crime Delinq.* 40(2):291–321

Terry v. Ohio, 392 U.S. 1 (1968)

Terry v. Ohio, 392 U.S. 1 (1968).

Tonry M. 1995. *Malign Neglect: Race, Crime, and Punishment in America*. New York: Oxford Univ. Press

Truman JL, Morgan RE. 2016. *Criminal victimization, 2015*. Bull. 250180, US Dep. Justice, Bureau Justice Stat., Washington, DC. http://www.bjs.gov/content/pub/pdf/cv15.pdf

Tyler TR. 2003. Procedural justice, legitimacy, and the effective rule of law. *Crime Justice* 30:283–357

Tyler TR. 2006. *Why People Obey the Law*. Princeton, NJ: Princeton Univ. Press. 2nd ed.

Tyler TR, Fagan J. 2008. Legitimacy and cooperation: Why do people help the police fight crime in their communities? *Ohio St. J. Crim. Law* 6(1):231–75

Tyler TR, Wakslak CJ. 2004. Profiling and police legitimacy: procedural justice, attributions of motive, and acceptance of police authority. *Criminology* 42(2):253–82

Unnever JD, Gabbidon SL. 2011. *A Theory of African-American Offending*. New York: Routledge

US Dep. Justice, Fed. Bureau Investig. 2016. *Crime in the United States, 2015*. Rep., US Dep. Justice, Washington, DC. https://ucr.fbi.gov/crime-in-the-u.s/2015/crime-in-the-u.s.-2015/home

Vitale AS. 2017. *The End of Policing*. New York: Verso

Voigt R, Camp NP, Prabhakaran V, Hamilton WL, Hetey RC, et al. 2017. Language from police body camera footage shows racial disparities in officer respect. *PNAS* 114(25):6521–26

Wacquant L. 2003. America's new "peculiar institution": on the prison as surrogate ghetto. In *Punishment and Social Control*, ed. TG Blomberg, S Cohen, pp. 471–82. New York: Aldine de Gruyter. 2nd ed.

Wacquant L. 2005. The great penal leap backward: incarceration in America from Nixon to Clinton. In *The New Punitiveness: Trends, Theories, Perspectives*, ed. J Pratt, D Brown, M Brown, S Hallsworth, W Morrison, pp. 3–26. Devon, UK: Willan

Weaver VM. 2007. Frontlash: race and the development of punitive crime policy. *Stud. Am. Political Dev.* 21:230–65

Weisburd DL. 2015. The law of crime concentration and the criminology of place. *Criminology* 53(2):133–57

Weisburd DL, Telep C, Hinkle J, Eck J. 2010. Is problem-oriented policing effective in reducing crime and disorder? *Criminol. Public Policy* 9(1):139–72

Weitzer R, Brunson RK. 2009. Strategic responses to the police among inner-city youth. *Sociol. Q.* 50:235–56

Weitzer R, Brunson RK. 2015. Policing different racial groups in the United States. *Cahiers Politiestud.* 35:129–45

Weitzer R, Tuch SA. 2006. *Race and Policing in America: Conflict and Reform.* New York: Cambridge Univ. Press

Weitzer R, Tuch SA, Skogan WG. 2008. Police–community relations in a majority-black city. *J. Res. Crime Delinq.* 45:398–428

Western B. 2006. *Punishment and Inequality in America.* New York: Russell Sage Found.

Wolfgang ME, Figlio R, Sellin T. 1972. *Delinquency in a Birth Cohort.* Philadelphia: Univ. Pennsylvania Press

Young KM, Petersilia J. 2016. Keeping track: surveillance, control, and the expansion of the carceral state. *Harv. Law Rev.* 129(7):1318–60

Questions for Critical Thinking

1. How does the authors' discussion impact your own understanding of the ways in which the problems between the police and the Black and Indigenous people of color communities that they serve are rooted in a long history of discriminatory practices and contemporary proactive policing strategies?

2. The authors argue that to be effective in controlling crime and holding offenders accountable, the police need public support and cooperation? How might they go about achieving this?

3. The authors offer some strategies that could improve police–community relations and enrich police effectiveness. What do you think of their strategies? What strategies would you offer?

THE TREACHEROUS TRIANGLE

Justice, Immigration Enforcement, and Child Welfare

○ *Seth Freed Wessler*

The following essay, by investigative reporter Seth Freed Wessler, describes the intersections of the criminal justice system, immigration enforcement, and the family court systems as "a treacherous triangle" for a child that leads to the destruction of families. Through his discussion he illustrates how the everyday decisions taking place in criminal and immigration courts have real impacts on the relationships between parents and children.

Roberta's story starts when she was pulled over by local police in Phoenix, Arizona, while driving three of her five children home from a family party where she admits she had one too many beers. Local police administered a Breathalyzer and put her under arrest for drunken driving. Roberta was shuttled to the county jail and her three children were immediately placed in temporary foster care. She expected to bond out and quickly return to her children. And, if Roberta were a citizen, that's probably exactly what would have happened. But Roberta is not a citizen. She's an undocumented immigrant. So, despite the fact that she's a single mother of five who lived in the United States without any previous run-ins with law enforcement, Roberta was flagged for deportation by federal immigration authorities and moved to an immigration detention center in the desert an hour and a half south of her home. She lost contact with her children, all five of whom were placed in foster care, and after seven months inside the detention center, Roberta was deported to Mexico without her children.

Roberta's story is not unique. Federal data obtained by the Applied Research Center (ARC)

through a Freedom of Information Act (FOIA) request, and first published in *Shattered Families; The Perilous Intersection of Immigration Enforcement and the Child Welfare System,* shows that in the six month period between January and June 2011, the federal government deported over 46,000 parents of U.S. children.[1] In December 2012, ARC obtained additional federal data through another FOIA request that reveals that the federal government deported nearly 205,000 parents of U.S. citizen children during the time period between July 1, 2010, and September 30, 2012.[2] The number accounts for 23 percent of all deportations in that period.[3]

One of the most troubling effects of this mass deportation of parents and separation of families is that thousands of children languish in foster care for long periods and are sometimes put up for adoption, at least in part because of the deportation of their mother or father. Based on surveys with child welfare caseworkers, attorneys who represent parents and children in juvenile courts, and analyses of data from 22 states, the *Shattered Families* report conservatively estimated that as of late 2011, there were at least 5,100 foster children around the country who faced barriers to reunifying with their families because their mothers or fathers had been detained or deported by the federal government. These families are often separated for long periods of time, and sometimes children are permanently separated from their parents.

Although U.S. Immigration and Customs Enforcement (ICE) issued a memo in 2011 instructing its agents to use discretion to focus immigration enforcement efforts on people with "serious" criminal convictions while avoiding the deportation of people charged with low level crimes, or whose sole violation is that they lack proper immigration documentation, the most up-to-date data reveal that this discretion has scarcely been applied and many of those deported as a result of involvement with the criminal justice system have been convicted of minor violations.[4] Meanwhile, the ICE memo on prosecutorial discretion enumerated a set of factors to weigh while making deportation decisions. One of these factors is whether a potential deportee is a parent to a U.S. citizen child.[5] The recent data on parental deportations suggest that the memo has not significantly changed ICE practice. Indeed for Roberta, a DUI charge, the first blemish she's ever had on her record, made her subject to rapid movement into deportation. The consequences for her and her children are Spartan: they may never see each other again.

Expanded Role of Local Law Enforcement in Federal Immigration Enforcement

In recent years, there has been an expanding conflation of immigration and criminal laws and the systems that enforce them and, as a result, a growing proportion of deportees now come to the attention of federal immigration authorities through county and state criminal justice systems. The federal government's flagship deportation program, Secure Communities, is broadening jail-based immigration enforcement, creating a treacherous triangle of the criminal justice, immigration, and child welfare systems. The federal government under the Obama

Administration rapidly expanded collaboration with and use of local law enforcement departments to identify noncitizens for deportation. If the Bush Administration's immigration enforcement strategy can be defined by its focus on workplace immigration raids, Obama's enforcement approach is defined by its focus on local law enforcement and jails. The Obama Administration has extended its enforcement infrastructure deeply into local jails in a strategic shift putatively aimed at deporting "criminal aliens" (noncitizens convicted of criminal offenses) rather than on immigrants who have only violated noncriminal immigration laws.

Secure Communities was piloted in 2008 and rapidly expanded under the Obama Administration. The deportation program uses local jails to identify immigrants for deportation. Currently, any time someone is booked into a local jail in the United States, his or her fingerprint data are automatically run through an FBI database. In jails where Secure Communities has been implemented, the FBI forwards that same data to ICE, which then determines the person's immigration status. ICE can issue a detainer to put an immigration hold on any arrested individual who is not a citizen, including lawful permanent residents of the United States, asking the local jail to continue detaining the arrested person until ICE arrives to move him or her to an immigration detention center. Secure Communities now operates in nearly all jails in the country and is scheduled to be implemented in all remaining counties by 2013.[6] Localities have no choice whether to participate in the program; it is mandatory and, as a partnership between the FBI and ICE, functions automatically.

President Obama and the heads of his U.S. Department of Homeland Security (DHS) and ICE regularly claim that they have deported record numbers of "criminal aliens," largely as a result of this program. And, they claim that the program is colorblind, immune from the racial profiling that's plagued previous federal-local immigration partnerships. However, both claims are shaky. Well over one-quarter of deportees who come to the attention of ICE through Secure Communities have no criminal conviction at all and are deported simply for violating immigration laws, like entering the United States without authorization.[7] Another 30 percent involve minor charges, including violations like driving without a license, a common charge against undocumented immigrants who, because of laws in most states, cannot obtain drivers' licenses.[8] In fact, fewer than 30 percent of Secure Communities deportations since the program was implemented have been a result of what ICE calls "level 1" convictions, or felonies.[9] As for the claim of color-blindness, although ICE may be correct that database immigration checks are run without regard for identity, the program cannot control for the discretion local police exercise in who they arrest and book into jail. In a jurisdiction where police are interested in targeting people who they think are immigrants, Secure Communities provides a surefire mechanism for getting people deported. Rather than apprehending people who have been convicted of serious criminal offenses, Secure Communities is much more akin to a dragnet that feeds off of local police practices. The result is that any non-citizen who comes into contact with local police for whatever reason is at risk of deportation.

Increased Risk of Separation

DHS' widespread use of local jails to detain noncitizens puts families at particular risk of separation. In jurisdictions where local police aggressively participate in immigration enforcement through programs like Secure Communities, children are more likely to be separated from their parents and face barriers to reunification. ARC measured the impact of a similar local immigration enforcement program called 287(g)—the name refers to a section of the Immigration and Nationality Act. Through 287(g), ICE deputized local police and jails to act as federal immigration agents, giving them authority to arrest and detain noncitizens.

The impact of aggressive policing and local enforcement is clear when comparing counties that are otherwise similar except for 287(g) programs.[10] In counties surveyed by ARC where local police signed 287(g) agreements with ICE, children in foster care were about 29 percent more likely to have detained or deported parents than in other counties (an average of 4.9 percent of foster care kids in 287(g) counties compared to 3.8 percent in others). The difference was statistically significant when variation in the size of counties' noncitizen populations and their proximity to the border were taken into account.

An attorney for children in Tucson, Arizona, explained to the author the impact of jail-based immigration enforcement while describing a current foster care case in which a mother was picked up on charges that were entirely unrelated to the children. Considering the nature of the relatively minor allegations, had she been a citizen, the attorney had little doubt that she would have bonded out of jail in a day or two.

The attorney described a mother who was otherwise "fit" to parent, but was separated from her children for an extended period because of the federal government's use of local jails as staging grounds for deportation. The mother was not released after a day or two, but rather moved to an immigration detention center and deported.

"In this particular case, it was her inability to be with her kids because of detention and deportation that got them into care. The kids are a little older and if she had been a citizen, the children would have made do for a day and then she would have been out and back with them."

The period of separation that was caused by the mother's detention and deportation, the attorney explained, "means it's considered to be neglect now by our state's statutory regime. This case has been open two months and the kids are still in foster care."[11]

Barriers to Reunification

Once parents with children in foster care are moved to federal immigration detention centers, they are severed from the vital lines of communication that connect them with their children, the child welfare system, juvenile court, and the court-appointed attorney. According to the ARC study, ICE has categorically refused to transport parents to their juvenile court hearings. While parents are sometimes able to appear telephonically in these hearings, all of the dozens of detained parents interviewed for *Shattered Families* missed at least one hearing because they were detained.

Moreover, detained mothers and fathers are nearly always denied access to the services they need to comply with their child welfare reunification plans. In general, jails and prisons provide few parenting, drug and alcohol, and other programs for parents. The federal immigration authorities, and the counties and private prison contractors paid to run many immigration detention centers, are even less likely to provide these services. Indeed, none of the six detention centers visited during the *Shattered Families* investigation made services available to detainees. And, ARC heard reports of county jails that provide some access to services to "regular" inmates, but refused similar access to ICE detainees held in the same facility.

In the Baker County jail in Florida, which has a contract with the federal government to hold ICE detainees, a British immigrant mother of a young daughter who was in foster care received a letter from her child welfare caseworker listing tasks she was required to complete to reunify with her daughter.

> The letter read as follows: This letter is to advise you that as part of your outstanding dependency case plan tasks, you are court ordered to complete:
>
> 1. Parent Educational Training for Teens
> 2. Psychological Evaluation and follow all Court approved recommendations
> 3. Substance Abuse Evaluation and follow all Court approved recommendations
> 4. Family Counseling upon release
> 5. Stable Housing and Income. ...[12]

The mother could complete none of these requirements from within detention. The document that the caseworker sent her went on to read, "One of the tasks in your case plan is to visit with your child," but the caseworker would not drive the daughter to see her mother in the detention center located four hours away. According to a 2011 report by Human Rights Watch, detainees are on average transferred to detention centers 370 miles from their initial arrest or apprehension by immigration authorities.[13]

Paths of Separation

Detained and deported parents' children enter foster care for a variety of reasons, and the child welfare and immigration enforcement systems can intersect in a number of ways. Some children enter into the child welfare system solely because their parents are detained. Other families already have child welfare system involvement, but immigration enforcement derails the family reunification process. Though every case bares a unique set of facts, there are a number of common routes leading to the separation of families at the intersection of parental deportation and the children welfare system. In each of these scenarios, detention and deportation result in extended family separation.

Straight Path

One route is that children enter foster care as a direct result of their parents' arrest or detention. In these cases, when parents are detained by ICE directly or are arrested by police and then shuffled to immigration authorities through Secure Communities or another program, parents are not able to care for their children and their children enter into foster care.

Even if parents in these cases are eventually released from immigration detention through the discretion of immigration authorities, the fact that their children are in the custody of the child welfare system can mean that the family will not be immediately reunified. In Phoenix, Arizona, an attorney told the author of a case in which a 2-year-old girl was placed in foster care when her mother was pulled over by police and arrested because she was undocumented and was driving without a license. The author spoke with the girl's foster care provider who said without equivocation, "The only reason they're not back together yet is the bureaucracy of the system. Before they can return her to her mother, they have to verify that the mom has a stable home, everyone else in the home passes background checks and that takes time" He added that if the mother had not been detained, the child welfare system would never have been involved in this family's life. "None of these were made into problems until she was detained"

Parallel Path

The second common route entails ostensibly "normal" allegations of child maltreatment that first bring a family to the attention of the child welfare department, but because the mother or father is detained, reunification is not immediately possible. In some cases, when police are involved in child welfare investigations, a case that might have resulted in prompt reunification for a citizen parent leads instead to detention and extended separation. Parents in detention are often denied the due process right to advocate for themselves in juvenile court, and the child welfare system poses obstacles to reunifying families.

In many cases, children enter into the child welfare system after a parent is deported following abuse or neglect allegations against a remaining parent or relative. In Alleghany County, North Carolina, for example, Felipe Montes, the father of three young U.S. citizens, was deported to Mexico in late 2010 because of repeated driving violations.[14] His kids remained with their mother, Marie Montes, a U.S. citizen. Marie struggled to take care of the children alone. Her husband had been the primary wage earner and caregiver in their family and she had long struggled with mental health and substance abuse issues. The local child welfare department quickly removed the three young children from their mother, deeming her neglectful. Rather than quickly reuniting the boys with their father, a man who had never been found to be neglectful, the boys were placed in foster homes. The child welfare department refused to consider placing the children with their father in Mexico. Even after Marie and Felipe told the department that they wanted the children sent to live with their father, who now lived with an uncle and aunt in Tamaulipas, Mexico, the child welfare system continued to move toward terminating both Felipe and Marie's parental rights. After nearly two years of separation, in November 2012, Felipe regained custody of his three children on a "trial" basis and as of the writing of this article, he expects the child welfare case to be fully closed in early 2013.[15]

Interrupted Path
The third route involves families that were already involved with the child welfare system when parents are detained. Immigration enforcement can interrupt the reunification process for families that are already involved with the child welfare system when parents are taken to detention facilities. A mother, a green card holder from Portugal who we'll call Magda, interviewed by the author in a Florida detention center, was just weeks away from fully reunifying with her son. The boy had been removed from her custody previously because of child maltreatment allegations stemming from substance abuse, but the family was

well on its way to reuniting. Magda and her son were spending the afternoon together on one of their unsupervised biweekly visits when her son soiled his pants. With little money to spare, Magda walked across the street to a dollar store and stole the set of clothes he needed. She wanted to avoid taking her son back to the foster home without changing his clothes first. She didn't make it out the door. The security guard called the police, who arrested the mother for petty theft. The officers drove her son back to his foster home and the mother was placed in deportation proceedings because of the theft charge. From detention, she could do little to maintain contact with her son, and their path to reunification was interrupted. Though it's likely an arrest of this kind during a visit would interrupt any reunification process, the difference for Magda was that detention denied her the chance to continue efforts to reunify.

Child Welfare Practice after Parental Deportation
The intersection of child welfare and immigration enforcement is treacherous from all directions. Though detention and deportation separate families on the front end, once parents are deported, child welfare departments often lack clear policies to facilitate the reunification of children with their parents in other countries.

Currently, few child welfare departments systematically contact consulates when child welfare departments take custody of U.S. citizen children of a noncitizen parent. This lack of communication is significant because when foreign consulates are involved in these cases, children are sometimes reunified with their deported parents. Consulates can serve as a bridge between parents and child welfare departments. They can help mothers and fathers access case plan services in other countries, facilitate home studies, conduct searches for parents who may have been deported leaving behind children in foster care, and process passports so that children are allowed to leave the United States. Based on interviews, the practice of involving consulates when a foreign national is involved in a case is increasing in some jurisdictions, but in too many instances, parental deportation leads directly to extended and sometimes permanent family separation.

Without explicit policies to facilitate reunification with detained or deported parents, reunification decisions may be driven by systemic bias against placing children with their parents in other countries. One common barrier to the reunification of children with parents who have been deported is bias in child welfare systems, which manifests as a belief that children are better off in the United States, even if it means they will be in foster homes or placed for adoption. This bias can supersede the child welfare system's mandate to reunify families whenever possible.

Many of the attorneys, social workers, children's advocates, and judges interviewed in the *Shattered Families* investigation raised questions about prejudice against reunifying U.S. citizen children with their deported noncitizen parents. According to the *Shattered Families* research, these biases were especially pronounced from many children's attorneys, advocates, and caseworkers. A parent and child attorney in Brownsville, Texas, said,

> With the climate in Mexico, nobody wants to send any of the kids to that—it's unsafe there now. Most of the attorneys don't want to send the kids back to Mexico and their arguments are, one, poor conditions in that county and, two, they only get public education up to a certain age before the parents have to pay for it. Most of our parents don't have education themselves; they are poor and they don't have the ability to pay for further education.

Because child welfare systems are tasked primarily with reunifying children with "fit" parents, the impact of this bias raises serious due process questions about how poverty, immigration status, and national origin may be used inappropriately to determine parental fitness.

These biases can compound anxieties among child welfare attorneys and courts about giving up jurisdiction over a dependency case, even if that case was near closure. A judge in Pima County took this position explicitly: "As a general matter, everyone is hesitant about placing a kid in another country because, from a practical standpoint, we are going to lose control of the case. Once I place the child [in another country], the judge basically ends up being asked to dismiss the

dependency." Without clear agreements with foreign consulates to take part in the transition of children from the United States to reunify with their parents, there's nothing to soothe these anxieties, and children can remain in foster care that might otherwise be reunified with their parents.

Recommendations

If the number of deported parents remains anywhere near the 2011 level, families will continue to be separated and children will continue to become stuck in foster care. This year, the Obama Administration offered a reprieve from deportation and work permits to young immigrants who entered or were brought into the United States without authorization before they were age 16 and who do not have criminal convictions. The deferred action for childhood arrivals policy could protect hundreds of thousands of young people from deportation. Yet some have asked, "What about these young immigrants' parents?" In September during a forum aired on Univision, the president was asked directly if he would consider granting a similar deferral of removal to parents of U.S. citizen children. President Obama did not offer a clear response, but the question placed such a policy shift on the table.[16]

Suspend Secure Communities
Meanwhile, immigrant rights advocates around the country are advocating for a suspension of the Secure Communities program. As *Shattered Families* found, the use of local jails in identifying non-citizens puts families at risk of separation and increases the chances that children in foster care will have parents who are detained and deported. Advocates call for an end to Secure Communities on the grounds that it is not the selective, targeted enforcement program that the administration claims it to be and that it separates families. In California, the legislature passed a bill that would have instructed local jails to refuse to participate in the program. The bill, called the TRUST Act, was ultimately vetoed by California Governor Jerry Brown, but a number of counties, including Cook County, home to Chicago, and Washington, D.C., have passed ordinances similar to the TRUST Act. By interrupting the pipeline from local jails to

deportation, families might be spared separation or allowed the time and space to reunite.

Minimize the Use of Detention before Deportation
If the federal government ultimately decides to deport parents, minimizing the use of detention before deportation could help reduce the prevalence of foster care cases. Were mothers and fathers released on their own recognizance while their immigration cases proceed, they could fully participate in decision-making about their children. As things stand, detention often makes this nearly impossible.

Train Child Welfare Departments and Attorneys
Short of changing immigration policy, child welfare departments around the country are the frontline in preventing the prolonged separation of children from their deported parents. These departments, however, often lack clear policies and guidelines to ensure that detained immigrant parents are provided with appropriate due process. Child welfare departments and juvenile courts can implement trainings for child welfare staff and attorneys who represent children and parents in juvenile dependency hearings to improve their understanding of the circumstances facing detained immigrant parents.

Legislative and Administrative Policy Reforms
Child welfare policies, protocols, and guidelines can be developed to specifically address detained and deported immigrant parents. The California legislature recently passed two pieces of legislation that would help reunify families separated by immigration enforcement and the child welfare system. California legislation, the Reuniting Immigrant Families Act (SB 1064) would authorize juvenile court judges to provide detained or deported parents additional time to reunify with their children and require state child welfare authorities to offer guidance to counties about how to establish agreements with foreign consulates.[17] The bill would also prohibit child welfare departments from considering immigration status when making foster care placement decisions. A similar federal bill, the Help Separated Families Act (H.R. 6128), was introduced, but not yet passed in Congress.

Most components of the California and federal legislation could be adopted via administrative reforms at the state or federal level. For example, a number of county and state child welfare departments around the country have had Memorandum of Understanding (MOU) with foreign consulates for a number of years, most often with the Mexican consulate. These MOUs could be adopted without legislative action. Similarly, at least one state, Illinois, has a clear policy that excludes immigration status from consideration in potential kinship placements.[18] In addition to child welfare departments, juvenile courts could also enter into MOUs with foreign consulates directly, such as the agreement developed by Los Angeles County Juvenile Court and the Mexican consulate.

A second California bill, the Call for Kids Act (AB 2015), would provide incarcerated immigrant parents with clear information in their native language about their right to make two phone calls at the time of arrest, clearly post this right in the jail/police location, and provide an additional two phone calls at the time of their transfer from local law enforcement to a federal detention facility.[19] Because immigrants in the criminal justice system are often moved quickly to immigration detention, the additional phone calls could help parents with childcare arrangements at the time of transfer so that they do not simply disappear into detention. This bill will also help incarcerated parents in general, by providing all parents in the criminal justice system with greater access to the world outside their cells.

Roberta, the mother whose case was described at the opening of this chapter, was deported late last year and has still not been reunified with her children. According to a local legal services provider who has intermittent contact with Roberta, two of the kids have now been placed in the care of relatives, while three remain in foster care with nonrelatives. With no likely route for her to return to the United States given the mandatory ten-year bar for illegal entry and lack of responsiveness from the child welfare department, she and her children will likely be separated for years. The policy and practice changes discussed here could help to keep other families from facing a similar fate.

Notes

1. Wessler, S. F. (2012). *Shattered families: The perilous intersection of immigration enforcement and the child welfare system.* Applied Research Center. Retrieved from http://www.arc.org/shatteredfamilies.
2. U.S. Immigration and Customs Enforcement. *Deportation of Parents of U. C. Citizen Children July 1, 2010-September 30, 2013.* Accessed by Colorlines.com on December 12, 2012. http://colorlines.com/archives/2012/12/deportations of parents of us-born citizens 122012.html.
3. *Ibid.*
4. Preston, J. (June 6, 2012). Deportations continue despite U.S. review of backlog, *New York Times,* Retrieved from http://www.nytimes.com/2012/06/07/us/politics/deportations-continue-despite-us-review-of-backlog.html?r=2&smid=tw-share.
5. Morton, J. (2012). ICE Memorandum. *Exercising prosecutorial discretion consistent with the civil immigration enforcement priorities of the agency for the apprehension, detention, and removal of aliens.* Retrieved from http://www.icc.gov/doclib/secure-communities/pdf/prosecutrial-discretion-memo.pdf.
6. U.S. Immigration and Customs Enforcement. *Secure Communities: Activated jurisdictions.* Retrieved from http://www.ice.gov/doclib/secure-communities/pdf/sc-activated.pdf.
7. U.S. Immigration and Customs Enforcement. *Secure Communities: Monthly statistics through April 30, 2012.* Retrieved from http://www.icc.gov/doclib/foia/sc-stats/nationwide_interop_ stats-fy2012-to-date.pdf.
8. *Ibid. 6.*
9. *Ibid. 6.*
10. *Ibid. 1.*
11. Anonymous interview by author, Tucson, Arizona. July 7, 2011.
12. Documents provided to author.
13. Human Rights Watch. *A costly move: Far and frequent transfers impede hearings for immigrant detainees in the United States.* Retrieved from http://www.htw.org/reports/2011/06/14/costly-move-0.<CE: Invalid URL - http://www.htw.org/reports/2011/06/14/costly-move-0. Please check.><ED: Is there another way to access this source, since the URL is invalid indeed?>
14. Seth Freed Wessler. "Deported Dad Begs North Carolina to Give Him Back His Kids," Colorlines. com, February 14, 2012. http://colorlines.com/archives/2012/02/deported_dad_begs_north_carolina_not_put_kids_into_adoption.html.
15. Seth Freed Wessler, "A Deported Father Wins a Long, Painful Fight to Keep His Kids," Colorlines. com November 28, 2012. http://colorlines.com/archives/2012/n/pc_judge_reunites_deported_father_with_three_us_citizen_children.html.
16. Rivas, J. (September 21, 2012). *Univision anchor cites Colorlines.com deportation investigation.* Colorlines. com. Retrieved from http://colorlines.com/archives/2012/09/univision_anchor_cites_colorlinescom_deportation_investigation_to_obama.html.
17. SB 1064, 2011–2012 Leg., Reg. Sess. (CA 2012). Retrieved from http://legiscan.com/gaits/text/574600. Illinois Department of Children and Family Services. *Licensing, payment and placement of children with undocumented relatives. III. Policy guide* 2008.01. Retrieved from http://www.f2f.ca.gov/res/pdf/PolicyGuideLicensing.pdf.
18. Illinois Department of Children and Family Services. Licensing, payment and placement of children with undocumented relatives. III. Policy guide 2008.01. Retrieved from http://www.f2f.ca.gov/ res/pdf/PolicyGuideLicensing.pdf.
19. AB 2015, 2011–2012 Leg., Reg Sess. (CA 2012). http://loginfo.legislature.ca.gov/faces/billText-Client.xhtml; jsessionid=fb26709e73be6c01b88669 26a8c2?bill_2011 20120AB2015.

Questions for Critical Thinking

1. Wessler asserts that, although instructed to focus on immigration enforcement on people with serious criminal convictions, agents of Immigration and Customs Enforcement often target those with minor convictions. Why do you think this is? How does this reality reinforce or counter your own assumptions about immigration enforcement?

2. What policy changes do you see as necessary in our policies around immigration enforcement? How might these changes impact inequality on the basis of immigration status in the United States?

3. Wessler offers several recommendations to help alleviate the inequality that results from current immigration enforcement policies. What do you think of these? What additional recommendations do you have to offer?

Social Institutions: Media

THE DIGITAL REPRODUCTION OF INEQUALITY

* *Eszter Hargittai*

The following essay, by communication studies professor and sociologist Eszter Hargittai, explores the notion of digital inequality, represented by differential access to online resources and technology depending on one's class position. As the author illustrates, differential access results in exacerbating social inequalities.

By the beginning of the twenty-first century, information and communication technologies (ICT) had become a staple of many people's everyday lives. The level of instantaneous connectivity—to others and to an abundance of information—afforded by advances in ICT is unprecedented. With economies increasingly dependent on knowledge-intensive activities, the unequal distribution of knowledge and information access across the population may be linked increasingly to stratification. No sooner did the Internet start diffusing to the general population in the mid-1990s than did debates spring up about its implications for social inequality. From the perspective of social mobility, digital media could offer people, organizations, and societies the opportunity to improve their positions regardless of existing constraints. From the point of view of social reproduction, however, ICT could exacerbate existing inequalities by increasing the opportunities available to the already privileged while leading to the growing marginalization of the disadvantaged.

Most initial attention concerning ICT's implications for social stratification focused on what segments of the population have access to the Internet or are Internet users (e.g., Bimber 2000; Hoffman and Novak 1998). Access is usually defined as having a network-connected machine in one's home or workplace. Use more specifically refers to people's actual use of the medium beyond merely having access to it. The term "digital divide" became a popular expression to sum up concerns about the unequal diffusion of the medium. The concept is most often understood in binary terms: someone either has access to the medium or does not, someone either uses the Internet or does not.

However, as an increasing portion of the population has gone online, a dichotomous approach is no longer sufficient to address the different dimensions of inequality associated with digital media uses.

Originally appeared as Hargittai, E. (2008). The Digital Reproduction of Inequality. In *Social Stratification*. Edited by David Grusky, Boulder, CO: Westview Press. 936–44. © 2008 Eszter Hargittai.

The term *digital inequality* better captures the spectrum of differences associated with ICT uses (DiMaggio et al. 2004). A more refined approach considers different aspects of the divide, focusing on such details as quality of equipment, autonomy of use, the presence of social support networks, experience and user skills, in addition to differences in types of uses (Barzilai-Nahon 2006; Dewan and Riggins 2006; DiMaggio et al. 2004; Mossberger, Tolbert, and Stansbury 2003; Norris 2001; van Dijk 2005; Warschauer 2003).

Variation in basic usage rates continues to exist, so considering the core digital divide of access versus no access remains an important undertaking. However, to understand in a nuanced manner the implications of ICT for social inequality, it is important to analyze differences among users as well. This chapter will do both, starting with a historical look at connectivity patterns by population segments. This discussion is then followed by an explanation of why it is important to distinguish among users of digital media. A conceptual framework lays out the processes through which users' social position influences their ICT uses and how this in turn may contribute to social inequality even among the connected. Although the primary focus here is on Internet use in the United States, the main arguments made can be extended to the use of other digital devices in other national contexts as well.

The Haves and Have Nots

In 1995, the National Telecommunications Information Administration of the U.S. Department of Commerce published a report entitled "Falling Through the Net: A Survey of the 'Have Nots' in Rural and Urban America" in which policy makers analyzed data from the Current Population Survey about computer and modem use among Americans. Findings suggested that different segments of the population were using digital technologies at varying rates. In subsequent years, these reports began to focus increasingly on Internet access as opposed to computer use only, documenting continued differences among various population groups (NTIA 1998, 1999, 2000). The reports' titles highlighted concerns about inequality as they all began with the phrase "Falling Through the Net."

Breaking with tradition, the fifth report of the NTIA published in 2002, based on data collected in 2001, was called "A Nation Online: How Americans Are Expanding Their Use of the Internet" (NTIA 2002). The title of this last report no longer focused on differences. Rather, it highlighted the fact that more and more Americans were going online. While significant differences remained among various population segments regarding their rates of connectivity, the report focused on the growing number of people accessing the Internet through high-speed connections. This change in focus may imply that Internet use had reached universal levels, but that was not the case.

Overall findings from the reports suggested that while the Internet may have been spreading to an increasing portion of the American population, certain segments were much more likely to be online than others. In particular, men, younger people, whites, non-Hispanics, urban residents, the more highly educated, and those with higher income were more connected than their counterparts. Gender differences leveled off after a few years with respect to basic access (Ono and Zavodny 2003) although not regarding amount of use and skill (Hargittai and Shafer 2006). In contrast, all other differences in access among different population segments remained throughout the years.

Looking at adoption figures over time, we find that while all segments increased their participation significantly, disparities continued to persist. Figures 1 and 2 illustrate this point for income and education, respectively. As Figure 1 shows, people in all income brackets increased their participation over time, but the slopes in the higher income brackets are somewhat steeper, leading to an increased gap among groups over time. The data points in Figure 2 tell a similar story. Although the gap between those who have a college degree and graduate education narrowed over the years, all other gaps widened over time. In particular, the least educated—those with less than a high school degree—increased their connectivity minimally over the eight-year period. Overall, these trend data suggest that while all population segments may have become increasingly connected, serious divides persist with the most disadvantaged trailing behind the more privileged in significant ways.

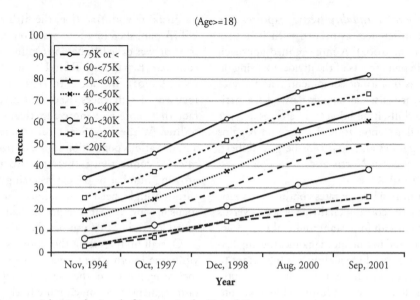

FIGURE 1.   Internet Adoption by Level of Income in the United States, 1994–2001.

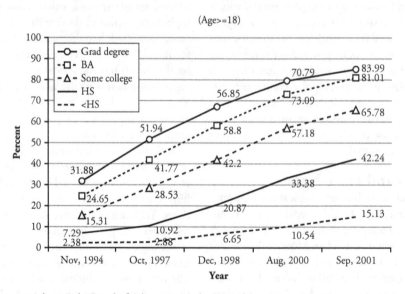

FIGURE 2.   Internet Adoption by Level of Education in the United States, 1994–2001.

We have less data on the diffusion of cell phones, but the little evidence that has surfaced suggests similar patterns of unequal distribution among the population. Looking at the earlier years of diffusion using data from 1994–1998, researchers found that mobile technology adoption was positively related to both income and education (Wareham, Levy, and Shi 2004). Based on data from 2006, Horrigan showed that people with lower levels of income were less likely to be users (Horrigan 2006). Analyses (by Hargittai for this chapter) of these same data collected by the Pew Internet and American Life Project also found that those with higher levels of education were more likely to own cell phones, and these

findings are robust (also for income) when controlling for other factors. Moreover, those with higher income tend to own cell phones with more functionality (e.g., the ability to send and receive text messages, take photos and go online). While this literature is not as elaborate as the one on different rates of Internet connectivity, these findings clearly suggest that the digital divide expands beyond Internet use into the domain of mobile technology adoption as well.

Differences among the Connected

The uses of ICT can differ considerably with divergent outcomes for one's life chances. Therefore, it is imperative to examine variations in use among those who have crossed the digital divide fault line to the land of the connected. Baseline Internet use statistics do not distinguish among those who go online for no more than checking sports scores or TV schedules and those who use the medium for learning new skills, finding deals and job opportunities, participating in political discussions, interacting with government institutions, and informing themselves about health matters. Yet such differentiated uses can have significant implications for how ICT uses may relate to life outcomes. This section describes how various user characteristics and one's social surroundings influence digital media uses.

People's Internet uses do not happen in isolation of their societal position and the social institutions they inhabit. A refined approach to digital inequality recognizes that people's socioeconomic status influences the ways in which they have access to and use ICT. In addition to factors such as age, gender, race, ethnicity, disability status, education, and wealth, one's social surroundings are also relevant to one's ICT experiences. Figure 3 presents a graphical representation of this framework.

The basic premise is that the societal position that users inhabit influences aspects of their digital media uses, such as the technical equipment to which they have access and the level of autonomy they possess when using the medium. Autonomy of use is understood as the freedom to use digital media when and where one wants to. Twenty-four-hour access at home can yield a much more autonomous user experience than having to drive half an hour to a public library where one competes with others for usage time and

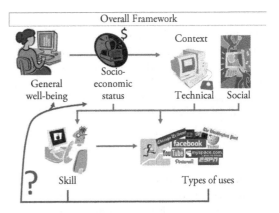

FIGURE 3. **Framework for Studying the Implications of ICT Use for Social Inequality.**

where filtering software limits the types of materials within reach. Similarly, a workplace that allows Web use without constraints results in a very different experience from a job environment where one's online actions are constantly monitored. Quality of equipment (available hardware, software, and connection speed) and autonomy of use can both be a function of one's socioeconomic status.

The use of and learning about digital media both happen in social contexts. In addition to autonomy of use, which itself is a certain social context, the availability of other users in one's social circles can have important implications for one's online experiences. The relevant mechanisms through which social networks matter can be grouped into two main categories: informal and more directed information exchange. The former refers to knowledge one amasses through everyday discussions with peers about digital media uses and includes suggestions passed along by others through email or at the water cooler. The latter highlights the importance of support networks when users encounter a specific problem during their experiences with ICT. When faced with a difficulty, it makes a difference to have access to knowledgeable networks that help in finding a solution.

All of these factors then influence users' online abilities and what they are able to accomplish using digital media. While many online actions may seem trivial to the experienced user, most activities require some level of know-how. From recognizing what material is available online to being able to find it efficiently, from knowing how to contribute to online content production to knowing where to find relevant networks, from having the ability to evaluate content credibility to being vigilant about privacy and security concerns, informed uses of digital media rely on many important skills (Hargittai 2007b).

One's social position, the context of one's use, and one's online abilities then all have the potential to influence the types of uses to which one puts the medium. Some uses are more likely to yield beneficial outcomes than others. The next section will enumerate the ways in which ICT uses may improve, or in some cases impede, one's life chances.

How ICT Use Matters

The most pressing question for students of social inequality is whether the usage dimensions described above then loop back and translate into differences in users' socioeconomic position. What are the processes through which more informed and frequent uses of ICT may privilege some users over others? There are several ways in which differential ICT uses may influence access to the types of assets, resources, and valued goods that underlie stratification systems (Grusky 2008). The overarching idea is that certain types of ICT uses can result in increased human capital, financial capital, social capital, and cultural capital while other types of uses may outright disadvantage the uninformed.

With more and more jobs requiring the synthesis and analysis of varying types of information, employees with advanced Internet user skills can perform their jobs more effectively and efficiently. The Internet makes vast amounts of information available *so long as* one knows how to locate desired material. While theoretically all public Web pages are equally available to all users, not everybody possesses the necessary skills to (1) recognize in all situations the types of content relevant to a task that can be found online; (2) find the information; (3) do so efficiently; and (4) carefully evaluate the results to avoid misinformation or, worse, fraudulent outcomes.

Even if people do not know how to perform certain tasks, advanced skills will allow them to find assistance online. Since skill encompasses the ability to find others who may have the desired information

and efficiently contact them for guidance, even when lacking know-how most relevant to the task at hand, the skilled user can benefit through informed use of the medium. This all leads to more tasks getting done quicker and more efficiently with possibly higher-quality results than would be possible if relying on fewer resources. In addition to helping with the performance of on-the-job tasks, ICT also allow people to develop additional skills that may advantage them in the labor market. Free tutorials exist online for training in a myriad of domains from foreign languages to software applications, from design skills to networking to productivity enhancement tips.

Enterprising ways of using the Internet can save a person significant amounts of money. Several services exist that make comparison shopping very easy, allowing the user to find the best deals on an item without spending money on gas and time on driving from one store to the next. The use of auction sites expands options even further. Moreover, the especially knowledgeable can take advantage of other people's mistakes by searching for items with spelling mistakes thereby avoiding bidding wars given that misspelled items are seen by few (Hargittai 2006). In addition to savings through informed purchasing, people can also make money by selling products on the Web. While putting one's items on the market used to require significant upfront investment, ICT have lowered the barriers to entry for putting things up for sale accessible to a large buyer base, assuming one knows what services help with reaching the largest or most relevant purchasers.

The potential of ICT for expanding one's social networks is enormous, although efficient and relevant ways of doing so are not trivial and require some amount of know how. In some cases the Internet simply complements more traditional methods of networking while in others the medium is the main facilitator of a new relationship. The former refers to use of the tool to contact people who are already in one's extended network. The latter occurs thanks to various online interactions that can range from the exchange of information on a mailing list to the exchange of goods and services extending well beyond the Web. People find rides, coordinate meetings, and get emotional support from others online. But as with all other aspects of Internet use, skill matters. Finding the relevant communities and being sufficiently vigilant not to place oneself in harm's way are all important aspects of building social capital on the Web.

Familiarity with the latest trends can serve as status markers. Being able to discuss special topics in depth can help create bonds between people. Thanks to the Internet, certain subjects formerly much less accessible to the general public are more widely available. It is no longer necessary to go see a museum's special exhibition to have the facility to discuss what is on display since many galleries now put their pieces online. It is possible to develop a reasonably informed opinion about a restaurant halfway across the world simply by reading the many reviews available and constantly updated online. Knowing how to locate information about travel destinations—from driving directions to entertainment options—can yield more influence to the informed. Being able to draw on a myriad of topics while conversing with higher-ups can leave a good impression. While resources about diverse topics have long been available to the public, the ease and speed with which the Internet delivers information are unprecedented.

Informed users can be more engaged in the political process than those who rely exclusively on broadcast media for their political information seeking. Whether finding like-minded people or informing oneself in depth about the other side's perspective, the Internet allows for the exchange of political opinions much more than any other medium. Creating petitions and mobilizing others around a cause can be facilitated significantly with various online tools. Again, however, knowledge of what is available in this domain and how one can implement the services to benefit one's specific needs and interests is an essential part of any such undertaking.

The above are examples of how informed uses can have beneficial outcomes. There is another side to online actions, however. Uninformed uses may have outright problematic if not detrimental consequences. Do users stop to think about the context of, for example, an email message that requests confidential information from them? If everyone was aware of

these issues, then phishing emails—messages that pretend to be from a reputable source to extract confidential information from users—would not lead to people giving up their passwords to Web sites that contain private information such as their bank accounts. Yet, we know that even among young adults—the generation that is growing up with these media—many lack the necessary knowledge to approach possibly malicious email with care (Hargittai 2008). While fraud has always existed, the scope of malicious activities and their consequences have skyrocketed.

Related to online social interactions discussed above, but sufficiently distinct to merit its own discussion, is one's reputation developed from one's online pursuits. Sending emails from the privacy of one's home or office leads many to behave less carefully than they would in a public social setting. Few interactions on the Web are truly anonymous yet many people do not realize this when sending critical messages or posting comments on Web sites. An unwelcome remark can have negative consequences if targeting the wrong person. Alternatively, critical comments by others can tarnish the reputation of the person under attack. In contrast, a well-thought-out online presence can result in significant benefits. Those who participate regularly in online discussions and maintain Web sites frequented by many can amass fame that can later translate into fortune as well.

Generally speaking, many of the skills needed to reap the benefits listed here—or sidestep negative implications—can be learned from one's immediate networks. Growing up in a household that has the latest gadgets and digital media resources will make a difference when a student then encounters these tools in the classroom. Having siblings who can navigate the technologies will help in the transfer of relevant know-how. Living in neighborhoods where many in one's proximity are also discovering the latest ICT options will allow for more opportunities to develop savvy in the domain of digital media than a situation in which one is isolated without access to relevant technologies and knowledgeable networks. Bourdieu's cultural capital (1973) applied to the twenty-first century must incorporate the differential exposure to, understanding, and use of ICT.

Work looking at young adults' digital literacy has found a statistically significant positive relationship between Internet savvy and the parental education of respondents (Hargittai 2007b).

Overall, it is important to recognize that ICT do not nullify the effects of other variables on one's life chances. People's ICT uses happen in the context of their lives, influenced by their socioeconomic status and social surroundings. The question is whether ICT uses have an independent effect on life outcomes. Given the relative newness of the Internet and other digital media uses at a mass societal level, this field is in its infancy and lacks the longitudinal data necessary to answer many of the questions raised here. Nonetheless, preliminary findings seem to suggest that ICT reinforce inequalities more than alleviating differences. Although not without its critics (DiNardo and Pischke 1997), the general consensus seems to be that skill-biased technological change, and especially computerization, is an important source of the rise in earnings inequality in recent years (Krueger 1993). A more recent study found Internet use to have an independent effect on wage differences, suggesting tangible outcomes of being among the connected (DiMaggio and Bonikowski 2006).

Luxury Good or Essential Tool?

In 2001, then chair of the Federal Communication Commission Michael Powell likened the digital divide to a luxury car divide, stating: "I think there is a Mercedes divide, I would like to have one, but I can't afford one" (quoted in Clewley 2001).

Is Internet use simply a luxury item with people's connectivity—or lack thereof—merely a reflection of their preferences for the medium? As ICT become ever more central to our social infrastructure one can no longer participate meaningfully in our society without deep and ongoing usage of digital media. Once an entire society is built around these tools, they can no longer be considered simply as luxury goods. While the car and the telephone may have, at one time, been regarded as extravagant expenditures of the wealthy, once contemporary society was thoroughly built around these innovations they became necessities for operating in society and those who lacked them were socially excluded.

While it may be that some people opt out of ICT use based on an informed understanding of all that the Internet has to offer, much more likely is that people do not realize the many necessities and benefits of digital media. As an increasing number of activities between institutions and individuals move online—concerning both the public and the private sector—being a nonuser will have growing implications for people's access to various services. If government institutions assume a familiarity with and access to the medium, then lacking access to and understanding of such resources, some will be unable to interact with and navigate the system optimally.

Take, for example, the case of Medicare Part D in 2006. The government introduced a new system and required the elderly to make important choices about their health insurance. In response to concerns about the difficulty of navigating the system, the administration created a Web site and directed people to it for assistance with the program (Freese, Rivas, and Hargittai 2006). However, the resource was very complicated to navigate for many and the assumption that the elderly could access and understand the site was unfounded, as many were uninformed about or confused by the system. Similarly, more and more commercial services make material available on the Web and charge extra fees to those who interact with the company offline. When important government services are primarily accessible online and when there is an extra financial cost to handling matters with businesses offline, then having access to the Internet and knowing how to use it can no longer be considered an optional luxury item.

Conclusion

Disparities in people's Web-use abilities and uses have the potential to contribute to social inequalities rather than alleviate them. Those who know how to navigate the Web's vast landscape and how to use digital media to address their needs can reap significant benefits from it. In contrast, those who lack abilities in these domains may have a harder time dealing with certain logistics of everyday life, may miss out on opportunities, and may also obtain incorrect information from unreliable sources or come to rely on unsubstantiated rumors. Differentiated uses of digital media have the potential to lead to increasing inequalities benefiting those who are already in advantageous positions and denying access to better resources to the underprivileged. Merton's (1973) observation "Unto every one who hath shall be given"

applies to this domain. Preliminary findings from this emerging field suggest that initial advantages translate into increasing returns over time for the digitally connected and digitally skilled.

References

Barzilai-Nahon, Karine. 2006. "Gaps and Bits: Conceptualizing Measurements for Digital Divide/s" *Information Society* 22: 269–78.

Bimber, B. 2000. "The Gender Gap on the Internet" *Social Science Quarterly* 81: 868–76.

Bourdieu, Pierre. 1973. "Cultural Reproduction and Social Reproduction." Pp. 71–112 in *Knowledge, Education, and Cultural Change*, edited by Richard Brown. London: Tavistock.

Clewley, Robin. 2001. "I Have a (Digital) Dream." In *Wired*, http://www.wired.com/politics/law/news/2001/04/43349.

Dewan, S., and F. Riggins. 2006. "The Digital Divide: Current and Future Research Directions." *Journal of the Association of Information Systems* 6: 298–337.

DiMaggio, Paul and Bart Bonikowski. 2006. "Make Money Surfing the Web? The Impact of Internet Use on the Earnings of U.S. Workers." *American Sociological Review* 73(2): 227–250.

DiMaggio, Paul, Eszter Hargittai, Coral Celeste, and Steven Shafer. 2004. "Digital Inequality: From Unequal Access to Differentiated Use." Pp. 355–400 in *Social Inequality*, edited by Kathryn Necker-man. New York: Russell Sage Foundation.

DiNardo, John E., and Jorn-Steffen Pischke. 1997. "The Returns to Computer Use Revisited: Have Pencils Changed the Wage Structure Too?" *Quarterly Journal of Economics* 112: 291–303.

Freese, Jeremy, Salvador Rivas, and Eszter Hargittai. 2006. "Cognitive Ability and Internet Use Among Older Adults." *Poetics* 34: 236–49.

Grusky, David B. 2008. *Social Stratification: Class, Race, and Gender in Sociological Perspective*. Boulder, CO: Westview Press.

Hargittai, Eszter. 2006. "Hurdles to Information Seeking: Explaining Spelling and Typographical Mistakes in Users' Online Search Behavior." *Journal of the Association of Information Systems* 7. http://jais.aisnet.org/articles/default.asp?vol=7&art=1.

_____. 2007b. "A Framework for Studying Differences in People's Digital Media Uses." In *Cyberworld*

Unlimited?, edited by Nadia Kutscher and Hans-Uwe Otto. Wiesbaden: VS Verlag für Sozialwissenschaften/GWV Fachverlage GmbH. Pp. 121–37.

_____. 2008. "The Role of Expertise in Navigating Links of Influence." In *The Hyperlinked Society*, edited by Joseph Turow and Lokman Tsui. Ann Arbor: University of Michigan Press. Pp. 85–103.

Hargittai, Eszter and Steven Shafer. 2006. "Differences in Actual and Perceived Online Skills: The Role of Gender" *Social Science Quarterly* 87(2): 432–48. June.

Hoffman, D. L., and T. P. Novak. 1998. "Bridging the Racial Divide on the Internet" Pp. 390–91 in *Science* 280(5362).

Horrigan, John. 2006. "Tech Users: What They Have, How It Matters." In *KMB Video Journal Conference*. St. Petersburg Beach, Florida.

Krueger, Alan. 1993. "How Computers Have Changed the Wage Structure: Evidence from Microdata, 1984–1989" *Quarterly Journal of Economics* 108: 33–60.

Merton, R. K. 1973. *The Sociology of Science: Theoretical and Empirical Investigations*. Chicago: University of Chicago Press.

Mossberger, Karen, Caroline J. Tolbert, and Mary Stansbury. 2003. *Virtual Inequality: Beyond the Digital Divide*. Washington, DC: Georgetown University Press.

National Telecommunications and Information Administration. 1998. *"Falling Through the Net II: New Data on the Digital Divide."* Washington, DC: NTIA.

_____. 1999. *"Falling Through the Net: Defining the Digital Divide."* Washington, DC: NTIA.

_____. 2000. *"Falling Through the Net: Toward Digital Inclusion."* Washington, DC: NTIA.

_____. 2002. *"A Nation Online: How Americans Are Expanding Their Use of the Internet."* Washington, DC: NTIA.

Norris, P. 2001. *Digital Divide: Civic Engagement, Information Poverty and the Internet in Democratic Societies*, New York: Cambridge University Press.

Ono, Hiroshi, and Madeline Zavodny. 2003. "Gender and the Internet." *Social Science Quarterly* 84: 111–21.

van Dijk, Jan A. G. M. 2005. *The Deepening Divide.* London: Sage Publications.

Wareham, Jonathan, Armando Levy, and Wei Shi. 2004. "Wireless Diffusion and Mobile Computing: Implications for the Digital Divide." *Telecommunications Policy* 28: 439–57.

Warschauer, M. 2003. *Technology and Social Inclusion.* Cambridge, MA: MIT Press.

Questions for Critical Thinking

1. Hargittai asserts that the use of information and communication technologies exacerbates social inequality, granting even greater benefits to those who already have access to a greater amount of resources. How does this occur?

2. Many have long argued that technologies like the internet will help to alleviate inequality because of the availability and accessibility of information to everyone. How does Hargittai's argument support or refute this assertion?

3. To alleviate inequality with regard to information and communication technologies, what policy changes do you think need to occur? Would it be possible to achieve these changes?

WINNEBAGOS, CHEROKEES, APACHES, AND DAKOTAS

The Persistence of Stereotyping of American Indians in American Advertising Brands

• *Debra Merskin*

The following essay by journalism professor Debra Merskin examines how stereotypes of Native Americans are created and used in advertising to perpetuate stereotypes. The author asserts that these images build on long-standing assumptions about Native Americans by whites and reinforce an ideology that has resulted in many consumers failing to see this form of racism.

From early childhood on, we have all learned about "Indianness" from textbooks, movies, television programs, cartoons, songs, commercials, fanciful paintings, and product logos.[1] Since the turn of the century, American Indian images, music, and names have been incorporated into many American advertising campaigns and product images. Whereas patent medicines of the past featured "coppery, feather-topped visage of the Indian" (Larson, 1937, p. 338), butter boxes of the present show the doe-eyed, buckskin-clad Indian "princess" These stereotypes are pervasive, but not necessarily consistent—varying over time and place from the "artificially idealistic" (noble savage) to present-day images of "mystical environmentalists or uneducated, alcoholic bingo-players confined to reservations" (Mihesuah, 1996, p. 9). Yet today a trip down the grocery store aisle still reveals ice cream bars, beef jerky, corn meal, baking powder, malt liquor, butter, honey, sour cream, and chewing tobacco packages emblazoned with images of American Indians. Companies that use these images of Indians do so to build an association with

an idealized and romanticized notion of the past through the process of branding (Aaker & Biel, 1993). Because these representations are so commonplace (Land O' Lakes maiden, Jeep Cherokee, Washington Redskins logo), we often fail to notice them, yet they reinforce long-held stereotypical beliefs about Native Americans.

Trade characters such as Aunt Jemima (pancake mix), Uncle Rastus (Cream of Wheat), and Uncle Ben (rice) are visual reminders of the subservient occupational positions to which Blacks often have been relegated (Kern-Foxworth, 1994). Similarly, Crazy Horse Malt Liquor, Red Chief Sugar, and Sue Bee Honey similarly remind us of an oppressive past. How pictorial metaphors on product labels create and perpetuate stereotypes of American Indians is the focus of this study. McCracken's (1993) Meaning Transfer Model and Barthes's (1972) semiotic analysis of brand images serve as the framework for the analysis of four national brands. The following sections discuss how stereotypes are constructed and how they are articulated in, and perpetuated through, advertising.

Background

To understand how labels on products and brand names reinforce long-held stereotypical beliefs, we must consider beliefs already in place that facilitated this process. Goings (1994), in his study of African American stereotypes, points out that, "Racism was not a byproduct of the Civil War; it had clearly been around since the founding of the nation" (p. 7). Similarly, anti-Indian sentiments did not begin with the subjugation and dislocation efforts of the 1800s. Racial and ethnic images, part of American advertising for more than a century, were created in "less enlightened times" but have become a part of American popular culture and thought (Graham, 1993, p. 35) and persist today. The system of representation thereby becomes a "stable cultural convention that is taught and learned by members of a society" (Kates & Shaw-Garlock, 1999, p. 34).

Part of the explanation for the persistent use of these images can be found in the power and persuasiveness of popular culture representations. Goings's (1994) analysis of Black collectibles and memorabilia from the 1880s to the 1950s is a useful analogy for understanding the construction of Native American stereotypes in popular culture. He suggests that "collectible" items such as salt and pepper shakers, trade cards, and sheet music with images of happy Sambos, plump mammies, or wide-eyed pickaninnies served as nonverbal articulations of racism made manifest in everyday goods. By exaggerating the physical features of African American men and women, and making them laughable and useable in everyday items, these household objects reinforced beliefs about the place of Blacks in American society. Aunt Jemima, the roly-poly mammy; and Uncle Rastus, the happy slave chef (ironically both remain with us today) helped make Whites feel more comfortable with, and less guilty about, maintenance of distinctions on the basis of race well after Reconstruction.

These items were meant for daily use, hence constantly and subtly reinforcing stereotypical beliefs.

Similarly, Berkhofer (1979) suggests that "the essence of the white image of the Indian has been the definition of American Indians in fact and in fancy as a separate and single other. Whether evaluated as noble or ignoble, whether seen as exotic or downgraded, the Indian as image was always alien to white" (p. xv). White images of Native Americans were similarly constructed through children's games, toys, tales, art, and theater of the 1800s. Whereas "Little Black Sambo" tales reinforced the construction of racist beliefs about Blacks, songs such as "Ten Little Indians" or "cowboy and Indian" games similarly framed Indian otherness in the White mind. Goings (1994) makes an important point about the source of the construction of objects that represent this way of thinking:

> It is important to note that Black memorabilia are figures from white American history. White Americans developed the stereotypes; white Americans produced the collectibles; and white American manufacturers and advertisers disseminated both the images and the objects to a white audience. (p. xix)

The maintenance of these kinds of beliefs satisfies the human need for psychological equilibrium and order, finding support and reinforcement in ideology. Defined as "typical properties of the 'social mind' of a group" (van Dijk, 1996, p. 56), ideologies provide a frame of reference for understanding the world. *Racist* ideologies serve several social functions operating to reproduce racism by legitimating social inequalities, thereby justifying racially or ethnically constructed differences. Racist ideology is used to (1) organize specific social attitudes into an evaluative framework for perceiving otherness, (2) provide the basis for "coordinated action and solidarity among whites," and (3) define racial and ethnic identity of the dominant group (van Dijk, 25–27). These beliefs and practices are thereby articulated in the production and distribution of racist discourse.

Theoretical Foundation

To every ad they see or hear, people bring a shared set of beliefs that serve as frames of reference for understanding the world around them. Beyond their obvious selling function, advertising images are about making meaning. Ads must "take into account not only the inherent qualities and attributes of the products they are trying to sell, but also the way in which they can make those properties mean something to us" (Williamson, 1978, p. 12).

Barthes (1972) describes these articulations as myth, that is, "a type of speech" or mode of signification that is conveyed by discourse that consists of many possible modes of representation including, but not limited to, writing, photography, publicity, and advertising. Myth is best described by the process of semiology (Barthes, 1972). Semiology "postulates a relation between two terms, a signifier and a signified" (Barthes, 1972, p. 112). The correlation of the terms *signifier, signified,* and *sign* is where associative meaning is made. What we see in an advertisement or product label, at first glance, are basic elements composed of linguistic signs (words) and iconic signs (visuals). Barthes (1972) uses a rose, for example, as a symbol of passion. Roses are not passion per se, but rather the roses (signifier) + concept of passion (signified) = roses (sign). He states that "the signifier is empty, the sign is full, it is a meaning" (Barthes, 1972, p. 113). Another example that involves race is the use of Aunt Jemima for maple syrup. We see the representation of a bandana-clad Black woman who suggests the mammy of the Deep South (signified). When placed on the bottle of syrup (sign), meaning is transferred to the otherwise ambiguous product—care giving, home cooking, and food sharing. The sign is formed at the intersection between a brand name and a meaning system that is articulated in a particular image. Quite simply, a sign, whether "object, word, or picture," has a "particular meaning to a person or group of people. It is neither the thing nor the meaning alone, but the two together" (Williamson, 1978, p. 17).

McCracken (1993, p. 125), who defines a brand as a "bundle or container of meaning," expanded on the Barthesian analysis and developed a framework for understanding the cultural relationship that brands have within society. His anthropological model (Figure 1) illustrates the meanings of brands. McCracken shows how brands assume meaning through advertising, combined with consumption behavior, and the nature of common knowledge that

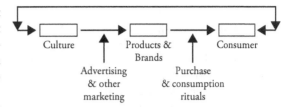

FIGURE 1. Meaning Model of Brand.
(*Source:* Revised from McCracken, 1993, p. 125.)

consumers bring to this system. The present study expands on this process by adding a reinforcement loop from consumer back to the culture where stereotypes are experienced and recirculated through the system.

A brand can have gendered meaning (maleness/femaleness), social standing (status), nationality (country meaning), and ethnicity/race (multicultural meaning). A brand can also stand for notions of tradition, trustworthiness, purity, family, nature, and so on. McCracken (1993) uses the Marlboro man as an example of these components with which a simple red and white box came to signify freedom, satisfaction, competence, maleness, and a quintessentially American, Western character. The product becomes part of the constellation of meanings that surrounds it and thereby "soaks up" meanings. When the rugged Marlboro man is situated on his horse, on the open plain, almost always alone, the meanings of the constellation become clear—freedom, love of the outdoors, release from the confines of industrialized society—he is a "real man," self-sufficient and individualistic. These meanings become part of a theme made up of prototypical content while simultaneously being "idealizations and not reality itself" (Schmitt & Simonson, 1997, p. 124).

Advertisements are created in such a way as to boost the commodity value of brand names by connecting them to images that resonate with the social and cultural values of a society. These images are loaded with established ideological assumptions that, when attached to a commodity, create the commodity sign. Tools of branding are thereby used to create a particular image in the mind of the consumer. According to van Dijk (1996), this pattern often serves to present an US versus THEM dichotomy, with US being White, "positive, tolerant, modern," and THEM being minorities who are "problematic, deviant and threatening" (pp. 26–27). Hence, attitudes, beliefs, and behavior that are racist serve to support a dominant ideology that focuses on difference and separatism.

These ideas and values are articulated through the construction, maintenance, and perpetuation of stereotypes. Stereotypes are overgeneralized beliefs that

> get hold of the few simple, vivid, memorable, easily grasped, and widely recognized characteristics about a person, reduce everything about the person to those traits, exaggerate and simplify them, and fix them without change or development to eternity. (Hall, 1997, p. 258)

An example is the way the "Indian problem" of the 1800s has been shown in "cowboy and Indian" films. In his analysis of the representation of Indians in film, Strickland (1998, p. 10) asks, "What would we think the American Indian was like if we had only the celluloid Indian from which to reconstruct history?" (Strickland, 1998, p. 10). The cinematic representation includes the Indian as a

> bloodthirsty and lawless savage; the Indian as enemy of progress; the Indian as tragic, but inevitable, victim; the Indian as a lazy, fat, shiftless drunk; the Indian as oil-rich illiterate; the Indian as educated half-breed unable to live in either a white or Indian world; the Indian as nymphomaniac; the Indian as noble hero; the Indian as stoic and unemotional; the Indian as the first conservationist. (Strickland, 1998, p. 10)

Champagne's (1994) analysis of Indians in films and theater suggests that the longevity of James Fenimore Cooper's *Last of the Mohicans,* evidenced by its many film treatments, demonstrates that "Hollywood prefers to isolate its Indians safely within the romantic past, rather than take a close look at Native American issues in the contemporary world" (p. 719).

Natty Bumpo, in James Fenimore Cooper's *Deerslayer*, is a literary example of the male who goes from a state of "uncultured animality" to a state of "civilization and culture" (Green, 1993, p. 327). Larson (1937) describes how this stereotype was translated into a tool for marketing patent medicines:

> No sooner had James Fenimore Cooper romanticized the Indian in the American imagination in his novels than patent-medicine manufacturers, quick to sense and take advantage of this new enthusiasm, used the red man as symbol and token for a great variety of ware. How the heart of the purchaser—filled, like as not, with the heroic exploits of Cooper's Indians—must have warmed as he gazed at the effigy, symbolic of "Nature's Own Remedy." (p. 338)

The female savage becomes an Indian princess who "renounces her own family, marries someone from the dominate culture and assimilates into it" (Green, 1993, p. 327), for example, Pocahontas. From this perspective, Indians are thought of as childlike and innocent, requiring the paternalistic care of Whites; that is, they are tamable. In her study of Indian imagery in *Dr. Quinn, Medicine Woman,* Bird (1996, p. 258) suggests that what viewers see is a White fantasy filled with White concerns around "guilt and retrospective outrage." Green's (1993) analysis of the use of male Indian images in ads posits that Natives continue to be portrayed according to stereotypical images: (1) noble savage (the stoic, innocent, child of nature), (2) civilizable savage (redeemable, teachable), and (3) bloodthirsty savage (fierce, predatory, cultureless, animalistic). Taken together, these studies suggest that historically constructed images and beliefs about American Indians are at the essence of stereotypical thinking that is easily translated into product images.

Method

To study the articulation of racist ideology in brand images, four currently available national products (Land O' Lakes butter, Sue Bee Honey, Big Chief [Monitor] Sugar, and Crazy Horse Malt Liquor) were analyzed according to Barthes's (1972) semiotic analysis. First, the material object was identified (signifier); second, the associative elements were identified (signified); and, third, these were brought together in what we as consumers recognize as the sign. Company websites, press releases, and product packages were used for visual and textual information. Several attempts to communicate directly with the companies yielded no response. Through this method of analysis we can see how these meanings are transferred to the different products on the basis of both race and gender.

Results

The following section presents a descriptive analysis of Land O' Lakes, Sue Bee Honey, Big Chief (Monitor) Sugar, and Crazy Horse Malt Liquor brand images.

Land O' Lakes

Although not the first national manufacturer to draw on the mystique of Indianness (that honor goes to Red Man Tobacco in 1904), Land O' Lakes is certainly one of the more prominent. In 1921, the Minnesota Cooperative Creameries Association opened for business in Arden Hills, Minnesota. This company served as the central shipping agent for a small group of small, farmer-owned dairy cooperatives (Morgan, 1986, p. 63). In 1924, the group wanted a different name and solicited ideas from farmers. Mrs. E. B. Foss and Mr. George L. Swift came up with the winning name—Land O' Lakes, "a tribute to Minnesota's thousands of sparkling lakes" (p. 63). The corporate website opens with a photograph of a quiet lake amid pine trees and blue sky. The copy under the photograph reads:

> Welcome to Land O' Lakes. A land unlike anywhere else on earth. A special place filled with clear, spring-fed lakes. Rivers and streams that dance to their own rhythms through rich, fertile fields. It's the land we call home. And from it has flowed the bounty and goodness we bring to you, our neighbors and friends. (Land O' Lakes, 2000)

In addition, "The now famous Indian maiden was also created during the search for a brand name and trademark. Because the regions of Minnesota and Wisconsin were the legendary lands of Hiawatha and Minnehaha, the idea of an Indian maiden took form" (Land O' Lakes, 2000). A painting was sent to the company of an Indian maiden facing the viewer, holding a butter carton with a background filled with lakes, pines, flowers, and grazing cows.

At the Land O' Lakes corporate website, the director of communications includes a statement about the maiden image, where he agrees that the logo, the "Indian Maiden," has powerful connotations (Land

O' Lakes). Hardly changed since its introduction in the 1920s, he says that Land O' Lakes has built on the "symbolism of the purity of the products" (Burnham, 1992). The company "thought the Indian maiden would be a good image. She represents Hiawatha and the Land of Gitchgoomee [sic] and the names of Midwest towns and streets that have their roots in the American Indian population" (Burnham, 1992).

The signifier is thereby the product, be it butter, sour cream, or other Land O' Lakes products. The Indian woman on the package is associated with youth, innocence, nature, and purity. The result is the generic "Indian maiden." Subsequently, the qualities stereotypically associated with this beaded, buckskinned, doe-eyed young woman are transferred to the company's products. Green's "noble savage" image is extended to include the female stereotype.

Sue Bee Honey

The Sioux Honey Association, based in Sioux City, Iowa, is a cooperative of honey producers, yielding 40 million pounds of honey annually (Sioux Honey Association, 2000). Corporate communications describe a change of the product name in 1964 from Sioux Bee to Sue Bee, "to reflect the correct pronunciation of the name" (Sioux Honey Association, 2000). The brand name and image are reinforced on trucks (both real and toys), on the bottles and jars in which the honey is sold, and through collectibles such as coffee mugs and recipe books.

Sue Bee Honey also draws upon the child-of-nature imagery in an attempt to imbue qualities of purity into their products. If we were to view Sue Bee in her full form (as she is shown on many specialty items such as mugs, glasses, and jars) we would see that she is an Indian maiden on top, with braided hair and headband, and a bee below the waist. Changing the spelling of her name from "Sioux Bee" to "Sue Bee" could be interpreted in a variety of ways—possibly simply as a matter of pronunciation, as the company asserts, or as an effort to draw attention away from the savage imagery stereotypically attributed to members of this tribe and more toward the little girlishness of the image. In this case, the product is honey, traditionally associated with trees and forests and natural places. This association works well with the girl-child Indian stereotype. By placing the girl bee on the package of honey, consumers can associate the innocence, purity, and naturalness attributed to Native American females with the quality of the product.

In the tradition of Pocahontas, both the Land O' Lakes and the Sue Bee maidens symbolize innocence, purity, and virginity—children of nature. The maiden image signifies a female "Indianness." She is childlike, as she happily offers up perhaps honey or butter (or herself) that "is as pure and healthy as she is" (Dotz & Morton, 1996, p. 11). The maiden's image is used to represent attempts to get back to nature, and the association is that this can be accomplished through the healthy, wholesome products of Land O' Lakes. Both images are encoded with socially constructed meanings about female Indian sexuality, purity, and nature.

Monitor Sugar Company

Founded in 1901, the Monitor Sugar Company processes approximately 4% of U.S. beet production into sugar (granulated, powdered, brown, and icing; Monitor Sugar Company, 2000). For 60 years the company has been producing sugar from beets, relying on the image of an American Indian in full headdress to sell the sugar goods. The products are available on grocery store shelves and in bulk for institutions, delivered by trucks with the Big Chief logo emblazoned on the sides.

So, who is this Chief said to represent? Is he a bona fide tribal leader or a composite Indian designed to communicate naturalistic characteristics associated with Indians with the sugar? Green's (1993) savage typology suggests that this individual is a combination of the noble savage (natural) and the bloodthirsty savage (ferocious). He is proud, noble, and natural and yet he is wearing a ceremonial headdress that communicates strength and stoicism.

Crazy Horse Malt Liquor

A 40-ounce beverage that is sold in approximately 40 states (Metz & Thee, 1994), Crazy Horse Malt Liquor is brewed by the Heilman Brewing Company of Brooklyn, New York. Crazy Horse Malt Liquor employs the image of Tasunke Witko (Crazy Horse) on the label of its malt liquor. On the front of the bottle

is an American Indian male wearing a headdress that appears to be an eagle feather bonnet, and there is a symbol representing a medicine wheel—both sacred images in Lakota and other Native cultures (Metz & Thee, 1994).

Image analysis shows that the sign is that of an actual Indian chief. Signified, however, are beliefs about Indians as warriors, westward expansion, how mighty the consumer might be by drinking this brand, and wildness of the American Western frontier.

This brand, perhaps more than any other, has come under public scrutiny because it is the image of a particular person. A revered forefather of the Oglala Sioux tribe of South Dakota, Crazy Horse died in 1877 (Blalock, 1992). The labels feature the prominent image of Chief Crazy Horse, who has long been the subject of stories, literature, and movies. Larger than life, he has played a role in American mythology.

Signifying Green's (1993) bloodthirsty savage image, Crazy Horse Malt Liquor makes use of American myths through image and association. Ironically, Crazy Horse objected to alcohol and warned his nation about the destructive effects of liquor (Specktor, 1995). As a sign, Crazy Horse represents a real symbol of early American life and westward expansionism. He was, according to the vice president of the Oglala Sioux Tribe, a "warrior, a spiritual leader, a traditional leader, a hero who has always been and is still revered by our people" (Hill, 1992; Metz & Thee, 1994, p. 50). This particular image brings together some interesting aspects of branding. Not only is the noble and bloodthirsty savage stereotype brought together in a proud, but ultimately defeated, Indian chief, but also this is an image of a real human being. The association of alcohol with that image, as well as targeting the Indian population, draws on assumptions of alcohol abuse.[2]

Discussion and Conclusions

Although there are dozens of possible examples of Native images on product labels, ranging from cigarette packages to sports utility vehicles, the examples discussed above illustrate the principles behind semiotics. The four presented here are significant examples of national brands employing stereotypical representations. When people are made aware of these products, they see how these images are consistently found in many products that employ Indian stereotypes either in product names or in their logos.

Many of these signs and symbols have been with us so long we no longer question them. Product images on packages, in advertisements, on television, and in films are nearly the only images non-Indians ever see of Native Americans. The covers of romance novels routinely feature Indian men sweeping beautiful non-Indian women off their feet as their bodices are torn away. These stereotypical representations of American Indians denies that they are human beings, and presents them as existing only in the past and as single, monolithic Indians (Merskin, 1998).

American Indians are certainly not the only racial or ethnic group to be discriminated against, overtly or covertly. Aunt Jemima and Rastus certainly have their origins in dehumanizing, one-dimensional images based on a tragic past. Yet, like Betty Crocker, these images have been updated. Aunt Jemima has lost weight and the bandana, and the Frito Bandito has disappeared (Burnham, 1992). But the Indian image persists in corporate marketing and product labeling.

These are highly visible and perhaps more openly discussed than images that appear on the products we see in grocery store aisles. An Absolut Vodka ad shows an Eskimo pulling a sled of vodka and a Grey Owl Wild Rice package features an Indian with braids, wearing a single feather, surrounded by a circle that represents (according to Grey Owl's distribution manager) the "oneness of nature" (Burnham, 1992). A partial list of others includes Apache helicopter, Jeep Cherokee, Apache rib doormats, Red Man Tobacco, Kleek-O the Eskimo (Cliquot Club ginger ale), Dodge Dakota, Pontiac, the Cleveland Indians, Mutual of Omaha, Calumet Baking Powder, Mohawk Carpet Mills, American Spirit cigarettes, Eskimo pies, Tomahawk mulcher, Winnebago Motor Homes, Indian Motorcycles, Tomahawk missiles, many high school sports teams, and the music behind the Hamm's beer commercials that begins "From the land of sky blue waters." And the list goes on.

Change is coming, but it is slow. For one thing, American Indians do not represent a significant target audience to advertisers. Representing less than 1% of the population, and the most economically destitute of all ethnic minority populations, American Indians are not particularly useful to marketers. Nearly 30% live below the official poverty line, in contrast with 13% of the general U.S. population (Cortese, 1999, p. 117). Without the population numbers or legal resources, it is nearly impossible for the voices of Natives to be heard, unlike other groups who have made some representational inroads. According to Westerman (1989), when minority groups speak, businesses are beginning to listen: "That's why Li'l Black Sambo and the Frito Bandito are dead. They were killed by the very ethnic groups they portrayed" (p. 28).

Not only does stereotyping communicate inaccurate beliefs about Natives to Whites, but also to Indians. Children, all children, are perhaps the most important recipients of this information for it is during childhood that difference is first learned. If, during the transition of adolescence, Native children internalize these representations that suggest that Indians are lazy, alcoholic by nature, and violent, this misinformation can have a lifelong impact on perceptions of self and others. As Lippmann (1922/1961) wrote,

> The subtlest and most pervasive of all influences are those which create and maintain the repertory of stereotypes. We are told about the world before we see it. We imagine most things before we experience them. (p. 89)

By playing a game of substitution, by inserting other ethnic groups or races into the same situation, it becomes clear that there is a problem. Stereotypical images do not reside only in the past, because the social control mechanisms that helped to create them remain with us today.

Future research should continue to examine how the advertising and marketing practice of branding contributes to the persistent use of racist images on product labels. This study adds to the sparse literature on media representations of Native Americans in general and adds to Green's (1993) typology by including female counterparts to the male savage stereotypes. Future research could explore more images of Native Americans in ads and on products. Qualitative research with members of different tribes would add depth to this area of study.

Notes

1. Many people have preferences about terms used to describe America's indigenous peoples. "American Indian" is commonly used, as is "Native American, Native, and Indian." These terms are used interchangeably in recognition of individual preferences, without disregarding the weight each Heileman word carries.

2. Lawsuits are currently under way to limit Heilman Breweries' use of the name Crazy Horse Malt Liquor (Specktor, 1995). Several states have outlawed the sale of this beverage (Specktor, 1995). Also under review are important legal issues such as a tribe's sovereign power to exercise civil jurisdiction and the Witko family's right to protect the image of their ancestor.

References

Aaker, D., & A. L. Biel. (1993). *Advertising's role in building strong brands*. Mahwah, NJ: Lawrence Erlbaum.

Barthes, R. (1972). *Mythologies*. New York: The Noonday Press.

Berkhofer, R., Jr. (1979). *The white man's Indian: Images of the American Indian from Columbus to the present*. New York: Vintage Books.

Bird, S. E. (1996). Not my fantasy: The persistence of Indian imagery in Dr. Quinn, Medicine Woman. In S. E. Bird (Ed.), *Dressing in feathers: The construction of the Indian in American popular culture* (pp. 245–62). Boulder, CO: Westview Press.

Blalock, C. (1992). Crazy Horse controversy riles Congress: Controversies over Crazy Horse Malt Liquor and Black Death vodka. *Beverage Industry*, 83(9), 1–3.

Burnham, P. (1992, 27 May). Indians can't shake label as guides to good buys. *The Washington Times*, p. El.

Champagne, D. (1994). *Native America: Portrait of the peoples*. Detroit: Visible Ink.

Cortese, A. J. (1999). *Provocateur: Images of women and minorities in advertising*. New York: Rowman & Littlefield Publishers, Inc.

Dotz, W., & Morton, J. (1996). *What a character! 20th century American advertising icons*. San Francisco: Chronicle Books.

Goings, K. W. (1994). *Mammy and Uncle Mose: Black collectibles and American stereotyping*. Bloomington, IN: Indiana University Press.

Graham, R. (1993, 6 January). Symbol or stereotype: One consumer's tradition is another's racial slur. *The Boston Globe*, p. 35.

Green, M. K. (1993). Images of American Indians in advertising: Some moral issues. *Journal of Business Ethics*, 12, 323–30.

Hall, S. (1997). *Representation: Cultural representations and signifying practices*. London: Sage.

Hill, R. (1992). The non-vanishing American Indian: Are the modern images any closer to the truth? *Quill* (May), 35–7.

Kates, S. M., & Shaw-Garlock, G. (1999). The ever-entangling web: A study of ideologies and discourses in advertising to women. *Journal of Advertising* 28(2), 33–49.

Kern-Foxworth, M. (1994). *Aunt Jemima, Uncle Ben, and Rastus: Blacks in advertising yesterday, today, and tomorrow*. Westport, CT: Praeger.

Land O' Lakes. (2000). [On-line]. Available: http://www.landolakes.com.

Larson, C. (1937). Patent-medicine advertising and the early American press. *Journalism Quarterly*, 14(4), 333–39.

Lippmann, W. (1922/1961). *Public opinion*. New York: McMillan & Company.

McCracken, G. (1993). The value of the brand: An anthropological perspective. In D. Aaker & A. L. Biel (Eds.), *Brand equity in advertising: Advertising's role in building strong brands*. Mahwah, NJ: Lawrence Erlbaum.

Merskin, D. (1998). Sending up signals: A survey of American Indian media use and representation in the mass media. *The Howard Journal of Communications*, 9, 333–45.

Metz, S., & Thee, M. (1994). Brewers intoxicated with racist imagery. *Business and Society Review*, 89, 50–1.

Mihesuah, D. A. (1996). *American Indians: Stereotypes and realities*. Atlanta, GA: Clarity Press.

Monitor Sugar Company. (2000). [On-line]. Available: http://members.aol.com/asga/mon.htm.

Morgan, H. (1986). *Symbols of America*. New York: Penguin Books.

Schmitt, B., & Simonson, A. (1997). *Marketing aesthetics: The strategic management of brands, identity, and image*. New York: The Free Press.

Sioux Honey Association. (2000). [On-line]. Available: http://www.suebeehoney.com.

Specktor, M. (1995, January 6). Crazy Horse exploited to peddle liquor. *National Catholic Reporter*, 31(10), 3.

Strickland, R. (1998). The celluloid Indian. *Oregon Quarterly* (Summer), 9–10.

van Dijk, T. A. (1996). *Discourse, racism, and ideology.* La Laguna: RCEI Ediciones.

Westerman, M. (1989, March). Death of the Frito bandito: Marketing to ethnic groups. *American Demographics*, 11, 28–32.

Williamson, J. (1978). *Decoding advertisements: Ideology and meaning in advertising.* New York: Marion Boyars.

Questions for Critical Thinking

1. Merskin offers numerous examples of the continued misrepresentation of American Indians in advertising brands. Why do you think such distorted images continue?

2. Do you think that the stereotypes that Merskin discusses maintain the continued oppression of American Indians in the United States? Why or why not?

3. What will bring about more positive images of American Indians in advertising and other media? What obstacles prevent such positive portrayals?

ASIAN AMERICAN MEDIA REPRESENTATION

A Film Analysis and Implications for Identity Development

• *Tiffany Besana, Dalal Katsiaficas, and Aerika Brittian Loyd*

This essay by educational psychologists Tiffany Besana, Dalal Katsiaficas, and Aerika Brittian Loyd examines representation of Asian Americans in the media, focusing on how media can positively and negatively impact identity development. Further, it explores how misrepresentations can shape intergroup interactions, particularly important as hate incidents against Asian American and Pacific Islanders have risen since the start of the COVID-19 pandemic. Through a film analysis of representations of Asian Americans in the media, the authors found that although the frequency of lead roles increased over the last 25 years, along with more frequency of stereotype-resisting representations, stereotype-confirming representations remained prevalent, thus reinforcing the historic trend of misrepresentation of Asian Americans in film.

Asian Americans are among the fastest-growing racial groups in the U.S. (Census, 2017), yet they remain limitedly represented and are often misrepresented in U.S. media. Media consumption is a common experience in U.S. life and such media use can influence one's overall sense of who they are and where they fit in society—also known as *identity* (Erikson, 1968). The process of establishing one's sense of identity is an especially significant aspect of human development that tends to take center stage during adolescence and continues throughout the lifespan. Film representations of Asian Americans can influence development in significant ways by shaping both how individuals view themselves and how other groups view Asian Americans. Yet, there has been little attention to the role of media as it relates to identity development, especially for Asian Americans.

Ecological Systems, Human Development, and Media

Although identity development continues throughout the lifespan, Erikson's (1968) theory of psychosocial development highlighted adolescence as a particularly critical time for individuals to form their identity and for healthy ego development to occur. The bioecological model augments Erikson's notions of identity development, as it allows us to consider human development as a continuous process that exists within a person and between a person and their environment over time (Bronfenbrenner & Morris, 2006). Based in this perspective, development occurs in various settings ranging from a person's immediate environments (e.g., family and peers; also known as microsystems) to larger cultural contexts (e.g., societal values and beliefs; also known as the

Research in Human Development, 16: 201–225, 2019
ISSN: 1542-7609 print/1542-7617 online
DOI: https://doi.org/10.1080/15427609.2020.1711680

macrosystem). Media, currently the mass means of communication in the U.S. (e.g., television, film, advertisements, news articles, etc.), is often considered a part of the macrosystem. However, research indicates media manifests across all levels of the ecological system, extending from daily activities to broader cultural contexts that impact development (McHale, Dotterer, & Kim, 2009).

Culture encompasses the shared beliefs and practices of humans and influences the development of the self (Kagitçibasi, 2007). In contemporary U.S. society, media communicates and further enforces shared understandings, and can influence whether the messages are positive or negative, and confirm, perpetuate, or resist stereotypes. Likewise, the content of media representations can also shape how society views certain racial groups. Consequently, messages from the media can affect both an individual's sense of self and how society interacts with members of that group.

Taken together, identity formation occurs through interactions with the various levels of the system individuals are embedded within (e.g., family, school, culture), yet media exists at multiple levels of the system and can play a potent role in shaping human development. The role that media plays in shaping societal beliefs is especially important because people develop their identity in relation to how society views them. Therefore, examining media is one way to better understand the social ecology that individuals live in and identify possible implications of the social context for human development.

Media and Identity

Media plays a critical role in adolescents' and young adults' lives, especially since young people of today value social media as an opportunity to express one's self and develop one's identity (Manago, 2015). As well, young people make meaning of the social experiences they are having through interactions with media, as those experiences shape identity development; it is indeed a bidirectional process (Velez & Spencer, 2018). While social media is a key platform that provides young people with the agency in developing their own self-representation, other forms of media, such as film, contain messages that are derived by others and may spread across a larger audience.

These media images are significant in shaping identity development, as they can act as a powerful socializing agent and serve as a context that shapes how people view themselves and each other within social systems (Mok, 1998). This process may occur through a concept known as *social mirroring* (Cooley, 1902).

Scholars define social mirroring as the ways in which people internalize others' perceptions of one's self based on the views of society (Cooley, 1902). Authentic representations of minority groups reflect favorable societal images and endorse positive social mirroring (Suárez-Orozco & Qin-Hilliard, 2004). However, when the dominant group is exposed to negative media representations of minority groups, this can induce negative attitudes about individuals from those groups and can confirm negative stereotypes. These attitudes can then precipitate acts of discrimination toward individuals from minority groups (Buchanan & Settles, 2018; Jaspal & Cinnirella, 2010). Absence of any representation of one's group also affects individuals from that group, since invisibility assumes that their community is not fully recognized nor valued in society (Buchanan & Settles, 2018).

Many minorities receive messages from society that are predominantly negative via perpetuation of inaccurate media portrayals or lack of portrayals. Oftentimes these media portrayals are damaging by creating a dialectic of both hypervisibility and concurrent invisibility. These media portrayals lead to hypervisibility in that they perpetuate negative stereotypes, while also simultaneously rendering many of the nuances of their personhood wholly invisible (Buchanan & Settles, 2018; Jaspal & Cinnirella, 2010). These distortions can affect how young people form their identity through the eyes of others and through discrimination and invalidation, which are especially detrimental experiences for those who are exploring their ethnic and racial identity (Suárez-Orozco & Qin-Hilliard, 2004; Torres & Ong, 2010; Yip, 2018).

Ethnic and Racial Identity and Identity Threats

Ethnic and racial identity (ERI), one domain of a person's overall sense of identity that is associated with ethnicity and race, and ethnic and racial group membership, has been identified as a particularly important psychological and psychosocial construct that is often linked to healthy development for individuals from minority groups (Umaña-Taylor et al., 2014). In Western cultural contexts, identity exploration often involves sorting through a variety of identity elements before committing to certain features of their identity (Schwartz, Zamboanga, Weisskirch, & Rodriguez, 2009). Those who remain in the stage of ERI exploration tend to be negatively impacted by experiences of discrimination (Torres & Ong, 2010). In contrast, those whose ERI is resolved and established are often protected from the detrimental effects of discrimination (Yip, 2018).

Complicating the process of ERI formation for many Asian Americans is the *perpetual foreigner* stereotype, which positions Asian Americans as an "other" in the mainstream (White) culture of the U.S. (Huynh, Devos, & Smalarz, 2011). For Asian Americans, being aware of the perpetual foreigner stereotype is a significant predictor of identity conflict and a low sense of belonging to American culture (Huynh et al., 2011). This particular stereotype does not acknowledge the nuanced realities of Asian Americans who come from a multitude of ethnic backgrounds and immigration statuses; many are U.S.-born while many others have immigrated to the U.S. (Huynh et al., 2011; Teranishi, 2010).

Acculturative stress is another social risk factor for Asian American individuals, especially those from immigrant backgrounds. Acculturative stress refers to the psychological burden that stems from acquiring the cultural characteristics of the new country one immigrates to (Hwang & Ting, 2008). Intercultural contacts are often associated with perceived cultural incompatibilities rooted in language and cultural values between the host (American) and heritage (Asian) cultures (Keum, 2016). Researchers have found links between acculturative stress and psychological distress in Asian Americans (Hwang & Ting, 2008). For some Asian Americans, feelings of cultural incompatibility may be further emphasized by experiencing acts of discrimination that can create a sense of rejection from the dominant group. Extant research indicates this is a common experience for ethnic and racial minority youth, particularly those from Asian backgrounds (Yip, 2018).

The *model minority myth*, a stereotype that positions Asian Americans as academically and economically more successful than other racial minority groups because of their values of hard work and perseverance, individual effort, and support of American meritocracy, is another issue that can affect identity development for Asian Americans (Lee, 2009). From as early as the 1960s, American news articles have perpetuated this myth by commending the accomplishments of Asian Americans and claiming that there are no racial barriers to success for this group (Atkin, Yoo, Jager, & Yeh, 2018). However, this stereotype does not accurately represent or portray the experiences of all Asian Americans and often limits the identity options available to them. This myth can have detrimental effects for Asian American adolescents and young adults, since the internalization of this stereotype may lead to psychological distress from unrealistic expectations and pressure to succeed (Atkin et al., 2018). Asian American youth who do not neatly fit into the high-achieving stereotype assigned to Asians may also feel out of place, as though they do not belong to their ethnic and racial group (Atkin et al., 2018). The disconnect from ethnic and racial group belonging can negatively impact ERI development and also lead to feelings of rejection and isolation within their ethnic and racial group (Atkin et al., 2018). Furthermore, Asian Americans have drastically different experiences navigating academic and economic success with varying backgrounds regarding family income level, country of origin, immigration status, and reason for immigration to the U.S., which this myth fails to recognize (Teranishi, 2010).

Presently, media is a major socializing force that can sustain and perpetuate these stereotypes, and can positively or negatively impact Asian Americans' identity development. Representations in media can also serve as a tool that assists Asian American adolescents and young adults in exploring their identity. Current literature, however, is limited in exploring media as a source of discrimination against Asian Americans. This major gap in research has failed to highlight the historic struggle Asian Americans experience in navigating their identity in the face of poor media representation. Poor and inaccurate representations of Asian Americans in the film can negatively affect ERI development in young Asian Americans. For example, when the reflected image is overall positive, individuals may experience a high sense of self-efficacy, but when the depiction is generally negative, they may experience low self-worth (Suárez-Orozco & Qin-Hilliard, 2004).

Therefore, it is critical to consider the implications that discrimination through media can have on Asian American identity development.

Representations of Asian Americans in Media

Although media has become an especially influential social context in recent years for adolescents and young adults (Manago, 2015), poor media representation of Asian Americans is unfortunately not a new concept. Mok (1998) established the groundwork for examining how the U.S. has historically portrayed negative media images and stereotypes of Asian Americans, how such representation leaves a lasting effect on psychological well-being, and how mental health professionals must remain educated and sensitive to the needs of a diverse clientele affected by stereotypical media images of their group.

Media rarely reflects the diversity that is evident within Asian American cultures (Mok, 1998). Although Asian American is a panethnic term that encompasses over 50 ethnic groups from the continent of Asia including those of Southeast Asian, East Asian, and South Asian descent who reside in the U.S., Asian Americans as a group tend to be homogenized in U.S. media (Mok, 1998; Census, 2018). The notion of Asian American as a cultural group also permeates research, since Asian American psychology has often focused on the cross-cultural experience the group shares between the U.S. and Asian nations and navigating constructs such as individualism-collectivism and independent-interdependent cultural orientations (Okazaki, Lee, & Sue, 2007). While the Asian American experience is culturally diverse, nuanced, and complex, media portrayals of Asian Americans often lack such depth and diversity (Mok, 1998). Such one-dimensional representations can negatively affect Asian Americans as they form their identities, since receiving these distorted messages can induce feelings of not being fully recognized or valued in society (Buchanan & Settles, 2018; Suárez-Orozco & Qin-Hilliard, 2004; Torres & Ong, 2010; Yip, 2018).

There has been a historic trend in the underrepresentation of minorities in U.S. media, especially in the case of Asian Americans (Mok, 1998; Qiu & Muturi, 2016). For instance, research has demonstrated that differences between Asian American stereotypes and favorability of stereotypes differ by gender, specifically

regarding sexual desirability depicted in the film (Mok, 1998). While Asian American women are typically depicted as helpless, dependent, servile, docile, and submissive, Asian American men are often portrayed as reserved, studious, and socially awkward (Mok, 1998; Said, 1978). Consequently, some Asian Americans may see their race as a limiting factor in their perception of their own attractiveness (Mok, 1998). This is especially true for men who are often portrayed as emasculate in media (Keum, 2016). Scholars assert the desexualization of Asian men is historically rooted in neutralizing concerns against mainstream fear of a "yellow peril," a racist sentiment that cast Asians as a threat to the Western world (Han, 2006; Said, 1978). We also rarely see media images of Asian women in U.S. media beyond exotic and overly sexualized representations (Mok, 1998; Said, 1978). These limited media messages can negatively affect Asian Americans' self-esteem and body image, which are two important aspects involved in identity formation (Baumeister, 1999; Keum, 2016; Mok, 1998).

Since Mok's seminal work, the Asian American population in the U.S. has grown rapidly, and adolescents and young adults receive more exposure to media (Census, 2017; Pasch & Velazquez, 2013). These conditions precipitate the importance to assess the changes that the social landscape has made on Asian American media representation. Have more Asian American actors been cast as lead characters or do they remain in supporting roles as the population of Asian Americans has increased? Are Asian American characters still commonly written to abide by racialized and gendered stereotypes or are more diverse character traits and stories more prevalent? Are Asian Americans writing and directing the stories themselves or are the stories being told by people not within the Asian American community? Answers to these questions would contemporize previous literature on the topic of Asian American media representation while focusing on content in films. Answers to these questions would also address Asian American's lack of and need for positive role models in media that reflect the increasing diversity within the Asian American community in recent years. Moreover, this investigation would tell us more about opportunities for positive social mirroring, indicating ways in which Asian American portrayal in media may improve to illuminate current beliefs of their group and promote internalization of more authentic representations. . . .

TABLE 1   **Film List by Year, Genre, Character, and Gender Listed in Chronological Order**

Film	Year	Genre	Character	Gender
Mortal Kombat	1995	Action, adventure	Liu Kang	Male
			Shang Tsung	Male
Mortal Kombat: Annihilation	1997	Action, adventure, science fiction/ adventure	Liu Kang	Male
Rush Hour	1998	Action-comedy, thriller	Chief Inspector Lee	Male
			Soo Yung	Female
			Consul Han	Male
Shanghai Noon	2000	Action-comedy, adventure	Chon Wang	Male
			Princess Pei-Pei	Female
			Lo Fong	Male
Rush Hour 2	2001	Action-comedy, thriller	Chief Inspector Lee	Male
			Hu Li	Female
			Ricky Tan	Male
Kill Bill: Volume 1	2003	Action, mystery-thriller	Oren Ishii	Female
			Gogo Yobari	Female
			Johnny Mo	Male
			Hattori Hanzo	Male
			Sofie Fatale	Female
Akeelah and the Bee	2006	Drama	Dylan	Male
			Mr. Chiu	Male
Rush Hour 3	2007	Action-comedy, thriller	Chief Inspector Lee	Male
			Kenji	Male
			Soo Yung	Female
			Mr. Han	Male
			Dragon Lady	Female
			Jasmine	
Gran Torino	2008	Drama	Thao Vang Lor	Male
			Sue Lor	Female
			Spider	Male
			Smokie	Male
The Karate Kid	2010	Action-comedy, adventure, drama	Mr. Han	Male
			Meiying	Female
Scott Pilgrim vs. the World	2010	Action-comedy, romance	Knives Chau	Female
			Matthew Patel	Male
			Kyle Katayanagi	Male
			Ken Katayanagi	Male
Cloud Atlas	2012	Science-fiction/adventure, drama	Sonmi	Female

Continued

TABLE 1   *Continued*

Film	Year	Genre	Character	Gender
			Yoona	Female
			Hae Joo Chang	Male
The Conjuring	2013	Horror, mystery/thriller	Drew Thomas	Male
Rogue One: A Star Wars Story	2016	Science-fiction/adventure, action	Bodhi Rock	Male
			Chirrut Imwe	Male
			Baze Malbus	Male
Guardians of the Galaxy Vol. 2	2017	Action-comedy, science-fiction/adventure	Mantis	Female
Star Wars: The Last Jedi	2017	Science-fiction/adventure, action	Rose Tico	Female
The Foreigner	2017	Action, mystery/thriller	Quan Ngoc Minh	Male
			Fan	Female
Spider-Man: Homecoming	2017	Action-comedy, science-fiction/adventure	Ned	Male
The Big Sick	2017	Romantic comedy, drama	Kumail	Male
			Azmat	Male
			Sharmeen	Female
			Naveed	Male
To All the Boy's I've Loved Before	2018	Romantic comedy	Lara Jean	Female
			Margot	Female
			Kitty	Female
Bird Box	2018	Horror, drama, mystery/thriller, science fiction	Greg	Male
Crazy Rich Asians	2018	Romantic comedy	Rachel Chu	Female
			Nick Young	Male
			Peik Lin Goh	Female
			Eleanor Young	Female
			Astrid Young Leong	Female
			Ah Ma	Female
			Wye Mun Goh	Male
			Araminta Lee	Female
			Colin Khoo	Male
The Darkest Minds	2018	Science-fiction/adventure, thriller	Suzume (Zu)	Female
Searching	2018	Mystery/thriller, drama	David Kim	Male
			Peter Kim	Male
			Margot Kim	Female
			Pamela Nam Kim	Female
The Princess Switch	2018	Romantic comedy	Stacy De Novo	Female
			Lady Margaret	Female

TABLE 2   Excluded Films by Year and Reason for Exclusion

Film	Year	Reason for Exclusion
The Killing Fields	1984	Produced prior to 1993, not a U.S. film
Legacy of Rage	1986	Produced prior to 1993, not a U.S. film
Full Metal Jacket	1987	Produced prior to 1993
The Joy Luck Club	1993	Produced in 1993
Rumble in the Bronx	1995	Not a U.S. film
Who Am I?	1998	Not a U.S. film
Crouching Tiger, Hidden Dragon	2000	A Chinese film
Lion	2016	Not a U.S. film
Train to Busan	2016	Not a U.S. film
Bleeding Steel	2017	Not a U.S. film

TABLE 3   Themes from Film Analysis

Theme	Description	Example
Colored streak of hair	Female character exhibited a symbolic strip of bright color in their hair	Knives Chau in *Scott Pilgrim Vs. the World* (2010) dyed a section of her hair bright blue as a redefining moment of her new confidence
Comedic	Character's key trait was their sense of humor	Chirrut Imwe in *Rogue One: A Star Wars Story* (2016) often showcased wit and humor
Family oriented	Character focused family at the center of their values	Eleanor Young in *Crazy Rich Asians* (2018) sacrificed her own personal ambition and education to raise her family
Foreigner	Character was described as an "other" who was foreign to the U.S.	Thao Vang Lor and Sue Lor in *Gran Torino* (2008) were victims of racial slurs and mocked for following traditional Hmong customs in their Minnesotan neighborhood
Dragon lady	Female character was cruel, evil, and gruesomely violent yet with sex appeal	O-Ren Ishii in *Kill Bill: Vol I* (2003) was a sadistic villain, yet was characterized as alluring
Martial artist	Male character was revealed as a skilled martial artist in an action film	Liu Kang in *Mortal Combat* (1995) displayed great strength, athleticism, and skill in fighting
Mischievous	Character was portrayed a playful rule breaker	Lady Margaret in *The Princess Switch* (2018) embarked on a journey to switch identities with her doppelgänger for fun
Nerd	Character's high level of intellect was one of their key and only qualities, sometimes paired with quirkiness	Ned from *Spider-Man: Homecoming* (2017) was the "guy in the chair" who served as the smart, tech guru sidekick of Spider-Man
Timid, soft-spoken woman	Female character presented submissiveness and lack of confidence	Sonmi in *Cloud Atlas* (2012) was a meek, submissive slave and lacked confidence

Results

Descriptive Findings

Character Roles

There were 70 Asian characters identified among the 25 films in the analytic sample. Fourteen characters served lead roles, while 56 served supporting roles (Figure 1). Five of the lead roles were from films produced earlier than 2002. Another lead role was present in 2007. Lead roles did not reemerge until 2017 (2 films) and peaked in 2018 (6 films). Supporting roles were consistent with a generally increasing trend over time and peaked in 2017 (7 films) and 2018 (14 films).

The trends of roles also differed based on the gender of the actor (Figure 2): 44.3% (n = 31) of the Asian actors were female, while 55.7% (n = 39) were male. None of the actors publicly identified as non-binary or non-gender conforming, and none of the characters were described as non-binary or non-gender conforming; 28.6% (n = 4) of lead characters were female, and 71.4% (n = 10) of leads were male; 48.2% (n = 27) of supporting characters were female, and 51.8% (n = 29) were male. Female actors served lead roles in 12.9% (n = 4) of the films and supporting roles in 87.1% (n = 27) of the films. Male actors served lead roles in 74.4% (n = 29) of the films and supporting roles in 25.6% (n = 10) of the films.

Age of Actors

The age of the actors at the time the films were produced ranged from 11 to 64 years old, with one outlier at 91 years old (Figure 3). The age also varied based on gender and type of role. Age of female actors ranged from 11 to 56 years old with one outlier at 91 years old, while the age of male actors ranged from 17 to 64 years old. Female lead actors were all within the 20–39 age range, while male leads varied between the 30–69 age range. Female supporting actors varied between the 11–59 age range with one outlier at 91, while male supporting actors varied between the 17–69 age range. The greatest number of female actors were within the 30–39 age range (n = 9) followed by the 20–29 range (n = 8) and the 11–19 range (n = 6). Male actors were more evenly distributed across the 17 to 64 age range.

Ethnicities of Actors

The films represented a diverse array of ethnicities. The actors' ethnicities (which were identified from online databases such as IMDb and Wikipedia) included Southeast Asian (Filipino, Hmong, Malaysian and Vietnamese), East Asian (Chinese, Hongkonger, Japanese, Korean, and Taiwanese), and South Asian

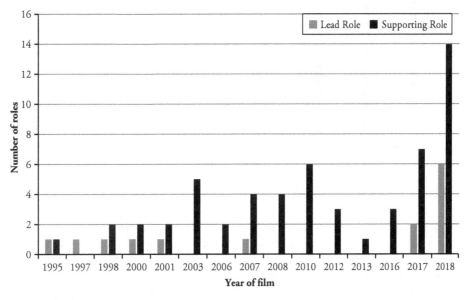

FIGURE 1. Type of role by year.

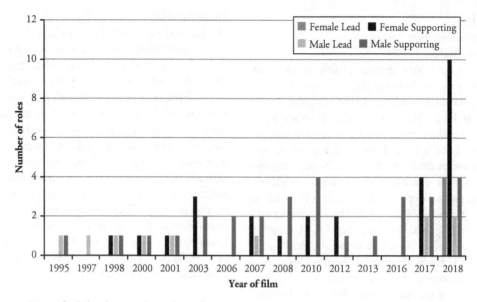

FIGURE 2. Type of role by character's gender and year.

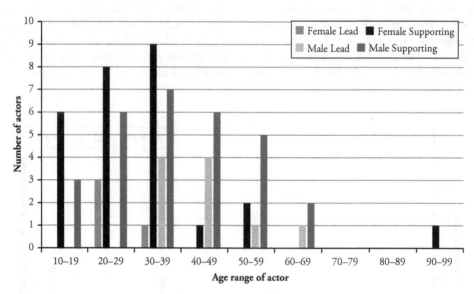

FIGURE 3. Age of actors by role type and gender.

(Indian, Pakistani, and Parsi). There were two outliers in the sample who were not racially Asian, yet they played Asian roles. In *Kill Bill: Volume 1* (2003), a French actor who is White played an Asian character named Sofie Fatale who was described as half-Japanese, half-French. In *Cloud Atlas* (2012), a British actor who is White played an Asian character named Hae Joo Chang. The character was described as ethnically Korean by using special effects to alter his face with more typically Asian features (i.e., smaller eyes, flatter face), despite objections by the Media Action Network for Asian Americans (Brooks, 2012).

Film Genres

The sample included films of multiple genres, ranging from action-comedy, drama, horror, mystery/thriller, science-fiction/adventure, and romantic comedy films. Some films were only categorized into one genre. However, others had aspects of multiple genres, so they were counted under multiple genres. For example, *Gran Torino* (2008) is a drama, while *Cloud Atlas* (2012) is considered both science-fiction/adventure and drama. Most common were action comedy (n = 12), science-fiction/adventure (n = 9), and drama (n = 7) films. Mystery/thriller (n = 4), romantic comedy (n = 4), and horror (n = 2) films were the least common genres. Between 1995 and 2005, action-comedy films were the most common genre, and they remained consistent across the years assessed (Figure 4). There were a few science-fiction/adventure films pre-2000; however, the reemergence of science-fiction/adventure occurred after 2010. Mystery/thrillers emerged in 2003 and then reemerged in 2013. Dramas began to emerge after 2005. Horror films emerged after 2010. Romantic comedies emerged in 2017. Only after 2005 did film genres begin to diversify, with 2018 as the most diverse year, having films of all categories.

Race/Ethnicity of Directors

The analytic sample included 27 directors. Each of the 25 films had one director, with the exception of *Cloud Atlas* (2012), which had three directors. Out of all directors, four were Asian while 23 were White. Among the Asian directors, one was female (3.7%) and three were male (11.1%). There were four White female directors (14.8%), but the majority of films had White male directors (70.4%). None of the directors publicly identified as non-binary or non-gender conforming.

Stereotype-Resisting Representations

There were many ways in which representations of Asian Americans in the films resisted stereotypes that are documented in previous literature. These diverse representations were noted across films and genres. While Asian women have historically been regarded as menacing, timid, and submissive (Mok, 1998; Said, 1978), stereotype-resisting female characters in this sample exemplified opposing traits such as compassionate, brave, and mischievous. In particular, female lead roles emerged in 2018. Those characters were all featured in romantic comedies and were partnered with male leads, including Rachel Chu in *Crazy Rich Asians* (2018), Lara Jean in *To All the Boys I've Loved*

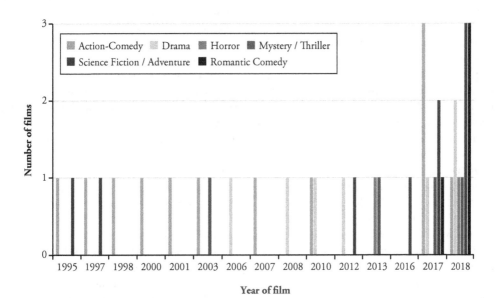

FIGURE 4.   Film genres by year.

Before (2018), and both Stacy De Novo and Lady Margaret in *The Princess Switch* (2018). These characters exhibited a variety of traits including compassionate, playful, humorous, romantic, and courageous, resisting the stereotype of Asian women as menacing and timid (Mok, 1998; Said, 1978). For example, all of these female-lead characters showcased the playful trait when bantering with their male romantic interests. Mischievous female characters also challenged the idea of Asian women as submissive (Mok, 1998; Said, 1978). These included Yoona from *Cloud Atlas* (2012), Kitty in *To All the Boys I've Loved Before* (2018), and Lady Margaret from *The Princess Switch* (2018). For example, Yoona broke the strict slave rules of exploring the building past curfew, entering a prohibited closet, and viewing restricted films.

Regarding male stereotype-resisting characters, films with male romantic interests as vital characters challenged the historic representation of Asian males as emasculate and lacking in sexual desirability (Han, 2006; Keum, 2016; Mok, 1998; Said, 1978). These male characters appeared in more recent films including Hae Joo Chang, a supporting character in *Cloud Atlas* (2012), Kumail, the lead in *The Big Sick* (2017), and Nick Young, the lead in *Crazy Rich Asians* (2018). In particular, the casting of Nick Young was met with praise from audiences, and the character was identified as a sex symbol (France, 2018).

Other stereotype-resisting characters were portrayed as loyal, countering the stereotype of Asians as manipulative and inscrutable (Mok, 1998; Qiu & Muturi, 2016). Characters displaying this trait included Liu Kang in *Mortal Kombat* (1995) and *Mortal Kombat: Annihilation* (1997), Chief Inspector Lee in *Rush Hour* (1998), *Rush Hour 2* (2001), and *Rush Hour 3* (2007), Gogo Yobari, Johnny Mo, and Sofie Fatale in *Kill Bill: Volume 1* (2003), Thao Vang Lor in *Gran Torino* (2008), Knives Chau in *Scott Pilgrim Vs. the World* (2010), Sonmi and Hae Joo Chang in *Cloud Atlas* (2012), Kumail in *The Big Sick* (2017), Peik Lin and Colin Koo in *Crazy Rich Asians* (2018), and Suzume in *The Darkest Minds* (2018). For example, Peik Lin was a loyal friend to Rachel Chu, offering her a place to stay, food to eat, and words of encouragement while she grieved the fate of her romantic relationship.

Characters coded as "down to earth" defied the image of Asians as greedy and elitist (Lee, 2009; Qiu & Muturi, 2016). They included Sue Lor in *Gran Torino* (2008), Nick Young, Astrid, and Colin in *Crazy Rich Asians* (2018), Stacy De Novo in *The Princess Switch* (2018), and Margot Kim in *Searching* (2018). Though very affluent, the characters in *Crazy Rich Asians* (2018) did not let money get to their head; instead, they remained humble and conscious of the valuable things in life that do not require money such as love.

Stereotype-Confirming Representations

The films also contained stereotype-confirming representations of Asian Americans. There was a plethora of lead male martial artists, yet films also exhibited nerdy and emasculate male side characters (Keum, 2016; Mok, 1998). The Asian-lead roles in the 1990s and early to mid-2000s were dominated by men in the action-comedy genre and in martial arts films (Figure 4). These characters starred in the films *Mortal Combat* (1995), *Mortal Kombat: Annihilation* (1997), *Rush Hour* (1998), *Shanghai Noon* (2000), *Rush Hour 2* (2001), and *Rush Hour 3* (2007). Notably, Jackie Chan played the lead role in four of the six martial arts films. The male-lead characters in action films displayed similar traits: brave, heroic, athletic, yet emasculate at times (e.g., being oblivious to women or not desired by female characters). As such, the representations contributed to the trope of athletic Asian men in martial arts films yet also confirmed the stereotype of Asian men as emasculate (Keum, 2016; Mok, 1998). For example, Liu Kang in *Mortal Combat* (1995) was teased by his peer, Johnny Cage, for not understanding the romantic stare and aroma of Kitana, the attractive female romantic interest.

Unfortunately, there was a common trope of a timid, soft-spoken female Asian supporting character who required the assistance or influence of a (often White) male lead to gain confidence. This observation reaffirmed the notion of Asian women as feeble and submissive, especially to a White male partner (Mok, 1998; Said, 1978). A few characters who succumbed to this trope included Knives Chau from *Scott Pilgrim vs. the World* (2010), Sonmi in *Cloud Atlas* (2012), Mantis in *Guardians of the Galaxy Vol.*

2 (2017), and Suzume from *The Darkest Minds* (2018). For example, only by the aid of Hae Joo Chang, a White actor playing an ethnically Korean character, did Sonmi in *Cloud Atlas* (2012) break out of her shell, build confidence, and become a charismatic leader who proclaimed many anti-slavery speeches such as, "You can maintain power over people as long as you give them something. Rob a man of everything and that man will no longer be in your power." In addition, Suzume from *The Darkest Minds* (2018) had no speaking lines yet built her confidence and strength after being saved from a mob by Liam, a White man.

Dylan from *Akeelah and the Bee* (2006), Ken and Kyle Katayanagi in *Scott Pilgrim vs. the World* (2010), and Ned in *Spider-Man: Homecoming* (2017) were all male characters who displayed high levels of intelligence as one of their key and only qualities, upholding the nerdy mold of Asian men in media (Mok, 1998). For example, Ned in *Spider-Man: Homecoming* (2017) expressed excitement for being the "guy in the chair" who served as the intelligent, tech guru sidekick of Spider-Man himself. Interestingly, Ned was also the only character in the sample with a large physical build.

Comedic characters were present across films as well. Portrayal of Asian characters as comedic relief was a common typecast implying Asians as fools (Mok, 1998). These characters included Chief Inspector Lee in *Rush Hour* (1998), *Rush Hour 2* (2001), and *Rush Hour 3* (2007), Chon Wang in *Shanghai Noon* (2000), Sue Lor in *Gran Torino* (2008), Drew Thomas in *The Conjuring* (2013), Bodhi Rock and Chirrut Imwe in *Rogue One: A Star Wars Story* (2016), Kumail in *The Big* Sick (2017), Mantis in *Guardians of the Galaxy Vol. 2* (2017), Ned in *Spider-Man: Homecoming* (2017), Lara Jean and Kitty in *To All the Boys I've Loved* Before (2018), Peik Lin, Rachel Chu, and Wye Mun Goh in *Crazy Rich* Asians (2018), and Lady Margaret in *The Princess Switch* (2018). For example, Chirrut Imwe in *Rogue One: A Star Wars Story* (2016) was kidnapped with a bag over his head and he said, "Are you kidding me? I'm blind!"

There were characters whose main characteristics were coded as sadistic and evil, as exemplified by gruesome acts of violence, enforcing the stereotype of Asians as dangerous and menacing (Mok, 1998). Female characters with these traits included Hu Li in

Rush Hour 2 (2001), O-Ren Ishii and Gogo Yobari from *Kill Bill: Volume 1* (2003), and Dragon Lady Jasmine in *Rush Hour 3* (2007). Male characters with these traits included Shang Tsung in *Mortal Kombat* (1995), Ricky Tan in *Rush Hour 2* (2001), Johnny Mo in *Kill Bill: Volume 1* (2003), and Spider and Smokie in *Gran Torino* (2008). Characters that were aggressive but not necessarily evil included Hattori Hanzo in *Kill Bill: Volume 1* (2003) who angrily scolded his restaurant worker and Rose Tico in *Rogue One: A Star Wars Story* (2016) who stated "I wish I could put my fist through this whole lousy town."

A number of film representations also confirmed the perpetual foreigner stereotype through interactions involving White characters who taunted Asian characters for their cultural background, therefore othering them. Characters that were stereotyped as foreigners included Chief Inspector Lee in *Rush Hour* (1998) and *Rush Hour 2* (2001), Chon Wang in *Shanghai Noon* (2000), Thao Vang and Sue Lor, Spider, and Smokie in *Gran Torino* (2008), and Quan Ngoc Minh in *The Foreigner* (2017). For example, Walt Kowalski in the beginning of *Gran Torino* (2008) constantly spewed racial slurs at his Hmong neighbors and scoffed at their traditional customs of family parties, cultural food, and excessive gift-giving.

Across the variety of film genres, characters also displayed a family-oriented trait, which is related to the model minority myth (Atkin et al., 2018; Lee, 2009; Mok, 1998). These characters included Liu Kang in *Mortal Kombat* (1995), Consul Han in *Rush Hour* (1998) and *Rush Hour 3* (2007), Thao Vang and Sue Lor in *Gran Torino* (2008), Meiying in *The Karate Kid* (2010), Kumail, Azmat, Sharmeen, and Naveed in *The Big Sick* (2017), Nick, Eleanor, and Ah Ma Young in *Crazy Rich Asians* (2018), David Kim in *Searching* (2018), and Lara Jean, Margot, and Kitty in *To All the Boys I've Loved Before* (2018). For example, Meiying in *The Karate Kid* (2010) felt pressured to respect and obey her parents' wishes, no matter how restrictive their orders were to her freedom. Strict Asian parental figures were also present in some of films, again exhibiting the idea of Asians having strong family values (Atkin et al., 2018; Lee, 2009). These included in Azmat and Sharmeen in *The Big Sick* (2017), as well as Eleanor Young and Ah Ma in *Crazy Rich Asians* (2018). For example, Kumail's parents in *The Big Sick* (2017) strongly encouraged him to pursue an arranged marriage as in line with their Pakistani-Muslim identity and in contrast to Kumail's personal interests. Azmat and Sharmeen were explicitly upset when their efforts did not prevail. Eleanor and Ah Ma in *Crazy Rich Asians* (2018) also forbade and nearly sabotaged Nick's romantic relationship that opposed their family's tradition. These examples confirm the concept of Asian families having a strong parental influence on their children's life decisions (Lee, 2009).

Intersections of Gender and Sexuality
Some representations neither resisted nor confirmed stereotypes regarding Asians. Rather, they portrayed commonalities that reflect the intersections of gender and sexuality. These themes included a scarcity of same-sex relationships, female Asian characters with bright strips color in their hair, and physically petite female characters.

Female actors, whether in lead or supporting roles, were often cast as heterosexual romantic interests in films. This characteristic was observed in all female lead characters in the sample and supporting characters such as Princess Pei-Pei in *Shanghai Noon* (2000), Knives Chau in *Scott Pilgrim vs. the World* (2010), Meiying in *The Karate* Kid (2010), Sonmi from *Cloud Atlas* (2012), and Rose Tico in *Star Wars: The Last Jedi* (2017). Out of the sample of films only one character, Greg from *Bird Box* (2018), was in a same-sex relationship. The remaining films portrayed their characters as heterosexual with heterosexual romantic pairings or they did not specify the character's sexuality.

There were female characters who wore a strip of bright color in their black hair including Knives Chau in *Scott Pilgrim Vs. the World* (2010) and both Sonmi and Yoona from *Cloud Atlas* (2012). Sonmi's colorful orange streak signified her initial status as a slave, as all of the female slaves shared a colorful hair streak; she eventually cut off the strand as a symbol of her rebelliousness and liberation. In contrast, Knives dyed a section of her hair blue as a redefining moment and symbol of her character development and newfound confidence.

Female characters were also often physically petite such as Soo Young in *Rush Hour* (1998) and *Rush Hour 3* (2007), Princess Pei-Pei in *Shanghai*

Noon (2000), Hu Li in *Rush Hour 2* (2001), Gogo Yobari in *Kill Bill: Volume 1* (2003), Dragon Lady Jasmine in *Rush Hour 3* (2007), Sue Lor in *Gran Torino* (2008), Meiying from *The Karate Kid* (2010), Knives Chau from *Scott Pilgrim vs. the World* (2010), Sonmi and Yoona in *Cloud Atlas* (2012), Mantis in *Guardians of the Galaxy Vol. 2* (2017), Fan in *The Foreigner* (2017), Rachel, Peik Lin, Astrid, and Araminta in *Crazy Rich* Asians (2018), Suzume from *The Darkest Minds* (2018), Lara Jean, Margot, and Kitty in *To All the Boys I've Loved Before* (2018), and Margot and Pamela Kim in *Searching* (2018). However, Rose Tico from *Star Wars: The Last Jedi* (2017) was not a typically petite female character, as she had a slightly larger build than the others.

Discussion

The results of this film analysis provided an interesting look at the nuanced and complex progression of Asian American media representation in recent years. Across the years, the sample showed an increase in the number of Asian characters in films, aligning with the recent increase in the Asian American population (Census, 2017). Representations that resisted stereotypes were present in the sample, especially in more recent films. However, stereotype confirming representations remained prevalent, which affirms the historic trend of misrepresentation of Asian Americans in media (Mok, 1998; Qiu & Muturi, 2016). Although there was a diversification of roles and genres in the films over time, stories about Asian Americans were widely not told by Asian Americans themselves (i.e., most directors were not Asian American). Analyzing the pattern of representations in the film sample illuminates commonly held beliefs about Asian Americans and could spark discussion on how to promote the internalization of more authentic representations for positive identity development.

As a socializing agent, media representations exhibited in the film sample might serve as a context for Asian American adolescents and young adults to view themselves and others within social systems (Mok, 1998). Moreover, the content of these representations varied across roles, gender, and genres over time, and can frame how Asian Americans are perceived in broader society. Stereotype-resisting representations in the films included playful female romantic interests and male romantic interests along with mischievous, loyal, and down to earth characters. These categorizations appeared to resist and challenge racial stereotypes regarding Asian women as menacing and timid and Asian men as undesirable (Mok, 1998; Said, 1978). They also countered the stereotype of greedy and elitist Asians (Lee, 2009; Qiu & Muturi, 2016). Such representations reflect the diversity within Asian American individuals and can provide opportunities for positive social mirroring and support how Asian Americans view themselves (Mok, 1998; Suárez-Orozco & Qin-Hilliard, 2004). In addition, media representations that challenge racial stereotypes can positively influence how society views Asian Americans by defying stereotypes (Cooley, 1902; Mok, 1998).

On the other hand, stereotype-confirming representations included emasculate men, martial artists, timid women, nerdy sidekicks, characters for comedic relief, sadistic aggressors, perpetual foreigners, family-focused characters (without any other nuanced characteristics), and overly strict parental figures. These categorizations came about due to their nature of endorsing rigid racial stereotypes typically imposed on Asian characters and upholding the commonly perceived homogeneity of Asian Americans (Mok, 1998; Rogers & Way, 2016). There arises the danger of negative social mirroring and an internalization of the stereotypical portrayals of one's own racial group when in-group members view negative representation of their group through the film (Cooley, 1902). Furthermore, stereotypical representations can reinforce negative attitudes and behaviors from out-group members (both the dominant group and other minority groups) toward Asian Americans. In this way, exposure to media representations that confirm stereotypes of Asian Americans can promote problematic intergroup behavior in the form of discrimination, microaggressions, and othering (Buchanan & Settles, 2018; Jaspal & Cinnirella, 2010). These acts of discrimination can negatively impact Asian American adolescents and young adults who are still exploring and developing their ERI (Erikson, 1968; Suárez-Orozco & Qin-Hilliard, 2004; Torres & Ong, 2010). Therefore, one direction for future research is to examine the range of effects that viewing stereotypical representations in media can

have for out-group members, including White youth and youth from other racial minority groups.

Dylan from *Akeelah and the Bee*, Ken and Kyle Katayanagi in *Scott Pilgrim vs. the World* (2010), and Ned in *Spider-Man: Homecoming* were all characters who displayed high levels of intelligence. Notably, Ned was also the only character in the sample with a large physical build, further demonstrating a physical difference of him compared to average-sized, conventionally attractive characters. Many Asian male supporting characters in the sample were portrayed solely as nerdy, dorky, and awkward without any other qualities or character development. Although intellect can be considered a positive trait, these characters reinforced the model minority myth with intelligence as one of their key and only qualities, further disregarding the range of academic experiences and personalities of Asian Americans (Mok, 1998; Teranishi, 2010). The model minority myth positions Asian Americans as the most academically successful racial minority group without considering the diverse experiences Asian Americans of varying ethnicities have navigating academia (Lee, 2009; Teranishi, 2010). The myth can also impact in-group members by causing psychological distress stemming from the pressure to adhere to unrealistic expectations and the pressure to succeed (Atkin et al., 2018). Failure to conform to the stereotype may negatively impact one's ERI development by promoting feelings of rejection and isolation within their ethnic and racial group (Atkin et al., 2018). The model minority myth also implies an asexual quality for Asian American men, further affecting self-esteem in a negative manner (Keum, 2016; Liu & Chang, 2007).

Another notable key finding was that representations of Asian characters differed greatly based on gender. Asian male stereotypes were presented in a very contrasting way, leaning toward nerdiness or extreme athleticism in the case of the martial arts films. However, what remained common among these characters was their emasculate traits, which is a racial stereotype of Asian American men that can have negative effects on self-esteem and body image, two important aspects of identity formation (Baumeister, 1999; Han, 2006; Keum, 2016). Scholars propose the desexualization of Asian men serves the purpose of neutralizing concerns against mainstream fear of a yellow peril (Han, 2006; Said, 1978).

Asian female characters, on the other hand, more frequently served the role of a romantic interest (i.e., object). Such was the case for all of the female lead roles and the five female supporting roles in the sample. Asian women were often cast as romantic interests, while Asian males scarcely served the romantic interest roles; there were only three accounts of male romantic interests in the sample, which appeared in more recent years (Hae Joo Chang in *Cloud Atlas* [2012], Kumail in *The Big Sick* [2017], and Nick Young in *Crazy Rich Asians* [2018]). Due to the previously established practice of desexualizing Asian men, it was especially impressive and groundbreaking for Nick Young from *Crazy Rich Asians* (2018) to earn status as a sex symbol in the film.

While this study identified an increase in Asian male romantic interests in the film by year, it is important to consider the nuances of the character Nick Young being played by a multiracial actor who is half-White. The casting of Nick Young and his appealing portrayal could be discussed in relation to colorism (or pigmentocracy) in the Asian community, in which lighter skin is often considered more attractive and high class than darker skin (Jones, 2013). The concept of pigmentocracy may also explain the casting of a White actor to play an Asian character Sofie Fatale in *Kill Bill: Volume 1* (2003). The effect of pigmentocracy on casting may feed into many Asian Americans' preexisting insecurities in seeing their race as a limiting factor in the perception of their own attractiveness (Keum, 2016; Mok, 1998). Future research should consider the further investigation of the impact that colorism in the Asian American community and in media may have on identity development among adolescents and young adults.

Furthermore, even though Asian Americans are often excluded in media (Mok, 1998), Hae Joo Chang from *Cloud Atlas* (2012) is an Asian character who was played by a White actor in *yellowface*, using special effects to alter their face with more typically Asian features (i.e., smaller eyes, flatter face). This decision was protested by the Media Action Network for Asian Americans who acknowledged this cinematic choice as yet another example of racially offensive depictions of Asians in media (Brooks, 2012).

Use of yellowface is particularly harmful to Asian Americans as it reinforces notions of white superiority, emphasizes the perpetual foreigner stereotype, turns Asian culture into a spectacle, and further limits Asian Americans' opportunities for authentic representations in media (Huynh et al., 2011; Vats & Nishime, 2013). Future research should further explore the use of yellowface by White actors in media portrayals of Asian characters and its impact on the racial identity development of Asian American adolescents and young adults.

Gendered representations were also present for female characters. Results suggested a common trope of timid, soft-spoken Asian women who required the assistance or influence of a White male character in order to gain confidence. This helpless, servile characterization has been attributed to why Asian women are more greatly accepted on-screen (Mok, 1998). A few characters who succumbed to this trope include Meiying from *The Karate Kid*, Knives Chau from *Scott Pilgrim vs. the World* (2010), Sonmi in *Cloud Atlas* (2012), Mantis in *Guardians of the Galaxy Vol. 2* (2017), and Suzume from *The Darkest Minds* (2018). Of these characters, Knives and Sonmi both also displayed the cliché of Asian female characters with a streak of color in their hair. Sonmi's colorful orange streak signified her initial slavery, as all the female slaves shared a colorful hair streak; she eventually cut off the strand as a symbol of her rebelliousness. Contrastingly, Knives dyed a section of her hair blue as a redefining moment and symbol of her character development and newfound confidence. Although for opposite reasons, both women utilized colorful hair to symbolize a shift in their identity. Future avenues for research might explore the implications of this common trope for Asian women in media and its possible links to the historic portrayal of their exoticism.

Most female characters were physically petite, and their physical build conformed to the conventionally attractive "slim" body weight. However, Asian women's body dissatisfaction and self-esteem may be affected by Western culture and values, such as those portrayed in media (Mok, 1998; Tsai, Hoerr, & Song, 1998). Notably, however, Rose Tico from *Star Wars: The Last Jedi* (2017) was not a typically petite female character. She had a slightly larger build than the others, serving as one example of a diverse body shape. Viewing different types of body shapes that represent a more diverse population may positively affect one's self-esteem and body image, therefore impacting identity formation especially among Asian American adolescents and young adults who are socialized by media messages at this critical time of their development. Future studies should explore how female characters with different body types (e.g., those who are strong and brave without body shapes that conform to stereotypes about Asian women) could impact youth's self-esteem.

The descriptive findings revealed the ages of the Asian actors differed by gender. Female actors' ages were mostly skewed toward younger ages (10 to 30), while male actors were more evenly distributed across the wide age range (17 to 64). It was interesting to see how the concentration of Asian women was nested within the younger age range, which is also the period when adolescents' and young adults' identities and perception of themselves are particularly sensitive to media messages (Erikson, 1968; Manago, 2015). Future research should explore the intersections of race and gender and the value placed on youthfulness in order to understand more fully the role of media on identity development.

The reemergence of lead roles in the late 2010s included a more diverse set of genres and character traits. Such genres included not only action but also drama, horror, mystery, science fiction, and romantic comedy films. This finding reflects the increased diversity in films with Asian characters over time in U.S. films. With a newfound increase in representation, Asian American adolescents and young adults have more opportunities to observe a diverse array of role models and engage in positive social mirroring (Suárez-Orozco & Qin-Hilliard, 2004), which can promote positive ERI development. Exploring the societal factors that contributed to an increase in lead roles in the late 2010s (e.g., pressure from Asian American actors or advocacy groups) may also be an interesting avenue for future research.

Notably, the four films that were in the romantic comedy genre (*The Big Sick* [2017], *To All the Boys I've Loved Before* [2018], *The Princess Switch* [2018], and *Crazy Rich Asians* [2018]) all centered around heterosexual coupling, with no representation of other forms of coupling. Importantly, in the entire sample only one character, Greg from *Bird Box*, was mentioned as engaging in a same-sex relationship, while other characters were either explicitly heterosexual or did not specify a sexual orientation. The invisibility of sexuality in Asian characters, especially males, perpetuates the stereotype of Asian American men as asexual by way of the model minority myth, and can contribute to low self-esteem and poor body image (Keum, 2016; Liu & Chang, 2007). As well, Han (2006) explores how media images and popular narratives gender Asian characters, particularly men, and how heterosexual discourse dominates media. A lack of diverse sexualities represented in these romance films in media may feed young lesbian, gay, and bisexual Asian Americans' feelings of isolation and lack of value in society (Bond, 2015). Scarce representations may also reduce this group's access to information about sexual minorities, therefore hindering sexual identity exploration and development (Bond, 2015; Buchanan & Settles, 2018). Future studies should explore the erasure of sexuality among depictions of Asian Americans and the impact of heteronormative narratives portrayed in media on Asian Americans.

Another notable but not necessarily surprising finding was that the vast majority of directors appeared to be White. Mok (1998) described how an inherent issue with media images of Asians is the stress and discomfort of dealing with images that have been defined by others, in this case, White directors, rather than self-defined messages by those within the community. It is dangerous and problematic for out-group directors to write inaccurate portrayals of minorities, since it maintains negative racial stereotypes rather than resisting and challenging said stereotypes (Rogers & Way, 2016; Shaheen, 2003). The perpetual foreigner stereotype is one particularly harmful stereotype that out-group members may perpetuate. For example, *Gran Torino* (2008) had a White director, and the film's main character initially supported the perpetual foreigner stereotype by spouting racial slurs and othering his Hmong neighbors, Thao Vang and Sue Lor. Exposure to this stereotype in media may lead to identity conflict and a low sense of belonging for Asian Americans living in American culture (Huynh et al., 2011). This finding illuminates the shortcomings of American media and the potential damage done when members of dominant groups write and direct the experiences of minority groups. This work points to the critical need to support the work of minorities, particularly Asian Americans, to be able to tell their own stories in authentic, nuanced, and meaningful ways.

Limitations

While this research contributes to a growing body of literature investigating the ways in which Asian Americans are portrayed in the media, there were limitations. Primarily, this study focused on providing a descriptive picture of the media representations of Asian Americans. Future work should examine the impact these media messages have on Asian Americans with samples of Asian American adolescents and young adults through experimental methods. An additional avenue for future research is to consider how Asian American parents discuss media representations with their youth through racial socialization (e.g., Juang et al., 2018).

Additionally, coding the representations portrayed by Asian characters as stereotype confirming or resisting proved challenging due to the subjectivity of such categorization and the complexity of each character's role. We also acknowledge the complexity of coding the depictions. For example, some representations can be both positive and stereotype-confirming when they are void of other character development (e.g., family-oriented with strict parents). At times, these contradictions were displayed by the same character (e.g., Chief Inspector Lee was depicted as loyal, athletic, and asexual). Thus, we challenge future research to grapple with these complexities and consider how youth make meaning of the content they are viewing. Future research might also consider larger teams of researchers to establish reliable coding schemes across multiple social positionalities (e.g., ethnicity, gender, sexual orientation).

Lastly, the sample was limited as it consisted of 25 films that were not evenly distributed over time. Future studies should explore a wider and more contemporary range of films that better represent the historic trend of media representations of Asian Americans in U.S. films. Although beyond the scope of the current project, an additional avenue for research is to explore how exposure to foreign media (e.g.,

streaming from Asian countries is increasingly available and popular) may impact Asian American adolescents' and young adults' identity development.

Implications for Parenting and Education

Findings from this work provide real-world implications for those who interact with Asian American adolescents and young adults. For example, caretakers of Asian American children can consider intentionally choosing films with diverse Asian characters to view as a family and discuss the different roles they see, and what they may not see, since familial ethnic socialization is positively related to ERI development (Umaña-Taylor & Guimond, 2010). Educators should also be mindful about the films they choose to present in their classrooms by being aware of the negative impact that distorted and stereotypical representations can have on young people (Buchanan & Settles, 2018). Instead of reinforcing one-dimensional notions about Asian Americans, educators can select media that includes ethnically, racially, and qualitatively diverse characters as a way to expose young people to positive role models in media that better reflect the nuances within racial groups (Suárez-Orozco & Qin-Hilliard, 2004). These activities serve as a few examples of how to promote positive identity development among Asian American adolescents and young adults through film.

Conclusion

This study investigated representations of Asian Americans in U.S. films over the last 25 years. Stereotype-confirming representations were found in some films that are harmful and can promote negative attitudes about individuals from already minoritized groups and confirm racial stereotypes. While more diverse representations of Asian Americans in film has increased in recent years, there is still much room for improved positive, stereotype-resisting representations. The results of this study indicate that the current landscape of media is on the cusp of more diverse and nuanced media representations, which should provide more opportunities for positive social mirroring and positive identity development. Additional research is needed to understand the wider scope of films that exist and the impact that Asian American representation in U.S. media will continue to have on adolescents' and young adults' identity development, and human development more broadly (e.g., intergroup attitudes and behaviors). As well, it is important for authentic stories to be told that showcase a wide array of representations and depict the rich diversity of Asian American life.

Disclosure Statement

No potential conflict of interest was reported by the authors.

Note

Address correspondence to Tiffany Besana, Department of Educational Psychology, University of Illinois at Chicago, Chicago, IL, USA. E-mail: tbesan2@uic.edu

References

Atkin, A. L., Yoo, H. C., Jager, J., & Yeh, C. J. (2018). Internalization of the model minority myth, school racial composition, and psychological distress among Asian American adolescents. *Asian American Journal of Psychology*, 9(2), 108–16. doi:10.1037/aap0000096

Baumeister, R. F. (1999). Self-concept, self-esteem, and identity. In V. J. Derlega, B. A. Winstead, & W. H. Jones (Eds.), *Nelson-hall series in psychology. Personality: Contemporary theory and research* (pp. 339–75). Chicago, IL: Nelson-Hall Publishers.

Bond, B. J. (2015). The mediating role of self-discrepancies in the relationship between media exposure and well-being among lesbian, gay, and bisexual adolescents. *Media Psychology*, 18(1), 51–73. doi:10.1080/15213269.2014.917591

Bronfenbrenner, U., & Morris, P. A. (2006). The bioecological model of human development. *Handbook of Child Psychology*. doi:10.1002/9780470147658.chpsy0114

Brooks, X. (2012, October 26). Cloud Atlas under fire for casting white actors in "yellowface" makeup. *The Guardian*. Retrieved from https://www.theguardian.com/film/2012/oct/26/cloud-atlas-under-fire-yellowface

Buchanan, N. T., & Settles, I. H. (2018). Managing (in)visibility and hypervisibility in the workplace. *Journal of Vocational Behavior* 113:1–5. Advanced online publication. doi: 10.1016/j.jvb.2018.11.001.

Cooley, C. H. (1902). *Human nature and the social order*. New York, NY: Charles Scribner & Sons.

Erikson, E. H. (1968). *Identity: Youth and crisis*. New York, NY: W. W. Norton.

France, L. R. (2018, August 20). "Crazy rich Asians" proves Asian men can be leading men. *CNN Entertainment*. Retrieved from https://www.cnn.com/2018/08/20/entertainment/crazy-rich-asian-sex-symbols/index.html

Han, C. (2006). Geisha of a different kind: Gay Asian men and the gendering of sexual identity. *Sexuality & Culture: An Interdisciplinary Quarterly*, 10(3), 3–28. doi:10.1007/s12119-006-1018-0

Huynh, Q.-L., Devos, T., & Smalarz, L. (2011). Perpetual foreigner in one's own land: Potential implications for identity and psychological adjustment. *Journal of Social and Clinical Psychology*, 30(2), 133–62. doi:10.1521/jscp.2011.30.2.133f

Hwang, W. C., & Ting, J. Y. (2008). Disaggregating the effects of acculturation and acculturative stress on mental health of Asian Americans. *Cultural Diversity & Ethnic Minority Psychology*, 14, 147–54. doi:10.1037/1099-9809.14.2.147

Jaspal, R., & Cinnirella, M. (2010). Media representations of British Muslims and hybridised threats to identity. *Contemporary Islam*, 4(3), 289–310. doi:10.1007/s11562-010-0126-7

Jones, T. (2013). The significance of skin color in Asian and Asian-American communities: Initial reflections. *UC Irvine Law Review*, 3(4), 1105–23.

Juang, L. P., Park, I., Kim, S. Y., Lee, R. M., Qin, D., Okazaki, S., . . . Lau, A. (2018). Reactive and proactive ethnic–Racial socialization practices of second-generation Asian American parents. *Asian American Journal of Psychology*, 9(1), 4–16. doi:10.1037/aap0000101

Kagitçibasi, C. (2007). *Family, self, and human development across cultures: Theory and applications*. Mahwah, NJ: Erlbaum.

Keum, B. T. (2016). Asian American men's internalization of Western media appearance ideals, social comparison, and acculturative stress. *Asian American Journal of Psychology*, 7(4), 256–64. doi:10.1037/aap0000057

Lee, S. J. (2009). *Unraveling the "model minority" stereotype: Listening to the Asian American youth.* New York, NY: Teachers College Press.

Liu, W. M., & Chang, T. (2007). Asian American masculinities. In F. T. L. Leong, A. Ebreo, L. Kinoshita, A. G. Inman, L. H. Yang, & M. Fu (Eds.), *Handbook of Asian American psychology* (2nd ed., pp. 197–211, Chapter x, 515 Pages) Sage Publications, Inc, Thousand Oaks, CA. Retrieved from http://proxy.cc.uic.edu/login?url=https://search-proquest-com.proxy.cc.uic.edu/docview/621431632?accountid=14552

Manago, A. M. (2015). Media and the development of identity. *Emerging Trends in the Social and Behavioral Sciences*, 1–14. doi:10.1002/9781118900772.etrds0212

McHale, S. M., Dotterer, A., & Kim, J.-Y. (2009). An ecological perspective on the media and youth development. *American Behavioral Scientist*, 52(8), 1186–203. doi:10.1177/0002764209331541

Mok, T. A. (1998). Getting the message: Media images and stereotypes and their effect on Asian Americans. *Cultural Diversity & Mental Health*, 4(3), 185–202. doi:10.1037/1099-9809.4.3.185

Okazaki, S., Lee, R. M., & Sue, S. (2007). Theoretical and conceptual models: Toward Asian Americanist psychology. In F. T. L. Leong, A. Ebreo, L. Kinoshita, A. G. Inman, L. H. Yang, & M. Fu (Eds.), *Handbook of Asian American psychology* (2nd ed., pp. 29–46). Thousand Oaks, CA: Sage Publications.

Pasch, K. E., & Velazquez, C. E. (2013). Alcohol advertising and underage drinking. In P. M. Miller, S. A. Ball, M. E. Bates, A. W. Blume, K. M. Kampman, D. J. Kavanagh, & P. De Witte (Eds.), *Comprehensive addictive behaviors and disorders, vol. 3: Interventions for addiction* (pp. 917–23, Chapter xvi, 983 Pages) San Diego, CA: Elsevier Academic Press. doi:10.1016/B978-0-12-398338-1.00092-0

Qiu, J., & Muturi, N. (2016). Asian American public relations practitioners' perspectives on diversity. *Howard Journal of Communications*, 27(3), 236–49. doi:10.1080/10646175.2016.1172527

Rogers, L. O., & Way, N. (2016). "I have goals to prove all those people wrong and not fit into any one of those boxes": Paths of resistance to stereotypes among black adolescent males. *Journal of Adolescent Research*, 31(3), 263–98. doi:10.1177/0743558415600071

Said, E. (1978). *Orientalism.* London, UK: Penguin.

Schwartz, S. J., Zamboanga, B. L., Weisskirch, R. S., & Rodriguez, L. (2009). The relationships of personal and ethnic identity exploration to indices of adaptive and maladaptive psychosocial functioning. *International Journal of Behavioral Development*, 33(2), 131–44. doi:10.1177/0165025408098018

Shaheen, J. G. (2003). Reel bad arabs: How hollywood vilifies a people. *The ANNALS of the American Academy of Political and Social Science*, 588(1), 171–93. doi:10.1177/0002716203588001011

Suárez-Orozco, M. M., & Qin-Hilliard, D. B. (2004). *Globalization: Culture and education in the new millennium.* Berkeley: University of California Press.

Teranishi, R. T. (2010). *Asians in the ivory tower: Dilemmas of racial inequality in american higher education.* New York, NY: Teachers College Press.

Torres, L., & Ong, A. D. (2010). A daily diary investigation of Latino ethnic identity, discrimination, and depression. *Cultural Diversity & Ethnic Minority Psychology*, 16, 561–8. doi:10.1037/a0020652

Tsai, C., Hoerr, S. L., & Song, W. O. (1998). Dieting behavior of Asian college women attending a US university. *Journal of American College Health*, 46(4), 163–8. doi:10.1080/07448489809595604

U.S. Census Bureau. (2017). Quickfacts. Retrieved from https://www.census.gov/quickfacts/fact/table/US/PST045218

U.S. Census Bureau. (2018). Race. Retrieved from https://www.census.gov/topics/population/race/about.html

Umaña-Taylor, A. J., & Guimond, A. B. (2010). A longitudinal examination of parenting behaviors and perceived discrimination predicting Latino adolescents' ethnic identity. *Developmental Psychology*, 46(3), 636–50. doi:10.1037/a0019376

Umaña-Taylor, A. J., Quintana, S. M., Lee, R. M., Cross, W. E., Jr., Rivas-Drake, D., Schwartz, S. J. & Ethnic and Racial Identity in the 21st Century Study Group. (2014). Ethnic and racial identity revisited: An integrated conceptualization. *Child Development*, 85, 21–39. doi:10.1111/cdev.12196

Vats, A., & Nishime, L. (2013). Containment as neocolonial visual rhetoric: Fashion, yellowface, and Karl Lagerfelds "Idea of China". *Quarterly Journal of Speech*, 99(4), 423–47. doi:10.1080/00335630.2013.833668

Velez, G., & Spencer, M. B. (2018). Phenomenology and intersectionality: Using PVEST as a frame for adolescent identity formation amid intersecting ecological systems of inequality. In C. E. Santos & R. B. Toomey (Eds.), Envisioning the Integration of an Intersectional Lens in Developmental Science. *New Directions for Child and Adolescent Development* (Vol. 161, pp. 75–90).

Yip, T. (2018). Ethnic/racial identity—A double-edged sword? associations with discrimination and psychological outcomes. *Current Directions in Psychological Science*, 27(3), 170–75. doi:10.1177/0963721417739348

Questions for Critical Thinking

1. The authors discuss the ways in which misrepresentation of Asian Americans and Pacific Islanders in media remains prevalent. How does their discussion help you to understand the portrayal of Asian American and Pacific Islanders in new and different ways?

2. Many of the ideas discussed by the authors can be applied to the ways in which the media represent a variety of marginalized groups in the United States. How does this reading help you to understand the ways in which the media influence your perceptions of others?

3. Understanding the role of the media in influencing our perceptions of ourselves and others helps us to become more media literate. How is this useful in understanding how to address problems of social inequality?

Language and Culture

HOW THE RIGHT MADE RACISM SOUND FAIR—AND CHANGED IMMIGRATION POLITICS

• *Gabriel Thompson*

The following essay, by journalist Gabriel Thompson, explores the power of language in constructing representations of immigrants in news media. As the author illustrates, these representations help to justify the continued inequality experienced by people of color, often regardless of their immigration status. Further, this essay demonstrates the powerful nature of language in influencing public perceptions and public policy.

In June of 2009, Sen. Charles Schumer took the stage in front of a capacity crowd at the Georgetown Law Center. The event was billed as "Immigration: A New Era," and Schumer, who chairs the Subcommittee on Immigration, Refugees and Border Security, was on campus to unveil his seven principles for a reform bill.

The first principle set the tone for his speech. "Illegal immigration is wrong, plain and simple," he said, before moving on to a linguistic primer for attendees. "People who enter the United States without our permission are illegal aliens. When we use phrases like 'undocumented workers,' we convey a message to the American people that their government is not serious about combating illegal immigration"

In total, Schumer used the term "illegal" 30 times and "alien" 9 times. It was a far cry from just three years earlier, when Schumer instead talked repeatedly about "undocumented" immigrants when speaking to a group of Irish Americans. But as the senator explained in 2009, he's choosing his words more purposefully these days.

And he is not alone. In the decade since the September 11 attacks, there has been a steady increase in language that frames unauthorized immigrants as a criminal problem. References to "illegals" "illegal immigrants" and their rhetorical variants now dominate the speech of both major political parties, as well as news media coverage of immigration.

In fact, Colorlines.com reviewed the archives of the nation's largest-circulation newspapers to compare how often their articles describe people as "illegal" or "alien" versus describing them as "undocumented" or "unauthorized." We found a striking and growing imbalance, particularly at key moments in the immigration reform debate. In 2006 and 2007, for example, years in which Congress engaged a pitched battle over immigration reform, the New York Times published 1,483 articles in which *people* were labeled as "illegal" or "alien"; just 171 articles used the adjectives "undocumented" or "unauthorized."

That imbalance isn't coincidental. In the wake of 9/11, as immigration politics have grown more heated and media organizations have worked to codify language they deem neutral, pollsters in both parties have pushed their leaders toward a punitive framework for discussing immigration. Conservatives have done this unabashedly to rally their base; Democrats have shifted rhetoric with the hopes that it will make their reform proposals more palatable to centrists. But to date, the result has only been to move the political center ever rightward—and to turn the conversation about immigrants violently ugly.

Calling someone "illegal" or an "alien" has a whole host of negative connotations, framing that person as a criminal outsider, even a potential enemy of the state. But it does more, by also setting the parameters of an appropriate response. To label unauthorized immigrants as criminals who made an immoral choice suggests that they should be further punished—that their lives be made harder, not easier. Not surprisingly, then, as rhetoric has grown harsher on both sides (or "tougher," in the words of pollsters), legislation has followed suit. Border walls have been constructed, unmanned drones dispatched. Deportation numbers have continued a steady, record-breaking climb, while states pass ever-harsher laws.

These policy developments reflect—and find reflection in—a segment of the broader culture that is struggling with uneasy feelings about race and the ongoing transformation of the nation. When immigrants are targeted and murdered because of their status, and politicians joke about shooting them as livestock, we've moved to something beyond a simple policy debate. And at its swirling center is "the illegal"—a faceless and shadowy character who, it can be hard to remember, is actually a person.

The Language of Lawmaking

The art of choosing words has become big business in politics, for good reason. How a problem or solution is framed can be key to its chances of success.

Take, for example, Bush's plan in 2005 to privatize Social Security. Republicans trumpeted the idea, with Bush repeatedly referring to the creation of private accounts for individuals. Democrats campaigned vigorously to label the proposal as too risky and support for the idea plummeted; *privatizing* Social Security, it turned out, made Americans uneasy. The Republicans then switched words. They talked about *personal* rather than private accounts and called media outlets to complain when they didn't adopt the new language. But by then it was too late and the proposal died.

That a single word can reframe an entire debate points to the power of language in evoking broad, often unexamined feelings. A *public* library or park may sound like a welcoming place to pass an afternoon; a *government* (or even worse, *government-run*) library or park, on the other hand, can bring to mind images of dull texts and rusty equipment.

"Words have entire narratives that go with them," says Geoffrey Nunberg, a linguist at University of California, Berkeley. "Government has acquired negative connotations, so public is what we call government when we don't want to say 'government.'"

When President Obama unveiled his health care proposal, he was careful to call the creation of a government-managed plan the "public option." As Republican strategist and pollster Frank Luntz told Fox News, "If you call it a 'public option,' the American people are split," but "if you call it the 'government option,' the public is overwhelmingly against it."

While language is always important, it has a special prominence when the discussion turns to immigration—and race. As Nunberg noted about the charged vocabulary around the topic: "The words refuse to be confined to their legal and economic senses; they swell with emotional meanings that reflect the fears and passions of the time."

Wetback. Alien. Illegal immigrant. These are powerful words, each of which has, at different times in our recent history, been the most popular term used to describe unauthorized immigrants. And while some anti-immigrant activists claim that words like "alien" or "illegal immigrant" are neutral, each conjures up a whole host of associations. Nunberg noted that in 1920 a group of college students was asked to define the word alien, and what they came up with— "a person who is hostile to this country," "an enemy from a foreign land"—hardly qualified as meeting its legal definition.

The same dynamic occurs today with illegal, especially when used to define a person rather than an action, such as working in the U.S. without authorization. "When two things bear the same name, there is a sense that they belong to the same category," Nunberg told me. "So when you say 'illegal,' it makes you think of people that break into your garage and steal your things"

"These are not small questions" agreed Frank Sharry, the executive director of America's Voice, a prominent immigrant advocacy group that has been a key player in Washington, D.C.'s word games. "The language, and who wins the framing of the language, likely will win the debate"

Prop 187: Before and After

The widespread belief that there is an "illegal immigrant" problem is a relatively recent phenomenon, according to Joseph Nevins, author of "Operation Gatekeeper: The Rise of the Illegal Alien and the making of the US-Mexico Boundary" As Nevins notes, the national platform of the Republican Party didn't mention a concern over "illegal immigration" until 1986. The Democrats— characteristically late and in a reactive mode— followed suit in 1996, adopting a similar stance as their counterparts.

That's one of the key patterns to understand in immigration debates over the past 15 years: Republicans take a stand; Democrats respond by agreeing with the critique but offering a slightly less harsh solution; Republicans get most of what they want.

It wasn't always that way. Back in the 1970s, the Carter administration, under INS Commissioner Leonel Castillo, sent out a directive forbidding the use of "illegal alien" and replaced it with "undocumented workers" or "undocumented alien" But as Nevins writes, "that linguistic sensitivity quickly disappeared"

The most significant turning point came in 1994 with the debate over California's Proposition 187, which barred undocumented immigrants from public schools and non-emergency health care. Today, Prop 187 is best remembered for propelling Republican Gov. Pete Wilson into the national spotlight, but what's often overlooked is the Democratic response to the immigrant-bashing ballot measure—and the party's striking departure from Carter's framing of the debate.

First Democrats ignored Prop 187, then came out against it without much conviction. "I simply do not believe it will work" California's Democratic Sen. Dianne Feinstein explained. President Bill Clinton, fearing that he could lose the crucial state of California in 1996, responded to Prop 187 by dramatically beefing up border security and promising to crack down on "illegal aliens," while Feinstein proposed a toll for legal crossers and made repeated visits to the border to highlight her determination in sealing it.

A look at the Los Angeles Times' archives during the years of this debate shows an eruption in the use of "illegal" and "alien" to describe immigrants themselves. In 1994, the year Californians voted on Prop 187, the Times published 1,411 articles that labeled people "illegal" or "alien" either as an adjective or, in some cases, as a noun—as in "illegals." The same year, the Times published just 218 articles that used "undocumented" or "unauthorized" to describe people living in the country without papers.

When the Prop 187 dust settled, the immigration reform landscape had been dramatically altered. The law did not stand up to court challenge and was ultimately thrown out without being implemented. But the framework it ushered in proved lasting.

"The fact is, they agreed on all of the fundamentals with the Republicans," Nevins says of the Democratic response. "If you accept the framing that your opponents put forth, then you've lost the debate. And this helped lay the groundwork for the situation in which we find ourselves today"

Within two years, Clinton had signed two sweeping bills into law that would do "much of what Prop 187 called for," according to Andrew Wrote, author of "The Republican Party and Immigration Politics: From Proposition 187 to George W. Bush" The Illegal Immigration Reform and Immigrant Responsibility

Act was enforcement-only legislation that, among other things, vastly expanded the grounds for deporting immigrants with legal status. The second bill, the Welfare Reform Act, stripped all non-citizens of many federal benefits. The pragmatist could argue that Clinton got in front of the issue by adopting harsh language and signing the bills; the pragmatist would also have to acknowledge, however, that Clinton got in front of the issue by signing strikingly anti-immigrant legislation.

Fifteen years later, President Obama, like Clinton, is still trying to appeal to the center by proving that he is serious about securing the border. In 2010, he sent 1,200 members of the National Guard to the border and signed a bill allocating $600 million to border enforcement, adding another 1,500 agents along with additional surveillance drones. At the same time, he has deported a record number of immigrants—many of whom have either no criminal record or low-level offenses, such as a traffic violation. And many of the enforcement tools Obama is currently flexing—from partnerships between ICE and local police to the flawed E-Verify program—actually have their roots in Clinton's 1996 bill.

"Changes on enforcement is the medicine that folks on our side have to accept," says Jeffrey Parcher, the communications director for the Center for Community Change, which helped coordinate an ultimately unsuccessful grassroots reform campaign in 2010. "The current narrative is that amnesty is some kind of gift, and in exchange for the gift we have to have enforcement. That is not a frame that we agree with, or that we endorse. But in the universe in which enough legislators sit in that box to prevent anything from passing, it's what we have to work with."

If true, it's a deliberately constructed universe. "Amnesty" became a bad word and "illegal" a good one because strategists on both sides of the partisan aisle assigned them those meanings.

"Words That Work"

For supporters of immigration reform, there was some reason for optimism during President George W. Bush's second term. Despite the House's passage of HR 4437 in 2005—a harsh bill introduced by Wisconsin Republican James Sensenbrenner that would have turned all unauthorized immigrants into

felons—there was momentum among key Republicans for a comprehensive solution.

In 2006, the Senate passed a reform measure that offered a path to citizenship for most undocumented immigrants, provided that they enrolled in English classes and paid fines, as well as back taxes. The citizenship provisions, which did not include unauthorized immigrants who had been in the country for less than two years, were coupled with significant enforcement measures, including the doubling of border patrol agents within five years and more than 800 miles of border fencing and vehicle barriers. Among the bill's supporters were 23 Republicans.

Vocal members in the House, though, were quick to criticize the bill's citizenship provisions, limited as they were. "Amnesty is wrong because it rewards someone for illegal behavior," said Sensenbrenner. "And I reject the spin that the senators have been putting on their proposal. It is amnesty." The House stuck to its talking point, killing the measure and seeing Bush sign instead a bill adding 700 miles of border fencing.

"The right was defining the debate; the amnesty charge just killed us," Sharry concludes. "Their top line beat our top line. We said fix a broken immigration system and they said amnesty rewards lawbreakers. They had a visceral argument and we had something wonkish. We came to a gunfight with a knife."

A 2005 memo by GOP strategist Luntz perfectly captures the talking points relied upon by anti-reform Republicans to kill any reform measures. Luntz is known as a word genius for popularizing terms like "death tax" for estate tax and turning oil drilling into the friendlier-sounding "energy exploration." In his immigration memo, he instructed Republicans to "always refer to people crossing the border illegally as 'illegal immigrants'—NOT as 'illegals.'"

This was a nod to the long-term danger Republicans faced in demonizing undocumented immigrants: losing the Latino vote. As Luntz wrote, "Republicans have made significant inroads into the Hispanic community over the past decade, and it would be a shame if poorly chosen words and overheated rhetoric were to undermine the credibility the party has built within the community." (Remember, this was 2005—pre–Tea Party.)

Such niceties aside, Luntz's memo was otherwise unrestrained in its attack on undocumented immigrants. In segments he labeled "Words That Work," he counseled Republicans to emphasize the following points:

Let's talk about the facts behind illegal immigrants. They do commit crimes. They are more likely to drive uninsured. More likely to clog up hospital waiting rooms. More likely to be involved in anti-social behavior because they have learned that breaking the law brings more benefit to them than abiding by it.

Here was the Prop 187 argument rehashed, with an added pathology—that undocumented immigrants were prone to even broader criminal behavior. And now, one could also throw in the fear of terrorism. Another talking-point section advised Republicans to use the following phrases: "Right now, hundreds of illegal immigrants are crossing the border almost every day. Some of them are part of drug cartels. Some are career criminals. Some may even be terrorists."

The 25-page document is full of the same "overheated rhetoric" Luntz cautioned against and, importantly, became a playbook for Republicans' immigration politics moving forward, "If it sounds like amnesty, it will fail," promised Luntz—and he was right. He was also right to be concerned about just how far his party would go with his vitriolic ideas about brown-skinned immigrants.

But notably, Luntz's message is also the lesson many pro-reform politicians and advocates took from the 2006–2007 debate. Sharry joined forces with John Podesta at the Center for American Progress and enlisted a crew of top Democratic pollsters to work on messaging. Their first report, "Winning the Immigration Debate," was based on polling by Guy Molyneux of Peter Hart Associates and shared with politicians in 2008.

The report argued that Democrats should adopt a tougher tone when discussing reform. Instead of "offering a path to citizenship," which sounded to some like a giveaway, Democrats should use more coercive terms: immigrants would be *required* to pay taxes, learn English and pass criminal background checks. As the report states: "This message places the focus where voters want it, on what's best for the United States, not what we can/should do for illegal immigrants."

"Rather than educate [the public], you can convince them to do the right thing if you call it a requirement," Cecilia Munoz of the National Council of La Raza, told the Huffington Post. Her statement amounted to a strategic retreat: Democrats ought to focus less on challenging anti-immigrant claims (educating) and instead use messages that implicitly reinforce those claims (co-opting).

Sharry and Podesta also enlisted Stanley Greenberg to hone the message. Greenberg, a former Clinton pollster and influential Democratic strategist, was initially skeptical: in 2006 and 2007, his polling had shown that when Democrats discussed immigration reform they were vulnerable to attack. But the new framework, when presented to center and center-right voters, seemed to diffuse the amnesty charge.

Another person involved in the framing was Drew Westen, a psychology professor at Emory University and director of Westen Strategies, a messaging consulting firm, who was brought in by Media Matters for America. One of his conclusions echoed Schumer: Democrats should drop the words "undocumented worker" from their lexicon and instead use "illegal immigrant." Westen, who didn't respond to requests for an interview, told Politico that his advice to progressives is, "If the language appears fine to you, it is probably best not to use it. You are an activist, and by definition, you are out of the mainstream."

After the polls and focus groups, the messaging was in place. Democrats should lead with border security and enforcement, frame the legalization process as a requirement, and call people "illegal immigrants" instead of "undocumented." It was to be tough but not "overly punitive"—and it was notable in that it made no reference to any positive attributes undocumented immigrants might bring to the country.

Not everyone was pleased with the new framework. "This is oppressive language—punitive and restrictive," says Oscar Chacon, executive director of the National Alliance of Latin American & Caribbean Communities. According to Chacon, the 2008 report was "nothing but an effort by D.C. groups to justify their views with a public opinion survey" and it highlighted the Democrats' tendency to "accept more and more of the premises of the anti-immigrant lobby."

"We should be trying to change the way people think about the situation," contends Chacon, "instead of finding a way to make anti-immigrant sentiments tolerable."

Even among people involved in the Beltway Democrats' polling project there was dissension. "It's one thing to say that enforcement has to be a part of the solution, and another to say we have to call people illegal," says David Mermin of Lake Research Partners, who has been polling on immigration for a decade and worked with Sharry on honing the message. "We think there's a more nuanced way of saying it."

Journalism's Objective Bias
Whatever nuance is possible, it's increasingly missing from the public conversation on immigration.

A major turning point in news media's own language came in the wake of the September 11 attacks, as editors for the first time looked closely at how their publications described immigrants. Until then, the Associated Press Stylebook—a language bible for newsrooms—didn't have any entries related to unauthorized immigrants. But in 2003, reflecting government concerns about border security following 9/11, the AP determined it needed to come with up a specific term. According to AP Deputy Standards Editor David Minthorn, the organization underwent extensive discussions, which included "reporters specializing in immigration and ethnic issues who are versed in the positions of all groups," as well as an overview of government and legal terminology. The AP settled on "illegal immigrant" as the "neutral" and preferred term, while noting that "illegal alien" and the shortened term of "illegal" should be avoided. Interestingly, that's precisely the message Luntz suggested in 2005.

The AP's decision locked in an industry standard for so-called neutral language on unauthorized immigration—and it focused on the person, not just the act. The Los Angeles Times' style book, for instance, calls for "illegal immigrant" as "the preferred, neutral, unbiased term that will work in almost all uses," as assistant managing editor

Henry Fuhrmann recently explained to the paper's ombudsman. As a consequence, that "unbiased" language dominates news coverage of big immigration battles. In 2010, as Congress debated the DREAM Act and immigration became a leading issue in midterm elections, four of the five largest-circulation newspapers published a combined 1,549 articles that referred to people as "illegal" or "alien" in the headline or at least once in the text of the story; they published just 363 articles that referred to "undocumented" or "unauthorized" immigrants. (The four papers, in order of 2011 circulation numbers, include USA Today, the New York Times, the Los Angeles Times and the Washington Post; we did not search the archives of the Wall Street Journal, which is the largest paper, because it does not make the full text of its archives available on the database we used.)

In recent years, there has been push back on the criminalizing framework from journalists of color. In 2006 the National Association of Hispanic Journalists launched a campaign pressuring media agencies to stop using the term "illegal" to describe unauthorized immigrants. It was a time of raucous protest, with millions of immigrants across the country marching against Sensenbrenner's draconian House bill. (Notably, the bill's title—the Border Protection, Anti-Terrorism, and Illegal Immigration Control Act—perfectly captured the conflation of undocumented immigrants with terrorists that became common after 9/11.)

"Politicians and others were taking the rhetoric of the anti-immigrant groups, and using 'illegal' as a noun," says Ivan Roman, NAHJ's executive director. "We don't like the term illegal alien and we prefer not to use illegal immigrant—we prefer undocumented immigrant. And we think the news media needs to think critically about the terminology they use"

A more recent campaign, Drop the I-word, is being coordinated by Colorlines.com's publisher, the Applied Research Center. The campaign, which asks news organizations to not use the term "illegal" when discussing unauthorized migrants, finds inspiration from Holocaust survivor Elie Wiesel's phrase "no person is illegal" which he coined during the 1980s Central American sanctuary movement. (The British were the first to use "illegal" as a noun to refer to people, when describing Jews in the 1930s who entered Palestine without official permission.)

"Getting rid of the i-word is about our society asserting the idea that migrants are human beings deserving of respect and basic human rights," says Monica Novoa, coordinator of the campaign. She says she has been disappointed with the number of otherwise sensitive journalists who continue to use the word, which she argues "points to how normalized the language has become."

And as the language has normalized, the broader public dialogue has grown increasingly harsh—and dangerous.

Part of the shift can be seen in the way formerly moderate Republicans have begun navigating political waters using the Tea Party as their compass.

In 2007, Republican Sen. Lindsey Graham was adamant in his support of reform, arguing that, "We're not going to scapegoat people. We're going to tell the bigots to shut up." By last year, however, he'd moved to discussing an overhaul of the 14th Amendment to end birthright citizenship for U.S.-born children of undocumented immigrants. Sen. John McCain has undergone a similar transformation: once a key proponent of reform, earlier this year he blamed wildfires in Arizona on undocumented immigrants, an absurd claim quickly refuted by the U.S. Forest Service. Longtime hardliners like Rep. Steve King of Iowa, who has called immigration a "slow moving Holocaust" and compared immigrants to livestock, are now finding more friends in Congress.

The new batch of Tea Party members openly use threatening images of brown-skinned immigrants to rally their base—in just the way Luntz warned against as he crafted the language politicians now hurl at immigrants. Sharron Angle, in an infamous commercial from her 2010 campaign against Nevada Sen. Harry Reid, featured Latinos ("illegals") sneaking along a border fence "putting our safety at risk" and labeled Reid as "the best friend an illegal alien ever had."

Angle lost, due in large measure to the Latino vote. But her campaign waged an unexpectedly meaningful threat to the long-term senator and Democratic leader. More and more people seem to believe

that, with "illegals putting our safety at risk" drastic words (and actions) are needed.

In March, Kansas State Rep. Virgil Peck, during a debate about the use of gunmen in helicopters to kill wild hogs, suggested that such a tactic could also be a solution "to our illegal immigration problem." His statement was followed by Rep. Mo Brooks of Alabama, who made repeated calls for doing "anything short of shooting" undocumented immigrants.

In November 2008, that's just what a group of Long Island, N.Y., teenagers did when they stabbed Marcelo Lucero to death. Lucero, an undocumented immigrant from Ecuador, was the target of what the teens called "beaner hopping"—in which they roamed the streets searching for Latinos to attack. In the wake of the murder it was discovered that other immigrants had been beaten but not come forward due to fears about their immigration status. Another streak of violence targeting Latinos occurred in New York City's Staten Island in 2010, which included 10 attacks within a six-month period.

As the situation in Long Island attests, taking an accurate stock of hate crimes is a difficult task, as many undocumented immigrants are hesitant to report crimes to authorities. Existing statistics do point to an increase in attacks on Latinos during much of the last decade: from 2003–2007 the FBI reported hate crimes against Latinos increased by 40 percent, and last month California released data showing anti-Latino crimes jumped by nearly 50 percent from the previous year.

For Novoa, these types of statistics highlight the urgency behind the call to stop using "illegal" to describe unauthorized immigrants. "We need to change the current debate. It's hate-filled, racially charged, and inhumane—and it's driving up violence."

And all of this points to perhaps the greatest weakness in the Democratic response to Luntz's message. When one side is framing immigrants as criminals and potential terrorists, with some "joking" about slaughtering them like hogs, the other side likely needs to do more than co-opt poll-tested talking points. There's more at stake than votes. The Democratic strategy also holds a contradiction at its core: The more focus that is placed on the illegality of immigrants and the problems they cause, the less it makes sense to offer a path to legalization.

"All of that [polling] work is based on an assumption that this is a policy argument," Sharry acknowledges. "This is looking more like a front in a culture war, in which a rabid, well organized part of the Republican Party wants to expel millions of brown people from this country."

Questions for Critical Thinking

1. Thompson discusses the ways in which language is used to frame discussions and influence public policy around immigration. How does his discussion help you to better understand your own perceptions of immigrants and immigration?

2. How does your membership in a particular race category influence your understanding of or level of agreement with the author's discussion?

3. Considering the author's discussion, do you think it is possible to reduce or eliminate immigration stereotypes in our language?

"STRONG BLACK WOMEN"

African American Women with Disabilities, Intersecting Identities, and Inequality

- *Angel Love Miles*

In the following article, author Angel Love Miles, policy analyst specializing in disability policy advocacy, explores how the trope of the "Strong Black Woman" and associated expectations had cultural and material relevance for African American women with disabilities. Through her mixed-methods study of the barriers and facilitators to homeownership, she argues that participants' relationships to care strongly contributed to their self-concept.

Compared to their white counterparts, African Americans have higher rates of poverty, lower rates of educational attainment, and are more likely to be employed in jobs that put their health and bodies at greatest risk (Schulz and Mullings 2006; Seabury, Terp, and Boden 2017; Smart and Smart 1997). All of these factors limit their social and economic opportunities and make it harder to prevent the onset of a disability and/or manage or rehabilitate a disability, if acquired. It is therefore not surprising that African Americans have significantly higher rates of disability and of severe disabilities than the white majority population (Beatty 2003; Drum et al. 2011; Smart and Smart 1997). Although African Americans have one of the highest rates of disability, 29 percent of African Americans versus 20 percent of white Americans, there is a dearth of recent statistical data describing their social and economic characteristics (Courtney-Long et al. 2015). The research that does exist suggests significant race and gender disparities among the disabled population, for example, that African American women with disabilities particularly face multiple barriers to resources and equitable treatment in society (Alston and McCowan 1994; Balcazar et al. 2010; Beatty 2003; Oberoi et al. 2015). Despite this, very little has been written about the multiple inequalities that African American women with disabilities or other disabled women of color experience.

The limited studies that discuss the implications of having to confront multiple and compounding systems of racism, ableism, and sexism in the united States context were written primarily by and for service providers who aim to document the racial and gender disproportionality in the quantity and quality of services that women and minorities with disabilities receive (e.g., Alston and McCowan 1994; Balcazar et al. 2012; Wilson 2004). This literature suggests that race, class, and gender biases contribute significantly to how the needs, capabilities, and desires of clients with disabilities are assessed and

GENDER & SOCIETY, Vol 33 No. 1, February, 2019 41–63

DOI: 10.1177/0891243218814820

© 2018 by The Author(s)

Article reuse guidelines: sagepub.com/journals-permissions

interpreted by disability service providers who are also more likely to be white, able-bodied, and male (Balcazar et al. 2010). These studies show persistent gender and racialized disparities in the delivery, quality, and outcomes of disability-related services, resulting in African American women with disabilities benefiting significantly less from disability policy than white disabled males (Balcazar et al. 2010; Oberoi et al. 2015). Still, studies conducted from a service provider perspective are more likely to focus on impairment prevention, cure, and expert advice rather than societal change or the lived experiences of African American women with disabilities (Linton 1998). Little is known about how African American women with disabilities experience these barriers, or how their multiple minority identities impact how they are perceived by themselves and others.

This article addresses these gaps in the literature by presenting findings from a study of the barriers and facilitators to homeownership for African American women with physical disabilities. The data provides insight on how African American women with physical disabilities perceived themselves and negotiated how they were perceived by others. Through examining social and economic opportunities via homeownership, distinct themes related to self-concept emerged. For the purposes of this study, I draw on Rosalyn Benjamin Darling's (2013) use of the term *self-concept*. For Benjamin Darling, self-concept refers to how people come to define their personal and social characteristics, such as race and disability, and their self-esteem. Self-esteem is defined as judgments about the self that are based on personal and social characteristics and are influenced by interactions between the self and society (Benjamin Darling 2013). The analysis reveals that the social implications of being an African American woman with a disability are in many ways different from white men and women with or without disabilities and African American men and women without disabilities. Attention to the multiple forms of oppression that impact African American women with disabilities in varying contexts is needed to understand not only their barriers and facilitators to homeownership but their full access to society. Hence, this article examines the self-concept of African American women with physical disabilities through the lens of the "Strong Black Woman" schema.

Controlling Images and African American Women with Disabilities

Black feminists have documented the significant role that the controlling image or trope of the Strong Black Woman (also called "Super Woman") has played in the social construction of African American womanhood (Collins 2000; Wallace 1999; Woods-Giscombe 2010). This image grew out of the history of African American women's exploitation as unpaid laborers during slavery, and later as underpaid workers and service providers. Their positionality as laborers both inside and outside the home conflicted with the traditional white American family ideal that suggested that women's roles should be restricted primarily to wife and mother. Because their positionality did not allow them to conform to white standards of womanhood and femininity, African American women were ridiculed and objectified through stereotypical images such as mammies and jezebels. These images dehumanized African American women and constructed them as hypersexual and as simple minded; the images also often connected their worth to their physical and emotional labor (Collins 1990).

The Strong Black Woman ideal acts as a counternarrative that celebrates characteristics in African American women who demonstrate their devotion to African American men and families, and to the African American community. These celebrated traits include being selfless, nurturing, resilient, independent, and exemplifying a physical and emotional will to endure great difficulties. More specifically, Strong Black Women are glorified in the African American community for their ability to persevere in a racist and sexist society. Research suggests that for African American women, aspiring to conform to the Strong Black Woman image can be simultaneously empowering and detrimental to their health and self-concept (Collins 1990; Wallace 1999; Woods-Giscombe 2010).

In the pivotal text *Women and Disability*, Fine and Asch (1985) argued that women with disabilities particularly experience a type of gender "rolelessness."

This "rolelessness" results from a society that tends to construct women with disabilities "as inadequate for economically productive roles (traditionally considered appropriate for males) and for the nurturant [sic], reproductive roles considered appropriate for females" (1985, 6). On account of their gender and disability, women with disabilities are socially constructed as weak, dependent, and unfit as providers, and they are considered unable to fulfill their gender expectations as mothers. Therefore, if the characteristics of a Strong Black Woman include being hardworking, independent, and caregiving, then the presence of a disability is in direct conflict with traditional ideals of African American womanhood. In addition, while there is growing literature that identifies the impact of the Strong Black Woman schema on African American women's health (Woods-Giscombe 2010), this research does not recognize that the schema itself is embedded in an ableist ideology that values independence over interdependence and caregiving over self-care. Moreover, this literature tends to include a narrow conception of strength and resilience that devalues and pathologizes those that are perceived as weak. . . .

Feminist Intersectional Disability Framework

For this study, I utilize a *feminist intersectional disability framework*. Intersectional research requires recognition of the distinct aspects of identity and systems of inequality, such as race, class, gender, and ability, and how they mutually constitute one another. In this way, it demands of its practitioners integrative thinking throughout theory development and research production (Conner 2008; Schulz and Mullings 2006). Feminist intersectional disability framework is grounded in the following assumptions: First, race, class, gender, and other markers of difference, and the associated systems of oppression, collectively contribute to how disability is acquired, experienced, and socially constructed. Second, the intersection of race, class, gender, and ability oppression contribute to disabled women of color's differential access to resources, opportunities, and treatment in society. Third, disabled women of color experience marginalization within dominant majority communities (i.e., white, able-bodied,

middle-class communities), as well as within their minority communities (i.e., black, disabled, poor communities). Finally, ableism is commonly an unaccounted predictor of structural inequality. Because many social problems examined by researchers exclude disability inquiry and its intersections, the conclusions developed to rectify these problems are often incomplete and inadequate.

Thus, in applying a feminist intersectional disability analysis to the housing experiences of African American women with physical disabilities, this study examines how these women discuss their self-concept as multiple minorities and its meaning for their lives. In addition, their interviews illustrate some of the ways that systems based on race, class, gender, and ability interact to produce deleterious outcomes.

Methods

The major research question guiding the impetus for this study was, "What are the barriers and facilitators to homeownership for African American women with physical disabilities?" However, this article only focuses on a portion of the study based on a subresearch question: "What is the self-concept of participants in a study on the barriers and facilitators to homeownership for African American women with physical disabilities?" The results shared in this article are based on the participant responses to the follow-up interview portion of the larger mixed methods study, and the quantitative sample description is based on the self-administered questionnaire. . . .

Care Work and African American Women With Disabilities

These African American women with disabilities internalized, resisted, and negotiated multiple intersecting structural and attitudinal barriers and expectations related to care work as part of their self-concept. Participants described some of the constraints they encountered in participating in care work as African American women with disabilities, and the ways in which those constraints impacted how they understood themselves and their position in society. I define "care work" as participating in the social, emotional, intellectual, and physical labor associated with identifying, requesting, denying, and managing the people, services, and resources that enable individuals to advance and maintain their health, well-being, and overall way of life. This care work includes participating in labor associated with providing and receiving care not only for self but also for others. The participants' experiences suggest that the intersectional barriers associated with the care work these women confront require them to exemplify Strong Black Woman characteristics (i.e., resilience, independence, sacrifice, endurance, etc.) because of having to go beyond what is generally required of more privileged others to access equitable resources, opportunities, and treatment. In this way, the Strong Black Woman trope has a material reality that is perpetuated not only through Black cultural expectations, but also through institutional structures that affect one's access to resources and life chances. While most of the interviews discussed self-concept, the stories highlighted here best exemplify the theme of how self-concept was expressed in relationship to care throughout the study.

The participants juggled multiple responsibilities related to care for self and others. Their relationship to care work was both a contributor to and outcome of their self-concept. For instance, Monica, a homeowner with arthritis, lymphedema, and a heart condition, described herself as someone who had based her self-concept on her ability to help others and be financially and socially independent throughout her life. Becoming a homeowner was among the achievements in her life in which she took great pride. However, in addition to having childhood-onset arthritis, she also was diagnosed with lymphedema and a heart condition three years prior to this study. During her interview, she suggested that she struggled with coping with her new limitations and accepting help from others at work or at home, both places that had become increasingly less accessible to her. For example, when asked why she resisted asking family or friends for assistance with minor chores and maintenance she had difficulty completing around the house, she responded:

> I like helping other people physically, spiritually, and financially. And so, you know, I like being able to pay people to do things for me. You know? I'm not a person

that always has to have something done for you for free. I would love to have the money so that anytime anything was broken in my home I could have it fixed.

While Monica took pride in her ability to provide care, she resisted receiving the same type of assistance from others without compensating them. Instead, Monica emphasized throughout her interview that she feared becoming a burden on the ones she loved, and she expressed that feelings of shame and embarrassment often prevented her from requesting help from others. This interpretation of her disability affected her personal relationships and ability to advocate for herself at home and work. For example, she had not requested work accommodations that she believed could help alleviate some of her physical pain and work stress because she feared that her coworkers and employer would then view her as a less productive and less valuable employee. However, in reflecting during the interview upon her patterns of resistance to requesting help, she suggested that this was an attitude that she may need to change. She said, "[I]n talking to you and actually talking to a few friends lately, I do think I need to become more open to let people come in and help me . . . Even though you try to portray yourself as a strong person, sometimes you do have little insecurities that you suppress." Monica's interview suggests that she associated strength with not needing or requesting care while simultaneously being freely available and able to provide care to others. Like Monica, other participants shared moments where they had to discern when they believed it was in their best interests to request, receive, and refuse care, and how to manage the care and help they did receive.

After receiving personal care assistance from her grandmother most of her life, Mary, a homeowner with a spinal cord injury, became aware in her adulthood that she could be eligible for personal care assistant services funded through the state and her medical insurance and decided to apply. After applying for these services, she waited quite some time to find out if her requests for supports were approved, only to learn that her grandmother had been intercepting her phone calls:

> I didn't know my grandma was sabotaging the phone calls. 'Cause I was calling every day; 'cause there wasn't

nobody callin' me back. And then I finally got a call, and she was tellin' me how she'd been callin' me, but my grandma been tellin' her, "We ain't need no services, I take care of her very well!"

Mary's grandmother was initially very resistant to Mary accepting personal care assistance from anyone other than herself. Mary argued that her grandmother initially interpreted her attempts to gain independence as a personal attack on the quality of care she provided. She did not trust others to provide Mary the same level of care, believing strongly that her care could only be provided by trusted loved ones. Mary further argued:

[B]elieve it or not, the people that take care of you, especially if they a relative, like, they got a system. That's something they had to do, so they more dependent on us than we are on them! 'Cause she upset if she can't do something for me. And if I go out, she stay up until I get there. And I know that's a mom thing, but, it's like, they get so used to doin' it. And then if you try to get your freedom and independence a little bit, they lookin' like, "Well what's gonna happen to me if you go?" . . . I'm like, "You're supposed to have your own identity." . . . I told her I can't be responsible for that, 'cause everybody in charge for themselves.

Although Mary's grandmother was initially resistant to her receiving outside care, after Mary applied for and received funding, for the first time her grandmother began receiving financial compensation for the personal care she had been providing Mary for most of her life. In addition, Mary was able to hire a close friend to assist her more regularly, relieving her grandmother of the workload.

Indeed, the women interviewed frequently argued that the cost of managing care for self and others was a major barrier to their ability to own a home. Carol, a nonhomeowner with muscular dystrophy, specifically highlighted the intersecting barriers to economic advancement she believed she confronted as an African American woman with a disability:

I'm not, as a female, as an African American, making as much money as my white male counterpart. Even still, disability-wise, I think—and when it comes to things like care, those are things that—they are extra expenses that I have to pay for. So even something as simple as my shower chair or showerhead or Depends underwear or anything like that, that are extra expenses of a disability, they're still extra expenses . . . and then paying a caregiver out of my pocket; those are all things that are taking my money in other ways. So that makes it less available for things like, you know, paying a mortgage.

Camille, a nonhomeowner with cerebral palsy and low vision, also argued that she had fewer opportunities for economic advancement as an African American woman with a disability. Camille is a retired worker from a government agency whose mission is to advance the full inclusion of people with disabilities through employment, education, and independent living. As such, there were many people who identified as having a disability who worked in Camille's office. Nevertheless, Camille argued that she observed significant race-, gender-, and disability-related differences in the way employee positions were organized and advanced in her department:

The white women that I've known on the job with disabilities have a much easier time accessing housing, employment in general. They have higher incomes. . . . African American women with disabilities on the job— we sometimes felt we were way at the bottom of the totem—of the pole—way at the bottom because you're black, you're female, you have a disability. So, everybody was on top of you. That's the way it pretty much worked; you weren't able to get promoted. The African American women without disabilities were promoted before you, even if you went back to school and got a degree. They were promoted before you. Then, the women that were non–African American—not just Caucasian—any ethnicity that was not African American—were promoted before you. So, it got to be kind of discouraging for a lot of women. They would just leave the job, and go out on disability.

According to Camille, her African American women coworkers with disabilities tended to be in low-level positions with little chance of career advancement. Despite being employed, they still struggled to pay their bills because of the added disability-related costs they experienced. Yet, they were not qualified to benefit from government assistance such as food stamps or Medicaid because of their employment earnings. With no perceived job advancement opportunities, some choose to leave work and go back on government assistance where they could cover their medical bills and have rent control. Throughout the study, the most frequently stated barrier to homeownership that participants gave was economics. Without economic parity, African American women with disabilities are less able to do the care work they need to maintain their way of life and fully participate in society.

In addition to tending to have to manage the cost and logistics of their care with fewer economic resources, multiple participants had children or other loved ones that they provided care for. These participants frequently discussed the structural and attitudinal barriers they confronted in being acknowledged and respected as not only receivers but also providers of care. These barriers hindered their access to the resources and opportunities that would enable them to receive and provide the best care.

In addition to being a retired government worker, Camille was also a mother of two adult children, including an 18-year-old daughter with mental health disabilities who had just started college, and her oldest, a son who had been incarcerated multiple times in the past for drug dealing and was a recovering drug and alcohol addict. As a consequence of her son's difficulties, Camille also had custody of his 11-year-old daughter, whom she had been raising since she was two years old. At the time of the study, Camille was also in love and busy managing the medical care of her fiancé, who had multiple disabilities and was in the hospital. Despite the multiple ways in which Camille successfully provided care to her loved ones, she argued that her competence and ability to take care of herself and others was constantly questioned by service providers and others in her community. When discussing her experience with assisting with the management of her fiancé's care, she shared:

My fiancé's been in the hospital for a while, so I've just spent a lot of time running back and forth trying to deal with the physicians with him, and that's difficult because they see a wheelchair and they assume ignorance . . . what gets me is the prevailing feeling that people with disabilities are not cognizant, they don't

know anything, and "What can you do?" You don't talk to them, you talk over them. In fact, I went once when he was in one nursing home with my granddaughter. They were talking to my granddaughter, and I said, "Why are you talking to her?"

When managing care, services or business of any kind, participants frequently shared that that they confronted a pervasive attitude from others that they did not belong, were not competent, and that their presence and contributions were consistently unacknowledged and/or treated as inconsequential. When discussing the barriers to getting the social services, care, and supports African American women with disabilities need, Mary exclaimed, "Being disabled, you got to fight harder. 'Cause you're female, I'm thinking matters what color and you're disabled, so you got to go that extra mile for them to even pay attention to you." Jessica, a homeowner with multiple sclerosis similarly discussed having to confront assumptions that she was incompetent in the context of advocating for the modifications she needed in her home and negotiating the terms for closing the purchase of her condo. However, she attributed the attitudinal barriers she faced in this process to her race and gender. She said:

It's always the perception, in my opinion, that as African American female, I'm not knowledgeable. So I play along . . . because it typically works in my favor . . . . . . They think I don't know. I let them think I don't know.

Jessica argued that she was able to use to her advantage the low expectations of the lawyers, realtors, and contractors she interacted with in the building and around the purchasing of her condo. Because they were underprepared for how knowledgeable she was about the home purchasing process, and the American with Disabilities Act (ADA) regulations for builders, she strategically used their ignorance as leverage during price and construction negotiations.

Multiple participants expressed concern that assumptions about their capabilities to care for and/or worthiness to have access to the housing they desired may lead to discrimination against them. Tameeka, who was born with arthrogryposis and lived in an apartment of her own with her son, explained,

"Most people, when they see me by myself, they probably think that I couldn't keep up a house and keep it clean, keep it modified to my needs, or to their expectations." African American women with disabilities have to contend with racial, gendered, and ability biases that may deter people from renting or selling a home to them. These intersecting biases include a lack of acknowledgment that African American women with disabilities can and do care for themselves and others and that the care they provide is laborious and valuable. Furthermore, intersecting biases construct African American women with disabilities as unfit, inadequate, deviant, and otherwise undesirable and incapable providers, managers, and receivers of care. These biases also impact the policies and practices of the institutions that serve them and the resources that they are able to access. When Donna, a nonhomeowner with cerebral palsy learned that her daughter's kindergarten class was assigned to a third floor classroom in a building with no elevator, she experienced significant resistance from school administrators to her request for accommodation. however, because of Donna's persistent advocacy on behalf of herself and her daughter, her daughter's class was eventually moved to the first floor. She explained:

> I want to see her teacher; want to see her classroom. So on the first floor . . . that's where they do have accessible things. So I just roll up there and drop her off or pick her up from her class and see how she's doing, see how she interacts with the other kids and that's it.

The interviewees confronted intersecting systemic burdens and social cultural expectations that produced a heavier demand for them to care for themselves and others. They managed these multiple and competing tasks with typically fewer resources and less acknowledgment of their needs and labor compared to their more privileged counterparts. The ability to discern when it is in one's best interests to ask for assistance and care, and to advocate for the right to give and receive care, are skills that participants displayed various degrees of mastery regardless of homeownership status. However, homeowners especially suggested that they had to display a command for these skills in the context of gaining and maintaining an owned home. Having a command for

assessing their needs, and the ability to identify the people, resources, and networks that can help meet them, was shown to be a strong facilitator of homeownership.

Do African American Women With Disabilities "Care"?

One of the primary characteristics of the Strong Black Woman schema is being a caregiver. Most participants shared multiple ways in which they managed and negotiated their care, and many shared multiple ways in which they were caregivers. This care work was a primary aspect of their self-concepts. Despite this reality, they described encountering a society that does not acknowledge or accommodate the ways they received, provided, and managed care. This lack of recognition and accommodation created greater social and structural barriers for them. Feminists have successfully brought to light the many ways in which women's labor is not valued as much as men's or even recognized as work (Kemp 1994). Similarly, the intensive labor often involved in people with disabilities receiving and/or managing care, and the ways in which the care received is an interdependent process, tends to go unrecognized. These excerpts highlight that for African American women with disabilities, this is also a racialized, classed, and gendered experience, with social and material consequences.

Monica's interpretation of her disability and its meaning for her life threatened her self-concept. It led her to question if others would perceive her as a competent, valuable, and desirable employee and individual. This internalization led her to resist assistance and support from others in ways that she described made her daily life more difficult to manage at home, at work and in her community. Given the strong messages of worthiness being connected to labor, it is not surprising that Monica would interpret her disability as making her a less desirable employee and person in society. The high unemployment rate of people with disabilities alone suggests that her fears were not unfounded. Still, her story suggests that she interpreted her disability as a limitation that interfered with her ability to perform in ways consistent with her ideal—someone who is strong, physically and economically independent, hardworking, and helpful to others. These characteristics are associated with the Strong Black Woman ideal. As can be understood from the Strong Black Woman trope, associating strength with not needing or requesting help can be detrimental to one's well-being. For African American women with disabilities, it may be especially damaging because of the social, economic, and health disparities they are more likely to experience. The consequences of the type of internalized ableism, racism, and sexism that Monica described can be loss of work or home, exacerbation of illness and/or impairment, and isolation. Internalized oppression is more than a bad or negative "feeling" about oneself or one's identity, but it has social and material consequences for the people affected by it because it also affects the decisions people make.

Mary's experience with her grandmother highlights the multiple complexities and interdependent nature of the relationship between people with disabilities and their caregivers, especially when a caregiver is a family member. Caregivers can be both an asset and hindrance to people with disabilities asserting their autonomy, and to the type of care they would like to receive. However, Mary resisted internalizing her grandmother's desires and expectations for her care. Instead, Mary argued that her grandmother also depended on her for her identity and sense of purpose in ways that also resemble the Strong Black Woman schema. As previously discussed, Strong Black Women are revered for being caregivers or accomplishing in other ways while enduring great difficulties. While this identity is developed to help cope with scarce and inequitable resources, it also becomes a barrier when resources do become available and fear and mistrust of systems that have historically failed marginalized people drive present decision making. Persistent and repeated experiences of oppression can lead to identifying with struggle in such a way that once relief becomes available, it is not recognizable or desirable for fear it will change or threaten one's current way of life, however difficult. While Mary's grandmother was likely participating in protective practices that African Americans have unfortunately found necessary in a racist world, she also was participating in

ableist practices by not informing Mary of the phone calls and making decisions for Mary without her input or consent. Mary suggested that her grandmother's self-concept as caregiver was threatened when Mary worked to gain more independence. After all, how could she be a Strong Black Woman without someone to rescue and care for? Although Mary's grandmother may not have viewed her as competent enough to decide the type of care she wanted, Mary's persistence to follow through with the application for services despite her grandmother's opposition suggests that she perceived herself as capable of making the best decision for her life.

In addition to experiencing constraints from caregivers to accessing the type of care they need and desire, the women in this study experienced significant financial constraints to funding that care. Carol stressed the ways in which African American women with disabilities confront multiple axis of wage inequality based on race, gender, and disability, while simultaneously experiencing higher economic cost. Similarly, Camille clearly delineated that she observed that others had social and economic advantages over African American women with disabilities in her workplace based on their race, class, gender and ability privilege. Camille's interview also reveals the ways in which the presence of a disability does not absolve African American women with disabilities from being impacted by the same social problems affecting the rest of the African American community, such as the prison industrial complex. In this way, participants consistently demonstrated that, compared to their counterparts, African American women with disabilities tend to have greater need and demand to manage and provide care for self and others, with fewer resources, accommodations, or acknowledgment of their needs and capabilities. These disparities, as Carol and Camille pointed out, reduce access to housing, homeownership, and other resources and create barriers to care work.

Camille, Jessica, Tameeka, and Donna's excerpts demonstrate how institutions and their policies reflect attitudinal biases about African American women with disabilities' capabilities and worthiness for access to resources and opportunities. Medical, housing, and educational policies are constructed to meet the needs and expectations of dominant groups.

They were created in a context that assumes male, white, able-bodied, heterosexual, cisgender competence and marginalizes the existence of others. When this happens, other perspectives and bodies are literally left outside of institutions and unable to enter, such as the case with Donna and her daughter's inaccessible public school. Or they may be left completely ignored and excluded, such as with Camille's experience with medical providers. Or they may be underestimated, such as with Jessica and Tameeka.

Despite these constraints, most participants demonstrated a certain amount of self-efficacy, self-awareness, and confidence, which may not have always reduced but at least helped them manage the inequities they encountered. Because the participants were recruited through a snowball sample of members associated with disability rights and advocacy organizations, they were more likely to have been exposed to disability and civil rights empowerment principles and connected to other disabled communities of color. Their proximity to other African American women with disabilities may have enabled them to identify how multiple and intersectional areas of marginalization impact their life. Having access to this community can help reveal common experiences and social patterns associated with their identities which are harder to identify in isolation. In this way, issues that might otherwise be ascribed solely to the individual can be understood as larger social problems.

However, most people with disabilities do not identify with other people with disabilities as a social political group or minority identity (Linton 1998) and African Americans even less so (Bell 2011). Thus, one of the primary barriers to integrating a positive self-concept is the limited access to other African American women with disabilities in contexts that provide opportunities to learn from shared experiences. It is not enough to be near other African American women with disabilities, as may be the case in a nursing home serving predominately African American women. Purposeful opportunities created for community building, empowerment, affirmation, and exchange are important for marginalized people because these can enable the sharing of resources, coping strategies, and collective resistance to oppressive systems and ideologies.

Unfortunately, however, African American women with disabilities are underrepresented and/or misrepresented in research and in U.S. culture, and this creates barriers for them to identify shared interests and develop community. Lack of representation or community leads to experiencing oppression in isolation and enables the internalization of oppression, just as Monica's experience suggests. Imani, a homeowner with cerebral palsy, argued, "More white women with disabilities are, uh, they get more attention than we do . . . when they put a face on a disability it's typically not a black face, it's typically a white one." When asked how she thought this exclusion affected African American women with disabilities, she responded,

> Adversely, because we don't get as much help. What's that saying? . . . The squeaky . . . wheel gets the oil, gets the grease? If you don't know we exist and you don't know what it is we need, how can you help us?

This study demonstrates the ways African American women with disabilities exhibit and identify with Strong Black Women characteristics of resilience, independence, sacrifice, endurance and more. It shows how characteristics and social expectations associated with the Strong Black Woman schema can be both an asset and hindrance to their empowerment. It demonstrates how even when African American women with disabilities perceive themselves as capable of managing, providing, and receiving care, they constantly confront a society that does not view them the same. This lack of recognition and accommodation creates greater social and structural barriers for them to confront. Hence, the Strong Black Woman ideal and expectation had cultural and material relevance for how participants interpreted themselves, were perceived by others, and accessed resources. In addition, exploring how African American women with disabilities experience the Strong Black Women schema makes evident that it is embedded in an ableist ideology that values independence over interdependence, and caregiving over self-care, and includes a narrow conception of strength and resilience that devalues and pathologizes those who are perceived as weak (i.e., African American women with disabilities). Not only are ableist structures not conducive to people with disabilities, but they tend to exacerbate and/or produce impairment. It is not surprising then that research is increasingly linking the Strong Black Women schema to health disparities for African American women (Woods-Giscombe 2010).

More research is needed to learn about the social construction of disability in the African American community, especially as it relates to gender, care work, and women with disabilities. Through using a feminist intersectional disability framework, this study offers a model for how to explore these intersections. African American women with disabilities' self-concept and relationships to their stigma management strategies, access to resources, and integration in society also need to be further explored. While participants expressed that housing and ability to live independently affected their self-concepts, the material reality of owning or not owning a home did not reveal significant differences between homeowners and nonhomeowners. Rather, it was through conversations about homeownership that this data around self-concept was revealed. The fields that have the most advanced theoretical and methodological tools to further speak to the positionalities of African American women with disabilities, that is, women's studies, disability studies, African American studies, and other areas in the social sciences and humanities, have failed to significantly recognize the need for inquiry about their lives. As suggested by Balcazar et al. (2010), the dominance of medical, rehabilitation, and other deficit models of disability, the limited acknowledgment of disability as a social, political, and minority identity, and the large absence of minorities with disabilities as researchers and scholars, are likely primary barriers to this subject of inquiry. This article intends to help spark the interests of future studies to come. It is clear that the particular configuration of ableism, white supremacy, and misogyny in society has created barriers to inquiring about certain marginalized bodies. These structures of power render African American women with disabilities as unknowable and unrecognized as a marginalized group worthy of exploration. One must wonder, who else is our scholarship and activism forgetting or ignoring? More importantly, what will we do about it?

References

Alston, Reginald J., and Carla J. McCowan. 1994. African American women with disabilities: Rehabilitation issues and concerns. *Journal of Rehabilitation* 60 (1): 36–40.

Balcazar, Fabrico, Ashmeet K. Oberoi, Yolanda Suarez-Balcazar, and Francisco Alvarado. 2012. Predictors of outcomes for African Americans in a rehabilitation state agency: Implications for national policy and practice. *Rehabilitation Research, Policy, and Education* 26 (1): 43–54.

Balcazar, Fabricio, Yolanda Suarez-Balcazar, Tina Taylor-Ritzler, and Christopher B. Keys, eds. 2010. *Race, culture, and disability: Rehabilitation science and practice.* Boston, MA: Jones and Bartlett.

Beatty, Lula. A. 2003. Substance abuse, disabilities, and Black women: An issue worth exploring. *Women & Therapy* 26 (3): 223–36.

Bell, Christopher, ed. 2011. *Blackness and disability: Critical examinations and cultural interventions.* East Lansing: Michigan State University Press.

Benjamin Darling, Rosalyn. 2013. *Disability and identity: Negotiating self in a changing society.* Boulder, CO: Lynne Rienner.

Collins, Patricia Hill. 1990. *Black feminist thought: Knowledge, consciousness, and the politics of empowerment.* Boston: Hyman

Collins, Patricia Hill. 2000. *Black feminist thought: Knowledge, consciousness, and the politics of empowerment,* 2nd ed. New York: Routledge.

Conner, David. J. 2008. *Urban narratives, portraits in progress: life at the intersections of learning disabilities, race and social class.* New York: Peter Lang.

Courtney-Long, Elizabeth A., Dianna D. Carroll, Qing C. Zhang, Alissa C. Stevens, Shannon Griffin Blake, Brian S. Amour, and Vincent A. Campbell. A. 2015. Prevalence of disability and disability type among adults—United States, 2013. *Morbidity and Mortality Weekly Report* 64 (29): 777–83.

Drum, Charles, Monica R. McClain, Willi Horner-Johnson, and Genia Taitano. 2011. Health disparities chartbook on disability and racial and ethnic status in the United States. *Institute on Disability, University of New Hampshire.* https://sph.umd.edu/sites/default/files/files/Healthpercent20Disparitiespercent20Chart-percent20Book_080411.pdf.

Fine, Michelle, and Adrienne Asch. 1985. Disabled women: Sexism without a pedestal. In *Women and disability: The double handicap,* edited by Mary J. Deegan and Nancy A. Brooks. New Brunswick, NJ: Oxford Transaction Books.

Kemp, Alice Abel. 1994. *Women's work: Degraded and devalued.* Englewood Cliffs, NJ: Prentice Hall.

Linton, Simi. 1998. *Claiming disability: Knowledge and identity.* New York: New York University Press.

Oberoi, Ashmeet Kaur, Fabricio E. Balcazar, Yolanda Suarez-Balcazar, Fredrik G. Langi, and Valentina Lukyanova. 2015. Employment outcomes among African American/Black and white women with disabilities: Examining the inequalities. *Journal of Women, Gender, & Families of Color* 3 (2): 144–64.

Schulz, Amy, and Leith Mullings. 2006. *Gender, race, class and health: Intersectional approaches.* San Francisco, CA: Jossey-Bass.

Seabury, Seth A., Sophie Terp, and Leslie I. Boden. 2017. Racial and ethnic differences in the frequency of workplace injuries and prevalence of work-related disability. *Health Affairs (Millwood)* 36 (2): 266–73.

Wallace, Michele. 1999. *Black macho and the myth of the superwoman.* New York: Verso.

Wilson, Keith. 2004. Vocational rehabilitation acceptance in the USA: Controlling for education, type of major disability, severity of disability and socioeconomic status. *Disability and Rehabilitation* 26:145–56.

Woods-Giscombe, Cheryl L. 2010. Superwoman schema: African American women's views on stress, strength, and health. *Qualitative Health Research* 20 (5): 668–83.

Questions for Critical Thinking

1. The author discusses the ways in which African American women with disabilities particularly face multiple barriers to resources and equitable treatment in society? How did this reading expand your understanding of this issue? What information was new to you? What information did you already know?

2. This article highlights persistent gender and racialized disparities in the delivery, quality, and outcomes of disability-related services, resulting in African American women with disabilities benefiting significantly less from disability policy than white disabled males. How can this inequity be addressed and alleviated? What solutions would you offer?

3. The author highlights the role of controlling images, such as the "strong Black woman" trope contributes to the inequities experienced by African American women. What will bring about more positive and accurate images of African American women? What obstacles prevent such positive portrayals?

THE FLORIDA STATE SEMINOLES

The Champions of Racist Mascots

• *Dave Zirin*

In this essay, sports editor David Zirin takes on the controversial topic of offensive mascots. Focusing primarily on the example of the Florida State Seminoles, he debunks the myth that this misrepresentation of Native Americans in sports imagery is endorsed by the Seminole Nation. Through his examination, he illustrates that this continued practice turns our attention away from dismantling the institutionalized racism that Native Americans continue to face.

It's easy to oppose the name of the Washington Redskins and call for owner Dan Snyder to change his beloved bigoted brand. After all, it's a dictionary-defined slur bestowed on the NFL franchise by their arch-segregationist, minstrel-loving founder. When you have Native American organizations, leading sportswriters, Republicans as well as Democrats in Congress and even the president say the time has come to change the name, it is not exactly difficult to get on board.

But what about the Florida State Seminoles, whose football team on Monday night won the Vizio/Dow Chemical/Blackwater/Vivid Video BCS National Championship Game? The NCAA, since 2005, has had formal restrictions against naming teams after Native American tribes, and yet there were the Seminole faithful: thousands of overwhelmingly Caucasian fans with feathers in their hair, doing the Tomahawk chop and whooping war chants on national television. Their passions were stirred into a frenzy by a white person, face smeared with war paint, dressed as the legendary chief Osceola riding out on a horse. As Stewart Mandel of *Sports Illustrated*

gushed, "Chief Osceola plants the flaming spear in the Rose Bowl. Awesome." (Osceola was adopted after the school quietly retired their previous Native American mascot "Sammy Seminole.")

I have been to dozens of Redskins game and have never seen anything close to this kind of mass interactive minstrelsy. Yet there are no protests against this spectacle, no angry editorials and no politicians jumping on the issue. Why is that? Because as any Florida State fanatic will shout at you, the university has "a formal agreement with Seminole Nation" and that makes everything all right. Fans treat this much-touted agreement like they have a "racism amnesty card" in their back pocket. The approval of the Seminole Nation, they will tell you makes it all A-okay. Actually it doesn't. It doesn't first and foremost because the existence of this "agreement with the Seminole Nation" is a myth.

The agreement is with the Florida Seminole Tribal Council and not the Seminole Nation. The majority of Seminoles don't even live in Florida. They live in Oklahoma, one of the fruits of the Seminole Wars, the Indian Removal Act and The Trail of Tears. These Oklahoma Seminoles—who, remember, are the majority—oppose the name. On October 26, 2013, the Seminole Nation of Oklahoma's governing body passed a resolution that read in part, "The Seminole Nation condemns the use of all American Indian sports team mascots in the public school system, by college and university level and by professional teams."

As for the Florida Seminole Tribal Council, it is the owner of a series of luxury casino hotels throughout the state where the Seminole "brand" is prominently on display. The Tribal Council also bought the Hard Rock Cafe for $965 million in cash in 2006, which thanks to the Seminoles' "first-nation status" now also offers gambling in its Florida locales. Hard Rock corporate called this "the perfect marriage of two kindred spirits." Seminole Nation Hard Rock Hotel and Casino T-shirts are available for purchase.

For the wealthy and powerful Florida Seminole tribal leaders, the cultural elevation of the football program is a part of their extremely lucrative gaming operation. Defending the school's use of the name is about defending its brand. That is why the chairman of the Florida Seminole Tribe of Florida, James Billie, said, "Anybody come here into Florida trying to tell us to change the name, they better go someplace else, because we're not changing the name."

Some might say that this is fine with them. After all, given the incalculable wealth stolen from Native American tribes over the centuries, what is wrong with them getting some of it back? That would be fine, except for the stubborn fact that gambling wealth flows into very few hands. The majority of Native Americans languish in dire poverty, with reservation poverty listed at 50 percent in the last census.

Another argument for the Florida State Seminoles' keeping their name is that it actually educates people and keeps the history from being eradicated. This is self-serving codswallop, like saying a Muhammad Ali mousepad teaches people about his resistance to the war in Vietnam. Branding and cultural appropriation is not history. It's anti-history. Take school mascot Chief Osceola as an example. If people in the stands and at home actually knew who Osceola was,

the ritual of his riding a horse and throwing a spear before games would be an outrage, and not just because the Seminoles, who lived and fought in swampy everglades, tended not to ride horses. Chief Osceola was a great resistance fighter and leader of the Second Seminole War in Florida.

As written in the terrific book *101 Changemakers: Rebels and Radicals who Changed US History*, "Osceola became an international symbol of the Seminole Nation's refusal to surrender. He was a renowned public speaker and a fierce fighter who was also an opponent of the US slave system. One of his two wives was a woman of African descent and it was not uncommon for escaped slaves to become a part of Seminole Nation. Osceola's army frustrated the entire US Government, five separate Army generals, at a cost to the US Treasury of more than 20 million dollars. . . . On October 21, 1837, Osceola met with US government officials to discuss a peace treaty. When he arrived, he was captured and imprisoned. Osceola's respect was so widespread that this maneuver was widely condemned and viewed as a dishonorable way to bring down the great warrior."

Osceola was nothing less than the American Mandela, but a Nelson Mandela who did not survive Robben Island. Imagine before a South African soccer game, a white person in black face, dressed like Mandela, running out to midfield to psyche up the crowd. Not even Rick Reilly would say that this was somehow educating people about African resistance to apartheid. No one is getting educated about Osceola or the Seminole Wars. Instead their heroic resistance has been translated for football purposes to being "tough." This "respect" for their toughness not only reduces a rich and varied Seminole culture to a savage culture of war, it is also an unspoken way to praise our own ability to engineer their conquest.

The last argument, which is perhaps the most common, is, "Changing the name of the Redskins or the Seminoles . . . where does the politically correct madness end? Do we stop using 'Giants' because it offends tall people? Or 'Cowboys' because it offends cowboys?" This kind of witticism is actually profoundly insulting because there was this thing called "history" that happened, and in this "history" giants were not subject to mass displacement and genocide. Once 100 percent of this country, Native Americans are now 0.9 percent, and we play sports on their graves. Their rituals and dress are our own commercialized entertainment. We turn our eyes to the field and away from the way institutionalized racism continues to define the lives of the overwhelming majority to Native Americans who do not own a stake in the Hard Rock Cafe. That gets us to the final problem with Seminole nation and all Native American mascoting. It makes us more ignorant about our own collective history. I'm not sure we can afford it.

Questions for Critical Thinking

1. How did reading this article help you to see the issue of sports symbols and mascots in new and different ways?
2. Do you think the use of American Indian/Native American mascots is problematic? Why or why not? How do you think your own status in society impacts your opinion?
3. What will bring about more positive images of American Indians in sports, advertising, and other media? What obstacles prevent such positive portrayals?

Violence and Social Control

CLIMATE OF FEAR

* *Southern Poverty Law Center*

The following essay comes from the Southern Poverty Law Center, an organization that is dedicated to fighting inequality and seeking justice for oppressed groups and individuals. The focus of this piece is on the experiences of Latino immigrants following a violent incident that highlighted a growing national problem—violent hatred directed at all suspected undocumented immigrants, Latinos in particular. This essay demonstrates that the actions of people in social institutions, such as the criminal justice system and the government, often contribute to the creation of a climate of hate directed at immigrants.

Suffolk County, N.Y.—The night of Nov. 8, 2008, seven teenage males gathered in a park in Medford, N.Y., to drink beer and plot another round of a brutal pastime they called beaner-hopping. It consisted of randomly targeting Latino immigrants for harassment and physical attacks.

Five days earlier, three of them had gone on the hunt and beaten a Latino man unconscious, they later told police. "I don't go out and do this very often, maybe once a week," one of them said.

Two of the youths in the park had started their day just after dawn by firing a BB gun at Latino immigrant Marlon Garcia, who was standing in his driveway. Garcia was hit several times.

After leaving the park, the pack of seven drove around Medford. Unable to locate a victim, they set off for Patchogue, a nearby seaside village. Both communities are in Suffolk County, which occupies the eastern, less urban half of Long Island. In Patchogue, they caught sight of Hector Sierra walking

downtown. They ran up to Sierra and began to punch him, but Sierra was able to flee.

Then, just before midnight, according to prosecutors, they spotted Ecuadorian immigrant Marcelo Lucero walking with a friend, Angel Loja. Lucero, 37, had come to the United States in 1992. He worked at a dry cleaning store and regularly wired money home to his ailing mother.

The seven teenagers jumped out of their vehicles and began taunting the two men with racial slurs. Loja fled, but the attackers surrounded Lucero and began punching him in the face. Trying to defend himself, Lucero removed his belt and swung it, striking one of the teens in the head. Enraged by that blow, 17-year-old Jeffrey Conroy, a star high school football and lacrosse player, allegedly pulled a knife, charged forward and stabbed Lucero in the chest, killing him.

All seven attackers were arrested a short time later. Conroy was charged with second-degree murder and manslaughter as a hate crime. The other six were charged with multiple counts of gang assault and hate crimes.

The local and national media gave the murder of Lucero extensive coverage. This was in part because it occurred less than four months after the highly publicized slaying of a Mexican immigrant in Shenandoah, Pa. Luis Ramírez, 25, was beaten to death by drunken high school football players in a case that sparked a national discussion and heightened awareness of the rising tide of anti-immigrant violence.[1]

In few places is that trend more viciously evident than in Suffolk County, where anti-immigrant sentiment has long run deep, and where a fast-growing Latino immigrant population has been victimized by a continuing epidemic of anti-immigrant hate crimes since the late 1990s.

In recent months, Southern Poverty Law Center (SPLC) researchers interviewed more than 70 Latino immigrants living in Suffolk County, along with more than 30 local religious leaders, human rights activists, community organizers and small business owners. Their accounts are remarkably consistent and demonstrate that although Lucero's murder represented the apex of anti-immigrant violence in Suffolk County to date, it was hardly an isolated incident.

Latino immigrants in Suffolk County live in fear. Low-level harassment is common. They are regularly taunted, spit upon and pelted with apples, full soda cans, beer bottles and other projectiles. Their houses and apartments are egged, spray-painted with racial epithets and riddled with bullets in drive-by shootings. Violence is a constant threat. Numerous immigrants reported being shot with BB or pellet guns, or hit in the eyes with pepper spray. Others said they'd been run off the road by cars while riding bicycles, or chased into the woods by drivers while traveling on foot. The SPLC recorded abundant firsthand accounts of immigrants being punched and kicked by random attackers, beaten with baseball bats or robbed at knifepoint.

Political leaders in the county have done little to discourage the hatred, and some have actively fanned the flames. County Executive Steve Levy, Suffolk's top elected official, has made hostile policies targeting undocumented immigrants a central theme of his administration since he was first elected in 2003. Others have done worse, with public statements that all but endorsed violence. At a public hearing on immigration in August 2001, County Legislator Michael D'Andre of Smithtown said that if his own town should ever experience an influx of Latino day laborers like that of nearby communities, "We'll be up in arms; we'll be out with baseball bats." In March 2007, County Legislator Elie Mystal of Amityville said of Latino immigrants waiting for work on street corners, "If I'm living in a neighborhood and people are gathering like that, I would load my gun and start shooting, period. Nobody will say it, but I'm going to say it."

Most immigrants said they do not dare travel alone at night. Few let their children play outside unattended.

"We live with the fear that if we leave our houses, something will happen," said Luis, a Mexican who migrated to Suffolk County three years ago. "It's like we're psychologically traumatized from what happens here."

Like all but two immigrants contacted by the SPLC, Luis spoke for this report on the condition that, to avoid retaliation, he would be identified only by his first name and country of origin.

At best, the immigrants said, the police seem indifferent to their plight. At worst, the police contribute to it, in the form of racial profiling, selective enforcement and outright bullying. A detailed account provided by Agosto, a Guatemalan immigrant, was typical. Agosto said that in early 2008, he was waiting for work at *la placita* (little plaza), a day labor pick-up point in Brentwood, when a police car pulled up. The two officers inside told him he wasn't allowed to stand there and demanded to see his identification. When he replied that he didn't have his I.D. with him, the officers told him to get in the back of the squad car. "I thought they were giving me a ride home," he said. But when they arrived at his residence, the police officers got out of the car and told Agosto to find his I.D. When he unlocked the front door, he said, the officers barged in without asking permission to enter. The police ransacked his living quarters, rifling through drawers and knocking items off shelves.

"I was very nervous," Agosto said. "They kept pushing me and telling me to hurry up. I got even more nervous so it took me awhile to find my I.D. When you are undocumented, you get scared." When Agosto finally located his *cédula de identidad*, a Guatemalan government-issued I.D. card, the police looked it over then left. "I felt bad, like they were treating me like I was less than they were," he said. "It felt racist."

No immigrants reported serious physical abuse at the hands of Suffolk County law enforcement authorities. But time after time, they gave similar accounts of being pulled over for minor traffic violations and then interrogated, or being questioned harshly at nighttime checkpoints after watching Anglo drivers being waved through. A few said they'd been arrested for driving under the influence or for refusing to take a Breathalyzer test even though in fact they'd submitted to the test and registered well below the legal limit.

Evidence suggesting unequal enforcement of the motor vehicle code in Suffolk County is easily observed in the local courts that handle minor offenses. Latinos account for roughly 14% of Suffolk County's population, but on a typical day in a Suffolk County justice court, they make up nearly half the defendants appearing for motor vehicle violations. A review of the police blotters printed in Suffolk County daily newspapers yields similarly suggestive demographic evidence: almost every day, around 50% of the drivers listed as having been fined for a motor vehicle violation have Latino surnames.

The most common violation that Latino immigrants are tagged with is violation 509, for unlicensed driving. It carries a $185 fine on top of a $150 vehicle impound charge and $25 a day for vehicle storage. Failure to appear in court or to pay a fine leads to arrest warrants.

Law enforcement officers in Suffolk County tend not to exhibit the same enthusiasm for investigating hate crimes against Latinos as they do writing them tickets, according to immigrants and other county residents interviewed for this report.

Immigrants in Suffolk County don't trust the police. They say there's no point in reporting bias-motivated harassment, threats or assaults, even severe beatings, because from what they can tell, the police take the report and then do nothing. They say that when the police arrive on the scene of a hate crime, they often accept the version of events given by the assailant or assailants, even to the point of arresting the true victim in response to false claims that the immigrant started a fight. And they say that officers discourage hate crime victims from making formal complaints by questioning them about their immigration status.

In the days following the murder of Marcelo Lucero, the Congregational Church of Patchogue invited immigrants to the church to speak about hate crimes. In all, more than 30 Latino immigrants in Suffolk County came forward with detailed accounts of their own victimization. In response, the Suffolk County Legislature formed a task force to investigate the sources of racial tension in the county. To date, the task force has held one of at least four planned hearings.

Prosecutors, meanwhile, have announced new indictments that accuse the defendants in the Lucero murder of assaulting or menacing a total of eight other Latino immigrants.

On June 24, 2008, according to prosecutors, the teenagers set upon Robert Zumba, kicking him and pinning his arms while Conroy, the alleged knife-wielder in the Lucero slaying, sliced Zumba with a blade. Members of the group repeatedly victimized another man, José Hernández, in December 2007, prosecutors said. During one attack, Conroy allegedly held a pipe in one hand and smacked it against his opposite palm, threatening, "We're going to kill you."

Immigrants who have been the victims of hate-crime violence in Suffolk County report that in most cases the attackers are white males in their teens or 20s. A few reported being attacked by African-American males, or being lured by a white female to a nearby "party" where assailants lay in wait. Almost always, the reported attackers were young.

All seven youths accused of participating in the attack on Lucero reside in Patchogue or Medford—predominantly middle-class towns whose strip malls and pizzerias appear in sharp contrast to the lavish wealth on display elsewhere in the county. Suffolk

County has one of the steepest wealth gradients in the country. Six of its ZIP codes are among the 100 wealthiest in the United States. The village of Sagaponack, one of a group of seaside communities collectively known as the Hamptons, is the most expensive ZIP code in the nation, with a median home sale price in 2005 of $2.8 million. It's home to investment bankers and real estate tycoons.

The parents of the alleged Lucero attackers include a teacher, a butcher, a store clerk, a deli owner and a former K-Mart operations manager. Latino immigrants may find work in Suffolk County's rich seaside communities, but they live in the more affordable inland towns, alongside middle–and working-class American families who are more likely to view the brown-skinned newcomers as competitors for jobs than hired help.

Immigrant advocates say that the violence committed by high school students and their slightly older peers is fueled by the immigrant-bashing rhetoric they absorb in the hallways and classrooms at school, in the news media, or in conversations at home.

Demographic change in Suffolk County has been rapid over the previous two decades. Some towns have gone from being practically all white to having a 15% Latino population, made up mostly of immigrants from Central America and Mexico, according to the latest census statistics. In Patchogue and Medford, the Latino population is 24%.

Although this influx has slowed since the U.S. economy faltered last year, the nativist backlash continues. It began in earnest in the late 1990s, when about 1,500 Mexican workers showed up over the course of a few years in the small, majority-white, middle-class hamlet of Farmingville. The hamlet's central location made it ideal for contractors looking to hire day laborers for jobs throughout the county. That in turn made it attractive to immigrants drawn to the area by then-abundant employment opportunities in the landscaping, restaurant, and construction industries.

In 1998, a militant nativist group called Sachem Quality of Life formed in Farmingville and began disseminating propaganda that accused undocumented Latino immigrants of being inherently prone to rape, armed robbery, and other violent crimes. Although Sachem Quality of Life is now defunct, the group, along with the Federation for American Immigration Reform and a smaller nativist group called American Patrol, heavily influenced the tone for public discourse on immigration in the area.

Nativist ideology now permeates many levels of society and government in Suffolk County. County Executive Levy in June 2006 mocked activists demonstrating against hate crime violence and the mass eviction of Latino immigrants based on the selective enforcement of zoning laws. "I will not back down to this one percent lunatic fringe," he said. "They evidently do not like me much because I am one of the few officials who are not intimidated by their politically correct histrionics."

That same year, a school board member in the Hamptons distributed an online petition to parents, teachers, and a school principal calling for undocumented immigrants to be prevented from receiving any "free services" in the U.S.

"Look, we need you to continue sending this around ... [G]et as many viable names on here so that someone hears our voices," the E-mail read. "It seems the only voices they hear are the illegal immigrants who say 'foul play,' or the agencies backing them. We need to stop this and stop it in the bud!"

Also in 2006, the same official distributed an E-mail containing a "hilarious" mock description of a doll called Brentwood Barbie. "This Spanish-speaking only Barbie comes with a 1984 Toyota with expired temporary plates & 4 baby Barbies in the backseat (no car seats)," it read. "The optional Ken doll comes with a paint bucket lunch pail & is missing 3 fingers on his left hand. Green cards are not available for Brentwood Barbie or Ken."

In a February 2007 public hearing on proposed legislation, County Legislator Jack Eddington of Brookhaven singled out two immigration advocates who were speaking from the podium in Spanish and demanded to know if they were in the country legally. Eddington also warned undocumented immigrants, "You better beware" and "Suffolk County residents will not be victimized anymore."

Later in 2007, Levy was reelected with 96% of the vote.

Over the years, immigrant advocates have built an energetic movement in Suffolk County. Earlier this year, on the six-month anniversary of Lucero's murder, the Long Island Immigrant Alliance and

The Workplace Project organized a vigil at the site of the killing. The event featured speakers from an array of groups, including the Fundación Lucero de América (Lucero Foundation America), along with Marcelo Lucero's brother, Joselo.

A few months before the vigil, some residents of eastern Long Island formed Neighbors in Support of Immigrants, in part to counter what they perceived as a takeover of local town council and community meetings by anti-immigrant zealots. In Patchogue, residents formed the Unity Coalition with the help of the New York Division of Human Rights to work to ease tensions in that community. A more established grassroots organization, Farmingdale Citizens for Viable Solutions, runs La Casa Comunal, a community center that serves Latino day laborers. The group also documents hate crimes.

Immigrant advocates cheered the news earlier this year that the Department of Justice had begun a criminal investigation into hate crimes against Latinos in Suffolk County. The federal agency also launched a probe into the way the Suffolk County Police Department, the main law enforcement agency in the county, has handled such crimes.

Nevertheless, the Latino immigrants interviewed for this report expressed little optimism that attitudes will change. If anything, they said, their situation is growing more perilous by the day. The weak economy means that more residents are out of work and looking for someone to blame. And many of the jobs for immigrants have dried up, forcing day laborers to spend more time traveling to and from their residence or waiting for work on street corners, making them all the more vulnerable.

Although most of the Latino immigrants who are victimized in Suffolk County are undocumented, their attackers have no way of knowing their immigration status. "They don't know if I'm legal or not so it must be because we're [Latino]," said Orlando, a Guatemalan immigrant who came to Suffolk County in 2005. "The racist people aren't going to change just because we get papers."

Note

1. On May 26, 2010, Jeffrey Conroy, age 19, was sentenced to 25 years in prison for the first-degree manslaughter as a hate crime of Marcelo Lucero.

Questions for Critical Thinking

1. As this article demonstrates, the actions of people in social institutions such as the criminal justice system and the government often contribute to the creation of a climate of hate directed at immigrants. What do you see as the responsibilities of these officials in creating a safe and fair environment for all persons living in our communities?

2. As illustrated in the report, economic difficulties faced by middle–and working-class individuals often result in misplacing blame on immigrants. Where do you think such blame should be more appropriately placed?

3. The United States is a country made up largely of immigrants and the descendants of immigrants, and yet recent immigrants face increasing resistance in their efforts to be included in society. What do you see as solutions to this resistance?

"RAPE IS A MAN'S ISSUE"

Gender and Power in the Era of Affirmative Sexual Consent

• *Julia Metz, Kristen Myers, and Patricia Wallace*

As the authors of the following article explain, the #MeToo movement has highlighted the social problem of sexual harassment and assault, creating new avenues for survivors to seek justice outside of the justice system. In response, U. S. universities have established affirmative consent policies. Through their analysis of data from interviews to understand how gender frames the negotiation of consent, they explore the gendered power dynamics in subjects' reported negotiations of sexual consent. They found that affirmative consent was mediated through gender frameworks that stressed men's sexual entitlement and conclude that sexual assault intervention strategies need to be reworked to address systemic, cultural, and individual-level issues.

Introduction

The #MeToo movement, started by sexual assault survivor Tarana Burke in 2006, has shined new light on sexual harassment and sexual assault, calling the public's attention to high-profile men who have allegedly committed sexual assault and/or harassment. The movement stresses that "rape is a man's issue." The argument is this: Because men are (usually) the ones committing sexual assault, they should be held responsible for ending rape by educating themselves about gendered power, changing their behavior, and holding other men accountable (metoomvmt.org). An important and contentious aspect of the #MeToo movement is that it circumvents the justice system, which has historically protected sexual aggressors (Lonsway & Archambault, 2012). Instead, #MeToo makes accusations public, encouraging public and private sectors to mete out other forms of justice, such as being publicly shamed or "cancelled," removed from public office, and/or "red from paid employment. Survivors have newfound avenues for telling their stories, and they are being heard. As Gilmore (2019) explains in her description of Bret Kavanaugh's hearings for the US Supreme Court, "#MeToo testimony broke through mechanisms of silencing that operate as structure and stricture (620)." The Chicago Tribune created an online timeline of the #MeToo movement (https://www.chicagotribune.com/lifestyles/ct-me-too-timeline-20171208-htmlstory.html). The list of accused offenders includes familiar figures: Justice Kavanaugh, US Vice President Joe Biden, Dr. Larry Nassar, television host Matt Lauer, movie mogul Harvey Weinstein, actor Bill Cosby, and musician R Kelly, among others. As the list continues to grow, concerns about a lack of due process for the accused have made many uncomfortable, including US President Donald Trump, who said, "It is a very scary time for young men in America, where you can be guilty of something you may not be guilty of" (Diamond, 2018). People are engaging in

JOURNAL OF GENDER STUDIES 2021, VOL. 30, NO. 1, 52–65
https://doi.org/10.1080/09589236.2020.1834367

important conversations about what constitutes consent, whose experiences are credible and legitimate, and who is most vulnerable.

Although #MeToo has paved new avenues for survivors to respond to sexual assault, feminist activists have been working for decades to prevent sexual assault from occurring in the first place. Focusing on the importance of consent, many have sought to change culture and practices. As a result of these efforts, there have been modifications to sexual assault training on US college campuses (Dyhouse, 2013). Grounded in sex-positivity, new policies often require affirmative, sober, and enthusiastic consent from all involved parties before and during sexual intimacy.

Within this larger context, we ask, How are university students navigating new affirmative consent policies? How does gender frame the negotiation of consent (Ridgeway, 2011)? As Pascoe and Hollander (2016) argue, all sexual assault intervention strategies are hindered by the larger gendered order in which many men still have power over women and other men. Is affirmative consent a panacea for gendered power in sexual intimacy? In a qualitative interview project (N = 45), we explored these research questions at one university that recently adopted an affirmative consent policy. In this particular paper, we focus primarily on the ways that subjects' conceptualizations of manhood shaped negotiations of sexual consent. Here, we present findings on gendered power dynamics that appeared to impact both men's and women's understandings of and responses to affirmative consent practices and sexual assault.

Through our systematic analysis of data, we found that participants' understandings of consent reinforced—rather than destabilized—hegemonic gendered systems of power. We conclude that affirmative consent policies alone are not capable of dismantling the systems of power that facilitate sexual violence and men's dominance. To prevent future sexual assault, we must go beyond trainings that focus on bodily autonomy and affirmative consent to incorporate lessons about gender and power.

Affirmative Consent

Although it has only recently gained traction, the concept of affirmative consent is not new. In the 1990s, a group of women at Antioch College in Ohio

were dismayed to learn about the prevalence of and weak response to sexual assault on their campus. Because consent was defined as "no means no," sexual assaults were going unpunished even in cases when a clear "no" was established. Students fought to change the way that sexual consent was defined at Antioch College. Through their activism, they developed the concept of affirmative consent and successfully lobbied to make it an official college policy, adopted in 1991. Since then, Antioch College has expanded its sex-positive consent policy and practices, and the concept has gained popularity across the US. California became the first state to enact an affirmative consent law in 2014, defined thusly:

> Affirmative, conscious, and voluntary agreement to engage in sexual activity. It is the responsibility of each person involved in the sexual activity to ensure that he or she has the affirmative consent of the other or others to engage in the sexual activity. Lack of protest or resistance does not mean consent, nor does silence mean consent. Affirmative consent must be ongoing throughout a sexual activity and can be revoked at any time. The existence of a dating relationship between the persons involved, or the fact of past sexual relations between them, should never by itself be assumed to be an indicator of consent.

Affirmative consent has been made into law in three more states: New York, Connecticut, and Illinois. Affirmative consent policies aim to prevent sexual assault from happening by improving communication and respect for bodily autonomy and personal boundaries. Rather than relying on outdated oppressor/victim frameworks, affirmative consent arguments focus on sexual empowerment and women's "bad assness" grounded in "girl power" (Dyhouse, 2013). Instead of shaming women or creating the illusion that women are not actively engaged in sex, affirmative consent intentionally emphasizes all participants' enthusiasm for and active role in sexual encounters, no matter their gender. Affirmative consent necessitates that women also have an active and eager role in their own sexual experiences.

The wisdom of shifting from "no means no" to affirmative consent continues to be debated for its legal (Soave, 2019), political (Saul & Taylor, 2017), and practical (Bauer-Wolf, 2018; Halley, 2015) implications. US Secretary of Education, Betsy DeVos, has pushed back, seizing upon false narratives claiming that women misuse affirmative consent policies and falsely accuse men of sexual assault if the sex was regrettable or unpleasurable (Fischel, 2019). To prevent men from being victimized by lying women—an anti-feminist concern that has no basis in evidence (Belknap, 2010; Lisak, Gardinier, Nicksa, & Cote, 2010)—DeVos developed several proposals that require "clear and convincing evidence" that the accused has committed sexual assault, weaken the power that universities have to address o#-campus assault, and provide a new, stricter definition of sexual harassment (Rhodes, 2019). These rollbacks may make it even more difficult for survivors of sexual assault to get justice (Meckler, 2019). Although the overhaul of these policies is being done in the name of due process, the deeper message seems to be: men need to be protected.

Rape as a Man's Problem

In efforts to prevent sexual violence, institutions including universities and the military have focused on training men not to sexually assault women. They have employed three main approaches: 1) addressing men as potential perpetrators; 2) explaining that men can also be victims of sexual assault; and 3) carrying out bystander awareness trainings (Scheel, Johnson, Schneider, & Smith, 2001, p. 258). Although these initiatives seem to embody feminist goals—ending the sexual assault of women—they can quickly become problematic. While they focus on men's role in sexual assault prevention, these programmers have not typically done anything to interrupt men's sexual dominance over women. Instead, they reinforce it through emphasizing a) men's need to protect women by asking for consent (because it is assumed that men are the initiators of sex), and b) men's responsibility in monitoring other men. This dynamic is most clear in bystander awareness programs that are geared towards men and reinforce men's role as protectors of women.

Women, conversely, are cast as passive objects for men to save. Saving women confers the status of a "good" man (Weitz, 2015).

In her study of sexual violence prevention within the military, Weitz (2015) revealed gendered messages

and strategies inherent in the U.S. military's training. For example, trainings argued that men should protect their women comrades because "male comrades . . . embodied a superior type of hyper- masculinity that could be harnessed for good" (175). Trainings idealized qualities associated with hegemonic masculinity (beliefs of ownership over women, aggression, and physical power) including the requirement of protecting women. This ideal masked an underlying chronic problem of sexual assault within the military: "Good men" were raping their colleagues with impunity while the military focused on protecting women from a foreign enemy. Weitz said, "Ironically, reinforcing the ubiquity of male predators, combined with reinforcing women's vulnerability, can reinforce (other) men's role as protector" (172).

Ridgeway (2011) argues that "gender frames" are important because they organize social relations and inform social and personal identities across gender, race, class, and sociopolitical lines. They persist over time despite social movements and larger structural shifts. Predominant gender frames in US society, such as the belief that men should protect and economically provide for women and children (Demantas & Myers 2015), stress men's dominance. Through everyday "manhood acts" (Schrock & Schwalbe, 2009), gender frames that benefit men over women are reinforced and reproduced. Importantly for this paper, systems of gendered power, heteronormativity, and patriarchy frame the ways in which we understand and practice sexual intimacy—and ultimately—consent (Connell, 1987; Hlavka, 2014; Moore & Reynolds, 2004; Risman, 2018). Ironically, when doing masculinity "correctly" is tied to enacting dominance (Connell, 1987; Pascoe 2012), even men with good intentions commit sexual assault (Pascoe & Hollander, 2016).

Weitz (2015) explored the link between protection and hegemonic masculinity, or the ultimate, most dominant form of masculinity in society at any given time (Connell, 1987). Weitz explains that, historically, masculinity in the US has been shaped through expectations of men defending the nation and serving as guardians over women. By enacting the role of protector, men access a higher level of status within society. Protectors are given permission to assert dominance over women and other men through physical violence and the close monitoring of others (Weitz, 2015).

The gender frame of men as protectors has currency because women are assumed to be in constant danger (Weitz, 2015). But, where does this danger come from? Ironically, it comes from men. Sexual coercion of women by men has been normalized in the US. This is especially clear on college campuses in the "Greek" or fraternity scene. Hattery and Smith (2019) explore this phenomenon within fraternities in which beliefs about consent are frequently manipulated and distorted. Hattery and Smith explain that there are multiple methods in which men use coercion while claiming that the sexual experience is consensual because they eventually get a "yes." These methods include "riffing, working a 'yes' out, and rape baiting" (27–28). The riffing strategy refers to a technique in which men talk their way into a situation where they will be able to have sex with a woman. Working a "yes" out refers to ways that men try to "seduce" women after they refuse to have sex with them the first time, such as by giving them something else to drink (27). Finally, men use rape baiting– or strategies to increase their probability of having sex— to identify women with whom they can easily talk into having sex, such as specifically targeting naïve first-year students. In their interviews, men argued that working out a yes was not sexual assault as long as women finally "gave in" (28). Men in their study constructed their own definition of consent to ensure their sexual gratification, and they used coercion through their role as the initiator of sex to make this happen.

Pascoe and Hollander (2016) work is particularly useful in teasing out these complexities. They argue that rape is normalized in society through a process that they call "mobilizing rape." They conceptualize sexual assault as more than individual-level incidents between perpetrators and their victims. Instead, sexual assault is only possible due to the array of cultural values and behaviors that underpin sexual violence, such as gender inequality and dominance. Importantly, multiple masculinities—not just hegemonic masculinity—are grounded in dominance. Men may participate in and benefit from traditional systems of gendered power and sexual dominance, even while subscribing to feminist ideals.

In this paper, we explore the ways that manhood framed subjects' navigation of affirmative consent in their intimate encounters, affecting both women and men. Many of the men in our study espoused pro-feminist rhetoric about women's empowerment. They took seriously the message that rape is a man's problem. However, most interpreted that message differently than it was intended by feminists in the #MeToo movement. Rather than taking responsibility for and rejecting nonconsensual sexual practices, they pivoted, finding a way to look like good guys while maintaining their gendered power in sexual situations. They redefined affirmative consent to suit their own purposes. Ultimately, they protected themselves and other men, contributing to rather than interrupting the mobilization of rape (Pascoe & Hollander, 2016).

Research Methods

This project is part of a larger study designed to understand college students' knowledge of changing definitions of consent, use of consent practices, and experiences with consensual and nonconsensual sex, including hook ups. To date, we have completed 45 face-to-face semi-structured interviews and eight focus group interviews with 23 subjects, and we received responses from 14 survey participants. The data for this paper come from the face-to-face interviews only. The sample size was larger than required for code saturation in qualitative analysis (Hennink, Kaiser, & Marconi, 2017), but we wanted to recruit as diverse a sample as possible. Semi-structured interviews enabled participants to answer questions openly while also giving interviewers the ability to direct the flow of conversation (Hesse-Biber & Leavy, 2012, p. 474). This method was particularly useful in this project for the following reasons: First, face-to-face interviews allowed for students to give in-depth, highly detailed descriptions of their sexual encounters and their understandings of consent. Second, we were better able to understand the processes through which students developed their understanding of consent over time. Third, these in-depth interviews revealed experiences with nonconsensual sex and sexual violence that students possibly had not self-identified as such outside of the interview context.

The interview guide was five pages long, and questions focused on the following: participants' experiences with casual hook-ups (Allison & Risman, 2014; Bogle, 2008) [e.g., Can you tell me what hooking up is to you? Let's focus on your most recent hook-up; can you describe the atmosphere? Was alcohol involved?]; understandings of consent [e.g., How would you define consent? What do you typically do to show that you are consenting to sexual activity? Have you ever had a sexual encounter where you or the other person did not give verbal consent?]; and understandings of and experiences with sexual assault [e.g., Since being in college, have you helped others who were dealing with their own experiences with sexual assault? Did the person consider reporting the incident to university authorities? How have you changed your daily routine after hearing about the event?]. The interview guide included numerous probes to encourage subjects to share details. Interviews were conducted from April 2018 to October 2018. Each lasted about an hour. Participants were offered 10 USD for their participation in the study. The interviews were audio-recorded and then transcribed. The average transcription was 12 pages long, single spaced, and about 10,000 words each.

Sample and Research Context

Data were collected at a midsized (about 17,000 students) public university in the Midwest. College campuses are a particularly important location to explore issues of consent. Despite having to complete trainings that focus on sexual assault prevention and Title IX policies, campuses continue to be sites in which students are constantly surrounded by messages that condone or ignore sexual violence (Hattery & Smith, 2019). This combination creates conflicting messages about consent and sexual assault. Furthermore, studies find that at least one in five bachelor's degree-seeking women will experience sexual assault before graduating from a four-year university (Muehlenhard, Peterson, Humphreys, & Jozkowski, 2017). Although men are also sexually assaulted, the incidence is less frequent, and regardless of whom is targeted, men are usually the perpetrators (Krebs, Lindquist, Warner, Fisher, & Martin, 2007). Many campaigns that are focused on sexual assault awareness and prevention (e.g., the No More Campaign

and It's On Us Campaign) have specifically targeted universities as sites for focusing their efforts. The university where we collected data for this current study requires all students to complete a Title IX training course at the beginning of the fall semester. These trainings cover the university's new affirmative definition of consent, the definition of sexual assault, bystander awareness, safety practices, and resources on campus. The university also posts messages about Title IX and consent on flyers around campus. This site was selected because participants had been exposed to (at least one) unifying message(s) about consent and affirmative consent policies.

Subjects were recruited in various ways. Professors from Sociology, Psychology, and Women, Gender, and Sexuality Studies departments advertised the study with their students in classes. We posted advertisements on social media platforms such as Facebook and Instagram. We gave out flyers and small recruitment cards announcing the study and the contact email address for anyone interested in participating. After students emailed the researchers expressing interest in participating in the study, we sent them a follow-up email explaining that the interview would discuss consensual and nonconsensual sexual experiences. Potential participants were informed that we would also ask them about experiences with assault. Interviews were scheduled based on participants' availability. Interviews took place in private offices or meeting rooms on campus. At the start of the interview, participants were given a consent form that reiterated the research purpose and included crisis hotlines for those who felt any distress after completing the interview. We assured participants that interviews would be confidential. Each subject created their own pseudonym.

All researcher conducted interviews over the course of the study, but no one interviewed a subject with whom she had a personal or professional relationship. For the larger study, we interviewed a diverse group of students: 27 identified as women (one a transwoman) and 18 identified as men. They had different majors and academic backgrounds. Most participants (N = 39) were undergraduate students. Three were graduate students, and three had recently graduated. The overall sample was diverse along several other dimensions, as well. The average age of participants was 23.8, ranging from 18 to 47 years old. Racially, 22 subjects identified as white, 9 were Latinx/Hispanic, 7 were Black, 4 identified as biracial, and 3 participants were Asian- American. Rather than asking participants to categorize their sexuality, which may be fluid, we collected data on the reported gender of their sexual partners (Manning, Longmore, Copp, & Giordano, 2014). Three women discussed having sex with both men and women, 22 women reported having sex with only men, and one woman reported only having sex with women. Among the men, 14 reported having sex with only women, three reported having sex with only men, and two participants only used gender-neutral pronouns to describe their partners.

Analysis

For the larger study, we used a grounded theory method of analysis (Charmaz, 1996; Corbin & Strauss, 1990), creating "analytic codes and categories developed from data, not from preconceived hypothesis" (Charmaz, 1996, p. 28). We began by identifying a list of broad but relevant codes/themes from within the interview guide, and transcriptions were coded using NVivo software. Several important codes emerged in this open coding phase: coercion, reason for use of consent, misconceptions about consent/sexual assault, feelings of safety. Next, we began axial coding, in which "categories are related to their subcategories, and the relationships tested against data" (Corbin & Strauss, 1990, p. 13). The use of axial coding was particularly helpful for establishing relationships and patterns within each of the codes and allowed for deeper investigation of the conditions in which the patterns arose. In this stage of the research, several patterns emerged. For this paper, we focus on only one major pattern: participants perceptions about consent were mediated by beliefs about gender. Here, we explore the ways in which men's negotiations of consent and discourse around sexual violence were mediated through gender frames about men as protectors. Although the data presented here focus primarily on the men's interviews, a small group of women expressed views similar to the men's. Those data are included here as well. It is important to note that findings from qualitative data analyses, although empirically grounded, are not generalizable.

Nonetheless, findings can be used to help us derive deeper understanding of social processes related to gender and power in different contexts.

Ethical Considerations

Although many students reported that the interview helped them gain insight into their own beliefs about consent, others compared the interview to talk to a therapist. During the interviews themselves, we noticed a pattern of misinformation about sexual assault among students. Many reported events that involved sexual assault without recognizing that what they described was assault until they discussed it in the interview context. When this occurred, we deviated from the interview schedule to say things like, "We need to talk about that some more." We took time after the interview to review the university's definitions and policies on consent and sexual assault with the participants, and occasionally we referred subjects to counselling. As feminist interviewers (Hesse-Biber & Leavy, 2012:), we believe that this step was crucial in practicing ethical research. Misinformation about sexual assault and confusion about resources on campus could potentially lead to further violence against students or prevent them from accessing resources that may be crucial for dealing with sexual violence. As such, our debriefing process involved an educational component.

Findings

Based on our systematic analysis of data, we found that men in this study had learned the lessons of affirmative consent training. Receiving the message that "rape is a man's problem," men reported changing their approaches to sexual encounters. Some men understood that men can stop rape by not raping women. However, many more conceptualized rape as a man's problem through a hegemonic-gendered frame. These men operationalized rape as a man's problem in three ways: 1) men need to protect women; 2) men need to avoid being accused of rape; 3) men need to protect each other from being accused of rape. We found that participants' understandings of consent reinforced—rather than destabilized—hegemonic systems of power within sex. Men used their understandings of affirmative consent to display their dominance over women and other men, while also appearing to maintain seemingly progressive, liberal, and even feminist values.

Protecting Women

In the current study, the ideal of men as protectors was expressed in a variety of ways. Some participants discussed how fraternities and masculine institutions have addressed sexual violence in their experiences. For example, Rick (age 24, Latino) stated:

> One of [my fraternity's] national events is "Rape is a Man's Issue." . . . We've been hosting it for the last three to four years. And it's shed light on, you know, consent . . . So, what we do is we tailor it to the guys, you know, we invite the girls too, but in a way so the guys can understand . . . And it gets really intense because a lot of times, the guys that will be in there, they feel like it's just another one of those . . . trainings. But you know, what's crazy is the girls that come—like we had one girl, a couple of girls actually—just break down and start crying because it's such a heavy topic. And I think—not that it's a good thing you know? They shouldn't be crying. But I think that it really does do a good job of showing the guys like, "Damn. This is for real. . . ." And we tell them too: everybody has a mother, everybody has a sister, everybody has a cousin. You know, something like this can happen to anybody who you know.

Rick's fraternity focused on men being the agents of change for sexual assault prevention and encouraged men to ensure they were getting consent from their partners before having sex. They appealed to men's pathos in order to get men to take the issue seriously. By emphasizing the vulnerability of women with whom men might have close relationships, Rick believed that men were made more aware of sexual assault, and thus, better equipped to protect women. Rick elaborated later in the interview, when he discussed his experiences coaching a powder puff football team, or football team for women. Rick recalled:

> During Homecoming and stuff, with those girls, we're on a Group Me [a social media communication platform]. And then right before Homecoming . . . I was like, "Look guys, be careful this weekend, you know, a lot of things can happen. Don't go anywhere alone."

> And they really appreciated that because I looked at them all like my little sisters. I was like you know, "just be safe."

Once again, Rick drew on the vulnerability of women. Despite all the women on the powder puff team being college-aged adults, he infantilized them by implying that it was his job as an older brother figure to warn them about the possibility of assault. By warning women about the threat of sexual assault and by framing sexual assault as a "man's issue," Rick applied ostensibly feminist tactics to maintain his image as a "good" man (Pascoe & Hollander, 2016). Rick thought that the women appreciated his protective stance and used their approval as evidence of its value.

Other participants discussed strategies they used in their own sexual experiences to help protect women. Jason (age 24, bi-racial), for example, described a routine he used to hook up with women. He said he would initiate the consent process by texting women before they came over and straightforwardly asking them, "Do you want to hook up?" He said:

> If they say, "yeah," and they show up to my house, then I take that in the context of consent. But, at any point in time—that's why the hang out period is so important too. At any point in time you can like—I wish people would understand that they have the right and ability and all that stuff to say, "Nope this is not for me, I'm fucking leaving."

Jason asked for consent via text before meeting up with his hook-ups, but he never verbally confirmed consent in person. He wanted to have sex, and he did not want to jeopardize that outcome by opening the topic for discussion. Instead, he built a waiting period into his routine to allow women to feel more comfortable. During this time, they watched TV, occasionally had a drink, and talked. He asserted that this waiting period showed respect for women's right to bodily autonomy and their own right and responsibility to say no if they changed their minds. Jason described himself as an active agent who protected women by giving them the time to say no before they begin to have sex. At the same time, his sexual partners were construed as passive participants: If they stayed, then they necessarily consented to having sex. To Jason, affirmative consent was measured by staying rather than leaving. The sentiment of a woman's passivity being a sign of consent was affirmed throughout his interview, for example, as he discussed negotiating consent and pleasure during sexual encounters:

> I mean aside from like, hit this way or hit that way, like that's about the most micro that I would understand. If she's like, [in terms of] communication—like, if she's giving me the eye thing, that means nothing to me. Like, I frankly don't care [laughter]. "If you can't verbalize it to me that I'm doing something wrong, or like you want me to do something else? Then it's just not important enough to you," is what I kind of take from that. Because I know what I like, and I tell them what I like. So, they would do that I suppose. And I would hope they would do the same.

Jason felt as though he created a safe space in which his partner could and should verbalize her desires (as he would do). He openly discounted non-verbal cues. While seeing himself as an active agent in promoting his partner's and his own pleasure, he continued to interpret non-verbal communication as a passive action that he could choose to ignore. Jason was able to simultaneously engage in progressive, feminist conversations about consent that made him a "good" man (Pascoe & Hollander, 2016), while prioritizing his own pleasure during sexual encounters.

Prevention strategies that rely on men serving as bystanders (situations in which men monitor other men's suspicious behaviors) also emphasize men's protector status. As Weitz (2015) argued in her research on sexual violence prevention work within the military, stressing the need for men to protect women from other men reinforces the dominance of men, in general. Men often monitor the actions of other men who they deem as less safe than they and their friends are. For example, men in this study discussed their experiences with bystander awareness and about how they have protected women from other men. Recalling an experience at a local bar, Charlie (age 22, Latinx) described how he and his friend, Billy (a man), saved their friend, Jenny (a woman), from a man who seemed to be bothering her. He explained that whenever he goes out and

sees Jenny, he "always [tries to] be mindful of her because she . . . does drink whenever she goes out." That night, Charlie noticed Jenny was drunk and "storming o#" from a man who seemed to insist that she follow him. He explained:

> So I literally just turned to the guy and I made it seem like I was in his way. Like "ohh" (shifting his body to right side). "Ope" (shifting his body to the left side). "Oh, ohh" (shifting body to right side again). Like "oh, excuse me." "Oh Sorry!" But I was doing it on purpose. I just I didn't want him to follow her. And it was cool because . . . one of my other homies [Billy] came next to me. And then he looked at the guy, and he's like, "No, just turn around." And the guy turned around. And then I looked at my boy and I gave him a big hug 'cause like man, like that was love! I knew he had my back and he understood. He understood intersectionalities that were happening within that situation and it felt good to know that I wasn't the only one, who you know, that was mindful of that.

While Charlie physically prevented the stranger from following Jenny, Billy noticed and came to help. The experience ended with a celebratory hug between the two men. Charlie beamed with a sense of pride he felt, bonding with one man to protect a woman from another man. In each of these examples, men expressed concern for women being sexually assaulted in seemingly progressive ways: making anti-sexual violence work a "men's issue," expressing value for bodily autonomy, and being good bystanders. It should be noted, though, that they concomitantly emphasize embodying masculine skills, such as assertiveness and leadership.

Some women in our study held similar beliefs about men's role in protecting women from other men. Erica (age 23, Asian) recalled her most recent hook-up, after which she felt her partner deliberately got her drunk in order to sway her into having sex. Erica explained:

> He knew I was interested in someone else and I felt like he got me drunk maybe on purpose or something . . I actually had invited the guy I was more interested in over that night to like hang out with all of us together.

He couldn't make it and I remember kind of saying how I was hoping he was there to make sure something else like that didn't happen.

Erica went on to describe feeling taken advantage of after this encounter and described her participation as, "I pretty much just laid there, let him have his way." Although she did not identify this experience as sexual assault, Erica believed the situation could have been prevented if the other, more desirable man had come. Erica's story reflects how messages about masculinities and men's ability to protect women from other, less desirable men are also subscribed to by women.

In recounting these experiences, the participants relied on old tropes about men's status as being "protectors of women" and framed women as passive actors within these situations (Weitz, 2015). Participants' discussions focused on the importance of men establishing dominance over women and other men whom they believe are strange or dangerous, unlike them, all under a veneer of feminist ideals.

Protecting Themselves

Although participants discussed men protecting women from sexual assault, they also expressed the need to protect men from being falsely accused of perpetrating assault. Thus, men simultaneously needed to protect women and to be protected from women. Underlying beliefs about false accusations of sexual assault complicated participants' discussions around sexual violence. Men and women in our study overwhelmingly expressed the importance of believing survivors who come forward, but often qualifying these statements with comments about false accusations. Alexis (bi-racial, 22) explained that thanks to the #MeToo movement: "Everyone's coming out more. And it's like, oh, I'm going to believe you. Why am I not going to believe you? But also, some people are just lying to get money." Julia (white, 24) had similar views about the effects of the #MeToo movement, explaining:

I think more people speak up if it happens to them from the movement. But then I feel like it could also cause some more problems that might- you know, if it

actually didn't happen and someone wants to get somebody in trouble for whatever reason, I feel like it could lead to kind of problems like that. But more obviously, more often [sexual assault] happens than not. But I just think with all like the people coming out about it now, I feel it'll led to a lot more cases of it.

Both women reported feeling that the #MeToo movement would help cultivate a culture in which survivors could more easily be believed, while concurrently highlighting that the movement may result in false accusations against men.

Men expressed these beliefs too. One participant, Ryan (age 21, White), talked about the effects of the #MeToo movement and recent pushes towards affirmative consent, saying:

A lot of guys are actually worried they will be accused of rape one day. Like, that they'll misinterpret a type of social cue. Or the social cues will be there, but a woman will say "Oh I changed my mind mid-way through" and [the man] wouldn't have known. I don't know how legitimate of a worry this is, but the worry is still there. I feel like there are different types of populations that are interpreting it in different ways and one population could be hurt or worried by this.

Ryan was not sure his worry was "legitimate," but he thought men's decisions were affected, nonetheless. The need to protect potential victims of false accusations was reiterated in many ways throughout the study. For example, Ghost (age 36, White) explained that while he was in the US Navy, he and his colleagues attended intense training courses on affirmative consent and sexual violence protection, so that when they had opportunities to hook up with women while bar hopping, service members would be sure to get affirmative consent. Ghost also said:

There was a lot of times when there was a possibility of taking someone home from the bar but, to me, there were very little coherences in our conversations. So, to me . . . it sounds bad [chuckles] but it was more of a cover- my-own-ass situation, right? If I'm not going to get a clear and concise "okay" with this, [then I'm not going to do it]. There were a lot of people who would say, "Oh I didn't have fun last night, so now I'm going to say I didn't want that." It happened a lot to guys on the base. So it was a very big cue that you better know what you're doing . . . So it was a lot more scary.

Ghost would not go home with intoxicated women from the bar out of fear that they would "consent" initially, but then disavow consent if the sex was not pleasurable. Ghost highlighted that this, indeed, was a "scary" time for men in the Navy. He related his motivation for getting clear, un-intoxicated consent, not out of the belief that it was a healthy part of sexual communication, but rather to ensure he was "covering his own ass." Ghost ensured his own safety and well-being by attaining affirmative consent.

Similarly, Paul (age 28, Asian) shared his fears that someone might accuse him of sexual assault based on things he did in the past. Paul recounted being at a party in his early 20s during which a woman led him into a room where people were already having sex. Paul said, I don't think there was ever consent there . . . yeah. It wasn't like "Hey, let's do this." It was like, take your hand and walk you into this room, sit you down, and just start blowing you, while other people were already fucking.

Paul did not seem worried that he had not verbally consented to having oral sex performed on him. He was worrying that the woman who performed the sex might later argue that she had not consented, making him responsible for sexual assault. Paul went on to explain how training in "the business world" changed his perspective on consent. He stated,

> [After working in the business world] I learned how to manage down and up. I just started managing everyone that I came in contact with after that . . . "this has to be done by the book." I didn't worry about that before. I mean . . . what if, what if that group of people [at that party] called the cops on the group of guys that were part of that. Would they call that rape? Because no one really talked about consent [then], and because I worked for a corporation, I reflected on that . . . It scares me.

In hindsight, despite his description of these women actively initiating sexual acts, Paul did not conceptualize initiation as affirmative consent. He was scared that he could be punished retro-actively. His new

training and responsibility taught him to start using affirmative consent because if he did not do things "by the book," there could be serious consequences for him. While sexual violence intervention tactics at universities are created to protect those most likely to be victimized by sexual violence—typically women (Armstrong, Hamilton, & Sweeney, 2006; Fedina, Holmes, & Backes, 2018)—in these situations, men incorporated their newfound understanding of these strategies into behaviors that they believed would protect themselves from being falsely accused of sexually assaulting women. Strategies that were originally intended to hold perpetrators accountable for a crime morphed into tools used to underscore women's untrustworthiness and men's vulnerability.

Protecting Other Men

Some men in our study used sexual violence prevention techniques to protect other men—not from being sexually assaulted, but from accidentally committing sexual assault. For example, Charlie (age 22) described parties at which he observed his friends talking to women who seemed too drunk to consent to hooking up. He explained:

> Like if . . . one of my boys is dancing with some girl who was getting heavily intoxicated then we're going to let him know, like "yo, bro chill . . . relax, she's drinking. Her friends are over there. Just watch out," you know, . . . And usually after that, he just calms down . . . Like, it doesn't get weird, like my friend isn't rubbing up on a girl. And it's not looking chaotic, in a sense that they're . . . making a scene. Does that make sense? In terms of getting people to look at them, and then grabbing other people's attention.

Here, like before, Charlie acted as a bystander and expressed pride that he was "protecting women" who might be too drunk to consent to intimate contact; however, there is a distinct difference in his descriptions of these two situations. In the first situation, Charlie focused on his and Billy's ability to force a strange man to turn around and leave the woman alone. In this second situation, Charlie expressed concern for protecting his friend. He warned his friend that he needed to "watch out" because the girl's friends were nearby, and he should not "make a scene." Charlie's worry was not that the woman could not consent because she was intoxicated. He was worried that his friend was in jeopardy. Charlie described his role as a bystander in two somewhat incompatible ways: he protected women from men he did not trust, and he protected men he did trust from women.

Equipped with seemingly progressive, feminist initiatives of sexual assault prevention, men in this study affirmed themselves as "good" and safe men, while using sexual assault prevention strategies to protect themselves, their friends, and the institutions where they belonged from false accusations of assault. This strategy impressed some women and made them feel safer. Maddie (age 18, White) talked about a fraternity house that she visited often, saying that they call themselves a gentlemen's fraternity. She explained that they used many strategies to prevent nonconsensual experiences. For instance:

> The fraternity that [my friends and I] always go to, they always provide rides for us to go back and forth from Greek Row. So that's always nice. They always have one designated driver who drives everyone home. They always have that one guy who's like, "Okay, you're taking all these people home at the same time." But they never let the guy be alone with one girl, or like the guy be alone with two girls . . . So they'll never allow the driver to take advantage, I guess. Even though he wouldn't . . . Like if he were to do that, he would get kicked out of the fraternity 'cause that's how they do it at their fraternity. But other fraternities, I bet they don't even care.

Maddie ranked this fraternity over others because its members tried to prevent unwanted, nonconsensual experiences by having a designated driver, ensuring women had safe rides home, and preventing men from being alone with one or two women. She claimed that these practices made women safer; however, these practices are consistent with fraternities' routine rituals of hypermasculinity. For example, being the designated driver is the job of pledges who are still trying to prove themselves to earn their place in the fraternity. Furthermore, as Hattery and Smith (2019) explain, having one pledge who is in charge of picking up and dropping off women at the end of the night actually helps create an

environment in which sexual assault is easier to facilitate because women are completely reliant on the pledge to help them get home. Women in these scenarios often end up stuck at the fraternity house with no idea when they will be picked up or where the pledge is. Rape is mobilized through a gentlemanly guise.

Bystander strategies can be used by men who want to appear to be protecting women from sexual assault, while ultimately protecting other men from accusations of sexual assault. For example, Eric (age 21, White) talked about his fraternity having a policy in which women were not allowed to be left alone with one man. Eric said:

> [My fraternity] had the system of cues that you would basically be able to give to your brother's that like, if they're doing something that you think is going in a bad direction. Like if they look like they're hitting on a girl that's super uncomfortable, you can give a cue, "Hey, slow down, take a step back." And stuff like that. . . . There was a conversation about how, if we were to ever walk somebody home, we would have to have a buddy in addition to whoever we were walking home. Especially if that person was like a drunk woman, we had to have that buddy. I'm pretty sure that was mostly for legal reasons. Like you need somebody to corroborate that nothing happened.

Maddie thought fraternity men cared about protecting women who attend their parties. Eric, a fraternity member himself, surmised that men sought to protect themselves for "legal reasons." Fraternities' strategies facilitated sex with women while protecting the credibility of the institution and its members. As stated by another participant, MJ (age 28, White), "No one wants to be seen as the rape house." Bystander strategies allowed fraternity members to appear chivalrous by protecting women from sexual assault while actually protecting themselves from being accused of sexual assault.

Discussion

At the surface level, it seems that men in this study took seriously the charge that rape is a man's issue and that men can and must end sexual assault by not raping people (Pascoe & Hollander, 2016). Ideally, this would involve a society in which women are viewed as equal, autonomous agents in sexual interactions, and to some extent, this was realized: our data showed that the men understood their role as "potential perpetrators" and their ability to be allies—or bystanders—for women (Scheel et al., 2001). Upon deeper analysis, however, we discovered that participants had employed affirmative consent behaviors in two ways that undermine their potential for eradicating sexual assault in the future. First, they upheld and asserted men's dominance over women and other men in the name of "protecting women." Second, they emphasized myths about false accusations and men's perceived vulnerability within the issue of sexual assault. Using seemingly progressive language and strategies surrounding sexual violence prevention that have grown out of the #MeToo movement, men in our study reframed gendered meanings in ways that ultimately benefitted themselves, reaffirming traditional manhood and masculine institutions.

In their critique of the ways that rape is normalized in society, Pascoe and Hollander (2016) said, "At first glance this may seem like a "damned if you do, damned if you don't" situation, where men reinforce gender inequality both by engaging in sexual assault and by not engaging in those same behaviors (76). We were left with a similar question: Does it matter that men are reproducing masculine privileges if their protective actions actually reduce the incidence of sexual assault in the end? Men who intervene with aggressive men may prevent the victimization of women. Men who personally opt-out of drunk sex in a self-motivated 'cover your ass" situation do prevent sexual assault. So why do we care about their motivations? We care because these actions are episodic rather than systemic. They do not interrogate or undo the underlying power imbalance. Ultimately, sexual assault persists despite progressive policies and practices because of stable gendered hierarchies and gender frames in society. Although affirmative consent conversations prevent some sexual assaults, sexual assault will not be eradicated without a more serious, culturally engrained shift in gendered meanings, structures, and practices. As Pascoe and Hollander wrote:

> When we attend to the way in which we provide avenues to oppose rape, we must combat normative masculinity as a mode of domination, rather than relying on tactics that render opposing gendered sexual violence part of that very system of domination (76).

Thus, we must care about these underlying issues.

Conclusion

Is rape a man's issue? As long as men continue to search for ways to maintain their gendered power in sexual intimacy, then yes it is. Can men work to stop sexual assault? Yes they can. We are currently in a time in which gendered power dynamics surrounding sexual intimacy are rapidly changing. Perhaps because of the mainstreaming of the feminist and #MeToo movements, many young women in the US express their own sexuality more freely and discourage men from blatantly engaging in sexually violent behaviors—or at least force them to find covert ways of engaging in it (Dyhouse, 2013; Pascoe & Hollander, 2016). Problems related to nonconsensual sexual intimacy and sexual coercion are at the forefront of political, social, and personal discussions. More men are embracing gender equity in their personal lives (Risman, 2018). The time seems ripe to make real systemic change.

Instituting new policies is an important part of this change, but it does not go far enough. Culture and individuals' practices must change as well. Affirmative consent grew out of a feminist goal to reduce the incidence of sexual violence. Affirmative consent policies are indeed useful in that they promote verbal consent, enthusiasm, and the freedom to say "no." Based on this study, however, we are skeptical that relying on affirmative consent policies will prevent sexual violence.

Affirmative consent policies alone do not interrupt persistent gender frames that help mobilize rape. This failure to dismantle the systems of power that facilitate sexual violence and reinforce men's dominance makes affirmative consent policies and practices only somewhat effective. Because negotiations of affirmative consent are mediated through gender frames that stress men's sexual entitlement, we must continue to work to disrupt those frames, while also finding new ways to educate men so that consensual sexual intimacy can become normative for all.

References

Allison, R., & Risman, B. (2014). It goes hand in hand with the parties:' Race, class, and residence in college student negotiations of hooking up. *Sociological Perspectives*, 57, 102–123.

Armstrong, E., Hamilton, L., & Sweeney, B. (2006). Sexual assault on campus: A multilevel, integrative approach to party rape. *Social Problems*, 53, 483–499.

Bauer-Wolf, J. (2018, October 22). Careful consent. Inside Higher Ed. https://www.insidehighered.com/news/2018/10/22/author-discusses-how-realistic-campus-consent-policies-are.

Belknap, J. (2010). Rape: Too hard to report and too easy to discredit victims. *Violence against Women*, 16, 1335–44.

Bogle, K. (2008). *Hooking up*. New York: NYU Press.

Charmaz, K. (1996). The search for meanings: grounded theory. In J. A. Smith, R. Harre, & L. Van Langenhove (Eds.), *Rethinking Methods in Psychology* (pp. 27–49). London: Sage.

Connell, R. W. (1987). *Gender and Power*. Stanford, CA: Stanford University Press.

Corbin, J., & Strauss, A. (1990). Grounded theory research: Procedures, canons, and evaluative criteria. *Qualitative Sociology*, 13, 3–21.

Demantas, I. and K. Myers. (2015). "Step up and be a man in a different manner:" Unemployed men re-framing masculinity. *Sociological Quarterly*. 56: 640–664.

Diamond, J. (2018, October 2). Trump says it's "a very scary time for young men in America." *CNN*. https://www.cnn.com/2018/10/02/politics/trump-scary-time-for-young-men-metoo/index.html.

Dyhouse, C. (2013). *Girl Trouble: Panic and Progress in the History of Young Women*. Chicago, IL: The University of Chicago Press.

Fedina, L., Holmes, J., & Backes, B. (2018). Campus sexual assault: A systematic review of prevalence research from 2000 to 2015. *Trauma, Violence, & Abuse*, 19, 76–93.

Fischel, J. J. (2019). *Screw Consent: A Better Politics of Sexual Justice*. Oakland, CA: University of California Press.

Gilmore, L. (2019). Frames of witness: The Kavanaugh hearings, survivor testimony, and #MeToo. *Biography*, 42, 610–623.

Halley, J. (2015). The move to affirmative consent. *Signs*, 42, 257–279.

Hattery, A. J., & Smith, E. (2019). *Gender, Power, and Violence: Responding to Sexual and Intimate Partner Violence in Society Today*. Lanham, MD: The Rowman and Littlefield Publishing Group.

Hennink, M. M., Kaiser, B. N., & Marconi, V. C. (2017). Code saturation versus meaning saturation: How many interviews are enough? *Qualitative Health Research*, 27(4), 591–608.

Hesse-Biber, S., & Leavy, P. L. (2012). *Feminist Research Practice: A Primer*. London: Sage Publications Inc.

Hlavka, H. (2014). Normalizing sexual violence: Young women account for harassment and abuse. *Gender & Society*, 28(3), 337–358.

Krebs, C., Lindquist, C., Warner, T., Fisher, B., & Martin, S. (2007). *The campus sexual assault (CSA) study. Final report to the US Department of Justice*. NIJ Grant No. 2004-WG-BX-0010.

Lisak, D., Gardinier, L., Nicksa, S. C., & Cote, A. M. (2010). False allegations of sexual assault: An analysis of ten years of reported cases. *Violence against Women*, 16, 1318–1334.

Lonsway, K., & Archambault, J. (2012). The "justice gap" for sexual assault cases: Future directions for research and reform. *Violence against Women*, 18(2), 45–68.

Manning, W., Longmore, M., Copp, J., & Giordano, P. (2014). The complexities of adolescent dating and sexual relationships: Fluidity, meaning(s), and implications for young adults' well-being. *New Directions for Child and Adolescent Development*, 144, 53–69.

Meckler, L. (2019, November 25). Betsy DeVos poised to issue sweeping rules governing campus sexual assault. *The Washington Post*, https://www.washingtonpost.com/local/education/betsy-devos-poised-to-issue-sweeping-rules-governing-campus-sexual-assault/2019/11/25/f9c21656-0f90-11ea-b0fc-62cc38411ebb_story.html.

Moore, A., & Reynolds, P. (2004). Feminist approaches to sexual consent: A critical assessment. In M. Cowling & P. Reynolds (Eds.), *Making Sense of Sexual Consent* (pp. 29–44). Burlington, VT: Ashgate.

Muehlenhard, C., Peterson, Z., Humphreys, T., & Jozkowski, K. (2017). Evaluating the one-in-five statistic: Women's risk of sexual assault while in college. *Journal of Sex Research*, 54, 549–576.

Pascoe, C. J., & Hollander, J. A. (2016). "Good guys don't rape": Gender domination, and mobilizing rape. *Gender & Society*, 30(1), 67–79.

Pascoe, C. J. (2012). *Dude, You're a Fag: Masculinity and Sexuality in High School*. Berkeley, CA: University of California Press. doi:10.1525/9780520950696

Rhodes, D. (2019, February 26). De Vos overhaul could make campus sex misconduct harder to prove. *Will that protect the accused or silence accusers? Chicago Tribune*, Chicago, Illinois. https://www.chicagotribune.com/news/breaking/ct-met-illinois-campus-sex-assault-title-ix-guidelines-devos-20190123-story.html

Ridgeway, C. (2011). *Framed by Gender*. New York: Oxford University Press.

Risman, B. (2018). *Where Will the Millennials Take Us? A New Generation Wrestles with the Gender Structure*. New York: Oxford University Press.

Saul, S., & Taylor, K. (2017, September 22). Betsy DeVos reverses Obama-era policy on campus sexual assault investigations *New York Times*, https://www.nytimes.com/2017/09/22/us/devos-colleges-sex-assault.html.

Scheel, E., Johnson, E., Schneider, M., & Smith, B. (2001). Making rape education meaningful for men: The case for eliminating the emphasis on men as perpetrators, protectors, or victims. *Sociological Practice*, 3(4), 257–278.

Schrock, D., & Schwalbe, M. (2009). Men, masculinity, and manhood acts. *Annual Review of Sociology*, 35, 277–295.

Soave, R. (2019, August 13). In win for due process, American Bar Association voted against affirmative consent. Reason. https://reason.com/2019/08/13/a!rmative-consent-aba-american-bar/.

Weitz, R. (2015). Vulnerable warriors: Military women, military culture, and fear of rape. *Gender Issues*, 32(3), 164–183.

Questions for Critical Thinking

1. Issues of rape and sexual assault are of particular concern on college campuses. Why do you think this is? What steps can all members of campus communities take to reduce or eliminate this concern?

2. The authors reference how U. S. universities have established affirmative consent policies. Do you have such policies on your campus? How, if at all, do you think such policies help to address the social problem of rape and sexual assault?

3. Gendered expectations of sexuality often contribute to an environment that fosters sexual assault. How might gender equality among college women and men in their sexual behavior reduce the incidence of rape?

CYBERBULLYING, SCHOOL BULLYING, AND PSYCHOLOGICAL DISTRESS

A Regional Census of High School Students

Shari Kessel Schneider, Lydia O'donnell, Ann Stueve, and Robert W. S. Coulter

Drawing on data from a regional census of high school students, the following essay documents the prevalence of cyberbullying, school bullying victimization, and negative consequences for the targets of that bullying. The authors' findings demonstrate that those students perceived to be gay, lesbian, bisexual, and/or transgendered were more likely to be targets of this form of violence and that such bullying had negative consequences for the school performance and mental health of these students. The conclusions of the authors confirm the need to establish structural changes to prevent this trend from continuing.

Recent national attention to several cases of suicide among youth victims of cyberbullying[1,2] has raised concerns about its prevalence and psychological impact. Most states now have legislation in place that requires schools to address electronic harassment in their antibullying policies,[3] yet schools lack information about cyberbullying correlates and consequences and how they may differ from those of school bullying. To inform schools' efforts, research is needed that examines the overlap between cyberbullying and school bullying and identifies which youths are targeted with either or both types of bullying. It is also necessary to understand whether the psychological correlates of cyberbullying are similar to those of school bullying and whether students targeted with both forms of bullying are at increased risk of psychological harm.

With reports indicating that 93% of teens are active users of the Internet and 75% own a cell phone, up from 45% in 2004,[4] there is great potential for cyberbullying among youths. Yet the extent of cyberbullying victimization and its prevalence relative to school bullying is unclear. Studies have found that anywhere from 9% to 40% of students are victims of cyberbullying,[5-7] and most suggest that online victimization is less prevalent than are school bullying and other forms of offline victimization.[8,9] Strikingly few reports provide information on youths' involvements in bullying both online and on school property.

Cyberbullying has several unique characteristics that distinguish it from school bullying. Electronic communications allow cyberbullying perpetrators to maintain anonymity and give them the capacity to post messages to a wide audience.[10] In addition, per-

Shari Kessel Schneider, Lydia O'Donnell, Ann Stueve, and Robert W. S. Coulter. "Cyberbullying, School Bullying, and Psychological Distress: A Regional Census of High School Students," *American Journal of Public Health*, 102(1), pp. 171–77. © 2017. Reprinted with permission of Sheridan Content Solutions on behalf of the *American Journal of Public Health*.

petrators may feel reduced responsibility and accountability when online compared with face-to-face situations.[11,12] These features suggest that youths who may not be vulnerable to school bullying could, in fact, be targeted online through covert methods. The limited number of studies that address the overlap between school and cyberbullying victimization has wide variation in findings, indicating that anywhere from about one third to more than three quarters of youths bullied online are also bullied at school.[11,13,14]

The distinct features of cyberbullying have led to questions about the sociodemographic characteristics of cyberbullying victims compared with those of school bullying victims. Although numerous studies of school bullying have found that boys are more likely to be victims,[15,16] the extent of gender differences in cyberbullying is unclear.[5] Some studies have found that girls are more likely to be victims of cyberbullying,[9,10] yet other studies have found no gender differences.[8,17,18] Age is another characteristic in which cyberbullying patterns may differ from traditional bullying. Although there is a decreasing prevalence of traditional bullying from middle to high school,[16] some studies suggest that cyberbullying victimization increases during the middle school years,[8,10] and others have found no consistent relationship between cyberbullying and age.[11,19] Sexual orientation has been consistently linked with traditional bullying.[20-22] Despite recent media attention to cases of suicide among sexual minority youths who have been cyberbullied,[23] accounts of the relationship between cyberbullying and sexual orientation are primarily anecdotal, with little documentation of the extent to which nonheterosexual youths are victimized. The wide range of definitions and time frames used to assess cyberbullying complicates the comparison of the prevalence and correlates of cyberbullying across studies, and rapid advances in communications technology render it difficult to establish a comprehensive and static definition. Furthermore, there is wide variation in the age and other demographic characteristics of the samples, with many studies employing small, nonrepresentative samples.

In addition to comparing the sociodemographics of cyberbullying victims with those of school bullying victims, it is important to understand whether cyberbullying is linked with negative school experiences, as is the case with school bullying. School bullying is widely known to be associated with many negative indicators, including lower academic achievement, lower school satisfaction, and lower levels of attachment and commitment to school, known as school bonding.[24,25] Because most cyberbullying occurs outside school,[19,26] it is uncertain whether a similar relationship exists for cyberbullying. A few studies have linked cyberbullying to negative school experiences, such as lower academic performance[27] and negative perceptions of school climate.[8] Although these studies suggest that cyberbullying may be a contributing factor, more research is needed to determine the extent to which school attachment and performance are related to cyberbullying experiences.

The known link between school bullying and psychological harm, including depression and suicidality,[28-31] has also raised concerns about how cyberbullying is related to various forms of psychological distress. An emerging body of research has begun to identify psychological correlates of cyberbullying that are similar to the consequences of traditional bullying, including increased anxiety and emotional distress.[6,11,32] There are also reports that online victimization may be linked with more serious distress, including major depression,[33,34] self-harm, and suicide.[31,35,36] Although studies consistently identify a relationship between cyberbullying and psychological distress, it is not known whether reports of psychological distress are similar among cyberbullying and school bullying victims or what levels of distress are experienced by those who report being victimized both online and at school.

In this study, we used data collected from more than 20 000 students from the second wave of the MetroWest Adolescent Health Survey to examine patterns and correlates of bullying victimization. We first examined the prevalence of cyberbullying and school bullying and the degree of overlap between the 2 forms of victimization. Next, looking at youths who experienced cyberbullying only, school bullying only, or both types of bullying, we identified sociodemographic and individual-level school characteristics associated with each type of victimization. Finally, we analyzed the relationship between type of bullying victimization and multiple indicators of psychological distress, ranging from depressive symptoms to suicide attempts.

Methods

The MetroWest Adolescent Health Survey is a biennial census survey of high school students in the western suburbs and small cities of the Boston metropolitan area that has the goal of monitoring trends to inform local and regional school and community policies and practices. The region is home to 26 high schools serving predominantly middle- and upper-middle class families. The survey employs a census rather than sampling procedure so that each district can monitor student behaviors and identify health issues that may vary by grade, gender, and other sociodemographic characteristics.

In fall 2008, 22 of 26 high schools in the region participated in the survey; these schools serve 86% of all public high school students in the region. Pencil and paper, anonymous surveys were conducted with all 9th- through 12th-grade students present on the day of administration. Parents and guardians were notified in advance and given the opportunity to view the survey and opt out their child(ren); students also provided assent. Youths (n = 20 406) completed the surveys, for a participation rate of 88.1% (range, 75.2%–93.7%). Reflecting differences in school size, the number of students participating at each site ranged from 303 to 1815.

Measures

To facilitate comparison with state and national data, most items in the Metro-West Adolescent Health Survey were drawn from the Centers for Disease Control and Prevention's Youth Risk Behavior Survey[37] and the Massachusetts Youth Risk Behavior Survey.[38]

Bullying.

Students were asked about cyberbullying victimization and school bullying victimization in the past 12 months. Cyberbullying was measured with the following question: "How many times has someone used the Internet, a phone, or other electronic communications to bully, tease, or threaten you?" School bullying was measured by the following question: "During the past 12 months, how many times have you been bullied on school property?" with bullying defined as "being repeatedly teased, threatened, hit, kicked, or excluded by another student or group of students." Responses from these 2 questions were categorically grouped into 4 categories of bullying victimization: cyberbullying victim only, school bullying victim only, both cyber and school bullying victim, and neither.

Psychological distress.

Depressive symptoms, suicidal ideation (seriously considering suicide), and suicide attempts (any attempt and an attempt requiring medical treatment) were measured using items about behavior in the past 12 months.[37] Self-injury was assessed by the item "How many times did you hurt or injure yourself on purpose? (For example, by cutting, burning, or bruising yourself on purpose)."[38] Responses were dichotomized into yes or no categories.

Sociodemographics.

Sociodemographic characteristics included gender, grade (9–12), race/ethnicity (Asian, African American or Black, Hispanic or Latino, Caucasian or White, or mixed or other), and sexual orientation (responses grouped as "heterosexually identified" vs "nonheterosexually identified," the latter of which encompassed gay or lesbian, bisexual, other, and not sure).

Individual-level school characteristics.

School performance was measured through self-reported grades coded as "mostly As," "mostly Bs," "mostly Cs," and a combined category encompassing "mostly Ds," "mostly Fs," and ungraded or other. School attachment was measured using a 5-item scale from the National Longitudinal Study of Adolescent Health[39]; scale scores were divided into tertiles (low, medium, high).

School size.

Schools were grouped into 3 categories on the basis of the size of student enrollment: <750 students, 750–1250 students, and >1250 students.

Results

Table 1 presents the sociodemographic characteristics of participants. Three quarters (75.2%) of the youths were non-Hispanic White, consistent with regional demographics. About 6% of youths reported that they were gay or lesbian, bisexual, other, or not sure (nonheterosexually identified youths).

TABLE 1   Sociodemographics and School-Related Characteristics of Study Sample: MetroWest Adolescent Health Survey, Massachusetts, 2008

Characteristics	No. (%)
Sociodemographics	
Gender	
Girl	10 218 (50.4)
Boy	10 050 (49.6)
Grade	
9th	5446 (26.8)
10th	5312 (26.2)
11th	5075 (25.0)
12th	4458 (22.0)
Race/ethnicity	
Asian	786 (3.9)
African American	564 (2.8)
Hispanic	1186 (5.8)
White	15 265 (75.2)
Mixed/other	2497 (12.3)
Sexual orientation	
Heterosexually identified	18 795 (93.7)
Nonheterosexually identified	1261 (6.3)
School-related Characteristics	
Self-reported school performance	
Mostly As	6072 (31.0)
Mostly Bs	9947 (50.8)
Mostly Cs	2477 (12.6)
Mostly Ds or Fs	1090 (5.6)
Self-reported school attachment	
Highest tertile	7066 (35.1)
Medium tertile	5953 (29.6)
Lowest tertile	7095 (35.3)
School enrollment	
< 750 students	2402 (11.8)
750–1250 students	8576 (42.0)
> 1250 students	9428 (46.2)

Prevalence and Overlap of Cyberbullying and School Bullying Victimization

Overall, 15.8% of students reported cyberbullying, and 25.9% reported school bullying in the past 12 months. The overlap between cyberbullying and school bullying was substantial: 59.7% of cyberbullying victims were also school bullying victims, and 36.3% of school bullying victims were also cyberbullying victims. When categorized into 4 groups on the basis of reports of cyber and school bullying victimization, one third of all students were bullying victims: 6.4% were victims of cyberbullying only, 16.5% of students were victims of school bullying only, and 9.4% were victims of both school and cyberbullying.

Correlates of Bullying Victimization

Regarding overall cyberbullying and school bullying victimization, reports of cyberbullying were higher among girls than among boys (18.3% vs 13.2%), whereas reports of school bullying were similar for both genders (25.1% for girls, 26.6% for boys). Although cyberbullying decreased slightly from 9th grade to 12th grade (from 17.2% to 13.4%), school bullying decreased by nearly half (from 32.5% to 17.8%). Nonheterosexually identified youths were far more likely than were heterosexually identified youths to report cyberbullying (33.1% vs 14.5%) and school bullying (42.3% vs 24.8%). There were no differences in overall reporting of cyberbullying or school bullying by race/ethnicity.

Table 2 displays the sociodemographic and individual-level school correlates of bullying victimization when categorized into the following 4 groups: cyberbullying victim only, school bullying victim only, both, and neither. Whereas there was little difference by gender, race/ethnicity, and grade, nonheterosexually identified youths were more likely to be victims of cyberbullying only, compared with those who self-identify as heterosexual (10.5% vs 6.0%). Youths who reported lower school performance and lower school attachment were also more likely to be victimized with cyberbullying only; for example, students who received mostly Ds and Fs were twice as likely to be cyber-only victims compared with students who received mostly As (11.3% vs 5.2%).

In contrast to reports of the cyber-only group, victimization on school property decreases substantially from 21.4% in 9th grade to 10.6% in 12th grade. There was little difference by gender or race/ethnicity. Consistent with the cyber-only group, nonheterosexually identified youths were at higher risk of school-only

TABLE 2 Sociodemographic and Individual-Level School-Related Correlates of Bullying Victimization: MetroWest Adolescent Health Survey, Massachusetts, 2008

Characteristics	Cyberbullying Victim Only, No. (%)	School Bullying Victim Only, No. (%)	Cyber and School Bullying Victim, No. (%)	Neither, No. (%)
Sociodemographics correlates				
Gender*				
Girl	723 (7.2)	1564 (15.5)	1118 (11.1)	6697 (66.3)
Boy	546 (5.6)	1718 (17.5)	751 (7.6)	6812 (69.3)
Grade*				
9th	327 (6.1)	1146 (21.4)	596 (11.1)	3293 (61.4)
10th	329 (6.3)	961 (18.4)	554 (10.6)	3376 (64.7)
11th	335 (6.7)	724 (14.5)	411 (8.2)	3529 (70.6)
12th	275 (6.3)	463 (10.6)	310 (7.1)	3324 (76.0)
Race/ethnicity*				
White	858 (5.7)	2474 (16.4)	1400 (9.3)	10332 (68.6)
Non-White/mixed	413 (8.4)	822 (16.8)	481 (9.8)	3179 (64.9)
Sexual orientation*				
Heterosexually identified	1125 (6.0)	3046 (16.3)	1583 (8.5)	12888 (69.1)
Nonheterosexually identified	131 (10.5)	243 (19.5)	282 (22.7)	589 (47.3)
Individual-level school-related correlates				
School performance*				
Mostly As	312 (5.2)	1002 (16.6)	448 (7.4)	4266 (70.8)
Mostly Bs	598 (6.1)	1642 (16.7)	896 (9.1)	6679 (68.0)
Mostly Cs	191 (8.0)	399 (16.6)	293 (12.2)	1516 (63.2)
Mostly Ds and Fs	117 (11.3)	145 (14.0)	167 (16.1)	606 (58.6)
School attachment*				
Highest tertile	364 (5.2)	891 (12.7)	393 (5.6)	5385 (76.6)
Medium tertile	348 (5.9)	965 (16.3)	435 (7.3)	4174 (70.5)
Lowest tertile	552 (7.9)	1442 (20.6)	1048 (14.9)	3974 (56.6)
Total	1275 (6.4)	3311 (16.5)	1889 (9.4)	13582 (67.7)

Note. All measures are for the past 12 months.*$P <. 001$ for association between bullying victimization and sociodemographic or student-level school correlate.

victimization (19.5% vs 16.3%); school-only victimization was also associated with lower school attachment.

Although there was little difference by gender for the other victimization groups, girls were more likely than were boys to be victims of both types of bullying (11.1% vs 7.6%). Like the cyber-only and school-only

groups, sexual orientation was associated with reports of both cyber and school victimization; 22.7% of nonheterosexually identified youths were victims of both types of bullying compared with 8.5% of heterosexually identified youths. In addition, the associations between dual forms of victimization and school variables were stronger: students who received mostly

Ds and Fs were more than twice as likely as were students who received mostly As to be victims of both forms of bullying (16.1% vs 7.4%), and students in the lowest school attachment tertile were nearly 3 times as likely to report both forms of victimization than were students in the highest tertile (14.9% vs 5.6%). Thus, youths who were in lower grades and nonheterosexually identified youths were more likely to be victims of one or both types of bullying, as were students who reported lower grades and lower levels of school attachment.

Bullying Victimization and Psychological Distress
Table 3 presents bivariate associations between types of bullying victimization (cyber-only, school-only, both, or neither) and 5 indicators of psychological distress. Bullying victimization was consistently and robustly associated with an increased likelihood of psychological distress across all measures from depressive symptoms and suicidal ideation to reports of self-injury and suicide attempts. Furthermore, the relationship between victimization and distress was strongest among students who were victims of both cyber and school victimization, followed by victims of cyberbullying only and then victims of school bullying only. For example, reports of depressive symptoms were highest among victims of both cyber and school bullying (47.0%), followed by cyber-only victims (33.9%), and school-only victims (26.6%) compared with 13.6% of nonvictims. Similarly, attempted suicide

was highest among victims of both cyber and school bullying (15.2%); however, it was also elevated among cyber-only victims (9.4%) and school-only victims (4.2%) compared with students reporting neither form of victimization (2.0%).

Table 4 displays logistic regressions modeling the relationship between type of bullying victimization and psychological distress, adjusting for the sociodemographic and individual-level school variables identified earlier as significant correlates of victimization. Consistent with the bivariate associations, there were strong relationships between bullying victimization and psychological distress across all indicators of distress. Overall, the risks of experiencing psychological distress were greatest for victims of both cyber and school bullying. For example, compared with nonvictims, victims of both cyber and school bullying were more than 4 times as likely to report depressive symptoms (adjusted odds ratio (AOR) = 4.38; 99% CI = 3.76, 5.10), suicidal ideation (AOR = 4.51; 99% CI = 3.78, 5.39), and self-injury (AOR = 4.79; 99% CI = 4.06, 5.65), and more than 5 times as likely to report a suicide attempt (AOR = 5.04; 99% CI = 3.88, 6.55) and a suicide attempt requiring medical treatment (AOR = 5.42; 99% CI = 3.56, 8.26). Victims of cyberbullying only were also at a heightened, but somewhat lower risk of psychological distress (AORs from 2.59 to 3.44). The risk was still notable, but even lower, among victims of school bullying only (AORs from 1.51 to 2.20) compared with nonvictims.

TABLE 3   **Psychological Correlates of Bullying Victimization: MetroWest Adolescent Health Survey, Massachusetts, 2008**

Bullying Victimization	Depressive Symptoms,* No. (%)	Suicidal Ideation,* No. (%)	Self-Injury,* No. (%)	Suicide Attempt,* No. (%)	Suicide Attempt With Medical Treatment,* No. (%)
Cyber victim only	429 (33.9)	228 (18.1)	305 (24.0)	119 (9.4)	42 (3.3)
School victim only	878 (26.6)	464 (14.1)	511 (15.5)	138 (4.2)	45 (1.4)
Both cyber and school victim	884 (47.0)	561 (30.0)	712 (37.8)	286 (15.2)	123 (6.6)
Neither	1839 (13.6)	836 (6.2)	1102 (8.1)	275 (2.0)	86 (0.6)
Total	4030 (20.2)	2089 (10.5)	2630 (13.2)	818 (4.1)	296 (1.5)

Note. All measures are for the past 12 months.
*P < .001 for association between victimization and indicator of psychological distress.

TABLE 4 Associations of Bullying Victimization and Psychological Distress among High School Students: MetroWest Adolescent Health Survey, 2008

Characteristics	Depressive Symptoms, No. or OR (95% Ci)	Suicidal Ideation, No. or OR (95% Cf)	Self-Injury, No. or OR (95% CI)	Suicide Attempt, No. or OR (95% CI)	Suicide Attempt With Medical Treatment, No. or OR (95% CI)
Unadjusted					
Students	19 990	19 953	19 975	19 988	19 877
Bullying victimization					
Cyber victim only	3.26 (2.76, 3.85)	3.35 (2.71, 4.13)	3.56 (2.95, 4.29)	5.00 (3.73, 6.71)	5.36 (3.28, 8.75)
School victim only	2.31 (2.04, 2.60)	2.49 (2.13, 2.92)	2.07 (1.78, 2.40)	2.11 (1.60, 2.77)	2.16 (1.34, 3.48)
Both cyber and school victim	5.64 (4.93, 6.46)	6.52 (5.56, 7.64)	6.86 (5.92, 7.94)	8.64 (6.88, 10.86)	10.93 (7.57, 15.80)
Neither (Ref)	1.00	1.00	1.00	1.00	1.00
Adjusted					
Students	18 815	18 784	18 796	18 812	18 735
Bullying victimization					
Cyber victim only	2.61 (2.17, 3.13)	2.59 (2.06, 3.25)	2.83 (2.30, 3.48)	3.44 (2.48, 4.76)	3.39 (1.99, 5.77)
School victim only	2.19 (1.92, 2.50)	2.20 (1.86, 2.62)	1.84 (1.57, 2.17)	1.63 (1.20, 2.20)	1.51 (0.89, 2.55)
Both cyber and school victim	4.38 (3.76, 5.10)	4.51 (3.78, 5.39)	4.79 (4.06, 5.65)	5.04 (3.88, 6.55)	5.42 (3.56, 8.26)
Neither (Ref)	1.00	1.00	1.00	1.00	1.00
Gender					
Girl	2.19 (1.97, 2.44)	1.59 (1.39, 1.82)	2.34 (2.05, 2.66)	1.29 (1.04, 1.59)	1.11 (0.79, 1.57)
Boy (Ref)	1.00	1.00	1.00	1.00	1.00
Grade					
9th	0.70 (0.60, 0.81)	0.76 (0.63, 0.93)	0.96 (0.80, 1.15)	1.04 (0.77, 1.42)	0.81 (0.50, 1.30)
10th	0.82 (0.71, 0.95)	0.92 (0.76, 1.11)	1.18 (0.98, 1.41)	1.06 (0.78, 1.44)	0.82 (0.51, 1.33)
11th	1.02 (0.88, 1.18)	0.93 (0.77, 1.13)	1.13 (0.94, 1.35)	1.05 (0.77, 1.44)	0.79 (0.48, 1.30)
12th (Ref)	1.00	1.00	1.00	1.00	1.00
Race/ethnicity					
White (Ref)	1.00	1.00	1.00	1.00	1.00
Non-White/mixed	1.25 (1.12, 1.41)	1.15 (0.99, 1.33)	1.02 (0.89, 1.18)	1.55 (1.25, 1.94)	1.38 (0.97, 1.98)
Sexual orientation					
Heterosexually identified (Ref)	1.00	1.00	1.00	1.00	1.00
Nonheterosexually identified	2.36 (1.97, 2.83)	3.43 (2.83, 4.16)	4.12 (3.42, 4.96)	5.17 (4.05, 6.60)	5.34 (3.69, 7.74)
School performance					
Mostly As (Ref)	1.00	1.00	1.00	1.00	1.00
Mostly Bs	1.44 (1.27, 1.63)	1.28 (1.09, 1.52)	1.27 (1.10, 1.48)	1.64 (1.22, 2.21)	1.21 (0.75, 1.96)
Mostly Cs	2.17 (1.83, 2.58)	1.70 (1.37, 2.12)	1.82 (1.49, 2.23)	2.79 (1.98, 3.94)	2.05 (1.19, 3.55)
Mostly Ds and Fs	2.71 (2.17, 3.38)	2.41 (1.85, 3.14)	2.28 (1.77, 2.94)	3.90 (2.67, 5.71)	3.31 (1.87, 5.87)

Continued

TABLE 4 *Continued*

Characteristics	Depressive Symptoms, No. or OR (95% Ci)	Suicidal Ideation, No. or OR (95% Cf)	Self-Injury, No. or OR (95% CI)	Suicide Attempt, No. or OR (95% CI)	Suicide Attempt With Medical Treatment, No. or OR (95% CI)
School attachment					
Highest tertile (Ref)	1.00	1.00	1.00	1.00	1.00
Medium tertile	1.23 (1.07, 1.43)	1.26 (1.03, 1.53)	1.18 (0.99, 1.40)	1.09 (0.78, 1.52)	0.98 (0.55, 1.75)
Lowest tertile	2.69 (2.36, 3.07)	2.50 (2.10, 2.98)	2.12 (1.81, 2.47)	2.09 (1.58, 2.77)	2.11 (1.33, 3.37)

Note. CI—confidence interval; OR—odds ratio. All measures are for the past 12 months.

Discussion

We examined data from a large, school-based census of more than 20 000 youths to document the co-occurrence of cyberbullying and school bullying and their association with psychological distress. We have provided evidence of a substantial overlap between cyberbullying and school bullying victimization and called attention to particularly vulnerable populations, including nonheterosexually identified youths. We also found an association between both types of bullying and indicators of school success. Finally, we have highlighted the relationship between victimization and psychological distress, documenting a substantially elevated risk of distress among victims of both cyber and school bullying. These findings show a clear need for prevention efforts that address both forms of victimization.

Although almost all states now mandate schools to address cyberbullying in their anti-bullying policies,[3] there is great flexibility in how much emphasis schools place on efforts to prevent cyberbullying, which occurs mostly outside school.[19,26] We found substantial overlap between cyberbullying and school bullying: nearly two thirds of all cyberbullying victims reported they were also bullied at school, and conversely, more than one third of school bullying victims also reported cyberbullying. This indicates the importance of prevention approaches that address both modes of victimization.

Another important reason for schools to address cyberbullying is the link between victimization and school attachment and self-reported school performance. This is true even for the 6% of students who were victimized only through cyberbullying.

Although this cross-sectional survey cannot make attributions of causality, cyberbullying may be a contributing factor to negative school experiences, suggesting the need for schools to incorporate cyberbullying into their antibullying programs and policies. Efforts to increase student engagement in school, connectedness to peers and teachers, and academic success may also promote a climate in which school and cyberbullying are less likely to occur.

Our findings identified several groups that were particularly susceptible to victimization. It is not surprising to learn that cyberbullying victimization and dual victimization were more prevalent among nonheterosexually identified youths, who are known to suffer from higher rates of victimization in school settings.[20–22] Nearly one quarter (23%) were victims of both cyber and school bullying, compared with only 9% of heterosexually identified youths. These disproportionate reports of bullying involvement, combined with the high prevalence of psychological distress among nonheterosexually identified youths,[40] show a clear need for antibullying programs and policies to address and protect students who identify as gay, lesbian, or bisexual or who may be questioning their sexual orientation. We also noted gender differences in victimization patterns. Girls were more likely than were boys to report cyberbullying, especially in combination with school bullying. Several other studies support the higher prevalence of cyberbullying victimization among girls.[9,10]

There is a robust relationship between cyberbullying victimization and all forms of psychological distress along the continuum from depression to suicide attempts. Importantly, whereas all 3 victim groups examined in this study reported elevated psychological distress, victims of cyberbullying alone reported more distress than did victims of school bullying alone. Moreover, the risk of psychological distress was most marked for victims of both cyber and school bullying, who were more than 4 times as likely to experience depressive symptoms and more than 5 times as likely to attempt suicide as were nonvictims. Our study not only provides further evidence of the link between cyberbullying and psychological distress[30,34,36] but also points to an even greater need to identify and support victims of both cyber and school bullying.

This study has several limitations. First, cyberbullying and school victimization were assessed using self-reported single items. There is no current consensus among researchers on how to measure cyberbullying, and the changing nature of communications technology makes it difficult to establish a fixed definition. In addition, some youths reporting both cyberbullying and school bullying may have answered positively to both questions because they were victims of cyberbullying that occurred on school property. The psychological distress indicators were also assessed using single self-report items; although these items are widely used, they are not diagnostic. The cross-sectional nature of the analysis means that we cannot attribute causality or temporality to the relation between bullying and distress. Furthermore, this study does not consider students' roles as perpetrators. These involvements may also be associated with increased psychological distress and negative school factors.[41,42] We also did not explore contextual influences on these behaviors and the complex roles that bystanders—students and parents and adults in the school community—play in escalating, condoning, tolerating, or preventing cyberbullying and school bullying. These are important areas for further research.

Despite these limitations, our study has several unique strengths. Many studies of cyberbullying are conducted online and, therefore, may have a bias toward the experiences of students who use the Internet more frequently. In fact, time spent online and computer proficiency have been related to cyberbullying behavior.[17] This school-based study included a more diverse group of students in terms of exposure to and use of electronic media. In addition, the sample size was large, permitting examination of behaviors within relatively small subgroups, such as nonheterosexually identified youths, and of infrequent forms of psychological distress, such as suicide attempts. At the same time, however, the results are regional, and generalizability to other populations, including youths in urban and rural schools, may be limited.

In summary, our study provides a better understanding of cyberbullying and its relationship to school bullying, which is critical to informing school-based prevention efforts and engaging parents and other community members in combating this significant public health issue. Our findings underscore the need for prevention efforts that address all forms of bullying victimization and their potential for harmful consequences both inside and outside school.

References

1. Deutsch L. Prosecutors: cyber law applies to suicide case. *Associated Press*. August 13, 2008. Available at: http://www.usatoday.com/news/nation/2008-08-12-327594069_x.htm. Accessed September 8, 2011.

2. Kennedy H. Phoebe Prince, South Hadley High School's "new girl" driven to suicide by teenage cyber bullies. *New York Daily News*. March 29, 2010.

3. Hinduja S, Patchin JW. *State Cyberbullying Laws: A Brief Review of State Cyberbullying Laws and Policies*. Cyberbullying Research Center. Available at: http://cyberbullying.us/Bullying_and_Cyberbullying_Laws.pdf. Accessed February 9, 2011.

4. Lenhart A, Purcell K, Smith A, Zickuhr K. *Social Media and Mobile Internet Use Among Teens and Adults*. Pew Research Center Publications; 2010. Available at: http://pewinternetorg/~/media//Files/Reports/2010/PIP_Social_Media_and_Young_Adults_Report_Final_with_toplines.pdf. Accessed February 9, 2011.

5. Tokunaga RS. Following you home from school: a critical review and synthesis of research on cyberbullying victimization. *Comput Human Behav*. 2010;26(3): 277–87.

6. Ybarra ML, Mitchell KJ, Wolak J, Finkelhor D. Examining characteristics and associated distress

related to Internet harassment: findings from the second Youth Internet Safety Survey. *Pediatrics.* 2006;118(4): et169–et177.

7. David-Ferdon C, Hertz MF. *Electronic Media and Youth Violence: A CDC Issue Brief for Researchers.* Atlanta, GA: Centers for Disease Control and Prevention; 2009.

8. Williams KR, Guerra NG. Prevalence and predictors of Internet bullying. *J Adolesc Health.* 2007;41(6 suppl 1): S14–S21.

9. Wang J, Iannotti RJ, Nansel TR. School bullying among adolescents in the United States: physical, verbal, relational, and cyber. *J Adolesc Health.* 2009;45(4):368–75.

10. Kowalski RM, Limber SP. Electronic bullying among middle school students. *J Adolesc Health.* 2007;41(6 suppl 1):S22–S30.

11. Juvonen J, Gross EF. Extending the school grounds?—Bullying experiences in cyberspace. *J Sch Health.* 2008;78(9): 496–505.

12. Mishna F, Saini M, Solomon S. Ongoing and online: children and youth's perceptions of cyber bullying. *Child Youth Serv Rev.* 2009;31(12):1222–8.

13. Twyman K, Saylor C, Taylor LA, Comeaux C. Comparing children and adolescents engaged in cyberbullying to matched peers. *Cyberpsychol Behav Soc Netw.* 2010; 13(2):195–9.

14. Ybarra ML, Diener-West M, Leaf PJ. Examining the overlap in Internet harassment and school bullying: implications for school intervention. *J Adolesc Health.* 2007;41(6 suppl 1):S42–S50.

15. Carlyle KE, Steinman KJ. Demographic differences in the prevalence, co-occurrence, and correlates of adolescent bullying at school. *J Sch Health.* 2007;77(9):623–9.

16. Nansel TR, Overpeck M, Pilla RS, Ruan WJ, Simons-Morton B, Scheidt P. Bullying behaviors among US youth: prevalence and association with psychosocial adjustment. *JAMA.* 2001;285(16):2094–100.

17. Hinduja S, Patchin JW. Cyberbullying: an exploratory analysis of factors related to offending and victimization. *Deviant Behav.* 2008;29(2):129–56.

18. Ybarra ML, Mitchell KJ. Youth engaging in online harassment: associations with caregiver–child relationships, Internet use, and personal characteristics. *J Adolesc.* 2004;27(3):319–36.

19. Smith PK, Mahdavi J, Carvalho M, Fisher S, Russell S, Tippett N, Cyberbullying: its nature and impact in secondary school pupils. *J Child Psychol Psychiatry.* 2008;49(4): 376–85.

20. Birkett M, Espelage DL, Koenig B. LGB and questioning students in schools: the moderating effects of

homophobic bullying and school climate on negative outcomes. *J Youth Adolesc.* 2009;38(7):989–1000.

21. Espelage DL, Aragon SR., Birkett M, Koenig BW. Homophobic teasing, psychological outcomes, and sexual orientation among high school students: what influence do parents and schools have? *School Psych Rev.* 2008;37(2):202–16.

22. Berlan ED, Corliss HIL, Field AE, Goodman E, Austin SB. Sexual orientation and bullying among adolescents in the Growing Up Today study. *J Adolesc Health.* 2010; 46(4);366–71.

23. Schwartz J. Bullying, suicide, punishment *New York Times.* October 2, 2010.

24. Dake JA, Price JK, Telljohann SK. The nature and extent of bullying at school. *J Sch Health.* 2003;73(5): 173–80.

25. Spriggs AL, Iannotti RJ, Nansel TR, Haynie DL. Adolescent bullying involvement and perceived family, peer and school relations: commonalities and differences across race/ethnicity. *J Adolesc Health.* 2007;41(3):283–93.

26. Agatston PW, Kowalski R, Limber S. Students' perspectives on cyber bullying. *J Adolesc Health.* 2007;41(6 suppl 1):S59–S60.

27. Beran T, Qing L. The relationship between cyberbullying and school bullying. *J Student Wellbeing.* 2007;1(2):15–33.

28. Brunstein Klomek A, Marrocco F, Kleinman M, Schonfeld IS, Gould MS. Bullying, depression, and suicidality in adolescents. *J Am Acad Child Adolesc Psychiatry.* 2007;46(1):40–9.

29. Klomek AB, Marrocco F, Kleinman M, Schonfeld IS, Gould MS. Peer victimization, depression, and suicidality in adolescents. *Suicide Life Threat Behav.* 2008;38(2):166–80.

30. Kim YS, Leventhal B., Bullying and suicide. A review. *Int J Adolesc Med Health.* 2008;20(2):133–54.

31. Brunstein Klomek A, Sourander A, Gould M. The association of suicide and bullying in childhood to young adulthood: a review of cross-sectional and longitudinal research findings. *Can J Psychiatry.* 2010;55(5):282–8.

32. Tynes B, Giang M. P01–298 online victimization, depression and anxiety among adolescents in the US. *Eur Psychiatry.* 2009;24(suppl 1):S686.

33. Ybarra ML, Mitchell KJ. Online aggressor/targets, aggressors, and targets: a comparison of associated youth characteristics. *J Child Psychol Psychiatry.* 2004;45(7): 1308–16.

34. Mitchell KJ, Ybarra M, Finkelhor D. The relative importance of online victimization in understanding

depression, delinquency, and substance use. *Child Maltreat.* 2007;12(4):314–24.

35. Hay C, Meldrum R. Bullying victimization and adolescent self-harm: testing hypotheses from general strain theory. *J Youth Adolesc.* 2010;39(5): 446–59.

36. Hinduja S, Patchin JW. Bullying, cyberbullying, and suicide. *Arch Suicide Res.* 2010;14(3):206–21.

37. Centers for Disease Control and Prevention. 2007 *Youth Risk Behavior Survey.* Available at: https://www.cdc.gov/mmwr/preview/mmwrhtml/ss5704a1.htm.

38. Massachusetts Department of Elementary and Secondary Education and Massachusetts Department of Public Health. Health and Risk Behaviors of Massachusetts Youth, 2007: The Report, 2008. Available at: https://www.mass.gov/doc/health-and-risk-behaviors-of-massachusetts-youth-2007/download.

39. Harris KM, Halpern CT, Whitsel E, et al. The National Longitudinal Study of Adolescent Health: Research Design. Available at: http://www.cpc.unc.edu/projects/addhealth/design. Accessed April 26, 2010.

40. Mustanski BS, Garofalo R, Emerson EM. Mental health disorders, psychological distress, and suicidality in a diverse sample of lesbian, gay, bisexual, and transgender youth. *Am J Public Health.* 2010;100(12): 2426–32.

41. Kaltiala-Heino R, Rimpelä M, Rantanen P, Rimpelä A. Bullying at school—an indicator of adolescents at risk for mental disorders. *J Adolesc.* 2000;23(6):661–74.

42. Juvoven J, Graham S, Schuster MA. Bullying among young adolescents: the strong, the weak, and the troubled. *Pediatrics.* 2003;112(6 pt 1):1231–7.

Questions for Critical Thinking

1. The authors of this essay illustrate how school bullying and cyberbullying are becoming more prevalent in society. What factors do you think contribute to their growth?

2. How is violence or the threat of violence used to maintain the status quo? For example, have you seen homophobia used to reinforce rigid gender roles?

3. What are some ways in which we can work toward eliminating school bullying and cyberbullying?

PART III

Experiencing Difference and Inequality in Everyday Life

Introduction

In Part I we examined the ways in which categories of difference are constructed and then transformed into systems of inequality. We continued this discussion in Part II with an exploration of how systems of inequality are maintained as oppression and privilege through the role of social institutions, language, and violence. In this section we will gain a more thorough understanding of the construction and maintenance of these systems by examining the experiences of difference and inequality in everyday life.

The Importance of Hearing Personal Accounts

The readings in this section help to put a face on what we have discussed thus far. Although theoretical explanations and statistical information can help us to understand the prevalence of inequality in our society, as well as the ways in which systems of oppression and privilege interconnect, the picture that they offer is far from complete. Through the examination of lived experiences we gain a more complete awareness of how categories of difference are constructed and how systems of oppression and privilege are manifested in everyday life.

Stephanie M. Wildman and Adrienne D. Davis's discussion on the existence of systems of privilege in "Making Systems of Privilege Visible" (Reading 35)—particularly around whiteness—shows us the effect of **privilege** on one's **life chances.** By reading Jon Ronson's encounters with negative stereotypes in "You May Know Me from Such Roles as Terrorist #4" (Reading 36), we gain a greater understanding of how attitudes about oppressed groups become internalized. Furthermore, the stories of living life as a member of a marginalized group and its accompanying stereotypes allow us to more fully comprehend how such **internalized oppression** results in the desire to **pass**—to deny one's membership in an oppressed group and to attempt to portray oneself as a member of a less stigmatized group. Each of the readings in this section demonstrates the daily grind of oppression and the perks of privilege and deepens our understanding of these issues.

Additional readings in this section demonstrate the impact of the structural factors that construct and maintain inequality, discussed in Parts I and II, on the everyday experiences of individuals. For example, Tressie McMillan Cottom illustrates the effect of the racialized aspects of the US health care system in her article "Dying to Be Competent" (Reading 37). Further, Kong Pheng Pha articulates the effect of discrimination and stereotypes on Hmong Americans, particularly as a result of the rise in hate against Asian American Pacific Islander communities during the COVID-19 pandemic in her article "Two Hate Notes" (Reading 39). These and other readings in this section bring into graphic detail the everyday consequences of systems of inequality.

It is important to point out that, although each of us experiences oppression and privilege each day, to examine the various factors of our own experiences while simultaneously living them is like a fish trying to examine the water in which it swims. To fully understand experiences of oppression and privilege, we must stand at a distance from these experiences. The accounts in this section provide us with the opportunity to stand outside and to look in on the experiences of others. By reading the stories in this section we will gain a greater understanding of the impact of oppression and privilege, not only on the lives of others but also on our own lives.

Personal Accounts and "Deconstructing" Stereotypes

At the foundation of our prejudice regarding those whom we see as different from ourselves are **stereotypes**—rigid, oversimplified, and often exaggerated beliefs that are applied both to a category of people and to each individual in the category. We learn these stereotypes through the process of socialization. They are fostered by the policies and practices of social institutions, as well as by our tendency to interact with people like ourselves, and we often have difficulty deconstructing or exposing the falsehoods in these stereotypes. Generally, it is not until we have frequent contact with those about whom we possess stereotypes that we are able to debunk them—but sometimes not even then. Through the sharing of personal experiences, the readings in this section provide a great deal of information that will serve to counter our stereotypes. As you read, be aware of the stereotypes that you possess and note your reactions when you encounter new information that challenges them.

The Lived Experience of the Matrix of Domination

To this point we have engaged in a primarily theoretical discussion of the matrix of domination. In examining the ways in which categories of difference are constructed and transformed into systems of inequality, we have noted some of the commonalities in the ways in which these categories are constructed. Further, our examination of the role of social institutions, language, and violence in maintaining systems of oppression and privilege has helped us to understand the similar foundations on which such systems rest. The readings in this section reveal the interrelationships of systems of oppression and privilege by providing us with an opportunity to witness the matrix of domination as lived experience. As you read the selections in this section, look closely to see how different systems of oppression and privilege interrelate in the stories the authors share. In addition, notice how some experience both oppression and privilege and how many experience more than one form of oppression simultaneously.

Keep This in Mind

Although reading personal accounts can serve to further our understanding of systems of oppression and privilege, it is important not to overgeneralize. The anecdotal evidence of a personal story does not in and of itself prove anything. Indeed, it is often anecdotal evidence that gets in the way of our fully seeing and accepting that systems of oppression and privilege exist. In addition, when we read the personal experiences of a member of a marginalized group, there is often the danger of expecting the writer to speak for the experiences of all members of that group. To avoid these pitfalls, it is important to keep in mind the readings of the previous two sections. By understanding the experiences of the different groups examined in previous sections, we will better understand the experiences of the individuals discussed here. In addition, the readings here confirm the theoretical and statistical discussions elsewhere in this text.

A Final Note

As stated in Part I, a fundamental component to understanding the impact of systems of inequality is to employ our **empathy** skills—the ability to understand the experiences of others, although you have not shared those experiences. The readings in this section are provided to aid you in honing your empathy skills. As you read these accounts, be mindful of how they increase your understanding of experiences with which you are not familiar. As you become more informed about the experiences of others, you will further your understanding of the construction, maintenance, and impact of systems of oppression and privilege.

MAKING SYSTEMS OF PRIVILEGE VISIBLE

Stephanie M. Wildman with Adrienne D. Davis

The following essay, written by law professors Stephanie Wildman and Adrienne Davis, discusses the existence of systems of privilege, often rendered invisible in our language. Through their discussion, they reveal these privileges, illustrating their effect on one's life chances.

The notion of privilege, although part of the consciousness of popular culture, has not been recognized in legal language and doctrine. This failure to acknowledge privilege, to make it visible in legal doctrine, creates a serious gap in legal reasoning, rendering us unable to address issues of systemic unfairness.

The invisibility of privilege strengthens the power it creates and maintains. The invisible cannot be combated, and as a result privilege is allowed to perpetuate, regenerate, and re-create itself. Privilege is systemic, not an occasional occurrence. Privilege is invisible only until looked for, but silence in the face of privilege sustains its invisibility.

Silence is the lack of sound and voice. Silence may result from a desire for quiet; it may signify intense mental concentration; it may also arise from oppression or fear. Whatever the reason, when there is silence, no criticism is expressed. What we do not say, what we do not talk about, allows the status quo to continue. To describe these unspoken systems means we need to use language. But even when we try to talk about privilege, the language we use inhibits our ability to perceive the systems of privilege that constitute the status quo.

How Language Veils the Existence of Systems of Privilege

Language contributes to the invisibility and regeneration of privilege. To begin the conversation about subordination, we sort ideas into categories such as race and gender. These words are part of a system of categorization that we use without thinking and that seems linguistically neutral. Race and gender are, after all, just words.

Yet when we learn that someone has had a child, our first question is usually "Is it a girl or a boy?" Why do we ask that, instead of something like "Are the mother and child healthy?" We ask, "Is it a girl or a boy?" according to philosopher Marilyn Frye, because we do not know how to relate to this new being without knowing its gender.[1] Imagine how long you could have a discussion with or about someone without knowing her or his gender. We place people into these categories because our world is gendered.

Similarly, our world is also raced, and it is hard for us to avoid taking mental notes as to race. We use our language to categorize by race, particularly, if we are white, when that race is other than white. Marge Shultz has written of calling on a Latino student in her class.[2] She called him Mr. Martínez, but his name was Rodríguez. The class tensed up at her error; earlier that same day another professor had called him Mr. Hernández, the name of the defendant in the criminal law case under discussion. Professor Shultz talked with her class, at its next session, about her error and how our thought processes lead us to categorize in order to think. She acknowledged how this process leads to stereotyping that causes pain to individuals. We all live in this raced and gendered world, inside these powerful categories, that make it hard to see each other as whole people.

But the problem does not stop with the general terms "race" and "gender." Each of these categories contains the images, like an entrance to a tunnel with many passages and arrows pointing down each possible path, of subcategories. Race is often defined as Black and white; sometimes it is defined as white and "of color." There are other races, and sometimes the categories are each listed, for example, as African American, Hispanic American, Asian American, Native American, and White American, if whiteness is mentioned at all. All these words, describing racial subcategories, seem neutral on their face, like equivalent titles. But however the subcategories are listed, however neutrally the words are expressed, these words mask a system of power, and that system privileges whiteness.

Gender, too, is a seemingly neutral category that leads us to imagine subcategories of male and female. A recent scientific article suggested that five genders might be a more accurate characterization of human anatomy, but there is a heavy systemic stake in our image of two genders.[3] The apparently neutral categories male and female mask the privileging of males that is part of the gender power system. Try to think of equivalent gendered titles, like king and queen, prince and princess, and you will quickly see that male and female are not equal titles in our cultural imagination.

Poet and social critic Adrienne Rich has written convincingly about the compulsory heterosexuality that is part of this gender power system.[4] Almost everywhere we look, heterosexuality is portrayed as the norm. In Olympic ice-skating and dancing, for example, a couple is defined as a man partnered with a woman.[5] Heterosexuality is privileged over any other relationship. The words we use, such as "marriage," "husband," and "wife," are not neutral, but convey this privileging of heterosexuality. What is amazing, says Rich, is that there are any lesbians or gay men at all.[6]

Our culture suppresses conversation about class privilege as well as race and gender privileges. Although we must have money or access to money to obtain human necessities such as food, clothing, and shelter, those fundamental needs are recognized only as an individual responsibility. The notion of privilege based on economic wealth is viewed as a radical, dangerous idea, or an idiosyncratic throwback to the past, conjuring up countries with monarchies, nobility, serfs, and peasants. Yet even the archaic vocabulary makes clear that no one wants to be categorized as a have-not. The economic power system is not invisible—everyone knows that money brings privilege. But the myth persists that all have access to that power through individual resourcefulness. This myth of potential economic equality supports the invisibility of the other power systems that prevent fulfillment of that ideal.

Other words we use to describe subordination also mask the operation of privilege. Increasingly, people use terms like "racism" and "sexism" to describe disparate treatment and the perpetuation of power. Yet this vocabulary of "isms" as a descriptive shorthand for undesirable, disadvantaging treatment creates several serious problems.

First, calling someone a racist individualizes the behavior and veils the fact that racism can occur only where it is culturally, socially, and legally supported. It lays the blame on the individual rather than the systemic forces that have shaped that individual and his or her society. White people know they do not want to be labeled racist; they become concerned with how to avoid that label, rather than worrying about systemic racism and how to change it.

Second, the isms language focuses on the larger category, such as race, gender, sexual preference. Isms language suggests that within these larger categories two seemingly neutral halves exist, equal parts in a mirror. Thus Black and white, male and female, heterosexual and gay/lesbian appear, through the linguistic juxtaposition, as equivalent subparts. In fact, although the category does not take note of it, Blacks and whites, men and women, heterosexuals and gays/lesbians are not equivalently situated in society. Thus the way we think and talk about the categories and subcategories that underlie the isms allows us to consider them parallel parts, and obscures the pattern of domination and subordination within each classification.

Similarly, the phrase "isms" itself gives the illusion that all patterns of domination and subordination are the same and interchangeable. The language suggests that someone subordinated under one form of oppression would be similarly situated to another person subordinated under another form. Thus, a person subordinated under one form may feel no need to view himself/herself as a possible oppressor, or beneficiary of oppression, within a different form. For example, white women, having an ism that defines their condition—sexism—may not look at the way they are privileged by racism. They have defined themselves as one of the oppressed.

Finally, the focus on individual behavior, the seemingly neutral subparts of categories, and the apparent interchangeability underlying the vocabulary of isms all obscure the existence of systems of privilege and power. It is difficult to see and talk about how oppression operates when the vocabulary itself makes these systems of privilege invisible. "White supremacy" is associated with a lunatic fringe, not with the everyday life of well-meaning white citizens. "Racism" is defined by whites in terms of specific, discriminatory racist actions by others. The vocabulary allows us to talk about discrimination and oppression, but it hides the mechanism that makes that oppression possible and efficient. It also hides the existence of specific, identifiable beneficiaries of oppression, who are not always the actual perpetrators of discrimination. The use of isms language, or any focus on discrimination, masks the privileging that is created by these systems of power.

Thus the very vocabulary we use to talk about discrimination obfuscates these power systems and the privilege that is their natural companion. To remedy discrimination effectively we must make the power systems and the privileges they create visible and part of the discourse. To move toward a unified theory of the dynamics of subordination, we have to find a way to talk about privilege. When we discuss race, sex, and sexual orientation, each needs to be described as a power system that creates privileges in some people as well as disadvantages in others. Most of the literature has focused on disadvantage or discrimination, ignoring the element of privilege. To really talk about these issues, privilege must be made visible.

What Is Privilege?

What then is privilege? We all recognize its most blatant forms. "Men only admitted to this club." "We will not allow African Americans into that school." Blatant exercises of privilege certainly exist, but they are not what most people think of as our way of life. They are only the tip of the iceberg, however.

When we try to look at privilege we see several elements. First, the characteristics of the privileged group define the societal norm, often benefiting those in the privileged group. Second, privileged group members can rely on their privilege and avoid objecting to oppression. Both the conflation of privilege with the societal norm and the implicit option to ignore oppression mean that privilege is rarely seen by the holder of the privilege.

A. The Normalization of Privilege

The characteristics and attributes of those who are privileged group members are described as societal norms—as the way things are and as what is normal in society.[7] This normalization of privilege means that members of society are judged, and succeed or fail, measured against the characteristics that are held by those privileged. The privileged characteristic is the norm; those who stand outside are the aberrant or "alternative."

For example, a thirteen-year-old-girl who aspires to be a major-league ballplayer can have only a low expectation of achieving that goal, no matter how superior a batter and fielder she is. Maleness is the foremost "qualification" of major-league baseball players. Similarly, those who legally are permitted to marry are heterosexual. A gay or lesbian couple, prepared to make a life commitment, cannot cross the threshold of qualification to be married.

I had an example of being outside the norm recently when I was called to jury service. Jurors are expected to serve until 5 P.M. During that year, my family's life was set up so that I picked up my children after school at 2:40 and made sure that they got to various activities. If courtroom life were designed to privilege my needs, then there would have been an afternoon recess to honor children. But in this culture children's lives and the lives of their caretakers are the alternative or other, and we must conform to the norm.

Even as these child care needs were outside the norm, I was privileged economically to be able to meet my children's needs. What many would have described as mothering, not privilege—my ability to pick them up and be present in their after-school lives—was a benefit of my association with privilege.

Members of the privileged group gain many benefits by their affiliation with the dominant side of the power system. This affiliation with power is not identified as such; often it may be transformed into and presented as individual merit. Legacy admissions at elite colleges and professional schools are perceived to be merit-based, when this process of identification with power and transmutation into qualifications occurs. Achievements by members of the privileged group are viewed as the result of individual effort, rather than privilege . . . .

B. Choosing Whether to Struggle against Oppression
Members of privileged groups can opt out of struggles against oppression if they choose. Often this privilege may be exercised by silence. At the same time that I was the outsider in jury service, I was also a privileged insider. During *voir dire*, each prospective juror was asked to introduce herself or himself. The plaintiff's and defendant's attorneys then asked additional questions. I watched the defense attorney, during *voir dire*, ask each Asian-looking male prospective juror if he spoke English. No one else was asked. The judge did nothing. The Asian American man sitting next to me smiled and flinched as he was asked the questions. I wondered how many times in his life he had been made to answer such a question. I considered beginning my own questioning by saying, "I'm Stephanie Wildman, I'm a professor of law, and yes, I speak English." I wanted to focus attention on the subordinating conduct of the

attorney, but I did not. I exercised my white privilege by my silence. I exercised my privilege to opt out of engagement, even though this choice may not always be consciously made by someone with privilege.

Depending on the number of privileges someone has, she or he may experience the power of choosing the types of struggles in which to engage. Even this choice may be masked as an identification with oppression, thereby making the privilege that enables the choice invisible . . . . Privilege is not visible to its holder; it is merely there, a part of the world, a way of life, simply the way things are. Others have a *lack*, an absence, a deficiency.

Systems of Privilege

Although different privileges bestow certain common characteristics (membership in the norm, the ability to choose whether to object to the power system, and the invisibility of its benefit), the form of a privilege may vary according to the power relationship that produces it. White privilege derives from the race power system of white supremacy. Male privilege[8] and heterosexual privilege result from the gender hierarchy.[9] Class privilege derives from an economic, wealth-based hierarchy.

Visualizing Privilege

For me the struggle to visualize privilege has most often taken the form of the struggle to see my white privilege. Even as I write about this struggle, I fear that my own racism will make things worse, causing me to do more harm than good. Some readers may be shocked to see a white person contritely acknowledge that she is racist. I do not say this with pride. I simply believe that no matter how hard I work at not being racist, I still am. Because part of racism is systemic, I benefit from the privilege that I am struggling to see.

Whites do not look at the world through a filter of racial awareness, even though whites are, of course, members of a race. The power to ignore race, when white is the race, is a privilege, a societal advantage. The term "racism/white supremacy" emphasizes the link between discriminatory racism and the privilege held by whites to ignore their own race.

As bell hooks explains, liberal whites do not see themselves as prejudiced or interested in domination through coercion, yet "they cannot recognize the

ways their actions support and affirm the very structure of racist domination and oppression that they
profess to wish to see eradicated."[10] The perpetuation
of white supremacy is racist.

All whites are racist in this use of the term, because
we benefit from systemic white privilege. Generally

whites think of racism as voluntary, intentional conduct, done by horrible others. Whites spend a lot of
time trying to convince ourselves and each other that
we are not racist. A big step would be for whites to
admit that we are racist and then to consider what
to do about it.[11]

Notes

1. See Marilyn Frye, *The Politics of Reality: Essays in Feminist Theory*, 19–34 (1983) (discussing sex marking, sex
   announcing, and the necessity to determine gender).
2. Angela Harris and Marge Shultz, *"A(nother) Critique
   of Pure Reason": Toward Civic Virtue in Legal Education*, 45 Stan. L. Rev. 1773, 1796 (1993).
3. Anne Fausto-Sterling, *The Five Sexes: Why Male and
   Female Are Not Enough*, Sciences, Mar./Apr. 1993.
   (Thanks to Gregg Bryan for calling my attention to
   this article.) See also Frye, *The Politics of Reality*, 25.
4. Adrienne Rich, *Compulsory Heterosexuality and Lesbian Existence*, in Blood, Bread, and Poetry, Selected
   Prose 1979–1985 (1986).
5. See Stephanie M. Wildman and Becky Wildman-
   Tobriner, *Sex Roles Iced Popular Team?* S.F. Chron.,
   Feb. 25, 1994, at A23.
6. Rich, *supra* note 4, at 57 ("Heterosexuality has been
   both forcibly and subliminally imposed on women").
7. Richard Delgado and Jean Stefancic, *Pornography and
   Harm to Women: "No Empirical Evidence?"* 53 Ohio St.

   L. J. 1037 (1992) (describing this "way things are." Because the norm or reality is perceived as including
   these benefits, the privileges are not visible.)
8. Catharine A. MacKinnon, Toward a Feminist Theory
   of the State 224 (1989).
9. Sylvia Law, *Homosexuality and the Social Meaning of
   Gender*, 1988 Wis. L. Rev. 187, 197 (1988); Marc Fajer,
   *Can Two Real Men Eat Quiche Together? Storytelling,
   Gender-Role Stereotypes, and Legal Protection for Lesbians and Gay Men*, 46 U. Miami L. Rev. 511, 617 (1992).
   Both articles describe heterosexism as a form of gender
   oppression.
10. bell hooks, *Overcoming White Supremacy: A Comment*,
    in Talking Back: Thinking Feminist, Thinking Black
    113 (1989).
11. See also Jerome McCristal Culp Jr., *Water Buffalo and
    Diversity: Naming Names and Reclaiming the Racial
    Discourse*, 26 Conn. L. Rev. 209 (1993) (urging people
    to name racism as racism).

Questions for Critical Thinking

1. Wildman and Davis discuss the ways in which
   language hides systems of privilege in the United
   States. What are some of the ways in which you are
   privileged by your class, race, gender, education,
   etc.? What makes it difficult to recognize this
   privilege?
2. How is the invisibility of white privilege a privilege in and of itself?
3. How might recognizing the various ways that we are
   privileged help to reduce or eliminate inequality?

YOU MAY KNOW ME FROM SUCH ROLES AS TERRORIST #4

* *Jon Ronson*

The following essay offers a reflection on the negative stereotypes experienced by Muslim American actors in the United States. Through the author's discussion, we gain an understanding of how the media plays a significant role in the perpetuation of false images of Muslim Americans.

The right-wing action hero gave Maz Jobrani hope. This was 2001. Maz had been trying to make it as an actor in Hollywood for three years, but things were going badly for him. He was earning peanuts as an assistant at an advertising agency. But then his agent telephoned: Did Maz want to play a terrorist in a Chuck Norris movie? So Maz read the screenplay for The President's Man: A Line in the Sand, and he found within it a moment of promising subtlety.

"Chuck Norris plays a professor of Middle Eastern studies," Maz tells me. We're sitting in a coffee shop in Westwood, Los Angeles. Maz is a goateed man in his early forties who was born in Tehran but moved with his family to the San Francisco Bay Area when he was 6. "There's a scene where he's talking to his students about Afghanistan. One of the students raises his hand and says something like, 'Uh, professor, they're all fanatics, so why don't we just kill them all?' And the Chuck Norris character goes, 'Now, now. They're not all bad.' And I thought, 'Wow! A nuance!'"

The nuance gave Maz hope. Did this mean they'd allow him to make his character nuanced? Maz was aware that fixating on this one line might have been

self-deluding, like a drowning man clutching driftwood in a hurricane. But he agreed to take the part.

Then, at the wardrobe fitting, they handed him his turban.

"I said, 'Whoa, whoa! No! Afghans in America don't wear turbans. Plus, this guy's a terrorist. He's not going to draw attention to himself. You tell the producers I want to bring authenticity to this character.' The wardrobe supervisor replied, 'All right, all right, I'll talk to them.'"

The message came back from Chuck Norris's people that the turban was mandatory.

And then came Maz's death. It was the one thing he'd been excited about, because the script alluded to a short fight immediately preceding it. Hand-to-hand combat with Chuck Norris!

"But on the day of the scene," Maz says, "Chuck Norris told his son, who was the director, 'Oh, I'll just take a gun and I'll shoot him.' Oh, great! I don't even get a fight!"

"So how exactly did you get shot?" I ask Maz.

"Okay, so I'm about to set off a bomb at a refinery," he replies. "Chuck Norris runs in. I run away, because

I'm scared. He gets behind the computer and starts dismantling the bomb, because he's a genius. I come running back in carrying an Uzi. And I try to shoot him. But he takes out his gun and shoots me." Maz shrugs. "I start to yell, 'Allah—' Bang! I'm down. I don't even get 'Allahu Akbar!' out. It was horrible, man."

Maz shakes his head at the memory. It was humiliating. Actually, it was worse than humiliating—it was a harbinger. Maz understood, as he lay dead in that refinery, that Hollywood didn't want him to be an actor. Hollywood wanted him to be a caricature. "I started acting in junior high," he says. "I was in Guys and Dolls. I was Stanley Kowalski. In my head, before coming to Hollywood, I thought, 'I can play anything.'" But instead he'd become the latest iteration in Hollywood's long history of racist casting, reducing his religion and culture to a bunch of villainous, cartoonish psychopaths. He knew he had to get out.

I glance at my phone. It's 1 p.m. We're running late to meet three of Maz's friends at a nearby Lebanese restaurant. We jump into Maz's car.

Maz refuses to take terrorist parts nowadays. He's primarily a stand-up comedian instead, a very funny and successful one. In fact, he's just published a memoir, I'm Not a Terrorist, But I've Played One on TV. But Maz's friends at the restaurant haven't been so lucky. They still make their livings as actors, which means they still play terrorists all the time.

Maz and I hurry into the restaurant, apologizing for being late. We order a mezze plate for five. These men have been killed while committing acts of terrorism on Homeland and 24, in The Kingdom and Three Kings and True Lies, and in too many other films and shows to list. We've barely sat down when Waleed Zuaiter, a Palestinian-American actor in his early forties, recounts for me his death scene on Law & Order: Criminal Intent. This was about a year after September 11. "I play a guy from a sleeper cell," Waleed says. "I'm checking my e-mails. I hear the cops come in, and the first thing I go for is my box cutter. There's literally a box cutter in the scene."

"Was this in an office?" I ask Waleed.

"It was in my home!" he replies. "I just happened to have a box cutter lying around." Waleed shakes his head, bemused. "The cops burst in, and next thing you know I've got the box cutter to some guy's neck. And then one of the cops shoots me."

"I die in Iron Man," says Sayed Badreya, an Egyptian man with a salt-and-pepper beard. "I die in Executive Decision. I get shot at by—what's his name?—Kurt Russell. I get shot by everyone. George Clooney kills me in Three Kings. Arnold blows me up in True Lies . . ."

As Sayed and Waleed and the others describe their various demises, it strikes me that the key to making a living in Hollywood if you're Muslim is to be good at dying. If you're a Middle Eastern actor and you can die with charisma, there is no shortage of work for you.

Here's another irony in the lives of these men: While they profoundly wish they didn't have to play terrorists, much of our lunch is taken up with them swapping tips on clever ways to stand out at terrorist auditions.

"If I'm going in for the role of a nice father, I'll talk to everybody," Sayed tells the table. "But if you're going for a terrorist role, don't fucking smile at all those white people sitting there. Treat them like shit. The minute you say hello, you break character."

"But it's smart at the end of the audition to break it," adds Hrach Titizian, who at 36 is the youngest actor here. "'Oh, thanks, guys.' So they know it's okay to have you on set for a couple of weeks."

Then Waleed says something you don't often hear actors say, because most actors regard their competition with dread: "Whenever it's that kind of role and we see each other at the auditions, it's so comforting. We're not in this alone. We're in this together."

We're in this together. By this Waleed is referring to a uniquely demeaning set of circumstances. I'm sure practically all actors, Muslim or otherwise, feel degraded. Most have no power over their careers—what roles they can play, how their performances are edited. But Muslim actors are powerless in unusually hideous ways. The last time one became a big star in America was back in 1962—Omar Sharif in Lawrence of Arabia. These days they get offered terrorist roles and little else. And we—the paying public—barely even notice, much less worry about it. Where's the outrage? There is none, except from the actors themselves. These roles are ethically nightmarish for them, and the stress can wreak havoc on their lives. Waleed's father, for instance, threatened never to talk to him again if he ever played a terrorist. I thought that was bad enough. But then I meet another actor who had it much worse.

Ahmed Ahmed was raised a strict Muslim in Riverside, California, by his Egyptian-immigrant parents—a mother who learned English from watching soap operas, and a gas-station-attendant father who ended up buying an automotive shop. The day Ahmed told them he was quitting college to try his luck in Hollywood, his father asked if he was gay and didn't speak to him for seven years.

When I meet Ahmed at the French Roast Café in downtown New York City, he echoes Waleed's thoughts about the camaraderie among these actors. "It's always the same guys at every audition. Waleed, Sayed Badreya . . . You're all sitting in a row in the waiting room. Oftentimes the casting office is right next to you. The door's shut, but you can hear what's going on."

"What do you hear?" I ask him.

"Oh, you know," he says. "'ALLAHU AKBAR!' And then . . .'" Ahmed switches to the voice of a bubbly casting director. "'Thank you! That was great!' And the guy walks out, sweating. And you walk in and they're, 'Hey! Thanks for coming in! Whenever you're ready!' And you're thinking, 'How do I do it differently from the guy before me? Do I go louder?'"

When he auditioned for Executive Decision, he went louder. Executive Decision is, I realize as I talk to people from this world, considered the ground zero (as it were) of ludicrous portrayals of Islamic terrorists. This was 1996, and Ahmed was in his mid-twenties. "My agent had called me. 'There's this film. It's a $55 million action suspense thriller starring Kurt Russell, Halle Berry, and Steven Seagal. They want to bring you in to read for one of the parts.' I said, 'What's the part?' She said, 'Terrorist Number Four.' I said, 'I don't want to do it.' She said, 'It's three weeks of work. It pays $30,000.'"

And so Ahmed read for the part. "My lines were 'Sit down and obey or I will kill you in the name of Allah.' And the director goes, 'Brilliant! Do it again. But this time, can you give me more of that Middle Eastern, you know . . .' I go, 'Anger?' He goes, 'Yes! Yes! Angry!'"

Feeling a flash of actual anger, Ahmed decided to ridicule the process by going stupidly over-the-top.

"And the next day," he says, "my agent calls me up: 'You booked it.'"

By the time Executive Decision came out later that year, Ahmed says, his life had "become dark. Boozing on the Sunset Strip. After-hours parties. I'd wake up at 2 p.m. and do it all over again. It's the same people in the clubs every night. Everyone's trying to fill a void."

"Were you doing all that boozing because you felt guilty for playing terrorists?" I ask him.

"There was an element of that," he replies. "There was an element of not working between those parts. And then I had an epiphany. I called my agent: 'Hey! Don't send me out on these terrorist parts anymore. I'll be open for anything else, but not the terrorist stuff.'" Ahmed pauses. "After that, she never called."

"How often did she call before then?" I ask him.

"Oh, three or four times a week."

And so Ahmed made a decision: "Get the fuck out of Hollywood." He went to Mecca. And what he saw there were "four and a half million people dressed in white—rich, poor, walking side by side, asking for blessings from God."

For ten solid years after his trip to Mecca, Ahmed quit acting and became a stand-up comedian. He still performs regularly, but he says he'll take a terrorist role from time to time if a good one comes along. After all, he notes, nobody accuses Robert De Niro of betraying other Italian-Americans when he plays a mobster.

The evening after our lunch in Westwood, I visit Sayed Badreya, the older Egyptian actor, at his Santa Monica apartment. When I arrive, he's online, looking at photographs of Arabian horses.

"I'm involved in breeding them," he says, "because I don't know if I can keep playing these same parts." He says his daughter was once asked at school what her father did for a living and she replied, "He hijacks airplanes."

Sayed takes his work seriously and has always gone to great lengths to research his roles. In 1991, he started attending a mosque in Culver City, one that was known to attract some militant worshippers, so he could study Islamic radicalism up close. A few years later, some of the mosque's worshippers went to a movie and recognized Sayed. Back at the mosque after Friday prayers, they surrounded him. "They were yelling, right in my face: 'You're helping the Zionist Jews of Hollywood in their agenda to make Islam look bad. For money, you're giving up your heritage.'"

"How were you responding?" I ask.

"I felt guilty," he says. "I knew they were sort of right. But I yelled back at them, 'We have to take their money to make our own movie and tell our own story!' We were yelling so hard we were showering each other with spit."

"What was the movie of yours they saw?" I ask him.

"Executive fucking Decision," he says.

Sayed says he does all he can to intersperse his terrorist roles with more helpful portrayals of Muslims. He wrote and starred in a well-regarded film, AmericanEast, charting the struggles of Muslims in America post-9/11. But he has to play terrorists to pay the bills, so he at least tries to be a realistic one. He does side work as a technical consultant, advising directors on the accuracy of their films. He worked in this capacity on Executive Decision. "We had a really beautiful moment in an Arabic wedding scene," Sayed says. "And the producer, Joel Silver, saw it and said, 'No, no. This is nice. I want a fucking bad Arab. We don't want a good Arab.'"

Almost all of the wedding scene was cut from the film, Sayed says. But here's a scene that wasn't cut: One of the terrorists takes a quick break from killing people to read the Koran. "If I'm playing a guy chosen to hijack a plane, that means I'm one of the top soldiers. I'm going on a mission. I'm not going to Mecca. He might recite something in his head if he's religious, but he's not going to open the Bible. But producers get really sensitive if you say, 'No, that's not accurate.'"

In an e-mailed statement, Joel Silver denied the "bad Arab" incident, adding, "Any editorial decisions, made twenty years ago, were strictly creative, and not to perpetuate any stereotypes." I didn't hear back from any of the other producers or directors I approached. Not Peter Berg (The Kingdom, another film that has a bad reputation with Muslim actors for its portrayal of the Islamic world), nor Stephen McEveety (Mel Gibson's collaborator on The Passion of the Christ and the producer of The Stoning of Soraya M., in which an Iranian husband has his wife stoned to death), nor Joel Surnow, the co-creator of 24. Maz told me that his most offensive acting offer ever was for a Joel Surnow production—Fox's short-lived comedy The 1/2 Hour News Hour. Maz says he was asked to audition for a sketch about a Middle Eastern architect pitching to rebuild the twin towers. The joke was that his design included a bull's-eye right on the building. Howard Gordon, the man behind Homeland and 24, is the only producer I persuade to talk to me. He calls me from his car.

"I came to this issue when I was accused of having Islamophobia in 24," he says. "We had a family, essentially, of terrorists on the show. The Muslim Public Affairs Council provided an education for me on the power of images."

"What did they say?"

"They asked me to imagine what it might be like to be a Muslim, to have people fear my faith," he replies. "I felt very sympathetic. I didn't want to be a midwife to xenophobia."

Since then, he says, he has done his best. And people have noticed. When I was having lunch with Maz and the other actors at the Lebanese restaurant in Westwood, Howard was one of the only mainstream producers they praised. (Three Kings' David O. Russell was another.)

"Anyone with a conscience has to take this seriously," Howard tells me. "I'd often hidden behind the defense that 24 was a counterterrorism show. We rationalized to ourselves that our primary task was to tell a compelling story." But the truth, he knew, was darker than that: "We all have our personal biases and fears—I suspect we're wired to feel threatened by the 'other.' And I include myself in that category."

In the lobby of a chichi old hotel in Midtown Manhattan, Anthony Azizi warns me that this interview might get heated. And indeed it does. If you want to know the impact that a lifetime of doing these movies can have on a man, spend some time with Anthony Azizi.

Anthony is a veteran of various CSIs and NCISs and 24. His death scene in 24, he says, made it onto a Yahoo list of best deaths ever. (His throat gets slit with a credit card.) He's a big, handsome, intense man who is not, by the way, a Muslim. He's a member of the Iranian spiritualist faith the Bahá'í.

"Hollywood has the power to snap its fingers and make whoever it wants a star," he begins. "It specifically and purposefully doesn't want to see an Arab or a Middle Eastern star. There's too much prejudice and racism—and the people running it, I don't need to go into the specifics of their backgrounds. . . ."

I think I know what he's getting at. But all sorts of producers—not just Jews—are behind insensitive movie portrayals of Muslims. There's Chuck Norris. There's John Musker, director of 1992's Aladdin, in which all the "good Arabs" have American accents and all the "bad Arabs" have pseudo-Middle Eastern accents. Stephen McEveety (The Stoning of Soraya M.) is Catholic.

Anthony carries on, turning his anger toward Jon Stewart's Rosewater, in which the Mexican actor Gael García Bernal plays the Iranian-Canadian reporter Maziar Bahari. "Man, if I saw Jon Stewart, you'd have to hold me back. How dare you hire a Mexican-American to play an Iranian-American, with all these amazing Iranian-American artists. I can't stand it. I'm sick of it. I speak Spanish fluently. . . ."

He effortlessly slides into perfect Spanish for a few seconds, then returns to being Anthony. "Why am I not being hired for Mexican or Latino roles?" he says. "You play my roles, but I can't play yours, and I speak Spanish just as well? Go fuck yourself." Anthony picks up my recorder. "Go fuck yourself, Jon Stewart!" he yells. "Have me on your show if you have the balls! You don't have the balls!"

He's really shouting now. The hotel receptionists keep glancing nervously over at us, wondering whether to intervene. "Hollywood people are pussies!" he rants. "They're racist! They don't want to say, 'I just built a Middle Eastern star!' Here's how I see it—and this is probably the most controversial thing I'll ever say: The only Middle Eastern star was Omar Sharif. The minute he had a relationship with a Jewish-American woman named Barbra Streisand was the death knell for any other Arab-American actor's career. Hear it again! The minute he had a sexual relationship with a Jewish . . ."

"I don't underst—" I start to say.

"How dare you make that an incident where no Arab-American actor can ever get a career again!"

Finally I get my question out, or at least some of it: "But what's the connection between Omar Sharif purportedly having an affair with Barbra Streisand and—"

"I think there's a certain type of producer that doesn't want to see that happen," he says. "They don't want their gem—Barbra Streisand was the gem of the Jewish community—sleeping with the Arab heathen! It caused huge riots in Egypt, too. I'd say the same thing to the Egyptian community. . . ."

Sure, Anthony's Barbra Streisand outburst is crazy. If there is a racist conspiracy in Hollywood to rob Middle Eastern actors of roles, it's not a great idea to rail against it with a racist-conspiracy theory of one's own. But think about what Anthony has been subjected to in his career. He and the other men in this story are going through something that future generations will regard as outrageous. They're the bloodthirsty Red Indians surrounding the settlers' wagons in Stagecoach. They're the black savages in The Birth of a Nation (who were played by white actors in blackface). They are the people Hollywood will be apologizing to tomorrow.

"Don't question my talent," Anthony says. "I should be a star by now. But I'm not. So you explain why."

Perhaps the closest this community has to a star is Navid Negahban. He played, most famously, Abu Nazir in Homeland and also the Iraqi in American Sniper who helps the U.S. military locate "the butcher." He was Ali, the stoner in The Stoning of Soraya M.

"Everyone I've met seems really talented," I tell Anthony. "So why do you think Navid, of all of you. . . .?"

"He's hot right now, playing bad guys," Anthony replies. "He loves to play those roles. I love Navid. He's my brother. But there's no longevity in those roles. You always get whacked. Everybody who's still alive in Homeland is white! Where is Abu Nazir? He got whacked, 'cause he's brown."

Getting to meet Navid isn't easy. One minute he's filming in upstate New York, the next he's doing motion capture as a video-game character in Los Angeles before flying off to shoot a movie in Morocco. But I manage to catch him for an hour at a coffee shop near Columbus Circle in New York City.

He's already there, chatting with another on-screen terrorist, Herzl Tobey (The Shield, 24, Homeland). They've been working on a movie together upstate, so Navid has brought him along to meet me. Navid is very dashing, with an old-fashioned matinee-idol air to him.

"I'm sure you've had a few of the others say, 'I won't do terrorists anymore,'" he says as I sit down.

"Yes," I say.

"I've told them that's the biggest mistake," says Navid. "If we don't play those roles, the character becomes a caricature. [The producers] might get some actor from a different background who looks Middle Eastern." Herzl nods, adding, "The writer is sitting here in America, writing about a world he's completely unfamiliar with. So of course he won't be able to write it with the full depth and sensuality that

comes with that world. It's up to us to bring that depth."

I tell Navid that I've noticed that the more prominent the Middle Eastern actor, the more awesome the death. Back when Maz was just starting out, he barely got "Allah" out before Chuck Norris shot him. But Navid is at the top of the pecking order, the closest thing we have to Omar Sharif. I ask him to remind me how Abu Nazir died on Homeland.

"Oh, he was graceful," Navid replies. "It was so . . ." He smacks his lips. "He's sitting very gracefully on the floor. On his knees. He's ready. The soldiers run in. Everybody's yelling. But he's calm. He's just looking at all of them very, very calmly. And then he reaches into his pocket and they shoot him. And there's a Koran in his pocket." Navid smiles wistfully. "That was beautiful," he says. "I die well."

Questions for Critical Thinking

1. How does the author's discussion of negative stereotypes experienced by Muslim American actors in the United States help you to understand the impact of these stereotypes?
2. What are the sources of your own perceptions of Muslims? How has this impacted your reactions to media and other coverage of incidents involving terrorism?
3. How do US foreign policy and other practices shape perceptions of Arabs, Arab Americans, and those that follow Islam? How have these things impacted the overall reaction in the United States to violent events and whether to label them terrorism?

DYING TO BE COMPETENT

Tressie Mcmillan Cottom

The following essay by professor of sociology and award-winning author Tressie McMillan Cottom offers a reflection on ways in which structural racism is pervasive in the U.S. health care system. Through recounting her own personal experience and incorporating data, she illustrates how the medical system dismissed her symptoms and pain, resulting in the miscarriage of her daughter. Through this powerful essay, she exposes how the medical system and other forms of structural racism harms black women. She also clearly demonstrates their capacity for self-advocacy.

> Recording my debut album, "I don't work here." Featuring the hit singles, "Yes, I do have a ticket. I'm the keynote speaker." and "Yes, I know this is the line for First Class." Droppin straight FIRE bars!
>
> —*@aryanwashere, tweet,* January 29, 2018

> . . . the most murderous states are also the most racist.
>
> —Michel Foucault

I never dreamed about weddings or boyfriends or babies. The first dream for my imagined future self that I can recall starts with a sound. I was maybe five years old and I wanted to click-clack. The click-clack of high heels on a shiny, hard floor. I have a briefcase. I am walking purposefully, click-clack-click-clack. That is the entire dream.[1]

At various times in my life I have interpreted that dream in different ways. It could be that I wanted the money someone with a briefcase and purpose would presumably earn. For a while I worried that it meant I did not have the heart required for committed love because my early, simple lessons of work were that it precludes anything soft. Now I have settled on competency. I dreamed of being competent.

Tressie Mcmillan Cottom

I am writing this in a freezing house in Virginia during a bitterly cold winter, because my heat is off.

I have three space heaters ordered in a pique from Amazon Prime and the oven door open. The oven door is country. The Amazon Prime is so middle class. All in all, it is very me. For perhaps the first season in my life I can afford heat *and* food *and* transportation *and* housing *and* the consumption of a good middle-class person. My heat is not off because I cannot pay, but because I forgot to pay. No matter that I can pack my overnight bag like a winning game of Tetris or that I keep receipts for tax season, competency will always be a ritual in wish fulfillment.

I am not the only one in love with the idea of competence. It is a neoliberal pipe dream that generates no end of services, apps, blogs, social media stars, thought leaders, and cultural programming, all promising that we can be competent. If you are

New York: The New Press. *Thick: And Other Essays* by Tressie McMillan Cottom. Copyright © 2019 working irregular shifts like an estimated 3.2 million people in the United States are, you cannot control your time. The instability of constant work without a constant employer can make it hard to plan your life. Thriving in liberal capitalism requires planning for eventualities that you cannot control. You have to plan for when you will be sick, when your children will go to daycare, when you will spend a week at the beach and how long you might live. Productivity tools promise you control where the political economy says you cannot have any. You cannot predict how well the State or your family will care for you when you are old, but you can schedule to the minute how much time you spend this week reallocating your retirement account.

My favorite of all of these tools is LinkedIn.[2] LinkedIn is the dumbest of all the dumb websites created during our new digital age. That is my expert opinion. LinkedIn is dumb. The interface is bad. The platform architecture cannot figure out how to facilitate networking *and* self-promotion *and* neoliberal branding *and* presentation of self, so it just does all of those things badly. It isn't dynamic. It isn't quite static. It is the worst of each. You know a website is bad when its founder proclaims that "people use the website wrong!" He thinks you should only "endorse" people you know, but everyone who uses LinkedIn accepts any request for a connection or an endorsement, because I have to believe deep down we know that it doesn't matter. Despite being dumb and poorly designed and having a founder who blames the users for the site's bad architecture, people are strangely defensive about LinkedIn. I made a joke about it on Twitter once and five years later people are still responding to that tweet, angry that I would even mildly disparage it. I made myself a promise that I would never again publicly make light of LinkedIn, once I realized why people were so defensive.

LinkedIn is an exemplar of the promises technology makes but that neoliberalism can never fulfill. By all accounts, all workers feel increasingly anxious about their job security, income mobility, and quality of life. Poor workers and middle-class workers and even highly paid elite workers in western economies are anxious because of the demands that our accelerated digital society make of us. We know that we could be outsourced, downsized, and eased out of a

job or a career or an entire industry at a moment's notice. Despite our shared anxiety not all of us believe in a collective response to what is fundamentally a collective problem. The only thing we mostly agree on is that we are individuals with the "freedom" to be anxious as we please. What pleases us is any technocratic fairytale of how we can network enough to offset unstable employment.

Who needs a promotion when you can add fifty endorsements to your LinkedIn or five new connections to your third-grade best friend's brother? All the busywork produced by the technological society perversely creates new ways for technology to make our anxiety a profitable extractive regime. It is a vicious cycle. Such is the foolishness of wanting to be competent in a political economy that can only sell you ways to *feel* competent, but does not offer sufficient ways to enact competency.

That is a problem for us all, to a certain degree. But for some of us being competent has always been an illusion. Now, it is the nature of global capital and inequality to make us structurally incompetent. For black women, racism, sexism, and classism have always made us structurally incompetent. To a black woman living global inequality and technological change, the competency trap is a cumulative multi-fold iron cage of network effects in oppressive regimes.

I have never felt more incompetent than when I was pregnant. Pregnancy is not just resistant to the dictates of capitalism, it is hell on competency. I was four months or so pregnant, extremely uncomfortable, and at work when I started bleeding. Bleeding is against company policy almost everywhere. When you are black woman, having a body is already complicated for workplace politics. Having a bleeding, distended body is especially egregious. When I started bleeding, I waited until I filed my copy, by deadline, before walking to the front of the building, where I called my husband to pick me up.

An hour or so later, I was in the waiting room of my obstetrics office on the good side of town. I chose the office based on the crude cultural geography of choosing a good school or which TJ Maxx to go to: if it is on the white, wealthy side of town, it must be good. For many people I am sure that the medical practice was actually good. The happy, normal, thin white women in the waiting room every time I visited seemed pleased enough. The office staff was effective. The nurses' hands were always warm when they stuck one up your vagina. The doctors were energetic. All in all, it was all I knew to ask for.

Until I started bleeding. That day I sat in the waiting room for thirty minutes, after calling ahead and reporting my condition when I arrived. After I had bled through the nice chair in the waiting room, I told my husband to ask them again if perhaps I could be moved to a more private area to wait. The nurse looked alarmed, about the chair, and eventually ushered me back. When the doctor arrived, he explained that I was probably just too fat and that spotting was normal and he sent me home. Later that night my ass started hurting, the right side. Just behind the butt muscle and off a bit to the side. I walked. I stretched. I took a hot bath. I called my mother, The Vivian. Finally, I called the nurse. She asked me if my back hurt. I said no, which was true. My back was fine. It was my butt that hurt. The nurse said it was probably constipation. I should try to go to the bathroom. I tried that for all the next day and part of another. By the end of three days, my butt still hurt and I had not slept more than fifteen minutes straight in almost seventy hours.

I went to the hospital. Again, they asked about my back, implied that I had eaten something "bad" for me and begrudgingly, finally decided to do an ultrasound. The image showed three babies, only I was pregnant with one. The other two were tumors, larger than the baby and definitely not something I had eaten. The doctor turned to me and said, "If you make it through the night without going into preterm labor, I'd be surprised." With that, he walked out and I was checked into the maternity ward. Eventually a night nurse mentioned that I had been in labor for three days. "You should have said something," she scolded me.

I asked for pain medication, but I would have to wait until it was bad enough to warrant what they kept calling "the narcotic." After a week of labor pains that no one ever diagnosed, because the pain was in my butt and not my back, I could not hold off labor anymore. I was wheeled into a delivery operating room, where I slipped in and out of consciousness. At one point I awoke and screamed, "motherfucker."

The nurse told me to watch my language. I begged for an epidural. After three eternities an anesthesiologist arrived. He glared at me and said that if I wasn't quiet he would leave and I would not get any pain relief. Just as a contraction crested, the needle pierced my spine and I tried desperately to be still and quiet so he would not leave me there that way. Thirty seconds after the injection, I passed out before my head hit the pillow.

When I awoke I was pushing and then my daughter was here. Barely breathing and four days too early for the Catholic hospital to try any medical intervention, she died shortly after her first breath. The nurse wheeled me out of the operating room to take me back to recovery. I held my baby the whole way, because apparently that is what is done. After making plans for how we would handle her remains, the nurse turned to me and said, "Just so you know, there was nothing we could have done, because you did not tell us you were in labor."

Everything about the structure of trying to get medical care had filtered me through assumptions of my incompetence. There it was, what I had always been afraid of, what I must have known since I was a child I needed to prepare to defend myself against, and what it would take me years to accept was beyond my control. Like millions of women of color, especially black women, the healthcare machine could not imagine me as competent and so it neglected and ignored me until I was incompetent. Pain short-circuits rational thought. It can change all of your perceptions of reality. If you are in enough physical pain, your brain can see what isn't there. Pain, like pregnancy, is inconvenient for bureaucratic efficiency and has little use in a capitalist regime. When the medical profession systematically denies the existence of black women's pain, underdiagnoses our pain, refuses to alleviate or treat our pain, healthcare marks us as incompetent bureaucratic subjects. Then it serves us accordingly.

The assumption of black women's incompetence—we cannot know ourselves, express ourselves in a way that the context will render legible, or that prompts people with power to respond to us as agentic beings—supersedes even the most powerful status cultures in all of neoliberal capitalism: wealth and fame. In 2017 Serena Williams gave birth to her daughter. She celebrated with an interview, as is the ritual custom of celebrity cultures. In the interview, Serena describes how she had to bring to bear the full force of her authority as a global superstar to convince a nurse that she needed a treatment. The treatment likely saved Serena's life. Many black women are not so lucky.

In the wealthiest nation in the world, black women are dying in childbirth at rates comparable to those in poorer, colonized nations. The World Health Organization estimates that black expectant and new mothers in the United States die at about the same rate as women in countries such as Mexico and Uzbekistan.[3] The difference in rates is attributable, in large degree, to the high mortality rate of black women in the United States. The CDC says that black women are 243 percent more likely to die from pregnancy- or childbirth-related causes than are white women.[4]

These are not new data. They aren't hard-to-find, if hard-to-accept, data. Medical doctors surely know about these disparities, right? Why, then, would a global superstar have to intervene so directly in her own postnatal care, and what does that say about how poorer, average black women are treated when they give birth? There is surely something to be said about black women's structural oppression and cumulative disadvantage that conditions our physical responses to pregnancy. But there is also something to say about a healthcare system's assumptions regarding competency when it comes to the delivery of care that is killing black women.

The evidence in healthcare is some of the most dire, but examples of racialized, gendered competence abound because we rely on organizations to allocate the resources that govern our human rights. Healthcare is a lot like education, in that it is primarily delivered through bureaucracy. People in the bureaucracies make decisions, but many of the decisions are made for people by the rules attached to every role and every routine interaction. All of those rules are assumptions, derived from cultural beliefs about people, bodies, illness, and health.

To get the "healthcare" promised by the healthcare bureaucracy, it helps tremendously if the bureaucracy assumes that you are competent. When I called the nurse and said that I was bleeding and in pain,

the nurse needed to hear that a competent person was on the phone in order to process my problem for the crisis that it was. Instead, something about me and the interaction did not read as competent. That is why I was left in a general waiting room when I arrived, rather than being rushed to a private room with the equipment necessary to treat a pregnancy crisis. When my butt hurt, the doctors and nurses did not read that as a competent interpretation of contractions and so no one addressed my labor pains for over three days. At every step of the process of having what I would learn later was a fairly typical pregnancy for a black woman in the United States, I was rendered an incompetent subject with exceptional needs that fell beyond the scope of reasonable healthcare.

"Black babies in the United States die at just over two times the rate of white babies in the first year of their life," says Arthur James, an OB-GYN at Wexner Medical Center at Ohio State University in Columbus.[5] When my daughter died, she and I became statistics.

What I remember most about the whole ordeal, groggy from trauma and pain and narcotics, is how nothing about who I was in any other context mattered to the assumptions of my incompetence. I was highly educated. I spoke in the way one might expect of someone with a lot of formal education. I had health insurance. I was married. All of my status characteristics screamed "competent," but nothing could shut down what my blackness screams when I walk into the room. I could use my status to serve others, but not myself.

Sociologists try to figure out how ideologies like race and gender and class are so *sticky*. How is it that we have laid bodies down in streets, challenged patriarchy in courts, bled for fair wages, and still inequalities persist? The easiest answer is that racism and sexism and class warfare are resilient and necessary for global capitalism. The easy answer is not wrong, but it does not always tell us the whys and what-fors of how a middle-class black woman getting care in the good part of town in the United States of America has the same health outcome as a black woman anywhere in the colonized world.

Of course, black women know why intuitively. Patricia Hill Collins once called on the idea of controlling images, those stereotypes that are so powerful they flatten all empirical status differences among a group of people to reduce them to the most docile, incompetent subjects in a social structure.[6] Those are the memes of the fat black woman, gesticulating with the text "I'm a strong black woman I don't need no man" that circulate throughout our digital media culture. Controlling images have fallen a bit out of favor in the feminist literature, sometimes thought to be a taken-for-granted relic of older theory. But that is only if we confine our analysis to popular culture, where negative stereotypes do seem pedestrian. When we broaden our field of analysis to the political economy of incompetence—who is and who is not structurally viable as an agentic being across the domains of social life—controlling images regain some of their explanatory power.

Controlling images were never just about the object of study—popular culture memes or characters from movies and television shows—but about the process of reproducing structural inequalities in our everyday lives. Social psychologists study how we acknowledge and reproduce status groups like "man," "woman," "black," "white," "Asian," "poor," "rich," "novice," and "expert" in routine interactions. These are statuses of people that we recognize as meaningful categories. When we interact with someone, a few things happen. We size up the person we are engaging with, scanning for any risks to our own social status. You don't want to be the person who mistakes the company president for the janitor, for example. We also scan others' perception of us. This is how all kinds of impromptu moments of cooperation make our day go smoothly. It's the guy who sees you struggling to get something on the bus and coordinates the four people around you to help you get on. Or it's the three women in a fast food line who all grab for a baby's bottle just before it hits the floor. We cooperate in micromoments and in longer settings like the waiting room of a doctor's office. And, when we are cooperating with strangers or near strangers, we are using all kinds of ideas about status to make the interaction work to our benefit.

Let's take a small detour to get something out of the way. The prevalent perception of black women as unruly bodies and incompetent caretakers overrules even the most dominant stereotype about us, namely that we are superhuman. The image of black women as physically strong without any emotions vulnerable enough to warrant consideration is one of the greatest cultural exports from the racist, sexist U.S. hierarchy. We are undisciplined yet steadfastly committed to the care of others. At one time we were good nannies until global anti-blackness made the world's immigrant brown women cheaper to import. Even as black women caregivers became less desirable as actual emotional labor-for-hire, we have remained firmly lodged in the cultural imagination as "superwomen." It might seem that the culture's perennial strong woman would also be *competent*. But incompetent and superhero do not actually conflict in the context of essential notions about gender, race, class, and hierarchy.

Black women are superheroes when we conform to others' expectations of us. When we are sassy but not smart; successful but not happy; competitive but not actualized—then, we have some inherent wisdom. That wisdom's value is only validated by our culture when it serves someone or something else. We must inspire or provide the emotional release of "calling out" someone afflicted by the guilt of their unearned privilege. When we perform some existential service to men, to capital, to political power, to white women, and even to other "people of color" who are marginally closer to white than they are to black, then we are superwomen.[7] We are fulfilling our purpose in the natural order of things. When, instead, black women are strong in service of themselves, that same strength, wisdom, and wit become evidence of our incompetence.

The structural incompetence of black women is how we were made into property makers without any rights to property during slavery; into Patrick Moynihan's ghosts of black family deviance in the 1960s; and today into icons whose embodiment of authentic emotion is transmuted into digital memes meant to show you're woke in the 2000s. As objectified superhumans, we are valuable. As humans, we are incompetent.

Back to how status works. The big categories that work in almost any context are diffuse status characteristics. Our beliefs about those categories are so rich, deep, historical, omnipresent, and shared by others whose esteem we value that they show up in almost any social interaction. Those are the categories on which organizations like schools and hospitals base their bureaucratic assumptions. Who is a doctor? Man, white, maybe Asian (East not South and god knows rarely Southeast). Who is a nursing assistant? Woman, brown, black. Of course, values come with those assumptions. Doctors are good. Man, white, maybe Asian (East not South and god knows rarely Southeast) is also good. And so forth and so on. The great promise of social progress is that we can each earn other status descriptors like "expert" or "medical professional." You go to school. You deny yourself a little fun here and there. You sacrifice. You conform. And people out there recognizing your specific status characteristics is supposed to be the reward. In interactions someone might assume a woman cannot do math, but learn that she is an engineer. The question is, which status characteristic will win out?

More often than not the hierarchy of diffuse status characteristics overpowers any status characteristics that we earn. Patricia Hill Collins's matrix of domination, the intersecting planes of privilege and domination, still matters.[8] If we read that oeuvre more deeply, attuned to the ways that capital and neoliberalism have inculcated greater incompetence for more and more people, we find that what black feminists promised all along was true: to know the most present marginalized oppressions is to know the future.

Being structurally incompetent injects friction into every interaction, between people, and between people and organizations, and between organizations and ideologies. Frictionless living is the promise of neoliberal capital—that is, if you are on the winning side of power. But when black women in the United States are dying trying to give birth and their babies are dying trying to get born, not simply because of poverty but because of the grotesque accumulation of

capital in the West is predicated on our structural incompetence, then we can see the ends of hypercapitalism in daily life.

This moment of global inequality demands incompetent subjects. The status quo and ever-intensifying versions of it require incompetent consumers who will learn to want technological solutions to their political problems. Are you starving even though there is food? Here is an app to connect you with the charity that is filling that hole in our ragged social safety net. Are global profits being extracted by the financial class while driving down wages and quality of work, even for people with expensive college educations? Here is a website where you can purchase a credential that might help you get a new job, one where you will likely be in the same position again in eighteen months. Your structural incompetence generates ever more sophisticated consumption goods, goods that reinforce status games of who is deserving and who is not.

Did you use the app to get a job or to become an entrepreneur? Do you use social media like a customer or a producer? Are you surveilled by the state like poor people or do you surveil yourself like the middle class? These gradations of difference are meaningless if the question is which consumption status group has power over their political incompetence. All of them are incompetent; they only differ in how they can afford to lie to themselves about it.

What so many black women know is what I learned as I sat at the end of a hallway with a dead baby in my arms. The networks of capital, be they polities or organizations, work most efficiently when your lowest status characteristic is assumed. And once these gears are in motion, you can never be competent enough to save your own life.

That is how black feminism knows the future.

Notes

1. The quoted phrase from Foucault is from Michel Foucault, *Society Must Be Defended: Lectures at the Collège de France, 1975–76*, trans. David Macey (New York: Picador, 2003).
2. Speaking with a business writer, LinkedIn founder Reid Hoffman intimated that many people use the platform wrong when they automatically accept any

request. See more at http://www.businessinsider.com/reid-hoffman-how-to-use-linkedin-2017-4.
3. World Health Organization, "World Health Statistics 2014: A Wealth of Information in Global Public Health" (2014).
4. "Pregnancy Related Mortality," Centers for Disease Control and Prevention, May 9, 2018, http://wwww.

cdc.gov/reproductivehealth/maternalinfanthealth/
pregnancy-relatedmortality.htm.

5. "Infant Mortality," Centers for Disease Control and
Prevention, August 3, 2018, http://wwww.cdc.gov/re-
productivehealth/maternalinfanthealth/infantmor-
tality.htm.

6. More than just stereotypes, controlling images are racialized, gendered, and classed ideologies produced by
and through social institutions such as the media but
also through political bodies, educational institutions, and courts.

7. Because I refuse to believe in the concept as anything
other than a political designation, I use it here the way
it is used loosely in popular culture—amorphous,
apolitical, and ambivalent about the project of ending
anti-blackness. Tamara K. Nopper has great work on
how the idea of "people of color" as a category marshals important resources to the detriment of small
black business owners: "Minority, Black, and Non-
Black People of Color: 'New' Color-Blind Racism and
the US Small Business Administration's Approach to
Minority Business Lending in the Post-Civil Rights
Era," *Critical Sociology* 37, no. 5 (2011): 65–71. And sociologist Jared Sexton called the erasure of anti-blackness that can be embedded in the elisions of "people of
color" endemic to the political construct of the term:
"People-of-Color-Blindness Notes on the Afterlife of
Slavery," *Social Text* 28, no. 2 (2010): 31–56.

8. Patricia Hill Collins, "Black Feminist Thought in the
Matrix of Domination," Social Theory: The Multicultural and Classic Readings (1993): 615–25.

Questions for Critical Thinking

1. The experiences of the author illustrate the how
the medical system and other forms of structural
racism harms black women. How did this reading expand your understanding of this issue?

2. In addition to presenting her own experiences,
the author incorporates statistics to illustrate the
ways in which structural racism is pervasive in
the U.S. health care system? How does viewing
issues of health care as matters of personal choices
rather than structural practices perpetuate health
care inequalities?

3. What solutions do you see to the social problems
the author highlights? What would need to take
place in order to implement such solutions?

THE STORY OF MY BODY

Judith Ortiz Cofer

In the following essay, author Judith Ortiz Cofer recounts her experiences as a Puerto Rican child coming to the United States and the impact that constructions of race and beauty had on her perceptions of self. At one moment literally learning to become invisible, Cofer demonstrates the impact of societal constructions of difference and inequality on the individual.

> Migration is the story of my body.
>
> —VICTOR HERNÁNDEZ CRUZ

Skin

I was born a white girl in Puerto Rico but became a brown girl when I came to live in the United States. My Puerto Rican relatives call me tall; at the American school, some of my rougher classmates called me Skinny Bones, and the Shrimp because I was the smallest member of my classes all through grammar school until high school, when the midget Gladys was given the honorary post of front row center for class pictures and scorekeeper, bench warmer, in P.E. I reached my full stature of five feet in sixth grade.

I started out life as a pretty baby and learned to be a pretty girl from a pretty mother. Then at ten years of age I suffered one of the worst cases of chicken pox I have ever heard of. My entire body, including the inside of my ears and in between my toes, was covered with pustules which in a fit of panic at my appearance I scratched off my face, leaving permanent scars. A cruel school nurse told me I would always have them— tiny cuts that looked as if a mad cat had plunged its claws deep into my skin. I grew my hair long and hid behind it for the first years of my adolescence. This was when I learned to be invisible.

Color

In the animal world it indicates danger: the most colorful creatures are often the most poisonous. Color is also a way to attract and seduce a mate. In the human world color triggers many more complex and often deadly reactions. As a Puerto Rican girl born of "white" parents, I spent the first years of my life hearing people refer to me as *blanca*, white. My mother insisted that I protect myself from the intense island sun because I was more prone to sunburn than some of my darker, *trigueño*[1] playmates. People were always commenting within my hearing about how my black hair contrasted so nicely with my "pale" skin. I did not think of the color of my skin consciously except when I heard the adults talking about complexion. It seems to me that the subject is much more common in the conversation of mixed-race peoples than in mainstream United States society, where it is a touchy and sometimes even embarrassing topic to discuss, except in a political context. In Puerto Rico I heard many conversations about skin color. A pregnant woman could say, "I hope my baby doesn't turn out *prieto*" (slang for "dark" or "black") "like my husband's grandmother, although she was a good-looking *negra*[2] in her time." I am a combination of both, being olive-skinned—lighter than my mother yet darker than my fair-skinned father. In America, I am a person of color, obviously a Latina. On the Island I have been called everything from a *paloma blanca*,[3] after the song (by a black suitor), to *la gringa*.[4]

My first experience of color prejudice occurred in a supermarket in Paterson, New Jersey. It was Christmastime, and I was eight or nine years old. There was a display of toys in the store where I went two or three times a day to buy things for my mother, who never made lists but sent for milk, cigarettes, a can of this or that, as she remembered from hour to hour. I enjoyed being trusted with money and walking half a city block to the new, modern grocery store. It was owned by three good-looking Italian brothers. I liked the younger one with the crew-cut blond hair. The two older ones watched me and the other Puerto Rican kids as if they thought we were going to steal something. The oldest one would sometimes even try to hurry me with my purchases, although part of my pleasure in these expeditions came from looking at everything in the well-stocked aisles. I was also teaching myself to read English by sounding out the labels in packages: L&M cigarettes, Borden's homogenized milk, Red Devil potted ham, Nestle's chocolate mix, Quaker oats, Bustelo coffee, Wonder bread, Colgate toothpaste, Ivory soap, and Goya (makers of products used in Puerto Rican dishes) everything—these are some of the brand names that taught me nouns. Several times this man had come up to me, wearing his blood-stained butcher's apron, and towering over me had asked in a harsh voice whether there was something he could help me find. On the way out I would glance at the younger brother who ran one of the registers and he would often smile and wink at me.

It was the mean brother who first referred to me as "colored." It was a few days before Christmas, and my parents had already told my brother and me that since we were in Los Estados[5] now, we would get our presents on December 25 instead of Los Reyes, Three

Kings Day, when gifts are exchanged in Puerto Rico. We were to give them a wish list that they would take to Santa Claus, who apparently lived in the Macy's store downtown—at least that's where we had caught a glimpse of him when we went shopping. Since my parents were timid about entering the fancy store, we did not approach the huge man in the red suit. I was not interested in sitting on a stranger's lap anyway. But I did covet Susie, the talking schoolteacher doll that was displayed in the center aisle of the Italian brothers' supermarket. She talked when you pulled a string on her back. Susie had a limited repertoire of three sentences: I think she could say: "Hello, I'm Susie Schoolteacher," "Two plus two is four," and one other thing I cannot remember. The day the older brother chased me away, I was reaching to touch Susie's blond curls. I had been told many times, as most children have, not to touch anything in the store that I was not buying. But I had been looking at Susie for weeks. In my mind, she was my doll. After all, I had put her on my Christmas wish list. The moment is frozen in my mind as if there were a photograph of it on file. It was not a turning point, a disaster, or an earth-shaking revelation. It was simply the first time I considered—if naively—the meaning of skin color in human relations.

I reached to touch Susie's hair. It seems to me that I had to get on tip-toe, since the toys were stacked on a table and she sat like a princess on top of the fancy box she came in. Then I heard the booming "Hey, kid, what do you think you're doing!" spoken very loudly from the meat counter. I felt caught, although I knew I was not doing anything criminal. I remember not looking at the man, but standing there, feeling humiliated because I knew everyone in the store must have heard him yell at me. I felt him approach, and when I knew he was behind me, I turned around to face the bloody butcher's apron. His large chest was at my eye level. He blocked my way. I started to run out of the place, but even as I reached the door I heard him shout after me: "Don't come in here unless you gonna buy something. You PR kids put your dirty hands on stuff. You always look dirty. But maybe dirty brown is your natural color." I heard him laugh and someone else too in the back. Outside in the sunlight I looked at my hands. My nails needed a little cleaning as they always did, since I liked to paint with watercolors, but I took a bath every night. I thought the man was dirtier than I was in his stained apron. He was also always sweaty—it showed in big yellow circles under his shirt-sleeves. I sat on the front steps of the apartment building where we lived and looked closely at my hands, which showed the only skin I could see, since it was bitter cold and I was wearing my quilted play coat, dungarees, and a knitted navy cap of my father's. I was not light pink like my friend Charlene and her sister Kathy, who had blue eyes and light brown hair. My skin is the color of the coffee my grandmother made, which was half milk, *leche con café* rather than *café con leche*.[6] My mother is the opposite mix. She has a lot of café in her color. I could not understand how my skin looked like dirt to the supermarket man.

I went in and washed my hands thoroughly with soap and hot water, and borrowing my mother's nail file, I cleaned the crusted watercolors from underneath my nails. I was pleased with the results. My skin was the same color as before, but I knew I was clean. Clean enough to run my fingers through Susie's fine gold hair when she came home to me.

Size

My mother is barely four feet eleven inches in height, which is average for women in her family. When I grew to five feet by age twelve, she was amazed and began to use the word tall to describe me, as in "Since you are tall, this dress will look good on you." As with the color of my skin, I didn't consciously think about my height or size until other people made an issue of it. It is around the preadolescent years that in America the games children play for fun become fierce competitions where everyone is out to "prove" they are better than others. It was in the playground and sports fields that my size-related problems began. No matter how familiar the story is, every child who is the last chosen for a team knows the torment of waiting to be called up. At the Paterson, New Jersey, public schools that I attended, the volleyball or softball game was the metaphor for the battlefield of life to the inner city kids—the black kids versus the Puerto Rican kids, the whites versus the blacks versus the

Puerto Rican kids; and I was 4F,[7] skinny, short, bespectacled, and apparently impervious to the blood thirst that drove many of my classmates to play ball as if their lives depended on it. Perhaps they did. I would rather be reading a book than sweating, grunting, and running the risk of pain and injury. I simply did not see the point in competitive sports. My main form of exercise then was walking to the library, many city blocks away from my barrio.

Still, I wanted to be wanted. I wanted to be chosen for the team. Physical education was compulsory, a class where you were actually given a grade. On my mainly all A report card, the C for compassion I always received from the P.E. teachers shamed me the same as a bad grade in a real class. Invariably, my father would say: "How can you make a low grade for *playing games?*" He did not understand. Even if I had managed to make a hit (it never happened) or get the ball over that ridiculously high net, I already had a reputation as a "shrimp," a hopeless nonathlete. It was an area where the girls who didn't like me for one reason or another—mainly because I did better than they on academic subjects—could lord it over me; the playing field was the place where even the smallest girl could make me feel powerless and inferior. I instinctively understood the politics even then; how the not choosing me until the teacher forced one of the team captains to call my name was a coup of sorts—there, you little show-off, tomorrow you can beat us in spelling and geography, but this afternoon you are the loser. Or perhaps those were only my own bitter thoughts as I sat or stood in the sidelines while the big girls were grabbed like fish and I, the little brown tadpole, was ignored until Teacher looked over in my general direction and shouted, "Call Ortiz," or, worse, "Somebody's *got* to take her."

No wonder I read Wonder Woman comics and had Legion of Super Heroes daydreams. Although I wanted to think of myself as "intellectual," my body was demanding that I notice it. I saw the little swelling around my once-flat nipples, the fine hairs growing in secret places; but my knees were still bigger than my thighs, and I always wore long- or half-sleeve blouses to hide my bony upper arms. I wanted flesh on my bones—a thick layer of it. I saw a new product advertised on TV. Wate-On.

They showed skinny men and women before and after taking the stuff, and it was a transformation like the ninety-seven-pound-weakling-turned-into-Charles-Atlas ads that I saw on the back covers of my comic books. The Wate-On was very expensive. I tried to explain my need for it in Spanish to my mother, but it didn't translate very well, even to my ears—and she said with a tone of finality, eat more of my good food and you'll get fat—anybody can get fat. Right. Except me. I was going to have to join a circus someday as Skinny Bones, the woman without flesh.

Wonder Woman was stacked. She had a cleavage framed by the spread wings of a golden eagle and a muscular body that has become fashionable with women only recently. But since I wanted a body that would serve me in P.E., hers was my ideal. The breasts were an indulgence I allowed myself. Perhaps the daydreams of bigger girls were more glamorous, since our ambitions are filtered through our needs, but I wanted first a powerful body. I daydreamed of leaping up above the gray landscape of the city to where the sky was clear and blue, and in anger and self-pity, I fantasized about scooping my enemies up by their hair from the playing fields and dumping them on a barren asteroid. I would put the P.E. teachers each on their own rock in space too, where they would be the loneliest people in the universe, since I knew they had no "inner resources," no imagination, and in outer space, there would be no air for them to fill their deflated volleyballs with. In my mind all P.E. teachers have blended into one large spiky-haired woman with a whistle on a string around her neck and a volleyball under one arm. My Wonder Woman fantasies of revenge were a source of comfort to me in my early career as a shrimp.

I was saved from more years of P.E. torment by the fact that in my sophomore year of high school I transferred to a school where the midget, Gladys, was the focal point of interest for the people who must rank according to size. Because her height was considered a handicap, there was an unspoken rule about mentioning size around Gladys, but of course, there was no need to say anything. Gladys knew her place: front row center in class photographs. I gladly moved to the left or to the right of her, as far as I could without leaving the picture completely.

Looks

Many photographs were taken of me as a baby by my mother to send to my father, who was stationed overseas during the first two years of my life. With the Army in Panama when I was born, he later traveled often on tours of duty with the Navy. I was a healthy, pretty baby. Recently, I read that people are drawn to big-eyed round-faced creatures, like puppies, kittens, and certain other mammals and marsupials, koalas, for example, and, of course, infants. I was all eyes, since my head and body, even as I grew older, remained thin and small-boned. As a young child I got a lot of attention from my relatives and many other people we met in our barrio. My mother's beauty may have had something to do with how much attention we got from strangers in stores and on the street. I can imagine it. In the pictures I have seen of us together, she is a stunning young woman by Latino standards: long, curly black hair, and round curves in a compact frame. From her I learned how to move, smile, and talk like an attractive woman. I remember going into a bodega[8] for our groceries and being given candy by the proprietor as a reward for being *bonita*, pretty.

I can see in the photographs, and I also remember, that I was dressed in the pretty clothes, the stiff, frilly dresses, with layers of crinolines underneath, the glossy patent leather shoes, and, on special occasions, the skull-hugging little hats and the white gloves that were popular in the late fifties and early sixties. My mother was proud of my looks, although I was a bit too thin. She could dress me up like a doll and take me by the hand to visit relatives, or go to the Spanish mass at the Catholic church and show me off. How was I to know that she and the others who called me "pretty" were representatives of an aesthetic that would not apply when I went out into the mainstream world of school?

In my Paterson, New Jersey, public schools there were still quite a few white children, although the demographics of the city were changing rapidly. The original waves of Italian and Irish immigrants, silk-mill workers, and laborers in the cloth industries had been "assimilated." Their children were now the middle-class parents of my peers. Many of them moved their children to the Catholic schools that proliferated enough to have leagues of basketball teams. The names I recall hearing still ring in my ears: Don Bosco High versus St. Mary's High, St. Joseph's versus St. John's. Later I too would be transferred to the safer environment of a Catholic school. But I started school at Public School Number 11. I came there from Puerto Rico, thinking myself a pretty girl, and found that the hierarchy for popularity was as follows: pretty white girl, pretty Jewish girl, pretty Puerto Rican girl, pretty black girl. Drop the last two categories; teachers were too busy to have more than one favorite per class, and it was simply understood that if there was a big part in the school play, or any competition where the main qualification was "presentability" (such as escorting a school visitor to or from the principal's office), the classroom's public address speaker would be requesting the pretty and/or nice-looking white boy or girl. By the time I was in sixth grade, I was sometimes called by the principal to represent my class because I dressed neatly (I knew this from a progress report sent to my mother, which I translated for her) and because all the "presentable" white girls had moved to the Catholic schools (I later surmised this part). But I was still not one of the popular girls with the boys. I remember one incident where I stepped out into the playground in my baggy gym shorts and one Puerto Rican boy said to the other: "What do you think?" The other one answered: "Her face is OK, but look at the toothpick legs." The next best thing to a compliment I got was when my favorite male teacher, while handing out the class pictures, commented that with my long neck and delicate features I resembled the movie star Audrey Hepburn. But the Puerto Rican boys had learned to respond to a fuller figure: long necks and a perfect little nose were not what they looked for in a girl. That is when I decided I was a "brain." I did not settle into the role easily. I was nearly devastated by what the chicken pox episode had done to my self-image. But I looked into the mirror less often after I was told that I would always have scars on my face, and I hid behind my long black hair and my books.

After the problems at the public school got to the point where even nonconfrontational little me got beaten up several times, my parents enrolled me at St. Joseph's High School. I was then a minority of one among the Italian and Irish kids. But I found several good friends there—other girls who took their studies seriously. We did our homework together and talked about the Jackies. The Jackies were two popular girls, one blonde and the other red-haired, who had women's bodies. Their curves showed even in the blue jumper uniforms with straps that we all wore. The blonde Jackie would often let one of the straps fall off her shoulder, and although she, like all of us, wore a white blouse underneath, all the boys stared at her arm. My friends and I talked about this and practiced letting our straps fall off our shoulders. But it wasn't the same without breasts or hips.

My final two and a half years of high school were spent in Augusta, Georgia, where my parents moved our family in search of a more peaceful environment. Then we became part of a little community of our Army-connected relatives and friends. School was yet another matter. I was enrolled in a huge school of nearly two thousand students that had just that year been forced to integrate. There were two black girls and there was me. I did extremely well academically. As to my social life, it was, for the most part, uneventful—yet it is in my memory blighted by one incident. In my junior year, I became wildly infatuated with a pretty white boy. I'll call him Ted. Oh, he was pretty: yellow hair that fell over his forehead, a smile to die for—and he was a great dancer. I watched him at Teen Town, the youth center at the base where all the military brats gathered on Saturday nights. My father had retired from the Navy, and we had all our base privileges—one other reason we moved to Augusta. Ted looked like an angel to me. I worked on him for a year before he asked me out. This meant maneuvering to be within the periphery of his vision at every possible occasion. I took the long way to my classes in school just to pass by his locker, I went to football games, which I detested, and I danced (I too was a good dancer) in front of him at Teen Town—this took some fancy footwork, since it involved subtly moving my partner toward the right spot on the dance floor. When Ted finally approached me, "A Million to One" was playing on the jukebox, and when he took me in his arms, the odds suddenly turned in my favor. He asked me to go to a school dance the following Saturday. I said yes, breathlessly. I said yes, but there were obstacles to surmount at home. My father did not allow me to date casually. I was allowed to go to major events like a prom or a concert with a boy who had been properly screened. There was such a boy in my life, a neighbor who wanted to be a Baptist missionary and was practicing his anthropological skills on my family. If I was desperate to go somewhere and needed a date, I'd resort to Gary. This is the type of religious nut that Gary was: when the school bus did not show up one day, he put his hands over his face and prayed to Christ to get us a way to get to school. Within minutes a mother in a station wagon, on her way to town, stopped to ask why we weren't in school. Gary informed her that the Lord had sent her just in time to find us a way to get there in time for roll call. He assumed that I was impressed. Gary was even good-looking in a bland sort of way, but he kissed me with his lips tightly pressed together. I think Gary probably ended up marrying a native woman from wherever he may have gone to preach the Gospel according to Paul. She probably believes that all white men pray to God for transportation and kiss with their mouths closed. But it was Ted's mouth, his whole beautiful self, that concerned me in those days. I knew my father would say no to our date, but planned to run away from home if necessary. I told my mother how important this date was. I cajoled and pleaded with her from Sunday to Wednesday. She listened to my arguments and must have heard the note of desperation in my voice. She said very gently to me: "You better be ready for disappointment." I did not ask what she meant. I did not want her fears for me to taint my happiness. I asked her to tell my father about my date. Thursday at breakfast my father looked at me across the table with his eyebrows together. My mother looked at him with her mouth set in a straight line. I looked down at my bowl of cereal. Nobody said anything. Friday I

tried on every dress in my closet. Ted would be picking me up at six on Saturday: dinner and then the sock hop at school. Friday night I was in my room doing my nails or something else in preparation for Saturday (I know I groomed myself nonstop all week) when the telephone rang. I ran to get it. It was Ted. His voice sounded funny when he said my name, so funny that I felt compelled to ask: "Is something wrong?" Ted blurted it all out without a preamble. His father had asked who he was going out with. Ted had told him my name. "Ortiz? That's Spanish, isn't it?" the father had asked. Ted had told him yes, then shown him my picture in the yearbook. Ted's father had shaken his head. No. Ted would not be taking me out. Ted's father had known Puerto Ricans in the Army. He had lived in New York City while studying architecture and had seen how the spics lived. Like rats. Ted repeated his father's words to me as if I should understand *his* predicament when I heard why he was breaking our date. I don't remember what I said before hanging up. I do recall the darkness of my room that sleepless night and the heaviness of my blanket in which I wrapped myself like a shroud. And I remember my parents' respect for my pain and their gentleness toward me that weekend. My mother did not say "I warned you," and I was grateful for her understanding silence.

In college, I suddenly became an "exotic" woman to the men who had survived the popularity wars in high school, who were not practicing to be worldly: they had to act liberal in their politics, in their lifestyles, and in the women they went out with. I dated heavily for a while, then married young. I had discovered that I needed stability more than social life. I had brains for sure and some talent in writing. These facts were a constant in my life. My skin color, my size, and my appearance were variables—things that were judged according to my current self-image, the aesthetic values of the time, the places I was in, and the people I met. My studies, later my writing, the respect of people who saw me as an individual person they cared about, these were the criteria for my sense of self-worth that I would concentrate on in my adult life.

Notes

1. *trigueño:* Brown-skinned.
2. *negra:* Black.
3. *paloma blanca:* White dove.
4. *la gringa:* A white, non-Latina woman.
5. *Los Estados:* "The States"—that is, the United States.
6. *leche con café . . . café con leche:* Milk with coffee (light brown) . . . coffee with milk (dark brown).
7. 4F: Draft-board classification meaning "unfit for military service"; hence, not physically fit.
8. *bodega:* Market.

Questions for Critical Thinking

1. Cofer's discussion illustrates that the way we see our bodies is influenced by dominant societal values and beliefs. How do you see your own perceptions of your body influenced by societal beliefs and values? How do these perceptions change in different situations?
2. Cofer experiences particular difficulties with regard to her body and dominant attitudes about gender. Do you think males experience similar problems? Why or why not?
3. Are the experiences Cofer relates simply examples of childhood difficulties everyone experiences or are they examples of larger issues? What makes you think this?

TWO HATE NOTES

Deportations, COVID-19, and Xenophobia against Hmong Americans in the Midwest

Kong Pheng Pha

In the following essay, assistant professor of Critical Hmong Studies and Women's, Gender, and Sexuality Studies Kong Pheng Pha shares a personal experience of receiving a xenophobic hate note in response to President Donald Trump's negotiations with the Lao government to deport Hmong living in the United States back to Laos. This experience was further exacerbated not only by lack of knowledge among the majority of people in the U.S. regarding the Hmong presence in the United States as forcibly displaced political refugees, but also as hate incidents against Asian American and Pacific Islanders increased with the start of the COVID-19 pandemic. She responds with a discussion of how the collective survival of Hmong Americans, and of Southeast Asian Americans and Asian Americans more broadly, depends on systems of mutual aid that take into account the everyday lived experiences of the most vulnerable within our society.

In February 2020, I received a xenophobic hate note in my campus mailbox regarding President Donald Trump's negotiations with the Lao government to deport Hmong living in the United States back to Laos. The hate note read: "Deport all Hmongs, Deport all illegal aliens HMONGS, ICE & CBP are law enforcement and should be obeyed, No room for criminals, No Amnesty ever." I was shaken and unsettled. The xenophobic hate note created intense anxiety for me because I know that my advocacy as a Hmong American scholar and professor teaching and speaking to the media about the deportation issues rendered me a vulnerable target for racists and xenophobes. In the following days, I discussed the deportation negotiations with Laos at length in my course, "Hmong American Experiences in the U.S." My students were furious about the larger American public's ahistorical, inaccurate, and misguided readings regarding the Hmong presence in the United

States as forcibly displaced political refugees who fought as proxy soldiers for the Central Intelligence Agency's secret war in Laos in the 1960s and 1970s. One Hmong American student commented that the deportation negotiations made her feel unwanted in the United States. How can I convey that I care about her? My spirit was shattered; I was on edge, demoralized, and fearing for my safety.

The news reports, activism, and social discourse surrounding the deportation negotiations came to a screeching halt when news of COVID-19 broke out all over the world just one month later, in March 2020. While still recovering from a traumatic racist experience with the hate note, I was thrust into another world of racism and xenophobia amidst the

Pha, Kong Pheng. 2020. "Two Hate Notes: Deportations, COVID-19, and Xenophobia against Hmong Americans in the Midwest." *Journal of Asian American Studies* (23)2: 335–39.

rapidly spreading global pandemic. A familiar wave of anti-Asian racism swept across the United States, as reckless as the virus itself. I was struck by another racist and xenophobic incident when a hate note was taped onto a Hmong American couple's apartment door in Woodbury, Minnesota. The note read: "We're watching you fucking chinks take the Chinese virus back to china. We don't want you hear infecting us with your diseases!!!!!!!!!! –your friendly neighborhood."1 The explosion of racist violence against Asians during the outbreak of COVID-19 exacerbated my fears of being Asian American in western, mostly rural Wisconsin. For my students, the couple, and myself, it is difficult to shake off that unsettling feeling of being targeted by both the U.S. settler state and racists on the ground. I find myself asking how we can turn to each other for support and care in these times of heightened racism.

There is one strand of social discourse that connects the two hate notes directed against me in Wisconsin and the Hmong American couple in Minnesota. The first note conflates Hmong as "illegals" and renders invisible the specific historical context that was the caveat to Hmong political migration to the United States. The second note conflates Hmong Americans with Chinese and China, and renders Hmong Americans invisible and anything but Americans. In the note that I received, the writer deployed the concept of "illegal aliens" towards Hmong to justify our deportation. "Illegal aliens" are understood pejoratively to be subjects whose presence in the United States is unlawful and thus whose existence in and of itself constitutes criminality. The "illegal alien" is reduced to a condition of statelessness because they do not belong in the U.S. nation-state via their lack of legal citizenship and/or formal recognition of their presence. For Hmong, the deployment of "illegal aliens" feels familiar due to the Hmong's historical and political conditions as stateless refugees. Although different from the position of the "illegal alien," nonetheless our deportability even as political refugees serves to remind us that we are neither citizens nor Americans, if not in the legal sense, then certainly in the social sense.

The Woodbury note contained an equally pernicious undertone. It aligns closer to the yellow peril discourse attributed to Asians as diseased invaders.

Hmong Americans are effaced by racism, even though Hmong Americans make up the largest group of Asian Americans in the state of Minnesota. Woodbury, a suburb of Saint Paul, is only fifteen minutes from the Twin Cities, the location of the largest enclave of Hmong Americans in the United States. We may conclude that the conflation of Hmong simply as "Chinese" or "Asian" is similar to the ongoing experiences of anti-Asian racism that all Asian Americans are facing within the U.S. nation at large. Yet, I contend that even the proximity of Woodbury to the Twin Cities could not secure a Hmong American visibility in the time of COVID-19. This invisibility thus rejects the larger and longer history of Hmong American structural eradication within U.S. history from the American imagination through war and militarism. But it all makes sense: erasing Hmong Americans, even though the COVID pandemic has rendered "Chinese" as dehumanizingly hyper-visible, is an intentional way to dehumanize us. And dehumanization enables the exteriorization of the threat as not American, but as Asian (read: disease).

Stamping Out Hate, Creating Care

While the two hate notes have presented palpable systemic and visceral violence for Hmong Americans in the Midwest, Hmong Americans are also forging more ethical formations of care to reclaim our humanity from xenophobic violence and confront the challenges posed during the COVID pandemic. The challenges of creating more sensible forms of care that lie ahead for Asian American studies scholars and activists in the time of intensifying racism—evidenced by the two hate notes—are twofold. First, we need to imagine decolonized ways of care and security that consider the multigenerational and non-nuclear familial structures within diverse Asian American communities. My own family represents a case of this non-nuclear and multigenerational family structure. I live simultaneously in and travel to and from Minneapolis and Eau Claire, a college city in Western Wisconsin. My mother lives with three of my younger siblings and my brother-in-law in an impoverished neighborhood on the north side of Minneapolis, and my father lives and works in a small rural town outside Oklahoma City with his sister (my aunt) and her husband. And lastly, my paternal grandparents, who have lived with my family for nearly ten years, relocated to a Saint Paul suburb to live with my father's brother (my uncle), his wife, and their two small children, while also traveling back and forth between their other adult children's homes both in Minnesota and Oklahoma. In these times, we are creating family and community models of care and security for our complex family structure that reject the impulses of individualism and neoliberal self-care management.2 In another instance of community care, the Hmong Medical Association created videos in the Hmong language to educate elders about the COVID pandemic and the social distancing mandates of the state while collaborating with a Hmong American tailor shop, City Tailor, to hand-sew and distribute over eight hundred protective masks to elder care centers and community clinics across the Twin Cities metropolitan area. In a world where hegemonic structures of knowledge around health and disease prevention preclude refugee and immigrant communities of color from accessing life-saving medical knowledge and social care, Hmong Americans are enacting forms of radical care that uplifts and ensures the collective survival.3

Second, there needs to be conjoined intellectual and activist efforts to situate racism both within the physical violence of everyday culture and within public policies in order to facilitate comparative and intersectional organizing. Such connective formulation enables an intersectional approach to anti-racist activism and links the racist and xenophobic discourses of the infectious and diseased "Other" with the undeserving noncitizen deportable subject. Various examples are seen in the activist efforts of ReleaseMN8, a campaign to stop the unjust deportations of eight Cambodian Americans, which has since become a national model for anti-deportation activism. A coalition of Southeast Asian American community organizations, including ReleaseMN8, rallied in solidarity with Hmong Americans opposing President Trump's negotiations with Laos on the deportation of Hmong. ReleaseMN8 has since assembled the Southeast Asian American Solidarity Toolkit: A Guide to Resisting Deportations and Detentions from the #ReleaseMN8 Campaign to assist vulnerable communities in combating immigration injustice and to prevent families from being broken apart by the White supremacist U.S. immigration

apparatus. Freedom Inc., a Hmong American, Black, and queer social justice organization additionally has organized against unjust deportations of Southeast Asian Americans for nearly a decade. In the weeks in which the media comprehensively covered the deportation negotiations against Hmong in the United States, activists from Freedom Inc. organized to set up legal clinics for those affected by unjust deportations, just as they have for issues such as domestic violence. Thus, the inhumanity of family separation within deportations is directly relational to the strict social distancing mandates that were implemented in the wake of the COVID-19 outbreak in that both scenarios work, explicitly or implicitly, to alienate marginalized communities.

Our collective survival as Hmong Americans, and as Southeast Asian Americans and Asian Americans more broadly, depends on systems of mutual aid that take into account the everyday lived experiences of the most vulnerable within our society.4 Hmong Americans have, since the beginning of our resettlement in the 1970s and up to the 2020s, relied on one another to care for our communities in times of crisis. Hmong American health and healing systems rely not on neoliberal forms of self-sufficiency, personal responsibility, or state-based care, but on consultation with elders and extended-family members in order to reconcile the arbitrary boundaries of both physical and spiritual health. The COVID-19 pandemic is killing us physically, but racism is also killing us spiritually. As news of the pandemic stretched across the United States, my mother tied two sets of black, green, and red fabric on our doors to protect our family from malevolent spiritual energies. A shaman had advised all families to immediately safeguard the home in order to negate the physical and spiritual deaths imminent amidst the global pandemic. In profound ways, Hmong ontologies of health have anticipated that physical welfare always entails affective, emotional, and spiritual welfare. Ultimately, we need to (re)create models of care that resist historical erasure as evidenced by the two hate notes that we received, while complicating the social distancing orders and deportation negotiations that inadvertently or otherwise work to disintegrate non-nuclear, nontraditional, and nonnormative families in ways that foster physical and spiritual well-being.

Notes

1. Maya Rao, "Asian Americans in Minnesota Face Insults, Hostility during Virus Outbreak, Star Tribune, March 28, 2020. https://www.startribune.com/local-asian-americans-face-insults-hostility/569178982.

2. Jade Begay, "Decolonizing Community Care in Response to COVID-19," NDN Collective, March 13, 2020. https://ndncollective.org/indigenizingand-decolonizing-community-care-in-response-to-co-vid-19.

3. Hi'ilei Julia Kawehipuaakahaopulani Hobart and Tamara Kneese, "Radical Care: Survival Strategies for Uncertain Times," Social Text 38, no. 1 (March 2020): 5.

4. Dean Spade, "Solidarity Not Charity: Mutual Aid for Mobilization and Survival," Social Text 38, no. 1 (2020): 134–39.

Questions for Critical Thinking

1. The experiences of the author illustrate the ways in which violence is used as a form of social control. What are some of the ways in which violence is used against Asian American and Pacific Islanders as well as Black and Indigenous people of color?

2. Beyond the direct violence exhibited in this essay, what are some of the barriers that Asian American and Pacific Islanders continue to face in society? How do these barriers impact all of us, regardless of our race?

3. The author references that the majority of people in the U.S. are ignorant of the history that resulted in the Hmong presence in the United States as forcibly displaced political refugees. How might a more complete education of history of Asian American and Pacific Islanders as well as Black and Indigenous people of color lead to greater racial equity in the United States?

"GEE, YOU DON'T SEEM LIKE AN INDIAN FROM THE RESERVATION"

· *Barbara Cameron*

In the following essay, author Barbara Cameron recounts her experiences growing up Native American in South Dakota. Her encounters with racism and racial violence had long-lasting and penetrating impacts on her sense of self.

One of the very first words I learned in my Lakota language was *wasicu*, which designates white people. At that early age, my comprehension of wasicu was gained from observing and listening to my family discussing the wasicu. My grandmother always referred to white people as the "wasicu sica" with emphasis on *sica*, our word for terrible or bad. By the age of five I had seen one Indian man gunned down in the back by the police and was a silent witness to a gang of white teenage boys beating up an elderly Indian man. I'd hear stories of Indian ranch hands being "accidentally" shot by white ranchers. I quickly began to understand the wasicu menace my family spoke of.

My hatred for the wasicu was solidly implanted by the time I entered first grade. Unfortunately in first grade I became teacher's pet so my teacher had a fondness for hugging me, which always repulsed me. I couldn't stand the idea of a white person touching me. Eventually I realized that it wasn't the white skin that I hated, but it was their culture of deceit, greed, racism, and violence.

During my first memorable visit to a white town, I was appalled that they thought of themselves as superior to my people. Their manner of living appeared devoid of life and bordered on hostility even for one another. They were separated from each other by their perfectly, politely fenced square plots of green lawn. The only lawns on my reservation were the lawns of the BIA[1] officials or white Christians. The white people always seemed so loud, obnoxious, and vulgar. And the white parents were either screaming at their kids, threatening them with some form of punishment or hitting them. After spending a day around white people, I was always happy to go back to the reservation where people followed a relaxed yet respectful code of relating with each other. The easy teasing and joking that were inherent with the Lakota were a welcome relief after a day with the plastic faces.

I vividly remember two occasions during my childhood in which I was cognizant of being an Indian. The first time was at about three years of age when my family took me to my first pow-wow. I kept asking my grandmother, "Where are the Indians?

431

Where are the Indians? Are they going to have bows and arrows?" I was very curious and strangely excited about the prospect of seeing real live Indians even though I myself was one. It's a memory that has remained with me through all these years because it's so full of the subtleties of my culture. There was a sweet wonderful aroma in the air from the dancers and from the traditional food booths. There were lots of grandmothers and grandfathers with young children running about. Pow-wows in the Plains usually last for three days, sometimes longer, with Indian people traveling from all parts of our country to dance, to share food and laughter, and to be with each other. I could sense the importance of our gathering times and it was the beginning of my awareness that my people are a great and different nation.

The second time in my childhood when I knew very clearly that I am Indian occurred when I was attending an all-white (except for me) elementary school. During Halloween my friends and I went trick or treating. At one of the last stops, the mother knew all of the children except for me. She asked me to remove my mask so she could see who I was. After I removed my mask, she realized I was an Indian and quite cruelly told me so, refusing to give me the treats my friends had received. It was a stingingly painful experience.

I told my mother about it the next evening after I tried to understand it. My mother was outraged and explained the realities of being an Indian in South Dakota. My mother paid a visit to the woman, which resulted in their expressing a barrage of equal hatred for one another. I remember sitting in our pick-up hearing the intensity of the anger and feeling very sad that my mother had to defend her child to someone who wasn't worthy of her presence.

I spent a part of my childhood feeling great sadness and helplessness about how it seemed that Indians were open game for the white people, to kill, maim, beat up, insult, rape, cheat, or whatever atrocity the white people wanted to play with. There was also a rage and frustration that has not died. When I look back on reservation life, it seems that I spent a great deal of time attending the funerals of my relatives or friends of my family. During one year I went to funerals of four murder victims. Most of my non-Indian friends have not seen a dead body or have not been to a funeral. Death was so common on the reservation that I did

not understand the implications of the high death rate until after I moved away and was surprised to learn that I've seen more dead bodies than my friends will probably ever see in their lifetime.

Because of experiencing racial violence, I sometimes panic when I'm the only non-white in a roomful of whites, even if they are my closest friends; I wonder if I'll leave the room alive. The seemingly copacetic gay world of San Francisco becomes a mere dream after the panic leaves. I think to myself that it's truly insane for me to feel the panic. I want to scream out my anger and disgust with myself for feeling distrustful of my white friends and I want to banish the society that has fostered those feelings of alienation. I wonder at the amount of assimilation which has affected me and how long my "Indianness" will allow me to remain in a city that is far removed from the lives of many Native Americans.

"Alienation" and "assimilation" are two common words used to describe contemporary Indian people. I've come to despise those two words because what leads to "alienation" and "assimilation" should not be so concisely defined. And I generally mistrust words that are used to define Native Americans and Brown People. I don't like being put under a magnifying glass and having cute liberal terms describe who I am. The "alienation" or "assimilation" that I manifest is often in how I speak. There isn't necessarily a third world language but there is an Indian way of talking that is an essential part of me. I like it, I love it, yet I deny it. I "save" it for when I'm around other Indians. It is a way of talking that involves "Indian humor" which I know for sure non-Indian people would not necessarily understand.

Articulate. Articulate. I've heard that word used many times to describe third world people. White people seem so surprised to find brown people who can speak fluent English and are even perhaps educated. We then become "articulate." I think I spend a lot of time being articulate with white people. Or as one person said to me a few years ago, "Gee, you don't seem like an Indian from the reservation."

I often read about the dilemmas of contemporary Indians caught between the white and Indian worlds. For most of us, it is an uneasy balance to maintain. Sometimes some of us are not so successful with it. Native Americans have a very high suicide rate.

When I was about 20, I dreamt of myself at the age of 25–26, standing at a place on my reservation, looking to the North, watching a glorious, many-colored horse galloping toward me from the sky. My eyes were riveted and attracted to the beauty and overwhelming strength of the horse. The horse's eyes were staring directly into mine, hypnotizing me and holding my attention. Slowly from the East, an eagle was gliding toward the horse. My attention began to be drawn toward the calm of the eagle but I still did not want to lose sight of the horse. Finally the two met with the eagle sailing into the horse causing it to disintegrate. The eagle flew gently on.

I take this prophetic dream as an analogy of my balance between the white [horse] and Indian [eagle] worlds. Now that I am 26, I find that I've gone as far into my exploration of the white world as I want. It doesn't mean that I'm going to run off to live in a tipi. It simply means that I'm not interested in pursuing a society that uses analysis, research, and experimentation to concretize their vision of cruel destinies for those who are not bastards of the Pilgrims; a society with arrogance rising, moon in oppression, and sun in destruction.

Racism is not easy for me to write about because of my own racism toward other people of color, and because of a complex set of "racisms" within the Indian community. At times animosity exists between half-breed, full-blood, light-skinned Indians, dark-skinned Indians, and non-Indians who attempt to pass as Indians. The U.S. government has practiced for many years its divisiveness in the Indian community by instilling and perpetuating these Indian versus Indian tactics. Native Americans are the foremost group of people who continuously fight against premeditated cultural genocide.

I've grown up with misconceptions about Blacks, Chicanos, and Asians. I'm still in the process of trying to eliminate my racist pictures of other people of color. I know most of *my* images of other races come from television, books, movies, newspapers, and magazines. Who can pinpoint exactly where racism comes from? There are certain political dogmas that are excellent in their "analysis" of racism and how it feeds the capitalist system. To intellectually understand that it is wrong or politically incorrect to be racist leaves me cold. A lot of poor or working class white and brown people are just as racist as the "capitalist pig." We are *all* continually pumped with gross and inaccurate images of everyone else and we *all* pump it out. I don't think there are easy answers or formulas. My personal attempts at eliminating my racism have to start at the base level of those mindsets that inhibit my relationships with people.

Racism among third world people is an area that needs to be discussed and dealt with honestly. We form alliances loosely based on the fact that we have a common oppressor, yet we do not have a commitment to talk about our own fears and misconceptions about each other. I've noticed that liberal, consciousness-raised white people tend to be incredibly polite to third world people at parties or other social situations. It's almost as if they make a point to SHAKE YOUR HAND or to introduce themselves and then run down all the latest right-on third world or Native American books they've just read. On the other hand it's been my experience that if there are several third world gay people at a party, we make a point of avoiding each other, and spend our time talking to the whites to show how sophisticated and intelligent we are. I've always wanted to introduce myself to other third world people but wondered how I would introduce myself or what would I say. There are so many things I would want to say, except sometimes I don't want to remember I'm Third World or Native American. I don't want to remember sometimes because it means recognizing that we're outlaws.

At the Third World Gay Conference in October 1979, the Asian and Native American people in attendance felt the issues affecting us were not adequately included in the workshops. Our representation and leadership had minimal input, which resulted in a skimpy educational process about our struggles. The conference glaringly pointed out to us the narrow definition held by some people that third world means black people only. It was a depressing experience to sit in the lobby of Harambee House with other Native Americans and Asians, feeling removed from other third world groups with whom there is supposed to be this automatic solidarity and empathy. The Indian group sat in my motel room discussing and exchanging our experiences within the third world context. We didn't spend much time in workshops conducted by other third world people because of feeling unwelcomed at the conference and demoralized by having an invisible presence. What's worse than being invisible among your own kind?

It is of particular importance to us as third world gay people to begin a serious interchange of sharing and educating ourselves about each other. We not only must struggle with the racism and homophobia of straight white America, but must often struggle with the homophobia that exists within our third world communities. Being third world doesn't always connote a political awareness or activism. I've met a number of third world and Native American lesbians who've said they're just into "being themselves," and that politics has no meaning in their lives. I agree that everyone is entitled to "be themselves" but in a society that denies respect and basic rights to people because of their ethnic background, I feel that individuals cannot idly sit by and allow themselves to be co-opted by the dominant society. I don't know what moves a person to be politically active or to attempt to raise the quality of life in our world. I only know what motivates my political responsibility . . . the death of Anna Mae Aquash— Native American freedom fighter—"mysteriously" murdered by a bullet in the head; Raymond Yellow Thunder—forced to dance naked in front of a white VFW club in Nebraska—murdered; Rita Silk-Nauni—imprisoned for life for defending her child; my dear friend Mani Lucas-Papago—shot in the back of the head outside of a gay bar in Phoenix. The list could go on and on. My Native American History, recent and past, moves me to continue as a political activist.

And in the white gay community there is rampant racism which is never adequately addressed or acknowledged. My friend Chrystos from the Menominee Nation gave a poetry reading in May 1980, at a Bay Area feminist bookstore. Her reading consisted of poems and journal entries in which she wrote honestly from her heart about the many "isms" and contradictions in most of our lives. Chrystos' bluntly revealing observations on her experiences with the white-lesbian-feminist community are similar to mine and are probably echoed by other lesbians of color.

Her honesty was courageous and should be representative of the kind of forum our community needs to openly discuss mutual racism. A few days following Chrystos' reading, a friend who was in the same bookstore overheard a white lesbian denounce Chrystos' reading as anti-lesbian and racist.

A few years ago, a white lesbian telephoned me requesting an interview, explaining that she was taking Native American courses at a local university, and that she needed data for her paper on gay Native Americans. I agreed to the interview with the idea that I would be helping a "sister" and would also be able to educate her about Native American struggles. After we completed the interview, she began a diatribe on how sexist Native Americans are, followed by a questioning session in which I was to enlighten her mind about why Native Americans are so sexist. I attempted to rationally answer her inanely racist and insulting questions, although my inner response was to tell her to remove herself from my house. Later it became very clear how I had been manipulated as a sounding board for her ugly and distorted views about Native Americans. Her arrogance and disrespect were characteristic of the racist white people in South Dakota. If I tried to point it out, I'm sure she would have vehemently denied her racism.

During the Brigg's initiative scare, I was invited to speak at a rally to represent Native American solidarity against the initiative. The person who spoke prior to me expressed a pro-Bakke sentiment which the audience booed and hissed. His comments left the predominantly white audience angry and in disruption. A white lesbian stood up demanding that a third world person address the racist comments he had made. The MC, rather than taking responsibility for restoring order at the rally, realized that I was the next speaker and I was also T-H-I-R-D-W-O-R-L-D!! I refused to address the remarks of the previous speaker because of the attitudes of the MC and the white lesbian that only third world people are responsible for speaking out against racism. *It is inappropriate for progressive or liberal white people to expect warriors in brown armor to eradicate racism.* There must be co-responsibility from people of color and white people to equally work on this issue. It is not just MY responsibility to point out and educate about racist activities and beliefs.

Redman, redskin, savage, heathen, injun, american indian, first americans, indigenous peoples, natives, amerindian, native american, nigger, negro, black, wet back, greaser, mexican, spanish, latin, hispanic, chicano, chink, oriental, asian, disadvantaged, special interest group, minority, third world, fourth world, people of color, illegal aliens—oh, yes, about them, will the U.S. government recognize that the Founding Fathers (you know George Washington and all those guys) are this country's first illegal aliens.

We are named by others and we are named by ourselves.

Epilogue . . .

Following writing most of this, I went to visit my home in South Dakota. It was my first visit in eight years. I kept putting off my visit year after year because I could not tolerate the white people there and the ruralness and poverty of the reservation. And

because in the eight years since I left home, I came out as a lesbian. My visit home was overwhelming. Floods and floods of locked memories broke. I rediscovered myself there in the hills, on the prairies, in the sky, on the road, in the quiet nights, among the stars, listening to the distant yelps of coyotes, walking on Lakota earth, seeing Bear Butte, looking at my grandparents' cragged faces, standing under wakiyan, smelling the Paha Sapa [Black Hills], and being with my precious circle of relatives.

My sense of time changed, my manner of speaking changed, and a certain freedom with myself returned.

I was sad to leave but recognized that a significant part of myself has never left and never will. And that part is what gives me strength—the strength of my people's enduring history and continuing belief in the sovereignty of our lives.

Note

1. Bureau of Indian Affairs.

Questions for Critical Thinking

1. Cameron discusses the hatred that she felt toward white people at a very early age. How is this hatred different from the racism that whites direct at American Indians?
2. What are some ways of eliminating the hatred that Cameron felt?
3. How does equating the contempt members of marginalized groups possess for whites with the racism that whites direct at people of color keep us from finding solutions to racism?

THE TRANSGENDER CRUCIBLE

Sabrina Rubin Erdely

The following essay details the experiences of CeCe McDonald, a transgender woman who endured homelessness and other hardships as a teen and was later charged with murder when defending herself from an attacker. Her experiences of survival despite the violence she has faced have helped to transform her into a hero for the rights of transgender people.

Dozen eggs, bacon, maybe some biscuits: CeCe McDonald had a modest shopping list in mind, just a few things for breakfast the next day. It was midnight, the ideal time for a supermarket run. Wearing a lavender My Little Pony T-shirt and denim cutoffs, CeCe grabbed her purse for the short walk to the 24-hour Cub Foods. She preferred shopping at night, when the darkened streets provided some relief from the stares, whispers and insults she encountered daily as a transgender woman. CeCe, 23, had grown accustomed to snickers and double takes—and was practiced in talking back to strangers who'd announce, "That's a man!" But such encounters were tiring; some days a lady just wanted to buy her groceries in peace.

And so it was that on a warm Saturday night in June 2011, CeCe and four friends, all African-Americans in their twenties, found themselves strolling the tree-lined streets of her quiet working-class Longfellow neighborhood in Minneapolis, toward a commercial strip. Leading the way was CeCe's roommate Latavia Taylor and two purse-carrying gay men—CeCe's makeshift family, whom she called "cousin" and "brothers"—with CeCe, a fashion student at a local community college, and her lanky boyfriend trailing behind. They were passing the Schooner Tavern when they heard the jeering.

"Faggots."

Gathered outside the dive bar were a handful of cigarette-smoking white people, looking like an aging biker gang in their T-shirts, jeans and bandannas, motorcycles parked nearby. Hurling the insults were 47-year-old Dean Schmitz, in a white button-down and thick silver chain, and his 40-year-old ex-girl-friend Molly Flaherty, clad in black, drink in hand. "Look at that boy dressed as a girl, tucking his dick in!" hooted Schmitz, clutching two beer bottles freshly fetched from his Blazer, as CeCe and her friends slowed to a stop. "You niggers need to go back to Africa!"

Chrishaun "CeCe" McDonald stepped in front of her friends, a familiar autopilot kicking in, shunting fury and fear to a distant place while her mouth went into motion. "Excuse me. We are people, and you need to respect us," CeCe began in her lisping delivery, one acrylic-nailed finger in the air, her curtain of orange microbraids swaying. With her caramel skin, angled jaw and square chin, friends called her "CeCe" for her resemblance to the singer Ciara; even her antagonist Flaherty would later describe CeCe as "really pretty." "We're just trying to walk to the store," CeCe continued, raising her voice over the blare of Schmitz and Flaherty's free-associating invective: "bitches with dicks," "faggot-lovers," "niggers," "rapists." The commotion was drawing more patrons out of the bar—including a six-foot-eight, 310-pound biker in leather chaps—and CeCe's boyfriend, Larry Thomas, nervously called to Schmitz, "Enjoy your night, man—just leave us alone." CeCe and her friends turned to go. Then Flaherty glanced at Schmitz and laughed.

"I'll take all of you bitches on!" Flaherty hollered, and smashed CeCe in the side of her face with a glass tumbler.

Just like that, a mundane walk to the store turned into a street brawl, in a near-farcical clash of stereotypes. Pandemonium erupted as CeCe and Flaherty seized each other by the hair; the bikers swung fists and hurled beer bottles, hollering "beat that faggot ass!"; and CeCe's friends flailed purses and cracked their studded belts as whips. When the two sides separated, panting and disoriented, Flaherty was curled up amid the broken glass screaming, mistakenly, that she'd been knifed, and CeCe stood over her, her T-shirt drenched with her own blood. Touching her cheek, CeCe felt a shock of pain as her finger entered the open wound where Flaherty's glass had punctured her salivary gland. Purse still over her shoulder, CeCe fast-walked from the scene. She'd made it more than a half-block away when she heard her friends calling, "Watch your back!"

CeCe whirled around to see Schmitz heading toward her: walking, then running, his face a twist of wild, unrestrained hatred. CeCe felt terror burst out from that remote place where she normally locked it away. She didn't know that Schmitz's veins were pounding with cocaine and meth. She didn't know of his lengthy rap sheet, including convictions for assault. Nor did she know that under Schmitz's shirt, inked across his solar plexus, was a four-inch swastika tattoo. All CeCe needed to see was the look on his face to know her worst fears were coming true: Her young life was about to end as a grim statistic, the victim of a hate crime.

"Come here, bitch!" Schmitz roared as he closed in. CeCe pedaled backward, blood dripping from her slashed face.

"Didn't y'all get enough?" CeCe asked, defiant and afraid, while her hand fished into her large handbag for anything to protect herself. Her fingers closed on a pair of black-handled fabric scissors she used for school. She held them up high as a warning, their five-inch blades glinting in the parking-lot floodlights. Schmitz stopped an arm's length away, raising clenched fists and shuffling his feet in a boxing stance. His eyes were terrible with rage.

"Bitch, you gonna stab me?" he shouted. They squared off for a tense moment: the furious white guy, amped up on meth, Nazi tattoo across his belly; the terrified black trans woman with a cartoon pony on her T-shirt; the scissors between them. CeCe saw Schmitz lunge toward her and braced herself for impact. Their bodies collided, then separated. He was still looking at her.

"Bitch—you stabbed me!"

"Yes, I did," CeCe announced, even as she wondered if that could possibly be true; in the adrenaline of the moment, she'd felt nothing. Scanning Schmitz over, she saw no sign of injury—though in fact he'd sustained a wound so grisly that CeCe would later recall to police that the button-down shirt Schmitz wore that night was not white but "mainly red. Like one of them Hawaiian shirts." CeCe waited until he turned to rejoin his crowd. Then she and Thomas ran arm in arm down the block toward the nearly empty Cub Foods parking lot, where they waited for police to arrive.

They didn't see the scene unfolding behind them: how Schmitz took a few faltering steps, uttered, "I'm bleeding," then lifted his shirt to unleash a geyser of blood. CeCe had stabbed him in the chest, burying the blade almost three and a half inches deep, slicing his heart. Blood sprayed the road as Schmitz staggered, collapsed and, amid his friends' screams, died. When CeCe and Thomas waved down a police car minutes later, she was promptly handcuffed and arrested.

Given the swift political advances of the transgender movement, paired with its new pop-culture visibility, you'd be forgiven for believing that to be gender-nonconforming today is to be accepted, celebrated, even trendy—what with trans models in ads for American Apparel and Barneys; Facebook's more than 50 gender options for users to choose from; and

Eurovision song-contest winner Conchita Wurst, who accepted the trophy in an evening gown and a full beard. When this spring Secretary of Defense Chuck Hagel recommended a review of the military's ban on allowing trans people to serve openly—by one estimate, trans people are as much as twice as likely as the general U.S. population to serve in the armed forces—his announcement seemed to herald a new era of recognition. But the appearance of tolerance belies the most basic day-to-day reality: No community living in America today is as openly terrorized as transgender women, especially trans women of color. "Every day a trans person says, 'I may die today,'" says trans woman Miasha Forbes. "You ready yourself for war each day." Leaving the house on a typical day, a trans woman prepares herself to endure indignities unimaginable to most of us: to be pelted by rocks, called slurs or referred to not as "she" or even "he," but rather as "it."

"Just being trans out on the street is cause for our lives to be in danger," says trans actress Laverne Cox, who says she envisioned her Orange Is the New Black character, Sophia Burset, as a homage to CeCe McDonald. "So many times I've been walking on the street as a trans woman and been harassed, called a man—one time I was kicked," she adds. "Any of them could have escalated into someone doing me harm. I very easily could be CeCe."

Living with a gender identity different from one's birth anatomy (a phenomenon thought to affect as many as one in 10,000 people) means that trans women live with constant anxiety of being recognized as trans—"getting spooked" or "getting clocked"—because reactions can be harsh to the extreme. Though transgender people make up perhaps 10 percent of the LGBT community, they account for a shocking proportion of its hate-crime statistics, with trans people nearly twice as likely to be threatened as their LGB peers. And trans people all too often meet with violent deaths: Of the 25 reported anti-LGBT homicides in 2012, according to the National Coalition of Anti-Violence Programs, transgender people accounted for more than half of the victims. All of those trans homicide victims were trans women of color.

Highlighting the danger, transgender murders tend to be gruesome, often involving torture and mutilation, as in the 2012 California murder of 37-year-old Brandy Martell, who was shot in the genitals; or the brutal hatchet slaying last July in Philadelphia of 31-year-old Diamond Williams, whose body was hacked to pieces and strewn in an overgrown lot. After Williams' alleged killer reportedly confessed that he'd killed Williams, a prostitute he'd solicited, when he'd realized she was trans—commonly known as the "trans panic defense"—online commenters were quick to agree "the cross-dresser had it coming": that Williams' transgender status was an act of duplicity whose logical punishment was death. "It's socially sanctioned to say that," says Cox. "If a guy is even attracted to her, then she has to die. What is that?" And when these cases go unresolved, as they often do—like last summer's vicious Harlem beating death of 21-year-old Islan Nettles, reportedly after a catcalling admirer turned vengeful—the lack of resolution seems a further reminder to trans women of their own disposability. It's telling that the closest thing the trans community has to a long-running Pride event is Transgender Day of Remembrance, a day of mourning for victims of violence.

"It takes a toll. This life is not an easy life," says trans woman Anya Stacy Neal. "Trust me, if this was a choice, I would have packed it up a long time ago."

As the sisterhood is picked off one by one, each gets a chilling vision of her own fate. "You rarely hear of a trans woman just living a long life and then dying of old age," says CeCe today, seated at a friend's Minneapolis dining-room table with her legs crossed ladylike at the knee. Wearing a striped cardigan that she opens to reveal, laughing, a T-shirt reading IT'S ALL ABOUT ME, CeCe's an animated run-on talker with a lip ring and a warm, open nature, whose cadences recall the church days of her youth, mouth opening wide to flash a tongue stud. "You never hear, 'She passed on her own, natural causes, old age,' no, no, no," she continues, ticking off on her fingers. "She's either raped and killed, she's jumped and killed, stalked and killed—or just killed." Which is why, amid all the death and sorrow, CeCe, whose jagged life experience embodies the archetypal trans woman's in so many ways, has become an LGBT folk hero for her story of survival—and for the price she paid for fighting back.

***

By age eight, CeCe McDonald was fascinated by the beauty rituals of the women in her family. Watching reverently from a doorway as her mother and aunts clucked over outfits, swiped on lipstick and examined themselves in the mirror—casually engaged in the intimate, luxuriant rites of femininity—she ached to join them someday. "Even seeing my grandma get ready for church, putting on her pearl earrings and her White Diamonds perfume, it was really powerful," remembers CeCe. "I felt like I was a guest in their presence, these superwomen who are fucking fabulous and have these great shoes and cute clothes. And I thought, 'Yeah! That's the person that I am.'"

From earliest childhood CeCe had felt at odds with her boy's body, boyish clothes and boy's name (a name that she still can't discuss without anguish). She'd always felt such an irrepressible girlishness. In grade school she walked with graceful wrists and swishing hips, to the consternation of her family. CeCe was the oldest of seven, raised on Chicago's gritty South Side by a single mother; a dozen family members crammed under one roof, where no one could fail to notice young CeCe sashaying in her mother's heels. "You need to pray that out of you," her religious family instructed, and at night, CeCe tearfully pleaded with God to take away her sinful attraction to boys. Better yet, she prayed to awaken a girl, in the body He had surely meant for her.

She redoubled her prayers as other kids began to mock her femininity, and their taunts turned violent. CeCe was chased through the neighborhood, beaten up and, around seventh grade, attacked by five high schoolers yelling "kill that faggot," who kicked her in the mouth so savagely that her incisor tore through the skin above her lip. Such bullying is the norm for transgender kids, nearly nine out of 10 of whom are harassed by peers, and 44 percent of whom are physically assaulted. But no number of beatings could change CeCe. In school she'd dash into the girls' bathroom when the coast was clear, frightened of being seen in the boys' room sitting down to pee. She joined the cheer-leading squad—gleefully doing splits at basketball games—coming to class in her mom's blouse or platform shoes, though she'd change back into boy clothes before returning home, fearful of her family's wrath, and of losing the love of her mother,

who was trying to persuade CeCe onto a more traditional path.

"It kind of scared me," says mom Christi McDonald of CeCe's femininity. "I know it's a cruel world, and if you're different it's hard for people to accept you." Christi bought CeCe baggy jeans and dropped hints about cute girls, just as when CeCe was smaller Christi had urged her to draw pictures of Superman instead of sketching dresses. "I kept questioning him, 'Why are you doing this?'" Christi says, adjusting her pronouns to add, "I just wanted a peaceful life for her."

CeCe had always tried staying in her mom's good graces by being a responsible, diligent child, constantly neatening the house, making the beds and whipping up recipes inspired by cooking shows, but nonetheless she felt her mother grow distant. CeCe was unable to find sanctuary with her family, and tensions grew in the crowded three-bedroom house. One day, an uncle found an undelivered love note she'd written to a boy and, CeCe says, knocked her to the kitchen floor and choked her. She ran away from home, never to return. She was 14.

She crashed with friends before taking up residence in a glorified drug den where other runaways congregated. CeCe tried to see the bright side of her family's rejection: She was finally free to be herself. The first time she tried on a bra and panties, she felt a shiver of recognition that she was headed in the right direction. Instead, she fell right through a trapdoor. She'd reached a crucial point in the too-typical trans woman's narrative, in which, cut loose at a young age from family, she falls directly into harm's way. Up to 40 percent of U.S. homeless youth are LGBT. Adrift without money, shelter, education or a support system, they're exposed to myriad dangers. According to one study, 58 percent of LGBT homeless youth are sexually assaulted (compared with 33 percent of their hetero peers). Drug and alcohol use is rampant. CeCe grew up fast. "Honey, I think there's not too much in this world that I haven't heard or seen or done," she tells me. "And a lot of that is sad."

She learned to sell crack and marijuana. Out in the streets, her appearance in girls' clothing was met with outbursts of violence, as when a man once threw an empty 40-ounce bottle at her head, knocking her unconscious; another time, a stranger pulled a knife.

Even more traumatic, a handsome man lured CeCe into his home with an invitation to smoke weed—"I was like, 'Oh, my goodness, this is so cool.' Very naive, thinking everybody is good"—then pushed her face-forward onto his bed and anally raped her. The assault changed CeCe profoundly, crystallizing how expendable she was in the eyes of the world. Never had she felt so degraded, and so certain no one would care. Living in poverty and unpredictability so extreme that she sometimes found herself sleeping on park benches and eating grass to fill her belly, CeCe decided to offer herself in the one last arena where she felt she had worth.

At 15, CeCe was a child prostitute working the strip off Belmont Avenue in Boys-town, climbing into men's cars to earn up to $1,000 on a Saturday night. In choosing the sex trade, CeCe was heading down a well-worn path. Studies of urban trans-gender women have found that upward of 50 percent had engaged in sex work. It's a risky job, in which the threat of violence is only one hazard. Transgender women are considered the fastest-growing HIV-positive population in the country, with a meta-analysis showing that nearly 28 percent of trans women in America have the virus. Bearing the highest risk are trans women in sex work, who are four times more likely to be living with HIV than other female sex workers.

CeCe got through each sex act by thinking about the cash, which not only kept her and her friends stocked with food and weed and liquor, but granted her the illusion of power. No longer merely a homeless trans teen, she recast herself as a fierce independent woman getting her coin, a sexy Donna Summer lyric sprung to life. "There is some type of pride in that," says CeCe. "I felt like, 'No bitch can touch me, I gets all the men, with all the money, and who gonna do something about it?' And that made me feel like I was on top." She also reveled in the ego boost of having her femininity affirmed for the very first time, her paying clientele proof of her irresistibility. But despite the pep talks she gave herself, CeCe was sickened by the way she'd turned her own body into a commodity available to anyone. "They saw me as an object; they saw me as their fantasy. And for a long time that's how I viewed myself, as a fantasy." She set a price on her own life, permitting sex without condoms for a premium.

"I became this soulless drone," says CeCe. She entertained a dim hope she'd get AIDS and die. She was tired of internalizing hostility and worthlessness, mentally exhausted from constantly scanning for danger. Such daily burdens take a heavy toll: Though the suicide-attempt rate in the general population is estimated to be 4.6 percent, the National Transgender Discrimination Survey found that an extraordinary 41 percent of trans respondents had attempted suicide, with the rate soaring to 64 percent for sexual-assault victims. The first time CeCe attempted suicide, it was with pills washed down with a bottle of NyQuil. The second time, she crushed up a pile of pills and drank it down with juice. Asked how many times she tried to kill herself, CeCe has to think for a long moment; it's hard to sort out, since her late teens were basically an extended death wish. So much so that when one night a man on a street corner pointed a gun at her, shouting, "Faggot, I'll kill you," CeCe just looked at him and said, "Shoot me."

Surely it would have been far easier for CeCe if she'd given up, renounced her womanhood and opted to live life as a gay man. And yet even in her darkest despair, CeCe never considered retreat an option. If she was going to continue living, it was going to be as a lady. For her there was no decision-making; she felt she couldn't "choose" to be a man, because she'd never been male to begin with.

"I wasn't born a boy," she says heatedly. "I was born a baby." Like many trans women, CeCe disputes her basic narrative as that of a boy who grew up to be a woman. Rather, hers is a story of mistaken identity, of a person assigned the wrong gender at birth. She doesn't know why she was created with a boy's anatomy but with the mind and soul of a girl; all she could do was work with the mixed-up results. "If the Creator, whoever He-She-They are, wanted me to be a certain way, that's how They would've made me," CeCe declares at the bohemian Minneapolis coffee shop Cafe South-Side, which serves as a local LGBT hub. "But until then, until all this shit is figured out? I'm-a rock this. Till the wheels fall off," she says, one balletic hand in the air testifying, flashing electric-yellow fingernails. Across the table a friend, a lesbian poet in Buddy Holly glasses, laughs with appreciation, as does the proprietress behind the cash register. "Till the wheels fall off. Mmmph!" CeCe exclaims with a flourish. "Crop tops and all, trust and believe that!"

That unflagging enthusiasm for her feminine identity, fused with her magnetic talent for making friends, helped push CeCe forward through her teenage years, until in 2008 she found herself as a 20-year-old living in St. Paul. "Hiiii! Y'all taking job applications?" she'd sing as she strode into yet another retail store or restaurant. Reluctantly checking "male" on her application, CeCe would subtly scan people's faces for that telltale twinge of discomfort, a sure sign that no job would be forthcoming; trans people have reported twice the unemployment rate as the general population. She tried not to let her spirits sink when she didn't get a callback. CeCe was intent on finding a job, which was a cornerstone of her plan to turn her life around.

She'd taken a Greyhound bus to the Twin Cities two years earlier on a whim, hoping to escape her Chicago misery and start anew. Instead she'd been floundering, in and out of shelters, flirting with coke and meth addictions, jailed for shoplifting and other misdemeanors, and hospitalized for suicidal ideation. But she'd also started visiting a drop-in youth center, where she learned how to regain control of her life bit by bit. "CeCe caught my attention right away," says her case manager Abby Beasley. "Her energy, she's just so bubbly, laughing constantly, just a real loving person. I put more work into her than I did anybody else, trying to help her stabilize her life."

Education was a first step: CeCe earned her GED, then enrolled in Minneapolis Community and Technical College, focusing on fashion design. Estrogen came next. A doctor diagnosed CeCe with gender dysphoria—determining that there was an incongruity between her biological sex and her gender identity—after which she started wearing a hormone patch on her hip, the cost covered by state medical assistance. CeCe watched with amazement as over the following months she developed smooth skin, fuller hips and, most fulfilling of all, breasts. Finally seeing her outer self match her inner self "was definitely something like a relief," she remembers. In an important move for CeCe, she called her mother to re-establish ties after years of separation. "Are those real?" Christi exclaimed when she finally got her first glimpse of CeCe post-hormones, and CeCe laughed in reply.

A legal name change tied a ribbon on CeCe's transition, a bureaucratic process that yielded a government ID identifying her by her carefully chosen new name: Chrishaun Reed Mai'luv McDonald. It was a name she liked for its mystique and personality; Chrishaun was also her aunt's name, keeping her tethered just a little bit to her past.

Secure in her identity at last, CeCe felt something free up within herself. And with confidence also came a new ability to stand up to street harassment; for perhaps the first time, she felt herself truly worth defending. "It's not OK that you called me a tranny," she'd lecture a surprised heckler. "You're gonna apologize, and then you're gonna go home and think about why you turned my pretty smile into an ugly mug." Satisfied, she'd coolly walk on, her self-respect growing with each small triumph.

"She looked like someone who knew where she was heading in life," says Larry Thomas, who caught sight of CeCe at a corner store and, knowing full well she was trans, gave her his phone number—thus beginning, in fits and starts, that thing that eludes so many trans women: an actual in-the-daylight relationship. Thomas was a straight man who usually kept his "flings" with trans women on the down-low. But CeCe began occupying much of his time, and she started to wonder if she wasn't doomed to live a lonely life after all.

Then came more good fortune, when in May 2011, after a decade of couch-surfing homelessness, CeCe moved into the very first apartment of her own. It was a two-bedroom oasis she shared with a roommate. Though still unemployed—CeCe paid her rent with general assistance and SSI—she was certain now that she was a college student with a permanent address, that remaining piece of the puzzle would be forthcoming.

"I was feeling really accomplished," remembers CeCe wistfully as she stands on the sidewalk looking up at the weather-beaten three-story brick apartment building on an early spring day. She tries flashing her patented wide smile, but it evaporates. We're taking a tour through her old neighborhood, and in skinny jeans, cropped jacket and a colorful head scarf, CeCe points at the second-floor window where she once lived, so full of potential and promise—a period that lasted for a single, shining month.

"I was just so happy with myself," she says, taking a fretful pull off her Newport. "I was unstoppable." She stubs out her cigarette and heads resolutely toward the passenger seat of my car for the next, most difficult stop on this sightseeing trip.

We drive slowly down East 29th Street, tracing the path CeCe walked just after midnight on June 5th, 2011. CeCe hasn't been back here since that fateful night, and as a maroon brick building with neon Bud Light signs comes into view, she clamps a hand to her belly. "Oooh, Jesus. I just get that little feeling inside," she says. We pull up alongside Schooner Tavern. "So. This is the bar," CeCe says, then in a sudden panic buries her face in her hands and hyperventilates, whispering, "Oh, my God. Oh, Lord, Lord, Lord. Oh, my goodness, Jesus Christ." A half-block past the bar CeCe speaks again, her voice trembling. "And somewhere at this point," she says, "is where I stabbed him."

In a police interrogation room hours after the stabbing, CeCe had given a full confession. "I was only trying to defend myself," CeCe sobbed. Police interviews with nearly a dozen witnesses would paint a consistent picture of the events of that night: Dean Schmitz and Molly Flaherty started the confrontation, Flaherty had triggered the fight by breaking a glass on CeCe's face, and Schmitz had pursued CeCe when she'd tried to escape—all precisely the way CeCe recounted in her confession. But no witness had seen exactly how the stabbing had transpired. "I didn't jab him; I didn't force the scissors into him; he was coming after me," CeCe insisted to detectives. "He ran into the scissors." And yet in Hennepin County Jail, CeCe was shocked to learn she was charged with second-degree murder. She faced up to 40 years in prison.

Dressed in orange scrubs, CeCe would cry and stare at the white brick walls of her cell for hours on end, her thoughts a tangle. There was the horrific knowledge that someone had died by her hand. And there was the agony that the life she'd been trying so hard to build had been decimated in an instant. "There wasn't a moment when I wasn't in pain mentally and spiritually, and even beating myself up for defending myself," CeCe says. She had nothing but time to obsess because she was locked alone in her cell for 23 hours a day. The jail had determined that for her own safety, she be held in solitary confinement.

Trans women have a difficult time behind bars, where they show up in disproportionate numbers; one survey found 16 percent of trans women had been to jail, compared to 2.7 percent of the general population. Once in prison they pose a dilemma, because, as a study of seven California prisons revealed, 59 percent of transgender inmates reported being sexually abused, compared to 4.4 percent of the general inmate population. A common solution, then, is to put them in solitary. For CeCe, who'd previously spent short stints in men's jails, the brain-racking isolation was a form of confinement she'd never known before. "There's no room for sanity," she says of her subsequent mental collapse. When her former caseworker Abby Beasley visited, Beasley was shocked at the sight of CeCe on the other side of the glass, scared and shaken, her left cheek swollen to the size of a golf ball.

"Whatever you can do to help me, please," CeCe begged.

Beasley notified the Trans Youth Support Network, a Minneapolis organization, which secured CeCe a pro bono lawyer. The case immediately galvanized the local trans and queer community, who saw CeCe's attack as something that could easily have happened to any of them, and hailed her as a hero. "CeCe was attacked in a racist, transphobic incident that could have killed her," says Billy Navarro Jr. of the Minnesota Transgender Health Coalition, who helped found the Free CeCe campaign. "And then how is she treated? She is prosecuted for having the audacity to survive."

Her support base grew after the Florida shooting death of Trayvon Martin, which stoked a national debate over race, self-defense and justice. CeCe's supporters argued that unlike George Zimmerman, who would be acquitted of all charges, CeCe had been faced with an actual threat, against which she had stood her ground. But they feared the justice system would view CeCe, as a black trans woman, unkindly. A petition advocating for CeCe's release gathered more than 18,000 signatures from across the country. As supporters in FREE CECE T-shirts held rallies outside the jail and packed the courthouse for each hearing, defense lawyer Hersch Izek set about building a case.

"CeCe was defending herself against a racist, a bigot, someone who had all sorts of issues against the LGBT community," says Izek, an aging hippie with long, sparse gray hair, a tie-dyed tie and a Bob Marley poster on his office wall. "And you couldn't understand what she did, and what this so-called victim did, without that context." The Hennepin County Attorney's Office, however, presented the scenario as simply the slaying of an unarmed man by a person with a weapon—who had a legal obligation to flee the scene. Minnesota forbids the use of deadly force in self-defense if you can avoid being harmed, for example, by running away. Prosecutors speculated that what had in fact occurred between CeCe and Schmitz was the very definition of intentional, unprovoked murder. "CeCe took shears and thrust them into his heart and killed him," says Hennepin County Attorney Michael Freeman. "We try to treat every case being blind to sex, sexual orientation, economic status. And it's not being insensitive to CeCe to say this was a bar fight. The bottom line is, did her actions result in the death of another? The answer is yes."

The months leading to trial saw the judge's rulings laying waste to CeCe's defense case. Evidence of Schmitz's swastika tattoo was deemed inadmissible, since CeCe never saw the tattoo—it had no bearing on her mindset at the time of the killing—and because, Judge Daniel Moreno wrote, "the tattoo does not establish that [Schmitz] intended to threaten, fight or kill anyone." Schmitz's prior assault convictions were deemed irrelevant, and the judge would allow only limited testimony about the toxicology report showing Schmitz was high on meth, feeding his aggression. The defense's bid to include expert testimony about the lives of transgender women also failed. "The idea was to show the violence transgender individuals face, to bolster the self-defense claim," says Izek. "We'd have to be educating the jury about what it meant to be transgender. That would be difficult. Most wouldn't even know what that meant."

Seated at the defense table with a headache on the morning of the trial, May 2nd, 2012, CeCe looked at the mostly white jury staring back at her. She knew those expressions all too well. She'd been intent on seeing her case through, but glancing at those tasked with deciding her fate, she gave up. "These people weren't going to let me win," she says. She accepted a deal and pleaded guilty to second-degree manslaughter. Her supporters in the courtroom cried as the judge led her through her admission of guilt.

CeCe tried her best to choke back tears as she was led from the courtroom, overwhelmed by what was next for her: A 41-month sentence in a state men's prison.

In a tiny office that serves as the de facto Free CeCe headquarters, Navarro, a burly, bearded trans man in overalls, checks his computer for CeCe's fan mail. "Somebody wants to know if you got a tank top?" he asks.

"Oh, T-GIRLS ROCK?" CeCe asks, distracted by her phone.

"Yeah. Can you tweet a picture of you wearing it?" Navarro shoots her an adoring grin. This crammed room tucked next door to Cafe SouthSide is known as the "Shot Clinic" for its main attraction: a brightly lit closet, inside of which a volunteer is currently administering a hormone injection to a trans man. This building serves as headquarters for three Minnesota transgender organizations. Together, the groups have knitted a vibrant infrastructure for the local trans community: improving health care access, arranging support groups, promoting trans artists and hosting parties and concerts. Their grassroots efforts have created a trans refuge, and have earned the Twin Cities a reputation as two of the nation's most trans-friendly, alongside San Francisco, New York and Seattle, each of which boasts similar community-driven hubs tailored around its members' unique needs. The idea for this Shot Clinic, for example, was born of a rather specific need. "Billy's scared of needles," Navarro says of himself faux-bashfully. So he implemented a program that trains volunteers to administer hormones to the squeamish. Fifteen to 20 patients now come in each week; bags of oranges lay around the office for those wanting to perfect their needle-stick technique.

A patient emerges from the closet, face slack with relief, and reports of today's injection volunteer: "He seems to know what he's doing!" Everyone laughs, with CeCe's guffaw, as always, loudest of all. Here, CeCe has found sanctuary. Everyone who bustles through the tiny office pauses to beam at her or give her a squeeze, and she opens her arms to each. She's at home in this space, cherished and protected, but also a star; no matter where she's standing, everyone aligns in her direction.

"She's legendary," one friend says later, and CeCe lets out an open-mouthed cackle. "I like that! Legendary," she repeats.

CeCe was released from the Minnesota Correctional Facility in St. Cloud in January after 19 months, her sentence reduced for good behavior and for the 275 days she'd served prior to trial. While in prison she'd been intent on staying positive and grateful for having continued access to her hormones, and having her own cell with a TV, where she'd escape the hyper-masculinity of her fellow inmates for Sex and the City marathons on E!. She says she never encountered violence, kept mostly to herself and even made a couple of friends. Mostly, she tried to work on recovering, and on remaining sane. When she was notified that Molly Flaherty was being prosecuted for attacking her, CeCe declined to testify, viewing it as a pointless act of vengeance potentially bad for her own mental health. (Flaherty pleaded guilty to third-degree assault and was sentenced to six months in jail.) "It's easy, especially for a person who's been through so much, to be a cruel and coldhearted person. But I chose not to be," CeCe says.

Outside encouragement helped. During her incarceration, the Free CeCe campaign continued spreading via social media, with chapters as far-off as Paris and Glasgow sending her mail. Upon CeCe's release, prominent trans activist Janet Mock asked her Twitter followers to tweet about what CeCe meant to them, and the outpouring of responses sent the hashtag #BecauseOfCeCe trending. CeCe is a little awestruck by her celebrity status. She's been stunned to come across a photo online of her own face tattooed upon a stranger's arm. She's been asked to help lead Seattle's Pride parade. Her parole officer has let her travel to New York and San Francisco to parlay her fame into activism and to film a documentary, Free CeCe, co-produced by Laverne Cox.

And yet to see CeCe trudging down the street from the Shot Clinic to the place she's calling home, you'd never know she's having her moment. Despite a strong network of friends, and the continued affections of her boyfriend—both lifelines to her—she's struggling. She has residual PTSD and trust issues. She's unemployed, and with a felony on her record, she's less hopeful about the job applications she's been filling out. For now, CeCe is living on food stamps and the remaining funds raised by the Free CeCe campaign; for her housing, she's crashing with a kind supporter in a small spare bedroom.

"My story wouldn't have been important had I been killed. Because it's like nobody cares," CeCe says forcefully at her dining-room table, as day turns to evening. A shiny, sickle-shaped scar cuts across the jawbone of her left cheek, a permanent reminder of her tragic walk to the supermarket. "But fortunately for me, I'm a survivor. I'm not gonna beat myself up for being a woman, I'm not gonna beat myself up for being trans, I'm not gonna beat myself up for defending myself." She smacks her lips for punctuation. "'Cause I am a survivor," she repeats in a voice sharp with conviction, while watching carefully for my assent. CeCe's still trying to come to terms with the way that evening disrupted her life, and the ground she must regain. Underneath her aura of loving positivity, she's angry as she grapples to understand her significance to a community that needs her inspiration so badly, and what it means to be heralded as a survivor, when her day-to-day survival feels so frustratingly precarious. She still has to get to the grocery store, after all, and despite all CeCe has been through, she still waits until nightfall.

Questions for Critical Thinking

1. The experiences of CeCe McDonald illustrate the ways in which violence is used as a form of social control. What are some of the ways in which violence is used against people of color and those who identify as transgender to maintain stratification based on race, sex, and gender?

2. Beyond the direct violence exhibited in this essay, what are some of the barriers that people who identify as transgender continue to face in society? How do these barriers impact all of us, regardless of our gender identity?

3. How might the acceptance of people who identify as transgender help to reduce problems of inequality based on sex and gender in society?

NICKEL-AND-DIMED

On (Not) Getting by in America

* *Barbara Ehrenreich*

The following essay is an excerpt from the book *Nickel and Dimed: On (Not) Getting by in America* by journalist Barbara Ehrenreich. In this ethnographic study on low-wage jobs in America, Ehrenreich's experiences illustrate the complexity of barriers faced by workers in such occupations in the United States.

At the beginning of June 1998 I leave behind everything that normally soothes the ego and sustains the body—home, career, companion, reputation, ATM card—for a plunge into the low-wage workforce. There, I become another, occupationally much diminished "Barbara Ehrenreich"—depicted on job-application forms as a divorced homemaker whose sole work experience consists of housekeeping in a few private homes. I am terrified, at the beginning, of being unmasked for what I am: a middle-class journalist setting out to explore the world that welfare mothers are entering, at the rate of approximately 50,000 a month, as welfare reform kicks in. Happily, though, my fears turn out to be entirely unwarranted: during a month of poverty and toil, my name goes unnoticed and for the most part unuttered. In this parallel universe where my father never got out of the mines and I never got through college, I am "baby," "honey," "blondie," and, most commonly, "girl."

My first task is to find a place to live. I figure that if I can earn $7 an hour—which, from the want ads, seems doable—I can afford to spend $500 on rent, or maybe, with severe economies, $600. In the Key West area, where I live, this pretty much confines me to flophouses and trailer homes—like the one, a pleasing fifteen-minute drive from town, that has no air-conditioning, no screens, no fans, no television, and, by way of diversion, only the challenge of evading the landlord's Doberman pinscher. The big problem with this place, though, is the rent, which at $675 a month is well beyond my reach. All right, Key West is expensive. But so is New York City, or the Bay Area, or Jackson Hole, or Telluride, or Boston, or any other place where tourists and the wealthy compete for living space with the people who clean their toilets and fry their hash browns.[1] Still, it is a shock to realize that "trailer trash" has become, for me, a demographic category to aspire to.

So I decide to make the common trade-off between affordability and convenience, and go for a $500-a-month efficiency thirty miles up a two-lane highway from the employment opportunities of Key West, meaning forty-five minutes if there's no road construction and I don't get caught behind some sundazed Canadian tourists. I hate the drive, along a roadside studded with white crosses commemorating the more effective head-on collisions, but it's a sweet little place—a cabin, more or less, set in the swampy back yard of the converted mobile home where my landlord, an affable TV repairman, lives with his bartender girlfriend. Anthropologically speaking, a bustling trailer park would be preferable, but here I have a gleaming white floor and a firm mattress, and the few resident bugs are easily vanquished.

Besides, I am not doing this for the anthropology. My aim is nothing so mistily subjective as to "experience poverty" or find out how it "really feels" to be a long-term low-wage worker. I've had enough unchosen encounters with poverty and the world of low-wage work to know it's not a place you want to visit for touristic purposes; it just smells too much like fear. And with all my real-life assets—bank account, IRA, health insurance, multiroom home—waiting indulgently in the background, I am, of course, thoroughly insulated from the terrors that afflict the genuinely poor.

No, this is a purely objective, scientific sort of mission. The humanitarian rationale for welfare reform—as opposed to the more punitive and stingy impulses that may actually have motivated it—is that work will lift poor women out of poverty while simultaneously inflating their self-esteem and hence their future value in the labor market. Thus, whatever the hassles involved in finding child care, transportation, etc., the transition from welfare to work will end happily, in greater prosperity for all. Now there are many problems with this comforting prediction, such as the fact that the economy will inevitably undergo a downturn, eliminating many jobs. Even without a downturn, the influx of a million former welfare recipients into the low-wage labor market could depress wages by as much as 11.9 percent, according to the Economic Policy Institute (EPI) in Washington, D.C.

But is it really possible to make a living on the kinds of jobs currently available to unskilled people? Mathematically, the answer is no, as can be shown by taking $6 to $7 an hour, perhaps subtracting a dollar or two an hour for child care, multiplying by 160 hours a month, and comparing the result to the prevailing rents. According to the National Coalition for the Homeless, for example, in 1998 it took, on average nationwide, an hourly wage of $8.89 to afford a one-bedroom apartment, and the Preamble Center for Public Policy estimates that the odds against a typical welfare recipient's landing a job at such a "living wage" are about 97 to 1. If these numbers are right, low-wage work is not a solution to poverty and possibly not even to homelessness.

It may seem excessive to put this proposition to an experimental test. As certain family members keep unhelpfully reminding me, the viability of low-wage work could be tested, after a fashion, without ever leaving my study. I could just pay myself $7 an hour for eight hours a day, charge myself for room and board, and total up the numbers after a month. Why leave the people and work that I love? But I am an experimental scientist by training. In that business, you don't just sit at a desk and theorize; you plunge into the everyday chaos of nature, where surprises lurk in the most mundane measurements. Maybe, when I got into it, I would discover some hidden economies in the world of the low-wage worker. After all, if 30 percent of the workforce toils for less than $8 an hour, according to the EPI, they may have found some tricks as yet unknown to me. Maybe—who knows?—I would even be able to detect in myself the bracing psychological effects of getting out of the house, as promised by the welfare wonks at places like the Heritage Foundation. Or, on the other hand, maybe there would be unexpected costs—physical, mental, or financial—to throw off all my calculations. Ideally, I should do this with two small children in tow, that being the welfare average, but mine are grown and no one is willing to lend me theirs for a month-long vacation in penury. So this is not the perfect experiment, just a test of the best possible case: an unencumbered woman, smart and even strong, attempting to live more or less off the land.

On the morning of my first full day of job searching, I take a red pen to the want ads, which are auspiciously numerous. Everyone in Key West's booming "hospitality industry" seems to be looking for someone like me—trainable, flexible, and with suitably humble expectations as to pay. . . .

Most of the big hotels run ads almost continually, just to build a supply of applicants to replace the current workers as they drift away or are fired, so finding a job is just a matter of being at the right place at the right time and flexible enough to take whatever is being offered that day. This finally happens to me at one of the big discount hotel chains, where I go, as usual, for housekeeping and am sent, instead, to try out as a waitress at the attached "family restaurant," a dismal spot with a counter and about thirty tables that looks out on a parking garage and features such tempting fare as "Polish [sic] sausage and BBQ sauce" on 95-degree days. Phillip, the dapper young West Indian who introduces himself as the manager, interviews me with about as much enthusiasm as if he were a clerk processing me for Medicare, the principal questions being what shifts can I work and when can I start. I mutter something about being woefully out of practice as a waitress, but he's already on to the uniform: I'm to show up tomorrow wearing black slacks and black shoes; he'll provide the rust-colored polo shirt with HEARTHSIDE embroidered on it, though I might want to wear my own shirt to get to work, ha ha. At the word "tomorrow," something between fear and indignation rises in my chest. I want to say, "Thank you for your time, sir, but this is just an experiment, you know, not my actual life."

So begins my career at the Hearthside, I shall call it, one small profit center within a global discount hotel chain, where for two weeks I work from 2:00 till 10:00 P.M. for $2.43 an hour plus tips.[2] In some futile bid for gentility, the management has barred employees from using the front door, so my first day I enter through the kitchen, where a red-faced man with shoulder-length blond hair is throwing frozen steaks against the wall and yelling, "Fuck this shit!" "That's just Jack," explains Gail, the wiry middle-aged waitress who is assigned to train me. "He's on the rag again"—a condition occasioned, in this instance, by the fact that the cook on the morning shift had forgotten to thaw out the steaks. For the next eight hours, I run after the agile Gail, absorbing bits of instruction along with fragments of personal

tragedy. All food must be trayed, and the reason she's so tired today is that she woke up in a cold sweat thinking of her boyfriend, who killed himself recently in an upstate prison. No refills on lemonade. And the reason he was in prison is that a few DUIs caught up with him, that's all, could have happened to anyone. Carry the creamers to the table in a monkey bowl, never in your hand. And after he was gone she spent several months living in her truck, peeing in a plastic pee bottle and reading by candlelight at night, but you can't live in a truck in the summer, since you need to have the windows down, which means anything can get in, from mosquitoes on up.

At least Gail puts to rest any fears I had of appearing overqualified. From the first day on, I find that of all the things I have left behind, such as home and identity, what I miss the most is competence. Not that I have ever felt utterly competent in the writing business, in which one day's success augurs nothing at all for the next. But in my writing life, I at least have some notion of procedure: do the research, make the outline, rough out a draft, etc. As a server, though I am beset by requests like bees: more iced tea here, ketchup over there, a to-go box for table fourteen, and where are the high chairs, anyway? Of the twenty-seven tables, up to six are usually mine at any time, though on slow afternoons or if Gail is off, I sometimes have the whole place to myself. There is the touch-screen computer-ordering system to master, which is, I suppose, meant to minimize server–cook contact, but in practice requires constant verbal fine-tuning: "That's gravy on the mashed, okay? None on the meatloaf," and so forth—while the cook scowls as if I were inventing these refinements just to torment him. Plus, something I had forgotten in the years since I was eighteen: about a third of a server's job is "side work" that's invisible to customers—sweeping, scrubbing, slicing, refilling, and restocking. If it isn't all done, every little bit of it, you're going to face the 6:00 P.M. dinner rush defenseless and probably go down in flames. I screw up dozens of times at the beginning, sustained in my shame entirely by Gail's support—"It's okay, baby, everyone does that sometime"—because, to my total surprise and despite the scientific detachment I am doing my best to maintain, I care. . . .

On my first Friday at the Hearthside there is a "mandatory meeting for all restaurant employees," which I attend, eager for insight into our overall marketing strategy and the niche (your basic Ohio cuisine with a tropical twist?) we aim to inhabit. But there is no "we" at this meeting. Phillip, our top manager except for an occasional "consultant" sent out by corporate headquarters, opens it with a sneer: "The break room—it's disgusting. Butts in the ashtrays, newspapers lying around, crumbs." This windowless little room, which also houses the time clock for the entire hotel, is where we stash our bags and civilian clothes and take our half-hour meal breaks. But a break room is not a right, he tells us. It can be taken away. We should also know that the lockers in the break room and whatever is in them can be searched at any time. Then comes gossip; there has been gossip; gossip (which seems to mean employees talking among themselves) must stop. Off-duty employees are henceforth barred from eating at the restaurant, because "other servers gather around them and gossip." When Phillip has exhausted his agenda of rebukes, Joan complains about the condition of the ladies' room and I throw in my two bits about the vacuum cleaner. But I don't see any backup coming from my fellow servers, each of whom has subsided into her own personal funk; Gail, my role model, stares sorrowfully at a point six inches from her nose. The meeting ends when Andy, one of the cooks, gets up, muttering about breaking up his day off for this almighty bullshit.

Just four days later we are suddenly summoned into the kitchen at 3:30 P.M., even though there are live tables on the floor. We all—about ten of us—stand around Phillip, who announces grimly that there has been a report of some "drug activity" on the night shift and that, as a result, we are now to be a "drug-free" workplace, meaning that all new hires will be tested, as will possibly current employees on a random basis. I am glad that this part of the kitchen is so dark, because I find myself blushing as hard as if I had been caught toking up in the ladies' room myself: I haven't been treated this way—lined up in the corridor, threatened with locker searches, peppered with carelessly aimed accusations—since junior high school. Back on the floor, Joan cracks, "Next they'll be telling us we can't have sex on the job."

When I ask Stu what happened to inspire the crackdown, he just mutters about "management decisions" and takes the opportunity to upbraid Gail and me for being too generous with the rolls. From now on there's to be only one per customer, and it goes out with the dinner, not with the salad. He's also been riding the cooks, prompting Andy to come out of the kitchen and observe—with the serenity of a man whose customary implement is a butcher knife—that "Stu has a death wish today."

The other problem, in addition to the less-than-nurturing management style, is that this job shows no sign of being financially viable. You might imagine, from a comfortable distance, that people who live, year in and year out, on $6 to $10 an hour have discovered some survival stratagems unknown to the middle class. But no. It's not hard to get my co-workers to talk about their living situations, because housing, in almost every case, is the principal source of disruption in their lives, the first thing they fill you in on when they arrive for their shifts. After a week, I have compiled the following survey:

- Gail is sharing a room in a well-known downtown flophouse for which she and a roommate pay about $250 a week. Her roommate, a male friend, has begun hitting on her, driving her nuts, but the rent would be impossible alone.
- Claude, the Haitian cook, is desperate to get out of the two-room apartment he shares with his girlfriend and two other, unrelated, people. As far as I can determine, the other Haitian men (most of whom only speak Creole) live in similarly crowded situations.
- Annette, a twenty-year-old server who is six months pregnant and has been abandoned by her boyfriend, lives with her mother, a postal clerk.
- Marianne and her boyfriend are paying $170 a week for a one-person trailer.
- Jack, who is, at $10 an hour, the wealthiest of us, lives in the trailer he owns, paying only the $400-a-month lot fee.
- The other white cook, Andy, lives on his dry-docked boat, which, as far as I can tell from his loving descriptions, can't be more than twenty feet long. He offers to take me out on it, once it's repaired, but the offer comes with inquiries

as to my marital status, so I do not follow up on it.

- Tina and her husband are paying $60 a night for a double room in a Days Inn. This is because they have no car and the Days Inn is within walking distance of the Hearthside. When Marianne, one of the breakfast servers, is tossed out of her trailer for subletting (which is against the trailer-park rules), she leaves her boyfriend and moves in with Tina and her husband.
- Joan, who had fooled me with her numerous and tasteful outfits (hostesses wear their own clothes), lives in a van she parks behind a shopping center at night and showers in Tina's motel room. The clothes are from thrift shops.[3]

It strikes me, in my middle-class solipsism, that there is gross improvidence in some of these arrangements. When Gail and I are wrapping silverware in napkins—the only task for which we are permitted to sit—she tells me she is thinking of escaping from her roommate by moving into the Days Inn herself. I am astounded: How can she even think of paying between $40 and $60 a day? But if I was afraid of sounding like a social worker, I come out just sounding like a fool. She squints at me in disbelief, "And where am I supposed to get a month's rent and a month's deposit for an apartment?" I'd been feeling pretty smug about my $500 efficiency, but of course it was made possible only by the $1,300 I had allotted myself for start-up costs when I began my low-wage life: $1,000 for the first month's rent and deposit, $100 for initial groceries and cash in my pocket, $200 stuffed away for emergencies. In poverty, as in certain propositions in physics, starting conditions are everything.

There are no secret economies that nourish the poor; on the contrary, there are a host of special costs. If you can't put up the two months' rent you need to secure an apartment, you end up paying through the nose for a room by the week. If you have only a room, with a hot plate at best, you can't save by cooking up huge lentil stews that can be frozen for the week ahead. You eat fast food, or the hot dogs and styrofoam cups of soup that can be microwaved in a convenience store. If you have no money for health insurance—and the Hearthside's niggardly plan kicks in only after three months—you go without routine care or prescription drugs and end up paying the price. Gail, for example, was fine until she ran out of money for estrogen pills. She is supposed to be on the company plan by now, but they claim to have lost her application form and need to begin the paperwork all over again. So she spends $9 per migraine pill to control the headaches she wouldn't have, she insists, if her estrogen supplements were covered. Similarly, Marianne's boyfriend lost his job as a roofer because he missed so much time after getting a cut on his foot for which he couldn't afford the prescribed antibiotic.

My own situation, when I sit down to assess it after two weeks of work, would not be much better if this were my actual life. The seductive thing about waitressing is that you don't have to wait for payday to feel a few bills in your pocket, and my tips usually cover meals and gas, plus something left over to stuff into the kitchen drawer I use as a bank. But as the tourist business slows in the summer heat, I sometimes leave work with only $20 in tips (the gross is higher, but servers share about 15 percent of their tips with the busboys and bartenders). With wages included, this amounts to about the minimum wage of $5.15 an hour. Although the sum in the drawer is piling up, at the present rate of accumulation it will be more than a hundred dollars short of my rent when the end of the month comes around. Nor can I see any expenses to cut. True, I haven't gone the lentil-stew route yet, but that's because I don't have a large cooking pot, pot holders, or a ladle to stir with (which cost about $30 at Kmart, less at thrift stores), not to mention onions, carrots, and the indispensable bay leaf. I do make my lunch almost every day—usually some slow-burning, high-protein combo like frozen chicken patties with melted cheese on top and canned pinto beans on the side. Dinner is at the Hearthside, which offers its employees a choice of BLT, fish sandwich, or hamburger for only $2. The burger lasts longest, especially if it's heaped with gut-puckering jalapenos, but by midnight my stomach is growling again.

So unless I want to start using my car as a residence, I have to find a second, or alternative, job. I call all the hotels where I filled out housekeeping applications weeks ago—the Hyatt, Holiday Inn, Econo Lodge, Hojo's, Best Western, plus a half dozen or so locally run guesthouses. Nothing. Then I start making the rounds again, wasting whole mornings waiting for some assistant manager to show up, even dipping into places so creepy that the front-desk clerk greets you from behind bulletproof glass and sells pints of liquor over the counter. But either someone has exposed my real-life housekeeping habits—which are, shall we say, mellow—or I am at the wrong end of some infallible ethnic equation: most, but by no means all, of the working housekeepers I see on my job searches are African Americans, Spanish-speaking, or immigrants from the Central European post-Communist world, whereas servers are almost invariably white and monolingually English-speaking. When I finally get a positive response, I have been identified once again as server material. Jerry's, which is part of a well-known national family restaurant chain and physically attached here to another budget hotel chain, is ready to use me at once. The prospect is both exciting and terrifying, because, with about the same number of tables and counter seats, Jerry's attracts three or four times the volume of customers as the gloomy old Hearthside. . . .

I start out with the beautiful, heroic idea of handling the two jobs at once, and for two days I almost do it: the breakfast/lunch shift at Jerry's, which goes till 2:00, arriving at the Hearthside at 2:10, and attempting to hold out until 10:00. In the ten minutes between jobs, I pick up a spicy chicken sandwich at the Wendy's drive-through window, gobble it down in the car, and change from khaki slacks to black, from Hawaiian to rust polo. There is a problem, though. When during the 3:00 to 4:00 P.M. dead time I finally sit down to wrap silver, my flesh seems to bond to the seat. I try to refuel with a purloined cup of soup, as I've seen Gail and Joan do dozens of times, but a manager catches me and hisses "No eating!" though there's not a customer around to be offended by the sight of food making contact with a server's lips. So I tell Gail I'm going to quit, and she hugs me and says she might just follow me to Jerry's herself.

But the chances of this are minuscule. She has left the flophouse and her annoying roommate and is back to living in her beat-up old truck. But guess what? she reports to me excitedly later that evening:

Phillip has given her permission to park overnight in the hotel parking lot, as long as she keeps out of sight, and the parking lot should be totally safe, since it's patrolled by a hotel security guard! With the Hearthside offering benefits like that, how could anyone think of leaving? . . .

Management at Jerry's is generally calmer and more "professional" than at the Hearthside, with two exceptions. One is Joy, a plump, blowsy woman in her early thirties, who once kindly devoted several minutes to instructing me in the correct one-handed method of carrying trays but whose moods change disconcertingly from shift to shift and even within one. Then there's B.J., a.k.a. B.J.-the-bitch, whose contribution is to stand by the kitchen counter and yell, "Nita, your order's up, move it!" or, "Barbara, didn't you see you've got another table out there? Come on, girl!" Among other things, she is hated for having replaced the whipped-cream squirt cans with big plastic whipped-cream-filled baggies that have to be squeezed with both hands—because, reportedly, she saw or thought she saw employees trying to inhale the propellant gas from the squirt cans, in the hope that it might be nitrous oxide. On my third night, she pulls me aside abruptly and brings her face so close that it looks as if she's planning to butt me with her forehead. But instead of saying, "You're fired," she says, "You're doing fine." The only trouble is I'm spending time chatting with customers: "That's how they're getting you." Furthermore I am letting them "run me," which means harassment by sequential demands: you bring the ketchup and they decide they want extra Thousand Island; you bring that and they announce they now need a side of fries; and so on into distraction. Finally she tells me not to take her wrong. She tries to say things in a nice way, but you get into a mode, you know, because everything has to move so fast . . . .[4]

I make the decision to move closer to Key West. First, because of the drive. Second and third, also because of the drive: gas is eating up $4 to $5 a day, and although Jerry's is as high-volume as you can get, the tips average only 10 percent, and not just for a newbie like me. Between the base pay of $2.15 an hour and the obligation to share tips with the busboys and dishwashers, we're averaging only about $7.50 an hour. Then there is the $30 I had to spend on the regulation tan slacks worn by Jerry's servers—a set-back it could take weeks to absorb. (I had combed the town's two downscale department stores hoping for something cheaper but decided in the end that these marked-down Dockers, originally $49, were more likely to survive a daily washing.) Of my fellow servers, everyone who lacks a working husband or boyfriend seems to have a second job: Nita does something at a computer eight hours a day; another welds. Without the forty-five-minute commute, I can picture myself working two jobs and having the time to shower between them.

So I take the $500 deposit I have coming from my landlord, the $400 I have earned toward the next month's rent; plus the $200 reserved for emergencies, and use the $1,100 to pay the rent and deposit on trailer number 46 in the Overseas Trailer Park, a mile from the cluster of budget hotels that constitute Key West's version of an industrial park. Number 46 is about eight feet in width and shaped like a barbell inside, with a narrow region—because of the sink and the stove—separating the bedroom from what might optimistically be called the "living" area, with its two-person table and half-sized couch. The bathroom is so small my knees rub against the shower stall when I sit on the toilet, and you can't just leap out of the bed; you have to climb down to the foot of it in order to find a patch of floor space to stand on. Outside, I am within a few yards of a liquor store, a bar that advertises "free beer tomorrow," a convenience store, and a Burger King—but no supermarket or, alas, laundromat. By reputation, the Overseas park is a nest of crime and crack, and I am hoping at least for some vibrant, multicultural street life. But desolation rules night and day, except for a thin stream of pedestrian traffic heading for their jobs at the Sheraton or 7-Eleven. There are not exactly people here but what amounts to canned labor, being preserved from the heat between shifts.

In line with my reduced living conditions, a new form of ugliness arises at Jerry's. First we are confronted—via an announcement on the computers through which we input orders—with the new rule that the hotel bar is henceforth off-limits to restaurant employees. The culprit, I learn through the grapevine, is the ultra-efficient gal who trained me—another trailer-home dweller and a mother of three.

Something had set her off one morning, so she slipped out for a nip and returned to the floor impaired. This mostly hurts Ellen, whose habit it is to free her hair from its rubber band and drop by the bar for a couple of Zins before heading home at the end of the shift, but all of us feel the chill. Then the next day, when I go for straws, for the first time I find the dry-storage room locked. Ted, the portly assistant manager who opens it for me, explains that he caught one of the dishwashers attempting to steal something, and, unfortunately, the miscreant will be with us until a replacement can be found—hence the locked door. I neglect to ask what he had been trying to steal, but Ted tells me who he is—the kid with the buzz cut and the earring. You know, he's back there right now.

I wish I could say I rushed back and confronted George to get his side of the story. I wish I could say I stood up to Ted and insisted that George be given a translator and allowed to defend himself, or announced that I'd find a lawyer who'd handle the case pro bono. The mystery to me is that there's not much worth stealing in the dry-storage room, at least not in any fenceable quantity: "Is Gyorgi here, and am having 200—maybe 250—ketchup packets. What do you say?" My guess is that he had taken—if he had taken anything at all—some Saltines or a can of cherry-pie mix, and that the motive for taking it was hunger.

So why didn't I intervene? Certainly not because I was held back by the kind of moral paralysis that can pass as journalistic objectivity. On the contrary, something new—something loathsome and servile—had infected me, along with the kitchen odors that I could still sniff on my bra when I finally undressed at night. In real life I am moderately brave, but plenty of brave people shed their courage in concentration camps, and maybe something similar goes on in the infinitely more congenial milieu of the low-wage American workplace. Maybe, in a month or two more at Jerry's, I might have regained my crusading spirit. Then again, in a month or two I might have turned into a different person altogether—say, the kind of person who would have turned George in.

But this is not something I am slated to find out. When my month-long plunge into poverty is almost over, I finally land my dream job—housekeeping. I do this by walking into the personnel office of the only place I figure I might have some credibility, the hotel attached to Jerry's, and confiding urgently that I have to have a second job if I am to pay my rent and, no, it couldn't be front-desk clerk. "All right," the personnel lady fairly spits, "so it's housekeeping," and she marches me back to meet Maria, the housekeeping manager, a tiny, frenetic Hispanic woman who greets me as "babe" and hands me a pamphlet emphasizing the need for a positive attitude. The hours are nine in the morning till whenever, the pay is $6.10 an hour, and there's one week of vacation a year. I don't have to ask about health insurance once I meet Carlotta, the middle-aged African-American woman who will be training me. Carla, as she tells me to call her, is missing all of her top front teeth.

On that first day of housekeeping and last day of my entire project—although I don't yet know it's the last—Carla is in a foul mood. We have been given nineteen rooms to clean, most of them "checkouts," as opposed to "stay-overs," that require the whole enchilada of bed-stripping, vacuuming, and bathroom-scrubbing. When one of the rooms that had been listed as a stay-over turns out to be a checkout, Carla calls Maria to complain, but of course to no avail. "So make up the motherfucker," Carla orders me, and I do the beds while she sloshes around the bathroom. For four hours without a break I strip and remake beds, taking about four and a half minutes per queen-sized bed, which I could get down to three if there were any reason to. We try to avoid vacuuming by picking up the larger specks by hand, but often there is nothing to do but drag the monstrous vacuum cleaner—it weighs about thirty pounds—off our cart and try to wrestle it around the floor. Sometimes Carla hands me the squirt bottle of "BAM" (an acronym for something that begins, ominously, with "butyric"; the rest has been worn off the label) and lets me do the bathrooms. No service ethic challenges me here to new heights of performance. I just concentrate on removing the pubic hairs from the bathtubs, or at least the dark ones that I can see. . . .

When I request permission to leave at about 3:30, another housekeeper warns me that no one has so far succeeded in combining housekeeping at the hotel with serving at Jerry's: "Some kid did it once for five days, and you're no kid." With that helpful information in mind, I rush back to number 46,

down four Advils (the name brand this time), shower, stooping to fit into the stall, and attempt to compose myself for the oncoming shift. So much for what Marx termed the "reproduction of labor power," meaning the things a worker has to do just so she'll be ready to work again. The only unforeseen obstacle to the smooth transition from job to job is that my tan Jerry's slacks, which had looked reasonably clean by 40-watt bulb last night when I hand-washed my Hawaiian shirt, prove by daylight to be mottled with ketchup and ranch-dressing stains. I spend most of my hour-long break between jobs attempting to remove the edible portions with a sponge and then drying the slacks over the hood of my car in the sun.

I can do this two-job thing, is my theory, if I can drink enough caffeine and avoid getting distracted by George's ever more obvious suffering.[5] The first few days after being caught he seemed not to understand the trouble he was in, and our chirpy little conversations had continued. But the last couple of shifts he's been listless and unshaven, and tonight he looks like the ghost we all know him to be, with dark half-moons hanging from his eyes. At one point, when I am briefly immobilized by the task of filling little paper cups with sour cream for baked potatoes, he comes over and looks as if he'd like to explore the limits of our shared vocabulary, but I am called to the floor for a table. I resolve to give him all my tips that night and to hell with the experiment in low-wage money management. At eight, Ellen and I grab a snack together standing at the mephitic end of the kitchen counter, but I can only manage two or three mozzarella sticks and lunch had been a mere handful of McNuggets. I am not tired at all, I assure myself, though it may be that there is simply no more "I" left to do the tiredness monitoring. What I would see, if I were more alert to the situation, is that the forces of destruction are already massing against me. There is only one cook on duty, a young man named Jesus ("Hay-Sue," that is) and he is new to the job. And there is Joy, who shows up to take over in the middle of the shift, wearing high heels and a long, clingy white dress and fuming as if she'd just been stood up in some cocktail bar.

Then it comes, the perfect storm. Four of my tables fill up at once. Four tables is nothing for me now, but only so long as they are obligingly staggered. As I bev table 27, tables 25, 28, and 24 are watching enviously. As I bev 25, 24 glowers because their bevs haven't even been ordered. Twenty-eight is four yuppyish types, meaning everything on the side and agonizing instructions as to the chicken Caesars. Twenty-five is a middle-aged black couple, who complain, with some justice, that the iced tea isn't fresh and the tabletop is sticky. But table 24 is the meteorological event of the century: ten British tourists who seem to have made the decision to absorb the American experience entirely by mouth. Here everyone has at least two drinks—iced tea and milk shake, Michelob and water (with lemon slice, please)—and a huge promiscuous orgy of breakfast specials, mozz sticks, chicken strips, quesadillas, burgers with cheese and without, sides of hash browns with cheddar, with onions, with gravy, seasoned fries, plain fries, banana splits. Poor Jesus! Poor me! Because when I arrive with their first tray of food—after three prior trips just to refill bevs—Princess Di refuses to eat her chicken strips with her pancake-and-sausage special, since, as she now reveals, the strips were meant to be an appetizer. Maybe the others would have accepted their meals, but Di, who is deep into her third Michelob, insists that everything else go back while they work on their "starters." Meanwhile, the yuppies are waving me down for more decaf and the black couple looks ready to summon the NAACP.

Much of what happened next is lost in the fog of war. Jesus starts going under. The little printer on the counter in front of him is spewing out orders faster than he can rip them off, much less produce the meals. Even the invincible Ellen is ashen from stress. I bring table 24 their reheated main courses, which they immediately reject as either too cold or fossilized by the microwave. When I return to the kitchen with their trays (three trays in three trips), Joy confronts me with arms akimbo: "What is this?" She means the food—the plates of rejected pancakes, hash browns in assorted flavors, toasts, burgers, sausages, eggs. "Uh, scrambled with cheddar," I try, "and that's . . ." "NO," she screams in my face. "Is it a traditional, a super-scramble, an eye-opener?" I pretend to study my check for a clue, but entropy has been up to its tricks, not only on the plates but in my head, and I

have to admit that the original order is beyond reconstruction. "You don't know an eye-opener from a traditional?" she demands in outrage. All I know, in fact, is that my legs have lost interest in the current venture and have announced their intention to fold. I am saved by a yuppie (mercifully not one of mine) who chooses this moment to charge into the kitchen to bellow that his food is twenty-five minutes late. Joy screams at him to get the hell out of her kitchen, please, and then turns on Jesus in a fury, hurling an empty tray across the room for emphasis.

I leave. I don't walk out; I just leave. I don't finish my side work or pick up my credit-card tips, if any, at the cash register or, of course, ask Joy's permission to go. And the surprising thing is that you can walk out without permission, that the door opens, that the thick tropical night air parts to let me pass, that my car is still parked where I left it. There is no vindication in this exit, no fuck-you surge of relief, just an overwhelming, dank sense of failure pressing down on me and the entire parking lot. I had gone into this venture in the spirit of science, to test a mathematical proposition, but somewhere along the line, in the tunnel vision imposed by long shifts and relentless concentration, it became a test of myself, and clearly I have failed. Not only had I flamed out as a housekeeper/server, I had even forgotten to give George my tips, and, for reasons perhaps best known to hardworking, generous people like Gail and Ellen, this hurts. I don't cry, but I am in a position to realize, for the first time in many years, that the tear ducts are still there, and still capable of doing their job.

When I moved out of the trailer park, I gave the key to number 46 to Gail and arranged for my deposit to be transferred to her. She told me that Joan is still living in her van and that Stu had been fired from the Hearthside. I never found out what happened to George.

In one month, I had earned approximately $1,040 and spent $517 on food, gas, toiletries, laundry, phone, and utilities. If I had remained in my $500 efficiency, I would have been able to pay the rent and have $22 left over (which is $78 less than the cash I had in my pocket at the start of the month). During this time I bought no clothing except for the required slacks and no prescription drugs or medical care (I did finally buy some vitamin B to compensate for the lack of vegetables in my diet). Perhaps I could have saved a little on food if I had gotten to a supermarket more often, instead of convenience stores, but it should be noted that I lost almost four pounds in four weeks, on a diet weighted heavily toward burgers and fries.

How former welfare recipients and single mothers will (and do) survive in the low-wage workforce, I cannot imagine. Maybe they will figure out how to condense their lives—including child-raising, laundry, romance, and meals—into the couple of hours between full-time jobs. Maybe they will take up residence in their vehicles, if they have one. All I know is that I couldn't hold two jobs and I couldn't make enough money to live on with one. And I had advantages unthinkable to many of the long-term poor—health, stamina, a working car, and no children to care for and support. Certainly nothing in my experience contradicts the conclusion of Kathryn Edin and Laura Lein, in their recent book *Making Ends Meet: How Single Mothers Survive Welfare and Low-Wage Work,* that low-wage work actually involves more hardship and deprivation than life at the mercy of the welfare state. In the coming months and years, economic conditions for the working poor are bound to worsen, even without the almost inevitable recession. As mentioned earlier, the influx of former welfare recipients into the low-skilled workforce will have a depressing effect on both wages and the number of jobs available. A general economic downturn will only enhance these effects, and the working poor will of course be facing it without the slight, but nonetheless often saving, protection of welfare as a backup.

The thinking behind welfare reform was that even the humblest jobs are morally uplifting and psychologically buoying. In reality they are likely to be fraught with insult and stress. But I did discover one redeeming feature of the most abject low-wage work—the camaraderie of people who are, in almost all cases, far too smart and funny and caring for the work they do and the wages they're paid. The hope, of course, is that someday these people will come to know what they're worth, and take appropriate action.

Notes

1. According to the Department of Housing and Urban Development, the "fair-market rent" for an efficiency is $551 here in Monroe County, Florida. A comparable rent in the five boroughs of New York City is $704; in San Francisco, $713; and in the heart of Silicon Valley, $808. The fair-market rent for an area is defined as the amount that would be needed to pay rent plus utilities for "privately owned, decent, safe, and sanitary rental housing of a modest (non-luxury) nature with suitable amenities."

2. According to the Fair Labor Standards Act, employers are not required to pay "tipped employees," such as restaurant servers, more than $2.13 an hour in direct wages. However, if the sum of tips plus $2.13 an hour falls below the minimum wage, or $5.15 an hour, the employer is required to make up the difference. This fact was not mentioned by managers or otherwise publicized at either of the restaurants where I worked.

3. I could find no statistics on the number of employed people living in cars or vans, but according to the National Coalition for the Homeless's 1997 report "Myths and Facts about Homelessness," nearly one in five homeless people (in twenty-nine cities across the nation) is employed in a full- or part-time job.

4. In *Workers in a Lean World: Unions in the International Economy* (Verso, 1997), Kim Moody cites studies finding an increase in stress-related workplace injuries and illness between the mid-1980s and the early 1990s. He argues that rising stress levels reflect a new system of "management by stress," in which workers in a variety of industries are being squeezed to extract maximum productivity, to the detriment of their health.

5. In 1996, the number of persons holding two or more jobs averaged 7.8 million, or 6.2 percent of the workforce. It was about the same rate for men and for women (6.1 versus 6.2), though the kinds of jobs differ by gender. About two thirds of multiple jobholders work one job full-time and the other part-time. Only a heroic minority—4 percent of men and 2 percent of women—work two full-time jobs simultaneously. (From John F. Stinson Jr., "New Data on Multiple Jobholding Available from the CPS," in the *Monthly Labor Review,* March 1997.)

Questions for Critical Thinking

1. In this reading, the author illustrates some of the factors that perpetuate social stratification on the basis of class in the United States. How did the author's experiences broaden your understanding of these factors? What information did you already know?

2. Reflecting on what you read, how do you think factors of race influence the author's experiences?

   In other words, would her experiences have been similar if she were a woman of color?

3. Economic policymakers in the United States rarely have had experience in trying to live on low-wage employment. Do you think their actions as policymakers would be influenced if they had the opportunity to have the experiences Ehrenreich did in this experiment?

NOT POOR ENOUGH

* *Susan Sheehan*

The following essay details the experiences of an elderly woman named Cassie Stromer. Living on less than $10,000 annually, Stromer is above what the US government has established as the threshold for poverty. As a result, she does not qualify for full Medicaid benefits. Her experiences provide a clear illustration of how constructions of poverty do not adequately reflect the everyday realities of the poor.

Cassie Stromer, a petite seventy-six-year-old woman with bottle-blond hair and off-blue eyes, lives in Mount Vernon House, a pleasant four-story red brick apartment complex in Alexandria, Virginia. She has good memories of a colorful past—three husbands, numerous boyfriends, five children, lots of jobs—but her current life is not so good. She was reared in rural Tennessee, and first came to Virginia to work when she was fifteen. She never finished high school. For a short period after separating from the father of her children, she went on welfare, but she found it demeaning. For a while, she worked two full-time jobs, from which she got home at midnight. Cassie doesn't brood over a past marked by poverty. She liked her jobs—at drugstores, at doughnut shops, waiting on tables in restaurants, serving as a hostess at hotels, working in the advertising department of a local newspaper, babysitting.

Cassie is fortunate to live at Mount Vernon House, which opened in 1983; it is one of the few privately owned and operated buildings in northern Virginia subsidized by the Department of Housing and Urban Development. To apply for an apartment there, a single person must be at least sixty-two or disabled and have an annual income no higher than $30,450. Cassie was sixty-eight when she moved there, in 1996. This year,

her income will be $9,654—$686 from Social Security every month and a monthly pension of $118.51 from the newspaper, for which she worked for twenty years.

Last year, Cassie's rent was seventy-two dollars a month. "That's on the low end of what our hundred and forty-one residents pay," the property manager for Mount Vernon House, La-Rita Timberlake, says. "As a general rule, residents pay about thirty per cent of their income minus medical bills for rent. HUD makes up the difference."

Cassie Stromer's income puts her in the lowest third of women over sixty-five living alone in America. The official poverty level is $9,310 a year. As it happens, Cassie would be better off if her income were considerably below that amount, rather than some three hundred dollars above it, because her income is regarded as too high for her to receive full Medicaid benefits.

Cassie suffers from neuropathy, a dysfunction of the peripheral nerves, which typically causes numbness or weakness. The neuropathy began in Cassie's big toe ten or twelve years ago; it has spread to her legs, arms, and hands. "I can't do much with my hands," she says. "I can't peel potatoes. When water hits my fingers, they hurt. I can walk, but standing hurts. The tops of my feet feel like people are pouring hot water on them and the bottoms feel like I'm stepping on coals."

In 2003, this is where Cassie's monthly income of $790.51 went after she paid her rent: about $66 for electricity; $50 for her telephone; and $45 for her cable TV. (Television is Cassie's primary form of recreation: she watches several daytime soaps, listens to the news, sometimes looks at the country-music channel, and in the evening watches one or two favorite shows, like "NYPD Blue" or "Law & Order.") Her prescription-drug bills averaged $328 a month. These expenses left Cassie with $230, which was supplemented with ten dollars a month in food stamps, the amount given to individuals who have a net income between $434 and $1,236 a month. Ten dollars has been the monthly minimum payment since 1978; advocates for the poor have been trying, without success, to raise it to twenty-five dollars.

In Alexandria, the Rising Hope United Methodist Mission Church and the United Community Ministries provide bags of groceries for residents who sign up. Still, Cassie estimates that she spends more than a hundred dollars a week on food and other products not covered by food stamps—paper towels, Kleenex, toilet tissue, laundry and cleaning products, toothpaste, shampoo, deodorant, vitamins, and other personal-care items.

"I've gotten away from eating bacon and eggs in the morning," Cassie says. "But I have to start the day with breakfast-type food, like cold cereal. I try to eat a nutritious dinner." She likes to drink juice and milk—and one cup a day of Dunkin' Donuts coffee—and to eat fresh fruit and vegetables, salads, and meat or chicken several evenings a week. A recent dinner consisted of a baked potato with sour cream, a can of asparagus, and some fresh tomatoes (the vegetables were donated by Rising Hope and the United Community Ministries). When her prescription bills and her medical co-payments are on the low side in a given month, she has ten dollars a week to spend on quarters for the washer and dryer, and bus fare. A friend drives her to church most Sundays, and she puts a dollar in the collection plate when she can.

Cassie was born in Harlan, Kentucky, on February 20, 1928, and moved with her parents to the small town of Sneedville, Tennessee, in the early nineteen-thirties. She was the sixth of seven children born to Henry Monroe Depew, a Baptist minister and a farmer, and Mahalie Seals Depew. A sister died as an infant about two years before Cassie's birth, and her younger brother died when she was five.

The family was poor, and one winter, Cassie recalls, "there wasn't enough to eat, so my grandmother stepped in and helped, because she always did a lot of canning." Cassie didn't feel poor, however. Few people in Sneedville were much better off than the Depews, and she didn't resent those who were.

As a child, Cassie had her share of chores—setting out tobacco, chopping chicken heads off with an axe, planting corn—but most of her early memories are warm ones. "I didn't start school until I was eight," she says. That wasn't unusual in the nineteen-thirties. June Seal, a childhood friend, recalls her as an attractive, slender girl with brown hair. Cassie likes to talk about the year she was "the most popular girl in the school." She was a good student.

In 1943, when Cassie was fifteen, she spent the summer in northern Virginia, where an older sister, who was married to a bus driver, was living. For the next several summers, Cassie worked at drugstores in or near Alexandria, staying either with her sister or at a Y or sharing an apartment with a friend. She returned to high school each fall, but stopped going six weeks before graduation. "I'd had enough of geometry and chemistry by then," she says. "I'd learned that poetry was easy to remember, and words that didn't rhyme—I think they call it prose—was hard. I had my high-school ring, and it never mattered that I didn't graduate. When anyone asked me how many years of school I'd done, I said twelve. No one ever asked to see my diploma."

While still in high school, Cassie married a sailor from North Carolina, but after he got out of the Navy she refused to move there with him, and the marriage was annulled. A few years later, she married again. Cassie's second husband, Bob, was a baker. Their first daughter was born in 1951, when Cassie was twenty-three, and their second in 1955. Cassie made babysitting arrangements for her daughters and kept working at a drugstore. Ten days after the birth of her first son, in 1956, she moved with her family from an apartment to a small house that the couple had bought for $13,750 in the Virginia Hills section of Alexandria, and she stopped working. A third daughter was born in 1958, a second son in 1961. "There were no birth-control pills back then," she says. "I guess if pills had been available I'd have had only two children. But once they were born I was glad to have all five."

Cassie enjoyed being home with the children. "I remember watching the first episode of 'General Hospital,' in 1963, while I was ironing clothes for the five kids," she says. For some months, Cassie babysat for another woman's four children in her house. At another point, when Cassie couldn't pay the pediatri-cian, she took a job at a doughnut shop, working the evening shift until 1 A.M. The marriage deteriorated as Bob began drinking heavily, and she left him, she says, after he hit her during a quarrel. "I took my five kids and my three cents to the house of friends across the street, and they let us stay overnight," she says. Social workers found a house for her to rent in Falls Church, Virginia, but although Cassie occasionally worked part time as a waitress while the older girls took care of their younger siblings, she couldn't make ends meet and had to go on welfare. Bob paid only forty dollars a week in child support. The house in Virginia Hills had appreciated in value, but she learned that her husband had borrowed money against it and hadn't paid the water bills. "There were so many liens against the house I wound up with less than a thousand dollars after it was sold," she says. "I put it in savings accounts in the kids' names and gradually spent it on clothes for them." She lived for a while in a rented house in a run-down neighbor-hood, and then moved to a series of apartments. She eventually got off welfare, and worked at a variety of jobs. "I'm pretty sure I married Bernie Stromer while I was a keypunch operator," she says. Stromer was the manager of a small hotel in Alexandria. "I'm certain I was attracted to him mostly because he didn't drink. I can't stand alcohol or cigarettes."

Cassie then got a job in the advertising depart-ment of the Alexandria *Gazette*. When she was at the newspaper, she was often away from her desk. Stromer would call and then accuse her—falsely, she says—of carrying on a romance with an advertising salesman there. "The one thing worse than a drinking man is a jealous man," she says. "I got a divorce after six years. I sold my three engagement rings and wedding bands to a gold dealer." After the divorce, Cassie worked at the *Gazette* from 7 A.M. to 4 P.M. and at a Peoples Drug from 4:30 P.M. until 11 P.M.

There are eight photograph albums on the top shelf of one of the two closets in Cassie's bedroom at Mount Vernon House. Taped to the pages are pho-tographs of Cassie, starting at the age of seven, and of her children and grandchildren. "My oldest daugh-ter was awarded a full scholarship to Barnard and later graduated from law school," she says. "She never wanted to practice law, so she prepares cases for a law firm in Washington, D.C. My second daughter is divorced. She lives with her older sister and works as a legal secretary. My older son works as a security guard in Tennessee, and he's studying accounting. He has two daughters. One is away at college, the other lives with him and is in high school. My third daughter is happily married. She and her husband have lived in Virginia, California, Mississippi, and Delaware. They've settled in Florida with their two children. They both work. My younger son is single. He's a land surveyor in Virginia." Here and there in the pages of the albums are photographs of Cassie taken at the weddings of her children.

Cassie's children help her out when they can. One of her daughters buys her shoes and also sends her padded socks, which are much more expensive than regular socks but are more comfortable for those suf-fering from neuropathy. She also sends Cassie checks from time to time, and gave her a forty-dollar Wal-Mart gift certificate last Christmas. One of her sons sent her a check for forty dollars for Christmas. An-other daughter is especially helpful, Cassie says, in situations where "there is an emergency or I let her know I really want to do something and I ask her ahead of time"—buying her a hundred and thirty-seven dollars' worth of groceries, for instance, one month when Cassie was out of money. A third daugh-ter telephones often, visits weekly, shops for her, and writes out her checks and mails them, saving Cassie from having to buy stamps. And each week, if there is enough in Cassie's bank account, she withdraws twenty-five dollars for her mother to use as spending money. "The kids got their own lives," Cassie says. "Mortgages or rent, house repairs, car payments, school bills, and vet bills. There's an old saying: 'It takes one mother to take care of five children, but oftentimes five children can't take care of a mother.'"

In one album is the business card of Cassie Stromer, Advertising Manager of the *Gazette*, "America's Oldest Daily Newspaper, Established in 1784," which was still a daily when Cassie went to work there, in 1970. The *Gazette* later merged with the Alexandria *Port Packet*, and became a weekly. "The company published seven other small papers, and I laid out the ads for the *Walter Reed Stripe*, the *Bolling Beam*, the *Pentagram News*, and the others," she says. In another album is a clipping from the *Gazette* with a photograph of Cassie and a number of her colleagues, taken on the occasion of their production of "14 prize-winning advertisements in the 1988 Newspaper Advertising Contest sponsored by the Virginia Press Association."

Two years later, when Cassie was sixty-two, she returned to work from a vacation and received unwelcome news. "My boss handed me a long list of additional jobs he wanted me to do," she says. "I was already doing the work of two people, so I told him he could take his list and shove it. I quit and gave him an hour and a half's notice."

Cassie worked for a time at an apartment-building switchboard, and then, finally, retired. To supplement her retirement income, she took a job babysitting for the six-week-old twins of a prosperous couple. "Some nights, I also took care of another couple's two children from 6 P.M. until midnight," she says. "They paid me more than I'd ever been paid in my life—sometimes even a hundred dollars a night." Frightened by a number of burglaries in her apartment building, she moved to Mount Vernon House in 1996. She was dating a retired Army enlisted man, and they enjoyed travelling together.

"We often flew, but one time he rented a Lincoln Town Car," she says. "He treated me better than any man I've ever known. He paid for everything. We took trips to Las Vegas, we went to Florida to visit my daughter, to Virginia Beach to visit his daughter, and to Kentucky to visit his son." Eventually, the man decided to move to another part of Virginia. Cassie didn't want to leave Alexandria, and the relationship ended. Afterward, Cassie became depressed, and sought help from a local mental-health

center. She continues to see a therapist every two weeks. "I find it easier to talk to psychologists and psychiatrists than to most of my friends," she says. "They listen better." With the therapist's help, Cassie has received prescriptions at nominal cost for Paxil, an anti-depressant, and Trazadone, another anti-depressant. Virginia law requires that everyone taking medication under the aegis of a mental-health agency be seen every three months by a psychiatrist. "I look forward to his visits," Cassie says. "He's handsome."

In 1991, Catherine Cole, a spirited woman now in her early fifties, was hired to be the director of resident services at Mount Vernon House. "Most people who live there are in situations similar to Cassie's," she says. "They weren't born with advantages. They didn't become doctors or lawyers or business executives. They were hair-dressers, food-service workers, private-school teachers, auto mechanics, and housekeepers. Some owned homes but couldn't afford to keep them up. Some moved here from trailer parks. The majority have spent most of their adult lives in Fairfax County. A fair number knew at least one other person before they moved here."

There are residents who are less healthy than Cassie. Some women walk around carrying oxygen tanks, a few men and women use wheelchairs. The *Mount Vernon Post*, a monthly newsletter for the residents, recently published a "Lobby Do's and Don'ts" that included "DO NOT BLOW YOUR HORN on motorized scooters in the lobby."

Part of the service director's job is providing entertainment for the residents, and this includes organizing parties to celebrate holidays. At the most recent Halloween party, Cole told Halloween jokes she had found on the Internet, passed out slices of pumpkin pie to the thirty people gathered for the occasion, and handed out prizes for the best costumes. Cassie was wearing a peach-colored top, jacket, and slacks—the closest color she had to orange. She was not among the fifteen residents who showed up, the following week, for a presentation by the Cunningham Funeral Home of Alexandria on the subject of funeral planning.

Regular activities are listed on the calendar published in the *Mount Vernon Post*. At 9:30 A.M. on Tuesdays, the Mount Vernon House van takes residents to a Wal-Mart or a shopping center. On Fridays, Fastran, a Fairfax County shuttle service for the elderly and the handicapped, takes them to a grocery store. Cassie, who doesn't feel well most mornings, prefers to go grocery shopping on weekend afternoons with one of her daughters. She does use Fastran for medical appointments.

A Bible-study group meets at Mount Vernon House on Tuesdays at 4 P.M., and bingo is played at 7 P.M. Movies are often shown on Wednesday evenings. For a while, a swing band rehearsed on Monday evenings in the lobby. The service director arranges occasional trips to dinner theatres in the Washington area and to the American Music Theatre, in Lancaster, Pennsylvania. "The Lancaster trip costs forty-six dollars, but you can pay in installments," Cassie says. "Two of my daughters will pay for me to go on outings, but the bus ride to Lancaster is long and it shakes you to pieces."

Each year, the Mount Vernon House Tenants' Association raises money for a Christmas dinner by holding a bazaar. The most recent dinner included ham, turkey, stuffing, succotash, green beans, sweet potatoes, mashed potatoes, gravy, cranberry sauce, rolls, apple crisp, and pumpkin pie with whipped cream. Cassie observed that most of the Asian residents sat at one long table and most of the Latinos at another, and that the two or three people who hang out together every day in the lobby sat together and didn't talk to anyone else. "This place is more clannish than junior high school," she said. Still, when a friend came over to her apartment to address Christmas cards to people from Sneedville, the *Gazette*, and other chapters of her life (Cassie's ability to write is limited by her neuropathy and by macular degeneration), she studied the Mount Vernon House directory and chose cards for forty-nine residents, and signed "Love, Cassie" on each card. Cassie keeps the cards that she receives each Christmas until she has dispatched her cards the following December. She was sad when she came across the card that her friend Lucille had sent her. Seven or eight residents of Mount Vernon House, among them Lucille, died the previous year. "I miss Lucille," Cassie says. She also misses another friend, named Warren, who left her his collection of Beanie Babies. Cassie can't afford to send her grandchildren birthday and Christmas

presents, but she has been sending Beanie Babies to her youngest granddaughter, who wrote her a thank-you note.

Ellen Cook, a large cheerful woman with only two upper front teeth, is among a handful of original residents, as is Cassie's friend Rachel Tucker, a lively, hundred-and-one-year-old African-American woman, who goes out nearly every day to visit one of her sons, who is blind. "Rachel can still thread a needle without using glasses," Cassie says admiringly. Rachel is the only resident with a key to Cassie's apartment. When Cassie prepares a dinner of baked chicken, egg noodles, and canned kale, she delivers a plate to Rachel. When Rachel fixes ribs, cabbage, or tapioca pudding, she takes some to Cassie.

Mount Vernon House is not an assisted-living facility. Its residents must be able to fend for themselves. Housekeeping help is provided by a county program called Share Care, and, once every week or so, someone comes to change Cassie's bed, scrub her bathroom and kitchen, and vacuum the worn indoor–outdoor carpeting that covers the concrete floor in the bedroom, living room, and hall.

"It's enlightened fiscal policy to enable residents to stay at Mount Vernon House," Cathy Cole says. "Assisted-living facilities are far more expensive, and they're rarely subsidized."

The medical needs of most of this country's old or disabled citizens fall under the jurisdiction of two Great Society programs created in 1965, Medicare and Medicaid. Medicare, a federal system of health insurance available to old people generally, does not provide full medical coverage. Medicaid is jointly administered by the federal government and the states, and covers medical costs for individuals and families with low incomes or with disabilities. Within broad national guidelines, each of the fifty states determines the income at which its residents become eligible for Medicaid. In Virginia, an old person with insignificant assets is eligible for comprehensive Medicaid benefits only if her personal income is no higher than eighty per cent of the poverty level, or $7,448. For those whose income, like Cassie's, is no higher than a hundred and twenty per cent of the poverty level, Medicaid does pay some of the Medicare premiums, but not the first hundred dollars in doctor bills that Cassie incurs each year, and she has to pay twenty per cent of the "usual and customary" fees that doctors charge for their services or, if she is admitted to a hospital, the $876 deductible for a hospital stay of up to sixty days.

Last November, after much debate, Congress significantly modified the Medicare program, authorizing it, for the first time in its history, to bear some of the costs of prescription drugs. The bill doesn't go into effect until 2006, but people whose income is less than $12,576 are now eligible to apply for an annual transitional benefit amounting to a six-hundred-dollar credit on various prescription cards. The new prescription-card system is cumbersome, however, and many of those who are eligible for the cards, including Cassie, find the application process too complicated to follow. Even with the cards, Cassie would be left with the prospect of having to pay thousands of dollars in additional prescription bills this year and next year.

On one visit to the pharmacy, Cassie had five prescriptions filled. Three were to alleviate the pain of neuropathy—Ultram, Keppra, and lidocaine patches (which she applies to the tops of her feet for twelve-hour periods). The fourth, Patanol drops, soothes her eyes, easing the unpleasantness of macular degeneration. The fifth, potassium pills, relieves cramps in her legs. The pharmacy bill that day came to $562.45. Last year, Cassie's entire pharmacy bill was $3,940.50.

"Up until I retired, my health was pretty good," Cassie says. "I was busy working and raising five children and putting one foot in front of the other, and I think it's lucky I couldn't see further down the road, to where I am today—on the borderline of Medicare and Medicaid, which ain't a nice place to be."

"I'd estimate that about one-third of Mount Vernon House's residents are eligible for Medicaid and another few have private health insurance," Cathy Cole says. "The majority, however, fall between the cracks. Their income is a couple of hundred dollars a month too high for them to qualify for Medicaid, and with Medicare alone they cannot afford to pay for all of their medical costs."

Cassie's only hope of qualifying for comprehensive Medicaid—and then only for a period of up to six months at a time—is to be placed on a "spend-down." Mount Vernon House gives residents like Cassie a plastic envelope and tells them to put all their medical bills in it—their co-pays, their prescription bills, and their receipts for all out-of-pocket medical expenses, including transportation to medical appointments. The spend-down is calculated by taking Cassie's monthly income—$790.51 in 2003—and first subtracting a twenty-dollar "disregard." $770.51 is multiplied by six, which amounts to $4,623.06. That figure is then compared with the "medically needy" figure for a single person in northern Virginia, which is $2,071 for a six-month period. The difference, $2,552.06, is Cassie's spend-down. If, in a six-month period, she has $2,552.06 in medical expenses, she will qualify for Medicaid for the remainder of that six-month period. In the eight years that Cassie has been at Mount Vernon House, she has met the Medicaid spend-down once. "It was wonderful to have a Medicaid card," Cassie says. "Prescriptions cost me only a dollar or two apiece. But, by the time I'd met the spend-down amount, the six months of Medicaid coverage was almost up, and before I knew it I was without Medicaid again." A friend remembers coming to visit Cassie at Mount Vernon House. "She was in pain, but she cut one of the pills she took for neuropathy in half, because it was expensive," the friend says.

"People like Cassie believe that their problem lies in having too much income," Steven L. Myers, the executive director of the Virginia Poverty Law Center, says. "In my opinion, the problem is, rather, that Virginia's Medicaid eligibility—eighty per cent of poverty—is too low. We struggled to get the General Assembly to raise it from seventy-four per cent to eighty per cent. That six-per-cent increase was helpful to thousands of people. I know of one woman who spent down and qualified for Medicaid a few years ago. She was on that spend-down long enough to get a free pair of prescription eyeglasses. Now Virginia Medicaid no longer covers eye-glasses. Spend-downs work for some people with catastrophic illnesses. They don't work for people with chronic health problems. I'm convinced that most upper-income people in the country don't know that our safety-net programs aren't as generous as they believe them to be. They assume that the aged, the blind, and the disabled receive Medicaid at a hundred per cent of poverty. Virginia is a very bad place in which to be elderly and poor."

Cassie Stromer is a fastidious person. After she makes coffee, she doesn't simply rinse out the drip machine's glass carafe; she fills it with fresh water, puts a filter in the plastic cone, and boils the water. Every couple of months, she pours vinegar into the carafe, boils the vinegar, and then repeats the process with water to get rid of the vinegar's pungent odor. She changes her towels and bed linens frequently. The laundry room at Mount Vernon House is less than ideal, she says. "Just four washers and dryers, and sometimes one is broken."

Before Cassie puts fifty cents in a washer, she sprays Lysol in it, and before inserting coins in the dryer she empties the lint tray. She usually doesn't leave the laundry room until her clothes are dry. "People waiting for a machine will change the delicate cycle to high heat so your clothes will be done faster, and that'll ruin them," she says. "Other times, they'll take out your things when they're still wet and they'll use what's left of your money to dry their own clothes."

That happened one day last year, when Cassie left her quilt in a dryer unattended and returned to her apartment. She was already upset because earlier in the day someone had reported her for using two machines at a time and she had been reprimanded. "If I use one machine at a time, I'll be in the laundry room for seven hours," she says. "That's my whole day. And that's the only rule I ever break. Everyone should be allowed to break one goddam rule. I've never reported anyone for using two machines." When Cassie discovered the damp quilt on top of the dryer, she carried it back to her apartment, hung it over the shower rod in her bathroom, and turned on the heat lamp. She owned only one quilt and wanted it on her bed by evening. She started to walk toward her La-Z-Boy recliner in the living room and collided with a small table in the hall that held her microwave. She fell, bumping her head. She lost consciousness briefly, came to, picked herself up, and made it to the recliner. A friend stopped by, saw the bump, and dialled 911. An ambulance took her to a nearby hospital, where she spent six days, returning to Mount Vernon House the day before Thanksgiving. She had been "peeked at and poked at" by numerous doctors—all of whom subsequently sent bills—and had had many X-rays and CAT scans. She

had not broken any bones, but she had broken her lower denture. The denture had been made some fifteen or twenty years earlier, when she was still at the *Gazette* and had dental insurance. There is virtually no dentistry that the poor can afford in Virginia; even Medicaid offers dental benefits only to children.

When Cassie received an unexpected rent rebate check from Fairfax County for a hundred dollars later that month, she cashed the check and stashed the hundred dollars in her bedroom, thinking that she might be able to save up for new dentures. Her mouth felt uncomfortable without the lower plate, and she couldn't easily chew meat or raw broccoli, celery, and carrots, which are among her favorite foods.

In January, Cassie's ophthalmologist prescribed TobraDex drops to relieve some irritation in her left eye. When a neighborhood pharmacy delivered the prescription, the bill was $63.23. Cassie had only seventeen dollars. "Shit, shit, shit," she said as she walked to the bedroom and took out fifty dollars of the squirrelled-away hundred dollars. She gave the delivery boy sixty-five dollars—the sum she owed and a tip.

As Cassie's birthday approached, in February, she had only twenty dollars left in her bedroom cache: she had dipped into the denture fund to buy groceries. She telephoned the dentist who had made her original dentures and learned that new ones would cost twenty-seven hundred dollars, but he encouraged her to bring in the broken lower denture. "If the break is clean, I can glue it together and that would last for a while," he said. Cassie had him do the glue repair.

In May, Cassie got some good news. Because of a formula involving her medical expenses, her rent was being reduced from $72 a month to $42. In September, however, she received a notice from the state, telling her that her $58 Medicare premium would no longer be covered, meaning that she would have to pay it herself.

Earlier this month, Cassie's lower denture broke again. "This time it shattered," she says. "It's harder to eat now. I can't really chew anything." She has to cut her food up into small pieces. She says there's nothing she can do about it. "I don't have any more money today than I did last February, and I won't have any more tomorrow."

Questions for Critical Thinking

1. The experiences of Cassie Stromer illustrate that current definitions of what is considered poor are inadequate. Despite this, official definitions of poverty remain relatively unchanged. Why do you think this is?

2. What are some of your own assumptions about the poor? How does Stromer's experience affirm or challenge these assumptions? How is your reaction impacted by your own class position?

3. What are some ways that the definitions of poverty can be changed to provide aid to those who need it?

THE MISEDUCATION OF THE AMERICAN BOY

Peggy Orenstein

The essay that follows explores the concept of toxic masculinity that is deeply engrained in contemporary U.S. culture, even if the idea is, as the author argues, outdated. Drawing on her book *Boys & Sex: Young Men on Hookups, Love, Porn, Consent, and Navigating the New Masculinity*, Peggy Orenstein argues that we need to give boys new and better models of masculinity.

I knew nothing about Cole before meeting him; he was just a name on a list of boys at a private school outside Boston who had volunteered to talk with me (or perhaps had had their arm twisted a bit by a counselor). The afternoon of our first interview, I was running late. As I rushed down a hallway at the school, I noticed a boy sitting outside the library, waiting—it had to be him. He was staring impassively ahead, both feet planted on the, floor, hands resting loosely on his thighs.

My first reaction was *Oh no.*

It was totally unfair, a scarlet letter of personal bias. Cole would later describe himself to me as a "typical tall white athlete" guy, and that is exactly what I saw. At 18, he stood more than 6 feet tall, with broad shoulders and short-clipped hair. His neck was so thick that it seemed to merge into his jawline, and he was planning to enter a military academy for college the following fall. His friends were "the jock group," he'd tell me. "They're what you'd expect, I guess. Let's leave it at that." If I had closed my eyes and described the boy I imagined would never open up to me, it would have been him.

But Cole surprised me. He pulled up a picture on his phone of his girlfriend, whom he'd been dating for the past 18 months, describing her proudly as "way

smarter than I am," a feminist, and a bedrock of emotional support. He also confided how he'd worried four years earlier, during his first weeks as a freshman on a scholarship at a new school, that he wouldn't know how to act with other guys, wouldn't be able to make friends. "I could talk to girls platonically," he said. "That was easy. But being around guys was different. I needed to be a 'bro,' and I didn't know how to do that."

Whenever Cole uttered the word bro, he shifted his weight to take up more space, rocking back in his chair, and spoke from low in his throat, like he'd inhaled a lungful of weed. He grinned when I pointed that out. "Yeah," he said, "that's part of it: seeming relaxed and never intrusive, yet somehow bringing out that aggression on the sports field. Because a 'bro'"—he rocked back again—"is always, always an athlete."

Cole eventually found his people on the crew team, but it wasn't a smooth fit at first. He recalled

Section 1.01 This article is adapted from Peggy Orenstein's book *Boys & Sex: Young Men on Hookups, Love, Porn, Consent, and Navigating the New Masculinity.* Harper Collins, 2021.
This article has been updated to reflect that the organization Plan International USA commissioned the 2018 survey of 10-to-19-year-olds conducted by the polling firm PerryUndem.

an incident two years prior when a senior was bragging in the locker room about how he'd convinced one of Cole's female classmates—a young sophomore, Cole emphasized—that they were an item, then started hooking up with other girls behind her back. And the guy wasn't shy about sharing the details. Cole and a friend of his, another sophomore, told him to knock it o-. "I started to explain why it wasn't appropriate," Cole said, "but he just laughed."

The next day, a second senior started talking about "getting back at" a "bitch" who'd dumped him. Cole's friend spoke up again, but this time Cole stayed silent. "And as I continued to step back" and the other sophomore "continued to step up, you could tell that the guys on the team stopped liking him as much. They stopped listening to him, too. It's almost as if he spent all his social currency" trying to get them to stop making sexist jokes. "Meanwhile, I was sitting there"—Cole thumped his chest—"too afraid to spend any of mine, and I just had buckets left.

"I don't know what to do," he continued earnestly. "Once I'm in the military, and I'm a part of that culture, I don't want to have to choose between my own dignity and my relationship with others I'm serving with. But . . ." He looked me in the eye. "How do I make it so I don't have to choose?"

I've spent two years talking with boys across America—more than 100 of them between the ages of 16 and 21—about masculinity, sex, and love: about the forces, seen and unseen, that shape them as men. Though I spoke with boys of all races and ethnicities, I stuck to those who were in college or college-bound, because like it or not, they're the ones most likely to set cultural norms. Nearly every guy I interviewed held relatively egalitarian views about girls, at least their role in the public sphere. They considered their female classmates to be smart and competent, entitled to their place on the athletic field and in school leadership, deserving of their admission to college and of professional opportunities. They all had female friends; most had gay male friends as well. That was a huge shift from what you might have seen 50, 40, maybe even 20 years ago. They could also easily reel off the excesses of masculinity. They'd seen the headlines about mass shootings, domestic violence, sexual harassment, campus rape, presidential Twitter tantrums, and Supreme Court confirmation hearings. A

Big Ten football player I interviewed bandied about the term toxic masculinity. "Everyone knows what that is," he said, when I seemed surprised.

Yet when asked to describe the attributes of "the ideal guy," those same boys appeared to be harking back to 1955. Dominance. Aggression. Rugged good looks (with an emphasis on height). Sexual prowess. Stoicism. Athleticism. Wealth (at least some day). It's not that all of these qualities, properly channeled, are bad. But while a 2018 national survey of more than 1,000 10-to-19-year-olds commissioned by Plan International USA and conducted by the polling from PerryUndem found that young women believed there were many ways to be a girl—they could shine in math, sports, music, leadership (the big caveat being that they still felt valued primarily for their appearance)—young men described just one narrow route to successful masculinity.

One-third said they felt compelled to suppress their feelings, to "suck it up" or "be a man" when they were sad or scared, and more than 40 percent said that when they were angry, society expected them to be combative. In another survey, which compared young men from the U.S., the U.K., and Mexico, Americans reported more social pressure to be ever-ready for sex and to get with as many women as possible; they also acknowledged more stigma against homosexuality, and they received more messages that they should control their female partners, as in: Men "deserve to know" the whereabouts of their girlfriends or wives at all times.

Feminism may have provided girls with a powerful alternative to conventional femininity, and a language with which to express the myriad problems-that-have-no-name, but there have been no credible equivalents for boys. Quite the contrary: The definition of masculinity seems to be in some respects contracting. When asked what traits society values most in boys, only 2 percent of male respondents in the PerryUndem survey said honesty and morality, and only 8 percent said leadership skills—traits that are, of course, admirable in anyone but have traditionally been considered masculine. When I asked my subjects, as I always did, what they liked about being a boy, most of them drew a blank. "Huh," mused Josh, a college sophomore at Washington State. (All the teenagers I spoke with are identified by pseudonyms.)

"That's interesting. I never really thought about that. You hear a lot more about what is wrong with guys."

While following the conventional script may still bring social and professional rewards to boys and men, research shows that those who rigidly adhere to certain masculine norms are not only more likely to harass and bully others but to themselves be victims of verbal or physical violence. They're more prone to binge-drinking, risky sexual behavior, and getting in car accidents. They are also less happy than other guys, with higher depression rates and fewer friends in whom they can confide.

It wasn't always thus. According to Andrew Smiler, a psychologist who has studied the history of Western masculinity, the ideal late-19th-century man was compassionate, a caretaker, but such qualities lost favor as paid labor moved from homes to factories during industrialization. In fact, the Boy Scouts, whose creed urges its members to be loyal, friendly, courteous, and kind, was founded in 1910 in part to counter that dehumanizing trend. Smiler attributes further distortions in masculinity to a century-long backlash against women's rights. During World War I, women proved that they could keep the economy humming on their own, and soon afterward they secured the vote. Instead of embracing gender equality, he says, the country's leaders "doubled down" on the inalienable male right to power, emphasizing men's supposedly more logical and less emotional nature as a prerequisite for leadership.

Then, during the second half of the 20th century, traditional paths to manhood—early marriage, breadwinning—began to close, along with the positive traits associated with them. Today many parents are unsure of how to raise a boy, what sort of masculinity to encourage in their sons. But as I learned from talking with boys themselves, the culture of adolescence, which fuses hyperrationality with domination, sexual conquest, and a glorification of male violence, fills the void.

For Cole, as for many boys, this stunted masculinity is a yardstick against which all choices, even those seemingly irrelevant to male identity, are measured. When he had a choice, he would team up with girls on school projects, to avoid the possibility of appearing subordinate to another guy. "With a girl, it feels safer to talk and ask questions, to work together or to admit that I did something wrong and want help," Cole said. During his junior year, he briefly suggested to his crew teammates that they go vegan for a while, just to show that athletes could. "And everybody was like, 'Cole, that is the dumbest idea ever. We'd be the slowest in any race. That's somewhat true—we do need protein. We do need fats and salts and carbs that we get from meat. But another reason they all thought it was stupid is because being vegans would make us pussies.'"

Learning to "Man Up"

There is no difference between the sexes' need for connection in infancy, nor between their capacity for empathy—there's actually some evidence that male infants are more expressive than females. Yet, from the get-go, boys are relegated to an impoverished emotional landscape. In a classic study, adults shown a video of an infant startled by a jack-in-the-box were more likely to presume the baby was "angry" if they were first told the child was male. Mothers of young children have repeatedly been found to talk more to their girls and to employ a broader, richer emotional vocabulary with them; with their sons, again, they tend to linger on anger. As for fathers, they speak with less emotional nuance than mothers regardless of their child's sex. Despite that, according to Judy Y. Chu, a human-biology lecturer at Stanford who conducted a study of boys from pre-K through first grade, little boys have a keen understanding of emotions and a desire for close relationships. But by age 5 or 6, they've learned to knock that stuff off, at least in public: to disconnect from feelings of weakness, reject friendships with girls (or take them underground, outside of school), and become more hierarchical in their behavior.

By adolescence, says the Harvard psychologist William Pollack, boys become "shame-phobic," convinced that peers will lose respect for them if they discuss their personal problems. My conversations bore this out. Boys routinely confided that they felt denied—by male peers, girlfriends, the media, teachers, coaches, and especially their fathers—the full spectrum of human expression. Cole, for instance, spent most of his childhood with his mother, grandmother, and sister—his parents split up when he was 10 and his dad, who was in the military, was often away. Cole spoke of his mom with unbridled love and respect. His father was another matter. "He's a nice guy," Cole said—caring and involved, even after the divorce—"but I can't be myself around him. I feel like I need to keep everything that's in here"—Cole tapped his chest again—"behind a wall, where he can't see it. It's a taboo—like, not as bad as incest, but . . ."

Rob, an 18-year-old from New Jersey in his freshman year at a North Carolina college, said his father would tell him to "man up" when he was struggling in school or with baseball. "That's why I never talk to anybody about my problems." He'd always think, If you can't handle this on your own, then you aren't a man; you aren't trying hard enough. Other boys also pointed to their fathers as the chief of the gender police, though in a less obvious way. "It's not like my dad is some alcoholic, emotionally unavailable asshole with a pulse," said a college sophomore in Southern California. "He's a normal, loving, charismatic guy who's not at all intimidating." But "there's a block there. There's a hesitation, even though I don't like to admit that. A hesitation to talk about . . . anything, really. We learn to confide in nobody. You sort of train yourself not to feel."

I met Rob about four months after he'd broken up with his high-school girlfriend. The two had dated for more than three years—"I really did love her," he said—and although their colleges were far apart, they'd decided to try to stay together. Then, a few weeks into freshman year, Rob heard from a friend that she was cheating on him. "So I cut her off," he said, snapping his fingers. "I stopped talking to her and forgot about her completely." Only . . . not really. Although he didn't use the word, Rob became depressed. The excitement he'd felt about leaving home, starting college, and rushing a fraternity all drained away, and, as the semester wore on, it didn't come back.

When I asked whom he talked to during that time, he shrugged. If he had told his friends he was "hung up" on a girl, "they'd be like, 'Stop being a bitch.'" Rob looked glum. The only person with whom he had been able to drop his guard was his girlfriend, but that was no longer an option.

Girlfriends, mothers, and in some cases sisters were the most common confidants of the boys I met. While it's wonderful to know they have someone to talk to—and I'm sure mothers, in particular, savor the role—teaching boys that women are responsible for emotional labor, for processing men's emotional lives in ways that would be emasculating for them to do themselves, comes at a price for both sexes. Among other things, that dependence can leave men unable to identify or express their own emotions, and ill-equipped to form caring, lasting adult relationships.

By Thanksgiving break, Rob was so distraught that he had what he called a "mental breakdown" one night while chatting in the kitchen with his mom. "I was so stressed out," he said. "Classes. The thing with my girlfriend." He couldn't describe what that "breakdown" felt like (though he did say it "scared the crap" out of his mom, who immediately demanded, "Tell me everything"). All he could say definitively was that he didn't cry. "Never," he insisted. "I don't cry, ever."

I paid close attention when boys mentioned crying—doing it, not doing it, wanting to do it, not being able to do it. For most, it was a rare and humiliating event—a dangerous crack in a carefully constructed edifice. A college sophomore in Chicago told me that he hadn't been able to cry when his parents divorced. "I really wanted to," he said. "I needed to cry." His solution: He streamed three movies about the Holocaust over the weekend. That worked.

As someone who, by virtue of my sex, has always had permission to weep, I didn't initially understand this. Only after multiple interviews did I realize that when boys confided in me about crying—or, even more so, when they teared up right in front of me—they were taking a risk, trusting me with something private and precious: evidence of vulnerability, or a desire for it. Or, as with Rob, an inability to acknowledge any human frailty that was so poignant, it made me want to, well, cry.

Bro Culture

While my interview subjects struggled when I asked what they liked about being a boy, the most frequent response was sports. They recalled their early days on the playing field with almost romantic warmth. But I was struck by how many had dropped athletics they'd enjoyed because they couldn't stand The Lord of the Flies mentality of teammates or coaches.

Perhaps the most extreme example was Ethan, a kid from the Bay Area who had been recruited by a small liberal arts college in New England to play lacrosse. He said he'd expected to encounter the East Coast "'lax bro' culture," but he'd underestimated its intensity. "It was all about sex" and bragging about hooking up, and even the coaches endorsed victim-blaming, Ethan told me. "They weren't like that in class or around other people; it was a super-liberal school. But once you got them in the locker room . . ." He shook his head. "It was one of the most jarring experiences of my life."

As a freshman, Ethan didn't feel he could challenge his older teammates, especially without support from the coaches. So he quit the team; not only that, he transferred. "If I'd stayed, there would've been a lot of pressure on me to play, a lot of resentment, and I would've run into those guys all the time. This way I didn't really have to explain anything." At his new school, Ethan didn't play lacrosse, or anything else.

What the longtime sportswriter Robert Lipsyte calls "jock culture" (or what the boys I talked with more often referred to as "bro culture") is the dark underbelly of male-dominated enclaves, whether or not they formally involve athletics: all-boys' schools, fraternity houses, Wall Street, Silicon Valley, Hollywood, the military. Even as such groups promote bonding, even as they preach honor, pride, and integrity, they tend to condition young men to treat anyone who is not "on the team" as the enemy (the only women who ordinarily make the cut are blood relatives—bros before hos!), justifying any hostility toward them. Loyalty is paramount, and masculinity is habitually established through misogynist language and homophobia.

As a senior in high school, Cole was made captain of the crew team. He relished being part of a unit, a band of brothers. When he raced, he imagined pulling each stroke for the guy in front of him, for the guy behind him—never for himself alone. But not everyone could muster such higher purpose. "Crew demands you push yourself to a threshold of pain and keep yourself there," Cole said. "And it's hard to find something to motivate you to do that other than anger and aggression."

I asked him about how his teammates talked in the locker room. That question always made these young men squirm. They'd rather talk about looking at porn, erectile dysfunction, premature ejaculation—anything else. Cole cut his eyes to the side, shifted in his seat, and sighed deeply. "Okay," he finally said, "so here's my best shot: We definitely say fuck a lot; fuckin' can go anywhere in a sentence. And we call each other pussies, bitches. We never say the N-word, though. That's going too far."

"What about fag?" I asked.

"No," he said, shaking his head firmly.

"So why can't you say fag or the N-word but you can say pussy and bitch? Aren't those just as offensive?"

"One of my friends said we probably shouldn't say those words anymore either, but what would we replace them with? We couldn't think of anything that bites as much."

"Bites?"

"Yeah. It's like . . . for some reason pussy just works. When someone calls me a pussy— 'Don't be a pussy! Come on! Fuckin' go! Pull! Pull! Pull!'—it just flows. If someone said, 'Come on, Cole, don't be weak! Be tough! Pull! Pull! Pull!,' it just wouldn't get inside my head the same way. I don't know why that is." He paused. "Well," he said, "maybe I do. Maybe I just try not to dig too deeply."

Although losing ground is more progressive circles, like the one Cole runs in, fag remained pervasive in the language of the boys I interviewed—including those who insisted that they would never use the word in reference to an actual homosexual. Fag has become less a comment on a boy's sexuality, says the University of Oregon sociology professor C. J. Pascoe, than a referendum on his manhood. It can be used to mock anything, she told me, even something as random as a guy "dropping the meat out of his sandwich." (Perhaps oddest to me, Pascoe found that one of the more common reasons boys get tagged with fag is for acting romantically with a girl. That's seen as heterosexual in the "wrong" way, which explains why one high-school junior told me that having a girlfriend was "gay.") That fluidity, the elusiveness of the word's definition, only intensifies its power, much like slut for girls.

Recently, Pascoe turned her attention to no homo, a phrase that gained traction in the 1990s. She sifted through more than 1,000 tweets, primarily by young men, that included the phrase. Most were expressing a positive emotion, sometimes as innocuous as "I love chocolate ice cream, #nohomo" or "I loved the movie The Day After Tomorrow, #nohomo." "A lot of times they were saying things like 'I miss you' to a friend or 'We should hang out soon,'" she said. "Just normal expressions of joy or connection." No homo is a form of inoculation against insults from other guys, Pascoe concluded, a "shield that allows boys to be fully human."

Just because some young men now draw the line at referring to someone who is openly gay as a fag doesn't mean, by the way, that gay men (or men with traits that read as gay) are suddenly safe. If anything, the gay guys I met were more conscious of the rules of manhood than their straight peers were. They had to be—and because of that, they were like spies in the house of hypermasculinity.

Mateo, 17, attended the same Boston-area high school as Cole, also on a scholarship, but the two could not have presented more differently. Mateo, whose father is Salvadoran, was slim and tan, with an animated expression and a tendency to wave his arms as he spoke. Where Cole sat straight and still, Mateo crossed his legs at the knee and swung his foot, propping his chin on one hand.

This was Mateo's second private high school. The oldest of six children, he had been identified as academically gifted and encouraged by an eighth-grade teacher to apply to an all-boys prep school for his freshman year. When he arrived, he discovered that his classmates were nearly all white, athletic, affluent, and, as far as he could tell, straight. Mateo—Latino and gay, the son of a janitor—was none of those things. He felt immediately conscious of how he held himself, of how he sat, and especially of the pitch of his voice. He tried lowering it, but that felt unnatural, so he withdrew from conversation altogether. He changed the way he walked as well, to avoid being targeted as "girly." "One of my only friends there was gay too," he said, "and he was a lot more outward about it. He just got destroyed."

Guys who identify as straight but aren't athletic, or are involved in the arts, or have a lot of female friends, all risk having their masculinity impugned. What has changed for this generation, though, is that some young men, particularly if they grew up around

LGBTQ people, don't rise to the bait. "I don't mind when people mistake me for being gay," said Luke, a high-school senior from New York City. "It's more of an annoyance than anything, because I want people to believe me when I say I'm straight." The way he described himself did, indeed, tick every stereotypical box. "I'm a very thin person," he said. "I like clothing. I care about my appearance in maybe a more delicate way. I'm very in touch with my sensitive side. So when people think I'm gay?" He shrugged. "It can feel like more of a compliment. Like, 'Oh, you like the way I dress? Thank you!'"

One of Luke's friends, who was labeled "the faggot frosh" in ninth grade, is not so philosophical. "He treats everything as a test of his masculinity," Luke told me. "Like, once when I was wearing red pants, I heard him say to other people, 'He looks like such a faggot.' I didn't care, and maybe in that situation no one was really harmed, but when you apply that attitude to whole populations, you end up with Donald Trump as president."

W's and L's

Sexual conquest—or perhaps more specifically, bragging about your experiences to other boys—is, arguably, the most crucial aspect of toxic masculinity. Nate, who attended a public high school in the Bay Area, knew this well. At a party held near the beginning of his junior year of high school, he sank deep into the couch, trying to look chill. Kids were doing shots and smoking weed. Some were Juuling. Nate didn't drink much himself and never got high. He wasn't morally opposed to it; he just didn't like the feeling of being out of control.

At 16, reputation meant everything to Nate, and certain things could cement your status. "The whole goal of going to a party is to hook up with girls and then tell your guys about it," he said. And there's this "race for experience," because if you get behind, by the time you do hook up with a girl "she'll have hit it with, like, five guys already. Then she's going to know how to do things" you don't—and that's a problem, if she tells people "you've got, floppy lips" or "don't know how to get her bra off."

A lanky boy with dark, liquid eyes and curly hair that resisted all attempts at taming, Nate put himself in the middle of his school's social hierarchy: friends with both the "popular" and "lower" kids. Still, he'd hooked up with only three girls since ninth grade—kissing, getting under their shirts—but none had wanted a repeat. That left him worried about his skills. He is afraid of intimacy, he told me sincerely. "It's a huge self-esteem suck."

It would probably be more accurate to say that Nate was afraid of having drunken sexual interactions with a girl he did not know or trust. But it was all about credentialing. "Guys need to prove themselves to their guys," Nate said. To do that, "they're going to be dominating." They're going to "push." Because the girl is just there "as a means for him to get off and to brag."

Before the start of this school year, Nate's "dry spell" had seemed to be ending. He'd been in a relationship with a girl that lasted a full two weeks, until other guys told him she was "slutty"—their word, he hastened to add, not his. Although any hookup is marginally better than none, Nate said, you only truly earn points for getting sexual with the right kind of girl. "If you hook up with a girl below your status, it's an 'L,'" he explained. "A loss. Like, a bad move." So he stopped talking to the girl, which was too bad. He'd really liked her.

After a short trip to the kitchen to watch his friend Kyle stand on a table and drunkenly try to pour Sprite from a can into a shot glass, Nate returned to the couch, starting to relax as people swirled around him. Suddenly Nicole, the party's host and a senior, plopped onto his lap, handing him a shot of vodka. Nate was impressed, if a little confused. Usually, if a girl wanted to hook up with you, there were texts and Snapchats, and if you said yes, it was on; everyone would be anticipating it, and expecting a postmortem.

Nate thought Nicole was "pretty hot"—she had a great body, he said—though he'd never been especially interested in her before this moment. Still, he knew that hooking up with her would be a "W." A big one. He glanced around the room subtly, wanting to make sure, without appearing to care, that everyone who mattered—everyone "relevant"—saw what was going down. A couple of guys gave him little nods. One winked. Another slapped him on the shoulder. Nate feigned nonchalance. Meanwhile, he told me, "I was just trying not to pop a boner."

Nicole took Nate's hand and led him to an empty bedroom. He got through the inevitable, cringey moments when you actually have to talk to your partner, then, finally, they started kissing. In his anxiety, Nate bit Nicole's lip. Hard. "I was thinking, Oh God! What do I do now?" But he kept going. He took off her top and undid her bra. He took off his own shirt. Then she took off her pants. "And that," he said, "was the first time I ever saw a vagina. I did not know what to do with it." He recalled that his friends had said girls go crazy if you stick your fingers up there and make the "come here" motion, so he tried it, but Nicole just lay there. He didn't ask what might feel better to her, because that would have been admitting ignorance.

After a few more agonizing minutes, Nicole announced that she wanted to see what was going on upstairs, and left, Nate trailing behind. A friend handed him a bottle of Jack Daniel's. Another high-fived him. A third said, "Dude, you hit that!" Maybe the hookup hadn't been a disaster after all: He still had bragging rights.

Then he heard a senior, a guy Nate considered kind of a friend, loudly ask Nicole, "Why would you hook up with Nate?"

She giggled. "Oh, I was drunk!" she said. "I was so drunk!" They were calling him an "L."

By Monday morning, Nicole had spread the word that Nate was bad at hooking up: that he'd bit her lip, that he didn't know how to finger a girl.at his nails were ragged. The stereotype is that guys go into gory detail," Nate said, but "it's the other way around." Guys will brag, but they're not specific. Girls will go into "what his penis looked like," every single thing he did.

Nate said he felt "completely emasculated," so mortified that he told his mom he was sick and stayed home from school the next day. "I was basically crying," he said. "I was like, Shit! I fucked up."

No question, gossip about poor "performance" can destroy a guy's reputation almost as surely as being called a "slut" or a "prude" can destroy a girl's. As a result, the boys I talked with were concerned with female satisfaction during a hookup; they just didn't typically define it as the girl having an orgasm. They believed it to be a function of their own endurance and, to a lesser extent, penis size. A college freshman in Los Angeles recalled a high-school classmate who'd had sex with a girl who told everyone he'd ejaculated really quickly: "He got the nickname Second Sam. That basically scared the crap out of all the other guys." A college senior in Boston recounted how he would glance at the clock when he started penetration. "I'd think, I have to last five minutes, minimum," he said. "And once I could do that, I'd think, I need to get to double digits. I don't know if it's necessarily about your partner's enjoyment. It's more about getting beyond the point where you'd be embarrassed, maintaining your pride. It turns sex into a task one I enjoy to a certain degree, but one where you're monitoring your performance rather than living in the moment."

Eventually, Nate decided that he had to take a stand, if only to make returning to school bearable. He texted Nicole and said, "'I'm sorry that you didn't enjoy it, [but] I would never roast you. Why are you doing this?'" She felt "really bad," he said. "She stopped telling people, but it took me until the next semester to recover."

How Misogyny Becomes "Hilarious"

No matter how often I heard it, the brutal language that even a conscientious young man like Nate used to describe sexual contact—you hit that!—always unnerved me. In mixed-sex groups, teenagers may talk about hooking up (already impersonal), but when guys are on their own, they nail, they pound, they bang, they smash, they hammer. They tap that ass, they tear her up. It can be hard to tell whether they have engaged in an intimate act or just returned from a construction site.

It's not like I imagined boys would gush about making sweet, sweet love to the ladies, but why was their language so weaponized? The answer, I came to believe, was that locker-room talk isn't about sex at all, which is why guys were ashamed to discuss it openly with me. The (often clearly exaggerated) stories boys tell are really about power: using aggression toward women to connect and to validate one another as heterosexual, or to claim top spots in the adolescent sexual hierarchy. Dismissing that as "banter" denies the ways that language can desensitize—abrade boys' ability to see girls as people deserving of respect and dignity in sexual encounters.

For evidence, look no further than the scandals that keep popping up at the country's top colleges: Harvard, Amherst, Columbia, Yale (the scene of an especially notorious 2010 fraternity chant, "No means yes; yes means anal").

Most recently, in the spring of 2019, at the politically progressive Swarthmore College, in Pennsylvania, two fraternities disbanded after student-run publications released more than 100 pages of "minutes" from house meetings a few years earlier that included, among other things, jokes about a "rape attic" and the acquiring of roofies, "finger blasting" a member's 10-year-old sister, and vomiting on women during sex.

When called out, boys typically claim that they thought they were just being "funny." And in a way that makes sense—when left unexamined, such "humor" may seem like an extension of the gross-out comedy of childhood. Little boys are famous for their fart jokes, booger jokes, poop jokes. It's how they test boundaries, understand the human body, gain a little cred among their peers. But, as can happen with sports, their glee in that can both enable and camouflage sexism. The boy who, at age 10, asks his friends the difference between a dead baby and a bowling ball may or may not find it equally uproarious, at 16, to share what a woman and a bowling ball have in common (you can Google it). He may or may not post ever-escalating "jokes" about women, or African Americans, or homosexuals, or disabled people on a group Snapchat. He may or may not send "funny" texts to friends about "girls who need to be raped," or think it's hysterical to surprise a buddy with a meme in which a woman is being gagged by a penis, her mascara mixed with her tears. He may or may not, at 18, scrawl the names of his hookups on a wall in his all-male dorm, as part of a year-long competition to see who can "pull" the most. Perfectly nice, bright, polite boys I interviewed had done one or another of these things.

How does that happen? I talked with a 15-year-old from the East Coast who had been among a group of boys suspended from school for posting more than 100 racist and sexist "jokes" about classmates on a group Finsta (a secondary, or "fake," Instagram account that is in many cases more genuine than a "Rinsta," or "real" account). The Finsta became very competitive," he said. "You wanted to make your friends laugh, but when you're not face-to-face," you can't tell whether you'll get a reaction, "so you go one step beyond." It was "that combination of competitiveness and that. , , disconnect that triggered it to get worse and worse."

At the most disturbing end of the continuum, "funny" and "hilarious" become a defense against charges of sexual harassment or assault. To cite just one example, a boy from Steubenville, Ohio, was captured on video joking about the repeated violation of an unconscious girl at a party by a couple of high-school football players. "She is so raped," he said, laughing. "They raped her quicker than Mike Tyson." When someone off camera suggested that rape wasn't funny, he retorted, "It isn't funny—it's hilarious!"

"Hilarious" is another way, under the pretext of horseplay or group bonding, that boys learn to disregard others' feelings as well as their own. "Hilarious" is a haven, offering distance when something is inappropriate, confusing, depressing, unnerving, or horrifying; when something defies boys' ethics. It allows them to subvert a more compassionate response that could be read as unmasculine—and makes sexism and misogyny feel transgressive rather than supportive of an age-old status quo. Boys may know when something is wrong; they may even know that true manhood—or maybe just common decency—compels them to speak up. Yet, too often, they fear that if they do, they'll be marginalized or, worse, themselves become the target of derision from other boys. Masculinity, then, becomes not only about what boys do say, but about what they don't—or won't, or can't—say, even when they wish they could. The psychologists Dan Kindlon and Michael Thompson, the authors of Raising Cain: Protecting the Emotional Life of Boys, have pointed out that silence in the face of cruelty or sexism is how too many boys become men. Charis Denison, a sex educator in the Bay Area, puts it another way: "At one time or another, every young man will get a letter of admission to 'dick school.' The question is, will he drop out, graduate, or go for an advanced degree?"

Midway through Cole's freshman year in military college, I FaceTimed him to see how he'd resolved the conflict between his personal values and those of the culture in which he found himself. As he'd expected, most of his classmates were male, and he said there was a lot of what passed for friendly ribbing: giving one another "love taps" on the back of the head; blocking one another's paths, then pretending to pick a fight; grabbing one another's asses; pretending to lean in for a kiss. Giving someone a hard time, Cole said, was always "easy humor," but it could spiral into something more troubling pretty quickly. When one of his dorm mates joked to another, "I'm going to piss on you in your sleep," for instance, the other boy shot back, "If you do, I'll fucking rape you." For better or worse, Cole said, that sort of comment no longer rattled him.

Although he had been adamantly against the epithet fag when we met, Cole found himself using it, reasoning, as other boys did, that it was "more like 'You suck' or 'You're lame.'" However, at least one of his friends had revealed himself to be legitimately homophobic, declaring that being gay was un-American ("I didn't know that about him until after we became friends," Cole insisted). And Cole had not met a single openly LGBTQ student at the school. He certainly wouldn't want to be out in this environment if he were gay. Nor, he said, would he want to be Asian—the two Asian American boys in his dorm were ostracized and treated like foreigners; both seemed miserable.

"I do feel kind of like a cop-out for letting all the little things slide," Cole said. "It's a cop-out to not fight the good fight. But, you know, there was that thing I tried sophomore year . . . It just didn't work. I could be a social-justice warrior here, but I don't think anyone would listen to me. And I'd have no friends."

The #MeToo movement has created an opportunity, a mandate not only to discuss sexual violence but to engage young men in authentic, long-overdue conversations about gender and intimacy. I don't want to suggest that this is easy. Back in the early 1990s, when I began writing about how girls' confidence drops during adolescence, parents would privately tell me that they were afraid to raise outspoken daughters, girls who stood up for themselves and their rights, because they might be excluded by peers and called "bossy" (or worse). Although there is still much work to be done, things are different for young women today. Now it's time to rethink assumptions about how we raise boys. That will require models of manhood that are neither ashamed nor regressive, and that emphasize emotional, flexibility—a hallmark of mental health. Stoicism is valuable sometimes, as is free expression; toughness and tenderness can coexist in one human. In the right context, physical aggression is fun, satisfying, even thrilling. If your response to all of this is Obviously, I'd say: Sure, but it's a mistake to underestimate the strength and durability of the cultural machinery at work on adolescent boys. Real change will require a sustained, collective effort on the part of fathers, mothers, teachers, coaches. (A study of 2,000 male high school athletes found significantly reduced rates of dating violence and a greater likelihood of intervening to stop other boys' abusive conduct among those who participated in weekly coach-led discussions about consent, personal responsibility, and respectful behavior.)

We have to purposefully and repeatedly broaden the masculine repertoire for dealing with disappointment, anger, desire. We have to say not just what we don't want from boys but what we do want from them. Instructing them to "respect women" and to "not get anyone pregnant" isn't enough. As one college sophomore told me, "That's kind of like telling someone who's learning to drive not to run over any little old ladies and then handing him the car keys. Well, of course you think you're not going to run over an old lady. But you still don't know how to drive." By staying quiet, we leave many boys in a state of confusion—or worse, push them into a defensive crouch, primed to display their manhood in the one way that is definitely on offer: by being a dick.

During our first conversation, Cole had told me that he'd decided to join the military after learning in high-school history class about the My Lai massacre—the infamous 1968 slaughter by U.S. troops of hundreds of unarmed Vietnamese civilians along with the mass rape of girls as young as 10. "I want to be able to be in the same position as someone like that commanding officer and not order people to do something like that," he'd said. I'd been impressed. Given that noble goal, was a single failure to call out sexism a reason to stop trying? I understood that the personal cost might be greater than the impact. I also understood that, developmentally, adolescents want and need to feel a strong sense of belonging. But if Cole didn't practice standing up, if he didn't figure out a way to assert his values and find others who shared them, who was he?

"I knew you were going to ask me something like that," he said. "I don't know. In this hyper-masculine culture where you call guys 'pussies' and 'bitches' and 'maggots'—"

"Did you say 'maggots,' or 'faggots?'" I interrupted.

"Maggots. Like worms. So you're equating maggots to women and to women's body parts to convince young men like me that we're strong. To go up against that, to convince people that we don't need to put others down to lift ourselves up . . . I don't know. I would need to be some sort of superman."

Cole fell silent.

"Maybe the best I can do is to just be a decent guy," he continued. "The best I can do is lead by example." He paused again, furrowed his brow, then added, "I really hope that will make a difference."

Questions for Critical Thinking

1. The author argues that, while feminism has provided girls with an alternative to conventional femininity, contemporary ideals about masculinity seem to be given less alternatives to conventional masculinity, ultimately being harmful to those who adhere to its ideals. Do you find her description to be accurate in your experience? What examples can you offer??

2. What functions are served by socializing boys to the conventional script of toxic masculinity? Why do you think such ideals are perpetuated?

3. What would men's relationships (to other men as well as to women) look like if they were socialized to into broader expectations regarding what it means to be a boy/man? Would the prevalence of social inequality be impacted in any way? If so, how? If not, why not?

PART IV

Resistance and Social Change

Introduction

Throughout this text we have explored how elements of the social structure construct categories of difference with regard to race, class, gender, and sexuality and transform them into systems of oppression and privilege. In Part I we examined why such categories are constructed, as well as the social factors involved in the process of transforming them into systems of inequality. In Part II we explored the significance of social institutions in maintaining these systems of inequality as systems of oppression and privilege. The readings in Part III provided us with personal representations illustrating how such systems impact daily lives. The readings in each of the preceding sections have prepared us for the task of this one—to understand the ways in which we can work toward the transformation of systems of oppression and privilege into a system of equal access to opportunity.

Beginning the work of transforming systems of oppression and privilege is often difficult. When we first become aware of systems of inequality, many of us are overwhelmed and do not have a clear idea of where to begin to bring about positive social change. Furthermore, as we discuss later in this section, many of us are motivated to work for social change because of the pain that we or someone close to us experienced as a result of systems of oppression. Because of our proximity to the injustice, we may not feel physically or emotionally capable of challenging the system.

Starting to transform systems of oppression and privilege is also hindered by the role of social institutions in maintaining these systems. As discussed in Part II, social institutions work to maintain systems of inequality based on ideologies that endorse and justify the interests of the dominant group. As a result, they are not likely to be open to challenges. Actions to bring about positive social change are therefore met with resistance on the parts of these institutions and discredited, if not omitted from history altogether. For example, in April 1989 in Beijing, China, a massive demonstration of Chinese students for democratic reform began on Tiananmen Square. Joined by workers, intellectuals, and civil servants until over one million people filled the square, the protestors demanded that the leadership of the country resign. The government responded on June 3 and 4 with troops and tanks, killing thousands to quell a "counter-revolutionary rebellion." Government reaction to these protests has been followed by silence. There is no public discussion of the incident in China, except for occasional government accounts defending the actions of the military. Editors of newspapers in China delete even vague references to the protests. Groups and individuals protesting injustice in the United States have been met with similar acts of resistance and attempts to render their political activism invisible. For example, there have been numerous anti-protest legislation efforts since the uprisings that occurred around the world in response to the murder of George Floyd in Minneapolis in May of 2020. In Indiana, a Republican proposal would block anyone convicted of unlawful assembly from holding state employment, including elected office. A bill in Minnesota would prohibit those convicted of unlawful protesting from receiving student loans, unemployment benefits or housing assistance. In Florida, Governor DeSantis signed legislation that reinforced existing laws governing public disorder and created a new level of infractions. In all, Republican lawmakers in 34 states have introduced 81 anti-protest bills during the 2021 legislative session—more than twice as many proposals as in any other year. Meanwhile, Republican legislators in Oklahoma and Iowa have passed bills granting immunity to drivers whose vehicles strike and injure protesters in public streets (Epstein and Mazzei 2021). Faced with the possibility of opposition and, moreover, lacking an awareness of previous efforts to transform systems of oppression and privilege, those who would begin work toward positive social change face major difficulty.

Finally, beginning the work of transforming systems of oppression and privilege into systems of equal access to opportunity is often difficult because we underestimate our ability to impact these systems. In essence, we doubt that we will be able to bring about change. However, as Margaret Mead said, "Never doubt that a small group of thoughtful, committed citizens can change the world; indeed, it's the only thing that ever has." Efforts to create social equality are often begun by everyday individuals.

The readings in this section examine the various ways individuals and groups have worked to create positive social change. Those who bring about social change come from all walks of life. As you read these selections, consider the systems of oppression and privilege that you would like to see change—and the ways in which you would like to go about working for this change. Create your own image of what a system of equal access to opportunity would look like.

Before beginning this process, it is important to remember that difference is not always negative. On the contrary, the preservation of a distinct identity is often central to working toward positive social change. Differences are not problematic; rather, as stated in Part I of this text, it is when the meanings and values applied to these *differences* transform them into systems of *inequality* that such constructs become problematic. As we work to find solutions to inequality, it is important that we seek not to eliminate difference but rather to transform the ways in which difference has been established into a system where each individual is seen as valuable.

What Is Social Change?

To transform systems of oppression and privilege into systems of equality, it is important that we understand the concept of social change. **Social change**—fundamental alterations in the patterns of culture, structure, and social behavior over time—is always occurring. It can result from a variety of actions and can be inspired from a number of motivations. From individual actions to collective behavior, efforts and movements to transform systems of oppression and privilege work toward **positive social change**—changing patterns of the social structure and social behavior in an effort to reduce oppression and increase inclusion for all members of society.

Such efforts often involve conflicts in **ideology.** As we discussed in Part II, the maintenance of systems of oppression depends on the presence of ideologies that provide the basis of inequality. The clash in ideology that results from challenging beliefs, values, and attitudes that see members of certain groups as inferior or superior is generally seen as disruptive to the social order and may result in strong reactions on the part of those interested in maintaining the power of the dominant group. For example, on November 14, 1960, Ruby Bridges became the first black child in the history of the US South to enter an all-white school. Although only in first grade and six years old, she was an agent for social change—and also represented a clash in ideology with the racially segregated South. As a result, she needed to be escorted by US marshals on the first day of school and spent her first year in that school in a class of one because all the parents pulled their children out of school to protest the integration. Although such clashes in ideology may act as deterrents for those wanting to transform systems of oppression, the reality that dominant ideologies do not always win out in the end can also serve as encouragement.

What Are the Goals of Social Change?

When seeking positive social change, we must have a clear idea of the goals we are working toward. Just as there are divergent approaches to positive social change, there are also many goals. The general goal in seeking to transform systems of oppression is to develop systems in which all have access to important resources and none is advantaged at the expense of others, but specific goals of positive social change are defined by those who seek them. As you read this section, consider the injustices that have come to matter to you and imagine how you would like to see these injustices transformed.

For some, discussions of social change are centered around a goal of creating a society based on a system of **social justice**—a system in which each member of society has the opportunity and power to fully participate in the social system. As mentioned in Part I, in the United States we have a system based on a **civil rights** framework. Such a framework is based on the concept of majority rule, where the will of the majority becomes the will for all, with some people inevitably losing. A *social justice* framework stands in contrast to such a system and provides the opportunity for each member of society to benefit. It relies on three principles.

The first principle is that *people have options.* These options relate to having access to resources and can include opportunity for work, adequate health care, access to housing, freedom from harassment or discrimination, and so on. In some ways, the United States can be seen as meeting this principle, in that with our vast resources it appears that we all have the *option* of access to these resources. For example, with regard to opportunity for work and career choice, many of us who grew up in the United States were presented with the notion that anyone has the option to be president. You do not need to be of any particular race, class, gender, or sexuality to have this option.

The second principle of a social justice framework is that *people are aware of their options.* In such a framework we must be made aware of our opportunities to access important resources such as attending college, applying for jobs, purchasing property, and receiving adequate health care. Considering again the opportunity to become president, many of us who grew up in the United States heard that this was a possibility and thus we were aware of this option. Indeed, we often heard such messages along with Horatio Alger stories and notions of achieving the "American Dream." Many of these messages were rooted in the assumption that the United States is a **meritocracy**—a system in which people's success is a result of their talents, abilities, and efforts. However, the notion of a meritocracy ignores the advantages that are given to some and denied to others. In a socially just system, people are aware of their options and their opportunities and are not hindered by unfair disadvantages.

The third and final principle of a socially just system is that *people have the power to act on their options.* This is where the system of civil rights—and thus the system of the United States— departs from that of a social justice framework. As noted above, the assumption of a meritocracy sits at the core of the American Dream. A system of oppression and privilege that derives from the social construction of difference results in an unequal distribution of power. Because of this unequal distribution, it is not our individual talents, abilities, and efforts that lead to our ability to succeed, but our access to power. Power, typically viewed as an ability to control people or things, can be defined in many ways. In the case of running for president, one's power directly relates to the amount of money one is able to raise to run a successful campaign. For example, according to the *United States Federal Elections Commission* in 2020, the two major presidential candidates for president (Biden and Trump) spent in excess of $1 billion and $808 million, respectively. From our discussion in Part II of the distribution of income and wealth in the United States, it is obvious that there are few people, particularly African Americans and other people of color, who possess or have access to the financial resources and other forms of power to be able to act on their option to become president. Considering this, it is clear that a civil rights system departs from one based on social justice.

A social justice framework is one of many possibilities in framing our efforts to transform systems of oppression and privilege. Another possible framework relies on **empowerment**—a process of defining ourselves rather than being defined by others. In a system based on empowerment, those who have experienced oppression are given the opportunity to create their own power in improving their own circumstances. Whatever specific goal each of us sets our sights on, we must establish our own strategies for working toward that goal. Many of the readings in this section offer insights that may be useful in establishing these strategies. These strategies include the importance of integrating issues of racial and class inequality, as in Eric Holt-Giménez and Yi Wang's exploration of the role of food justice to address issues of hunger and food insecurity in "Reform or Transformation? The Pivotal Role of Food Justice in the U.S. Food Movement" (Reading 48) and the role of a human rights framework in the Black Lives Matter movement, rooted in the history of the black freedom struggle as explained by Fredrick C. Harris in "The Next Civil Rights Movement?" (Reading 50). These examples are intended to broaden our understanding of how to build effective movements to bring about positive social change.

What Motivates Work for Social Change?

Much work has been done in a variety of contexts to bring about positive social change to transform systems of oppression and privilege. The factors that precipitate such work come from a variety of sources. Work for positive social change can be motivated by personal experiences; at other times, it is motivated by dissatisfaction with social systems on the part of large groups of people. To understand how to create positive social change, it is important to understand what has motivated others to become involved in such efforts.

Motivation for working toward positive social change can come from factors related to the social system. For example, according to Neil Smelser (1962), when important aspects of a social system appear to be out of joint, such as when standards of living are not what people expect them to be, people may experience **structural strain.** As an illustration, consider the notion that the United States is thought to be an affluent society. Whether our economy is in a state of recession or boom, poverty rates continue to be high. Further, as illustrated in Part I, such poverty rates are arbitrarily determined and do not necessarily reflect the experience of poverty accurately. According to Smelser, as the strain from this situation accumulates over time, individuals become motivated to use courses of action not defined by existing institutional arrangements. As people begin to see the strain as a problem in need of a solution, they develop shared ideas about how they should respond to it.

At other times, motivation for working toward positive social change requires precipitating factors, such as the recent mobilization on many campuses and in numerous cities to work for peace in response to the war in Iraq and Afghanistan. Other precipitating factors can be hearing stories of social injustice experienced on the part of individuals. For example, the Matthew Shepard and James Byrd, Jr. Hate Crimes Prevention Act passed in 2009. Much of the motivation for working on such legislation arose from the brutal killings of James Byrd,[1] Matthew Shepard,[2] Billy Jack Gaither,[3] Juana Vega,[4] and Scotty Joe Weaver.[5] Indeed, increasing incidents of antigay hate crimes were reported after the narrow passage in 2008 of Proposition 8 in California, an antigay piece of legislation that provides that only marriage between a man and a woman is valid or recognized in California. According to the Stop AAPI Hate coalition, between March 2020 and March 2021 the number of hate incidents directed at those who were or were perceived to be Asian, Asian American, or Pacific Islander increased significantly, largely as a result of misinformation related to the COVID-19 pandemic. Acts of brutality such as these, motivated by hatred for someone seen as different or other, have motivated individuals, organizations, and government officials to work to enact legislation to reduce the likelihood that hate crimes will continue to occur.

Whether the motivation for working toward positive social change comes from witnessing inconsistencies between structural values, hearing stories of violence committed by those who hate, our own personal experiences with inequality, or some other source, taking on the challenge of working to improve our social environment does not occur unless we can imagine a reality that differs from what already exists. Returning to Part I, one of the fundamental aspects of critical thinking is the ability to imagine alternative ways of thinking. For example, if children experienced an inclusive representation of history, how might that positively impact their perceptions of their own race as well as those of others? What lasting impact might that have on constructions of race and the interactions of those who identify as belonging to different race categories? Critical thinking is a fundamental tool for those desiring to create positive social change. Imagining alternatives to the current social order can provide us not only with the motivation to work for positive social change but also with a goal and some strategies for achieving that goal.

Who Creates Positive Social Change?

When we think of positive social change, we often think of large **social movements**—sustained, organized collective effort. In addition, we tend to think of those who work toward such change as being charismatic leaders with large groups of followers. Thus, if asked who were great makers of social justice, we may mention names such as Martin Luther King, Malcolm X, Emma Goldman, Gandhi, Cesar Chavez, and Jane Addams. Moreover, many of us may imagine activists as fitting a radical image that we do not see ourselves fitting into. In any event, we rarely identify ourselves when describing agents of change.

Although it is true that a great deal of the positive social change that has occurred in our society has involved the organization of movements and the participation of great leaders, the earlier example of Ruby Bridges illustrates that such social transformation has also involved the actions of a wide array of individuals coming from all walks of life. Thus, there is no model activist. An activist can be anyone with the motivation and ideas of how to transform a situation of inequality.

For example, in 1996 Kelli Peterson, a Salt Lake City East High School student, created a group that provided safe space for support and dialogue for lesbian, gay, and bisexual students and their allies at her school. Many studies and reports have indicated the need for such a group. For example, a study conducted by the Gay, Lesbian, and Straight Education Network found that

> 84 percent of LGBT students reported that they have been verbally harassed; 82.9 percent stated that teachers or administrators rarely, if ever, intervened when they witnessed homophobic comments; 55 percent of transgender students reported being physically harassed because of their gender identity; 41 percent of lesbian, gay and bisexual students said that they had been physically harassed because of their sexual orientation; and 64.3 percent of LGBT students reported that, because of their sexual orientation, they felt unsafe at school.

When Kelli attempted to establish a gay/straight alliance, the school board voted to ban all noncurricular clubs rather than allow the alliance to be formed. Through her commitment and motivation, however, she worked to organize students, faculty, and community members to overturn the decision. The gay/straight alliance now meets regularly at Salt Lake City East High School, offering a safer environment for lesbian, gay, bisexual, and transgender students and their allies.

Just as each of us participates in constructing categories of difference and systems of oppression and privilege, we can also participate in transforming them into systems of equality. Once we locate our source of motivation and establish a new vision of what is possible, we are well on our way toward creating this change.

Where Does Positive Social Change Occur?

Just as a vast array of social activists and endless contributing factors transform categories of difference, there are also a large number of contexts within which we can enact positive social change. Further, as categories of difference are constructed and transformed into systems of inequality in a variety of contexts—institutional, interpersonal, and internal—so, too, can we work to transform systems of oppression in all contexts.

The first site of working toward positive social change is often the internal context—within ourselves. We are able to begin this work once we are able to transform how we view ourselves and our memberships within a system of oppression. To be effective agents for social change, we often must transform the negative perceptions we have of ourselves before we are able to effectively work at transforming systems of oppression in other contexts. This often involves a transformation of identity through the restoration of dignity and overcoming a previously stigmatized status.

Transforming systems of oppression within ourselves requires that we examine not only our own internalized oppression but also how we have internalized oppressive attitudes about others. One of the reasons systems of oppression persist is that individuals in those systems, regardless of their location in them, internalize the ideas of the dominant group. As Patricia Hill Collins notes in "Toward a New Vision" (Reading 45), we often fail to see how our own ideas and behaviors perpetuate someone else's subjugation. She quotes Audre Lorde as saying,

> The true focus of revolutionary change is never merely the oppressive situations which we seek to escape but that piece of the oppressor which is planted deep within each of us. (1984, 123)

As this quote illustrates, if we desire to engender positive social change, we must first examine not only the ideas we have internalized that oppress ourselves but also those notions that perpetuate the oppression of others.

Transformations of systems of oppression and privilege can also occur in interpersonal contexts. Indeed, it is at this level that a great deal of positive social change begins. Here we can often use the dynamics of our interpersonal relationships as a source of leverage in seeking to transform inequality. Love between family members, commitment between spouses/partners, philosophical or religious alliances between members of communities, political coalitions between members of an organization, and so on can all provide a foundation that makes challenges regarding oppressive or discriminatory behavior more likely to be heard and seen as valid.

We can also seek to transform systems of oppression and privilege within institutional contexts. This can involve seeking to transform the institution from within, with members of the institution using their power to create change in individuals and policies. For example, a teacher can use their position within the institution to change students through using a curriculum that is inclusive and focuses on transformation rather than perpetuation of systems of oppression. Additionally, a social scientist can use knowledge and skills as a researcher and status as a member of an academic institution to demonstrate the importance of transforming difference within other institutions. Further, institutions can establish policies and procedures that set precedents for the more inclusive treatment of marginalized groups. For example, when President Harry S. Truman officially desegregated the military in 1948, he helped to establish a precedent for future inclusion of blacks and African Americans in the United States.

Transforming systems of oppression and privilege within institutional contexts also involves individuals outside the institution who use a variety of means to pressure it to change. The use of methods such as protests, boycotts (withdrawal of support, usually through money), and informing the public of the institution's discriminatory policies and practices have been effective in bringing about change within these contexts.

It is important to note here, however, that institutions in the United States are generally organized around systems of oppression and privilege, as the readings in this text have made clear. As a result, we are often limited in the amount of change that can occur within these structures. For example, a woman who works in a large corporation that is dominated by males may risk loss of advancement, if not job security, if she challenges the institution's sexist hiring and operating practices. In addition, we should not expect that positive change will result merely because members of marginalized groups are present in powerful positions within these organizations. The success of marginalized *individuals* within an organization should not be assumed to reflect a positive change in institutional policies toward that *group*. We often assume that gender inequality will cease to exist in the workplace as more women obtain positions of prestige and authority. As illustrated in Part II, however, social policies that ignore the patriarchal structure on which they are built and assume that institutional changes will occur on the individual level will inevitably fail. These failures, in turn, will be blamed on the subordinated individual rather than on the social structure itself.

Regardless of the context within which we focus our efforts to generate positive social change, such change is possible from a variety of starting points. As you read this section, take note of the strategies and tools used and think critically about the possibilities that they reveal for you to transform systems of oppression and privilege in your own social world.

Strategies: The Importance of Coalition

As the previous discussion indicates, there are a variety of ways in which we can work to transform systems of oppression and privilege. However, it is difficult, and perhaps dangerous, to try to discern which is the *best* strategy. Indeed, such debates over strategies for generating positive social change have often stood in the way of creating any change at all and have generally only served to perpetuate inequality. However, it is important to note here that, regardless of the strategies we choose to use in the formation of positive social change, it is important to build coalitions and work across categories of difference.

Throughout this text, the connections between forms of oppression have been made clear. Systems of oppression share similarities in how they are established and maintained as well as in their effect. Thus, if we seek to transform such systems, we need to examine their foundations and the underlying aspects of the social structure that serve to perpetuate them. Such a *system-based rather* than *issue*-based focus not only enables us to build coalitions but also *requires* us to do so.

As Collins notes in "Toward a New Vision" (Reading 45), we often get caught up in asserting that there is one type of oppression that is most important, and all others, as a result, become less important. As mentioned earlier, such a debate is not only endless but also likely to defeat all efforts to transform systems of oppression and privilege. Rather than focusing on ranking oppressions, Collins argues, we need to focus on how systems of stratification interconnect. As we discussed in Parts I and II, Collins sees these systems as operating within a matrix of domination. Significant problems occur when we miss these parallels and interconnections. Understanding the interconnections among various forms of oppression will help us to forge stronger alliances and coalitions. In addition, it is important that we understand the ideological foundations shared by various forms of stratification. We cannot hope to eradicate one form of inequality if others remain intact. While these alliances and coalitions may be difficult to develop and maintain, they are necessary if we are to eradicate all forms of domination.

Further Barriers to Creating Positive Social Change

While coalition building presents an effective strategy for transforming categories of difference, it also can present a variety of barriers, institutional as well as personal, to bringing about positive social change. In addition to these barriers, we may face other obstacles in both interpersonal and institutional contexts.

Social control mechanisms, which reward conformity and punish or discourage nonconformity, are effective means of regulating the behavior of societal members. These mechanisms also create barriers to transforming systems of oppression by thwarting efforts to bring about positive social change. Anne Wilson Schaef (1981) offers an example of one such mechanism. Focusing on the social control of women, she uses the term *stoppers* to refer to anything that keeps women where the dominant group wants them to be. People seeking to create positive social change often face such stoppers, regardless of the form of oppression that they may be seeking to transform. For example, heterosexual men who challenge other men on their sexism may experience challenges to their masculinity or have their heterosexuality called into question by other men. Women who speak out against sexism risk being called lesbians or facing physical violence. People of color who speak out about racism in their workplace face accusations of being too angry or having an agenda. People who speak out against the war risk being called un-American or having their civil liberties curtailed.[6]

Stoppers also exist within institutional contexts and can have a more severe impact than those that occur on an individual level. As mentioned at the beginning of this essay, efforts to transform systems of oppression and privilege are often met with resistance on the part of institutions. For example, the social institution of the state may enact policies seeking to repress the efforts of those working to transform systems of oppression and privilege. The experiences of political prisoners, including Angela Davis[7] and Leonard Peltier,[8] offer clear examples of the ways in which institutions may work to prevent the transformation of systems of oppression.

Again, to effectively transform systems of oppression and privilege, it is important to be aware of individual as well as institutional barriers. Having this awareness will enable us to create effective strategies for moving beyond them.

Conclusion

Despite the barriers we face when seeking to transform systems of oppression and privilege, opportunities for bringing about such change continually present themselves. As mentioned earlier, there is no single cause for inequality, and thus there is no single solution. Thinking critically about categories of difference and structures of inequality can present us with endless options for generating positive social change. By challenging our assumptions and being aware of our own standpoint, we can become more aware of how our own ideas perpetuate someone else's subjugation. By imagining alternative ways of constructing our social world, we are able to establish goals for our social action. Finally, by employing a reflexive analysis, we are able to challenge dominant ideas and question rigid belief systems. Such questions and challenges will provide a good foundation for creating a structure where each individual is seen as valuable. As you read the selections in the final chapters of this text, take note of how your process of critical thinking helps you to become aware of your own goals for transforming systems of oppression and privilege.

Notes

1. James Byrd, forty-nine, was beaten unconscious and then dragged by a chain to his death from the back of a pickup truck after accepting a ride from three white men in Jasper, Texas, in June 1998. One of the men, John William King, was found guilty and given the death penalty for his role in the killing. Another man, Lawrence Brewer, was also found guilty and sentenced to death. The third suspect, Shawn Berry, was sentenced to life in prison. Byrd's body was dismembered in the

assault and many of his body parts were found about a mile from his torso. When he was found, his body was so badly disfigured that Byrd had to be identified by fingerprints.

2. Matthew Shepard, a University of Wyoming student, was lured from a bar and attacked by two men, allegedly because they presumed he was gay. He was struck eighteen times in the head with a pistol and left to die on a fence outside Laramie in October 1998. He was found unconscious eighteen hours after he was kidnapped and died five days later. One of his attackers, Russell Henderson, was sentenced to two consecutive life sentences after pleading guilty. The other man accused in the murder, Aaron McKinney, was sentenced to life without parole.

3. The body of Billy Jack Gaither, a thirty-nine-year-old textile worker, was found in rural Sylacauga, Alabama, some forty miles southeast of Birmingham, on February 20, 1999. Two men, Steven Eric Mullins and Charles Monroe Butler Jr., confessed to the killing in early March after waiving their right to counsel. After bludgeoning Gaither with an axe handle, the men burned the victim's remains. They then drove his car to a deserted location and burned it as well.

4. Juana Vega was murdered in November 2001 by Pablo Parrilla, the brother of her partner. Upset about his sister's relationship with a woman, he shot Vega five times and then repeatedly hit her with the gun and kicked her motionless body. Parrilla confessed to the killing, and following a seven-day trial, a jury found him guilty. He was sentenced to life imprisonment with extended supervision eligibility after forty-five years. Parrilla has appealed this decision.

5. The severely burned and decomposed body of Scotty Joe Weaver was found in July 2004 by a man driving an all-terrain vehicle in Minnette, Alabama. Christopher Gaines, twenty; Nichole Kelsay, eighteen; and Robert Porter, eighteen, were arrested on July 24 and charged with capital murder, according to the Associated Press. Police say they robbed Weaver of $65.00 to $85.00 and then beat, cut, and strangled him before setting him on fire. The district attorney argues that Weaver's identity as a gay man played a key role in the killing.

6. Armed government agents detained Nancy Oden, Green Party USA coordinating committee member, on November 1, 2001, at Bangor International Airport in Bangor, Maine, as she attempted to board an American Airlines flight to Chicago. Her name had been flagged by airport computers because of the Green Party's opposition to the war in Afghanistan.

7. A retired professor of history at the University of California–Santa Cruz, Davis was placed on the FBI's Ten Most Wanted list in 1970, after she was accused of planning the kidnapping of three imprisoned African American activists in San Quentin and supplying the gun that killed four people during the incident. She was incarcerated on charges of murder, kidnapping, and conspiracy, and her case was taken up by supporters across the country. In 1972, after eighteen months in jail, she was tried and acquitted of all crimes.

8. On June 26, 1975, two FBI agents and one Native American were killed in a shootout on the Pine Ridge Indian Reservation. This firefight led to what many see as the false incarceration of American Indian Movement member Leonard Peltier. Now fifty-four years old, Peltier is serving his twenty-fourth year of incarceration in Leavenworth Penitentiary in Kansas. He stands accused of the murders of the two FBI agents. To date, no credible evidence has been presented to suggest that he is guilty. All others who have been brought to trial regarding this incident were acquitted on the basis of self-defense.

References

Epstein, Reid J. and Patricia Mazzei. 2021 "G.O.P. Bills Target Protestors (and absolve Motorists Who Hit Them)." *New York Times*, April 21. https://www.nytimes.com/2021/04/21/us/politics/republican-anti-protest-laws.html

Lorde, Audre. 1984. *Sister Outsider*. Trumansberg, NY: Crossing Press.

Schaef, Anne Wilson. 1981. *Women's Reality: An Emerging Female System in the White Male Society*. Minneapolis, MN: Winston Press.

Smelser, Neil J. 1962. *Theory of Collective Behavior*. New York: Free Press.

TOWARD A NEW VISION

Race, Class, and Gender as Categories of Analysis and Connection

• *Patricia Hill Collins*

The following essay, written by sociologist Patricia Hill Collins, considers a challenge faced by those working for positive social change: while we are often aware of our own situations and where we lack privilege, we often fail to see how our own ideas and behaviors perpetuate someone else's inequality. Collins calls on us to consider reconceptualizing categories of race, class, and gender and to overcome the barriers of our own experiences of inequality to build the coalitions necessary to bring about social justice.

> The true focus of revolutionary change is never merely the oppressive situations which we seek to escape, but that piece of the oppressor which is planted deep within each of us.
>
> —AUDRE LORDE, *Sister Outsider* (1984, 123)

Audre Lorde's statement raises a troublesome issue for scholars and activists working for social change. While many of us have little difficulty assessing our own victimization within some major system of oppression, whether it be by race, social class, religion, sexual orientation, ethnicity, age or gender, we typically fail to see how our thoughts and actions uphold someone else's subordination. Thus, white feminists routinely point with confidence to their oppression as women but resist seeing how much their white skin privileges them. African-Americans who possess eloquent analyses of racism often persist in viewing poor white women as symbols of white power. The radical left fares little better. "If only people of color and women could see their true class interests," they argue, "class solidarity would eliminate racism and sexism." In essence, each group identifies the type of oppression with which it feels most comfortable as being fundamental and classifies all other types as being of lesser importance.

Oppression is full of such contradictions. Errors in political judgment that we make concerning how we teach our courses, what we tell our children, and which organizations are worthy of our time, talents and financial support flow smoothly from errors in theoretical analysis about the nature of oppression and activism. Once we realize that there are few pure victims or oppressors, and that each one of us derives varying amounts of penalty and privilege from the multiple systems of oppression that frame our lives, then we will be in a position to see the need for new ways of thought and action.

Patricia Hill Collins. "Toward a New Vision: Race, Class, and Gender as Categories of Analysis and Connection." *Race, Sex, and Class*, Vol. 1, No. 1, Fall 1993. Reprinted with permission of the author.

To get at that "piece of the oppressor which is planted deep within each of us," we need at least two things. First, we need new visions of what oppression is, new categories of analysis that are inclusive of race, class, and gender as distinctive yet interlocking structures of oppression. Adhering to a stance of comparing and ranking oppressions—the proverbial, "I'm more oppressed than you"—locks us all into a dangerous dance of competing for attention, resources, and theoretical supremacy. Instead, I suggest that we examine our different experiences within the more fundamental relationship of damnation and subordination. To focus on the particular arrangements that race or class or gender takes in our time and place without seeing these structures as sometimes parallel and sometimes interlocking dimensions of the more fundamental relationship of domination and subordination may temporarily ease our consciences. But while such thinking may lead to short-term social reforms, it is simply inadequate for the task of bringing about long-term social transformation.

While race, class, and gender as categories of analysis are essential in helping us understand the structural bases of domination and subordination, new ways of thinking that are not accompanied by new ways of acting offer incomplete prospects for change. To get at that "piece of the oppressor which is planted deep within each of us," we also need to change our daily behavior. Currently, we are all enmeshed in a complex web of problematic relationships that grant our mirror images full human subjectivity while stereotyping and objectifying those most different than ourselves. We often assume that the people we work with, teach, send our children to school with, and sit next to . . . will act and feel in prescribed ways because they belong to given race, social class or gender categories. These judgments by category must be replaced with fully human relationships that transcend the legitimate differences created by race, class, and gender as categories of analysis. We require new categories of connection, new visions of what our relationships with one another can be . . . .

[This discussion] addresses this need for new patterns of thought and action. I focus on two basic questions. First, how can we reconceptualize race, class, and gender as categories of analysis? Second, how can we transcend the barriers created by our experiences with race, class, and gender oppression in order to build the types of coalitions essential for social exchange? To address these questions I contend that we must acquire both new theories of how race, class, and gender have shaped the experiences not just of women of color, but of all groups. Moreover, we must see the connections between the categories of analysis and the personal issues in our everyday lives, particularly our scholarship, our teaching and our relationships with our colleagues and students. As Audre Lorde points out, change starts with self, and relationships that we have with those around us must always be the primary site for social change.

How Can We Reconceptualize Race, Class, and Gender as Categories of *Analysis*?

To me, we must shift our discourse away from additive analyses of oppression (Spelman, 1982; Collins, 1989). Such approaches are typically based on two key premises. First, they depend on either/or, dichotomous thinking. Persons, things and ideas are conceptualized in terms of their opposites. For example, Black/White, man/woman, thought/feeling, and fact/opinion are defined in oppositional terms. Thought and feeling are not seen as two different and interconnected ways of approaching truth that can coexist in scholarship and teaching. Instead, feeling is defined as antithetical to reason, as its opposite. In spite of the fact that we all have "both/ and" identities (I am both a college professor and a mother—I don't stop being a mother when I drop my child off at school, or forget everything I learned while scrubbing the toilet), we persist in trying to classify each other in either/or categories. I live each day as an African-American woman—a race/gender specific experience. And I am not alone. Everyone has a race/gender/class specific identity. Either/or, dichotomous thinking is especially troublesome when applied to theories of oppression because every individual must be classified as being either oppressed or not oppressed. The both/ and position of simultaneously being oppressed and oppressor becomes conceptually impossible.

A second premise of additive analyses of oppression is that these dichotomous differences must be ranked. One side of the dichotomy is typically labeled dominant and the other subordinate. Thus, Whites rule Blacks, men are deemed superior to women, and reason is seen as being preferable to emotion. Applying this premise to discussions of oppression leads to the assumption that oppression can be quantified, and that some groups are oppressed more than others. I am frequently asked, "Which has been most oppressive to you, your status as a Black person or your status as a woman?" What I am really being asked to do is divide myself into little boxes and rank my various statuses. If I experience oppression as a both/and phenomenon, why should I analyze it any differently?

Additive analyses of oppression rest squarely on the twin pillars of either/or thinking and the necessity to quantify and rank all relationships in order to know where one stands. Such approaches typically see African-American women as being more oppressed than everyone else because the majority of Black women experience the negative effects of race, class, and gender oppression simultaneously. In essence, if you add together separate oppressions, you are left with a grand oppression greater than the sum of its parts.

I am not denying that specific groups experience oppression more harshly than others—lynching is certainly objectively worse than being held up as a sex object. But we must be careful not to confuse this issue of the saliency of one type of oppression in people's lives with a theoretical stance positing the interlocking nature of oppression. Race, class, and gender may all structure a situation but may not be equally visible and/or important in people's self-definitions. In certain contexts, such as the antebellum American South and contemporary South America, racial oppression is more visibly salient, while in other contexts, such as Haiti, El Salvador and Nicaragua, social class oppression may be more apparent. For middle-class White women, gender may assume experiential primacy unavailable to poor Hispanic women struggling with the ongoing issues of low-paid jobs and the frustrations of the welfare bureaucracy. This recognition that one category may have salience over another for a given time and place does not minimize the theoretical importance of assuming that race, class, and gender as categories of analysis structure all relationships.

In order to move toward new visions of what oppression is, I think that we need to ask new questions. How are relationships of domination and subordination structured and maintained in the American political economy? How do race, class, and gender function as parallel and interlocking systems that shape this basic relationship of domination and subordination? Questions such as these promise to move us away from futile theoretical struggles concerned with ranking oppressions and towards analyses that assume race, class, and gender are all present in any given setting, even if one appears more visible and salient than the others. Our task becomes redefined as one of reconceptualizing oppression by uncovering the connections among race, class, and gender as categories of analysis.

1. The Institutional Dimension of Oppression

Sandra Harding's contention that gender oppression is structured along three main dimensions—the institutional, the symbolic and the individual—offers a useful model for a more comprehensive analysis encompassing race, class, and gender oppression (Harding 1986). Systemic relationships of domination and subordination structured through social institutions such as schools, businesses, hospitals, the workplace and government agencies represent the institutional dimension of oppression. Racism, sexism and elitism all have concrete institutional locations. Even though the workings of the institutional dimension of oppression are often obscured with ideologies claiming equality of opportunity, in actuality, race, class, and gender place Asian-American women, Native American men, White men, African-American women and other groups in distinct institutional niches with varying degrees of penalty and privilege.

Even though I realize that many . . . would not share this assumption, let us assume that the institutions of American society discriminate, whether by design or by accident. While many of us are familiar with how race, gender and class operate separately to structure inequality, I want to focus on how these three systems interlock in structuring the institutional dimension of oppression. To get at the interlocking nature of race, class, and gender, I want you to think about the antebellum plantation as a guiding metaphor for a variety of American social institutions. Even though slavery is typically analyzed as a racist institution, and occasionally as a class institution, I suggest that slavery was a race, class, gender specific institution. Removing any one piece from our analysis diminishes our understanding of the true nature of relations of domination and subordination under slavery.

Slavery was a profoundly patriarchal institution. It rested on the dual tenets of White male authority and White male property, a joining of the political and the economic within the institution of the family. Heterosexism was assumed and all Whites were expected to marry. Control over affluent White women's sexuality remained key to slavery's survival because property was to be passed on to the legitimate heirs of the slave owner. Ensuring affluent White women's virginity and chastity was deeply intertwined with maintenance of property relations.

Under slavery, we see varying levels of institutional protection given to affluent White women, working class and poor White women and enslaved African women. Poor White women enjoyed few of the protections held out to their upper class sisters. Moreover, the devalued status of Black women was key in keeping all White women in their assigned places. Controlling Black women's fertility was also key to the continuation of slavery, for children born to slave mothers themselves were slaves.

African-American women shared the devalued status of chattel with their husbands, fathers and sons. Racism stripped Blacks as a group of legal rights, education and control over their own persons. African-Americans could be whipped, branded, sold, or killed, not because they were poor, or because they were women, but because they were Black. Racism ensured that Blacks would continue to serve Whites and suffer economic exploitation at the hands of all Whites.

So we have a very interesting chain of command on the plantation—the affluent White master as the reigning patriarch, his White wife helpmate to serve him, help him manage his property and bring up his heirs, his faithful servants whose production and reproduction were tied to the requirements of the capitalist political economy and largely propertyless, working class White men and women watching from

afar. In essence, the foundations for the contemporary roles of elite White women, poor Black women, working class White men and a series of other groups can be seen in stark relief in this fundamental American social institution. While Blacks experienced the most harsh treatment under slavery, and thus made slavery clearly visible as a racist institution, race, class, and gender interlocked in structuring slavery's systemic organization of domination and subordination.

Even today, the plantation remains a compelling metaphor for institutional oppression. Certainly the actual conditions of oppression are not as severe now as they were then. To argue, as some do, that things have not changed all that much denigrates the achievements of those who struggled for social change before us. But the basic relationships among Black men, Black women, elite White women, elite White men, working class White men and working class White women as groups remain essentially intact.

A brief analysis of key American social institutions most controlled by elite White men should convince us of the interlocking nature of race, class, and gender in structuring the institutional dimension of oppression. For example, if you are from an American college or university, is your campus a modern plantation? Who controls your university's political economy? Are elite White men overrepresented among the upper administrators and trustees controlling your university's finances and policies? Are elite White men being joined by growing numbers of elite White women helpmates? What kinds of people are in your classrooms grooming the next generation who will occupy these and other decision-making positions? Who are the support staff that produce the mass mailings, order the supplies, fix the leaky pipes? Do African-Americans, Hispanics or other people of color form the majority of the invisible workers who feed you, wash your dishes, and clean up your offices and libraries after everyone else has gone home?

If your college is anything like mine, you know the answers to these questions. You may be affiliated with an institution that has Hispanic women as vice-presidents for finance, or substantial numbers of Black men among the faculty. If so, you are fortunate. Much more typical are colleges where a modified version of the plantation as a metaphor for the institutional dimension of oppression survives.

2. The Symbolic Dimension of Oppression

Widespread, societally sanctioned ideologies used to justify relations of domination and subordination comprise the symbolic dimension of oppression. Central to this process is the use of stereotypical or controlling images of diverse race, class, and gender groups. In order to assess the power of this dimension of oppression, I want you to make a list, either on paper or in your head, of "masculine" and "feminine" characteristics. If your list is anything like that compiled by most people, it reflects some variation of the following:

Masculine	Feminine
aggressive	passive
leader	follower
rational	emotional
strong	weak
intellectual	physical

Not only does this list reflect either/or dichotomous thinking and the need to rank both sides of the dichotomy, but ask yourself exactly which men and women you had in mind when compiling these characteristics. This list applies almost exclusively to middle class White men and women. The allegedly "masculine" qualities that you probably listed are only acceptable when exhibited by elite White men, or when used by Black and Hispanic men against each other or against women of color. Aggressive Black and Hispanic men are seen as dangerous, not powerful, and are often penalized when they exhibit any of the allegedly "masculine" characteristics. Working class and poor White men fare slightly better and are also denied the allegedly "masculine" symbols of leadership, intellectual competence, and human rationality. Women of color and working class and poor White women are also not represented on this list, for they have never had the luxury of being "ladies." What appear to be universal categories representing all men and women instead are unmasked as being applicable to only a small group.

It is important to see how the symbolic images applied to different race, class, and gender groups interact in maintaining systems of domination and subordination. If I were to ask you to repeat the same assignment, only this time, by making separate lists for Black men, Black women, Hispanic women and Hispanic men, I suspect that your gender symbolism would be quite different. In comparing all of the lists, you might begin to see the interdependence of symbols applied to all groups. For example, the elevated images of White womanhood need devalued images of Black womanhood in order to maintain credibility.

While the above exercise reveals the interlocking nature of race, class, and gender in structuring the symbolic dimension of oppression, part of its importance lies in demonstrating how race, class, and gender pervade a wide range of what appears to be universal language. Attending to diversity in our scholarship, in our teaching, and in our daily lives provides a new angle of vision on interpretations of reality thought to be natural, normal and "true." Moreover, viewing images of masculinity and femininity as universal gender symbolism, rather than as symbolic images that are race, class, and gender specific, renders the experiences of people of color and of nonprivileged White women and men invisible. One way to dehumanize an individual or group is to deny the reality of their experiences. So when we refuse to deal with race or class because they do not appear to be directly relevant to gender, we are actually becoming part of someone else's problem.

Assuming that everyone is affected differently by the same interlocking set of symbolic images allows us to move forward toward new analyses. Women of color and White women have different relations to White male authority and this difference explains the distinct gender symbolism applied to both groups. Black women encounter controlling images such as the mammy, the matriarch, the mule and the whore, that encourage others to reject us as fully human people. Ironically, the negative nature of these images simultaneously encourages us to reject them. In contrast, White women are offered seductive images, those that promise to reward them for supporting the status quo. And yet seductive images can be equally controlling. Consider, for example, the views of Nancy White, a 73-year-old Black woman, concerning images of rejection and seduction:

> My mother used to say that the black woman is the white man's mule and the white woman is his dog.

Now, she said that to say this: we do the heavy work and get beat whether we do it well or not. But the white woman is closer to the master and he pats them on the head and lets them sleep in the house, but he ain't gon' treat neither one like he was dealing with a person. (Gwaltney 1980, 148)

Both sets of images stimulate particular political stances. By broadening the analysis beyond the confines of race, we can see the varying levels of rejection and seduction available to each of us due to our race, class, and gender identity. Each of us lives with an allotted portion of institutional privilege and penalty, and with varying levels of rejection and seduction inherent in the symbolic images applied to us. This is the context in which we make our choices. Taken together, the institutional and symbolic dimensions of oppression create a structural backdrop against which all of us live our lives.

3. The Individual Dimension of Oppression

Whether we benefit or not, we all live within institutions that reproduce race, class, and gender oppression. Even if we never have any contact with members of other race, class, and gender groups, we all encounter images of these groups and are exposed to the symbolic meanings attached to those images. On this dimension of oppression, our individual biographies vary tremendously. As a result of our institutional and symbolic statuses, all of our choices become political acts.

Each of us must come to terms with the multiple ways in which race, class, and gender as categories of analysis frame our individual biographies. I have lived my entire life as an African-American woman from a working class family and this basic fact has had a profound impact on my personal biography. Imagine how different your life might be if you had been born Black, or White, or poor, or of a different race/class/gender group than the one with which you are most familiar. The institutional treatment you would have received and the symbolic meanings attached to your very existence might differ dramatically from that you now consider to be natural, normal and part of everyday life. You might be the same, but your personal biography might have been quite different.

I believe that each of us carries around the cumulative effect of our lives within multiple structures of oppression. If you want to see how much you have been affected by this whole thing, I ask you one simple question—who are your close friends? Who are the people with whom you can share your hopes, dreams, vulnerabilities, fears and victories? Do they look like you? If they are all the same, circumstance may be the cause. For the first seven years of my life I saw only low income Black people. My friends from those years reflected the composition of my community. But now that I am an adult, can the defense of circumstance explain the patterns of people that I trust as my friends and colleagues? When given other alternatives, if my friends and colleagues reflect the homogeneity of one race, class, and gender group, then these categories of analysis have indeed become barriers to connection.

I am not suggesting that people are doomed to follow the paths laid out for them by race, class, and gender as categories of analysis. While these three structures certainly frame my opportunity structure, I as an individual always have the choice of accepting things as they are, or trying to change them. As Nikki Giovanni points out, "we've got to live in the real world. If we don't like the world we're living in, change it. And if we can't change it, we change ourselves. We can do something" (Tate 1983, 68). While a piece of the oppressor may be planted deep within each of us, we each have the choice of accepting that piece or challenging it as part of the "true focus of revolutionary change."

How Can We Transcend the Barriers Created by Our Experiences with Race, Class, and Gender Oppression in order to Build the Types of Coalitions Essential for Social Change?

Reconceptualizing oppression and seeing the barriers created by race, class, and gender as interlocking categories of analysis is a vital first step. But we must transcend these barriers by moving toward race, class, and gender as categories of connection, by building relationships and coalitions that will bring about social change. What are some of the issues involved in doing this?

1. Differences in Power and Privilege

First, we must recognize that our differing experiences with oppression create problems in the relationships among us. Each of us lives within a system that vests us with varying levels of power and privilege. These differences in power, whether structured along axes of race, class, gender, age or sexual orientation, frame our relationships. African-American writer June Jordan describes her discomfort on a Caribbean vacation with Olive, the Black woman who cleaned her room:

> . . . even though both "Olive" and "I" live inside a conflict neither one of us created, and even though both of us therefore hurt inside that conflict, I may be one of the monsters she needs to eliminate from her universe and, in a sense, she may be one of the monsters in mine. (1985, 47)

Differences in power constrain our ability to connect with one another even when we think we are engaged in dialogue across differences. Let me give you an example. One year, the students in my course "Sociology of the Black Community" got into a heated discussion about the reasons for the upsurge of racial incidents on college campuses. Black students complained vehemently about the apathy and resistance they felt most White students expressed about examining their own racism. Mark, a White male student, found their comments particularly unsettling. After claiming that all the Black people he had ever known had expressed no such beliefs to him, he questioned how representative the viewpoints of his fellow students actually were. When pushed further, Mark revealed that he had participated in conversations over the years with the Black domestic worker employed by his family. Since she had never expressed such strong feelings about White racism, Mark was genuinely shocked by class discussions. Ask yourselves whether that domestic worker was in a position to speak freely. Would it have been wise for her to do so in a situation where the power between the two parties was so unequal?

In extreme cases, members of privileged groups can erase the very presence of the less privileged. When I first moved to Cincinnati, my family and I went on a picnic at a local park. Picnicking next to us was a family of White Appalachians. When I went

to push my daughter on the swings, several of the children came over. They had missing, yellowed and broken teeth, they wore old clothing and their poverty was evident. I was shocked. Growing up in a large eastern city, I had never seen such awful poverty among Whites. The segregated neighborhoods in which I grew up made White poverty all but invisible. More importantly, the privileges attached to my newly acquired social class position allowed me to ignore and minimize the poverty among Whites that I did encounter. My reactions to those children made me realize how confining phrases such as "well, at least they're not Black," had become for me. In learning to grant human subjectivity to the Black victims of poverty, I had simultaneously learned to demean White victims of poverty. By applying categories of race to the objective conditions confronting me, I was quantifying and ranking oppressions and missing the very real suffering which, in fact, is the real issue.

One common pattern of relationships across differences in power is one that I label "voyeurism." From the perspective of the privileged, the lives of people of color, of the poor, and of women are interesting for their entertainment value. The privileged become voyeurs, passive onlookers who do not relate to the less powerful, but who are interested in seeing how the "different" live. Over the years, I have heard numerous African-American students complain about professors who never call on them except when a so-called Black issue is being discussed. The students' interest in discussing race or qualifications for doing so appear unimportant to the professor's efforts to use Black students' experiences as stories to make the material come alive for the White student audience. Asking Black students to perform on cue and provide a Black experience for their White classmates can be seen as voyeurism at its worst.

Members of subordinate groups do not willingly participate in such exchanges but often do so because members of dominant groups control the institutional and symbolic apparatuses of oppression. Racial/ethnic groups, women, and the poor have never had the luxury of being voyeurs of the lives of the privileged. Our ability to survive in hostile settings has hinged on our ability to learn intricate details about the behavior and world view of the powerful and adjust our behavior accordingly. I need only point to the difference in perception of those men and women in abusive relationships. Where men can view their girlfriends and wives as sex objects, helpmates and a collection of stereotypes—categories of voyeurism—women must be attuned to every nuance of their partners' behavior. Are women "naturally" better in relating to people with more power than themselves, or have circumstances mandated that men and women develop different skills? . . .

Coming from a tradition where most relationships across difference are squarely rooted in relations of domination and subordination, we have much less experience relating to people as different but equal. The classroom is potentially one powerful and safe space where dialogues among individuals of unequal power relationships can occur. The relationship between Mark, the student in my class, and the domestic worker is typical of a whole series of relationships that people have when they relate across differences in power and privilege. The relationship among Mark and his classmates represents the power of the classroom to minimize those differences so that people of different levels of power can use race, class, and gender as categories of analysis in order to generate meaningful dialogues. In this case, the classroom equalized racial difference so that Black students who normally felt silenced spoke out. White students like Mark, generally unaware of how they had been privileged by their whiteness, lost that privilege in the classroom and thus became open to genuine dialogue . . . .

2. Coalitions around Common Causes

A second issue in building relationships and coalitions essential for social change concerns knowing the real reasons for coalition. Just what brings people together? One powerful catalyst fostering group solidarity is the presence of a common enemy. African-American, Hispanic, Asian-American, and women's studies all share the common intellectual heritage of challenging what passes for certified knowledge in the academy. But politically expedient relationships and coalitions like these are fragile because, as June Jordan points out:

> It occurs to me that much organizational grief could be avoided if people understood that partnership in misery does not necessarily provide for partnership for change. When we get the monsters off our backs all of us may want to run in very different directions. (1985, 47)

Sharing a common cause assists individuals and groups in maintaining relationships that transcend their differences. Building effective coalitions involves struggling to hear one another and developing empathy for each other's points of view. The coalitions that I have been involved in that lasted and that worked have been those where commitment to a specific issue mandated collaboration as the best strategy for addressing the issue at hand.

Several years ago, master degree in hand, I chose to teach in an inner-city parochial school in danger of closing. The money was awful, the conditions were poor, but the need was great. In my job, I had to work with a range of individuals who, on the surface, had very little in common. We had White nuns, Black middle class graduate students, Blacks from the "community," some of whom had been incarcerated and/or were affiliated with a range of federal antipoverty programs. Parents formed another part of this community, Harvard faculty another, and a few well-meaning White liberals from Colorado were sprinkled in for good measure.

As you might imagine, tension was high. Initially, our differences seemed insurmountable. But as time passed, we found a common bond that we each brought to the school. In spite of profound differences in our personal biographies, differences that in other settings would have hampered our ability to relate to one another, we found that we were all deeply committed to the education of Black children. By learning to value each other's commitment and by recognizing that we each had different skills that were essential to actualizing that commitment, we built an effective coalition around a common cause. Our school was successful, and the children we taught benefited from the diversity we offered them . . . . None of us alone has a comprehensive vision of how race, class, and gender operate as categories of analysis or how they might be used as categories of connection. Our personal biographies offer us partial views. Few of us can manage to study race, class, and gender simultaneously. Instead, we each know more about some dimensions of this larger story and less about others . . . . Just as the members of the school had special skills to offer to the task of building the school, we have areas of specialization and expertise, whether scholarly, theoretical, pedagogical or within areas of race, class or gender. We do not all have to do the same thing in the same way. Instead, we must support each other's efforts, realizing that they are all part of the larger enterprise of bringing about social change.

3. Building Empathy

A third issue involved in building the types of relationships and coalitions essential for social change concerns the issue of individual accountability. Race, class, and gender oppression form the structural backdrop against which we frame our relationship— these are the forces that encourage us to substitute voyeurism . . . for fully human relationships. But while we may not have created this situation, we are each responsible for making individual, personal choices concerning which elements of race, class, and gender oppression we will accept and which we will work to change.

One essential component of this accountability involves developing empathy for the experiences of individuals and groups different than ourselves. Empathy begins with taking an interest in the facts of other people's lives, both as individuals and as groups. If you care about me, you should want to know not only the details of my personal biography but a sense of how race, class, and gender as categories of analysis created the institutional and symbolic backdrop for my personal biography. How can you hope to assess my character without knowing the details of the circumstances I face?

Moreover, by taking a theoretical stance that we have all been affected by race, class, and gender as categories of analysis that have structured our treatment, we open up possibilities for using those same constructs as categories of connection in building empathy. For example, I have a good White woman friend with whom I share common interests and beliefs. But we know that our racial differences have provided us with different experiences. So we talk about them. We do not assume that because I am Black, race has only affected me and not her or that because I am a Black woman, race neutralizes the effect of gender in my life while accenting it in hers. We take those same categories of analysis that have created cleavages in our lives, in this case, categories of race and gender, and use them as categories of connection in building empathy for each other's experiences.

Finding common causes and building empathy is difficult, no matter which side of privilege we inhabit. Building empathy from the dominant side of privilege is difficult, simply because individuals from privileged backgrounds are not encouraged to do so. For example, in order for those of you who are White to develop empathy for the experiences of people of color, you must grapple with how your white skin has privileged you. This is difficult to do, because it not only entails the intellectual process of seeing how whiteness is elevated in institutions and symbols, but it also involves the often painful process of seeing how your whiteness has shaped your personal biography. Intellectual stances against the institutional and symbolic dimensions of racism are generally easier to maintain than sustained self-reflection about how racism has shaped all of our individual biographies. Were and are your fathers, uncles, and grandfathers really more capable than mine, or can their accomplishments be explained in part by the racism members of my family experienced? Did your mothers stand silently by and watch all this happen? More importantly, how have they passed on the benefits of their whiteness to you?

These are difficult questions, and I have tremendous respect for my colleagues and students who are trying to answer them. Since there is no compelling reason to examine the source and meaning of one's own privilege, I know that those who do so have freely chosen this stance. They are making conscious efforts to root out the piece of the oppressor planted within them. To me, they are entitled to the support of people of color in their efforts. Men who declare themselves feminists, members of the middle class who ally themselves with anti-poverty struggles, heterosexuals who support gays and lesbians, are all trying to grow, and their efforts place them far ahead of the majority who never think of engaging in such important struggles.

Building empathy from the subordinate side of privilege is also difficult, but for different reasons.

Members of subordinate groups are understandably reluctant to abandon a basic mistrust of members of powerful groups because this basic mistrust has traditionally been central to their survival. As a Black woman, it would be foolish for me to assume that White women, or Black men, or White men or any other group with a history of exploiting African-American women have my best interests at heart. These groups enjoy varying amounts of privilege over me and therefore I must carefully watch them and be prepared for a relation of domination and subordination.

Like the privileged, members of subordinate groups must also work toward replacing judgments by category with new ways of thinking and acting. Refusing to do so stifles prospects for effective coalition and social change. Let me use another example from my own experiences. When I was an undergraduate, I had little time or patience for the theorizing of the privileged. My initial years at a private, elite institution were difficult, not because the coursework was challenging (it was, but that wasn't what distracted me) or because I had to work while my classmates lived on family allowances (I was used to work). The adjustment was difficult because I was surrounded by so many people who took their privilege for granted. Most of them felt entitled to their wealth. That astounded me.

I remember one incident of watching a White woman down the hall in my dormitory try to pick out which sweater to wear. The sweaters were piled up on her bed in all the colors of the rainbow, sweater after sweater. She asked my advice in a way that let me know that choosing a sweater was one of the most important decisions she had to make on a daily basis. Standing knee-deep in her sweaters, I realized how different our lives were. She did not have to worry about maintaining a solid academic average so that she could receive financial aid. Because she was in the majority, she was not treated as a representative of her race. She did not have to consider how her classroom comments or basic existence on campus contributed to the treatment her group would receive. Her allowance protected her from having to work, so she was free to spend her time studying, partying, or in her case, worrying about which sweater to wear. The degree of inequality in our lives and her unquestioned sense of entitlement concerning that inequality offended me. For a while, I categorized all affluent White women as being superficial, arrogant, overly concerned with material possessions, and part of my problem. But had I continued to classify people in this way, I would have missed out on making some very good friends whose discomfort with their inherited or acquired social class privileges pushed them to examine their position.

Since I opened with the words of Audre Lorde, it seems appropriate to close with another of her ideas . . . .

> Each of us is called upon to take a stand. So in these days ahead, as we examine ourselves and each other, our works, our fears, our differences, our sisterhood and survivals, I urge you to tackle what is most difficult for us all, self-scrutiny of our complacencies, the idea that since each of us believes she is on the side of right, she need not examine her position. (Lorde 1985)

I urge you to examine your position.

References

Collins, Patricia Hill. 1989. "The Social Construction Feminist Thought." *Signs* 14(4): 745–773.

Gwaltney, John Langston. 1980. *Drylongso: A Self-Portrait of Black America*. New York: Vintage.

Harding, Sandra. 1986. *The Science Question in Feminism*. Ithaca, New York: Cornell University Press.

Jordan, June. 1985. *On Call: Political Essays*. Boston: South End Press.

Lorde, Audre. 1984. *Sister Outsider*. Trumansberg, New York: The Crossing Press.

————. 1985. "Sisterhood and Survival." *Keynote address, conference on the Black Woman Writer and the Diaspora*, Michigan State University.

Spelman, Elizabeth. 1982. "Theories of Race and Gender: The Erasure of Black Women." *Quest* 5: 36–62.

Tate, Claudia. ed. 1983. *Black Women Writers at Work*. New York: Continuum.

Questions for Critical Thinking

1. Collins argues that we often fail to see how our own ideas and behaviors perpetuate someone else's oppression. What are some ideas or behaviors that you possess that perpetuate the inequality of others?

2. What makes it difficult to recognize the ways that we participate in transforming difference into inequality?

3. How can recognizing the ways we participate in perpetuating inequality move us toward a more equal society?

#FEMINISTANTIBODIES

Asian American Media in the Time of Coronavirus

* *Rachel Kuo, Amy Zhang, Vivian Shaw, and Cynthia Wang*

The following essay explores the creative ways and processes that can be considered for making productive social change across differences. Responding to the "mediatization of 'Asian-ness' as contagion" the authors discuss the Asian American Feminist Collective's zine *Asian American Feminist Antibodies: Care in the Time of Coronavirus* and corresponding #FeministAntibodies Tweetchat and their use of digital media-making in the midst of the COVID-19 pandemic.

> "For me, this space of radical openness is a margin—a profound edge. Locating oneself there is difficult yet necessary. It is not a 'safe' place. One is always at risk. One needs a community of resistance."
>
> —bell hooks, "Choosing the margin as a space of radical openness," *Framework 36*, 206, 1989

The mediatization of "Asian-ness" as contagion has been a large part of the information environment surrounding the 2020 COVID-19 pandemic. Mainstream media outlets have used generic images of Chinatowns and East Asian people in masks without context; racist comments and false information about avoiding Asian businesses have spread on social media platforms; and continuing communication from the Trump administration racializes the virus as the "Chinese virus." Simultaneously, in the United States, media coverage of coronavirus-related racism toward Asians and Asian Americans have reinforced perceptions of Asian America as both monolithic and East Asian/Chinese-centric. In anticipating and responding directly to a racially hostile media and information environment, digital media created by Asian American organizers, community groups, and artists in the midst of the COVID-19 crisis have grappled with tensions between forging collective politics while also pushing

Social Media + Society

October-December 2020: 1–11

© The Author(s) 2020

Article reuse guidelines:

sagepub.com/journals-permissions

DOI: 10.1177/2056305120978364

journals.sagepub.com/home/sms

against presumptions of racial homogeneity. Backlash from some Asian Americans against shirts proclaiming "I am not Chinese" and former Democratic presidential hopeful Andrew Yang's call for Asians to be "more American" demonstrate the contentious politics of Asian American identity (Kuo, 2018).

In the early stages of the pandemic, a multitude of digital outputs began making up a rich media ecosystem, demonstrating the depth and breadth of Asian American knowledges, histories, and experiences in making meaning and living through the COVID-19 pandemic. Alice Wong, Director of the Disability Visibility Project, curated a sample of 1,299 tweets (Wong, 2020) about coronavirus from the perspectives of homebound, chronically ill, and immunosuppressed people. Writer Leah Lakshmi Piepzna-Samarasinha (2020) published emergency preparation tips from her survival experiences of being poor and disabled. Artist Monyee Chau (2020a) created a comic on Yellow Peril and community resilience to share the history of Seattle's International District to generate donations for the Wing Luke Museum of the Asian Pacific American Experience. These resources and more draw on community-based knowledge to distribute information and identify historical and political frameworks for understanding state-based and racial violence.

The New York City-based Asian American Feminist Collective's (AAFC) digital zine *Asian American Feminist Antibodies: Care in the Time of Coronavirus* curated different media artifacts created prior to and during the crisis as an archive of Asian American political mobilization. In early March 2020, AAFC, along with community partner Bluestockings Bookstore, Cafe, and Activist Center, initiated a call to collect firsthand accounts of experiences with racism connected to COVID-19, resulting in 36 unique stories of varying lengths describing the feelings and experiences of public harassment and targeting in grocery stores, schools, public transport, and other sites of daily encounter. As an example of media-based organizing, which is a collaborative process using media, art, and technology to envision solutions to interconnected systemic issues (Allied Media Projects, 2020), the zine connected these firsthand accounts with analyses from community organizers and activists. Furthermore, the zine emphasizes that despite this moment of precarity, there is both "deep collective knowledge" and "radical possibilities" toward realizing "dreams, visions, and desires for an alternative world" and building "interdependent communities of resistance" (Bhaman et al., 2020, p. 3).

Later, on 10 April 2020, AAFC and Bluestockings hosted a community Tweetchat with 12 invited participants representing different organizations and campaigns under the hashtag #FeministAntibodies. The Tweetchat was organized around seven different questions, offering the invited participants a space to discuss Asian American experiences of the pandemic through the frameworks of community and care, reflect on historical parallels, and share resources. This coordinated effort to bring different actors into a shared space and time also afforded the opportunity for other people to join the conversation using the #FeministAntibodies hashtag. These media practices function as rapid response strategies with a vision of longer term movement building. Drawing on different perspectives across different community groups and movements, the zine and corresponding Tweetchat aimed to foster political alignments across differential experiences of crisis—thus, these digital materials help facilitate what bell hooks (1990) calls a "homeplace," a communal site of resistance.

This article looks to the technological infrastructures, social economies, and material forms of Asian American digital media-making in the midst of the COVID-19 pandemic. Focusing on AAFC's zine *Care in the Time of Coronavirus* and the corresponding hosted Tweetchat #FeministAntibodies, this article highlights the tensions, communal processes, and narrative frameworks behind producing collective racial politics across differences. We write from an autoethnographical perspective as the zine's creators and Tweetchat's organizers, use collaborative qualitative discursive methods as Asian American feminist scholars, media practitioners, and interlocuters, and bring ground our study of digital texts (Brock, 2016). Through CTDA, we demonstrate how digital discursive practices constitute and evolve identity-based political positionality. In examining both the media-making process and content within the zine and Tweetchat, we found three emergent themes in how different actors understand, define, and mobilize Asian American collective politics: (1) as intersectional and diverse, (2) as constituted interdependently, and (3) as a site for imagining political possibility through different histories. This study extends scholarship on the cultural and racial politics of media, including Lisa Lowe's (1998) discussion of cultural production and subjectivity and Lori Kido Lopez's (2016) discussion of Asian American media activism as cultural citizenship; the uses of social media to develop counter narratives and build networks of dissent (Jackson et al., 2020), and contributes to discussions of how race "works" online (Nakamura & Chow-White, 2013).

In the ways that COVID-19 has been described through the language and narratives of contagion, it is apt that the collective political uses and circulation of hashtags by Asian Americans on Twitter and other social media platforms create what Sanjay Sharma (2013) describes as the "contagious effects of networked relations" (p. 48) in producing politics. This article begins with an overview of Asian American cultural politics and the mediation of race in online platforms, followed by a discussion of political formation and temporality in the time of crisis to contextualize Asian American digital organizing in the midst of COVID-19. We then discuss our methodological approaches in the creation and analysis of digital text. In our findings, we argue that processes of digital organizing offer a means to articulate Asian America as a political formation through navigating uneven social differences.

Asian American Cultural Politics and Digital Production

Tweeting as a political act, or what feminist scholar bell hooks (1989) calls "the margins," showcases digital media-making as sites of "radical possibility, a space of resistance" (p. 149). Digital media outputs, such as zines, short illustrated comics posted to Instagram, and tweets constitute "minor objects . . . marginal forms, persons and worlds mobilized in narrative (including archival) constructions to designate moments of crisis" (Nguyen, 2015, p. 12). Similarly, these objects extend Lisa Lowe's (1996) discussion of Asian women's' worker testimonials as "crucial media that connect subjects to social relations" (p. 33). In other words, these digital records can organize collective politics. Asian American digital media production extends from print technologies and movement

media histories of grassroots publications of newsletters, circulars, pamphlets, and zines (Kuo, 2017). For example, during 1960s and 1970s, leftist Asian critical technocultural discourse analysis (CTDA) to American organizations produced and circulated their own movement media, such as *Gidra* and Basement Workshop's *Bridge Magazine* (Ishizuka, 2016). Deepa Iyer (2017) describes grassroots media as utilizing the stories from the lived experiences and leadership of those facing multiple levels of injustice and inequities to equip and mobilize people around campaigns. Part of an alternative, progressive media ecosystem, independently published media circulated movement discourse to develop shared political imagination, build political vision, challenge dominant paradigms, and construct solidarities.

Asian American feminism as politics is also constructed through ongoing technological discourse. For example, since 2018, AAFC has created digital and print zines and facilitated online discussions to interrogate and reflect upon feminism as an ever-evolving political practice and approach. Such acts of media-making inherit both longer and more recent histories of feminist media artifacts, from the Third World Women's Alliance's *Triple Jeopardy* newsletters in the 1970s to hashtags such as #SolidarityisforWhiteWomen and #NotYourAsianSidekick in 2013 (Kuo, 2017). Scholarship of digital activism has shown us how marginalized groups excluded from mainstream media spaces have used digital technologies for counter narratives, "talking back" (Jackson et al., 2020; Steele, 2017), political debate, and building movement networks. However, Black feminist scholars have also challenged neoliberal narratives of digital technologies/social media as sources of liberation and empowerment (Noble, 2016). Different users are valued differently by corporate platforms based on social difference—for example, racial ideologies embedded within algorithms play a role in facilitating disparate systems of value in how information is accessed and circulated online (McIlwain, 2017). In the adaptation of Asian American cultural politics in digital spaces, Victor Bascara and Lisa Nakamura (2014) point us toward the significance of how different digital platforms transform cultural and political formations. They argue that beyond a narrow focus on representation through text and image, engaging how platforms intersect and shape racial processes and relations enable us to see the capacities, exclusions, and surveillance of racial bodies in digital space.

In beginning to write this article in early May 2020, because of city and state social distancing and shelter-in mandates due to COVID-19, many of the social and political spaces we collectively inhabit are virtual. Yet, as much as digital media platforms have enabled Asian American media production, systems of oppression including vitriolic hate speech and harassment continue to propagate in online spaces. COVID-19 has exposed rampant existing inequalities of people's access to safety, including digital safety. The idea of "free speech" becomes complicated when corporate platforms like Twitter become weaponized for harassment and abuse, disproportionately against women and communities of color. The same technological affordances for political mobilization and expression can also be used by White supremacists and hate groups, with "Zoom bombings" entering the digital space as a racist tool of abuse. Digital organizing tactics, such as Tweetchats and Tweetstorms, or multitudes of Tweets posted all at once using a hashtag identifier, have extended and corresponded with analog forms of movement strategy through the act of reclaiming space in an exhausting, relentlessly racist digital media environment.

Organizing in the Time of Crisis

Feminist organizing during a pandemic is fraught with social and political imperatives that preceded COVID-19. Frames of crisis that position this moment as new and temporary camouflage systems of power and exploitation that are operating as designed. Instead, we understand the crisis as a consolidating moment of racial capitalism. As activists in #FeministAntibodies and *Care in the Time of Coronavirus* have suggested, the US President Trump's stoking of anti-Asian racism through disinformation and Sino phobic monikers, such as "Kung Flu" and "Chinese virus," operate alongside the shock doctrine of eroding environmental protections through COVID-19 recovery legislation. For as long as they remain unresolved, crises portend a multiplicity of potential outcomes. These uncertainties influence activism and organizing, as well as the documentation of these efforts (Gilmore, 2007).

The neoliberal logics that enable states to avoid responsibilities during disasters such as Hurricane Katrina, Hurricane Maria, and now COVID-19 ironically underscore the necessity of mutual aid and other community-based political alternatives. When states dismiss their obligation to protect and care for vulnerable groups as "voluntary," they create a vacuum for activists to fill (Nickel & Eikenberry, 2007). For example, the Japanese government's misinformation about the Fukushima nuclear disaster in 2011, combined with its retrenchment of civil liberties and endorsement of ultralight militarism in the years following, catalyzed a durable network of activists (Shaw, 2020). As these activists connected the rise of anti-Korean hate speech in 2013 to the state's failure to protect multiple groups of vulnerable people, they began to envision antiracism as central to their task of rebuilding their communities (Shaw, 2017). Moreover, they prioritized their own social connections above recognition from the state as a source of legitimacy. In this example, activists re-centered political membership around "obligation, mutual protection, and struggle—which not only includes the disaster but also refers to the temporality of protests themselves—as a collective experience" (Shaw, 2017, p. 73). In moments when states use disasters to levy additional harms on already injured communities, activists sometimes create new political coalitions (Tang, 2011).

Methodologies: On Process, Collaboration, and Making Data

Focusing on the zine *Care in the Time of Coronavirus* and #FeministAntibodies Tweetchat, this article brings together autoethnographic reflections on media-based organizing with qualitative discourse analysis of text. Together, these methods intervene upon "big data" approaches to studies of digital media through "deeper" data by offering an intimate way to study, understand, and contextualize processes of media production (Brock, 2015). Furthermore, these methods also unveil a process of data-making—how datasets are co-produced through research interventions (Vis, 2013). Our process-oriented approach also draws upon Dorothy Kim and Eunsong Kim's (2014) #TwitterEthicsManifesto, which rejects object-oriented and birds-eye approaches to digital research, and instead foregrounds circular and participatory systems. In using an autoethnographic approach that draws on personal experience and position (Bailey, 2015; Korn, 2017), author Rachel Kuo writes from the reflexive position of facilitating the zine's creation and organizing the Tweetchat as one of the co-leaders of the Asian American Feminist Collective in collaboration with author Vivian Shaw in the zine's editorial process.

We invited authors Amy Zhang and Cynthia Wang as feminist interlocutors with these digital texts. Together, we coded the tweets through a qualitative inductive process, using observations of the Tweetchat's process and content to find emergent themes about Asian American collective politics in these digital narratives. We see the process of collaboration as feminist methodology—working and thinking together to think as integral to intellectual and political inquiry. In collaborating remotely, we developed an infrastructure of digital documents, messaging channels, and scheduling meetings that enabled collective discussion of the findings. As scholars across the fields of communication, media studies, and sociology, beyond the content of the digital materials themselves, we also discussed our shared (and also divergent) theories of race and methodological approaches to learn cross-disciplinarily from each other.

To incorporate critical race and feminist theory and center the "epistemological standpoint" of underserved users, we bring CTDA to our qualitative study of digital text (Brock, 2016). As a technique, CTDA assesses user discourse alongside the technological and material specificities of media platforms, connecting together form, function, and meaning. For example, CTDA considers how differences between mobile and desktop uses of Twitter—the holding of a handheld device with fingers brushing the screen versus typing at a laptop—change how a user may participate in a digital space, including different forms of political participation. As a method, CTDA seeks to reveal the political meanings embedded within technologies through examining their situated uses. Taking Asian American feminism as a grounding point—specifically, how it becomes articulated, defined, and operationalized within technocultural spaces—we use CTDA to inform an understanding

of the *making* of collective politics by different actors across discursive platforms during a particular point in time. In this way, CTDA connects with our autoethnographic and collaborative approaches to critically consider how our own position and practices as Asian American feminists on Twitter and other digital platforms also inform our interactions with and understandings of our research materials.

As a field site for examining Asian American politics, hashtags "performatively frame" racial meaning as well as archiving and indexing racial discourses in an "intertextual chain" (Bonilla & Rosa, 2015). The #FeministAntibodies Tweetchat generated over 300 original tweets (not including social engagement, such as retweets, likes, or shares). Kuo created a public archive of the chat using Wakelet, a visual content platform for organizing and curating online information. Wakelet functions as a substitute to Storify, a narrative timeline platform that was shut down in May 2018, leaving people scrambling to download their stories or risk them disappearing forever. The #FeministAntibodies Wakelet archive includes 315 different posts organized by the seven questions posed by AAFC during the chat (Asian American Feminist Collective, 2020a). Using a platform external to Twitter allows for both a re-evaluation and temporal re-organization of information, since the search functions on Twitter only easily afford reading the most recent posts first and also prioritizing posts with the highest engagement.

In late April, the four authors coded all of the tweets from Wakelet, organized by the Tweetchat's seven questions to identify emergent themes. The questions, edited for length, include the following: (1) How are Asian American communities experiencing the pandemic? (2) What kinds of community resources are missing in this moment for Asian American communities and individuals? (3) What practices of care are fueling you and providing you solace in this difficult moment? (4) What does revolutionary love and care mean for you? (5) What parallels in history are we seeing? (6) What mutual aid funds should we be supporting? and (7) What kind of world would you like to build for the future? These questions invited participants to both make sense of the pandemic through historical contexts as well as circulate and construct shared political visions.

After the coding process, the authors discussed themes they observed in their reading and interpretation, arriving at three emergent themes that revealed how political actors within the Tweetchat were understanding and defining "Asian American collective politics": (1) assertions that Asian American identities are intersectional and diverse, (2) narratives of interdependency within Asian American communities as well as solidarity with other marginalized communities, and (3) using historical and contemporary critiques of systems of violence to imagine future possibilities. In the findings and analysis that follow, we first share details from the coordination and curation process of both the zine and Tweetchat. Rather than solely focus on movement outputs, such as the tweets themselves, we emphasize the immaterial and feminized labor in processes of movement building across different digital architectures. We then turn to a discussion of the emergent themes from the #FeministAntibodies Tweetchat and implications of these themes in Asian American cultural production and politics.

Care in the Time of Coronavirus: Making Asian American Feminist Media

Before its final form as a digital PDF, the AAFC's zine *Asian American Feminist Antibodies: Care in the Time of Coronavirus* existed over messy notes, emails, and Google documents. Media coverage and scholarship of social movements often fail to acknowledge the mundane and quotidian processes of media-making and the feminized and devalued administrative and technical labor of creating digital media outputs. Matilda Sabal, a volunteer for Bluestockings Bookstore, originally reached out to AAFC to volunteer their time, resources, and labor after witnessing multiple incidents of anti-Asian racism in their local community. After several email exchanges, plans were drafted for an open submissions call. The zine's editorial team drew primarily on their existing networks, reaching out to friends they had previously organized and worked alongside; later, they also privately messaged poets, artists, and writers. Most contributors were quick to reply, generously lending their work and perspectives to the zine and expressing ways this

project felt meaningful to them. One user on Twitter regularly messaged AAFC directly to share posts from their feed where Asian Americans were discussing instances of racism. These acts of reaching out to one another and bringing people in function as gestures for connection. These acts of extending the reach of the self into space forge meaningful political coalitions—"bring[ing] into the possibility of a 'we'" (Rodriguez, 2014, p. 2). The ways we touch, reach, make space, and connect reveal how we relate to those with whom we build community.

There are many limits to and critiques of using corporate technologies such as Google Drive to develop community-based communications infrastructures, such as data surveillance and the overvaluation of productivity. However, we might also consider how feminist uses of these technologies can reappropriate capitalist logics embedded within these technologies. This might include using the comments feature in Google Docs to offer expressions of gratitude, ask if someone needs support, or think and learn new histories and languages alongside other people. The zine itself functioned as a means to bring people into space together through the figurative and literal space of a digital object. The proximities forged through the use of space—the alignment of text and images—reflect and express political alignments and orientations.

To generate further conversation from the zine and create additional space for dialogue, AAFC and Bluestockings hosted an hour-long Tweetchat on community care on 10 April 2020 using the hashtag #FeministAntibodies (Asian American Feminist Collective, 2020b). Different leaders within AAFC took on different tasks: generating questions, designing graphics, and pre-writing tweets to post during the event. AAFC also reached out to community partners. In addition to individual contributors, invited participants represented leftist and anti-authoritarian organizations, groups, and campaigns such as Equality Labs, Nodutdol, Red Canary Song, and Free Them All for Public Health. Partners received questions in advance to allow for preparation in addition to a timeline for when questions for the chat would be posted; this is reflected in the flow of the Tweetchat itself, as the majority of the content comes from invited partners. The shared labor of preparation affords a dynamism within the conversation itself as an illusion of live-ness that invites other interlocutors to participate.

During the Tweetchat, Kuo posted from AAFC's and her individual user account, using Twitter on different browsers to participate as both the organization and herself. She used a Google doc of pre-written tweets and also participated in a live video chat with other AAFC leaders. Another leader of the collective spent the entire hour using Tweetdeck, a browser extension, to retweet and engage posts from other users participating in the conversation. The uses of different platforms adjusted for limitations on interfaces. Emphasizing the collective work behind producing the Tweetchat, such as assembling together notes and threading together information, reveals laboring figures behind the machine (Green, 2011; Nakamura, 2011).

Organizing within the context of the COVID-19 pandemic demonstrates the milieu of ways we bring movement work home. Prior to the pandemic, AAFC's monthly Sunday meetings rotated between different collective leaders' homes. bell hooks (1989) describes a homeplace as one about building a safe space for healing, affirmation, and growth within racist systems. Or, as Barbara Smith (1989) describes of the Kitchen Table Press, the kitchen is the center of a home for work and communication and the kitchen table represents a grassroots operation. The table can also be the site of a feminist point, a surface for political work. The table and the home have often been the site of "networking" space to foster belonging—collectively, it is a place for relationship building and gathering together. The next section turns toward the digital discourses circulating within the #FeministAntibodies chat to consider how perspectives, orientations, and inheritances of political and intellectual worlds and histories mobilize a particular orientation to Asian American collective politics.

#FeministAntibodies Tweetchat: Collective Orientations

This section discusses the three emergent themes from the coordinated #FeministAntibodies Tweetchat, interpreting how different political actors understand and define "Asian America" as a political formation that is (1) intersectional (or "not a monolith"), (2) interdependent, and (3) with

interconnected histories. The Tweetchat offers a specific discursive articulation of Asian American collective politics within a technocultural space as a way to intervene upon and remediate the racialization of Asian-ness during the COVID-19 pandemic.

Together, the three themes challenge neoliberal norms in both our technological and political culture, which fragment identity-based differences into discrete, individual categories by instead emphasizing difference as the foundation toward building collective politics. The neoliberalization of identity politics has reduced identity onto the level of the individual, rather than membership in collective struggles against oppressive systems and structures. Capitalism has been a medium in which community enacts itself (Joseph, 2002), and digital platforms function as a site to both produce and consume identity. For example, Wendy Hui Kyong Chun (2016) discusses how digital networks generate a neoliberal "you," rather than a collective "we" through a market of information. However, feminist and queer uses of platforms can reflexively use neoliberal logics embedded into platforms to circulate alternative imaginings. Rather than address anti-Asian racism during the COVID-19 pandemic at the level of individual injury, we interpret the Tweetchat's themes as challenging dominant discourses around recognition based on individual difference to instead re-imagine difference as a building block for mass opposition against racism and capitalism. In this vein, the Tweetchat also demonstrates Asian American feminism as entangled with discursive media technologies.

"Not a Monolith"—A Call for Intersectionality

AsAm communities are not experiencing this as a monolith. Asians who are East/SE Asian, incarcerated, Muslim, working class, undocumented, queer&trans, survivors, houseless are facing racialized violence & need intra-community support & solidarity. (Sharma, 2020a, April 10)

Participants in the Tweetchat identified a necessity in extending and expanding the reach of Asian American collective formation. They stressed the need to push against the construction of Asian America as a "monolith," a specific intervention given the disproportionate focus on East Asian populations by both mainstream news media coverage of COVID-19 as well as Asian American media responses to this coverage. They also highlighted the importance of intersectionality as a framework for building collective politics given differential experiences of disaster under multiple systems of power. While some early media accounts of the pandemic expressed hope for shared unity, the crisis exposed how combined factors including race, ethnicity, religion, class, gender, and other defining factors (Collins, 2015) differentially shape people's experiences. For example, people of color are infected and dying at faster rates during the pandemic, have less access to health care resources, and experience greater job instability (Devakumar et al., 2020). Participants emphasized the different ways particular groups were facing racialized violence; for example, Equality Labs (2020), a Dalit-led South Asian feminist organization, observed, "Bangladeshi communities have to close their shops and have no access to aid" as well as a "huge uptick in hate-speech connecting Muslim people to COVID-19" (@Equality Labs, April 10).

Participants cited differential access to resources as well as unequally distributed exposure to state violence, testifying to how the social and economic ramifications of COVID-19 impacted Asian populations in different ways. The potential for harassment, coupled with increased stress regarding potential economic loss, escalates during times of crisis (Peek, 2011), as testified to by Tweetchat participants who mentioned immigrant-owned stores, such as groceries, nail salons, and restaurants, in their communities closing. Red Canary Song (2020), a grassroots collective organizing Asian sex workers, highlighted how informal sector workers lack an unemployment safety net: ". . . Street vendors, day laborers, domestic workers & sex workers put themselves at risk. While there are few funds for gig workers, criminalized & undocumented workers esp. need more support & solidarity" (@RedCanarySong, April 10).

Long-standing stereotypes and biases in the mainstream media landscape, such as the model minority myth which casts Asians as upwardly mobile and economically successful, have tended to depict Asian Americans as homogeneous. However, Asian American activists have long worked to counter these perceptions—as a collective identity, Asian America was formed out of political movements during the Civil Rights era, in solidarity with Black liberation movements. In emphasizing intersectionality and challenging Asian America as a monolith, participants also called for building intra-community and cross-community solidarities. During the Tweetchat, rather than approach the lack of resources from tenets of individualism premised upon scarcity and intra-group competition, participants observed that pan-Asian collective action would benefit all Asian Americans during this time. For example, Nodutdol (2020), a grassroots Korean organization against war and militarism, shared that the pandemic "cuts across race and class . . . As anti-Asian racism is on the rise again, we also need to acknowledge how Black and Brown communities are disproportionately being affected [—] to build cross-community solidarity" (@Nodutdol, 2020, 10 April). Rather than take individual identity and recognition as a starting point, intersectional methods countering oppressive structures produce community formations in spite of (or because of) difference (Nash, 2019).

Participants identified racial tensions between communities of color, including how anti-Blackness within Asian American communities remains conspicuous during a time when Asian Americans are targets of racial hostility—the perspectives of Black Asians are notably largely missing from this dialogue. Participants stressed the need to "show up" for other impacted communities, highlighting the need for solidarity work between Asian Americans and medically vulnerable populations disproportionately impacted by COVID-19. Under externalized stress and grief during the coronavirus pandemic, this moment has seen tensions between narrow bids for inclusion and access to resources as well as calls to build across differences. In foregrounding difference, participants within the #FeministAntibodies Tweetchat outlined a vision for collective formation that emphasized community interdependence.

"Community is Growing"—Collectivity and Interdependence

It means breaking social norms instilled in us, embracing intimacy, sharing vulnerable spaces. It means re-centering collectivism and making sure everyone has a space in the world we want to create together. (Chau, 2020b, April 10)

The Tweetchat highlighted interdependence between individuals, families, and communities despite government neglect. Participants emphasized the importance of community-based mutual aid networks in responding to governmental indifference and emphasized models of caring for each other by sharing resources and support. For example, Shahana Hanif (2020), a language justice advocate, highlighted the importance of community translation and interpretation to not only expand immigrant access to resources but also "create a culture of shifting power, expand democratic participation, and [center] the wellness and survival of the most disenfranchised communities" (@ShahanaFromBK, 10 April).

In addition, in a moment of social and economic crisis, participants countered neoliberal individualism, which values individual responsibility, by presenting a feminist framework of interdependency and collective accountability to one another. Many acknowledged the need to carve out a space to heal, while asserting that productivity did not equate to worth—a direct critique of and movement against capitalist notions of labor which alienates workers from their own humanity in service of economic profit (hooks, 1990). Disabled artist and activist and Bluestockings volunteer Matilda Sabal (2020) highlighted practices of interdependency to build intimacy across distance and isolation, drawing on the long legacy of disability justice movements: "calling friends & comrades, coworking over Zoom, building space for rest and joy . . . the revolutionary work can be done anywhere, even your bed" (@fierce_invalids, 10 April). The emphasis on creating space for rest and joy through the uses of different technologies decenters notions of individual productivity. Such a pivot counters social relations structured by capitalism. In this vein, participants also emphasize care work and reproductive labor in their digital practices as a means of community support—the work of physically, materially, and emotionally preparing people to continue revolutionizing (Federici, 2012). Participants stressed the need to prioritize health and wellness as an essential part of organizing, as no activist movement can function if its members are burnt out.

Participants also spoke of feeling politically re-energized to mobilize with other people during this time. Scholar and activist Kim Tran (2020) shared the hope that people "(re) commit to movement work . . . and focus on building people power, building with each other" (@but_im_kim_tran, 10 April). The theme of interdependence in this Tweetchat draws heavily from Leah Lakshmi Piepzna-Samarasinha, whose writing on building care webs and mutual aid networks is also heavily featured within AAFC's zine. Drawing from the disability justice movement, Piepzna-Samarasinha (2018) intervenes on crash-and-burn emergency models of rapid response, often deployed in the midst of crisis, by highlighting the necessity for models of collective organizing that center "sustainability, slowness, and building for the long haul" (p. 53). Participants observed that in the wake of disaster, rather than formal institutions responding directly or quickly to community needs, local grassroots organizations led community recovery. These groups have few resources but hold deep knowledge of a specific neighborhood and build infrastructures and networks for aid and support (Hong, 2012).

"A World Built for All of Us"—Connecting Pasts, Presents, Futures

Community care over capital gain . . . A world built for all of us and run by all of us. (Asian American Feminist Collective, 2020c, April 10)

Participants discussed how histories of racial violence have facilitated the creation of spaces where disabled, trans, and economically disadvantaged people were not prioritized. The third theme that we identified from the Tweetchat highlighted how participants relied on their historical knowledge to make sense of the current COVID-19 outbreak, using history to drive their analyses and articulate their political positioning. They drew on these histories to generate imaginations for future worlds and possibilities. For example, Lausan (2020), a Hong Kong magazine, described the trauma of the SARS outbreak in 2003 and how mutual care practices undertaken during coronavirus are in our collective "muscle memory" (@LausanHK, April 10). Alison Roh Park (2020), a poet and writer, shared that she woke up feeling "intergenerational aches in my bones" (@alisonrohpark, April 10). The description of bodily memory as a visceral response to this moment demonstrates the embodiment of geohistorical politics of knowledge (Yoneyama, 2016). As people detailed the increase in harassment in their communities, they traced these painful experiences to transnational histories of colonization. For example, Heena Sharma (2020b) reflects on histories of genocide between Asian communities that has led to present-day "Hindu nationalist rhetoric further endangering the lives of Muslims who are being used as a scapegoat for this pandemic" (Sharma, 2020b, April 10). Participants reconstructed trauma narratives that transcend generations as embedded in collective memory, and share creative strategies of remembering (Kwan, 2020).

For many participants, the fear-mongering racist language from the Trump administration "blam[ing] China for their own mishandling of the pandemic" and observations that "Asian Americans are bearing the brunt of xenophobic attacks" (@DrHStilley, Kelly, 2020, 10 April) extended a long history of xenophobic racism in the United States, marked by the passage of events such as the Page Act, the Chinese Exclusion Act of 1882, and the Japanese internment during the Second World War, where Asian bodies represented a threat to the purity of (White) Western society in the form of "Yellow Peril" (Lee, 2007; Shah, 2001). In these cases, the circulation of information about who is deemed undesirable and unassimilable, from the stereotyping of Chinese immigrants as more likely to carry disease to the racialized constructions of Asians as threats and terrorists, has furthered racist projects of exclusion through anti-immigration and carceral policies. Drawing on the longer history of how Asians have been racialized as scapegoats in times of crisis, participants underlined a commonality of experience while also attempting to problematize the "perpetual foreigner" trope that reinforces the superiority and nativism of Eurocentric whiteness (Cheryan and Monin, 2005).

The Wing Luke Museum (2020) described the present moment as "American cultural amnesia in action" (@winglukemuseum, April 10). Here, the museum counters liberal erasures of historical violence in the pursuit of limited freedoms. Participants interrogated the present by calling attention to past conditions of injustice, as well imagining future possibilities, or "freedoms yet to come" (Lowe, 2015). The Tweetchat offered what Betina Hsieh (2020) described as an "affinity space" that allowed participants to unpack histories of oppression that make the disparities in this moment "historically predictable and not an anomaly" (@ProfHsieh, 10 April). Hsieh also added that we can only build solidarities if we know our own histories, "the ways in which we've bought into white supremacy, benefited from privilege and known oppressions" (@ProfHsieh, 10 April). In this vein, Tweetchat participants use historical recovery as a means to hold institutions of power more accountable. As historian Salonee Bhaman (2020) tweeted, "We have to build a language of solidarity and find a way to hold power accountable to those who are most vulnerable" (@saloneee, 10 April).

Discussion: Making Feminist Politics

The #FeministAntibodies Tweetchat offered a particular alignment of race in a technocultural space, namely a specific orientation to Asian American collective politics. As information environments, digital platforms offer a site of political performance for collectives and individual actors to articulate politics (Hall & Grossberg, 1986) and draw connections across differences at a particular conjuncture. The ways specific organizations, campaigns, and individuals mediate Asian American politics through discursive uses of platforms across different epistemological standpoints (Brock, 2016) demonstrate a particular orientation to Asian America as a political home and identity as well as the making and remaking of identity through technologies.

Facilitating together-ness in the midst of the COVID-19 pandemic has also shifted how digital connections become materialized. Recounting coordinating efforts to "be together" online with other people at a given time reveals the work involved in building a shared political home in digital space. By highlighting the friendships and relationships embedded within social movements and across technologies, we can see that digitally networked communications are not moments of seemingly spontaneous eruption, but instead involve both coordination work and deeper relationship building over time.

An observation and corresponding question that continues to emerge is the following: our current society is broken—so what is the society we desire for the future? This present moment of crisis and instability reveals a lot about what possibilities the future can hold, or how systems and institutions can and must be transformed. During the pandemic, social movements that have often been deemed as impractical or impossible suddenly seem within reach: free Internet, decarceration, eviction moratoriums, rent freezes, and loan payment suspensions can be possible. Through the discussion of intersectionality and interdependence, participants offered a critique of power, identifying the multiple ways that systems of racism and capitalism harm people collectively and how we might work together to imagine new systems.

Furthermore, bringing different histories together under the #FeministAntibodies hashtag discursively mobilizes solidarities across differences. For example, Asian communities are often excluded from dominant discourses on incarceration, preventing cross-community solidarity. Free Them All (2020), a decarceration campaign, pointed out, "all forms of incarceration harm all of us" (Free Them All for Public Health, 2020, April 10). Participants drew upon different histories of state violence as a means toward building future coalitions. The Tweetchat ended with a question prompting participants to imagine future worlds, where participants brought together their previous discussions of intersectionality, interdependence, and history. Many posts focused on community-based organizing as a strategy toward abolishing and transforming present institutions and systems.

With an economy of hearts and likes, activism on digital spaces can sometimes be a "humming positivity machine" (Ryan, 2016) through the discursive circulation of happy words about community. As an immersive information environment that encourages infinite scrolling, Twitter also functions as a medium of compression, transmitting ideas in 280 characters or less. However, looking beyond the content of the Tweets themselves to bring in both historical context as well as discussion of the labor and process that generated them emphasizes how digital objects function as a medium where questions of identity and inequality are worked out and how relationships are made and built through conceptualizing and circulating writing and ideas. The level of curation and moderation of the Tweetchat does not afford for broad representations of Asian America, but instead articulates a specific vision of what Asian American collective politics might be.

Conclusion

The Asian American Feminist Collective's zine and corresponding Tweetchat digitally circulate the intergenerational arguments, histories, languages, and ideas that have shaped Asian American movement building and Asian American studies across multiple decades. Initiated alongside the "ethnic studies" as part of social justice movements in the 1960s and 1970s, Asian American studies originated as an academic field of study in the midst of racial and political crisis (Suyemoto & Liu, 2018). Yet, as a field and as a political concept, "Asian American" also faced critical problems, including the tension between homogenizing "Asian American" and navigating internal diversity. The contradictions surrounding Asian American collective politics in the larger digital information environment during the COVID-19 pandemic indicate political and intellectual tensions around how we build collective politics in ways that continue to account for uneven differences. As a political orientation and political "home," Asian America is continuously in the midst of rebuilding—and now, rebuilding across digital platforms. The recursive pull of Asian American political identity in navigating differences in the process of narrating collective politics has been central to how "Asian America" continues to form and reform, including in our digital spaces.

As examples of cultural politics across platforms, the zine and Tweetchat demonstrate an orientation to Asian America that reflects upon and responds to sociocultural and political histories. The process of political expression and content circulation through the curation of particular interlocutors across different technological and discursive forms produced a specific vision of Asian American politics. The threads emerging from these conversations function as forms of alignment and "being in line with others" (Ahmed, 2006, p. 15). As highlighted by both contributors to the zine and participants in the Tweetchat, the COVID-19 pandemic has revealed both the ongoing precarities of everyday existence in our communities as well as exposing who is unevenly at risk when social safety nets fail. While this moment is unique, activists and community organizers emphasize that "we" have also been here before. As expressed in the manifold community resources that circulate online, people marginalized by state violence hold extensive experience and knowledge on how to survive despite precarity and scarcity. Furthermore, these forms of knowledge also envision ideas on how to radically change systems so they no longer continue to render particular communities and people disposable.

As scholars and media-makers using collaboration as a feminist method, we emphasize the necessity of community-based research projects that interrogate ongoing inequalities at the intersection of race, technology, labor, and migration. Continuing to extend scholarly arguments on the relationship between media and politics, we see community forms of knowledge production as central to intellectual and political inquiry. This study focuses on organizing during March and April 2020; with the long-lasting duration of the pandemic, future studies can further investigate shifts in processes of community organizing during crisis. Significantly, with uprisings beginning at the end of May 2020 in the wake of continued police violence against Black people and ongoing structural anti-Black racism, further attention should be paid to relational theorizations of race, including in studies of technology and social movements. This particular study also focuses on a small network of Asian American feminist media practitioners. As a distinctly Asian *American* form of media production, this particular study does not include critical engagements with Asian migrant and diasporic communities. Given how immigrants are uniquely positioned as vulnerable during this time, with matters such as immigration status and visas becoming increasingly politicized,

future research in this sphere should engage these communities. To further understand and study the digital information environment in which Asian and Asian American politics form during the ongoing pandemic, future research could also look to media practices across diasporic platforms and networks. For example, the Chinese social media app WeChat functions as an alternative site to further examine collective politics. Furthermore, the intersectionality of Asian America could also be seen through testimonials and other media practices by domestic workers and taxi drivers impacted by the gig economy, sharing economy, and on-demand service apps.

As revealed by yet-increasing cases, hospitalizations, and deaths across the United States, the COVID-19 pandemic will have long-lasting implications on our communities, and we are only beginning to see the devastating social and economic impacts of the crisis. If we are pedagogically committed to redressing unequal differences in service of future world-building, this requires building alongside grassroots communities on the frontlines in shaping the meaning of Asian America as a formation.

Acknowledgements

The authors would like to extend a thank you to the "Care in the Time of Coronavirus" zine co-editors, Salonee Bhaman (AAFC), Matilda Sabal (Bluestockings), and Tiffany Diane Tso (AAFC), as well as additional co-leaders of the Asian American Feminist Collective, Julie Ae Kim and Senti Sojwal. They appreciate the time and contributions of all participants in the #FeministAntibodies Tweetchat. In addition, they would like to thank other members of the AAPI COVID-19 Project collaborative research group, including Catherine Nguyen, Christina Ong, Susanna Park, Kara Takasaki, Mu Wu, and Liwei Zhang, as well as Jason Beckfield for ongoing support of their research.

Corresponding Author
Rachel Kuo, Center for Information, Technology, and Public Life, The University of North Carolina at Chapel Hill, 100 Manning Hall, CB 3360, Chapel Hill, NC 25799, USA.

Email: rskuo@email.unc.edu; @rachelkuo

Declaration of Conflicting Interests

The author(s) declared no potential conflicts of interest with respect to the research, authorship, and/or publication of this article.

Funding

The author(s) received no financial support for the research, authorship, and/or publication of this article.

References

Ahmed, S. (2006). *Queer phenomenology: Orientations, objects, others.* Duke University Press.

Allied Media Projects. (2020). Media-based organizing. https://www.alliedmedia.org/media-based-organizing

Asian American Feminist Collective. (2020a, April). #FeministAntibodies Tweetchat: Care in the time of coronavirus. *Wakelet.* bit.ly/feministantibodies

Asian American Feminist Collective. (2020b, April 6). [@aafcollective]. Twitter. https://twitter.com/aafcollective/status/1247173433231839234

Asian American Feminist Collective. (2020c, April 10). [@aafcollective]. Twitter. https://twitter.com/aafcollective/status/1248670749793095681

Bailey, M. (2015). #Transform(ing)DH writing and research: An autoethnography of digital humanities and feminist ethics. *Digital Humanities Quarterly,* 9(2), Article 1.

Bascara, V., & Nakamura, L. (2014). Adaptation and its discontents: Asian American cultural politics across platforms. *Amerasia Journal,* 40(2), ix–xviii.

Bhaman, S. (2020, April 10). @saloneee. Twitter. https://twitter.com/saloneee/status/1248659432940228610

Bhaman, S., Kuo, R., Sabal, M., Shaw, V., & Tso, T. D. (2020). Care in the time of coronavirus. In Asian American Feminist Collective (Ed.), *Asian American feminist antibodies: Care in the time of coronavirus.* https://digitalcommons.wcl.american.edu/wlpanalyses/9/

Bonilla, Y., & Rosa, J. (2015). #Ferguson: Digital protest hashtag ethnography and the racial politics of social media. *American Ethnologist,* 42(1), 4–17.

Brock, A. (2015). Deeper data: A response to Boyd and Crawford. *Media, Culture, and Society,* 37(7), 1084–88.

Brock, A. (2016). Critical technocultural discourse analysis. *New Media & Society,* 20(3), 1012–30.

Chau, M. (2020a, March 19). A comic on resiliency. *Wing Luke Museum Newsletter.* https://bit.ly/2yYKbF6

Chau, M. (2020b, April 10). [@monyeeart]. Twitter. https://twitter.com/monyeeart/status/1248663472788762624

Cheryan, S., & Monin, B. (2005). Where are you really from? Asian Americans and identity denial. *Journal of Personality and Social Psychology,* 89(5), 717–30.

Chun, W. H. K. (2016). *Habitual new media.* MIT Press

Collins, P. H. (2015). Intersectionality's definitional dilemmas. *Annual Review of Sociology,* 41, 1–20.

Devakumar, D., Shannon, G., Bhopal, S. S., & Abubakar, I. (2020). Racism and discrimination in COVID-19 responses. *The Lancet,* 395(10231), Article 1194.

Equality Labs. (2020, April 10). [@equalitylabs]. https://twitter.com/EqualityLabs/status/1248658596117831680

Federici, S. (2012). *Revolution at point zero: Housework, reproduction, and feminist struggle.* PM Press.

Free Them All for Public Health. (2020, April 10). [@freethemall2020]. Twitter. https://twitter.com/FreeThemAll2020/status/1248660261445271552

Gilmore, R. W. (2007). *Golden gulag: Prisons, surplus, crisis, and opposition in globalizing California.* University of California Press.

Green, V. (2011). *Race on the line: Gender, labor, and technology in the Bell System, 1880–1980.* Duke University Press.

Hall, S., & Grossberg, L. (1986). On postmodernism and articulation: An interview with Stuart Hall. *Journal of Communication,* 10(45), 45–60.

Hanif, S. B. K. (2020, April 10). [@ShahanafromBK]. Twitter. https://twitter.com/ShahanaFromBK/status/1248672500550164483

Hong, S. (2012, November 7). *Left in the dark: Inside the buildings of Chinatown after Hurricane Sandy.* Asian American Writers Workshop. https://aaww.org/left-in-the-dark/

hooks, b. (1989). Choosing the margin as a space of radical openness. *Framework: The Journal of Cinema and Media,* 36, 15–23.

hooks, b. (1990). Homeplace: A site of resistance. In b. hooks (Ed.), *Yearning: Race, gender, and cultural politics* (pp. 41–49). South End Press.

Hsieh, P. (2020, April 10). [@ProfHsieh]. Twitter. https://twitter.com/ProfHsieh/status/1248660271716950016

Ishizuka, K. (2016). *Serve the people: Making Asian America in the long sixties.* Verso Books.

Iyer, D. (2017). *We too sing America: South Asian, Arab, Muslim, and Sikh immigrants shape our multiracial future.* The New Press.

Jackson, S. J. M., Bailey, M., & Foucault Welles, B. (2020). *#HashtagActivism: Networks of race and gender justice.* MIT Press.

Joseph, M. (2002). *Against the romance of community*. University of Minnesota Press.

Kelly, H. S. (2020, April 10). [@DrHStilley]. Twitter. https://twitter.com/DrHStilley/status/124973288 2878345221

Kim, D., & Kim, E. (2014). The #TwitterEthics Manifesto. *Model View Culture*. https://modelviewculture.com/pieces/the-twitterethics-manifesto

Korn, J. (2017). Expecting penises in Chatroulette: Race, gender, and sexuality in anonymous online spaces. *Popular Communication*, 15(2), 95–109.

Kuo, R. (2017). Reflections on #solidarity: Intersectional movements in APIA communities. In L. K. Lopez & V. Pham (Eds.), *Routledge companion to Asian American media*. Routledge. https://www.routledgehandbooks.com/doi/10.4324/9781315727745.ch16

Kuo, R. (2018). Visible solidarities: #Asians4BlackLives and affective racial counterpublics. *Studies of Transition States and Societies*, 10(2), 40–54.

Kwan, Y. Y. (2020). Time-image episodes and the construction of transgenerational trauma narratives. *Journal of Asian American Studies*, 23(1), 29–59.

Lausan, H. K. (2020, April 10). [@lausanhk]. Twitter. https://twitter.com/lausanhk/status/124866082 0030087171

Lee, E. (2007). "The Yellow Peril" and Asian exclusion in the Americas. *Pacific Historical Review*, 76(4), 537–62.

Lopez, L. K. (2016). *Asian American media activism: Fighting for cultural citizenship*. New York University Press.

Lowe, L. (1996). *Immigrant acts: On Asian American cultural politics*. Duke University Press.

Lowe, L. (1998). Work, immigration, gender: New subjects of cultural politics: Social justice: crossing lines: Revisioning U.S. *Race Relations*, 25(3), 31–49.

Lowe, L. (2015). History hesitant. *Social Text*, 125, 85–107.

McIlwain, C. (2017). Racial formation, inequality and the political economy of web traffic. *Information, Communication & Society*, 20(7), 1073–89.

Nakamura, L. (2011). Economies of digital production in East Asia: iPhone girls and the transnational circuits of cool. *Media Fields Journal*, 2. http://mediafieldsjournal.org/economies-of-digital/

Nakamura, L., & Chow-White, P. (Eds.). (2013). *Race after the Internet*. Routledge.

Nash, J. (2019). *Black feminism reimagined: After intersectionality*. Duke University Press.

Nguyen, M. T. (2015). Minor threats. *Radical History Review*, 122, 11–24.

Nickel, P. M., & Eikenberry, A. M. (2007). Responding to "natural" disasters: The ethical implications of the voluntary state. *Administrative Theory & Praxis*, 29(4), 534–45.

Noble, S. N. (2016). A future for intersectional black feminist technology studies. *Scholar & Feminist Online*, 13(3), 1–8.

Nodutdol. (2020, April 10). [@nodutdol]. Twitter. https://twitter.com/nodutdol/status/1248659624779223041

Park, A. (2020, April 10). [@alisonrohpark]. Twitter. https://twitter.com/alisonrohpark/status/124865933 1115102209

Peek, L. (2011). *Behind the backlash: Muslim Americans after 9/11*. Temple University Press.

Piepzna-Samarasinha, L. L. (2018). *Care work: Dreaming disability justice*. Arsenal Pulp Press.

Piepzna-Samarasinha, L. L. (2020, March 9). Half-assed disabled prepper tips for preparing for a coronavirus quarantine. *Google Docs*. bit.ly/preppertips

Red Canary Song. (2020, April 10). [@redcanarysong]. Twitter. https://twitter.com/RedCanarySong/status/1248663620902359041

Rodriguez, J. M. (2014). *Sexual futures, queer gestures, and other Latina longings*. New York University Press.

Ryan, E. G. (2016, December 21). Pantsuit nation is the worst: Why a book of uplifting Facebook posts won't heal America. *Daily Beast*. https://www.thedailybeast.com/pantsuit-nation-is-the-worst-why-a-book-of-uplifting-facebook-posts-wont-heal-america

Sabal, M. (2020, April 10). [@fierce_invalids]. Twitter. https://twitter.com/fierce_invalids/status/124866 1850474061827

Shah, N. (2001). *Contagious divides: Epidemics and race in San Francisco's Chinatown*. University of California Press.

Sharma, H. (2020a, April 10). [@heenasharma]. Twitter. https://twitter.com/heenasharma_/status/12486682 77129216001

Sharma, H. (2020b, April 10). [@heenasharma]. Twitter. https://twitter.com/heenasharma_/status/124867 0419114131461

Sharma, S. (2013). Black Twitter? Racial hashtags, networks and contagion. *New Formations*, 78, 46–64.

Shaw, V. (2017). We are already living together. In D. Goh & C.-M. Wang (Eds.), *Precarious belongings: Affect and nationalism in Asia* (pp. 59–76). Rowman & Littlefield.

Shaw, V. (2020). Strategies of ambivalence: Cultures of liberal Antifa in Japan. *Radical History Review*, 138, 145–70.

Smith, B. (1989). A press of our own kitchen table: Women of color press. *Frontiers: A Journal of Women Studies*, 10(3), 11–13.

Steele, C. K. (2017). Black bloggers and their varied publics: The everyday politics of black discourse online. *Television and New Media*, 19(2), 112–27.

Suyemoto, K. L., & Liu, C. M. (2018). Asian American students in Asian American studies: Experiences of racism-related stress and relation to depressive and anxious symptoms. *Journal of Asian American Studies*, 21(2), 301–26.

Tang, E. (2011). A gulf unites us: The Vietnamese Americans of Black New Orleans East. *American Quarterly*, 63(1), 117–49.

Tran, K. (2020, April 10). [@but_im_kim_tran]. Twitter. https://twitter.com/but_im_kim_tran/status/124867062853142528o

Vis, F. (2013). A critical reflection on Big Data: Considering APIs, researchers and tools as data makers. *First Monday*, 18(10). https://firstmonday.org/ojs/index.php/fm/article/view/4878

Wing Luke Museum. (2020, April 10). [@winglukemuseum]. Twitter. https://twitter.com/winglukemuseum/status/1248657324043993088

Wong, A. (2020). #Coronavirus and the disability community. Wakelet. https://wakelet.com/wake/1633ef52-2ade-43a9-b118-50d19f821cb7

Yoneyama, L. (2016). *Cold War ruins: Transpacific critique of American justice and Japanese war crimes*. Duke University Press.

Questions for Critical Thinking

1. As the authors discuss their collective action utilizing digital media was a response to the "mediatization of 'Asian-ness' as contagion" during the COVID-19 pandemic. What examples did you see of such mediatization?

2. How did this reading expand your ideas of the tools that can be used for positive social change?

3. What lessons can movements for social justice learn from the people involved in this movement?

SEEING MORE THAN BLACK AND WHITE

Latinos, Racism, and the Cultural Divides

* *Elizabeth Martinez*

In the essay that follows, sociologist Elizabeth Martinez offers some explanations for the difficulty the United States has with viewing issues of race beyond a black–white dichotomy and calls for inclusion when discussing racial issues. Especially keeping in mind our increasing diversity as a nation and the ever-growing complexity of race, she asserts that our effectiveness in working toward racial justice will only come when we move beyond black and white.

A certain relish seems irresistible to this Latina as the mass media have been compelled to sit up, look south of the border, and take notice. Probably the Chiapas uprising and Mexico's recent political turmoil have won us no more than a brief day in the sun. Or even less: liberal Ted Koppel still hadn't noticed the historic assassination of presidential candidate Colosio three days afterward. But it's been sweet, anyway.

When Kissinger said years ago "nothing important ever happens in the south," he articulated a contemptuous indifference toward Latin America, its people, and their culture which has long dominated U.S. institutions and attitudes. Mexico may be great for a vacation, and some people like burritos, but the usual image of Latin America combines incompetence with absurdity in loud colors. My parents, both Spanish teachers, endured decades of being told kids were better off learning French.

U.S. political culture is not only Anglo-dominated but also embraces an exceptionally stubborn national self-centeredness, with no global vision other than relations of domination. The U.S. refuses to see itself as one nation sitting on a continent with 20 others all speaking languages other than English and having the right not to be dominated.

Such arrogant indifference extends to Latinos within the U.S. The mass media complain, "people can't relate to Hispanics"—or Asians, they say. Such arrogant indifference has played an important role in invisibilizing La Raza (except where we become a serious nuisance or a handy scapegoat). It is one reason the U.S. harbors an exclusively white-on-Black concept of racism. It is one barrier to new thinking about racism which is crucial today. There are others.

Good-bye White Majority

In a society as thoroughly and violently racialized as the United States, white–Black relations have defined racism for centuries. Today the composition and culture of the U.S. are changing rapidly. We need to consider seriously whether we can afford to maintain an exclusively white/Black model of racism when the population will be 32 percent Latin/Asian/Pacific American and Native American—in short, neither Black nor white—by the year 2050. We are challenged to recognize that multi-colored racism is mushrooming, and then strategize how to resist it. We are challenged to move beyond a dualism comprised of two white supremacist inventions: Blackness and Whiteness.

At stake in those challenges is building a united anti-racist force strong enough to resist contemporary racist strategies of divide-and-conquer. Strong enough in the long run, to help defeat racism itself. Doesn't an exclusively Black/white model of racism discourage the perception of common interests among people of color and thus impede a solidarity that can challenge white supremacy? Doesn't it encourage the isolation of African Americans from potential allies? Doesn't it advise all people of color to spend too much energy understanding our lives in relation to Whiteness, and thus freeze us in a defensive, often self-destructive mode?

No "Oppression Olympics"

For a Latina to talk about recognizing the multi-colored varieties of racism is not, and should not be, yet another round in the Oppression Olympics. We don't need more competition among different social groupings for that "Most Oppressed" gold. We don't need more comparisons of suffering between women and Blacks, the disabled and the gay, Latino teenagers and white seniors, or whatever. We don't need more surveys like the recent much publicized Harris Poll showing that different peoples of color are prejudiced toward each other—a poll patently designed to demonstrate that us coloreds are no better than white folk. (The survey never asked people about positive attitudes.)

Rather, we need greater knowledge, understanding, and openness to learning about each other's histories and present needs as a basis for working together. Nothing could seem more urgent in an era when increasing impoverishment encourages a self-imposed separatism among people of color as a desperate attempt at community survival. Nothing could seem more important as we search for new

social change strategies in a time of ideological confusion.

My call to rethink concepts of racism in the U.S. today is being sounded elsewhere. Among academics, liberal foundation administrators, and activist-intellectuals, you can hear talk of the need for a new "racial paradigm" or model. But new thinking seems to proceed in fits and starts, as if dogged by a fear of stepping on toes, of feeling threatened, or of losing one's base. With a few notable exceptions, even our progressive scholars of color do not make the leap from perfunctorily saluting a vague multi-culturalism to serious analysis. We seem to have made little progress, if any, since Bob Blauner's 1972 book *Racial Oppression in America*. Recognizing the limits of the white–Black axis, Blauner critiqued White America's ignorance of and indifference to the Chicano/a experience with racism.

Real opposition to new paradigms also exists. There are academics scrambling for one flavor of ethnic studies funds versus another. There are politicians who cultivate distrust of others to keep their own communities loyal. When we hear, for example, of Black/Latino friction, dismay should be quickly followed by investigation. In cities like Los Angeles and New York, it may turn out that political figures scrapping for patronage and payola have played a narrow nationalist game, whipping up economic anxiety and generating resentment that sets communities against each other.

So the goal here, in speaking about moving beyond a bipolar concept of racism is to build stronger unity against white supremacy. The goal is to see our similarities of experience and needs. If that goal sounds naive, think about the hundreds of organizations formed by grassroots women of different colors coming together in recent years. Their growth is one of today's most energetic motions and it spans all ages. Think about the multicultural environmental justice movement. Think about the coalitions to save schools. Small rainbows of our own making are there, to brighten a long road through hellish times.

It is in such practice, through daily struggle together, that we are most likely to find the road to greater solidarity against a common enemy. But we also need a will to find it and ideas about where, including some new theory.

The West Goes East

Until very recently, Latino invisibility—like that of Native Americans and Asian/Pacific Americans—has been close to absolute in U.S. seats of power, major institutions, and the non-Latino public mind. Having lived on both the East and West Coasts for long periods, I feel qualified to pronounce: an especially myopic view of Latinos prevails in the East. This, despite such data as a 24.4 percent Latino population of New York City alone in 1991, or the fact that in 1990 more Puerto Ricans were killed by New York police under suspicious circumstances than any other ethnic group. Latino populations are growing rapidly in many eastern cities and the rural South, yet remain invisible or stigmatized—usually both.

Eastern blinders persist. I've even heard that the need for a new racial paradigm is dismissed in New York as a California hang-up. A black Puerto Rican friend in New York, when we talked about experiences of racism common to Black and brown, said "People here don't see Border Patrol brutality against Mexicans as a form of police repression," despite the fact that the Border Patrol is the largest and most uncontrolled police force in the U.S. It would seem that an old ignorance has combined with new immigrant bashing to sustain divisions today.

While the East (and most of the Midwest) usually remains myopic, the West Coast has barely begun to move away from its own denial. Less than two years ago in San Francisco, a city almost half Latino or Asian/Pacific American, a leading daily newspaper could publish a major series on contemporary racial issues and follow the exclusively Black–white paradigm. Although millions of TV viewers saw massive Latino participation in the April 1992 Los Angeles uprising, which included 18 out of 50 deaths and the majority of arrests, the mass media and most people labeled that event "a Black riot."

If the West Coast has more recognition of those who are neither Black nor white, it is mostly out of fear about the proximate demise of its white majority. A second, closely related reason is the relentless campaign by California Gov. Pete Wilson to scapegoat immigrants for economic problems and pass racist, unconstitutional laws attacking their health, education, and children's future. Wilson has almost single-handedly made the word "immigrant" mean Mexican

or other Latino (and sometimes Asian). Who thinks of all the people coming from the former Soviet Union and other countries? The absolute racism of this has too often been successfully masked by reactionary anti-immigrant groups like FAIR blaming immigrants for the staggering African-American unemployment rate.

Wilson's immigrant bashing is likely to provide a model for other parts of the country. The five states with the highest immigration rates—California, Florida, New York, Illinois and Texas—all have a governor up for re-election in 1994. Wilson's tactics won't appear in every campaign but some of the five states will surely see intensified awareness and stigmatization of Latinos as well as Asian/Pacific Islanders. *Editor's Note:* While the specific references are dated, the larger reality is still true: immigration remains a controversial issue in local and regional elections.

As this suggests, what has been a regional issue mostly limited to western states is becoming a national issue. If you thought Latinos were just "Messicans" down at the border, wake up—they are all over North Carolina, Pennsylvania and 8th Avenue Manhattan now. A qualitative change is taking place. With the broader geographic spread of Latinos and Asian/Pacific Islanders has come a nationalization of racist practices and attitudes that were once regional. The west goes east, we could say.

Like the monster Hydra, racism is growing some ugly new heads. We will have to look at them closely.

The Roots of Racism and Latinos

A bipolar model of racism—racism as white on Black—has never really been accurate. Looking for the roots of racism in the U.S. we can begin with the genocide against American Indians which made possible the U.S. land base, crucial to white settlement and early capitalist growth. Soon came the massive enslavement of African people which facilitated that growth. As slave labor became economically critical, "blackness" became ideologically critical; it provided the very source of "whiteness" and the heart of racism. Franz Fanon would write, "colour is the most outward manifestation of race."

If Native Americans had been a crucial labor force during those same centuries, living and working in the white man's sphere, our racist ideology might have evolved differently. "The tawny," as Ben Franklin dubbed them, might have defined the opposite of what he called "the lovely white." But with Indians decimated and survivors moved to distant concentration camps, they became unlikely candidates for this function. Similarly, Mexicans were concentrated in the distant West; elsewhere Anglo fear of them or need to control was rare. They also did not provide the foundation for a definition of whiteness.

Some anti-racist left activists have put forth the idea that only African Americans experience racism as such and that the suffering of other people of color results from national minority rather than racial oppression. From this viewpoint, the exclusively white/Black model for racism is correct. Latinos, then, experience exploitation and repression for reasons of culture and nationality—not for their "race." (It should go without saying that while racism is an all-too-real social fact, race has no scientific basis.)

Does the distinction hold? This and other theoretical questions call for more analysis and more expertise than one article can offer. In the meantime, let's try on the idea that Latinos do suffer for their nationality and culture, especially language. They became part of the U.S. through the 1846–48 war on Mexico and thus a foreign population to be colonized. But as they were reduced to cheap or semi-slave labor, they quickly came to suffer for their "race"—meaning, as non-whites. In the Southwest of a super-racialized nation the broad parallelism of race and class embrace Mexicans ferociously.

The bridge here might be a definition of racism as "the reduction of the cultural to the biological," in the words of French scholar Christian Delacampagne now working in Egypt. Or: "racism exists wherever it is claimed that a given social status is explained by a given natural characteristic." We know that line: Mexicans are just naturally lazy and have too many children, so they're poor and exploited.

The discrimination, oppression and hatred experienced by Native Americans, Mexicans, Asian/Pacific Islanders, and Arab Americans are forms of racism. Speaking only of Latinos, we have seen in California and the Southwest, especially along the border, almost 150 years of relentless repression which today includes Central Americans among its targets. That history

reveals hundreds of lynchings between 1847 and 1935, the use of counterinsurgency armed forces beginning with the Texas Rangers, random torture and murder by Anglo ranchers, forced labor, rape by border lawmen, and the prevailing Anglo belief that a Mexican life doesn't equal a dog's in value.

But wait. If color is so key to racial definition, as Fanon and others say, perhaps people of Mexican background experience racism less than national minority oppression because they are not dark enough as a group. For White America, shades of skin color are crucial to defining worth. The influence of those shades has also been internalized by communities of color. Many Latinos can and often want to pass for whites; therefore, White America may see them as less threatening than darker sisters and brothers.

Here we confront more of the complexity around us today, with questions like: What about the usually poor, very dark Mexican or Central American of strong Indian or African heritage? (Yes, folks, 200,000–300,000 Africans were brought to Mexico as slaves, which is far, far more than the Spaniards who came.) And what about the effects of accented speech or foreign name, characteristics that may instantly subvert "passing"?

What about those cases where a Mexican-American is never accepted, no matter how light-skinned, well-dressed or well-spoken? A Chicano lawyer friend coming home from a professional conference in suit, tie and briefcase found himself on a bus near San Diego that was suddenly stopped by the Border Patrol. An agent came on board and made a beeline through the all-white rows of passengers direct to my friend. "Your papers." The agent didn't believe Jose was coming from a U.S. conference and took him off the bus to await proof. Jose was lucky; too many Chicanos and Mexicans end up killed.

In a land where the national identity is white, having the "wrong" nationality becomes grounds for racist abuse. Who would draw a sharp line between today's national minority oppression in the form of immigrant-bashing, and racism?

None of this aims to equate the African American and Latino experiences; that isn't necessary even if it were accurate. Many reasons exist for the persistence of the white/Black paradigm of racism; they include numbers, history, and the psychology of whiteness.

In particular they include centuries of slave revolts, a Civil War, and an ongoing resistance to racism that cracked this society wide open while the world watched. Nor has the misery imposed on Black people lessened in recent years. New thinking about racism can and should keep this experience at the center.

A Deadly Dualism

The exclusively white/Black concept of race and racism in the U.S. rests on a western, Protestant form of dualism woven into both race and gender relations from earliest times. In the dualist universe there is only black and white. A disdain, indeed fear, of mixture haunts the Yankee soul; there is no room for any kind of multi-faceted identity, any hybridism.

As a people, La Raza combines three sets of roots—indigenous, European, and African—all in widely varying degrees. In short we represent a profoundly un-American concept: *mestizaje* (pronounced mess-tee-zah-hey), the mixing of peoples and emergence of new peoples. A highly racialized society like this one cannot deal with or allow room for *mestizaje*. It has never learned to do much more than hiss "miscegenation!" Or, like that Alabama high school principal who recently denied the right of a mixed-blood pupil to attend the prom, to say: "your parents made a mistake." Apparently we, all the millions of La Raza, are just that—a mistake.

Mexicans in the U.S. also defy the either–or, dualistic mind in that, on the one hand, we are a colonized people displaced from the ancestral homeland with roots in the present-day U.S. that go back centuries. Those ancestors didn't cross the border; the border crossed them. At the same time many of us have come to the U.S. more recently as "immigrants" seeking work. The complexity of Raza baffles and

frustrates most Anglos; they want to put one neat label on us. It baffles many Latinos too, who often end up categorizing themselves racially as "Other" for lack of anything better. For that matter, the term "Latino" which I use here is a monumental simplification; it refers to 20-plus nationalities and a wide range of classes.

But we need to grapple with the complexity, for there is more to come. If anything, this nation will see more *mestizaje* in the future, embracing innumerable ethnic combinations. What will be its effects? Only one thing seems certain: "white" shall cease to be the national identity.

A glimpse at the next century tells us how much we need to look beyond the white/Black model of race relations and racism. White/Black are real poles, central to the history of U.S. racism. We can neither ignore them nor stop there. But our effectiveness in fighting racism depends on seeing the changes taking place, trying to perceive the contours of the future. From the time of the Greeks to the present, racism around the world has had certain commonalties but no permanently fixed character. It is evolving again today, and we'd best labor to read the new faces of this Hydra-headed monster. Remember, for every head that Hydra lost it grew two more.

Sometimes the problem seems so clear. Last year I showed slides of Chicano history to an Oakland high school class with 47 African Americans and three Latino students. The images included lynchings and police beatings of Mexicans and other Latinos, and many years of resistance. At the end one Black student asked, "Seems like we have had a lot of experiences in common—so why can't Blacks and Mexicans get along better?" No answers, but there was the first step: asking the question.

Questions for Critical Thinking

1. Martinez offers some explanations for the difficulty the United States has with viewing issues of race beyond a black–white dichotomy. What do you think of her explanations?

2. Has the reality that whites will no longer be a majority in the United States impacted race relations positively or negatively?

3. How might expanding issues of race beyond the black–white dichotomy help us to move toward a system of equal access to opportunity with regard to race?

REFORM OR TRANSFORMATION?

The Pivotal Role of Food Justice in the U.S. Food Movement

* *Eric Holt-Giménez and Yi Wang*

A sixth of the world's population is now hungry, just as a sixth of the US population is "food insecure." These severe levels of hunger and insecurity share root causes, located in the political economy of a global, corporate food system. As the authors illustrate, food justice is centrally positioned to influence the direction of a change in this system. What will be of particular importance is how addressing issues of racial and class inequality is integrated into this change.

The global food crisis has pushed the U.S. food movement to a political juncture. A sixth of the world's population is now hungry—just as a sixth of the U.S. population is "food insecure." These severe levels of hunger and insecurity share root causes, located in the political economy of a global, corporate food regime. Because of its political location between reformist calls for food security and radical calls for food sovereignty, food justice is pivotally placed to influence the direction of food-systems change. This placement subjects the concept of food justice to multiple claims, definitions, and practices that tend either to affirm a structural focus on resource redistribution, or to dilute its political meaning by focusing on food access. How issues of race and class are resolved will influence the political direction of the food justice movement's organizational alliances: toward reform or toward transformation. How the food justice movement "pivots" may determine the degree to which it is able to bring about substantive changes to the U.S. food system.

Background: The Global Food Crisis, Hunger, and Food Security

The global food price crisis of 2008 ushered in record levels of hunger for the world's poor at a time of record global harvests as well as record profits for the world's major agrifoods corporations (Lean 2008). The combination of increasing hunger in the midst of wealth and abundance unleashed a flurry of worldwide "food riots" (including in the United States) not seen for many decades. In June 2008, the World Bank reported that global food prices had risen 83 percent in three years and the Food and Agriculture Organization of the United Nations (FAO) cited a 45 percent increase in their world food price index in just nine months (Wiggins and Levy 2008). Despite a brief drop in the

"Reform or Transformation? The Pivotal Role of Food Justice in the U.S. Food Movement," Eric Holt-Giménez and Yi Wang, published in *Race/Ethnicity: Multidisciplinary Global Contexts* (published by Indiana University Press); Kirwan Institute for the Study of Race and Ethnicity at The Ohio State University.

food price index, retail food prices remained high through 2010 and into 2011 when the index spiked again to record levels (FAO 2011). According to the United Nations World Food Program, more than 90 percent of the world's hungry—most of whom are peasant farmers—are simply too poor to buy enough food (WFP 2011). Some of the planet's hungry people live in the Global North, though hunger is measured as "food insecurity" and social safety nets are more readily available. Levels of food insecurity in the United States mirror global patterns; more than 50 million people are now food insecure and one in nine Americans are on food stamps (Nord et al. 2010).

Food insecurity in the United States is characterized by a nationwide epidemic of diet-related diseases that result in an estimated $240 billion a year in health costs (Schlosser 2001) that fall disproportionately on low-income communities of color (Baker et al. 2006). In these neighborhoods, food access is often limited to the cheap, high-fat, high-salt, high-calorie, processed food available at gas stations, liquor stores, corner stores, and fast food outlets (Herrera, Khanna, and Davis 2009; Mamen 2007; Morton and Blanchard 2007; Parker 2005). When available, fruits, vegetables, and low-fat dairy products are often of inferior quality and are more expensive at these establishments than in supermarkets and grocery stores (Perry and Harries 2007). Lack of access to affordable, fresh, and healthy food, when combined with preexisting health disparities in regions with high socioeconomic inequality, has led to a dramatic increase in obesity, heart disease, cancer, diabetes, immunity disorders, and hypertension (Alkon and Norgaard 2009).

Dealing with what food-systems analyst Raj Patel (2007) describes as crises of the "stuffed and starved" has produced a wide array of initiatives that, while linked through their focus on food, are largely divided between those who want to preserve the political economy of the existing global food system and those who seek to change it. The former tend to be from government and industry; the latter make up the global "food movement." The food movement itself, however, is diverse and subject to social divides.

The Rise and Divides of Food Movements

Even before the onset of the current food price crisis, the decades-long increase in hunger, food insecurity, diet-related diseases—fueled by low-nutrient, highly processed food—gave rise to social movements for community food security and food justice (Winne 2008), food sovereignty (Wittman, Desmarais, and Wiebe 2010), food democracy (Lang 2005), new agrarianism (Jackson, Berry, and Coleman 1984), food safety (Nestle 2002), anti-hunger (Berg 2008), and Slow Food that is "good, clean and fair" (Petrini 2005). This past decade has seen a boom in documentaries that both attack the industrial agrifoods complex and champion local, organic, sustainable food systems. These titles include Super Size Me (Spurlock 2004), The Future of Food (Garcia 2004), The World According to Monsanto (Robin 2008), Food Inc. (Kenner 2009), and King Corn (Woolf 2007).

These efforts have loosely come to be identified as the "food movement." Journalism professor Michael Pollan, one of the mainstream media's prominent food celebrities, asserts that "[t]he food movement coalesces around the recognition that today's food and farming economy is 'unsustainable'—that it can't go on in its current form much longer without courting a breakdown of some kind, whether environmental, economic, or both. . . ." For Pollan, the food movement is "splintered" in its origins, "[unified] as yet by little more than the recognition that industrial food production is in need of reform because its social/environmental/ public health/animal welfare/ gastronomic costs are too high" (Pollan 2010).

This recognition leads to calls for quality, environmental sustainability, and safety of food (e.g., fresh, organic, local) as well as for the reaffirmation of environmental values and community relationships associated with halcyon days of a reconstructed agrarian past. These make up what Alkon and Agyeman (2011a) refer to as the dominant food-movement narrative. Grounded in the social base of predominantly white, middle-class consumers, this narrative has become an important reference in the mainstream media. However, it also tends to render the food histories and realities of low-income people and people of color invisible.

An emblematic example of this narrative at work is the ubiquitous food-movement adage to fix the food system by "voting with your fork" (Pollan 2006). This strategy not only takes the access and purchasing power of the predominantly white, middle-class consumer for granted, but also it assumes that our food system can be reformed through informed consumer choice, and ignores the ways working-class and people of color have historically brought about social change (Guthman 2008). But, as one Slow Food leader counsels, "If dinner is a democratic election . . . in many electoral districts . . . there are no polling stations [and] there is only one candidate, the incumbent: fast food" (Viertel 2011). The notion that the food system can be transformed through individual acts of consumption—rather than through lobbying, organizing, boycotts, mobilization, or direct action—fits nicely within the prevailing neoliberal economic rhetoric: that unregulated capitalist markets yield the most efficient allocation of resources (Harvey 2005). The prominence of the privileged in the food-movement narrative, along with its "whiteness" (Slocum 2007), reflects the uneasy dualism between the trend of "quality food" for higher-income consumers and "other food" consumed by the masses (Goodman and Goodman 2008 6).

On the ground, the food movement's dominant narrative is, arguably, skin deep. Its widespread growth through farmers' markets, Community Supported Agriculture (CSAs), and high-end organic/"locavore" restaurants and retail chains has also been paralleled by less-celebrated expansions of the community food security movement (CFS), the food justice movement (FJ), and the food-sovereignty movement (FS) over the last ten years. While not rejecting the need for "good," "real," sustainable, or organic food, the agendas of these movements are focused on the lack of good food access, social and distributional inequities, institutional racism and classism, and the need to address labor, gender, and human rights in the food system (Holt-Giménez, Patel, and Shattuck 2009; Gottlieb and Joshi 2010 Alkon and Agyeman 2011a,b).

These developments suggest that below the surface of its amorphous "splintering," the food movement is segmented in ways that reflect social hierarchies of race and class in the food system. As we will explore further in this article, this segmentation has important implications for movement-based strategies for food-systems change.

Community Food Security, Food Justice, and Food Sovereignty: Adding Voices, Being Heard, or Forging a New Narrative?

The CFS is a broad-based movement that grew to national prominence with the formation of the Community Food Security Coalition (CFSC), a nonprofit group founded in 1994. With more than 250 affiliated organizations, the CFSC is representative of the diversity within the U.S. food movement. The CFSC refers to Hamm and Bellows's (2003) definition of community food security as "a condition in which all community residents obtain a safe, culturally acceptable, nutritionally adequate diet through a sustainable food system that maximizes community self-reliance and social justice" (CFSC 2004; 2010). The Coalition supports food-system alternatives by advocating for new business models, cooperative ownership of retail outlets, direct marketing, urban agriculture, community gardens and urban greening projects, community nutrition education, and community-driven agricultural research (Pothukuchi and Kaufman 1999). By focusing on community, the CFSC takes the notion of food security beyond long-standing governmental programs that typically focus on individual and household food access (Mooney and Hunt 2009).

The CFS framework also calls for increased funding to safety-net welfare programs such as the federal Supplemental Nutrition Assistance Program (food stamps); school lunch and breakfast programs; the Special Supplemental Nutrition Program for Women, Infants, and Children; the Child and Adult Care Food Program; and food banks (Anderson and Cook 1999; McCullum et al. 2004).

CFS frames food-system inequities in terms of food production and acquisition rather than structural inequality, resulting in an emphasis on enhancing food skills and alternative means of food access for low-income households, coupled with a

Washington D.C.–focused lobbying effort for increased forms of food aid and support for community food systems (Tarasuk 2001; McCullum et al. 2004). Politically, CFS seeks strategic partnerships with government, industry, and major anti-hunger organizations to enhance food security programs, food access, and to promote anti-poverty measures (NAHO 2009). By working actively for government reforms and industry partnerships to improve the "other food" consumed by low-income people, CFS movement strives to mainstream food security into the existing food system.

CFS's efforts to incorporate food-security issues into the dominant food-movement narrative is not without its contradictions. While the movement has gained political currency with the Obama administration's initiative for Healthy Food Financing and First Lady Michelle Obama's "Let's Move" campaign against childhood obesity, many food activists feel the administration's staunch support for agribusiness and food retail monopolies (reaching new heights with the Let's Move/Walmart partnership) goes against CFS's core principles of self-reliance and social justice:

> Imagine if the national answer to the food crisis took the form of a huge, publicly financed flood of corporations like WalMart and Tesco opening up stores in inner city neighborhoods using the exact same economic model they're using now. We could expect low wages, the destruction of small businesses and local economies, and all of the awful labor and supply chain practices we're familiar with. . . . [We need] good, living-wage jobs that pay meaningful earnings and teach meaningful skill sets. . . . [Instead] poor urban communities will see their economies tied to the wealth and resource extraction from rural communities with the usual negative consequences for local economies and the environment. (Ahmadi 2011)

The Food Justice movement (FJ) overlaps broadly with CFS, but tends to be more progressive than reformist in that it addresses specifically the ways in which people of color in low-income communities are disproportionately and negatively impacted by the industrial food system. In their recent book on the movement, Gottlieb and Joshi (2010, 229) describe FJ as a social movement with "multiple layers . . . [of]

producers, processors, workers, eaters, or communities," for whom race, ethnicity, class, and gender issues are at the forefront of an agenda that includes a mix of "producing food, local preference, environment, economic development, healthy food for all, preparing, cooking & eating, and public health & nutrition."

The food-justice movement emerged from several corners, including movements for environmental justice (Bullard 1994), working-class communities of color dealing with diet-related diseases (Herrera, Khanna, and Davis 2009), critiques of racism in the food system (Self 2003; Allen 2008) as well as critiques of racism in the food movement itself (Slocum 2007; Guthman 2008). Food justice formulates its food-security discourse in the "context of institutional racism, racial formation, and racialized geographies" (Alkon and Norgaard 2009). The Detroit Black Community Food Security Network, for example, articulates an explicit analysis of structural racism in the food system and a policy platform that includes eliminating "barriers to African-American participation and ownership in all aspects of the food system," as well as a "re-distribution of wealth through cooperative community ownership" (Detroit Black Community Food Security Network 2010). According to FJ advocate Brahm Ahmadi of the People's Community Market in Oakland, California:

> Food justice asserts that no one should live without enough food because of economic constraints or social inequalities. . . . The food justice movement is a different approach to a community's needs that seeks to truly advance self-reliance and social justice by placing communities in leadership of their own solutions and providing them with the tools to address the disparities within our food systems and within society at large. (Ahmadi 2010)

In a debate on COMFOOD, a popular food security/food justice list-serve, Hank Herrera, another longtime FJ advocate from Dig Deep Farms in Oakland, California, offers up the following principles:

> Food justice must address structural inequity, structural violence and structural racism. Food justice work must result in ownership of the means of production and exchange of food by the people who consume the

food. Food justice work is the incredibly difficult work of building new local healthy food systems, not opposing the global food industry. Food justice emerges from the economic justice work of Dr. King and represents the next wave of the civil rights movement. Food justice cannot reproduce systems of power, privilege and capital that create and maintain food apartheid. (Herrera 2011)

As Herrera's principles suggest, many food-justice activists engaged in the hard, grassroots work of building new food systems simply do not have the time, resources, or inkling to actively oppose the global food industry. Nonetheless, many see a role for food justice in addressing systemic change by engaging in political and policy processes as well as activism and movement mobilization (Steel 2010; Wekerle 2004).

In its more radical forms, FJ asserts economic democracy for underserved communities of color, including the transfer of ownership, property, and leadership to those most negatively affected by the industrial food System.1 FJ's radical roots reflect the community work of the Black Panther Party nearly half a century ago. According to Black Panther cofounder Bobby Seale:

> One of the party's important lasting legacies is grassroots programmatic organizing such as the Free Breakfast for Children Program which evolved to a point where forty-nine Black Panther chapters and branches in association with many other organizations across the United States were feeding 250,000 kids five days a week each morning before school. We had no government money or War on Poverty money to start the programs—we did it ourselves with donations. (Shames 2006, 12–13)

Accomplished long before community organizing developed its dependence on funding from philanthropic foundations, the Black Panther's free breakfast program predated the nation's school breakfast legislation of 1973. Food was part of a much larger program for black liberation and community autonomy as expressed in the October 1966 Black Panther Party Platform and Program. The first point in the program demanded freedom and the power for the black community to determine its own destiny. The last point, invoking the Declaration of Independence and calling for a black plebiscite, was introduced with the statement

> "We want land, *bread*, housing, education, clothing, justice and peace. . . ." (Shames, 13–14, emphasis added)

The platform was radical not only because it addressed the egregious manifestations of racism, such as underemployment, economic exploitation, police brutality, and a skewed criminal justice system (and suggested black communities might secede from the United States), but because the Black Panthers sought to dismantle the capitalist structures of racism.

The call among many of today's FJ activists for local control over food and dismantling racism in the food system echoes some of the liberation politics of the Black Panthers. Less common today are the structural critiques of capitalism and racism that were integral to the Black Panther's political work.

The food-justice movement confronts both the effects of structural racism on the ground and the failure of the dominant social change paradigms to take structural racism into account. Its discourse invokes the notion of a grassroots-driven transition to a more equitable and sustainable food system. Thus, just as the Environmental Justice Paradigm established at the People of Color Environmental Leadership Summit in 1991 sought to emphasize the issues of race, class, and leadership in the face of the mainstream "New Environmental Paradigm" dominated by middle-class white activists (Taylor 2000; Bullard 2010), FJ struggles to make its voice heard above the mainstream food-movement narrative.

Food sovereignty is another radical trend for food-system transformation based on the notion of entitlement and redistribution of food-producing resources. The discourse is framed by a more radical interpretation of food justice that sees access to food, land, and water as a human right, works for the democratization of the food system in favor of the poor and underserved, and specifically advocates dismantling the present global food system (Patel 2009; Wittman, Desmarais, and Wiebe 2010).

While the food-sovereignty movement has its origins in the peasant struggles for land and livelihoods in the Global South, the call has been increasingly taken up by family farms and the more radical food justice organizations in the United States and Europe. The draft mission statement of the recently formed U.S. Food Sovereignty Alliance states as follows:

> The US Food Sovereignty Alliance works to end poverty, rebuild local food economies, and assert democratic control over the food system. We believe all people have the right to healthy, culturally appropriate food, produced in an ecologically sound manner. As a US-based food justice, anti-hunger, labor, environmental, and faith-based alliance, we uphold the right to food as a basic human right and work to connect our local and national struggles to the international movement for food sovereignty. (U.S. Food Sovereignty Alliance 2010)

The food-sovereignty movement seeks to dismantle global markets and the monopoly power of corporations at local, national, and international scales, and advocates redistributing and protecting productive assets such as seeds, water, land, and processing and distribution facilities. The rights of labor and immigrants figure prominently in this trend, as advocated by the national Food Chain Workers Alliance and the Community to Community Alliance of Washington state. Direct action is practiced by organizations like the Coalition of Immokalee Workers and Students for Fair Food. Reminiscent of the United Farm Worker (UFW) mobilizations of the 1960s, these groups seek to achieve labor justice and an end to modern-day slavery in the tomato fields through student–farmworker coalitions and national boycotts.

Poverty, hunger, and community demands for healthy food access continually pull low-income communities of color toward food aid and food-access solutions coming from mainstream food security and anti-hunger groups, as well as toward the cheap industrial food solutions offered by low-end food retail chains such as Walmart, Food 4 Less, and Dollar Stores (Holt-Giménez, Wang, and Shattuck 2011). While anti-hunger and food-security advocates often prefer affordable access to bad food over no food at all, this puts them at odds with food-justice and food-sovereignty groups who distrust these large agrifood corporations (Gottlieb and

Joshi 2010, 215). Indeed, because they produce poor health outcomes and drain precious local food dollars from underserved communities, the pervasiveness of programs that channel surplus industrial food to low-income people of color could itself be considered an insidious form of racism. They also tend to divert attention from the structural causes of food insecurity and diet-related disease, and can bind local food-security efforts to the very industrial food system that is making their community members sick.

Caught between the urgency of access and the imperative of equity, the food-justice movement shifts, overlaps, and bridges with the efforts of the CFS and food-sovereignty movements, attempting to address racism and classism on one hand while trying to fix a broken food system on the other. This produces a "both/and" food justice narrative in which "the lack of fresh food access [is seen as] both an equity disparity and a system failure" (Gottlieb and Joshi 2010, 299).

One difficulty with this narrative—fairly generalized within the food-justice movement—is that it separates the system from the disparity. The food system may be dysfunctional in that it does not serve the better interests of the environment, peasants, family farmers, or low-income people of color, but it is certainly not broken. During the food crisis of 2008, and again in 2010, quarterly profits for the world's agrifood monopolies (seed and input suppliers, grain traders, retailers) grew by some 80 percent, so the system clearly works well for those who run it (Holt-Giménez, Patel, and Shattuck 2009). "Equity disparity" and "system failure" do not sufficiently describe the profound, ongoing systemic exploitation that girds the global food system.

But understanding that racial and class disparities are a structurally integrated part of the present food system does not, in and of itself, resolve the strategic problem of how to proceed—practically and politically. In the following sections, we construct a "regime/movement" framework for understanding food systems and food movements, taking into account the historical tendencies of capitalist food systems and the strategic importance of alliance building to overcome the system/disparity dilemma.

The Corporate Food Regime

Our food systems are part of a corporate food regime[2] that is performing exactly as a late-capitalist system would be expected: it efficiently creates and concentrates wealth through market expansion, compound economic growth, technological innovation, and, increasingly, financial speculation (Magdoff and Tokar 2010; Harvey 2010). In addition to noting the cornucopian abundance frequently associated with the corporate food regime, it is important to recall that it was built over two centuries of violent, global-scale dispossession, and accumulation, a good part of which took place in North America. The regime continues to rely extensively on the direct and indirect appropriation and exploitation of land, labor, and capital, both at home and abroad.

A food regime is a "rule-governed structure of production and consumption of food on a world scale" (McMichael 2009). The first global food regime spanned the period from the late 1800s through the Great Depression and linked food imports from southern and American colonies to European industrial expansion. The second food regime began after World War II and reversed the flow of food from the northern to the southern hemisphere to fuel Cold War industrialization in the Third World.

Today's corporate food regime, ushered in by the neoliberal policies of Ronald Reagan and Margaret Thatcher in the 1980s, is characterized by the monopoly market power of agrifood corporations, globalized grain-fed meat production, giant retail, and growing links between food and fuel. This regime is controlled by a far-flung agrifood industrial complex made up of huge oligopolies including Monsanto, Archer Daniels Midland, Cargill, Conagra, and Walmart. Together, these corporations dominate the government agencies and multilateral organizations that make and enforce the regime's rules, regulations, and projects for trade, labor, property, and technology, including the World Bank and International Monetary Fund (IMF), the UN World Food Program, USAID, the USDA, and big philanthropy.

Liberalization and Reform

Like the capitalist economic system of which they are a part, global food regimes historically alternate between periods of economic liberalization characterized by unregulated markets, privatization, and massive concentrations of wealth, followed by devastating economic and financial busts—the costs of which are socialized and paid for by citizens, consumers, workers, and taxpayers. This eventually leads to social unrest, which, when sufficiently widespread, threatens profits and governability. Governments then usher in reformist periods in which markets, supply, and consumption are re-regulated to stem the crisis and restore stability to the regime. In cases where governments are incapable of reform—as witnessed in 2011 in Egypt and other countries in northern Africa—rebellion and revolution can become likely avenues of social change.

Infinitely unregulated markets would eventually destroy both society and the natural resources that the regime depends on for its reproduction. Therefore, while the "mission" of reform is to mitigate the social and environmental externalities of the corporate food regime, its "job" is identical to that of the liberal trend: preserving the corporate food regime. Though liberalization and reform may appear politically distinct, they are actually two phases of the same system. While both tendencies exist simultaneously, they are rarely ever in equilibrium, with either liberalization or reform hegemonic at any period of time. Reformists dominated the global food regime from the New Deal in the 1930s until our current era of neo-liberal "globalization" in the 1980s. The current neo-liberal phase has been characterized by deregulation, privatization, and the growth and consolidation of global corporate monopoly power in food systems around the globe.

With the recurrent global food crises, desperate calls for reform have sprung up worldwide. However, less than 5 percent of the US$22 billion in promised aid to end the crisis has actually been committed, and most government and multilateral solutions (e.g., Feed the Future, Global Agriculture and Food Security Program, Global Harvest) simply call for more of the same policies that brought about the crisis to begin with: extending liberal (free) markets, privatizing common resources (including forests and the atmosphere), proprietary technological "fixes" including genetically modified seeds, and protecting monopoly concentration. Collateral damage to community food systems is mitigated by weak safety nets—including food aid from the World Food Program and U.S. food banks or food stamps. Unless there is strong pressure from civil society, reformists will not likely affect (much less reverse) the present neo-liberal direction of the corporate food regime.

From Coping to Regime Change: The Pivotal Role of Food Justice

The current food and health crises reflect a socially inequitable and economically volatile corporate food regime. Unless there are profound changes to this regime, it will repeat its cycles of liberalization and reform, plunging neighborhood food systems, rural communities, and the environment into ever graver crises. While moderate food system reforms—such as increasing food stamps or relocating grocery stores—are certainly needed to help vulnerable communities cope with crises, because they address the proximate rather than the root causes of hunger and food insecurity (Holt-Giménez, Patel, and Shattuck 2009), they will not alter the fundamental balance of power within the food system and in some cases may even reinforce existing, inequitable power relations. Fixing the dysfunctional food system—in any sustainable sense—requires regime change.

If the history of U.S. capitalism and social change is a reliable guide, we can be assured that substantive changes to the corporate food regime will not come simply from within the regime itself, but from a combination of intense social pressure and political will. Today's food-system "reforms" and the rush of anti-hunger alliances between agrifood monopolies, government, and big philanthropy (Global Harvest, AGRA, AGree, etc.) are attempts to mitigate the negative effects of food price volatility, not end global hunger or substantively challenge neo-liberal control over the food system. Food-system change will come from powerful and sustained social pressure that forces reformists to roll back neo-liberalism in the food system. Much of this pressure could come from the food movement—if it overcomes its divides.

As we indicated earlier in this article, the food-sovereignty movement and some food-justice organizations have a radical critique of the corporate food regime. These groups call for structural, redistributive reforms of basic entitlements, for example, for property, labor, capital, and markets. Other food-justice groups (and some CFS organizations) advance a progressive agenda on the basis of sustainable family farming and rights of access to healthy food. These radical and progressive trends overlap significantly in their approaches, demographics, and types of organization (e.g., CFS, FJ, and FS). While the progressive trend focuses on local ownership of production and on improving the service and delivery aspects of the food system, the radical trend directs more of its energy at structural changes to capitalist food systems. When taken together, both trends seek to change the rules and practices of food systems, locally, nationally, and internationally. In this regard they are two sides of the same food movement. Their strategic alliance could go a long way toward overcoming the food movement's system/disparity dilemma.

Food-movement organizations are fluid and have different and changing positions on food-system issues such as GMOs, domestic hunger programs, food aid, supply management, land reform, and trade. Depending on their ideology, political awareness, support base, and funding, food-movement organizations will adopt a range of stances and will consciously (or unconsciously) form alliances with groups and institutions across regime and movement trends. While some organizations are solidly neo-liberal, reformist, progressive, or radical, others are much harder to categorize because they adopt politically divergent positions on different issues (for example, a reformist position on labor, but a radical position on GMOs). Some organizations say one thing, yet do another. Rather than ascribing fixity to organizations, an appreciation of their heterogeneous and fluid political nature, coupled with an analysis of their positions on specific issues, can help identify opportunities for alliance building for food-system change.

As the world's fuel, financial, and climate crises exacerbate the food crisis, the systemic differences between the food regime and food movements will likely deepen. However, unlike the symbiotic relationship between neo-liberal and reformist trends in the food regime, in which the latter helps to stabilize the food regime following a crisis caused by the former, there is nothing intrinsically stable about the relationship between the progressive and radical trends that will keep them from splitting under pressure. The fragmentation and segmentation of the U.S. food movement already cedes political ground to the corporate food regime, whose reformist trends are busy co-opting food security and its related terms, among them "community," "organic," "local," and "fair."

Overcoming the present (and future) divisions within the food movement will require strong alliances and the clarity to distinguish superficial change from structural change. This in turn depends not only on clear vision and practice of the desired changes, but also means making strategic and tactical sense of the matrix of actors, institutions, and projects at work within local–global food politics. The dominant food-movement narrative is not only color-blind, but it also does not distinguish between the neo-liberal/reformist trends in the food regime (of which it is unconsciously a part) and the progressive and radical trends of the food movement itself. The challenge for building a powerful food movement is to reach beyond the dominant (and depoliticizing) food-movement narrative to build strategic political alliances and construct a new narrative. But who should reach; to whom; and on what basis?

Addressing this challenge, Gottlieb and Joshi (2010, 232–33) identify FJ as a key political trend within the U.S. food movement and claim it is facing a "pivotal moment" that requires an "overarching theory of food system change." They call on FJ to organize existing food groups into a larger social movement, to develop a theory of change, an agenda that is both incremental and structural, and to link to other social movements, worldwide.

We agree with this assessment, and suggest that in addition to its pivotal moment, because it is located between, and in many ways also spans, radical and progressive trends within the food movement, the food-justice movement occupies a "pivotal position." The way FJ organizations organize, theorize, set agendas, and build alliances will have a direct influence on the balance of forces that will serve to stabilize, reform, or transform the corporate food regime. If FJ organizations build reformist alliances, the corporate food regime will be strengthened. If they build radical alliances, the food movement will be strengthened. The former scenario will not lead to regime change, while the latter at least opens the possibility of a strong food movement capable of pushing substantive reforms.

On what basis could these alliances be built? The structural exploitation of resources, markets, and communities—at home and abroad—is foundational to the corporate food regime. Racial disadvantages are structured into the corporate food regime, reproducing a hierarchical social structure into our food systems (Winant 2001). The flood of cheap, unhealthy, and fast food into the void left by the exodus of food retail outlets from low-income communities of color is part of the racialized dispossession affecting immigrants and people of color in both rural and urban areas (Minkoff-Zern et al. 2011). For example, the recent drive by monopoly food retailers to gobble up real estate in underserved urban communities follows on this trend (Holt-Giménez, Wang, and Shattuck 2011). These racialized enclosures are no less structural issues than the wholesale dispossession of peasants occurring as a result of the massive global land grabs exploding across the Global South (Grain 2008). Land itself is one basis for local–global alliance building.

Engaging with the structural aspects of food justice requires addressing race and class in relation to dispossession and control over land, labor, and capital in the food system. For reforms to actually reverse the trends of dispossession and concentration—and lead to transformation—they must be redistributive (Borras 2007). This means that FJ needs to build alliances to address ownership and redistribution over the means of production and reproduction, including credit, land, processing, markets, and retail as well as labor and immigrant rights—all areas of dispossession within the food-value chain of the corporate food regime. The most likely partners for these structural alliances are in local and international food-sovereignty movements and other organizations working within the radical trend of the food movement.

Granted, no amount of fresh produce will solve the underlying socioeconomic problems of chronic unemployment, labor exploitation, crumbling public education, land and real estate speculation, and violence visited upon underserved communities of color.

But within a historicized framework of structural racism, the centrality of food to a community's collective cultural identities provides links between racial identity and activism (Pulido 2000). Food-justice activism is an important social change driver that, if allied with other, radical social movements, could seriously challenge the corporate food regime's structural inequities.

Solving the food crisis requires dismantling racism and classism in the food system and transforming the food regime. This challenges the food-justice movement to forge alliances that advance equitable and sustainable practices on the ground while mobilizing politically for broad, redistributive reforms. This pivotal praxis may yet produce a new, powerful food movement narrative: the narrative of liberation.

Notes

We would like to thank Annie Shattuck for her work on earlier versions of this paper, as well as the three anonymous reviewers for their helpful comments. All the usual disclaimers apply.

1.. These demands have a solid material basis. In West Oakland, California, one of the city's lowest-income neighborhoods, an estimated $65 million per year is spent on food, $48 million of which "floats" out of the community (People's Community Market 2009). This amount represents some 1,000 potential jobs paying $45,000 a year. Figures are similarly high for other low-income urban communities in which grocery stores have abandoned the inner city for the suburbs (Mamen 2007). This is one reason many FJ activists prefer the term "food apartheid" over "food deserts," as the former provides a more accurate description of the political–economic depth of structural racism in the U.S. food system (Ahmadi 2010; Cook 2010; Workman 2010).

2.. For a more extensive, global analysis of the corporate food regime and its relation to the global food movement, see Holt-Giménez and Shattuck (2011).

Works Cited

Ahmadi, Brahm. 2011. Racism and food justice: The case of Oakland. In *Food Movements Unite!*, ed. Eric Holt-Giménez, 149–62. Oakland, CA: Food First Books.

_____. 2010. Structural Racism in the U.S. *Food System*. Oakland, CA: Food First Books.

Alkon, Alison Hope, and Julian Agyeman. 2011a. Introduction: The food movement as polyculture. In *Cultivating Food Justice: Race, Class, and Sustainability*, 1–20. Food, Health and Environment; series ed. Robert Gottlieb. Cambridge, MA: MIT Press.

_____, eds. 2011b. *Cultivating food justice: Race, class, and sustainability.* Cambridge, MA: MIT Press.

Alkon, Alison Hope, and Kari Marie Norgaard. 2009. Breaking the food chains: An investigation of food justice activism. *Sociological Inquiry* 79: 289–305.

Allen, Patricia. 2008. Mining for justice in the food system: Perceptions, practices, and possibilities. *Agriculture and Human Values* 25: 157–61.

Anderson, Molly, and John T. Cook. 1999. Community food security: Practice in need of theory? *Agriculture and Human Values* 16: 141–50.

Baker, Elizabeth A., Mario Schootman, Ellen Barnidge, and Cheryl Kelly. 2006. The role of race and poverty in access to foods that enable individuals to adhere to dietary guidelines. *Preventing Chronic Disease* 3: 1–11.

Berg, Joel. 2008. *All you can eat: How hungry is America?* New York: Seven Stories Press.

Borras, Saturnino M. Jr. 2007. *Pro-poor land reform: A critique.* Ottawa: University of Ottawa Press.

Bullard, Robert D. 1994. *Unequal protection: Environmental justice and communities of color.* San Francisco: Sierra Club Books.

_____. 2010. Environmental justice in the 21st Century. http://www.ejrc.cau.edu/ejinthe21century. htm (accessed June 30, 2011).

CFSC Community Food Security Coalition. 2004. About CFSC. http://www.foodsecurity.org/aboutcfsc.html (accessed June 30, 2011).

_____. 2010. What is community food security? http://www.foodsecurity.org/views_cfs_faq.html (accessed June 30, 2011).

Cook, Christopher. 2010. Covering food deserts. University of Southern California Annenberg School for Communication. http://www.reportingonhealth.org/resources/lessons/covering-food-deserts (accessed June 30, 2011).

Detroit Black Community Food Security Network. 2010. A City of Detroit policy on food security: "Creating a food-secure Detroit." http://detroitblackfoodsecurity. org/policy.html (accessed June 30, 2011).

FAO. 2011. FAO Food Price Index. Food and Agriculture Organization of the United Nations, March 7. http:// www.fao.org/worldfoodsituation/wfs-home/foodpric-esindex/en/(accessed June 30, 2011).

Garcia, Deborah Koons. 2004. The future of food. Documentary. Lily Films.

Goodman, David, and Michael K. Goodman. 2008. "Alternative food networks," in Rob Kitchin and Nigel Thrift, *Encyclopedia of Human Geography*. Oxford: Elsevier.

Gottlieb, Robert, and Anupama Joshi. 2010. *Food justice*. Cambridge, MA: MIT Press.

Grain. 2008. Seized: The 2008 landgrab for food and financial security. Grain Briefing. http://www.grain.org/ briefings/?id=212 (accessed June 30, 2011).

Guthman, Julie. 2008. "If only they knew": Color blindness and universalism in California alternative food institutions. *The Professional Geographer* 60: 387–97.

Hamm, Michael W., and Anne C. Bellows. 2003. Community food security and nutrition educators. *Journal of Nutrition Education and Behavior* 35: 37–43.

Harvey, David. 2005. *A brief history of neoliberalism*. Oxford: Oxford University Press.

_____. 2010. *The enigma of capital: And the crises of capitalism*. Oxford: Oxford University Press.

Herrera, Henry. Unpublished correspondence. Oakland, California, April 24, 2011.

Herrera, Henry, Navina Khanna, and Leon Davis. 2009. Food systems and public health: The community perspective. *Journal of Hunger & Environmental Nutrition* 4: 430–45.

Holt-Giménez, Eric, and Annie Shattuck. 2011. "Food Crises, Food Regimes and Food Movements: Rumblings of Reform or Tides of Transformation?" *Journal of Peasant Studies* 38(1): 109–44.

Holt-Giménez, Eric, Raj Patel, and Annie Shattuck. 2009. *Food rebellions! Crisis and the hunger for justice*. Oakland: Food First Books.

Holt-Giménez, Eric, Yi Wang, and Annie Shattuck. 2011. "The urban and northern face of global land grabs." Paper presented at the presented at the International Conference on Global Land Grabbing, Brighton, UK, April 6–8.

Jackson, Wes, Wendell Berry, and Bruce Coleman, eds. 1984. *Meeting the expectations of the land: Essays in sustainable agriculture and stewardship*. San Francisco: North Point Press.

Kenner, Robert. 2009. Food, Inc. Documentary. Magnolia Pictures, Participant Media.

Lang, Tim. 2005. Food control or food democracy? Reengaging nutrition with society and the environment. *Public Health Nutrition* 8(6A): 730–37.

Lean, Geoffrey. 2008. Multinationals make billions in profit out of growing global food crisis. *The Independent*, May 4.

Magdoff, Fred, and Brian Tokar. 2010. *Agriculture and food in crisis: Conflict, resistance, and renewal*. New York: Monthly Review Press.

Mamen, Katy. 2007. Facing Goliath: Challenging the impacts of supermarket consolidation on our local economies, communities, and food security. Oakland, CA: The Oakland Institute.

McCullum, Christine, David Pelletier, Donald Barr, Jennifer Wilkins, and Jean-Pierre Habicht. 2004. Mechanisms of power within a community-based food security planning process. *Health Education & Behavior* 31: 206–22.

McMichael, Philip. 2009. A food regime genealogy. *Journal of Peasant Studies* 36: 139–69.

Minkoff-Zern, Laura-Anne, Nancy Peluso, Jennifer Sowerwine, and Christy Getz. 2011. Race and regulation: Asian immigrants in California agriculture. In *Cultivating Food Justice: Race, Class, and Sustainability*, ed. Alison Alkon and Julian Agyeman, 65–86. Cambridge, MA: MIT Press.

Mooney, Patrick H., and Scott A. Hunt. 2009. Food security: The elaboration of contested claims to a consensus frame. *Rural Sociology* 74: 469–97.

Morton, Lois Wright, and Troy C. Blanchard. 2007 *Starved for access: Life in rural America's food deserts*. Columbia, MO: University of Missouri Press.

NAHO. 2009. Roadmap to end childhood hunger in America by 2015. National Anti-Hunger Organizations. http://www.foodsecurity.org/policy/NAHO-Road-map_to_End_Hunger.pdf (accessed June 30, 2011).

Nestle, Marion. 2002. Food politics: How the food industry influences nutrition and health. In *California Studies in Food and Culture*. Berkeley: University of California Press.

Nord, Mark, Alisha Coleman-Jensen, Margaret Andrews, and Steven Carlson. 2010. Household food security in the United States, 2009. Economic Research Report. U.S. Department of Agriculture, November 10. http:// www.ers.usda.gov/publications/err108/(accessed June 30, 2011).

Parker, Lynn. 2005. Obesity, food insecurity and the federal child nutrition programs: Understanding the linkages. Food Research and Action Center.

Patel, Raj. 2007. *Stuffed and starved: Markets, power and the hidden battle for the world food system*. London: Portobello Books.

_____. 2009. Food Sovereignty. *Journal of Peasant Studies* 36: 663–706.

People's Community Market. 2009. Market Gap Study. Unpublished.

Perry, Duane, and Caroline Harries. 2007. The need for more supermarkets in Chicago. Philadelphia: The Food Trust.

Petrini, Carlo. 2005. *Slow food nation: Why our food should be good, clean, and fair.* Bra, Italy: Slow Food Editore.

Pollan, Michael. 2006. Voting with your fork. http://pollan.blogs.nytimes.com/2006/05/07/voting-with-your-fork/(accessed June 30, 2011).

_____. 2010. The food movement, rising. *New York Review of Books,* June 10. http://www.nybooks.com/articles/archives/2010/jun/10/food-movement-rising/ (accessed June 30, 2011).

Pothukuchi, Kameshwari, and Jerome Kaufman. 1999. Placing the food system on the urban agenda: The role of municipal institutions in food systems planning. *Agriculture and Human Values* 16: 213–24.

Pulido, Laura. 2000. Rethinking environmental racism: White privilege and urban development in Southern California. *Annals of the Association of American Geographers* 90: 12–40.

Robin, Marie-Monique. 2008. The world according to Monsanto. Documentary. National Film Board of Canada, ARTE France, Image & Compagnie, WDR, and Les Productions Thalie.

Schlosser, Eric. 2001. *Fast food nation: The dark side of the all-American meal.* New York: Harper Perennial.

Self, Robert O. 2003. *American Babylon: Race and the struggle for postwar Oakland.* Princeton, NJ: Princeton University Press.

Shames, Stephen. 2006. *The Black Panthers.* New York: Aperture Foundations Books.

Slocum, Rachel. 2007. Whiteness, space and alternative food practice. *Geoforum* 38: 520–33.

Spurlock, Morgan. 2004. *Super size me.* Documentary. Samuel Goldwyn Films; Roadside Attractions.

Steel, Anim. 2010. Youth and food justice: Lessons from the Civil Rights movement. Food First/Institute for Food and Development Policy.

Tarasuk, Valerie. 2001. A critical examination of community-based responses to household food insecurity in Canada. *Health Education & Behavior* 28: 487–99.

Taylor, Dorceta E. 2000. The rise of the environmental justice paradigm: Injustice framing and the social construction of environmental discourses. *American Behavioral Scientist* 43: 508–80.

U.S. Food Sovereignty Alliance. 2010. Food sovereignty PMA resolution. http://www.usfoodsovereigntyalliance.org/foodsovereigntypma/food-sovereignty-pma-resolution (June 30, 2011).

Viertel, Josh. 2011. Beyond voting with your fork: Moving past enlightened eating, to movement building. In *Food Movements Unite!,* ed. Eric Holt-Giménez, 137–48. Oakland, CA: Food First Books.

Wekerle, Gera R. 2004. Food justice movements: Policy, planning, and networks. *Journal of Planning Education and Research* 23: 378–86.

WFP. 2011. Hunger FAQs. World Food Program. http://www.wfp.org/hunger/faqs (accessed June 30, 2011).

Wiggins, Steve, and Stephanie Levy. 2008. Rising food prices: A global crisis. *Briefing Paper #37.* Overseas Development Institute. London. http://www.odi.org.uk/resources/download/1009. pdf (accessed June 30, 2011).

Winant, Howard. 2001. *The world is a ghetto: Race and democracy since World War II.* New York: Basic Books.

Winne, Mark. 2008. *Closing the food gap.* Boston: Beacon Press.

Wittman, Hannah, Annette Aurelie Desmarais, and Nettie Wiebe. 2010. *Food sovereignty: Reconnecting food, nature and community.* Oakland, CA: Food First Books.

Woolf, Aaron. 2007. King Corn. Mosaic Films.

Workman, Mandy Lynn. 2010. Food deserts & growing hunger in the US: The USDA's response, Oakland Food Policy Council, http://www.oaklandfood.org/blog/entry/587521/-food-deserts-growing-hunger-in-the-us-the-usda%E2%80%99s-response%C2%A0ID-177 (accessed June 30, 2011).

Questions for Critical Thinking

1. In this article, the authors discuss the important topic of food justice. In what ways is this issue new to you? Can you think of examples of barriers to food access in your own communities?

2. The authors discuss the root causes of severe levels of hunger in our communities. How does their discussion inform your understanding of how to go about making structural change to achieve food justice?

3. What new insights does this reading give you with regard to personally being involved in making social change around issues of food justice?

VOICES OF A NEW MOVIMIENTO

• *Roberto Lovato*

The final essay in this text, written by Robert Lovato, discusses why it is important to organize for change. Highlighting the ways in which this new movimiento goes beyond single-minded organizing tactics, the author provides examples of how activists merge traditional labor and civil rights strategies and tactics with more global, networked—and personalized—ones.

Under cover of an oak tree on a tobacco farm deep in the heart of rural North Carolina, Leticia Zavala challenges the taller, older male migrant farm workers with talk of a boycott and *legalización*.

"We will not get anything without fighting for it," declares the intense 5-foot-1 organizer with the Farm Labor Organizing Committee (FLOC). Pen and notebook in hand, Zavala hacks swiftly through the fear and doubt that envelop many migrants. She speaks from a place, an experience, that most organizers in this country don't know: Her earliest childhood and adolescent memories are of migrating each year with her family between Mexico and Florida. "We have five buses and each of you has to decide for yourselves if you want to go to Washington with us," she says. After some deliberation most of the workers, many of whom have just finished the seven-day trek from Nayarit, Mexico, opt to get on another bus and join the May 1 *marcha* and boycott. They trust her, as do the more than 500 other migrant workers from across the state who heed the call from one of the new leaders of the *movimiento* that is upon us.

Asked why she thinks FLOC was so successful in mobilizing farm workers (the union made history after a stunning 2004 victory that secured representation and a contract for more than 10,000 H-2A

"guest" workers who labor on strawberry, tobacco, yam, cucumber and other farms), Zavala talks about "the importance of networks" and the need to respond to the globalization of labor through the creation of a "migrating union." She and other FLOC organizers have followed migrant workers to Mexico, where the organization has an office—and then have followed them back over several months. She also points to the vision, strategies, and tactics shared by her mentor, FLOC founder Baldemar Velásquez, who passed on to her the advice that Martin Luther King Jr. gave him during the Poor People's Campaign in 1967: "When you impact the rich man's ability to make money, anything is negotiable."

But when you ask her what is most important in the twenty-first-century matrix of successful organizing, the bespectacled, bright-eyed Zavala will bring you back to basics: "One of the biggest successes of the union is that it takes away loneliness."

The 26-year-old Zavala's vision, experience, and learning are a telling reflection of how the leaders of the *movimiento* merge traditional labor and civil rights strategies and tactics with more global, networked—and personalized—organizing to meet the challenges of the quintessentially global issue of immigration. While it's important to situate the immigrant struggle within the context of the ongoing freedom struggles of African-Americans, women (like Zavala, an extraordinary number of *movimiento* leaders are *mujeres*) and others who have fought for social justice in the United States, labeling and framing it as a "new civil rights movement" risks erasing its roots in Latin American struggles and history.

The mainstream narrative of the movement emphasizes that single-minded immigrants want legalization—and how "angry Hispanics" and their Spanish-language radio DJ leaders mobilized in reaction to HR 4437 (better known as the Sensenbrenner immigration bill, which would criminalize the undocumented). But Zavala and other *movimiento* leaders across the country say that while it's true that the Sensenbrenner bill provided a spark, explaining this powerful movement of national and even global significance as a reaction to DJ-led calls to "*marchar!*" leaves many things—and people—out of the picture.

This time, there is no Martin Luther King or César Chávez centering and centralizing the movement. Instead, grassroots leaders like Zavala mix, scratch, and dub different media (think MySpace.com and text messaging, radio and TV, butcher paper and bullhorns) while navigating the cultural, political, and historical currents that yoke and inspire the diverse elements making up this young, decentralized, digital-age *movimiento*.

At the older end of the age and experience spectrum (the average Latino is 26) is 44-year-old Juan José Gutiérrez. He started organizing in the late 1970s, distributing mimeographed copies of the radical newspaper *Sin Fronteras* to immigrant workers in the face of hostility from the anti-Communist right. The director of Latino Movement USA and a key figure in the recent (and, to some, controversial) May 1 boycott, Gutiérrez has logged thousands of miles and met hundreds of leaders in his efforts to build one of many vibrant movement networks.

"Since January, I've been to about thirty-five different cities and seen old and new leadership coming together to create something that has never been seen before," says Gutiérrez, who migrated to

Los Angeles from Tuxpan, Jalisco, Mexico, when he was 11. "The [Spanish-language] DJs played a role, an important role, but they let us put our message in their medium. You can trace this movement all the way back to 1968."

Unlike the *movimiento* leaders who cut their teeth organizing in left-leaning Latin America, Gutiérrez traces his political roots to post–civil rights East LA; he and many of the most important Mexican and Chicano immigrant rights leaders in LA—including union leader Maria Elena Durazo, longtime activist Javier Rodriguez, and LA Mayor Antonio Villaraigosa—came out of the Centro de Acción Social Autónomo (Center for Autonomous Social Action), or CASA, a seminal Chicano political organization founded by legendary leaders Bert Corona and Soledad "Chole" Alatorre in 1968. One of the central tasks of CASA, which from its inception had a strong working-class and trade union orientation, was organizing undocumented workers. Gutiérrez and others who have covered the country spiderlike for years see a direct line from the organizing around the amnesty law of 1986, which legalized 3 million undocumented workers, to immigrant rights organizing in California (home to one of every three immigrants in the United States), the fight against Proposition 187 of 1994 (which tried to deny health and education benefits to the children of the undocumented) and the historic shift of the AFL–CIO in 2000, when it decided to undertake immigrant organizing.

Having hopped back and forth among many of the more than 200 cities and towns that staged actions in April and May, Gutiérrez sees different kinds of leaders emerging from the grassroots: "There are, of course, the undocumented, who are also leading things in local communities; there are legal immigrants getting involved, because they have friends and family who are affected by the anti-immigrant policies; and there are immigrants from different countries who bring their own political, sometimes radical, experiences from places like Guatemala and El Salvador."

One of the "radical" legacies that New York immigrant rights leader Miguel Ramírez has carried with him since fleeing El Salvador is an intensely collective outlook on personal and political identity. Ramírez, who heads the Queens-based Centro

Hispano Cuzcatlán, recalls how one of his US-born colleagues told him to "correct" the résumé he used to apply for his first organizing job in New York. "He [the friend] told me I had to take out the 'we,'" says 53-year-old Ramírez, whose bushy mustache often lifts to reveal a disarming smile. "I didn't know it was wrong to write, 'We organized a forum, we organized a workshop, we organized a network.'"

The experience and approach of Ramírez, who left his homeland in 1979 after many of his fellow students at the University of El Salvador were persecuted and killed, show that the US *movimiento* is as much the northernmost expression of a resurgent Latin American left as it is a new, more globalized, human rights–centered continuation of the Chicano, civil rights and other previous struggles that facilitated immigrant rights work here.

Ramírez, who estimates that since migrating he's helped organize more than 100 marches—all of them "very disciplined and without incidents"—is informed by the experience of organizing students, campesinos, and others in revolutionary El Salvador, where one of every three Salvadorans adopted radicalized politics during the war. Lacking the wealth and pro-US government politics of Cuban-Americans and other, more conservative immigrant groups, Ramírez and many Salvadoran immigrants (most of whom were denied legal status and benefits granted to Cubans, Vietnamese, and others) created organizations that then formed vast multi-issue, mass-based networks challenging the foreign and domestic policies of the most powerful country on earth.

This robust legacy energizes Ramírez and Centro Hispano Cuzcatlán, which organizes around worker rights, housing, and immigration, as they play definitive roles in the construction of local networks like the Immigrant Communities in Action coalition. Through the coalition, Centro joined Indian, Pakistani, Korean, Filipino, Bangladeshi, Indonesian and other groups that have organized some of the country's most diverse marches.

Reflecting the historic and ongoing tensions between more election- and legislative-focused immigrant rights advocates in Washington and local and regional players, Ramírez, like the younger Zavala, calmly insists the *movimiento* must look beyond the upcoming elections and even the pending immigration bill. "In the end, it's an issue of power, one that can only be addressed by constant organizing."

US-born Latinos also feel Ramírez's urgency about organizing around immigration. Their ranks include teens and twentysomethings relatively new to politics, along with veterans like Wisconsin's Christine Neumann-Ortiz, who was influenced by several Latin American movements as well as the struggle against California's Proposition 187.

"To see those thousands of people marching against Prop 187 was an inspiration," says Ortiz, who heads Voces de la Frontera, an immigrant worker center in the belly of the anti-immigrant beast, James Sensenbrenner's Milwaukee. "I was very impressed that there was that kind of response [to Prop 187]. We used that as a lesson," says Ortiz, who was one of the main organizers of marches of 30,000 and 70,000 people, some of the largest marches ever in a state with a storied progressive past.

Ortiz was not caught off guard by the *movimiento*. "I'm happy to be alive to see this shift," she states from one of Voces's three offices in Wisconsin, "but I'm not at all surprised. We've been building up networks of people over many years."

She and other activists point to years of service and advocacy on behalf of immigrants, which built up good will and trust in the community, as being defining factors in the ability to rally people into political action.

Founded in Austin, Texas, with a mission to build solidarity between US and Mexican maquiladora workers following the signing of the NAFTA accords in nearby San Antonio in 1994, Voces de la Frontera embodies a local–global sensibility. Ortiz started the Milwaukee Voces in November 2001 in response to the growing needs of Milwaukee's fast-growing Latino immigrant population. Like the settlement houses and mutual aid societies and other organizations that supported German and other white European immigrant workers of previous, more progressive eras in Wisconsin and elsewhere, Voces provides a critical support structure for the mostly Mexican and Central American workers in the agricultural, hotel and restaurant, construction, and manufacturing industries in HR 4437 country.

Sensenbrenner "wants to leave a legacy. So did McCarthy. Immigrants in Wisconsin know his hypocrisy better than anyone," says Ortiz, whose German and Mexican immigrant heritage portends the not-so-distant future of once wholly white Wisconsin. "He is encroaching on his own base. Dairy farmers in his own district are revolting because he's attacking their economic base. This can't last in the long term," she says, as if eyeing developments in post-Prop 187 California, where short-term anti-immigrant backlash led to a longer-term movement that gave Los Angeles its first Latino (and progressive) mayor—and gave the *movimiento* a vision of its potential.

Like organizers in Los Angeles, Chicago, and other cities, Ortiz and Voces have built strong and deep relationships with the local Spanish-language media. But they're also keenly aware of who's leading the charge. "We had lists of more than 4,000 workers before the radio stations or Sensenbrenner came into the picture," Ortiz explains.

As they continue to organize and lobby around the immigration debate in Congress, around the inevitable backlash at the local and state levels and around a more proactive agenda, Ortiz and many of the other leaders of the immigrant rights movement are keeping their eyes on a larger prize, beyond the issue of immigration. "We're going to change this country," she says, adding, "We've gained public sympathy for immigrants. We've gained recognition and power, and we are an inspiration to the larger movement for change." She is especially motivated when she describes the effect of the *movimiento* on the generations to come. Like the "Hmong students who went to a Sensenbrenner town hall meeting in South Alice [a Milwaukee suburb] and chanted 'Si se puede, Si se puede' at him." Asked if the backlash will damage the *movimiento*, Ortiz responds, "In the long run this will make us stronger and build our movement."

Questions for Critical Thinking

1. Lovato discusses the reasons that it is important to organize for change beyond electoral politics. Why does he think this is so important?

2. As is often said, the United States is made up predominantly of immigrants and their descendants. In what ways are recent immigrants treated in similar ways to those of the past? In what ways are they treated differently? What do you think needs to occur to provide more access to equal opportunity for recent waves of immigrants?

3. After reading this text, what do you see as important issues of social inequality? What are you willing to do to address these issues?

THE NEXT CIVIL RIGHTS MOVEMENT?

• *Fredrick C. Harris*

In the essay that follows, author Fredrick Harris, professor of political science and director of the Center on African-American Politics and Society at Columbia University, discusses how the Black Lives Matter movement's appeal to human rights has deep roots in the history of the black freedom struggle. As he illustrates, black America's struggle for human rights is once again gaining strength and will, hopefully, result in long-lasting positive social change.

Kareem Jackson, a St. Louis hip-hop artist who goes by the name Tef Poe, was interviewed this February by a BBC talk show host about why the Black Lives Matter movement was necessary. A leader in the organization Hands Up United, which was founded in the wake of Michael Brown's murder, Poe explained: "One of the negligent areas of the civil rights movement is that we did not move the moral compass of racism to the right direction."

Though the 1960s movement addressed the civil and political rights that were denied to black people—access and use of public accommodations, the right to vote, and ensuring fair employment and housing opportunities—it did not directly confront the racialized degradation black people endured, and many continue to endure, at the hands of the police. What the Black Lives Matter protests have done, however, is not only put police reform on the policy agenda but demanded that American society reconsider how it values black lives.

Tef Poe had not been directly involved in politics until Brown's death. He was a struggling hip-hop artist who occasionally wrote a column for the *Riverfront Times*, an independent newspaper in St. Louis. One day, while checking his Instagram account, Poe noticed a post that shook him. It was a photograph of Brown's stepfather holding up a hand-written sign that read simply, "My unarmed child has been murdered by the Ferguson police." As he watched the wave of anger, disgust, and disbelief mount on his social media feed within hours of the shooting, Tef Poe knew he had to go to Ferguson. This is how he—along with legions of people across the country—was transformed into an activist, not just concerned with civil and political rights but with black humanity.

The protests that have erupted since the deaths of Brown and other casualties of police brutality have been extraordinary. Seemingly out of nowhere, a multiracial, multigenerational movement asserting black humanity in response to racist police killings and vigilante violence has ripped across the country. The police brutality and killings are not, to be sure, new; the emerging movement against them, however, is. The upsurge in anti-racist organizing is a break from what we normally consider black activism in the United States. Each periodic wave of activism for the last half century—whether centered on electoral politics or protests—has traced its lineage to the "golden age" of the 1960s. But while there is a great deal of nostalgia in these comparisons, core activists of the Black Lives Matter movement have been quick to remind us that this current wave of protest "is not your grandmamma's civil rights movement."

In a purely tactical sense, that assessment is correct. The movement's use of technology to mobilize hundreds of thousands of people through social media is light years away from the labor that was once required to mobilize black people and their allies during the 1960s or even a few years ago. Jo Ann Robinson of the all-black Women's Political Council in Montgomery, for instance, spent hours using a hand-driven mimeograph machine to crank out over 52,000 leaflets that announced a mass protest after Rosa Parks's arrest in 1955.

Today, social media—particularly Twitter—can reach individuals throughout the nation and across the world in milliseconds, drastically slashing the time it takes to organize protests. As a recent *New York Times Magazine* spread noted, through Twitter, core Black Lives Matter activists like Johnetta Elzie and DeRay Mckesson, who are based in St. Louis, now have the ability to frame events and direct the actions of hundreds of thousands of people across the nation at their fingertips. Not only is social media a tool for mobilization, but the intense reporting on police brutality via social media also influences print and television coverage, which means that attention to such incidents has multiplied. Twitter and Facebook have, in this way, become documentary tools for Black Lives Matter activists, a way for them to become citizen journalists capturing the protests and police responses in almost real time. Indeed, for this reason, the spontaneity and the intensity of Black Lives Matter is more akin to other recent movements—Occupy Wall Street and the explosive protests in Egypt and Brazil—than 1960s activism.

Similarly, images of police violence are helping put pressure on municipal police departments to address these issues. Unlike the images of brutality that sparked outrage in the past—photographs of lynch victims hanging from trees during the age of Jim Crow or newspaper images of brutalized black bodies lying in a coroner's office—we are now able to witness and document police violence as it happens. Videos

from handheld phones and surveillance cameras have shown Marlene Pinnock being beaten by a California highway patrol officer, the ambush police shooting of John Crawford at a Walmart in Ohio, the chokehold death of Eric Garner in Staten Island, the drive-by police shooting of twelve-year-old Tamir Rice in Cleveland, and the crippling condition of Freddie Gray as he was arrested in Baltimore, before he eventually died.

But it is not only technological and tactical differences that separate Black Lives Matter activists from their civil rights predecessors. When activists remind us that the Black Lives Matter movement is different from the civil rights movement, they are making a conscious decision to avoid mistakes from the past. They are rejecting the charismatic leadership model that has dominated black politics for the past half century, and for good reason.

This older model is associated with Martin Luther King and the clergy-based, male-centered hierarchal structure of the organization he led, the Southern Christian Leadership Conference. In the ensuing years, this charismatic model has been replicated, most notably through organizations like Jesse Jackson's Rainbow PUSH Coalition and Al Sharpton's National Action Network, but also by hundreds of other locally based activist organizations across the country. But Black Lives Matter activists today recognize that granting decision-making power to an individual or a handful of individuals poses a risk to the durability of a movement. Charismatic leaders can be co-opted by powerful interests, place their own self-interest above that of the collective, be targeted by government repression, or even be assassinated, as were Martin Luther King and Malcolm X. The dependence of movements on charismatic leaders can therefore weaken them, even lead to their collapse.

Instead, core activists of the Black Lives Matter movement have insisted on a group-centered model of leadership, rooted in ideas of participatory democracy. The movement has modeled itself after the Student Nonviolent Coordinating Committee (SNCC), the 1960s organization that helped black Americans gain legal access to public spaces and the right to vote. Black Lives Matter organizers also operate on the principle that no one person or group of individuals should speak for or make decisions on behalf of the movement. They believe, as the legendary civil rights activist Ella Baker believed, that "strong people don't need strong leaders."

In some ways, the new tools of technology—particularly social media and especially Twitter—have facilitated the emergence of just such a bottom-up insurgency led by ordinary people, and have displaced the top-down approach of old guard civil rights organizations. But this model has also been adopted by design. For many young black Americans, leaders like Jesse Jackson and Al Sharpton, as well as heads of civil rights organizations such as the NAACP and the National Urban League, are no longer seen as the gatekeepers of the movement's ideals or the leaders who must broker the interests of black communities with the state or society. Additionally, with the exception of Al Sharpton's National Action Network, which has represented families of victims but has been less effective accomplishing police and prison reform, policing and mass incarceration have not been aggressively pursued by these more traditional organizations. And none, certainly, have adopted the disruptive protest tactics—the street marches, die-ins, bridge and tunnel blockades, and the intense publicity campaigns—that have helped Black Lives Matter force these issues onto the national political agenda.

Unlike the civil rights movement, the focus of Black Lives Matter—on policing in black and brown communities, on dismantling mass incarceration—is also being articulated less as a demand for specific civil or political rights, and more as a broader claim for "black humanity." This insistence on black humanity has repeatedly been used by Black Lives Matter activists as a catalyst for political action. "If you can see a dead black boy lie in the street for four and a half hours and that doesn't make you angry, then you lack humanity," said Ashley Yates, a Ferguson activist and co-founder of Millennial Activists United, at a rally last October. Evoking humanity is used to express communal anger against police brutality, but also to mobilize those who aren't acting. Yates explained further:

> And at the very core of this is humanity—Black Lives Matter. We matter. We matter. Black lives matter

because they are lives. Because we are human. Because we eat. Because we breathe. Because he [Michael Brown] had a dream, because he made rap songs, they may have had cuss words in them. Yeah. He was human. And when we neglect to see that we end up where we are today.

Activists like Yates have also used the claim of humanity to challenge the politics of respectability, a black middle-class ideology that has its origins in the turn-of-the-twentieth century response to black people's loss of civil and political rights following Reconstruction's collapse. The politics of respectability is invested in changing the personal behavior and culture of poor and working-class black people, rather than squarely addressing the structural barriers that keep them locked into a perpetual state of marginality.

This appeal to humanity too has deep—though hidden—roots in the history of the black freedom struggle. The eighteenth-century anti-slavery campaign roused the consciousness of nations by pleading to those who kept them and profited from their bondage, "Am I Not a Man and a Brother?" The agitation of the anti-lynching campaigns of the first half of the twentieth century highlighted the inhumanness of mob violence against black people. Striking garbage workers fighting for a living wage in Memphis in 1968 carried with them placards proclaiming, "I am a Man." But with the successful passage of major civil rights legislation—specifically the 1964 Civil Rights Act, 1965 Voting Rights Act, and the 1968 Fair Housing Act—and the expansion of these laws in subsequent decades, the language of civil rights came to dominate both the ideas and the strategies of leaders and organizations concerned with racial inequality.

With Black Lives Matter, we now have a revival of these historical roots. Its recognition that all black lives deserve humanity, regardless of their gender, class, or sexual orientation, has breathed new life into the legacy of the black freedom struggle. Today's new—and much larger—movement is also articulating the national struggle for racial justice as a broader one for human rights.

In 1951, the "We Charge Genocide" campaign—which included William Patterson, Paul Robeson, W. E. B. Du Bois, Claudia Jones, and family members of victims of racial violence such as Josephine Grayson and Rosalie McGee—petitioned the United Nations to examine human rights abuses against black Americans. The petitioners sought to frame their claims—that African Americans were being persecuted, denied the right to vote, and "pauperized" because of their race—as a question of both black humanity and as a human rights issue: "[A]bove all we protest this genocide as human beings whose very humanity is denied and mocked."

The horrific evidence compiled for the petition, culled from stories in black newspapers and accounts collected by civil rights and labor organizations from 1945 to 1951, is eerily similar to the accounts we hear today. We may be more familiar with the evidence that petitioners document in the Jim Crow South, but the incidents recorded outside it are especially revealing. In many pockets of the urban North, the policing of black migrants was merely a parallel to the Jim Crow violence that terrorized them in the South.

For instance, in February 1946 in Freeport, Long Island, a policeman shot and killed two unarmed black men, wounded a third, and arrested a fourth for "disorderly conduct." The men had objected to being denied service in a café. The Freeport police, in a move that resembles the police's response to protesters in Ferguson, "threw a cordon around the bus terminal and stationed men with tommy guns and tear gas there, saying that they wanted to 'prevent a possible uprising of local Negroes.'"

Three months later in Baltimore, police shot and killed Wilbur Bundley. "Nine witnesses stated that he was shot in the back while running," the petition reports. In July, Lucy Gordy James, a member of a prominent family of "Negro business people in Detroit," was "beaten severely" by three police officers. "She sued the officers for $10,000 damages, charging illegal arrest, assault, and maltreatment." And in 1951 in Philadelphia, "forty police officers killed an unarmed 21-year-old Negro youth, Joseph Austin Conway, allegedly being sought for questioning in a robbery. He died in a hail of bullets while seeking to draw fire away from his family and neighbors." This catalogue of disaster—to quote James Baldwin—is documented in over 200 pages.

In the 1950s, Malcolm X and Martin Luther King also used the language of human rights to internationalize the issue of racial inequality in the United States. During his travels abroad, Malcolm X enlisted the assistance of heads of states in Africa and the Middle East to condemn the United States for their treatment of black Americans. He discovered that by framing the mistreatment of black Americans as an international human rights issue instead of a national civil rights one, "those grievances can then be brought into the United Nations and be discussed by people all over the world." For him, as long as the discussion was centered on civil rights, "your only allies can be the people in the next community, many of whom are responsible for your grievance." Malcolm X wanted "to come up with a program that would make our grievances international and make the world see that our problem was no longer a Negro problem or an American problem but a human problem."

In framing racial discrimination in human rights terms, the Black Lives Matter movement is today picking up the baton of civil rights activists before them. The parents of Trayvon Martin and Jordan Davis have raised the issue of discriminatory policing with members of the UN Committee on the Elimination of All Forms of Racial Discrimination in Geneva. The parents of Mike Brown along with representatives of organizations in Ferguson and Chicago traveled to Geneva to share information about their cases with the UN Committee Against Torture in November 2014. Brown's parents submitted a statement to the Committee that read in part, "The killing of Mike Brown and the abandonment of his body in the middle of a neighborhood street is but an example of the utter lack of regard for, and indeed dehumanization of, black lives by law enforcement personnel." Following its examination of the United States, the Committee Against Torture recommended that it undertake independent and prompt investigations into allegations of police brutality and expressed concerns about racial profiling and the "growing militarization of policing activities." After it reviewed the human rights record of the United States, a review procedure of the UN Human Rights Council recommended strengthening legislation to combat racial discrimination and addressing excessive use of force by the police.

When Anthony Scott saw the video of his brother Walter Scott being shot as he fled a North Charleston police officer, he remarked, "I thought that my brother was gunned down like an animal." It is a curious thing for black people in the twenty-first century to once again have to claim their humanity.

We live in a society where people are more likely to be convicted of animal cruelty than police officers are likely to be charged for the murder of unarmed black, brown, and poor people. But with the Black Lives Matter movement, black America's struggle for human rights is once again gaining strength. Hopefully this time, we can win the more than century-long campaign that has demanded of our nation simply to see us as human.

Questions for Critical Thinking

1. In this essay, Fredrick Harris discusses how the Black Lives Matter movement's appeal to human rights has deep roots in the history of the black freedom struggle. How did his argument help you to understand this movement in new and different ways?

2. Harris points to the importance of recognizing that this movement is less about a demand for specific civil or political rights and more about a broader claim for "black humanity." Why is this an important distinction?

3. What are the conditions necessary for building effective coalitions to bring about positive social change for all with regard to the Black Lives Matter movement?